For Reference

Not to be taken from this room

HISTORICAL DICTIONARIES OF WAR, REVOLUTION, AND CIVIL UNREST
Edited by Jon Woronoff

Historical Dictionary of the Civil War

Volume 1
A–L

Terry L. Jones

Historical Dictionaries of War,
Revolution, and Civil Unrest, No. 18

The Scarecrow Press, Inc.
Lanham, Maryland, and London
2002

SCARECROW PRESS, INC.

Published in the United States of America
by Scarecrow Press, Inc.
A Member of the Rowman & Littlefield Publishing Group
4720 Boston Way, Lanham, Maryland 20706
www.scarecrowpress.com

4 Pleydell Gardens, Folkestone
Kent CT20 2DN, England

British Library Cataloguing in Publication Information Available

Library of Congress Cataloging-in-Publication Data

Jones, Terry L., 1952–
    Historical dictionary of the Civil War / Terry L. Jones.
        p. cm. — (Historical dictionaries of war, revolution, and civil unrest ; no. 18)
        Includes bibliographical references (p.).
        Contents: v. 1. A–L — v. 2. M–Z.
        ISBN 0-8108-4112-6 (alk. paper)
        1. United States—History—Civil War, 1861–1865—Dictionaries. I. Title. II. Series.
E468 .J777 2002
973.7'03—dc21   20010491616

♾™ The paper used in this publication meets the minimum requirements of
American National Standard for Information Sciences—Permanence of
Paper for Printed Library Materials, ANSI/NISO Z39.48-1992.
Manufactured in the United States of America.

In Memory of James and June Janette

Contents

Editor's Foreword

The Civil War has left a particularly deep mark on the collective conscience of the American people because it was so long and so bitter and because, unlike other wars, it pitted Americans against fellow Americans and not foreigners. This also explains why, although the Civil War was waged almost a century and a half ago, countless books and articles have been written, are still being written, and will continue to be written to explain, justify, analyze, and rationalize this war. The purpose of a historical dictionary like this is to present the facts that can be marshaled, and to trace the general current of events—in other words, to present in one place a solid base from which students and other researchers can generate their own conclusions.

That task has been carefully and clearly achieved in this *Historical Dictionary of the Civil War*. The introduction provides a broad overview of the war, its origins, and consequences. The dictionary entries then go into greater detail about the people, places, institutions, military engagements, weapons, and so on that played a part in this great conflict. In this 18th volume of the Historical Dictionaries of War, Revolution, and Civil Unrest series, the dictionary portion is necessarily large, in order to remind us of these many actors and events. A chronology has been included to assist readers in understanding the order in which these events took place. Those who wish more in-depth information should consult the bibliography for further sources on points of special interest.

This was probably the most difficult volume of the series to write, because so much of the available information remains controversial. Terry L. Jones has done an uncommonly good job of digging and getting at the data and has presented them both objectively and neutrally. The caliber of the research and the presentation is a result of several decades of studying, teaching, and writing. Dr. Jones is currently a professor of history at the University of Louisiana at Monroe. He has published three significant books on the American Civil War: *Lee's Tigers, The Civil War Memoirs of*

Capt. William J. Seymour, and *Campbell Brown's Civil War.* Thanks to his extensive experience, Dr. Jones was able to produce in this *Historical Dictionary of the Civil War* an excellent reference work that fills in so many of the essential details of an unforgettable war.

—Jon Woronoff
Series Editor

Preface

The American Civil War was one of the largest wars of the 19th century and was, perhaps, the most important episode in the history of the United States. Although a daunting endeavor, this historical dictionary is an attempt to provide in two concise volumes detailed information on all aspects of the war. Included is an overview of the conflict; entries on nearly 1,300 personalities, and almost 400 entries on campaigns and battles, weapons, and terminology; a chronology of important events; and a bibliography.

The introduction is a general overview of the Civil War. Although it includes information on the causes of the conflict and on wartime political and diplomatic events, the introduction stresses the military aspects of the war. It is not an in-depth study but rather is designed to give the reader a general understanding of the war. More detailed information on individual topics mentioned in the introduction can be found in the dictionary proper.

The dictionary itself concentrates on personalities, campaigns and battles, terminology, weapons, and military organizations. All general grade officers who were commissioned before Robert E. Lee's surrender at Appomattox Court House, Virginia, are included, as well as the wartime governors and other prominent military personnel, politicians, and civilians. The initials USA or CSA are assigned to each personality to indicate their affiliation with either the United States or Confederate States, respectively. For military ranks, there sometimes is confusion over dates given for commissions. For seniority purposes, some officers' commissions were made effective from a date prior to their actual appointment. Unless otherwise stated, dates cited in the dictionary are when the person was appointed to that rank, not their effective dates. As for battles, not all of the war's several thousand armed clashes could be included in the dictionary. Only the larger ones or ones that had a strategic effect on military operations are included. Also, no attempt has been made to distinguish between battles, engagements, and skirmishes—all of the armed clashes are listed as battles for simplicity.

A few remarks are appropriate regarding use of the dictionary. For cross-referencing, bold type has been used to denote subjects that have separate entries. Also, some entries have notations at the end of the narrative to guide the reader to further information on the topic. Some Civil War battles have different names and spellings, since the Union tended to name battles after bodies of water and the Confederacy after towns. Stones River is also known as Murfreesboro, and Jonesboro is sometimes spelled Jonesborough, for example. To be consistent, I have generally used the names and spellings found in Frances H. Kennedy, ed., *The Civil War Battlefield Guide,* 2nd edition (New York: Houghton Mifflin, 1998). Finally, pronunciation of some entries is cited directly after the term within parentheses. Most of these pronunciations come from Robert D. Quigley, *Civil War Spoken Here: A Dictionary of Mispronounced People, Places and Things of the 1860's* (Collingswood, N.J.: C. W. Historicals, 1993).

A number of people have given their time and expertise to this project. Many thanks go to Jon Woronoff, series editor, who exhibited great understanding and patience over the several years it took to complete the dictionary. I would also like to thank Crystal Clifton of Scarecrow Press for her work in editing the manuscript. Arthur W. Bergeron Jr., of Pamplin Historical Park and the National Museum of the Civil War Soldier in Petersburg, Virginia; Richard Lowe of North Texas State University in Denton, Texas; and my colleagues Marshall Scott Legan and Rory Cornish of the University of Louisiana at Monroe read parts of the manuscript and greatly strengthened it through their expert knowledge and insightful comments. Any errors of fact or interpretation, however, are mine alone. To Gary Joiner of Precision Cartographics, Shreveport, Louisiana, I am indebted for the maps. Finally, my wife, Carol, and daughters Laura and Amie, as usual, were understanding when I tied up the computer or was preoccupied by long ago events. To them I owe everything.

Abbreviations and Acronyms

Brig. Gen.	Brigadier General
Capt.	Captain
Cmdr.	Commander
Col.	Colonel
CSA	Confederate States of America
CSS	Confederate States Ship
ft.	feet
GAR	Grand Army of the Republic
Gen.	General
Gens.	Generals
Gov.	Governor
lbs.	pounds
Lt.	Lieutenant
Lt. Col.	Lieutenant Colonel
Lt. Comdr.	Lieutenant Commander
Lt. Gen.	Lieutenant General
Maj.	Major
Maj. Gen.	Major General
oz.	ounces
Pvt.	Private
Repr.	Representative
Sen.	Senator
Sens.	Senators
Sgt.	Sergeant
UCV	United Confederate Veterans
U.S.	United States
USA	United States of America
USS	United States Ship
VMI	Virginia Military Institute

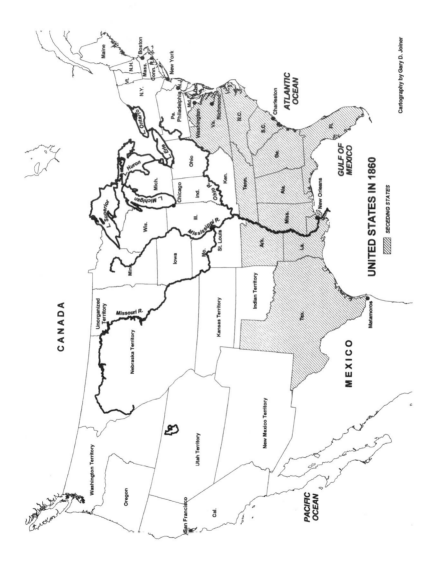

CANADA

ATLANTIC OCEAN

GULF OF MEXICO

MEXICO

PACIFIC OCEAN

UNITED STATES IN 1860

SECEDING STATES

Cartography by Gary D. Joiner

Maine

N.H.

Vt.

Mass.

Boston

Conn.

R.I.

New York

N.Y.

Ontario

Erie

Pa.

Philadelphia

N.J.

Del.

Md.

Washington

Va.

Richmond

N.C.

Charleston

S.C.

Fla.

Ga.

Huron

Mich.

Ohio

Ken.

Tenn.

Ala.

New Orleans

L. Michigan

L. Superior

Chicago

Ind.

Ohio R.

Wis.

Ill.

Miss.

La.

Minn.

Iowa

Mo.

St. Louis

Mississippi R.

Ark.

Indian Territory

Tex.

Matamoros

Unorganized Territory

Missouri R.

Nebraska Territory

Kansas Territory

New Mexico Territory

Washington Territory

Utah Territory

Oregon

Cal.

San Francisco

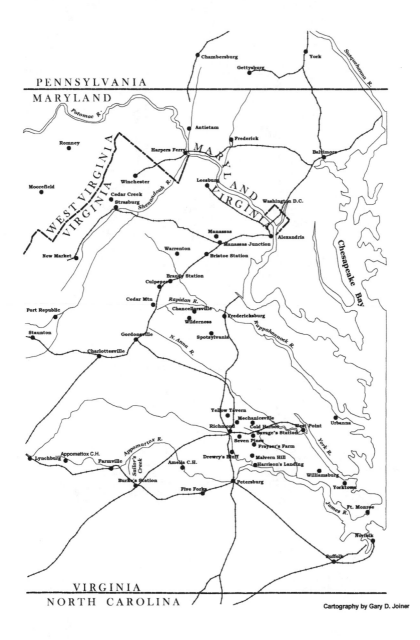

EASTERN THEATER OF WAR WITH MAJOR RAILROADS

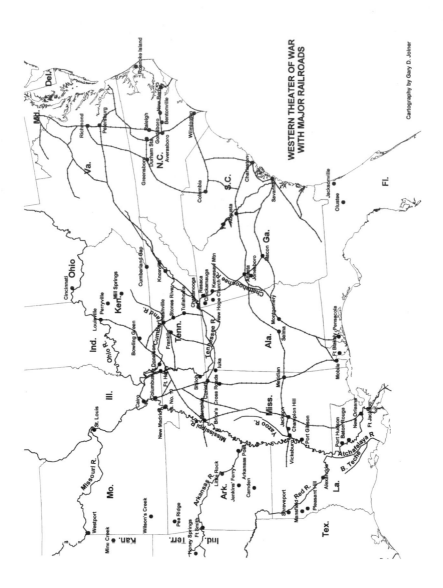

WESTERN THEATER OF WAR
WITH MAJOR RAILROADS

Cartography by Gary D. Joiner

Civil War Chronology

1820 **March 2:** Missouri Compromise was passed by the U.S. Congress.

1828 **May 11:** Tariff of 1828 (Tariff of Abomination) was passed by Congress.

1832 **July 14:** Congress passed the Tariff of 1832. **November 24:** South Carolina nullified the Tariff of 1832 and began the Nullification Crisis.

1833 **January 21:** South Carolina suspended its nullification act. **March 1:** Congress passed Force Act and Henry Clay's compromise tariff.

1836 **May 26:** Congress adopted the "gag rule" on slavery.

1846 **May 13:** Mexican War began when the United States declared war on Mexico. **August 8:** Wilmot Proviso was first introduced.

1848 **February 2:** Treaty of Guadalupe Hidalgo was signed, ending the Mexican War.

1850 **June 3–12:** First Nashville Convention was held. **September 17:** Congress passed last measures of the Compromise of 1850. **November 11–18:** Second Nashville Convention was held.

1852 **March:** *Uncle Tom's Cabin* was published.

1854 **February:** Republican Party was formed. **May 22:** Congress passed Kansas-Nebraska Act.

1857 **March 6:** U.S. Supreme Court issued the Dred Scott decision.

1857–58: Utah Expedition.

1858 **August 21–October 15:** Lincoln-Douglas debates were held in Illinois.

1859 **October 16–18:** John Brown's Raid on Harpers Ferry, Virginia, occurred.

1860 **April 23:** Democratic National Convention met in Charleston, South Carolina, but the Southern delegates walked out in protest over the slavery issue. **May 9:** Constitutional Union Party opened its convention in Baltimore, Maryland, and later nominated John Bell for president and Edward Everett for vice president. **May 18:** Republican National Convention opened in Chicago, Illinois, and later nominated Abraham Lincoln for president and Hannibal Hamlin for vice president. **June 18:** A second Democratic National Convention was held in Baltimore, Maryland, but Southern delegates again walked out four days later. **June 23:** In Baltimore, the Northern Democratic Party nominated Stephen Douglas for president and Benjamin Fitzpatrick for vice president (Fitzpatrick declined and was replaced by Herschel V. Johnson); Southern Democratic Party in Baltimore nominated John C. Breckinridge for president and Joseph Lane for vice president. **November 6:** Abraham Lincoln was elected president. **December 6:** Committee of Thirty-three was appointed by Congress to try to preserve the Union. **December 7:** Secretary of the Treasury Howell Cobb resigned to join South Carolina. **December 14:** Secretary of State Lewis Cass resigned because President James Buchanan would not reinforce federal installations in the South. **December 17:** A secession convention was held in Columbia, South Carolina. **December 20:** South Carolina seceded. **December 22:** Committee of Thirteen met in Washington, D.C. **December 26:** Major Robert Anderson moved his men from Fort Moultrie to Fort Sumter in Charleston Harbor, South Carolina. **December 27:** South Carolina seized Castle Pinckney and Fort Moultrie. **December 29:** Secretary of War John B. Floyd resigned. **December 30:** South Carolina seized the U.S. arsenal in Charleston.

1861 **January 3:** Crittenden Compromise was considered; Delaware legislature refused to join seceding states. **January 5:** Alabama militia seized Forts Morgan and Gaines in Mobile Bay; *Star of the West* sailed from New York City to Charleston to reinforce Fort Sumter. **January 6:** Georgia seized Fort Pulaski. **January 8:** Secretary of the Interior Jacob Thompson resigned. **January 9:** Mississippi seceded; *Star of the West* was fired on and prevented from reinforcing Fort Sumter. **January 10:** Florida seceded; Union garrison of Fort Barrancas, Florida, transferred to Fort Pickens near Pensacola; Louisiana militia seized the Baton Rouge arsenal and Forts Jackson and St. Philip. **January 11:** Alabama seceded; Gov. Francis W. Pickens demanded the surrender of Fort Sumter, but Major Anderson refused. **January 12:** Florida seized Barrancas Barracks, the U.S. Naval Yard, and Forts Barrancas and McRee at Pensacola. **January 16:** U.S. Senate rejected the Crittenden Compromise. **January 19:** Georgia seceded. **January 24:** Georgia seized the U.S. arsenal at Augusta. **January 26:** Louisiana seceded. **January 29:** Kansas was admitted to the Union as the 34th state; USS *Brooklyn* arrived with reinforcements at Fort Pickens, Florida. **February 1:** Texas seceded; Louisiana seized the U.S. Mint and Customs House in New Orleans. **February 4:** Washington Peace Conference met; delegates from seceding states met in the Montgomery, Alabama, Convention and became the Provisional Confederate Congress. **February 5:** Resolution was made at the Montgomery Convention to form a confederacy of seceding states. **February 8:** Montgomery Convention adopted a constitution for the Confederate States of America; Arkansas seized the U.S. arsenal at Little Rock. **February 9:** Confederate Provisional Congress elected Jefferson Davis the provisional president of the Confederate States of America and Alexander Stephens the vice president. **February 18:** Davis was inaugurated as president of the Confederacy; Gen. David E. Twiggs surrendered to Texas all U.S. military positions in the state. **February 23:** Lincoln entered Washington incognito for his inauguration. **February 24:** Texas voters approved secession. **February 27:** Washington Peace Conference recommended the adoption of a constitutional amendment, but Congress later refused to adopt it. **February 28:** Missouri State Convention met in Jefferson City to consider secession. **March 2:** Texas was admitted to the Confederacy. **March 3:** Brigadier General P. G. T. Beauregard assumed command of the Confederate forces at Charleston. **March 4:** Lincoln was inaugurated. **March 6:** Provisional Confederate Congress passed law to establish an army. **March 11:** Provisional Confederate Congress adopted the Confederate Constitution. **March 18:** Texas Gov. Sam Houston resigned after refusing to swear loyalty to the Confederacy. **March 29:** Lincoln decided to resupply Fort Sumter and prepared a naval expedition with supplies. **April 1:** Lincoln received and rejected a memorandum by Secretary of State William Seward proposing to unify the country by provoking a war with Spain and Great Britain. **April 6:** Federal government informed South Carolina of its intention to resupply Fort Sumter. **April 8:** Federal naval supply expedition departed from New York City for Fort Sumter. **April 11:** Beauregard demanded the surrender of Fort Sumter, but Major Anderson refused. **April 12:** Anderson again refused a Confederate surrender demand, and Beauregard began an artillery bombardment at 4:30 A.M.; Fort Pickens, Florida, was reinforced by Union troops from the USS *Brooklyn*. **April 13:** Major Anderson surrendered Fort Sumter at 2:30 P.M. **April 14:** Anderson evacuated Fort Sumter and was replaced by Confederate troops. **April 15:** Lincoln declared the Southern states to be in rebellion and called for 75,000 volunteers. **April 17:** Virginia seceded; *Star of the West* was captured by Confederates in Texas; more Union reinforcements landed at Fort Pickens; Davis called for 32,000 troops to defend the Confederacy and offered letters of marque to privateers. **April 18:** Union forces abandoned and burned the Harpers Ferry Arsenal in Virginia. **April 19:** Lincoln announced a blockade of Confederate ports; Baltimore Riot occurred in Maryland. **April 20:** Norfolk Navy Yard in Virginia and the USS *Merrimack* were burned by Federals. **April 22:** Arkansas Gov. Henry M. Rector refused Lincoln's request for volunteers; former U.S. Army officer Robert E. Lee was appointed major general of Virginia's troops. **April 23:** Robert E. Lee was given command of Virginia's forces. **April 25:** Arkansas seized Fort Smith; Tennessee legislature voted to secede. **April 27:** Lincoln suspended the writ of habeas corpus in the area between Washington, D.C., and Philadelphia, Pennsylvania. **April 29:** Maryland legislature rejected secession. **May 3:** Gen. Winfield Scott unveiled the "Anaconda Plan"; Lincoln called for 40,000 more volunteers. **May 6:** Arkansas; Jefferson Davis signed a bill recognizing a state of war with the United States. **May 7:** Union forces crossed the Potomac River and occupied Arlington Heights, Virginia; Virginia was admitted to the Confederacy. **May 10:** Union troops forced the surrender of pro-Confederate militia at Camp Jackson, Missouri, sparking the St. Louis Riot; Robert E. Lee assumed command of all Confederate forces in Virginia. **May 11:** St. Louis Riot continued. **May 13:** Great Britain declared neutrality in the American conflict; Union Brig. Gen. Benjamin Butler occupied Baltimore, Maryland. **May 16:** Tennessee was admitted into the Confederacy. **May 18:** The *Savannah* was commissioned a Confederate privateer in Charleston, South Carolina. **May 20:** North Carolina seceded; Provisional Confederate Congress agreed to move its capital to Richmond, Virginia; Kentucky declared its neutrality. **May 23:** Virginia voters approved secession; Joseph E. Johnston assumed command of Confederates in the Shenandoah Valley. **May 24:** When Union troops occupied Alexandria, Virginia, Col. Elmer Ellsworth was killed for taking down a Confederate flag. **May 26:** The United States stopped postal service to the Confederate states; U.S. Navy blockaded Mobile, Alabama, and New Orleans, Louisiana. **May 27–29:** Union forces occupied Newport News, Virginia. **May 28:** Union Brig. Gen. Irvin McDowell assumed command of the Department of Northeastern Virginia; Savannah, Georgia, was blockaded. **May 30:** Confederates raised the USS *Merrimac* at Norfolk, Virginia. **June 2:** Beauregard took command of Confederate forces in Northern Virginia. **June 3:** Battle of Philippi, Virginia; Sen. Stephen A. Douglas, of Illinois, died. **June 8:** Tennessee voters approved secession. **June 10:** Battle of Big Bethel, Virginia. **June 11:** Unionist citizens in western Virginia met in Wheeling to form a loyal state government. **June 12:** Secessionist Missouri Gov. Claiborne Jackson called for 50,000 volunteers to protect the state from Union aggression. **June 14:** Approaching Union troops forced Governor Jackson to flee Jefferson City with his supporters. **June 19:** Unionist voters in western Virginia elected Francis H. Pierpont governor of a loyal Virginia government. **July 2:** Unionist Virginia legislature assembled in Wheeling. **July 4:** Special session of U.S. Congress met. **July 5:** Battle of Carthage, Missouri. **July 11:** Battle of Rich Mountain, Virginia. **July 13:** Battle of Carrick's Ford, Virginia. **July 16:** Irvin McDowell began his advance from Washington, D.C., against P. G. T. Beauregard's Confederates at Manassas, Virginia. **July 17:** Confederate forces under Joseph E. Johnston in the Shenandoah Valley were ordered to join Beauregard at Manassas. **July 18:** Battle of Blackburn's Ford, Virginia; Johnston began moving his men from the Shenandoah Valley to Manassas. **July 20:** Johnston's command began arriving at Manassas to reinforce Beauregard. **July 21:** First Battle of Manassas; U.S. Navy blockaded Wilmington, North Carolina. **July 22:** Convention in Jefferson City, Missouri, voted to uphold the Union and to establish a loyal government in St. Louis. **July 25:** U.S. Senate passed resolutions declaring the war's goal was to preserve the Union and enforce the Constitution, not to interfere with slavery; Confederate Col. John R. Baylor's "buffalo hunt" reached Fort Fillmore, New Mexico Territory, and Union garrison evacuated the fort after a skirmish. **July 26:** Baylor occupied Fort Fillmore. **July 27:** Maj. Gen. George B. McClellan replaced McDowell in command of Union forces around Washington, D.C. **July 31:** Unionist convention in Jefferson City, Missouri, elected Hamilton Gamble governor of the new loyal state government. **August 1:** Baylor established the Confederate Territory of New Mexico; Brazil granted belligerent status to the Confederacy. **August 2:** Union troops evacuated Fort Stanton, New Mexico Territory. **August 5:** U.S. Congress passed the first federal income tax. **August 6:** U.S. Congress passed the First Confiscation Act. **August 10:** Battle of Wilson's Creek, Missouri; Union Brig. Gen. John C. Frémont issued an order freeing all slaves within his Western Department. **August 15:** Union Department of the Potomac was created, with its Army of the Potomac placed under George B. McClellan's command. **August 26:** Battle of Kessler's Cross Lanes, Virginia; Union Maj. Gen. Benjamin F. Butler led expedition from Hampton Roads, Virginia, for Hatteras Inlet, North Carolina. **August 28:** Union fleet under Silas H. Stringham bombarded Fort Hatteras, and Butler landed troops. **August 29:** Stringham resumed bombardment of Fort Hatteras, and the Confederates surrendered.

August 30: In Missouri, Frémont declared martial law and, without authorization, approved the confiscation of secessionist property. **August 31:** Robert E. Lee was given command of Confederate forces in western Virginia. **September 3:** Confederate Maj. Gen. Leonidas Polk advanced into Kentucky without authorization, thus violating Kentucky's neutrality. **September 6:** Union Brig. Gen. Ulysses S. Grant advanced his troops to Paducah, Kentucky, to counter Polk's intrusion. **September 10:** Battle of Carnifex Ferry, Virginia; Robert E. Lee advanced against Union forces at Cheat Mountain, Virginia. **September 11:** Skirmishing began around Cheat Mountain; Lincoln ordered Frémont to cancel his orders confiscating property and freeing slaves in Missouri. **September 12:** Lee closed in on an inferior enemy force at Cheat Mountain; secessionist troops under Sterling Price began siege of Lexington, Missouri. **September 13:** Battle of Cheat Mountain, Virginia; Confederates skirmished with Federals at Lexington, Missouri. **September 15:** Lee withdrew from Cheat Mountain. **September 17:** U. S. Navy occupied Ship Island, Mississippi; Battle of Liberty, Missouri. **September 18:** Confederates under Simon Buckner occupied Bowling Green, Kentucky. **September 18–19:** Fighting continued at Lexington, Missouri. **September 20:** Union forces surrendered Lexington, Missouri. **September 24:** Lincoln suspended the writ of habeas corpus nationwide. **October 3:** Battle of Greenbrier River, Virginia. **October 8:** Union Brig. Gen. William T. Sherman was put in command of the Department of the Cumberland. **October 9:** Battle of Santa Rosa Island at Pensacola, Florida. **October 16:** Union troops recaptured Lexington, Missouri. **October 21:** Battle of Ball's Bluff, Virginia; Battle of Camp Wildcat, Kentucky; Battle of Fredericktown, Missouri. **October 23:** Lincoln suspended the writ of habeas corpus in Washington, D.C. **October 25:** First Battle of Springfield, Missouri. **October 28:** Confederate Gen. Albert Sidney Johnston took command of the Army of Central Kentucky. **October 29:** Union forces captured Hampton Roads, Virginia; Union fleet under Samuel du Pont sailed from Hampton Roads for Port Royal, South Carolina. **November 1:** Union Gen. Winfield Scott resigned as general-in-chief and was replaced by Maj. Gen. George B. McClellan. **November 3:** Frémont was removed from command in Missouri and was replaced by David Hunter; at Neosho, Missouri, the secessionist legislature voted to secede and join the Confederacy. **November 6:** Jefferson Davis and Alexander Stephens were elected Confederate president and vice president, respectively; Thomas J. Jackson took command of the Confederate Valley District in Virginia; Union Brig. Gen. U. S. Grant left Cairo, Illinois, for Belmont, Missouri. **November 7:** Union forces captured Port Royal, South Carolina; Battle of Belmont, Missouri.

November 8: Confederate commissioners James Mason and John Slidell were seized by the U.S. Navy in the *Trent* Affair. **November 18:** Kentucky secessionists created their own government in Russellville and voted to secede. **November 21:** Judah P. Benjamin was named Confederate secretary of war. **November 24:** Captured Confederate envoys Mason and Slidell were placed in Fort Warren, Massachusetts. **November 26:** A Unionist convention in Wheeling, Virginia, adopted its own constitution to create the state of West Virginia. **November 28:** Missouri was admitted to the Confederacy. **December 2:** Lincoln authorized the suspension of the writ of habeas corpus in the Department of Missouri. **December 9:** U.S. Senate established the Committee on the Conduct of the War to investigate the war's prosecution; Battle of Chusto-Talasah, Indian Territory. **December 10:** U.S. House of Representatives concurred with the Senate to create the Committee on the Conduct of the War; Kentucky was admitted to the Confederacy. **December 14:** Henry Hopkins Sibley joined forces with John R. Baylor at Fort Bliss (El Paso), Texas, to begin his New Mexico Campaign. **December 17:** Battle of Rowlett's Station, Kentucky. **December 19:** Great Britain formally protested the seizure of Mason and Slidell and demanded an apology and their immediate release. **December 20:** Battle of Dranesville, Virginia; committee on the Conduct of the War was formed. **December 26:** St. Louis, Missouri, was placed under martial law; Battle of Chustenahlah, Indian Territory; U.S. government agreed to release Confederate envoys Mason and Slidell. **December 28:** Battle of Mount Zion Church, Missouri.

1862   January 1: Mason and Slidell were released and allowed to continue their mission to Europe. **January 2:** Union Brig. Gen. Ambrose Burnside's expedition left Fort Monroe, Virginia, for Roanoke Island, North Carolina. **January 11:** Union Secretary of War Simon Cameron resigned. **January 15:** Edwin Stanton was confirmed as the new Union secretary of war. **January 18:** Confederates formed the Territory of Arizona. **January 19:** Battle of Mill Springs, Kentucky. **January 24:** Frustrated at Union military inactivity, Lincoln issued president's General War Orders No. 1 that all Union forces were to advance against the Confederates on February 22, 1862. **February 2:** U. S. Grant and Andrew Foote left Cairo, Illinois, to begin the Forts Henry and Donelson Campaign. **February 6:** Foote's gunboats forced the surrender of Fort Henry, Tennessee. **February 7:** U.S. Navy bombarded Roanoke Island, North Carolina. **February 8:** Burnside attacked and captured Roanoke Island. **February 9:** Union Brig. Gen. Charles P. Stone was arrested for his role in the Ball's Bluff, Virginia, defeat. **February 11:** Grant began his advance from Fort Henry toward Fort Donelson, Tennessee, causing Confederate General Albert Sidney Johnston to evacuate Bowling Green, Kentucky; Union forces under Samuel Curtis began an advance against Sterling Price in northwest Arkansas. **February 12:** Grant began investing Fort Donelson. **February 13:** Fighting began around Fort Donelson as Grant continued to surround it. **February 14:** Lincoln offered amnesty to those who took an oath of allegiance to the Constitution; Union gunboats were repulsed at Fort Donelson. **February 15:** Confederate forces failed in an attempt to break out of Fort Donelson. **February 16:** Confederate Maj. Gen. Simon Buckner surrendered Fort Donelson to Grant. **February 18:** In Richmond, the permanent Confederate Congress met for the first time. **February 20:** With Forts Henry and Donelson lost, Confederate forces withdrew from Columbus, Kentucky, and virtually abandoned Kentucky. **February 20–21:** Battle of Valverde, New Mexico Territory. **February 23:** First Union troops arrived at Nashville, Tennessee. **February 27:** Confederate Congress authorized Jefferson Davis to suspend the writ of habeas corpus. **February 28:** Union forces under John Pope began an advance from Commerce, Missouri, toward New Madrid, Missouri. **March 2:** Union forces occupied Columbus, Kentucky; in Arkansas, Earl Van Dorn's Confederates joined forces with Sterling Price and Ben McCulloch. **March 3:** Pope began siege of New Madrid, Missouri. **March 4:** Tennessee Sen. Andrew Johnson was appointed the Union military governor of Tennessee; Robert E. Lee was appointed Davis's military adviser; Van Dorn began advancing toward Curtis at Pea Ridge, Arkansas; Union troops completed evacuation of Albuquerque, New Mexico Territory. **March 5:** Sibley's Confederates occupied Albuquerque. **March 7:** George B. McClellan finally advanced his Army of the Potomac out of Washington, D.C., toward Manassas. **March 7–8:** Battle of Pea Ridge, Arkansas. **March 8–9:** Battle of Hampton Roads, Virginia. **March 10:** Sibley's Confederates occupied Santa Fe, New Mexico Territory. **March 11:** Lincoln removed McClellan as general-in-chief but kept him as commander of the Army of the Potomac; McClellan's army reached Manassas Junction, Virginia, only to find that Joseph E. Johnston's Confederates had retreated; Union Maj. Gen. Ambrose Burnside left Roanoke Island for an attack on New Bern, North Carolina. **March 13:** Burnside began attack on New Bern; Confederates evacuated New Madrid, Missouri. **March 14:** Burnside captured New Bern; Pope captured New Madrid. **March 17:** McClellan began moving troops to Fort Monroe, Virginia, for his Peninsula Campaign. **March 23:** Battle of Kernstown, Virginia. **March 26–28:** Battle of Glorieta Pass, New Mexico Territory.

March 29: Union troops began landing to capture Fort Macon, North Carolina. **April 1:** Army of the Potomac began arriving at Fort Monroe, Virginia. **April 3:** Unionist voters ratified constitution for the new state of West Virginia; Albert Sidney Johnston began marching his Confederate army from Corinth, Mississippi, to attack U. S. Grant's position at Shiloh, Tennessee. **April 4:** Andrew Foote's Union fleet began bypassing the Mississippi River's Island No. 10 near New Madrid, Missouri, through a canal on the river's west bank. **April 5:** McClellan began siege of Yorktown, Virginia. **April 6:** Battle of Shiloh, Tennessee, began when Johnston attacked Grant's encampment; Johnston was killed in the fighting; Grant was reinforced this night by Don Carlos Buell's command. **April 7:** Grant assumed the offensive and counterattacked the Confederates, now led by Beauregard; Beauregard retreated to Corinth; Pope captured Island No. 10. **April 8:** Shiloh Campaign ended when Nathan Bedford Forrest's cavalry stopped the pursuing Union troops. **April 10:** Union forces began bombarding Fort Pulaski, at Savannah, Georgia. **April 11:** Union forces captured Fort Pulaski. **April 12:** Union forces began digging siege lines at Fort Macon, North Carolina; the "Great Locomotive Chase" began at Big Shanty, Georgia, during James Andrews's Raid. **April 16:** Lincoln signed bill abolishing slavery in Washington, D.C.; Jefferson Davis signed America's first military conscription act. **April 18–23:** David Farragut's Union fleet bombarded Forts Jackson and St. Philip, Louisiana. **April 19:** Battle of South Mills, North Carolina. **April 24:** Farragut's fleet successfully passed Forts Jackson and St. Philip during predawn hours. **April 25:** Union forces bombarded Fort Macon, North Carolina, and forced its surrender; Farragut's fleet arrived at New Orleans. **April 26:** Joseph E. Johnston assumed command of Confederate forces confronting McClellan on the Virginia Peninsula. **April 27:** Confederate garrison at Fort Jackson, Louisiana, mutinied. **April 28:** Forts Jackson and St. Philip surrendered to Union fleet. **April 29:** Union forces began advance from Shiloh, Tennessee, toward Corinth, Mississippi. **May 1:** Union Maj. Gen. Benjamin Butler occupied New Orleans, Louisiana. **May 3:** This night, Joseph E. Johnston began evacuating Yorktown, Virginia. Stonewall Jackson's Shenandoah Valley Campaign began. **May 4:** Henry Hopkins Sibley reached Fort Bliss, Texas, ending his New Mexico Campaign. **May 5:** Battle of Williamsburg, Virginia. **May 7:** Battle of Eltham's Landing, Virginia. **May 8:** Battle of McDowell, Virginia. **May 9:** David Hunter ordered the emancipation of all slaves in his Department of the South; Confederates evacuated Virginia's Norfolk Navy Yard and Pensacola, Florida; Farragut's ships captured Baton Rouge, Louisiana. **May 10:** Union forces occupied Portsmouth and Norfolk, Virginia; Battle of Plum Run Bend, Tennessee. **May 11:** The CSS *Virginia* was blown up near Norfolk, Virginia, to keep it from falling into enemy hands. **May 12:** Farragut's ships captured Natchez, Mississippi; Union forces occupied Pensacola, Florida. **May 15:** First Battle of Drewry's Bluff, Virginia; Butler issued his "Woman's Order" in New Orleans; CSS *Alabama* was launched in Great Britain. **May 19:** Lincoln countermanded Hunter's emancipation of slaves in the Department of the South. **May 20:** Lincoln signed the Homestead Act. **May 23:** Battle of Front Royal, Virginia. **May 25:** First Battle of Winchester, Virginia. **May 27:** Battle of Hanover Court House, Virginia. **May 29:** This night, Beauregard's Confederates began evacuating Corinth, Mississippi. **May 30:** Stonewall Jackson began his retreat from Harpers Ferry, Virginia, back up the Shenandoah Valley; Beauregard completed his evacuation of Corinth. **May 31:** Battle of Seven Pines, Virginia, began, and Joseph E. Johnston was severely wounded. **June 1:** Battle of Seven Pines ended, and Davis appointed Robert E. Lee to replace the wounded Johnston in command of what became the Army of Northern Virginia. **June 3:** Confederates evacuated Fort Pillow, Tennessee, leaving Memphis unguarded. **June 6:** Battle of Memphis, Tennessee; Memphis surrendered to Union forces. **June 7:** Benjamin Butler hanged William B. Mumford, a New Orleans civilian, for tearing down a U.S. flag; James Andrews was executed for his role in April's "Great Locomotive Chase." **June 8:** Battle of Cross Keys, Virginia. **June 9:** Battle of Port Republic, Virginia, ending Stonewall Jackson's Shenandoah Valley Campaign. **June 12:** Confederate Brig. Gen. J. E. B. Stuart's Ride began. **June 13:** Nathan Bedford Forrest's Confederate cavalry raided Murfreesboro, Tennessee. **June 15:** Stuart arrived in Richmond after completing his ride around McClellan's army. **June 16:** Battle of Secessionville, South Carolina. **June 17:** Jackson's command left the Shenandoah Valley to join Lee at Richmond; Battle of St. Charles, Arkansas. **June 18:** Seven of James Andrews's comrades were executed for their role in the "Great Locomotive Chase." **June 19:** Lincoln signed into law a bill abolishing slavery in the territories. **June 20:** Union forces under David Farragut and Brig. Gen. Thomas Williams bombarded Vicksburg, Mississippi. **June 25:** Seven Days Campaign began with Battle of King's School House, Virginia. **June 26:** Battle of Mechanicsville, Virginia; this night McClellan began his fighting retreat down the Virginia Peninsula. **June 27:** Battle of Gaines' Mill, Virginia; McClellan continued his retreat. **June 27–28:** Battle of Garnett's and Golding's Farms, Virginia. **June 28:** McClellan continued his retreat down the Peninsula. **June 29:** Battle of Savage's Station, Virginia; McClellan continued his retreat. **June 30:** Battle of Frayser's Farm, Virginia; McClellan continued his retreat. **July 1:** Battle of Malvern Hill, Virginia; Lincoln signed into law the first federal income tax. **July 2:** McClellan stopped his retreat at Harrison's Landing, Virginia, ending the Seven Days Campaign. **July 4:** Confederate cavalryman Col. John Hunt Morgan began his first Kentucky Raid. **July 7:** Battle of Hill's Plantation, Arkansas. **July 9:** Morgan's raiders captured Tompkinsville, Kentucky; Forrest's Confederate cavalry left Chattanooga, Tennessee, for a raid on Murfreesboro, Tennessee. **July 10:** Morgan's raiders captured Glasgow, Kentucky. **July 11:** Lincoln appointed Maj. Gen. Henry Halleck general-in-chief; Morgan's raiders captured Lebanon, Kentucky. **July 13:** Lee began moving Stonewall Jackson off the peninsula toward northern Virginia to stop the advance of John Pope's Union Army of Virginia; Forrest defeated the Union garrison at Murfreesboro, Tennessee. **July 14:** Morgan's raiders reached Cynthiana, Kentucky. **July 15:** CSS *Arkansas* steamed out of the Yazoo River into the Mississippi River and caused havoc in the Union fleet near Vicksburg, Mississippi. **July 16:** France's Napoleon III denied a request by Confederate commissioner John Slidell to recognize the Confederacy; U.S. Congress passed the Second Confiscation Act. **July 17:** Morgan's raiders defeated the Union garrison and captured Cynthiana, Kentucky. **July 20:** Morgan's raiders were defeated at Owensville, Kentucky. **July 22:** Lincoln presented the Emancipation Proclamation to the Cabinet but was persuaded to delay its announcement until a major Union victory was won. **July 29:** CSS *Alabama* sailed from Liverpool, England. **August 1:** Morgan's raiders returned to Tennessee, ending his first Kentucky Raid. **August 5:** Battle of Baton Rouge, Louisiana; CSS *Arkansas* was blown up to prevent its capture. **August 6–9:** Battle of Kirksville, Missouri. **August 9:** Battle of Cedar Mountain, Virginia. **August 10:** Battle of Nueces River, Texas. **August 11:** First Battle of Independence, Missouri. **August 12:** Confederate cavalryman John Hunt Morgan raided and captured Gallatin, Tennessee. **August 13:** Union forces forced Morgan's raiders out of Gallatin. **August 14:** Confederate Maj. Gen. Edmund Kirby Smith left Knoxville, Tennessee, to begin the Kentucky Campaign. **August 15–16:** Battle of Lone Jack, Missouri. **August 16:** McClellan began evacuating Harrison's Landing, Virginia, to reinforce John Pope's Army of Virginia. **August 17:** Sioux uprising began in Minnesota. **August 19:** Horace Greeley published his "The Prayer of Twenty Millions." **August 21:** Union forces evacuated Baton Rouge, Louisiana, after looting and burning much of the city. **August 22:** J. E. B. Stuart raided Catlett's Station, Virginia; Lincoln's answer to Greeley's "Prayer of Twenty Millions" was published, in which he stated his goal was to save the Union, not to free the slaves.

August 25: Union Secretary of War Stanton authorized the enlistment of black troops; Second Manassas Campaign began with Stonewall Jackson marching from the Rappahannock River to get into the rear of Pope's Army of Virginia. **August 26:** Jackson captured Pope's supply base at Manassas Junction, Virginia. **August 27:** Jackson burned Pope's supplies at Manassas Junction, and his men repulsed a Union probe at Kettle Run; Lee moved from the Rappahannock River to join Jackson. **August 28:** Battle of Groveton, Virginia; Lee forced his way through Thoroughfare Gap on his way to join Jackson; Confederate Maj. Gen. Braxton Bragg left Chattanooga, Tennessee, to begin his part of the Kentucky Campaign. **August 29–30:** Second Battle of Manassas; Battle of Richmond, Kentucky. **September 1:** Battle of Chantilly, Virginia; Kirby Smith approached Lexington, Kentucky, forcing the state legislature to evacuate the city. **September 2:** Lincoln ordered McClellan to take command of all Union troops around Washington, D.C. **September 3:** Kirby Smith captured Frankfort, Kentucky. **September 4:** Lee crossed the Potomac River into Maryland to begin the Antietam Campaign. **September 5:** Pope was relieved of command, and his Army of Virginia was consolidated with McClellan's Army of the Potomac. **September 7:** Lee began concentrating his army at Frederick, Maryland; McClellan marched out of Washington, D.C., in pursuit of Lee. **September 9:** Lee issued Special Order No. 191 (the "Lost Order") outlining his invasion plans. **September 10:** Lee marched out of Frederick, Maryland; Jackson began his advance on Harpers Ferry, Virginia. **September 12:** McClellan entered Frederick, Maryland. **September 13:** At Frederick, Union soldiers discovered Lee's "Lost Order"; Jackson began investing Harpers Ferry; Confederates arrived at Munfordville, Kentucky. **September 14:** Battle of South Mountain, Maryland. **September 14–17:** Battle of Munfordville, Kentucky. **September 15:** Jackson captured Harpers Ferry; Lee began consolidating his army at Sharpsburg, Maryland, along Antietam Creek. **September 16:** Jackson joined Lee at Antietam Creek. **September 17:** Battle of Antietam, Maryland. **September 18:** After remaining on the Antietam battlefield all day, Lee withdrew from Maryland and returned to Virginia that night. **September 19:** Lee continued to retreat across the Potomac River; Battle of Iuka, Mississippi. **September 19–20:** Battle of Shepherdstown, Virginia. **September 21:** Bragg occupied Bardstown, Kentucky. **September 22:** Lincoln issued the Preliminary Emancipation Proclamation. **September 23:** Sioux uprising in Minnesota was put down. **September 24:** Lincoln suspended the writ of habeas corpus in cases involving people interfering with the war effort. **September 27:** Confederate Congress passed the Second Conscription Act; in New Orleans, Louisiana, the Louisiana Native Guards became the first government-sanctioned black troops to join the Union army. **September 28:** Confederate forces under Earl Van Dorn and Sterling Price united to attack Corinth, Mississippi. **September 29:** Union forces under Don Carlos Buell reached Louisville, Kentucky, to confront Kirby Smith's Confederates. **September 30:** Battle of Newtonia, Missouri. **October 3–4:** Battle of Corinth, Mississippi. **October 4:** Confederates installed a Confederate governor at Lexington, Kentucky. **October 6:** Battle of Davis Bridge, Tennessee. **October 8:** Battle of Perryville, Kentucky. **October 10–11:** J. E. B. Stuart's Confederate cavalry made the Chambersburg, Pennsylvania, Raid. **October 13:** Before adjourning, the Confederate Congress renewed a law suspending the writ of habeas corpus; John C. Pemberton took command of the Confederates at Vicksburg, Mississippi. **October 16:** U. S. Grant took command of the Department of the Tennessee and what became the Army of the Tennessee. **October 17:** Confederate cavalryman John Hunt Morgan began his second Kentucky Raid. **October 18:** Morgan defeated a Union force near Lexington, Kentucky. **October 20:** Lincoln authorized Maj. Gen. John McClernand to raise troops in the Midwest for an attack on Vicksburg, Mississippi. **October 22:** Battle of Old Fort Wayne, Indian Territory. **October 24:** Union Maj. Gen. Don Carlos Buell was relieved of command in Kentucky and Tennessee for failing to pursue Bragg and was replaced by Maj. Gen. William Rosecrans. **October 26:** McClellan finally crossed the Potomac River into Virginia after the Battle of Antietam; Bragg retreated into Tennessee and ended the Kentucky Campaign. **October 27:** Battle of Georgia Landing, Louisiana. **November 1:** Morgan's raiders reached Springfield, Tennessee, ending his second Kentucky Raid. **November 5:** Lincoln removed McClellan from command of the Army of the Potomac. **November 9:** Lincoln appointed Maj. Gen. Ambrose Burnside to command the Army of the Potomac. **November 15:** Burnside advanced from Warrenton, Virginia, toward Fredericksburg to begin the Fredericksburg Campaign. **November 17:** Burnside's vanguard reached Falmouth, Virginia, but could not cross the Rappahannock River for a lack of pontoon boats. **November 18:** Lee's Army of Northern Virginia began arriving at Fredericksburg. **November 19:** Burnside's army was finally concentrated at Falmouth. **November 26:** Grant began his Overland Vicksburg Campaign from Grand Junction, Tennessee. **November 28:** Battle of Cane Hill, Arkansas. **December 4:** Confederate Gen. Joseph E. Johnston was put in command of the Department of the West. **December 5:** Battle of Coffeeville, Mississippi. **December 6:** Confederate cavalryman John Hunt Morgan left Baird's Mill, Tennessee, on a raid to Hartsville, Tennessee. **December 7:** Morgan captured a large Union force at Hartsville; Battle of

Prairie Grove, Arkansas. **December 10:** U.S. Congress passed a bill creating the state of West Virginia; Confederate forces captured Plymouth, North Carolina. **December 11:** Burnside crossed the Rappahannock River under heavy fire and occupied Fredericksburg, Virginia; Forrest's Confederate cavalry began a raid from Columbia, Tennessee, against Grant's supply line during the Overland Vicksburg Campaign. **December 12:** Union troops looted Fredericksburg and prepared to attack Lee; USS *Cairo* sank in the Yazoo River, near Vicksburg, Mississippi, after striking two torpedoes. **December 13:** Battle of Fredericksburg, Virginia; U.S. Congress passed a bill admitting West Virginia. **December 14:** First Battle of Kinston, North Carolina. **December 15:** Burnside withdrew across the Rappahannock River to Falmouth. **December 16:** Maj. Gen. Nathaniel Banks replaced Benjamin Butler in command of New Orleans, Louisiana; Battle of White Hall, North Carolina. **December 15–17:** Forrest crossed the Tennessee River near Clifton, Tennessee, on his raid against Grant's supply line; Confederate cavalryman Earl Van Dorn left Grenada, Mississippi, for his raid on Holly Springs, Mississippi. **December 17:** Grant issued General Order No. 11, expelling all Jews from the Department of the Tennessee; Union forces reoccupied Baton Rouge, Louisiana; Battle of Goldsboro Bridge, North Carolina. **December 18:** Forrest defeated Union cavalry at Lexington, Tennessee. **December 19:** Forrest's cavalry destroyed the railroad near Jackson, Tennessee. **December 20:** Van Dorn's Confederate cavalry destroyed Grant's supply base at Holly Springs, Mississippi; William T. Sherman left Memphis, Tennessee, for his attack against Chickasaw Bayou, Mississippi. **December 21:** Confederate cavalryman John Hunt Morgan began his Christmas Raid from Alexandria, Tennessee. **December 26:** Sherman landed his troops at Chickasaw Bayou, Mississippi. **December 26–28:** Confederate cavalryman J. E. B. Stuart made his Dumfries Raid in Virginia. **December 27:** Morgan raided Elizabethtown, Kentucky. **December 27–29:** Battle of Chickasaw Bayou, Mississippi. **December 31:** Battle of Parker's Cross Roads, Tennessee; in the predawn hours, the USS *Monitor* sank in a storm off Cape Hatteras, North Carolina. **December 31, 1862–January 2, 1863:** Battle of Stones River, Tennessee.

1863   January 1: Lincoln signed the Emancipation Proclamation; Forrest recrossed the Tennessee River at Clifton, Tennessee, ending his raid; Morgan's raiders reached Columbia, Tennessee, ending the Christmas Raid; Battle of Galveston, Texas. **January 2:** Battle of Stones River, Tennessee, ended; Sherman withdrew from Chickasaw Bayou, Mississippi, ending Grant's Overland Vicksburg Campaign. **January 3:** This night, Bragg retreated from Stones River. **January 4:** Union Maj. Gen. John McClernand began a movement with William T. Sherman against Confederate forces at Arkansas Post, Arkansas. **January 8:** Joseph Wheeler's Confederate cavalry began a raid into Tennessee; Second Battle of Springfield, Missouri. **January 9:** Sherman landed his troops near Arkansas Post; Confederates captured Hartville, Missouri. **January 9–11:** Battle of Hartville, Missouri. **January 10–11:** Battle of Arkansas Post, Arkansas. **January 11:** CSS *Alabama* sank the USS *Hatteras* near Galveston, Texas. **January 13:** Union naval and land forces unsuccessfully attacked Fort Fisher, North Carolina. **January 16:** CSS *Florida* escaped from Mobile, Alabama, and began a cruise in which she took 15 Union vessels. **January 18:** Massacre of Shelton Laurel, North Carolina; Grant issued orders to begin the Vicksburg Campaign. **January 20:** In Virginia, Ambrose Burnside began the "Mud March." **January 23:** Heavy rains forced Burnside to abandon the "Mud March." **January 25:** Lincoln removed Burnside from command of the Army of the Potomac. **January 26:** Maj. Gen. Joseph Hooker took command of the Army of the Potomac. **January 31:** CSS *Chicora* and CSS *Palmetto State* captured one Union vessel and disabled another at Charleston, South Carolina. **February 2:** USS *Queen of the West* ran past Vicksburg, Mississippi; Union preparations began for the Yazoo Pass Expedition. **February 3:** Battle of Dover, Tennessee; USS *Queen of the West* captured three Confederate supply vessels below Vicksburg. **February 12:** USS *Indianola* ran past the Vicksburg batteries. **February 14:** USS *Queen of the West* was captured by Confederates in Louisiana's Red River. **February 22:** Battle of Okolona, Mississippi. **February 24:** USS *Indianola* was captured by the Confederates in the Mississippi River. **February 25:** U.S. Congress completed passage of the Conscription Act. **February 26:** *Indianola* was destroyed by its Confederate crew when a mock Union gunboat approached it. **March 2:** Union Maj. Gen. Nathaniel P. Banks left New Orleans, Louisiana, to begin the Bayou Teche Campaign. **March 3:** Lincoln signed the Conscription Act. **March 5:** Battle of Thompson's Station, Tennessee. **March 7:** Confederate Lt. Gen. Edmund Kirby Smith took command of the Trans-Mississippi Department; Yazoo Pass Expedition began in Mississippi. **March 8:** John S. Mosby's Confederate partisans captured Union Brig. Gen. Edwin Stoughton and 32 men at Fairfax Court House, Virginia. **March 10:** Lincoln issued an amnesty proclamation to Union deserters and soldiers absent without leave if they would return to their units. **March 10–April 5:** Federals on the Yazoo Pass Expedition unsuccessfully attacked Fort Pemberton, Mississippi. **March 13–15:** Confederate raid on New Bern, North Carolina. **March 14:** USS *Hartford* and USS *Albatross* ran past

Confederate batteries at Port Hudson, Louisiana, but another ship was destroyed and two others were forced back; Steele's Bayou Expedition began in Mississippi. **March 17:** Battle of Kelly's Ford, Virginia. **March 20:** Battle of Vaught's Hill, Tennessee. **March 25:** Ambrose Burnside assumed command of the Army of the Ohio; David Porter abandoned the Steele's Bayou Expedition; Battle of Brentwood, Tennessee. **March 26:** Confederate Congress passed the Impressment Act. **March 29:** U. S. Grant began moving his Union army down the right bank of the Mississippi River to New Carthage, Louisiana. **March 30–April 20:** Battle of Washington, North Carolina. **April 2:** Bread riot erupted in Richmond, Virginia. **April 5:** Union forces abandoned the Yazoo Pass Expedition. **April 6:** Grant's army began arriving at New Carthage, Louisiana. **April 7:** Samuel du Pont's Union fleet unsuccessfully attacked Forts Sumter and Moultrie in Charleston Harbor, South Carolina. **April 10:** Earl Van Dorn's Confederate cavalry raided Franklin, Tennessee. **April 11–May 3:** Siege of Suffolk, Virginia. **April 12–13:** Battle of Fort Bisland, Louisiana. **April 14:** *Queen of the West* was destroyed by Federals in Grand Lake, Louisiana; Battle of Irish Bend, Louisiana. **April 15:** CSS *Alabama* captured two Union whalers off Brazil. **April 16:** This night, David Porter successfully ran 11 vessels past Vicksburg batteries. **April 17:** Union Col. Benjamin H. Grierson's Raid began from La Grange, Tennessee. **April 19:** Battle of Fort Huger, Virginia. **April 20:** William E. "Grumble" Jones and John Imboden's Raid began in western Virginia; Nathaniel P. Banks captured Opelousas, Louisiana; Lincoln signed bill to admit West Virginia. **April 21:** Union Col. Abel D. Streight's Raid began from Eastport, Mississippi. **April 22:** This night, 11 of 18 Union ships ran past the Vicksburg batteries. **April 24:** Confederate Congress passed controversial tax that included taxes on income, certain profits, and agricultural products. **April 26:** Streight's raiders left Tuscumbia, Alabama; Battle of Cape Girardeau, Missouri. **April 27:** Joseph Hooker began the Chancellorsville Campaign by marching the Army of the Potomac up the Rappahannock River from Falmouth, Virginia. **April 28:** Hooker began crossing the Rappahannock River. **April 29:** Maj. Gen. John Sedgwick's Union forces in Fredericksburg, Virginia, crossed the Rappahannock River to threaten Robert E. Lee's position and to divert attention from Hooker's crossing upstream; Union Maj. Gen. George Stoneman's Raid began in Virginia; Union gunboats bombarded Grand Gulf, Mississippi. **April 29–May 1:** William T. Sherman demonstrated against Snyder's Bluff, Mississippi, to divert attention from Grant's river crossing downstream. **April 30:** Grant's army began crossing the Mississippi River near Bruinsburg, Mississippi, to begin the Vicksburg Campaign in earnest; Streight's raiders escaped Forrest's pursuing cavalry at Day's Gap, Alabama. **May 1:** Battle of Chancellorsville, Virginia, began; Battle of Port Gibson, Mississippi. **May 1–2:** Battle of Chalk Bluff, Arkansas. **May 2:** Stonewall Jackson crushed Hooker's right flank at Chancellorsville but was mortally wounded that night; Grierson's raiders reached Baton Rouge, Louisiana. **May 3:** Lee continued attacking Hooker at Chancellorsville; Sedgwick attacked Jubal Early's Confederates in the Second Battle of Fredericksburg; Stonewall Jackson's left arm was amputated; Longstreet abandoned the siege of Suffolk, Virginia; Confederates evacuated Grand Gulf, Mississippi; Streight's raiders surrendered to Forrest at Cedar Bluff, Alabama. **May 3–4:** Battle of Salem Church, Virginia. **May 4:** Sedgwick's Federals began retreating across the Rappahannock River this night. **May 5:** Hooker withdrew the Army of the Potomac across the Rappahannock River this night, ending the Chancellorsville Campaign. **May 8:** Grant began his advance on Jackson, Mississippi, from Port Gibson. **May 9:** Nathaniel P. Banks's Union army captured Alexandria, Louisiana. **May 10:** Stonewall Jackson died from pneumonia. **May 12:** Battle of Raymond, Mississippi. **May 13:** Confederate Lt. Gen. John C. Pemberton moved out of Vicksburg, Mississippi, to attack Grant's supply line. **May 14:** Grant captured Jackson, Mississippi; Banks abandoned Alexandria, Louisiana, and marched for Port Hudson, Louisiana. **May 15:** Grant advanced toward Vicksburg from Jackson to engage Pemberton. **May 16:** Battle of Champion Hill, Mississippi. **May 17:** Pemberton was defeated at the Battle of Big Black River Bridge and withdrew inside Vicksburg's defenses. **May 18:** Grant arrived at Vicksburg. **May 19:** Grant unsuccessfully attacked Vicksburg. **May 21:** The Port Hudson Campaign began in earnest with the Battle of Plains Store, Louisiana. **May 22:** Grant made a second unsuccessful attack against Vicksburg; Banks surrounded Port Hudson. **May 27:** Banks unsuccessfully attacked Port Hudson; Jones and Imboden's Raid came to an end in West Virginia. **June 3:** Gettysburg Campaign began when Lee's Army of Northern Virginia marched from Fredericksburg toward Culpeper, Virginia. **June 5:** Battle of Franklin's Crossing, Virginia. **June 7:** Battle of Milliken's Bend, Louisiana. **June 9:** Battle of Brandy Station, Virginia. **June 10:** Lee marched from Culpeper toward the Shenandoah Valley. **June 13:** Lee's vanguard under Richard S. Ewell reached Winchester, Virginia; Confederate Maj. Gen. Franklin Gardner refused Banks's surrender demand at Port Hudson, Louisiana. **June 14:** Second Battle of Winchester, Virginia; Banks unsuccessfully attacked Port Hudson. **June 15:** Battle of Stephenson's Depot, Virginia; Ewell's corps began crossing the Potomac River into Maryland. **June 16:** Hooker's Army of the Potomac reached Fairfax Court House, Virginia, in pursuit of Lee; Lee crossed the Potomac River into Maryland. **June 17:** Battle of Aldie, Virginia. **June 17–19:** Battle of Middleburg, Virginia. **June 20:** West Virginia was admitted as the 35th state. **June 20–21:** Battle of Lafourche Crossing, Louisiana. **June 21:** Battle of Upperville, Virginia. **June 22:** Lee's army entered Chambersburg, Pennsylvania. **June 23:** Hooker crossed the Potomac River into Maryland in cautious pursuit of Lee; Union Maj. Gen. William Rosecrans began the Tullahoma Campaign in Tennessee. **June 24–25:** The last of Lee's Army of Northern Virginia crossed the Potomac River. **June 24–26:** Battle of Hoover's Gap, Tennessee. **June 25:** J. E. B. Stuart's Confederate cavalry began Stuart's Gettysburg Raid; at Vicksburg, the Federals exploded a mine under the Confederate defenses, but the subsequent attack failed. **June 26:** Elements of Ewell's Confederate corps entered Gettysburg, Pennsylvania. **June 27:** Hooker submitted his resignation as Army of the Potomac commander when his recommendation to evacuate Harpers Ferry, Virginia, was not followed; Lee entered Chambersburg, Pennsylvania; in the Tullahoma Campaign, Union troops attacked Guy's Gap, Tennessee, and entered Manchester. **June 28:** Lincoln accepted Hooker's resignation and appointed George Gordon Meade to command the Army of the Potomac; upon learning that Meade was advancing toward him through Maryland, Lee decided to concentrate his army around Gettysburg and Cashtown, Pennsylvania; Stuart captured 125 Union wagons at Rockville, Maryland; Battle of Fort Butler, Louisiana. **June 29:** Stuart's cavalry destroyed the Baltimore & Ohio Railroad at Hood's Mill, Maryland, and engaged the Union cavalry at Westminster, Maryland; Meade's army advanced toward Pennsylvania. **June 29–30:** Battle of Goodrich's Landing, Louisiana. **June 30:** Stuart clashed with Union cavalry at Hanover, Pennsylvania; the Tullahoma Campaign ended when Braxton Bragg's Confederate Army of Tennessee evacuated Tullahoma, Tennessee, and retreated across the Elk River. **July 1:** Battle of Gettysburg, Pennsylvania, began with Confederates successfully driving the Federals out of Gettysburg and killing Maj. Gen. John Reynolds; Grant exploded a second mine under the Vicksburg defenses without success; Johnston's Confederate force left Jackson, Mississippi, and moved toward Vicksburg. **July 1–2:** Battle of Cabin Creek, Indian Territory. **July 2:** At Gettysburg, Lee launched unsuccessful attacks against Meade's flanks; Confederate cavalryman John Hunt Morgan began his Ohio Raid by crossing the Cumberland River at Burkesville, Kentucky. **July 3:** At Gettysburg, Lee unsuccessfully attacked Meade's center in Pickett's Charge; at Vicksburg, Pemberton asked for a truce to discuss surrender terms with Grant.

July 4: At Gettysburg, Lee began his retreat to Virginia; Pemberton formally surrendered his nearly 30,000 men at Vicksburg; Battle of Helena, Arkansas. **July 5:** William T. Sherman left Vicksburg to attack Jackson, Mississippi; Morgan's raiders recaptured Lebanon, Kentucky. **July 6:** Lee reached the Potomac River but could not cross because of high water; Battle of Williamsport, Maryland. **July 7:** Bragg concentrated his army around Chattanooga, Tennessee; Morgan's raiders crossed the Ohio River into Indiana. **July 8:** Opposing officers at Port Hudson, Louisiana, met to discuss Confederate surrender terms. **July 8–14:** Battle of Falling Waters, Maryland. **July 9:** Gardner surrendered Port Hudson to Nathaniel Banks; Battle of Corydon, Indiana. **July 10:** Union forces established a beachhead on Morris Island and began a siege of Fort Wagner near Charleston, South Carolina. **July 11:** In New York City, the draft lottery began; at Charleston, Union forces unsuccessfully attacked Fort Wagner. **July 12:** Sherman clashed with Joseph E. Johnston's Confederates at Jackson, Mississippi. **July 13:** During the night, Lee began to retreat across the Potomac River; Battle of Bayou Lafourche, Louisiana; Morgan's raiders entered Ohio. **July 13–16:** New York City Draft Riot. **July 14:** Lee completed his retreat across the Potomac River, ending the Gettysburg Campaign. **July 15:** Elements of the Army of the Potomac arrived in New York City to quell the draft riot. **July 16:** Johnston abandoned Jackson, Mississippi. **July 17:** Morgan's raiders rode through the outskirts of Cincinnati, Ohio; Battle of Honey Springs, Indian Territory. **July 18:** In Charleston, Col. Robert Gould Shaw of the 54th Massachusetts Colored Infantry was killed during an unsuccessful attack on Fort Wagner. **July 19:** Meade crossed the Potomac River into Virginia in pursuit of Lee; most of Morgan's raiders were captured at Buffington Island, Ohio. **July 23:** Battle of Manassas Gap, Virginia. **July 24:** Sherman returned to Vicksburg after his raid on Jackson, Mississippi. **July 26:** Morgan and his surviving men were captured near Salineville, Ohio. **August 10:** Frederick Steele's Union forces marched from Helena, Arkansas, toward Little Rock. **August 12:** Union forces began bombarding Confederate positions around Charleston, South Carolina. **August 16:** William Rosecrans's Army of the Cumberland left Tullahoma, Tennessee, in pursuit of Braxton Bragg's Army of Tennessee; Union Brig. Gen. Charles P. Stone was released from prison after being detained for the Ball's Bluff defeat. **August 17:** Union forces began a heavy bombardment of Fort Sumter at Charleston, South Carolina. **August 20:** Kit Carson began a campaign against the Navajo Indians in New Mexico. **August 21:** Rosecrans reached the Tennessee River; Confederate guerrilla William Quantrill raided Lawrence, Kansas. **August 25:** Union forces again unsuccessfully attacked Fort Wagner outside Charleston; to punish guerrillas, Union Brig. Gen. Thomas Ewing issued General Orders No. 11, evicting thousands of civilians from Missouri. **August 26:** Union forces captured some Confederate positions near Fort Wagner; Battle of Rocky Gap, West Virginia. **August 29:** In Charleston, the Confederate submarine *H. L. Hunley* sank with the loss of five men. **September 1:** Union forces heavily bombarded Fort Sumter; Rosecrans began crossing the Tennessee River. **September 5:** John A. B. Dahlgren's Union fleet began bombarding Fort Wagner, South Carolina, as the Federals inched closer to the Confederate position; Rosecrans divided his army into three columns and moved into mountainous north Georgia; under pressure from the United States, British officials seized the "Laird rams" being constructed in Liverpool for Confederate service. **September 6–7:** On this night, Confederates abandoned Fort Wagner, South Carolina. **September 7:** Bragg began withdrawing from Chattanooga, Tennessee, to concentrate his army in northern Georgia; Union forces arrived off Sabine Pass, Texas, in preparation for a Texas invasion. **September 8:** Confederates at Fort Sumter repelled a nighttime attack; Battle of Sabine Pass, Texas. **September 9:** Rosecrans's Army of the Cumberland occupied Chattanooga; Bragg began concentrating his army to crush Rosecrans's widely scattered Union army that was advancing into Georgia; in Virginia, James Longstreet's corps embarked by rail to reinforce Bragg. **September 10:** Union forces won Battle of Bayou Fourche, Arkansas, and occupied Little Rock. **September 10–11:** Battle of McLemore's Cove, Georgia. **September 12:** Rosecrans began concentrating his army in northern Georgia to confront Bragg's Confederates. **September 17:** Rosecrans began positioning his army along Chickamauga Creek. **September 18:** Longstreet's corps began arriving at Chickamauga Creek as Bragg planned to attack Rosecrans. **September 19:** Bragg attacked Rosecrans and began the Battle of Chickamauga, Georgia; Longstreet arrived on the battlefield. **September 20:** Rosecrans was defeated at Chickamauga, but George H. Thomas's stand on Snodgrass Hill allowed the army to retreat to Chattanooga, Tennessee. **September 21:** Rosecrans took up a strong defensive position around Chattanooga. **September 22:** Bragg occupied Lookout Mountain and Missionary Ridge, effectively besieging Rosecrans in Chattanooga; Battle of Blountsville, Tennessee. **September 25:** Joseph Hooker was sent from Virginia with two corps to reinforce Rosecrans. **September 29:** Battle of Stirling's Plantation, Louisiana. **October 1:** Joseph Wheeler's Confederate cavalry began a raid to disrupt Rosecrans's supply line. **October 2:** Hooker's two corps began arriving at Bridgeport, Alabama, to support Rosecrans; Wheeler's cavalry destroyed a Union wagon train at Anderson's Cross Roads, Tennessee. **October 3:** Union forces in south Louisiana began the Texas Overland Expedition. **October 5:** Wheeler's cavalry under John A. Wharton raided Murfreesboro, Tennessee. **October 6:** Massacre at Baxter Springs, Kansas. **October 9:** Bristoe Station Campaign began in Virginia when Lee advanced to turn Meade's flank; Wheeler's cavalry recrossed the Tennessee River near Rogersville, Alabama, ending its raid. **October 10:** Jefferson Davis arrived in Chattanooga, Tennessee, to restore harmony to a fractious Army of Tennessee; Battle of Blue Springs, Tennessee. **October 12:** Meade withdrew in Virginia as Lee marched north in the Bristoe Station Campaign. **October 13–14:** Battle of Auburn, Virginia. **October 14:** Battle of Bristoe Station, Virginia. **October 15:** Confederate submarine *H. L. Hunley* sank again, drowning its inventor, Horace L. Hunley, and seven crewmen. **October 17:** Lee retreated from Bristoe Station. **October 18:** Grant was put in command of the Military Division of Mississippi. **October 19:** Battle of Buckland Mills, Virginia; Nathan Bedford Forrest left Corinth, Mississippi, on his Johnsonville Raid. **October 20:** Bristoe Station Campaign ended in Virginia when Lee retreated across the Rappahannock River; Grant relieved Rosecrans from command of the Army of the Cumberland and replaced him with George H. Thomas. **October 23:** Grant arrived in Chattanooga, Tennessee, and began the Chattanooga Campaign. **October 25:** Battle of Pine Bluff, Arkansas. **October 27:** Union forces again bombarded Fort Sumter, South Carolina. **October 28:** Battle of Wauhatchie, Tennessee, occurred this night; Forrest attacked Union shipping on the Tennessee River near Fort Heiman, Tennessee. **October 29:** Fort Sumter was again heavily shelled by Union forces. **October 30:** A supply ship arrived in Chattanooga, ending the near starvation conditions for the Union soldiers. **November 2:** Nathaniel P. Banks's Union force landed at Brazos Santiago Island, Texas, to isolate Brownsville. **November 3:** Union navy again bombarded Fort Sumter; Battle of Collierville, Tennessee; Battle of Bayou Bourbeau, Louisiana. **November 4:** Knoxville Campaign began when Bragg sent Longstreet's corps and Wheeler's cavalry from Chattanooga to attack Ambrose Burnside's Union force at Knoxville, Tennessee; Forrest attacked Union supply base at Johnsonville, Tennessee. **November 6:** Battle of Droop Mountain, West Virginia; Banks captured Brownsville, Texas. **November 7:** Battle of Rappahannock Station, Virginia. **November 10:** Forrest returned to Corinth, Mississippi, from his Johnsonville Raid. **November 16:** Battle of Campbell's Station, Tennessee. **November 17:** Union forces reached New Iberia, Louisiana, ending the Texas Overland Expedition. **November 19:** Lincoln gave the Gettysburg Address. **November 23:**

Union forces captured Orchard Knob, outside Chattanooga. **November 24:** Battle of Lookout Mountain, Tennessee. **November 25:** Grant forced Bragg to withdraw from Chattanooga by winning the Battle of Missionary Ridge, Tennessee. **November 26:** Mine Run Campaign began in Virginia when Meade advanced to turn Lee's right flank; Bragg retreated to Ringgold, Georgia. **November 27:** Lee blocked Meade's maneuver at Mine Run, resulting in the Battle of Payne's Farm; John Hunt Morgan escaped from the Ohio State Penitentiary; Battle of Ringgold Gap, Georgia. **November 29:** Battle of Fort Sanders, Tennessee. **November 29–30:** Lee and Meade skirmished at Mine Run. **November 30:** Davis accepted the resignation of Braxton Bragg as commander of the Army of Tennessee. **December 1:** This night, Meade abandoned the Mine Run entrenchment and retreated across the Rapidan River; **December 2:** Lee halted after a brief pursuit of Meade, ending the Mine Run Campaign; Bragg relinquished command of the Army of Tennessee to Lt. Gen. William H. Hardee. **December 4:** Longstreet abandoned his attempt to capture Knoxville, Tennessee, and retreated this night toward Rogersville, Tennessee, with Burnside in cautious pursuit. **December 8:** Lincoln issued the Proclamation of Amnesty and Reconstruction, which offered to pardon most Confederates who took an oath of allegiance, and set forth his Ten Percent Plan for Reconstruction. **December 11:** Union forces heavily bombarded Fort Sumter, South Carolina. **December 14:** Battle of Bean's Station, Tennessee, ended Knoxville Campaign. **December 16:** Joseph E. Johnston was put in command of the Army of Tennessee. **December 27:** Johnston arrived at Dalton, Georgia, to assume command of the Army of Tennessee. **December 29:** Battle of Mossy Creek, Tennessee.

1864   **January 2:** Dalton Conference was held in Georgia concerning the enlistment of slaves into the Confederate army. **January 11:** The 13th Amendment was proposed in the U.S. Senate to abolish slavery. **January 13:** Lincoln ordered Nathaniel P. Banks in Louisiana and Quincy A. Gillmore in Florida to help Unionist citizens organize loyal state governments. **January 17:** Battle of Dandridge, Tennessee. **January 19:** In Little Rock, Arkansas, a Unionist constitutional convention adopted a resolution abolishing slavery; Lincoln ordered Maj. Gen. Frederick Steele in Arkansas to hold immediate elections to establish a loyal government. **January 22:** Unionist Isaac Murphy was appointed provisional governor of Arkansas until elections could be held. **January 26–27:** Battle of Fair Gardens, Tennessee. **January 28–February 1:** Confederate Brig. Gen. Thomas Rosser's Moorefield, West Virginia, Raid occurred. **February 1:** Lincoln issued a call for 500,000 additional conscripts. **February 1–2:** Confederates under George E. Pickett raided New Bern, North Carolina. **February 2:** Pickett's Confederates captured and burned the USS *Underwriter*. **February 3:** Sherman began his Meridian Campaign in Mississippi. **February 5:** Sherman occupied Jackson, Mississippi. **February 6–7:** Battle of Morton's Ford, Virginia. **February 9:** 109 Union officers escaped from Libby Prison in Richmond, Virginia. **February 11:** Sooy Smith's Expedition left Colliersville, Tennessee, to join Sherman at Meridian, Mississippi. **February 13:** Battle of Middle Boggy, Indian Territory. **February 14:** Confederate Lt. Gen. Leonidas Polk evacuated Meridian, Mississippi, and Sherman occupied the town. **February 17:** Confederate Congress suspended the writ of habeas corpus in certain authorized arrests; the submarine CSS *H. L. Hunley* sank the USS *Housatonic* in Charleston harbor, but it also was lost. **February 20:** Sherman withdrew from Meridian and headed back to Vicksburg; Nathan Bedford Forrest's Confederate cavalry began skirmishing with Sooy Smith near West Point, Mississippi; Battle of Olustee, Florida. **February 21:** Forrest's cavalry stopped Sooy Smith's Expedition at West Point, Mississippi, and Smith began to withdraw. **February 22:** Battle of Okolona, Mississippi; "Pomeroy Circular" was circulated in Washington, D.C.; a Union force advanced on Joseph E. Johnston's Confederate position at Rocky Face Ridge near Dalton, Georgia. **February 24–25:** Battle of Tunnel Hill, Georgia. **February 26:** Sooy Smith's Expedition returned to Colliersville, Tennessee. **February 27:** The Confederate prison Camp Sumter, or Andersonville, Georgia, received its first prisoners. **February 28:** Kilpatrick-Dahlgren Raid began in Virginia. **February 29:** Kilpatrick and Dahlgren separated at Spotsylvania, Virginia, with Kilpatrick heading for Richmond, while Dahlgren rode for Goochland; U.S. Congress passed a bill reviving the rank of lieutenant general. **March 1:** Kilpatrick reached Richmond but withdrew after deciding it was too well defended to attack; Dahlgren reached the outskirts of Richmond and withdrew as well. **March 2:** Kilpatrick and Dahlgren continued their retreat, but Dahlgren was killed at Walkerton, and the Dahlgren Papers were discovered; the Senate confirmed Grant as lieutenant general. **March 4:** Kilpatrick returned to Union lines; Sherman reached Vicksburg after his Meridian Campaign. **March 9:** Grant was commissioned lieutenant general and joined the Army of the Potomac at Brandy Station, Virginia. **March 10:** Union Maj. Gen. Franz Sigel took command of the Army of West Virginia in the Shenandoah Valley; Union Maj. Gen. Andrew J. Smith left Vicksburg, Mississippi, with his division on David Porter's ships to join Nathaniel P. Banks in the Red River Campaign. **March 12:** Porter and Smith arrived at the mouth of the Red

River, near Simmesport, Louisiana, to begin the Red River Campaign; Sherman was given command of the Military Division of the Mississippi; Henry Halleck stepped down as Union general-in-chief and was made chief of staff. **March 14:** Smith captured Fort De Russy, Louisiana, on the Red River. **March 16:** Porter's fleet arrived at Alexandria, Louisiana. **March 17:** Grant assumed command of all Union forces and met with Sherman at Nashville, Tennessee, to plan a spring offensive. **March 18:** Loyal citizens held a convention in Arkansas that adopted a pro-Union constitution and abolished slavery. **March 21:** Battle of Henderson's Hill, Louisiana. **March 23:** Union forces under Frederick Steele left Little Rock, Arkansas, on the Camden Expedition. **March 24:** Nathan Bedford Forrest's Confederate cavalry captured Union City, Tennessee; Banks's Union army reached Alexandria, Louisiana. **March 25:** Forrest occupied Paducah, Kentucky. **March 26:** Forrest left Paducah and rode toward Fort Pillow, Tennessee; Union Maj. Gen. James McPherson took command of the Army of the Tennessee. **March 28:** Banks left Alexandria and marched for Natchitoches, Louisiana. **March 29:** Steele reached Arkadelphia, Arkansas. **April 2:** Banks's army reached Natchitoches, Louisiana. **April 3:** Porter's fleet left Alexandria and steamed toward Grand Ecore, Louisiana. **April 4:** Union Maj. Gen. Philip Sheridan was put in command of the Army of the Potomac's cavalry. **April 6:** Banks left Natchitoches and marched toward Shreveport, Louisiana; Unionist citizens met in New Orleans, Louisiana, and adopted a constitution that abolished slavery. **April 7:** Longstreet's Confederate corps rejoined the Army of Northern Virginia at Fredericksburg, Virginia, after detached duty in the west; Porter's fleet left Grand Ecore and steamed for Shreveport. **April 8:** Richard Taylor's Confederate army stopped Banks's invasion at the Battle of Mansfield, Louisiana; U.S. Senate passed the 13th Amendment. **April 9:** Battle of Pleasant Hill, Louisiana; this night Banks retreated toward Natchitoches; John Thayer's Union command joined Frederick Steele at Elkin's Ferry, Arkansas. **April 10–13:** Battle of Prairie D'Ane, Arkansas. **April 11:** Porter was forced to retire toward Natchitoches after Confederates blocked the Red River; a Unionist government was installed in Arkansas. **April 12:** Battle of Blair's Landing, Louisiana; Forrest's cavalry massacred black troops at the Battle of Fort Pillow, Tennessee. **April 14:** Much of Taylor's Confederate army was sent from Louisiana to Arkansas to stop Steele's Camden Expedition; part of Forrest's cavalry raided Paducah, Kentucky. **April 15:** Porter reunited with Banks at Grand Ecore, Louisiana; USS *Eastport* was damaged by a torpedo on the Red River; Steele occupied Camden, Arkansas. **April 17:** Grant severely restricted the exchanging of prisoners; CSS *Albemarle* was commissioned and participated in an attack on Plymouth, North Carolina, with Robert Hoke. **April 18:** Battle of Poison Spring, Arkansas. **April 19:** The CSS *Albemarle* rammed and sank the USS *Smithfield* and damaged another ship at Plymouth, North Carolina. **April 20:** Hoke's Confederates captured Plymouth. **April 21:** Banks and Porter left Grand Ecore, Louisiana, and began a retreat to Alexandria. **April 22:** The motto "In God We Trust" began appearing on U.S. coins. **April 23:** Battle of Monett's Ferry, Louisiana. **April 25:** Banks arrived at Alexandria, Louisiana; Battle of Marks' Mills, Arkansas. **April 26:** Porter's fleet began arriving at Alexandria; Union Lt. Col. Joseph Bailey recommended building Bailey's Dam to get Porter's fleet over the rapids; the USS *Eastport* was blown up when its crew was unable to keep it afloat; the USS *Cricket* was attacked on the Red River and lost over half of its crew, while the USS *Champion 3* had 200 men killed when its boiler exploded from a Confederate shell; Steele left Camden, Arkansas, this night when he learned of the Union defeats at Marks' Mills and Mansfield. **April 27:** Grant issued orders for the spring offensive, calling for simultaneous advances on all fronts. **April 28:** Union forces began a new bombardment of Fort Sumter, South Carolina. **April 30:** Battle of Jenkins' Ferry, Arkansas; Jefferson Davis's five-year-old son, Joe, was killed by an accidental fall from the president's house; Banks's army began building Bailey's Dam at Alexandria, Louisiana. **May 2:** Union Maj. Gen. Franz Sigel left Winchester, Virginia, for his raid into the Shenandoah Valley. **May 3:** Steele arrived at Little Rock, Arkansas, ending the Camden Expedition. **May 4:** Grant began the Overland Campaign in Virginia by crossing the Rapidan River into the area known as the Wilderness. **May 5:** Benjamin Butler began the Bermuda Hundred Campaign outside Petersburg, Virginia; Battle of Albemarle Sound, North Carolina. **May 5–6:** Battle of the Wilderness, Virginia; Confederate Lt. Gen. James Longstreet was seriously wounded on the second day. **May 6:** Butler entrenched at Bermuda Hundred, Virginia, and made a foray against the railroad at Port Walthall Junction. **May 7:** Grant withdrew from the Wilderness this night and headed for Spotsylvania to outflank Lee; Confederates repulsed Butler's attack at Port Walthall Junction; Sherman attacked Joseph E. Johnston's positions at Rocky Face Ridge, Georgia, beginning the Atlanta Campaign; James B. McPherson began his move toward Snake Creek Gap, Georgia, on a turning movement against Johnston. **May 8:** Battle of Spotsylvania, Virginia, began as Confederates arrived there first and held the crossroad in heavy fighting; Sherman continued pressuring Johnston at Rocky Face Ridge. **May 9:** At Spotsylvania, Union Maj. Gen. John Sedgwick was killed by a sharpshooter; Philip Sheridan's Union cavalry left

Spotsylvania on Sheridan's Richmond Raid to draw J. E. B. Stuart into battle; Butler continued to advance against the railroad outside Petersburg and engaged in the Battles of Swift Creek and Fort Clifton, Virginia; P. G. T. Beauregard arrived at Petersburg with Confederate reinforcements; Battle of Cloyd's Mountain, Virginia; Union probes continued at Rocky Face Ridge, Georgia, but McPherson outflanked the Confederates at Snake Creek Gap; Porter's fleet began passing through Bailey's Dam at Alexandria, Louisiana. **May 10:** Union Col. Emory Upton led an attack that briefly broke Lee's Spotsylvania line at a salient known as the Mule Shoe; Sheridan destroyed Confederate railroad cars and supplies at Beaver Dam Station; Battles of Chester Station and Cove Mountain, Virginia; McPherson failed to seize Resaca, Georgia, and retreated back into Snake Creek Gap. **May 11:** Stuart was mortally wounded at Yellow Tavern, Virginia; Grant wired Lincoln that he proposed fighting it out on the Virginia line if it took all summer; Sherman began moving his armies from Rocky Face Ridge to Snake Creek Gap; Porter continued through Bailey's Dam. **May 12:** Grant launched a massive attack against Spotsylvania's Mule Shoe that led to vicious fighting at the "Bloody Angle"; Stuart died from the wound he received the previous day; Butler began an advance against Drewry's Bluff, Virginia; Johnston evacuated Dalton, Georgia, this night and retreated to Resaca. **May 13:** John C. Breckinridge's Confederates engaged Franz Sigel north of New Market, Virginia; Sherman moved through Snake Creek Gap and skirmished with Johnston around Resaca; Porter's fleet completed passage through Bailey's Dam; Banks retreated from Alexandria, Louisiana, and the city was burned. **May 14:** Sheridan's cavalry reached Butler at Bermuda Hundred; Sherman unsuccessfully attacked Johnston at Resaca. **May 15:** Battle of New Market, Virginia; Sherman continued to attack unsuccessfully at Resaca but laid pontoon bridges across the Oostanaula River below town, forcing Johnston to retreat this night. **May 16:** Second Battle of Drewry's Bluff, Virginia. **May 17:** Butler reached Bermuda Hundred and was bottled up there by Beauregard; Battle of Adairsville, Georgia; Banks reached the Atchafalaya River in Louisiana. **May 18:** Battle of Yellow Bayou, Louisiana; Gold Hoax occurred. **May 19:** At Spotsylvania, Richard S. Ewell attacked Grant's right flank at the Harris Farm; subordinates failed to carry out Johnston's planned counterattack at Cassville, Georgia; Johnston retreated this night toward Allatoona. **May 19–20:** Banks crossed the Atchafalaya River, ending the Red River Campaign. **May 20:** Battle of Ware Bottom Church, Virginia; Grant began disengaging from Spotsylvania to make another flanking march to the southeast. **May 21:** Lee withdrew from Spotsylvania to match Grant's march; Union

Maj. Gen. David Hunter replaced Franz Sigel in command of the Shenandoah Valley. **May 22:** Lee's army blocked Grant at the North Anna River and entrenched. **May 23:** Sherman crossed the Etowah River and marched toward Marietta, Georgia, by way of Dallas, turning Johnston out of his position at Allatoona Pass. **May 23–25:** Grant and Lee skirmished along the North Anna River. **May 24:** Battle of Wilson's Wharf, Virginia; Sheridan rejoined the Army of the Potomac after his raid; Johnston retreated from Allatoona, Georgia, and moved toward Dallas to confront Sherman. **May 25–27:** Battle of New Hope Church, Georgia. **May 26:** Grant withdrew from the North Anna River and began another attempt to turn Lee's right flank; Union Maj. Gen. David Hunter began his Shenandoah Valley Campaign; Lincoln issued a second amnesty proclamation offering pardons to Southern civilians. **May 27:** Battle of Pickett's Mill, Georgia. **May 28:** In Virginia, Grant crossed the Pamunkey River, while Lee moved to intercept him; Battle of Haw's Shop, Virginia; Battle of Dallas, Georgia. **May 28–31:** Battle of Totopotomoy Creek, Virginia. **May 30:** Confederate cavalryman John Hunt Morgan began a raid to Cynthiana, Kentucky. **May 31:** Sheridan's cavalry seized Old Cold Harbor, Virginia. **June 1:** Battle of Cold Harbor began; George Stoneman's Union cavalry captured Allatoona Pass, Georgia; Sherman shifted his armies to the east to threaten Johnston's right flank. **June 2:** Lee and Grant consolidated their positions at Cold Harbor; Union Brig. Gen. Samuel Sturgis left Memphis, Tennessee, to engage Nathan Bedford Forrest in northern Mississippi. **June 3:** At Cold Harbor, Grant ordered an ill-advised attack on Lee that cost him 7,000 men. **June 4:** Sherman concentrated Allatoona Pass, Georgia, and Johnston withdrew from the Dallas-New Hope Church area and retreated east to a line along Lost and Brushy Mountains. **June 5:** Battle of Piedmont, Virginia; Union forces under Andrew J. Smith left La Grange, Tennessee, to engage Forrest. **June 6:** Hunter occupied Staunton, Virginia; Lincoln's National Union Party began its convention in Baltimore, Maryland; Battle of Ditch Bayou, Arkansas. **June 7:** A truce was agreed to at Cold Harbor, allowing Grant to recover his wounded, most of whom had died; Sheridan began his Trevilian Station Raid to join Hunter; Sturgis reached Ripley, Mississippi. **June 8:** Morgan seized Mount Sterling, Kentucky, and robbed its bank; National Union Party nominated Lincoln, with Andrew Johnson as his running mate. **June 9:** Butler made an unsuccessful attack on Petersburg, Virginia; Sherman advanced against the Confederates on Lost and Brushy Mountains in Georgia. **June 10:** After repairing the railroad, Sherman resumed his advance toward Atlanta, Georgia; Forrest defeated Sturgis at the Battle of Brice's Crossroads, Mississippi; Morgan's troopers raided Lexington,

Kentucky. **June 11:** Hunter reached Staunton; Morgan's raiders occupied Cynthiana, Kentucky; the CSS *Alabama* entered Cherbourg, France. **June 11–12:** Battle of Trevilian Station, Virginia; Battle of Cynthiana, Kentucky. **June 12:** Grant withdrew from Cold Harbor and marched for Petersburg; Sheridan rode to rejoin Grant rather than link up with Hunter; Morgan retreated toward Virginia; Hunter burned the Virginia Military Institute in Staunton. **June 13:** Lee sent Jubal Early's corps from Cold Harbor to reinforce Lynchburg, Virginia. **June 14:** The Army of the Potomac crossed the James River, and Grant joined Butler near Petersburg with reinforcements; unaware of Grant's whereabouts, Lee shifted his army to Richmond; Confederate Lt. Gen. Leonidas Polk was killed at Pine Mountain, Georgia; this night, Johnston abandoned Pine Mountain and consolidated his position on Lost and Brushy Mountains. **June 15:** With a much smaller force, Beauregard repulsed attacks by Grant against Petersburg; Sherman unsuccessfully attacked Johnston at Gilgal Church; Sturgis retreated from Tupelo, Mississippi. **June 16:** Grant renewed his attacks against Petersburg, with only limited success; Sherman attacked Johnston and advanced toward Lost Mountain, causing Johnston to retreat that night. **June 17:** Fighting continued at Petersburg; finally realizing the location of Grant's army, Lee sent his army to join Beauregard. **June 17–18:** Battle of Lynchburg, Virginia, with Early arriving on the second day. **June 18:** Lee's army began arriving at Petersburg as Grant again unsuccessfully attacked there; Hunter began retreating this night from Lynchburg, ending his Shenandoah Valley Campaign. **June 19:** Early pursued Hunter in the Shenandoah Valley; before daylight, Johnston withdrew to Kennesaw Mountain, Georgia; the CSS *Alabama* was sunk by the USS *Kearsarge* off Cherbourg, France. **June 20:** John Hunt Morgan reached Abingdon, Virginia, ending his Kentucky Raid. **June 21:** Lincoln visited Grant at Petersburg; Andrew J. Smith returned to La Grange, Tennessee. **June 21–23:** Battle of Jerusalem Plank Road, Virginia. **June 22:** Union forces began moving against Virginia's Weldon Railroad. Wilson-Kautz Raid began in Virginia; Battle of Kolb's Farm, Georgia. **June 23:** Wilson and Kautz destroyed the railroad at Burkeville, Virginia; Federals secured a foothold on the Jerusalem Plank Road near Petersburg. **June 24:** Battle of Samaria Church, Virginia. **June 25:** Soldiers under Union Maj. Gen. Ambrose Burnside began digging a mine under the Confederate defenses at Petersburg; Battle of Staunton River Bridge, Virginia. **June 27:** Battle of Kennesaw Mountain, Georgia. **June 28:** Sheridan rejoined Grant after his Trevilian Station Raid. **June 29:** U.S. Secretary of the Treasury Salmon Chase offered his resignation. **June 30:** Early reached New Market, Virginia, as he moved down the Shenandoah Valley to begin his Washington Raid; Lincoln accepted Chase's resignation. **July 1:** Wilson returned to Union lines, ending the Wilson-Kautz Raid. **July 2:** Johnston retreated from Kennesaw Mountain to the north side of the Chattahoochee River; U.S. Congress passed the Wade-Davis Bill. **July 4:** Early occupied Harpers Ferry, West Virginia; Johnston retreated to the Chattahoochee River in Georgia; Lincoln pocket vetoed the Wade-Davis Bill. **July 5:** Early crossed the Potomac River into Maryland; Sherman began moving against Johnston's flanks at the Chattahoochee River; Union forces under Maj. Gen. Andrew J. Smith left La Grange, Tennessee, in a move against Nathan Bedford Forrest's Confederate cavalry; Lincoln proclaimed martial law in Kentucky and suspended the writ of habeas corpus there. **July 6:** Early occupied Hagerstown, Maryland, and demanded $20,000 from its citizens. **July 8:** Sherman began crossing the Chattahoochee River upstream to threaten Johnston's right rear. **July 9:** Battle of the Monocacy, Maryland; Early occupied Frederick, Maryland, and demanded $200,000 from its citizens; Johnston began retreating across the Chattahoochee River this night; Union Maj. Gen. Lowell Rousseau's Alabama Raid began from Decatur, Alabama, against the Montgomery & West Point Railroad. **July 10:** Early advanced on Washington, D.C.; Johnston retreated across the Chattahoochee River. **July 11:** Early reached the outskirts of Washington, D.C., skirmishing with Union troops at Fort Stevens; Lincoln visited Fort Stevens during the skirmishing; Union reinforcements from the VI Corps in Virginia began arriving in Washington, D.C.; Smith reached Pontotoc, Mississippi. **July 12:** Early withdrew from the Washington area. **July 13:** Smith reached Tupelo, Mississippi. **July 14:** Early recrossed the Potomac River into Virginia; Battle of Tupelo, Mississippi. **July 15:** Smith began a retreat from Tupelo. **July 16:** Sherman's main force crossed the Chattahoochee River. **July 17:** Jefferson Davis relieved Johnston from command of the Army of Tennessee and replaced him with John Bell Hood; Major General Lovell H. Rousseau destroyed the Montgomery & West Point Railroad at Opelika, Alabama. **July 17–18:** Battle of Cool Spring, Virginia. **July 19:** Early continued a fighting retreat through Berryville, Virginia, and moved toward Strasburg. **July 20:** Battle of Rutherford's Farm, Virginia; Battle of Peachtree Creek, Georgia. **July 21:** Smith reached La Grange, Tennessee; Battle of Leggett's Hill, Georgia. **July 22:** Union Maj. Gen. James McPherson was killed in the Battle of Atlanta. **July 24:** Union Brig. Gen. George Crook was defeated at the Battle of Kernstown, Virginia. **July 25:** Early pursued the retreating Federals from Kernstown. **July 27:** Crook reached Harpers Ferry, West Virginia; Oliver O. Howard assumed command of the Union Army of the Tennessee. **July 27–29:** First Battle of Deep Bottom,

Virginia. **July 27–31:** George Stoneman and Edward McCook's Raid occurred in Georgia. **July 28:** Battle of Ezra Church, Georgia. **July 29:** Jubal A. Early crossed the Potomac River into Maryland, with his cavalry reaching Pennsylvania. **July 30:** Battle of the Crater, Virginia; Early's men burned Chambersburg, Pennsylvania, after its citizens failed to pay a $500,000 ransom; at Macon, Georgia, Confederates defeated and captured Union cavalryman George Stoneman; at Newman, Georgia, Confederates also defeated Edward McCook. **August 3:** Union forces landed on Dauphin Island to attack Fort Gaines, Alabama; Battle of Jug Tavern, Georgia. **August 4–7:** Federals attacked Fort Gaines, Alabama. **August 5:** Battle of Mobile Bay, Alabama; this night Confederates evacuated and destroyed Fort Powell, Alabama. **August 5–6:** Battle of Utoy Creek, Georgia. **August 6:** CSS *Tallahassee* escaped from Wilmington, North Carolina, and began raiding Union shipping. **August 7:** Philip Sheridan was put in command of the Middle Military Division to destroy the Shenandoah Valley and Jubal Early's Confederate army; Robert E. Lee sent two divisions under Richard H. Anderson to reinforce Early; Battle of Moorefield, West Virginia. **August 8:** Fort Gaines, Alabama, surrendered to Federals. **August 9:** Sherman began bombarding Atlanta, Georgia; Confederate agents caused a devastating explosion at Grant's supply base at City Point, Virginia; Federals began siege of Fort Morgan, Alabama. **August 10:** Sheridan left Harpers Ferry, West Virginia, to begin his Shenandoah Valley Campaign; Joseph Wheeler's Confederate cavalry began a raid from Covington, Georgia, against Sherman's supply line. **August 12:** CSS *Tallahassee* raided the coast of New York and New Jersey, capturing seven ships. **August 14:** Federals at Petersburg, Virginia, began another advance against the Weldon Railroad; Wheeler attacked Dalton, Georgia. **August 13–20:** Second Battle of Deep Bottom, Virginia. **August 15:** CSS *Tallahassee* captured six Union ships; Union reinforcements forced Wheeler to withdraw from Dalton and move into Tennessee. **August 16:** Battle of Guard Hill, Virginia; CSS *Tallahassee* captured five ships. **August 18:** Union cavalry under Judson Kilpatrick left Sandtown, Georgia, on a raid against Confederate railroad at Lovejoy's Station, Georgia. **August 18–21:** Battle of Globe Tavern, Virginia, occurred during the Union operation against the Weldon Railroad. **August 19:** Kilpatrick destroyed the Macon Railroad at Jonesboro, Georgia. **August 20:** Battle of Lovejoy's Station, Georgia. **August 21:** Battles of Summit Point and Cameron's Depot, Virginia; Confederate cavalry under Forrest raided Memphis, Tennessee; Federals bombarded Fort Morgan, Alabama. **August 23:** Union forces captured Fort Morgan, Alabama; Kilpatrick returned to Sherman, ending his raid. **August 24:** Union Maj. Gen.

Winfield S. Hancock advanced on Reams' Station, Virginia, and destroyed the railroad there. **August 25:** Battle of Reams' Station, Virginia; Sherman began moving his armies to the south side of Atlanta; CSS *Tallahassee* arrived at Wilmington, North Carolina. **August 27:** Sherman marched his armies south of Atlanta. **August 28:** Sherman's armies cut the Macon & Western Railroad south of Atlanta; Confederate Maj. Gen. Sterling Price left Camden, Arkansas, to begin Price's Missouri Raid. **August 28–29:** Battle of Smithfield Crossing, West Virginia. **August 29:** Democratic National Convention convened in Chicago, Illinois; Sherman cut the Atlanta & West Point Railroad south of Atlanta. **August 30:** Sherman cut one of the last railroads into Atlanta around Jonesboro, Georgia; Hood sent part of his army south to defend Jonesboro. **August 31:** George McClellan was nominated for president at the Democratic National Convention. **August 31–September 1:** Battle of Jonesboro, Georgia. **September 1:** Hood evacuated Atlanta this night. **September 2:** Union forces entered Atlanta, while Hood retreated to Lovejoy's Station. **September 3–4:** Battle of Berryville, Virginia. **September 4:** Confederate cavalryman John Hunt Morgan was killed at Greeneville, Tennessee; Union forces bombarded Fort Sumter, South Carolina. **September 5:** Unionist citizens in Louisiana ratified a state constitution abolishing slavery. **September 6:** Union forces bombarded Fort Sumter, South Carolina; Maryland voters approved a new constitution abolishing slavery. **September 8:** McClellan accepted the Democratic presidential nomination but repudiated the peace platform; Sherman ordered all civilians out of Atlanta, Georgia. **September 10:** Wheeler recrossed the Tennessee River at Tuscumbia, Alabama, ending his raid. **September 12:** Southern civilians began evacuating Atlanta, Georgia, in compliance with Sherman's orders. **September 14–17:** "Beefsteak Raid" in Virginia. **September 16:** Nathan Bedford Forrest began a raid from Verona, Mississippi, against Sherman's supply line in Alabama and Tennessee. **September 19:** Third Battle of Winchester, Virginia; Sterling Price entered Missouri on his Missouri Raid. **September 20:** Early retreated up the Shenandoah Valley after his defeat at Winchester. **September 21:** Early halted his retreat at Fisher's Hill. **September 22:** Battle of Fisher's Hill, Virginia. **September 23:** Early retreated toward New Market, Virginia. **September 26:** Forrest attacked Union forces near Pulaski, Tennessee. **September 26–28:** Battle of Pilot Knob, Missouri; Confederate guerrillas under William "Bloody Bill" Anderson raided Centralia, Missouri. **September 29:** Battle of New Market Heights, Virginia. **September 29–30:** Battle of Fort Harrison, Virginia. **September 30–October 2:** Battle of Peebles' Farm, Virginia. **October 1:** Union raiders under Stephen Burbridge reached Saltville, Virginia;

Confederate spy Rose O'Neal Greenhow drowned when her blockade-runner ran aground near Fort Fisher, North Carolina. **October 2:** Massacre at Saltville, Virginia; Beauregard was given command of the Confederate armies in the West; Wheeler destroyed a railroad bridge at Resaca, Georgia. **October 3:** George H. Thomas arrived in Nashville, Tennessee, to prepare its defense against Hood, who was moving north with the Army of Tennessee. **October 4:** Sherman arrived at Kennesaw Mountain, Georgia, in cautious pursuit of Hood. **October 5:** Battle of Allatoona Pass, Georgia. **October 6–8:** Sheridan retreated down the Shenandoah Valley from Harrisonburg, Virginia, destroying the Valley in "The Burning." **October 7:** Battle of Darbytown and New Market Heights, Virginia; CSS *Florida* was captured by the USS *Wachusett* at Bahia, Brazil. **October 8:** CSS *Shenandoah* made maiden voyage from London, England. **October 9:** Battle of Tom's Brook, Virginia; Price occupied Boonville, Missouri. **October 10:** Sheridan camped at Cedar Creek, Virginia. **October 12:** David D. Porter took command of the North Atlantic Blockading Squadron. **October 13:** John S. Mosby made his Greenback Raid; Battle of Darbytown Road, Virginia; Hood captured Union garrison at Dalton, Georgia; Maryland voters abolished slavery in that state. **October 14:** Hood marched for Gadsden, Alabama. **October 15:** Price's cavalry captured Glasgow and Sedalia, Missouri. **October 16:** Sheridan left Virginia to meet with Lincoln and Grant to plan strategy. **October 17:** Hood moved toward Gadsden, Alabama, planning to invade Tennessee and force Sherman out of Georgia. **October 19:** Battle of Cedar Creek, Virginia; Confederate agents raided St. Albans, Vermont; Nathan Bedford Forrest left Corinth, Mississippi, on a three-week raid into Tennessee; Battle of Lexington, Missouri. **October 20:** Lincoln issued a proclamation establishing Thanksgiving as a national holiday for feasting and thanking God for Union victories. **October 21:** Battle of Little Blue River, Missouri. **October 22:** Hood left Gadsden, Alabama, for Decatur, Alabama, to cross the Tennessee River; Second Battle of Independence, Missouri, and Battle of Big Blue River, Missouri. **October 23:** Battle of Westport, Missouri. **October 24:** Price began a retreat south along the Missouri-Kansas border. **October 25:** Battles of Mine Creek and Marais des Cygnes, Kansas. **October 26:** William "Bloody Bill" Anderson was killed near Richmond, Missouri. **October 26–28:** Hood skirmished around Decatur, Alabama, but was unable to cross the Tennessee River; Hood marched for Florence, Alabama. **October 27:** Battles of Burgess' Mill and Darbytown Road, Virginia. **October 28:** CSS *Albemarle* was sunk in the Roanoke River, North Carolina. **October 29:** Forrest captured a Union vessel on the Tennessee River. **October 30:** CSS *Olustee* left Wilmington,

North Carolina, to begin a cruise; Hood entered Tuscumbia and Florence, Alabama; Forrest captured three more Union vessels on the Tennessee River. **October 31:** Union naval forces captured Plymouth, North Carolina; Nevada was admitted as the 36th state. **November 3:** Forrest reached Johnsonville, Tennessee, and set up artillery on the Tennessee River. **November 4:** Forrest bombarded Johnsonville, destroying several Union boats. **November 6:** Confederate agents attempting to free prisoners at Camp Douglas were arrested in Chicago, Illinois. **November 8:** Lincoln defeated George B. McClellan for the presidency. **November 10:** Forrest returned to Corinth, ending his Johnsonville Raid. **November 11:** Union forces destroyed railroads and mills at Rome, Georgia. **November 11–14:** Battle of Bull's Gap, Tennessee. **November 13:** Sherman burned public and commercial buildings in Atlanta, Georgia, in preparation for abandoning the city. **November 15:** Sherman left Atlanta, Georgia, and began his March to the Sea. **November 16–21:** Hood crossed the Tennessee River near Tuscumbia, Alabama, and began the Franklin and Nashville Campaign. **November 17:** William J. Hardee was put in command of Confederate forces in Georgia. **November 21–22:** Battle of Griswoldville, Georgia. **November 22:** John M. Schofield withdrew his Union troops from Pulaski, Tennessee, and began racing Hood to Columbia; Sherman's troops captured the Confederate capital of Georgia at Milledgeville. **November 24:** Schofield reached Columbia, Tennessee; Sherman left Milledgeville, Georgia, with Kilpatrick riding toward Millen to destroy railroad track and free Union prisoners. **November 25:** Confederate agents set fires in a number of New York City hotels. **November 26:** Hood's main force arrived at Columbia, Tennessee. **November 27:** In Virginia, Union Gen. Benjamin Butler's headquarters ship was blown up in the James River apparently by Confederate agents. **November 28:** Hood occupied Columbia, Tennessee, and marched north to cut off Schofield from Nashville; Battle of Buck Head Creek, Georgia. **November 29:** Hood failed to block Schofield's escape in the Spring Hill Incident; Sand Creek Massacre, Colorado. **November 30:** Battle of Franklin, Tennessee; Battle of Honey Hill, South Carolina. **December 1:** Schofield reached Nashville, Tennessee. **December 2:** Hood reached Nashville and took up a position south of the city; Price reached Laynesport, Arkansas, after his unsuccessful Missouri Raid. **December 4:** Battle of Waynesborough, Georgia. **December 6:** Lincoln appointed Salmon Chase chief justice of the Supreme Court. **December 7:** Forrest and William Bate unsuccessfully attacked Murfreesboro, Tennessee, but did destroy some railroad track. **December 8:** Benjamin Butler left the Petersburg, Virginia, area to join an operation against Fort Fisher, North Carolina; ice storm paralyzed armies at

Nashville, Tennessee. **December 9:** Sherman arrived outside Savannah, Georgia. **December 10:** George Stoneman's Union cavalry left Knoxville, Tennessee, to begin a raid into southwest Virginia. **December 13:** Butler's Expedition against Fort Fisher, North Carolina, left Fort Monroe, Virginia; Sherman attacked and captured Fort McAllister near Savannah. **December 15–16:** Battle of Nashville, Tennessee. **December 16:** Hood retreated from Nashville. **December 16–18:** Battle of Marion, Virginia. **December 17:** Hood continued a fighting retreat toward Franklin, Tennessee; Sherman demanded the surrender of Savannah, Georgia. **December 18:** Union Adm. David Porter's fleet and Butler's Expedition arrived at Wilmington, North Carolina; Hood reached Columbia, Tennessee; at Savannah, Confederate Gen. William J. Hardee refused Sherman's surrender demand; Lincoln called for 300,000 more volunteers. **December 19:** Butler left Wilmington to secure more provisions and coal. **December 20:** Hardee evacuated Savannah. **December 20–21:** Second Battle of Saltville, Virginia. **December 21:** Sherman occupied Savannah. **December 22:** Sherman wired Lincoln to present him Savannah as a Christmas present. **December 24:** At Wilmington, Porter exploded a powder-laden ship near Fort Fisher in the predawn hours, but it failed to inflict any major damage; Porter bombarded the fort during the day; Butler arrived at sunset. **December 25:** Hood reached the Tennessee River near Florence, Alabama; Butler advanced against Fort Fisher and captured the outer works but withdrew after deciding the fort was too strong to assault. **December 26–27:** Hood ended the Franklin and Nashville Campaign when he crossed the Tennessee River. **December 27:** Butler canceled his Fort Fisher operation and returned to Fort Monroe, Virginia. **December 30:** Francis P. Blair wrote Jefferson Davis requesting a meeting to discuss peace.

1865   January 3: Sherman moved part of his force from Savannah, Georgia, to Beaufort, South Carolina. **January 4:** Union Brig. Gen. Alfred H. Terry's command left Bermuda Hundred, Virginia, to join David Porter for an attack on Fort Fisher, North Carolina. **January 7:** Benjamin Butler was relieved of command of the Army of the James and the Department of Virginia and North Carolina and was replaced by Maj. Gen. E. O. C. Ord; Confederate Maj. Gen. Thomas Rosser and his cavalry raided Beverly, West Virginia. **January 9:** Hood reached Tupelo, Mississippi, after his retreat from Nashville. **January 11:** Bosser raided Beverly and captured a large number of prisoners; Missouri abolished slavery in a constitutional convention. **January 12:** Francis P. Blair met with Jefferson Davis in Richmond on a peace mission; Porter's and Terry's forces arrived at Fort Fisher,

North Carolina. **January 13:** Porter's fleet began bombarding Fort Fisher, while Terry's infantry landed near the fort; Hood asked to be relieved as commander of the Army of Tennessee. **January 14:** Porter continued to bombard Fort Fisher. **January 15:** Terry's troops attacked and captured Fort Fisher. **January 16:** The Confederate Senate passed a resolution recommending that Davis appoint Robert E. Lee as general-in-chief; Union forces suffered heavy casualties at Fort Fisher when a powder magazine accidentally exploded; at Savannah, Georgia, Sherman ordered abandoned or confiscated land along the Georgia coast be set aside for the use of freedmen. **January 23:** Davis signed a law creating the position of general-in-chief; Confederate Lt. Gen. Richard Taylor assumed command of the Army of Tennessee. **January 25:** CSS *Shenandoah* arrived in Melbourne, Australia. **January 28:** Thomas Rosser's Moorefield, West Virginia, Raid began from New Market, Virginia; Jefferson Davis appointed three commissioners to discuss peace with Union authorities. **January 30:** Rosser captured a Union wagon train at Medley, West Virginia; elements of the Army of Tennessee arrived at Augusta, Georgia, to reinforce Hardee. **January 31:** Robert E. Lee was named general-in-chief of the Confederate armies; Rosser captured Petersburg, West Virginia; U.S. Congress passed the 13th Amendment. **February 1:** Rosser captured Patterson's Creek, West Virginia; Sherman left Savannah, Georgia, and began the Carolinas Campaign by advancing on Rivers' Bridge, South Carolina. **February 2:** Lincoln left Washington, D.C., to attend the Hampton Roads Conference. **February 2–3:** Battle of Rivers' Bridge, South Carolina. **February 3:** Lincoln and Secretary of State William Seward met with Confederate Vice President Alexander Stephens and two other delegates at the Hampton Roads Conference. **February 4:** Lincoln returned to Washington from the Hampton Roads Conference. **February 5–7:** Battle of Hatcher's Run, Virginia. **February 9:** Lee assumed the position of Confederate general-in-chief. **February 14:** After frequent skirmishing, Sherman crossed the Congaree River in South Carolina and marched for Columbia. **February 16:** Confederate Gen. P. G. T. Beauregard began evacuating Columbia, South Carolina, and Sherman entered the city; Union Maj. Gen. John Schofield advanced on Fort Anderson near Wilmington, North Carolina, while Porter bombarded the fort. **February 17:** During this night, fires broke out in Columbia and burned much of the city; Hardee began evacuating Charleston, South Carolina. **February 18:** The last Confederates evacuated Charleston, and the Federals occupied the city; Sherman's men began destroying Columbia's railroads and public property; CSS *Shenandoah* sailed from Melbourne, Australia. **February 18–19:** This night, Confederates abandoned Fort Anderson, North Carolina. **February 20:** Confederate Congress passed a law authorizing the enlistment of slaves into the army; Sherman left Columbia, South Carolina, and marched for Goldsboro, North Carolina. **February 21:** Confederates under Braxton Bragg evacuated Wilmington, North Carolina. **February 22:** Union forces occupied Wilmington, North Carolina; Confederate partisans captured Union Maj. Gen. George Crook in Maryland. **February 25:** Joseph E. Johnston assumed command of the Confederate Army of Tennessee. **February 27:** Union cavalry under Wesley Merritt began a raid into Virginia; Philip Sheridan left Winchester, Virginia, to begin Sheridan's Virginia Raid. **March 1:** Sheridan reached Staunton, Virginia. **March 2:** Lee sent a message to Grant proposing a meeting to discuss peace; Battle of Waynesboro, Virginia, ended Sheridan's Shenandoah Valley Campaign. **March 3:** Grant was ordered by Lincoln to meet with Lee only if Lee was surrendering the Army of Northern Virginia; Sheridan's cavalry occupied Charlottesville, Virginia; U.S. Congress established the Freedmen's Bureau. **March 4:** Grant informed Lee that there could be no meeting to discuss peace; Lincoln was sworn in for his second term as president. **March 6:** Joseph E. Johnston took command of all Confederate forces south of Petersburg, Virginia; Battle of Natural Bridge, Florida. **March 7:** Elements of the Army of Tennessee arrived at Kinston, North Carolina, to reinforce Joseph E. Johnston. **March 7–10:** Battle of Wyse Fork, North Carolina. **March 8:** Sherman entered North Carolina. **March 8–10:** Second Battle of Kinston, North Carolina. **March 10:** Battle of Monroe's Cross Roads, North Carolina; Bragg withdrew from Kinston and moved toward Goldsboro to join Johnston. **March 11:** Sherman occupied Fayetteville, North Carolina; Lincoln issued his second wartime amnesty proclamation to bring deserters and soldiers absent without leave back to their units. **March 13:** Davis signed into law the bill allowing the enlistment of slaves into the Confederate army. **March 15:** Sherman left Fayetteville, North Carolina, marching toward Averasboro. **March 16:** Battle of Averasboro, North Carolina; Hardee withdrew to Bentonville to join forces with Joseph E. Johnston. **March 17:** Union Maj. Gen. Edward R. Canby began the Mobile Campaign. **March 19–21:** Battle of Bentonville, North Carolina. **March 20:** George Stoneman's Union cavalry left Jonesboro, Tennessee, on a raid into North Carolina. **March 22:** James Wilson's Selma, Alabama, Raid began from Gravelly Springs, Alabama. **March 23:** Sherman joined forces with John Schofield at Goldsboro, North Carolina. **March 24:** Lincoln joined Grant at Fort Monroe, Virginia, for a conference. **March 25:** Battle of Fort Stedman, Virginia. **March 27:** Lincoln met with Grant, Sherman, and Porter at City

Point, Virginia; Union forces began siege of Spanish Fort, Alabama. **March 28:** Sheridan's cavalry joined Grant near Petersburg, ending Sheridan's Virginia Raid. **March 29:** Sheridan began moving around Lee's right flank near Five Forks to force the Confederates from Petersburg, Virginia; Battles of Lewis's Farm and Quaker Road, Virginia. **March 30:** Fighting erupted around Dinwiddie Court House, Hatcher's Run, and Gravelly Run, Virginia; Wilson occupied Elyton (Birmingham), Alabama. **March 31:** Battles of Dinwiddie Court House and White Oak Road, Virginia. **April 1:** Battle of Five Forks, Virginia; Battle of Ebenezer Church, Alabama. **April 2:** A general Union assault against Fort Gregg, Sutherland Station, and other Confederate defenses at Petersburg killed Confederate Lt. Gen. A. P. Hill; Lee informed Jefferson Davis of the necessity of evacuating Petersburg and Richmond, forcing the Confederate government to flee this night; Lee began evacuating the two cities and started the Appomattox Campaign; Battle of Selma, Alabama; Canby began siege of Fort Blakely, Alabama. **April 3:** Davis and the Confederate cabinet arrived in Danville, Virginia; Union forces occupied Richmond and Petersburg. **April 4:** Lincoln toured Richmond, Virginia; Lee retreated west; Sheridan cut off Lee's escape route to the south at Jetersville, Virginia. **April 5:** Lee retreated toward Farmville, Virginia; Battle of Amelia Springs, Virginia. **April 6:** Battles of Sailor's Creek and Rice's Station, Virginia; Lee reached Farmville. **April 6–7:** Battle of High Bridge, Virginia. **April 7:** Grant asked Lee to surrender, and Lee refused but asked about terms; Battle of Cumberland Church, Virginia. **April 8:** Lincoln returned to Washington, D.C., from Richmond; Sheridan blocked Lee's retreat at Appomattox Court House, Virginia, and captured a Confederate wagon train; Canby attacked Spanish Fort, Alabama, and the Confederates evacuated the fort this night. **April 9:** After failing to cut his way out of the encirclement, Lee met with Grant at Appomattox Court House and agreed to surrender the Army of Northern Virginia; Canby attacked and captured Fort Blakely, Alabama; Wilson left Selma, Alabama, and headed for Montgomery. **April 10:** Lee issued his Farewell Address to the Army of Northern Virginia; Davis and his cabinet left Danville, Virginia, and headed for Greensboro, North Carolina. **April 11:** Davis arrived at Greensboro, North Carolina. **April 12:** Army of Northern Virginia was formally surrendered at Appomattox Court House, Virginia; Sherman approached Raleigh, North Carolina; Confederates evacuated Mobile, Alabama, and Union forces occupied the city; Wilson's cavalry occupied Montgomery, Alabama. **April 13:** Sherman occupied Raleigh, North Carolina. **April 14:** This night, John Wilkes Booth mortally wounded Lincoln in Ford's Theater, Washington, D.C.; Lewis Payne attacked and wounded Secretary of State William Seward; Johnston contacted Sherman near Raleigh to request a truce until peace could be established; Robert Anderson raised the Union flag over Fort Sumter, South Carolina; CSS *Shenandoah* sailed from the East Caroline Islands on a raid against Union Pacific whalers. **April 15:** Lincoln died in Washington, and Andrew Johnson was sworn in as president. **April 16:** Wilson's cavalry occupied Columbus and West Point, Georgia. **April 17:** Sherman and Johnston met near Durham Station; North Carolina, to discuss Johnston's surrender. **April 18:** Johnston surrendered to Sherman at Bennett's Farm, near Durham Station; Davis reached Charlotte, North Carolina. **April 19:** Lincoln's funeral was held in the White House. **April 20:** Wilson's cavalry captured Macon, Georgia, ending his Selma Raid. **April 21:** Lincoln's body was put aboard a train for transport back to Springfield, Illinois; John Mosby disbanded his partisan force in Northern Virginia; Wilson occupied Macon, Georgia. **April 22:** Booth and David Herold crossed the Potomac River near Port Tobacco, Maryland, and entered Virginia; Wilson's cavalry occupied Talladega, Alabama. **April 24:** Grant met with Sherman in Raleigh, North Carolina, and told him the government had rejected his peace terms with Johnston. **April 25:** Sherman and Johnston met again to negotiate Johnston's surrender. **April 26:** In Virginia, either Union cavalry killed Booth or he committed suicide, and Herold was captured; Johnston surrendered to Sherman on the same terms as Lee received. **April 27:** The steamboat *Sultana* exploded and sank in the Mississippi River killing hundreds of Union soldiers. **April 30:** Canby and Confederate Lt. Gen. Richard Taylor conferred near Mobile, Alabama, and arranged a truce until a Confederate surrender could be arranged in Alabama and Mississippi. **May 2:** Johnson offered a $100,000 reward for the capture of Jefferson Davis. **May 3:** Lincoln's body arrived in Springfield, Illinois; surrender ceremony was held for Johnston's army. **May 4:** Taylor surrendered to Canby all Confederates in Alabama, Mississippi, and East Louisiana; Lincoln was buried in Springfield. **May 5:** Slavery was officially abolished in the U.S. when Connecticut ratified the 13th Amendment. **May 8:** Taylor's Confederates were paroled and allowed to return home. **May 9:** Nathan Bedford Forrest disbanded his Confederate cavalry. **May 10:** Union cavalry captured Davis and his entourage near Irwinville, Georgia; Confederate guerrilla William Quantrill was mortally wounded near Taylorsville, Kentucky. **May 11:** M. Jeff Thompson surrendered his Confederates at Chalk Bluffs, Arkansas. **May 12–13:** Last battle of the war was fought at Palmito Ranch, Texas. **May 19:** Confederate raider CSS *Stonewall* surrendered at Havana, Cuba. **May 21:** CSS *Shenandoah* entered the Sea of Okhotsk to raid Union whalers. **May 22:** Davis arrived at Fort Monroe, Virginia, and was put in prison. **May 23–24:** The Grand Review was held in Washington, D.C., and the Army of the Potomac was disbanded on May 23. **May 26:** At New Orleans, Louisiana, Lt. Gen. Simon Buckner arranged the surrender of the Confederates in the Trans-Mississippi Department. **May 27:** Andrew Johnson ordered the release of most military and political prisoners. **May 29:** Johnson issued a general amnesty to most men who served in or cooperated with the Confederacy on the condition they take an oath of allegiance. **June 2:** Confederate Gen. Edmund Kirby Smith approved the terms of surrender of his Trans-Mississippi Department at Galveston, Texas. **June 6:** Quantrill died in Louisville, Kentucky, from wounds received on May 10. **June 22:** CSS *Shenandoah* captured two ships in the Bering Sea. **June 23:** In Indian Territory, Stand Watie surrendered the last major Confederate force; Johnson ended the blockade against Southern ports. **June 26:** CSS *Shenandoah* captured six whaling ships in the Bering Sea. **June 28:** CSS *Shenandoah* captured 11 more ships. **June 30:** Eight of Booth's coconspirators were found guilty in Lincoln's assassination. **July 7:** Four convicted Booth conspirators, including Mary Surratt, were hanged in Washington, D.C. **August 1:** Union Army of the Tennessee was disbanded. **August 2:** CSS *Shenandoah*, cruising the Bering Sea, learned the war was over. **November 6:** CSS *Shenandoah* surrendered to British authorities at Liverpool, England.

Introduction

COMING OF THE CIVIL WAR

It has been said that if the United States were an individual, the Civil War would have been the great traumatic event of its adolescence that haunted its adulthood. Much of the nation's history over the last 137 years has been affected by the war, and the American people still are struggling with its aftermath. The Civil War was arguably the greatest single event in American history.

Numerous books have been written about the causes of the Civil War, and it still is a much-debated topic. Whether or not the war was inevitable is also disputed, but it is a fact that from the founding of the first successful English colony at Jamestown, Virginia, in 1607, the nation's southern and northern sections developed differently, thus creating separate economies, labor systems, and political philosophies that made conflict more likely. Because of its fertile soil and warm climate, the South created an almost exclusively agricultural economy, while Northern colonies were colder, with less-fertile soil, and were forced to develop a more diverse economy. Southerners needed an abundant, stable labor supply to work the plantations and at first depended on white indentured servants. But this system broke down by the late 17th century, and the planters turned to African slaves. Although slavery also existed in the North and it was Northern traders who supplied most of the slaves to the South, the North did not need large numbers of slaves since its economy was not as labor intensive. Instead, it developed a system based on wages, or free labor (as opposed to slave labor), as it came to be called. Also, in the North there were more religious sects, such as Quakers, who viewed slavery as a sin and were able to turn public opinion against it. These abolitionists were always a minority, but they were vocal, well financed, and often held important political and social positions that allowed them to act as the conscience of the people.

As the nation spread westward and better agricultural land was found in the North, a majority of the people there (later known as Free-Soilers) became

1

more opposed to slavery. Like most white Americans at the time, they believed in white supremacy and generally did not think of slavery in terms of it being immoral and did not oppose slavery in the South. They did fear that their wage labor system and small farms could not compete with slavery and thus did not want it to spread outside the South. The image of slavery moving into new territories and Southern planters taking over the best farmland became a nightmare for most Free-Soilers.

Thus the spread of slavery became the most important political issue in the antebellum United States, but it was not the only issue. The sections also bitterly argued over tariffs, particularly protective tariffs. A protective tariff was a high tax placed on imported goods to make them more expensive and thus protect American industrial jobs by encouraging consumers to buy domestic products. Since most of the nation's industry was located above the Mason-Dixon Line, Northerners generally supported protective tariffs. Southerners had few industrial jobs to protect, yet they were consumers of foreign-made products. Protective tariffs provided little benefit to them, generally made goods more expensive, and were seen as discriminatory because they forced the South to pay for the protection of Northern jobs. Also, European nations retaliated by placing high tariffs on American exports, which, for the most part, were Southern agricultural products.

Homesteading, or the practice of gaining free land from the government by living on it and making improvements over a certain number of years, later became another divisive issue. Northerners supported homesteading because the expansive and unsettled Great Plains lay due west, directly in the path of their migration route. Southerners feared homesteading because it could lead to Northerners gaining a population majority in the western territories. The Free-Soil faction could then create antislavery governments and upset the precarious balance of power between free and slave states in the U.S. Senate when they were admitted to the Union.

At the heart of the slavery and tariff issues was the constitutional debate of states rights versus federal power. It is difficult in the 21st century to understand the importance that antebellum Americans placed on state power and state identity. Today, most Americans think of themselves as being first and foremost citizens of the United States and then residents of the states in which they live. In antebellum days, however, it was the reverse. States rights was closely associated with having a strict constructionist's view of the Constitution, that is, believing that federal government authority was limited to those areas that the Constitution specifically granted to it. The individual states, being sovereign entities, reserved all other powers. This philosophy could be traced back to the beginning of the republic. Under the Articles of Confederation, for example, the states reserved the right to print money and had the sole right to tax. When the Constitution was ratified in 1787, the federal government took on these powers, but the Bill of Rights (adopted in 1791) included the 10th Amendment, which reserved for the states those powers not delegated to the federal government. This gave the state governments authority over such things as citizenship, voting rights, and slavery within a state's borders. James Madison and Thomas Jefferson argued in the Virginia and Kentucky Resolutions, respectively, that the Union was a "compact," or partnership, that was created by the 13 original states, with the states being the principals, the federal government their agent, and the Constitution the contract binding them together. States rights philosophy stated that as the principals, the individual states had the right to judge for themselves if the compact was being violated by the national government, and, therefore, could decide for themselves the constitutionality of federal laws and "nullify" them if need be. It is important to note that while Madison and Jefferson supported this theory of nullification, they did not advocate secession. Their writings, however, were used by those who did.

Most Americans at the end of the 18th century adhered to some form of states rights philosophy, but in the 19th century it was the Southerners who took it to heart. The industrialized Northern states came to see the advantage of a powerful national government that could pass protective tariffs, regulate overseas trade, contain the spread of slavery, and use tax revenues to build roads, canals, railroads, and other internal improvements to facilitate commerce. Southerners realized that as the North gained in population and states, it eventually would dominate the federal government and could force its will on the South. States rights came to be seen as the only way the South could protect its minority rights from a tyrannical majority. This states rights philosophy caused many Southern politicians to oppose internal improvements because that was seen as the domain of state governments, even though the undeveloped South would benefit most from such federally funded projects.

A fundamental aspect of states rights consisted of the constitutional questions of nullification and secession, which Vice President John C. Calhoun popularized in his "South Carolina Exposition and Protest," a pamphlet written in protest to the Tariff of 1828. Expanding on Madison's and Jefferson's Virginia and Kentucky Resolutions, Calhoun argued that the people of each state had the right to decide for themselves which federal laws were constitutional. If a state decided to "nullify" a federal law, Congress would be forced to secure an amendment to make it constitutional. If Congress so acted, Calhoun believed the state then could decide either to obey the law or pass an ordinance of secession. Although, he saw secession as the ultimate states right, Calhoun did not advocate its use. He was actually trying save the Union by keeping the federal government within its prescribed limits and make secession unnecessary. Madison, who was still alive when Calhoun wrote his "Exposition and Protest," also opposed the idea of secession.

Although not widely accepted at first, the philosophy of secession actually had been debated for some time. To protect its diminishing political influence and economy, the New England states threatened it twice in response to the Louisiana Purchase and the War of 1812. It was the South, however, that came to embrace secession. States rights philosophy argued that the Union was a confederation of individual states that had voluntarily joined an association where the national government was given only certain limited powers. The people were sovereign and held ultimate power, and the state government was the people's sole representative government. This, fundamentally, was the original Union created during the Revolutionary War, when the term *united states* was used more as a description than a proper name. Southerners, therefore, viewed themselves as keeping alive the original intent of the Founding Fathers. They also believed that a state had the right to leave, or secede from, the Union any time it felt its sovereignty was threatened. Most Northerners agreed that the people were sovereign but did not believe that state governments were their sole representatives. They viewed the Union as indivisible and the national government as the superior government, with a state government accepting a subservient position when it was admitted to the Union. Northerners argued that the Founding Fathers would never have envisioned a Union where each state could arbitrarily leap in and out at will. To do so would be unthinkable, since some states likely would secede every time their political party or presidential candidate lost an election. Secession, therefore, was unconstitutional, and it would mean the destruction of the nation. What made this debate so acrimonious was that the Founding Fathers did not address secession when they wrote the Constitution; without a definitive guide on the subject, the sections became polarized around their own interpretation of what the Founding Fathers intended. In short, both sides believed they were protecting the intent of the Founders and were the true torchbearers of liberty and freedom.

One of the most serious incidents of the antebellum period involving these philosophies occurred in 1832 when South Carolina voted to nullify the 1832 tariff and created the Nullification Crisis. Tension rose as President Andrew Jackson had Congress pass the Force Act, authorizing him to use the military to enforce the tariff. Neither side wanted war, and South

Carolina and the federal government accepted a compromise tariff proposed by Henry Clay that provided for a declining tariff rate over a number of years. South Carolina rescinded its nullification act but defiantly voted to nullify the Force Act. Thus civil war was avoided, but radical Southerners—who came to be known as fire-eaters—still maintained that they had the right to nullify unconstitutional laws, and secession became more and more an acceptable solution to the South's growing political problems.

Ultimately, the Civil War was fought over constitutional rights, but the argument over what those rights entailed almost always revolved around the spread of slavery. Until 1818, this issue was never very volatile because there was an uneasy balance of power in the U.S. Senate between the slave and free states, and thus neither section could force its will on the other. When Missouri petitioned to be admitted as a slave state in 1818, this balance of power was threatened, and a bitter political battle ensued. The 1820 Missouri Compromise settled the issue temporarily and led to a shaky truce by admitting Maine as a free state and Missouri as a slave state to maintain the balance of power and by partitioning the Louisiana Purchase at 36°30' N and agreeing that future territories north of this Missouri Compromise Line would be free and those south of it would be slave. In spite of the compromise, such abolitionists as William Lloyd Garrison kept pressure on slavery afterward, and Congress was so flooded with antislavery petitions that in 1836 a gag rule was adopted to prevent the slavery debate from tying up congressional sessions.

It was not until the 1846–48 Mexican War that the slavery issue exploded again. From the war's beginning, Americans were confident of victory and expected to gain California and the American Southwest. By that time, Southern agricultural lands were becoming exhausted and world competition more threatening, and many planters were facing an uncertain financial future. They saw the West as an area of opportunity, either by moving there themselves to start new plantations or by making a profit by selling slaves to other planters who moved there.

Such Northerners as the Free-Soilers bitterly opposed the westward spread of slavery because it would threaten their plans to move west to establish homesteads, family farms, and wage labor. They looked to Congress to make the West safe for free labor, relying on Article 4 of the Constitution, which gave Congress the power to "make all needful rules and regulations respecting the territory or other property belonging to the United States." Southerners who supported the spread of slavery claimed that the 5th Amendment's "due process" clause guaranteed a citizen his property rights and that Congress could no more interfere with a slave owner's right to take his slaves to a territory than it could prevent a Northerner from taking his livestock. Since both sides recognized that states had the right to prohibit slavery, the crucial point was whether slave owners would be given the opportunity to populate a territory before it achieved statehood and thus have a chance to affect its decision.

In 1846, Pennsylvania congressman David Wilmot introduced the Wilmot Proviso, banning slavery in any territory the United States might win in the Mexican War. Most Northerners saw the bill as a way to ensure that slavery would not spread out of the South, while most Southerners bitterly opposed it because they believed it denied them the spoils of war and violated their constitutional rights. With a majority in the House of Representatives, Northerners could pass the proviso there, but it always failed in the Senate, where a balance of power was maintained. The acrimonious debate over the proviso helped lead to sectional polarization, caused many Southerners to think more about secession, and helped create the Free-Soil Party.

Soon after the Mexican War ended, the slavery debate was aggravated by a series of political problems: California petitioned to be admitted as a free state, New Mexico and Utah asked to be admitted as territories, Texas and New Mexico were embroiled in a boundary dispute, abolitionists wanted to abolish the slave auctions in Washington, D.C., and Southerners demanded the federal government help return runaway slaves. Henry Clay proposed the Compromise of 1850 to temporarily settle these issues: California was admitted as a free state, the two territories were organized but with no mention of slavery's status, the boundary dispute was settled in favor of New Mexico (with Texas being compensated $10 million), the capital's slave auctions were abolished, and a Fugitive Slave Act was passed to help return runaways. Clay was unable to get the compromise passed and died soon after proposing it. It was left to Sen. Stephen A. Douglas of Illinois to get the measure through Congress.

Soon after the Compromise of 1850 was passed, the Southern states held the Nashville Convention to discuss a strategy to defend slavery. Earlier Calhoun had called for such a meeting during the congressional debates over the Wilmot Proviso. Interest waned after the passage of the Compromise of 1850, and only nine slave states attended the June 1850 meeting. Moderate delegates won control of the convention from the radical South Carolina fire-eaters who wanted immediate secession. The convention passed a resolution calling for the opening of all territories to slavery, but in a cooperative spirit agreed to settle for the extension of the Missouri Compromise Line to the Pacific Ocean. A small number of fire-eaters returned to Nashville some months later and reiterated the right of secession. In the end, the Nashville Convention had no great impact on the country except to bring Southerners together to discuss secession and to demonstrate to the North that the South was contemplating extreme measures to protect its interests.

The 1850s were the critical years that decided the nation's fate. The antislavery faction gained significant support in 1852 when Harriet Beecher Stowe published her powerful *Uncle Tom's Cabin*. The novel convinced many Northerners that slavery, indeed, was an evil that should be contained, if not abolished. Southerners were outraged that so much credence was given to a fictitious piece written by someone who had never actually witnessed the slave system. Two years later, it was the Northerners' turn to be outraged when the 1854 Ostend Manifesto was publicized. In hopes of gaining Cuba (a Spanish colony where slavery flourished), President Franklin Pierce secretly had three American diplomats draw up a plan to acquire it. This plan, which became known as the Ostend Manifesto, stated that the United States should first try to buy Cuba from Spain, but if the Spanish refused, Pierce had the right to take it by force. It so happened that two of the three diplomats were Southerners, and it seemed to the North that the South was willing to plunge the nation into war just to add more slave territory.

One of the most critical events leading up to civil war also occurred in 1854. In an attempt to build a Northern transcontinental railroad and to better his chances of being elected president, Illinois Sen. Stephen A. Douglas was able to pass the Kansas-Nebraska Act. This act organized the territories of Kansas and Nebraska to allow the federal government to give land grants to the railroads involved in the project. To gain Southern support, Douglas had to include in the bill the replacement of the Missouri Compromise Line with popular sovereignty (allowing voters to decide the issue) as a means to determine the status of slavery in these territories. Douglas did not believe slavery could survive on the arid Great Plains, and, therefore, the two new territories naturally would be populated by antislavery people. He underestimated how controversial his bill would become and was taken aback when Free-Soilers and other Northerners vehemently criticized him for opening the way for slavery's spread. Although Douglas may have been confident that slave owners would never be a majority of the territories' voters, most Northern people did not want to take that risk.

As a result of the Kansas-Nebraska Act, the Republican Party was formed in the North to oppose the spread of slavery. Made up of former Whig, Democratic, Free-Soil, and Liberty Party members, the Republicans were a fractious group who often quarreled among themselves. Some were abolitionists who wanted to free the slaves and grant freedmen certain rights. Others were racists and did not care if the South had slaves but simply did not want to see slavery spread into areas where they might live. About this time, the Whig Party also died out in the South, leaving only the Democratic Party there. The nation thus became even more polarized, with most Democrats in the South believing all Republicans were abolitionists who were out to destroy the Southern socioeconomic system, while Republicans viewed Southerners as being determined to spread slavery across the nation.

Another result of the Kansas-Nebraska Act was the first outbreak of widespread violence over the slavery issue. Nebraska was located so far to the north, that there was never any doubt it would be populated by antislavery people. On the other hand, Kansas was a different matter. Located adjacent to the slave state of Missouri, it was populated by both proslavery and abolitionist settlers. The two factions quickly clashed as each attempted to win the territory for its side. Proslavery "Border Ruffians" from Missouri fought abolitionists armed with rifles known as "Beecher's Bibles." In 1856, proslavery forces attacked the town of Lawrence, which led to the retaliatory murder of five proslavery men at Pottawatomie Creek by John Brown and his followers. As the violence escalated to near civil war, Kansas became known as Bleeding Kansas. Elections held to decide the territory's fate were marred by violence and corruption, although it was clear that the majority of voters opposed slavery. Voters rejected the proslavery Lecompton Constitution in 1858, but turmoil continued for years.

With the nation being torn apart by the slavery issue, in early 1857, President-elect James Buchanan encouraged the U.S. Supreme Court to use the Dred Scott case to make a sweeping ruling on the matter. This case dragged through the lower courts for 10 years before reaching the Supreme Court. It involved the slave Dred Scott, who was suing for his freedom because he had been taken into Illinois and the Wisconsin Territory, where slavery was outlawed. Chief Justice Roger Taney handed down the much-awaited decision in March 1857. In a 7–2 ruling, the Court stated that Negroes were not citizens of the United States and therefore could not sue in federal court; that slaves were like any other property, and the 5th Amendment's "due process" clause guaranteed a slave owner's right to carry his property into any territory; and that the Missouri Compromise Line was unconstitutional. The decision also implied that territories could not use popular sovereignty as a means to outlaw slavery. The decision was a major victory for the radical Southern slave owners, but it outraged most Northerners because the vote followed sectional lines, with all of the majority Southern justices voting for it. The Dred Scott decision was one of the major disrupting factors prior to the Civil War and led to the Republican Party gaining significant strength in the North.

Just when it appeared the North had no way in which to fight the spread of slavery legally, Douglas proposed his Freeport Doctrine during the 1858 Lincoln-Douglas debates. He noted that while the Dred Scott decision prevented territories from outlawing slavery, they could still keep it out by requiring slave owners to pay taxes or post bonds on all their slaves and make it too expensive to bring them in. This ingenious policy won back for Douglas much of the support he had lost because of the Kansas-Nebraska Act.

John Brown's 1859 Raid on Harpers Ferry, Virginia, was the last major event involving slavery before the 1860 presidential election. On October 16, 1859, abolitionist John Brown and 18 followers (with the secret financial support of several other prominent abolitionists) attacked Harpers Ferry, Virginia, to steal rifles with which to arm runaway slaves and form a new free black nation in the Appalachian Mountains. Several people were killed in the raid, but it ultimately failed, and Brown and a number of his accomplices were captured by Col. Robert E. Lee. Brown and eight followers were convicted of treason against Virginia, insurrection, and murder, and Brown was hanged on December 2. The raid greatly increased sectional tension. Southerners viewed Brown and his supporters as typical abolitionists who intended to end slavery through violent insurrection and murder. Most Northerners condemned Brown's methods but admired his goal and made him a martyr.

By 1860, the United States was on the verge of splitting apart over slavery, and everyone knew the presidential election might be the last chance to prevent disunion. Most hopes lay with the Democratic Party, the only truly national party in 1860. The Republican Party, on the other hand, was purely a Northern party devoted to stopping the spread of slavery. The Democrats split along sectional lines when the nominating convention failed to agree on a platform. Southern delegates at Charleston, South Carolina, and at Baltimore, Maryland, walked out in protest after the Northern delegates refused to support a platform calling for congressional protection of slavery in the territories. As a result, the Northerners formed the Northern Democratic Party and nominated Stephen A. Douglas, who pledged not to interfere with slavery in the South but promised to support his Freeport Doctrine to prevent its spread into the territories. The Southerners formed the Southern Democratic Party and nominated John C. Breckinridge, who insisted the Dred Scott decision gave slave owners the constitutional right to take their slaves into any territory. Thus, the only national party—and the nation's last hope for avoiding disaster—ceased to exist.

The Republicans held their convention next and nominated Abraham Lincoln. Lincoln also promised not to interfere with slavery in the South, but he, too, was determined to prevent its spread. He also supported homesteads and a higher tariff to provide better protection for Northern industrial workers.

Some border states leaders realized that any conflict between the North and South would consume them, so they formed the new Constitutional Union Party to provide a candidate who was neither pro-North nor pro-South. John Bell of Tennessee was nominated, and he adopted a platform that was vague and noncontroversial so as not to offend any voters. Bell called on everyone to support the Union, obey the law, and uphold the Constitution. This was a platform all Americans could support, but how they supported it depended on one's interpretation of the Union, the law, and the Constitution.

Realizing the South's political power was waning as the North's advantage in population and states grew, Southerners greatly feared a Republican victory. Despite Lincoln's promises to the contrary, they were convinced that he was an abolitionist and if elected would stop the spread of slavery, if not destroy it outright. Such a view of Lincoln was incorrect and ignored the political reality that Lincoln probably could never convince Congress to abolish slavery. To do so would have required a constitutional amendment and the approval of two-thirds of the states. This would have been impossible, since well over one-third of the states supported slavery. It was perception, however, not reality that was important, and in the face of this perceived threat, the fire-eaters believed only secession would protect the South against tyranny by the majority. They openly warned the nation that Lincoln's election would lead to disunion.

THE SECESSION CRISIS

In the election on November 6, 1860, Lincoln carried about 40 percent of the popular vote but won 180 electoral votes. Breckinridge won 72 electoral votes, while Bell took 39 and Douglas 12. Lincoln's victory and the fire-eaters' rhetoric greatly diminished the influence of moderate Southerners who wished to find a compromise to save the nation. As a result, South Carolina radicals carried out their disunion threat when the state seceded on December 20, 1860. Other Deep South states followed, and by the end of

January 1861, Mississippi, Florida, Alabama, Georgia, and Louisiana also had seceded. To prevent the nation's permanent breakup, moderate politicians desperately tried to find a solution agreeable to all parties.

After Kentucky's Sen. John J. Crittenden proposed a series of resolutions to prevent disunion, the Senate formed the Committee of Thirteen on the same day South Carolina seceded. Crittenden was appointed chairman of the so-called Crittenden Committee, and the members were charged with finding a compromise that would save the nation. Crittenden's resolutions were used as the basis for the committee's work, and they became known as the Crittenden Compromise. The Crittenden Compromise recommended the passage of six constitutional amendments to settle the slavery issue permanently. The most important of these were the extension of the Missouri Compromise Line to the Pacific Ocean (with new states having the right of popular sovereignty to decide the slavery issue) and prohibiting Congress from ever abolishing slavery in the territories. No future constitutional amendment could interfere with these amendments. The committee voted down the compromise, partly because President-elect Lincoln let it be known he would refuse to compromise on containing the spread of slavery. Despite the committee's lack of endorsement, the compromise was presented to the Senate on January 3, 1861, but it failed on January 16 by a vote of 25–23.

Virginia also called for a peace conference to be held in Washington, D.C., and received the strong support of the border states. The Washington Peace Conference opened on February 4, 1861, with 21 states participating, and it used the Crittenden Compromise as the basis for negotiations, but no one was in a mood to make any real concessions. The conference finally adopted seven recommendations similar to the Crittenden Compromise, to be enacted as a constitutional amendment, and submitted them to Congress on February 27. Both the House and Senate rejected the proposals, and this last major attempt to avoid disunion failed.

On February 4, 1861—the same day the Washington Peace Conference convened—the six seceding Southern states (with Texas joining them later) met in the Montgomery, Alabama, Convention to form the Confederate States of America. The 50 delegates organized a Provisional Confederate Congress; created a new government; adopted a Confederate Constitution; elected Jefferson Davis and Alexander Stephens as provisional president and vice president, respectively; adopted a flag; authorized a Confederate army; issued $15 million in treasury bonds; and created a cabinet. The Confederate government made Montgomery its capital until May, when it was moved to Richmond, Virginia.

THE OUTBREAK OF WAR

Even before the Confederate government was established, the seceding states began seizing all U.S. installations within their borders. By March 1861, Fort Pickens at Pensacola, Florida, and Fort Sumter at Charleston, South Carolina, were among the few federal properties still in Union hands. At Fort Sumter, Maj. Robert Anderson had approximately 80 officers and men and about 40 civilian workers inside the fort, but he was surrounded by several thousand Confederates under Brig. Gen. P. G. T. Beauregard. When Lincoln took office on March 4, 1861, he decided to hold both Sumter and Pickens. At Charleston, a standoff continued for weeks, with Anderson refusing all calls to surrender. When the Confederates learned on April 8 that a relief expedition was being sent from New York City to aid Anderson, they made one last surrender demand. Anderson again refused on April 11.

At 4:30 A.M., April 12, Beauregard opened fire on Fort Sumter. Anderson, recognizing the futility of resistance, protected his men and only occasionally fired back. After a 33-hour bombardment, in which approximately 4,000 shells were fired, Anderson surrendered the badly battered fort. No deaths had been suffered on either side, but war soon followed, when Lincoln quickly declared the South was in rebellion, instituted a blockade around Southern ports, and called for 75,000 volunteers to put down the insurrection. In response to his actions, Arkansas, Tennessee, Virginia, and North Carolina not only refused the call for volunteers but seceded and joined the Confederacy.

Both sides quickly mobilized for war and thousands of eager recruits answered the call for men. No one expected the war to last long, and many men wanted to be in on the excitement before it ended. The Union and Confederate armies essentially were organized in the same way. Men usually volunteered for a specific length of time, such as 90 days or one year, but three years or the war's duration eventually became a standard. Volunteer companies of about 100 men each were raised in communities, usually by some prominent figure who was elected captain, and 10 companies normally formed a regiment, commanded by a colonel. The soldiers elected all officers up to the rank of colonel, which did not ensure that the most qualified men became officers. Several regiments formed a brigade, several brigades formed a division, and, later in the war, several divisions formed a corps. Armies were formed around a number of divisions early in the war, and later around corps. The government appointed the general grade officers who commanded the brigades (sometimes a colonel commanded a brigade), divisions, corps, and armies.

When the Civil War began, the U.S. Army was very small, and most of its fighting force was posted on the frontier guarding against Indian attacks. In 1861, the army had a strength of only 16,367 officers and men distributed among 19 regiments of infantry, cavalry, artillery, and various bureaus and agencies (313 of its officers joined the Confederacy). This regular army was kept intact during the war and even was expanded by creating more units, but the vast majority of Union soldiers who fought the Confederates belonged to the huge volunteer army that was created. Thus, the Union fought the war with two armies, the regulars and the volunteers. One mistake made in creating this fighting force was in not distributing the trained regular officers and men among the volunteers to establish discipline and training more quickly. Instead, the regulars remained in their separate regiments, although a number of the officers were assigned to volunteer units, and the regular regiments were placed in divisions and corps that were largely made up of volunteers.

The Union's volunteer army was much larger than the regular army, for after the firing on Fort Sumter, 300,000 recruits responded to Lincoln's call for men. Even this was not enough, and as the war continued more troops were raised through conscription and the offer of bounties. During the four years of war, some 2.3 million men served in the Union's volunteer army.

On March 6, 1861, the Provisional Confederate Congress created a regular army called the Army of the Confederate States of America, which was intended to be the nation's permanent army. It never became a real functioning entity, however, because it quickly became apparent that volunteers would constitute the main fighting force. As a result, only 12 cavalry and seven infantry regiments, one artillery battery, and a number of independent companies were ever authorized in the regular army, for a total of about 1,750 officers and men. For its defense, the Confederacy depended on a temporary volunteer Provisional Army of the Confederate States that was created by congressional acts on February 28 and March 6, 1861. These volunteers first entered the state militia and then were mustered into Confederate service and placed under the authority of the president. It is estimated that 850,000–900,000 men served in the Confederate armies.

As both sides mobilized for war, it appeared the Union had an overwhelming advantage, with 22 states against 11. The Union had a population of approximately 22,340,000, while the Confederacy had approximately 9,105,000 people. Even more important, nearly the entire Union population was white, from which the military would draw most of its soldiers, while only about 5,585,000 of the Confederate population was white. The 3,520,000 slaves in the Confederacy were an important labor source but provided virtually no soldiers. On the other hand, during the war's second half these slaves volunteered in great numbers to serve in the Union army.

The Union also had a huge advantage in railroads, and the Civil War was the first war in which they played a vital role. In virtually all of the major campaigns, the armies depended on railroads to bring supplies and men to the front and to evacuate the wounded. When the war began, the Union had about 20,000 miles of track, while the Confederates had approximately 9,000 miles. Northern states also possessed 24 times the number of locomotives as the South. Not only did the Confederacy have inadequate amounts of track, in many cases the lines were of different gauge, or tracks in and out of such towns as Petersburg, Virginia, did not actually connect. This meant that great delays were caused when trains frequently had to stop and transfer their cargo or men to another train. The Confederacy's small industrial base also made it difficult to build new tracks, and it could do little to straighten out rails that became damaged in cavalry raids. The Confederate government also did not take steps to control what track it did have. Unlike the Union, which created the U.S. Military Railroads System, the Confederates never placed the railroads under government control to facilitate their use. By war's end, the Confederate railway system lay in shambles from enemy raids and a lack of rails and rolling stock. This helped weaken the Confederate armies, because despite there being plenty of food in the countryside late in the war, the lack of a working transportation system prevented the government from getting it to the soldiers.

While the Confederacy did have the great Tredegar Iron Works and some other heavy industry in Virginia and Georgia, it was no match for the Union's industrial might. The Union produced more than 92 percent of the nation's gross national product in 1860. It contained 110,274 industrial establishments to the Confederacy's 18,026 (the states of New York and Pennsylvania individually had more industry than all of the seceding states combined) and produced 20 times the amount of pig iron and 17 times the amount of textiles as the Confederacy. In addition, the Union greatly outproduced the Confederacy in weapons manufacturing through its Springfield, Colt, and Remington companies. Other advantages the Union enjoyed at the war's beginning were a well-trained, albeit small, army and navy; a powerful, experienced national government; a sound financial and monetary system; and an established diplomatic service.

Despite the overwhelming advantage the Union had in war-making capabilities, success was not ensured. The burden of victory rested with the Union, and to win, it had to assume the offensive and conquer the Confederacy. In return, the Confederates simply had to defend their territory and survive to win. The vast expanse of the Confederacy, which was about the size of Western Europe, convinced many people that it could never be conquered. Even the huge Union population was not as threatening as it first seemed. A conventional rule of thumb in the 19th century was that to have a reasonable chance of victory, an attacking force had to be three times greater than the defending one. Thus, the four-to-one advantage the Union enjoyed in white population was not insurmountable, considering the Confederacy would be on the defensive. After all, not only were the Confederates convinced they were the superior soldiers, they also had a superb historical example of the weaker side emerging victorious. The odds George Washington and the Americans had faced against Great Britain in the Revolutionary War were probably greater than what the Confederacy faced in 1861, yet the Founding Fathers had won their struggle. And it was not forgotten that Washington, Thomas Jefferson, Patrick Henry, Francis Marion, Richard Henry Lee, Dan Morgan, and other colonial heroes were Southerners.

Although not as obvious, the Confederates did enjoy several advantages early in the war. These included the interior line that allowed the transportation of troops and material from point to point on a faster, shorter line than the Union's; numerous West Point-trained officers, who, in the eastern theater, at least, outclassed their Union counterparts; and fighting on their own soil, where local knowledge of the countryside was vital at a time when accurate maps still did not exist. There was also the possibility that through so-called Cotton Diplomacy, Great Britain and France would be forced to intervene in the war once cotton became scarce in Europe. Unfortunately for the Confederates, these strengths proved to be fleeting. The interior line soon broke down along with the Confederate transportation system; Union officers became progressively better, and many of the leading Confederate officers were killed; and fighting on home soil often meant one's home was destroyed. Although in late 1861, it appeared the much-anticipated foreign intervention was at hand when the Union seized two Confederate envoys from a British ship in the *Trent* Affair, the incident was settled peacefully. Confederate hopes for foreign aid later were dashed permanently when it became apparent that the cotton shortage was not nearly enough to make antislavery Europe become involved in the struggle.

Once war erupted, Lincoln asked General-in-Chief Winfield Scott to devise a grand strategy on how to achieve victory. Scott recommended a three-part plan: blockading the Southern ports to deny the Confederates supplies; seizing control of the Mississippi River to split the Confederacy in two; and, with the Confederacy then isolated, to halt operations and allow pro-Union Southerners to rise up in protest and force the enemy to come to terms. Scott's plan called for ending the rebellion by constricting and isolating the Confederacy, which reminded the public of an anaconda snake. The nickname "Anaconda Plan" was actually meant to ridicule, since it referred to a slow death for the rebellion and not the quick battlefield defeat people wanted.

The Confederacy, on the other hand, depended on a defensive-offensive strategy to conserve resources. Jefferson Davis believed the war could be won by emulating George Washington's Revolutionary War strategy: to defend as much territory as possible while avoiding catastrophic defeats on the battlefield. If an opportunity arose to take the offensive without too great a risk, Davis would do so, but his main objective was simply to survive and make the war so long and bloody that the Union eventually would exhaust itself and seek a negotiated settlement.

To achieve their strategies, both the Union and Confederacy divided their territories into military departments. Each department had its own commander and military force, which sometimes was an army named for the department, such as the Army of Northern Virginia, which defended the Confederate Department of Northern Virginia. These departments were very fluid and were created, disbanded, and redrawn according to military and political necessities. They also bred jealousy and caused poor coordination among the commanders. Since each officer was responsible for defending his department, there was often a reluctance to send reinforcements from one department to another or to cooperate in military campaigns involving more than one department. Despite its weaknesses, both sides continued to use this department system throughout the war.

Both armies also used the same type of weapons and followed identical military tactics. Although a few flintlock smoothbore muskets were used at the war's beginning, the single shot percussion rifle musket firing a minié ball became the standard long arm (repeating rifles were used more and more as the war progressed, especially by the Union). The infantry was the backbone of an army and was massed on a battlefield in tight formations, so the commander could maintain control and volleys of fire could be concentrated on the enemy. Artillery pieces such as Napoleons and Parrott rifles were positioned to rake advancing lines of infantry or to silence opposing batteries. The cavalry served as an army's eyes to provide intelligence, to protect the flanks against surprise attack, and to raid behind enemy lines to destroy railroads and lines of communication. Battlefield tactics were fundamentally the same as in the days of Napoleon and forced high-ranking officers to be on or very near the firing line so they could observe their units and keep control of them in the chaos of battle. Realizing that modern rifles and their increased accuracy and distance made frontal attacks dangerous, both sides used turning movements or flank attacks when possible to force the enemy from a position. By 1864, both armies also recognized the value of strong entrenchments, and generals began to lose some of their mobility as troops dug in and battlefields came to foreshadow those of World War I.

DOMESTIC EVENTS

One of the greatest problems both sides faced in the conflict was how to finance their war efforts. The Confederacy, especially, was at a disadvantage because it began the Civil War with no currency, tax structure, or other financial base, and only a few million dollars in specie that had been seized from federal mints. As a result, it was forced to finance the government and war through loans, taxes, and treasury notes (paper money).

Secretary of the Treasury Christopher G. Memminger first put the Confederacy deeply in debt by borrowing millions of dollars from private banks and by selling bonds. In October 1862, the Erlanger Loan, a cotton-backed loan, was also secured in France. It is estimated that the Confederate government raised about $700 million—or 39 percent of its revenue—through such borrowing.

On August 19, 1861, the Confederate Congress also authorized a direct tax on real estate, slaves, and other property. This tax was largely ineffective and only raised about $17.5 million. As the Confederacy's chance of victory dwindled in 1863, its people actually began demanding taxes as a way to strengthen the armies and turn the tide of battle. On April 23, 1863, the Confederate Congress passed a comprehensive tax bill that included taxes on certain products, income, and licenses. The products tax placed an 8 percent tax on many agricultural products (plus liquor, salt, and naval stores). The graduated income tax ranged from 1 to 15 percent on incomes over $1,000 per year, and the $50–500 license tax was placed on nearly all professions (including theater and circus owners and jugglers). The most unpopular Confederate tax was the tax-in-kind, which forced farmers to give the government 10 percent of their products. This tax was plagued by corrupt officials who seized an illegal amount of goods and by the wasteful rotting of food caused by the crumbling Confederate railway system, but an estimated $150 million in supplies were gathered. Overall, the Confederate tax system was a failure. Fearful of losing support among its people, the government never passed taxes sufficient enough to raise the large sums of money needed to fight the war. It is estimated that these taxes raised only about 7 percent of the government's revenue during the war, equaling approximately 1 percent of Confederate wealth.

The Confederate national and state governments also printed approximately $1.5 billion in paper money. Inflation set in almost immediately and was so rampant by 1864 that Davis replaced Secretary Memminger with George A. Trenholm in July. The change did not affect inflation, and by 1865 the Confederate dollar's value had shrunk to just 1.7 cents.

A chronic shortage of supplies was another huge problem for the Confederacy. At first the armies, and sometimes the state governments, took what was needed and only paid owners after they had filed a claim for their losses. A formal impressment system was adopted on March 26, 1863, when the Confederate Congress passed the Impressment Act. This law originally allowed the government to impress only goods needed to feed and sustain the military, but it was amended in April 1864 and March 1865 to allow it to take virtually anything that was needed for public use. Impressment agents scoured the countryside inspecting farms and businesses for potential goods and set fair prices for commodities impressed. Owners were either paid immediately in Confederate currency or were given certificates for later redemption. Protests soon began, because not only was impressment seen as a violation of states rights, but there were also many flaws in the system. Soaring inflation prevented the prices paid by the government from equaling the actual market value of the goods, and the law was not equally applied. Civilians living closest to the armies suffered much more impressment than people living far from the front. Many unscrupulous men also pretended to be impressment agents and used counterfeit certificates to steal goods. Even products legitimately obtained often spoiled before they could be delivered because either the agents did not make transportation arrangements or the deteriorating Confederate railroad system could not handle the traffic.

Slaves frequently were impressed for military labor early in the war, but after the Impressment Act was passed, their impressment had to conform to the law. Slave owners were paid $30 a month, or some other agreed upon price, and were reimbursed if the slave died during the work period. As with impressments of commodities, there was much protest against slave impressment. Owners accused the government of mistreating their property, always being late with payment, and keeping slaves longer than the agreed upon time.

The Confederate government impressed hundreds of millions of dollars' worth of supplies and slaves during the war. Just how much is unknown, but one source estimates 17 percent of the Confederacy's purchasing power, or more than $500 million, came through impressment. Opposition to the practice further weakened morale, and by war's end, the policy had largely been abandoned in favor of paying market value for seized goods.

Although in better financial condition than the Confederacy, the Union also had a difficult time paying its war costs and relied mostly on paper money, loans, and bonds. Taxes also were passed, but they were not an important source of income. In 1861, paper money in circulation had to be backed by gold in the U.S. treasury. However, the federal gold reserve quickly became depleted, and people began hoarding specie because they feared an economic collapse. By late 1861, the gold reserve was virtually exhausted, and the Union's money supply was severely limited. As a result, in December most major banks suspended paying specie to redeem their bank notes. In January 1862, the U.S. Congress proposed making paper money, without any specie backing, legal tender in the United States (except for paying tariffs or interest on the national debt). An intense congressional debate followed, but the government's staggering debt convinced Congress to pass the Legal Tender Act, and it was signed into law in February 1862. The bill provided the issuance of $150 million of Treasury notes, which became known as greenbacks, and it greatly improved the Union's ability to finance the war. Later acts in July 1862 and March 1863 increased the amount of greenbacks to $300 million, and by war's end, approximately $433 million had been issued. Drawbacks to the legislation were inflation and speculation, plus fluctuations in greenback value as the Union armies' battlefield success ebbed and flowed. Loans brought in about $2.2 billion for the Union, while millions more were raised when Secretary of the Treasury Salmon P. Chase gave financier Jay Cooke the sole right to sell U.S. bonds.

On August 5, 1861, the U.S. Congress passed two new tax laws. One was to raise $20 million through a direct tax that placed a revenue quota (based on population) on each state. Even the rebelling Southern states were included, but it raised only $17 million. The second tax was the nation's first income tax, which originally placed a flat 3-percent tax on incomes over $800 per year and later 5–7.5 percent on incomes of $600–10,000 per year, and 10 percent on incomes over $10,000. It raised about $55 million. The most comprehensive Union tax was an internal tax passed on July 1, 1862. This complex law included luxury taxes, taxes on raw materials and manufacturing, property taxes, professional licenses fees, and taxes on corporations. Overall, taxes did not play a very large role in financing the Union war effort. Whereas loans and treasury notes alone raised $2.6 billion, taxes provided the Union with only about $667 million.

Besides financial difficulties, another problem shared by the belligerents was a lack of manpower. As the war progressed and casualties mounted, both sides resorted to conscription to fill their ranks. The first military draft law in American history was the April 1862 conscription act passed by the Confederate Congress, which made all white males between 18 and 35 eligible for the draft. This was changed in subsequent laws to include those men between 17 and 50. The Union enacted its first conscription act in March 1863, making all white men between 18 and 35 eligible for military service. Both sides exempted men whose work was considered vital to the war effort, allowed the payment of commutation fees and the hiring of substitutes, and recognized certain religious conscientious objectors. Conscription mainly was seen as a way to encourage men to volunteer, since there was much stigma attached to being a draftee. Still, the conscription acts were very unpopular because people realized wealthy or politically connected men were able to avoid service by taking advantage of the laws' many loopholes. The war had become "a rich man's war and a poor man's fight." In the Union, there was even violent opposition, such as in the 1863 New York City draft riot.

While most Northerners and Southerners supported their respective governments during the war, each section had sizeable numbers of people who were either disloyal, conscientious objectors, neutral, or believed the cost in blood and money was not worth the price of victory. In the Confederacy, there had been opposition to secession from the beginning. Most of those opposed to secession simply wanted to be left alone and refused to support the war effort unless forced to do so. Others who were more vigorous in their opposition operated clandestinely to oppose conscription and harsh war measures and to return the South to the Union. Operating largely in North Carolina, Alabama, Tennessee, Texas, and Arkansas, such organizations as the Peace Society encouraged desertions, aided Union forces, and called for a peace settlement and a restoration of the Union. In October 1862, Confederates hanged a large number of Texas Unionists in what became known as the "Great Gainesville, Texas, Hanging."

Such disloyal activity was also found in the North, where many people — mostly Democrats — believed it was not worth war to force the South to remain a part of the Union, opposed freeing the slaves, or opposed such harsh war measures as the suspension of the writ of habeas corpus. Known as Copperheads, or Peace Democrats, they were most active in the old northwest states of Illinois, Indiana, and Ohio and operated such secret organizations as the Knights of the Golden Circle and the Sons of Liberty. Because of their antiwar activities and fear that they might aid the Confederacy,

Lincoln's administration took strong measures and began arresting their members and censoring their presses. One leading Copperhead, Clement L. Vallandigham, was arrested and exiled into Confederate territory.

The border states of Missouri and Kentucky especially suffered from split loyalties. Although the majority of their people supported the Union, each had a large number of secessionists, with Missouri's Gov. Claiborne F. Jackson being staunchly pro-Confederate. While both states formally rejected secession, the secessionists in each formed Confederate governments in exile and were admitted to the Confederacy (both were given stars in the Confederate flag). Thousands of Missouri and Kentucky men also served in both the Union and Confederate armies, and Missouri, especially, was wracked by vicious guerrilla warfare as neighbor turned on neighbor and families were split apart.

In Virginia, dissent by a minority of the population led to the creation of a new state. The mountainous western counties opposed secession in April 1861 because of political opposition to the rich, plantation tidewater region; the paucity of slaves in the western area; and the region's economic and family ties to Pennsylvania and Ohio. When these Unionist delegates were outvoted at the secession convention, representatives from 26 western counties met at Wheeling on June 11, 1861, to form a new state and to create a loyal government for Virginia. Ordinances were adopted two months later establishing the state of Kanawha, and Francis H. Pierpont was chosen the Unionist governor of Virginia. In November, a constitutional convention was held to finalize the creation of the new state. The name West Virginia was adopted, the constitution was ratified on April 3, 1862, by voters who had taken the oath of allegiance, and West Virginia was admitted to the Union on June 20, 1863.

To combat dissent, both sides took the drastic step of suspending the writ of habeas corpus. On April 27, 1861, Lincoln suspended it along the route between Washington, D.C., and Philadelphia, Pennsylvania, to facilitate the shipment of troops to the capital and to prevent Maryland from seceding. In September 1862, he suspended habeas corpus throughout the North as a wartime measure to allow the government to arrest and detain suspected disloyalists without having to prove a case against them. At first, the public supported such action, but as more and more people were arrested, it became a great controversy, because it was being used in states that remained loyal. As the war dragged on, the U.S. Congress passed the Habeas Corpus Act in March 1863 specifically authorizing its suspension and protecting military officers from being prosecuted for carrying out their duties. Arrests of suspected disloyalists resumed and continued until war's end.

In the Confederacy, Davis also suspended the writ of habeas corpus but to a lesser degree because of the states rights philosophy and congressional restrictions. The Confederate Congress first approved suspension in February 1862 to maintain civil order and to enforce the conscription act. In all, the Confederate Congress passed three acts suspending habeas corpus, the last one in February 1864, but each one expired after a certain period of time. The Confederates eventually became more and more discontented with such measures, because they saw them as an attempt by the central government to seize tyrannical powers. Although Davis requested another suspension in November 1864, Congress refused.

Perhaps the most important development during the war on the domestic scene was the shifting of the Union's war goals from simply preserving the Union to preserving the Union and abolishing slavery. Although personally opposed to slavery, even Lincoln had always maintained that the "peculiar institution" was guaranteed by the Constitution, and that the federal government had no authority to abolish it arbitrarily. Emancipation, however, inevitably became part of the war effort. Union generals David Hunter and John C. Frémont tried to force the issue early in the war by ordering slaves freed in their departments, but Lincoln reversed both actions. The U.S. Congress also became involved in 1861 when it passed a confiscation act that freed slaves that were being used to support the rebellion.

As the war continued and became increasingly bloody, Lincoln began to view emancipation as a way to weaken the Confederacy. It would deny the enemy much of the labor that was being used to construct fortifications and to raise food and would create internal chaos by encouraging slaves to escape to Union lines. The Confederate armies would also be weakened because more troops would have to remain behind the lines to guard against runaways. Emancipation would also help prevent the antislavery European nations from recognizing Confederate independence. Lincoln drafted the Emancipation Proclamation in July 1862, but the Cabinet convinced him to delay its release until a major victory had been won so the government would be issuing it from a position of strength rather than as an act of desperation. The Battle of Antietam served as that needed victory, and Lincoln issued the Preliminary Emancipation Proclamation on September 22, 1862. It stated that if the Confederates did not end the rebellion by January 1, 1863, all slaves then being held in Confederate territory would be free. The proclamation did not apply to slaves in the border states, to ensure those states' continued loyalty.

Thousands of Union soldiers at first protested this change in war goals, some even to the point of mutiny. But in the end, most came to recognize the military necessity of such action. Although the document actually freed slaves in areas over which Lincoln had no control, it did have the desired effect because slaves were freed as the Union armies advanced or as slaves ran away into Union lines. When Lincoln signed the Emancipation Proclamation on January 1, 1863, the war was changed from a conflict to preserve the Union to a war to preserve the Union without slavery.

After the Emancipation Proclamation, large numbers of blacks began to enlist in the Union army. The U.S. Congress had authorized the enlistment of black troops in July 1862, and such units as the 1st Kansas Colored Volunteers, the Louisiana Native Guards, and the 54th Massachusetts were organized. Despite this, Union officers did not believe blacks would make effective combat soldiers because it was thought they had an innate fear of whites and possessed inferior personal qualities. As a result, black Union soldiers usually were forced to have white officers, received less pay than their white counterparts, and suffered from open abuse and resentment within their own army. Instead of combat, they performed such menial tasks as digging ditches, building fortifications, or guarding prisoners and supply depots to free white soldiers to fight.

Attitudes toward black troops began to change in 1863 when they were first used in major combat. In May, the Louisiana Native Guards fought in the Port Hudson Campaign, and in June other blacks saw action at Milliken's Bend, Louisiana. The 54th Massachusetts then made its famous assault on Fort Wagner later that summer. These black soldiers proved their bravery and convinced officials to make better use of them. During the war, black Union soldiers engaged in 39 battles and 410 smaller engagements and suffered 68,178 casualties. Their use infuriated Confederates and led to massacres at such places as Baxter Springs, Fort Pillow, Poison Spring, Saltville, and the Crater. By war's end, approximately 180,000 black soldiers (or 10 percent of the Union army) had served in 139 regiments and 10 artillery batteries.

The Confederates made less use of blacks for obvious reasons. Thousands of slaves were used as laborers, teamsters, and servants, but most Confederates loathed the idea of using them as soldiers. This attitude began to change as some officers recognized slaves as a potential source of manpower and came to believe Europe would never recognize the Confederacy unless slavery was abolished, or at least radically altered. The idea of trading freedom for military service was first proposed in January 1864 by the Army of Tennessee's Maj. Gen. Patrick Cleburne at the so-called Dalton Conference. Cleburne met fierce resistance from other officers, and Jefferson Davis ordered the matter dropped for political reasons even though he personally thought the idea had some merit. Later in the war, as the Confederacy faced almost certain defeat, the plan gained support from such generals as Robert E. Lee. With Lee's backing, a bill finally was passed in the Confederate Congress in March 1865 allowing the enlistment of blacks. Soon, North Carolina and Georgia also authorized the enlistment of blacks into their units, but the change was too little too late. A small number of black troops were organized into a battalion at Richmond, Virginia, but they apparently were never used in combat since the war ended soon after the battalion was formed.

Since Lincoln fought the Civil War to maintain the Union, few domestic issues were as important as Reconstruction, or the process of reorganizing loyal governments in the seceding states and bringing them back into the Union. As soon as sizeable portions of the Confederacy were occupied by the Union army, Lincoln began experimenting with a Reconstruction policy that became known as the Ten Percent Plan. On December 8, 1863, he issued a Proclamation of Amnesty and Reconstruction, offering a pardon and the restoration of property (except slaves) to any supporter of the rebellion who took an oath of allegiance. Lincoln also declared that a seceded state could return to the Union when 10 percent of the 1860 voters took the oath of allegiance and established a loyal state government without slavery. This moderate policy reflected Lincoln's belief that most Southerners had been misled by the fire-eating slave owners and could be persuaded to abandon the fight.

The Radical Republicans opposed the plan because it was too lenient, did not provide for freedmen's rights, and was not controlled by Congress. In December 1863, Senator Benjamin F. Wade and Congressman Henry W. Davis unveiled their own harsh plan known as the Wade-Davis Bill. This legislation called for the seceding states to be ruled by provisionary governors appointed by the President once they were defeated and occupied. White male citizens were required to sign an oath of allegiance swearing to their past loyalty to the Union, and when a majority of voters had done so the state could hold a constitutional convention to reform its government. Former Confederate soldiers or politicians could not participate in the process or hold any state office. When the state adopted a constitution that abolished slavery, repudiated the Confederate debt, and barred former Confederates from ever holding significant state positions, the state could be readmitted to the Union. Lincoln supported parts of the bill but believed overall it was too vindictive. Thus, when the Wade-Davis Bill was passed on July 2, 1864, he used the pocket veto to prevent it from becoming law. Wade and Davis issued a manifesto condemning the action, but for the time being the Radicals were denied control of Reconstruction.

Lincoln began implementing his Ten Percent Plan in Louisiana, Arkansas, and Tennessee, but the process halted with Lincoln's assassination. President Andrew Johnson continued a lenient plan similar to Lincoln's, but he, too, ran afoul of the Radicals and was impeached. Afterward, the Radicals seized control of Reconstruction, passed the 1867 Military Reconstruction Act, and directed the reunion process until its end in 1877.

CIVIL WAR DIPLOMACY

During the Civil War, the Union and Confederate governments pursued foreign policies that in a sense were the reverse of their military strategies. Confederate diplomacy was offensive in nature, and the new nation actively sought diplomatic recognition and foreign military aid. Union foreign policy was more defensive, trying to prevent diplomatic recognition of the Confederacy and keeping Europe out of the war.

From the start, the Confederacy hoped for foreign aid and recognition. At first, there was reason for optimism because a permanently divided, and therefore weaker, America would benefit such countries as Great Britain and France in areas of trade and world politics. France, for example, would have had a freer hand to establish Maximilian's regime with a weak Confederacy on Mexico's border rather than a strong United States. Some Confederates also believed Europe would be forced to intervene because the Union blockade would create a cotton shortage that would damage its economies too badly for it to sit idly by. It also was well known that Great Britain's ruling aristocratic class had more in common with and was more sympathetic to the Confederacy. The British, French, and Russian ambassadors to the United States in 1861 actually favored recognizing the Confederacy, but they could not act independently of their governments. France would not act without British support, and British Prime Minister Palmerston favored nonintervention and a wait-and-see policy.

While the Confederates sought foreign support, the Lincoln administration took strong measures to prevent it. Its efforts at first were somewhat hampered by Secretary of State William Seward, whom the Europeans, particularly the British, distrusted. Before taking office, Seward had boasted that as secretary, he would twist the lion's tail, and in April 1861 he had remarkably proposed to create a crisis with Europe as a way to bring the South back into the Union. Fortunately for Lincoln, Seward's bombastic nature was offset by Charles Francis Adams, the diplomatic and astute ambassador to Great Britain.

Soon after the Confederate government was created in February 1861, President Jefferson Davis and Secretary of State Robert Toombs began formulating a foreign policy. Commissioners were sent to the major European powers with instructions to establish diplomatic relations and trade ties. The Confederates also were to convince the Europeans that Lincoln's blockade was illegal, since the 1856 Declaration of Paris (which the United States refused to sign) stated that a blockade had to be "effective" to be legal. William Lowndes Yancey and Pierre A. Rost met with British Foreign Secretary Lord John Russell in early May but were told the decision on recognition rested with the Cabinet. Shortly afterward, Great Britain announced its neutrality in the conflict but recognized the Confederacy as a belligerent, largely because Palmerston believed the Union blockade already bestowed that status. This was not the same as diplomatic recognition, but it did make the Confederacy a legitimate warring party and entitled it to buy war material in Great Britain. Seward protested the decision and argued that the war was an internal rebellion that did not warrant such foreign action. His protest was ignored, and France, Spain, and several other nations followed the British example.

Perhaps the most serious diplomatic event of the war was the 1861 *Trent* Affair when the USS *San Jacinto* seized Confederate diplomats James Mason and John Slidell from the British mail steamer *Trent*. Captain Charles Wilkes acted on his own accord but created a crisis because Prime Minister Palmerston demanded their return. The seizure was an act of piracy in British eyes and clearly was illegal, but, ironically, it was similar to the British impressment policy that had caused the War of 1812. With enthusiasm still running high early in the war, most Northerners applauded the seizure and viewed Wilkes as a hero, but the Lincoln administration was hard pressed to defend his actions. When Palmerston sent 8,000 troops to Canada, it appeared war might erupt, and Adams worried the British might expel him. In the end, Seward and Adams convinced the British that Wilkes had acted without orders, and the diplomats were released in January 1862. As a parting shot, Seward wrote the British that the United States was glad to see they finally had renounced the principle of impressment.

Mason and Slidell continued their mission to Europe and tried to convince Great Britain and France to declare the blockade illegal since it was ineffectual. The two powers refused, however, partly because the small amount of cotton reaching Europe as a result of Confederate policy proved the blockade was effective. Earl Russell also noted that while most blockade-runners succeeded in reaching Confederate harbors, there still was a great danger in the attempt, and Union warships were preventing Confederate commerce raiders from using their own ports. In short, the blockade was effective enough to be legitimate. Self-interest was another reason the British refused to declare the blockade illegal. By not contesting it or insisting on the right of trade as a neutral, Great Britain was looking to the future. Much of its military and diplomatic interests relied on the might of the British navy. By recognizing the legitimacy of the weak Union blockade, it set a precedent that could force the United States to reciprocate if roles were ever reversed in the future.

The Confederacy hoped that what became known as Cotton Diplomacy would win it foreign assistance. It was believed that if Europe's important textile mills ran out of cotton, the British would be forced to intervene and perhaps break the blockade to save its economy. To ensure such a shortage, the Confederates not only relied on the blockade cutting off trade but intentionally held back exports to create a cotton shortage as quickly as possible. This proved to be a mistake. A better policy would have been to ship as much cotton as possible overseas to establish collateral for loans and for the purchase of war material. A cotton surplus actually existed in Great Britain when the war began, and it took some time for the expected shortage to occur. In the end, Cotton Diplomacy failed because Europe was able to make up for the shortages with cotton from Egypt, Brazil, and India.

Confederate diplomatic hopes reached their zenith in the summer of 1862 when Lee defeated the Federals in Virginia in the Seven Days Campaign. A motion was made in Parliament in July to recognize the Confederacy, but Palmerston succeeded in having it withdrawn without a vote. A few months later when the Confederate armies were on the offensive in both the Antietam and Kentucky Campaigns, and it appeared the Union might lose the war, British and French diplomats increasingly considered recognition or attempting to mediate a settlement even though that might provoke war with the United States. However, Confederate defeats in both invasions caused them to hesitate. Foreign Secretary Lord Russell presented the Cabinet a memorandum proposing mediation in October 1862, but the Cabinet rejected it. Shortly afterward, France told Confederate envoys that while it was sympathetic to their cause, it could not take any action without British support. The devastating Confederate defeats the following year at Vicksburg and Gettysburg virtually ended the possibility of European intervention. The Confederates made one last attempt to win British support in 1865 when it offered to abolish slavery in return for recognition, but Palmerston refused.

While the Confederates failed to win foreign diplomatic recognition, propaganda efforts by such figures as Henry Hotze did win them much sympathy from the public. Agents also succeeded in gaining badly needed military aid and some financing. The Erlanger Loan provided several million dollars, and purchasing agents bought thousands of rifle muskets in Europe and successfully shipped them through the blockade. One of the most successful ventures was the acquisition of commerce raiders by James D. Bulloch. In March 1862, the *Oreto* sailed from Liverpool to Nassau and became the Confederate raider *Florida*. Adams had presented evidence to the British government of the ship's real mission, but the British took no action to detain it. When Adams learned that the *Enrica* was another would-be raider, he again notified the authorities. This time, Lord Russell ordered the ship detained, but it was too late, and the *Enrica* sailed from Liverpool to the Azores and became the CSS *Alabama*. The United States suspected Great Britain of intentionally allowing the ship to escape, and Adams increased his protests. When he learned that Bulloch had contracted for the Laird rams, Adams compiled irrefutable proof that they were intended for Confederate service and finally convinced authorities in 1863 to seize them. These commerce raiders became a serious issue between the United States and Great Britain after the war, when the United States filed the *Alabama* Claims to win financial compensation for the damages wrought by them.

1861 MILITARY CAMPAIGNS

After some initial skirmishing between the opposing sides, the war's first large battle took place in Northern Virginia. Lincoln had organized an army in Washington under the command of Brig. Gen. Irvin McDowell and was eager for it to engage P. G. T. Beauregard's Confederate army positioned just outside Washington at Manassas, Virginia. Although McDowell protested against a hasty advance because his troops were untrained, Lincoln argued that the Confederates were just as disorganized. As a result of this political pressure, McDowell reluctantly advanced toward Manassas on July 16, 1861.

After a small clash at Blackburn's Ford on July 18, McDowell attacked Beauregard on the morning of July 21. Unknown to McDowell, Joseph E. Johnston had secretly slipped away from Union forces in the Shenandoah Valley on July 18 and brought his army by railroad to reinforce Beauregard. Thus, after some initial success, McDowell found his men becoming more and more exhausted as the day wore on, while the Confederates continually brought in fresh troops. In the end, the Confederates won a decisive victory and forced the Federals to flee back to Washington.

Afterward, Lincoln relieved McDowell of command and replaced him with Maj. Gen. George B. McClellan, a highly respected officer who had won two minor victories at Philippi and Rich Mountain, Virginia. McClellan was given command of what was designated the Army of the Potomac and later was appointed general-in-chief of all Union forces. He proved to be an outstanding organizer, planner, and disciplinarian but was reluctant to advance against the enemy until he had attended to every detail. As a result, the war came to a standstill in Virginia, and Lincoln watched in disappointment as months passed without any further offensive action.

Meanwhile, the border states of Kentucky and Missouri became important areas of activity because of their split loyalties. The pro-Union Kentucky legislature declared its neutrality in May, hoping to avoid involvement in the war, and, at first, Union and Confederate troops respected the decision. In September, however, Confederate Maj. Gen. Leonidas Polk rashly occupied Columbus to more effectively defend the Mississippi River. The Union reacted by occupying Paducah, and soon Gen. Albert Sidney Johnston, who was in command of all the western Confederates, had advanced his entire force to establish a defensive line running from Columbus through Bowling Green.

To the west in Missouri, the situation was tense through the spring of 1861, and violence soon erupted. Secessionist Gov. Claiborne Fox Jackson assembled his militia outside St. Louis at Camp Jackson in May to seize the U.S. arsenal in the city. Captain Nathaniel Lyon, however, organized a large Unionist force and attacked the militia on May 10, capturing nearly 1,000 men. When the prisoners were marched through the city, the column was confronted by an angry mob, and 28 people were killed in the ensuing St. Louis Riot.

Lyon was promoted to brigadier general for his decisive action at St. Louis, formed a Union army, and occupied Springfield. In early August, Confederate Brig. Gen. Ben McCulloch advanced his 12,000 men against Lyon to win the state for the Confederacy. Learning of the enemy advance, Lyon struck first at Wilson's Creek in a two-pronged attack on the morning of August 10. The Confederates stopped one of the attacks and then repeatedly assaulted the other Union column. Lyon was killed in the fighting, but the Confederates were unable to overrun the enemy's position. Exhausted and low on ammunition, Maj. Samuel Sturgis withdrew the Union troops that night, but the Confederates were in no condition to follow. After resting, the Confederates advanced to occupy Springfield and then won a small victory at Lexington. This string of Confederate victories seemed to ensure secessionist control of Missouri, but the campaign season ended, and the state's fate was left undecided.

In the far west, the New Mexico Territory became a center of activity in late 1861, when Jefferson Davis authorized Brig. Gen. Henry H. Sibley to lead a Confederate column from Texas through New Mexico to occupy California. Confederate Col. John Baylor, however, took the initiative and in July led "Baylor's Buffalo Hunt" into New Mexico and captured Fort Fillmore. By the time Sibley arrived, Baylor had already created the Confederate Territory of Arizona in the southwest and appointed himself governor.

In January 1862, Sibley moved up the Rio Grande into New Mexico with 2,600 men. He defeated one Union command at Valverde on February 21 and occupied Albuquerque and Santa Fe in early March. A column sent out by Sibley then won a tactical victory at Glorieta Pass on March 28, but the invasion was blunted when the Confederates were forced to retreat after the Federals destroyed their supply train. Nearly out of supplies and threatened by Brig. Gen. Edward R. S. Canby's small Union army, Sibley retreated on April 12 and, after a harrowing, exhausting march, finally reached the safety of Texas. The Confederates never again made a serious attempt to seize the Southwest.

1862 MILITARY CAMPAIGNS

At the beginning of 1862, the opposing armies in Virginia were inactive, observing each other around Washington; the fate of Missouri still was uncertain; and Kentucky was occupied by both belligerents. Within a few months, the fortunes of war would swing greatly in favor of the Union.

In January 1862, two small armies under Union Maj. Gen. George H. Thomas and Confederate Maj. Gen. George B. Crittenden were positioned in eastern Kentucky. Fighting broke out at Mill Springs on the morning of January 19, 1862, during a fierce rainstorm. Crittenden advanced and drove back the Federals, but rain, smoke, and fog greatly confused the fighting, and the wet weather prevented many of the Confederates' obsolete flintlock muskets from firing. In the confusion, Confederate Brig. Gen. Felix Zollicoffer was killed when he mistakenly rode into the Union lines. After a fierce fight, Crittenden left behind his wounded and much of his equipment, retreated across the Cumberland River, and abandoned eastern Kentucky to the Federals.

Soon after this small victory, Union forces in the west began to make great strides against the Confederates. In February 1862, Union Brig. Gen. U. S. Grant, with the cooperation of Andrew Foote's fleet, moved against Forts Henry and Donelson, Tennessee, to gain control of the lower Tennessee and Cumberland Rivers. If Grant captured the forts, the Confederate defensive line anchored at Bowling Green, Kentucky, would be turned, and Albert Sidney Johnston would have to withdraw into Tennessee. The Union might then capture Nashville and Middle Tennessee, as well.

Foote's gunboats forced the surrender of Fort Henry on February 6, and Grant marched his 15,000 men east toward Fort Donelson. There Confederate Brig. Gen. John B. Floyd had about 21,000 men, but he made no attempt to engage the Federals before they reached the fort. In bitterly cold weather, Grant besieged Fort Donelson, while Foote attacked unsuccessfully from the river. In a daring escape attempt on February 15, Floyd successfully punched a hole through the Union lines but then lost his nerve and ordered his men back into the defenses. That night the Confederate generals decided to surrender, but Floyd and Maj. Gen. Gideon Pillow feared being captured and turned command over to Brig. Gen. Simon Buckner. Floyd and Pillow then escaped, as did Col. Nathan Bedford Forrest and his cavalry. On February 16, Buckner surrendered the fort, 65 cannons, 20,000 muskets, and 12,000 to 15,000 men. The capture of Fort Donelson forced the Confederates to abandon Kentucky, led to the Union occupation of Nashville on February 23, and made a hero out of Grant.

After the loss of Forts Henry and Donelson, the Confederates' defensive line on the Mississippi River centered on New Madrid, Missouri, and Island No. 10. On February 28, 1862, Union Maj. Gen. John Pope left Commerce, Missouri, with 18,000 men to seize New Madrid and open the way to Memphis, Tennessee. Reaching New Madrid on March 3, Pope forced Confederate Brig. Gen. John P. McCown to withdraw his garrison on March 13 to a peninsula across the river. Although he had saved his troops, McCown was replaced by William W. Mackall for abandoning New Madrid. Pope next cut a canal across the tip of land on the west bank facing Island No. 10 so Foote's gunboats could avoid running past the island's fortifications. The first of two of Foote's gunboats moved through the canal on April 4, and on April 7 Pope transferred his troops to the river's east bank, cutting off Mackall's line of retreat from the peninsula. Trapped, Mackall later that day surrendered Island No. 10, with his 6,000 men and heavy cannons. At a cost of about 50 men, Pope had successfully opened the river for a drive toward Memphis.

On the same day Pope captured Island No. 10, the fate of Tennessee also was being decided. After losing Forts Henry and Donelson, Albert Sidney Johnston retreated to the important railroad junction of Corinth, Mississippi. Grant's Union forces then advanced to Pittsburg Landing and Shiloh Church on the Tennessee River's west bank, just a few miles north of the

Tennessee-Mississippi state line. Meanwhile, Union Maj. Gen. Don Carlos Buell and his 36,000-man Army of the Ohio had occupied Nashville, Tennessee, and were preparing to join Grant at Shiloh for an advance on Corinth. Johnston knew his only hope of avoiding disaster was to strike Grant before Buell could reinforce him.

Johnston's 44,000-man Army of the Mississippi departed Corinth on April 3. Bad weather and the men's inexperience slowed the march, and by the time the Confederates reached Shiloh on April 5, Johnston's subordinates feared they had lost the element of surprise. Despite their concerns, Johnston decided to attack. Grant ignored warnings of Confederate troops in the area and was completely surprised when Johnston attacked early on the morning of April 6, 1862. At first the Confederates overran the Federals' camps, but the thick woods and pockets of stubborn Union resistance at the Hornets' Nest and Peach Orchard soon slowed the advance. Casualties were very high on both sides as the Confederates launched repeated frontal attacks. In one assault, Johnston was shot in the leg and bled to death before a tourniquet could be applied. Beauregard took command and stopped the advance in late afternoon after deciding nothing more could be gained that day. Grant was reinforced by Buell's army that night and assumed the offensive on the morning of April 7. After more vicious fighting, the now superior Union army battered back the Confederates until Beauregard finally ordered a withdrawal to Corinth.

The Battle of Shiloh was the war's first great clash of arms. Grant lost 13,047 men to the Confederates' 10,694, making the total casualties greater than all of America's combined war losses up to the Civil War. The battle did not enhance either Grant's or Beauregard's reputations. Grant was criticized for being surprised (and falsely accused of being drunk) and was replaced by Henry Halleck, who began a slow siege of Corinth. Beauregard, in turn, earned Jefferson Davis's wrath first by misleading him with a report that a great victory had been won and later by evacuating Corinth without a fight and taking an unauthorized leave of absence. He was soon replaced in command of the Confederate army by Braxton Bragg.

Meanwhile, Union forces also were gaining the upper hand west of the Mississippi River. Early in 1862, Confederate Maj. Gen. Sterling Price was in a threatening position in southwestern Missouri. When Union Brig. Gen. Samuel R. Curtis's Army of the Southwest advanced in February, Price withdrew into northwest Arkansas and joined forces with Brig. Gen. Benjamin McCulloch. Curtis's 10,250 men took up a defensive position near Pea Ridge, Arkansas, to block any move the Confederates might make against Missouri. Confederate Maj. Gen. Earl Van Dorn joined Price and

McCulloch in early March, combined their 16,500 men into the Army of the West, and advanced toward Missouri.

When Van Dorn divided his army to attack the Federals from the north and west, Curtis split his army to meet the threats. The resultant Battle of Pea Ridge actually was two distinct clashes nearly two miles apart. To the west, the Confederates at first drove the Federals back on March 7, but then McCulloch and Brig. Gen. James McIntosh were killed, and the assaults finally were repulsed. Around Elkhorn Tavern, the Confederates pushed the Federals back almost a mile in very heavy fighting before darkness ended the battle. That night, both Curtis and Van Dorn concentrated around Elkhorn Tavern, and on the morning of March 8, the Federals assumed the offensive. Exhausted and very low on artillery ammunition, the Confederate army broke and retreated in a disorganized fashion, giving Curtis a decisive victory that not only ended the Confederate threat to Missouri but also led to the Union occupation of much of Arkansas.

Union forces quickly followed up their victories at Shiloh and Pea Ridge with an attack on New Orleans, Louisiana, to seize control of the lower Mississippi River. An armada led by Flag Officer David Farragut assembled at the river's mouth in March 1862. The only obstacles facing Farragut were Forts Jackson and St. Philip, located about 12 miles above Head of Passes. The forts were manned by several hundred Confederates under the command of Brig. Gen. Johnson K. Duncan, but many of their cannons were antiquated, and the powder proved to be of poor quality. A large boom made by chaining schooners together also had been stretched across the river as a barrier, and a small River Defense Fleet of 12 Confederate gunboats was assembled to assist Duncan.

Farragut was reluctant to steam past the ominous forts and decided to use David Porter's mortar boats to reduce them. Beginning on April 18, the Federals bombarded the forts for a week and under the cover of darkness were able to cut a small hole in the boom to allow the fleet to pass through. When the bombardment proved ineffective, Farragut steamed past the forts in the predawn hours of April 24. A tremendous artillery engagement resulted, but he routed the Confederate River Defense Fleet and moved most of his ships above the forts with little loss. Farragut captured New Orleans on April 25 and took Baton Rouge a few days later. This stunning victory greatly demoralized the Confederates and placed the Federals in a position to gain complete control of the Mississippi River. After its capture, New Orleans was occupied by troops under Maj. Gen. Benjamin F. Butler, whose harsh rule soon earned him the nickname "Beast Butler." The city remained in Union hands for the remainder of the war.

On May 10, 1862, Capt. James E. Montgomery's small Confederate River Defense Fleet attempted to blunt the Union offensive on the upper Mississippi River by attacking Capt. Charles H. Davis's Union fleet at Plum Run Bend, Tennessee. Caught by surprise, the USS *Cincinnati* and USS *Mound City* were rammed and sunk, but the Confederates were forced to withdraw when the rest of the Union fleet arrived. Afterward, the Confederates abandoned Fort Pillow, Tennessee, and the River Defense Fleet retreated to Memphis. On June 6, 1862, a Union fleet under Col. Charles Ellet and Davis approached Memphis from upstream. In a short, decisive battle at daybreak, the Federals sank or captured all but one of the Confederate ships. Ellet, who was mortally wounded, was the only Union casualty in the battle, while the Confederates lost approximately 180 men. Federal troops then occupied Memphis and used it as a base for future operations on the river.

While the U.S. Navy slowly gained control of the Mississippi River, Union fortunes also were improving in the eastern theater. In February 1862, a combined force under Brig. Gen. Ambrose E. Burnside and Flag Officer Louis M. Goldsborough attacked the North Carolina coast to gain a foothold in the region and to establish coaling stations for the North Atlantic Blockading Squadron. After brushing aside a small Confederate fleet, the Federals captured Roanoke Island and 2,500 Confederate defenders on February 8 and New Bern on March 14.

Following these successes, and after much prodding from Lincoln, George B. McClellan unveiled his Urbanna Plan. This aimed to bypass the Confederate position at Manassas by ferrying the Army of the Potomac through the Chesapeake Bay to Urbanna, Virginia, located on the Rappahannock River's south bank only 50 miles east of Richmond. When Confederate Gen. Joseph E. Johnston evacuated his Manassas line in early March 1862 and retreated to the south side of the Rappahannock, McClellan's plan was ruined, for the Confederate army was in a position to block his advance from Urbanna to Richmond. McClellan then decided to transfer his army by sea to Fort Monroe, Virginia, located southeast of Richmond on the tip of the Virginia Peninsula. From there, he could move up the peninsula toward Richmond and have his flanks protected by the York and James Rivers and his waterborne supply line secured. Lincoln preferred an overland march toward Richmond so Washington would be protected but finally approved the plan on the condition McClellan leave enough troops behind to defend the capital. To ensure the campaign's success, Lincoln also removed McClellan as general-in-chief so he could concentrate on leading the Army of the Potomac to victory. Major General Henry Halleck was brought to Washington from the west to coordinate the Union war effort as general-in-chief.

As McClellan prepared to move his army to Fort Monroe, a historic encounter between the world's first iron battleships occurred. An important part of Virginia's coastal defenses was the CSS *Virginia*, an ironclad that had been constructed from the hulk of the USS *Merrimac* after it was burned when the Federals evacuated Norfolk, Virginia. Captain Franklin Buchanan took the *Virginia* out of Norfolk on March 8 to attack the Union fleet anchored at nearby Hampton Roads. Buchanan first rammed the USS *Cumberland* and sank it in shallow water, but his ram broke off inside the enemy ship. He then attacked the *Congress*, whose captain ran it aground while trying to escape, and set it ablaze. After Buchanan was wounded in the thigh by small arms fire, Lt. Catesby Ap Jones took command of the *Virginia* and withdrew.

On March 9, Jones steamed back to Hampton Roads to finish off the Union vessels. By then, the USS *Monitor*, the Union's first unique ironclad, had arrived and was protecting the *Minnesota*. The two ironclads engaged in a point-blank duel that lasted several hours. While the *Virginia* was larger and carried more guns, the *Monitor* was faster and more maneuverable, and the battle was a stalemate. Shortly after noon, both ships withdrew when a Confederate shell temporarily blinded Lt. John L. Worden, commander of the *Monitor*, and the *Virginia* suffered rudder damage. Neither ship suffered extensive damage in the historic battle, thus proving the protective value of the iron plates that revolutionized warships.

McClellan departed Washington with more than 100,000 men on March 17, 1862, and by April 4 had his army ashore at Fort Monroe, Virginia, to begin what became known as the Peninsula Campaign. Facing him were Maj. Gen. John B. Magruder and about 17,000 Confederates strongly entrenched in a line running across the Virginia Peninsula from Yorktown to the James River. Magruder's ingenious deception tactics, and faulty intelligence provided by Allan Pinkerton, caused McClellan to believe the Confederate line was too strong to assault. He began a long siege that allowed Johnston time to move his army from the Rappahannock River to the peninsula and assemble approximately 60,000 men to defend Richmond. Small but indecisive battles were fought at Yorktown and Williamsburg as McClellan pressed Johnston up the peninsula. When Union forces captured Norfolk on May 9, the Confederates were unable to withdraw the *Virginia* upriver because of its deep draft and had to destroy it on May 11 to keep it out of enemy hands.

Much to Jefferson Davis's chagrin, Johnston retreated to the outskirts of Richmond, but on May 31, 1862, he finally attacked two isolated Union corps on the south side of the Chickahominy River. In the two-day Battle of Seven Pines, the fighting again was indecisive, and Johnston was seriously wounded. Davis then placed Gen. Robert E. Lee, his military adviser, in command of the army, which Lee renamed the Army of Northern Virginia. Although he had not yet proven himself in the war, Lee was an aggressive officer and planned to take the offensive. To be successful, however, he needed the troops under Stonewall Jackson in the Shenandoah Valley as reinforcements.

Lee earlier had suggested to Jackson that he begin offensive operations in the Shenandoah Valley to prevent the Union forces there from reinforcing McClellan. In March 1862, Jackson's small Valley Army attacked the Federals at Kernstown. Although defeated, his aggressiveness alarmed Washington and caused Lincoln to withhold thousands of troops from McClellan. Jackson soon was reinforced, and in May he launched his famous Shenandoah Valley Campaign. Relying on surprise, aggressiveness, and swift marching, he attacked and defeated the enemy at McDowell, Front Royal, and the First Battle of Winchester and virtually cleared the Valley of Union troops. When three Federal columns began converging to trap him, Jackson retreated, defeated the enemy at Cross Keys and Port Republic, and made his escape. In the 30-day campaign, Jackson marched his nearly 17,000 men 350 miles, defeated three different Union commands in five battles, inflicted twice as many casualties as he suffered, captured tons of valuable supplies, and succeeded in his primary mission of occupying some 60,000 enemy troops that otherwise would have been sent to the peninsula.

In late June 1862, Lee ordered Jackson to Richmond to take advantage of a tactical mistake made by McClellan. The Union commander had kept his army split across the Chickahominy River after the Battle of Seven Pines, and Fitz John Porter's 30,000-man V Corps was isolated on the north side of the river. Lee decided to strike after J. E. B. Stuart's Ride revealed that Porter's right flank was "in the air." In a daring move, Lee left part of his army on the south side of the Chickahominy River to defend Richmond against McClellan's main force of 70,000 men, while massing the bulk of the army on the river's north side to crush Porter. The plan was risky, but Lee took into account McClellan's habit of slowness and his cautiousness. Jackson played the key role in the plan, for he was to march from the Valley and attack Porter from the north on June 26. When the other Confederate units heard Jackson attack, they would advance from the west.

Lee was startled when McClellan advanced south of the Chickahominy on June 25 as if he had learned of the plan and was attacking Richmond. The Battle of Oak Grove/King's School House proved to be only a reconnaissance in force, but it was the first battle in what became known as the Seven Days Campaign. The next day, Jackson failed to get into position on time, but the other Confederates attacked Porter at Mechanicsville. Porter skillfully held his position against repeated assaults and that night retreated to Gaines' Mill, where he again took up a strong position on high ground. Lee launched numerous attacks on June 27 and after very bloody fighting finally broke through the Union line and forced Porter to withdraw. Completely unnerved by the unexpected fighting, McClellan began a general retreat, claiming he simply was changing his base from the York River to the James River. In doing so, he virtually abandoned his responsibilities and provided little leadership during the difficult withdrawal.

June 28 was spent largely in maneuver, but on June 29 Lee attacked the Federals at Savage's Station with little success. The next day, he again was frustrated when he attacked at Frayser's Farm but was unable to crush the enemy. By July 1, McClellan had positioned his army in a very strong position at Malvern Hill, near the James River. There his artillery was massed to cover a deadly killing field, and Union gunboats were near enough to provide supporting fire. Believing the Federals were demoralized and that one more attack would finish them, Lee impatiently ordered his infantry to attack the nearly impregnable position. In a series of disjointed assaults, the Confederates were slaughtered by the Union artillery and failed to make any significant gains. The campaign ended the next day when McClellan fell back to a strong position at Harrison's Landing on the James River, which Lee wisely decided not to attack.

Although Richmond had been saved, Lee was frustrated with his officers for failing to carry out his plans effectively. The campaign was marred by a lack of coordination, poor staff work, and slowness on the part of several generals (most noticeably Jackson), but it still was a great Confederate victory and marked Lee's rise to prominence. On the Federal side, the Union soldiers had fought very well, and the army had carried out a skillful retreat. McClellan, on the other hand, had exercised little command over the army and at times could be accused of actually abandoning his men. In the weeklong campaign, Lee lost a staggering 20,141 men to McClellan's 15,849 casualties.

Although McClellan had been stopped, Virginia was quickly threatened by another Union army. After his victories at New Madrid and Island No. 10, Pope was ordered to Washington. Given command of the Army of Virginia in late June 1862, he was to protect the capital and the Shenandoah Valley and assist McClellan's advance on Richmond by threatening Charlottesville, Virginia. After McClellan was defeated in the Seven Days Campaign, Lincoln knew he would not soon resume the offensive and ordered him to send the Army of the Potomac to Washington to reinforce Pope. Lee realized that if McClellan's men joined Pope's 63,000 troops, the combined force would be much too large for his Army of Northern Virginia to stop. His only hope was to defeat Pope before McClellan could reinforce him.

Lee first sent Stonewall Jackson's 24,000 men northward, and Jackson defeated Pope's advance guard in a poorly managed battle at Cedar Mountain on August 9, 1862. Lee soon joined Jackson and in a bold plan divided his army into two wings under Jackson and James Longstreet. Leaving Longstreet to pin down Pope on the Rappahannock River, Lee sent Jackson and Stuart's cavalry upstream around the enemy's right flank and into Pope's rear to cut him off from Washington and force him to withdraw from the Rappahannock line. Lee and Longstreet then would follow Jackson's route, join him, and together fight the decisive battle.

Jackson began his march on August 25 and covered 54 miles in 36 hours. He captured Pope's supply base at Manassas Junction and burned it on August 27 before moving to Groveton and taking up a hidden position near the Warrenton Turnpike. Thinking the Confederates were simply a cavalry raid, Pope sent units to the rear to drive them off. Late in the afternoon of August 28, Jackson fought a furious but indecisive battle with Rufus King's Union division at Groveton. So intent was Pope on destroying the Confederates in his rear that he failed to take adequate steps to block Lee, who was able to follow Jackson's route unmolested.

After Groveton, Jackson took up a defensive position on the old Manassas battlefield along the cuts and embankments of an unfinished railroad. Pope concentrated his army there and throughout August 29 attacked Jackson, but he committed his men piecemeal and failed to dislodge the badly outnumbered Confederates. Lee arrived on the field about noon and placed Longstreet at nearly right angles with Jackson's right flank, positioning his army much like a trap ready to spring shut against the Federals. Pope ignored warnings from Fitz John Porter that Longstreet had arrived and later court-martialed Porter for failing to make an ordered flank attack. After Jackson again repulsed Union attacks on August 30, Lee finally sprang the trap by sending Longstreet in an attack that crushed Pope's left flank and drove the Federals from the field. The Second Battle of Manassas cost Pope 13,826 men to Lee's 8,353. Lee sent Jackson after the Federals to cut them off from Washington, and another bloody battle was fought on September 1 at Chantilly, but Pope escaped.

Pope bitterly blamed his subordinates for his defeat, particularly Porter, and accused McClellan of trying to win back command by withholding timely reinforcements so he would be defeated. Despite the accusation, Lincoln was desperate to restore order out of the chaos and placed McClellan back in command of the Union forces around Washington.

The late summer and autumn of 1862 found the Confederates on a surprising general offensive. In the west, two Confederate armies moved north in the Kentucky Campaign, and in Virginia, Lee held the initiative after his successful Second Manassas Campaign. Lee decided to invade Maryland to take the war out of Virginia during the crucial harvest season; to liberate Maryland to allow it and new recruits to join the Confederacy; to alarm the Union and strengthen the Northern peace movement; and to win European recognition and aid by defeating the Union Army of the Potomac on its own soil. After crossing the Potomac River on September 4, 1862, Lee concentrated his army at Frederick, Maryland, and divided it into two wings. Longstreet's three divisions accompanied Lee to Hagerstown, Maryland, while Jackson took six divisions to attack the 12,000-man Union garrison at Harpers Ferry, Virginia, so it would not threaten Lee's lines of communications. The invasion's success depended on the Federals being slow to react, thus giving Lee time to reconcentrate his army before battle was given.

McClellan responded to the enemy offensive cautiously. He did not begin his pursuit until September 7 and then was careful to remain in a position to protect both Washington and Baltimore, Maryland, from attack. On September 12, the Federals entered Frederick, and the next day two Union soldiers discovered the famous Lost Order, which detailed Lee's campaign strategy. Now knowing the enemy's disposition and plans, McClellan was in an excellent position to march swiftly and defeat the scattered Confederate army in detail. However, he believed Lee greatly outnumbered him and waited 16 hours before leaving Frederick. When Lee realized the Union army was marching more rapidly, he left one division to hold the South Mountain passes to delay McClellan's advance and ordered the army to concentrate near Sharpsburg, Maryland. Jackson was to hurry his Harpers Ferry operation and join Lee at Sharpsburg as soon as possible.

On September 14, McClellan moved against South Mountain, but Daniel H. Hill's Confederates held the passes until dark, and then Union Maj. Gen. William B. Franklin failed to push on to relieve Harpers Ferry as ordered. When the Union army advanced the next day, Lee was preparing to retreat to Virginia, but he decided to concentrate near Sharpsburg when he learned that Jackson would soon capture Harpers Ferry. When the enemy garrison surrendered on September 15, Jackson left behind Maj. Gen. A. P. Hill's division to parole the Union prisoners and hurriedly marched to join Lee.

On the morning of September 16, the superior Union force made contact with Lee near Sharpsburg, but McClellan failed to attack. When Jackson arrived later in the day, Lee had 40,000 men on hand and decided to make a stand along the west bank of Antietam Creek. To offer battle against the entire

Union army with the Potomac River in his rear was tactically unwise, but he had entered Maryland as a liberator and apparently believed he could not withdraw without a fight. McClellan soon had 75,000 men on hand, but he spent the rest of the day reconnoitering rather than attacking the thinly held Confederate line.

On September 17, the Federals attacked both Confederate flanks and the center but failed to coordinate their assaults. These disjointed attacks allowed Lee to take advantage of his interior line and skillfully move units to threatened points. Some of the bloodiest fighting of the war took place on the northern part of the field around the Miller cornfield and in the center along Bloody Lane. In the afternoon, the battle entered its third phase on Lee's right flank. There, after wasting much of the day, Ambrose Burnside finally forced his way across a stone bridge (known afterward as Burnside's Bridge) and was threatening to crush the Confederate flank when Hill dramatically arrived after a forced march from Harpers Ferry and stopped the Union advance. When the battle ended, the opposing armies were in much the same positions they had occupied that morning. After remaining on the field through September 18, Lee began recrossing the Potomac River into Virginia that night, and the Antietam Campaign ended.

The Battle of Antietam proved to be the bloodiest single day of the Civil War and in American history, with Lee losing approximately 10,300 men to McClellan's 12,400. It was a battle where Lee showed remarkable tactical skill by shifting troops from one threatened point to another. On the other hand, it also demonstrated his weakness for accepting battle at any odds. Lee risked his army for what, in the best case, could only have been a stalemate. McClellan's battle plan was sound, and his men fought bravely, but he showed no skill in directing the fight. Each of his attacks was launched piecemeal, and a large part of his army was never even engaged. Although tactically a stalemate, Antietam proved to be a strategic Union victory because it stopped Lee's invasion and kept Maryland firmly in the Union. It also changed the war itself, because Lincoln used the victory to announce his Emancipation Proclamation.

In the summer of 1862, the Union armies in the west were poised to continue their advance southward. At Corinth, Mississippi, Grant was threatening Vicksburg, Mississippi, and in northern Alabama, Buell's Army of the Ohio was menacing Chattanooga, Tennessee. The situation looked bleak for the western Confederates, but just as Lee was assuming the offensive in the east, they, too, took the war to the enemy. Bragg's Confederate Army of the Mississippi was at Tupelo, Mississippi, and Maj. Gen. Edmund Kirby Smith's small army was in Tennessee. In late July, Bragg decided to move swiftly to join Kirby Smith in Middle Tennessee, where together they could threaten the Union supply lines and force Grant and Buell to withdraw or, perhaps, even to defeat them in detail. Bragg left 16,000 men at Tupelo under Maj. Gen. Sterling Price to cooperate with Maj. Gen. Earl Van Dorn in an invasion of western Tennessee and then moved his army to Chattanooga. From there, he planned to join forces with Kirby Smith for an invasion of Middle Tennessee and Kentucky.

Bragg's plan was foiled by Kirby Smith, who was the commander of a separate department and not entirely under Bragg's jurisdiction. Kirby Smith decided to launch his own invasion of Kentucky, where it was believed large numbers of recruits were eager to join the Confederate army. Leaving part of his army to guard the Cumberland Gap, Kirby Smith advanced from Knoxville, Tennessee, on August 14, thus making it impossible for Bragg to join forces with him. Still hoping for a successful invasion, Bragg moved north, as well, on August 28 and followed a course parallel to Kirby Smith about 100 miles to the west. When Lee began the Antietam Campaign soon afterward, it appeared the Confederacy was about to strike two crippling blows against the Union.

On August 30, Kirby Smith attacked and defeated Maj. Gen. William Nelson at Richmond, Kentucky, and two days later, occupied Lexington. He then could have joined Bragg and formed a considerable invasion force, but, instead, he weakened Confederate strength by allowing his men to spread out from Cumberland Gap to Lexington. Elements of Bragg's army attacked the Union garrison at Munfordville, Kentucky, on September 14 and captured it after three days of sporadic fighting. Bragg then marched to Bardstown. Meanwhile, Buell had received reinforcements from Grant and had withdrawn into Kentucky on a nearly parallel course west of Bragg. If Bragg had used his cavalry more effectively, he would have been aware of Buell's location and perhaps could have broken up his long column. Instead, Buell reached Louisville unmolested on September 29 and received reinforcements. The tide now had turned, for the Confederates not only were outnumbered badly, but they also were scattered widely across the Kentucky countryside.

At Frankfort, Bragg installed a secessionist government under Gov. Richard Hawes to attract support for the Confederate cause. The dream of thousands of new recruits proved to be overly optimistic, because those Kentuckians who supported the Confederacy had already volunteered. As a result, the invasion brought little to the Confederacy in terms of fresh manpower.

On October 1, the Federals advanced against the Confederates in four columns. Bragg ordered Leonidas Polk, whom he had left in command at

Bardstown, to cooperate with Kirby Smith in an attack on Buell, but Polk claimed he was outnumbered and retreated, thus widening the distance between himself and Kirby Smith. Bragg then was forced to abandon Frankfort and rejoin the main army, bringing along with him the newly installed Confederate government. The two armies collided at Perryville on October 8. Buell at first was driven back, but he had reinforcements close at hand and finally stopped Bragg's attack. Although the battle had been a tactical stalemate, a number of factors convinced Bragg it was time to withdraw. He faced a superior, concentrated foe, while he had enjoyed little success in cooperating with Kirby Smith. Also, Van Dorn and Price had been defeated at Iuka and Corinth, Mississippi, and would not be able to support him by invading western Tennessee. Finally, a lack of supplies and drought conditions made it difficult to supply the army, and the lack of recruitment showed that Kentucky was not ready to join the Confederacy.

Bragg withdrew from Perryville on the night of October 8 and united with Kirby Smith at London, Kentucky. The combined Confederate force then retreated through Cumberland Gap and reentered Tennessee on October 26. The Kentucky Campaign had been a dismal failure and, together with Lee's retreat from Maryland, ruined what may have been one of the Confederacy's best chances to force the Union to the peace table. The campaign also ended Buell's career. His pursuit of the retreating Confederates was so feeble that he was removed from command, and William S. Rosecrans and his Army of the Cumberland became the main Union force in Tennessee.

Civil War armies usually did not campaign in the winter because it was nearly impossible to move over rain-soaked roads, but in December 1862, several campaigns were undertaken before the war took a respite. When McClellan failed to pursue the retreating Confederates after the Antietam Campaign, Lincoln replaced him in command of the Army of the Potomac in early November 1862 with Maj. Gen. Ambrose E. Burnside. Before winter ended the campaign season, Burnside marched the army rapidly to Falmouth, Virginia, where he planned to cross the Rappahannock River at Fredericksburg and advance toward Richmond before Lee could bring his scattered units into position to challenge him. Burnside had his 120,000 men concentrated at Falmouth by November 19 before Lee could respond. But his pontoon bridges failed to arrive on time, and Lee was able to assemble his army on the hills behind Fredericksburg. Burnside's pontoon bridges finally arrived on November 25, and engineers began laying them on December 11. After considerable fighting, in which Fredericksburg was wrecked by artillery fire and looted by the Federals, the bridges were completed, and Burnside crossed the river.

Burnside divided his army into the Left Grand Division, under William B. Franklin, and the Right Grand Division, under Edwin V. Sumner. He made a general advance on the morning of December 13, with Franklin attacking Jackson's position on the Confederate right and Sumner attacking Longstreet on the left. Franklin enjoyed some success when he briefly broke through Jackson's line at a point that had been left undefended, but Jackson rushed forward reinforcements and sealed the break. The battle then stagnated on the Confederate right but rose to a fury on the left, where Longstreet held an impregnable position behind a stone wall on Marye's Heights. Wave after wave of Union troops assaulted the hill, only to be shot down by the hundreds in front of the stone wall. The Irish Brigade particularly won acclaim in its brave, but unsuccessful, attack. When Burnside halted the bloodletting, the Federals had suffered one of their greatest disasters of the war, losing 12,653 men to Lee's 5,309 casualties (most of whom were on Jackson's front). Burnside retreated across the river on the night of December 15, but in January 1863, he marched upstream to turn Lee out of his formidable position. Tremendous winter rains turned the roads to quagmires, and Burnside's so-called Mud March finally was called off. Burnside bitterly blamed his subordinates for his failure at Fredericksburg and demanded that a number of officers be cashiered from the army. Ultimately, however, Lincoln held him responsible for the defeat and replaced him with Maj. Gen. Joseph Hooker.

In the west, two major campaigns occurred in late December 1862. Major General U. S. Grant, commander of the Department of the Tennessee, first launched his Overland Vicksburg Campaign to capture Vicksburg, Mississippi. Grant advanced from Tennessee through north-central Mississippi to draw the Confederate defenders away from the city, while William T. Sherman moved down the Mississippi River to attack the town itself. Grant was forced to retreat when Confederate cavalry under Nathan Bedford Forrest and Earl Van Dorn destroyed his supply line in Tennessee and at Holly Springs, Mississippi, respectively. Unaware that Grant's maneuver had failed to weaken the enemy's defenses, Sherman moved by transport up the Yazoo River and suffered a bloody repulse at Chickasaw Bayou when he attempted to take the Confederate-held high ground by storm.

In Middle Tennessee, Rosecran's Army of the Cumberland moved out of Nashville on December 26 to drive Bragg's Army of Tennessee from its base at Murfreesboro. To disrupt the advance, Bragg sent Joseph Wheeler's cavalry on a successful raid in the Federals' rear that captured a significant number of prisoners and wagons. Rosecrans reached Murfreesboro on December 30, but when he failed to attack, Bragg seized the initiative. At daylight on December 31, his entire left wing moved forward in an attack that made a giant right wheel. Fighting was vicious in dense cedar thickets that broke up the Confederate lines. Rosecrans's right flank took the brunt of the assault and was pushed back steadily. Philip Sheridan's Union division and other units made a desperate stand to slow the Confederates, but eventually they had to fall back, as well. The Union line came to resemble a *V*, with the angle located at the Round Forest or "Hell's Half Acre." The Confederates repeatedly charged the Round Forest in a piecemeal fashion, only to be annihilated by volleys of rifle fire and massed cannons. Unable to break the stubborn Union defense, the bloodied and exhausted Confederates finally ended their attacks about dark.

Neither side attacked on January 1, 1863, but the cavalry was active in raids and skirmishes behind Union lines. Bragg expected Rosecrans to retreat, but the Federals simply withdrew from the Round Forest to straighten out their line. By January 2, the bulk of both armies were on the west side of Stones River. John C. Breckinridge's Confederate division remained alone east of the river, as did one Union division under Col. Samuel Beatty. Bragg's main line west of the river could be enfiladed by the Federals on the east side so he ordered Breckinridge to attack and drive them back. Breckinridge vehemently protested the order because Union artillery on the west bank would enfilade his attacking line. Bragg insisted, however, and Breckinridge finally obeyed under protest. The Confederates advanced late in the afternoon and succeeded in driving the Federals back to the river. But then, as Breckinridge predicted, his men were cut down by the massed cannons on the west bank and were forced to retreat.

With his men exhausted and Stones River rising from recent rains and threatening to cut the army in two, Bragg reluctantly withdrew in a driving rain late on the night of January 3. Although he initially enjoyed great tactical success, his withdrawal allowed Rosecrans to claim final victory. The three-day battle had no strategic effect on the war, but it cost Bragg 10,266 men and Rosecrans 13,249.

1863 MILITARY CAMPAIGNS

As a new campaign season began, the Union had made significant gains in the west, but the war in the east was stalemated, and the issue was still very much in doubt. The year would close with the Union perhaps having turned the tide of battle against the Confederates.

January 1863 began promising for the Union when Rosecrans won the Battle of Stones River, Tennessee, but then a setback occurred in Texas. The

U.S. Navy had captured Galveston in October 1862 and closed its port to blockade-runners. To reopen it, Confederate Maj. Gen. John B. Magruder assembled two cottonclad gunboats and a small assault force and moved against the Federals before dawn on January 1, 1863. In a wild, bloody melee in Galveston Bay, Magruder captured the USS *Harriet Lane*, forced another Union ship to run aground, and caused the crew of a third to destroy their own vessel. At the cost of one cottonclad and 143 casualties, Magruder recaptured Galveston, and the port remained in Confederate hands until war's end.

Much of the western war in 1863 focused on the Mississippi River and the last two Confederate strongholds at Vicksburg, Mississippi, and Port Hudson, Louisiana. If the Union could capture them, it would gain control of the river, split the Confederacy in two, and accomplish one of the Anaconda Plan's major goals. In January 1863, Maj. Gen. John C. McClernand assumed command of the Union forces on the Mississippi River and successfully captured the Confederate garrison at Arkansas Post. Grant then took command of all the Union troops assigned for the Vicksburg operation and began a new campaign with his Army of the Tennessee.

Moving downriver from Memphis, Tennessee, with David Porter's fleet, Grant's immediate problem was how to get at Vicksburg. The city sat atop high river bluffs that were heavily defended by artillery, and Confederate Lt. Gen. John C. Pemberton had more than 40,000 men under his command. Sherman's earlier defeat at Chickasaw Bayou proved that a frontal attack against the high ground was impossible. Also, it seemed suicidal to run the ships past the bluffs to land troops below Vicksburg, but floodwater prevented any overland maneuver. Grant's solution to the dilemma was to bypass Vicksburg through Grant's Canals. By digging a canal across the peninsula fronting the city, he hoped to straighten out the river and take his troops below the city by transport without having to steam past the deadly bluffs, but poor canal placement and the falling Mississippi River doomed this project. Other canals were dug to connect the Mississippi River with inland bayous to allow ships to go from the Mississippi River through a series of Louisiana streams, and reenter the Mississippi below Vicksburg. These, too, failed because of river obstructions and the falling water level. Grant also tried similar projects in Mississippi. In early March, the Yazoo Pass and Steele's Bayou Expeditions moved troops by transports through levee cuts and into Mississippi's interior waterways to get into the rear of Vicksburg, but river obstructions and enemy opposition stopped both attempts.

All of these projects kept the Union army busy until April 1863, when the floodwater began to recede. Grant then marched his men downstream, and on the nights of April 16 and 22, Porter successfully ran several ships past Vicksburg. To divert the Confederates' attention away from the river during these operations, Sherman probed Snyder's Bluff on the Yazoo River, while Benjamin Grierson's and Abel Streight's Raids were launched in Mississippi and Alabama, respectively. McClernand's and James P. McPherson's corps marched to Hard Times, Louisiana, and Porter ferried them across the river to Bruinsburg, Mississippi, on April 30. Confused by Grant's strategy, Pemberton had few troops to counter the Federals' inland march from Bruinsburg.

On May 1, McClernand and McPherson defeated a small Confederate force under John Bowen at Port Gibson. Grant next decided to move against Jackson, Mississippi, to disperse a growing enemy army there before turning west to attack Vicksburg itself. This maneuver also would give him control of the vital railroad connecting Jackson and Vicksburg, over which Pemberton received supplies and reinforcements. Against the advice of his subordinates, Grant left the river, marched toward Jackson, and placed his 44,000 men deep inside Confederate territory.

Pemberton was taken by surprise by Grant's maneuver, for he expected the Federals to follow the retreating Bowen due north to Vicksburg. Sherman's corps joined Grant on May 8, and on May 12, McPherson's corps defeated a small Confederate detachment at Raymond and pushed it back toward Jackson. Joseph E. Johnston arrived at Jackson the next day to take command of the Confederates there, but he was defeated on May 14 and was forced out of the city. After leaving Sherman's corps to destroy the railroad and public property, Grant left Jackson and headed west toward Vicksburg. Throughout these maneuvers, Johnston ordered Pemberton to leave Vicksburg and engage the Federals while they were strung out on the roads and vulnerable. At the same time, Pemberton was ordered by Jefferson Davis to hold the city at all costs. Confused by conflicting orders, he took no decisive action to stop Grant until it was too late. Pemberton finally advanced from Vicksburg and engaged Grant at Champion Hill on May 16, but he was defeated in the campaign's largest battle and forced to retreat. The next day, the Federals brushed aside the Confederate rear guard at the Big Black River Bridge and reached Vicksburg on May 18.

Hills, gullies, and a tangle of abatis aided the 30,000 Confederates defending the city, and months had been spent preparing miles of trenches, earthworks, and fortifications around Vicksburg. After suffering heavy casualties in two unsuccessful frontal attacks on May 19 and May 22, Grant settled into a siege. Over the following weeks, while the Union army grew to 77,000 men, Pemberton's men began to suffer from sickness and shortages of food, medicine, and ammunition. Artillery and rifle fire were constant, and both sides (including many civilians who remained in the city) were forced to live in caves dug into the sides of hills enduring the misery of oppressive heat, water-filled ditches, and frequent thunderstorms. At night, the Federals dug their trenches closer to the Confederates, and during the day they shot at everything that moved. During these weeks, Johnston built up a large army near Jackson and urged Pemberton to break out of the city and join him. Pemberton refused, choosing to obey Davis's orders to hold Vicksburg, and Johnston took no steps to rescue him. The only Confederate attempt to raise the siege was a small, unsuccessful attack against a Union supply base at Milliken's Bend, Louisiana, in early June.

The strain of constant combat and supply shortages finally broke the spirit of many Confederates. With the situation hopeless, Pemberton surrendered the city and its garrison on July 4, 1863. Fearing Johnston might move against his rear, Grant then sent Sherman to the east in a short campaign that successfully besieged Jackson and forced Johnston to withdraw. The capture of Vicksburg ensured Grant's reputation as the Union's most successful general. As a result, in October 1863, he was put in command of the Military Division of the Mississippi and took charge of all the Union forces in the west.

While Grant besieged Vicksburg, to the south a similar siege was carried out at Port Hudson, Louisiana. Major General Nathaniel P. Banks had assumed the offensive early that spring and cleared the Confederates out of south Louisiana in the Bayou Teche Campaign. He then moved against Port Hudson on May 14, 1863. When he failed to take the fortress by storm, Banks settled into a siege with the aid of David Farragut's fleet. Confederate commander Maj. Gen. Franklin Gardner stoically held his position for weeks, but after learning of Vicksburg's surrender, he knew his position was untenable and surrendered his 6,500 men on July 9. With the capture of Port Hudson, the Union finally had won complete control of the Mississippi River and split the Confederacy in two.

To compound the twin Confederate disasters on the Mississippi River, the Army of Tennessee also was forced to abandon Tennessee in the summer of 1863. In June, Rosecrans skillfully maneuvered Bragg out of Middle Tennessee in the Tullahoma Campaign and forced him to retreat to Chattanooga. It was a major triumph for the Union, but it received little attention because of the more spectacular Union victories in Mississippi and Louisiana that summer.

In Virginia, 1863 began dreadfully for the Union. Major General Joseph Hooker had been put in command of the Army of the Potomac after Burnside's

"Mud March" debacle. Encamped across the Rappahannock River from Fredericksburg, he devised a bold plan to force Lee either to abandon his strong position on the heights south of town or be cut off from Richmond. Leaving 40,000 men under Maj. Gen. John Sedgwick to keep Lee's Army of Northern Virginia in position, Hooker took his other 75,000 men upriver on April 27. This column was to cross over the Rappahannock and Rapidan Rivers, march through a tangled region 12 miles west of Fredericksburg known as the Wilderness, and move into Lee's rear. At the same time, Maj. Gen. George Stoneman took his 10,000 cavalrymen and raided behind the Confederates to disrupt their lines of communication. Hooker believed Lee would be forced to abandon his strong defensive position at Fredericksburg and either retreat or fight on ground of Hooker's choosing. With Lt. Gen. James Longstreet's corps on detached duty at Suffolk, Virginia, Lee had only 60,000 men to fend off this deadly trap.

Hooker's plan began well, and he was deep inside the Wilderness before Lee realized what was happening. Largely ignoring Stoneman (who showed no initiative and caused little damage), Lee sent Stuart's cavalry toward Chancellorsville to engage Hooker and then boldly divided his infantry, leaving 10,000 men under Maj. Gen. Jubal A. Early to watch Sedgwick, while taking the other 50,000 toward the Wilderness. Lee's intentions were to stop Hooker in the tangle of woods before he could reach open ground where his superior numbers would be more decisive.

On May 1, the Confederates made contact with Hooker's advance guard. Surprised at the swift enemy response, Hooker suddenly lost his confidence and surrendered the initiative by ordering his men to halt and entrench around Chancellorsville. When Stuart learned that Hooker's right flank was "in the air," Lee decided to hold the front with only 20,000 men and to send Jackson's entire corps on a 14-mile march to attack this exposed flank. Late on the afternoon of May 2, Jackson launched a surprise attack that crushed Maj. Gen. Oliver O. Howard's XI Corps. The Union line was pushed back two miles, and only darkness and a determined stand by Hooker's men saved the Federals from complete disaster. That night, while beyond the lines reconnoitering for a possible night attack, Jackson was mortally wounded when his party was mistakenly fired upon by his own troops.

Throughout May 3, Lee launched numerous costly attacks but gained no appreciable results other than reuniting his separated wings. To relieve the pressure from his front, Hooker ordered Sedgwick to push aside the Confederates at Fredericksburg and threaten Lee's rear. That afternoon, Sedgwick attacked Early and in the Second Battle of Fredericksburg pushed him off Marye's Heights. Faced with this new threat, Lee once again divided his army by leaving Stuart with 25,000 men to contend with Hooker, while he took 20,000 back toward Fredericksburg to help stop Sedgwick. On May 4, Lee attacked Sedgwick near Salem Church, but after some initial success, the Confederate attack stalled. Sedgwick retreated across the river that night, and Hooker followed the next night.

The Chancellorsville Campaign is considered to be Lee's greatest victory. Faced with overwhelming odds, he divided his army three times, defeated two Union columns, and forced the enemy to retreat. The victory came at a very high cost, because Jackson died from his wounds, and the Confederates lost approximately 12,800 men. Once again, Lee had won a spectacular victory but had not struck a decisive blow against the enemy. These heavy casualties, especially in officers, also forced him to reorganize his army only weeks before the Gettysburg Campaign. Hooker suffered approximately 17,300 casualties in the campaign.

After Chancellorsville, Lee once again held the initiative in Virginia. Some government officials and military officers pressured him either to send troops to the west to regain lost territory or even go there himself to take command. Lee could also stay in Virginia to rest and resupply his men, or he could invade the Union and once again take the war to the enemy. Lee believed he could do more good for the Confederacy in the eastern theater and thus opposed all attempts to send him or part of his army to the west. Remaining on the defensive was also unappealing because he favored the offensive. Thus, Lee decided that an invasion of Pennsylvania was in order. Such a move, he argued, would take the war out of Virginia and allow him to gather supplies in rich Pennsylvania. If he could capture a major Northern city or win a large battle on the enemy's soil, an invasion also could strengthen the growing Northern peace movement and perhaps finally win the Confederacy foreign recognition.

On June 3, 1863, the 75,000-man Army of Northern Virginia began marching to Culpeper, Virginia, from where the campaign would begin. Suspecting Lee was planning an offensive, Hooker sent Maj. Gen. Alfred Pleasonton's cavalry across the Rapidan River to probe the Confederates' position. Pleasonton surprised Stuart's cavalry at Brandy Station, and on June 9 the war's largest cavalry battle was fought. In a bloody engagement, Stuart eventually forced Pleasonton to retire, but for the first time in the war, the Union troopers demonstrated they were becoming an equal match to the Confederate cavalry in skill and tenacity. Although it was a victory, Brandy Station tarnished Stuart's reputation because he had been taken by surprise.

Concerned that Hooker was aware of his intentions, Lee hurried Lt. Gen. Richard S. Ewell's corps to the Shenandoah Valley on June 10 to clear the way to the Potomac River. On June 14 and 15, Ewell defeated Maj. Gen. Robert H. Milroy at the Second Battle of Winchester and Stephenson's Depot, respectively, and moved into Maryland. Stuart's cavalry screened this march, and on June 24, one of the campaign's greatest controversies began to unfold. Stuart, embarrassed over the surprise he suffered at Brandy Station, received permission from Lee to raid behind Hooker's army and rejoin Lee later in Pennsylvania. Lee ordered him to leave behind enough cavalry to screen the invasion, to guard Ewell's right flank as he advanced, and to keep the army informed of Union activity. Stuart left his two weakest brigades with Lee and on June 25 began the raid, but he soon became trapped behind the advancing Union army. Unable to maintain communications with Stuart, Lee advanced into Pennsylvania virtually blind.

Hooker carefully kept his 93,500 men between Lee and Washington, D.C., and by June 28 was at Frederick, Maryland. Convinced that Lee outnumbered him, he complained that he was not being properly supported by the government. When his request to evacuate the Harpers Ferry garrison was refused by his superiors, Hooker resigned and was replaced on June 28 by V Corps commander, Maj. Gen. George G. Meade.

As they advanced, the Confederates seized horses and supplies, and the army's vanguard reached the outskirts of Harrisburg, Pennsylvania, by June 28. That same day, Lee learned from a spy for the first time that the Union army had pushed north of the Potomac River in pursuit. Alarmed that the enemy might cross west of South Mountain and threaten his lines of communications to the Shenandoah Valley, he ordered the army to concentrate at Cashtown, from which it could keep the enemy away from the rear by threatening both Baltimore, Maryland, and Harrisburg.

Meade advanced north along a 30-mile-wide front to cover Baltimore, and when he learned from his cavalry that Lee was at Cashtown, he decided to concentrate at Gettysburg, a small town where nine roads intersected. The two armies first made contact there on June 30, but the Confederates withdrew. On July 1, A. P. Hill sent two Confederate divisions back to Gettysburg to drive out John Buford's Union cavalry. Their orders were not to bring on a general engagement, since Lee did not want a battle until his army was completely concentrated. Buford recognized the importance of the high ground west of town and took up a position to defend it. At about 8:00 A.M., Henry Heth's division engaged Buford about four miles west of Gettysburg. Although outnumbered, Buford fought stubbornly until John F. Reynold's I Corps arrived on the scene at about 10:30 A.M. and relieved him.

The battle no one wanted quickly escalated as reinforcements were drawn in from both sides, and Reynolds's corps was forced back to Seminary Ridge. Oliver O. Howard's XI Corps arrived shortly after noon and went into action on the right of the I Corps, stretching the battle line north of town. Both sides suffered heavy casualties, and the fight was stalemated by mid-afternoon. By chance, Ewell's corps then approached the field from the northeast and launched a crushing attack against Howard's right flank. The XI Corps was routed, and when Hill renewed his attack, the entire Union line collapsed. By that time, Winfield Scott Hancock had arrived to take command on the field, and he rallied the retreating soldiers south of town on Cemetery and Culp's Hills. Lee ordered Ewell to advance and seize the hills if practicable, but in one of the battle's greatest controversies, he failed to do so.

Meade arrived that night and decided to stay and fight. He positioned his arriving corps in an inverted fishhook fashion along Cemetery Ridge, anchored on the left by Big and Little Round Tops and on the right by Culp's Hill. Although he did not initially intend to fight at Gettysburg, Lee accepted the battle and paralleled Meade's line. He ordered Longstreet to attack Meade's left flank the next day and Ewell to advance against Culp's and Cemetery Hills. Longstreet disapproved of the plan and, instead, advised circling behind the Union army and forcing Meade to attack on ground of Lee's choosing. Lee, reluctant to turn his back on the enemy without a decisive fight, rejected this advice and insisted the battle continue. Final plans for the attack were not made until late morning on July 2, and it took time for Longstreet to move his corps into position. After the war, he became another scapegoat for Lee's failure at Gettysburg when critics assailed him for being too slow to start this assault.

At about 4:00 P.M., Longstreet hit Daniel Sickles's III Corps holding Meade's left. Without orders, Sickles had advanced his corps far beyond the main Union line to take advantage of higher ground in his front. As a result, he abandoned Big and Little Round Tops just as the Confederates attacked. Longstreet smashed Sickles's corps and slowly pushed it back during vicious fighting in the Wheatfield, Devil's Den, and the Peach Orchard. Brigadier General Gouverneur K. Warren realized Little Round Top controlled the battlefield and ordered reinforcements to the hill. There Col. Joshua Lawrence Chamberlain and his 20th Maine put up a stubborn defense and repulsed numerous Confederate attacks. Longstreet battered the Union line, but it held as elements of the I, V, VI, and XI Corps were rushed into the gap formed by Sickles's untimely advance. In the bloody fighting, Confederate Maj. Gen. John Bell Hood was severely wounded in the arm, and Brig. Gen. William Barksdale was killed. On the Union side, Sickles lost a leg, Brig. Gen. Samuel K. Zook was killed, and Brig. Gen. Stephen H. Weed and Col. Strong Vincent were mortally wounded.

On the Union right, Ewell bombarded the Federal line with heavy artillery fire when he heard Longstreet attack and then advanced against Culp's and Cemetery Hills. In heavy fighting, the Confederates gained a foothold on Culp's Hill but were prevented from seizing the high ground by the stubborn defense of George S. Greene's lone Union brigade. Early's division managed briefly to seize two batteries atop Cemetery Hill, but a Union counterattack and the lack of Confederate support forced it to withdraw after dark. Throughout the fighting on July 2, Meade took advantage of his interior line and skillfully shifted needed reinforcements to the most threatened areas of the line.

Believing Meade had weakened his center to reinforce the flanks, Lee decided to make his main attack there the next day. He also ordered Stuart, who finally arrived on July 2, to raid behind Meade's line and Ewell to continue his assault on Culp's Hill. At daybreak on July 3, the Federals on Culp's Hill attacked Ewell first, and a fierce but indecisive battle raged there until about noon. Longstreet again opposed making a frontal attack against the Union center but was ordered to assemble a 13,000-man strike force around George Pickett's fresh division. At 1:00 P.M., the Confederates opened a heavy two-hour artillery bombardment on the Union line, but most of the shells overshot their targets and did little harm to the Federal batteries and frontline troops. At about 3:00 P.M., the Confederate infantry surged forward. Pickett's Charge was one of the war's most dramatic moments as the Confederates moved from Lee's position on Seminary Ridge across a mile of open ground. Raked by artillery fire and musketry, hundreds of men were shot down, but the assault continued. Although a few Confederates reached the Union line, Hancock (who was seriously wounded) stood firm and repulsed the charge. Pickett lost over half his men, including Generals Lewis Armistead, mortally wounded, and Richard Garnett, killed. At the same time, fierce cavalry actions took place on both flanks. Still seeking to gain an advantage, Lee remained in place on July 4 hoping in vain that Meade would attack him. Finally, he retreated that night and on July 6 reached Williamsport, Maryland, where he had to wait a few days for the river to recede from recent rains before crossing back into Virginia on July 13–14.

Gettysburg was the largest battle of the Civil War and the largest ever waged in the Western Hemisphere. More than 50,000 casualties were suffered in the battle, with Lee losing perhaps 28,000 men to Meade's 23,000. The Gettysburg Campaign also became one of the war's most controversial events, with Southerners especially seeking the causes of Lee's defeat. Although Stuart, Ewell, and Longstreet were singled out for criticism, Lee bore ultimate responsibility for insisting on fighting a battle where the enemy enjoyed a great tactical advantage. One point many Confederates failed to grasp was that at Gettysburg, Meade and the Army of the Potomac performed magnificently and essentially had outfought the Confederates. Sometimes called the "high water mark of the Confederacy," Gettysburg marked the zenith of Confederate power and later was viewed as the turning point of the war, since Lee's retreat occurred on the same day Vicksburg, Mississippi, was captured by U. S. Grant.

Following the Gettysburg Campaign, Lee and Meade rested their armies in Virginia, but in the west, the war continued unabated in late summer 1863. In the Tullahoma Campaign, Bragg's Army of Tennessee had been forced to withdraw to Chattanooga, Tennessee, an important railroad hub on the Tennessee River and one of the Confederacy's most strategic western towns. Lee finally agreed to send most of Longstreet's corps to reinforce the west, but before it arrived, Rosecrans advanced again and forced Bragg out of Chattanooga and into northern Georgia. The Federals occupied Chattanooga on September 9, and Rosecrans continued to push two other columns rapidly forward to cut Bragg's lines of communication. Nearly 20,000 fresh troops were stripped from the Deep South to reinforce Bragg and allow him to take the offensive. On September 10–11, he attempted to destroy an isolated part of Rosecrans's army at McLemore's Cove, but his subordinates failed to carry out his plans effectively. Bragg finally decided to concentrate his army between Chattanooga and Rosecrans's two southern corps, roll up the Union line, and push the Federals back into the mountains, where they could be destroyed. Bragg knew that Longstreet's two divisions were en route from Virginia but was uncertain whether they would arrive in time.

Realizing his dangerous position, Rosecrans concentrated his army near Lee and Gordon's Mill, Georgia. The vanguard of Longstreet's command began arriving on September 18, and fighting erupted early on September 19 when a Union division on Rosecrans's left flank advanced and encountered Confederate cavalry under Maj. Gen. Nathan Bedford Forrest. As each side called for reinforcements, the battle spread to the south and consumed the entire line. Throughout the day, both armies made charges and countercharges in the thick, confusing woods, but neither enjoyed any permanent success, and casualties were heavy.

During the night, Longstreet arrived on the field with two more brigades, and Bragg renewed his attacks on September 20. Just before noon, the Federals made a critical mistake, when a division mistakenly withdrew from the line. Longstreet attacked through the gap and shattered Rosecrans's right wing. George H. Thomas brought together various units and made a determined stand on Snodgrass Hill, but much of the army, including Rosecrans himself, fell back to Chattanooga in confusion. Thomas repulsed numerous Confederate attacks and was joined by Maj. Gen. Gordon Granger's reserve corps, which marched to his aid without orders. Together, they covered the army's withdrawal and then fell back to Chattanooga that night. For his heroic efforts, Thomas became known as the "Rock of Chickamauga."

Bragg had about 66,000 men in the battle and lost approximately 18,450. Rosecrans had about 58,000 engaged and lost approximately 16,150 men. Not only was the Battle of Chickamauga the largest Civil War battle in the west and the only decisive victory for the Army of Tennessee, it also was one of the few battles in which the Confederates outnumbered the Federals. Bragg failed to launch a vigorous pursuit of the defeated enemy, however, and was content to pin down Rosecrans in Chattanooga and await developments.

The situation at Chattanooga was a desperate one for the Federals, and Meade agreed to send two of his corps from Virginia to reinforce Rosecrans. When Lee learned of this in early October, he believed the time was right for offensive action. On October 9, 1863, he advanced, threatened Meade's flanks, and forced him to withdraw from his camps near Culpeper. On October 14, A. P. Hill's corps reached Bristoe Station and found the Union army crossing Broad Run. Hill attacked without proper reconnaissance, and his men were slaughtered by the unseen Union II Corps, which was concealed behind a railroad embankment. Meade then completed his crossing and took up a position near Centreville. After two days of skirmishing, Lee withdrew on October 17 and retreated behind the Rapidan River. Although Lee failed to damage Meade significantly in the Bristoe Station Campaign, he did force the Union army to withdraw 40 miles.

One more campaign took place in Virginia before winter ended maneuvers. In November 1863, Meade attempted to turn Lee's right flank to force him to abandon his position along the Rapidan River. In bitterly cold weather, the Union army crossed the Rapidan on November 26, but Lee quickly countered the move. After a short but fierce battle at Payne's Farm the following day, the two armies settled into earthworks along Mine Run. Heavy skirmishing continued for a couple of days, but Meade finally determined that Lee's position was too strong to attack and began withdrawing across the Rapidan on the night of December 1. The Mine Run Campaign ended, and both armies went into winter quarters to await spring.

While Lee and Meade sparred in Northern Virginia, events at Chattanooga came to a dramatic conclusion. Taking up dominating positions on Lookout Mountain and Missionary Ridge, Bragg blocked the Federals' main supply line. Rosecrans's army was saved from starvation only by a long, difficult wagon road from Chattanooga to Bridgeport, Alabama, that took 20 days to travel. When Grant was appointed commander of the Military Division of the West in October, he replaced Rosecrans with George H. Thomas and then went to Chattanooga himself to reopen the supply line. On October 27, Union troops drove the Confederates from Brown's Ferry and opened the so-called Cracker Line to Bridgeport. Meanwhile, Maj. Gen. Joseph Hooker, who commanded the two corps sent west from the Army of the Potomac, marched toward Chattanooga from Bridgeport with three divisions. He left one division at Wauhatchie to help guard the Cracker Line, but it was attacked by elements of Longstreet's command. In a vicious night battle on October 28–29, the Confederates were repulsed, and the Cracker Line was secured.

In early November, Bragg made a serious error by sending Longstreet to besiege Knoxville, Tennessee, just as Grant was receiving steady reinforcements at Chattanooga. Learning of Longstreet's departure, Grant attacked on November 23 and seized Orchard Knob, a prominent hill west of Missionary Ridge. The next day, Hooker attacked the Confederates on Lookout Mountain, and in a fight that became known as "The Battle above the Clouds" forced them to retreat to Missionary Ridge. On the morning of November 25, Grant moved against Missionary Ridge. Sherman first attacked Bragg's right flank, but he was repulsed by Maj. Gen. Patrick Cleburne's Confederate division. That afternoon, Grant sent Thomas forward against Bragg's center in what was intended to be only a demonstration to assist Sherman's flank attack. This demonstration, however, turned into a full-scale assault as the Union troops spontaneously broke into a charge. Caught by surprise, the Confederate center broke and ran. Bragg's disorganized army fell back into northern Georgia, and the siege of Chattanooga was lifted. After the Chattanooga Campaign, Bragg was relieved of command at his own request and was replaced by Joseph E. Johnston. To the northeast, Longstreet also was unsuccessful in the Knoxville Campaign when Ambrose Burnside repulsed his attack on Fort Sanders. After spending the winter in the area, Longstreet rejoined Lee in Virginia in the spring of 1864.

1864 MILITARY CAMPAIGNS

The last full year of war began with a small western campaign by William T. Sherman to destroy the Confederate railroads that linked Meridian, Mississippi, to Selma and Mobile, Alabama. This would greatly hamper the Confederacy's ability to move troops in Mississippi and thus secure for the

Union much of the territory along the Mississippi River's east bank. A byproduct of the raid would be to weaken Southern morale by creating havoc in the Confederacy's interior.

On February 3, 1864, Sherman took 26,000 men from the Army of the Tennessee's XVI and XVII Corps from Vicksburg, Mississippi, and marched east toward Jackson and Meridian. At the same time, William Sooy Smith was to take 7,000 cavalrymen from Tennessee to Meridian and destroy the Mobile & Ohio Railroad. The 13,500 Confederate troops in Mississippi under Leonidas Polk were unable to offer serious resistance to Sherman's march, and he made good headway. Through great effort, Polk removed most of Meridian's rolling stock and supplies and had sent them and his troops to Alabama by the time Sherman reached Meridian on February 14. To make matters worse for Sherman, Sooy Smith's Expedition never arrived from Tennessee. Longer than expected preparations delayed his leaving until February 11, and then his column was slowed by thousands of runaway slaves who joined it. After destroying 55 miles of track, Smith was turned back by Nathan Bedford Forrest at West Point. Unable to accomplish anything more in the largely unsuccessful Meridian Campaign, Sherman returned to Vicksburg after destroying more than 100 miles of track.

The same month Sherman launched his campaign, Florida experienced its largest Civil War battle. Northern Florida contained a sizeable number of Unionists, and in February 1864, Maj. Gen. Quincy A. Gillmore sent Brig. Gen. Truman A. Seymour's division to liberate them, cut Confederate supply lines, and recruit black troops among the area's slaves. When Seymour landed at Jacksonville on February 7, Gillmore ordered him to protect the town and not to advance beyond Baldwin. Seymour, however, disobeyed orders and moved his 5,500 men past Lake City to destroy the Florida, Atlantic & Gulf Railroad crossing over the Suwannee River. On February 20, Seymour engaged Joseph Finegan's 5,100 Confederates near Ocean Pond and Olustee on a narrow neck of land between two swampy areas. The limited field prevented Seymour from using all of his men, and the Federals were driven back with the loss of two cannons. After considerable skirmishing, the Confederates counterattacked, turned Seymour's right flank, and captured three more cannons. Seymour then began a withdrawal to Jacksonville at dusk. In the Battle of Olustee, Seymour lost 1,861 men to Finegan's 946. The Federals returned safely to Jacksonville and held it for the rest of the war, but the battle stopped the only major Union invasion of northern Florida and ensured Confederate control over the area.

One of the weaknesses that plagued both sides through much of the war was the lack of an effective general-in-chief who could coordinate all the armies. The Union rectified this in March 1864 when Congress reactivated the rank of lieutenant general and appointed U. S. Grant to fill the position as general-in-chief. Up to that time, the Union had never coordinated its offenses, thus allowing the Confederates to take advantage of their interior line and shift troops to threatened areas. Grant planned to change that by having several Union armies launch simultaneous offenses in the spring of 1864. His main goal was to destroy the Confederate armies, but major cities were targeted to draw the enemy into battle.

Grant's strategy called for George G. Meade's Army of the Potomac to advance toward Richmond and engage Robert E. Lee's Army of Northern Virginia; Benjamin F. Butler's Army of the James was to move up the James River from the Atlantic Ocean and threaten Richmond; Franz Sigel was to invade the Shenandoah Valley; Sherman was to move against Atlanta, Georgia, and destroy Joseph E. Johnston's Army of Tennessee; and Nathaniel P. Banks was to advance up Louisiana's Red River to threaten Shreveport. Since Lee's was the main Confederate army in the field, Grant decided to accompany and direct Meade's operation in Virginia.

Banks's Red River Campaign began first. With about 30,000 men and the support of David D. Porter's fleet, he hoped to confiscate much needed cotton, destroy Richard Taylor's small Confederate army, capture Shreveport, and open the way for a Texas invasion. At the same time, Frederick Steele was to advance on Shreveport from Little Rock, Arkansas, in what became known as the Camden Expedition.

Banks's campaign at first went well. Major General Andrew J. Smith and Porter captured Fort De Russy near the mouth of the Red River on March 14, 1864, and moved on to Alexandria, where they were joined by Banks. After stripping the countryside of cotton, the Federals then moved upriver to Grand Ecore, where Banks made a significant error by taking a narrow road that snaked west and north from Natchitoches to Shreveport rather than staying on the river road. This decision split the Federal force and made it impossible for Banks to receive any support from Porter's gunboats. Taylor had no choice but to retreat before the Union juggernaut, but reinforcements eventually brought his army up to about 8,800 men. On April 8, he attacked Banks's vanguard near Mansfield and won a stunning victory. Badly shocked by the encounter, Banks retreated to Pleasant Hill, where Taylor attacked again the next day. This time the Federals held their ground and repulsed the Confederates. Despite his tactical victory at Pleasant Hill, Banks abandoned the campaign and his wounded and withdrew to Natchitoches. Taylor intended to launch a vigorous pursuit, but his superior, Edmund Kirby Smith, ordered him to send nearly all of his infantry to

Arkansas to stop Steele's Camden Expedition. Outraged by the decision, Taylor could do little more than follow and harass the retreating enemy.

On Red River, Porter also had been stopped by steadily falling water and an obstructed river channel. Unable to proceed farther and learning of Banks's defeat, he withdrew as well. Confederate cavalry constantly harassed the ships and even made a significant attack at Blair's Landing. During the harrowing retreat, Porter lost several ships to torpedoes and artillery fire.

Banks's retreat became a frenzy of arson and looting, and numerous houses and several small towns were burned. Taylor tried to trap the Federals at Monett's Ferry, but the small Confederate force was unable to hold its ground, and Banks pushed through and reached Alexandria on April 25. At Alexandria, Porter's fleet was trapped by low water, but Lt. Col. Joseph Bailey constructed Bailey's Dam, raised the river, and dramatically saved the vessels. When Banks retreated from Alexandria on May 13, soldiers in Smith's command set fire to the town and completely destroyed it. The campaign's last battle was at Yellow Bayou, near the Atchafalaya River, where Banks fought a rear guard action while Bailey constructed a pontoon bridge across the river. The Federals then crossed over on May 20, and the campaign ended. Banks's campaign was a disaster, for it tied up troops that could have been used better in the Atlanta Campaign, and by being confined to the Trans-Mississippi Department, it allowed the Confederates to move 15,000 reinforcements east of the Mississippi River to defend Atlanta.

The Union had no better success in Arkansas, where Steele began the Camden Expedition from Little Rock on March 23. Joined by John M. Thayer's column from Fort Smith near Elkin's Ferry on April 9, he had about 10,400 men to face approximately 5,000 Confederates. A supply shortage forced Steele to put his men on half rations, and on April 10 a running four-day battle began at Prairie D'Ane as the Confederates contested his advance. The Federals occupied Camden on April 15, but the situation became precarious when the Confederates attacked and destroyed the Union supply train at Poison Spring on April 18. Two days later, Kirby Smith arrived from Louisiana with three divisions from Taylor's army, and on April 25 another of Steele's supply trains and approximately 1,700 men were captured at Marks' Mills. With no hope of reinforcements and out of supplies, he retreated to Little Rock. Skirmishing occurred daily, and on April 30 Steele fought a pitched battle while crossing the Saline River at Jenkins' Ferry. Exhausted and half-starved, the Union troops finally arrived at Little Rock on May 3. Steele lost 2,750 men, 650 wagons, and nine cannons in the campaign, while the Confederates suffered approximately 2,350 casualties.

As the two unsuccessful Union campaigns came to an end in the Trans-Mississippi Department, Grant was just beginning the Overland Campaign in Virginia. On May 4, 1864, he crossed the Rapidan River with 120,000 men and headed south to engage Lee's 60,000. The next day, the two armies collided in the Wilderness, where the thick woods largely negated Grant's superior numbers and artillery. Vicious fighting ended in a stalemate the first day. When Winfield Scott Hancock's II Corps renewed the assault on the morning of May 6, only the timely arrival of Longstreet's corps saved Lee's right wing from destruction. Just as Longstreet was making a successful flank attack about noon, he was accidentally shot by his own men and was put out of action for months. Grant withdrew on the night of May 7, but instead of retreating, he moved south to turn Lee's right flank at Spotsylvania Court House. Correctly guessing Grant's intentions, Lee rushed toward Spotsylvania and reached the crucial crossroads first. Heavy fighting occurred over the next several days, and while inspecting his line on May 9, Union VI Corps commander John Sedgwick was killed by a Confederate sharpshooter.

The Confederates constructed nearly impregnable earthworks, but a dangerous salient nicknamed the "Mule Shoe" extended toward the Union lines. On May 10, Grant attacked the Mule Shoe and temporarily broke through using a new tactic devised by Col. Emory Upton in which advancing troops were formed in a massed column instead of a battle line. Impressed with the result, Grant ordered a larger attack against the Mule Shoe on May 12. Led by Hancock's II Corps in a pouring rain, the assault at first succeeded, and much of Richard Ewell's Confederate corps was captured. Lee counterattacked and drove back the Federals. For the next 20 hours, some of the war's most horrific fighting took place at the Mule Shoe's apex as the armies slugged it out in a few acres of contested breastworks that became known as the Bloody Angle. Not until long after dark were the Confederates able to withdraw to a new line constructed farther to the rear. During the fighting at Spotsylvania, Union cavalry launched Philip Sheridan's Richmond Raid to draw out and destroy Stuart's cavalry. Sheridan burned a considerable amount of railroad stock, freed some prisoners, and generally raised havoc, but he failed to destroy the Confederate cavalry. In the raid's largest battle at Yellow Tavern on May 11, however, Stuart was mortally wounded.

Grant withdrew from Spotsylvania on May 20 and again moved around the enemy's right flank, but Lee once more successfully intercepted him at the North Anna River. Realizing he could not fight his way through the Confederates' defenses, Grant withdrew on May 26 and marched toward

Cold Harbor beyond Lee's right. When he found the Confederates once again entrenched in his front, Grant became frustrated and launched a disastrous frontal attack on June 3. In what was little more than a suicide charge, the Federals lost approximately 7,000 men in less than 30 minutes, while Lee suffered fewer than 1,500 casualties. This battle more than any other earned Grant the nickname of "Butcher."

By this time, both armies were exhausted, having been in almost constant combat for a month. Grant and Meade had lost an average of 2,000 men per day but were able to replace them with new, albeit, poorly trained troops. Lee had lost about half as many men, but he was unable to replace all of them. As a result, the Army of Northern Virginia quickly was being bled white, making it impossible to take the offensive. Developments in the Shenandoah Valley further weakened Lee during this crucial time. Sigel's Shenandoah Valley Campaign had been stopped by John C. Breckinridge at New Market, but David Hunter had taken over the Union forces and was threatening Lee's supply line at Lynchburg. While at Cold Harbor, Lee sent Jubal Early and the II Corps to drive back the Union raiders, and, if possible, to threaten Washington and force Grant to weaken his command by sending reinforcements to the capital.

On the night of June 12 (the same day Lee sent Early to the Valley), Grant made a bold move when he withdrew from Cold Harbor and over the next few days crossed the James River to attack Petersburg, an important rail center about 20 miles south of Richmond. By doing the unexpected and moving far to the south, he hoped to cut Richmond's supply line and force the Confederates to evacuate the city. By the time Grant made this river crossing, his other Virginia offensives had failed. In early May, Butler had landed on Bermuda Hundred, a neck of land between the James and Appomattox Rivers southeast of Richmond, to cut the railroad supplying the city. Over the next two weeks, the Bermuda Hundred Campaign was marked by Union cautiousness and confusion and stubborn resistance by Confederate Gen. P. G. T. Beauregard. Several significant battles were fought, and Butler temporarily damaged some track, but he eventually withdrew to Bermuda Hundred. Beauregard followed and built strong earthworks across the peninsula's western base, leaving Butler, according to Grant, as if in a "strongly corked" bottle.

In the Shenandoah Valley, Grant's other offensive also had been stopped. After Sigel's defeat at New Market, Hunter moved toward Staunton. William E. "Grumble" Jones attacked him at Piedmont on June 5, but Jones was killed, and his army was defeated. Hunter reached Staunton the next day and wrecked the Virginia Central Railroad, factories, stores, and other property before moving on to Lexington on June 11. There the Federals burned the Virginia Military Institute and the home of Gov. John Letcher, looted Washington College, and plundered and burned the entire region. It was then that Lee sent Early to confront the raiders. Hunter attacked Breckinridge at Lynchburg on June 18 but was driven back by Breckinridge and part of Early's corps that had just arrived. Learning that Early's entire corps was at hand, Hunter then withdrew and began a hurried retreat to West Virginia.

With the Shenandoah Valley temporarily safe, Early advanced into Maryland to threaten Washington. He first occupied Hagerstown and Frederick and forced their residents to pay $20,000 and $200,000 ransoms, respectively, to save the towns from destruction. Meanwhile, a small Union force under Maj. Gen. Lew Wallace took up a position near the Monocacy River to delay the Confederates. The Battle of the Monocacy on July 9 was fierce, and Wallace was forced to retreat, but he succeeded in delaying Early's march on Washington one crucial day. The Confederates reached the city's outskirts on July 11, and skirmishing began near Fort Stevens. By that time, elements of the Army of the Potomac's VI Corps had arrived from the Petersburg front and the XIX Corps from Louisiana. Early decided against attacking, withdrew on the night of July 12, and crossed back into Virginia on July 13–14. Early's Washington Raid succeeded in clearing the enemy from the Shenandoah Valley and drew some Union troops from Lee's front, but it had no impact on the war's outcome.

At Petersburg, Grant's plan to move swiftly at first worked, and he reached the city before Lee could react. Beauregard's small force, however, successfully held the Federals at bay until Lee arrived with the bulk of his army on June 18. Thus began the long and bloody Petersburg Campaign. Grant slowly extended his lines to the west over the next 10 months to cut the roads and railroads supplying the Confederates. Lee countered by stretching his lines thinner and thinner to block Grant. Soon there were miles of trenches, fortifications, abatis, and other obstructions ringing Richmond and Petersburg on their eastern and southern sides. The conflict deteriorated into trench warfare as maneuverability largely was lost. Despite the dangerous and dreary duty, the Union soldiers were kept supplied by ships on the James River, while the Confederates slowly ran out of essentials as Grant began cutting the remaining supply lines. Sharpshooter and artillery fire were constant, and large battles were fought at such places as the Weldon Railroad, Jerusalem Plank Road, the Crater, First and Second Deep Bottom, Globe Tavern, Reams Station, Fort Harrison, New Market Heights, and Hatcher's Run. By early 1865, the Federals had severed both the Weldon Railroad and the Boydton Plank Road, two of Lee's vital supply lines, and the Confederate situation was becoming desperate.

The string of Union failures in 1864 finally was broken in the west. In Georgia, Sherman's orders were to advance on Atlanta, "break up" Johnston's Army of Tennessee, and destroy Confederate war resources as he went. He had approximately 110,000 men in Maj. Gen. George H. Thomas's Army of the Cumberland, Maj. Gen. James B. McPherson's Army of the Tennessee, and Maj. Gen. John M. Schofield's Army of the Ohio. To oppose this massive invasion, Johnston's Army of Tennessee numbered only about 62,000 men, but it enjoyed the tactical advantage in both terrain and position. Northern Georgia was perfect for defense, being laced with rivers and mountain ranges that ran directly across Sherman's path. Also, as Johnston fell back toward Atlanta, he would draw closer to his base of supplies, while Sherman would be stretching his and be forced to detach soldiers to guard it.

On May 7, 1864, Sherman advanced toward the Confederate position at Rocky Face Ridge, Georgia. Knowing this was too strong to assault, he initiated a maneuver that set the tone for the entire campaign. Holding the Confederates in place with Thomas and Schofield, Sherman sent McPherson south to Snake Creek Gap to get into Johnston's rear and cut his line of retreat. McPherson marched through Snake Creek Gap on May 9 but unexpectedly met enemy resistance near Resaca. Believing he was outnumbered, he withdrew into the gap and entrenched instead of pressing on. Actually, the Confederate presence at Resaca was small, and McPherson missed one of the Union's best opportunities to destroy Johnston. On May 10, Sherman began moving the rest of his armies toward Snake Creek Gap, and Johnston withdrew to Resaca two days later.

Johnston was reinforced by Lt. Gen. Leonidas Polk and now had nearly 70,000 men. On May 14–15, attacks and counterattacks were made at Resaca, but neither side made much headway. On May 15, Sherman again turned the Confederate position by sending a division to cross the Oostanaula River south of Resaca and threaten Johnston's line of retreat. Johnston was forced to withdraw across the river on the night of May 15 and retreat to Kingston and Cassville. In his pursuit, Sherman made a tactical error by spreading his three armies widely apart and leaving Schofield in an isolated position to the east. Johnston took advantage of this mistake and positioned John Bell Hood's corps near Cassville on May 19 to crush Schofield. Hood proved too timid, the opportunity was lost, and Johnston withdrew that night across the Etowah River to Allatoona. Sherman found the Confederate defenses there too strong to attack. On May 23, he abandoned his railroad supply line and made another turning movement toward Marietta by way of Dallas, deep in Johnston's left rear. Johnston withdrew from Allatoona Pass the next day, reached Dallas first, and constructed strong entrenchments around it. Over the next few days, very intense fighting took place as Sherman futilely attacked the strong Confederate works around New Hope Church and Pickett's Mill.

On June 1, Sherman began shifting his armies to the east, and on June 4 his cavalry captured Allatoona Pass. This threatened Johnston's right rear and forced him to withdraw to near Marietta on June 4. For two weeks, the opposing armies fought along the Lost-Brushy Mountain line, and on June 14, Confederate General Polk was killed by an artillery shell. Johnston finally retreated to Kennesaw Mountain in the predawn hours of June 19. After engaging the Confederates at Kolb's Farm on June 22, Sherman blundered badly on June 27 by ordering a frontal attack against the Confederate entrenchments at Kennesaw Mountain. In the bloody repulse, he lost nearly 3,000 men to Johnston's 750–1,000.

While Sherman engaged Johnston along the Lost-Brushy Mountain line and at Kennesaw Mountain, another major battle associated with the campaign was fought in Mississippi. To protect his long supply line, Sherman ordered Brig. Gen. Samuel D. Sturgis to defeat Maj. Gen. Nathan Bedford Forrest's Confederate cavalry in northern Mississippi. Sturgis engaged Forrest at Brice's Cross Roads on June 10, but the outnumbered Forrest skillfully drew the Federals into an exhausting battle and then routed them after hard fighting. Besides inflicting more than 2,000 casualties on Sturgis, Forrest also captured 16 cannons, 192 wagons, and 1,500 rifles.

On July 2, Johnston withdrew from the Kennesaw Mountain line and fell back to the Chattahoochee River, the last natural barrier outside Atlanta. When Schofield crossed the river to his right a week later, Johnston retreated across the Chattahoochee and took up a new position behind Peachtree Creek. When Sherman crossed it on July 16, he was within seven miles of the city. Dismayed with Johnston's failure to stop the enemy and his lack of aggressiveness, Jefferson Davis replaced him with John Bell Hood on July 17. Hoping to catch Thomas's Army of the Cumberland in a vulnerable position astride Peachtree Creek, Hood attacked on July 20, but the attack came too late, and the Federals held their ground. Hood lost approximately 2,500 men in the bloody clash to Thomas's 1,800. Hood then withdrew into Atlanta's defenses, but on July 22, he attacked McPherson's Army of the Tennessee in the Battle of Atlanta. McPherson was killed in the fighting, but the Federals again repulsed the Confederates. Sherman lost approximately 3,700 men in this clash to Hood's 8,000.

His armies now positioned to the north and east of Atlanta, Sherman next tried to cut the railroads south of the city. In late July, Stoneman's and Mc-Cook's Raids took place, but Wheeler's Confederate cavalry defeated the scattered Union columns and saved the railroad (a later raid by H. Judson Kilpatrick met the same fate). At the same time, Sherman also began moving Oliver O. Howard, who had replaced the fallen McPherson at the head of the Army of the Tennessee, around Atlanta's west side to cut the Atlanta & West Point Railroad. On July 28, Hood attacked Howard at Ezra Church and saved the railroad but lost 5,000 men to Howard's 560. In early August, Sherman continued to move toward the railroads south of Atlanta, but Hood stopped him in a series of clashes along Utoy Creek. After a brief respite, Sherman continued the maneuver, and in late August he cut the Macon & Western Railroad at Rough and Ready and at Jonesboro. Hood shifted part of his army toward Jonesboro on August 30 and unsuccessfully engaged Howard there on August 31–September 1. With his last railroad cut, Hood evacuated Atlanta on the afternoon of September 1, and Sherman's troops occupied it the next morning.

The war now had reached a critical turning point. With the fighting in Virginia a bloody stalemate, the Northern people were becoming very weary, and there was a danger Lincoln would not be reelected that autumn. But in early August, Adm. David Farragut had successfully defeated the Confederates and taken control of Mobile Bay, Alabama, thus closing down one of the last major Confederate ports. Less than a month later, Sherman captured Atlanta. These victories greatly boosted Northern morale and helped reelect Lincoln, thus ensuring the war would continue until a final Union victory was achieved.

After the embarrassing defeats of Sigel and Hunter and Early's Washington Raid, Grant took decisive measures in early August 1864 to reverse Union defeats in Virginia's Shenandoah Valley. Major General Philip H. Sheridan was put in command of the Valley, and he created the 40,000-man Army of the Shenandoah to attack and defeat Early's 18,500-man Army of the Valley. Sheridan's Shenandoah Valley Campaign began on August 10 when he moved up the Valley toward the Confederates. On the morning of September 19, he attacked and defeated Early in very heavy fighting at the Third Battle of Winchester. Early fell back to a strong position at Fisher's Hill, but Sheridan attacked and crushed his left flank on September 22 and sent the Confederates in headlong flight. After pursuing Early to Staunton, the Federals withdrew to Strasburg and from October 6–8 destroyed everything that could be of use to the enemy. Besides killing and carrying off livestock, they burned hundreds of houses, barns, and mills along the 92-mile march in what became known in the Valley as "The Burning."

Confident that Early no longer posed a threat, Sheridan encamped near Middletown behind Cedar Creek and went to Washington to confer with officials on future operations. In an audacious move, Early launched a surprise attack at dawn of October 19, broke the Union left flank, and sent the Federals streaming in retreat. The attack then lost momentum, and the Federals were able to reorganize when many Confederates stopped to plunder the enemy camps. Sheridan, who was on his way back from Washington, rode furiously to the battlefield, skillfully launched a counterattack, and crushed Early that afternoon. After the Battle of Cedar Creek, both sides sent the bulk of their forces to Petersburg and went into winter camps. On March 2, 1865, the campaign ended when Sheridan annihilated Early's remaining 2,000 men at Waynesboro. Losing only 30 troopers, he inflicted 1,600 casualties on Early and virtually eliminated the Confederate presence in the Valley. Afterward, Sheridan led his cavalry east to join Grant at Petersburg. His successful campaign played a major role in the final destruction of Lee's army, for it denied the Confederates the important supplies that came from the Valley.

While the war in Virginia was static at Petersburg in late 1864, Sherman continued the Union offensive in Georgia. After evacuating Atlanta, Hood tried to lure the Federals away from the city by moving north and attacking their supply line. Sherman briefly gave chase but finally decided a better strategy was to leave George H. Thomas to stop Hood while he took the bulk of his armies back to Atlanta to prepare his next move. He then won approval from a reluctant Grant to march from Atlanta through Georgia's interior to the Atlantic coast, living off the land as he advanced. Besides destroying war-related industries and supplies, the raid would greatly demoralize Southern civilians and soldiers by demonstrating that the Confederacy was unable to protect even its heartland. Sherman promised to "make Georgia howl."

Sherman led 62,000 men out of Atlanta on November 15, 1864, and over the next five weeks cut a swath from Atlanta to Savannah, Georgia, in what became known as the March to the Sea. The only Confederates facing him were about 8,000 men in Gustavus W. Smith's Georgia militia and Joseph Wheeler's small cavalry corps. By placing his men in separate columns on roughly parallel roads, Sherman's front often was 60 miles wide. The Confederates were forced to spread thin their troops, and Sherman skillfully kept them off guard by waiting until the last possible moment before converging on a particular target. Forced to live off the land, he had regularly appointed commissary officers who took needed supplies, but they usually left enough food to feed the Southern families through the winter. Excessive confiscation, however, did come from "bummers," or unauthorized soldiers who left the ranks and frequently took everything they could carry.

Destruction was widespread during the march, but the number of private homes that were torched probably has been exaggerated. Public property and buildings were routinely destroyed (such as at the state capital of Milledgeville), as were railroads (which were turned into "Sherman's Neckties") and many barns and warehouses filled with supplies that could be useful to the Confederates. Private houses were rarely burned, although they often were vandalized by bummers. Personal violence, including rape—another evil associated with the march—was very rare and was aimed more at slaves than at whites.

After leaving Atlanta, Sherman was not heard from again until he reached Savannah on December 9. There he began encircling William J. Hardee's 18,000 Confederates and captured Fort McAllister, but Hardee escaped on the night of December 20. The following day, Sherman entered the city and jubilantly wired Lincoln that he was presenting Savannah to him as a Christmas present. The March to the Sea was a huge success. At a cost of approximately 2,200 men, Sherman destroyed much of the Confederacy's war-making capability and greatly demoralized Southern civilians and soldiers by demonstrating that Union armies could raid with impunity deep inside the Confederacy.

While Sherman was marching through Georgia, Hood launched one last desperate offensive to retrieve Confederate fortunes in the west. The Franklin and Nashville Campaign was intended to restore Confederate morale and force Sherman to abandon Georgia by threatening Nashville, Tennessee. Hood even entertained the possibility of marching to Virginia after securing Tennessee to join forces with Lee to defeat Grant. But Hood had to postpone the campaign until Forrest could join him in northern Alabama, and this delay gave Thomas time to assemble troops to meet the invasion. Hood's 40,000 Confederates finally crossed the Tennessee River near Tuscumbia, Alabama, on November 16–21, and the campaign began.

Thomas had placed Maj. Gen. John M. Schofield's 30,000 men at Pulaski, Tennessee, to delay the invasion while he assembled a force in Nashville. When the Confederates advanced, Schofield withdrew and marched toward Nashville by way of Spring Hill. Hood reached the Spring Hill area first on November 29 and was in a position to cut off and trap the Federals. Misunderstood orders and other blunders known as the Spring Hill Incident, however, prevented Hood from blocking the road effectively, and Schofield escaped to Franklin that night by marching right past the sleeping Confederates. Hood pursued the next morning and rashly ordered a frontal attack that afternoon when he found Schofield strongly entrenched at Franklin. Larger than Gettysburg's Pickett's Charge, this assault included

18 brigades and covered two miles of open ground. The Confederates briefly broke through Schofield's center, but the Federals sealed the break in bitter fighting and repulsed the attack at about 9:00 P.M. Hood lost 6,252 men and 12 generals, while Schofield lost 2,326 men.

Hood followed Schofield to Nashville and took up a defensive position south of the city in hope either of receiving reinforcements or luring Thomas into attacking his entrenched line. The methodical Thomas took his time gathering 70,000 men for a decisive blow despite orders from Grant to attack immediately. Grant was on the verge of removing him from command, when Thomas finally attacked on December 15, 1864. Hood's army was routed and withdrew a few miles to a new position, but the next day Thomas attacked again, crushed Hood's left flank with his cavalry, and sent the Confederates fleeing to the south. The Battle of Nashville essentially destroyed the Army of Tennessee. Hood's casualties are uncertain, but he probably lost about 6,000 men, while Thomas reported losing 2,562. When the Confederate rear guard crossed the Tennessee River into Alabama on December 27, Hood assembled his surviving men at Tupelo, Mississippi. Out of the 40,000 who began the campaign in November, only 18,708 reported for duty at Tupelo. In January 1865, Hood was relieved of command, and the army's remnants were scattered, with some units being sent to join Joseph E. Johnston for the Carolinas Campaign.

In the Trans-Mississippi Department, 1864 ended with another unsuccessful Confederate offensive when Confederate Maj. Gen. Sterling Price raided Missouri to capture St. Louis and carry the war into Illinois. Price entered southeastern Missouri on September 19 with 14 cannons and 12,000 mounted men and reached Fredericktown five days later. On September 26, he launched a bloody but unsuccessful attack on Pilot Knob and then abandoned his plan to seize St. Louis because of the large number of Union troops in the area. Price continued the raid in the belief he could gather thousands of recruits and perhaps demoralize the Union enough to defeat Lincoln in the November election. Moving up the Missouri River toward Jefferson City on September 30, the Confederates foraged off the land and destroyed railroad tracks and bridges, but the large number of expected recruits never materialized. Price bypassed Jefferson City because it was now heavily defended, and Alfred Pleasonton's Union cavalry was pressing his rear guard. After capturing Boonville on October 9, he sent Jo Shelby and M. Jeff Thompson on raids to Glasgow and Sedalia. Price then left Boonville on October 14 and headed northwest toward Waverly, but a long supply train and Pleasonton's harassing cavalry slowed his progress and allowed Union Maj. Gen. William S. Rosecrans to assemble enough troops to trap the Confederates. Samuel Curtis also gathered more than 15,000 men on the Missouri-Kansas border and sent 2,000 men under James G. Blunt to Lexington, Missouri, to assist Rosecrans.

Pushing back Blunt's vanguard at Lexington on October 18, Price turned to the southwest to get in between the two enemy forces and defeat them in detail. On October 21, Blunt was defeated at the Little Blue River and retreated to the Big Blue River to unite with Curtis. The next day, Price successfully forced a crossing of the Big Blue River, but Pleasonton's cavalry defeated his rear guard at the Little Blue River and Independence. On October 23, the Confederates attacked Curtis at Westport but were defeated, and this time Pleasonton defeated John Marmaduke's rear guard at Byram's Ford on the Big Blue River. Learning of Marmaduke's defeat, Price ordered Shelby to fight a delaying action while the rest of the army escaped to the south. With Confederate morale shattered, only Shelby's skillful rear guard action and Curtis's slow pursuit prevented the withdrawal from becoming a rout. Blunt and Pleasonton defeated the Confederates at Marais des Cygnes and Mine Run, Kansas, on October 25 and captured Marmaduke, William Cabell, and a large number of prisoners. Price burned many of his wagons to lighten his column, but the fighting retreat continued for several days, with the last battle occurring at Newtonia on October 28. The survivors of Price's Missouri Raid staggered back to Arkansas in early December.

The Confederates had fought 43 engagements, rode 1,488 miles, and suffered approximately 4,000 casualties (mostly to desertion). Although Price gathered a few thousand recruits and captured some prisoners, the raid was a failure because he did not liberate Missouri or inflict any serious damage on the Union army or its vital railroads. In addition, many of the recruits Price did gain were violent guerrillas, and their lawless activities made many Missourians abandon the Confederate cause. Price's Missouri Raid ended organized Confederate resistance in the Trans-Mississippi Department.

1865 MILITARY CAMPAIGNS

By 1865, the Confederacy was on the verge of collapse. Lee's army was pinned around Richmond and Petersburg, Virginia, unable to maneuver and slowly starving, and the Confederates in the Shenandoah Valley had been routed. In the west, the Confederate Army of Tennessee was wrecked after the disastrous Franklin and Nashville Campaign, and Sherman stood poised to wreak the same kind of havoc in the Carolinas as he had in Georgia. In the far west, the war virtually had ceased, following Sterling Price's failed Missouri Raid.

The Union offensive first renewed on the North Carolina coast at Wilmington. With its deepwater port and railroads to Virginia and South Carolina, the city was the Confederacy's last major port for blockade-runners. It also was the receiving point for meat rations sent to Robert E. Lee's Army of Northern Virginia and was critical for that army's survival. Wilmington was ringed by fortifications, and its two outlets to the Atlantic Ocean were guarded by Forts Fisher and Caswell. Fort Fisher, under the command of Col. William Lamb, guarded New Inlet and was the more important and larger of the two since most blockade-runners preferred using that inlet. Known as the Gibraltar of the Confederacy, it was manned by about 1,200 troops and had nearly 50 cannons. Supporting the fort was a small river fleet under the command of Flag Officer William F. Lynch.

Union forces had a difficult time blockading Wilmington because its two inlets forced warships to cover a 50-mile stretch of water. An attempt to capture Fort Fisher was made in December 1864 by Benjamin F. Butler and David Porter, but it ended in dismal failure because of poor coordination and Butler's lack of aggressiveness. As a result, Grant relieved Butler of his command and launched a second expedition under Brig. Gen. Alfred H. Terry. Terry and Porter arrived off Fort Fisher on January 12, 1865, and Terry landed his infantry the next day. Following a naval bombardment, Terry attacked on January 15 with 2,000 men. In fierce fighting, Confederate commander Maj. Gen. William H. C. Whiting was mortally wounded, and the fort was finally captured after dark. The fall of Fort Fisher effectively closed Wilmington as a port, but the city itself remained in Confederate hands.

Soon after Fort Fisher's capture, Sherman resumed his offensive. Ordered by Grant to move north from Savannah, Georgia, to Virginia to help in the Petersburg Campaign, he decided to march through the Carolinas. By continuing his March to the Sea strategy through the largely untouched regions of North and South Carolina, Sherman could disrupt the enemy's supply line and spread such terror and demoralization through Confederate ranks that the Southern people would lose their will to fight. At the same time, Maj. Gen. John M. Schofield was to provide Sherman a shorter line of communication to the sea by capturing Wilmington and New Bern, North Carolina, and marching inland to join him at Goldsboro.

On February 1, 1865, Sherman left Beaufort, South Carolina, with 62,000 men and advanced in two columns, with Slocum and Kilpatrick on the left and Howard on the right. Beauregard, the Confederate commander in the Carolinas, had only about 22,500 men to stop the invasion. This shortage of troops and Sherman's practice of using widespread columns to threaten several towns at once prevented Beauregard from seriously opposing the Federals. The Union advance quickly forced William J. Hardee

to abandon Charleston, South Carolina, and all of the Confederates retreated toward North Carolina.

Sherman's march proved destructive as the Union soldiers took
vengeance on the cradle of secession. Columbia was occupied on February
17 and was burned in a controversial incident in which both sides blamed
the other for its destruction. As Sherman approached Cheraw, Joseph E.
Johnston assumed command of the Carolinas and withdrew to Fayetteville,
North Carolina, but the Federals seized it on March 11 and over the next
five days destroyed much public and personal property there. Sherman next
headed for Averasboro to meet Schofield's column, which had forced the
Confederates to abandon Wilmington and New Bern. The small Army of
Tennessee was rushed to Kinston to help Bragg stop Schofield, but the Con-
federates were defeated at Wyse Fork on March 7–10 and retreated to
Goldsboro.

Rapidly running out of maneuvering room, Johnston decided to strike
the enemy before Sherman and Schofield could join forces. Hardee first
was ordered to Averasboro, where he fought a sharp battle on March 16 in
an unsuccessful attempt to stop Slocum's advance. As Slocum continued
toward Bentonville, Johnston concentrated 21,000 men near there hoping
to crush him on March 19, but poor maps and a lack of coordination prevented him from effectively springing the trap. In the largest battle of the
campaign, Johnston severely mauled Slocum on the first day of battle, but
Sherman arrived with reinforcements. The battle continued on March 21,
but the Confederates finally were forced to retreat. Sherman's and Slocum's
separate columns then united at Goldsboro on March 23, giving Sherman
an invincible army of 80,000 men.

By the spring of 1865, the Army of Northern Virginia was exhausted after 10 months of trench warfare in the Petersburg Campaign. On March 25,
a desperate Lee attempted to break through Grant's besieging army at Fort
Stedman and move to North Carolina to link up with Johnston. The breakout failed, and Grant counterattacked on April 1 by sending Sheridan's cavalry against the Confederate right flank at Five Forks. Sheridan crushed
George Pickett's command, and the next day Grant launched a general assault that forced Lee to abandon Petersburg and Richmond and begin a harrowing retreat to the west. In the Appomattox Campaign that followed, Lee
marched his 50,000 men toward Amelia Court House, where he planned to
collect supplies that had been ordered there and then use the Richmond &
Danville Railroad to move south to join Johnston. Speed was essential
since the 113,000-man Union Army of the Potomac was in rapid pursuit.

Lee reached Amelia Court House on April 4, but the supply trains were
not there. He waited in vain for an entire day, giving Sheridan's cavalry

time to cut the railroad to the south at Jetersville. Unable to use the railroad as planned, Lee then marched west on April 5 toward an alternate supply line at Lynchburg. On April 6, the Confederates reached Farmville, but almost the entire rear guard under Lt. Gen. Richard S. Ewell was cut off and captured at Sailor's Creek. Although he had lost a quarter of the army, Lee resumed the march on April 7. Fighting continued that day at High Bridge and Cumberland Church, and Lee rejected a surrender request from Grant (although he did ask about Grant's terms). A large Union cavalry and infantry force under Sheridan sprinted ahead and blocked the Confederate advance at Appomattox Court House. After sporadic fighting on April 8, Lee attacked Sheridan on April 9 to cut his way through the encirclement, but he quickly realized a breakout was impossible. Now blocked front and rear, he had no choice but to meet with Grant at the Wilmer McLean house that afternoon and surrender.

Conditions of the surrender were generous. After signing parole oaths promising not to take up arms again until exchanged and to obey lawful authority, the Confederates were released. Officers were allowed to keep their side arms, and those men owning their own horses and mules were allowed to keep them. On April 12, the 26,000 survivors of the Army of Northern Virginia were formally surrendered. During the Appomattox Campaign, another 25,000 Confederates had become casualties, while Grant lost an estimated 10,800 men.

While the war in Virginia was rapidly coming to an end, in the west another campaign and a cavalry raid were bringing the Union total victory. Farragut had captured Mobile Bay, Alabama, in August 1864, but the Federals were unable to seize the city itself because of the strong Confederate fortifications at Spanish Fort and Fort Blakely. It was not until March 1865 that a sufficient land and naval force had been assembled to overrun these Confederate strongholds in the Mobile Campaign. Supported by Adm. Henry K. Thatcher's 20 ships, Maj. Gen. E. R. S. Canby assembled 45,000 men for the operation. Defending Mobile were 10,000 Confederates and five gunboats under Maj. Gen. Dabney H. Maury. Canby ordered Frederick Steele from Pensacola, Florida, to attack Fort Blakely from the north, while he attacked Spanish Fort from the south. Canby bombarded the Confederate defenders from March 27 to April 8 and then launched an assault on the night of April 8 that overran and captured the fort. Five miles to the north, Steele had been engaged in siege work at Fort Blakely since April 1 and soon was reinforced by Canby's troops. The few thousand Confederate defenders under Brig. Gen. St. John R. Liddell held out until April 9. On that day (the same day Lee surrendered at Appomattox), the last major battle of the Civil War occurred when Canby attacked Fort Blakely and captured it in 20 minutes. Maury evacuated Mobile on the morning of April 12, and the Federals took possession of the city shortly after noon.

As Canby was closing in on Mobile, Union cavalryman Brig. Gen. James H. Wilson raided the important Confederate munitions depot and manufacturing center of Selma, Alabama. He led 13,500 troopers from Gravelly Springs, Alabama, on March 22, 1865, to confront Nathan Bedford Forrest's 7,000–8,000-member Confederate cavalry who were defending the area. On April 1, Wilson defeated Forrest in a wild, bloody melee at Ebenezer Church, and the Confederates retreated. Wilson attacked Selma the next day, defeated Forrest that afternoon, and captured 2,700 prisoners, 102 cannons, and an immense amount of supplies. Leaving Selma on April 9, he next headed for Montgomery, Alabama, and captured it on April 12. Advancing into Georgia, Wilson then occupied Columbus on April 16 and Macon four days later. During the raid, the Federals penetrated more than 300 miles into Confederate territory and lost 725 men, but they captured 6,820 prisoners and inflicted an estimated 1,200 casualties on the Confederates. Wilson's Selma Raid was one of the most successful cavalry raids of the war.

Lincoln was ecstatic to see these stunning Union victories, but he did not live to see the war's final conclusion. Since 1864, actor and Confederate supporter John Wilkes Booth had been involved with other conspirators in a plot to kidnap Lincoln and hold him hostage for the release of Confederate prisoners of war, but this plan failed because of Lincoln's ever-present armed escort. After Lee's surrender, Booth changed his plan from kidnapping Lincoln to murdering Lincoln, Vice President Andrew Johnson, and Secretary of State William H. Seward. It has generally been believed that Booth was motivated by revenge, but recent scholarship raises the possibility that the Confederate government might have been involved in the assassination to turn the tide of war by throwing the Union government into turmoil.

On the night of April 14, 1865, Booth mortally wounded Lincoln at Ford's Theater in Washington, and a fellow conspirator seriously wounded Seward. Lincoln died the next morning, but Booth and a companion escaped the city. Following a massive manhunt, the two finally were cornered by Union cavalry in a Virginia tobacco warehouse on April 26. Booth's companion surrendered, but Booth refused to do so and either was shot and killed or committed suicide. Federal authorities quickly arrested and tried eight other conspirators. Four, including Mary Surratt, were hanged; three were given life sentences; and one was sentenced to six years in prison. A ninth man escaped overseas but later was returned to the United States, where he was tried and acquitted.

In North Carolina at this time, Johnston was still confronting Sherman as he marched through the state. After learning of Lee's surrender and realizing there was now no hope of uniting their two armies, Johnston met with fleeing president Jefferson Davis at Greensboro on April 12 and received Davis's reluctant permission to begin surrender negotiations. He and Sherman met on April 17 at James Bennett's farmhouse near Durham Station. By the next day, they agreed that Johnston would surrender, but Sherman overstepped his authority and also agreed that the existing Confederate state governments would continue to function. President Andrew Johnson's administration rejected the agreement, and Grant ordered Sherman to offer only those terms that had been presented to Lee. As a result, Sherman and Johnston met at the Bennett home again on April 26 and agreed that Johnston would surrender his 30,000 men on those terms on May 3. Like falling dominoes, the other Confederate armies quickly surrendered from east to west. Richard Taylor, commander of the Department of Alabama, Mississippi, and East Louisiana, surrendered on May 4, at Citronelle, Alabama, and Trans-Mississippi Department commander Kirby Smith surrendered on June 2 in Galveston, Texas. The last Confederate ground troops to surrender were Brig. Gen. Stand Watie's Indians, who laid down their arms at Doaksville, Indian Territory, on June 23. The last surrender of all was the Confederate commerce raider *Shenandoah*, which steamed to Liverpool and surrendered to British authorities on November 6, 1865.

THE CIVIL WAR'S LEGACY

The Civil War was one of the largest wars of the 19th century and is considered to have been the first modern war. Among the "firsts" documented in the conflict were the first successful use of a submarine; ironclad warships; rotating gun turrets; trench warfare; widespread use of rifles, rifled cannons, and repeating weapons; reliance on railroads and telegraphs; airships; wire entanglements; and telescopic sights. The war also was the bloodiest in American history, but determining the precise number of casualties is difficult. A reasonable estimate would be 360,000 dead for the Union and 260,000 for the Confederacy. Of these, approximately 110,000 Union soldiers were killed or mortally wounded in battle, while at least 75,000 (and perhaps many more) Confederates suffered the same fate. Despite these high battle casualties, most of the war's fatalities were caused by disease, particularly typhoid and dysentery. In addition, approximately 275,000 Federals and up to 226,000 Confederates were wounded. The estimated 620,000 soldiers' deaths were more American dead than were suffered in all of the nation's other wars combined through World War II. It also is known that thousands of civilians died from disease, exposure, and wounds, but there is no accurate way even to estimate their number.

Thousands of soldiers also were taken prisoner during the war. The exact number is uncertain, but it is estimated that 211,411 Union soldiers were captured, and 30,218 died in captivity. Not counting those who were surrendered at war's end, approximately 220,000 Confederates were captured, with 25,976 dying in captivity. Since neither side had made any plans to handle large numbers of prisoners, releasing captives on parole was a common practice, but more than 150 sites did serve as prisons. Most were horrid places, with overcrowded, unsanitary conditions, and prisoners suffered from exposure, disease, and hunger. Some prisons like Andersonville and Point Lookout became infamous for cruel guards and scant food, but in most cases abuse was not intentional. For those who were sent to prisons, a formal exchange system was agreed to in July 1862. For two years, the belligerents swapped prisoners, although problems frequently arose over such issues as the exchange of black Union troops. This system benefited the Confederates since they suffered the most from manpower shortages, so U. S. Grant virtually stopped exchanges in 1864.

Two questions that are still debated by Civil War historians are whether or not the war was inevitable and could the Confederacy have won. Such what-if questions are unanswerable, and there will never be agreement on them. One could argue that the North and South developed into different socioeconomic regions that made conflict likely and that most nations engage in at least one civil war to settle the type of issues that were facing the United States in 1861. On the other hand, it is also true that during the crucial decade preceding the war, America's presidents and other political leaders were not of the same caliber as earlier ones. If there had been more capable men like George Washington and Henry Clay in the 1850s and fewer radicals like Charles Sumner and Robert Barnwell Rhett, perhaps an accommodation could have been reached that would have preserved the peace.

As for the Confederacy winning the war, it was possible but not probable. Certainly, history proves that in many conflicts, the weaker side often wins if its people are committed enough to wage a war of attrition and fight until the opponent tires of the struggle and quits. The American Revolution and America's experience in Vietnam are only two examples of this. Some historians argue that if the Confederacy had remained on the defensive, not wasted men in frontal attacks, or launched such costly invasions as the Antietam and Gettysburg Campaigns, it could have continued the struggle until the Union was forced to negotiate a peace. While this perhaps is true, it ignores the war's politics, and the fact the Union would have grown stronger as time passed. Like their leading general, Robert E. Lee, most Confederates expected to win the war on the battlefield. Would they have supported a purely defensive strategy and allowed the armies to remain inactive for long periods of time? Other historians believe the Confederate people were not committed to the cause and stopped supporting the war when conditions became difficult, which in turn led to poor morale and military defeats. There certainly was a weakening of morale as the war progressed but whether that led to military defeats or vice versa is debatable. Some historians believe that if the Confederacy could have held on to Mobile and Atlanta in 1864, Northern resolve would have weakened, Lincoln would have been defeated for reelection, and McClellan would have negotiated a peace when he became president. Such a scenario is unlikely, however, because McClellan repudiated the Democrats' peace plank, and Lincoln still would have had four months before inauguration to win the war against the exhausted Confederacy. He no doubt would have pressed the war vigorously, and even without such a concerted effort, the Union still essentially won the war only a month after the 1865 inauguration. Such what-if speculation is pointless, for even if events had occurred differently, all one can say for sure is that the Civil War would have been different, not that the Confederacy would have won.

When debating whether the Confederates could have won the war, there are an infinite number of scenarios. One thing is certain, however. The Civil War was won and lost in the west; the war in Virginia remained a stalemate until the bitter end. It was in the west at such places as New Orleans, Vicksburg, Chattanooga, Atlanta, and Nashville that the rebellion was broken, and from the west came the Union's best generals—Grant and Sherman—without whom the war's outcome could have been very different.

The Civil War's legacy goes beyond military history. The war transformed both the nation and the people's perspectives. Before the conflict, Americans identified more with their respective states, and the federal government intruded little on their lives. The Civil War laid to rest the philosophy of secession and never again has a section of the country entertained the notion that the Union can be dissolved. No longer is the United States viewed as a confederation of sovereign states, but rather it is seen as a nation where the federal government is supreme and state governments play a subordinate role. During the war, the federal government assumed much more power than it had previously, and that trend has continued—largely through constitutional amendments—until it has taken control of such issues as citizenship and voting rights, which previously were the states' domain.

Many other aspects of modern American life have been affected by the Civil War. The federal income tax and military draft, which were first used during the war, became acceptable. Because of the war and Reconstruction, the Southern states remained a solid Democratic Party stronghold until the 1970s. Modern race relations are also affected by the war. Even now, for example, there are frequent clashes over the public display of Confederate symbols. Many whites and most African-Americans oppose any such display because they believe the Confederacy was an evil entity that fought to maintain slavery. Also, some Southern states incorporated the Confederate battle flag into their state flags in the 1950s as a sign of opposition to the civil rights movement, and hate groups like the Ku Klux Klan and neo-Nazis have adopted the flag for their use. Other Americans, particularly white Southerners, argue that the war was over constitutional rights, not slavery; that most Confederate soldiers owned no slaves and should be honored for bravely defending their homes against invasion; and that the adoption of the Confederate battle flag by modern hate groups should not be confused with racially tolerant Americans displaying the flag to honor their ancestors. As a result of these conflicting viewpoints, there continues to be frequent turmoil over monuments honoring Confederate soldiers, the naming of schools after Confederate personalities, and the display of the Confederate battle flag or its incorporation into state flags.

Because of its drama and great impact on the United States, the Civil War is the most studied event in American history; more books have been written about it than any other topic, and scores continue to be released every year. It seems the public's appetite for information on the conflict is insatiable, and considering the significance of the conflict, that interest is well deserved.

THE DICTIONARY

– A –

ABATIS. Used to defend a position, an abatis (AH-buh-tee) is a tangle of trees felled so the branches, sometimes sharpened, face the attacking force.

ABERCROMBIE, JOHN JOSEPH (1798–1877) USA. A native of **Tennessee**, Abercrombie was the son-in-law of Union Maj. Gen. **Robert Patterson** and the brother-in-law of Brig. Gen. **Francis E. Patterson**. After graduating near the top of his 1822 **West Point** class, he served in the Black Hawk, **Seminole**, and **Mexican Wars**, winning a **brevet** against the Seminoles and being wounded and brevetted in Mexico.

Abercrombie was colonel of the 7th U.S. Infantry when the Civil War began. He was promoted to brigadier general of volunteers in August 1861 and was given a **brigade** in **Nathaniel P. Banks's** division of the **Army of the Potomac**. In April 1862, Abercrombie was sent to the **Shenandoah Valley**, where he served as a brigade commander during **Stonewall Jackson's 1862 Shenandoah Valley Campaign**. He then was transferred back to the Army of the Potomac and was wounded at **Seven Pines** while leading his brigade in the **Peninsula Campaign**. Abercrombie rejoined his men in time to serve in the closing days of the **Seven Days Campaign** and then was sent to command a **division** in the **Washington, D.C.**, defenses. After being declared unfit for field service in June 1863, he served the rest of the war on boards and commissions or commanding troops protecting Washington and **Fredericksburg**.

Abercrombie left the volunteer service in June 1864 but remained in the regular **army**. After being brevetted a brigadier general in March 1865, he retired in June and moved to **New York**.

ABOLITIONISTS. Composing a small minority of Northerners, abolitionists wanted to abolish **slavery** and grant some political and social rights to blacks. The abolitionists were particularly strong in New England and in parts of **Pennsylvania** and the Midwest where Quakers enjoyed influence. Originally vilified by other Northerners, the abolitionists enjoyed support from a number of wealthy and influential citizens and politicians and eventually converted many to their views. *See also* AMERICAN ANTI-SLAVERY SOCIETY; BEECHER, HENRY WARD; BROWN, JOHN; GARRISON, WILLIAM LLOYD; PHILLIPS, WENDELL; STOWE, HARRIET BEECHER.

ACCOUTERMENTS. This refers to the equipment, besides his weapon and clothing, a soldier carries. Examples would be canteen, **knapsack**, eating utensils, and cartridge box.

ACOUSTIC SHADOW. Particular atmospheric conditions or topography can lead to a phenomenon known as an acoustic shadow. During this condition, sound may not carry very far in one direction but may be heard a long distance away in another. Acoustic shadows sometimes caused commanders to be unaware a battle was raging only a short distance away. The phenomenon was noted at the battles of **Seven Pines**, and **Perryville**.

ADAIRSVILLE, GEORGIA, BATTLE OF (MAY 17, 1864). During the **Atlanta Campaign**, **William T. Sherman** had forced **Joseph E. Johnston** to retreat behind the Oostanaula River by mid-May 1864. Johnston took up a new defensive line near Adairsville, with Maj. Gen. **Benjamin F. Cheatham's division** occupying a position at the Saxon (Octagon) house. When **Oliver O. Howard's** Union IV Corps arrived on May 17, his lead **brigade** under Maj. Frank Sherman was hit by **artillery** and **sharpshooter** fire from Cheatham's Confederates. Sherman lost approximately 200 men during the fight, but Confederate losses are unknown. Howard made preparations to attack Cheatham's position the following day, but Johnston withdrew during the night to Cassville.

ADAMS, CHARLES FRANCIS, SR. (1807–1886) USA. A member of the famous **Massachusetts** Adams family, Charles Francis Adams Sr., was the son of former president John Quincy Adams. He began his political career with the **Whig Party** but later joined the **Republicans**. Adams served in the **U.S. Congress** from 1858 to 1861 and was appointed by **Abraham Lincoln** in early 1861 to be minister to Great Britain, a post he kept until 1868. His main mission was to keep the British from recognizing the Confederacy as a legitimate nation and from providing the Confederates war materials.

Adams earned the respect of the British with his calm and rational manner. He convinced the British foreign minister to discontinue meeting with Confederate envoys, helped persuade his own government to release Confederate commissioners **James Mason** and **John Slidell** during the *Trent* **Affair**, and prevented the Confederacy from purchasing two British-built **rams**. Adams also helped lay the groundwork for the *Alabama* **Claims**, which the United States pursued against Great Britain for the destruction caused by the British-built ram **CSS *Alabama***. During those talks, Adams served as one of five American negotiators.

ADAMS, DANIEL WEISIGER (1821–1872) CSA. A native of **Kentucky**, Adams was the brother of Confederate general **William Wirt Adams**. He moved with his family to **Mississippi** as a child and once killed a man in a duel for insulting his father. After studying law, Adams moved to **Louisiana** and began his practice. When the **secession** crisis began, he was appointed to the board that prepared the state for war.

Adams entered Confederate service as lieutenant colonel of the 1st Louisiana Regulars and was promoted to regimental colonel in October 1861. At **Shiloh**, he took command of the Louisiana Brigade when the commander was killed, but a wound cost him his right eye. Promoted to brigadier general in May 1862, Adams and his **brigade** fought at **Perryville** and **Stones River**, where he was wounded again. At **Chickamauga** with the **Army of Tennessee**, the brigade temporarily broke through the Union lines, but Adams was captured after being wounded for the third time. After being **exchanged**, he was given command of a cavalry brigade in **Alabama** and in the war's last year commanded various Alabama **districts**.

After the war, Adams lived in Great Britain for a while and then returned to Louisiana to practice law.

ADAMS, JOHN (1825–1864) CSA. A native of **Tennessee**, Adams graduated from **West Point** in 1844. During the **Mexican War**, he served under **Philip Kearny** and was **brevetted** for gallantry at the Battle of Santa Cruz de Rosales. Adams mostly served on the frontier with the 1st Dragoons during the 1850s and held the rank of captain when he resigned from the **U.S. Army** in May 1861.

Adams entered Confederate service as a captain of cavalry and was put in command of the garrison at Memphis, Tennessee. Promotion to colonel and brigadier general followed in May and December 1862, respectively, and in the spring of 1863, he assumed command of a **Mississippi brigade**. Adams served with **Joseph E. Johnston's** command during the **Vicksburg**

Campaign and later joined **Leonidas Polk's corps** in the **Army of Tennessee**. After the **Atlanta Campaign**, Adams participated in the **Franklin and Nashville Campaign**. At the Battle of Franklin on November 30, 1864, he was severely wounded in the right arm. Remaining with his men, Adams led them in an attack against the Union lines and was killed.

ADAMS, WILLIAM WIRT (1819–1888) CSA. The brother of Confederate general **Daniel Weisiger Adams**, Adams was born in **Kentucky** but grew up in **Mississippi**. He briefly served in the army of the Republic of Texas but returned to Mississippi to become a planter, banker, and two-term legislator.

In early 1861, Adams refused **Jefferson Davis's** offer of appointment as the Confederate postmaster general. Instead, he raised the 1st Mississippi Cavalry and was appointed its colonel in October 1861. After serving with **Albert Sidney Johnston** in Kentucky and **Tennessee**, Adams fought at **Shiloh** and at **Iuka** and **Corinth, Mississippi**. He then took part in pursuing **Benjamin Grierson's** raiders and skillfully opposed **William T. Sherman's** siege of **Jackson, Mississippi**, after the fall of **Vicksburg, Mississippi**, and was promoted to brigadier general in September 1863. With a **brigade** of cavalry, Adams again opposed Sherman during the **Meridian Campaign**. For the last year of war, he was attached to **Nathan Bedford Forrest's** command and surrendered with Forrest in May 1865.

Adams returned to Mississippi after the war and served as the state's revenue agent and postmaster of Jackson. He was killed on March 1, 1888, in a confrontation with a newspaper editor with whom he had been feuding.

AFRICAN-AMERICAN SOLDIERS, USE OF. *See* BLACK TROOPS, USE OF.

ALABAMA. On January 11, 1861, Alabama became the fourth Southern state to secede. Afterward, upon the invitation of the state's **secession** convention, the other seceding states met in the **Montgomery, Alabama, Convention**, on February 4 and created the **Confederate States of America**. Montgomery served as the Confederacy's first capital until the new government was moved to **Richmond, Virginia**, in May 1861. Although many people in mountainous northern Alabama opposed secession, the state served the Confederacy well. It produced large amounts of iron, and a number of ironworks produced ammunition. Also, it is estimated that 75,000–125,000 Alabama men served in the **Confederate army**, of whom 25,000–70,000 were casualties. *See also* BAT-

TLES OF DAY'S GAP, DECATUR, FORT BLAKELY, MOBILE BAY, SPANISH FORT; WILSON'S SELMA, ALABAMA RAID.

ALABAMA* CLAIMS.** One of the greatest diplomatic issues resulting from the war was the question of compensation for U.S. shipping destroyed or captured by British-built **Confederate commerce raiders**. The most successful, and famous, of these raiders was the **CSS *Alabama; thus, the claims were named for it. U.S. Minister **Charles Francis Adams Sr.** demanded compensation during the war, and soon after hostilities ended, Secretary of State **William Seward** continued to press the issue. The U.S. demanded payments totaling $19,021,000 for the losses inflicted by the Confederate raiders *Alabama*, *Florida*, and *Shenandoah*. An 1868 convention designed to settle all Anglo-American claims filed since 1853 failed to win Senate approval because it did not include the *Alabama* Claims.

The *Alabama* Claims became the most important diplomatic issue of President **Ulysses S. Grant's** administration and was not settled until Secretary of State Hamilton Fish took up the matter. In the 1871 Treaty of Washington, both sides finally agreed to submit the claims for arbitration. In 1872, an arbitration board composed of members from the United States (Adams), Great Britain, Italy, Switzerland, and Brazil awarded the United States $15,500,000 after ruling that Great Britain had not lived up to its neutrality responsibilities during the war. In turn, the United States had to pay $1,929,819 for losses British citizens suffered during the war.

ALABAMA*, CSS.** The *Alabama* became the most famous of the **Confederate commerce raiders**. Purchased from Great Britain, it was launched on May 15, 1862, in Liverpool as the *Enrica*. Despite the efforts of U.S. Minister **Charles Francis Adams Sr.** to prevent its departure, the ship sailed from Liverpool on July 29 on what was described as a shakedown cruise. It was commissioned the *Alabama* in the Azores under Capt. **Raphael Semmes** and received four cannons. In the next two years, the *Alabama* sailed the Atlantic, Caribbean, Gulf of Mexico, and even the Indian Ocean and the South China Sea. During its career, the vessel sailed nearly 75,000 miles and accounted for more than 66 enemy vessels (most of which were burned), including the **USS *Hatteras, which it engaged and sank near Galveston, Texas.

In June 1864 the *Alabama* was discovered at Cherbourg, France, by the **USS *Kearsarge***. On June 19, Semmes took the ship to sea and engaged the Union vessel despite the poor condition of his own ship. In a short battle, witnessed by hundreds of onlookers, the *Alabama* was sunk.

ALBEMARLE, **CSS.** This ship, built on the Roanoke River, **North Carolina**, was designed to operate in the shallow North Carolina inlets. Covered with four inches of iron plating, it was 152 feet in length, had a draft of nine feet, and was armed with two 6.4-inch **Brooke cannons**. Only two days after its launch in April 1864, the *Albemarle*, under Comdr. James W. Cooke, joined in an attack on **Plymouth**. During the engagement, it rammed and sank one Union gunboat and forced three others to withdraw. A month later, the *Albemarle* was damaged during action against Union gunboats at the mouth of the Roanoke River.

Greatly feared by Union commanders, the ship was sunk in a night raid by Lt. **William B. Cushing** and a small party of volunteers. Cushing and his men mounted a spar **torpedo** on a small boat, slipped up the Roanoke River on the night of October 28, 1864, and rammed the *Albemarle*. The torpedo detonated and sank the vessel in shallow water. When Plymouth later fell to Union forces, the *Albemarle* was raised and taken to **Norfolk** Navy Yard, where it was sold for scrap in 1867.

ALBEMARLE SOUND, NORTH CAROLINA, BATTLE OF (MAY 5, 1864). After capturing **Plymouth, North Carolina**, on April 20, 1864, Confederate Brig. Gen. **Robert F. Hoke** took the **ironclad CSS *Albemarle*** and two additional vessels and headed for New Bern on May 5. Upon reaching Albemarle Sound, he discovered a small seven-ship Union flotilla under Capt. Melancton Smith. After sending his troop transport to the rear to protect the infantry onboard, Hoke attacked with the *Albemarle* and the *Bombshell*, a steamer the Confederates had captured earlier. In the following engagement, Smith's ships pounded the *Albemarle* but inflicted no serious damage. That night, however, the Federals did manage to recapture the *Bombshell*. Hoke then retreated to Plymouth and soon departed with his men to reinforce Petersburg, Virginia. Total casualties for the action at Albemarle Sound are estimated at 88.

ALDIE, VIRGINIA, BATTLE OF (JUNE 17, 1863). As **Robert E. Lee** began his **Gettysburg Campaign** with the **Army of Northern Virginia** in June 1863, **Joseph Hooker**, commander of the **Army of the Potomac**, ordered his cavalry under Brig. Gen. **Alfred Pleasonton** to ascertain the Confederates' intentions. On June 17, 1863, Pleasonton's troopers rode from Manassas Junction to Aldie, Virginia. There they clashed with Confederate Col. Thomas T. Munford's cavalrymen, who were guarding a gap through the Bull Run Mountains. Union cavalry under Brig. Gen. **H. Judson Kilpatrick** charged Munford and was forcing him out of Aldie when the Confederates received help from the 5th Virginia Cavalry and, in turn, drove the Federals back. Kilpatrick and Munford continued a series of charges and countercharges west of town until Munford was ordered to withdraw about dark. Casualty figures are uncertain, but it is estimated that Munford lost about 100 men and Kilpatrick approximately 300.

ALEXANDER, EDWARD PORTER (1835–1910) CSA. A native of **Georgia**, Alexander was a member of a wealthy planter family and graduated near the top of his 1857 **West Point** class. Entering the **engineers**, he taught at the academy and briefly served in the **Utah Expedition**. Just prior to the Civil War, Alexander also helped develop the **signal** flag method of communication. Serving in **California** when Georgia seceded, he resigned his commission as first lieutenant in March 1861 and was appointed captain of Confederate engineers.

At **First Manassas**, Alexander served as **P. G. T. Beauregard's** chief signal officer; it was he who discovered and warned his chief of the Union **army** approaching the Confederate left flank early in the battle. Recognized as an excellent officer, Alexander was given the position of army chief of ordnance. He kept this position until November 1862, serving under Beauregard, **Joseph E. Johnston**, and **Robert E. Lee** in all of the major campaigns of the **Army of Northern Virginia**. Promotion to major of **artillery** came in April 1862 and to lieutenant colonel in July. In November 1862, Alexander was given command of an artillery battalion under **James Longstreet** and was promoted to colonel in March 1863.

Alexander served as nominal chief of Longstreet's artillery for the next year, although technically he was simply a battalion commander. His gift for artillery **tactics** was shown at **Fredericksburg**, where his guns decimated the attacking Union columns, and at **Chancellorsville**, where he took control of the high ground at Hazel Grove. At **Gettysburg**, Alexander was put in charge of silencing the Union batteries on Cemetery Ridge prior to **Pickett's Charge**, but disagreed with the tactics used there and was reluctant to assume such responsibility.

After serving with Longstreet at **Chickamauga** and **Knoxville**, Alexander was offered a promotion to brigadier general and to be appointed chief of artillery for the **Army of Tennessee**. Lee, however, refused to release him and instead helped secure his promotion to brigadier general in March 1864. Shortly afterward, Alexander was made chief of artillery for Longstreet's I Corps, and in that position, he continued his excellent service until the surrender at **Appomattox**. Few officers contributed as much to their army as did Alexander. Besides directing Longstreet's artillery, he also was involved in developing new weapons and a signal service, reorganizing the army's artillery units, operating signal **balloons**, engineering, and training.

After the war, Alexander was active in the **railroad** industry and upon President Grover Cleveland's request, served as an arbitrator in a boundary dispute between Costa Rica and Nicaragua from 1897 to 1900. His memoirs, published under the title *Fighting for the Confederacy*, are recognized as one of the best Civil War books written by a participant.

ALLATOONA PASS, GEORGIA, BATTLE OF (OCTOBER 5, 1864). After **William T. Sherman** captured Atlanta, Georgia, in September 1864, **John Bell Hood** attempted to force the Federals to evacuate the city by moving the **Army of Tennessee** northward to cut Sherman's supply line. Allatoona, garrisoned by a single Union **regiment**, was one of Sherman's largest supply bases and was attacked by Maj. Gen. **Samuel G. French's** Confederate **division**. Sherman expected such a move and ordered Brig. Gen. **John M. Corse** to reinforce Allatoona.

Telegraph wires had been cut, so on the afternoon of October 4, signal officers on Kennesaw Mountain sent to Allatoona encouraging messages that Sherman was coming and for the garrison to hold on. Corse arrived at Allatoona with Col. Richard Rowett's 1,100-man **brigade** shortly after midnight on October 5, 1864. Unaware of these reinforcements, French cut the roads into Allatoona after daylight and demanded its surrender, but Corse refused. French then attacked the town from three sides that morning, but Rowett's brigade repulsed the attacks, and French finally withdrew that afternoon. During the battle, Corse was grazed by a bullet. The following day he sent a grandiose message to Sherman declaring, "I am short a cheek-bone and an ear, but am able to whip all hell yet" (Warner, *Generals in Blue* '95).

During the short, fierce fight, Corse lost 707 men, while French reported 799 casualties, including Brig. Gen. **William H. Young**, who was wounded and captured. The dramatic fight became a famous Civil War story. The message sent by the Kennesaw Mountain signal station was, "Hold the fort; we are coming" and led to the popular hymn "Hold the Fort."

ALLEN, HENRY WATKINS (1820–1866) CSA. Born in **Virginia**, Allen grew up in **Missouri**. After graduating from Marion College, he worked as a **Mississippi** tutor and schoolteacher before becoming a lawyer and captain of a local militia **company**. Allen and his men volunteered for the **Texas** army in 1842 and saw some combat fighting Mexicans along the border. After marrying a Mississippi woman, Allen once fought a duel with her father, but the man did not hold a grudge and even gave Allen and his wife a plantation. Allen was elected to the Mississippi legislature in 1846 but in 1852 moved to **Louisiana** and became a sugar planter. After briefly studying at Harvard University, he entered politics and was elected to the Louisiana senate in 1859.

After helping raise several military companies, Allen was elected lieutenant colonel of the 4th Louisiana and entered Confederate service in May 1861. His **regiment** served at Ship Island and in southern Louisiana before joining **P. G. T. Beauregard's army** in 1862. Allen was promoted to colonel in March and gallantly led his regiment at **Shiloh**, where he suffered a wound to the face. After service at **Corinth** and **Vicksburg, Mississippi**, he again led his regiment at the **Battle of Baton Rouge, Louisiana**, and suffered such severe wounds to his legs that he walked on crutches for the rest of his life.

Allen became a major general of Louisiana state militia in February 1863 and was promoted to brigadier general of Confederate troops in August. After being elected Confederate governor of Louisiana in January 1864, he resigned his Confederate commission and assumed his civilian duties. Allen proved to be one of the best governors of the Confederacy. When the war ended, he went into exile to Mexico and became a newspaper publisher.

ALLEN, ROBERT (1811–1886) USA. A native of **Ohio**, Allen graduated from **West Point** in 1836 and was assigned to the **artillery**. He joined the quartermaster department in 1846, served in the **Seminole Wars**, and earned a **brevet** and promotion to captain during the **Mexican War**.

Allen was a major in 1861 and served in the quartermaster department for the entire Civil War. He was promoted to colonel in February 1862 and became chief quartermaster for the **Department of the Missouri**, with promotion to brigadier general following in May 1863. By 1864, the talented Allen was given responsibility for supplying all Union troops west of the Mississippi River (except for **California**). He was brevetted major general of volunteers in March 1865 and retired from the **U.S. Army** in 1878.

ALLEN, WILLIAM WIRT (1835–1894) CSA. A native of **New York**, Allen grew up in **Alabama**. After graduating from the College of New Jersey (Princeton) in 1854, he returned to Alabama and became a planter.

Allen entered Confederate service in early 1861 as a 1st lieutenant in a local volunteer **company** and served in **Pensacola, Florida**, before being elected major of the 1st Alabama Cavalry in March 1862. After fighting at **Shiloh**, he was promoted to colonel in July 1862 and was slightly wounded while leading the **regiment** at **Perryville**. Well respected, Allen commanded a **brigade** during the latter part of 1862 and was wounded again at the **Battle of Stones River** while fighting with the **Army of Tennessee**. After recuperating from the partial loss of his right hand, he was promoted to brigadier general in February 1864 and was given permanent command of one of **Joseph Wheeler's** cavalry brigades.

During the **Atlanta Campaign**, Allen helped capture **George Stoneman's** raiders near Macon, Georgia, and afterward was given command of a cavalry **division**. Wounded for a third time at **Waynesboro** in November 1864, he saw hard service opposing the enemy during the **March to the Sea** and in the **Carolinas Campaign**. Allen was promoted to major general in March 1865, but it is questionable whether the appointment was ever confirmed by the Senate. He was **paroled** at Salisbury, North Carolina, in May 1865 after having survived three wounds and the loss of 10 horses in combat.

After the war, Allen returned to Alabama and worked as a planter, businessman, Montgomery city official, Alabama adjutant general, and U.S. marshal. His bullet-riddled coat is now sealed in the cornerstone of a Confederate monument in Montgomery.

ALLEN'S FARM, VIRGINIA, BATTLE OF (JUNE 29, 1862). *See* SAVAGE'S STATION, VIRGINIA, BATTLE OF.

ALLIGATOR, **USS.** Although the **CSS** *H. L. Hunley* is the better known Civil War **submarine**, the Union developed one as well. The USS *Alligator* was designed by French engineer Brutus de Villeroi and was contracted by the **U.S. Navy** in November 1861. Built in Philadelphia, Pennsylvania, it was 45 feet long, 5½ feet in diameter, and was powered by 16 oars that folded onto the hull. Unlike its Confederate counterpart, the *Alligator*'s crew included two divers who were to swim out of the boat and attach electrically detonated mines onto enemy ships. In June 1862, the *Alligator* arrived for duty on the James River, Virginia, but was found to be unable to operate safely in the shallow tidal waters. It sank in a storm on April 2, 1863, while being towed to **Charleston, South Carolina**.

ALLISON, ALEXANDER (dates unknown) USA. An **Illinois** engraver, Allison became a partner of Louis Kurz in 1880 to form the famous lithograph firm of Kurz and Allison. Over the next 20 years, the firm produced

36 lithographs of Civil War battles. Although completely unrealistic in their depiction of warfare, the lithographs became very popular with the public.

ALTON PRISON, ILLINOIS. Located on the Mississippi River at Alton, Illinois, Alton Prison was the first state **prison** in **Illinois** and became notorious for its poor conditions. Although closed when the Civil War began, it was reopened in 1862 for use as a prison camp. Conditions were horrid, and when a smallpox epidemic broke out among the Confederate **prisoners**, many of the sick were moved to an isolated island in the river. Although a number of prisoners managed to escape, including 36 who tunneled their way out in 1862, untold numbers died of disease. No records were kept of the deaths, but it is believed that several thousand Confederate prisoners died at Alton or on the nearby island.

ALVORD, BENJAMIN (1813–1884) USA. Although not serving in combat, Alvord was an important officer in the **U.S. Army**. A native of **Maine**, he graduated from **West Point** in 1833 and served in the **Seminole** and **Mexican Wars** (where he won two **brevets**). Alvord was a major serving as paymaster of the Department of Oregon when the Civil War began. Promoted to brigadier general of volunteers in April 1862, he commanded the District of Oregon for the duration of the war. Alvord was known to be an excellent administrator, negotiated with the Nez Percé Indians, and was awarded three brevets for his service.

After the war, Alvord became paymaster general of the U.S. Army. Besides his military service, he also was a well-known botanist and mathematician.

AMBULANCE CORPS. When the Civil War began, neither side had any separate organization dedicated to the removal of wounded from the battlefield. The Confederacy never established any official military organization to assume this responsibility, relying instead on using ambulatory soldiers, musicians, cooks, and so on, on the **regiment** or **brigade** level as litter bearers. The Union, however, did eventually create a separate ambulance corps.

After the **First Battle of Manassas** demonstrated the complete lack of preparedness for casualty care, Surgeon General Charles S. Tripler began making changes in the **Army of the Potomac**. He adopted more comfortable ambulances, required drivers to be soldiers and not civilians, and began training ambulance crews.

In 1862, Tripler was replaced by Jonathan Letterman, who persuaded Maj. Gen. **George B. McClellan** to create a separate **army** ambulance corps. Training continued, and the corps became more and more efficient in the removal of wounded from the field. However, when the **U.S. Congress** addressed a bill designed to create an ambulance corps for all the armies, it was killed by the influence of Secretary of War **Edwin Stanton** and General-in-Chief **Henry Halleck**. It was not until March 1864 that the Ambulance Corps Act finally was passed, creating a separate ambulance corps for the armies. Under the new law, the Medical Department had the right to train its members and to dismiss those soldiers deemed unsuited for service. The Ambulance Corps proved a huge success and was copied by many nations after the war.

AMELIA SPRINGS, VIRGINIA, BATTLE OF (APRIL 5, 1865). When **Robert E. Lee** abandoned Petersburg and **Richmond, Virginia**, and began the **Appomattox Campaign**, he planned to reunite his scattered **Army of Northern Virginia** at Amelia Springs. There, he hoped to resupply the **army** from a supply train ordered to meet him there and then move southwest to join **Joseph E. Johnston** in **North Carolina**. When the train brought ammunition rather than supplies, Lee was forced to waste a day foraging in the Amelia Springs area. This delay gave **U. S. Grant** and the **Army of the Potomac** a chance to catch the Confederates.

On April 4, **Philip Sheridan** blocked Lee's advance to the southwest at Jetersville and the next morning sent Brig. Gen. **Henry E. Davies's** cavalry northward to Paineville. There Davies attacked a Confederate wagon train being escorted by **Martin W. Gary's brigade**. The Federals destroyed 200 wagons and captured numerous **prisoners** and mules and may have destroyed Lee's headquarters records. Gary then was reinforced by **Fitzhugh Lee's** cavalry, and together they attacked and drove Davies back through Amelia Springs. Confederate losses in the fight are unknown, but Davies lost 116 men. At Sheridan's request, Grant joined him at Jetersville that night and issued orders for the army to move in front of Lee and cut off his advance. The next day, the Federals attacked and captured a large part of Lee's army at **Sailor's Creek**.

AMERICAN ANTI-SLAVERY SOCIETY. William Lloyd Garrison and other **abolitionists** such as George C. Finney, Theodore D. Weld, and Arthur and Lewis Tappan were often at odds over how to end **slavery**. Egos, politics, and religion played major roles in keeping such abolitionists at odds. Tappan and others had begun making plans for a national antislavery society, but Garrison beat them to it by establishing the American Anti-Slavery Society in Philadelphia, Pennsylvania, in 1833. The more moderate abolitionists were alarmed at Garrison's radicalism, but they joined forces with him and made the society a potent force throughout the 1830s.

The society became widespread with hundreds of chapters and more than 250,000 members. Its main activities were petitioning the **U.S. Congress** for the abolition of slavery, spreading antislavery propaganda, and pushing for the immediate emancipation of slaves and the granting of complete equality to blacks. The society was cursed by proslavery factions, and its members were sometimes targeted for violence. Internal factionalism, decreasing popularity of abolitionism, and monetary problems led to its decline as a national force in the 1840s.

AMERICAN COLONIZATION SOCIETY. Founded in 1817, largely by slave owners, the American Colonization Society was dedicated to sending freed slaves to Africa. Some members viewed this as a means to protect **slavery** from the influence of freed slaves; others saw slavery as evil, albeit necessary, and believed the gradual emancipation and deportation of slaves was a way to wean the South from its grasp. After 1830, Northern **abolitionists** took over the society and used it to remove blacks from America and to give them an opportunity to establish their own republic. The society bought land in Liberia but found that few freed slaves wished to move there and by 1831 had resettled only 1,400 people. The controversial society was weakened by internal disputes, outside criticism, and financial problems and disappeared in the 1850s.

AMERICAN FLAG DISPATCH. During the tense days of January 1861, the U.S. Treasury Department sent W. Hemphill Jones to **Louisiana** to ensure that the department's revenue cutters were turned over to proper federal authorities and not to the seceding states. After Louisiana seceded on January 26, Jones informed Secretary of the Treasury **John A. Dix** that the captain of the cutter *McClelland* refused to obey the order. Dix sent Jones a dispatch ordering him to have the first officer arrest the captain and to treat the captain as a mutineer if he interfered. "If anyone attempts to haul down the American flag," Dix added, "shoot him on the spot" (Boatner, *Civil War Dictionary*, 11). Dix's strong statement angered the South and increased tensions during this volatile time, but it made him a hero in the North.

AMERICAN PARTY. *See* KNOW-NOTHING PARTY.

AMES, ADELBERT (1835–1933) USA. A native of **Maine**, Ames became a leading Union officer during the war. Abandoning a career as a clipper's mate, he entered **West Point** and graduated near the top of his class in 1861. An **artillery** lieutenant at **First Manassas**, Ames was seriously wounded in the thigh but refused to leave the field and continued to fight while perched on a caisson until he became too weak to continue. For his gallantry, he was **brevetted** major in the regular **army** (and in 1893 was awarded the **Medal of Honor**). Afterward, Ames commanded an artillery battery in the **Army of the Potomac** during the **Peninsula Campaign** and won another brevet to lieutenant colonel for his conduct at **Malvern Hill**.

Appointed colonel of the 20th Maine in August 1862, Ames led the **regiment** at **Antietam** and **Fredericksburg** and at **Chancellorsville** served as Maj. Gen. **George Meade's** aide. He won promotion to brigadier general of volunteers in May 1863 and received command of an infantry **brigade**. At **Gettysburg**, Ames served gallantly and assumed command of his **division** on the second day of battle. For the remainder of the war, he not only led his brigade, but frequently assumed division and even **corps** command. Ames also fought in **South Carolina**, and at **Cold Harbor**, **Petersburg**, and **Fort Fisher**. For this last battle, he was brevetted major general of volunteers and brigadier and major general in the regular army.

After the war, Ames became a controversial **Reconstruction** politician in the **Republican Party**. He was appointed provisional governor of **Mississippi** in 1868 and was elected to the U.S. Senate from Mississippi in 1870. That same year, Ames resigned from the army and married the daughter of former Union general **Benjamin Butler**. Elected governor in 1873, he resigned in 1876 rather than be impeached by the legislature. Ames then left Mississippi and lived in **Massachusetts** and **Florida**. He reentered the army as a brigadier general of volunteers in 1890 and served in Cuba during the Spanish-American War. Ames was one of the last surviving Civil War generals when he died in 1933 at the age of 97.

AMMEN, JACOB (1806–1894) USA. A native of **Virginia**, Ammen (AM-men) grew up in **Ohio** and graduated from **West Point** in 1831. After serving as a professor at the academy, he resigned from the **U.S. Army** in 1837 and became a mathematics professor and engineer.

When the Civil War began, Ammen became captain in the 12th Ohio in April 1861, was promoted to lieutenant colonel two weeks later, and in May was appointed colonel of the 24th Ohio. After leading his **regiment** in the **Battle of Cheat Mountain**, he was given command of a **brigade** in the **Army of the Ohio** in late 1861 and led it at **Shiloh** and **Corinth**. Ammen was promoted to brigadier general of volunteers in July 1862 and largely served as a **division** commander and administrator in rear areas until he resigned in January 1865.

After the war, Ammen resumed engineering, served on West Point's Board of Visitors, and helped investigate the best site for the Panama Canal.

AMNESTY PROCLAMATIONS. As the Civil War dragged on, both sides resorted to amnesty as a means to strengthen their cause. For the Union, **Abraham Lincoln** used amnesty both to encourage deserters to return to their military units and to encourage Southerners to abandon the rebellion. When **desertion** became a serious problem in early 1863, Lincoln issued an amnesty proclamation on March 10 that allowed all deserters and soldiers absent without leave to return to their units by April 1 without fear of punishment. Those returning after the deadline, however, faced possible court-martial. This proclamation brought back as many as 15,000 absent soldiers. Lincoln issued a second amnesty proclamation on March 11, 1865, to soldiers who returned to duty within 60 days.

Lincoln believed that many Southerners—particularly in the **border states** and in areas under Union control—had little loyalty to the Confederacy and thought an amnesty offer would encourage these reluctant **rebels** to abandon the fight. Since the **Confiscation Act** of 1862 authorized him to pardon secessionists, Lincoln issued an amnesty proclamation on December 8, 1863, offering a pardon to all who took an **oath of allegiance** (except certain political figures and those accused of mistreating Union **prisoners**). A second amnesty offer to Southern civilians was made on May 26, 1864.

After **Lincoln's assassination**, President **Andrew Johnson** issued a third amnesty proclamation on May 29, 1865, offering pardons to all Confederates under the rank of colonel (or navy lieutenant) or who had less than $20,000 in property. Those who were excluded by these conditions could individually request pardons from the president. The **Radical Republicans** became very angry with Johnson when thousands of former Confederates took advantage of his offer and quickly regained political control of their respective states. This helped lead to Johnson's impeachment, but he was undeterred and issued a final blanket pardon to all but the highest ranking former Confederates on December 25, 1868.

The Confederates also used amnesty proclamations to encourage absent soldiers back to the **army**. Sometimes these were issued by President **Jefferson Davis** and sometimes by individual generals (with government approval). On May 9, 1862, the War Department issued the first such measure when it ordered all absent soldiers back to their units. This order did not specifically offer amnesty to those who returned, but amnesty was implied. After desertions continued to mount, Davis issued a second proclamation on August 1, 1863, and this time he specifically offered amnesty to those (except multiple offenders) who returned within 20 days. Army and **department** commanders also offered similar proclamations, but generally such offers had little success.

Early in the war, the Confederates were reluctant to punish deserters harshly for fear of hurting morale. Having little fear of punishment, therefore, most absentees simply ignored the amnesty offers. Authorities resorted to punishment more as the war progressed, but generally the proclamations still had little success. The last general amnesty proclamation by the Confederates was issued by General-in-Chief **Robert E. Lee** in February 1865. Lee offered amnesty to all but multiple offenders and those who joined the enemy if they would return to their units, but the appeal was made too late and had no effect on the war's outcome.

ANACONDA PLAN. In the spring of 1861, Union General-in-Chief **Winfield Scott** drew up a grand **strategy** for winning the war, which became nicknamed the "Anaconda Plan." Scott devised a three-part strategy: **blockading** the Southern ports to deny the Confederacy supplies; seizing control of the Mississippi River to split the Confederacy in two; and, with the South then isolated, Scott recommended waiting to let the pro-Union Southerners rise up and force the Confederacy to come to terms. The plan called for ending the rebellion by constricting and isolating the Confederacy and reminded the public of the anaconda snake. The nickname was ridiculed, because it referred to a slow death for the rebellion, not the quick battlefield defeat that the public expected.

ANDERSON, GEORGE BURGWYN (1831–1862) CSA. A native of **North Carolina**, Anderson graduated first in his class at the University of North Carolina in 1847. He then entered **West Point**, graduated in 1852, and served in the antebellum **U.S. Army** as a lieutenant in the 2nd Dragoons.

In April 1861, Anderson resigned his commission and was made colonel of the 4th North Carolina. He served as post commander at Manassas Junction, Virginia, before being appointed a **brigade** commander and seeing his first combat at **Seven Pines** in May 1862. Although he lost 900 men in the battle, Anderson's actions won him promotion to brigadier general in June. Numerous biographical sketches incorrectly claim that he received this promotion when President **Jefferson Davis** witnessed a charge he made at the **Battle of Williamsburg**, but in fact, Anderson did not fight at Williamsburg.

Serving with the **Army of Northern Virginia**, Anderson led his North Carolina brigade at **Gaines' Mill** and **Malvern Hill**, where he was wounded in the hand and lost another 900 men. During the **Antietam Campaign**, he fought at **South Mountain** and was highly praised for holding his ground tenaciously at Antietam's Bloody Lane. In the latter fight, Anderson received an ankle wound that became infected. Surgeons were forced to amputate his leg, and Anderson died from complications on October 16, 1862. His wife gave birth to a daughter the next day.

ANDERSON, GEORGE THOMAS (1824–1901) CSA. A prosperous native of **Georgia**, Anderson left Emory College in 1847 to fight in the **Mexican War** as a lieutenant of volunteers. He again left civilian life in 1855 to accept an appointment as captain of the 1st U.S. Cavalry, but he resigned this commission in 1858 and returned to Georgia.

When the Civil War began, Anderson raised a **company** for the 11th Georgia and was elected regimental colonel in July 1861. Although his **regiment** knew him as "Tom," Anderson's best-known nickname was "Tige," an abbreviated version of "Tiger." The 11th Georgia became part of Brig. Gen. **Francis Bartow's** brigade, but was delayed by a **railroad** accident in reaching the **First Battle of Manassas** and thus did not participate in the fight that claimed Bartow's life. In the months that followed, Anderson often acted as **brigade** commander, a position that he filled permanently after March 1862.

Anderson fought in the **Peninsula**, **Seven Days**, **Second Manassas** (where he was severely wounded), and **Antietam Campaigns**. Well respected and liked by his men, he was recommended for promotion to brigadier general by his own officers. **Robert E. Lee** concurred, and in November 1862 Anderson received his promotion and official command of the brigade in the **Army of Northern Virginia**. Severely wounded in the thigh at **Gettysburg**, he returned to duty in time to fight with **James Longstreet** in the **Knoxville Campaign**. Anderson also fought in most of the 1864 **Overland Campaign** but was criticized during the **Petersburg Campaign** for attacking too early at **Fort Harrison**. He surrendered with his brigade at **Appomattox** at war's end.

After the war, Anderson served as the police chief of Atlanta, Georgia, before moving to **Alabama** in the 1880s to become Anniston's chief of police.

ANDERSON, JAMES PATTON (1822–1872) CSA. A native of **Tennessee**, Anderson attended **Pennsylvania's** Jefferson College before settling in **Mississippi** and becoming a physician. He also served as DeSoto County sheriff in the 1840s and became a lawyer in 1847. During the **Mexican War**, Anderson raised the 1st Battalion Mississippi Rifles and served as its lieutenant colonel. After the war, he entered politics and served one term in the Mississippi legislature. In 1853, Anderson was appointed U.S. marshal for the Washington Territory and became its first delegate to the **U.S. Congress** in 1855.

In 1861, Anderson was a **Florida** planter who served as a member of the state **secession** convention and in the Provisional **Confederate Congress**. He soon left the Congress and was elected colonel of the 1st Florida Infantry. After participating in **Braxton Bragg's** October attack on **Santa Rosa Island** and serving as a **brigade** commander, Anderson was promoted to brigadier general in February 1862.

Anderson's performance at **Shiloh** and Farmington earned him a **division** command. After the **Battle of Perryville**, the division was disbanded, and Anderson resumed commanding a brigade in the **Army of Tennessee**. He fought well at **Stones River**, where he captured three enemy batteries, and served as Bragg's rear guard when the **army** retreated. At **Chickamauga**, Anderson assumed command of the division when Maj. Gen. **Thomas Hindman** was wounded and led it through the **Chattanooga Campaign**. Promoted to major general in February 1864, he was put in command of the District of Florida but then rejoined the Army of Tennessee for the **Atlanta Campaign** in the spring of 1864. Anderson led his old division at **Ezra Church**, **Utoy Creek**, and **Jonesboro**, and was severely wounded in the chest in the last battle. Against his doctor's advice, he rejoined the army for the **Carolinas Campaign** and briefly led a division before surrendering with **Joseph E. Johnston** in April 1865.

After the war, Anderson's wound affected his productivity, but he managed to sell insurance in Tennessee, publish an agricultural newspaper, and serve as Shelby County's tax collector.

ANDERSON, JOSEPH REID (1813–1892) CSA. Graduating near the top of his 1836 **West Point** class, this **Virginia** native resigned from the **U.S. Army** after only 15 months' service. After serving as an engineer in the construction of the Shenandoah Valley Turnpike, Anderson bought the **Tredegar Iron Works** in 1848 and became a wealthy iron maker. Shortly before the Civil War began, he formed and commanded a militia **company** that became known as the Governor's Mounted Guard.

When war broke out, Anderson's ironworkers formed the 8th Virginia Infantry Battalion and elected him their major. After actively pursuing a higher commission, he was promoted to brigadier general in September 1861 and was given command of the District of Cape Fear. Anderson also briefly assumed command of the **Department of North Carolina** before he was given an infantry **brigade** and ordered to Fredericksburg,

Virginia. There he assembled a **division** and confronted Union Maj. Gen. **Irvin McDowell** until he was called to serve in the **Peninsula Campaign**. Back in command of a brigade in **A. P. Hill's Light Division**, Anderson fought through the **Seven Days Campaign** with the **Army of Northern Virginia** and was wounded in the head at **Frayser's Farm**.

Anderson resigned his commission in July 1862 and managed his ironworks for the rest of the war. He made his best contribution to the war effort by supplying the Confederacy with much of its weaponry and ordnance.

ANDERSON, RICHARD HERON (1821–1879) CSA. A native of **South Carolina**, Anderson graduated from **West Point** in 1842. Rising to the rank of captain, he fought **Indians** and then served in the **Mexican War** (where he won a **brevet**), the **Utah Expedition**, and in **Bleeding Kansas**.

Anderson resigned his commission in February 1861 and was appointed major of Confederate cavalry in March. At **Fort Sumter**, he was colonel of the 1st South Carolina Infantry and took command of Confederate troops in **South Carolina** when **P. G. T. Beauregard** left in May. Promoted to brigadier general in July, Anderson commanded a **brigade** at **Pensacola, Florida**, and was wounded in the arm when he led the assault against **Santa Rosa Island** in October. His superior, **Braxton Bragg**, accused him of being drunk in a later engagement, but Anderson transferred to the **Army of Northern Virginia** before any action was taken against him.

Assuming command of **David R. Jones's** old brigade, Anderson fought very well throughout the **Peninsula** and **Seven Days Campaigns**. Promoted to major general in July 1862, he led a **division** in **James Longstreet's** corps and performed admirably at **Second Manassas**. Anderson was wounded in the thigh at **Antietam** but saw little combat at **Fredericksburg**. At **Chancellorsville** in May 1863, his effective service brought praise from **Robert E. Lee**. After Chancellorsville, Anderson's division was transferred to **A. P. Hill's** corps and fought with it at **Gettysburg**.

In May 1864, after Longstreet was wounded in the **Wilderness**, Anderson assumed command of the I Corps and was given the temporary rank of lieutenant general the following month. His finest moment came on May 8, when he reached **Spotsylvania** first and held it against advancing Union troops. Anderson led the I Corps at the **North Anna River** and at **Cold Harbor**, but Longstreet resumed command in October 1864. Anderson then took command of Beauregard's forces around

Petersburg, Virginia, where he served most of the remaining months of war. After his **corps** was virtually annihilated at **Sailor's Creek** in April 1865, Anderson was relieved of duty.

Although competent, Anderson proved to be a less able corps commander than he was a brigade and division leader. After the war, he lived in near poverty until his death in South Carolina in 1879.

ANDERSON, ROBERT (1805–1871) USA. A native of **Kentucky**, Anderson was married to a Southerner, did not oppose **slavery**, and disapproved of using force against secessionists. Yet he became the North's first great hero in the Civil War. Graduating from **West Point** in 1825, Anderson became a career officer, serving in the Black Hawk, **Seminole**, and **Mexican Wars**. He was awarded **brevets** for the latter two conflicts and was severely wounded in Mexico. Known as something of an intellectual, Anderson translated into English several French **artillery** texts and was promoted to major in 1857. In November 1860, he took command of Union troops in **Charleston, South Carolina**.

After tense weeks confronting Confederate Brig. Gen. **P. G. T. Beauregard**, Anderson found himself surrounded in **Fort Sumter**. The Confederates began the Civil War by bombarding the fort on April 12, 1861, after Anderson refused Beauregard's surrender demand. After enduring a 33-hour bombardment, Anderson surrendered on April 14 and then was released and allowed to return north. Hailed as a hero, he was promoted to brigadier general in May and took command of the **Department of Kentucky**. In August, Anderson was put in charge of the **Department of the Cumberland**, a post he kept until poor health forced his retirement in 1863. At war's end, he was able to return to Fort Sumter to raise the Union **flag** back over the fort four years to the day after he surrendered it.

Anderson moved to France after the war. When he died there in 1871, his body was returned for burial at West Point.

ANDERSON, ROBERT HOUSTOUN (1835–1888) CSA. A native of **Georgia**, Anderson graduated near the bottom of his 1857 **West Point** class. He resigned his commission when Georgia seceded and became a lieutenant of Confederate **artillery** in March 1861. Anderson was promoted to major in September and briefly served on Brig. Gen. **William H. T. Walker's** staff. After Walker resigned in October, Anderson organized the 1st Battalion of Georgia Sharpshooters and commanded it until June 1862, when he transferred to the 5th Georgia Cavalry. In January 1863, he was promoted to regimental colonel and command of Confederate forces on the Ogeechee River, Georgia.

Anderson's defense of **Fort McAllister** in February 1863 won him praise, and in September he was put in command of Sullivan's Island, near **Charleston, South Carolina**. He was transferred to **Florida** in March 1864 but had returned to **South Carolina** by May. Throughout his service on the coast, Anderson politicked to get his **regiment** moved to a more active theater. He finally succeeded, and he and his men joined **Joseph Wheeler's** cavalry, where Anderson took command of a **brigade**.

Anderson was wounded while serving under Wheeler but also earned a promotion to brigadier general in July 1864. He continued to serve with Wheeler and fought **William T. Sherman's** armies in the **March to the Sea** and the **Carolinas Campaign**. During this service, Anderson was wounded again. Although recommended for promotion to major general, he remained a brigade commander for the rest of the war.

After the war, Anderson served as chief of police for Savannah, Georgia, and twice served on West Point's Board of Visitors.

ANDERSON, SAMUEL READ (1804–1883) CSA. A native of **Virginia**, Anderson settled in **Tennessee** and became a prominent citizen around Nashville. He fought in the **Mexican War** as lieutenant colonel of the 1st Tennessee Infantry and was serving as Nashville's postmaster when the Civil War began.

Anderson first was appointed major general of Tennessee volunteers when the state seceded and then to brigadier general of Confederate troops in July 1861. Commanding a **brigade** of Tennessee infantry, he participated in the **Battle of Cheat Mountain** and in **Stonewall Jackson's** expedition to Romney, Virginia. After brief service in the **Peninsula Campaign**, Anderson resigned his commission in the spring of 1862 because of poor health. He returned to service as a brigadier general in November 1864 and served for the remainder of the war as head of the Bureau of Conscription for Tennessee.

ANDERSON, WILLIAM "BLOODY BILL" (1840–1864) CSA. One of the most infamous Civil War guerrillas. He organized a guerrilla unit for the Confederacy after his sister was killed when a Kansas City, Missouri, **prison** collapsed onto Southern sympathizers housed there. Anderson first served with **William Quantrill** and participated in the 1863 **raid on Lawrence, Kansas**, earned a reputation for murder and brutality, and counted future outlaw Jesse James among his men.

Anderson left Quantrill's service in 1864 when Quantrill had one of his men shot for killing a civilian. Anderson's men then independently raided

Missouri before participating in **Sterling Price's 1864 Missouri Raid**. During his career, Anderson committed one of the war's worst atrocities in the **Centralia, Missouri, Massacre**. After looting the town, the guerrillas stopped a train and murdered 24 unarmed Union soldiers. When a column of Union infantry pursued the raiders, Anderson ambushed it and then attacked Union Soldiers in the town of Centralia, killing 116 men.

On October 24, 1864, Anderson was killed in a clash near Richmond, Missouri. His head was hacked off by the Federals and was mounted as a trophy on a nearby **telegraph** pole.

ANDERSONVILLE PRISON. Officially designated Camp Sumter, Georgia, Andersonville became the most notorious of the Civil War **prisons**. In 1863, so many Union **prisoners** were being held in **Richmond, Virginia**, that Confederate authorities found it difficult to care for them. In addition, there were fears of a Union attempt to free those prisoners (as occurred later in the 1864 **Kilpatrick-Dahlgren Raid**). Thus, Confederate officials decided to build a new prison camp in southwest **Georgia's** Sumter County near Andersonville.

The camp originally covered about 16 acres but was later enlarged to 26. The first Union prisoners arrived in February 1864, but their numbers swelled to nearly 33,000 by summer. Polluted drinking water, poor **rations**, and unsanitary, overcrowded living conditions led to nightmarish conditions and a high death rate. By war's end, at least 13,000 prisoners had died there. Although Northerners accused the Confederates of intentionally mistreating the prisoners, evidence indicates that this was not so. The Confederacy was simply unable to provide adequately for such large numbers of prisoners. Sadly, many of the prisoners who were released at war's end were killed in the *Sultana* **sinking**.

After the war, camp commandant **Heinrich (Henry) Wirz** was convicted of mistreating prisoners and was hanged. He supposedly was the only Civil War soldier to be executed for his wartime activities.

ANDREWS, CHRISTOPHER COLUMBUS (1829–1922) USA. A native of **New Hampshire**, Andrews became a **Massachusetts** lawyer after briefly attending Harvard Law School. In 1854, he moved to **Kansas** but quickly accepted an appointment in **Washington, D.C.**, as a Treasury Department clerk. Moving to **Minnesota** in 1857, Andrews was elected to the state senate in 1859.

When the Civil War began, Andrews volunteered as a private but in November 1861 was commissioned captain of the 3rd Minnesota. In one of the **regiment's** first actions, he was captured by **Nathan Bedford Forrest** near Murfreesboro, Tennessee, in July 1862 but was soon **ex-**

changed and appointed his regiment's lieutenant colonel in December. After briefly fighting the **Sioux uprising** in Minnesota, Andrews returned south to serve with the **Army of the Tennessee** during the **Vicksburg Campaign**. He was promoted to colonel in August 1863 and led his regiment in the 1863 expedition against **Little Rock, Arkansas**.

Promoted to brigadier general of volunteers in January 1864, Andrews briefly led a **brigade** in **Arkansas** that spring but in June was given command of a **division**. Sent to the **Department of the Gulf** in December 1864, he took command of a brigade for about a month before assuming command of a division in February 1865. Anderson fought well at **Fort Blakely** in the April 1865 **Mobile Campaign** and was **brevetted** major general of volunteers for his conduct there.

After leaving the service in January 1866, Andrews returned to Minnesota, reentered politics, and was appointed U.S. minister to Sweden and Norway in 1869 by President **U. S. Grant**. Returning to his home in St. Cloud in 1877, he served in numerous political posts, including a stint as consul general to Brazil, until his death in 1922.

ANDREWS, GEORGE LEONARD (1828–1899) USA. A native of **Massachusetts**, Andrews graduated first in his 1851 **West Point** class. After serving as an **engineer** and academy professor, he resigned his commission in 1855 to become a civil engineer.

When the Civil War began, Andrews became lieutenant colonel of the 2nd Massachusetts in May 1861 but was promoted to colonel in June 1862. After fighting at **First Winchester**, **Cedar Mountain**, and **Antietam**, he was given command of a **brigade** in the **Army of the Potomac** and was promoted to brigadier general of volunteers in November 1862.

In November 1862, Andrews was transferred to the **Department of the Gulf**, where he briefly commanded the defenses of **New Orleans, Louisiana**, before assuming command of a brigade in the XIX Corps. In March 1863, he was appointed Maj. Gen. **Nathaniel P. Banks's** chief of staff and served in that position through the **Bayou Teche** and **Port Hudson Campaigns**. Afterward, Andrews held several administrative posts in **Louisiana**, including commanding Port Hudson, **Baton Rouge**, and the **Corps d'Afrique**, before assuming command of the **department** in August 1864. He was appointed the department's provost marshal general in February 1865 and served in that position during the **Mobile Campaign** and until war's end, earning a **brevet** to major general of volunteers for his service.

After the war, Andrews became a **Mississippi** planter, a U.S. marshal in Massachusetts, and a West Point professor.

ANDREWS, JOHN ALBION (1818–1867) USA. A native of **Maine**, Andrews attended Bowdoin College before moving to **Massachusetts** in 1837 and becoming a lawyer. An **abolitionist**, he helped organize the **Free-Soil Party** in 1848 but later joined the **Republican Party**. Andrews was elected to the Massachusetts legislature in 1857 but decided to become a Republican Party leader rather than run for reelection. It was believed by many that he was a financial backer of **John Brown's Raid** on **Harpers Ferry**, **Virginia**, because Andrews raised money for Brown's defense fund and family. The U.S. Senate investigated his role in the raid, but nothing was proved.

After serving as a delegate for **Abraham Lincoln** at the 1860 Republican National Convention, Andrews was elected governor of Massachusetts the same year. He was reelected twice and served until 1866. One of the strongest wartime governors, Andrews was the first governor to send troops in response to Lincoln's call for volunteers in 1861. Being an abolitionist, he also strongly believed in the use of **black troops** and raised the famous **54th Massachusetts**. Despite his belief in vigorously prosecuting the war against the Confederacy, however, Andrews supported President **Andrew Johnson's** lenient **Reconstruction** policy. After leaving office in 1866, he resumed his law practice.

ANDREWS' RAID (APRIL 7–13, 1862). James J. Andrews, a mysterious Kentuckian, had served as a Union spy during the **Forts Henry and Donelson Campaign** and had unsuccessfully tried to sabotage a Confederate **railroad** prior to the **Battle of Shiloh**. On April 7, 1862, he was dispatched by Brig. Gen. **Ormsby M. Mitchel** with a band of 21 disguised soldiers from Shelbyville, Tennessee, to destroy railroad bridges in northern **Georgia**.

After making their way to Marietta, Georgia, the saboteurs boarded a train for Big Shanty on the night of April 12. When the passengers and crew debarked for breakfast, Andrews and his men stole the locomotive "The General" and several cars. Their plan was to take them to Chattanooga, Tennessee, and destroy the railroad along the way.

Unfortunately for the raiders, the train's conductor and a shop foreman immediately began pursuing them. First on foot, then by handcar, the tenacious Southerners finally found the locomotive "Texas" and used it in what became known as The Great Locomotive Chase. For 90 miles the chase continued, with the raiders unable to damage the railroad because rain had soaked the bridges. When only 18 miles outside of Chattanooga, "The General" ran out of fuel. Andrews's raiders fled into the woods but were soon captured.

Andrews and seven of his men were convicted of spying and were hanged in Atlanta, Georgia, in June; the others were imprisoned, but eight escaped in October 1862. The remaining six raiders were **paroled** the next year and released. Some of the men became the first soldiers to be awarded the **Medal of Honor**, but the raid itself was a failure, since no bridges were ever burned during the chase.

"ANGEL OF MARYE'S HEIGHTS." *See* KIRKLAND, RICHARD ROWLAND.

ANTIETAM, MARYLAND, CAMPAIGN AND BATTLE OF (SEPTEMBER 4–20, 1862). In September 1862, **Robert E. Lee** launched his first northern invasion. Following the **Second Manassas Campaign**, Lee held the initiative in **Virginia** and decided to invade **Maryland** for a variety of reasons: to take the war out of Virginia during the crucial harvest season; to liberate Maryland and allow it and new recruits to join the Confederacy; to alarm the North and strengthen the northern peace movement; and to win European recognition and aid by defeating the Union **Army of the Potomac** on its own soil.

After crossing the Potomac River near Leesburg, Virginia, on September 4, Lee concentrated his **Army of Northern Virginia** at Frederick, Maryland, on September 7. Two days later, in Special Order No. 191, he outlined a campaign **strategy** that eventually called for an invasion of **Pennsylvania**. Lee's first priority was to protect his line of communication that ran through the **Shenandoah Valley**. To do so, he had to eliminate the threat presented by the 12,000 Union soldiers stationed at **Harpers Ferry, Virginia**.

Lee divided his **army** into two wings. **Stonewall Jackson**, with his four **divisions** and those of **Lafayette McLaws** and **John G. Walker**, was to attack the Union garrison at Harpers Ferry. **James Longstreet's** three divisions would accompany Lee to Hagerstown, Maryland, with Jackson rejoining them once Harpers Ferry was captured. The audacious plan depended on the Federals being slow to pursue in order to give the Confederates time to concentrate before battle was given.

Meanwhile, on September 2, Maj. Gen. **George B. McClellan** had been restored to field command of the Army of the Potomac at **Washington, D.C.** Always slow, he did not begin pursuing Lee until September 7, the same day the Confederates reached Frederick. The pursuit was cautious, with McClellan being careful to remain in a position to protect both Washington and Baltimore, Maryland, from attack.

On September 12, McClellan entered Frederick, Maryland, where the next day two Union soldiers discovered Lee's Special Order No. 191 wrapped around three cigars. It is unclear which Confederate officer was responsible for dropping the **Lost Order**, but the intelligence coup was taken to McClellan. Now knowing Lee's disposition and plans, McClellan was in an excellent position to march swiftly and defeat the scattered Confederate army in detail. McClellan, however, believed Lee greatly outnumbered him and waited 16 hours before beginning his pursuit. Whether Lee, now at Hagerstown, was aware of McClellan's find is not certain, but when he realized that the Union army was moving more rapidly, he ordered the army to concentrate near Sharpsburg. **Daniel H. Hill's** division was ordered to hold the **South Mountain** passes at Fox's and Turner's Gaps and delay McClellan's advance. Longstreet was to concentrate at Sharpsburg, while Jackson was to hurry along his Harpers Ferry operation and rejoin Lee at Sharpsburg.

On September 14, McClellan moved against South Mountain in two wings. Major General **William B. Franklin's** VI Corps was ordered to push through **Crampton's Gap** and relieve the Harpers Ferry garrison, while the rest of the army seized South Mountain's Fox's and Turner's Gaps. In vicious fighting at South Mountain, Hill's division, with late-arriving reinforcements from Longstreet, delayed the advance of Maj. Gen. **Ambrose Burnside's** Union I and IX Corps until dark. Unable to hold out any longer, Hill's men then withdrew from the passes that night and marched for Sharpsburg. At Crampton's Gap, Franklin pushed out McLaws's defenders and was in a position to relieve Harpers Ferry but failed to press on because he believed the Confederates outnumbered him.

With the Union army advancing against him, Lee was preparing to retreat to Virginia when he learned that Jackson would force Harpers Ferry's surrender on September 15. Lee decided to concentrate near Sharpsburg instead of retreating and ordered Jackson to march there as soon as possible. When Harpers Ferry surrendered on the 15th, Jackson hurriedly marched to Sharpsburg after leaving Maj. Gen. **A. P. Hill's** division to **parole** the approximately 12,000 Union **prisoners**.

On the morning of September 16, Lee had only about 15,000 men facing McClellan's 60,000, but McClellan made no attempt to attack. With Jackson's arrival later that day, Lee had 40,000 men on hand and decided to make a stand along the west bank of Antietam Creek, just outside Sharpsburg. To offer battle against the entire Union army with the Potomac River in his rear was tactically unwise, but Lee had entered Maryland as a liberator and could hardly withdraw without a fight. McClellan soon had 75,000 men at hand but spent September 16 reconnoitering rather than attacking the thinly held Confederate line.

McClellan finally developed a battle plan calling for attacks against both of Lee's flanks and his center. At daylight on September 17, **Joseph Hooker's** I Corps opened the battle by attacking Jackson's troops on Lee's left. After an **artillery** bombardment, Hooker advanced through the Miller cornfield and managed to drive out Jackson's men after fierce fighting. Hooker then advanced along the Hagerstown Pike toward the Dunkard Church, but a devastating counterattack by Maj. Gen. **John Bell Hood's** division sent Hooker retreating back through the corn.

With Hooker's attack stalled and Hooker himself wounded, Maj. Gen. **Joseph Mansfield's** XII Corps advanced next from the northeast. Fierce fighting again broke out in the East Woods, cornfield, and West Woods, and Mansfield was mortally wounded. This action was soon followed by an attack from Maj. Gen. **Edwin Sumner's** II Corps. Jackson had received two more divisions from Lee, and when Sumner's lead division entered the West Woods it found itself nearly surrounded by Confederates. Walking into an ambush, the division suffered 2,200 casualties in 20 minutes, and Sumner was forced to withdraw.

All through the morning, attacks and counterattacks swirled around the cornfield, Dunkard Church, and the East and West Woods. Lee was able to take advantage of the **interior line** and shift his forces to meet the Union assaults because McClellan and his officers never coordinated their attacks. By mid-morning the fighting had ended on Lee's left with little change in the armies' positions.

A second phase of the battle began when Sumner's II Corps attacked Lee's center. There, fighting focused on a sunken farm road where Daniel H. Hill's Confederate division was positioned. For three hours, Hill held out against repeated enemy assaults from the Union divisions of Brig. Gens. **William H. French** and **Israel B. Richardson**. Then during one attack, a Confederate **regiment** mistakenly withdrew and created a gap in the line, through which the Union soldiers poured. Hill's line was **enfiladed**, and so many Confederates were shot down that the road became known as Bloody Lane. Lee's center had been pierced and an appeal went to McClellan for fresh reserves to exploit the breakthrough. McClellan refused to commit his reserves, and Hill was able to establish a new defensive position.

When fighting sputtered out in the center, the battle entered its third phase on Lee's right flank. There, Burnside's IX Corps was to cross Antietam Creek by the Rohrback Bridge and assault the enemy flank. Lee had stripped his right during the day to reinforce the left and center, and now barely 500 Confederates under **Robert Toombs** held the Confederate right. Despite repeated orders from McClellan to cross the creek, Burnside showed no imagination and became focused on taking the bridge rather than fording the narrow stream. Thus, for much of the day his entire **corps** was blocked by a handful of Confederates. In mid-afternoon, however, Burnside finally crossed the bridge, now known as Burnside's Bridge, and pushed the Confederates back.

By mid-afternoon the battle was at a critical stage, with Union troops pouring into Lee's right rear. But then A. P. Hill's division suddenly arrived after a forced march from Harpers Ferry and stopped the Union advance. The battle came to an end, with the opposing forces in much the same positions as they were at the beginning.

The Battle of Antietam proved to be the bloodiest single day of the Civil War and in American history, with Lee losing approximately 10,300 men to McClellan's 12,400. It was a battle in which Lee showed remarkable tactical skill by shifting troops from one threatened point to another. However, it also demonstrated his weakness for accepting battle at any odds. Lee risked his army for what, in the best case, could only have been a stalemate. McClellan's battle plan was sound, and his men fought bravely, but he showed no skill in carrying out the plan. Each of his attacks was launched piecemeal, and a large part of his army was never even engaged.

Although tactically a stalemate, Antietam proved to be a strategic Union victory because it stopped Lee's invasion and kept Maryland firmly in the Union. It also changed the war itself. Prior to the battle, the Northern war goal was simply to preserve the Union. **Abraham Lincoln**, however, who had been waiting for a victory before issuing the Preliminary **Emancipation Proclamation**, announced the new policy on September 22. The war then became a struggle to destroy **slavery**, as well as to preserve the Union.

Lee remained on the field throughout September 18 searching for a counterattack opportunity, but found none, and McClellan declined to initiate a battle. Accepting the inevitable, Lee recrossed the Potomac River into Virginia that night and the next day. McClellan launched a slow pursuit, and on September 20 Union cavalry and infantry engaged the Confederate rear guard at **Shepherdstown, Virginia**. A Union assault carried the Confederate position and threatened to capture a large number of artillery pieces. A swift counterattack by A. P. Hill's division, however, drove the Federals back across the river, thus ending the Antietam Campaign.

APACHE CANYON, NEW MEXICO TERRITORY, BATTLE OF (MARCH 26, 1862). *See* GLORIETA PASS, NEW MEXICO TERRITORY, BATTLE OF.

APPOMATTOX STATION AND APPOMATTOX COURT HOUSE, VIRGINIA, BATTLE OF (APRIL 8, 1865). On the afternoon of April 8, 1865, during the **Appomattox Campaign**, Union troops under **Philip Sheridan** managed to get ahead of **Robert E. Lee's** retreating **Army of Northern Virginia** and block its path around Appomattox Station and Appomattox Court House. Union cavalryman **George A. Custer** attacked and captured three enemy supply trains at the station and then rode on to the courthouse, where at 9:00 P.M. he attacked a large collection of Confederate **artillery** and wagons assembled under Brig. Gen. **R. Lindsay Walker.** Custer completely overwhelmed Walker's defenders and captured more than 25 cannons and most of the wagons. This action also succeeded in blocking Lee's escape route, leading to his surrender the following day. In the fight at Appomattox Station and Court House, Custer lost 48 men, while Confederate casualties are estimated at 1,000 (mostly taken **prisoners**).

APPOMATTOX, VIRGINIA, CAMPAIGN (APRIL 1–9, 1865). In late March 1865, **Robert E. Lee's Army of Northern Virginia** was exhausted after 10 months of trench warfare during the **Petersburg Campaign**. Lee planned to break through **U. S. Grant's** besieging force and move to **North Carolina** to link up with **Joseph E. Johnston's** Confederate **army**, which was being pushed northward by **William T. Sherman** in the **Carolinas Campaign**. On March 25, Lee's Army of Northern Virginia made its escape attempt by unsuccessfully attacking the Union lines at **Fort Stedman** outside Petersburg, Virginia.

On April 1, Grant counterattacked by sending **Philip Sheridan's** cavalry against Lee's right flank at **Five Forks**. Sheridan crushed the Confederates under **George Pickett**, and Grant then launched a general assault against the Petersburg lines on April 2, forcing Lee to abandon Petersburg and **Richmond** and begin a harrowing retreat westward. Lee planned first to march his 50,000 men to Amelia Court House to meet supplies that had been ordered sent there and then use the Richmond & Danville Railroad to move southward to join Johnston. Speed was essential since the 113,000-man Union **Army of the Potomac** was in rapid pursuit.

Lee reached Amelia Court House on April 4, but the supply trains were not there. He spent an entire day gathering supplies from the countryside, giving Sheridan's Union cavalry time to cut the **railroad** to the south at Jetersville. Unable to use the railroad as planned, Lee then marched westward on April 5 in hopes of reaching an alternate supply line at Lynchburg. Fighting erupted at **Amelia Springs** that day as Grant's army closed in. On April 6, Lee reached Farmville, but more clashes occurred at **Rice's Station** and **High Bridge** and almost the entire Confederate rear guard under Lt. Gen. **Richard S. Ewell** was cut off and captured at **Sailor's Creek**.

Although he had lost a quarter of his army, Lee resumed the march westward on April 7. Fighting continued that day at High Bridge and **Cumberland Church**, and Lee rejected a surrender request from Grant (although he did ask about Grant's terms). A large Union cavalry and infantry force under Sheridan sprinted ahead and managed to block the Confederate advance at Appomattox Court House. On April 8, fighting broke out at **Appomattox Station and Appomattox Court House**, with Union cavalry destroying one of Lee's wagon trains just as he arrived. The following day, Lee attacked Sheridan in an attempt to cut his way through the encirclement but quickly realized a breakout was impossible. Now blocked front and rear, Lee had no choice but to meet with Grant at the **Wilmer McLean** house that afternoon and sign a **surrender** document.

Conditions of the surrender were generous. After signing **parole** oaths promising not to take up arms again and to obey lawful authority, the Confederates were released. Officers were allowed to keep their side arms, and those men owning their own horses and mules were allowed to keep them. On April 12, the estimated 26,000 survivors of the Army of Northern Virginia were formally surrendered. During the campaign, another 25,000 Confederates had become casualties, and Grant lost an estimated 10,800 men.

ARCHER, JAMES JAY (1817–1864) CSA. A native of **Maryland**, Archer practiced law after graduating from the College of New Jersey (Princeton) in 1835. He served as a captain in the **Mexican War** and earned a **brevet** for gallantry at Chapultepec. In 1855, Archer rejoined the **U.S. Army** and was serving as a captain on the frontier when the Civil War began.

Archer resigned his commission and was appointed colonel of the 5th Texas in October 1861. After fighting at **Seven Pines**, he was appointed brigadier general in June 1862 and was given a **brigade** in **A. P. Hill's** famous **Light Division** of the **Army of Northern Virginia**. Archer earned high praise as his Tennessee brigade was heavily engaged during the **Seven Days** and **Second Manassas Campaigns**. At **Antietam**, he led his brigade in a charge that helped stop the advance of **Ambrose Burnside's corps**, even though Archer was so sick he had arrived on the battlefield in an ambulance. When **Robert E. Lee** retreated across the Potomac River after Antietam, Archer played a key role in throwing back a Union assault at **Shepherdstown**. At **Fredericksburg**, Archer again won great praise for holding his position after the Federals pierced **Stonewall Jackson's** line. His greatest moment came when his brigade charged and captured an enemy artillery battery at **Chancellorsville**, thus securing the high ground around Hazel Grove.

At **Gettysburg**, Archer's command was in **Henry Heth's division** and was badly shot up on the first day, and Archer was captured. This gave him the distinction of being the first general grade officer captured after Lee assumed command of the **army**. After being shuttled through several Northern **prisons**, Archer was **exchanged** a year later, but his health was ruined, and he died in **Richmond, Virginia**, on October 24, 1864.

ARKANSAS. Admitted to the Union in 1836 as a slave state, Arkansas was slow to secede. State officials seized the **Little Rock** federal arsenal in February 1861, but a March convention preferred a compromise solution to the crisis and rejected **secession**. After the fall of **Fort Sumter**, a second convention was held. Governor **Henry M. Rector** refused **Abraham Lincoln's** call for volunteers, and Arkansas became the eighth Southern state to leave the Union when the convention voted to secede on May 6.

Arkansas supplied Confederate troops to both the eastern and western theaters of war. Although no huge battles were fought in the state, there were such notable engagements as **Pea Ridge**, **Arkansas Post**, **Prairie Grove**, **Poison Spring**, and **Jenkins' Ferry**. Union advances forced the Confederate state government to flee Little Rock in 1863 and move to Washington.

Slavery was not strong in much of the mountainous parts of the state, and large numbers of Arkansans opposed the Confederacy. In early 1864, representatives from 23 counties formed a loyal government in Little Rock that represented much of the state lying north of the Arkansas River. These loyalists formed 17 military units that served in the Union **army**, as opposed to 70 units furnished the Confederacy by the secessionists. It is estimated that nearly 7,000 Arkansans died in Confederate service, while approximately 1,700 died for the Union. *See* *also* BATTLES OF BAYOU FOURCHE; CANE HILL; CHALK BLUFF; DITCH BAYOU; HELENA; HILL'S PLANTATION; MARKS' MILLS; PINE BLUFF; PRAIRIE D'ANE; ST. CHARLES.

ARKANSAS, CSS. Construction of the Confederate **ironclad** *Arkansas* was begun at Memphis, Tennessee, in October 1861 but was completed at Yazoo City, Mississippi, in July 1862. A large ship at 165 feet long, it carried 10 guns and a crew of 200.

On July 15, 1862, the *Arkansas* engaged three Union ships on the Yazoo River, disabling one and driving off the other two. It then entered the Mississippi River near **Vicksburg, Mississippi,** and battled its way through the fleets of **David Farragut** and **Charles Davis.** Anchoring at Vicksburg, the *Arkansas* again was engaged by Farragut's ships that night.

In August 1862, the *Arkansas* played a key role in Maj. Gen. **John C. Breckinridge's** attempt to capture **Baton Rouge, Louisiana.** Breckinridge planned to attack the city from the east with his small **army,** while the *Arkansas* sailed downstream and bombarded the enemy from the river. He attacked on August 5, but the *Arkansas*'s engines stalled before arriving at Baton Rouge. After Breckinridge was repulsed, the ship's crew prevented its capture by setting it on fire a few miles upstream from Baton Rouge on August 5 and abandoning ship. The *Arkansas* drifted downstream, exploded, and sank.

ARKANSAS POST, ARKANSAS, BATTLE OF (JANUARY 10–11, 1863). Arkansas Post was the site of Fort Hindman, a large, square bastion built by the Confederates on the Arkansas River, 50 miles upstream from its juncture with the Mississippi River. From this strong point, the Confederates could threaten any Union movement down the Mississippi, but it was seen as secondary in importance by the Union to the taking of **Vicksburg, Mississippi.**

Major General **John McClernand** took the initiative to attack the fort. He had been given authority to raise an **army** to attack Vicksburg, but **U. S. Grant** had allowed Maj. Gen. **William T. Sherman** to assume command of McClernand's men to use in the unsuccessful attack against **Chickasaw Bayou** in December 1862. In January 1863, McClernand took command from Sherman and made plans with **David Porter** to launch a combined land and water attack against Arkansas Post.

McClernand's 32,000 men were ferried up the Arkansas River by transports, escorted by Porter's warships. On January 9, 1863, McClernand's **Army of the Mississippi** was unloaded near Fort Hindman and got into position to attack. Porter began shelling the fort's defenses on the afternoon of January 10 to support an expected advance, but Mc-Clernand's troops were not yet in position. About noon on January 11, Porter again shelled the fort, which was manned by approximately 5,000 Confederates under Brig. Gen. **Thomas J. Churchill**. Porter knocked out the fort's **artillery**, but McClernand's men were repulsed when they attacked the outer defenses. A renewed naval bombardment in the afternoon finally forced the defenders along the river to begin surrendering without orders from Churchill. Churchill had repulsed every enemy attack but surrendered the rest of the garrison when he saw his river defenders raise the white flag.

The Confederates suffered few casualties in the battle but surrendered nearly 5,000 men. McClernand and Porter lost just over 1,000 men.

ARMISTEAD, LEWIS ADDISON (1817–1863) CSA. Armistead (ARM-sted) was a **North Carolina** native who entered **West Point** in 1834. In 1836, he was dismissed for breaking a plate over the head of fellow cadet and future Confederate general **Jubal A. Early**. Nonetheless, Armistead was appointed a lieutenant in the **U.S. Army** in 1839. He served in the **Seminole Wars**, was **brevetted** twice for gallantry during the **Mexican War**, and was wounded at Chapultepec.

Armistead resigned a captain's commission in May 1861 to join the Confederacy. First commissioned colonel of the 57th Virginia in September, he was promoted to brigadier general in April 1862. Armistead's **brigade** of Virginians fought at **Seven Pines**, and its advance was the signal for the general attack against **Malvern Hill** on July 1, 1862. In the thick of the fighting at **Antietam's** West Woods, Armistead was wounded while launching a counterattack.

After Antietam, Armistead joined **George Pickett's** division in the **Army of Northern Virginia** but did not see combat duty again until **Gettysburg**. On July 3, 1863, he formed the left of Pickett's **division** during **Pickett's Charge**, shouting to his men as they prepared to advance, "Men, remember your wives, your mothers, your sisters and your sweethearts! (Davis, ed., *The Confederate General*, vol. 1, 41). As his brigade approached the Union line, Armistead put his hat on his sword and ran for the stone wall. Shouting "Boys, give them the cold steel!" he led his men over the wall and into an enemy battery. As Armistead placed his hand on one cannon, he was cut down by bullets to his arm and leg. Captured when the Confederates retreated, Armistead was treated well by the Federals but died on July 5. His wounds at first were not considered mortal, and it was believed he died from exhaustion.

ARMSTRONG, FRANK CRAWFORD (1835–1909) CSA. The son of a U.S. Army officer and the brother-in-law of Confederate Brig. Gen. **Lucius M. Walker**, Crawford was a native of the **Indian Territory** and a graduate of **Massachusetts**'s Holy Cross Academy and College. In 1855, he was commissioned 2nd lieutenant in the U.S. Army after participating in a **New Mexico Territory** Indian fight with his stepfather, Gen. Persifor Frazer Smith. Afterward, Armstrong served in the **Utah Expedition**.

Armstrong was promoted to captain in June 1861 and commanded part of the Union 2nd Dragoons at the **First Battle of Manassas**. He resigned his commission in August and joined the Confederacy, making him a man who fought on both sides of the Civil War as an officer. Armstrong served as a volunteer aide to Brig. Gen. **Ben McCulloch** at **Wilson's Creek** in August and continued in a volunteer capacity in Indian Territory before accepting a commission as a lieutenant on Col. **James McIntosh's** staff in early 1862. After McIntosh was killed at **Pea Ridge** in March 1862, Armstrong served on Maj. Gen. **Earl Van Dorn's** staff before being appointed colonel of the 3rd Louisiana in May 1862.

In July 1862, Armstrong was made an acting brigadier general and took command of Maj. Gen. **Sterling Price's** cavalry. In this capacity, he excelled in launching raids into **Alabama** and **Tennessee** and in covering the Confederate retreats from **Iuka** and **Corinth, Mississippi**. Given a **brigade** in Van Dorn's cavalry command, Armstrong continued to serve well in numerous engagements.

Armstrong's permanent promotion to brigadier general came in April 1863, and he joined **Nathan Bedford Forrest's** cavalry. After the **Tullahoma Campaign**, he was given a **division** of Forrest's cavalry and fought dismounted at **Chickamauga**. Armstrong commanded another cavalry division during the **Knoxville Campaign**, but reverted to a brigade command in March 1864. He served admirably during both the **Atlanta Campaign** and the **Franklin and Nashville Campaign** and was considered to be one of the best Confederate cavalry commanders.

After the war, Armstrong was active in Indian affairs, serving as a U.S. Indian inspector and assistant commissioner of Indian affairs.

ARMSTRONG GUN. Designed by Englishman William George (later, baron) Armstrong in 1855, the Armstrong gun was a **rifled** cannon, which was cast in various sizes, with bores ranging from 3-inch to 13.3-

inch. Produced in both breech and muzzle loading styles, its shells had brass studs or lead sheathing to grip the barrel's rifling to give the shell spin and greater distance and accuracy. The Confederates imported a few of the guns, but they were never as popular as other models. *See also* ARTILLERY.

ARMSTRONG'S MILL, VIRGINIA, BATTLE OF (FEBRUARY 5–7, 1865). *See* HATCHER'S RUN, VIRGINIA, BATTLE OF.

ARMY. The **U.S. Army** consisted of 16,367 officers and men when the Civil War began, but the Confederacy had only state militia. Both sides quickly organized a volunteer force and divided it into armies, usually named for the **department** or geographical area in which they fought. The Union generally named its armies after bodies of water, while the Confederacy usually used state or regional names. During the war, the Union used 16 armies, with approximately 2,300,000 men. The Confederacy had 23 armies during the war, with a total number of soldiers estimated between 850,000 and 900,000.

Although with some variation, both sides generally organized their armies in the same way. The smallest official unit was the **company**, commanded by a captain and numbering approximately 100 men. Companies normally were raised from one town or county, so they were close-knit units. Although many (especially Confederate) companies had original names like the "Tiger Rifles," they were given letter designations within the **regiment**.

Four or five companies formed a **battalion**, commanded by a major, but battalions were too small for effective use, and many were phased out as the war progressed. Usually 10 companies formed a regiment (12 for cavalry and heavy **artillery**), commanded by a colonel and numbering approximately 1,000 men. Casualties, sickness, and detached duty severely reduced numbers, however, and in many cases regiments went into battle with only 300 to 400 men. Regiments were the backbone of the armies and were identified by their state and numbered according to the order in which they were accepted for service. In the first year of war, the soldiers themselves were allowed to elect the positions of corporal to captain, and the elected officers elected the regiment's field officers.

Four or six regiments formed a **brigade**, usually commanded by a brigadier general. Like regiments, brigades rarely went into battle full strength, so 1,500 men on the firing line was a respectable figure. Union armies numbered their brigades (1st Brigade, for example), but the

Confederates came to call their brigades by their commander's name (such as Early's brigade).

Two to four brigades formed a **division**, again with the Union using numerical designations, the Confederates using commanders' names. In the Union army, a brigadier general usually commanded a division, but the **Confederate army** used major generals in that capacity.

Two to four divisions usually formed a **corps**, with major generals usually commanding Union corps and lieutenant generals normally commanding Confederate corps. The respective armies followed their traditions of using numerical designations for Union corps and commanders' names for the Confederates (although the South also sometimes used numbers). Several corps composed each army, with a major general commanding Union armies and full generals commanding the Confederates.

ARMY OF EAST TENNESSEE (CONFEDERATE). In February 1862, the Confederates established the **Department of East Tennessee**. The scattered troops in the **department** were called the Army of East Tennessee until August 1862, when it was renamed the **Army of Kentucky** when Maj. Gen. **Edmund Kirby Smith** began the **Kentucky Campaign**. In November 1862, after retreating from **Kentucky**, the **army** reverted to its original name of the Army of East Tennessee. Afterward it remained scattered and played only a minor role in the war.

ARMY OF EASTERN KENTUCKY (CONFEDERATE). This Confederate **army** was created on November 1, 1861, as part of **Department No. 2**. Commanded by Brig. Gen. **Humphrey Marshall**, it defended eastern **Kentucky** and the Cumberland Gap until disbanded on March 8, 1862. Most of its units then were sent to the **Army of East Tennessee**.

ARMY OF GEORGIA (UNION). When Maj. Gen. **William T. Sherman** began his **March to the Sea**, his **army** was split between the Left Wing and Right Wing. The **Army of the Tennessee** formed the Right Wing, and the XIV and XX Corps (with Brig. Gen. **H. Judson Kilpatrick's** cavalry), formerly of the **Army of the Cumberland**, formed the Left Wing. Under the command of Maj. Gen. **Henry W. Slocum**, the Left Wing began to use the name Army of Georgia. During the March to the Sea, the Army of Georgia seized Milledgeville, Georgia, and formed Sherman's left when he invested **Savannah**. After fighting at **Averasboro** and **Bentonville** in the **Carolinas Campaign**, Slocum's wing was officially designated the Army of Georgia in March 1865. It was on hand for the surrender of Gen. **Joseph E. Johnston's** Confederate army in April 1865 and participated in the **Grand Review** in **Washington, D.C.**, on May 24. The army was disbanded on June 1, 1865.

ARMY OF KANSAS (UNION). The Union force within the **Department of Kansas** was sometimes referred to as the Army of Kansas. Created in November 1861, its commanders included Maj. Gen. **David Hunter** (November 1861–March 1862), Brig. Gen. **James Blunt** (May–September 1862), and Maj. Gen. **Samuel R. Curtis** (January 1864–January 1865). During the war, the **army** mostly served on frontier duty.

ARMY OF KENTUCKY (CONFEDERATE). When Confederate Maj. Gen. **Edmund Kirby Smith** began the **Kentucky Campaign** in August 1862, his **Army of East Tennessee** was redesignated the Army of Kentucky. Smith used it to win the **Battle of Richmond** and to control much of central **Kentucky**. After the Confederates were forced to retreat from the state, part of the **army** joined the **Army of Tennessee**, while the rest reverted to its old name of the Army of East Tennessee.

ARMY OF KENTUCKY (UNION). Formed in August 1862, this "army" was made up of troops raised early in the war by Brig. Gen. **William "Bull" Nelson** from around Danville and Louisville, Kentucky. Put under the command of Brig. Gen. **Gordon Granger**, its two **brigades** were assigned to the **Army of the Ohio** but were captured five days later at the **Battle of Richmond**.

After Richmond, the term *Army of Kentucky* was used for several forces under Granger's command. Such an **army** was formed around three **divisions** in October 1862, but was immediately disbanded. Granger then had overall command of the four brigades composing Brig. Gen. **Absalom Baird's** division. In June 1863, Granger led the Reserve Corps in the **Army of the Cumberland**. This **corps**, sometimes referred to as the Army of Kentucky, fought at **Chickamauga**. Its designation as an "army" ended in October 1863, when Granger took command of the IV Corps, Army of the Cumberland.

ARMY OF LOUISIANA (CONFEDERATE). At the beginning of the war, the **Louisiana** state troops were sometimes referred to as the Army of Louisiana.

ARMY OF MIDDLE TENNESSEE (CONFEDERATE). When the Confederates established the District of Middle Tennessee in September

1862, the troops within it were designated the Army of Middle Tennessee. Consisting of Brig. Gen. **Nathan Bedford Forrest's** cavalry and Maj. Gen. **John C. Breckinridge's** infantry, the 8,000-man **army** was under Breckinridge's command. The army was short-lived. After conducting some cavalry raids against Union supply lines, it was abolished when Gen. **Braxton Bragg** reorganized the **Army of Tennessee**. Forrest's cavalry joined the command of Maj. Gen. **Joseph Wheeler**, and Breckinridge's infantry became a **division** within Lt. Gen. **William J. Hardee's corps**.

ARMY OF MISSISSIPPI, OR ARMY OF THE MISSISSIPPI (CONFEDERATE). Three Confederate armies carried this designation. The first was formed by Gen. **P. G. T. Beauregard** in March 1862 from troops in the **Western Department**. Its two **corps** merged with Gen. **Albert S. Johnston's Central Army of Kentucky** and fought at **Shiloh** as the Army of Mississippi. After Johnston was killed there, the **army** went through a number of commanders, including Beauregard, **Leonidas Polk**, **William J. Hardee**, and **Braxton Bragg**. When the army joined part of the **Army of Kentucky** in November 1862, the two were merged to form the **Army of Tennessee**.

In December 1862, Maj. Gen. **Earl Van Dorn's Army of West Tennessee** joined Lt. Gen. **John C. Pemberton's** troops and formed the second Army of Mississippi. This army had a confusing array of names. **Sterling Price's** corps kept its identity as the **Army of the West**, and Van Dorn's and Price's combined corps continued to use the name Army of West Tennessee. When the two corps were changed into **divisions** in January 1863, the name Army of Mississippi was dropped.

In May 1864, Polk's corps joined forces with Gen. **Joseph E. Johnston's** Army of Tennessee, and the corps was referred to as the Army of Mississippi. When Polk was killed in June 1864, his corps lost its identity as an army and became known simply as Maj. Gen. **Alexander P. Stewart's** corps.

ARMY OF MISSOURI (CONFEDERATE). This was the name given to the Confederate **army** that participated in Maj. Gen. **Sterling Price's Missouri Raid**. With 12,000 men and 14 cannons, the army entered southeast **Missouri** in September 1864. Over the next 10 weeks, it marched 1,488 miles and fought in 43 engagements. The raid was a failure, however, and the Army of Missouri retreated into **Arkansas** with about half of its original strength. It lost its identity when the raid ended.

ARMY OF MOBILE (CONFEDERATE). Organized to defend Mobile, Alabama, the Army of Mobile was created in January 1862. Commanded by Brig. Gen. **Jones M. Withers**, a former Mobile mayor, the **army** fought at **Shiloh** as a **division** in the **Army of Mississippi**. On March 1, 1862, Withers was replaced by Col. **John B. Villepigue**, who in turn was replaced by Maj. Gen. **Samuel Jones** on March 15. The army ceased to exist shortly afterward as more and more of its men were sent to reinforce the Army of Mississippi.

ARMY OF NEW MEXICO (CONFEDERATE). In December 1861, all of the Confederate forces in the **New Mexico** and Arizona Territories and on much of the Rio Grande were formed into the Army of New Mexico. Commanded by Brig. Gen. **Henry Hopkins Sibley**, the **army** also was known as Sibley's Arizona Brigade. Sibley led the army in an invasion of New Mexico, defeated a Union force at **Valverde** in February 1862, and then captured Albuquerque and Santa Fe. Sibley's invasion was stopped when he was defeated at **Glorieta Pass** in March. The Army of New Mexico then made a long retreat to San Antonio, Texas, and was disbanded. Most of its men were **Texas** cavalry, and they came to make up the bulk of Brig. Gen. **Thomas Green's** cavalry **brigade**.

ARMY OF NORTHERN VIRGINIA (CONFEDERATE). This was the main Confederate **army** in the eastern theater of war. Identified with Gen. **Robert E. Lee**, it was also the most famous and successful of the Confederate armies. Previously known as the **Army of the Potomac (Confederate)**, it was first commanded by Gen. **Joseph E. Johnston**. After Johnston was wounded on May 31, 1862, at **Seven Pines**, Lee was put in command the next day. It is generally believed that the Army of the Potomac (Confederate) became known as the Army of Northern Virginia the day Lee took over.

Lee quickly counterattacked against **George B. McClellan** and pushed his **Army of the Potomac (Union)** down the Virginia Peninsula in the **Seven Days Campaign**. Lee then marched north and defeated **John Pope's Army of Virginia** in the **Second Manassas Campaign**. Having driven the Union armies out of **Virginia** in only three months, he next invaded **Maryland** but was stopped by McClellan in September 1862 at the **Battle of Antietam**. Retreating back to Virginia, Lee next handed the Union one of its worse defeats when **Ambrose Burnside** attacked his strong position at **Fredericksburg**.

In May 1863, **Joseph Hooker** launched a new advance against **Richmond, Virginia**, but was soundly defeated by Lee at **Chancellorsville**.

The Army of Northern Virginia then invaded **Pennsylvania**, but it was defeated by **George G. Meade** at **Gettysburg** in July 1863. Returning to Virginia, Lee sparred with Meade in the **Bristoe Station** and **Mine Run Campaigns** that autumn.

When **U. S. Grant** assumed command of the Union armies in the spring of 1864, the Army of Northern Virginia became locked in a prolonged struggle with the Army of the Potomac. In the **Overland Campaign**, Lee clashed with Grant at the **Wilderness, Spotsylvania, North Anna River**, and **Cold Harbor**. In each of these battles, Lee either gained a tactical victory or stalemate but suffered so many casualties that his army's effectiveness began to wane. In the summer of 1864, the Army of Northern Virginia was forced into the 10-month-long **Petersburg Campaign**.

In March 1865, Lee failed in an attempt to cut his way out of the Petersburg siege. When Grant broke through its lines in April 1865, the Army of Northern Virginia evacuated its positions around Petersburg and Richmond and began retreating west in the **Appomattox Campaign** in an attempt to join Gen. **Joseph E. Johnston's** army in **North Carolina**. After a weeklong running battle, Lee was finally trapped at Appomattox Court House. There on April 9, 1865, he was forced to surrender the 26,000 survivors of the Army of Northern Virginia.

The Army of Northern Virginia's many successes were largely due to the caliber of its officers. It contained a larger number of school-trained and college-educated officers than other Confederate armies. Lee's **corps** commanders included **Stonewall Jackson, James Longstreet, Richard Ewell, J. E. B. Stuart**, and **A. P. Hill**.

ARMY OF PENSACOLA (CONFEDERATE). Originally commanded by Brig. Gen. **Braxton Bragg**, this **army** was created in October 1861 to protect **Pensacola, Florida**. When Bragg joined Gen. **Albert Sidney Johnston's Army of Mississippi** for the **Battle of Shiloh**, the Army of Pensacola lost its identity. In March 1862, it became Bragg's **corps** in the Army of Mississippi.

ARMY OF RICHMOND (CONFEDERATE). This was an unofficial name sometimes used for the **Army of the Potomac (Confederate)**.

ARMY OF SOUTHWEST MISSOURI (UNION). This name was sometimes used in reference to the **Army of the Southwest (Union)**.

ARMY OF TENNESSEE (CONFEDERATE). This was the largest and most famous Confederate **army** in the western theater. In November 1862, the **Army of Kentucky (Confederate)** and the **Army of Mississippi** were merged to form the Army of Tennessee under Gen. **Braxton Bragg**. Under Bragg, the army was defeated at **Stones River** and was forced to withdraw from Middle **Tennessee** in the **Tullahoma Campaign**.

After retreating into northern **Georgia**, Bragg turned and defeated the **Army of the Cumberland** at **Chickamauga** in September 1863. He then besieged Chattanooga, Tennessee, until he was defeated in the November **Chattanooga Campaign** and was forced back into Georgia. Bragg was relieved of command in December 1863, and the army was temporarily led by **William J. Hardee** and **Leonidas Polk** before Gen. **Joseph E. Johnston** assumed command in late December.

Under Johnston, the Army of Tennessee fought Maj. Gen. **William T. Sherman's** armies during the 1864 **Atlanta Campaign**. Johnston repeatedly retreated during the campaign until he was relieved of command in July 1864. General **John B. Hood** replaced him and immediately took the offensive. At the battles of **Peachtree Creek**, **Atlanta**, and **Ezra Church** in July, Hood lashed out at Sherman but failed to win victory. The Army of Tennessee continued to hold on to Atlanta and engaged in bloody battles throughout the summer, but was finally forced to evacuate the city on September 2. In an attempt to draw Sherman out of Georgia, Hood then marched north against Sherman's supply line. Sherman refused to chase Hood for long and returned to Atlanta to prepare for his **March to the Sea**.

Hood next began his **Franklin and Nashville Campaign** but wrecked his army by rashly attacking Maj. Gen. **John Schofield's** army at Franklin. After Maj. Gen. **George Thomas** virtually destroyed Hood at Nashville in December 1864, Hood was relieved of command in January 1865. Lieutenant General **Richard Taylor** temporarily led the army until Johnston returned to command in February. Johnston opposed Sherman's **Carolinas Campaign** and fought one last battle at **Bentonville**, **North Carolina**. He was forced to surrender the approximately 30,000 survivors near **Durham Station**, **North Carolina**, on April 26, 1865.

ARMY OF THE ALLEGHENY (CONFEDERATE). This name was sometimes given to the force commanded by Brig. Gen. **Edward Johnson** in the upper **Shenandoah Valley** in early 1862.

ARMY OF THE CONFEDERATE STATES OF AMERICA. *See* CONFEDERATE ARMY.

ARMY OF THE CUMBERLAND (UNION). In October 1862, the Union **Department of the Cumberland** was recreated out of parts of

Tennessee, **Alabama**, and **Georgia**, and the **Army of the Ohio** was redesignated the Army of the Cumberland, under the command of Maj. Gen. **William S. Rosecrans**. Rosecrans led the **army** in the **Stones River**, **Tullahoma**, and **Chickamauga Campaigns**. In October 1863, Maj. Gen. **George H. Thomas** replaced Rosecrans and commanded the army through the **Chattanooga** and **Atlanta Campaigns**. After the fall of Atlanta, the army was broken up. Part of it, under Maj. Gen. **Henry W. Slocum**, accompanied **William T. Sherman** in the **Carolinas Campaign**. The rest retained the name Army of the Cumberland and served with Thomas in the **Franklin and Nashville Campaign**.

ARMY OF THE FRONTIER (UNION). On September 30, 1862, the Confederates defeated a Union force at **Newtonia, Missouri**. Union Maj. Gen. **John M. Schofield** assembled reinforcements from **Kansas** and **Missouri**, formed the Army of the Frontier in October, and forced the Confederates to retreat into northwestern **Arkansas**. Under Brig. Gen. **James G. Blunt**, the **army** won a strategic victory at **Prairie Grove, Arkansas**, on December 7 that prevented a new Confederate invasion of Missouri. After the battle, Schofield resumed command and was engaged in fighting Confederate guerrillas until he was relieved in March 1863. Major General **Francis Herron** then led the Army of the Frontier until it was disbanded in June 1863.

ARMY OF THE GULF (UNION). When the Union organized the **Department of the Gulf** in February 1862, the troops within it were designated the Army of the Gulf. Consisting mostly of New England **regiments**, the **army** was commanded by Maj. Gen. **Benjamin F. Butler** from March to December 1862; Maj. Gen. **Nathaniel P. Banks** from December 1862 to September 1864; Maj. Gen. **Stephen Hurlbut** from September 1864 to April 1865; Banks from April to June 1865; and Maj. Gen. **E. R. S. Canby** in June 1865. During its existence, the army fought in the **Bayou Teche**, **Port Hudson**, and **Red River Campaigns**, and the **Texas Overland Expedition**. The Army of the Gulf was disbanded in June 1865.

ARMY OF THE JAMES (UNION). Led by Maj. Gen. **Benjamin F. Butler**, this **army** was organized in April 1864 and saw service around **Richmond, Virginia**, in the **Bermuda Hundred Campaign**, when it attacked Richmond while **U. S. Grant** was engaged in the **Overland Campaign**. Defeated by Gen. **P. G. T. Beauregard** at **Second Drewry's Bluff**, Butler withdrew the army to Bermuda Hundred and entrenched.

The army continued to fight during the **Petersburg Campaign**, most notably at **Fort Harrison**, but in December 1864 it was detached for an unsuccessful attack against **Fort Fisher, North Carolina**. This failure led to Butler being relieved of command by Maj. Gen. **E. O. C. Ord** in January 1865. After finally capturing Fort Fisher later in the month, Ord took part of the army back to Petersburg and helped force **Robert E. Lee's** surrender during the **Appomattox Campaign**. The army was disbanded in June 1865.

ARMY OF THE KANAWHA (CONFEDERATE). On June 6, 1861, Confederate forces in western **Virginia's** Kanawha Valley were put under the command of Brig. Gen. **Henry Wise** and became known as the Army of the Kanawha (kan-NOW-wha). In August 1861, Brig. Gen. **John B. Floyd** was ordered to take command of the **army**, but Wise, a political foe of Floyd's, refused to cooperate and continued to act independently. Even after Gen. **Robert E. Lee** arrived to assume overall command of the area, Wise proved uncooperative. After being defeated at **Carnifex Ferry** in September, Wise was ordered by the secretary of war to relinquish command to Floyd. When Floyd failed to confront the Union forces in the area effectively, the army was abolished in November 1861. Floyd's **brigade** then was transferred to the **Central Army of Kentucky**.

ARMY OF THE MISSISSIPPI (UNION). There were two Union armies with this name. In February 1862, Brig. Gen. **John Pope** organized one such **army** for use along the Mississippi River at **New Madrid and Island No. 10**. After successfully capturing these strongholds, he was transferred to **Virginia**, and in June 1862 Maj. Gen. **William S. Rosecrans** assumed command. Under him, the army fought at **Iuka** and **Corinth, Mississippi**, in the autumn of 1862. The army was disbanded in October 1862 and became part of the **Army of the Tennessee**.

The second Army of the Mississippi was associated with Maj. Gen. **John A. McClernand**, who was authorized by **Abraham Lincoln** in 1862 to raise a force to attack **Vicksburg, Mississippi**. Major General **William T. Sherman** used some of these troops in his failed assault at **Chickasaw Bayou** in December 1862. Afterward, McClernand assumed command of the force, named it the Army of the Mississippi, and captured **Arkansas Post** in January 1863. Pope's army then ceased to exist when **U. S. Grant** assumed command of Union forces for the 1863 **Vicksburg Campaign**, and McClernand's troops were designated the XIII and XV Corps of the Army of the Tennessee.

ARMY OF THE MOUNTAIN DEPARTMENT (UNION). When the **Mountain Department** was created in western **Virginia** and eastern **Kentucky** in March 1862, the Union troops within it were referred to as the Army of the Mountain Department. Led by Maj. Gen. **John C. Frémont**, it was defeated by **Stonewall Jackson** at **McDowell** in May 1862 and at **Cross Keys** the following month. On June 26, 1862, the **department** and **army** were abolished, with the troops becoming the I Corps of the **Army of Virginia**.

ARMY OF THE NORTH (CONFEDERATE). This was the unofficial name used by President **Jefferson Davis** to refer to Confederate forces in **Virginia** along the Rappahannock River and in the **Shenandoah Valley** in early 1862.

ARMY OF THE NORTHWEST (CONFEDERATE). Created on June 8, 1861, under the command of Brig. Gen. **Robert S. Garnett**, this **army** was made up of the Confederate troops defending northwestern **Virginia**. It was defeated at **Rich Mountain** on July 11, and Garnett was killed at **Carrick's Ford** on July 13. After being temporarily commanded by Brig. Gen. **Henry R. Jackson**, the army was taken over by Brig. Gen. **William W. Loring** on July 20. After Loring was defeated at **Cheat Mountain** in September 1861, he took the army to Winchester, Virginia, and joined the command of **Stonewall Jackson**. Jackson failed in his expedition to Romney, Virginia, that winter, and he and Loring clashed.

Loring's Army of the Northwest was abolished on February 9, 1862, when Loring was transferred from Jackson's command. The soldiers then were absorbed into the **Army of Northern Virginia**. Afterward, the Confederate troops with Brig. Gen. **Edward Johnson** in the upper **Shenandoah Valley** were sometimes referred to as the Army of the Northwest.

ARMY OF THE OHIO (UNION). There were two Union armies by this name. On November 15, 1861, Maj. Gen. **Don Carlos Buell** took command of the forces within the **Department of the Ohio**, which was frequently abolished and recreated. Called the Army of the Ohio, these troops played a vital role at the **Battle of Shiloh** when they arrived on April 6, 1862, to reinforce Maj. Gen. **U. S. Grant**, and in the Kentucky Campaign on October 24, 1862, Buell was replaced by Maj. Gen. **William S. Rosecrans**, and the **army** was designated the XIV Corps but continued to refer to itself as the Army of the Ohio.

In August 1862, the Department of the Ohio was recreated after a five-month lapse. On March 25, 1863, Maj. Gen. **Ambrose Burnside**, who had arrived from **Virginia** with his IX Corps, assumed command. On April 27, his command was designated the XXIII Corps, but it was popularly known as the Army of the Ohio. Under Burnside, the army fought Confederate Lt. Gen. **James Longstreet** in the **Knoxville Campaign**.

When Burnside was transferred back to Virginia, the army went through a number of commanders. These included Maj. Gen. **John Gray Foster** (December 1863–February 1864); Maj. Gen. **John Schofield** (February–November 1864); and Maj. Gen. **George Stoneman** (November 1864–January 1865). The army became most famous under Schofield, under whom it fought in the **Knoxville, Atlanta,** and **Franklin and Nashville Campaigns**. In January 1865, Schofield's army was transferred east, where it captured **Wilmington, North Carolina,** in February. The army also participated in the **Carolinas Campaign** and fought at **Kinston, North Carolina,** in March. It remained in North Carolina until it was disbanded on June 27, 1865.

ARMY OF THE PENINSULA (CONFEDERATE). To guard against Union forces at **Fort Monroe, Virginia,** Col. **John B. Magruder** was given command of the Confederate **Department of the Peninsula** on May 26, 1861. His force became known as the Army of the Peninsula and won one of the first battles of the war at **Big Bethel, Virginia,** in June 1861. Promoted to brigadier general, Magruder then used his small **army** to prepare a series of defensive works on the Virginia Peninsula.

When **George B. McClellan** began the **Peninsula Campaign** in March 1862, only Magruder's Army of the Peninsula was in a position to stop him. Badly outnumbered, Magruder used his small army effectively to fight several small battles and delay McClellan's advance toward **Richmond**. When Gen. **Joseph E. Johnston** arrived and assumed command of the peninsula forces on April 26, Magruder's army lost its identity and became known as the Right Wing of Johnston's **Army of the Potomac (Confederate)**.

ARMY OF THE POTOMAC (CONFEDERATE). When Gen. **P. G. T. Beauregard** took command of the Confederate forces around Manassas, Virginia, on June 2, 1861, his command became known as the Army of the Potomac. It was joined by Gen. **Joseph E. Johnston's Army of the Shenandoah** to win the **First Battle of Manassas** on July 21. After the battle, the two Confederate forces combined under Johnston's command as the Army of the Potomac. Johnston took the **army** southward in the spring of 1862 to confront Maj. Gen. **George B. McClellan's** Union **Army of the Potomac** in the **Peninsula Campaign**. On June 1, 1862, when Gen. **Robert E. Lee** took command of the army after Johnston's wounding at **Seven Pines**, he first referred to it as the **Army of Northern Virginia**. It kept that name for the rest of the war.

ARMY OF THE POTOMAC (UNION). One of the most famous Civil War armies, the Army of the Potomac was the main Union **army** in the eastern theater. It was created on August 15, 1861, when the **Department of the Potomac** was established following the Union defeat at **First Manassas**. Placed under the command of Maj. Gen. **George B. McClellan**, it threatened **Richmond, Virginia**, during the **Peninsula Campaign** but was forced to retreat by **Robert E. Lee's Army of Northern Virginia** during the **Seven Days Campaign**. McClellan's failure in the latter campaign forced **Abraham Lincoln** to strip most of the troops from the peninsula and send them to Maj. Gen. **John Pope's Army of Virginia** in the summer of 1862. When Pope was defeated by Lee at **Second Manassas**, his army was disbanded, and McClellan again led the Army of the Potomac into **Maryland** to confront Lee in the **Antietam Campaign**. When McClellan failed to pursue Lee after the **Battle of Antietam**, he was replaced on November 9, 1862, by Maj. Gen. **Ambrose Burnside**.

After nearly wrecking the army by assaulting Lee's entrenched position at **Fredericksburg** and floundering in the **Mud March**, Burnside was replaced on January 26, 1863, by Maj. Gen. **Joseph Hooker**. Hooker did an admirable job reorganizing the army and improving morale, but he met defeat at the hands of Lee at **Chancellorsville**. When Lee began the **Gettysburg Campaign** in June 1863, Hooker demanded that **Harpers Ferry, Virginia**, be evacuated. When it was not, he submitted his resignation, which was accepted by Lincoln on June 28, 1863.

On that same day, Maj. Gen. **George G. Meade** became the last commander of the Army of the Potomac. Meade defeated Lee at **Gettysburg** and in the autumn of 1863 sparred with the Confederates in the **Bristoe Station** and **Mine Run Campaigns**. When **U. S. Grant** was made lieutenant general in March 1864, he accompanied and directed Meade's army during the **Overland Campaign**. After suffering horrendous casualties, the Army of the Potomac finally forced Lee into a siege during the **Petersburg Campaign**. Near continuous fighting occurred through the winter of 1864–65 as Grant tightened his grip on Petersburg.

After Lee unsuccessfully tried to break out of the Petersburg lines in March 1865, Grant sent the Army of the Potomac in a counterattack that broke through the Confederate lines. Then began the **Appomattox Campaign**, a running battle that culminated in Lee's surrender at Appomattox on April 9, 1865.

After the **Grand Review** in **Washington, D.C.**, the Army of the Potomac was disbanded on May 23, 1865. During the war, it was defeated time after time but continued to fight despite suffering terrible **losses**. The army's tenacity eventually wore down the Confederates until final victory was achieved.

ARMY OF THE SHENANDOAH (CONFEDERATE). In April 1861, **Virginia** state troops began assembling in the **Shenandoah Valley** near **Harpers Ferry**. Colonel **Thomas J. Jackson** assumed command of them on April 28 and continued raising troops until he was relieved by Gen. **Joseph E. Johnston** on May 23. Named the Army of the Shenandoah, this force of approximately 10,000 men **skirmished** with Maj. Gen. **Robert Patterson's** Union **army** around Harpers Ferry until slipping away on July 18 to join Gen. **P. G. T. Beauregard** for the **First Battle of Manassas**. At that time, Johnston's army was absorbed into the **Army of the Potomac (Confederate)**.

ARMY OF THE SHENANDOAH (UNION). There were two Union armies by this name. It first was used as an informal name for Maj. Gen. **Robert Patterson's** forces, which confronted **Joseph E. Johnston's** Confederates in the **Shenandoah Valley** in July 1861. The name more properly refers to the command led by Maj. Gen. **Philip H. Sheridan** in the Valley during 1864.

In August 1864, Sheridan assembled in the Valley a variety of troops from the **Army of the Potomac**, **Army of the Gulf**, and **Army of West Virginia**. Named the Army of the Shenandoah, these 60,000 men were to destroy Lt. Gen. **Jubal A. Early's** Confederate **army**. In **Sheridan's 1864 Shenandoah Valley Campaign**, the Army of the Shenandoah defeated Early in the battles of **Third Winchester**, **Fisher's Hill**, **Tom's Brook**, and **Cedar Creek** and then ravaged the Valley to destroy it as a source of supplies for **Robert E. Lee's Army of Northern Virginia** at Petersburg, Virginia.

From December 1864 to January 1865, elements of the Army of the Shenandoah were drawn off to reinforce **U. S. Grant** and **William T. Sherman**. When Sheridan was placed in command of a cavalry **corps**, Brig. Gen. **Alfred T. A. Torbert** assumed army command on February 28, 1865. He led the army until it was disbanded on June 27, 1865.

ARMY OF THE SOUTHWEST (UNION). This short-lived **army** was created on December 25, 1861, when the **Military Division of the Southwest** was established. It was mainly used as an occupation force for southwestern **Missouri**, and its original commander, Brig. Gen.

Samuel R. Curtis, led it to victory at the **Battle of Pea Ridge** in March 1862. This battle helped keep Missouri in the Union and was the army's greatest achievement. For the rest of the war, the Army of the Southwest mainly performed garrison duty. Its later commanders were Maj. Gen. **Frederick Steele** (August 29–October 7, 1862), Maj. Gen. **Eugene A. Carr** (October 7–November 12, 1862), and Maj. Gen. **Willis A. Gorman** (November 12–December 13, 1862). On December 13, 1862, the Division of the Southwest was merged with the District of Eastern Arkansas, and the army was absorbed into the **Army of the Tennessee**.

ARMY OF THE TENNESSEE (UNION). When the **Department of the Tennessee** was formed on October 16, 1862, its troops under Maj. Gen. **U. S. Grant** were designated the XIII Corps. When several **corps** were formed out of this one on December 18, the new organization was referred to as the Army of the Tennessee. Its commanders included Grant (October 16, 1862–October 24, 1863), Maj. Gen. **William T. Sherman** (October 24, 1863–March 26, 1864), Maj. Gen. **James B. McPherson** (March 26–July 22, 1864), Maj. Gen. **John A. Logan** (July 22–27, 1864, and May 19–August 1, 1865), and Maj. Gen. **Oliver O. Howard** (July 27, 1864–May 19, 1865).

The Army of the Tennessee was the war's most successful Union **army**. It captured **Vicksburg, Mississippi**; helped defeat the Confederates in the **Chattanooga Campaign**; and played an important role in the **Atlanta Campaign**, the **March to the Sea**, and the **Carolinas Campaign**. Except for its foray into the Carolinas at the end of the war, the army fought exclusively in the western theater. After participating in the **Grand Review** at **Washington, D.C.**, the army was disbanded on August 1, 1865.

ARMY OF THE TRANS-MISSISSIPPI (CONFEDERATE). This was the Confederate **army** that defended the **Trans-Mississippi Department**. It was created on May 26, 1862, and was first commanded by Maj. Gen. **Thomas C. Hindman** (May 31–July 30, 1862) and Maj. Gen. **Theophilus H. Holmes** (July 30, 1862–March 7, 1863). It was under Gen. **Edmund Kirby Smith** (March 7, 1863–June 2, 1865), however, that the army faced its greatest threat. After the fall of **Vicksburg, Mississippi**, in 1863, the Trans-Mississippi Department was cut off and isolated from the rest of the Confederacy. Kirby Smith was forced to supply and recruit his widely scattered 40,000-man army virtually without assistance from the government. Despite these problems, the army defeated its Union counterparts in the 1864 **Red River Campaign** and **Camden Expedition**.

Kirby Smith's army was the last Confederate army to surrender. On May 26, 1865, Kirby Smith's subordinate Lt. Gen. **Simon B. Buckner** surrendered the **department** in **New Orleans, Louisiana**, and on June 2, 1865, Kirby Smith approved the terms of surrender at Galveston, Texas.

ARMY OF THE WEST (CONFEDERATE). Major General **Earl Van Dorn**, commander of the **Trans-Mississippi District**, named his force the Army of the West on March 4, 1862. Four days later it was defeated at the **Battle of Pea Ridge**. The **army** then crossed the Mississippi River to participate in the **siege of Corinth, Mississippi**. When the Confederates retreated at the end of May 1862, Van Dorn's army contained 20,000 men.

Van Dorn was transferred on June 20, 1862, and Maj. Gen. **John P. McCown** assumed temporary command until Maj. Gen. **Sterling Price** took permanent command on July 3. Price fought at **Iuka, Mississippi**, and then joined Van Dorn's **Army of West Tennessee** for an unsuccessful assault on **Corinth** on October 3–4. Afterward, on November 26, 1862, Price's Army of the West was absorbed into the Army of West Tennessee as a **corps**, but it was still sometimes referred to as the Army of the West.

ARMY OF VICKSBURG (CONFEDERATE). On October 13, 1862, Lt. Gen. **John C. Pemberton** assumed command of the **Department of Mississippi and East Louisiana** and the troops defending **Vicksburg, Mississippi**. Pemberton's main force was Maj. Gen. **Earl Van Dorn's Army of West Tennessee**, which was renamed the **Army of Mississippi** on December 7, 1862. By January 1863, this name was discontinued, and Pemberton's soldiers became known as the Army of Vicksburg.

The Union's first major attempt to capture Vicksburg was in **Grant's Overland Vicksburg Campaign** in December 1862. The Army of Vicksburg repulsed Maj. Gen. **William T. Sherman** at **Chickasaw Bayou**, and the Confederate cavalry forced Maj. Gen. **U. S. Grant** to retreat in northern **Mississippi**. In the spring of 1863, Grant landed troops below the city in the **Vicksburg Campaign**. Rather than concentrating his **army** to meet Grant, Pemberton fought a series of small battles and finally was besieged in Vicksburg with 30,000 men. He held out for 47 days, but the Army of Vicksburg was forced to surrender on July 4, 1863.

ARMY OF VIRGINIA (UNION). The Army of Virginia was created on June 26, 1862, while Maj. Gen. **George B. McClellan's Army of the Potomac** was beginning the **Seven Days Campaign**. Placed under the command of Maj. Gen. **John Pope**, this **army** was a consolidation of troops from four separate commands—the **Mountain Department,**

Department of the Shenandoah, Department of the Rappahannock, and the Military District of Washington—and was created to bring unity of command to these scattered forces after **Stonewall Jackson's Shenandoah Valley Campaign**.

After the Seven Days Campaign, much of McClellan's command was transferred from the Virginia Peninsula to Pope as he took the army southward from near **Washington, D.C.** On August 9, 1862, the army was defeated by Jackson at **Cedar Mountain** and withdrew across the Rappahannock River. During the **Second Manassas Campaign**, it was involved in intense fighting at **Groveton, Second Manassas**, and **Chantilly**, with Pope being soundly defeated at Manassas. By the end of the campaign, McClellan had arrived in Washington and assumed command of the troops. The Army of Virginia was quickly assimilated into the Army of the Potomac, and Pope was relieved of command on September 12, 1862.

ARMY OF WEST TENNESSEE (CONFEDERATE). On September 28, 1862, the troops within Maj. Gen. **Earl Van Dorn's** District of the Mississippi were joined by Maj. Gen. **Sterling Price's Army of the West** for an attack on **Corinth, Mississippi**. The combined force was named the Army of West Tennessee (although Price's **army** was not officially absorbed until November 26) and fought under Van Dorn at Corinth on October 3–4, 1862. Van Dorn was repulsed, and his army was renamed the **Army of Mississippi** on December 7, 1862.

ARMY OF WEST TENNESSEE (UNION). This name was applied to the Union forces in the District of West Tennessee, which was created in February 1862 and placed under Maj. Gen. **U. S. Grant**. The name was short-lived, however, for in October 1862, the **district** was absorbed into the newly created **Department of the Tennessee**.

ARMY OF WEST VIRGINIA (UNION). When the **Department of West Virginia** was created on June 24, 1863, Union troops of the VIII Corps were used to form the Army of West Virginia. Put under the command of Brig. Gen. **Benjamin F. Kelly**, the **army** was to protect the newly created state of **West Virginia** and the Baltimore & Ohio Railroad. On March 10, 1864, Maj. Gen. **Franz Sigel** took command and moved up the **Shenandoah Valley**. After being defeated at **New Market**, Sigel was replaced on May 21, 1864, by Maj. Gen. **David Hunter**. The army defeated the Confederates at **Piedmont** during **Hunter's Shenandoah Valley Campaign** and then devastated the Valley. When Hunter was driven out of the Valley by **Jubal A. Early**, he was replaced by **George Crook** on August 8, 1864. Under Crook, the army participated in Maj. Gen. **Philip Sheridan's 1864 Shenandoah Valley Campaign**. After Crook was captured on February 22, 1865, the army was commanded first by Brig. Gen. **Samuel S. Carroll** (February 27–March 7, 1865) and then by Maj. Gen. **Winfield S. Hancock** until its disbandment on June 27, 1865.

ARNOLD, LEWIS GOLDING (1817–1871) USA. A native of **New Jersey**, Arnold graduated from **West Point** in 1837. His early military career included service in the **Seminole Wars**, the Cherokee **Indian** removal, and the **Mexican War** (where he suffered two wounds and was awarded two **brevets** for gallantry).

A major when the Civil War began, Arnold was stationed at **Fort Pickens, Florida**, with the 1st U.S. Artillery. He served there throughout its siege and was commanding that post when he was appointed brigadier general of volunteers in January 1862. Arnold was put in command of the **Department of Florida** in February and in September was placed in command of the **New Orleans, Louisiana**, defenses. In November 1862, he suffered a stroke while reviewing his troops and remained on sick leave until he retired in February 1864.

ARNOLD, RICHARD (1828–1882) USA. Related to Benedict Arnold, this **Rhode Island** native was the son of a prominent politician. Arnold graduated from **West Point** in 1850 and had a routine military career before the Civil War. At **First Manassas** he was a captain in the 5th U.S. Artillery and lost all of his guns during the retreat. During the **Peninsula Campaign**, Arnold served as chief of **artillery** for Brig. Gen. **William B. Franklin's** division in the **Army of the Potomac** and was the VI Corps' acting inspector general during the **Seven Days Campaign**. During the latter campaign, he was **brevetted** major for his actions at the **Battle of Savage's Station**.

Promoted to brigadier general of volunteers in November 1862, Arnold was appointed chief of artillery for the **Department of the Gulf** and saw service with Maj. Gen. **Nathaniel P. Banks** in the **Port Hudson Campaign**. In the 1864 **Red River Campaign**, he at first was Banks's chief of artillery but took command of a cavalry **division** in the latter part of the campaign. Arnold also played a role in the capture of **Fort Blakely, Alabama**, near war's end during the **Mobile Campaign**.

Arnold was mustered out of the volunteer service in August 1865 but remained in the **U.S. Army** as a captain even though he had received brevets of major general in both the regular and volunteer service. When he died in 1882, he held the rank of major.

ARNOLD, SAMUEL BLAND (1834–1906) CSA. A childhood friend of both **John Wilkes Booth** and **Michael O'Laughlin**, Arnold joined (and apparently deserted) the **Confederate army**. Booth then drew him into the circle of conspirators to kidnap **Abraham Lincoln**, even though Arnold had little faith in the plan. In March 1865, Arnold withdrew from the conspiracy but was arrested with the others after **Lincoln's assassination**. During the trial, Arnold admitted to being involved in the plot to kidnap the president but denied participating in the assassination. He was convicted anyway and was sentenced to life imprisonment at Dry Tortugas, Florida. After surviving a yellow fever epidemic, Arnold was pardoned, along with **Dr. Samuel Mudd**, by President **Andrew Johnson** in 1869.

ART. The Civil War was one of the first wars to be widely illustrated by artists. Such illustrated publications as *Frank Leslie's Illustrated Newspaper* and *Harper's Weekly* hired professional artists who accompanied the Union armies and provided illustrations that were converted into woodblock engravings for mass production. Some of the art had patriotic or political themes, but much of it depicted camp life and battle scenes. The Confederacy had few publications in which to offer art; therefore, illustrations depicting the Southern side of the conflict did not become widespread until after the war. Such artists as **Edwin Forbes**, **Alfred R. Waud**, and **Winslow Homer** provided illustrations for the Northern magazines, while **Allen C. Redwood's** and **Conrad W. Chapman's** Confederate works became popular after the conflict. Much of the Civil War art was reproduced in the popular postwar publication *Battles and Leaders of the Civil War* (The Century Co., 1888).

ARTILLERY. The Union and Confederate armies used the same type of artillery and organized their cannoneers in similar ways, with the battery being the basic organizational unit. A battery was supposed to include six cannons of the same caliber (although many, especially in the **Confederate army**, contained from four to six guns, sometimes of different calibers and types), with the accompanying limbers, caissons, battery forge, battery wagon (containing tools and equipment), a number of reserve limbers and caissons carrying reserve ammunition, and the crew. One gun and its accompanying limbers and caissons made up a gun platoon; two gun platoons made up a section. In the Union **army**, a battery had a standard crew of 123 officers and men, while the Confederates generally had fewer men. In both armies, captains commanded the battery.

At the start of the war, artillery batteries were assigned to each infantry **brigade**. This proved to be ineffective, however, since it spread the artillery out and often made it difficult to concentrate a large number of guns at a critical point on the battlefield. As the war progressed, batteries became more concentrated at the **division** and **corps** levels.

The war saw a wide variety of cannons used for different purposes. Civil War artillery pieces included both muzzle loaders and breech loaders and were made of iron, bronze, and steel. Smooth bores, such as the 1857 **Napoleon**, had a rather short range but were excellent against advancing infantry. **Parrotts** and other **rifled** guns had a longer range and were used against infantry, opposing batteries, ships, and fortifications. Field artillery, both smooth bore and rifles, fired a flat trajectory and were used against opposing armies and fortified walls. **Mortars** fired a very high trajectory and were used to lob shells over walls and earthworks into the troops positioned behind them. A **howitzer's** trajectory fell in between these two.

Artillery pieces were classified either by the weight of the projectile (12-pounder, for example) or the diameter of the bore (3-inch rifle, for example). The 12-pounder Napoleon was perhaps the most common cannon used by either side. Others included the **Armstrong**, Parrott, **Columbiad**, **Dahlgren**, **Blakely**, **Whitworth**, **Brooke**, **Ordnance Rifle**, and **Rodman**. Ammunition also varied greatly, depending on whether the target was a fort, ship, infantry, or something else, and included **solid shot**, **grape shot**, **canister**, **bar shot**, and **chain shot**.

Use of artillery was devastating to the enemy. Cannons were effective from 1,500 yards (smooth bores) to 2,500 yards (rifles), and could be fired two to three times per minute.

ASBOTH, ALEXANDER SANDOR (1811–1868) USA. A native of Hungary, Asboth was a trained engineer who supported Lajos Kossuth during the 1848 Hungarian Revolution. He moved to the United States with Kossuth in 1851 and became a naturalized citizen.

In July 1861, Asboth joined Maj. Gen. **John C. Frémont's** staff. Frémont appointed him brigadier general of volunteers in September 1861 and made him chief of staff. This appointment was not government sanctioned, however, and Asboth did not receive his official commission until March 1862. Despite his unofficial promotion, he was given command of a **division** in the **Army of Southwest Missouri** in February 1862 and was wounded while leading it at the **Battle of Pea Ridge**. After his commission was confirmed, Asboth led a division in the **Army of the Mississippi** in the summer of 1862 before being placed in charge of the District of Columbus, Kentucky. In August 1863, he was put in command of the District of West Florida. In October 1864, Asboth was badly wounded in the left cheek and left arm during a **skirmish** at Marianna, Florida, but managed to return to his command in the war's final days. **Brevetted** major general of volunteers in March 1865, he left the **army** in August.

After the war, Asboth underwent surgery in Paris, France, to have the bullet removed from his face. Returning to the United States, he was appointed minister to Argentina and Uruguay in 1866 and died in Buenos Aires in 1868 from his unhealed facial wound.

ASHBY, TURNER (1828–1862) CSA. A native of **Virginia**, Ashby was largely educated at home. He remained a lifelong bachelor, established a farm in his native county, and, as a militia captain, helped guard **John Brown's** execution in 1859.

Although a reluctant secessionist, Ashby joined Confederate service when his militia **company** became part of the 7th Virginia Cavalry in early 1861. He was promoted to lieutenant colonel in June and raised Chew's Horse Battery. Ashby became colonel of the 7th Virginia in October and compiled a mixed record while he commanded the cavalry in the **Valley District** during **Stonewall Jackson's 1862 Shenandoah Valley Campaign**. Although daring and brave, he was a poor disciplinarian and sometimes was unavailable at crucial times during Jackson's campaign. Faulty intelligence by him also helped lead to Jackson's defeat at **Kernstown**.

Jackson tried to break up Ashby's command but relented when Ashby threatened to resign. Without Jackson's endorsement, Ashby was promoted to brigadier general in May 1862 and fought well during Jackson's retreat back up the Valley. On June 6, 1862, while conducting a rear guard action at Harrisonburg, Ashby's horse was shot from under him but he continued to lead his men on foot until a shot to the chest killed him. Some of Ashby's men believed he was accidentally shot from behind by his own men, but there is no evidence to support that belief.

***ATLANTA*, CSS.** This Confederate **ironclad** was a former **blockade runner** named the *Fingal*. Ship builders N. and A. F. Tift converted the *Fingal* into a warship in 1862 at Savannah, Georgia. The finished ironclad was 204 feet long, with a 41-foot beam, and was armed with a spar **torpedo**, ram, and two 7-inch and two 6.4-inch **Brooke rifles**.

Commissioned the CSS *Atlanta* in November 1862, the ship remained in the Savannah River near the city until June 1863. At that time, Cmdr.

William A. Webb took it down the Wilmington River to enter the Atlantic Ocean and raise the **blockade**. Webb, however, ran aground and was attacked by the Union **monitor** *Weehawken*. After the *Atlanta* was hit several times and started to list, Webb surrendered. The Union navy refitted the *Atlanta* and used it in the James River until war's end. Afterward, it was sold for scrap.

ATLANTA, GEORGIA, BATTLE OF (JULY 22, 1864). Because of his failure to stop **William T. Sherman's** advance during the **Atlanta Campaign**, Gen. **Joseph E. Johnston** was replaced in command of the **Army of Tennessee** by **John Bell Hood** on July 17, 1864. Hood immediately took the offensive and unsuccessfully attacked Sherman at **Peachtree Creek** on July 20. Two days later, he attacked again when he learned that Maj. Gen. **James B. McPherson's Army of the Tennessee** was approaching Atlanta from Decatur, Georgia, with his left (or southern) flank exposed.

Hood left Lt. Gen. **Alexander P. Stewart's corps** to confront the Union forces north and northeast of Atlanta, while the corps of **William J. Hardee** and **Benjamin F. Cheatham** positioned themselves to attack McPherson. Cheatham was to hold the entrenchments in McPherson's front and attack due east, while Hardee circled to the south and attacked McPherson's left flank and rear. At the same time, Maj. Gen. **Joseph Wheeler's** cavalry would attack the enemy wagon train in McPherson's rear at Decatur.

This plan, however, soon fell apart. Hardee began his 15-mile march on the night of July 21 but did not get into position until midday. It was then discovered that Maj. Gen. **Grenville M. Dodge's** XVI Corps had extended the Union line farther east so that Hardee's attack struck the Union left-center rather than at the exposed flank as expected. The **divisions** of Maj. Gens. **William H. T. Walker** and **William B. Bate** made two attacks against Dodge but were repulsed with heavy losses, and Walker was killed.

McPherson arrived on the field as the Confederates were driven back and discovered a gap had opened between Dodge's right and Maj. Gen. **Francis P. Blair's** XVII Corps. He ordered Col. Hugo Wangelin's brigade to fill the hole and then rode toward Blair's position with an aide. The two suddenly encountered Confederate troops and were told to surrender. McPherson spurred his horse instead and was killed as he tried to escape.

Major Generals **Patrick R. Cleburne** and **George E. Maney** then poured their divisions into the gap and furiously assaulted Brig. Gen. **Giles Alexander Smith's** division, which held Blair's left flank. The flank was driven back until Wangelin's **brigade** arrived, stopped the Confederates, and sealed the gap. Meanwhile, Hood had failed to send Cheatham's corps against McPherson's front as planned. It was not until Hardee was being repulsed at about 3:00 P.M. that Hood finally ordered Cheatham and the **Georgia** militia under Maj. Gen. **Gustavus W. Smith** to advance against Maj. Gen. **John A. Logan's** XV Corps. In this attack, Brig. Gen. **Arthur Middleton Manigault's** brigade overran Logan's forward units and began driving in the Union line. However, massed **artillery** fire and a counterattack repulsed the Confederates. Cheatham continued to attack through the afternoon but was unable to break Logan's line. While these battles raged around Atlanta, Wheeler's cavalry attacked the Union wagon train at Decatur and captured more than 200 soldiers, but tenacious fighting and timely reinforcements enabled the defenders ultimately to drive off the cavalry.

Hood's failure to coordinate his two attacks at Atlanta led to his defeat. The Confederates lost approximately 8,000 men in the battle to McPherson's 3,700.

ATLANTA, GEORGIA, CAMPAIGN (MAY 7–SEPTEMBER 2, 1864). In the spring of 1864, Lt. Gen. **Ulysses S. Grant** became general-in-chief of the Union armies and planned simultaneous advances against the Confederacy on several fronts. One of the main offensives was to be carried out by Maj. Gen. **William T. Sherman**, commander of the **Military Division of the Mississippi**. Sherman's orders were to "break up" the Confederate **Army of Tennessee** under Gen. **Joseph E. Johnston** in northern **Georgia** and invade the interior, destroying Southern war resources as he went. Atlanta, Georgia, was a vital Confederate railhead and industrial center, and its loss would be a devastating blow to the South, so Sherman used it as a target to draw Johnston into battle.

For the campaign, Sherman had approximately 110,000 men and 254 cannons in Maj. Gen. **George H. Thomas's Army of the Cumberland** (73,000 men), Maj. Gen. **James B. McPherson's Army of the Tennessee** (24,500 men), and Maj. Gen. **John M. Schofield's Army of the Ohio** (11,500 men). Of these, approximately 99,000 men actually were available for the offensive. To oppose this massive force, Johnston's Army of Tennessee had approximately 62,000 men and 144 cannons. Although Johnston was outnumbered, he had the advantage of terrain and position. Northern Georgia was perfect for defense, being laced with rivers and mountain ranges that ran directly across the path of Sherman's march. Also, as Johnston fell back toward Atlanta, he would draw closer to his base of supplies, while Sherman would be stretching his line of communications farther and be forced to leave more and more men behind to guard it.

On May 7, 1864, Sherman left his camps and advanced to the southeast toward the Confederate position at **Rocky Face Ridge**, near Dalton, Georgia. Realizing these positions were too strong to assault, Sherman initiated a **turning movement** that would set the tone for the entire campaign. Holding the Confederates in place with Thomas and Schofield, Sherman sent McPherson to turn the enemy position by marching south to **Snake Creek Gap**. McPherson was to push through the gap into Johnston's rear and trap the Confederates by cutting their line of communication. McPherson marched through Snake Creek Gap on May 9 but unexpectedly ran into enemy resistance near **Resaca**. Believing he was outnumbered, he fell back into the gap and entrenched instead of pressing on. The Confederate presence at Resaca actually was small, and McPherson missed one of the Union's best opportunities to destroy Johnston. Meanwhile, Sherman began moving most of his force toward Snake Creek Gap on May 10, and Johnston withdrew on May 12 from near Dalton to Resaca.

After moving through Snake Creek Gap, Sherman confronted the well-entrenched enemy at Resaca on May 14. By this time Johnston had been reinforced by Lt. Gen. **Leonidas Polk** and had nearly 70,000 men. On May 14–15, Sherman and Johnston attacked and counterattacked at Resaca, but neither made much headway. On May 15, Sherman again turned the Confederate position by sending a **division** to cross the Oostanaula River downstream and threaten Johnston's line of retreat. At the same time, Union cavalry under Brig. Gen. **Kenner Garrard** headed farther south and captured the Confederate supply base at Rome. Johnston was forced to retreat across the river on the night of May 15 and fell back to Calhoun and **Adairsville**. During the fighting at Resaca, Sherman lost approximately 4,000 men to Johnston's 3,000.

Unable to hold his ground at Calhoun and Adairsville, Johnston withdrew again to near Kingston and Cassville. In following up the Confederates, Sherman made a tactical mistake by spreading his three armies over a wide front, with McPherson advancing on the Union right, Thomas in the center, and Schofield in an isolated position on the left. Taking advantage of this error, Johnston ordered **William J. Hardee's corps** and **Joseph Wheeler's** cavalry to engage McPherson and Thomas to the west and north, while **John Bell Hood's** corps smashed the isolated Schofield near Cassville. On May 19, a wayward Union cavalry unit on Hood's right flank convinced Hood that he was about to be attacked. Hood repositioned his corps to face this perceived threat instead of attacking Schofield, and Johnston's plan collapsed. Johnston then withdrew that night across the Etowah River to **Allatoona**.

Sherman continued on to Allatoona Pass but found the Confederate defenses there too strong to attack. He again made a turning movement on May 23 by abandoning his **railroad** line and moving to the west and south toward Marietta by way of Dallas to get behind Johnston's left flank. Johnston withdrew from Allatoona Pass the next day, reached **Dallas** first, and dug strong entrenchments around it and **New Hope Church**. On May 25–27, very intense fighting took place as Sherman futilely attacked these strong works. On May 25, Sherman's XX Corps lost 1,600 men at New Hope Church, and on May 27 the IV Corps lost 1,600 men at **Pickett's Mill**. Johnston's losses were light, but the following day he suffered approximately 1,000 casualties when **William Bate's** division attacked the entrenched Federals around Dallas.

On June 1, Sherman began shifting his armies to the east, and on June 4 his cavalry occupied Allatoona Pass. This threatened Johnston's right rear and forced him to withdraw on June 4 to near Marietta. For over a week the opposing armies fought along the **Lost Mountain-Brushy Mountain line**, and on June 14, Confederate Lt. Gen. Polk was killed by an **artillery** shell. Johnston finally retreated to **Kennesaw Mountain** in the predawn hours of June 19. After engaging the Confederates at **Kolb's Farm** on June 22, Sherman blundered badly on June 27 by ordering a **frontal attack** against the Confederate entrenchments at Kennesaw Mountain. In the fiasco, Sherman lost nearly 3,000 men to Johnston's nearly 1,000.

On July 2, Johnston withdrew from the Kennesaw Mountain line and fell back to near the Chattahoochee River at Smyrna. Two days later, he retreated to the river itself. On July 8, Sherman sent Schofield upstream on another turning movement to cross the river on Johnston's right. Johnston fell back across the river on July 10 and took up a new position behind **Peachtree Creek**. The Chattahoochee was the last natural barrier behind which Johnston could stop Sherman outside Atlanta. When Sherman crossed it with his main force on July 16, he was within seven miles of the city. Dismayed with Johnston's failure to stop the enemy and his lack of aggressiveness, **Jefferson Davis** relieved him of command on July 17 and replaced him with Hood.

Hood immediately attacked on July 20 when Sherman's armies crossed Peachtree Creek along three separate fronts. Striking Thomas on Sherman's right, Hood hoped to hit the Federals while they were astride the stream, but delays in the assault allowed Thomas time to cross over.

A vicious battle erupted between Thomas and Hardee's and **Alexander P. Stewart's** corps, but the Federals repulsed all advances. Hood lost approximately 2,500 men at Peachtree Creek to Thomas's 1,800.

After the defeat, Hood withdrew into Atlanta's defenses, but on July 21 he began concentrating his army against McPherson's front on Sherman's left with the intention of attacking McPherson's left flank and front simultaneously. In the **Battle of Atlanta** on July 22, Hood's battle plan fell apart when Hardee's attack missed the Union flank, and **Benjamin F. Cheatham** failed to coordinate his frontal attack with Hardee. McPherson was killed in the fighting, but the Federals again repulsed Hood. In the battle, the Federals lost approximately 3,700 men to Hood's 8,000.

In position north and east of Atlanta, Sherman next tried to cut the railroads leading into the city from the south with **Stoneman's and McCook's Raid**. The cavalry rode out on July 27, with George Stoneman moving to the east of Atlanta and Edward M. McCook to the west. They were to meet south of the city and destroy the Macon & Western Railroad. Stoneman, however, divided his command in an attempt to liberate **Andersonville prison**. As a result, Wheeler's Confederate cavalry was able to catch and defeat the scattered Union columns and save the railroad.

At the same time Sherman sent out Stoneman and McCook, he also began sliding **Oliver O. Howard** (who assumed command of McPherson's army) around the west side of Atlanta to cut the Atlanta & West Point Railroad. On July 28, Hood countered by attacking Howard at **Ezra Church** with part of **Stephen D. Lee's** and Stewart's corps. The Confederates attacked an entrenched enemy and lost 5,000 men to Howard's 562, but did manage to save the railroad. In early August, Sherman next sent Schofield to extend Howard's right to continue his move toward the railroads south of Atlanta. On August 5–6, Hood stopped this advance in a series of clashes along **Utoy Creek**.

After Wheeler stopped Stoneman's and McCook's Raid in early August, Hood sent him to raid Sherman's supply line to the north. The Confederate cavalry unsuccessfully attacked Dalton on August 14–15, but Wheeler continued his raid into **Tennessee**. The monthlong raid destroyed some railroads and bridges but did not affect the campaign other than deprive Hood of his cavalry during the campaign's last weeks. Sherman countered **Wheeler's Raid** by sending **H. Judson Kilpatrick's** cavalry on August 18 to destroy the Macon & Western Railroad near Jonesboro. Kilpatrick destroyed some track but was driven off by the Confederates at **Lovejoy's Station** on August 20 and had to flee back to Federal lines.

Sherman continued his southward movement, and on August 28 his infantry reached the Atlanta & West Point Railroad. Within days, Schofield and Thomas cut the Macon & Western track around Rough and Ready and **Jonesboro**, respectively, and Howard marched to near Jonesboro. Hood shifted Lee's and Hardee's corps toward Jonesboro on August 30 and unsuccessfully attacked Howard there on August 31. Lee then was returned to Atlanta, while Hardee fought off a Union counterattack on September 1.

With his last railroad cut, Hood evacuated Atlanta on the afternoon of September 1, and elements of Sherman's XX Corps occupied the city the next morning. Sherman pursued Hood to Lovejoy Station but found him too strongly entrenched to attack. He then returned to Atlanta, and the campaign ended.

The Atlanta Campaign proved to be a turning point of the war. The much-needed victory boosted Union morale and helped reelect **Abraham Lincoln**, thus ensuring that the war would continue until a final Northern victory was achieved.

ATZERODT, GEORGE A. (1835–1865) CSA. A German immigrant who settled in **Maryland**, Atzerodt (ATZ-uh-rot) was a part-time Confederate smuggler who first joined **John Wilkes Booth** in a plot to kidnap **Abraham Lincoln**. Remaining with Booth after the kidnapping plan changed to murder, he was ordered to kill Vice President **Andrew Johnson** on the night of **Lincoln's assassination** but failed to act and fled the city. After being captured near Rockville, Maryland, on April 20, 1865, Atzerodt was tried with the other conspirators and hanged on July 7.

AUBURN, VIRGINIA, BATTLE OF (OCTOBER 13–14, 1863). During the October 1863 **Bristoe Station Campaign, J. E. B. Stuart's** Confederate cavalry was sent on a **reconnaissance** toward Catlett's Station. On October 13, Stuart encountered elements of **William H. French's** Union III Corps at Auburn, Virginia, and engaged in some **skirmishing**. While hiding in woods observing the enemy, Stuart suddenly became surrounded when the Union II Corps arrived at Auburn. Trapped between two enemy columns marching on a parallel road and **railroad**, Stuart sent word to **Robert E. Lee** for help. The next morning, **Richard S. Ewell's** II Corps attacked the Federals at Auburn from the south, and Stuart came out of hiding and attacked from the north. Stuart thus managed to escape his predicament and gave Lee vital intelligence on the enemy movement. Using this information, Lee pushed on, and **A. P. Hill** engaged the Federals at **Bristoe Station** later that day. In the fighting around Auburn, the total casualties numbered approximately 163.

AUGUR, CHRISTOPHER COLUMBUS (1821–1898) USA. A native of **New York**, Augur grew up in **Michigan** and graduated from **West Point** in 1843. Serving in the **Mexican War** and on the frontier, he rose to the rank of captain and was commandant of cadets at West Point when the Civil War began.

In May 1861, Augur was promoted to major of the newly created 7th U.S. Infantry. Promoted to brigadier general of volunteers in November 1861, he received command of an infantry **brigade** in **Irvin McDowell's division** of the **Army of the Potomac** and captured **Fredericksburg, Virginia**, in April 1862. He then was given command of a division in the **Army of Virginia** in July and was severely wounded at **Cedar Mountain** in August while serving under **Nathaniel P. Banks**. Augur won promotion to major general, which was to date from his wounding, and followed Banks to **Louisiana**, where in January 1863 he assumed command of a division in the XIX Corps. He commanded **Baton Rouge** in early 1863 and led Banks's assault troops during the **Port Hudson Campaign** attack of May 27, 1863. During the remainder of the siege, Augur commanded Banks's left wing. After the capture of Port Hudson, Augur returned to **Washington, D.C.**, in October and commanded the XXII Corps and the **Department of Washington** until 1866.

Augur was mustered out of the volunteers in September 1866 but remained in the **U.S. Army** as a colonel. He retired in 1885 as a brigadier general.

AUGUSTA (GEORGIA) ARSENAL. Originally a U.S. arsenal, the Augusta Arsenal was seized by the **Georgia** militia on January 24, 1861. While under Confederate control, it not only stored weapons but also produced small arms ammunition and some **artillery** shells. At one time the arsenal produced nearly 30,000 rounds of **rifle** ammunition daily.

AUGUSTA (GEORGIA) POWDER WORKS. In September 1861, Col. **George W. Rains** began building a powder works near the **Augusta (Georgia) Arsenal** to produce gunpowder for the Confederacy. Rains's factory was two miles long by May 1863 and consisted of dozens of buildings that produced 5,000 pounds of powder per day. The Augusta Powder Works was one of the Confederacy's most important munitions plants, producing 2,750,000 pounds of powder by war's end.

AVERASBORO, NORTH CAROLINA, BATTLE OF (MARCH 16, 1865). One of the war's last major engagements, this battle was fought during **William T. Sherman's Carolinas Campaign**. In March 1865, Sherman was marching from Fayetteville, North Carolina, in two columns, with Maj. Gen. **Henry W. Slocum** on the left threatening Raleigh, and Maj. Gen. **Oliver O. Howard** on the right threatening Goldsboro. Confederate Lt. Gen. **William J. Hardee** blocked Slocum's route near Averasboro with 6,000 men positioned along a ridge between a swamp and the Black River. Sherman sent the XX Corps against Hardee's front, while Col. Henry Case's **brigade** attempted to turn the Confederate right flank. Case enjoyed some success, but the XX Corps was stopped in its attacks against the ridge. Fighting ended at dark, and Hardee withdrew during the night. Hardee is estimated to have lost 850 men during the battle, while Slocum counted 682 casualties. Although the Federals forced the Confederates to retreat, the battle delayed Slocum's march and left him isolated from Sherman's right wing. Three days later the Confederates again tried to destroy Slocum's column at the **Battle of Bentonville**.

AVERELL, WILLIAM WOODS (1832–1900) USA. A native of **New York**, Averell (AV-rul) graduated from **West Point** in 1855. Assigned to frontier duty, he was severely wounded while fighting the Navajo **Indians** in 1858.

Averell was still recuperating from his wound when the **secession** crisis began but returned to service and in early 1861 carried secret Union correspondence to posts in **Arkansas** and the **Indian Territory**. Promoted to 1st lieutenant in May, he then joined Brig. Gen. **Andrew Porter's** staff as assistant adjutant general. After fighting at **First Manassas**, Averell was promoted from 1st lieutenant to colonel of the 3rd Pennsylvania Cavalry in August 1861. He led a cavalry **brigade** in the **Army of the Potomac** during the **Peninsula Campaign** and was praised for covering **George B. McClellan's** retreat during the **Seven Days Campaign**.

Averell served in the **Antietam Campaign** and was promoted to brigadier general of volunteers in late September 1862. After leading a cavalry brigade at **Fredericksburg**, he was given command of a cavalry **division** in February 1863 and in March won the first significant victory by Union cavalry over **J. E. B. Stuart's** Confederate troopers at the **Battle of Kelly's Ford**. During the **Chancellorsville Campaign**, Averell took part in **Stoneman's Raid** but was called back to the **army** by **Joseph Hooker** after demonstrating a lack of aggressiveness. Hooker then removed Averell from command after Averell showed a similar lack of spirit at the **Battle of Chancellorsville**. He held brigade and division commands in **West Virginia** for the rest of the year and participated in **Phillip H. Sheridan's 1864 Shenandoah Valley Campaign** at the head of a cavalry division. Averell fought at **Third Winchester** but was removed from command in September 1864 after a lackluster performance at **Fisher's Hill**.

Averell resigned from the **army** in May 1865 after having received **brevets** to brigadier general in the regular army and major general of volunteers. After the war, he served as the American consul general to Canada and became a successful inventor.

AYRES, ROMEYN BECK (1825–1888) USA. A native of **New York**, Ayres (AIRZ) graduated from **West Point** in 1847. He saw non-combat duty in Mexico at the end of the **Mexican War** and was promoted to captain in the 5th U.S. Artillery in May 1861.

After fighting well with the **artillery** at **First Manassas**, Ayres served as chief of artillery for several **divisions** in the **Army of the Potomac**. His excellent service with the VI Corps at **Antietam** earned him appointment as the **corps'** chief of artillery and a promotion to brigadier general of volunteers in November 1862. Ayres commanded the corps' artillery at **Fredericksburg** but in April 1863 was given command of an infantry **brigade** in the V Corps' 2nd Division. After leading it at **Chancellorsville**, he was given command of the division in June and led it during the **Gettysburg Campaign**. Afterward, Ayres was called on to maintain order in New York City after the **New York City Draft Riot** that summer. In March 1864, he assumed a brigade command in the corps' 1st Division and fought with it through the **Overland Campaign**. In June, Ayres returned to a division command and remained in that position until war's end, suffering a severe wound during the **Petersburg Campaign**.

At war's end, Ayres held the **brevet** rank of brigadier general and major general in both the regular and volunteer **armies**. He assumed command of the **Shenandoah Valley** after the war ended and was mustered out of the volunteers in April 1866. Remaining in the **U.S. Army** as a lieutenant colonel, Ayres served on garrison duty in the South during **Reconstruction**. In 1879, he was promoted to colonel of the 2nd U.S. Artillery and was sent to **Florida**, where he died while on active duty.

– B –

BAGBY, ARTHUR PENDLETON (1832–1921) CSA. Born in **Alabama**, Bagby graduated from **West Point** in 1852. He entered Confederate service as lieutenant colonel of the 7th Texas Cavalry and rose to regimental colonel in 1862. Bagby participated in **Henry Sibley's New Mexico Campaign** and fought at the **Battle of Galveston**, **Texas**, and along the **Louisiana** coast. After the fall of **Vicksburg, Mississippi**, the **Trans-Mississippi Department** was so isolated that **department** commander Gen. **Edmund Kirby Smith** began appointing general grade officers on his own, without the approval of the president or senate. Bagby was so appointed to brigadier general on March 17, 1864, and led a cavalry **brigade** in the **Red River Campaign**. Kirby Smith promoted him again, this time to major general in May 1865, but the war ended in the department within a month.

BAILEY, JOSEPH (1825–1867) USA. Born in **Ohio**, Bailey grew up in **Illinois** and became a trained engineer before moving to **Wisconsin** to become a lumberman. He entered Union service in July 1861 as a **company** captain in the 4th Wisconsin Infantry. After participating in the capture of **New Orleans, Louisiana**, Bailey became the city's acting chief engineer. His service as a military **engineer** in the **Port Hudson Campaign** earned him promotions to major in May 1863 and to lieutenant colonel in July. Bailey's greatest service came while serving under **Nathaniel P. Banks**, during the 1864 **Red River Campaign**. During the retreat down the Red River, **David Porter's** fleet became trapped by low water at Alexandria, Louisiana. Bailey supervised the construction of "Bailey's Dam," a series of wing dams that deepened the water and allowed Porter to extract his ships. Later, Bailey also built what then was one of the longest **pontoon bridges** in American history across the Atchafalaya (uh-CHAF-uh-LIE-uh) River, which allowed Banks to retreat safely to **Baton Rouge**. Bailey received the **Thanks of Congress** for his service and was **brevetted** brigadier general of volunteers, with a regular appointment to that rank coming in November 1864. Afterward, he served as an engineer during the **Mobile Campaign** and was awarded a brevet to major general of volunteers.

After the war, Bailey became a sheriff in **Missouri** and was shot and killed in 1867 by two men he had arrested.

BAILEY, THEODORUS (1805–1877) USA. A native of **New York**, Bailey entered the **U.S. Navy** as a midshipman when he was 13. He rose through the ranks to command the USS *Lexington* during the **Mexican War** and was made captain in 1855 after having served on several world cruises.

Bailey was one of the best naval commanders of the Civil War. After **blockade** duty with the USS *Colorado* at **Pensacola, Florida**, he served as **David Farragut's** second in command during the 1862 **Siege of**

Forts Jackson and St. Philip and the capture of **New Orleans, Louisiana.** It was Bailey who recommended that Farragut run past the forts at night and, while commanding the *Cayuga*, helped destroy the Confederate **River Defense Fleet** during the battle. At New Orleans, Bailey and one other officer won much praise by walking unarmed through a hostile crowd to demand the city's surrender from authorities.

Bailey assumed command of the East **Gulf Blockading Squadron** in November 1862 and captured 150 vessels in 18 months. After that duty, he was put in command of the Portsmouth Navy Yard for the duration of the war and retired after being promoted to rear admiral in 1866.

BAILEY'S DAM. *See* BAILEY, JOSEPH; RED RIVER CAMPAIGN.

BAIRD, ABSALOM (1824–1905) USA. A native of **Pennsylvania**, Baird graduated from **West Point** in 1849. During his antebellum military career, he fought in the **Seminole Wars**, taught at West Point, and served on frontier duty.

A 1st lieutenant when the Civil War began, Baird was appointed a **brevet** captain in May 1861 and served at **First Manassas** as adjutant general for Brig. Gen. **Daniel Tyler**. After the battle, he and other officers received the president's thanks for protecting Confederate **prisoners** against an angry mob in **Washington, D.C.** Baird was promoted to the rank of captain and then major in the latter part of 1861 and in March 1862 was appointed inspector general and chief of staff for the **Army of the Potomac's** IV Corps. He then served through the **Peninsula Campaign** and was promoted to brigadier general of volunteers in April 1862.

Sent west, Baird commanded **divisions** in the **Army of Kentucky** before being given a division in the **Army of the Cumberland** in June 1863. As part of the **George H. Thomas's** XIV Corps, he participated in the **Tullahoma Campaign**, helped Thomas hold **Snodgrass Hill** at **Chickamauga**, and fought at **Missionary Ridge** during the **Chattanooga Campaign**, earning two brevets for the latter two battles. During the **Atlanta Campaign**, Baird was highly praised for leading the attack that finally defeated the Confederates at **Jonesboro**. His actions there also earned him the **Medal of Honor** in 1896. After the fall of Atlanta, Baird participated in the **March to the Sea** and the **Carolinas Campaign**.

Baird was considered to be one of the best Union division commanders of the war, and his superiors often recommended him for promotion, but he never received a higher commission. He ended the war as a brevet major general in both the regular and volunteer service and remained in the **U.S. Army**. Baird finally was promoted to brigadier general of regulars in 1885 and served as the army's inspector general. He also earned the French Legion of Honor while serving as an observer in France in 1887.

BAKER, ALPHEUS (1828–1891) CSA. Baker was a native of **South Carolina** and taught school in South Carolina, **Georgia**, and **Alabama** before passing the Alabama bar in 1849. In 1861, he briefly served as a delegate to Alabama's constitutional convention before resigning in January 1861 to join his hometown **company**, the Eufaula Rifles.

After being elected company captain, Baker served at **Pensacola, Florida**, before being sent to **Tennessee** in November 1861, where he was elected colonel of the 1st Alabama, Tennessee, Mississippi Regiment. Baker fought at **New Madrid, Missouri**, and was captured with his **regiment** at **Island No. 10**. After being **exchanged** in September, his regiment was reorganized as the 54th Alabama. During the **Vicksburg Campaign**, Baker was wounded in the foot at **Champion Hill**. After returning to duty, he took command of an Alabama **brigade** and was appointed brigadier general, probably in March 1864.

During the **Atlanta Campaign**, Baker had a horse killed under him at **Resaca** and was wounded again at **Ezra Church**. Although his **division** commander often praised his actions, **corps** commander **Stephen D. Lee** was critical of Baker for showing a lack of aggressiveness and indecisiveness. After the campaign, Baker's brigade briefly served at Mobile, Alabama, before participating in the **Carolinas Campaign** and capturing more than 200 **prisoners** at **Bentonville**.

After the war, Baker resumed his Alabama law practice before eventually moving to **Kentucky**.

BAKER, EDWARD DICKINSON (1811–1861) USA. Born in Great Britain, Baker moved to the United States as a child. He was a veteran of both the Black Hawk and **Mexican Wars** and served as an **Illinois** congressman, a **Republican Party** leader in **California**, and a U.S. senator from **Oregon**. A renowned speaker, Baker was a close friend of **Abraham Lincoln**, who named a son for him.

While still a senator, Baker organized the 71st Pennsylvania and was commissioned its colonel in June 1861. In September, Lincoln appointed him a major general of volunteers. Baker never officially accepted the appointment since it would have required him to resign his senate seat, but on October 21, 1861, he led a **brigade** in an attack on a Confederate position at Leesburg, Virginia. Through poor **reconnaissance** and planning, Baker's command was trapped and mauled at **Ball's Bluff, Virginia**. Baker was killed, and many of his men were lost. Because of his popularity, Baker became a hero, while his superior, Brig. Gen. **Charles P. Stone**, was blamed for the fiasco and ruined.

BAKER, LAFAYETTE CURRY (1826–1868) USA. Born in **New York**, Baker moved to **California** and became a member of the Vigilance Committee of San Francisco. Having an interest in intelligence gathering, he went east when the Civil War began and offered to spy on Confederate forces around Manassas, Virginia. Baker was captured during this endeavor but convinced Confederate authorities that he was actually pro-Southern. He then was sent North as a double agent but retained his Union loyalty and brought **Abraham Lincoln** valuable information about the Confederates. During the **Second Manassas Campaign**, Baker rode 100 miles to carry secret dispatches between **Edwin M. Stanton** and **Nathaniel P. Banks**.

In May 1863, Stanton commissioned Baker colonel of the 1st D.C. Cavalry, a special intelligence **regiment** that served the War Department. Working with William Wood to suppress Confederate activity around **Washington, D.C.**, Baker had numerous people imprisoned and became hated by frightened citizens. Since **Allan Pinkerton's** intelligence service was abolished when **George B. McClellan** was relieved of command of the **Army of the Potomac**, Stanton allowed Baker to establish the National Detectives, an intelligence organization that answered only to Stanton. Throughout the war, Baker hunted spies, disloyal citizens, counterfeiters, and corrupt contractors. He was greatly feared because of his almost unlimited power and had a reputation for being as corrupt as the criminals he hunted.

Baker headed the pursuit of **John Wilkes Booth** in 1865 and was present when Booth was killed. For his role in the hunt, Baker received $3,750 of the reward money and was appointed brigadier general of volunteers in April 1865. President **Andrew Johnson** finally dismissed him for being corrupt and for conducting secret operations against the White House. Baker testified against Johnson during the impeachment proceedings and later wrote the book *History of the United States Secret Service*.

After the Civil War, Baker lived in obscurity and died in Philadelphia, Pennsylvania. Some people believed he was murdered to cover up the illegal activities in which he had been involved.

BAKER, LAURENCE SIMMONS (1830–1907) CSA. A native of **North Carolina**, Baker graduated last in his 1851 **West Point** class and for the next 10 years served on the frontier, rising to the rank of 1st lieutenant.

Although Baker opposed **secession**, he resigned his commission in May 1861 and joined the Confederacy as lieutenant colonel of the 1st North Carolina Cavalry. During the **army's** reorganization in April 1862, he was elected regimental colonel. Baker fought in most of the major campaigns of the **Army of Northern Virginia** and earned special praise during the **Seven Days Campaign** and at **Second Manassas**, **Antietam**, and **Brandy Station**. Despite his skill on the battlefield, he had one weakness and was forced to sign a pledge for **J. E. B. Stuart** that he would abstain from alcohol for the war's duration.

Baker assumed command of **Wade Hampton's brigade** after Hampton was wounded at **Gettysburg**, even though Baker also had suffered a slight wound. After covering **Robert E. Lee's** retreat back to **Virginia**, he was promoted to brigadier general in late July 1863. Eight days later, Baker received a severe arm wound in a **skirmish**, but Lee also praised him for his leadership. Baker's shattered arm prevented him from returning to cavalry duty, so in June 1864 he was put in command of a **district** in the **Department of North Carolina**. He received another wound while serving there, and during the **Carolinas Campaign** he resumed command of his old brigade and fought at **Bentonville**. Absent from **Joseph E. Johnston's** army when it surrendered, Baker subsequently disbanded his brigade and was **paroled** at Raleigh, North Carolina, in May 1865.

BAKER'S CREEK, MISSISSIPPI, BATTLE OF (MAY 16, 1863). *See* CHAMPION HILL, MISSISSIPPI, BATTLE OF.

BALDWIN, WILLIAM EDWIN (1827–1864) CSA. A native of **South Carolina**, Baldwin moved to **Mississippi** as a child and there became a bookstore merchant. Having served in the state militia, he was commissioned a **company** captain in the 14th Mississippi and entered Confederate service in the spring of 1861.

After being ordered to **Pensacola, Florida**, Baldwin was elected regimental colonel. Later in the year, he was stationed in central **Kentucky** and in eastern **Tennessee** and in February 1862 earned praise for his role as a **brigade** commander at **Fort Donelson**. Baldwin was captured there and held **prisoner** until **exchanged** in August.

Commissioned a brigadier general in September 1862, Baldwin took command of an infantry brigade in the **Army of West Tennessee** and was commended for his service at **Coffeeville** and in the **Vicksburg Campaign**. He was wounded during the siege of **Vicksburg** and was the only general grade officer who opposed **John C. Pemberton's** surrender of the city. After being exchanged a second time, Baldwin was ordered to Mobile, Alabama. On February 19, 1864, he died near Dog River Factory, Alabama, from injuries received when he fell from his horse after a stirrup broke.

BALLOONS. Both the Union and Confederate armies used balloons for observation and intelligence gathering, but the Union was more successful. **Thaddeus S. C. Lowe** operated several balloons for **George B. McClellan's Army of the Potomac** during the 1862 **Peninsula Campaign**. The largest was a silk balloon 45 feet tall that was coated with linseed oil, benzine, and japan drier to make it air tight. The early balloons used hot air, although Lowe later turned to hydrogen, and were tethered to the ground by a rope, which was played out to allow the balloon to rise. Sometimes a **telegraph** wire was run into the basket to allow the observers to notify officers on the ground instantly of their findings as they scouted the enemy lines.

Captain **Edward Porter Alexander** also supervised a balloon for the **Confederate army** on the peninsula. His is the only documented time the Confederates used balloons. Alexander's was a gas-filled balloon that was tethered to a boat and used on the James River until the boat ran aground and was captured in July 1862. Another Confederate balloon was said to have been used at **Charleston, South Carolina**, but there is no firm documentation supporting its existence.

BALL'S BLUFF, VIRGINIA, BATTLE OF (OCTOBER 21, 1861). In the autumn of 1861, Union forces were attempting to force Confederate Col. **Nathan G. Evans** out of his Leesburg, Virginia, position by marching upriver from Dranesville. Brigadier General **Charles P. Stone** was ordered to assist in the operation by **demonstrating** against Evans from his headquarters near Poolesville, Maryland.

Stone ordered one of his **brigades** under Col. **Edward D. Baker** to cross the river and threaten Evans's left flank, while another brigade advanced against the Confederate right flank. On October 21, 1861, a patrol in the Union center was attacked at Ball's Bluff, prompting Baker to move his brigade across the Potomac River at Harrison's Island to reinforce it. Unfortunately, Baker did not carry out proper **reconnaissance** or assemble enough boats to cross the river quickly. As a result, he advanced against Evans's center rather than the left flank, as he believed he was doing. When the Union column from Dranesville turned back, the Confederates were able to concentrate their force at Ball's Bluff and attack Baker while he was still crossing the river and making his way up steep bluffs. Baker was killed in the fighting (which was also known as the Battle of Conrad's Ferry), and his brigade suffered 921 casualties (mostly captured) out of 1,700 men engaged. Evans lost just 155 men.

Since Baker was a close friend of **Abraham Lincoln** and a U.S. senator from **Oregon**, he escaped censure for the disaster. Instead, Stone was unfairly made the scapegoat, and the **Committee on the Conduct of the War** was formed to investigate this and other Union defeats. The Committee believed Stone was "unsound" on the **slavery** issue, and he was branded a traitor. He was arrested on February 9, 1862, and was imprisoned for over six months, spending 50 days in solitary confinement. Stone never was charged with a crime and finally was released on August 16, 1862.

BALTIMORE, MARYLAND, RIOT (APRIL 19, 1861). **Maryland** was a slave state whose loyalties were divided during the Civil War. After the firing on **Fort Sumter**, many Marylanders opposed **Abraham Lincoln's** call for volunteers, and tensions ran high when Union troops began passing through Baltimore on April 18, 1861, on their way to **Washington, D.C.** These first soldiers passed peacefully through town, but angry crowds were incited by pro-Confederate agitators and violence broke out on April 19 as the 6th Massachusetts marched through the city.

For its protection, the **regiment** remained on the **railroad** cars and was drawn by horses through the streets to the connecting railhead. A mob attacked one car with stones and obstructed the passage of another. The soldiers then disembarked and began marching through the city, with the mayor and police chief at their head trying to calm the situation. When more stones were thrown and shots rang out, the soldiers returned fire. Four **Massachusetts** soldiers were killed and 39 were injured in the riot. The number of civilian casualties is uncertain, but one report claimed 12 were killed and many more were wounded.

The city exploded in anti-Union sentiment, and Gov. **Thomas Hicks** threatened **secession**. City officials then burned railroad bridges north of town to cut railroad service with the North in an attempt to prevent further violence. For a few days, secessionists seemed in charge of the city, but passions calmed after a week or so, and the majority pro-Union citizens regained control. On the night of May 13, additional Union troops under Maj. Gen. **Benjamin F. Butler** arrived and ensured Union control of Baltimore. The riot was a traumatic event for the city and state and was memorialized in a verse in the state song, "Maryland, My Maryland."

BANKS, NATHANIEL PRENTISS (1816–1894) USA. A native of **Massachusetts**, Banks was a self-made man known as the "Bobbin Boy of Massachusetts" because he began work early in the state's textile industry. With little formal education, he became a lawyer and entered politics, running unsuccessfully for the legislature seven times before finally being elected. Banks became affiliated with five different parties during his career and served as the speaker of the house, president of the state's 1853 constitutional convention, and in the **U.S. Congress**. After an early career in the **Democratic Party**, he joined the **Republican Party** because of his opposition to the **Kansas-Nebraska Act** and was elected the U.S. Speaker of the House in 1856 on the 133rd ballot. A moderate on the **slavery** issue, Banks was elected governor of Massachusetts in 1858 but resigned in January 1861.

Abraham Lincoln appointed Banks a major general of volunteers in May 1861 because of his political influence, but Banks made a poor general. He briefly commanded the **Departments of Annapolis** and **of the Shenandoah** in the summer of 1861 but then was given command of a **division** in the **Army of the Potomac**. In March 1862, Banks was given command of the V Corps and the following month was returned to command the Department of the Shenandoah. Although he defeated **Stonewall Jackson** at the **First Battle of Kernstown** in March 1862, Banks later was chased out of the **Shenandoah Valley** in **Jackson's 1862 Shenandoah Valley Campaign**. Adding insult to injury, the Confederates captured so many Union supplies that they nicknamed Banks "Commissary Banks." In June 1862, Banks was given command of the **Army of Virginia's** II Corps and engaged Jackson at **Cedar Mountain** two months later but again was defeated. After briefly commanding the Military District of Washington that autumn, he was ordered in December to replace **Benjamin F. Butler** in command of the **Department of the Gulf**.

In the spring of 1863, Banks cleared out **Richard Taylor's** small **Confederate army** from south **Louisiana** in the **Bayou Teche Campaign** and then began his **Port Hudson Campaign**. In a long siege, interspersed with unsuccessful bloody assaults, he wore down the Confederates until the stronghold finally surrendered on July 9, 1863. For the victory, Banks received the **Thanks of Congress**. Later in 1863, Banks tried to establish a Union presence in **Texas** through the unsuccessful **Texas Overland Expedition**.

In the spring of 1864, Banks launched the **Red River Campaign** with Adm. **David Porter** in hopes of strengthening his political position by invading the Louisiana interior to capture cotton and the Confederate capital of Shreveport. He mishandled the invasion, however, and was stopped by Taylor at the **Battle of Mansfield**. Although Banks won a tactical victory the next day at **Pleasant Hill**, he abandoned the invasion and retreated unnecessarily. He then was replaced as **department** commander in September 1864 but returned as commander for a brief time at war's end.

Banks resigned from the army in August 1865 and resumed his political career in Massachusetts. He later served 12 years in Congress.

BAR SHOT. An obsolete type of **artillery** ammunition by the time of the Civil War, bar shot consisted of two iron balls connected by an iron shaft, resembling dumbbells. When fired, it whirled toward its target and was designed to destroy a ship's sails and rigging.

BARBETTE. This was a raised wooden platform, sometimes made of earth, on which an **artillery** piece was set in order to fire over a parapet instead of firing through the parapet's embrasure. Barbettes usually were found only in permanent or semipermanent fortifications.

BARHAMSVILLE, VIRGINIA, BATTLE OF (MAY 7, 1862). *See* ELTHAM'S LANDING, VIRGINIA, BATTLE OF.

BARKSDALE, WILLIAM (1821–1863) CSA. Barksdale was a **Tennessee** native who later moved to **Mississippi** and became a newspaper editor and **Mexican War** veteran. In 1852, he was elected to the **U.S. Congress**, where he became a strong defender of **slavery** and **states rights**.

Barksdale resigned his congressional seat in January 1861 and served as Mississippi's quartermaster general before being appointed colonel of the 13th Mississippi. After participating in the **First Battle of Manassas**, he was court-martialed for drunkenness but escaped punishment by taking a temperance oath. Barksdale's **regiment** then was sent to the Virginia Peninsula as part of a Mississippi **brigade** that joined the **Army of Northern Virginia**. During the **Seven Days Campaign**, he took over the brigade when its commander was killed. After being praised for his performance at **Malvern Hill**, Barksdale was promoted to brigadier general in August 1862 and took permanent command of **Barksdale's Mississippi Brigade**.

Barksdale's brigade helped capture **Harpers Ferry**, **Virginia**, during the **Antietam Campaign** and fought well at the Battle of Antietam. In December 1862, he earned his greatest fame when his brigade held up for an entire day the Union **Army of the Potomac's** crossing of the Rappahannock River at **Fredericksburg**. During the 1863 **Chancellorsville Campaign**, Barksdale remained at Fredericksburg holding Marye's Heights until forced to retreat on May 3. On July 2, 1863, his brigade participated in **James Longstreet's** attack against the Union left flank at **Gettysburg**. After pushing the Federals out of the **Peach Orchard**, Barksdale was shot in the lung and leg. Taken **prisoner** when his brigade was forced to fall back, he was carried to a field hospital and died on July 3.

BARKSDALE'S MISSISSIPPI BRIGADE. One of the famous fighting units in **Robert E. Lee's Army of Northern Virginia**, this **brigade** was commanded by Brig. Gen. **William Barksdale**. It contained the 13th, 17th, 18th, and 21st **Mississippi regiments** and served in **Lafayette McLaws's division** of **James Longstreet's corps**. The brigade was praised for its fighting ability in many battles, especially at **Antietam**, **Fredericksburg**, and **Gettysburg**. Its finest moment came on December 11, 1862, when it was positioned in Fredericksburg and prevented the Union crossing of the Rappahannock River for an entire day. After Barksdale was killed at Gettysburg, Brig. Gen. **Benjamin Grubb Humphreys** assumed command of the unit.

BARLOW, FRANCIS CHANNING (1834–1896) USA. A native of **New York**, Barlow grew up in **Massachusetts**, graduated from Harvard University, and became a lawyer. When the Civil War began, he quit his New York law practice in April 1861 to enlist as a private in the 90-day 12th New York. After his enlistment expired, Barlow returned to the **army** in August as lieutenant colonel of the 61st New York and was promoted to colonel in April 1862. As part of the **Army of the Potomac**, he fought in the **Peninsula Campaign** and then was severely wounded at **Antietam**.

Barlow was promoted to brigadier general of volunteers in September 1862 and was given command of a **brigade** in the Army of the Potomac's XI Corps. He led the brigade at **Chancellorsville** and the **division** in the **Gettysburg Campaign**. On the first day of battle at Gettysburg, Barlow was shot, temporarily paralyzed, and captured. After being **exchanged**, he was given command of a II Corps division, which he led in the 1864 **Overland Campaign**. At **Spotsylvania**, Barlow's division helped overrun the "Mule Shoe" and then engaged in fierce combat at the Bloody Angle. Barlow was on sick leave through much of the **Petersburg Campaign**, but he again commanded a division at **Sailor's Creek** in April 1865. He was promoted to major general in May but resigned his commission in November 1865 and resumed his law practice.

After the war, Barlow was elected New York's secretary of state twice, served as a U.S. marshal, and was elected state attorney general. He also helped prosecute the corrupt Tweed Ring and was a founder of the American Bar Association.

BARNARD, GEORGE N. (1819–1902) USA. An established **New York** photographer when the Civil War began, Barnard is said to have made the first news photograph when he documented an 1853 mill fire in Oswego, New York. He briefly joined **Mathew Brady** at the beginning of the war and photographed the **First Manassas** battlefield and the **Peninsula Campaign**. Barnard then left Brady and went west, where the government hired him as an official photographer.

Barnard photographed **Lookout Mountain** and other scenes of the **Chattanooga Campaign** and reportedly was present with **William T. Sherman's** armies during the **Atlanta Campaign**. After the war, he photographed many places associated with that campaign, the **March to the Sea**, and the **Carolinas Campaign**. The federal government also hired Barnard after the war to photograph the Confederate defenses of Atlanta, Georgia. These images were compiled in the 1866 book *Photographic Views of Sherman's Campaign*, and are included in Keith F. Davis, *George N. Barnard, Photographer of Sherman's Campaign*. Barnard continued his photography after leaving federal service and documented the Great Chicago Fire before briefly working with George Eastman.

BARNARD, JOHN GROSS (1815–1882) USA. A native of **Massachusetts**, Barnard graduated second in his 1833 **West Point** class. Assigned to the **engineers**, he worked on various construction projects before the Civil War and served as superintendent of the academy for one year.

In 1861, Barnard was a major of engineers and supervised the construction of the defenses of **Washington, D.C.** He then was appointed the **Army of the Potomac's** chief engineer in August 1861 and was promoted to brigadier general of volunteers the following month. After serving with **George B. McClellan** in the **Peninsula Campaign**, Barnard was placed in command of Washington's defenses from 1862 to 1864. In July 1864, he became **U. S. Grant's** chief engineer and served him well during the **Petersburg Campaign**. For his war service, Barnard was promoted to colonel in the regular **army** in December 1865 and was **brevetted** major general in both the regular and volunteer service.

After the war, Barnard became a renowned author in the field of science and helped organize the National Academy of Sciences. He was one of those soldiers who served in the Civil War with distinction and skill but is little known because his service was in the unglamorous engineers.

BARNES, JAMES (1801–1869) USA. A native of **Massachusetts**, Barnes graduated near the top of the **West Point** class of 1829. He then taught at the academy until resigning from the **U.S. Army** in 1836 to become a railroad engineer.

In July 1861, Barnes entered Union service as colonel of the 18th Massachusetts. After serving with distinction in the **Peninsula Cam-**

paign, he was given command of a **brigade** in the **Army of the Potomac's** V Corps in July 1862. Barnes led his brigade at **Antietam** and was promoted to brigadier general of volunteers in November 1862.

Barnes fought with his brigade in the battles of **Fredericksburg** and **Chancellorsville** and was elevated to a **division** command prior to the **Gettysburg Campaign**. At Gettysburg, he was wounded and did not perform particularly well, but one of his brigades under Col. **Strong Vincent** helped defend Little Round Top. Never fully recovering from his wound, Barnes served in various administrative positions for the remainder of the war and was **brevetted** major general of volunteers in March 1865 for his war service.

Barnes was mustered out of the service in January 1866. In 1868, he was appointed to the government commission investigating the building of a **railroad** and **telegraph** line by the Union Pacific Railroad.

BARNES, JOSEPH K. (1817–1883) USA. A native of **Pennsylvania**, Barnes attended Harvard University and graduated from the University of Pennsylvania's Medical School. He joined the **U.S. Army** in 1840 and served in the Medical Corps during the **Seminole** and **Mexican Wars**.

Stationed in the Pacific Northwest as a major when the Civil War began, Barnes returned east to serve as a surgeon. In 1862, he was seen as an effective and apolitical officer and was appointed acting surgeon general by Secretary of War **Edwin Stanton** after Surgeon General **William A. Hammond** was relieved of duty. Barnes was appointed medical inspector and was promoted to lieutenant colonel in February 1863 and to colonel in August 1863.

When Hammond left the **army** in August 1864, Barnes was promoted to brigadier general and was officially appointed surgeon general. He continued many reforms Hammond had begun and greatly improved the Medical Corps. For his valuable war service, Barnes was **brevetted** major general in the regular army in March 1865.

Barnes supervised the publishing of the *Medical and Surgical History of the War of the Rebellion* and provided medical attention for assassinated presidents **Abraham Lincoln** and **James Garfield**.

BARNWELL, ROBERT WOODWARD (1801–1882) CSA. A native of **South Carolina**, Barnwell graduated from Harvard University and became a prominent Southern politician. After serving in the state legislature, he was elected to the U.S. House of Representatives in 1829 and in 1831 and signed South Carolina's 1832 Ordinance of Nullification.

Barnwell left Congress in 1833 to become a planter and president of South Carolina College. When **John C. Calhoun** died in 1850, Barnwell was appointed to replace him in the U.S. Senate until 1853.

Although a moderate in 1861, Barnwell still supported **secession** and was a delegate to the state's secession convention. He also was a member of the Provisional **Confederate Congress**, where he supported **Jefferson Davis** for president and signed the **Confederate constitution**. Barnwell turned down Davis's offer to be appointed secretary of state but remained a Davis supporter in the Confederate Senate. As chairman of the Senate Finance Committee, he was an influential member of the Confederate government for most of the war.

Barnwell was appointed faculty chairman of the University of South Carolina in early 1865 and held that position until 1873. He then served as the university's librarian until his death in 1882.

***BARON DE KALB*, USS.** *See ST. LOUIS*, USS.

BARRINGER, RUFUS (1821–1895) CSA. A native of **North Carolina**, Barringer was a graduate of the University of North Carolina and the brother-in-law of Confederate generals **Stonewall Jackson** and **Daniel H. Hill**. He became a lawyer and was elected to the state assembly in 1848 and to the state senate in 1851.

Barringer opposed **secession** but when war came raised a **company** of cavalry and entered Confederate service in May 1861 as a captain in the 1st North Carolina Cavalry. He participated in most of the campaigns of the **Army of Northern Virginia** and was severely wounded in the face at **Brandy Station**. After winning commendations for his service at **Gettysburg**, Barringer was promoted to major in August 1863 and to lieutenant colonel in November. For meritorious service during the **Bristoe Station Campaign**, he was promoted to brigadier general in June 1864 and was given command of a North Carolina cavalry **brigade**. Barringer was consistently praised by his superiors and at times held temporary **division** command. When finally captured in April 1865, he was said to have been involved in 76 fights, had been wounded three times, and had two horses killed under him.

After the war, Barringer resumed his law practice and joined the **Republican Party** during **Reconstruction**.

BARRON, SAMUEL (1809–1888) CSA. A native of **Virginia**, Barron was the son of Commodore Samuel Barron and in honor of his father was appointed a midshipman in the **U.S. Navy** at age two. He began his own navy service in 1820, rose to the rank of captain by 1855, and became known to his colleagues as "Navy Diplomat."

After **Abraham Lincoln** was inaugurated in March 1861, Barron may have conspired to seize control of the Navy Department from **Gideon Welles**, but Welles dismissed him from service in April. Joining the Confederacy, Barron was appointed a captain in **Virginia's** navy and headed its Office of Naval Detail and Equipment. He assumed that same position with the **Confederate navy** when Virginia's naval forces were incorporated into it.

Barron was appointed commander in June 1861 and persuaded **Stephen R. Mallory** to put him in command of the naval defenses of Virginia and **North Carolina**. He arrived at Fort Hatteras just as Union forces were making their attack on **Hatteras Inlet**, **North Carolina**. At the request of the fort's commander, Barron took charge of the **artillery** on August 28, but he was forced to surrender the next day. After being **exchanged** 11 months later, Barron commanded naval forces in Virginia until he was sent on a mission to Great Britain in the summer of 1863 as a captain. There, he was to work with agent **James D. Bulloch**, appoint officers for the two **Laird rams** being built for the Confederacy, and inspect other ships being built for the navy. When British officials seized the two **rams**, Barron moved to France to continue efforts to acquire warships but had little success other than acquiring the CSS *Stonewall*. When ordered to return to the Confederacy, he resigned his position in late February 1865.

When the war ended, Barron returned to Virginia, retired, and died there in 1888.

BARRY, JOHN DECATUR (1839–1867) CSA. A native of **North Carolina**, Barry was a graduate of the University of North Carolina. He entered Confederate service as a private in the 8th North Carolina (later redesignated the 18th North Carolina) and was elected **company** captain in April 1862. Serving with the **Army of Northern Virginia**, Barry was severely wounded at **Frayser's Farm** during the **Seven Days Campaign** and after winning commendations for his service at **Antietam** was promoted to major in November 1862. On the night of May 2, 1863, at **Chancellorsville**, he ordered his men to fire on a group of horsemen he believed to be the enemy and mortally wounded **Stonewall Jackson**. Despite this tragic accident, Barry was promoted to regimental colonel, to rank from May 3, and temporarily led his **brigade** during **Pickett's Charge** at **Gettysburg**.

After earning more commendations for his service in the **Wilderness**, Barry took over the **brigade** after **James Lane** was wounded at **Cold Harbor** and led it for the remainder of the **Overland Campaign**. When he was given the temporary rank of brigadier general in August 1864,

Barry became one of the Confederacy's youngest generals. This temporary commission was canceled in September, when Lane returned to duty. Barry was also forced to leave the field at that time, having had two fingers shot off in July. He was able to return to duty in early 1865 as commander of the **Department of North Carolina**.

After the war, Barry settled in North Carolina, where he ran a newspaper.

BARRY, WILLIAM FARQUHAR (1818–1879) USA. A native of **New York**, Barry graduated from **West Point** in 1838. He rose to the rank of captain in the antebellum **U.S. Army** and served with the **artillery** in the **Seminole** and **Mexican Wars** and in **Bleeding Kansas**.

In May 1861, Barry was promoted to major in the 5th U.S. Artillery and served at **Fort Pickens, Florida**, before becoming chief of artillery for **Irvin McDowell** in June. He served well at **First Manassas** and in August 1861 was promoted to brigadier general of volunteers and was appointed chief of artillery for **George B. McClellan's Army of the Potomac**. Barry participated in the **Seven Days Campaign** but then asked to be reassigned. From September 1862 to March 1864, he served in various positions in the **Washington, D.C.**, defenses, including chief of artillery, and earned a promotion to lieutenant colonel of regulars in August 1863. In March 1864, Barry became **William T. Sherman's** chief of artillery and served with him throughout the **Atlanta Campaign**. This service earned him **brevets** of colonel in the regular **army** and major general of volunteers. Barry then accompanied Sherman on his **March to the Sea** and served under him throughout the **Carolinas Campaign**, earning brevets of brigadier general and major general in the regular army.

Barry remained in the army after the war with the permanent rank of colonel.

BARTLETT, JOSEPH JACKSON (1834–1893) USA. A native of **New York**, Bartlett became a lawyer in 1858 and was practicing law when the Civil War began. He enlisted in the 27th New York and was elected captain and then major in May 1861. At **First Manassas**, Bartlett took command of the **regiment** when the colonel was wounded and earned much praise for conducting a fighting retreat and helping to delay the Confederate pursuit. Promoted to colonel in September 1861 for this action, he was given command of a **brigade** in the **Army of the Potomac's** VI Corps in May 1862 and fought well at **Gaines' Mill, Crampton's Gap**, and **Antietam**.

Bartlett was promoted to brigadier general of volunteers in October 1862 and fought at **Salem Church** and **Gettysburg** the following year. In late 1863, he was transferred to the V Corps and for the remainder of the war often served as a temporary **division** commander. Bartlett served with distinction in nearly every campaign in the **Virginia** theater, including the **Overland** and **Petersburg Campaigns**, although he was forced to flee his camp in his underwear to avoid being captured during the **Mine Run Campaign**. He was **brevetted** major general of volunteers in August 1864 and was chosen to receive the surrendered arms of the Confederate **Army of Northern Virginia** at **Appomattox**.

Bartlett left the **army** in 1866 and later served as a diplomat to Sweden and Norway and as a deputy pension commissioner.

BARTLETT, WILLIAM FRANCIS (1840–1876) USA. A native of **Massachusetts**, Bartlett was enrolled at Harvard University when the Civil War began. He enlisted as a private in the 4th Massachusetts Battalion in April 1861 and became a **company** captain in the 20th Massachusetts in August. Bartlett fought at **Ball's Bluff** in October 1861 (where only he and one other regimental officer were able to report for duty afterward) and then lost a leg at **Yorktown** while serving with the **Army of the Potomac's** II Corps.

Bartlett graduated with his Harvard class in 1862 and in November was commissioned colonel of the nine-month 19th Massachusetts. Sent to **Louisiana**, he participated in the **Port Hudson Campaign**, where two wounds so badly injured him that he was forced to remain mounted in future battles. When his **regiment** was mustered out of service, Bartlett organized the 57th Massachusetts and was wounded a fourth time in the **Wilderness** while leading it during the **Overland Campaign**.

After fighting at **Cold Harbor**, Bartlett was promoted to brigadier general of volunteers in June 1864. The following month, he was captured during the **Petersburg Campaign** at the **Battle of the Crater** after receiving his fifth wound and having his cork leg destroyed by bullets. After spending two months in **Libby Prison**, Bartlett was **exchanged. Brevetted** major general of volunteers in March 1865, he briefly commanded the **division** after hostilities ended.

Bartlett was mustered out of the volunteers in July 1866 and remained in **Richmond, Virginia**, for a time working for the **Tredegar Iron Works**, where he used his position to help some of his former enemies. He eventually returned to Massachusetts and repeatedly refused entreaties to enter politics.

BARTON, CLARA HARLOWE (1821–1912) USA. A native of **Massachusetts**, Barton was home-educated and became a teacher at age 15. When the Civil War began, she was living in **Washington, D.C.**, and working in the Patent Office. In the spring of 1861, Barton organized a relief program for the soldiers of the 6th Massachusetts who had been attacked in the **Baltimore, Maryland, Riot**. Appalled that wounded soldiers suffered from a lack of supplies after **First Manassas**, she asked for donations in a Massachusetts newspaper and began distributing what she received. Barton's efforts were so successful that she received a pass from the Surgeon General to travel with **army** ambulances in order to dispense medical supplies and provide care for the patients. Known as the "Angel of the Battlefield," Barton became famous as she served in **Virginia** with the **Army of the Potomac** and with other Union forces at **Charleston, South Carolina**. The only formal relationship she ever had with the army was when she served as superintendent of nurses for Maj. Gen. **Benjamin F. Butler** at **Bermuda Hundred, Virginia**.

A less well-known aspect of Barton's work came at war's end when **Abraham Lincoln** commissioned her to identify those soldiers missing in action in order to inform the families of their loved ones' fates. After the war, she served with the International Red Cross in the Franco-Prussian War, and in 1881 organized the American Red Cross. Barton also helped get the United States to sign the Geneva Agreement and worked in Cuba during the Spanish-American War.

BARTON, SETH MAXWELL (1829–1900) CSA. A native of **Virginia**, Barton graduated from **West Point** in 1849 and was posted to the southwest. He was a captain when the Civil War began but in June 1861 accepted an appointment in the **Confederate army** as lieutenant colonel of the 3rd Arkansas. Barton resigned his **U.S. Army** commission three days later.

Barton fought at **Cheat Mountain, Virginia**, and was **Stonewall Jackson's** chief **engineer** during his expedition to Romney, Virginia. **Jefferson Davis** nominated him for brigadier general in January 1862 but then withdrew the nomination. In March, Davis resubmitted Barton's name, and he was commissioned a brigadier general effective March 1862. After serving in East **Tennessee**, his **brigade** transferred to **Mississippi**, where it fought at the **Battle of Chickasaw Bayou** in December 1862. Barton served throughout the **Vicksburg Campaign** and was captured when the city surrendered.

After being **exchanged**, Barton was given command of **Lewis Armistead's** brigade in **George Pickett's division** of the **Army of Northern**

Virginia. He led it at **New Bern, North Carolina**, but afterward was transferred to **Drewry's Bluff, Virginia**, because Pickett claimed he was uncooperative during the New Bern operation. When Maj. Gen. **Robert Ransom** accused Barton of poor leadership during fighting at **Second Drewry's Bluff** in May 1864, Barton was relieved of his command. This negative view of Barton's abilities was not shared by his officers, who petitioned for his return. Barton also demanded a court-martial to clear his name, but one was never held. In September 1864, he was given command of a brigade in the **Richmond** defenses and was captured at **Sailor's Creek** in April 1865.

After being released from **prison** in July 1865, Barton settled in Virginia, where he worked as a chemist.

BARTOW, FRANCIS STEBBINS (1816–1861) CSA. A native of **Georgia**, Bartow graduated from Yale Law School and became a prominent Savannah lawyer. He served in the state assembly and senate in the 1840s as a **Whig** and became a militia captain in the 1850s. Bartow came to support **secession** strongly and was on the committee that drew up Georgia's secession ordinance. His militia **company** helped seize **Forts Pulaski** and **McAllister** and claimed to have been the first militia company to volunteer for Confederate service. Elected to the Provisional **Confederate Congress**, Bartow served as chairman of the Committee on Military Affairs and succeeded in getting gray **uniforms** adopted for the **army**.

Bartow resigned his congressional seat in May 1861 and took his militia company to **Virginia**, where in June he was elected colonel of the 8th Georgia. He commanded a **brigade** at **First Manassas** and was wounded in the leg just before his horse was killed under him. While rallying his men on Henry House Hill, Bartow was shot in the chest and killed. He became one of the Confederacy's first heroes and Cass County, Georgia, was renamed Bartow County in his honor.

BATE, WILLIAM BRIMAGE (1826–1905) CSA. A native of **Tennessee**, Bate worked on a steamboat early in life and was a **Mexican War** veteran. After editing a newspaper and serving one term in the Tennessee legislature, he became a Nashville lawyer, was elected attorney general of the Nashville District in 1854, and was a **secession** supporter by 1861.

Bate first entered Confederate service as a private but then was elected **company** captain and finally colonel of the 2nd Tennessee in May 1861. He was severely wounded in the left leg at **Shiloh** and was said to have prevented its amputation by threatening the surgeon with a pistol. Bate took months to recover but won a promotion to brigadier general in October 1862.

In June 1863, Bate was nominated for governor of Tennessee but earned the respect of his men by refusing the nomination and staying in the **army**. As a **brigade** commander in **Alexander P. Stewart's** division of the **Army of Tennessee**, he fought in the **Tullahoma Campaign** and at **Chickamauga**, where he had two horses killed under him. During the retreat from **Missionary Ridge** in November 1863, Bate was praised by **Braxton Bragg** for his service in the army's rear guard.

Bate was promoted to major general effective February 1864 and was given command of a **division** for the rest of the war. He earned special praise at **Resaca** during the **Atlanta Campaign** and later at Franklin during the **Franklin and Nashville Campaign**. Bate was wounded three times during the war and had six horses shot from under him.

After the war, Bate was active in the **Democratic Party** and twice was elected Tennessee's governor. He was elected to the U.S. Senate in 1886 and served at that post until his death.

BATES, EDWARD (1793–1869) USA. A native of **Virginia**, Bates settled in St. Louis, Missouri, and became the city's prosecuting attorney. An active **Whig**, he also served both in the **U.S. Congress** and in the state legislature. Bates was a fierce antisecessionist and joined the **Republican Party** in the 1850s. He was in contention for the 1860 Republican presidential nomination but at the convention withdrew his name after one ballot and threw his support to **Abraham Lincoln**.

Bates became the first cabinet member from west of the Mississippi River when Lincoln appointed him U.S. attorney general in early 1861. He disliked many other cabinet members and had a contentious relationship with his colleagues. Bates opposed the emancipation of slaves and the admission of **West Virginia** but supported Lincoln's naval **blockade** and the **suspension of the writ of habeas corpus**. His inconsistency on policies caused difficulties with the **Radical Republicans** and led to his resignation in November 1864.

Bates returned to **Missouri**, where he again became involved in state politics and quarreled with the **Radical Republicans**.

BATON ROUGE, LOUISIANA. The capital of **Louisiana**, Baton Rouge had a population of 5,429 in 1860. As the **secession** crisis deepened, state militia peacefully seized the U.S. Arsenal there on January 10, 1861. Governor **Thomas O. Moore** then convened a secession convention on January 23, and on January 26 the delegates voted 113–17 for secession. After **New Orleans** fell to **David Farragut** in late April 1862, Union gunboats proceeded upriver to Baton Rouge and occupied it without resistance on May 9. When Confederate guerrillas fired on Union sailors a few weeks later, the gunboats shelled the city and Brig. Gen. **Thomas Williams** landed 2,600 soldiers to occupy the town. After the **Battle of Baton Rouge**, the Union soldiers looted and then briefly evacuated the city on August 21, 1862, but returned in force on December 16 under Brig. Gen. **Cuvier Grover**. Baton Rouge remained in Union hands for the rest of the war, forcing the Confederates to move the state capital first to Opelousas, then to Shreveport. During the war, Baton Rouge served as a major base for Union operations in Louisiana and suffered the burning of its statehouse. In 1879, a new state constitution provided for the state capital to return to Baton Rouge.

BATON ROUGE, LOUISIANA, BATTLE OF (AUGUST 5, 1862). After **Baton Rouge, Louisiana**, fell to Union forces on May 9, 1862, Confederate **district** commander Maj. Gen. **Earl Van Dorn** hoped to liberate it to pave the way for retaking **New Orleans** and lifting the enemy **blockade** of the Red River. Major General **John C. Breckinridge** was ordered to take his Confederate force from **Vicksburg, Mississippi**, by rail to Camp Moore, Louisiana. From there he was to attack Baton Rouge, while the gunboat **CSS *Arkansas*** came down the Mississippi River and attacked any enemy ships in the river.

Disease and exhaustion depleted Breckinridge's command to the point he could muster only 2,600 men for the attack on August 5, 1862. In Baton Rouge, Brig. Gen. **Thomas Williams** also had about 2,600 men. Breckinridge attacked from the east through an early morning fog and initially drove back the Federals. But the *Arkansas* developed engine trouble and never arrived, allowing the Union gunboats to pound the Confederates with their cannons. Breckinridge finally broke off the attack after suffering 467 casualties. Thomas was killed in the battle, and an additional 382 Union soldiers were lost. Unable to restart the engines, the crew of the *Arkansas* set the ship on fire and abandoned it.

BATTERY. *See* ARTILLERY.

BATTERY ROBINETTE AT BATTLE OF CORINTH, MISSISSIPPI (OCTOBER 3–4, 1862). *See* CORINTH, MISSISSIPPI, BATTLE OF.

BATTERY WAGNER, SOUTH CAROLINA, BATTLE OF (JULY 10–SEPTEMBER 6, 1863). *See* FORT WAGNER, SOUTH CAROLINA, BATTLE OF.

"BATTLE ABOVE THE CLOUDS" (NOVEMBER 24, 1863). *See* LOOKOUT MOUNTAIN, TENNESSEE, BATTLE OF.

BATTLE, CULLEN ANDREWS (1829–1905) CSA. A native of **Georgia**, Battle moved to **Alabama** as a boy and graduated from the University of Alabama. He became a lawyer, was involved in **Democratic Party** politics, was a noted speaker, and served as a presidential elector at the 1860 Democratic National Convention. An ardent secessionist, Battle formed a militia **company** in 1859 that became part of the 3rd Alabama in 1861.

Battle became major of his **regiment** and accompanied it to **Virginia**. There he was promoted to lieutenant colonel in July 1861 and took command of the regiment when Col. Tennent Lomax was killed at **Seven Pines** (Battle was wounded in the same fight). As part of the **Army of Northern Virginia**, Battle led the regiment at **South Mountain** and **Antietam** and was wounded at both, but his promotion to colonel did not come until March 1863. Injuries sustained in a riding accident kept him from playing any major role in the **Chancellorsville Campaign**. Numerous officers and politicians recommended Battle for further promotion, but his **division** commander preferred others over him. After fighting at **Gettysburg**, Battle finally did receive his promotion to brigadier general, effective August 1863.

Battle competently led **Robert Rodes's** old **brigade** through the **Overland** and **Philip Sheridan's Shenandoah Valley Campaigns** and received a fourth wound at **Cedar Creek**. He spent the rest of the war recuperating from this wound. Some sources claim Battle was promoted to major general late in the war, but it is unproven.

After the war, Battle was elected to the **U.S. Congress** in 1868 but was denied his seat because he refused to take the **Ironclad Oath**. He later moved to **North Carolina** and became a newspaper editor.

"BATTLE HYMN OF THE REPUBLIC." This song's tune originally was used in the popular Union marching tunes "John Brown's Body Lies a-Moulderin' in the Grave" and "We'll Hang Old Jeff Davis from a Sour Apple Tree." When **Julia Ward Howe** heard troops singing "John Brown's Body" in 1861, she disliked the lyrics and wrote a new set. Her new song, entitled "Battle Hymn of the Republic," was first published in February 1862 in *Atlantic Monthly* and quickly became popular with Northerners.

BAXLEY, CATHERINE VIRGINIA (1812–?) CSA. A **Virginia** native, Baxley was teaching school in Baltimore, **Maryland**, when the war began. She was arrested in December 1861 for smuggling messages from

Jefferson Davis and was placed in **prison** with famed Confederate spy **Rose O'Neal Greenhow**. Although an ardent secessionist with one son in the **Confederate army**, Baxley denied being a spy and claimed the papers she carried were personal, not official. **Paroled** with Greenhow on June 2, 1862, she was sent to **Richmond, Virginia**, and was paid $500 by the Confederate government for her courier service. In April 1865, Baxley was again briefly held by federal authorities for unknown reasons.

BAXTER, HENRY (1821–1873) USA. A native of **New York**, Baxter moved to **Michigan** as a boy. In 1849, he took a wagon train to **California** but then returned to Michigan three years later and worked in the milling business.

Baxter entered Union service in August 1861 when he was elected captain of a volunteer **company** that became part of the 7th Michigan. As part of the **Army of the Potomac**, he saw combat during the **Peninsula Campaign** and was severely wounded in the abdomen. Baxter was promoted to lieutenant colonel in July 1862 and at **Fredericksburg** was severely wounded in the shoulder while leading the amphibious assault that drove **Barksdale's Mississippi Brigade** from the riverfront.

Promoted to brigadier general of volunteers in March 1863, Baxter was given command of a **brigade** in the I Corps' 2nd Division the following month. He fought at **Chancellorsville** and at **Gettysburg** lost half of his men and every one of his staff officers. In April 1864, Baxter was transferred to a brigade command in the V Corps' 2nd Division and the following month suffered a third wound, this time to his leg, at the **Wilderness**. When he returned to duty in June, Baxter was given command of a brigade in the **corps'** 3rd Division and led it through the remainder of the **Petersburg Campaign** and in the **Appomattox Campaign**. After being **brevetted** major general of volunteers for the battles of the Wilderness and **Five Forks**, he was mustered out of the **army** in August 1865.

Baxter returned to Michigan after the war and served two years as register of deeds. President **U. S. Grant** appointed him minister to Honduras from 1869 to 1872, and he then returned to Michigan and worked in the lumber industry.

BAXTER SPRINGS, KANSAS, MASSACRE AT (OCTOBER 6, 1863). After attacking **Lawrence, Kansas**, on August 21, 1863, Confederate guerrilla **William C. Quantrill** took his command south toward **Indian Territory**. Along the way, he learned from two Union teamsters before murdering them that a Union garrison was at Baxter Springs. The garrison consisted of about 90 **black troops**, commanded by Lt. James B. Pond of the 3rd Wisconsin Cavalry. One column of Quantrill's force attacked Pond and caught his men at mealtime, unprepared to fight. Many of the black soldiers fled and were chased down and killed by the raiders. Pond prevented a worse **massacre** by manning a **howitzer** and holding off the Confederate force.

Meanwhile, Quantrill attacked an approaching wagon train led by Maj. Gen. **James G. Blunt**, commander of the **Army of the Frontier**, who was moving his headquarters. Blunt at first mistook Quantrill's approaching men for Federals since many of the guerrillas wore captured Union **uniforms**. When Quantrill attacked, Blunt managed to escape, but many of his men were slaughtered, with some being stripped, burned, and mutilated. Approximately 90 Union soldiers were killed at Baxter Springs, while Quantrill lost only three. Blunt was relieved of his command because of his poor performance in the incident.

BAYARD, GEORGE DASHIEL (1835–1862) USA. A native of **New York**, Bayard grew up in the **Iowa** Territory. After graduating from **West Point** in 1856, he fought **Indians** on the frontier while serving in the cavalry. During this service, Bayard was wounded in the face by a poisoned arrow and touched off an Indian uprising when he killed the Kiowa chief Big Pawnee.

In 1861, Bayard was a 1st lieutenant teaching at West Point, but in August he was promoted to captain in the 4th U.S. Cavalry. The following month, he was appointed colonel of the 1st Pennsylvania Cavalry. While serving in the **Washington, D.C.**, defenses, Bayard impressed his superiors by fighting his way out of a Confederate trap near Falmouth, Virginia.

Bayard was promoted to brigadier general of volunteers in April 1862 and was given a cavalry **brigade** in the **Department of the Rappahannock**. After fighting at **Port Republic**, he took command of a cavalry brigade in the **Army of Virginia's** III Corps and led it at **Cedar Mountain**. Bayard served in the Washington defenses for two months following the **Second Manassas Campaign** and then was appointed cavalry commander for the Left Grand Division in **Ambrose Burnside's Army of the Potomac**. At **Fredericksburg** on December 13, 1862, Bayard was mortally wounded by a shell while at **William B. Franklin's** headquarters. He died the next day.

BAYLOR, JOHN ROBERT (1822–1894) CSA. Born in **Kentucky**, Baylor grew up in the **Indian Territory** as part of a military family. At 17, he began earning a reputation as a respected **Texas** Indian fighter, which helped him win election to the Texas legislature in 1853. Afterward, Baylor briefly served as an Indian agent, but his fierce hatred of **Indians** ended that career.

After serving as a delegate to the Texas **secession** convention, Baylor raised approximately 1,000 men for **Baylor's "Buffalo Hunt,"** which actually was a planned invasion of **New Mexico**. His force became the 2nd Texas Mounted Rifles, with Baylor serving as lieutenant colonel. Baylor invaded New Mexico, captured the Union garrison at **Fort Fillmore**, and pronounced the creation of the Confederate Territory of New Mexico on August 1, 1861, with himself acting as governor. Afterward, however, Confederate authorities revoked his commission when it was discovered he planned to trap and annihilate the Apache Indians. After fighting at **Galveston, Texas**, as a private, Baylor was elected to the **Confederate Congress** in 1863, where he opposed all peace efforts and pressed authorities to allow him to invade New Mexico again.

After the war, Baylor returned to Texas and became a rancher.

BAYLOR'S "BUFFALO HUNT" (MAY 1–AUGUST 1, 1861). In the spring of 1861, Texan **John R. Baylor** raised about 1,000 men for what he claimed was to be a "buffalo hunt" out West. In reality, he was planning to invade the **New Mexico Territory** and capture it for the Confederacy. Organized into the 2nd Texas Mounted Rifles, Baylor's men left San Antonio, Texas, in May and made an exhausting march to Fort Bliss, near El Paso. The 250 or so men who made it that far then entered New Mexico and reached Union-held **Fort Fillmore** on July 25. Union Maj. Isaac Lynde had 700 men in the fort but proved to be a cautious fighter. He made one weak, unsuccessful attack against Baylor's outnumbered men on July 25 but then abandoned the fort that night and marched northeast toward Fort Stanton. The next day, Baylor set out in pursuit and captured Lynde and 500–600 of his men. The Federals evacuated Fort Stanton, and on August 1 Baylor declared the creation of the Confederate Territory of New Mexico (with himself as governor) out of that part of New Mexico south of the 34th parallel. In December 1861, Confederate Brig. Gen. **Henry Hopkins Sibley** arrived at Baylor's capital of Mesilla and took charge of Confederate troops for **Sibley's New Mexico Campaign**. For his poor showing at Fort Fillmore, Lynde was dismissed from the Union **army**.

BAYONET. Civil War soldiers used two types of bayonets. The sword bayonet was used on the **Mississippi**, **Sharps**, **Henry**, and some **Enfield rifles**. Sword bayonets were never popular, however, because of their large, cumbersome size, and the Confederates stopped making them in

1864. Most soldiers used the triangular bayonet, which fit the **Springfield** and 1853 Enfield **rifles**. Still, bayonets were never used in combat as often as imagined because the **rifle musket** allowed a soldier to kill his opponent at long range. Less than 0.004 percent of Union wounded were injured by bayonets. Soldiers generally found the bayonet more useful for holding candles or to serve as a roasting spit.

BAYOU BOURBEAU, LOUISIANA, BATTLE OF (NOVEMBER 3, 1863).

Following his repulse at **Sabine Pass**, **Texas**, Union Maj. Gen. **Nathaniel P. Banks** sent two **corps** under Maj. Gen. **William Franklin** up **Bayou Teche** (TESH) to Opelousas, Louisiana, in October 1863 on the **Texas Overland Expedition**. Opposing the movement was the small **army** of Confederate Maj. Gen. **Richard Taylor**. Franklin reached Opelousas without difficulty but was unable to continue westward because of poor roads over the difficult terrain and a lack of supplies. In late October, he retreated back down the Teche, and Taylor followed.

On November 3, Taylor launched a surprise attack against Brig. Gen. **Stephen G. Burbridge's division** near Grand Coteau, along Bayou Bourbeau (bore-BOW). Led by Brig. Gen. **Thomas Green**, the Confederates hit the Union front and flanks and drove the enemy back in confusion. When the 67th Indiana, holding Burbridge's left flank, was surrounded and captured, Burbridge ordered a retreat. He fell back three miles to another Union encampment and, with reinforcements, finally stopped Green's Confederates. In the engagement, Burbridge lost one cannon and 716 men, mostly taken **prisoners**. Green lost approximately 200 men.

BAYOU DE GLAIZE, LOUISIANA, BATTLE OF (MAY 18, 1864).

See YELLOW BAYOU, LOUISIANA, BATTLE OF.

BAYOU FOURCHE, ARKANSAS, BATTLE OF (SEPTEMBER 10, 1863).

In August 1863, Union Maj. Gen. **Frederick Steele** began an offensive in **Arkansas** to capture the Confederate capital of **Little Rock**. As the Federals approached Little Rock from Helena with 12,000 men, the Confederate state government relocated to Washington, and Confederate Maj. Gen. **Sterling Price** prepared to evacuate his 7,700 men. To prepare for battle, Price released Brig. Gen. **John S. Marmaduke** from arrest (a result of Marmaduke's killing Brig. Gen. **Lucius M. Walker** in a duel that took place on September 6) and placed him at the head of the cavalry.

When Steele reached the Arkansas River outside Little Rock on September 10, he was confronted by Confederate entrenchments on the north bank. Steele sent **John W. Davidson's** cavalry **division** across to the south bank to outflank the Confederates while he attacked the entrenchments on the north bank. While Price evacuated the city, Marmaduke engaged Davidson's cavalry a few miles to the east at Bayou Fourche (FOOSH). Outnumbered, Marmaduke was shelled by Union **artillery** on the north bank and quickly withdrew to Little Rock and retreated with the rest of Price's command. Later that day, Steele's Federals occupied the city. In the brief clash at Bayou Fourche, Marmaduke lost 64 men, while Davidson suffered 72 casualties.

BAYOU LAFOURCHE, LOUISIANA, BATTLE OF (JULY 13, 1863). After the **Port Hudson Campaign**, Union Maj. Gen. **Nathaniel P. Banks** sent the divisions of **Godfrey Weitzel** and **Cuvier Grover** to Donaldsonville, Louisiana, to oppose the Confederates along Bayou Lafourche (luh-FOOSH). After encountering Confederate cavalry under Brig. Gen. **Thomas Green**, each Union **division** sent a **brigade** sweeping along opposite banks of the bayou. Green took the initiative on the west bank and on July 13, 1863, led 750 cavalrymen and two guns against Weitzel's brigade, which was commanded by Col. Nathan A. M. Dudley. Green attacked Dudley's front and both flanks, capturing three cannons and forcing the Federals to flee up the bayou to the safety of a second Union brigade. On the east bank, Col. Joseph S. Morgan's brigade from Grover's division ran into another column of Green's cavalry. Although the superior force, Morgan's command panicked when hit by Col. **Walter P. Lane's** Confederates and also was chased up the bayou. During the rout, Lane was able to turn his guns on the west bank and help Green drive back Dudley's brigade.

After withdrawing to Donaldsonville, Morgan was court-martialed for his poor performance and was dismissed from the **army**. In the battle, also known as Cox's, or Kock's, or Saint Emma Plantation, Green's 1,200 troopers defeated a Union force three times its size. Green lost 33 men to the Federals' 459.

BAYOU RAPIDES, LOUISIANA, BATTLE OF (MARCH 21, 1864). *See* HENDERSON'S HILL, LOUISIANA, BATTLE OF.

BAYOU TECHE, LOUISIANA, CAMPAIGN (MARCH 25–MAY 7, 1863). Before Union Maj. Gen. **Nathaniel P. Banks** could begin his 1863 **Port Hudson Campaign**, he first needed to clear the small Confederate **army** of Maj. Gen. **Richard Taylor** out of the Bayou Teche (TESH) region and capture Alexandria, Louisiana, on the Red River to safeguard his flank and prevent the enemy from resupplying the Port Hudson garrison. On March 25, 1863, Banks began shifting his army from **Baton Rouge, Louisiana**, to Brashear City (BRA-shur, modern-day Morgan City). From there, he planned to send part of his force under Brig. Gen. **Cuvier Grover** by transports through Grand Lake to Irish Bend, located near Franklin behind Taylor's position on Bayou Teche. Banks then would accompany Brig. Gen. **Godfrey Weitzel's** command and move across Berwick Bay to Berwick City and then up Bayou Teche to attack Taylor. If coordinated properly, the Union forces would trap the enemy between them.

Banks and Weitzel left Berwick City on April 11 with two divisions, but delays prevented Grover's **division** from leaving until the next day. Encountering Taylor's two **brigades** and the Confederate gunboat *Diana* at **Fort Bisland** on Bayou Teche, Banks bombarded and probed the enemy position on April 12–13 but did not launch a major assault. Learning that Grover had pushed aside his small rear guard and had landed behind him at **Irish Bend**, Taylor began evacuating Fort Bisland on the night of April 13 to escape the closing trap. In the fighting at Fort Bisland, Banks lost 224 men to Taylor's are unknown.

On April 14, Taylor deployed part of his command and the *Diana* and attacked Grover at Irish Bend while the rest of the army escaped up Bayou Teche toward Vermilionville (modern-day Lafayette). After a short, sharp fight, the Confederates abandoned and blew up the *Diana* and then disengaged to follow Taylor upstream. In this clash, Grover suffered 353 casualties. Confederate losses are unknown. That same day, the Confederate *Queen of the West* was attacked and destroyed by the Union fleet in Grand Lake.

Taylor reached Vermilionville on April 17 and fought a brief rear guard action at Vermilion Bayou before continuing his retreat to Opelousas. Banks halted his pursuit at Opelousas to await expected reinforcements from Maj. Gen. **U. S. Grant** and allowed Taylor to escape to Alexandria. Resuming the chase, Banks finally reached Alexandria on May 7, only to find that **David D. Porter's** gunboats had taken possession of the town a few hours earlier.

Banks's Bayou Teche Campaign succeeded in clearing the area of the Confederates and cutting Port Hudson's supply line but failed to destroy Taylor's small army. Shortly after occupying Alexandria, Banks withdrew his army and began the Port Hudson Campaign.

BEAL, GEORGE LAFAYETTE (1825–1896) USA. A native of **Maine**, Beal was a bookbinder before the Civil War. He also joined a militia

company as a private in 1855 and rose to captain by 1861. Beal may have been the first Maine man mustered into Union service when his company became part of the 90-day 1st Maine in May 1861.

After serving three months in **Washington, D.C.**, the **regiment** was reorganized as the 10th Maine in August 1861, with Beal appointed its colonel in October. He led it through very bloody fighting at **Cedar Mountain** (where he lost 173 men in 30 minutes), and at **Antietam** he was wounded and had his horse killed under him. After the 10th Maine was mustered out of service in May 1863, Beal raised the 29th Maine and became its colonel in December. Sent to the **Department of the Gulf**, he was given command of a **brigade** in the XIX Corps' 1st Division in February 1864. Beal fought in **Nathaniel P. Banks's Red River Campaign** and often commanded the rear guard during Banks's retreat. Afterward, he accompanied the XIX Corps to **Virginia** and led his brigade in **Philip H. Sheridan's Shenandoah Valley Campaign**, seeing combat at **Third Winchester** and **Fisher's Hill**.

Beal was promoted to brigadier general of volunteers in November 1864 and was **brevetted** major general of volunteers in March 1865. Mustered out of the service in January 1866, he returned to Maine, where he served as Maine's adjutant general from 1880 to 1885 and as treasurer from 1888 to 1894.

BEALE, RICHARD LEE TURBERVILLE (1819–1893) CSA. A native of **Virginia**, Beale graduated from the University of Virginia Law School and practiced law before the Civil War. He also served one term in the **U.S. Congress** as a **Democrat** in 1847–49 and was a state senator from 1858–60.

Beale entered Confederate service in 1861 as a 1st lieutenant in a cavalry **company** and engaged in some **skirmishes** prior to **First Manassas** but missed that battle. He was promoted to captain in July, and when the company was converted into a battalion that October, he was appointed its major. When the battalion became part of the 9th Virginia Cavalry in April 1862, Beale was appointed lieutenant colonel. After fighting with the **Army of Northern Virginia** in the **Peninsula**, **Second Manassas**, and **Antietam Campaigns**, he was promoted to colonel in October 1862. In that capacity, Beale won the praise of **Robert E. Lee** by leading the **regiment** on a successful raid to Leeds' Ferry. In April 1863, he won **J. E. B. Stuart's** praise for helping stop **George Stoneman's Raid**. Beale then fought with Stuart at **Brandy Station** and at **Gettysburg** and accompanied him on his raid into **Maryland** afterward. In September 1863, he received a severe wound in a skirmish that put him out of action for the rest of the year.

After returning to duty, Beale led the cavalrymen who killed Col. **Ulric Dahlgren** during the 1864 **Kilpatrick-Dahlgren Raid** on **Richmond, Virginia**, and helped discover the **Dahlgren Papers** calling for **Jefferson Davis's** assassination. Afterward, he fought with distinction during the **Overland Campaign** and again earned more praise for his actions at **Reams' Station**. Despite the accolades he received, Beale often was dissatisfied and tendered his resignation three times between 1862 and 1863.

Beale was promoted to brigadier general effective January 1865 and led a cavalry **brigade** for the rest of the war. After surrendering with Lee at **Appomattox**, he resumed his law practice and was elected to the Congress in 1878.

BEALL, JOHN YATES (1835–1865) CSA. A native of western **Virginia**, Beall (BELL) studied law before the Civil War, but instead of opening a practice he became a "country gentleman." He entered Confederate service as a private with the 2nd Virginia in 1861 and fought at **First Manassas**, but in October, he was wounded so severely at **Harpers Ferry, Virginia**, that he had to leave the **army**.

Commissioned an acting master in the **Confederate navy**, Beall became known as "Captain Beall" and engaged in **privateering** on Chesapeake Bay in 1863. He was captured in November 1863 and was held at Fort McHenry, Maryland, before being **exchanged** in March 1864. In September 1864, Beall led a raid to free Confederate **prisoners** from **Johnson's Island** in Lake Erie. He and his 20 men captured two steamers and were outfitting a third when Canadian officials arrested one member of the expedition. The others refused to continue the mission when they failed to receive an agreed upon signal from shore. Later in the year, Beall participated in an attempt to free some imprisoned Confederate generals being transferred by rail, but he was captured on December 16 in **New York** near the Canadian border. A captured accomplice testified against him, and Beall was hanged as a spy on February 24, 1865.

BEALL, LLOYD JAMES (1808–1887) CSA. A native of **Rhode Island**, Beall (BELL) graduated from **West Point** in 1830 and fought in the **Seminole** and **Mexican Wars**. He resigned his major's commission in April 1861 and the following month was commissioned a colonel and commandant of the **Confederate Marine Corps**. Beall fought hard to maintain the Marine Corps' separate identity and made it into one of the Confederacy's best military units. He moved to **Richmond, Virginia**, after the war, where a house fire destroyed much of the records of the Confederate Marine Corps.

BEALL, WILLIAM NELSON RECTOR (1825–1883) CSA. A native of **Kentucky**, Beall (BELL) was the brother-in-law of Confederate Maj. Gen. **James F. Fagan**, by Fagan's first wife. After moving to **Arkansas** as a boy, Beall received an appointment to **West Point**, graduated in 1848, and served most of his antebellum career fighting **Indians** on the frontier. He rose to the rank of captain but resigned his commission in August 1861 and joined the Confederacy.

Beall entered Confederate service as a captain of cavalry and in early 1862 served as Maj. Gen. **Earl Van Dorn's** assistant adjutant general. He was promoted to major in the commissary department, and the **Confederate Congress** confirmed him as a brigadier general effective April 1862 after Van Dorn recommended his promotion to colonel. Beall first took command of the cavalry around **Corinth, Mississippi**, and then assumed command of the District of East Louisiana. He greatly improved the fortifications at Port Hudson and in early 1863 was given command of a **brigade** there after **Franklin Gardner** took over the **district**. During the **Port Hudson Campaign**, Beall commanded the center of the fortifications and performed admirably. After the garrison surrendered on July 9, 1863, he was imprisoned on **Johnson's Island** until 1864. Beall then was **paroled** and in an agreement with Union officials served as a special Confederate agent responsible for purchasing Northern supplies for Confederate **prisoners**. He was given an office in New York City and until August 1865 imported approved cotton from the South for sale in the North, with the proceeds being used to buy the necessary supplies.

After the war, Beall lived for a time in **Missouri** as a merchant.

BEAN'S STATION, TENNESSEE, BATTLE OF (DECEMBER 14, 1863). Late in the 1863 **Knoxville Campaign**, Confederate Lt. Gen. **James Longstreet** withdrew from Knoxville, Tennessee, on December 4, 1863, and marched northward. Union forces cautiously pursued him and encamped on the Holston River at Bean's Station. From Rogersville, Longstreet seized the opportunity to strike at the exposed Federals and sent **Bushrod R. Johnson's division**, plus cavalry and **artillery**, to cut off and destroy the enemy.

On the morning of December 13, Johnson drove back Union Brig. Gen. **James M. Shackelford**, but Shackelford took up a position at Bean's Station and fought off the Confederates. Longstreet had planned for cavalry under Maj. Gen. **William T. Martin** to outflank the enemy, but Martin failed to appear. After reinforcements arrived, Longstreet finally pushed Shackelford out of town, but the Federals managed to retreat through Bean's Gap before the Confederate cavalry could close it. The fighting was fierce, but each side lost only about 200 men. This fight ended the Knoxville Campaign.

BEARDSLEE TELEGRAPH. George W. Beardslee invented this portable **telegraph** system, which had a range of about five miles. The two telegraphers had identical dials that allowed the letter one operator pushed to be shown on the receiving end. The system's advantage was that it eliminated the need to know Morse Code and was lighter and easier to transport. The Beardslee Telegraph was effectively used by Union forces in the **Peninsula** and **Fredericksburg Campaigns** but was abandoned in late 1863 because of its limited range.

BEATTY, JOHN (1828–1914) USA. A native of **Ohio**, Beatty began a bank with his brother, William, in 1854 and served as a **Republican** elector in the **election of 1860.** When the Civil War began, the brothers decided that John would go to war while William would remain in Ohio to manage the bank.

Beatty entered Union service in April 1861 when he raised a **company** of volunteers that became part of the 3rd Ohio. He was elected lieutenant colonel that same month and served with the **regiment** in western **Virginia** under **George B. McClellan** before being promoted to colonel in February 1862. Sent to **Kentucky**, Beatty fought at **Perryville** and was promoted to brigadier general of volunteers in November 1862.

In December 1862, Beatty was given command of a **brigade** in the **Army of the Cumberland's** XIV Corps and led it in the **Stones River** (where two horses were killed under him), **Tullahoma**, **Chickamauga**, and **Chattanooga Campaigns**. He resigned his commission in January 1864 in order to manage the family's bank and to allow William to join the **army**.

After the war, Beatty remained in the banking business, was elected to the **U.S. Congress** in 1868, and was reelected twice. He also unsuccessfully ran for governor in 1884 and worked to preserve the Chickamauga and Chattanooga battlefields.

BEATTY, SAMUEL (1820–1885) USA. A native of **Pennsylvania**, Beatty moved to **Ohio** as a boy. After service in the **Mexican War** as a 1st lieutenant, he was elected county sheriff in 1857 and held that position until the outbreak of the Civil War.

Beatty was elected **company** captain in the 19th Ohio in April 1861 and then regimental colonel in May. After fighting at **Shiloh** and participating in the **siege of Corinth, Mississippi,** he was elevated to a **brigade** command in the **Army of the Ohio's** II Corps in May 1862 and led it at **Perryville.** In November, Beatty took command of a brigade in the **Army of the Cumberland's** XXI Corps, but at **Stones River** he temporarily led the **division.** His actions in the battle won him promotion to brigadier general of volunteers effective November 1862.

In April 1863, Beatty took command of a division in the XXI Corps but later reverted to a brigade command and led it in the **Chickamauga** and **Chattanooga Campaigns,** participating in the assault on **Missionary Ridge** in the latter. After service in the **Atlanta Campaign,** he was sent to **Tennessee** to stop **John Bell Hood's** invasion and was given a division command in the Army of the Cumberland's IV Corps for the **Battle of Nashville.**

After being **brevetted** major general of volunteers in March 1865 for his war service, Beatty left the **army** in January 1866 and returned to Ohio to farm. He had participated in most of the major western battles and proved to be one of the better Union commanders in that theater.

BEAUREGARD, PIERRE GUSTAVE TOUTANT (1818–1893) CSA. One of the Confederacy's most controversial generals, Beauregard was born into a prominent **Louisiana** Creole family and did not learn to speak English until he attended school in New York City. He graduated second in his 1838 **West Point** class and dropped both the name Pierre and a hyphen that had been present between his last two names. In the **Mexican War,** Beauregard was a 1st lieutenant of **engineers** and won three **brevets** while serving under **Winfield Scott.** Still, Beauregard became bitter toward Scott when the general did not give him the same recognition he did Beauregard's comrade **Robert E. Lee.** Promoted to captain in 1853, Beauregard performed engineering duties in **New Orleans, Louisiana,** and then was made West Point's superintendent in January 1861. He was a secessionist, however, and when Louisiana seceded that same day, Beauregard was ordered to relinquish his position five days later.

Beauregard resigned his commission in February 1861 and was made a brigadier general in the **Confederate army** effective March 1. He was assigned to command Confederate forces at **Charleston, South Carolina,** a few days later and became the South's first military hero when he forced **Fort Sumter** to surrender on April 13, 1861. Once the war began, Beauregard advocated abandoning territory to the enemy in return for concentrating Confederate strength at strategic points. His plans sometimes had merit, but Beauregard tended to overestimate the Confederacy's abilities, and often his plans were little more than wild fantasies.

Placed in command of Confederate forces around Manassas, Virginia, in June 1861, Beauregard formed the **Army of the Potomac (Confederate)**. In July, he again earned fame for directing the Confederate forces that won the **First Battle of Manassas**. Because of difficulty distinguishing friend from foe on that battlefield, Beauregard and **Joseph E. Johnston** designed the famous **Confederate** battle **flag** to give Confederate forces a more distinct banner.

In August 1861, Beauregard was promoted to full general and became the Confederacy's fifth ranking general. Transferred to the west, he played a key role at **Shiloh** by helping concentrate the Confederate **army** at **Corinth, Mississippi**; forming **Albert Sidney Johnston's** battle plan; and serving as Johnston's second in command. When Johnston was killed, Beauregard took command of the army and withdrew from Shiloh to Corinth after two days of fighting. By this time, Beauregard and **Jefferson Davis** had become bitter enemies. Beauregard earlier had claimed that Davis prevented him from making the victory at First Manassas more complete and was unhappy with his military ranking. At Shiloh, Beauregard also misled Davis by first sending a telegram claiming a great victory and then unexpectedly retreating. When Beauregard left the army without permission in June, Davis removed him from command and appointed him commander of the **Department of South Carolina and Georgia** two months later.

For the next 18 months, Beauregard served at Charleston, where he worked tirelessly to improve the city's defenses and fought off Union attacks. Transferred to the **Department of North Carolina** in April 1864, he became responsible for defending Petersburg, Virginia. In May 1864, Beauregard stopped the advance of **Benjamin F. Butler** in the **Bermuda Hundred Campaign** and the following month held off a much superior Union force at the **Second Battle of Drewry's Bluff** until Lee could arrive with his army. Despite these successes, Beauregard was never assigned another army command. Instead, Davis made him commander of the **Military Division of the West**. After the **Army of Tennessee** was wrecked at the **Battle of Nashville** in December 1864, Beauregard was transferred once again to **South Carolina** in February 1865. He spent the war's last months serving under Joseph E. Johnston in the **Carolinas Campaign**.

After the war, Beauregard was a **railroad** executive, a representative of the corrupt Louisiana Lottery Company, and Louisiana's adjutant general. He was a talented Civil War general but often an unrealistic one whose pride and pettiness prevented him from enjoying a cordial relationship with any of his superiors.

BEAVER DAM CREEK, VIRGINIA, BATTLE OF (JUNE 26, 1862). *See* MECHANICSVILLE, VIRGINIA, BATTLE OF.

BEE, BARNARD ELLIOTT (1824–1861) CSA. The younger brother of Confederate general **Hamilton Bee**, Bee was a native of **South Carolina**. While still a boy, he moved to **Texas** with his family to join his father, who served as Texas's secretary of state and treasury. From there, Bee secured an appointment to **West Point**, where he gained the nickname "Bubble," and graduated in 1845. He won two **brevets** in the **Mexican War** and was wounded once.

Although Bee was not a secessionist, he resigned his captain's commission in March 1861 and became lieutenant colonel of the 1st South Carolina Regulars (**artillery**) in June. He was promoted to brigadier general in June 1861 and was given command of a **brigade** under **Joseph E. Johnston** in the **Shenandoah Valley**. At the **First Battle of Manassas**, Bee's brigade saw heavy fighting, and during the battle he reportedly rallied part of his command by pointing to Brig. Gen. **Thomas J. Jackson's** brigade on Henry House Hill and crying out that Jackson was standing like a "stone wall," thus giving Jackson his famous nickname. It has sometimes been claimed, probably falsely, that this sobriquet was actually given in contempt by Bee because of Jackson's failure to advance. While leading one of his **regiments** back into the fight near Henry House Hill, Bee was mortally wounded, and he died the next morning. He was hailed a hero and was seen as one of the Confederacy's first martyrs, but some claimed that he was disoriented during the battle and may have been drinking.

BEE, HAMILTON PRIOLEAU (1822–1897) CSA. The older brother of Confederate general **Barnard Bee**, Bee was a native of **South Carolina**. He moved to **Texas** with his family while a young man to join his father, who served as Texas's secretary of state and treasury. Bee served on the Boundary Commission that set the Louisiana-Texas boundary, served as secretary of the Texas senate, fought in the **Mexican War**, and served with the Texas Rangers. After the Mexican War, he served in the Texas legislature and for a time was speaker of the house.

When the Civil War erupted, Bee first was appointed brigadier general of state troops and then received the same commission in the

Confederate army, effective March 1862. For most of the war, he served at Brownsville, Texas, overseeing trade entering the Confederacy through Mexico. In the spring of 1864, Bee was given command of a cavalry **division** during the **Red River Campaign** and fought at **Mansfield** (where he was slightly wounded), **Pleasant Hill**, and **Monett's Ferry**. Although his bravery was never questioned, Bee's leadership at Monett's Ferry was criticized by his superior, **Richard Taylor**. When **Thomas Green** was killed during this campaign, Bee took temporary command of the cavalry and remained in the **Trans-Mississippi Department** for the rest of the war. He was **paroled** in June 1865 as a major general, apparently having been appointed to that rank by **department** commander **Edmund Kirby Smith**, although there is no record of this rank having been confirmed by the Senate.

BEECH GROVE, KENTUCKY, BATTLE OF (JANUARY 19, 1862). *See* MILL SPRINGS, KENTUCKY, BATTLE OF.

BEECHER, HENRY WARD (1813–1887) USA. The brother of **Harriet Beecher Stowe**, Beecher was a native of **Connecticut** who became a popular Congregational minister involved in the antislavery movement. An excellent speaker, he was a popular lecturer, and his sermons were often printed in newspapers. Unlike his famous sister, Beecher was not an **abolitionist** before the Civil War. While he opposed the spread of **slavery** and wished it an early natural death, he did not think it was constitutional to abolish it outright. When fighting broke out in **"Bleeding Kansas,"** Beecher helped arm the antislavery settlers by smuggling in crates of **rifles** known as **"Beecher's Bibles."**

During the Civil War, Beecher became more of an abolitionist. He supported the **Emancipation Proclamation**, although he criticized **Abraham Lincoln's** slowness in issuing it, and pushed for black suffrage during **Reconstruction**. Beecher also believed in a moderate reconstruction policy that would allow the Southern states quick readmission. Much of his later career was in support of women's suffrage.

"BEECHER'S BIBLES." This was the nickname given to **rifles** smuggled by Congregational minister **Henry Ward Beecher** to antislavery forces during the fighting in **"Bleeding Kansas."** Beecher often hid the rifles in crates marked "Bibles" and justified his actions by claiming that one rifle held more "moral power" over slave owners than did a hundred Bibles.

"BEEFSTEAK RAID" (SEPTEMBER 14–17, 1864). During the 1864 **Petersburg Campaign**, a scout reported to Confederate cavalryman

Maj. Gen. **Wade Hampton** that a large herd of cattle was being held by Union forces at Coggins Point, Virginia. Hampton received permission to seize the herd and on September 14, 1864, led 4,000 cavalrymen from Petersburg toward Coggins Point, located near the Union headquarters at **City Point**. On the morning of September 16, Brig. Gen. **Thomas L. Rosser's brigade** routed the Union guards and captured 2,486 head of cattle. The Confederates then forced their Union **prisoners** to help drive the herd back to the Southerners' lines. While Rosser held off the pursuing enemy, Hampton took the badly needed cattle to Petersburg on September 17. Besides the valuable beef, Hampton also inflicted on the enemy 400 casualties at a loss of only 61 men.

BELKNAP, WILLIAM WORTH (1829–1890) USA. A native of **New York**, Belknap (BELL-nap) became a lawyer in 1851 after attending the College of New Jersey (Princeton University). After briefly practicing in **Washington, D.C.**, he opened a law office in **Iowa** and served one term in the Iowa legislature in 1857–58.

Belknap entered Union service in December 1861 when he was commissioned major of the 15th Iowa. After being wounded at **Shiloh**, he was promoted to lieutenant colonel in August 1862. Belknap was praised for his service at the **Battle of Corinth** and won promotion to colonel in June 1863. After meritorious service with the **Army of the Tennessee** in the **Vicksburg**, **Meridian**, and **Atlanta Campaigns** (particularly at the **Battles of Atlanta** and **Ezra Church**), he was commissioned brigadier general of volunteers in July 1864.

Belknap was given command of a **brigade** in the Army of the Tennessee's XVII Corps in July 1864 and led it during the latter part of the Atlanta Campaign. He sometimes led the **division** in the **March to the Sea** and the **Carolinas Campaign** and commanded the XVII Corps in the months following the Confederates' **surrender**. Belknap was **brevetted** a major general of volunteers and was mustered out of service in August 1865.

After the war, Belknap served as an Iowa tax collector until 1869, when President **U. S. Grant** appointed him secretary of war. He was accused of accepting bribes from post **sutlers**, and, although impeached in 1876, was allowed to resign his post. The Belknap scandal was an inglorious end to an officer who had fought in most of the Civil War's western battles and who frequently was commended for bravery. After leaving the government, Belknap returned to his law practice.

BELL, JOHN (1797–1869) USA. A native of **Tennessee**, Bell was a prominent politician during the antebellum years. After serving one term in the state senate, he was elected to the U.S. House of Representatives and served there for 14 years. A **Whig**, Bell also served briefly as President William Henry Harrison's secretary of war in 1841. Afterward, Bell entered the U.S. Senate, where he took a moderate stand on **slavery** even though he was a slave owner himself. He angered some Southerners by supporting Congress's right to regulate slavery in the territories and for voting against **Kansas's** admission as a state under a proslavery constitution.

In the **election of 1860**, the **Constitutional Union Party** nominated Bell as a compromise candidate. To win the moderate vote, he had a vague platform that promised to uphold the Constitution, obey the law, and support the Union, but he and running mate **Edward Everett** carried only Tennessee, **Kentucky**, and **Virginia**. Afterward, when all alternatives seemed gone, Bell supported Tennessee's **secession**.

BELL, TYREE HARRIS (1815–1902) CSA. A native of **Kentucky**, Bell grew up in **Tennessee** and became a planter. When the Civil War began in 1861, he formed a volunteer **company** that became part of the 12th Tennessee. Bell first was elected company captain in June and then was chosen regimental lieutenant colonel. Praised for his handling of the **regiment** at the **Battles of Belmont** and **Shiloh** (where he was slightly wounded), Bell was promoted to colonel in May 1862 and was put in command of his regiment and the 22nd Tennessee. After fighting in the battles of **Corinth**, **Richmond**, and **Perryville**, his regiments were absorbed into the 47th Tennessee, and Bell was sent to raise cavalry in Tennessee.

Bell eventually raised enough men to fill three regiments and spent the latter part of 1863 raiding Tennessee. These recruits were formed into Bell's Brigade, which joined **Nathan Bedford Forrest's** cavalry in January 1864. Although recommended for promotion to brigadier general by his commander, Bell remained a colonel but went on to win more accolades at **Fort Pillow**, **Brice's Crossroads**, and **Franklin**. He finally was promoted to brigadier general effective February 1865 and served in **Alabama** and **Georgia** for the rest of the war.

After the surrender, Bell moved to **California**.

BELLE GROVE, VIRGINIA, BATTLE OF (OCTOBER 19, 1864). *See* CEDAR CREEK, VIRGINIA, BATTLE OF.

BELLE ISLE PRISON. Belle Isle was an 80-acre island in the James River at **Richmond**, **Virginia**. A Confederate **prison** camp was put there in the summer of 1862 to accommodate the thousands of **prisoners** taken during the **Seven Days Campaign**. The prison briefly closed in late 1862 when **exchanges** had depleted the prisoner population, but it was reopened in January 1863. Commanded by Lt. Virginius Bossieux, Belle Isle was designed for only 3,000 prisoners but housed more than 8,000 by 1864, causing prisoners to suffer greatly from malnutrition, disease, and exposure. When the prisoners were sent to **Andersonville** in March 1864, Belle Isle was closed temporarily, but it was reopened that summer. In October 1864, these last prisoners were sent to other prisons, and Belle Isle was returned to its civilian owners in February 1865.

BELMONT, MISSOURI, BATTLE OF (NOVEMBER 7, 1861). In late 1861, Maj. Gen. **Leonidas Polk** held one of the Confederate strongholds on the Mississippi River at Columbus, Kentucky. Two Union forces were sent to harass the Confederates, one leaving from Paducah, Kentucky, and moving down the river's east bank toward Columbus and one under Brig. Gen. **U. S. Grant** moving down the Mississippi River from Cairo, Illinois. On November 6, Grant boarded 3,100 men onto transports and, with the gunboats *Lexington* and *Tyler*, moved downstream and landed above one of Polk's camps at Belmont, Missouri.

Grant advanced toward Belmont and encountered approximately 3,000 Confederates under Brig. Gen. **Gideon Pillow**. Pillow mishandled his men in the battle's opening phase and was pushed back, allowing Grant to capture the Confederate camp. Polk then sent reinforcements from across the river to cut Grant off from his transports, but Grant managed to fight his way through and escape. In the daylong fight, Grant lost 607 men to the Confederates' 641 casualties. This was Grant's first opportunity to command troops in battle, and it instilled in him needed confidence.

BENHAM, HENRY WASHINGTON (1813–1884) USA. A native of **Connecticut**, Benham graduated first in his 1837 **West Point** class. He served as an **engineer** in the antebellum **U.S. Army** and won one **brevet** and was wounded during the **Mexican War**.

In May 1861, Benham was promoted to captain and was made chief engineer for the **Department of the Ohio**. After leading the Union vanguard that pursued the retreating Confederates from **Rich Mountain** to **Carrick's Ford, Virginia**, that summer, he was promoted to major and then to brigadier general of volunteers in August 1861.

The new brigadier did not please his superior, **William Rosecrans**, and thus soon was transferred to **South Carolina**. After participating in the attack on **Fort Pulaski, Georgia**, Benham disobeyed orders and unsuccessfully attacked the Confederates at **Secessionville, South Carolina**, in June 1862. Because of his poor performance there, he was relieved of command and was placed under arrest for disobeying orders. Benham's promotion to brigadier general also was revoked in August 1862, but the revocation was canceled in February 1863. At that time, he was placed in command of the **Army of the Potomac's** engineering **brigade**. Benham redeemed himself by building **pontoon bridges** across the Rappahannock River during the 1863 **Chancellorsville Campaign** and for building the long James River pontoon bridge at the end of the 1864 **Overland Campaign**. By war's end, he was brevetted a major general in both the regular and volunteer forces.

Benham was mustered out of the volunteers in January 1866 but remained in the **army** as a lieutenant colonel. He retired as a colonel in 1882.

BENJAMIN, JUDAH PHILIP (1811–1884) CSA. Born in the Virgin Islands, Benjamin was the most prominent member of the **Confederate cabinet**. Of British-Jewish parentage, he grew up in **South Carolina** and entered Yale University at age 14. Benjamin dropped out of college when he was 17 and moved to **New Orleans, Louisiana**, where he became a law partner with **John Slidell**. He was elected to the U.S. Senate in 1852, the first known Jew to be so elected, but resigned his seat in February 1861 after **Louisiana** seceded.

Although Benjamin once challenged **Jefferson Davis** to a duel over a perceived insult, Davis appointed him the Confederate attorney general in February 1861. He held that post until Davis appointed him secretary of war in September 1861. Because many politicians blamed him for the Confederate defeats at **Port Royal**, **South Carolina**, and **Forts Henry and Donelson**, **Tennessee**, Benjamin finally resigned from the War Department in March 1862. On that same day, Davis appointed him secretary of state, a position he held for the rest of the war. Late in the war, Benjamin strongly supported the enlistment of **black troops** to fight for the Confederacy in return for their freedom.

Benjamin escaped capture at war's end and fled to Great Britain, where he became a wealthy barrister. He never returned to the United States. Benjamin had been a brilliant, but controversial Confederate figure, partly because of his Jewish heritage, partly because such mannerisms as a perpetual smile made him appear flippant.

BENNETT'S FARM, NORTH CAROLINA, SURRENDER AT (MAY 3, 1865). *See* DURHAM STATION, NORTH CAROLINA, SURRENDER AT.

BENNING, HENRY LEWIS (1814–1875) CSA. A native of **Georgia**, Benning graduated first in his Franklin College class. He then became a lawyer and served as a Georgia solicitor general and legislator. A secessionist, Benning was a delegate to the **Nashville Convention** and, while serving on the Georgia Supreme Court, wrote an opinion arguing that state supreme courts were on an equal footing with the **U.S. Supreme Court.** He also served as a delegate at both the 1860 **Democratic** National Convention and the 1861 Georgia **secession** convention.

After secession, Benning raised a **regiment** of volunteers and in August 1861 was elected colonel of the 17th Georgia. Sent to **Virginia**, he fought with the **Army of Northern Virginia** at **Malvern Hill** and **Second Manassas** and earned particular fame at **Antietam** when he defended Burnside's Bridge while in command of **Robert Toombs's brigade.** After commanding Toomb's brigade at **Fredericksburg**, Benning was promoted to brigadier general in March 1863 and took permanent command of the brigade.

Benning led his brigade with skill at **Gettysburg, Chickamauga** (where he lost three horses and captured eight cannons), **Wauhatchie**, and **Knoxville.** He then was severely wounded at the **Wilderness** and was out of action until the **Petersburg Campaign.** Benning returned to the **army** to lead his brigade in this campaign and surrendered with **Robert E. Lee** at **Appomattox** in April 1865. Benning was one of the best brigade commanders in the **Confederate army** and earned the nickname "Old Rock."

After the war, Benning resumed his Georgia law practice. Fort Benning, Georgia, is named in his honor.

BENTON, SAMUEL (1820–1864) CSA. A native of **Tennessee**, Benton was the nephew of Sen. Thomas Hart Benton. After working as a teacher, he moved to **Mississippi**, where he practiced law, served as a legislator, and became a prosecessionist delegate to the state's **secession** convention.

In 1861, Benton was appointed captain in the 9th Mississippi but in April 1862 was promoted to colonel of the 37th Mississippi (later redesignated the 34th Mississippi). He supposedly fought at **Shiloh** but is not mentioned in the official records and was absent from the **regiment** during the **Chickamauga Campaign.** After briefly commanding both the 24th and the 27th Mississippi in early 1864, Benton returned to his 34th Mississippi during the **Atlanta Campaign** and assumed command of the **brigade** in July 1864 when **Edward Walthall** was promoted to major general. At the **Battle of Atlanta**, Benton was mortally wounded by shell fragments that mangled his foot and pierced his chest. After his foot was amputated, he was promoted to brigadier general on July 26 but died two days later. Benton has the distinction of being the Confederate general who served the shortest length of time.

BENTON, USS. Constructed by James B. Eads at St. Louis, Missouri, the *Benton* was the largest and most powerful **ironclad** in **Andrew H. Foote's** Union fleet (conflicting figures of 633 and 1,033 tons are given for it), and Foote made it his flagship when it was assigned to his command in January 1862. The *Benton* saw much service at **Forts Henry and Donelson** and **Island No. 10**, but its heavy weight and weak engines made it slow and difficult to steer. While under **David D. Porter's** command, the *Benton* accompanied **William T. Sherman's** expedition to **Chickasaw Bayou** in December 1862 and was badly shot up by Confederate **artillery** fire. In this fight, the ship's commander, Lt. William Gwin, was killed and nine other men were killed or wounded. After being repaired, the *Benton* saw further service in the **Vicksburg** and **Red River Campaigns**. After surviving the war, it was sold for scrap in November 1865.

BENTON, WILLIAM PLUMMER (1828–1867) USA. A native of **Maryland**, Benton moved to **Indiana** when he was a boy. He fought in the **Mexican War** and then returned to Indiana and became a lawyer in 1851. In the 1850s, Benton served as a district attorney and judge and in 1861 was reportedly the first man of his county to enlist for the Union.

Benton was elected colonel of the 90-day 8th Indiana in April 1861 and again in September when the **regiment** reenlisted. After fighting at **Rich Mountain**, he and his men were sent to **Missouri** in September. Benton supposedly led a **brigade** at **Pea Ridge** but there is no record of his doing so.

In April 1862, Benton was promoted to brigadier general of volunteers and was given command of a **division** in October. In March 1863, he took command of a **brigade** in the **Army of the Tennessee's** XIII Corps and led it in the **Vicksburg Campaign**, being slightly wounded at **Jackson, Mississippi**. After the capture of **Vicksburg**, Benton led a division for a number of months in **Louisiana** and was commander of **Baton Rouge** from May to December 1864. In February 1865, he took over a division in the XIII Corps and led it in the **Mobile Campaign**, earning a **brevet** to major general of volunteers.

Benton was mustered out of the volunteers in July 1865 and returned to his law practice. The following year, however, he moved to Louisiana as a government agent and died there from yellow fever in 1867.

BENTONVILLE, NORTH CAROLINA, BATTLE OF (MARCH 19–21, 1865). One of the last major Confederate attacks of the war, this battle occurred during the 1865 **Carolinas Campaign**. From Fayetteville, North Carolina, **William T. Sherman** moved toward Goldsboro in two columns, led by Maj. Gens. **Henry Slocum** on the left and **Oliver O. Howard** on the right. At Goldsboro, Sherman was to link up with a third column marching from the coast. Confederate Gen. **Joseph E. Johnston** decided to attack Slocum's column before the two Union wings could unite.

After engaging Slocum at **Averasboro** on March 16, Johnston laid a trap near Bentonville in hopes of delaying or preventing him from reaching Goldsboro. He blocked the road with part of his **army**, while the rest took up a position perpendicular to his right flank in order to smash Slocum's left flank when he tried to push down the road. Contact was made on the afternoon of March 19, 1865, when Slocum pushed back **Wade Hampton's** cavalry and engaged Johnston's main line. The Confederates counterattacked and forced Slocum back, but poor maps, poor leadership, and confusion prevented Johnston from springing the devastating trap he had planned. The first day's fight was inconclusive, and Sherman arrived with Union reinforcements the next day.

Johnston decided to stay in place even though he had a sizeable stream known as Mill Creek in his rear. On March 21, Sherman attacked Johnston's center, while one **corps** tried to move around the Confederate left to cut Johnston's line of retreat. The Confederates, however, held on until dark and then withdrew. Sherman was criticized for not pursuing Johnston, but he believed the Confederate army posed no further threat. In the three-day battle, Sherman lost 1,455 men out of 16,127 engaged, while Johnston lost 2,606 out of 16,895.

BERDAN, HIRAM (1824–1893) USA. A New York City engineer, Berdan (bur-DAN) was an antebellum weapons inventor who patented a repeating **rifle** and was ranked the top amateur sport shooter for 15 years before the Civil War. Taking advantage of his fame when the war began, he organized two **regiments** of **sharpshooters** that became known as **Berdan's Sharpshooters**.

Berdan entered Union service in November 1861 when he was commissioned colonel of the 1st U.S. Sharpshooters. He rarely served with his regiment, however, instead concentrating on inventions and lobbying for contracts. One of Berdan's few actual combat experiences was at **Gettysburg**, where he led a **reconnaissance** on the second day. Overall, little respect was given to him either as a commander or as an honorable man. His regiment became famous for its skill and saw heavy combat with the **Army of the Potomac** in the **Peninsula**, **Chancellorsville**, and **Gettysburg Campaigns**. Despite his lackluster record, Berdan was **brevetted** brigadier general of volunteers for his service at Chancellorsville and major general for Gettysburg. He resigned from the **army** in January 1864.

After the war, Berdan continued to design such military innovations as a range finder and a torpedo boat.

BERDAN'S SHARPSHOOTERS. Organized by **Hiram Berdan** (bur-DAN) in 1861, the 1st and 2nd U.S. Sharpshooters became famous for their specialized service. Men had to qualify for membership by competing at marksmanship trials. Dressed in distinctive green **uniforms** and largely armed with .52-caliber **Sharps rifles** (some with telescopic sights), the men were used mostly as **skirmishers** and **sharpshooters** with the **Army of the Potomac**. The two **regiments** often were dispersed on the battlefield and performed valuable duty shooting artillerymen and officers or in slowing enemy advances with their rapid-firing **rifles**. They participated in most of the battles fought by the **army** and performed especially well at **Gettysburg** by slowing the Confederate advance on the second day. The regiments lost their identities late in the war when they were consolidated in December 1864. In February 1865, Berdan's Sharpshooters were disbanded, and the **companies** were dispersed among regular regiments. Out of 2,570 men, the two regiments lost 1,008 killed or wounded during the war.

BERMUDA HUNDRED CAMPAIGN (MAY 5–16, 1864). Named for the Bermuda Hundred Plantation, Bermuda Hundred was a peninsula formed by the confluence of the James and Appomattox Rivers about 15 miles southeast of **Richmond, Virginia**. It was an important strategic location since it lay between Richmond and Petersburg, and the vital Richmond & Petersburg Railroad linking the two cities ran across its western edge.

In May 1864, Union Maj. Gen. **Benjamin Butler** began the Bermuda Hundred Campaign as part of Lt. Gen. **U. S. Grant's** plan to advance against the Confederates on several fronts. In support of Grant's **Overland Campaign**, Butler was to land his **Army of the James** on Bermuda Hundred and cut the **railroad** supplying Richmond. Butler landed his troops by transports on May 5 and moved toward the railroad, but Confederate forces under **George Pickett** were rushed there by **department** commander **P. G. T. Beauregard**. Butler's advance was cautious, but his troops managed to gain a foothold on the railroad after fighting Pickett at **Port Walthall Junction** and **Swift Creek and Fort Clifton**. On May 10, an attack by the Confederates at **Chester Station** was repulsed, but the Federals withdrew to Bermuda Hundred after destroying some track.

On May 12, Butler advanced northward toward the Richmond defenses and touched off a series of battles over the next four days at **Second Drewry's Bluff**. Beauregard successfully massed troops in the area, and was able to hold the Federals in check. Butler then retreated back to Bermuda Hundred on May 16 and took up a defensive position behind a strong line of works that were built across the narrow neck of land. Beauregard followed and built his own line across the western base. Butler thus became, in the words of Grant, as if in a bottle "strongly corked." Union forces at Bermuda Hundred remained there through the **Petersburg Campaign**, until **Robert E. Lee** evacuated Richmond in April 1865.

BERRY, HIRAM GREGORY (1824–1863) USA. A native of **Maine**, Berry worked at numerous antebellum positions, including carpenter, bank president, state legislator, militia captain, and mayor.

Berry entered Union service in June 1861 when he was appointed colonel of the 4th Maine. After serving at **First Manassas**, he was promoted to brigadier general of volunteers in March 1862 and led a **brigade** in the **Army of the Potomac's** III Corps during the **Peninsula Campaign**. Illness kept Berry out of the **Antietam** and **Second Manassas Campaigns**, but in November 1862, he was promoted to major general of volunteers. Despite his recent promotion, he only led a brigade at **Fredericksburg** but in early 1863 was given command of **Joseph Hooker's** old III Corps **division**. At **Chancellorsville**, Berry was mortally wounded on the morning of May 3, 1863, and died within an hour. During the war, he was often commended by his superiors but remains a little known major general.

BERRYVILLE, VIRGINIA, BATTLE OF (SEPTEMBER 3–4, 1864). In August 1864, Maj. Gen. **Philip Sheridan**, newly appointed commander of Union forces in the **Shenandoah Valley**, began offensive operations against Lt. Gen. **Jubal A. Early's** Confederates, in what became known as **Sheridan's Shenandoah Valley Campaign**. Leaving **Harpers Ferry, West Virginia**, Sheridan **skirmished** with Early at **Summit Point and Cameron's Depot** and at **Smithfield Crossing** as Early retreated toward Winchester. On September 3, Sheridan moved toward Berryville from near Charles Town at the same time Early dispatched **Joseph B. Kershaw's** division eastward from Winchester down the Berryville Pike on a **reconnaissance**. Kershaw came upon Col. Joseph Thoburn's VIII Corps **division**, preparing to camp just west of Berryville, and attacked it at about 5:00 P.M. The Confederates crushed the Federal left flank, but darkness prevented them from following up the victory. That night both sides reinforced their positions, but the next morning Early decided to withdraw behind Opequon (oh-PEK-un) Creek rather than fight the now-superior enemy force. Thoburn lost 312 men at Berryville, while Kershaw's casualties were 195.

BETHEL CHURCH, VIRGINIA, BATTLE OF (JUNE 10, 1861). *See* BIG BETHEL, VIRGINIA, BATTLE OF.

BETHESDA CHURCH, VIRGINIA, BATTLE OF (MAY 28–30, 1864). *See* TOTOPOTOMOY CREEK, VIRGINIA, BATTLE OF.

BICKERDYKE, MARY ANN BALL (1817–1901) USA. A native of **Ohio**, "Mother Bickerdyke" was widowed before the Civil War and supported her family by becoming a "botanic physician." Living in **Illinois** when war erupted, her hometown of Galesburg began receiving soldiers' complaints of poor hospital conditions. Medical supplies soon were gathered, and Bickerdyke was chosen to take them to the **army**. She spent the war years working in field hospitals, finding medical supplies, cleaning up hospitals, and caring for soldiers. After Bickerdyke served **U. S. Grant's Army of the Tennessee** during the **Vicksburg Campaign**, **William T. Sherman** requested her services for his command. During the 1864 **Atlanta Campaign**, Bickerdyke served as the **U.S. Sanitary Commission's** field agent with Sherman's armies. Mother Bickerdyke claimed to have served in three armies and in 19 battles and became a beloved figure to Union soldiers. She rode in the **Grand Review** at war's end and was given a government pension in 1886.

BICKLEY, GEORGE WASHINGTON LAMB (1823–1867) CSA. A native of **Virginia**, Bickley moved to **Ohio** in the late 1840s and became a physician and political speaker. A rogue and scoundrel, he abandoned his family, always promoted himself, and greatly exaggerated perceived threats to the country. Bickley served on the faculty of Ohio's Eclectic Medical Institute from 1852 to 1859 but in 1857 organized the secret society **Knights of the Golden Circle**. This organization originally was devoted to spreading **slavery** by gaining American control of northern Mexico and attracted mostly Southern members. In 1860, the Knights of the Golden Circle recognized Bickley's weaknesses and removed him as their leader.

As the **secession** crisis deepened in early 1861, Confederate authorities began using the knights to promote their cause. The organization set up its headquarters at Montgomery, Alabama, but when civil war began, the knights believed their mission had been accomplished and disbanded. Bickley, who had lost control of his own organization, lived for a time in Knoxville, Tennessee, and tried to reorganize knights "castles" (or chapters) to secure the secession of **Kentucky**. When this failed, "Major General" Bickley briefly served in the **Confederate army** as a surgeon but was arrested by Union authorities when he entered **Indiana** in July 1863. Because of his association with the knights, he was held without trial and was not released until late 1865.

Upon his release from arrest, Bickley briefly made an unsuccessful speaking tour of Europe but then returned to the United States. In 1867, he died in obscurity and poverty in **Maryland**.

BIDWELL, DANIEL DAVIDSON (1819–1864) USA. A native of **New York**, Bidwell was a prominent militiaman and police justice before the war. He entered Union service as a private in the 65th New York, became **brigade** inspector, and eventually transferred to the 74th New York. In October 1861, Bidwell was appointed colonel of the 49th New York and led it in the **Army of the Potomac** through the **Peninsula Campaign**. He supposedly led a brigade during the **Seven Days** and **Antietam Campaigns**, but there is no official evidence to support the claim. Records do indicate Bidwell commanded his **regiment** at **Fredericksburg, Chancellorsville**, and **Gettysburg**. After commanding a brigade in the VI Corps' 2nd Division during the 1864 **Overland Campaign**, Bidwell was promoted to brigadier general of volunteers in August 1864. He fought with **Philip Sheridan** at **Third Winchester** and **Fisher's Hill** but was mortally wounded by a shell fragment early on the morning of October 19, 1864, at **Cedar Creek**.

BIERCE, AMBROSE GWINNETT (1842–1913?) USA. Born in **Ohio**, Bierce moved as a youngster to **Indiana**. He attended the Kentucky Military Institute for a while before beginning work for an **abolitionist** newspaper.

In April 1861, Bierce joined the 9th Indiana as a private and served in western **Virginia** with **George B. McClellan**. The **regiment** then was sent west, and he fought at **Shiloh, Corinth, Perryville, Stones River, Chickamauga**, and in the **Atlanta Campaign**, where he was wounded in the head at **Kennesaw Mountain**. During his service, Bierce rose from private to 1st lieutenant and topographical **engineer** for Maj. Gen. **William B. Hazen**.

During the postwar period, Bierce used his wartime experiences to become a famous writer and satirist. Promoted by William Randolph Hearst, he published *Tales of Soldiers and Civilians* (1891), *The Devil's Dictionary* (1906), and such short stories as "An Occurrence at Owl Creek Bridge" and "The Coup De Grace." Bierce's tales concentrated on the horrors of war and often had a surprise ending. While reporting on Mexican bandit Pancho Villa in 1913, he disappeared and is presumed to have been killed.

BIG BETHEL, VIRGINIA, BATTLE OF (JUNE 10, 1861). Also known as Bethel Church, this is generally considered to have been the Civil War's first battle after the bombardment of **Fort Sumter**. On June 9, 1861, Union Maj. Gen. **Benjamin Butler** sent a force of 4,400 men under Brig. Gen. Ebenezer Pierce, a **Massachusetts** militiaman, from Hampton and Newport News, Virginia, up the Virginia Peninsula to Big Bethel Church to probe the enemy entrenchments there held by **Daniel H. Hill's** 1st North Carolina. Because some Union soldiers wore gray **uniforms** and others forgot the watchword, there was much confusion that night, and some units fired into one another. After regrouping, the Federals advanced again against the now-alerted Confederates.

On the morning of June 10, a short, spirited fight erupted, but the Federals soon retired. Pierce lost 76 men, while the Confederates lost eight out of 1,200 men engaged. The "battle" was little more than a **skirmish** but received much attention, coming as it did so early in the war. The Union's poor showing confirmed Southern beliefs in their superiority as soldiers.

BIG BLACK RIVER BRIDGE, MISSISSIPPI, BATTLE OF (MAY 17, 1863). After its May 16, 1863, defeat at **Champion Hill**, **Mississippi**, during the **Vicksburg Campaign**, the Confederate **army** of Lt. Gen. **John C. Pemberton** retreated toward **Vicksburg**. Upon reaching the bridge across the Big Black River, Pemberton ordered Brig. Gen. **John Bowen** to man the breastworks on the river's east bank with three **brigades** and 18 cannons and to hold the bridge until Maj. Gen. **William Loring's** division crossed. Loring's **division**, however, took a circuitous rout to Jackson, Mississippi, instead of following Pemberton.

On May 17, Maj. Gen. **John McClernand's** Union **corps** arrived at the river leading **U. S. Grant's Army of the Tennessee**. While Grant sent **William T. Sherman's** and **James B. McPherson's** corps to flank the Confederates, Brig. Gen. **Michael Lawler's** brigade of McClernand's corps rushed across the river. Having already suffered a string of defeats, the Confederates panicked and fled after setting fire to the bridge. In the rout, Pemberton lost 1,700 men and 18 cannons captured, while Grant suffered 279 casualties. The disaster forced Pemberton to fall back into the Vicksburg defenses and set the stage for the protracted siege to come.

BIG BLUE RIVER, MISSOURI, BATTLE OF (OCTOBER 22–23, 1864). By late October 1864, Maj. Gen. **Sterling Price's Missouri Raid** was drawing to a close as the Confederates headed west toward **Kansas**. To protect Kansas, Maj. Gen. **Samuel Curtis's** Army of the Border drew up in a defensive position along the Big Blue River. When he approached the main ford and found the Federals there, Price sent Brig. Gen. **Joseph O. Shelby** south to locate another ford, while he kept the enemy in place. Shelby successfully crossed the Big Blue River at Byram's Ford on October 22, turned Curtis's right flank, and forced him to fall back to **Westport**.

Crossing the river, Price sent his wagon train southward with a strong guard the next morning while **John S. Marmaduke's** cavalry guarded Byram's Ford. Later that day, Union cavalryman **Alfred Pleasonton**, who had been chasing Price, sent **John McNeill's brigade** down the east bank of the river to cross over and intercept the Confederate wagon train while Pleasonton attacked Marmaduke at Byram's Ford. Pleasonton defeated Marmaduke and sent the Confederates fleeing to the west. Following up his victory, Pleasonton then attacked Price's rear and right flank. Meanwhile, McNeill caught up with the wagon train but decided its 5,000-man guard was too strong to attack. Casualties for the fighting along the Big Blue River are unknown, but afterward Pleasonton court-martialed McNeill for his lack of aggressiveness.

BIG ROUND TOP AT BATTLE OF GETTYSBURG, PENNSYLVANIA (JULY 2, 1863). *See* GETTYSBURG, PENNSYLVANIA, CAMPAIGN AND BATTLE OF.

BIRD CREEK, INDIAN TERRITORY, BATTLE OF (DECEMBER 9, 1861). *See* CHUSTO-TALASAH, INDIAN TERRITORY, BATTLE OF.

BIRGE, HENRY WARNER (1825–1888) USA. A native of **Connecticut**, Birge was a merchant and governor's staff member when the Civil War began.

Birge helped raise the 4th Connecticut and entered Union service as its major in May 1861. After serving with **Robert Patterson** in the **Shenandoah Valley** and in **Washington, D.C.**, he resigned his commission in November to raise the 13th Connecticut (Connecticut's first three-year **regiment**) and was appointed its colonel in February 1862. After accompanying the expedition that captured **New Orleans**,

Louisiana, Birge served in **Louisiana**, first under **Benjamin F. Butler** and later **Nathaniel P. Banks**. In January 1863, he was given a **brigade** in the XIX Corps' 4th Division and led it during the 1863 **Port Hudson Campaign** and was preparing to lead a last desperate assault against the Confederates when Port Hudson's surrender made it unnecessary.

In September 1863, Birge was promoted to brigadier general of volunteers and commanded the **Bayou Lafourche** region until the spring of 1864. He then participated in Banks's **Red River Campaign** and sometimes led a **division** during the operation. After the campaign, Birge's brigade was sent to **Virginia**, where it was attached to **Philip H. Sheridan's** command and fought at **Third Winchester**, **Fisher's Hill**, and **Cedar Creek**. His last active service was in command of the X Corps during the **Carolinas Campaign**. Birge was **brevetted** major general of volunteers in February 1865 and was mustered out of the **army** in October.

After the war, Birge was involved in several business ventures, including cotton and timber, and finally settled in New York City.

BIRNEY, DAVID BELL (1825–1864) USA. The son of antislavery leader **James G. Birney** and the younger brother of Union general **William Birney**, Birney was born in **Alabama**. He moved to **Ohio** as a boy and finally settled in **Pennsylvania**, where he became a prominent lawyer and businessman.

Birney entered Union service in April 1861 as lieutenant colonel of the 23rd Pennsylvania (which he largely recruited) and was commissioned its colonel in August. Promoted to brigadier general of volunteers in February 1862, he led a **brigade** in the **Army of the Potomac's** III Corps during the **Peninsula Campaign**. Partly because he was a supporter of controversial **army** commander **George B. McClellan**, Birney was disliked by some regular officers. He was accused of misconduct at **Williamsburg** and was court-martialed (and acquitted) for failing to engage the enemy at **Seven Pines**. At **Chantilly**, Birney assumed command of the **division** when Maj. Gen. **Philip Kearny** was killed. More controversy occurred at **Fredericksburg**, where he was accused of dereliction of duty. Still, Birney remained in division command and was praised for his efforts to halt the Confederate flank attack at **Chancellorsville**.

After being promoted to major general of volunteers in May 1863, Birney led his III Corps division at **Gettysburg**. When **Daniel Sickles** was wounded there, he assumed command of the **corps** even though he had received two slight wounds himself. After fighting through much of the 1864 **Overland Campaign**, Birney was given command of the X

Corps in May. He soon contracted malaria, and died after being taken back to Pennsylvania. Just before his death, Birney is said to have cried out, "Keep your eyes on that flag, boys!" (Faust, ed., *Historical Times Illustrated Encyclopedia of the Civil War*, 61)

BIRNEY, JAMES GILLESPIE (1792–1857) USA. The father of Union generals **David Bell Birney** and **William Birney**, Birney was an **Alabama** slave owner turned **abolitionist**. Before the Civil War, he freed his slaves in northern Alabama, moved to **Ohio**, and worked for both the **American Colonization Society** and the **American Anti-Slavery Society**. Unlike abolitionist **William Lloyd Garrison**, Birney supported political action to abolish **slavery**. He once was arrested for violating the **Fugitive Slave Act** and ran for president on the Liberal Party ticket in 1840 and 1844.

BIRNEY, WILLIAM (1819–1907) USA. The son of **abolitionist James G. Birney** and older brother of Union general **David B. Birney**, Birney was born in **Alabama** but moved to **Ohio** as a young man. After becoming a lawyer, he moved to Europe in 1848 and participated in that year's French revolution. Birney returned to the United States in 1853, started a **Pennsylvania** newspaper that year, and ran it until the outbreak of civil war.

Birney entered Union service in May 1861 as a captain in the 1st New Jersey. After fighting at **First Manassas**, he was appointed major of the 4th New Jersey in September and colonel in January 1863. Birney fought with this **regiment** and the **Army of the Potomac** at **Seven Pines**, **Second Manassas**, **Antietam**, **Fredericksburg**, and **Chancellorsville**. In May 1863, he was given simultaneous appointments as colonel of the 22nd U.S. Colored Troops and brigadier general of volunteers.

Birney raised seven regiments of **black troops** for the Union; freed the slaves being held in Baltimore, Maryland's, slave prison; and helped end **slavery** in **Maryland**. He commanded the **districts** of Florida and Hilton Head from April to June 1864 and then was given command of a **division** of black troops in the X Corps and returned to **Virginia**. There, Birney suffered a disastrous defeat in September 1864 when his division attacked the Confederate stronghold of Fort Gilmer near **Richmond's Fort Harrison**. In December 1864, Birney took command of a division in the **Army of the James's** XXV Corps and led it until war's end. He was **brevetted** major general of volunteers in March 1865 and was present for **Robert E. Lee's** surrender at **Appomattox**.

After the war, Birney lived in **Florida** for a while and then settled in **Washington, D.C.** There he served as a U.S. attorney, practiced law, and wrote a number of works, including a biography of his father.

BISLAND, LOUISIANA, BATTLE OF (APRIL 12–13, 1863). *See* FORT BISLAND, LOUISIANA, BATTLE OF.

BLACK HAT BRIGADE. *See* IRON BRIGADE.

BLACK HAWK, **USS.** Originally named the *New Uncle Sam*, this ship was purchased by the Union government in November 1862 at Cairo, Illinois. Commissioned and renamed the *Black Hawk*, it served as Adm. **David Porter's** flagship. Armed with eight cannons, the gunboat was 260 feet long and saw action at **Arkansas Post** and in the **Vicksburg** and **Red River Campaigns**. The *Black Hawk* burned and sank on April 22, 1865, in the Ohio River near Cairo.

BLACK REPUBLICANS. This was the nickname given by Southerners to members of the **Republican Party**. The name derived from the Southern belief that Republicans were **abolitionists** who desired racial equality. Although used in the 1860 presidential campaign, the term became most popular during **Reconstruction** when the Republicans labored to protect **freedmen** and to gain the black vote. *See also* ELECTION OF 1860.

BLACK TROOPS, USE OF. When the Civil War began, neither **army** allowed blacks to enlist; the Union because of racism and the fear of angering the slave-owning **border states**, and the Confederacy because of racism and its support of **slavery**. As the war dragged on, however, casualties mounted and white enlistments plummeted. Forced to accept blacks into the army in order to maintain strength, the **U.S. Congress** officially authorized their enlistment in July 1862. The following month recruitment began in **Kansas** for the **1st Kansas Colored Volunteers**, and some of the men became the first black Union soldiers to see combat when they engaged in a small battle at Island Mount, Missouri, in October. This **regiment** was not officially mustered into service, until January 1863, so the first sanctioned black Union regiment was the 1st Regiment of **Louisiana Native Guards**, which entered service at **New Orleans, Louisiana**, in September 1862 under Maj. Gen. **Benjamin F. Butler**. Union officers did not believe that blacks would make effective combat soldiers because it was believed they had an innate fear of whites and inferior personal qualities. As a result, black Union soldiers were used to perform such menial tasks as digging ditches, building fortifications, or guarding **prisoners** and supply depots in order to free up white soldiers to fight. These "U.S. Colored Troops" also were forced to have white officers (except the Louisiana Native Guards), received less pay than their white counterparts, and suffered from open abuse and resentment within their own army.

Attitudes toward black soldiers began to change in 1863 when they were first used in major combat. In May, the Louisiana Native Guards fought in the **Port Hudson Campaign**, and other blacks saw action at **Milliken's Bend, Louisiana**, in June before the **54th Massachusetts** made its famous assault against **Fort Wagner, South Carolina**, later that summer. These black soldiers proved their bravery and skill and convinced officials to make better use of them. In all, black Union soldiers engaged in 39 battles and 410 small clashes, suffering 68,178 casualties. Among their battles were **Fort Blakely, Goodrich's Landing, New Market Heights, Cabin Creek, Honey Springs**, Fort Clifton, **Fort Fisher, Nashville, Natural Bridge, Olustee, Palmito Ranch**, Milliken's Bend, and **Tupelo**. Their use infuriated Confederates and led to **massacres** at such places as **Baxter Springs, Fort Pillow, Poison Spring, First Saltville**, and the **Crater**. By war's end, approximately 180,000 blacks had served in 139 regiments and 10 **artillery** batteries. By 1865, nearly 10 percent of the Union army was black.

Confederate authorities used thousands of slaves as laborers, teamsters, and servants, but most loathed the idea of using blacks as soldiers. This attitude began to change as some officers recognized slaves as a potential source of manpower for the dwindling armies and realized that European powers would never recognize the Confederacy unless slavery was abolished or at least radically altered. The idea of trading freedom for military service was first proposed in January 1864 at the so-called **Dalton Conference**. While in winter camp at Dalton, Georgia, Maj. Gen. **Patrick Cleburne** of the **Army of Tennessee** wrote a paper proposing the enlistment of slaves with a promise of freedom if they loyally served. Cleburne had the support of his subordinates but met bitter opposition when he presented the paper to other army officers. **Jefferson Davis** was informed of the conference and ordered the matter dropped for political reasons, even though he personally thought the idea had some merit. Later in the war, as the Confederacy faced almost certain defeat, the idea gained new support from such generals as **Robert E. Lee**. With Lee's backing, a bill finally was passed in the **Confederate Congress** in March 1865 allowing the enlistment of slaves. Although no promise was made of freedom for those who served, the promise was implied. In **Richmond, Virginia**, Lee put Lt. Gen. **Richard S. Ewell** in charge of raising the black recruits, but Ewell ran into stiff opposition from slave owners and had little success. Following **Virginia's** lead, **North Carolina** and **Georgia** then authorized the enlistment of blacks into their units, but the move was too little too late. A small number of blacks were organized into a battalion at Richmond, but it apparently was never used in combat since the war ended soon after it was formed.

BLACKBURN'S FORD, VIRGINIA, BATTLE OF (JULY 18, 1861).
When Union Brig. Gen. **Irvin McDowell** marched out of **Washington, D.C.**, in July 1861 to begin the **First Manassas Campaign**, Brig. Gen. **Daniel Tyler** commanded the advance. At Centreville on July 18, Tyler learned that the Confederates had withdrawn across Bull Run and decided to feel their positions at Blackburn's and Mitchell's Fords. The Union **brigade** of Col. **Israel B. Richardson** and the Confederate brigade of Col. **James Longstreet** clashed at Blackburn's Ford. The opposing brigades clung to opposite sides of the stream and exchanged musketry and **artillery** fire for more than an hour. Longstreet was reinforced by Col. **Jubal Early's** brigade but was unable to dislodge Richardson. Under orders not to bring on a general engagement, Tyler finally withdrew his command. Tyler lost 83 men in the sharp fight, while the Confederates suffered 68 casualties. A prelude to the **First Battle of Manassas**, this battle served no real purpose other than to confirm that the Confederates were in position behind Bull Run.

BLACKFORD'S FORD, VIRGINIA, BATTLE OF (SEPTEMBER 19–20, 1862). *See* SHEPHERDSTOWN, VIRGINIA, BATTLE OF.

BLAIR, AUSTIN (1818–1894) USA. A native of **New York**, Blair became a **Michigan** lawyer and was elected to the state legislature as a **Whig** in 1845. After joining the **Republican Party**, he was elected governor in 1860 and held that position until January 1865. As governor, Blair strongly supported the Union war effort and made sure Michigan met its troop quota. After the war, he served three terms in the **U.S. Congress** during **Reconstruction**.

BLAIR, FRANCIS PRESTON, JR. (1821–1875) USA. A member of the prominent Blair family of **Missouri**, Francis Preston Jr. was the son of **Francis Preston Blair Sr.** and the brother of **Mongtomery Blair**. Born in **Kentucky**, Blair graduated from Princeton University and fought in the **Mexican War** before serving as the attorney general of the **New Mexico Territory**. Returning to Missouri, he helped organize the **Free-Soil Party** and was elected to the U.S. House of Representatives in 1856. Blair was defeated for reelection in 1858 but won back his seat in 1860 as a **Republican**. As a member of Congress during the **secession** crisis, he chaired the Committee on Military Defense.

Blair entered Union service in April 1861 when he was appointed colonel of the 1st Missouri (Union). Working hard to keep Missouri in the Union, he aided **Nathaniel Lyon** in seizing the St. Louis arsenal to prevent the secessionists from taking over the city. After raising seven **regiments** in the summer of 1862, Blair was commissioned brigadier general of volunteers in August and became one of the better political generals in the **army**. Promoted to major general of volunteers in November, he led a **brigade** in the attacks on **Chickasaw Bayou** and **Arkansas Post**. In January 1863, Blair assumed command of a brigade in the **Army of the Tennessee's** XV Corps and led it during the early stages of the **Vicksburg Campaign**. In April he was elevated to **division** command and remained there for the remainder of the campaign.

In October 1863, Blair was given command of the **corps** and led it through the **Chattanooga Campaign**. He then took over the army's XVII Corps in April 1864 and commanded it during the **Atlanta Campaign**. During this time, Blair also was a member of Congress, having regained his seat in March 1863 but losing it in June 1864 after a candidate contested the election. Blair went on to lead the X Corps through the **Carolinas Campaign** and then resigned his commission in November 1865. A close friend of both **U. S. Grant** and **William T. Sherman**, Blair had served his country well, but the war ruined him financially.

After the war, Blair was a moderate Republican during **Reconstruction**. Because of this, **Radical Republicans** rejected his nomination as minister to Austria. Becoming disgruntled with the Republican Party, Blair then reestablished the **Democratic Party** in Missouri and served as the unsuccessful Democratic vice presidential candidate in 1868. He fulfilled an uncompleted term in the U.S. Senate from 1871 to 1873 but failed to be reelected.

BLAIR, FRANCIS PRESTON, SR. (1791–1876) USA. Born in **Virginia**, Blair was the patriarch of the influential Missouri Blair family and the father of **Francis Preston Blair Jr.** and **Montgomery Blair**. An influential force in the antebellum **Democratic Party**, he was a friend of Andrew Jackson and served as the editor of the Washington *Globe*, the official newspaper of Jackson's administration. Although a slave owner, Blair was a staunch Unionist and joined the **Republican Party** in the 1850s. He supported the presidential nomination of **Abraham Lincoln** at the 1860 Republican National Convention and became one of Lincoln's close advisers.

During the Civil War, Blair met with **Jefferson Davis** in **Richmond, Virginia**, in December 1864 and proposed a truce, with the Union and Confederacy jointly enforcing the Monroe Doctrine to remove the French from Mexico. Blair hoped that such a **strategy** would lure the Southern states back into the Union. Although his ploy failed, it did lead to the **Hampton Roads Conference** in February 1865.

After the war, Blair's moderate **Reconstruction** views clashed with those of the **Radical Republicans**, and he rejoined the Democratic Party.

BLAIR, MONTGOMERY (1813–1883) USA. Born in **Kentucky**, Blair was the son of **Francis Preston Blair Sr.** and the brother of **Francis Preston Blair Jr.** He graduated from **West Point** in 1835 but resigned from the **U.S. Army** less than a year later, after serving in the **Seminole Wars**. Blair then practiced law under Thomas Hart Benton in **Missouri** and was elected the Democratic mayor of St. Louis in 1842. Moving to **Maryland**, he joined the **Republican Party** and argued the **Dred Scott** case before the **U.S. Supreme Court**. After serving as a delegate at the 1860 Republican National Convention, Blair was appointed to **Abraham Lincoln's** cabinet as postmaster general.

During the **secession** crisis, Blair strongly advised Lincoln to hold Union forts against Confederate seizure. He also ran the postal department with efficiency during the war but was opposed by **Radical Republicans** who disliked his moderate views. These Radicals finally forced Blair out of the cabinet in 1864 by pressuring Lincoln to ask for his resignation in return for Radical Republican support of Lincoln's reelection.

After the war, Blair supported President **Andrew Johnson's** lenient **Reconstruction** policy and rejoined the **Democratic Party**.

BLAIR'S LANDING, LOUISIANA, BATTLE OF (APRIL 12, 1864). Following the **Battles of Mansfield** and **Pleasant Hill** during the 1864 **Red River Campaign**, Union Maj. Gen. **Nathaniel P. Banks** abandoned his advance on Shreveport, Louisiana, and began retreating. Admiral **David Porter** had taken his fleet of gunboats up the Red River toward Shreveport, but low water, river obstructions, and the news of Banks's retreat forced him to withdraw as well. Confederate Maj. Gen. **Richard Taylor** sent his cavalry under Brig. Gen. **Thomas Green** to engage the fleet as it steamed back down the river.

On April 12, 1864, Green found several gunboats and transports either run aground or struggling through shallow water at Blair's Landing. He attacked, pitting dismounted cavalrymen against **ironclad** gunboats, and Union Brig. Gen. **Thomas Kilby Smith** disembarked part of his XVII Corps to engage the Confederates. Green, who some falsely claimed was drinking, was leading his troopers against four gunboats when he was nearly decapitated by an **artillery** shell. After a brief but fierce fight, the Confederates withdrew, and Porter continued his retreat. It is estimated that the Confederates lost about 300 men in the clash.

BLAKELY RIFLE. Invented by British Capt. Theophilus Alexander Blakely, the Blakely rifle was a **rifled** cannon used mostly by the Confederates. It was an accurate **artillery** piece that was made in various calibers and fired shells ranging from 10 to 470 lbs. Most of the guns were muzzle loaders, but a few were breech loading. The Blakely had a reputation for having a very high recoil, and its carriage often was damaged during firing.

BLANCHARD, ALBERT GALLATIN (1810–1891) CSA. A native of **Massachusetts**, Blanchard graduated from **West Point** in 1829. After resigning from the **U.S. Army** in 1840, he became a merchant in **New Orleans, Louisiana**, and served as the state's director of public schools. Blanchard led a volunteer **company** in the **Mexican War** and won an appointment to major in the 12th U.S. Infantry.

Blanchard entered Confederate service in 1861 when he was elected colonel of the 1st Louisiana. Sent to **Virginia**, he was appointed brigadier general in September and commanded a **brigade**, but **Robert E. Lee** released him from duty in June 1862 when he took command of the **Army of Northern Virginia**. Blanchard returned to Louisiana and was given command of the northern part of the state but was criticized for failing to prevent Union raids into his area. His superior, Maj. Gen. **Richard Taylor**, accused him of incompetence and the War Department relieved him of command in February 1863. After failing to be reassigned, Blanchard moved his family to **North Carolina**. He briefly led a brigade there in the war's final months and then returned to New Orleans, where he became a city surveyor.

BLAZER'S SCOUTS. Organized in August 1864 by Maj. Gen. **George Crook** to fight **John S. Mosby's Rangers** in Northern **Virginia**, this Union unit officially was known as the Independent Scouts. When it was put under the command of Capt. Richard Blazer, it became known as Blazer's Scouts. Although numbering only 100 men, the Scouts were armed with **Spencer rifles** and at first enjoyed some success in fighting Mosby. Mosby, however, lured them into open battle near Myerstown on November 18 and effectively wiped them out. Out of 62 men, the Scouts lost 33 killed, wounded, or captured, including Blazer taken **prisoner**.

"BLEEDING KANSAS." After the passage of Sen. **Stephen A. Douglas's Kansas-Nebraska Act** in 1854, both proslavery and **abolitionist** settlers moved into **Kansas**. The two factions quickly clashed as each attempted to win the territory for its side. Proslavery "Border Ruffians" from **Missouri** clashed with abolitionists armed with **"Beecher's Bibles."** In

1856, proslavery forces attacked the town of Lawrence, which led to the retaliatory murder of five proslavery men at Pottawatomie Creek by **John Brown** and his followers. As the violence escalated to near civil war, Kansas became known as "Bleeding Kansas." Elections held to decide the fate of Kansas were marred by violence and corruption, although it was clear that the majority of voters opposed **slavery**. Voters rejected the proslavery Lecompton Constitution in 1858, but turmoil continued for years. Kansas finally was admitted as a free state in 1861.

BLENKER, LOUIS (1812–1863) USA. A German native, Ludwig Blenker immigrated to the United States after participating in the 1848 German revolution. Adopting the name Louis, Blenker became a New York City merchant and in 1861 used his fame as a revolutionary to organize the 8th New York and become its colonel.

Blenker was given command of a **brigade** in June 1861 and at **First Manassas** commanded the retreating **army's** rear guard and won promotion to brigadier general of volunteers in August 1861. He took command of a brigade in **Joseph Hooker's** division of the **Army of the Potomac** in October and took charge of a **division** of mostly German immigrants in December. In March 1862, Blenker was sent to reinforce Maj. Gen. **John C. Frémont** in western **Virginia**. His division suffered from exposure and privations, and Blenker was injured in a fall from his horse, but the division finally joined Frémont in time to fight **Stonewall Jackson** at the **Battle of Cross Keys**, **Virginia**. Blenker, who did not perform particularly well in the battle, suffered heavy casualties and was relieved of command in June. Discharged from service in March 1863, he returned to **New York** and soon died from injuries sustained in the previous fall from his horse.

BLOCKADE. On April 19, 1861, **Abraham Lincoln** declared a naval blockade against the Confederate states. The blockade's goals were to prevent the Confederate **blockade runners** from exporting cotton and importing needed war material and to prevent **privateers** from raiding Union shipping. The blockade was the largest ever attempted up to that time but at first existed only on paper. There were more than 3,500 miles of southern coastline and nearly 200 points of entry to guard, but the **U.S. Navy** had fewer than 50 commissioned vessels. By 1862, however, the navy had organized four blockading squadrons (the **North** and **South Atlantic Blockading Squadrons**, and the East and West **Gulf Blockading Squadrons**) and by war's end had some 600 vessels enforcing the blockade. Combined Union forces gradually captured the Confederacy's major ports, and the blockade tightened around the fewer available ports. By 1865, only **Wilmington, North Carolina**, remained open, and it finally fell in mid-January. The blockade officially was lifted by President **Andrew Johnson** on June 23, 1865.

Just how effective the blockade was is debatable. As late as 1865 at least half of all blockade runners made it to port. While it is true that the blockade weakened the Confederacy, Confederate armies continued to receive supplies from overseas until war's end. By 1865, the Confederates actually had huge amounts of supplies stockpiled (although the distribution system often failed to deliver them). A lack of manpower and a poor transportation system were greater causes of Confederate defeat than the lack of supplies. Simply put, the Confederacy never lost a major battle because of a lack of arms or ammunition.

BLOCKADE RUNNERS. After **Abraham Lincoln** declared a naval **blockade** against the Confederacy on April 19, 1861, numerous Confederate ships began running the blockade to Europe, Bermuda, Cuba, and the Bahamas to bring back vital supplies. Early in the war, it was easy to penetrate the blockade, but the growing presence of the **U.S. Navy** made this task increasingly difficult, and by 1865 nearly half of those ships attempting to run it were captured. During the war, approximately 300 vessels tried to run the blockade, with 1,000 out of 1,300 attempts being successful. Of the 300 blockade runners, 136 were captured by the U.S. Navy, and 85 others were destroyed.

Many blockade runners were sleek and fast steam-powered vessels that usually were painted gray for camouflage. Early in the war, most were privately owned vessels, but later both state governments and the Confederate government purchased their own ships. Government-owned vessels usually concentrated on bringing war-related material from Europe, while private ships often brought luxury items that would bring the most profit. Depending on the cargo, as much as $100,000 profit could be made from a single voyage. Recognizing that this profit seeking hurt the war effort, the Confederate government in 1863 began forcing blockade runners to reserve part of their cargo space for war material. The following year, a law was passed allowing the government to reserve up to half of a ship's cargo space for its own use.

Most of the government supplies brought in by blockade runners were purchased through the use of cotton bonds. These certificates could either be redeemed with interest at a later date or used to purchase stockpiled Confederate cotton for transport and sale (at a high profit) in Europe. Approximately 1,250,000 bales of cotton were taken out of the Confederacy by blockade runners.

Blockade runners proved invaluable to the Confederacy. During the war, they provided 60 percent of its arms, 30 percent of its lead, 75 percent of its saltpeter, and most of its paper for cartridges, plus medicine, clothing, and food.

"BLOODY ANGLE" AT BATTLE OF SPOTSYLVANIA, VIRGINIA (MAY 12, 1864). *See* SPOTSYLVANIA, VIRGINIA, BATTLE OF.

"BLOODY LANE" AT BATTLE OF ANTIETAM, MARYLAND (SEPTEMBER 17, 1862). *See* ANTIETAM, MARYLAND, CAMPAIGN AND BATTLE OF.

"BLOODY POND" AT BATTLE OF SHILOH, TENNESSEE (APRIL 6, 1862). *See* SHILOH, TENNESSEE, CAMPAIGN AND BATTLE OF.

BLOUNTSVILLE, TENNESSEE, BATTLE OF (SEPTEMBER 22, 1863). To gain control of East **Tennessee**, where Union sentiment was strong, Maj. Gen. **Ambrose E. Burnside** and his **Army of the Ohio** seized control of Knoxville and the Cumberland Gap in September 1863 at the beginning of the **Knoxville Campaign**. Afterward, Col. John W. Foster's cavalry **brigade** was sent on a successful mission on September 19 to burn the **railroad** bridges above Bristol. On his return, Foster encountered at Blountsville elements of Confederate Maj. Gen. **Samuel Jones's** command under Col. James E. Carter of the 1st Tennessee Cavalry. After **artillery** shelling set fire to much of the town, Foster was able to drive the Confederates out of Blountsville. He then rejoined Burnside at Knoxville and allowed the Confederates to reoccupy the area. In the small action at Blountsville, Foster lost 27 men while the Confederate casualties are estimated at 165.

BLUE SPRINGS, TENNESSEE, BATTLE OF (OCTOBER 10, 1863). Just prior to the 1863 **Knoxville Campaign**, Confederate forces in East **Tennessee** were maneuvering to retake Cumberland Gap. Major General **Robert Ransom** dispatched 1,700 cavalry under Brig. Gen. **John S. Williams** to **demonstrate** near Bull's Gap along the East Tennessee & Virginia Railroad. Williams advanced farther than Ransom had intended and **skirmished** with Union cavalry under Brig. Gen. **Samuel P. Carter** at Blue Springs on October 3–9, 1863. Major General **Ambrose Burnside** reinforced Carter with more cavalry and infantry and advanced against Williams's isolated force on October 10. Williams began a fighting retreat but was vigorously attacked late in the afternoon. The Confederates inflicted heavy casualties on the Federals, and forced them to withdraw. Williams then discovered that the Cumberland Gap operation had been canceled and withdrew into **Virginia**, skirmishing frequently with the enemy as he went. Williams reported losing 216 men at Blue Springs, while Burnside counted 100 casualties.

BLUNT, JAMES GILLPATRICK (1826–1881) USA. A native of **Maine**, Blunt went to sea for five years when he was 15. Afterward, he graduated from an **Ohio** medical college and began a practice there before moving to **Kansas** in 1856. Blunt became a staunch supporter of **abolitionist John Brown** in **"Bleeding Kansas"** and, when civil war erupted, served as a regimental commander in **James H. Lane's Jayhawker** command. This unit participated in some **skirmishes** around Kansas and in the **Indian Territory**, but it was not officially mustered into Union service until April 1862.

In April 1862, Blunt was appointed brigadier general of volunteers and was put in command of the **Department of Kansas**. After winning a victory at **Old Fort Wayne**, he was promoted to major general of volunteers in March 1863. Given command of a **division**, Blunt then won victories at **Cane Hill** and **Prairie Grove**. In October 1863, however, Confederate guerrilla **William Quantrill massacred** the escort of one of Blunt's wagon trains near **Baxter Springs**, and Blunt was relieved of command. After service as a recruiter of **black troops**, he was given command of the District of Upper Arkansas in July 1864, as well as the District of South Kansas in October, and helped defeat Maj. Gen. **Sterling Price's Missouri Raid**.

Blunt was mustered out of service in July 1865 and resumed his Kansas medical practice. He moved to **Washington, D.C.**, in 1869 to take a position as a government claims agent and later worked in a government hospital for the insane.

BOGGS, WILLIAM ROBERTSON (1829–1911) CSA. A native of **Georgia**, Boggs graduated near the top of his 1849 **West Point** class and rose to the rank of 1st lieutenant while serving in the **engineers** and Ordnance Bureau. Resigning his commission in February 1861, he entered Confederate service as a captain on **P. G. T. Beauregard's** staff.

In April 1861, Boggs joined Maj. Gen. **Braxton Bragg's** staff and served as his chief of engineers and **artillery** at **Pensacola, Florida**. Although Bragg recommended Boggs for promotion to brigadier general, Boggs clashed with his superior and resigned his position in December 1861 to become Georgia's chief engineer. Promoted to brigadier general in November 1862, he then became Gen. **Edmund Kirby Smith's** chief of staff in 1863. After quarreling with Kirby Smith, Boggs again resigned his commission in the spring of 1865, but he briefly served as commander of the **Louisiana** District.

After the war, Boggs worked as an architect, **railroad** engineer, and professor in **Missouri** before moving to **Virginia** and becoming a professor of mechanics and drawing.

BOHEMIAN BRIGADE. This was a nickname adopted by Union **war correspondents** because of the close-knit and unusual lifestyle they followed.

BOHLEN, HENRY (1810–1862) USA. A German native, Bohlen immigrated to **Pennsylvania** as a boy and became a wealthy liquor dealer. He claimed to have served in the **Mexican War** and, when the Civil War began, helped raise the German-dominated 75th Pennsylvania. Bohlen was appointed colonel of the **regiment** in September 1861 and served with other German regiments in **Louis Blenker's division** of the **Army of the Potomac.**

Bohlen was given command of a **brigade** in Blenker's division in December 1861 and was promoted to brigadier general of volunteers in April 1862. After fighting at **Cross Keys**, his division was attached to the **Army of Virginia** and covered the Union retreat at **Cedar Mountain.** While on **reconnaissance** on August 22, 1862, Bohlen was killed when his brigade was forced to retreat across the Rappahannock River at Freeman's Ford.

BOMBPROOF. This was the Civil War term for a bunker or bomb shelter.

BONHAM, MILLEDGE LUKE (1813–1890) CSA. A native of **South Carolina**, Bonham (BONE-um) practiced law after graduating from South Carolina College. He also served as an officer in the **Seminole Wars** and became the state adjutant general, a major general of militia, and a legislator. Bonham fought in the **Mexican War** as lieutenant colonel of the 12th U.S. Infantry and served as governor of a Mexican province. In 1857, he assumed the congressional seat vacated by his cousin Preston Brooks as a result of the Brooks-Sumner Affair and remained in the **U.S. Congress** until South Carolina seceded in 1860.

After assuming command of the state militia in **Charleston**, Bonham was commissioned a Confederate brigadier general in April 1861. He led an infantry **brigade** at **First Manassas**, but his argumentative and temperamental nature led to his resigning his commission in January 1862 in a dispute with **Jefferson Davis** over seniority. Bonham quickly was elected to the **Confederate Congress** and served on the House Ways and Means Committee, where he championed **states rights**. He was elected governor of South Carolina in 1862 and served two years, but he reentered the **army** in February 1865 as a brigadier general and led cavalry under **Joseph E. Johnston** during the **Carolinas Campaign**.

After the war, Bonham was elected to one term in the state legislature, worked in insurance, and served as the state **railroad** commissioner.

"BONNIE BLUE FLAG, THE." Written in 1861 by English immigrant Harry McCarthy, "The Bonnie Blue Flag" was a popular patriotic tune in the Confederacy. Almost as popular as **"Dixie,"** the song supposedly referred to a pre-Confederate **flag** that had a blue field with one star representing **South Carolina**, the first state to secede. The field of stars then grew to eleven to represent the 11 states that officially seceded. At least 11 versions of the song were published by war's end. Despite its patriotic tone, the song's composer deserted the Confederate cause and moved to **Pennsylvania** during the war.

BOONSBORO, MARYLAND, BATTLE OF (JULY 8–14, 1863). *See* FALLING WATERS, MARYLAND, BATTLE OF.

BOOTH, JOHN WILKES (1838–1865) CSA. Born in **Maryland**, Booth was the member of a prominent acting family who took to the stage at age 15 and toured much of the United States. A staunch Southerner, he was in the **Virginia** militia during **John Brown's Raid** and witnessed Brown's hanging.

Despite his Southern bias, Booth did not join the **Confederate army** when civil war began, pursuing instead his acting career. In 1864, while in **Washington, D.C.**, he assembled a loose collection of associates and planned to kidnap **Abraham Lincoln** and hold him hostage for the release of Confederate **prisoners**. One attempt was made on March 17, 1865, but the presence of guards foiled the try. When news came of **Robert E. Lee's** surrender in April, Booth changed his plan to murder. His motive for **Lincoln's assassination** apparently was revenge, although there is some circumstantial evidence indicating Booth may have been working with the Confederate government in an attempt to win the war by throwing the Union government into disarray.

While Booth targeted Lincoln, two coconspirators were to kill Vice President **Andrew Johnson** and Secretary of State **William Seward**. Being a well-known actor, Booth had easy access to **Ford's Theater** on the night of April 14, 1865, where he shot Lincoln in the head. After slashing one of Lincoln's companions with a knife, Booth jumped to the stage from the presidential box, screaming the Virginia state motto "Sic Semper Tyrannis" ("Thus Always to Tyrants!"). Breaking his left leg when he hit the stage, Booth managed to escape the city with coconspirator **David Herold**. Seward was wounded in another attack, but Johnson's assassin lost his nerve and failed to carry out his part of the plan. Lincoln died the next morning from his wound.

While attempting to escape, Booth and Herold were cornered by Federal troops in a barn near Bowling Green, Virginia, on April 26. Booth refused to surrender, and the barn was set afire. Moments later, U.S. cavalry Sgt. Boston Corbett supposedly shot and mortally wounded Booth with his carbine, but an autopsy showed he had been shot with a pistol. Some people believed Booth actually had committed suicide.

BORDER STATES. Delaware, **Maryland**, **Kentucky**, and **Missouri** were considered to be the border states during the Civil War period. Although slave states, these four were split as to their loyalties, since the people had economic and family ties to both the North and South. Even those who eventually favored **secession** often did so reluctantly, realizing that any war would likely be fought on their soil. **Abraham Lincoln** struggled to keep the border states in the Union and even exempted them from the **Emancipation Proclamation**. Of the four states, Delaware was most loyal to the Union and never considered secession.

Many Marylanders joined the Union **army**, but there was also a large pro-Confederate population, which was greatly aroused after **Massachusetts** troops became involved in the 1861 **Baltimore Riot**. The pro-Union governor refused to call a secession convention. Numerous Marylanders joined the **Confederate army**, but occupation by Union troops prevented secession. The state was the scene of considerable military activity, including the **Antietam Campaign** and **Jubal A. Early's Washington Raid**.

Kentucky declared its neutrality at the war's beginning but could not maintain it. When Confederate forces under **Leonidas Polk** entered the state in 1861, the Union responded in kind. A pro-Confederate government was soon established, and Kentucky was admitted to the Confederacy, but it was in name only (although the Confederate **flag** did contain a star for the state), and the Confederate state government operated in exile. Kentuckians served on both sides during the war, and Kentucky was invaded by the Confederates in the 1862 **Kentucky Campaign**, but the state was occupied by Union troops for nearly the entire war.

Missouri suffered the greatest hardships of the border states. It rejected secession in 1861, but Gov. **Claiborne Jackson**, numerous officials, and many of its citizens were pro-Confederate. Jackson led a state government in exile that was admitted to the Confederacy (with a star in the flag, as well), but as with the other border states, Missouri was occupied by Union troops during most of the war. Besides furnishing troops to both sides, Missouri also suffered great devastation and loss of life from guerrilla activity and was the scene of **Sterling Price's Missouri Raid**.

BOREMAN, ARTHUR INGRAM (1823–1896) USA. A native of **Pennsylvania**, Boreman moved to western **Virginia**, where he became involved in politics and served three terms in the state legislature. He attended the Virginia **secession** convention in 1861 as a Unionist and refused to accept secession. Joining those Unionists who wished to create a separate state of **West Virginia**, Boreman presided over the Wheeling Convention, which named **Francis H. Pierpont** governor of a loyal Virginia government in June 1861.

Boreman served as a judge until the new state of West Virginia was admitted to the Union in June 1863, at which time, he was elected the first state governor. As governor, he confronted guerrilla violence and occasional Confederate cavalry raids. After being reelected twice, he retired from office in 1869, but then entered the United States Senate. Boreman served only one term and then practiced law and again served as a judge.

BORMANN FUSE. Developed by a Belgian military officer, this was an **artillery** time **fuse** that had a five-second limit. After screwing the fuse into the tip of a shell, the gunner punched out the appropriate length of time (which was marked in quarter seconds) in which the shell was to explode. Powder in the fuse was ignited when the cannon discharged, which in turn set off a charge at the appropriate time delay and exploded the shell.

BOTELER'S FORD, VIRGINIA, BATTLE OF (SEPTEMBER 19–20, 1862). *See* SHEPHERDSTOWN, VIRGINIA, BATTLE OF.

BOUNTIES. After the initial flourish of volunteers in 1861, both the Union and Confederacy found it increasingly difficult to entice men to join the service. One method of encouragement, used more by the Union than the Confederates, was the paying of bounties. Under this system, a recruit was paid a certain amount of money for enlisting. Later, bounties were also used to encourage veterans to reenlist. The system was often used by individual states struggling to meet their quota of men, but the federal and local governments resorted to it as well. Union bounties usually ran from $25.00 to as high as $1,500 for a three-year enlistment, with Confederate bounties rarely rising over $50. It is estimated that the U.S. government paid out $300,000,000 in bounties, with state and local governments probably paying an equal amount. These large sums of money led to "bounty-jumping," a process whereby unscrupulous men would enlist in one area, claim their bounty, and then promptly desert and do it all over again somewhere else.

BOUTWELL, GEORGE SEWALL (1818–1905) USA. A native of **Massachusetts**, Boutwell was largely a self-educated man who was elected governor in 1851 after serving seven terms in the legislature. A **Democrat**, he opposed **slavery** and received much of his support from the **Free-Soil Party**.

By 1861, Boutwell had joined the **Republican Party** and was appointed commissioner of internal revenue by **Abraham Lincoln**. He successfully developed an internal revenue system and allied himself with the **Radical Republicans** during the Civil War. Elected to the **U.S. Congress** in 1863, Boutwell served on the Joint Committee on Reconstruction, opposed President **Andrew Johnson**'s lenient **Reconstruction** policies, and served as a prosecutor in Johnson's impeachment trial. Afterward, Boutwell served as President **U. S. Grant's** secretary of the treasury and as a U.S. senator.

BOWEN, JAMES (1808–1886) USA. A prominent native of New York City, Bowen was president of the Erie Railroad, served as a **New York** legislator from 1848 to 1849, and in 1855 was president of New York City's first board of police commissioners.

After helping to organize a number of **regiments** when the Civil War began, he was commissioned a brigadier general of volunteers in October 1862. Because his age prevented him from performing field service, Bowen was appointed provost marshal for the **Department of the Gulf** in December 1862. He was relieved of duty along with his superior **Nathaniel P. Banks** after the disastrous 1864 **Red River Campaign** and then resigned his commission in July 1864. Bowen returned to New York City, where he became very active in charities and clubs.

BOWEN, JOHN STEVENS (1830–1863) CSA. A native of **Georgia**, Bowen graduated from **West Point** in 1853. He resigned from the **U.S. Army** in 1856 and moved to **Missouri**, where he joined the state militia. As a colonel, Bowen guarded the western border against **Jayhawkers**

and was captured along with other prosecessionists at **Camp Jackson** in May 1861.

When he was released, Bowen organized the 1st Missouri (Confederate) and became its colonel in June 1861. After service in **Kentucky**, he was promoted to brigadier general in March 1862 and was wounded at **Shiloh** while in command of a **brigade** in the **Army of Mississippi**. Rejoining his brigade in time for the battles of **Iuka** and **Corinth**, Bowen accused his commander **Earl Van Dorn** of misconduct during the latter battle. A court of inquiry cleared Van Dorn. Placed under Lt. Gen. **John C. Pemberton**, Bowen strongly fortified Grand Gulf, Mississippi, to defend the Mississippi River against **U. S. Grant** in the **Vicksburg Campaign**.

By April 1863, Bowen had been given command of a **division** under Pemberton. He fought off a Union navy attack on **Grand Gulf** that month and held a superior enemy force at bay at **Port Gibson** when Grant crossed the river into **Mississippi**. At **Champion Hill**, Bowen again fought with great skill, although his division was routed the next day at **Big Black River Bridge**. During the siege of **Vicksburg**, his division was held in reserve and often was put where the line was most threatened. Bowen's skillful actions won him promotion to major general in May 1863. Bowen's health was broken during the siege, and he died on July 13, 1863, just nine days after the city's surrender.

BOYD, BELLE (1843–1900) CSA. A native of the **Shenandoah Valley**, **Virginia**, Boyd was one of the most famous Confederate spies. She once killed a Union soldier who broke into her home and was captured and held **prisoner** a number of times. Boyd entertained Union officers in her home in order to gain military information, served as a courier for Generals **Stonewall Jackson** and **P. G. T. Beauregard**, and was able to bring important intelligence to Jackson minutes before he attacked **Front Royal, Virginia**, in May 1862. Jackson appointed her a captain and made her an honorary member of his staff. In 1863, Boyd was captured on a **blockade runner** and the next year married the Union officer who had been put in charge of her captured ship. Her husband later was cashiered from the **army** for allowing her to proceed to Great Britain. After the war, Boyd became an actress, married twice more, and published her memoirs.

BOYDTON PLANK ROAD, VIRGINIA, BATTLE OF (OCTOBER 27, 1864). *See* BURGESS' MILL, VIRGINIA, BATTLE OF.

BRADLEY, LUTHER PRENTICE (1822–1910) USA. A native of **Connecticut**, Bradley served in the state's militia before moving to **Illinois** in

1855 and becoming lieutenant colonel of a militia unit there. He also worked as a bookkeeper and salesman.

In November 1861, Bradley entered Union service as lieutenant colonel of the 51st Illinois. After fighting at **New Madrid and Island No. 10**, he became regimental colonel in October 1862. At **Stones River**, Bradley assumed command of his **Army of the Cumberland** brigade when his superior was killed, but in January 1863, he took command of another **brigade** in the XX Corps and led it through the **Tullahoma Campaign**. At **Chickamauga**, Bradley was badly wounded but earned a **brevet** for gallantry. He returned to his **regiment** in the IV Corps for the early part of the **Atlanta Campaign**, won another brevet for **Resaca**, and again assumed command of the brigade when his superior was killed at **Kennesaw Mountain**.

In July 1864, Bradley was promoted to brigadier general of volunteers. After the fall of Atlanta, his brigade was sent to defend **Tennessee** during the **Franklin and Nashville Campaign**, and he was wounded again at the **Battle of Franklin**. This wound kept Bradley off duty until after the war was over.

Bradley was mustered out of the volunteers in 1866 but remained in the regular **army** as lieutenant colonel of the 27th U.S. Infantry. He retired a colonel in 1886.

BRADY, MATHEW (1823?–1896) USA. A **New York** native, Brady was a popular photographer before the Civil War with studios in **Washington, D.C.**, and New York City. He accompanied Union forces at the **First Battle of Manassas** and became the first person to photograph a Civil War battlefield. Brady and his photographers **Alexander Gardner** and **Timothy O'Sullivan** took thousands of photographs during the war using a cumbersome camera and a wagon darkroom. In 1875, he sold his collection of 5,712 negatives to the federal government for $25,000 but died impoverished in a charity hospital. The Library of Congress houses the Brady photographs today.

BRAGG, BRAXTON (1817–1876) CSA. One of the most controversial Civil War generals, Bragg was a native of **North Carolina** and the brother of Confederate general **Thomas Bragg**. After graduating from **West Point** in 1833, Bragg served in the **Seminole** and **Mexican Wars** (distinguishing himself in the latter at Buena Vista), but then resigned his captain's commission in 1856 to become a **Louisiana** sugar planter. In 1860, he was put in charge of organizing the Louisiana militia and seized the Baton Rouge Arsenal in early 1861.

After Louisiana seceded in January 1861, Bragg was commissioned major general and was put in command of the Louisiana militia, but in March he entered Confederate service as a brigadier general. After defending Mobile, Alabama, and **Pensacola, Florida**, he was promoted to major general and led a **corps** under **Albert Sidney Johnston** at **Shiloh**. After the battle, Bragg was promoted to general and took command of the **Army of Tennessee** in June 1862. Under his leadership, the **army** launched the **Kentucky Campaign** in late summer and installed a Confederate governor in **Kentucky**. Although Bragg won a tactical victory at **Perryville** in October, he became embroiled in controversy when he withdrew back to **Tennessee**. In late December, he attacked William S. Rosecran's Union army at **Stones River**. After winning the first day's battle, Bragg failed in his subsequent attempts to crush the enemy and again retreated.

In the summer of 1863, Bragg was maneuvered out of Tennessee by Rosecrans in the **Tullahoma Campaign** but then counterattacked at **Chickamauga** in September. Rosecrans was defeated and retreated to Chattanooga, Tennessee, where Bragg took up positions on the surrounding high ground in an attempt to starve the enemy into surrender. In November 1863, however, **U. S. Grant** counterattacked and defeated Bragg at **Lookout Mountain** and **Missionary Ridge** in the **Chattanooga Campaign**. Bragg was forced to retreat into northwest **Georgia** and in December asked to be relieved of command. **Jefferson Davis** then brought him to **Richmond, Virginia**, where he served as the president's general-in-chief until he transferred to North Carolina late in the war and saw his final service under **Joseph E. Johnston** at **Bentonville**. As a general, Bragg was an exceptional organizer, administrator, and disciplinarian, but he also was argumentative, unpopular with his troops, and lacked decisiveness.

After the war, Bragg worked mainly as an engineer. Modern-day Fort Bragg, North Carolina, is named for him.

BRAGG, EDWARD STUYVESANT (1827–1912) USA. A native of **New York**, Bragg attended what is now Hobart College before becoming a lawyer in 1848. He moved to **Wisconsin** in 1850, became active in **Democratic** politics, and served both as a district attorney and a delegate to the 1860 Democratic National Convention.

Bragg entered Union service as a captain in the 6th Wisconsin in July 1861 and was promoted to major in September. Sent to **Virginia**, the **regiment** became part of the famous **Iron Brigade** in the **Army of the**

Potomac. After service around **Washington, D.C.**, and Fredericksburg, Bragg was promoted to lieutenant colonel in June 1862 and fought with the regiment at **Groveton**, **Antietam**, and **Fredericksburg**. In March 1863, he was appointed colonel of the 6th Wisconsin and led it at **Chancellorsville**. Illness forced Bragg to miss the **Gettysburg Campaign**, but when he returned to duty, he was put in command of a **brigade** in the V Corps' 3rd Division. He led it through most of the 1864 **Overland Campaign** but was put in command of what was left of the Iron Brigade in June. Later in June 1864, Bragg was promoted to brigadier general of volunteers. He continued to lead the brigade through the **Petersburg Campaign** to the final surrender at **Appomattox**. During his career, Bragg participated in every major battle fought by the Army of the Potomac except Gettysburg.

After being mustered out of the **army** in October 1865, Bragg returned to Wisconsin and was elected to the state senate in 1867. He also served eight years in the **U.S. Congress**, was a delegate to the Democratic National Convention three times, and was President Grover Cleveland's minister to Mexico. Breaking with the Democrats over the "free silver" issue, Bragg joined the **Republican Party** at the turn of the 20th century and served as Theodore Roosevelt's consul general to Hong Kong.

BRAGG, THOMAS (1810–1872) CSA. The brother of Confederate Gen. **Braxton Bragg**, Thomas Bragg was a native of **North Carolina**. After attending **Vermont's** Norwich Military Academy, he returned to his native state and became a lawyer in 1832. Becoming active in **Democratic Party** politics, Bragg was elected county attorney and in 1842 to one term in the state legislature. In 1854, he was elected governor and won reelection two years later. Elected to the U.S. Senate in 1859, Bragg did not believe in **secession** but did resign his seat in March 1861 as the Southern states left the Union.

In November 1861, Bragg was appointed Confederate attorney general to replace **Judah P. Benjamin** when he became secretary of war. Although he had serious reservations about the Confederacy's chance of victory, Bragg served his country well. He insisted that impressed supplies be paid for, tried unsuccessfully to establish a **Confederate supreme court**, and generally got along with **Jefferson Davis**. In March 1862, Bragg resigned from his post for unknown reasons and returned to **North Carolina**. After the war, he continued to practice law and be active in the Democratic Party.

BRAMLETTE, THOMAS E. (1817–1875) USA. A native of **Kentucky**, Bramlette worked as a lawyer before the Civil War and served in both the state legislature and as a commonwealth attorney. He became a judge in 1856 but resigned that position and raised the 3rd Kentucky (Union) when civil war came. Appointed regimental colonel in October 1861, Bramlette served in Kentucky and **Tennessee** before resigning in 1862 to become a district attorney. Elected governor of Kentucky in August 1863 as a **War Democrat**, he took office the following month. During his term of office, Bramlette refused an opportunity to enter the **U.S. Congress** and to run as **George B. McClellan's** vice president in the 1864 presidential election. He also was appointed a brigadier general of volunteers in April 1863 but refused the commission. Still serving as governor when the war ended, Bramlette was praised for treating with equal respect both Union and Confederate veterans. After leaving office in 1867, he resumed his law practice and unsuccessfully ran for the U.S. Senate.

BRANCH, LAWRENCE O'BRYAN (1820–1862) CSA. Orphaned in his native **North Carolina** at an early age, Branch was raised by his politician uncle and graduated from the College of New Jersey (Princeton). He then became a lawyer in **Florida** and served briefly in the **Seminole Wars** before returning to North Carolina to engage in the **railroad** business. Branch served in the **U.S. Congress** from 1852 to 1861 and turned down offers to serve as President **James Buchanan's** postmaster general and secretary of the treasury.

After **secession**, Branch first served as North Carolina's quartermaster general and then was appointed colonel of the 33rd North Carolina in September 1861. In November, he was promoted to brigadier general and led a famous North Carolina **brigade** in the **Army of Northern Virginia**. Branch fought losing battles against superior enemy forces at **New Bern, North Carolina**, and at **Hanover Court House, Virginia**, but then served well during the **Seven Days Campaign** and played a key role in winning the **Battle of Cedar Mountain**. After fighting at **Second Manassas**, he entered the **Battle of Antietam** and was killed by a shot to the cheek. Although he frequently complained about his superiors and his position in the **army**, Branch was seen as one of the army's most dependable brigade commanders.

BRANDON, WILLIAM LINDSAY (1800 or 1802–1890) CSA. A native of **Mississippi**, Brandon attended the College of New Jersey (Princeton) and became a Mississippi planter. He also served in the state legislature in the 1820s and became major general of the state militia.

Brandon entered Confederate service in June 1861 as a major but was promoted to lieutenant colonel and command of the 1st Mississippi Battalion in July. When the battalion was reorganized as the 21st Mississippi, he became its second in command. Joining the **Army of Northern Virginia**, Brandon led the **regiment** with skill at **Malvern Hill**, but he also received a wound that required the amputation of his right leg. He was promoted to regimental colonel in August 1863 and participated in the **Battle of Chickamauga**, but his unhealed wound forced him to resign from his position in October 1863. Nonetheless, Brandon was promoted to brigadier general in June 1864 and was given command of Mississippi's reserve troops. In this position, he often quarreled with Gov. **Charles Clark** over control of the militia, but he remained in command until war's end.

After the war, Brandon retired to his Mississippi plantation and served one term as lieutenant governor.

BRANDY STATION, VIRGINIA, BATTLE OF (JUNE 9, 1863). When **Robert E. Lee** and the **Army of Northern Virginia** prepared to launch the **Gettysburg Campaign** in June 1863, Maj. Gen. **Joseph Hooker** sent his Union cavalry from the **Army of the Potomac** to probe Lee's position to gather intelligence. Early on June 9, Union Maj. Gen. **Alfred Pleasonton** led 11,000 cavalrymen across the Rappahannock River at Beverly and Kelly's Fords. Pushing aside the Confederate **pickets**, the Union troopers soon ran into considerable opposition from **J. E. B. Stuart's** Confederate cavalry. Fighting raged up and down Fleetwood Hill near Brandy Station, with charges and countercharges being made. Lee sent **Richard S. Ewell's corps** to support Stuart, but Pleasonton withdrew before it arrived.

This battle was the largest cavalry battle of the war and marked a new beginning for the Union cavalry. Repeatedly outmatched by the Confederates in previous encounters, the Union troopers demonstrated at Brandy Station that they had become a force to be reckoned with. Although losing the fight, Pleasonton succeeded in learning that the Confederates were on the move. Being caught by surprise also embarrassed Stuart and may have contributed to his poor performance in the Gettysburg Campaign. In the fight, Pleasonton lost 936 men, including Brig. Gen. **Benjamin F. "Grimes" Davis** killed. Stuart reported a loss of 523 men.

BRANNAN, JOHN MILTON (1819–1892) USA. A native of **Washington, D.C.**, Brannan graduated from **West Point** in 1841 and won a

brevet and received a wound during his **artillery** service in the **Mexican War**. In September 1861, he was promoted from captain in the **U.S. Army** to brigadier general of volunteers and was sent to **Florida**. There he commanded the District of Key West in the summer of 1862 before taking temporary command of the **Department of the South** in August. For more than a year, Brannan remained in the **department**, sometimes in department command and sometimes in command of Beaufort, **South Carolina**. In a small **skirmish** at Jacksonville, Florida, in March 1863, he won another brevet for gallantry.

In April 1863, Brannan was transferred to the **Army of the Cumberland** and was given command of a **division** in the XXI Corps. The following month, he took a division in the XIV Corps and led it in the **Tullahoma** and **Chickamauga Campaigns**. In the latter campaign, Brannan helped **George H. Thomas** make the desperate defensive stand on **Snodgrass Hill** that allowed the Union **army** to retreat to Chattanooga, Tennessee. In October 1863, he was appointed chief of artillery for the Army of the Cumberland and remained in that position until war's end, fighting throughout the **Chattanooga** and **Atlanta Campaigns**.

Brannan earned brevets in the regular army from lieutenant colonel to major general. He remained in the army with the artillery as a major and retired as a colonel in 1881.

BRANTLEY, WILLIAM FELIX (1830–1870) CSA. Born in **Alabama** and raised in **Mississippi**, Brantley was a lawyer who served as a prosecession delegate at the Mississippi **secession** convention. Elected captain of a volunteer **company** in 1861, he became part of the 15th Mississippi. Brantley soon was promoted to major and fought at **Mill Springs** and **Shiloh**. In May 1862, he was promoted to lieutenant colonel of the 29th Mississippi and fought with it at **Corinth** and **Munfordville** in what became the **Army of Tennessee**. After being promoted to regimental colonel, Brantley led the unit at **Stones River**, where he was stunned by a shell. At times consolidated with other Mississippi units, Brantley's **regiment** fought well at **Chickamauga**, **Lookout Mountain**, and in the **Atlanta Campaign**.

In July 1864, Brantley was promoted to brigadier general and assumed command of his **brigade**. He led his men at **Ezra Church**, **Jonesboro**, **Franklin**, and **Nashville**, and surrendered with **Joseph E. Johnston** in **North Carolina** in 1865.

Although a very capable commander, Brantley was one of the lesser-known Confederate generals. In 1870, he was murdered in Mississippi by an unknown assailant.

BRATTON, JOHN (1831–1890) CSA. A native of **South Carolina**, Bratton graduated from South Carolina College and became a physician. Entering Confederate service in 1861 as a private, he was elected **company** captain and participated in the bombardment of **Fort Sumter**. Afterward, Bratton organized another company and became a 2nd lieutenant in the 6th South Carolina. He was elected the **regiment's** colonel in the spring of 1862 and fought at the **Battles of Williamsburg** and **Seven Pines**. Wounded and captured in the latter battle, Bratton was **exchanged** in time to fight with the **Army of Northern Virginia** at **Fredericksburg**. He temporarily commanded **Micah Jenkins's brigade** at the siege of **Suffolk** and in the **Chattanooga Campaign** and led it in a charge at the **Battle of Wauhatchie**. Bratton then assumed permanent brigade command after Jenkins's death and led it with skill at **Spotsylvania**. Promoted to brigadier general in June 1864, he fought in several battles during the **Petersburg Campaign** and became nicknamed "Old Reliable." Bratton surrendered his command with the rest of the **army** at **Appomattox**.

After the war, Bratton was active in South Carolina politics. He served as a state senator and congressman and unsuccessfully ran for governor.

BRAWNER'S FARM, VIRGINIA, BATTLE OF (AUGUST 28, 1862). *See* GROVETON, VIRGINIA, BATTLE OF.

BRAYMAN, MASON (1813–1895) USA. A native of **New York**, Brayman served as a distinguished newspaper editor and lawyer before moving to **Michigan** and becoming a city attorney. He then moved to **Illinois** in 1842, where he served as a regent for the University of Illinois, became reporter for the 1847 constitutional convention, worked as a **railroad** lawyer, and tried to maintain peace during the turmoil that led to the removal of Mormons from the state.

Brayman entered Union service in August 1861 as major of the 29th Illinois. After fighting at **Belmont, Fort Donelson**, and **Shiloh**, he was promoted to colonel in April 1862. Promotion to brigadier general of volunteers followed in September, and in March 1863, he was given command of a **brigade** in the **Army of the Tennessee's** XVI Corps. Brayman commanded Cairo, Illinois, in March–April 1864 and then was placed in charge of the Natchez, Mississippi, **district** for the remainder of the war.

Brayman was **brevetted** major general of volunteers for his war service and was mustered out of the volunteers in August 1865. He then became involved with railroads in **Missouri** and **Arkansas** before resuming his work as a newspaper editor in Illinois. Brayman moved to **Wisconsin** in 1873 but in 1876 was appointed governor of Idaho.

BREAD RIOT, RICHMOND, VIRGINIA (APRIL 2, 1863). On April 2, 1863, a large crowd of mostly women and boys marched through **Richmond, Virginia**, to demand bread at a time when food shortages were becoming chronic in the Confederacy. The crowd grew to more than 1,000 and soon began looting stores in the business district. President **Jefferson Davis** confronted the mob with a militia **company** and tried to persuade it to disperse, even throwing what little money he had to the people. When this failed, he ordered the mob to disperse in five minutes or he would order the soldiers to open fire. The crowd then retreated, and order was restored. Later, some of the mob's leaders were convicted of rioting and were imprisoned.

BRECKINRIDGE, JOHN CABELL (1821–1875) CSA. Born into a prominent **Kentucky** family, Breckinridge was the cousin of **Margaret E. Breckinridge**. After attending several colleges, he practiced law in his native state and served as a major in the **Mexican War** but was not in combat. A member of the **Democratic Party**, Breckinridge served in the state legislature and was elected to the U.S. House of Representatives in 1851. In 1856, he was elected **James Buchanan's** vice president. A moderate, Breckinridge reluctantly ran for president on the Southern Democratic ticket in 1860 and placed second in the election. Since he already had been elected to the U.S. Senate, he took his seat there in 1861. In the Senate, Breckinridge defended the South's rights, but he opposed war. The federal government believed he was dangerous and planned to arrest him, but Breckinridge escaped and accepted a brigadier general's commission in the **Confederate army** in November 1861.

Breckinridge commanded a **division** in the **Army of Mississippi** at **Shiloh** and won promotion to major general in April 1862. In August, he led a small force in the **Battle of Baton Rouge**, **Louisiana**, and then withdrew to Port Hudson, Louisiana, where he began building fortifications. Breckinridge's division saw heavy fighting at **Stones River** with the **Army of Tennessee**, and he served under **Joseph E. Johnston** during the **Vicksburg Campaign**. At **Chickamauga**, Breckinridge's division played a major role in breaking the Union line, and he temporarily led a **corps** during the **Chattanooga Campaign**. After the enemy broke his line at **Missionary Ridge**, Breckinridge was accused by **Braxton Bragg** of being drunk during the battle. **Jefferson Davis** then transferred him to an independent command in southwest **Virginia**, where he won a major victory at **New Market** in May 1864. Joining **Robert E. Lee's Army of Northern Virginia**, Breckinridge led a division at **Cold Harbor**, where he was injured when his horse was killed. Afterward, he was sent back to defend the **Shenandoah Valley** and led a corps under **Jubal Early** during **Philip H. Sheridan's Shenandoah Valley Campaign**.

In February 1865, Breckinridge was appointed the Confederacy's last secretary of war. He served well with the resources available and in 1865 counseled for an honorable surrender. Breckinridge participated in the **surrender** negotiations between **William T. Sherman** and Johnston in April 1865 and essentially disbanded the Confederate government soon afterward.

Escaping to Cuba after the war, Breckinridge stayed in Europe and Canada but returned to the United States in 1868 and settled in Kentucky.

BRECKINRIDGE, MARGARET E. (1832–1864) USA. A cousin of **John C. Breckinridge**, Breckinridge left her **New Jersey** home in 1862 and became a nurse in the Union hospital at Lexington, Kentucky. She soon became an agent for the **U.S. Sanitary Commission** and in 1863 served on boats ferrying Union sick and wounded from **Vicksburg, Mississippi**, to St. Louis, Missouri. Breckinridge became exhausted and sick during this time and died in Niagara, New York, in 1864, perhaps from typhoid fever. Because of her Confederate relations, she attracted a great deal of publicity during the war.

BRENTWOOD, TENNESSEE, BATTLE OF (MARCH 25, 1863). After the **Battle of Stones River**, opposing cavalry were very active in the Middle Tennessee region in early 1863, leading to clashes at **Dover**, **Thompson's Station**, and **Vaught's Hill**. On March 15, Maj. Gen. **Nathan Bedford Forrest** led his **division** in an attack on Brentwood, a station on the Nashville & Decatur Railroad. After destroying some track and cutting the **telegraph** wire, Forrest surrounded the town with his **artillery** on March 25. The small Union garrison under Lt. Col. Edward Bloodgood surrendered, however, before Forrest opened fire. In the small clash, Forrest lost only three men, but he captured 529 **prisoners**. He then continued on to **Franklin**, where he captured 230 more Federals.

BREVARD, THEODORE WASHINGTON (1835–1882) CSA. A native of **Alabama**, but raised in **Florida**, Brevard was a lawyer and Florida's adjutant general and inspector general before the Civil War. He entered Confederate service in early 1861 when he was elected captain of a **company** he raised.

Joining the 2nd Florida, Brevard saw combat at the **Battle of Williamsburg, Virginia**, but then returned to Florida in 1862 after he failed to be reelected captain. In October, Brevard was appointed major of the 2nd Florida Partisan Ranger Battalion, which was reorganized in 1863 as the 2nd Florida Infantry Battalion. He participated in operations against Jacksonville that year and was promoted to lieutenant colonel in August. In 1864, Brevard was sent to reinforce **Joseph Finegan's** Florida **brigade** in the **Army of Northern Virginia**. Appointed colonel of the 11th Florida in June 1864, he remained in **Virginia** and generally was viewed as a competent officer.

In March 1865, Brevard was appointed brigadier general and was to be given command of the Florida brigade, but in the chaos of the war's final days, he never received his commission and was forced to serve under the brigade's senior colonel. Brevard was captured at **Sailor's Creek** and returned to his Florida law practice after being released from **prison**.

BREVET RANK. Essentially an honorary rank, the brevet (bruh-VET) was given in the **U.S. Army** for brave or meritorious service. When brevetted, an officer was allowed to use the title of that rank but did not receive its pay or authority. It led to much confusion, because an officer might be known as "colonel," when his actual rank was captain. During the Civil War, approximately 1,700 Union officers were brevetted brigadier general or major general. Perhaps the best-known example of the brevet rank was **George A. Custer**. Although a lieutenant colonel in the regular **army**, he had been brevetted major general for his Civil War service. Thus at the time of his death at the Little Big Horn, Custer was referred to as General Custer.

BRICE'S CROSS ROADS, MISSISSIPPI, BATTLE OF (JUNE 10, 1864). During the 1864 **Atlanta Campaign**, Maj. Gen. **William T. Sherman** ordered Brig. Gen. **Samuel D. Sturgis** to engage and defeat Maj. Gen. **Nathan Bedford Forrest's** Confederate cavalry in northern **Mississippi** to keep Forrest from interfering with Sherman's long supply line in northern **Georgia** and **Tennessee**. Sturgis left Memphis, Tennessee, on June 2, 1864, with 8,500 men. Slowed by rain, he camped June 9 about nine miles northwest of Brice's Cross Roads, Mississippi, where Forrest had ordered his 3,500 cavalry to concentrate.

On June 10, Brig. Gen. **Benjamin Grierson's** cavalry led Sturgis's column toward Brice's Cross Roads. By mid-morning, Grierson had pushed back Forrest's **videttes**, crossed over Tishomingo Creek, and engaged Forrest about a mile beyond the crossroads. Forrest's **tactical** plan was based on his knowledge of the roads and weather. He knew that once battle was joined, the Union infantry would be hurried to the front over the muddy roads in killing heat and humidity. Forrest planned first to defeat Grierson's cavalry and then turn on the exhausted Union infantry once they arrived.

The plan worked flawlessly. Although outnumbered three to one, Forrest defeated Grierson by noon. Reinforced by a fresh cavalry **brigade**, he then attacked Sturgis's exhausted infantry as it came onto the field and in bitter fighting pushed Sturgis back across Tishomingo Creek. The retreat then became a rout, and much of Sturgis's **artillery** and wagons were abandoned. Forrest continued the pursuit the next day.

In the fight, which is also known as the Battle of Guntown or Tishomingo Creek, Forrest lost 492 men to Sturgis's 2,240, most of whom were captured. In addition, Forrest captured 16 cannons, 192 wagons, and 1,500 **rifles**. The battle ruined Sturgis's career, and he never again held a field command.

BRIGADE. A brigade was a military unit generally consisting of four to six infantry or cavalry **regiments**, with two to four brigades making up a **division**. In theory, a brigade was supposed to number from 4,000 to 6,000 men, but casualties, sickness, and detached duty greatly reduced a brigade's strength. Most brigades actually went into battle with 1,000 to 1,500 men. A brigade usually was commanded by a brigadier general but sometimes was led by a colonel—especially in the Union **army**. The Confederates referred to their brigades by the commander's name, such as "Early's brigade," while the Federals referred to theirs by numbers, such as the "1st Brigade." Also, Confederate brigades usually were made up of regiments from one state, while the Federals more often brigaded together regiments from different states.

BRIGGS, HENRY SHAW (1824–1887) USA. A native of **Massachusetts**, Briggs was the son of a congressman and governor. After graduating from Williams College in 1844, he became a lawyer in 1848 and was elected to the state legislature in 1856.

Briggs entered Union service as a militia **company** captain in April 1861 and became part of the 8th Massachusetts Militia. When his 90-day company was mustered out of service, he was commissioned colonel of the 10th Massachusetts in June. Sent to **Washington, D.C.**, the **regiment** performed garrison duty and drilled before becoming part of the **Army of the Potomac**. Briggs temporarily took command of a **brigade** in the IV Corps' 1st Division in the spring of 1862, but he then returned to the regiment and was severely wounded in both thighs at **Seven Pines** during the **Peninsula Campaign**.

Promoted to brigadier general of volunteers in July 1862 while still recovering from his wounds, Briggs physically was unable to perform much field service for the duration of the war. He was put in command of a brigade garrisoning **Maryland** in February 1863 and later ran a camp for **conscripts** in **Virginia**.

After being mustered out of service in December 1865, Briggs returned to Massachusetts. He continued to be active in state politics, served as the state's auditor until 1869, became a judge, and worked as an appraiser at the Boston Custom House.

BRISTOE STATION, VIRGINIA, CAMPAIGN AND BATTLE OF (OCTOBER 9–22, 1863). Following the **Gettysburg Campaign**, the **Army of Northern Virginia** and the **Army of the Potomac** recuperated in their **Virginia** camps. In early October 1863, **Robert E. Lee** learned that Maj. Gen. **George G. Meade** had sent two of his **corps** to reinforce the beleaguered Union garrison at Chattanooga, Tennessee. Although Lt. Gen. **James Longstreet's** corps also was in **Tennessee**, Lee decided the time was right for offensive action.

On October 9, 1863, Lee marched his two remaining corps west and north from his camps south of the Rapidan River to turn Meade's right flank and to threaten **Washington, D.C.** Meade was forced to withdraw from his camps near Culpeper, which was occupied by Lee on October 11. From Culpeper, Lee sent **A. P. Hill's** corps on a wide westerly march in an attempt to get into Meade's rear, while **Richard Ewell's** corps followed the Union retreat along the Orange & Alexandria Railroad. On October 14, a small battle was fought at **Auburn, Virginia**, and Hill learned that Meade was to his east along the Orange & Alexandria Railroad. He quickly turned to cut Meade's line of retreat at Bristoe Station.

Upon arriving at the station, Hill saw that the Union **army** was in the process of crossing Broad Run and decided to attack. He hurried Maj. Gen. **Henry Heth's division** into action and sent two **brigades** forward without proper **reconnaissance**. Unknown to Hill, Maj. Gen. **Gouverneur K. Warren's** Union II Corps (temporarily commanded by Brig. Gen. **John C. Caldwell**) was posted behind the **railroad** embankment that ran at an angle across Heth's front. Warren's men opened a furious fire on the Confederate right flank and forced Heth to angle his attack toward the railroad. In short time, Heth's two brigades were repulsed with 1,300 casualties. Among the Confederate wounded were Brig. Gens.

John R. Cooke, **William W. Kirkland**, and **Carnot Posey**, the last being mortally wounded. Warren reported losing 548 men. This battle was the largest of the Bristoe Station Campaign, and Lee held Hill responsible for the debacle. Afterward, Meade completed his crossing and took up a position near Centreville.

After two days of **skirmishing**, Lee began withdrawing Behind the Rapidan River on October 17. Meade cautiously pursued and numerous skirmishes occurred over the next few days. On October 19, Maj. Gen. **J. E. B. Stuart's** Confederate cavalry lured the Union cavalry under Maj. Gen. **H. Judson Kilpatrick** into an ambush at **Buckland Mills** and routed it in an action the Confederates called the "Buckland Races." Lee then crossed the Rappahannock River, and the campaign ended.

The campaign was marked by two significant battles and almost constant skirmishing. Lee lost 1,381 men—nearly all of them at Bristoe Station—while Meade suffered 2,292 casualties. Although Lee failed to damage Meade significantly, he did force the Union army to withdraw 40 miles.

BROOKE CANNON. Invented during the Civil War by Cmdr. **John Mercer Brooke** of the Confederate Bureau of Ordnance and Hydrography, the Brooke cannon was one of the war's best **rifled** cannons. Manufactured at the **Tredegar Iron Works** in **Richmond**, **Virginia**, it was made of cast iron and had one to three iron reinforcing bands encircling its breech to reinforce it and thus allow the cannon to fire heavy rounds. It differed from the **Parrott rifle** in that the bands were not welded together. Made in 3-inch to 11-inch bores for rifled guns and 10-inch and 11-inch smooth bores, the rifles were used in both fortifications and ironclads.

BROOKE, JOHN MERCER (1826–1906) CSA. A native of **Florida**, Brooke graduated from the **U.S. Naval Academy** in 1847. He sailed with Commodore Matthew Perry to Japan in 1854 and spent much of his antebellum career surveying the ocean floor with a sounding device he invented.

After resigning his lieutenant's commission in April 1861, Brooke entered first the **Virginia** navy and then the **Confederate navy** as a lieutenant. A proponent of **ironclads**, he served as inspecting officer during the conversion of the *USS Merrimac* into the ironclad **CSS *Virginia***. Placed in charge of the ship's armor and guns, Brooke was credited with the idea of angling the iron plating on ironclads to deflect enemy shot. In September 1862, he was promoted to commander and in March 1863 was appointed chief of the Bureau of Ordnance and Hydrography, a position he held until war's end. During the war, Brooke invented the **Brooke cannon**, a powerful **rifled** cannon that had reinforcing metal bands around its breech.

After the war, Brooke taught geography, meteorology, and astronomy at the **Virginia Military Institute**.

BROOKS-SUMNER AFFAIR. *See* SUMNER, CHARLES.

BROOKS, WILLIAM THOMAS HARBAUGH (1821–1870) USA. A native of **Ohio**, Brooks graduated from **West Point** in 1841. He served in both the **Seminole** and **Mexican Wars** and twice was **brevetted** for gallantry in the latter. After Mexico, Brooks served as a staff officer for **David E. Twiggs** and on frontier duty.

In September 1861, Brooks was promoted from captain to brigadier general of volunteers and the following month was given command of the **Army of the Potomac's Vermont brigade**. He fought well at the **Battle of Williamsburg** and in the **Seven Days Campaign**, suffering a leg wound during the latter at **Savage's Station** but remaining on the field. After being wounded again at **Antietam**, Brooks was given a **division** in the VI Corps in October 1862 and led it at **Fredericksburg** and **Chancellorsville**. His role in the former was criticized by Maj. Gen. **Ambrose Burnside**, who unsuccessfully tried to have Brooks dismissed from the service for speaking ill of government policy and demoralizing his command.

In June 1863, Brooks was promoted to major general and was put in command of the **Department of the Monongahela**. His previous clash with Burnside, however, led to the commission being revoked in April 1864. Brooks was given command of a division in the **Army of the James's** XVIII Corps that same month and led it at **Cold Harbor** and in the **Bermuda Hundred Campaign**. In June, he was given command of the X Corps but was forced to resign from the **army** the following month because of poor health.

After the war, Brooks became a farmer in **Alabama** and was accepted into society by his Southern neighbors. Oddly, he was buried with a Confederate emblem on his tombstone.

BROUGH, JOHN (1811–1865) USA. A native of **Ohio**, Brough became a prominent politician and newspaper editor before the Civil War. A **Democrat**, he owned three newspapers, served in several state positions (including the legislature), and was president of three different **railroads**.

Switching to the **Republican Party** during the war, Brough was elected governor of Ohio in 1863, defeating the **Peace Democrat**, **Clement Vallandigham**. Although a supporter of **Abraham Lincoln**, Brough was not popular and did not seek reelection. He died in office after developing gangrene in a sprained ankle.

BROWN, EGBERT BENSON (1816–1902) USA. A **New York** native, Brown sailed on a whaling ship as a young man before settling in Toledo, New York, in the 1840s. He worked as a grain dealer, built the city's first steam-powered grain elevator, and served as city clerk, councilman, and mayor before moving to **Missouri** in the 1850s to engage in the **railroad** industry.

A staunch Unionist, Brown entered Union service as lieutenant colonel of the 7th Missouri (Union) in August 1861. Resigning his commission in May 1862 to accept an appointment to brigadier general in the Missouri militia, he was put in command of the District of Southwest Missouri in June and spent his time fighting guerrillas.

In November 1862, Brown was commissioned a brigadier general of volunteers and two months later was severely wounded in the shoulder (losing the use of his arm) and hip at the **Second Battle of Springfield**. In June 1864, he was put in command of the District of Central Missouri. There, Brown again fought guerrillas and led a cavalry **brigade** during Confederate Maj. Gen. **Sterling Price's Missouri Raid**. During the campaign, Brown showed a lack of aggressiveness, and his failure to obey an order to attack at **Westport** led to his arrest. The matter apparently was not pursued, and he was put in command of the District of Rolla in January 1865. Brown remained in that position until he resigned from the **army** in November 1865.

After the war, Brown worked as a pension agent in Missouri from 1866 to 1868 and then became a farmer in **Illinois**.

BROWN, JOHN (1800–1859) USA. Born in **Connecticut**, Brown lived in **Ohio** and **Pennsylvania** as a young man and engaged in such unsuccessful financial ventures as tanning hides, raising sheep, and selling land. Twice married, he fathered 20 children. Brown also was deeply religious, abhorred **slavery** (once living in a community of free blacks), and came from a family where insanity was common. Brown probably was not insane, but he did come to view himself as God's instrument in helping end slavery and punishing slaveholders.

After moving to **"Bleeding Kansas"** with his sons in the 1850s, Brown became active with the **abolitionist** forces. When Southerners raided Lawrence in 1856, he led his followers in a raid on Pottawatomie Creek and murdered five proslavery men. Afterward, Brown began forming a plan to help free the slaves. With financial backing from some prominent abolitionists, he planned to attack the U.S. Arsenal at **Harpers Ferry, Virginia**, and steal weapons with which he could arm runaway slaves and start a general slave uprising.

With 18 followers, Brown attacked the arsenal on the night of October 16, 1859. The plan soon broke down when Brown was confronted by militia and later became surrounded in a brick firehouse by **U.S. Marines** under the command of Col. **Robert E. Lee**. This building finally was stormed, and Brown was wounded and captured. In **John Brown's Raid on Harpers Ferry**, 10 of Brown's men were killed, along with several civilians. Convicted of treason against **Virginia**, he was hanged on December 2, 1859, in Charles Town, Virginia, (modern-day **West Virginia**).

Brown's raid and martyr-like death further split apart the North and South. Southerners viewed him as a typical abolitionist who encouraged murder and rebellion. Most abolitionists denounced his methods but praised Brown for his lofty ideals.

BROWN, JOHN CALVIN (1827–1889) CSA. A **Tennessee** native, Brown was the brother of Tennessee Gov. Neill S. Brown. After graduating from Jackson College, Brown studied law with his brother and then began his own law practice. Opposed to **secession**, he served as a **John Bell** elector in the **election of 1860**.

In May 1861, Brown volunteered for Confederate service as a private but was quickly elected captain and then colonel of the 3rd Tennessee. In September, he was put in command of an infantry **brigade** and fought with it at **Fort Donelson** in February 1862. Brown played an important role in the attempted breakout there and then surrendered with the other troops.

A month after being **exchanged**, Brown was promoted to brigadier general in September 1862. He led an infantry brigade in **James P. Anderson's division** at **Perryville** and was severely wounded there. As part of the **Army of Tennessee**, Brown temporarily commanded **Alexander P. Stewart's** division in early 1863 and then returned to his brigade. At its head, he served in the **Tullahoma Campaign** and was wounded at **Chickamauga**. During the November 1863 **Chattanooga Campaign**, Brown temporarily commanded **Carter Stevenson's** division, and throughout the 1864 **Atlanta Campaign**, he often temporarily led different divisions while replacing wounded or absent commanders. In August 1864, Brown was promoted to major general and took command of **William B. Bate's** division. He received his third wound of the war while leading it at **Franklin**. Because of his wound, Brown was unable to rejoin his division until April 1865. He returned to the **army** in **North Carolina** just days before the final **surrender**.

Viewed as one of the Confederates' best fighting generals, Brown returned to Tennessee after the war. There he became involved in the **railroad** industry and twice was elected governor.

BROWN, JOSEPH EMERSON (1821–1894) CSA. Born in **South Carolina**, Brown moved to **Georgia** with his family as a boy. After working as a laborer and teacher, he graduated from Yale Law School, began a Georgia law practice, and entered **Democratic** politics. Strongly influenced by Andrew Jackson and **John C. Calhoun**, Brown began his political career in 1849 when he was elected to the state senate. In 1855, he was elected a circuit court judge and in 1857 won the gubernatorial race as a compromise candidate. A popular governor, Brown was reelected in 1859, 1861, and 1863.

A **secessionist**, Brown led Georgia out of the Union in 1861, seized **Forts Pulaski** and Jackson, and then personally took control of the **Augusta (Georgia) Arsenal**. During the Civil War, he often clashed with President **Jefferson Davis** over **states rights**. Believing the Confederate government was gaining too much power from the states, Brown fought with Davis over such issues as **conscription**, the **impressment** of slaves and supplies, the naming of officers, **tax** laws, the **suspension of the writ of habeas corpus**, and the use of Georgia troops. Captured near war's end, Brown was briefly imprisoned.

Upon his release from **prison**, Brown angered his supporters by advocating cooperation with the federal government and joining the **Republican Party**. He engaged in a number of business ventures and soon convinced many Georgians that cooperation was the correct path to follow. In 1868, Brown became Georgia's chief justice and in 1880 was appointed by the governor to the U.S. Senate, where he served two terms.

BROWNE, WILLIAM MONTAGUE (1823–1883) CSA. A native of Ireland, Browne was the son of a Parliament member who served in the British diplomatic service and in the Crimean War before moving to the United States in the 1850s. He became an editor of New York City and **Washington, D.C.**, newspapers but moved to Washington in 1859 and became a supporter of **secession**.

After moving to the South in early 1861, Browne was appointed Confederate assistant secretary of state in February 1861 by President **Jefferson Davis**. He served in that capacity until 1862 and actually was secretary of state for about a month in early 1862 before **Judah P. Benjamin** was finally appointed to that post. Browne's contributions to the state department are debated, and he resigned his post in April 1862 after being appointed colonel of cavalry and an aide-de-camp to Davis. Besides carrying out special duties for the president, he led a cavalry battalion on the **Virginia** Peninsula in 1863 and in April 1864 was appointed temporary superintendent of **conscription** in **Georgia**. There, Browne clashed with Gov. **Joseph E. Brown** over conscription until December 1864, when Browne was appointed brigadier general by Davis and was given command of local troops. After his **brigade** participated in the defense of **Savannah**, the Senate rejected Browne's nomination to brigadier general in February 1865, probably as an act of protest against Davis. He then returned to his position as head of Georgia conscription. Even though his nomination to brigadier general had been rejected, Browne was **paroled** as a brigadier general.

After the war, Browne farmed, practiced law, worked in the newspaper business, and taught history and political science at the University of Georgia.

BROWNELL, FRANCIS EDWIN (?–1894) USA. The first soldier to earn the **Medal of Honor**, Brownell was a private in Col. **Ephraim Elmer Ellsworth's** 11th New York Fire **Zouaves (Ellsworth's Zouaves)**. On May 24, 1861, Brownell accompanied Ellsworth to the Marshall Hotel in Alexandria, Virginia, to remove a Confederate **flag** from its roof. After Ellsworth removed the flag, the hotel's owner, James T. Jackson, confronted him on the stairway. Jackson shot and killed the colonel with a shotgun, but then Brownell killed Jackson by shooting and bayoneting him. Ellsworth was a personal friend of **Abraham Lincoln** and was the first Union officer to be killed in the war. Brownell was promoted to 2nd lieutenant but retired from the **army** in 1863. After several unsuccessful applications, he was finally awarded the Medal of Honor in 1877.

BROWNELL, KADY (1842–?) USA. Born in Africa to a British soldier, Brownell was married to a sergeant in the 5th Rhode Island. She became a **vivandière** and served as the **regiment's** color bearer at **First Manassas**. Brownell later served with the regiment at **New Bern, North Carolina**, and it was claimed that she carried the colors again in a charge there. Brownell's husband was wounded and disabled at New Bern, and Kady returned to **Rhode Island** when he was discharged.

BROWNLOW, WILLIAM GANNAWAY (1805–1877) USA. A native of **Virginia**, Brownlow grew up near Knoxville, Tennessee. Orphaned as a boy, he received little formal education but taught himself and became a Methodist minister and a **Whig** newspaper editor. Known as "Parson" Brownlow, he was a staunch Unionist, although he did support **slavery**. Brownlow continued his pro-Union writings even after **Tennessee's secession**, and in October 1861 his Knoxville newspaper was closed by the Confederate government and eventually sacked. When he continued to speak out and fly a Union **flag** over his house, Brownlow was arrested by the authorities. He was exiled to Union territory and became a popular speaker for the Union cause. In 1863, Brownlow returned to Knoxville when it was occupied by Union troops during the **Knoxville Campaign** and began publishing a new newspaper.

Brownlow supported Tennessee's reentry into the Union under a loyal government and was elected the Unionist governor in 1865. He was vilified by former Confederates during **Reconstruction** because of his harsh rule, but Brownlow was reelected in 1867. He then served one term in the U.S. Senate.

BRYAN, GOODE (1811–1885) CSA. A native of **Georgia**, Bryan graduated from **West Point** in 1834, but he served in the **U.S. Army** for only five months before resigning his commission. He then became a **railroad** engineer and moved to **Alabama**, where he became a planter and a colonel in the state militia. After serving in the **Mexican War** as a major, Bryan moved back to Georgia and became a prosperous planter, a captain in the Georgia militia, and a delegate to the state **secession** convention.

Bryan entered Confederate service in July 1861 as lieutenant colonel of the 16th Georgia. He was promoted to colonel in February 1862 and fought with the **Army of Northern Virginia** through the **Peninsula**, **Seven Days**, **Second Manassas**, **Fredericksburg**, **Chancellorsville**, and **Gettysburg Campaigns**. At Gettysburg, Bryan temporarily took command of **Paul J. Semmes's** brigade when Semmes was mortally wounded. Bryan's reputation as a competent regimental commander led to several recommendations for promotion.

In August 1863, Bryan was commissioned a brigadier general and took command of Semmes's **brigade** in **James Longstreet's corps**. He missed **Chickamauga** but led the brigade in the **Knoxville Campaign** and in the early stages of the **Overland Campaign**. Chronically plagued by poor health and often absent from his brigade, Bryan gave up command in July 1864 and then resigned his commission in September because of "gouty diathesis, complicated with great derangement of the kidneys" (Davis, ed., *The Confederate General*, vol. 1, 137).

After the war, Bryan served as a local politician in Augusta, Georgia.

BUCHANAN, FRANKLIN (1800–1874) CSA. A native of **Maryland**, Buchanan entered the **U.S. Navy** as a midshipman at age 14. In 1861, he was a captain and had served as the **U.S. Naval Academy's** first superintendent, fought in the **Mexican War**, sailed with Matthew Perry to Japan, and commanded the Washington Navy Yard. Believing his native state was about to secede, Buchanan resigned his commission in April 1861. When Maryland remained in the Union, however, he unsuccessfully tried to cancel the resignation, but Secretary of the Navy **Gideon Welles** dismissed him from the service.

Buchanan joined the **Confederate navy** as a captain in September 1861 and was appointed chief of the Bureau of Orders and Detail. He left that post in February 1862 and took command of the Chesapeake Bay Squadron. Serving as commander of the **CSS *Virginia***, Buchanan was wounded by small arms fire on the first day of the fight at **Hampton Roads** and had to relinquish command before the famous duel with the **USS *Monitor***. In August 1862, he was promoted to admiral and took command of the naval forces defending Mobile, Alabama. At the **Battle of Mobile Bay** in August 1864, he fought courageously against superior forces. Onboard the **CSS *Tennessee***, Buchanan again was seriously wounded and was finally forced to surrender. **Exchanged** in February 1865, he was reassigned to Mobile but did not reach the city before its surrender in April.

After the war, Buchanan served as president of the Maryland Agricultural College. *See also* MOBILE BAY, BATTLE OF.

BUCHANAN, JAMES (1791–1868) USA. A native of **Pennsylvania**, Buchanan served in the War of 1812 and had a long, impressive antebellum political career as a **Democrat**. He served in the U.S. House of Representatives from 1821 to 1831, was the minister to Russia from 1832 to 1834, served in the U.S. Senate from 1834 to 1845, was secretary of state from 1845 to 1849, and was minister to Great Britain from 1853 to 1856.

Buchanan was elected president in 1856, and the political strife between North and South consumed his administration. During his term, Buchanan frequently supported the South on such major issues as **Kansas's** proslavery Lecompton Constitution. When the **secession** crisis erupted in 1860–61, he struggled to avoid taking any action that might cause war and seemed content to just survive his term until **Abraham Lincoln** took office. As a result, events swirled out of control during the critical months before the 1861 inauguration. Despite his pro-Southern administration, Buchanan supported the Union during the war. Confederate Brig. Gen. **Charles S. Winder** was the son of Buchanan's sister-in-law.

BUCHANAN, ROBERT CHRISTIE (1811–1878) USA. A native of **Maryland**, Buchanan graduated in the 1830 **West Point** class and married the niece of President John Quincy Adams. A career officer, he rose to the rank of captain in the 4th U.S. Infantry and saw service in this Black Hawk, **Seminole**, and **Mexican Wars**, winning two **brevets** in the last. While stationed in the Pacific Northwest in 1854, Buchanan accepted Capt. **U. S. Grant's** resignation from his command. Grant despised Buchanan, but it was probably Grant's drinking that led Buchanan to ask for the resignation.

Buchanan was a major when the Civil War began, and his **regiment** was stationed in **Washington, D.C.**, for the first year of fighting. He was promoted to lieutenant colonel in September 1861 and in May 1862 was given command of a **brigade** of regulars in the **Army of the Potomac's** V Corps. During the **Seven Days Campaign**, Buchanan won two more brevets for his excellent service at **Gaines' Mill** and **Malvern Hill**. His brigade saw further combat at **Second Manassas** (where **John Pope** highly praised his service), but it was only lightly engaged at **Antietam**.

In November 1862, Buchanan was commissioned brigadier general of volunteers and fought at **Fredericksburg** the following month. He was brevetted major general of regulars for his service at Second Manassas and Fredericksburg, but the Senate refused to confirm his appointment to brigadier general. This slight was probably due to politics, since Buchanan was close to Maj. Gen. **Fitz John Porter**, the scapegoat of Second Manassas. After his commission expired in March 1863, Buchanan took command of **Fort Delaware**, and in February 1864, he was appointed colonel of the 1st U.S. Infantry.

After the war, "Old Buck," as Buchanan was known, worked with the **Freedmen's Bureau** and served as commander of the Department of Louisiana before retiring in 1870.

BUCK AND BALL. A musket load used for close-quarter fighting, the buck and ball was a paper cartridge containing one large **rifle** ball and three smaller buckshot.

BUCK AND GAG. This was one of several forms of corporal punishment used by both sides to **discipline** their soldiers during the Civil War. To be bucked and gagged was both humiliating and painful. The victim was forced to sit on the ground with his hands tied to his feet and his knees slightly bent. A stick then was inserted behind his knees, resting on his arms. Another stick or **bayonet** was inserted in his mouth as a gag and tied to his head. Thus "bucked and gagged," the offender was usually forced to endure his punishment for hours in full view of his comrades.

BUCK HEAD CREEK, GEORGIA, BATTLE OF (NOVEMBER 28, 1864). During **William T. Sherman's March to the Sea**, Union forces left Milledgeville, Georgia, on November 24, 1864. While the main **army** moved eastward, Brig. Gen. **H. Judson Kilpatrick's** cavalry moved northeastward toward Augusta, then eastward, to destroy the **railroad** near **Waynesborough** and to release Union **prisoners** held at Millen. On November 26, Confederate cavalry under Maj. Gen. **Joseph Wheeler** attacked the rear of Kilpatrick's column and prevented him from destroying a key railroad bridge across Briar Creek. Kilpatrick destroyed some track and then headed southwest to rejoin Sherman when he learned the prisoners had already been moved.

On the morning of November 28, Wheeler surprised Kilpatrick's camp near Buck Head Creek and almost captured Kilpatrick himself. The Union troopers held off the Confederates at the creek's bridge and then burned it. Another Confederate charge was repulsed a few miles beyond the bridge at Reynolds's Plantation. Wheeler finally withdrew, and Kilpatrick rejoined Sherman.

BUCKINGHAM, CATHARINUS PUTNAM (1808–1880) USA. A native of **Ohio**, Buckingham graduated in the 1829 **West Point** class along with his friend **Robert E. Lee**. He then served on topographical duty and taught at the academy, but he resigned his commission in 1831. Buckingham next taught mathematics and natural philosophy at Ohio's Kenyon College and became the owner of an ironworks before the Civil War.

In May 1861, Buckingham was appointed Ohio's assistant adjutant general and commissary general and was made adjutant general two months later. Appointed brigadier general of volunteers in July 1862, he was attached to the War Department and personally carried the orders relieving **George B. McClellan** of command of the **Army of the Potomac** in November 1862.

Buckingham resigned his commission in February 1863 and eventually moved to Chicago, Illinois, where he rebuilt the Illinois Central grain elevators after the Great Chicago Fire. He also wrote two works on mathematics and served as president of the Chicago Steel Works.

BUCKINGHAM, WILLIAM ALFRED (1804–1875) USA. A native of **Connecticut**, Buckingham was a successful businessman and local **Whig** politician who served as a Norwich town councilman and treasurer before joining the **Republican Party**. He then ran for mayor and was successfully elected four times before the Civil War.

In 1858, Buckingham was elected governor (and subsequently was re-elected to seven more one-year terms), and **Abraham Lincoln** sought his advice in 1860 as he prepared to enter the presidential race. The only Union governor to serve throughout the entire war, Buckingham strongly supported Lincoln's administration. He raised 54,882 volunteers out of a population of only 80,000 registered voters, sometimes having to use his own money to **finance** the recruitment. Buckingham refused to run for reelection in 1866 and briefly returned to his business interests. In 1868 he returned to politics and was elected to the U.S. Senate. Buckingham died while in office.

BUCKLAND MILLS, VIRGINIA, BATTLE OF (OCTOBER 19, 1863). As the Confederates retreated after the Battle of Bristoe Station during the 1863 **Bristoe Station Campaign**, Maj. Gen. **J. E. B. Stuart** personally commanded Maj. Gen. **Wade Hampton's** cavalry **division**. On October 18, Stuart was attacked by Union troopers under Maj. Gen. **Alfred Pleasonton** and took up a defensive position on the south side of Broad Run to await the arrival of Maj. Gen. **Fitzhugh Lee's** division. On October 19, Stuart repulsed some weak advances by Brig. Gen. **H. Judson Kilpatrick** and received word from Lee that he was nearby and could attack the enemy's flank if Stuart could draw Kilpatrick southward. Stuart withdrew a couple of miles to Chestnut Hill, drawing Kilpatrick after him. The Confederates then took up a defensive position, and when Kilpatrick approached, Lee launched a surprise attack against the Union flank. Kilpatrick's men fled in panic and were chased five miles by the Confederates. In what the Confederates called the "Buckland Races," 150 Union **prisoners** were captured.

"BUCKLAND RACES." *See* BUCKLAND MILLS, VIRGINIA, BATTLE OF.

BUCKLAND, RALPH POMEROY (1812–1892) USA. It is not certain whether Buckland was born in **Massachusetts** or **Ohio**, but he grew up in the latter. After living in **Louisiana** for three years, he returned to Ohio and became a prominent lawyer and state **Whig** politician, serving as mayor and as a delegate to the 1848 Whig National Convention. After joining the **Republican Party** in the 1850s, Buckland served two terms in the state senate.

Buckland entered Union service as colonel of the 72nd Ohio in January 1862. In March 1862, he was given command of a **brigade** in **William T. Sherman's division** and was commended by Sherman for his service at **Shiloh**. After serving in the **siege of Corinth, Mississippi**, Buckland was appointed brigadier general of volunteers in November 1862. He was given command of a brigade in the 3rd Division of the **Army of the Tennessee's** XVI Corps in December 1862 and led it during the early part of the **Vicksburg Campaign**. In April, Buckland transferred to a XV Corps division and commanded it until he went on leave in June 1863 and thus missed the surrender at **Vicksburg**. In January 1864, Buckland assumed command of the District of Memphis and became responsible for contesting **Nathan Bedford Forrest's** cavalry raids in the area. He remained in Memphis until he resigned his commission in January 1865 to accept a seat in the **U.S. Congress**. In March, Buckland took his seat and was **brevetted** major general of volunteers for his war service.

Buckland served two terms in Congress and afterward was active in business, politics, **railroads**, and veterans' activities. In 1876, he actively campaigned for his former law partner, **Rutherford B. Hayes**, for president.

BUCKNER, SIMON BOLIVAR (1823–1914) CSA. Known by his middle name, Buckner was a native of **Kentucky**. He graduated from **West Point** in 1844, served as a professor at the academy, and won two **brevets** in the **Mexican War** while serving under **Winfield Scott**. After Mexico, Buckner again taught at West Point and served on the frontier. He was a captain serving in a New York City regimental commissary when he resigned his commission in 1855. While working in **Illinois**, Buckner became active in the state militia and served as the state's adjutant general in 1857–58. He then moved to Kentucky and became that state's inspector general.

Although he opposed **secession**, Buckner resigned his position after Kentucky's pro-Union legislature interfered with his duties. He then rejected an appointment to brigadier general of volunteers from **Abraham Lincoln** and accepted a commission as a Confederate brigadier general in September 1861. As a result, Buckner was indicted for treason in Kentucky. During the February 1862 **Forts Henry and Donelson Campaign**, he assumed command of Fort Donelson, Tennessee, when the two ranking generals fled, and surrendered the fort to his friend Brig. Gen. **U. S. Grant**.

After being **exchanged** in August 1862, Buckner was promoted to major general. He commanded a **division** under **Braxton Bragg** during the 1862 **Kentucky Campaign** and played a key role in capturing **Mun-fordville**. Afterward, Buckner commanded the District of the Gulf and the **Department of East Tennessee** (later renamed the District of East Tennessee). After commanding a **corps** in Bragg's **Army of Tennessee** at **Chickamauga**, he became one of Bragg's critics and supported his removal from **army** command. Bragg then reduced Buckner to a division command and abolished his **district**. Illness forced Buckner to relinquish field command until 1864. Afterward, he again commanded the Department of East Tennessee, and in August he assumed command of the District of West Louisiana. In September, Buckner was promoted to lieutenant general and became Gen. **Edmund Kirby Smith's** chief of staff. While serving in that position, he surrendered the **Trans-Mississippi Department** in May 1865.

After the war, Buckner regained property that had been confiscated from him during the war, returned to Kentucky in 1868, and became a newspaper editor. Entering politics, he was elected governor in 1887 and unsuccessfully ran for vice president on the "Gold Democrat" ticket in 1896. When he died in 1914, Buckner was the last of the high-ranking Confederate generals.

"BUCKTAILS." *See* "PENNSYLVANIA BUCKTAILS."

BUELL, DON CARLOS (1818–1898) USA. A native of **Ohio**, Buell grew up in **Indiana** and graduated from **West Point** in 1841. He served in the **Seminole** and **Mexican Wars** (being severely wounded in the latter) and was awarded two **brevets** for gallantry. Buell then served as a staff officer with the adjutant general's department until the Civil War began.

Buell was promoted from lieutenant colonel of regulars to brigadier general of volunteers in May 1861 and was transferred from San Francisco, California, to the **Washington, D.C.**, defenses. **George B. McClellan** gave him a **division** command in the **Army of the Potomac** in October, but the following month Buell was transferred west to take command of the **Department of the Ohio**.

Promoted to major general in March 1862, Buell was expected to liberate pro-Union East **Tennessee**, but instead, he disappointed **Abraham Lincoln** by occupying Nashville, Tennessee. He then marched his **Army of the Ohio** from Nashville and arrived at **Shiloh** in time to reinforce

U. S. Grant and ensure a Union victory. Afterward, Buell participated in the **siege of Corinth**, **Mississippi**, and in June 1862 was sent to Middle Tennessee with four divisions to advance on Chattanooga, repairing the **railroad** as he went. Confederate cavalry raided his supply line and forced him to abandon the advance. In September, Buell withdrew his force from Tennessee and went to **Kentucky** to protect that state during the **Kentucky Campaign**. He attacked **Braxton Bragg** at **Perryville** and forced the Confederates to retreat, but his lack of pursuit led to his being relieved of command in October 1862. An investigation brought no recommendations against him, but Buell spent the next 18 months waiting for new orders that never came. Besides his lack of aggressiveness, his friendship with the controversial **George B. McClellan** may also have hurt his military career.

Buell was mustered out of the volunteers in May 1864 and resigned his regular **army** commission in June. Grant later recommended that he be restored to duty, but no action was taken, and Buell settled in Kentucky, where he became involved in the iron and coal industry.

BUFFINGTON ISLAND, OHIO, BATTLE OF (JULY 19, 1863). By mid-July 1863, Brig. Gen. **John Hunt Morgan's Ohio Raid** was in trouble. Having accomplished little more than spreading fear in enemy territory, the exhausted Confederate raiders were being hotly pursued by the Federals. Riding eastward, they passed north of Cincinnati, Ohio, on July 13–14 and reached a guarded ford across the Ohio River at Buffington Island on July 18. After resting his men, Morgan attacked the Union infantry on the morning of July 19. By that time, Union cavalry under Brig. Gen. **Edward H. Hobson** and Brig. Gen. **Henry M. Judah** had arrived on the scene by horseback and steamboat, respectively. Caught between a gunboat in the river and cavalry in their rear, most of the Confederates were captured. Morgan and about 400 men escaped by riding through a ravine to the north, but they, too, were caught on July 26 at **Salineville**. At a cost of only 25 casualties, the Federals captured about 900 raiders.

BUFORD, ABRAHAM (1820–1884) CSA. A native of **Kentucky**, Buford was a cousin of Union generals **John Buford** and **Napoleon Bonaparte Buford** and at 320 pounds possibly was the largest Confederate general. He graduated from **West Point** in 1841 and served on the frontier before fighting in the **Mexican War** and winning one **brevet** for gallantry. Buford resigned his captain's commission in 1854 and returned to Kentucky, where he raised livestock and served as a **railroad** president.

Although a supporter of **states rights**, he opposed **secession** and supported Kentucky's neutrality early in the Civil War. It was not until the Confederates invaded Kentucky in the 1862 **Kentucky Campaign** that Buford decided to cast his lot with the Confederacy.

Buford was appointed brigadier general in November 1862 and quickly organized a cavalry **brigade** for the **Army of Tennessee**. After fighting at **Stones River**, he was transferred to **Mississippi** in January 1863 to serve under Lt. Gen. **John C. Pemberton**. Pemberton sent Buford to **Port Hudson, Louisiana**, where Maj. Gen. **Franklin Gardner** created a brigade for him and put him into the Confederate defenses. In the spring of 1863, Buford's mounted brigade was ordered back to **Tennessee** but then was diverted to Pemberton when **U. S. Grant** threatened the Confederates in the **Vicksburg Campaign**. Joining **William W. Loring's division**, Buford fought at **Champion Hill** and in the siege of **Jackson**.

In March 1864, Buford was given command of a cavalry brigade under **Nathan Bedford Forrest**. He fought at **Fort Pillow**, was given credit by Forrest for the victory at **Brice's Cross Roads**, and participated in several raids, including Forrest's attack on **Johnsonville, Tennessee**. During the **Franklin and Nashville Campaign** in late 1864, Buford participated in the Spring Hill Incident and was severely wounded at Richland Creek while covering Hood's retreat from the Battle of Nashville. In February 1865, he was put in command of the cavalry in **Alabama** and fought his last battle at **Selma** in April 1865.

After the war, Buford resumed breeding horses and promoted reconciliation between the North and the South. He served one term in the Kentucky legislature but committed suicide in 1884 after suffering financial problems.

BUFORD, JOHN (1826–1863) USA. Born in **Kentucky**, Buford was a half-brother of Brig. Gen. **Napoleon Bonaparte Buford** and a cousin of Confederate Brig. Gen. **Abraham Buford**. He moved as a child to **Illinois** and graduated from **West Point** in 1848. Buford was assigned to the dragoons and served on the frontier, where he fought **Indians**, garrisoned **Kansas**, and participated in the **Utah Expedition**.

When the Civil War began, Buford was a captain in the 2nd U.S. Cavalry. His **regiment** was sent to **Washington, D.C.**, where in November 1861 he was promoted to major and was made assistant inspector general of the city's defenses. Upon taking command of the **Army of Virginia**, Maj. Gen. **John Pope** rescued Buford from his lowly post, had him promoted to brigadier general of volunteers in July 1862, and placed him in command of a cavalry **brigade**. Buford's duty with the dragoons made him an excellent officer, and he served Pope well in the **Second Manassas Campaign**, where he was severely wounded and for a time was thought to have been killed. He then served as **George B. McClellan's** and **Ambrose Burnside's** chief of cavalry for the **Army of the Potomac** in late 1862, but he assumed command of the **army's** reserve cavalry brigade in February 1863. During the **Chancellorsville Campaign**, Buford participated in **George Stoneman's Raid** against **Richmond, Virginia**.

In May 1863, Buford was put in command of a cavalry **division** and performed his most valuable wartime service at **Gettysburg**. There he fought his cavalry dismounted on July 1, 1863, and slowed the Confederate advance into town long enough for Union reinforcements to arrive. During the **Bristoe Station Campaign**, Buford contracted typhoid fever and was forced on sick leave in November 1863. He died on December 16 but was appointed major general of volunteers posthumously.

BUFORD, NAPOLEON BONAPARTE (1807–1883) USA. A half-brother of Union Brig. Gen. **John Buford** and a cousin of Confederate Brig. Gen. **Abraham Buford**, Buford was a **Kentucky** native who graduated from **West Point** in 1827. After serving in the **artillery** and as an instructor at the academy, he resigned his lieutenant's commission in 1835 and became a civil engineer. Buford moved to **Illinois** in 1843 and became a successful merchant, banker, and **railroad** president.

After going bankrupt in 1861, Buford raised the 27th Illinois and entered Union service as its colonel in August. He fought with his **regiment** at **Belmont** and **Island No. 10** before being promoted to brigadier general of volunteers in April 1862. Given command of a **brigade** in the **Army of the Mississippi's** 3rd Division, Buford participated in the **Battle of Corinth** and was appointed major general of volunteers in November. The U.S. Senate, however, did not confirm the appointment, and Buford's commission expired in March 1863 during the **Vicksburg Campaign**. He reverted to the rank of brigadier general and was made commander of the District of East Arkansas in September. Buford served there for the rest of the war.

Buford was mustered out of service in August 1865 with a **brevet** of major general of volunteers. He worked as a minor government appointee afterward.

BULLOCH, JAMES DUNWODY (1823–1901) CSA. A native of **Georgia**, Bulloch entered the **U.S. Navy** as a midshipman when he was 16 but resigned his lieutenant's commission in 1853 to begin a maritime mail delivery service.

When Georgia seceded in early 1861, Bulloch returned his boat to **New York** and joined the Confederacy as a civilian naval agent in May to secure ships and equipment in Great Britain. In 1862, he worked secretly with **Fraser, Trenholm & Co.** to obtain and outfit the **commerce raiders** *Florida* and *Alabama*. Bulloch then returned to the Confederacy in command of a **blockade runner**. Rewarded with a commander's commission, he went back to Britain and secured several blockade runners and the two **Laird rams**. Bulloch also worked with the French but was able to obtain only one ship in France, which never saw service. In 1864, he secured another raider that was christened the *Shenandoah* and became the last Confederate ship to surrender.

Bulloch remained in Great Britain after the war, became a cotton merchant, and wrote the book *The Secret Service of the Confederate States in Europe*.

BULLOCH, ROBERT (1828–1905) CSA. A native of **North Carolina**, Bulloch moved to **Florida** as a young man, where he worked as a teacher and raised a **company** of volunteers that served in the **Seminole Wars**.

After the Civil War began, Bulloch raised another company of volunteers in April 1862 and was elected its captain. He soon was elected lieutenant colonel of the 7th Florida when it was organized later that month. The **regiment** was sent to Chattanooga, Tennessee, and served with Maj. Gen. **Edmund Kirby Smith** during the **Kentucky Campaign**. Bulloch was promoted to regimental colonel in June 1863 and led his men into battle with the **Army of Tennessee** at **Chickamauga**. While serving with the Florida Brigade at **Missionary Ridge**, he was captured and held **prisoner** until March 1864. After being **exchanged**, Bulloch fought in the **Atlanta Campaign** and temporarily commanded the **brigade** after Brig. Gen. **Jesse J. Finley** was wounded at **Resaca**. When Finley was wounded again at **Jonesboro**, Bulloch took permanent command of the brigade, even though he also had been wounded at **Utoy Creek**. After receiving a second wound at **Franklin**, he was promoted to brigadier general in January 1865. Bulloch received his third wound while serving with Lt. Gen. **Nathan Bedford Forrest** near Murfreesboro, Tennessee. This wound prevented him from performing any further field service.

After the war, Bulloch practiced law in Florida and became active in politics, serving as a state legislator, U.S. congressman, and circuit judge.

BULL'S GAP, TENNESSEE, BATTLE OF (NOVEMBER 11–14, 1864). One of the strategic areas of East **Tennessee** was Bull's Gap, a mountain gap 25 miles northeast of Knoxville where the East Tennessee

& Virginia Railroad and the Knoxville Road passed through Bay Mountain. In November 1864, the 2,500-man "Governor's Guard" under Union Brig. Gen. **Alvan C. Gillem** guarded the gap after having chased away a Confederate garrison a few weeks earlier. To regain control of the vital position, Maj. Gen. **John C. Breckinridge** led about 3,000 men from Abingdon, Virginia, into Tennessee. After taking possession of Greeneville, Breckinridge attacked Gillem at Bull's Gap on November 11.

Breckinridge opened an **artillery** barrage on Gillem and sent troops into the Federals' rear and against their left flank. Confederate attacks on November 12 were unsuccessful, and Breckinridge spent November 13 **skirmishing** rather than making a **frontal attack**. By nightfall, Gillem was nearly out of ammunition and withdrew toward Morristown, where he expected to be reinforced. Breckinridge sent his men hurrying after the enemy and threw them into confusion with a night attack near Strawberry Plains. Gillem and most of his command escaped, but he lost all of his artillery and about 300 men taken **prisoner**. In the fighting at Bull's Gap, Gillem suffered only 24 casualties, while inflicting about 100 on Breckinridge.

BUMMERS. This was the nickname given to the soldiers who **foraged** without permission from Maj. Gen. **William T. Sherman** during his **March to the Sea** and in the **Carolinas Campaign**.

BURBRIDGE, STEPHEN GANO (1831–1894) USA. A native of **Kentucky**, Burbridge attended the Kentucky Military Institute and became a lawyer and farmer. He entered Union service in August 1861 when he raised the 26th Kentucky (Union) and became its colonel.

After fighting at **Shiloh**, Burbridge was promoted to brigadier general of volunteers in June 1862, and in October, he was given command of an infantry **brigade** in the **Army of Kentucky**. The following month, he was given command of a brigade that became part of the 10th Division in the **Army of the Tennessee's** XIII Corps. After fighting at **Chickasaw Bayou**, Burbridge joined the **Army of the Mississippi** for the operation against **Arkansas Post**. Returning to the Army of the Tennessee, he led his brigade throughout the **Vicksburg Campaign** and in the siege of **Jackson, Mississippi**. In August 1863, Burbridge accompanied his **corps** to the **Department of the Gulf**, where he commanded the **division** from September through December and fought at **Bayou Bourbeau, Louisiana**, during the **Texas Overland Expedition**.

Burbridge took command of the District of Kentucky in April 1864, but Kentuckians quickly came to despise him for his harsh rule. He did enjoy some military success and won a **brevet** for his role in defeating Brig. Gen. **John Hunt Morgan's** Confederate raiders in June 1864. In October, Burbridge led an unsuccessful raid against **Saltville, Virginia**, in which many of his **black troops** were **massacred**. Charged with interfering with the 1864 election, he was removed from command in early 1865 and resigned from the **army** in December.

After the war, Burbridge was forced to move from his native state because of the animosity he had stirred among its people during the conflict. He finally settled in **New York**.

BURGESS' MILL, VIRGINIA, BATTLE OF (OCTOBER 27, 1864). During the **Petersburg Campaign**, Lt. Gen. **U. S. Grant** sent three **corps** and some cavalry from the **Army of the Potomac** to his left on October 27, 1864, to cut the vital Boydton Plank Road and South Side Railroad that supplied Gen. **Robert E. Lee's Army of Northern Virginia**. Major General **Winfield Scott Hancock's** II Corps reached the Boydton Plank Road near Burgess' Mill at midday, but the two corps advancing on his right were stopped by the Confederates near Hatcher's Run. Major General **A. P. Hill's** Confederate corps and Brig. Gen. **Wade Hampton's** cavalry **division** then attacked Hancock and his accompanying cavalry at Burgess' Mill. The Confederates enjoyed some success against Hancock's flanks, but a Union counterattack was able to stabilize the line. Because he was in an isolated position without supports, Hancock withdrew the next day. In the operation, the Union forces lost 1,758 men, and Confederate casualties were about 1,800.

BURNHAM, HIRAM (1814?–1864) USA. A native of **Maine**, Burnham worked as a lumberman before the Civil War and served as a county commissioner and coroner. He entered Union service in July 1861 as lieutenant colonel of the 6th Maine, a **regiment** he helped recruit. Promoted to colonel in December, Burnham joined **Winfield S. Hancock's brigade** in the **Army of the Potomac** and fought very well in the **Peninsula** and **Seven Days Campaigns**. After seeing action at **Antietam**, he temporarily led the brigade at **Fredericksburg** but saw no significant combat there. During the **Chancellorsville Campaign**, Burnham commanded a large brigade in the VI Corps known as the **Light Division** and suffered heavy losses at **Second Fredericksburg**. His regiment was held in reserve at **Gettysburg**, but it served in the **Bristoe Station** and **Mine Run Campaigns** in the autumn of 1863.

Promoted to brigadier general of volunteers, effective April 1864, Burnham took command of a brigade in XVIII Corps' 1st Division and joined **Benjamin F. Butler's Army of the James** for the **Bermuda Hundred Campaign**, but he soon was sent to reinforce **U. S. Grant** and fought at **Cold Harbor**. Returning to Butler, Burnham was killed at **Fort Harrison** on September 29, 1864, during the **Petersburg Campaign**.

BURNS, JOHN (1789–1872) USA. Nicknamed "The Old Hero of Gettysburg," Burns was a veteran of the War of 1812. During the **Battle of Gettysburg**, he appeared on the field and fought alongside Union troops in the **Army of the Potomac**, despite their attempts to send him to a safer position. Wounded three times and briefly held **prisoner**, Burns became a folk hero for his bravery, and there is a statue of him on the battlefield today.

BURNS, WILLIAM WALLACE (1825–1892) USA. A native of **Ohio**, Burns graduated from **West Point** in 1847. He first served as a recruiter during the **Mexican War** and then fought **Indians** on the frontier. Burns was a commissary captain in early 1861 and in March was made chief commissary for the **Department of the Ohio**. He served Maj. Gen. **George B. McClellan** during his successful operation in western **Virginia** and earned promotion to major in August.

Promoted to brigadier general of volunteers in September 1861, Burns was given command of **Edward Baker's brigade** in the **Army of the Potomac** after Baker was killed at the **Battle of Ball's Bluff**. He served in the 2nd Division of the **army's** II Corps during the **Peninsula Campaign** and was shot in the face at **Savage's Station** during the **Seven Days Campaign**. Burns was awarded two **brevets** for his service during the Seven Days, but he was forced to go on extended sick leave afterward. He returned to duty in November 1862 and was given command of a IX Corps **division**, which he led at **Fredericksburg** and in the **Mud March**. Burns resigned his volunteer commission in March 1863, resumed duties as a major in the **U.S. Army**'s commissary department, and served the remainder of the war in the **Department of the Northwest**.

Burns was brevetted brigadier general of regulars for his wartime service and remained on duty after the war. He retired in 1889 as a colonel.

BURNSIDE, AMBROSE EVERETT (1824–1881) USA. A native of **Indiana**, Burnside was the son of a **South Carolina** slave owner who freed his slaves and moved north. After graduating from **West Point** in 1847, he served with the **artillery** on garrison duty during the **Mexican War** but in 1849 was wounded while fighting Apache **Indians** in **New Mexico**. Burnside resigned his commission in 1853 and became a **Rhode**

Island firearms manufacturer to produce the **Burnside carbine** that he had designed. Failure to secure a government contract ultimately forced him into bankruptcy, but during the Civil War, 55,567 of the **rifles** were produced. Burnside then worked for his friend **George B. McClellan** with the Illinois Central Railroad and became major general of the Rhode Island militia.

When the Civil War began, Burnside raised the 1st Rhode Island Volunteers and became its colonel in May 1861. In June, he was given command of a **brigade** under Brig. Gen. **Irvin McDowell** and performed well enough at **First Manassas** to win promotion to brigadier general of volunteers in August. In December, Burnside was given command of a large force, with which he launched successful attacks on **Roanoke Island** and **New Bern, North Carolina**, in early 1862 that earned him a promotion to major general of volunteers in March.

After commanding the **Department of North Carolina** from January to July 1862, Burnside was sent back to **Virginia** to take command of the **Army of the Potomac's** IX Corps. His impressive career began to falter at **Antietam**, however, where he proved to be hesitant and unimaginative in carrying out orders to cross a stone bridge across Antietam Creek (renamed Burnside's Bridge) and attack the Confederate right flank. After Antietam, Burnside twice turned down **Abraham Lincoln's** offer to command the **Army of the Potomac**, but he finally accepted the position and replaced McClellan in November 1862.

Although well-liked personally, Burnside proved to be a failure as an **army** commander. At **Fredericksburg**, he unwisely launched a series of **frontal attacks** against the well-positioned **Army of Northern Virginia** that resulted in his men's slaughter. In January 1863, Burnside next marched up the Rappahannock River from Fredericksburg to turn the Confederates' left flank, but a drenching rain bogged down the movement and forced him to call off the so-called **Mud March**.

Discredited for his two failures, Burnside was replaced as army commander in late January 1863 by Maj. Gen. **Joseph Hooker**. In March, he was put in command of the **Department of the Ohio**, where he oversaw the arrest of **Clement L. Vallandigham** and the capture of Confederate Brig. Gen. **John Hunt Morgan**. In late 1863, Burnside regained some of his popularity and received the **Thanks of Congress** by successfully defending Knoxville, Tennessee, against Confederate Lt. Gen. **James Longstreet** during the **Knoxville Campaign**. Back in command of the IX Corps in the spring of 1864, he earned **U. S. Grant's** displeasure when he again proved to be slow and indecisive during the **Overland**

and **Petersburg Campaigns**. After poorly handling his men at Petersburg's **Battle of the Crater**, **Virginia**, Burnside was relieved of command and later resigned his commission in April 1865.

After the war, Burnside was elected governor of Rhode Island three times and served one term in the U.S. Senate. Although he had been one of the more important Civil War generals, Burnside perhaps is best remembered for his bushy side-whiskers, which became known as "sideburns."

BURNSIDE CARBINE. This breech-loading carbine was patented in 1856 by future Union Maj. Gen. **Ambrose E. Burnside**. His failure to win a government contract led to bankruptcy before the Civil War, but the carbine was adopted by the military during the war and ranked third, behind the **Spencer** and **Sharps**, as the most-used Union carbine. The first American-made military weapon to use metallic cartridges, the Burnside Carbine was made in four models. Using a .54-caliber metallic cartridge, it was a dependable weapon that was used mostly by cavalry units. During the Civil War, the U.S. government purchased 55,567 of the carbines.

BURNSIDE'S BRIDGE AT BATTLE OF ANTIETAM, MARYLAND (SEPTEMBER 17, 1862). *See* ANTIETAM, MARYLAND, CAMPAIGN AND BATTLE OF.

BURNSIDE'S NORTH CAROLINA EXPEDITION (JANUARY 2–MARCH 14, 1862). *See* ROANOKE ISLAND, BATTLE OF; NEW BERN, NORTH CAROLINA, CAPTURE OF.

BUSHWHACKER. This was the nickname commonly given to Civil War guerrillas.

BUSSEY, CYRUS (1833–1915) USA. Born in **Ohio**, Bussey (BUS-ee) moved to **Indiana** as a child. After establishing himself as a dry goods merchant when he was only 16, he moved to **Iowa** in 1855. There, Bussey became involved in **Democratic** politics, was elected to the state senate in 1858, and served as a delegate to the 1860 Democratic National Convention.

At the outbreak of the Civil War, Bussey was a colonel in the state militia. After seeing some minor combat, he was commissioned colonel of the 3rd Iowa Cavalry in September 1861 and led it at **Pea Ridge**. There, Bussey panicked, and the regiment's lieutenant colonel had to assume command. Despite his poor performance, Bussey was given command of a cavalry **brigade** in December 1862 and led it at **Arkansas Post**. During the 1863 **Vicksburg Campaign**, he was assigned to the **Army of the Tennessee's** XIII Corps and led a brigade, and sometimes the **division**, in eastern **Arkansas** before joining the main **army** at **Vicksburg** and leading a brigade in **Francis J. Herron's** division during the remainder of the campaign and in the siege of **Jackson, Mississippi**. Bussey was promoted to brigadier general of volunteers in January 1864. Returning to Arkansas, he led a brigade during the **Camden Expedition** and served in Arkansas as either a brigade or division commander for the remainder of the war.

After being **brevetted** major general of volunteers for his wartime service, Bussey left the army in August 1865. He then engaged in various business ventures in several cities before moving to **Louisiana** during **Reconstruction** and becoming involved in **Republican** politics. Bussey was appointed assistant secretary of the interior in 1889.

BUTLER, BENJAMIN FRANKLIN (1818–1893) USA. Born in **New Hampshire**, Butler moved to **Massachusetts** with his mother after his father died. After graduating from **Maine's** Colby College, he taught school for a time and then became a successful Massachusetts lawyer. A **Democrat**, Butler was elected to both the legislature and state senate in the 1850s and served as a delegate to the 1860 Democratic National Convention in **Charleston, South Carolina**. He believed that only a moderate southerner could keep the nation united and therefore voted 57 times to nominate **Jefferson Davis** for president. When the Southern Democrats bolted and held their convention in Baltimore, Maryland, Butler also attended and supported **John C. Breckinridge** for the nomination. Despite his pro-Southern politics in trying to save the Union, Butler opposed **secession** and immediately accepted an appointment as a brigadier general of the state militia when war began in April 1861.

Butler was put in command of the **Department of Annapolis** later in the month and used Massachusetts troops to secure safe passage through Baltimore after the **Baltimore Riot** erupted. Impressed with Butler's bold action, **Abraham Lincoln** appointed him the first Union major general of volunteers in May, making him the ranking volunteer general in the **army**, and placed him in command of the **Department of Virginia**, with his headquarters at **Fort Monroe, Virginia**. The following month, troops under Butler's command were defeated by the Confederates in the small engagement at **Big Bethel**. While at Fort Monroe, Butler became the first general to face the problem of runaway slaves.

Rather than return them to their owners, he declared the slaves were "**contraband** of war" and kept them within his lines. In August 1861, he also won an important victory when he cooperated with the **U.S. Navy** to capture **Hatteras Inlet, North Carolina**.

After some impressive accomplishments, Butler's career began to falter in 1862. In March, he was put in command of the **Department of the Gulf** and accompanied **David Farragut** to **Forts Jackson and St. Philip**. After Farragut captured **New Orleans, Louisiana**, Butler made his headquarters there and ruled harshly by censoring newspapers, confiscating secessionists' property, imprisoning Confederate sympathizers, and hanging **William Mumford** for taking down the U.S. **flag** from the mint building. He also was accused of corruption and earned the nickname "Spoons" for supposedly stealing silverware out of civilians' houses. It was his **"Woman's Order,"** however, that earned Butler the name "Beast." To stop women from insulting his soldiers, Butler declared that such women would not be viewed as ladies but instead be treated as if they were common prostitutes. Despite his having performed such admirable services as cleaning up the city, feeding the poor, and eradicating yellow fever, this order caused outrage in both the North and the South. Because of his controversial nature, Butler was relieved of command in December 1862.

In November 1863, Butler was put in command of the **Department of Virginia and North Carolina**, and in April 1864, he took command of the **Army of the James**. That spring he was to cooperate with Lt. Gen. **U. S. Grant's Overland Campaign** against **Robert E. Lee** by moving his army up the James River and cutting the **railroad** between Petersburg and **Richmond**. A small Confederate force under Gen. **P. G. T. Beauregard** defeated Butler in the **Bermuda Hundred Campaign** and effectively eliminated him as a threat. Grant removed Butler from **Virginia**, but in December 1864 Butler used his seniority to assume command of the force being sent to capture **Fort Fisher, North Carolina**. Failing to cooperate effectively with the navy, he handled the affair badly and retreated rather than laying siege to the fort as Grant had ordered. Grant then relieved Butler of duties and sent him back to Massachusetts, where he resigned his commission in November 1865.

After the war, Butler became a **Radical Republican**, was elected to the **U.S. Congress** four successive times beginning in 1866, and played a major role in the impeachment of President **Andrew Johnson**. He was elected again in 1878 as a Greenbacker (his third party affiliation) and served as that party's presidential candidate in 1884. After several unsuccessful attempts, Butler was elected Massachusetts's governor in 1882. *See also* BUTLER MEDAL.

BUTLER, MATTHEW CALBRAITH (1836–1909) CSA. A native of **South Carolina**, Butler was the son of a congressman and the nephew of Commodores Oliver Hazard Perry and Matthew Perry and South Carolina Senator Andrew Butler. He attended South Carolina College but dropped out of school and became a lawyer in 1857. The next year, Butler married the daughter of Gov. **Francis W. Pickens** and was elected to the legislature in 1860, but he resigned his seat after the state seceded and became captain of a volunteer cavalry **company** that became part of the **Hampton Legion**.

After fighting at **First Manassas**, Butler was promoted to major. His skillful service during the **Peninsula Campaign** earned him a promotion to colonel of the 2nd South Carolina Cavalry in August 1862. As part of the **Army of Northern Virginia**, Butler was praised for his actions at **Second Manassas** and **Antietam**. A severe wound suffered at **Brandy Station** cost him his right foot, but Butler was promoted to brigadier general in September 1863.

When Butler returned to duty in early 1864, he was given command of a cavalry **brigade** in **Wade Hampton's** division. He led it with skill during the **Overland Campaign**, earning promotion to major general in December 1864. Butler then was sent with a **division** to join Gen. **Joseph E. Johnston** in the Carolinas and spent the remainder of the war contesting the advance of Maj. Gen. **William T. Sherman** during the **Carolinas Campaign**.

After the war, Butler became active in **Democratic** politics and served three terms in the U.S. Senate beginning in 1877. He returned to the military during the Spanish-American War, when he again was commissioned a major general of volunteers.

BUTLER MEDAL. To honor his troops for their service in the **Petersburg Campaign**, Maj. Gen. **Benjamin F. Butler** had Tiffany's of New York City strike 200 medals, which were suspended on red, white, and blue ribbon. In May 1865, when he was preparing to run for the **U.S. Congress**, Butler presented some of the medals to **black troops** of the XXV Corps for their bravery in attacking **New Market Heights** and **Fort Harrison, Virginia**.

BUTLER'S NORTH CAROLINA EXPEDITION (DECEMBER 13–27, 1864). *See* FORT FISHER, NORTH CAROLINA, BATTLE OF; WILMINGTON, NORTH CAROLINA.

BUTTERFIELD, DANIEL (1831–1901) USA. A native of **New York**, Butterfield was the son of John Butterfield of Overland Mail Company fame. After graduating from Union College, he became a New York merchant and worked for the American Express Company.

Butterfield entered Union service as a sergeant in a **Washington, D.C.**, militia **company**, but in May 1861, he was appointed both colonel of the 12th New York Militia and lieutenant colonel of the 12th U.S. Infantry. Given command of a **brigade** in the **Department of Pennsylvania** in July, he served in the **Shenandoah Valley** before being promoted to brigadier general of volunteers in September.

In October 1861, Butterfield was given command of a brigade in **Fitz John Porter's division** of the **Army of the Potomac**. During the **Peninsula Campaign**, he first led a brigade in the III Corps but in May moved to the V Corps. Butterfield was wounded at **Gaines' Mill** during the **Seven Days Campaign**, and 30 years later he was awarded the **Medal of Honor** for his actions there. While encamped at **Harrison's Landing** at the end of the campaign, he made his most lasting contribution to the **army** when he composed the bugle call **"Taps."** After serving in the **Second Manassas** and **Antietam Campaigns**, Butterfield was given command of the V Corps in November 1862 and was promoted to major general of volunteers.

Butterfield led the **corps** at **Fredericksburg** but then became Maj. Gen. **Joseph Hooker's** chief of staff when Hooker took command of the Army of the Potomac in January 1863. While in that position, he assisted Hooker in designing the army's **corps badges**. Butterfield remained as army chief of staff when **George Meade** assumed army command in June 1863, and he was wounded a second time at **Gettysburg**. When he returned to duty, he joined Hooker as his chief of staff when Hooker was sent to the western theater at the head of the XI and XII Corps. In April 1864, Butterfield assumed command of a division in Hooker's XX Corps and led it during the **Atlanta Campaign**. After serving in most of the campaign's major battles, he fell ill in late June and had to relinquish command. Butterfield held no other field commands for the rest of the war.

Butterfield had been commissioned colonel of the 5th U.S. Infantry in July 1863 and was **brevetted** brigadier and major general in the regular army for his war service. He resigned from the army in 1870 and became a prominent American who often was involved in well-publicized ceremonies. Although never a cadet, special arrangements were made to have Butterfield buried at **West Point**.

BUTTERNUT. A yellowish-brown color created with dyes made from copperas and walnut hulls, this was not only the usual color of a Confederate **uniform**, but it was also a nickname given to Confederate soldiers themselves.

BUZZARD'S ROOST, GEORGIA, BATTLE OF (FEBRUARY 24–25, 1864). *See* TUNNEL HILL, GEORGIA, BATTLE OF.

BYRAM'S FORD, MISSOURI, BATTLE OF (OCTOBER 22–23, 1864). *See* BIG BLUE RIVER, MISSOURI, BATTLE OF.

– C –

CABELL, WILLIAM LEWIS (1827–1916) CSA. A native of **Virginia**, Cabell (KAB-ul) graduated from **West Point** in 1850 and served on the frontier for 10 years. He resigned his captain's commission when Virginia seceded and entered Confederate service in March 1861 as a major and the state's chief quartermaster. After serving at **First Manassas**, Cabell aided Gen. **P. G. T. Beauregard** in designing the Confederate battle **flag**.

Transferred west of the Mississippi River in January 1862, Cabell became Maj. Gen. **Earl Van Dorn's** chief quartermaster. He performed valuable service supplying Van Dorn's **army** after the **Battle of Pea Ridge** and was appointed brigadier general by **Jefferson Davis**. Cabell led a **brigade** at **Iuka** and was wounded in the foot when the Confederates attacked **Corinth, Mississippi**, in October. After being injured again when his horse fell on him during a **skirmish**, he had to relinquish field command and returned to **Arkansas**, where his rank reverted to major because the Senate failed to confirm his appointment to brigadier general.

Cabell continued to serve in the quartermaster department until April 1863, when he finally received his brigadier general's commission. In April 1864, he took command of a cavalry brigade, which he led during the **Camden Expedition** and was accused of murdering **black troops** at the **Battle of Poison Spring**. After being engaged in several more fights in Arkansas, Cabell participated in Maj. Gen. **Sterling Price's Missouri Raid**. He was praised for leading an assault at **Pilot Knob**, where his horse was killed, but then he was captured in October 1864 at **Marais des Cygnes, Kansas**.

Cabell moved to Dallas, Texas, after the war and served as mayor four times.

CABIN CREEK, INDIAN TERRITORY, BATTLE OF (JULY 1–2, 1863). In the summer of 1863, Union Maj. Gen. **James G. Blunt** was attempting to return pro-Union **Indians** to their homes in **Indian Territory** and had gathered a large number of Creeks and Seminoles at **Fort Gibson** under the protection of Col. William A. Phillips's **brigade**. To resupply the fort, Col. James A. Williams and his **1st Kansas Colored Infantry** escorted 300 wagons from Fort Scott, Kansas, into Indian Territory. Confederate Col. **Stand Watie** and his 2,000 Cherokees and Texans headed to Cabin Creek, where Watie hoped to stop Williams at the ford. However, expected reinforcements from **Arkansas** failed to arrive, and Watie was left to confront Williams alone.

Throughout July 1–2, Williams pounded Watie's position with **artillery** fire and launched two cavalry charges that finally drove the Confederates from the ford. Williams then continued on and successfully resupplied Phillips at Fort Gibson. In the two-day battle, Watie lost 59 men, while Williams counted 21 casualties. In September 1864, Watie successfully attacked another Union wagon train at Cabin Creek and captured 130 wagons.

CABINET, CONFEDERATE. The Confederate cabinet actually was an informal body since the **Confederate Constitution** did not provide for one, only the appointment of secretaries to head the six executive departments of attorney general, navy, postmaster general, state, treasury, and war. Fourteen secretaries served in these positions during the Civil War.

On February 8, 1861, the Provisional Confederate government became operational, with Attorney General **Judah P. Benjamin**, Secretary of the Navy **Stephen R. Mallory**, Postmaster General **John H. Reagan**, Secretary of State **Robert Toombs**, Secretary of the Treasury **Christopher G. Memminger**, and Secretary of War **Leroy P. Walker**. In appointing these men, **Jefferson Davis** was guided by both trying to fill the positions with capable people and trying to make the cabinet representative of the entire Confederacy. Most of his appointees fulfilled their duties as well as circumstances permitted, and they represented nine of the 11 Confederate states. The cabinet subsequently changed frequently, as some secretaries resigned for political or personal reasons and Davis replaced others. Mallory and Reagan were the only ones who kept their positions for the entire war. Others who served in the cabinet were, attorney general: **Thomas Bragg, Thomas H. Watts**, and **George Davis**; state: **R. M. T. Hunter** and Judah P. Benjamin; treasury: **George A. Trenholm**; and war: Judah P. Benjamin, **George W. Randolph, Gustavus W. Smith, James A. Seddon**, and **John C. Breckinridge**.

CABINET, UNION. In appointing his cabinet, **Abraham Lincoln** was guided by trying to fill the positions with skilled men and to bring the various political factions of the Union into the government. His choices usually were nationally known politicians who performed their duties skillfully. Lincoln's original cabinet consisted of Attorney General **Edward Bates**, Postmaster General **Montgomery Blair**, Secretary of the Interior **Caleb B. Smith**, Secretary of the Navy **Gideon Welles**, Secretary of State **William H. Seward**, Secretary of the Treasury **Salmon P. Chase**, and Secretary of War **Simon Cameron**. During the war, others who served on the cabinet were Attorney General **James Speed**, Postmaster General **William Dennison**, Secretary of the Interior **John P. Usher**, Secretaries of the Treasury **William P. Fessenden** and **Hugh McCulloch**, and Secretary of War **Edwin M. Stanton**. Only Seward and Welles kept their positions for the entire war.

CADWALADER, GEORGE (1806–1879) USA. A native of **Pennsylvania**, Cadwalader was a prominent antebellum lawyer and soldier and was the son-in-law of **South Carolina** Senator Pierce Butler. He served as a brigadier general in the state militia in the 1840s and quelled anti-immigrant riots in Philadelphia. During the **Mexican War**, Cadwalader served as a brigadier general of volunteers and was **brevetted** major general for his actions at Chapultepec.

Cadwalader was appointed major general of state troops in April 1861 and a week later was commissioned major general of volunteers. He served as a **division** commander under Maj. Gen. **Robert Patterson** in the **Shenandoah Valley** prior to the **First Battle of Manassas** and then was mustered out of the service in July. In April 1862, Cadwalader was appointed a major general of volunteers and served as a presidential adviser and in various administrative positions before becoming commander of Philadelphia in August 1863. In December 1864, he assumed command of the **Department of Pennsylvania** and remained in that position until war's end. Cadwalader resigned his commission in July 1865 and returned to his private life.

CAHABA (ALABAMA) PRISON. A converted cotton shed, this Confederate **prison** was made operational in early 1864. At its peak, the prison housed approximately 2,000 Union **prisoners**.

CAIRO, **USS.** Built by James B. Eads, the *Cairo* (KAIR-roh) was a 512-ton **ironclad** that was commissioned for the **U.S. Navy** in January 1862. Known as a **Pook Turtle** after its designer Samuel M. Pook, it was 175 feet long and carried eight assorted guns. Operating on the western waterways, the *Cairo* participated in the capture of **Fort Henry** and the naval battles at **Plum Run Bend** and **Memphis, Tennessee**. On December 12, 1862, it was part of a five-boat flotilla steaming up the Yazoo River in support of Maj. Gen. **William T. Sherman's** attack on **Chickasaw Bayou**, near **Vicksburg, Mississippi**. The Confederates detonated two electric **torpedoes** under it, sinking the ship in 12 minutes but with no loss of life. The *Cairo* was the first ship ever to be sunk by an electrically detonated mine. It was raised in the late 1950s and now is on display at the Vicksburg National Military Park.

CALDWELL, JOHN CURTIS (1806–1912) USA. A native of **Vermont** and a graduate of Amherst College, Caldwell left his position as a school principal when the Civil War began and entered Union service in November 1861 as colonel of the 11th Maine. After participating in the **Peninsula Campaign** with the **Army of the Potomac**, he was promoted to brigadier general of volunteers in April 1862 and led a **brigade** in the **army's** II Corps during the **Seven Days Campaign**.

Caldwell took temporary command of the **division** at **Antietam** and was wounded twice while leading his brigade in an attack at **Fredericksburg**. Following service at **Chancellorsville**, he temporarily commanded the II Corps at **Gettysburg** after Maj. Gen. **Winfield Scott Hancock** was wounded. Caldwell again commanded the **corps** temporarily in the **Mine Run Campaign** and was given command of the corps' 1st Division in January 1864. When the **army** was reorganized in March 1865, he was left without a command. Caldwell spent the rest of the war serving on a War Department board and was one of eight generals who formed an honor guard for **Abraham Lincoln's** body when it was transported from **Washington, D.C.**, to Springfield, Illinois.

Mustered out of service in January 1866, Caldwell moved to **Maine** and became a lawyer. He also served as state adjutant general; the U.S. consul to Valparaiso, Chile, and San Jose, Costa Rica; and the U.S. minister to Uruguay.

CALHOUN, JOHN CALDWELL (1782–1850) USA. A native of **South Carolina**, Calhoun became one of the leading Southern politicians before the Civil War. A slave owner and Yale University graduate, he served one term in the state legislature before being elected to the U.S. House of Representatives in 1810. A member of the War Hawks, Calhoun helped persuade Congress to declare war on Great Britain in 1812. He served as James Monroe's secretary of war from 1817 to 1825 and was elected John Quincy Adams's and Andrew Jackson's vice president in 1824 and 1828, respectively.

Known as a strong nationalist who supported internal improvements, a national bank, and a protective tariff during his early political career, Calhoun began to formulate a **states rights** philosophy in the late 1820s when the South began to blame protective tariffs for much of its economic woes. In protest to the Tariff of 1828, he anonymously wrote the *South Carolina Exposition and Protest*, which argued the right of nullification as a means to protect states rights. During the 1832 **Nullification Crisis**, Calhoun strongly supported South Carolina's position against the federal tariff and broke with President Jackson when he threatened to use force in South Carolina to enforce the tariff. Calhoun then resigned as vice president and was elected to the U.S. Senate.

Calhoun served in the Senate until 1843 and, after a brief retirement, served as President John Tyler's secretary of state from 1844 to 1845. He then was reelected to the Senate in 1845 and served there until his death. Throughout his senatorial career, Calhoun worked to unite the Southern states to protect their rights against what he saw as an increasingly tyrannical federal government. His last political activity was opposing the **Compromise of 1850**. Although a great orator, Calhoun was too sick to speak out against the compromise and had to have his speech read to the Senate. He died shortly afterward.

CALIFORNIA. California had a population that overwhelmingly supported the Union, but its small prosecession faction was very strong and vocal. During the 1861 **secession** crisis, the secessionists proposed a separate "Pacific Republic" and actually raised a flag at Stockton in January. Once war began, however, the state legislature took strong measures to ensure the loyalty of its people. It outlawed the display of the Confederate **flag** and prohibited secessionists from seeking redress in court, while local authorities closed secessionist newspapers. Amasa Leland Stanford, president of the Central Pacific Railroad, was elected governor in January 1862 and kept California firmly in the Union camp. No military action took place in the state, but California did raise 16,000 volunteers for state service, some of whom served in the **California Battalion** and in the **California Column** that went to **New Mexico** to oppose **Henry H. Sibley's New Mexico Campaign**. The state's abundant gold supply also helped **finance** the Union war effort.

CALIFORNIA BATTALION. When the Civil War began, approximately 500 Californians traveled east to join the Union war effort. Enlisted in the 2nd Massachusetts Cavalry, these men became known as the California Battalion and served with distinction in the **Army of the Potomac**.

CALIFORNIA COLUMN. When Confederate Col. **John R. Baylor** launched **Baylor's "Buffalo Hunt"** in 1861 and threatened the **New Mexico Territory**, Union Brig. Gen. **Edwin V. Sumner** sent Col. **James Henry Carleton** to guard southern **California**. When news arrived that Confederate Brig. Gen. **Henry Hopkins Sibley** had defeated Col. **E. R. S. Canby's** command at **Valverde**, Carleton was reinforced and took his 2,000-man California Column on an 859-mile march to drive a small Confederate occupation force out of modern-day Tucson, Arizona. The Confederates evacuated Tucson before Carleton arrived, and the colonel then moved on to occupy the rest of modern-day Arizona. Although the California Column never fought the Confederates, it did **skirmish** with **Indians** and helped prevent the Confederates from securing any kind of foothold in the Southwest.

CAMDEN, ARKANSAS, EXPEDITION (MARCH 23–MAY 3, 1864). When Union Maj. Gen. **Nathaniel P. Banks** began the **Red River Campaign** in the spring of 1864, Maj. Gen. **Frederick Steele** was ordered to cooperate by advancing his force in **Arkansas** toward Shreveport, Louisiana, to draw away as many of the Confederate defenders as possible. Although Steele opposed making the offensive because of bad roads, a lack of **forage**, and his vulnerable supply line, he led one infantry **division** and two cavalry **brigades** from **Little Rock** on March 23, a full three weeks behind schedule. This delay played a major role in the campaign, for it allowed the Confederates to first defeat Banks in **Louisiana** and then concentrate against Steele.

After numerous **skirmishes** with Confederate cavalry, Steele reached Arkadelphia on March 29. He was supposed to be met there by Brig. Gen. **John M. Thayer's** column from **Fort Smith**, but when Thayer failed to show up, Steele continued the advance despite a shortage of supplies. When Thayer finally linked up with Steele near Elkin's Ferry on April 9, Steele had a total of 10,400 men. As planned, many of Shreveport's defenders had moved to oppose Steele. Led by Brig. Gen. **John S. Marmaduke**, three Confederate brigades first began seriously contesting Steele's advance when he left Arkadelphia. Confederate Maj. Gen. **Sterling Price**, who commanded the District of Arkansas, then sent more troops, and soon approximately 5,000 Confederates had massed to oppose the invasion. On April 10, a running four-day battle began at **Prairie D'Ane**, as the Confederates attempted to prevent Steele from reaching Washington, his presumed destination. Actually, Steele was heading for Camden, which he intended to make his base of operations. By this time, he was running very short of supplies and had his men on half **rations** for three weeks. He also learned that Banks had been defeated at **Mansfield** and was retreating.

After a brief battle with Marmaduke's cavalry, Steele occupied Camden on April 15. His situation became precarious when the Confederates attacked and destroyed his supply train at **Poison Spring** on April 18. Two days later, Gen. **Edmund Kirby Smith** arrived from Louisiana with three Confederate divisions and soon had Steele effectively trapped in Camden. On April 25, another of Steele's supply trains and approximately 1,700 men were captured at **Marks' Mills** while on their way to Pine Bluff for supplies. With no hope of reinforcements and out of supplies, Steele began a retreat back to Little Rock. Skirmishing occurred daily, and on April 30 he fought a pitched battle at **Jenkins' Ferry**. While the bulk of his force crossed the Saline River on a **pontoon bridge**, Steele kept the pursuing Confederates at bay with 4,000 men. After successfully crossing the river, he abandoned his seriously wounded and continued the retreat. Exhausted and half-starved, the Union troops finally arrived at Little Rock on May 3. Steele lost 2,750 men, 650 wagons, and nine cannons in the campaign, while the Confederates suffered approximately 2,350 casualties.

CAMERON, ROBERT ALEXANDER (1828–1894) USA. Born in **New York**, Cameron moved with his parents to **Indiana** as a boy. Although he graduated from a medical college, he bought a newspaper instead of starting a practice and became active in **Republican** politics. Cameron served as a state legislator and was a delegate to the 1860 Republican National Convention.

Cameron entered Union service in April 1861 as a captain in the 9th Indiana and served with **George B. McClellan** in western **Virginia**. When this nine-month **regiment** was disbanded, he reenlisted as lieutenant colonel of the 19th Indiana in November and then became colonel of the 34th Indiana in June 1862. After leading the regiment at **New Madrid and Island No. 10** and in the **Vicksburg Campaign**, Cameron was promoted to brigadier general of volunteers in August 1863. He was given command of a **division** in the XIII Corps and participated in the 1864 **Red River Campaign**. At the **Battle of Mansfield**, Cameron assumed command of the **corps** and led it during much of the retreat. In June, he was given command of the District of La Fourche and remained there until war's end.

Cameron was **brevetted** major general of volunteers in March 1865 and resigned his commission in July. He then moved to **Colorado** and played an important role in settling that state, including founding the town that became known as Greeley.

CAMERON, SIMON (1799–1889) USA. A **Pennsylvania** native, Cameron owned the Harrisburg *Republican* before the Civil War, was very influential in **Democratic** politics, and became well known for putting together political coalitions and for corruption. He was elected to the U.S. Senate in 1845, but his tainted reputation prevented his reelection until 1857, when he returned to the Senate as a **Republican**. As a senator, Cameron built and controlled the Republican Party in Pennsylvania. In 1860, **Abraham Lincoln's** campaign managers promised him the position of secretary of war if he could carry Pennsylvania in the election. Cameron did so, and Lincoln reluctantly kept the promise, of which he knew nothing until after the election.

Cameron was a controversial cabinet member. There were so many accusations made against him for corruption, purchasing poor and overpriced equipment, appointing favorites to government positions, and maneuvering to run for president that he was censured by the **U.S. Congress**. In January 1862, Lincoln finally moved Cameron out of the cabinet by appointing him minister to Russia.

Cameron returned to Pennsylvania for an unsuccessful Senate race in 1863, but he did win back his seat in 1867. He remained in the Senate until 1877, at which time he was able to pass the seat on to his son. The Cameron machine dominated Pennsylvania politics until 1921.

CAMERON'S DEPOT, WEST VIRGINIA, BATTLE OF (AUGUST 21, 1864). *See* SUMMIT POINT AND CAMERON'S DEPOT, WEST VIRGINIA, BATTLE OF.

CAMPBELL, ALEXANDER WILLIAM (1828–1893) CSA. A native of **Tennessee** and college educated, Campbell was a Nashville lawyer when the Civil War began. He entered Confederate service as a private, but in May 1861, he was appointed colonel of Tennessee state troops and joined Brig. Gen. **Benjamin F. Cheatham's** staff. Appointed colonel of the 33rd Tennessee in October 1861, Campbell and his **regiment** garrisoned Columbus, Kentucky, before fighting at **Shiloh**. There, he commanded the 5th Tennessee as well as his own regiment and received a wound while leading his men in a charge. Campbell failed to be reelected when the regiment was reorganized in the spring of 1862, but he remained with the **army** in an unofficial capacity.

In December 1862, Campbell was appointed assistant adjutant general and inspector general for Lt. Gen. **Leonidas Polk's corps** of the **Army of Tennessee**. After serving with Polk at **Stones River**, he was captured in July 1863 while recruiting for Brig. Gen. **Gideon Pillow** in western Tennessee. **Exchanged** in late 1864, Campbell was assigned to **Nathan**

Bedford Forrest in February 1865 as acting inspector general. Soon, he was in the field commanding one of Forrest's cavalry **brigades**. Campbell was promoted to brigadier general in March 1865, but surrendered in May.

CAMPBELL, CHARLES THOMAS (1823–1895) USA. A native of **Pennsylvania**, Campbell entered the **Mexican War** as a lieutenant and rose to captain in the 11th U.S. Infantry. After the war, he became involved in politics and was elected to the state legislature in 1852.

Campbell entered Union service in May 1861 as a captain in the Pennsylvania Light Artillery but in August was promoted to lieutenant colonel of the 1st Pennsylvania Artillery. A month later, he was promoted again to colonel but resigned this commission in February 1862 to become colonel of the 57th Pennsylvania Infantry. As part of the **Army of the Potomac**, Campbell fought with this **regiment** at **Seven Pines**, where he was wounded three times and had his horse killed under him.

After being appointed brigadier general of volunteers in November 1862, Campbell led his regiment at **Fredericksburg** with one of his arms still in a sling. There, another horse was killed, and Campbell was wounded twice more. One of these wounds was through the liver and was believed to be mortal, but Campbell survived. The Senate never confirmed his appointment to brigadier general, but his commission was renewed when it expired in March 1863. This time it was confirmed, and Campbell was sent in May 1863 to command the District of Wisconsin until war's end.

Campbell remained in the **army** until 1866. He then served as an inspector of Indian agencies in South Dakota, ran a stage line, and helped found Scotland, South Dakota, where he became its mayor and operated a hotel. It was said that Campbell had survived seven wounds in the Mexican and Civil Wars, only to die in 1895 after falling on the steps of his hotel.

CAMPBELL, JOHN ARCHIBALD (1811–1889) CSA. Born in **Georgia**, Campbell was admitted to **West Point** but resigned upon the death of a parent. He then became a prominent **Alabama** lawyer and was elected to the state legislature.

In 1853, President Franklin Pierce appointed Campbell to the **U.S. Supreme Court**. Campbell freed his slaves before taking his seat and became known as a strict constructionist and a supporter of **states rights** but a moderate on the **slavery** issue. While on the Court, he sided with the majority in the **Dred Scott decision** and ruled that William Walker's filibustering expeditions in Latin America violated the nation's neutrality laws. Although he believed in the legality of **secession**, Campbell did not think it was the proper course of action for the South.

During the 1861 **Fort Sumter** crisis, Campbell served as a mediator between Secretary of State **William Seward** and Southern commissioners, telling the Southerners that Seward was adamant that the federal government would not try to reinforce the fort. When the Union ship *Star of the West* attempted to resupply Fort Sumter, the Southerners felt betrayed by Campbell, and Campbell himself felt that he may have been used by Seward. As a result, he resigned his Supreme Court seat and returned to Alabama.

In October 1862, Campbell was appointed Confederate assistant secretary of war under **George W. Randolph**. He was placed in charge of the nation's first military **conscription**, earned a reputation for being an influential force within the department, and participated in the **Hampton Roads Conference** in February 1865. When Union troops entered **Richmond, Virginia**, in April 1865, Campbell met with **Abraham Lincoln** and asked that the **Virginia** legislature be allowed to assemble and consider the Union's **Reconstruction** demands. Permission was at first given but then withdrawn. After **Lincoln's assassination**, Campbell was arrested and held in **Fort Pulaski** for four months before friends on the Supreme Court could win his release. He then moved to **New Orleans, Louisiana**, where he practiced law until his death.

CAMPBELL, WILLIAM BOWEN (1807–1867) USA. A **Tennessee** native, Campbell was a lawyer who had fought in the **Seminole Wars** as a captain in the 2nd Tennessee Mounted Volunteers. He was elected to the **U.S. Congress** as a **Whig** in 1837 and served three terms. In the **Mexican War**, Campbell served as colonel of the 1st Tennessee Infantry and fought in a number of major engagements. He was elected Tennessee's last Whig governor in 1851 and strongly opposed **secession** in 1861.

Both the North and South tried to win Campbell's support, and in June 1862, he finally accepted a commission of brigadier general of volunteers from the Union. He kept the commission only until January 1863, at which time he resigned, apparently never having held any command. Afterward, Campbell worked to get Tennessee readmitted to the Union and became a strong supporter of **Andrew Johnson**. This angered the **Radical Republicans**, and they refused to seat him when he won a congressional election in 1865.

CAMPBELL'S STATION, TENNESSEE, BATTLE OF (NOVEMBER 16, 1863). When Confederate Lt. Gen. **James Longstreet** moved from

Chattanooga, Tennessee, in November 1863 to begin the **Knoxville Campaign** against Maj. Gen. **Ambrose Burnside**, he threatened a Union garrison at Loudon, Tennessee. Burnside evacuated the town on November 16 and headed northeast along the East Tennessee & Georgia Railroad toward Knoxville, with Longstreet's superior force marching along a parallel road. This road and **railroad** intersected at Campbell's Station, about 10 miles southwest of Knoxville. Burnside won the footrace by only 15 minutes after sending units to **skirmish** with and slow down the Confederates.

Burnside left elements of the IX and XXIII Corps behind at Campbell's Station, under Brig. Gen. **Robert B. Potter** to fight a delaying action on November 16, while the main force continued toward Knoxville. Longstreet drew up opposite the Union defenders and sent one **brigade** to flank their left. This attack was mistakenly made against the main line, however, and failed, as did Confederate assaults against the Union right and center. The Federals then retreated almost a mile to a new position and repulsed another flank attack. During the night, Burnside withdrew his infantry and replaced them with cavalry, who skirmished with Longstreet over the next two days. In this rear guard action, Burnside lost 318 men to Longstreet's 174.

CAMP CHASE, OHIO. Located just west of Columbus, Ohio, Camp Chase was named in honor of Secretary of the Treasury **Salmon P. Chase**. It originally was used as a Union training camp but in 1863 became a major **prison** camp. At first the camp had rather lax security and **prisoners** were allowed unusual freedom of movement. As the war dragged on, security tightened and conditions deteriorated as the camp became overcrowded with 7,000 prisoners (it was designed to hold 4,000). Facilities were expanded, but by war's end it was estimated that 10,000 Confederate prisoners were housed there.

CAMP DOUGLAS, ILLINOIS. Located south of Chicago, Illinois, this camp originally was used to train Union recruits but was converted into a **prison** camp after the capture of **Forts Henry and Donelson** in early 1862. During the war, 30,000 Confederate **prisoners** were kept there before it was closed in November 1865.

CAMP FOLLOWER. When armies moved across the countryside, not only did they comprise soldiers but camp followers as well. *Camp follower* was a term applied to any civilian who accompanied an **army**, usually to make money. These included teamsters, laborers, **sutlers**, laundresses, **vivandières**, barbers, washerwomen, nurses, prostitutes, and others. Some, like laundresses, sutlers, and laborers, were recognized army employees and in some way regulated. Others, like prostitutes and runaway slaves, were not.

CAMP FORD, TEXAS. Located near Tyler, Texas, this Confederate **prison** camp, an open, square stockade, was the largest in **Texas** and became operational in August 1863. Its **prisoners** included both officers and enlisted men. The camp was relatively healthy, having good water and ground, and at times did not even have a hospital. Prisoners also reported they usually had adequate food and housing. When hundreds of new prisoners were brought in as a result of the 1864 **Red River Campaign**, however, conditions worsened. At its peak in July 1864, the camp contained 4,900 men. The camp released its last prisoners in May 1865 after an estimated 286 had died during the war.

CAMP GROCE, TEXAS. Located near Hempstead, Texas, Camp Groce was a Confederate **prison** camp, but little information is known of it. It simply was an open field with boundary lines drawn around it.

CAMP JACKSON, MISSOURI. Located on the western outskirts of St. Louis, Missouri, this camp was where Gov. **Claiborne Fox Jackson** assembled his prosecession militia in May 1861 in preparation to seize the U.S. arsenal in St. Louis. On the night of May 8, the militia under Brig. Gen. **Daniel Marsh Frost** received an illicit shipment of arms from Confederate authorities in **Baton Rouge, Louisiana**. Determined to foil the plot, Capt. **Nathaniel Lyon** led a large Unionist force and attacked Camp Jackson on May 10, capturing nearly 1,000 secessionists. As the **prisoners** were marched through the city, the **St. Louis Riot** was sparked when the column was confronted by an angry secessionist crowd, and 28 people were killed.

CAMP LAWTON, GEORGIA. Located at Millen, Georgia, this Confederate **prison** camp became operational in the summer of 1864 to take in some of the overflow from **Andersonville**. A square stockade, it covered about 42 acres and by November 1864 housed approximately 10,000 **prisoners**.

CAMP MORTON, INDIANA. Named for **Indiana** Gov. **Oliver P. Morton**, this camp near Indianapolis was first opened in 1861 as a training camp for state recruits. It was converted into a **prison** after the capture of **Forts Henry and Donelson** in February 1862 and took in 3,000 Confederates captured there. Morton personally supervised the camp, and it reverted to a training base in August 1862 after the **prisoners** were

exchanged. The camp changed back into a prison in early 1863 and became one of the better prison camps of the war, with a lower death rate than most. It usually housed more than 3,500 prisoners and reported 1,763 deaths.

CAMP SUMTER, GEORGIA. *See* ANDERSONVILLE PRISON.

CAMP WILDCAT, KENTUCKY, BATTLE OF (OCTOBER 21, 1861). During the Civil War, Cumberland Gap was an important strategic position because it allowed access to **Kentucky** from **Tennessee** by way of the Wilderness Road. After Confederate Brig. Gen. **Felix Zollicoffer** occupied the gap in mid-September 1861, Union Brig. Gen. **George H. Thomas** responded by sending Brig. Gen. **Albin F. Schoepf's brigade** to nearby Wildcat Mountain to block the Wilderness Road. On October 21, Zollicoffer attacked Schoepf's Camp Wildcat with 7,500 men, but the 5,400 Federals repulsed the assaults by fighting behind strong manmade and natural fortifications. Unable to dislodge the enemy, Zollicoffer retreated that night after losing 53 men. Schoepf's casualties numbered 43.

CANBY, EDWARD RICHARD SPRIGG (1817–1873) USA. Born in **Kentucky**, Canby moved as a boy to **Indiana**. He graduated from **West Point** in 1835 and served with distinction in the **Seminole** and **Mexican Wars**, receiving two **brevets** for gallantry in the latter. Canby had been promoted to major of the 10th U.S. Infantry and was stationed in the **New Mexico Territory** when the Civil War began.

Appointed colonel of the 19th U.S. Infantry in May 1861, Canby was named commander of the **Department of New Mexico** the following month. When Confederate Brig. Gen. **Henry Hopkins Sibley's New Mexico Campaign** began in 1862, Canby attempted to blunt the invasion but was defeated at **Valverde** in February. The Confederates finally were driven out of the territory after being defeated at **Glorieta Pass**, and Canby received a promotion to brigadier general of volunteers in March 1862.

Transferred east, Canby served over a year as an assistant adjutant general in **Washington, D.C.** After the **New York City Draft Riot** in the summer of 1863, he was sent to command the Union troops that were stationed there. Promoted to major general of volunteers in May 1864, Canby was sent west to take command of the **Military Division of West Mississippi**. After being severely wounded by guerrillas, he captured Mobile, Alabama, in the April 1865 **Mobile Campaign** and accepted the surrender of Confederate Lt. Gen. **Richard Taylor's Department of Al-**

abama, Mississippi, and East Louisiana, and Gen. **Edmund Kirby Smith's Trans-Mississippi Department** in May.

For his war service, Canby was brevetted both brigadier general and major general in the regular **army** and was promoted to brigadier general of regulars in July 1866. Given command of the Department of the Columbia in 1870, he was murdered by hostile Modoc Indians while on a **California** peace mission in April 1873.

CANE HILL, ARKANSAS, BATTLE OF (NOVEMBER 28, 1862). In November 1862, Union Brig. Gen. **James Gillpatrick Blunt** learned that approximately 8,000 Confederate cavalrymen under Brig. Gen. **John S. Marmaduke** were riding north from **Arkansas** toward **Missouri**. He took his 5,000 men to meet them and engaged Marmaduke on November 28 in northwest Arkansas at Cane Hill. In a brief battle, Blunt defeated the Confederates, who retreated into the Boston Mountains. Blunt reported losing 40 men in the clash and claimed Marmaduke lost 435.

CANE RIVER CROSSING, LOUISIANA, BATTLE OF (APRIL 23, 1864). *See* MONETT'S FERRY, LOUISIANA, BATTLE OF.

CANISTER. Often misidentified as **grape shot** or **case shot**, canister was **artillery** ammunition used against attacking infantry at a range of 100–400 yards. It consisted of a tin can filled with cast-iron or lead balls. When the cannon was fired, the can (or canister) peeled away, releasing the balls and producing an effect much like that of a shotgun.

CANNON. *See* ARTILLERY.

CANNON, WILLIAM (1809–1865) USA. Cannon was a **Delaware** merchant and active Methodist who was elected to the state legislature as a **Democrat** in 1844. He then became state treasurer in 1851 and participated in the 1861 **Washington Peace Conference**. Although he at first supported the **Crittenden Compromise**, Cannon came to believe that war was necessary after the firing on **Fort Sumter**.

After joining the **Republican Party**, Cannon was elected governor in 1862. He had a difficult administration because the legislature was hostile toward him, but he supported **Abraham Lincoln's** war effort and the **Emancipation Proclamation**. Cannon died in 1865, midway through his term of office.

CANTEY, JAMES (1818–1874) CSA. Born in **South Carolina**, Cantey graduated from South Carolina College and became a lawyer. He had served two terms in the state legislature by the outbreak of the **Mexican**

War but left his seat to serve as a lieutenant, and later captain, in the Palmetto Regiment. Wounded once in Mexico, Cantey moved to **Alabama** after the war and became a planter.

Cantey entered Confederate service in July 1861 when he was elected colonel of the 15th Alabama. After serving in **Stonewall Jackson's Shenandoah Valley Campaign** and with the **Army of Northern Virginia** in the **Seven Days Campaign**, he was transferred to Alabama and was put in command of an infantry **brigade**.

Promoted to brigadier general in January 1863, Cantey was sent to Mobile, Alabama, and in August became commander of the Eastern Division of the **Department of the Gulf (Confederate)**. He served in that capacity until the winter of 1864, when he joined the **Army of Tennessee** and became commander of the defenses of **Resaca, Georgia**. During the **Atlanta Campaign** in May 1864, Cantey's 4,000-man force repulsed an advance by Union Maj. Gen. **James McPherson** through **Snake Creek Gap**, but Cantey was criticized by one officer for remaining in a **bombproof** throughout the fight. During and after the Atlanta Campaign, he was frequently absent from his brigade because of sickness, but he did lead it during the **Franklin and Nashville Campaign** and at **Bentonville, North Carolina**. Cantey surrendered with **Joseph E. Johnston** in April 1865.

CAPE GIRARDEAU, MISSOURI, BATTLE OF (APRIL 26, 1863). In April 1863, Confederate Brig. Gen. **John S. Marmaduke** took his cavalry from **Arkansas** into **Missouri** and forced Brig. Gen. **John McNeill's** Federals to withdraw from Bloomfield to strong fortifications protecting Cape Girardeau. Marmaduke followed McNeill and demanded his surrender on April 26, but McNeill refused. Marmaduke then sent forward **Joseph O. Shelby's brigade** to probe the Union defenses. Shelby turned the probe into a full assault, but McNeill's men successfully drove back the Confederates. After receiving reports that Union reinforcements were on the way, Marmaduke hurriedly withdrew from Cape Girardeau and returned to Arkansas. In the battle, the Confederates suffered 325 casualties, while McNeill lost only 12 men.

CAPERS, ELLISON (1837–1908) CSA. A native of **South Carolina**, Capers graduated first in the South Carolina Military Academy class of 1857. He then taught at the academy until he was elected major of a volunteer **regiment** in December 1860. After commanding a battery of **artillery** on Sullivan's Island during the bombardment of **Fort Sumter**, Capers continued to serve around **Charleston, South Carolina**, until he helped raise the 24th South Carolina in April 1862. Elected lieutenant colonel, he served with the regiment the next year on the Carolina coast. Capers was praised for his actions at the **Battle of Secessionville**, where he took command of an artillery battery. Transferred west, his regiment joined **Joseph E. Johnston** during the **Vicksburg Campaign** and helped defend **Jackson, Mississippi**, in May 1863. Capers was wounded there and at **Chickamauga**, where his gallantry was again praised. Promoted to colonel in January 1864, he led his regiment throughout the **Atlanta Campaign** and sometimes acted as **brigade** commander with the **Army of Tennessee**. At **Franklin**, Capers received his third wound and assumed permanent command of his brigade when Brig. Gen. **States Rights Gist** was killed. Capers received his promotion to brigadier general in March 1865 and surrendered with Johnston in **North Carolina** the following month.

After the war, Capers briefly served as South Carolina's secretary of state in 1866 but then entered the ministry and resigned his position in 1868. He was active in the Episcopal Church, becoming assistant bishop of South Carolina, and was appointed chancellor of the University of the South in 1904.

CARLETON, JAMES HENRY (1814–1873) USA. A native of **Maine**, Carleton served in the state militia during the so-called Aroostook War of 1838. He was commissioned a lieutenant in the **U.S. Army** in 1839 and served in both Stephen Kearny's Rocky Mountain Expedition and in the **Mexican War**, where he earned one **brevet**.

When the Civil War began, Carleton was a captain in the 1st U.S. Cavalry, but he was promoted to colonel of the 1st California Infantry in August 1861. Placed in command of the District of Southern California, his moment of fame came in 1862 when he led the 2,000-man **California Column** 859 miles from southern **California** to the **New Mexico Territory** to prevent the Confederates from seizing the territory.

Carleton was promoted to brigadier general of volunteers in April 1862 and assumed command of the **Department of New Mexico** in September. His time there was marred by controversy as he declared martial law and arrested prominent Southern sympathizers. Carleton finally was relieved of command in September 1866.

For his war service, Carleton was brevetted major general in both the volunteers and the regular **army**. He had been appointed lieutenant colonel of the 4th U.S. Cavalry in July 1866 and still held that position when he died.

CARLIN, WILLIAM PASSMORE (1829–1903) USA. A native of **Illinois**, Carlin graduated from **West Point** in 1850 and spent his antebellum military career fighting **Indians** on the frontier and serving in the **Utah Expedition**. He was a captain in the 6th U.S. Infantry when the Civil War began but was appointed colonel of the 38th Illinois in August 1861. Carlin was engaged in several **skirmishes** in **Missouri** before being appointed to a **brigade** command in the **Army of the Mississippi** in June 1862. In September, he took command of a **brigade** in the **Army of the Ohio** and led it well at **Perryville**.

Carlin was promoted to brigadier general of volunteers in November 1862 and was given a brigade in the **Army of the Cumberland's** XIV Corps. He helped defend Hell's Half Acre at **Stones River**, served in the **Tullahoma** and **Chickamauga Campaigns**, and helped break the Confederate line at **Missionary Ridge** (for which he was **brevetted**) during the **Chattanooga Campaign**. Carlin took command of his **division** in August 1864 and led it during the latter part of the **Atlanta Campaign** (earning another brevet for **Jonesboro**) and through the **March to the Sea** and the **Carolinas Campaign**. He was promoted to major general of volunteers and was brevetted major general of regulars in March 1865.

Carlin was mustered out of the volunteers in August 1865 but continued to serve in the regulars as a major. During **Reconstruction**, he served with the **Freedmen's Bureau** in **Tennessee** and on garrison duty and rose to the rank of colonel in 1882. Carlin was appointed a brigadier general in 1893 and then retired.

CARNIFEX FERRY, VIRGINIA, BATTLE OF (SEPTEMBER 10, 1861). In August 1861, Confederate forces in western **Virginia** attempted to drive out the Union troops that had occupied the area. Brigadier General **John B. Floyd** led his men up the Kanawha (kan-NOW-wha) Valley and crossed the Gauley River at Carnifex Ferry to attack some small Union garrisons in the vicinity. Union Brig. Gen. **William S. Rosecrans** then advanced with 7,000 men and trapped Floyd at the ferry. A second Confederate force under Brig. Gen. **Henry A. Wise** was only 12 miles away, but Wise and Floyd were feuding, and Wise refused to send reinforcements. Rosecrans attacked Floyd on September 10 and captured his supplies, but the Confederates retreated to a strong fortified position at the ferry. Rosecrans delayed attacking again until the next day, giving Floyd time to slip across the river and escape. Rosecrans suffered approximately 150 casualties in the fight, while Floyd reported only 20 wounded.

CAROLINAS CAMPAIGN (FEBRUARY 1–APRIL 26, 1865). After Maj. Gen. **William T. Sherman** completed his **March to the Sea** in December 1864, Lt. Gen. **U. S. Grant** wanted him to move his armies north to **Virginia** to cooperate with Grant in the **Petersburg Campaign**. Given the choice on how to proceed to **Virginia**, Sherman decided to march his armies through the Carolinas. By continuing his March to the Sea **strategy** through the largely untouched regions of **North** and **South Carolina**, Sherman believed he not only could disrupt the supply line feeding Gen. **Robert E. Lee's Army of Northern Virginia** at Petersburg, Virginia, but also spread such terror and demoralization through Confederate ranks that the Southern people would lose their will to fight. In cooperation with the march, Maj. Gen. **John M. Schofield** was to capture **Wilmington** and **New Bern**, **North Carolina**, and then provide Sherman a shorter line of communication to the sea by marching inland and joining him at Goldsboro, North Carolina.

Bad weather delayed Sherman's march until February 1, 1865, when his veterans finally left Beaufort, South Carolina. He had with him approximately 62,000 men and 64 cannons, including Maj. Gen. **Oliver O. Howard's Army of the Tennessee**, Maj. Gen. **Henry W. Slocum's Army of Georgia**, and the cavalry of Brig. Gen. **H. Judson Kilpatrick**. Slocum and Kilpatrick moved directly into South Carolina, while Howard was carried by transports to Port Royal Sound and then marched inland. As a result, Sherman invaded South Carolina in two columns, with Howard on the right and Slocum and Kilpatrick on the left.

Confederate Gen. **P. G. T. Beauregard** arrived to take command of the Carolinas in February 1865 but was able to assemble only about 22,500 men. This lack of troops and Sherman's practice of using widespread columns to threaten several towns at once prevented Beauregard from seriously opposing the invasion. Major General **William J. Hardee**, who was defending **Charleston, South Carolina**, was threatened with being cut off from Beauregard as Sherman moved northward. As a result, Beauregard ordered Hardee to evacuate Charleston and take his force to Cheraw, on the North Carolina border, while the remnants of the **Army of Tennessee** assembled at Chester.

Sherman's entire march was marked by destruction as the Union soldiers took vengeance upon the cradle of **secession**. After fighting a small battle at **Rivers' Bridge** on February 2–3, Sherman occupied **Columbia, South Carolina**, on February 17. Retreating Confederates set fire to bales of cotton piled in the streets, and the flames spread because of high winds and with the help of arsonists. By the next day, half of the city had been destroyed. The burning of Columbia became a controversial event, with both sides blaming the other for the city's destruction.

As Sherman approached Cheraw, **Joseph E. Johnston** assumed overall command of the Carolinas from Beauregard and withdrew the Confederate forces to Fayetteville, North Carolina. Sherman pushed on into North Carolina, forcing Johnston to retreat once more. After part of the column survived a surprise attack at **Monroe's Cross Roads** on March 10, the Union soldiers seized Fayetteville on March 11. For five days the Federals ransacked or destroyed, among other things, an arsenal, newspaper offices, factories, mills, and a number of private dwellings.

On March 15, Sherman left Fayetteville and headed toward Averasboro, where he was to meet Schofield's column from New Bern. The Army of Tennessee was rushed to Kinston to join Gen. **Braxton Bragg** to stop Schofield. There Bragg engaged Schofield's forward units under Maj. Gen. **Jacob D. Cox** on March 7–10 at **Wyse Fork** but was forced to retreat to Goldsboro. Johnston had not yet seriously contested Sherman's march because of a lack of troops and uncertainty as to the enemy's objectives. Finally, he decided to strike before Sherman and Schofield could join forces. Hardee was ordered to **Averasboro**, where he fought a sharp battle on March 16 to stop Slocum's advance. Slocum defeated Hardee, however, and inflicted approximately 850 casualties, while losing about 682 men himself.

After Averasboro, Slocum continued on toward **Bentonville**, and Johnston gathered all the troops he could to crush him. With 21,000 men, Johnston set an ambush for Slocum just outside Bentonville on March 19. Poor maps and a lack of coordination prevented Johnston from effectively springing his trap. He severely mauled Slocum on the first day, but Sherman then arrived with reinforcements. This, the largest battle of the campaign, continued on March 21, when Johnston was forced to retreat. In the three-day clash, Johnston lost approximately 2,600 men to Slocum's nearly 1,500. Sherman and Slocum's separate columns then united and entered Goldsboro on March 23. This juncture gave Sherman an overwhelming army of 80,000 men. After Lee surrendered at the end of the **Appomattox Campaign** on April 9, Johnston and Sherman opened negotiations that led to Johnston's **surrender** at **Durham Station** on April 26.

CARONDELET, USS. Launched in October 1861, the *Carondelet* (ka-RON-da-LET) was designed by James B. Eads. Constructed near St. Louis, Missouri, it displaced 512 tons and carried 13 guns of assorted sizes. The ship participated in operations against **Forts Henry and Donelson, Island No. 10**, and in the **Vicksburg Campaign**. On July 15, 1862, it was disabled by the Confederate **ironclad** *Arkansas* and ran aground but survived to fight in the 1864 **Red River Campaign**, its last operation. The ship was sold for scrap after the war.

CARPETBAGGERS. This was a derisive nickname given either to Northerners who went to the South during **Reconstruction** or to Union soldiers who stayed there after the Civil War. Some of these people sought financial gain in rebuilding the devastated South, some worked for the **Freedmen's Bureau**, and others became involved in politics. Many carpetbaggers were honest men engaged in legitimate activities, but most white Southerners viewed them as corrupt interlopers who worked with **scalawags** and **freedmen** to control the Southern states. The name was a reference to "carpetbags," a type of luggage they inevitably carried.

CARR, EUGENE ASA (1830–1910) USA. A native of **New York**, Carr graduated from **West Point** in 1850. Assigned to the 3rd U.S. Cavalry, he served on the frontier and was wounded in 1854 while fighting **Indians** in **Texas**.

When the Civil War began, Carr was serving as a captain in the 1st U.S. Cavalry. Only days after fighting at **Wilson's Creek**, he was appointed colonel of the 3rd Illinois Cavalry in August 1861. Carr was put in command of a cavalry **brigade** in the **Army of the Southwest Missouri** in January 1862, but he took command of an infantry **division** for the **Battle of Pea Ridge**. At Pea Ridge, he was wounded three times and later was awarded the **Medal of Honor** for gallantry.

Commissioned a brigadier general of volunteers in March 1862, Carr commanded various divisions in **Missouri** over the next year and even the Army of the Southwest Missouri for a brief time that autumn. In March 1863, he was given command of an infantry division in the **Army of the Tennessee's** XIII Corps and led it during the **Vicksburg Campaign**, earning a **brevet** for his actions at **Big Black River Bridge**. Carr took over a cavalry division in **Arkansas** in February 1864 and led it in the capture of **Little Rock** and in the **Camden Expedition**. He commanded Little Rock from May to December 1864 and in March 1865 was given command of a XVI Corps infantry division, which he led in the **Mobile Campaign**.

For his war service, Carr was **brevetted** major general in both the volunteer and the regular **armies**. He was mustered out of the volunteers in January 1866 and resumed his rank of major in the 5th U.S. Cavalry. Carr became famous as an Indian fighter after the Civil War and finally retired from the army as a brigadier general in 1893 after 43 years of service. He was one of the army's most respected officers when he retired.

CARR, JOSEPH BRADFORD (1828–1895) USA. A native of **New York**, Carr worked in the tobacco industry before the Civil War and became a colonel in the state militia.

After helping raise the 2nd New York in 1861, Carr was appointed its colonel in May. He led a **brigade** at **Big Bethel** and then became part of the **Army of the Potomac's** III Corps. Carr commanded a brigade in the 2nd Division in the **Peninsula** and **Second Manassas Campaigns** and was promoted to brigadier general of volunteers in September 1862.

After leading the brigade competently at **Fredericksburg**, Carr had to be reappointed brigadier general in March 1863 because the U.S. Senate did not confirm his commission. He temporarily led the **division** several times in the first half of 1863 but was back at the head of his brigade at **Gettysburg**. In October 1863, Carr was placed in command of the division again and led it in the **Bristoe Station** and **Mine Run Campaigns**, but in May 1864, he was transferred to garrison duty on the **Virginia** Peninsula. In August, he joined **Benjamin F. Butler's Army of the James** and briefly commanded a division of **black troops** in the XVIII Corps. In October 1864, Carr was given a brigade in the Army of the James and remained with it until war's end. He was **brevetted** major general of volunteers for his war service and was mustered out of the volunteers in August 1865.

After the war, Carr operated a manufacturing business in New York, became active in **Republican** politics, served as New York's secretary of state from 1879 to 1885, and became a major general in the state militia.

CARRICK'S FORD, VIRGINIA, BATTLE OF (JULY 13, 1861). When **Virginia** seceded in 1861, the mountainous western counties remained loyal to the Union and eventually entered the Union as the state of **West Virginia**. In May 1861, Union Maj. Gen. **George B. McClellan** entered the region with 20,000 troops to defend it, but Confederate Brig. Gen. **Robert S. Garnett** confronted him with 4,500 men. On July 11, the Union forces defeated the Confederates on **Rich Mountain**, forcing Garnett to evacuate his position on Laurel Mountain. While attempting to withdraw from the area, Garnett was told, incorrectly, that Union troops occupied his intended route through Beverly. He then moved into the Cheat River Valley, with Union militiaman Brig. Gen. Thomas A. Morris in pursuit.

Rain and a wagon train slowed Garnett, and on July 13 Morris attacked his rear guard at Carrick's Ford. Garnett personally supervised a fighting withdrawal to another ford a short distance away. There, while commanding a small 10-man rear guard, Garnett was killed. The rest of the Confederates continued the retreat to Monterey. Besides Garnett, the Confederates lost about 70 men, one cannon, and 40 wagons in these actions, while Morris lost approximately 50 men. On the same day, 555 of the Confederates who had defended Rich Mountain also were captured. Although McClellan was not personally involved in the fighting at Rich Mountain or Carrick's Ford, he received recognition for the victories and was picked to assume command of the main Union **army** at **Washington, D.C.** Confederate authorities sent Gen. **Robert E. Lee** to western Virginia to try to salvage the bungled defense of that region.

CARRINGTON, HENRY BEEBEE (1824–1912) USA. A native of **Connecticut**, Carrington graduated from Yale University in 1845. A dedicated **abolitionist**, he then graduated from Yale Law School, moved to **Ohio**, and became law partner with **William Dennison**, Ohio's future Civil War governor. Also a friend of Gov. **Salmon Chase**, Carrington was appointed the state's adjutant general in 1857.

When the Civil War began, Carrington swiftly raised volunteer troops and sent them to reinforce Maj. Gen. **George B. McClellan** in western **Virginia**. He was rewarded in May 1861 by being commissioned colonel of the 18th U.S. Infantry. Promoted to brigadier general of volunteers in November 1862, Carrington supervised the raising and training of troops in nearby **Indiana**. There, he also tried to destroy the disloyal organization **Sons of Liberty**, which was active in Indiana and Ohio. The **U.S. Supreme Court**, however, ruled Carrington's military tribunals illegal since neither state was in rebellion.

After the war, Carrington fought **Indians** in the west and was in command of Fort Phil Kearny when the Fetterman Massacre occurred. Because of his incompetence, he was forced to resign from the **army** in 1870 and then began a successful career as a historian, teacher, and writer.

CARROLL, SAMUEL SPRIGG (1832–1893) USA. Born in **Washington, D.C.**, Carroll was the brother-in-law of Union general **Charles Griffin**. After graduating from **West Point** in 1856, he served on the frontier and at the academy. Carroll was promoted to 1st lieutenant in the 10th U.S. Infantry in April 1861 and then to captain in November.

In December 1861, Carroll was appointed colonel of the 8th Ohio. The following May, he was given command of a **brigade** in the **Shenandoah Valley** and led it at **First Kernstown** and **Port Republic**. Only days after fighting at **Cedar Mountain**, Carroll was wounded while on the **picket** line, but he recovered in time to lead a **brigade** in the **Army of the Potomac's** III Corps at **Fredericksburg**. In March 1863, he was transferred to a II Corps brigade and led it in the **Chancellorsville, Gettysburg, Bristoe Station**, and **Mine Run Campaigns** and at the beginning of the **Overland Campaign**. After receiving his second and third wounds at the **Wilderness** and **Spotsylvania**, respectively, Carroll was promoted to brigadier general of volunteers in May 1864. His last wound kept him out of action until December, at which time he took command of the **Department of West Virginia**. Carroll commanded the **department** until March 1865 and then took over a **division** in the Shenandoah Valley until war's end. He received **brevets** of brigadier general in the regular **army** and major general of volunteers.

Carroll was mustered out of the volunteers in January 1866 but remained in the army as lieutenant colonel of the 21st U.S. Infantry. His wounds forced his retirement as a major general in 1869.

CARROLL, WILLIAM HENRY (1810?–1868) CSA. The son of a **Tennessee** governor, Carroll was a **Mississippi** planter and Memphis, Tennessee, postmaster before the Civil War.

In 1861, Carroll was appointed brigadier general in the Tennessee provisional **army** and colonel of the 37th Tennessee. Sent to raise troops in eastern Tennessee in September 1861, he organized three **regiments** and was promoted to brigadier general of Confederate troops in October. Carroll took his three poorly armed regiments to Chattanooga, Tennessee, where one officer accused him of being a drunk. In November 1861, he was given command of 5,000 troops at Knoxville, Tennessee, and operated against Union guerrillas. Carroll's inability to arm his troops brought reprimands from the government, but in January 1862, he was sent to **Kentucky**, where he fought at **Mill Springs**. Continued complaints about Carroll finally led to his court-martial in April 1862 on charges of drunkenness, incompetence, and neglect of his command. The trial was delayed, but Gen. **Braxton Bragg** later listed him among general officers he deemed unfit for service. Under such pressure, Carroll resigned his commission in February 1863.

After quitting the service, Carroll moved to Canada to join his family there in exile and never returned to the United States.

CARSON, CHRISTOPHER "KIT" (1809–1868) USA. Born in **Kentucky**, Carson moved to **Missouri** as a boy. After being apprenticed to a saddler, he ran away to **New Mexico** and became a famous guide and mountain man, most notably guiding three Rocky Mountain expeditions for **John C. Frémont**. Praised for brave service in **California** during the **Mexican War**, Carson then became an Indian agent.

When the Civil War began, Carson was commissioned lieutenant colonel of the 1st New Mexico Infantry in July 1861 and then promoted to colonel in September. After participating in the **Battle of Glorieta Pass**, he carried out the government's plan to place the Southwest **Indians** on reservations. Carson rounded up Apaches and Navajos but protested the harsh treatment of the Indians and refused standing orders by his superior, Brig. Gen. **James H. Carleton**, to shoot any Indian who resisted resettlement. After bringing thousands of Indians to the reservations, Carson was appointed superintendent of the Bosque Redondo Reservation in July 1864. A few months later, he resumed operations against the Indians and in November fought a major battle with the Comanches at Adobe Wells, **Texas**. Despite little actual service against the Confederates, Carson was **brevetted** brigadier general of volunteers for his Civil War service. Carson was mustered out of service in 1867 and died the following year in **Colorado**.

CARTER, JOHN CARPENTER (1837–1864) CSA. A native of **Georgia**, Carter attended the University of Virginia and graduated from **Tennessee's** Cumberland University. Admitted to the bar, he began a practice in Tennessee, where in September 1861 he organized and became captain of a **company** in the 38th Tennessee.

Carter gallantly led his company at **Shiloh** and quickly moved up the ranks to become regimental colonel in May 1862. He again was praised for his conduct at **Perryville** and **Stones River**. At **Chickamauga** with the **Army of Tennessee**, Carter had command of his **regiment** and a battalion and saw heavy fighting on the first day. While the **army** was besieging **Chattanooga**, **Tennessee**, his **brigade** was sent to garrison Charleston, Tennessee, and Carter assumed command of that post in November 1863. After his service there, he fought through the 1864 **Atlanta Campaign** and was recommended for promotion.

Carter was made brigadier general in July 1864 and led a brigade in **Benjamin F. Cheatham's** division at **Peachtree Creek** and in the **Battle of Atlanta** and temporarily commanded the **division** at the **Battle of Jonesboro**. After the fall of Atlanta, he was placed in command of a brigade in **John C. Brown's** division and led it at the **Battle of Franklin**. During the battle, Carter was mortally wounded while bringing his brigade up to reinforce Brig. Gen. **States Rights Gist**. He died on December 10, 1864.

CARTER, SAMUEL POWHATAN (1819–1891) USA. Born in **Tennessee**, Carter attended both Washington College and the College of New Jersey. He joined the **U.S. Navy** as a midshipman in 1840 and served in the Pacific and Great Lakes before entering the **U.S. Naval Academy** and graduating in 1846. Afterward, Carter rose to the rank of lieutenant while serving in the Mediterranean and with the East India and Brazil squadrons.

When the Civil War began, Carter received some publicity for being a Southerner who remained loyal to the Union and was brought to **Washington, D.C.**, through the influence of Sen. **Andrew Johnson**. Dispatched to East Tennessee to raise Union troops, Carter was successful and was transferred from the navy to the **army**. He was put in command of a **brigade** in the **Army of the Ohio** in November 1861 and fought at **Mill Springs** in January 1862.

Carter was appointed a brigadier general of volunteers in May 1862 and helped seize Cumberland Gap the following month. In December 1862, he led what was claimed to be the first successful Union cavalry raid in the west when he raided the upper Tennessee Valley. Afterward Carter remained in **Tennessee** and during the **Knoxville Campaign** commanded **Ambrose Burnside's** cavalry **division**. During the **Carolinas Campaign**, he was given command of a division in March 1865 and commanded the Union army's left wing at **Wyse Fork**. Carter was **brevetted** major general of volunteers for his service and returned to the navy in January 1866.

While serving in the army, Carter also was promoted to the navy rank of lieutenant commander in 1862 and to commander in 1865. He retired as a commodore in 1881, but the following year was appointed a rear admiral on the retired list. Carter was the only person in American history to serve as both a major general and a rear admiral.

CARTHAGE, MISSOURI, BATTLE OF (JULY 5, 1861). Following the capture of his **Missouri** militia at **Camp Jackson** in May 1861, Gov. **Claiborne Jackson** and his secessionist legislature fled to southwestern Missouri. Union forces under Col. **Franz Sigel** pursued them and then encamped at Carthage. Having been reinforced by 4,000 militiamen, Jackson decided to attack Sigel's 1,100 men. When Jackson arrived outside Carthage, however, Sigel attacked him on July 5, 1861. There was a brief fight, but the outnumbered Sigel thought Jackson was moving against his left flank and retreated. After some rear guard action, Sigel entered Carthage but then continued the retreat that night. In the battle, Sigel lost 44 men to Jackson's 74. Although the clash was little more than a **skirmish**, it boosted Southern morale in Missouri.

CARUTHERS, ROBERT LOONEY (1800–1882) CSA. A **Tennessee** native, Caruthers served in the state legislature, the U.S. House of Representatives, and Tennessee Supreme Court before the Civil War. To prevent **secession**, he attended the **Washington Peace Conference** in February 1861, but when the conference failed, he accepted secession and was elected to the Provisional **Confederate Congress** in May 1861. Caruthers was not a very active congressman and was defeated for election to the Senate in October 1861. He was elected the Tennessee Confederate governor in 1863 but never actually carried out any duties since the Union occupation of the state prevented him from ever being inaugurated. After the war, Caruthers taught at Cumberland University.

CASCABEL. This is the large knob found at the end of a cannon's breech. It was used for hoisting and moving the heavy gun tube.

CASE SHOT. Used against advancing infantry, *case shot* was the generic name given to a type of **artillery** ammunition that released lead or cast-iron balls when fired. It included **grape shot**, **canister**, and spherical case shot. British officer Lt. Henry Shrapnel invented this type of ammunition in 1784, thus causing the term *shrapnel* also to be used to describe it.

CASEY, SILAS (1807–1882) USA. A native of **Rhode Island**, Casey graduated from **West Point** in 1826. He served in the **Seminole Wars** and was a captain in the 2nd U.S. Infantry during the **Mexican War**. In Mexico, Casey was severely wounded at Chapultepec and was **brevetted** major and lieutenant colonel for gallantry. After the war, he mostly served on the Pacific coast.

Casey was serving as a lieutenant colonel when the Civil War began. Commissioned a brigadier general of volunteers in August 1861 (and colonel of the 4th U.S. Infantry in October), he led a **division** in the **Army of the Potomac** at **Seven Pines** and won a brevet to brigadier general of regulars. In May 1862, Casey was promoted to major general of volunteers and served in **Washington, D.C.**, for the rest of the war. In 1862, he compiled the three-volume *Infantry Tactics*, a training manual used by most Union troops, as well as another edition for **black troops**. Known as *Casey's Tactics*, it was nearly identical to the one compiled in 1855 by future Confederate Lt. Gen. **William J. Hardee**. The Union **army** did not want to use a manual authored by a Confederate, so Casey's manual was the main one used on the Union side. Casey requested retirement in 1868 after 46 years of service.

CASHIER, ALBERT D. J. (1844–1915) USA. An Irish native who arrived in America as a stowaway, Cashier was actually a woman named Jennie Hodgers. She disguised herself as a man and joined the 95th Illiniois in August 1862. Hodgers kept her real identity a secret and served in the **Vicksburg**, **Red River**, and **Mobile Campaigns**, as well as in the battles of **Brice's Cross Roads** and **Nashville**. She was awarded a soldier's pension in 1899 (which required a medical examination), and her real identity was not discovered until she was injured in a 1911 automobile accident. After her accident, Hodgers lived for two years in an **Illinois** soldiers' and sailors' home and then was admitted to an insane asylum in 1913. Upon her death, she was buried in a **uniform** with full military honors by the local **Grand Army of the Republic**.

CASSVILLE, GEORGIA. *See* ATLANTA, GEORGIA, CAMPAIGN.

CASTLE PINCKNEY, SOUTH CAROLINA. Built as a fort after the Revolutionary War and named for **South Carolina** hero Gen. Charles C. Pinckney, Castle Pinckney was located in **Charleston** harbor. After the 1861 **First Battle of Manassas**, the fort was converted into a **prison** and began housing Union **prisoners**. The prisoners and their guards, the Charleston **Zouave** Cadets, treated each other with respect, and the prison became known as one of the better ones in the Confederacy. There was never a known escape made from it.

CASTLE THUNDER, VIRGINIA. Although there was another Castle Thunder in Petersburg, Virginia, so named by Union **prisoners** because of the loud roar of **artillery** fired during the **Petersburg Campaign**, the most famous **prison** by that name was located in **Richmond, Virginia**. It was a converted tobacco warehouse and was used to keep such non-military prisoners as spies, Unionists, and common criminals. The prison became notorious for its hardened criminals, bad conditions, and cruel guards. In 1863, the **Confederate Congress** investigated the prison commandant, Capt. George W. Alexander, for cruelty and dishonesty, but a majority of the investigators cleared him of any wrongdoing. After Richmond was captured in April 1865, Castle Thunder was used to house Confederates accused of war crimes.

CASUALTIES. *See* LOSSES.

CATLETT'S STATION, VIRGINIA, RAID ON (AUGUST 22–23, 1862). In mid-August 1862, prior to the **Second Battle of Manassas**, Gen. **Robert E. Lee** and his **Army of Northern Virginia** were maneuvering against Maj. Gen. **John Pope's Army of Virginia** along the Rappahannock River. On August 17, 1862, Maj. Gen. **J. E. B. Stuart** was nearly captured by Union cavalry at Verdiersville and lost his plumed hat, sash, and gloves. Worse, his adjutant was captured, along with papers revealing Lee's plan to move into Pope's rear. As a result, Pope retreated across the Rappahannock River.

His pride stung by the incident, Stuart received permission to raid behind Pope's line to cut the Orange & Alexandria Railroad, which kept Pope supplied. Taking two cannons and 1,500 cavalrymen from two **brigades**, Stuart crossed the Rappahannock on August 22 at Waterloo Bridge and Hart's Ford. Passing through Warrenton, he went around Pope's right flank and arrived outside Catlett's Station after dark. A captured slave informed Stuart that this was Pope's headquarters and agreed to guide the Confederates to his tent. In a driving rainstorm, Stuart quickly routed the Union soldiers. The raid resulted in the capture of several of Pope's staff officers, more than $500,000 in cash, and many of Pope's official papers and personal possessions. After attacking another Union encampment and unsuccessfully trying to burn the **railroad** bridge across Cub Run, Stuart retreated. The Confederates had covered 60 miles in 26 hours, brought back 300 **prisoners**, and Stuart put Pope's captured **uniform** on display in a Richmond shop window. Headquarters' papers brought back to Lee also provided important intelligence information that was useful in the upcoming Second Manassas Campaign.

CEDAR CREEK, VIRGINIA, BATTLE OF (OCTOBER 19, 1864). By October 1864, Maj. Gen. **Philip Sheridan** had defeated Lt. Gen. **Jubal Early's** Confederate forces in his **Shenandoah Valley Campaign** at the **Third Battle of Winchester** and **Fisher's Hill**. Believing Early's 18,000 men no longer posed a serious threat, Sheridan withdrew up the Valley and encamped his 31,000-man army along Cedar Creek, near Middletown. He then left Maj. Gen. **Horatio G. Wright** in command and went to **Washington, D.C.**, to attend **strategy** meetings. Early, however, left his camp at Fisher's Hill and launched a surprise attack at dawn of October 19 that came close to defeating Sheridan's **army**.

Following a plan developed by Maj. Gen. **John B. Gordon** and Maj. **Jedediah Hotchkiss**, Early sent three **divisions** under Gordon to cross the Shenandoah River and mass against Wright's left flank, while the rest of the Confederate army threatened his front. Attacking at dawn in a thick fog, Gordon's assault broke Wright's flank and sent it retreating. Despite valiant defenses by some isolated Union units, Early forced Wright back three miles in what was becoming a total rout. The Confederate pursuit slowed because of growing disorganization and because many famished Confederates began looting the Union camps. Despite Gordon's urging him to finish the victory, Early believed the enemy would abandon the field and was content to regroup his army and rest.

Meanwhile, Sheridan was returning from Washington and heard the battle when he reached Winchester. In a dramatic 14-mile ride, made famous by T. Buchanan Read's poem "Sheridan's Ride," Sheridan reached the field at mid-morning and rallied his men for a counterattack. At about 4:00 P.M., Sheridan crushed Early's left flank and sent the Confederates streaming back up the Valley to Fisher's Hill. Despite his initial success, Early suffered a major defeat and the loss of 5,700 men. Sheridan reported 2,900 casualties.

CEDAR MOUNTAIN, VIRGINIA, BATTLE OF (AUGUST 9, 1862). During the summer of 1862, Union Maj. Gen. **John Pope** was given command of the newly constituted **Army of Virginia**, with orders to defend both **Washington, D.C.**, and the **Shenandoah Valley.** When Pope moved his **army** to near Culpeper, Gen. **Robert E. Lee**, who had just defeated Maj. Gen. **George B. McClellan's Army of the Potomac** in the **Seven Days Campaign**, was forced to meet this threat against the vital **railroads** that supplied his **Army of Northern Virginia.** Lee dispatched Maj. Gen. **Thomas J.** "Stonewall" **Jackson** to Gordonsville in mid-July. When he advanced to Orange Court House on August 7, Pope countered by placing his army in a long defensive line covering both Madison Court House and Culpeper. Major General **Nathaniel P. Banks's** II Corps, numbering fewer than 15,000 men, held an advanced position outside Culpeper at Cedar Mountain. On the morning of August 9, Jackson moved his 24,000 men to Cedar Mountain and there hastily advanced against Banks without undertaking proper **reconnaissance.** With the **division** of Brig. Gen. **Charles S. Winder** on the left and Maj. Gen. **Richard S. Ewell** on the right, Jackson's line had large gaps in it and was poorly arranged. Winder was mortally wounded by a shell just before Banks launched a vicious attack that caught Jackson by surprise and drove back Winder's disorganized division. Jackson personally rallied the retreating men, while Ewell managed to hold his position. Reinforced by Maj. Gen. **A. P. Hill's** division, Jackson counterattacked as evening came and slowly forced Banks to retire.

Although a Confederate victory, the battle somewhat tarnished Jackson's reputation. He had rashly advanced without adequate knowledge of his opponent's numbers or disposition and was nearly defeated by a much smaller Union force. Jackson lost about 1,400 men to Banks's 2,600. The battle also was known as Slaughter Mountain or Cedar Run.

CEDAR RUN, VIRGINIA, BATTLE OF (AUGUST 9, 1862). *See* CEDAR MOUNTAIN, VIRGINIA, BATTLE OF.

CEMETERY HILL AT BATTLE OF GETTYSBURG, PENNSYLVANIA (JULY 1–3, 1863). *See* GETTYSBURG, PENNSYLVANIA, CAMPAIGN AND BATTLE OF.

CEMETERY RIDGE AT BATTLE OF GETTYSBURG, PENNSYLVANIA (July 1–3, 1863). *See* GETTYSBURG, PENNSYLVANIA, CAMPAIGN AND BATTLE OF.

CENSORSHIP. Reporters during the Civil War were not subjected to the same strong formal censorship that is common in modern wars. The

Union government did impose some censorship in August 1861 when it forbade **war correspondents** from telegraphing from **Washington, D.C.**, any information concerning **army** movements. The Confederates also took action in May 1861 when they censored the **telegraph** and authorized agents to monitor messages. The following month, the Confederate postal service also was authorized to censor the mail.

These measures were never enforced rigorously. Instead, both the Union and Confederate governments appealed to the press's sense of patriotism and requested restraint in printing sensitive information. When this did not work, both sides on occasion seized offending publications and shut down their presses. Two effective methods of censorship were **army** commanders controlling war correspondents' access to the telegraph and expelling offending correspondents from the front. Taking such action frequently earned Maj. Gen. **William T. Sherman** the reporters' wrath, and when Maj. Gen. **George G. Meade** expelled one reporter from the **Army of the Potomac**, war correspondents conspired to snub Meade by omitting his name from their stories. The lack of censorship often helped army commanders by allowing them to gain much military intelligence by reading the opposition's newspapers. **Robert E. Lee**, especially, made good use of Northern newspapers.

CENTRAL ARMY OF KENTUCKY (CONFEDERATE). This was the original Confederate **army** that was scattered throughout central **Kentucky** in September 1861. First commanded by Brig. Gen. **Simon B. Buckner**, it was taken over by Gen. **Albert Sidney Johnston** in October 1861. In March 1862, the army numbered approximately 23,000 men but lost its identity when it was merged with the **Army of Mississippi**.

CENTRALIA, MISSOURI, MASSACRE (SEPTEMBER 27, 1864). On the morning of September 27, 1864, Confederate guerrilla **William "Bloody Bill" Anderson** raided Centralia, **Missouri**, with about 225 men (including future outlaws Frank and Jesse James). After several hours of looting and robbing, the guerrillas surrounded a train when it pulled into the station and captured 25 unarmed Union soldiers who were on furlough. The guerrillas robbed the soldiers of their **uniforms**, burned the train, and then, on Anderson's orders, murdered 24 of them. Sergeant Thomas Goodman was the only one released, apparently in recognition of his bravery when he stepped forward after Anderson asked the **prisoners** if any were officers or noncommissioned officers. The guerrillas also stole $3,000 from the train and murdered two men who tried to hide their valuables.

That afternoon, the 39th Missouri Infantry arrived at Centralia under Maj. A. V. E. Johnson. Despite warnings, Johnson split his command by leaving part in town and taking the rest to pursue Anderson. The inexperienced Johnson rode into an ambush and was killed, along with nearly his entire command. The guerrillas then rode back to Centralia and attacked and killed nearly all of the soldiers there. In little more than an hour, the 39th Missouri lost 116 men killed, two wounded, and six missing.

CHAFFIN'S FARM, VIRGINIA, BATTLE OF (SEPTEMBER 29–30, 1864). *See* FORT HARRISON, VIRGINIA, BATTLE OF.

CHAIN SHOT. An obsolete **artillery** round that was rarely used in the Civil War, chain shot was designed to be used against the sails and riggings of an opposing ship. It consisted of two solid cannon balls that were connected by a length of chain. When fired, the balls whirled through the air, snaring and tearing down rigging. Chain shot was similar to **bar shot**, except a chain and not a bar connected the two balls.

CHALK BLUFF, ARKANSAS, BATTLE OF (MAY 1–2, 1863). After Confederate Maj. Gen. **John S. Marmaduke's** cavalry was driven out of **Missouri** at **Cape Girardeau** in April 1863, Brig. Gens. **William Vandever** and **John McNeill** pursued the raiders back into **Arkansas**. They caught up with Marmaduke at Chalk Bluff, where the Confederates were crossing the flooded St. Francis River on a rickety floating bridge. While the main Confederate body crossed the bridge, a small rear guard was left behind to keep the Federals at bay. After crossing over, Marmaduke's men cut the bridge supports and left 250 Texans stranded on the far side. The Texans managed to swim the river safely with their horses. In the rear guard action, combined casualties were estimated at fewer than 100.

CHALMERS, JAMES RONALD (1831–1898) CSA. Born in **Virginia**, Chalmers moved to **Mississippi** as a boy. He graduated from South Carolina College and became a Mississippi lawyer and district attorney.

After serving as a prosecession delegate to the state's **secession** convention, Chalmers was appointed colonel of the 9th Mississippi Infantry in April 1861 and served under **Braxton Bragg** at **Pensacola**, **Florida**. Promoted to brigadier general in February 1862, he skillfully led a **brigade** of infantry under Bragg at **Shiloh**. For a time, Chalmers commanded the Confederate cavalry in northern Mississippi, but he rejoined his brigade for Bragg's 1862 **Kentucky Campaign**. An ill-advised attack against a Union blockhouse near **Munfordville** led to heavy casualties and brought Chalmers one of the few censures he ever received from Bragg. A serious wound by shell fragments at **Stones River** ended Chalmers's infantry career.

In March 1863, Chalmers was given a cavalry brigade in northern Mississippi and joined **Nathan Bedford Forrest** in February 1864. Although the two sometimes clashed, he served Forrest well and was commanding one of his **divisions** by March. At **Fort Pillow**, Chalmers was implicated along with Forrest in the **massacre** of **black troops**, but he maintained that he and Forrest stopped the killings as soon as possible. Afterward his division served with Forrest at **Tupelo** and in the raid on **Johnsonville, Tennessee**. Joining **John Bell Hood's Army of Tennessee** for the 1864 **Franklin and Nashville Campaign**, Chalmers fought in the campaign's two major battles. At Nashville, he commanded Hood's left wing on the second day of battle and formed the rear guard when Hood retreated. Chalmers surrendered with Forrest in **Alabama** in May 1865.

Active in **Reconstruction** politics, Chalmers was elected to the Mississippi legislature and to the **U.S. Congress** as a **Democrat**, sometimes with the support of **Republicans**.

CHAMBERLAIN, JOSHUA LAWRENCE (1828–1914) USA. A native of **Maine**, Chamberlain's only military training was at a local military academy. After graduating from Bowdoin College and Bangor Theological Seminary, he returned to Bowdoin as a professor.

Taking a sabbatical in 1862 to study in Europe, Chamberlain instead offered his services to the governor. Commissioned lieutenant colonel of the 20th Maine in August, he fought with it and the **Army of the Potomac** at **Antietam, Fredericksburg** (where he was wounded), and **Chancellorsville** before being promoted to colonel in May 1863. Chamberlain's greatest moment came at **Gettysburg** on July 2, 1863, when his **regiment** held Little Round Top against repeated Confederate attacks. He was slightly wounded in the fight and was awarded the **Medal of Honor** in 1893. Since **brigade** commander **Strong Vincent** was mortally wounded at Gettysburg, Chamberlain temporarily took command of the brigade (in the V Corps' 1st Division) until November 1863. At that time, a bout of malaria forced him on extended sick leave. Chamberlain returned to his regiment, however, in time to lead it in the 1864 **Overland Campaign**.

In June 1864, Lt. Gen. **U. S. Grant** returned Chamberlain to his brigade command, but only 12 days later he was severely wounded through the hips during the **Petersburg Campaign**. The wound, which caused considerable internal damage, at first was believed to be mortal, but Chamberlain recovered, and Grant immediately promoted him to brigadier general of volunteers. Chamberlain returned to duty in November 1864 but soon was forced back to Maine because of his wound. He finally returned to his brigade in early 1865 and was wounded a fourth time in the fighting around Petersburg. He was **brevetted** major general of volunteers for his actions at **Five Forks** and was given the honor to accept the **surrender** of the **Army of Northern Virginia** at **Appomattox**.

Declining a commission in the regular **army**, Chamberlain left the service in 1866 and was elected governor of Maine. He was reelected three times and then became the president of Bowdoin College from 1870 to 1883. Fifty years after his wounding at Petersburg, Chamberlain finally died from the injury's effects.

CHAMBERS, ALEXANDER (1832–1888) USA. A **New York** native, Chambers graduated from **West Point** in 1849 and joined the 5th U.S. Infantry. He served at routine frontier posts and was a captain in the 18th U.S. Infantry when the Civil War began.

After serving on recruitment duty in **Iowa**, Chambers was appointed colonel of the 16th Iowa in March 1862. At **Shiloh**, he was wounded twice and won a **brevet** to major in the regular **U.S. Army**. Another wound was received at **Iuka**, and service there and in the **Vicksburg Campaign** won him brevets of lieutenant colonel and colonel in the regular **army**.

Chambers was appointed brigadier general of volunteers in August 1863, but the Senate revoked the appointment, perhaps because he was not a resident of Iowa. He recruited in Iowa for the remainder of the war and was brevetted brigadier general in the regular army in March 1865. Chambers remained in the army performing routine duties until his death.

CHAMBERSBURG, PENNSYLVANIA, BURNING OF (JULY 30, 1864). When Lt. Gen. **Jubal A. Early** operated in the **Shenandoah Valley** in the summer of 1864 after **Early's Washington Raid**, he sent 2,600 cavalrymen under Brig. Gen. **John McCausland** to Chambersburg, Pennsylvania, with orders to demand from the town $100,000 in gold or $500,000 in **greenbacks**. The demand was made to compensate Virginians who had suffered property losses during Union Maj. Gen. **David Hunter's Shenandoah Valley Campaign**. If the demand was not met, McCausland was to destroy the town.

McCausland reached Chambersburg on July 30 and gave the townspeople six hours to comply with the demand. While waiting, many Confederates robbed the civilians and looted their homes. When the town refused the demand, McCausland ordered it burned, destroying 400 buildings and causing nearly $1,500,000 in damages. One officer was temporarily arrested for refusing to carry out the order, and other Confederates who objected to the action managed to save several houses.

CHAMBERSBURG, PENNSYLVANIA, RAID ON (OCTOBER 10–11, 1862). After the **Battle of Antietam**, Gen. **Robert E. Lee** sent

Maj. Gen. **J. E. B. Stuart's** cavalry on a raid into **Maryland** and **Pennsylvania** to gather intelligence and to cut the Cumberland Valley Railroad, which supplied Maj. Gen. **George B. McClellan's Army of the Potomac.** Leaving camp on October 10, 1862, Stuart took 1,800 men across the Potomac River near **Harpers Ferry, Virginia,** rapidly rode through Maryland, and reached Chambersburg, Pennsylvania, that evening. After destroying part of the **railroad,** capturing a number of **prisoners,** and confiscating or destroying some supplies, Stuart left the next morning and rode east to Cashtown to escape the expected Union pursuit. From Cashtown, the Confederates turned south toward Emmitsburg, Maryland, and finally crossed the Potomac at White's Ferry. In two days, Stuart had ridden more than 100 miles and once again had embarrassed McClellan by riding completely around the Army of the Potomac. The raid proved too much for **Abraham Lincoln,** and he relieved McClellan of **army** command in November 1862. *See also* STUART's RIDE AROUND McCLELLAN (JUNE 12–15, 1862).

CHAMBLISS, JOHN RANDOLPH, JR. (1833–1864) CSA. A native of **Virginia,** Chambliss graduated from **West Point** in 1853. He resigned from the **U.S. Army** the following year and returned to **Virginia** to become a planter. After serving as a regimental colonel in the state's militia, Chambliss was commissioned colonel of the 41st Virginia in July 1861.

Chambliss led his **regiment** at **Seven Pines,** where his horse was shot from under him, and in the **Seven Days Campaign.** In July 1862, he was appointed colonel of the 13th Virginia Cavalry and conducted operations around Suffolk and Manassas, Virginia, before joining Brig. Gen. **William H. F. "Rooney" Lee's brigade** in November. As part of the **Army of Northern Virginia,** his regiment guarded the Rappahannock River during the **Fredericksburg** and **Chancellorsville Campaigns,** opposed Union Maj. Gen. **George Stoneman's Raid** to **Richmond,** and fought at **Brandy Station.** Chambliss was promoted to brigade commander after Lee was wounded and the senior brigade colonel was killed in the latter battle. During the **Gettysburg Campaign,** he rode with Maj. Gen. **J. E. B. Stuart** and captured a large number of **prisoners** in a clash at **Aldie, Virginia.** Chambliss saw continuous duty throughout 1863 and was highly praised by his commanders.

Promoted to brigadier general in January 1864, Chambliss saw hard service throughout the **Overland Campaign** and early in the **Petersburg Campaign.** On August 16, 1864, he was killed while fighting Union Brig. Gen. **David M. Gregg's** cavalry outside Richmond on the Charles City Road.

CHAMELEON, CSS. *See TALLAHASSEE, CSS.*

CHAMPION HILL, MISSISSIPPI, BATTLE OF (MAY 16, 1863). Also known as Baker's Creek, Champion Hill was the largest battle fought outside **Vicksburg, Mississippi**, during the **Vicksburg Campaign**. After **U. S. Grant** crossed the Mississippi River on April 30, 1863, Confederate Lt. Gen. **John C. Pemberton**, who was in command at Vicksburg, reacted timidly to the threat. When Gen. **Joseph E. Johnston** arrived at **Jackson, Mississippi**, to take command of the area, he ordered Pemberton on May 14 to attack Grant's rear as he advanced against Jackson. Unsure what to do, Pemberton instead decided to march southeast from Edward's Station to hit Grant's supply line. His movement was so slow that Grant had time to capture Jackson and then turn west toward Pemberton.

On May 16, Pemberton called off his movement and turned back toward Edward's Station to obey another order from Johnston to join forces with him. It was too late, because by then Grant had sent part of his **Army of the Tennessee** westward to confront Pemberton. The two **armies** collided at Champion Hill, a hill 18 miles east of Vicksburg that dominated the road. Pemberton positioned his 22,000 men on the hill to oppose the 29,000 men of Maj. Gens. **James B. McPherson's** and **John McClernand's corps**.

McClernand first made contact in the morning and was in a position to crush the Confederate right flank. Instead of attacking, he waited hours for orders. In the meantime, McPherson immediately attacked Pemberton's left flank held by Maj. Gen. **Carter L. Stevenson's division**, but the Confederates took advantage of McClernand's inactivity and shifted forces from the right to the left flank. In vicious fighting, the hill changed hands three times, but Pemberton was outmaneuvered and finally retreated. Pemberton blamed the defeat on Maj. Gen. **William W. Loring**, who failed to follow orders to attack McClernand's front and then reinforce Stevenson.

In the battle, Pemberton lost 3,851 men and 27 cannons, while Grant counted 2,441 casualties. Afterward, Pemberton fell back to the **Big Black River Bridge**, where he again was defeated the next day. Loring was cut off from Pemberton during the retreat and made a long circuitous march to join Johnston at Jackson.

CHAMPLIN, STEPHEN GARDNER (1827–1864) USA. A **New York** native, Champlin practiced law in his native state before moving to **Michigan** in 1853. There he became judge of the recorder's court and a district attorney.

In June 1861, Champlin entered Union service as major of the 3rd Michigan and was promoted to colonel in October. Joining the **Army of the Potomac**, he suffered a severe hip wound during the **Peninsula Campaign** at **Seven Pines** and was highly praised by his superiors. Champlin quickly returned to duty but during the **Second Manassas Campaign** became completely broken down by his unhealed wound. Afterward, he recruited in Michigan and was promoted to brigadier general of volunteers in November 1862. Champlin died from the effects of his wound in January 1864.

CHANCELLORSVILLE, VIRGINIA, CAMPAIGN AND BATTLE OF (APRIL 27–MAY 5, 1863). Following the **Battle of Fredericksburg**, Maj. Gen. **Joseph Hooker** was put in command of the **Army of the Potomac**, which was encamped at Falmouth, Virginia, across the Rappahannock River from Fredericksburg. On April 27, 1863, he made a bold move to force Gen. **Robert E. Lee** either to abandon his strong positions on the heights south of Fredericksburg or be attacked from the rear. Leaving 40,000 men under Maj. Gen. **John Sedgwick** at Falmouth to keep Lee's **Army of Northern Virginia** in position, Hooker took his other 75,000 men and marched upriver. This column crossed over the Rappahannock and Rapidan Rivers and began marching through a tangled region 12 miles west of Fredericksburg known as the Wilderness, from which it could move into Lee's rear. At the same time, Maj. Gen. **George Stoneman** took his 10,000 cavalrymen and rode into the Confederates' rear to threaten their lines of communication. Faced with these threats, Hooker believed Lee would be forced either to abandon his strong defensive position and retreat or fight on ground of his choosing.

By the time Lee realized what was happening, the Federals already were moving into the Wilderness. With Lt. Gen. **James Longstreet's corp** on detached duty at **Suffolk, Virginia**, Lee had only 60,000 men to counter Hooker. He largely ignored Stoneman's raiders and sent **J. E. B. Stuart's** cavalry toward the Wilderness to determine Hooker's intentions. When Stuart confirmed that Hooker was turning the flank, Lee reacted quickly. He divided his infantry and left 10,000 men under Maj. Gen. **Jubal A. Early** to watch Sedgwick, while he took the other 50,000 westward to stop Hooker in the Wilderness before he could reach the open ground beyond which his superior numbers would be more decisive.

On May 1, Lt. Gen. **Thomas J. "Stonewall" Jackson** made contact with Hooker's advance guard. Surprised at the swift Confederate response, Hooker lost his confidence and surrendered the initiative by ordering his men to halt and entrench rather than pushing on to the open ground. During the fighting on May 1, Stuart learned that Hooker's right flank was "in the air" and open to attack, and that night Lee and Jackson decided to strike.

While Lee held the front with only 20,000 men on May 2, Jackson took his 26,000-man corps on a 14-mile march toward Hooker's exposed flank. Hooker received reports during the day of a large Confederate movement, but he believed Lee was withdrawing. As a precaution, he did warn his right flank to be prepared for an attack but took no other measures to ensure his orders were carried out. Jackson finally got into position late in the afternoon and launched a surprise attack that crushed Maj. Gen. **Oliver O. Howard's** XI Corps. The Union line was pushed back two miles, and only darkness and a determined stand by Hooker's men saved the Federals from complete disaster. That night, while beyond the lines reconnoitering for a night attack, Jackson and his party were fired upon when they were mistaken for enemy cavalry. Jackson was mortally wounded, and several of his party were killed or wounded. Stuart then took command of Jackson's corps and led it during the remainder of the battle.

On the morning of May 3, Hooker withdrew from an open area near the center of the battlefield known as Hazel Grove. Confederate **artillery** then occupied it and used the strategic position to pound the Federals throughout the day. One shell severely stunned Hooker when it struck his headquarters. Stuart and Lee also launched costly **frontal attacks** and slowly reunited their forces but gained no appreciable results except to force Hooker to pull his **army** back closer to the river. While under such relentless attacks, Hooker ordered Sedgwick to come to his aid by attacking at Fredericksburg and threatening Lee's rear. On May 3, Sedgwick attacked Early in the **Second Battle of Fredericksburg** and forced him to abandon Marye's Heights and retreat. Faced with this new threat, Lee once again divided his army by leaving Stuart 25,000 men to contend with Hooker, while he took 20,000 back toward Fredericksburg to help Early stop Sedgwick.

On May 4, Lee attacked Sedgwick near **Salem Church**. After some initial success, the Confederate attack finally stalled, but Sedgwick chose to retreat across the river that night. Hooker then abandoned his campaign and retreated across the Rappahannock on the night of May 5. **Stoneman's Raid** had enjoyed no better success because of Stoneman's lack of aggressiveness.

Chancellorsville was Lee's greatest victory. Faced with overwhelming odds, he divided his army three times, defeated two Union forces, and forced the enemy to retreat. But the victory came at a very high cost, for

Jackson died from his wounds, and Lee lost approximately 12,800 men. The heavy casualties forced him to reorganize his army only weeks prior to the **Gettysburg Campaign** and meant that many of his units were being led by inexperienced officers during that crucial campaign. Hooker suffered approximately 17,300 casualties at Chancellorsville.

CHANDLER, ZACHARIAH (1813–1879) USA. A native of **New Hampshire**, Chandler moved to Detroit, **Michigan**, where he became a wealthy businessman and was elected mayor in 1851. Strongly opposed to **slavery**, he helped organize the **Republican Party** in Michigan, worked to send **abolitionist** settlers to **"Bleeding Kansas,"** and voted for **John C. Frémont** at the 1856 Republican National Convention.

Elected to the U.S. Senate in 1857, Chandler became a powerful **Radical Republican** during the Civil War and **Reconstruction**. As chairman of the Committee on Commerce, he worked to improve business and earned a reputation for being a tough-minded, but honest, politician. Chandler also became a member of the **Committee on the Conduct of the War**, helped pass the **confiscation acts**, opposed Maj. Gen. **George B. McClellan**, supported **greenbacks** and high tariffs, and played a key role in getting **Abraham Lincoln** reelected in 1864.

During Reconstruction, Chandler served as chairman of the Republican National Executive Committee and was an important figure in the impeachment of President **Andrew Johnson**. After being defeated for reelection in 1874, Chandler was appointed secretary of the interior by President **U. S. Grant**. He was returned to the Senate in 1879, but died shortly afterward.

CHANTILLY, VIRGINIA, BATTLE OF (SEPTEMBER 1, 1862). Also known as Ox Hill, this battle ended the **Second Manassas Campaign**. After defeating Maj. Gen. **John Pope's Army of Virginia** at Second Manassas, Gen. **Robert E. Lee** pursued the retreating Federals with his **Army of Northern Virginia**. Lee sent Lt. Gen. **Thomas J. "Stonewall" Jackson's corps** on a rapid march north of Pope's route to cut the Union line of retreat near Fairfax Court House.

On August 31, 1862, Jackson crossed Bull Run at Sudley Ford and headed toward Fairfax Court House. Rain turned the roads to mud and slowed the exhausted Confederate column. Meanwhile, Pope realized he was in danger and sent troops to block Jackson at a country mansion called Chantilly.

On September 1, Jackson made contact with two Union **divisions** under Maj. Gen. **Philip Kearny** and Brig. Gen. **Isaac Stevens**. A thunderstorm broke and drenched the battlefield as Jackson sent his troops in an attack. Vicious fighting erupted in the rainstorm as Jackson attacked various parts of the Union line without success. At times the Federals counterattacked, and in the fighting, both Kearny and Stevens were killed. The Federals finally withdrew about dark. In the short, but intense, battle, Jackson lost about 800 men but did not succeed in seriously interfering with Pope's retreat. Pope suffered approximately 1,300 casualties.

CHAPLAINS. When the Civil War began, neither side had any formal policy regarding the appointment, pay, or duties of **army** chaplains. Soon, the Union allowed its regimental commanders to appoint chaplains for their units. These chaplains were paid $100 per month and were expected to make reports on the moral and religious health of their men and to make suggestions on how to improve living conditions. It was not until 1864 that the **U.S. Congress** added chaplains to the regimental roster and made regular church services part of their duties.

The Confederates took chaplains more seriously than the Federals. At the war's beginning, the **Confederate Congress** authorized **Jefferson Davis** to appoint chaplains for each **regiment**, but he generally deferred to regimental commanders. These chaplains were paid $85 per month beginning in May 1861, but that was reduced to $50 a few weeks later.

Army chaplains on both sides performed many functions besides holding religious services. They also **foraged** for supplies, wrote letters for soldiers, tended the sick and wounded, and sometimes even went into battle. To win the soldiers' respect, chaplains not only had to be godly men, but they also had to be tolerant of minor moral infractions and show genuine concern for their charges. Letters and diaries show that while many chaplains failed to meet this test, others were highly regarded. In the Confederate armies, chaplains especially were valued in the winter of 1863–64 when a fervent religious revival swept through the winter camps.

Most chaplains were either Protestants or Catholics; Jews were not allowed to be chaplains in the Union army until September 1862 and apparently did not serve with the Confederates, even though they were allowed. Approximately 2,300 chaplains served in the Union army, of whom at least 66 died in service, and three received the **Medal of Honor**. Approximately 600 served the Confederates, of whom 25 died in service, and 14 were killed in battle.

CHAPLIN HILLS, KENTUCKY, BATTLE OF (OCTOBER 8, 1862). *See* PERRYVILLE, KENTUCKY, BATTLE OF.

CHAPMAN, CONRAD WISE (1842–1910) CSA. Born in **Washington, D.C.**, Chapman was the son of artist John Gadsby Chapman. Young

Chapman grew up in Rome, Italy, and studied art under his father, but when the Civil War began, he returned to the United States and joined the 3rd Kentucky (Confederate). He was wounded at **Shiloh** and then transferred to the 46th Virginia Volunteers at the request of family friend Brig. Gen. **Henry A. Wise**. Sent to **Charleston, South Carolina**, Chapman sketched the city's defenses at Gen. **P. G. T. Beauregard's** request so the illustrations could be included with a set of maps being prepared by his staff.

Learning that his mother was ill, Chapman got leave to return to Rome in 1864. While there, he painted a series of works depicting the Charleston area during the war. Returning to Galveston, Texas, about the time of the **surrender**, Chapman went with Maj. Gen. **John B. Magruder** to Mexico after the war. He then traveled in the United States and Europe and suffered a three-year period of insanity. Chapman's 31 paintings of Confederate topics made him the foremost Confederate artist. The paintings are now housed in the Valentine Museum at **Richmond, Virginia**.

CHAPMAN, GEORGE HENRY (1832–1882) USA. Born in **Massachusetts**, Chapman moved to **Indiana** as a boy. He was appointed a midshipman in the **U.S. Navy** in 1847 and served in the **Mexican War** but resigned his commission in 1851 to become an Indiana newspaper publisher. Chapman later became a lawyer and in November 1861 entered Union service as major of the 3rd Indiana Cavalry.

Chapman served with his **regiment** during the **Second Manassas** and **Antietam Campaigns** and was promoted to lieutenant colonel in October 1862. After fighting with the **Army of the Potomac** at **Fredericksburg**, he was appointed regimental colonel in March 1863. While serving in **John Buford's** division at **Gettysburg**, Chapman's was the first Union cavalry regiment to engage the Confederates on July 1, 1863. In September, he was given command of a cavalry **brigade** in the 1st Division but in April 1864 took command of a brigade in the 3rd Division. Chapman led this brigade through the **Overland Campaign** and in July 1864 was promoted to brigadier general of volunteers.

Chapman was sent to participate in **Philip Sheridan's Shenandoah Valley Campaign** in late 1864 and was wounded at the **Third Battle of Winchester**. He was put in command of a cavalry **division** in January 1865, but when Sheridan moved from the Valley to join **U. S. Grant** in the **Petersburg Campaign** in March, Chapman was left behind with a cavalry brigade and some **artillery**. Chapman was **brevetted** major general of volunteers for his service at Third Winchester but resigned his commission in January 1866.

After the war, Chapman served as an Indiana judge and in the state senate, and was involved in **railroads**.

CHARLES CITY CROSS ROADS, VIRGINIA, BATTLE OF (JUNE 30, 1862). *See* FRAYSER'S FARM, VIRGINIA, BATTLE OF.

CHARLESTON *MERCURY.* Founded in 1822, the *Mercury* became one of the South's leading newspapers and strongly supported both **slavery** and **secession**. Edited by Robert Barnwell Rhett Jr. during the war, the *Mercury* became one of the strongest critics of President **Jefferson Davis's** administration.

CHARLESTON, SOUTH CAROLINA. Charleston, South Carolina, was founded in 1670 and had a population of about 40,000 when the Civil War began. It was the focal point of the **secession** crisis in early 1861 when Maj. **Robert Anderson** refused to surrender **Fort Sumter** to Confederate Brig. Gen. **P. G. T. Beauregard**. In the predawn hours of April 12, Beauregard began shelling Fort Sumter and thus started the war. After enduring 33 hours of bombardment, Anderson finally surrendered the fort on April 13.

During the war, Charleston became a major port for **blockade runners** and was heavily defended by **torpedoes** hidden in the harbor and by **artillery** in Forts Sumter and **Wagner**. Several attempts were made by the Union to capture the city. The first came on June 16, 1862, at the **Battle of Secessionville**, when Union forces unsuccessfully attacked Confederate positions on James Island. On April 7, 1863, Rear Adm. **Samuel F. Du Pont** led seven **monitors** and two **ironclads** in an unsuccessful attack against Fort Sumter that led to his ships being riddled with shot and his being relieved of command. On July 10, 1863, Union forces landed on the south side of the harbor on Morris Island and began operations against Fort Wagner, while the **U.S. Navy** began a prolonged bombardment of the forts. In a siege that began in August 1863 and lasted 587 days, as many as 5,643 shells were fired into Charleston's fortifications in one seven-day period, but the Confederates continued to occupy the defenses. Furious, but unsuccessful, assaults were made on Fort Wagner on July 11 and 18, the famed **54th Massachusetts** participating in the attack on the latter day. Afterward, the Federals began digging trenches toward the fort in preparation for one final assault. The stubborn Confederate defenders held out until September 6, 1863, at which time they evacuated Wagner, and the Federals seized it the next day. The Confederates continued to hold Fort Sumter, and Charleston remained in Southern hands until 1865.

In February 1865, Maj. Gen. **William T. Sherman** approached the city from Savannah, Georgia, in his **Carolinas Campaign**. Marching west of Charleston, Sherman cut the defenders' lines of communication. Garrison commander Maj. Gen. **William J. Hardee** was ordered by Beauregard to evacuate the city, which he did on the night of February 17, and Union troops finally entered Charleston the following day. Robert Anderson returned to Fort Sumter and on April 14, 1865, raised the U.S. **flag** back over the fort, four years to the day from when he had taken it down.

CHASE. This is the formal name given to the main part of a cannon's tube, or barrel. It is the section of the gun between the breech and the point on the muzzle where the tube flares outward.

CHASE, KATE (1840–1899) USA. *See* SPRAGUE, KATE CHASE.

CHASE, SALMON PORTLAND (1808–1873) USA. Born in **New Hampshire**, Chase graduated from Dartmouth College and moved to **Ohio**, where he opened a law practice. An **abolitionist**, he became active in politics and supported the Liberty and **Free-Soil Parties**. In 1849, Chase was elected to the U.S. Senate and became active in the **Republican Party** when it was formed. He was elected Ohio's governor in 1855 and was later reelected. Chase's radical antislavery sentiment largely prevented his winning the Republican presidential nomination in 1860, but he returned to the Senate the next year. Although bitter that **Abraham Lincoln** won the nomination, he resigned his Senate seat in 1861 to become Lincoln's secretary of the treasury.

Chase clashed with Secretary of State **William H. Seward** and offered his resignation four times, but he also used his influence and political ability to win passage of important financial bills. Chase served Lincoln well, doing much to **finance** the war and succeeding in getting **greenbacks** accepted as legal tender. His political ambition remained unchecked, however, and he secretly agreed with **Radical Republicans**—who opposed Lincoln's **Reconstruction** plan—to run again for the nomination in 1864. The **Pomeroy Circular** exposed Chase's plans, and he was forced to offer his resignation. Lincoln refused to accept it, however, and Chase remained in the cabinet. Chase again offered his resignation in June 1864, and to his surprise Lincoln accepted it.

Despite their troubles, Lincoln appointed Chase chief justice of the **U.S. Supreme Court** in December 1864. While on the court, he angered Radicals by refusing to give in to their every whim during the impeachment of President **Andrew Johnson**. Because of this split, Chase became a **Democrat** and in 1870 reversed his opinion on the use of greenbacks as legal tender. The famous Washington hostess, **Kate Chase Sprague**, was his daughter.

CHASSEURS. Chasseurs (sha-SOGRZ) were French light infantrymen who dressed in colorful **uniforms** similar to those worn by **Zouaves**. When the Civil War began, it was popular in some areas to organize chasseur units. Among these were the 14th Brooklyn and Louisiana's Chasseurs-a-Pied Infantry Battalion.

CHATTANOOGA, TENNESSEE, CAMPAIGN (OCTOBER 23– NOVEMBER 25, 1863). Chattanooga, Tennessee, had a population of about 2,500 at the beginning of the Civil War and became a strategic point because it was the crossroads of important **railroads**—the East Tennessee & Georgia linking **Virginia** with the west, and the Nashville & Chattanooga linking **Kentucky** with the Deep South by way of the Western & Atlantic. Adding to the town's importance was the Tennessee River, which ran past it.

Union Maj. Gen. **William S. Rosecrans** and his **Army of the Cumberland** captured Chattanooga on September 9, 1863, after forcing Gen. **Braxton Bragg's Army of Tennessee** out of Middle **Tennessee** in the **Tullahoma Campaign**. Rosecrans then pursued Bragg into **Georgia**, only to be defeated in September at **Chickamauga**. Retreating back to Chattanooga, the 35,000 Federals then were besieged by Bragg.

Taking up dominating positions on Raccoon Mountain west of town, Lookout Mountain southwest of town, and Missionary Ridge east of town, the 46,000 Confederates cut the Federals' main supply line. Confederate cavalry under Maj. Gen. **Joseph Wheeler** also raided into Tennessee and burned Union wagon trains bringing in supplies. As a result, Union **rations** in Chattanooga were cut in half. The only thing that kept Rosecrans's **army** from starving completely was a long, difficult wagon road from Chattanooga to Bridgeport, Alabama, that took 20 days to travel.

After being appointed commander of the **Military Division of the West** in October, Maj. Gen. **U. S. Grant** took steps to save Chattanooga. Replacing Rosecrans with Maj. Gen. **George H. Thomas**, Grant arrived in town on October 23 and almost immediately reopened the supply line. On October 27, Union troops drove the Confederates from Brown's Ferry, a crossing on the Tennessee River west of Chattanooga at the point of Raccoon Mountain. This put the Chattanooga garrison within eight miles of Kelly's Ford, another crossing farther west, which was in Union hands. A "Cracker Line" thus was opened with steamboats running supplies from Bridgeport to Kelly's Ford, where they could be transferred to wagons for the short haul to Brown's Ferry.

Meanwhile, Maj. Gen. **Joseph Hooker** had left Bridgeport with three **divisions** and was marching to Chattanooga by way of Lookout Valley, just west of Lookout Mountain. Arriving on October 28, Hooker left one division at **Wauhatchie** to help guard the Cracker Line. That night, it was attacked by elements of Lt. Gen. **James Longstreet's** Confederate **corps**. In a vicious nighttime battle, the Confederates were repulsed, the Cracker Line was secured, and the first steamboat arrived at Kelly's Ford on November 1.

In early November, Bragg made a serious error by sending Longstreet's corps to besiege Knoxville, Tennessee, in an operation that became the **Knoxville Campaign**. While Bragg voluntarily was weakening his army at Chattanooga, Grant was receiving steady reinforcements that soon gave him 70,000 men, including 17,000 men under Maj. Gen. **William T. Sherman**. Upon learning of Longstreet's departure, Grant made plans to lift the siege of Chattanooga.

On November 23, Grant swiftly attacked and seized **Orchard Knob**, a prominent hill west of **Missionary Ridge**, and brought the troops out of Chattanooga and positioned them against the ridge. The next day, Hooker attacked the Confederate force on **Lookout Mountain**. In dense fog, the Federals fought their way up the steep slope in what became known as "The Battle above the Clouds" and finally forced the Confederates to retreat to Missionary Ridge. Bragg had lost all of his dominating positions except for Missionary Ridge, and Grant planned to take it by having Sherman attack Bragg's right (or northern) flank, while Hooker continued on from Lookout Mountain and attacked the Confederate's left flank. Thomas's army would threaten the Confederate center.

On the morning of November 25, Sherman launched an attack against Bragg's right but was repulsed by Maj. Gen. **Patrick Cleburne's** Confederate division. On the Confederate left, Hooker's advance stalled while waiting for a **pontoon bridge** to cross Chattanooga Creek. That afternoon, Grant sent Thomas forward against Bragg's center, in what he intended to be only a **demonstration** to assist the flank attacks. This demonstration, however, turned into a full-scale **frontal attack** as the Union troops spontaneously broke into a charge without orders. Caught by surprise, the Confederate center made a short stand but then broke and retreated, followed by the units holding the flanks. Bragg's disorganized army fell back into north Georgia, and the siege of Chattanooga was broken.

In the fighting on November 23–25, Grant lost approximately 5,800 men to Bragg's 6,650. Afterward, Sherman remained in Chattanooga to prepare for his **Atlanta Campaign**, and the town became a major part of his supply line.

CHEAT MOUNTAIN, VIRGINIA, BATTLE OF (SEPTEMBER 11-13, 1861). Although a minor affair, this battle is notable for being **Robert E. Lee's** first Civil War battle. After the Confederate defeats at **Philippi** and **Rich Mountain, Virginia**, in the summer of 1861, Lee was sent to western **Virginia** to retrieve Southern fortunes. There, he planned an attack against the Union position at Cheat Mountain, which controlled several strategic roads and mountain passes. Brigadier General **Joseph J. Reynolds** commanded the position with about 2,000 Union troops that were dangerously divided into two wings seven miles apart.

Taking command of the 15,000 Confederate troops under Brig. Gen. **William W. Loring**, Lee devised a complicated and unrealistic battle plan. He divided his command into five columns, planning not only to attack the Federals holding the mountain's summit and cut their line of retreat but also to envelope the other Union wing as well.

Lee began the movement on September 10, but rain hampered the march. On September 11, contact was made with the enemy, and on the next day one of the Confederate columns cut a road into the Union rear while another was pushing the enemy back. But Lee's main attack against the mountain's summit failed to materialize because the Confederate commander was convinced by **prisoners** that he was facing 4,000 Federals instead of the actual 300. After more probing on September 13, Lee realized the element of surprise was lost, and that the heavy rain prohibited further operations. He withdrew on September 15 and was nicknamed "Granny Lee" by newspapers for his poor performance. Total casualties in the operation amounted to approximately 100 for each side.

CHEATHAM, BENJAMIN FRANKLIN (1820-1886) CSA. A native of **Tennessee**, Cheatham fought in the **Mexican War**, where he served under **Winfield Scott** as a captain in the 1st Tennessee and colonel of the 3rd Tennessee. After participating in the **California** Gold Rush, he returned to Tennessee and became a planter and major general in the state militia.

Cheatham was appointed brigadier general in the Tennessee Provisional Army in May 1861. He then entered Confederate service in July, when **Jefferson Davis** appointed him brigadier general in the **Confederate army**. Cheatham's first action was at **Belmont**, where he played a major role in driving off the enemy.

Promoted to major general in March 1862, Cheatham led a **division** at **Shiloh**, where he was slightly wounded and had three horses shot from under him. Joining what became the **Army of Tennessee**, his division charged and nearly destroyed one Union division at the **Battle of Per-**

ryville during the 1862 **Kentucky Campaign**. Cheatham's performance at **Stones River** was less spectacular. There he was said to have been drunk and failed to use his division effectively. As a result, Gen. **Braxton Bragg** did not commend Cheatham in his report, causing Cheatham to become one of Bragg's critics. At **Chickamauga**, Cheatham regained his reputation for hard fighting when his division performed admirably. Still, his relationship with Bragg continued to deteriorate as Bragg reorganized Cheatham's close-knit Tennessee division. When the Confederate line was broken on **Missionary Ridge** in the November 1863 **Chattanooga Campaign**, Cheatham played an important role by fighting stubbornly in a delaying action that helped Bragg's **army** escape.

Throughout the 1864 **Atlanta Campaign**, Cheatham served admirably, especially at **Kennesaw Mountain** where his division repulsed several Union assaults. When **John Bell Hood** assumed command of the army in July 1864, Cheatham temporarily took command of Hood's **corps** during the **Battle of Atlanta**. During the **Franklin and Nashville Campaign**, he commanded **William J. Hardee's** corps. In the Spring Hill Incident, Cheatham failed to block the road on which **John Schofield's** Union command was retreating. Hood and Cheatham bitterly disagreed over who was at fault for allowing the enemy to escape, and responsibility for the error is still unclear. Cheatham's corps was badly shot up at Franklin, and at Nashville, after holding its ground the first day, it was routed on the second day of battle. After retreating to **Mississippi**, Cheatham took the survivors of his corps to **North Carolina** and fought his last battle at **Bentonville** during the **Carolinas Campaign**.

After surrendering with **Joseph E. Johnston**, Cheatham returned to Tennessee, married, and served as superintendent of the state prison and postmaster of Nashville. During the war, he had been a hard fighter, and drinker, and always was very popular with his Tennessee troops. Cheatham was one of the army's better commanders and was considered for command of the Army of Tennessee in 1864 but was passed over in favor of Hood.

CHESNUT, JAMES, JR. (1815–1885) CSA. A native of **South Carolina** and a first cousin of Confederate Brig. Gen. **Zachariah C. Deas**, Chesnut graduated with honors from Princeton University and became a South Carolina lawyer. In 1840, he married **Mary Boykin Miller (Chesnut)**, whose later Civil War diary became famous. Chesnut served in both houses of the state legislature and as a prosecession delegate to the **Nashville Convention** in 1850. In 1858, he was appointed to the U.S. Senate but resigned in 1860 after the election of **Abraham Lincoln**.

Chesnut helped draft South Carolina's Ordinance of Secession and served in the Provisional **Confederate Congress**. He entered Confederate service in April 1861 as a colonel on **P. G. T. Beauregard's** staff and personally took messages demanding **Fort Sumter's** surrender. After serving with Beauregard at **First Manassas**, Chesnut briefly left the **army** in early 1862 to serve on the South Carolina governor's staff as chief of militia. He then returned to Confederate service in November as a colonel of cavalry assigned to **Jefferson Davis's** staff.

Davis trusted Chesnut and sent him on a variety of missions, including asking governors for reinforcements and inspecting **Braxton Bragg's Army of Tennessee**, which was besieging Chattanooga, Tennessee. It was Chesnut who persuaded Davis to go to Chattanooga to try to solve the disputes wracking the army there. He also unsuccessfully advised that Bragg be reassigned to **Richmond, Virginia**. Tiring of his staff duties, Chesnut asked for field duty and was promoted to brigadier general in April 1863. For the remainder of the war, he commanded South Carolina's reserve forces and often was criticized by his superior for failing to cooperate against **William T. Sherman's** advancing armies during the **Carolinas Campaign**.

Chesnut remained in South Carolina after the war and became active in **Democratic** politics.

CHESNUT, MARY BOYKIN MILLER (1823–1886) CSA. A native of **South Carolina**, Chesnut wrote one of the most informative diaries of the Civil War. Well-educated, a member of one of the state's elite families, and the wife of Confederate Brig. Gen. **James Chesnut Jr.**, she was uniquely positioned to chronicle the war's social, political, and military activities. Chesnut lived in **Richmond, Virginia**, for much of the war and became a close friend of **Varina Davis**. After the war, Chesnut condensed and rewrote her diary, which was first published in 1905 as *A Diary from Dixie*.

CHESTER STATION, VIRGINIA, BATTLE OF (MAY 10, 1864). In early May 1864, Union Maj. Gen. **Benjamin F. Butler's Army of the James** attempted to cut the Richmond & Petersburg Railroad linking **Richmond** and **Petersburg, Virginia**, in the **Bermuda Hundred Campaign**. After arriving at Bermuda Hundred on May 5, Butler engaged Maj. Gen. **George Pickett's** Confederates at **Port Walthall Junction** and at **Swift Creek and Fort Clifton** and gained a position astride the **railroad** at the junction and at Chester Station. After Gen. **P. G. T. Beauregard** arrived at Petersburg on May 9 with **Robert Hoke's division**, he sent two **brigades** under Brig. Gen. **Robert Ransom Jr.** to dislodge

Quincy Adams Gillmore's Union X Corps from Chester Station. Ransom attacked at dawn on May 10, but he was badly outnumbered and soon was forced to withdraw. Gillmore retired back to Bermuda Hundred that afternoon after destroying the railroad tracks. Soon, the Confederates repaired the line and restored communications between Richmond and Petersburg. Total casualties for the battle are estimated at 569.

CHETLAIN, AUGUSTUS LOUIS (1824–1914) USA. Born in **Missouri**, Chetlain moved to **Illinois** as a child and became a prosperous Galena businessman. At the suggestion of fellow townsman **U. S. Grant**, he was elected captain of a volunteer **company** in 1861. The company joined the 12th Illinois in May, and the next day Chetlain was elected lieutenant colonel. He served as regimental commander at **Forts Henry and Donelson** and at **Shiloh**. Promoted to colonel in April 1862, Chetlain again led his **regiment** at **Iuka** and **Corinth**.

Commissioned brigadier general of volunteers in December 1863, Chetlain transferred to **Memphis, Tennessee**, where he recruited and organized **black troops**. In January 1865, he was put in command of the Memphis post. **Brevetted** major general of volunteers in June 1865, Chetlain resigned from the **army** in January 1866.

After the war, Chetlain served as a U.S. consul in Belgium and then moved to Chicago, Illinois, where he became a banker and served on the Chicago Stock Exchange and Board of Education.

CHEVAUX-DE-FRISE. Chevaux-de-frise (shuh-VOH-duh-FREEZ) were types of obstruction used to protect field fortifications. They consisted of logs with rows of sharpened stakes protruding from them. When lined up in front of a defensive position, they acted as a barriers, much like **wire entanglements**, and slowed or prevented attacking infantry from reaching the position.

CHICAGO CONSPIRACY. *See* NORTHWEST CONSPIRACY.

CHICKAHOMINY RIVER, VIRGINIA, BATTLE OF (JUNE 27, 1862). *See* GAINES' MILL, VIRGINIA, BATTLE OF.

CHICKAMAUGA, GEORGIA, CAMPAIGN AND BATTLE OF (AUGUST 16–SEPTEMBER 20, 1863). By late summer 1863, Gen. **Braxton Bragg's Army of Tennessee** had been forced to fall back from Tullahoma to Chattanooga, Tennessee, by Maj. Gen. **William S. Rosecrans's Army of the Cumberland** in the **Tullahoma Campaign**. On August 16, Rosecrans, positioned west of Chattanooga along the **Tennessee** and **Alabama** state line, moved against Bragg again. Dividing his

army into three columns, Rosecrans sent Maj. Gen. **Thomas L. Crittenden's** XXI Corps east toward Chattanooga, while Maj. Gen. **George H. Thomas's** XIV Corps moved to the southeast toward Steven's Gap, and Maj. Gen. **Alexander M. McCook's** XX Corps marched south to Alpine. Bragg withdrew from Chattanooga on September 7 and retreated into northern **Georgia** but made plans to counterattack. Having been reinforced with nearly 20,000 fresh troops from Knoxville, Tennessee, and **Mississippi**, he intended to **defeat in detail** the Federals as their widely scattered columns emerged from the mountain passes.

Crittenden occupied Chattanooga on September 9, and Rosecrans continued to push his other two columns rapidly forward to cut Bragg's lines of communication. On September 10–11, Bragg attempted to destroy an isolated part of Rosecrans's army at **McLemore's Cove**, but confusion and missteps by subordinates foiled his plans. He finally decided to concentrate his army between Chattanooga and Rosecrans's two southern **corps**. Bragg then would advance westward across Chickamauga Creek, turn south, and hit the corps' left flank, believed to be located about 10 miles south of Chattanooga on Chickamauga Creek at Lee and Gordon's Mill. Bragg could roll up the Union line and push Rosecrans back into the mountains, where he would be destroyed. Bragg knew that Lt. Gen. **James Longstreet** and two of his **divisions** were being sent from the **Army of Northern Virginia** to help but was uncertain whether he would arrive in time.

Meanwhile, Rosecrans became aware of his dangerous position and began concentrating his army near Lee and Gordon's Mill. Bragg planned to attack Rosecrans's left flank at dawn of September 18, but Union cavalry delayed the movement at the creek crossings, and it was late afternoon before the Confederates pushed across. During the day, three fresh **brigades** of Longstreet's vanguard arrived. By nightfall, Rosecrans had extended his left, or northern, flank three miles north of the Mill along the LaFayette Road. Bragg still assumed he was well to the north of Rosecrans's left flank, when actually the two armies were roughly parallel.

Fighting erupted early on September 19 when one of Thomas's divisions advanced eastward from Rosecrans's left flank to attack a Confederate brigade that had crossed the creek the day before. The Federals encountered Confederate cavalry under Maj. Gen. **Nathan Bedford Forrest**, and the battle was on. As each side called for reinforcements, the fighting spread southward to consume the entire line. The battle was fought largely in thick woods and in a few small fields, and confusion reigned on both sides. Attacks and counterattacks were made, with the

Confederates temporarily breaking through Rosecrans's right center. Both sides suffered heavy casualties.

During the night, Longstreet arrived on the field with two more brigades, and Bragg divided his army into two wings with Lt. Gen. **Leonidas Polk** commanding the right wing and Longstreet the left. Polk was to attack at daylight the next day. That same night, Rosecrans dismissed advice from his officers to withdraw to a more defensible position near Chattanooga and decided to stay and fight.

On September 20, Polk failed to attack until mid-morning (prompting Bragg to later place him under arrest), but savage fighting ensued, with the Confederates again making temporary gains. Just before noon, a critical mistake was made by the Federals. In the confusing fighting, Rosecrans ordered Brig. Gen. **Thomas John Wood's** division, located on the right, to fill a gap in the line Rosecrans thought was on Wood's immediate left. In fact, there was no gap. Wood dutifully pulled out of line to march left, creating a hole in Rosecrans's right wing. At that moment, Longstreet happened to attack through the opening left by Wood's departure and shattered Rosecrans's right wing. Thomas managed to bring together various units and make a determined stand on **Snodgrass Hill** near the center. Other officers and commands, including Rosecrans himself, fell back in confusion toward Chattanooga. Thomas's line was bent to form a *V* shape, pointing eastward, but he repulsed numerous Confederate attacks and finally was joined by the Reserve Corps under Maj. Gen. **Gordon Granger**, who marched to his aid without orders. Together, they covered the army's withdrawal and fell back to Chattanooga that night. For his heroic efforts, Thomas became known as the **"Rock of Chickamauga."**

Bragg had about 66,000 men in the battle and lost approximately 18,450. Rosecrans had about 58,000 engaged and lost approximately 16,150 men. Not only was the Battle of Chickamauga the largest Civil War battle in the west, it also was one of the few battles in which the Confederates outnumbered the Federals. Despite being an important victory for the Confederates, it proved to be of little long-term value. Bragg was unable to follow up the victory successfully and had to lay siege to Chattanooga. Two months later, he suffered a devastating defeat in the **Chattanooga Campaign**.

CHICKASAW BAYOU, MISSISSIPPI, BATTLE OF (DECEMBER 27–29, 1862). In December 1862, Maj. Gen. **U. S. Grant** made his first attempt to capture **Vicksburg, Mississippi**, in **Grant's Overland Vicksburg Campaign**. Grant advanced from **Tennessee** into northern

Mississippi with his **Army of the Tennessee** to engage Confederate Lt. Gen. **John C. Pemberton** and prevent him from reinforcing Vicksburg from his base at Grenada. At the same time, Maj. Gen. **William T. Sherman's** 32,000 men moved down the Mississippi River by transports and up the Yazoo River. Sherman was to attack the supposedly lightly defended Confederate position at Chickasaw Bayou, located northeast of Vicksburg, and take the city from the rear.

While Sherman was going down the river, Grant's advance was turned back when **Earl Van Dorn's** Confederate cavalry destroyed his supply base at **Holly Springs**, **Mississippi**, and **Nathan Bedford Forrest** raided his supply line in Tennessee. As a result, Pemberton was able to send 6,000 men to Vicksburg to join the 6,000 already there under Maj. Gen. **Martin L. Smith**. Sherman had no way of knowing about this development and continued on with the plan.

Sherman landed three **divisions** at Chickasaw Bayou (also known as Walnut Hills) on December 26, while Adm. **David D. Porter's** gunboats bombarded the enemy's batteries on nearby Haynes' Bluff. On December 27, Sherman heavily shelled the Confederate defenses and then advanced his infantry across a broad swamp to the base of the bluffs. The Confederates were well dug in and had every approach covered by **artillery**. Sherman's main attempt to carry the heights took place on December 29 when he sent forward two **brigades** that were riddled by the entrenched Confederates. Sherman finally disengaged, had his men back on the boats by January 2, 1863, and returned to the Mississippi River, where he joined Maj. Gen. **John C. McClernand** for an attack on **Arkansas Post**. The Federals lost 1,776 men at Chickasaw Bayou, while the Confederates lost only 207. After this failure, Grant moved down the Mississippi River in early 1863 and began the **Vicksburg Campaign**.

CHICORA, CSS. Commissioned in September 1862, the *Chicora* was a Confederate **ironclad** used to defend **Charleston**, **South Carolina**. Commanded by **John R. Tucker**, it was 150 feet long and was armed with six guns. The *Chicora* was joined by the ***Palmetto State*** on January 31, 1863, for an attack on the Union **blockading** fleet. The two ships captured one vessel and disabled another. The *Chicora*'s poor boilers limited its usefulness, and in February 1865, its crew was dispatched to **Wilmington**, **North Carolina**. The ship was blown up when Charleston was evacuated on February 18, 1865.

CHILTON, ROBERT HALL (1815–1879) CSA. A native of **Virginia**, Chilton graduated from **West Point** in 1837 and rose to the rank of captain in the 1st Dragoons. He was **brevetted** major during the **Mexican**

War for carrying a wounded **Jefferson Davis** to safety at Buena Vista. After the war, Chilton served on the frontier and as a paymaster and rose to the rank of major.

Chilton resigned his commission when Virginia seceded in April 1861 and entered Confederate service in May as a lieutenant colonel in the Adjutant and Inspector General's Office. In June 1862, he was appointed **Robert E. Lee**'s chief of staff and became the **Army of Northern Virginia's** inspector general in October.

Chilton was appointed brigadier general in October 1862. When the **Confederate Congress** rejected the appointment in April 1863, he immediately was promoted to colonel. Lee supported Chilton's efforts to be confirmed as a brigadier general, and Chilton learned that Congress's rejection stemmed from his having been critical of Maj. Gen. **John B. Magruder's** performance during the **Seven Days Campaign**. Chilton then was criticized for his role in the **Chancellorsville Campaign** when he poorly communicated Lee's orders to **Jubal A. Early** and nearly caused Early to withdraw prematurely from **Fredericksburg**.

Chilton finally was confirmed as brigadier general in February 1864 but was then reassigned to the Inspector General's Office in **Richmond, Virginia**. Knowing that the promotion was intended for him to serve as Lee's chief of staff, he resigned the commission in April. For the remainder of the war, Chilton served as a colonel in command of the Bureau of Inspection, but he did see combat when he helped repulse an enemy probe against Richmond in May 1864.

CHIMBORAZO HOSPITAL. This Confederate hospital was the largest and most famous of the Civil War. Built on a prominent plateau just east of **Richmond, Virginia**, Chimborazo (chim-buh-RAH-zoh) served as the prototype for future Confederate hospitals. It was directed by Dr. James Brown McCaw and began admitting patients in October 1861. Among the hospital's 120 buildings were soup houses, icehouses, kitchens, mess halls, morgues, bathhouses, a bakery, and even a brewery. It had a capacity of approximately 3,000 patients, and almost 78,000 Confederate sick and wounded soldiers were treated at Chimborazo during the war.

CHIVINGTON, JOHN MILTON (1821–1894) USA. A Methodist minister, Chivington was major of the 1st Colorado Volunteers. Known as the "Fighting Parson," he first earned fame when he led the charge that destroyed the Confederate supply train at the **Battle of Glorieta Pass**. Promoted to colonel in 1862, Chivington began to overly exaggerate **Colorado's** Indian threat to gain support for a congressional race whenever Colorado attained statehood. A new **regiment** named the 3rd Colorado was raised to fight **Indians** and was placed under Chivington's command. On November 29, 1864, he led this regiment of undisciplined men in an attack against Chief Black Kettle's defenseless Cheyenne village. In what became known as the **Sand Creek Massacre**, Chivington slaughtered 150–600 men, women, and children, while losing only about 50 men. The incident was investigated by the **U.S. Congress**, and Chivington resigned his commission rather than be court-martialed. The massacre also ruined any political career he might have had.

CHOCTAW, USS. Built in St. Louis, the *Choctaw* was a side-wheel steamer that was bought by the U.S. government in 1862 for conversion into an **ironclad ram**. It had seven guns of assorted size and was viewed as one of the Union's most powerful western gunboats. The *Choctaw*'s first combat was in April 1863 when it attacked Confederate batteries on the Yazoo River near **Vicksburg, Mississippi**. The following month, it participated in the capture of Yazoo City and in June performed valuable service helping repel a Confederate attack against **Milliken's Bend, Louisiana**. The *Choctaw* also served under Adm. **David D. Porter** during the **Red River Campaign**. After the war, it was sold as scrap in **New Orleans, Louisiana**, for $9,272.

CHRISTIAN COMMISSION, U.S. Organized in November 1861 by the New York City Young Men's Christian Association, the Christian Commission worked along with the **U.S. Sanitary Commission** to provide services for Union soldiers. The Commission gave out free meals and reading and writing material to front-line soldiers and performed nursing duties in hospitals. Being a Christian organization, the commission also worked to promote Christian values in the **armies**. The organization was phased out in early 1866.

CHRISTMAS RAID, JOHN HUNT MORGAN'S (DECEMBER 21, 1862–JANUARY 1, 1863). *See* MORGAN'S KENTUCKY RAIDS.

CHURCHILL, THOMAS JAMES (1824–1905) CSA. A native of **Kentucky** and the brother-in-law of a Kentucky governor, Churchill graduated from St. Mary's College and studied law at Transylvania University. He served as a lieutenant in the 1st Kentucky Mounted Riflemen during the **Mexican War** and was captured. After the war, Churchill moved to **Arkansas** and became postmaster of **Little Rock**.

When the Civil War began, Churchill raised a **regiment** of 12-month volunteers, which became the 1st Arkansas Mounted Rifles, and was elected colonel in June 1861. After fighting at **Wilson's Creek**, he was promoted to brigadier general in March 1862 and was engaged at **Pea**

Ridge the very next day. Churchill was given command of a **brigade** and led it in the 1862 **Kentucky Campaign**, where he was praised for his service at **Richmond**. Transferred back to **Arkansas**, he was in command of Fort Hindman at **Arkansas Post** when it was forced to surrender in January 1863. Many soldiers blamed Churchill for the fort's capture, and after being **exchanged** he found that a **Texas** cavalry brigade refused to serve under him. Given command of an infantry **division**, Churchill fought at **Pleasant Hill** during the 1864 **Red River Campaign** but did not perform particularly well. Afterward, his division marched to Arkansas and participated in the **Battle of Jenkins' Ferry** during the **Camden Expedition**. In March 1865, Churchill was promoted to major general and temporarily commanded the Confederate troops in southern Arkansas.

Churchill briefly fled to Mexico after the war, but he soon returned to Arkansas and was elected state treasurer three times before being elected governor in 1880. His governorship was marred, however, by charges of misconduct while he had been treasurer.

CHUSTENAHLAH, INDIAN TERRITORY, BATTLE OF (DECEMBER 26, 1861). After the **Battle of Chusto-Talasah**, Chief Opothleyahola and his pro-Union Creek and Seminole **Indians** retreated to a camp at Chustenahlah (CHOOS-tuh-NAH-lah). Confederate Col. **Douglas H. Cooper** was reinforced by Col. **James McQueen McIntosh's brigade** and followed Opothleyahola. On December 26, 1861, the Confederates attacked the Unionists at Chustenahlah and finally drove them away after heavy fighting. **Stand Watie**, who had joined Cooper and McIntosh after the battle began, then pursued Opothleyahola. The Unionists finally made it to **Kansas** and the protection of Federal troops, but many died from exposure during the trek. Opothleyahola lost 211 men at Chustenahlah, while the Confederates suffered 40 casualties. The Southern victory enabled the Confederates to solidify their hold on **Indian Territory**.

CHUSTO-TALASAH, INDIAN TERRITORY, BATTLE OF (DECEMBER 9, 1861). When the Civil War began, the Five Civilized Tribes of **Indian Territory** were divided in their loyalties, but many supported the Confederacy. Several thousand **Indians** joined Unionist Creek Chief Opothleyahola and accompanied him on a trek toward **Kansas** and Union protection. On November 19, 1861, Opothleyahola and his 3,500 followers were attacked at Round Mountain by a mixed force of approximately 1,400 Confederate Indians and whites under Col. **Douglas Cooper**. Opothleyahola retreated to Chusto-Talasah (CHOOS-toe-tuh-LAH-suh) and encamped on Bird Creek. Cooper eventually followed and arrived at Chusto-Talasah on December 8.

Neither leader had any desire to continue the fratricide, so a conference was arranged for the next day. That night, concern swept through Cooper's ranks as it became known that many of Opotheyahola's warriors were tired of running and were preparing to attack. This news unnerved the Confederate Cherokees, and many simply left the area. When no attack came, Cooper decided to attack Opothleyahola's camp first. His Creeks, Choctaws, and Cherokees attacked Opothleyahola's flanks, and **Texas** cavalry moved into his rear. The Unionist Creeks and Seminoles fell back fighting stubbornly, and the battle raged for about four hours. The fight eventually sputtered out, after Cooper lost 52 men and Opothleyahola an estimated 412. Cooper was able to claim victory when Opothleyahola withdrew during the night.

CITY POINT, VIRGINIA. During the **Petersburg Campaign**, City Point, Virginia, served as headquarters for Lt. Gen. **U. S. Grant** and was the main supply depot for the **Army of the Potomac**. Located on top of a bluff overlooking the confluence of the Appomattox and James Rivers, the small port town was transformed into a huge military base in the summer of 1864. Warehouses, hospitals, and wagon and **artillery** parks sprawled over the area, and ships of all sorts anchored in the James River. A newly laid **railroad** transported munitions and supplies from City Point to the soldiers besieging **Richmond** and Petersburg. City Point was the scene of one of the war's most spectacular incidents of sabotage. On August 9, 1864, two Confederate agents managed to place an explosive device disguised as a lump of coal onboard a munitions ship. The resulting explosion devastated the area, killing and wounding 169 men, and narrowly missed killing Grant.

CLANTON, JAMES HOLT (1827–1871) CSA. Born in **Georgia**, Clanton moved to **Alabama** as a boy and attended the University of Alabama. After serving in the **South Carolina** Palmetto Regiment during the **Mexican War**, he returned to Alabama and became a lawyer. Clanton was elected to the state legislature in 1855, where he opposed **secession**, and served as a **John Bell** elector in the **election of 1860**.

Clanton entered Confederate service in 1861 when he was elected captain of a volunteer cavalry **company** that he raised. After serving on the Florida coast, he was appointed colonel of the 1st Alabama Cavalry in November. At **Shiloh**, Clanton was praised by his superiors for his bravery and leadership. After fighting at **Corinth**, he resigned his commission (perhaps because of a clash with **Braxton Bragg**) and returned to Alabama, where he helped raise troops and served as the governor's aide-de-camp. In 1863, Clanton raised one infantry and three cavalry

regiments and an **artillery** battery at Montgomery and was sent to help defend the Gulf Coast.

Clanton was promoted to brigadier general in November 1863, but after a secret peace society was discovered among his men, his **brigade** was transferred in early 1864 to northern Alabama. While defending the Gadsden area, he was praised by his superior, **Leonidas Polk**, but **Joseph E. Johnston** thought he was incompetent and would not let Clanton join the **Army of Tennessee** in the spring of 1864. Instead, Clanton served as Polk's aide-de-camp during the **Atlanta Campaign**. His subsequent service was mostly spent skirmishing with the enemy in northern Alabama and guarding against Union raids. Returning to the Gulf Coast late in the war, Clanton was gravely wounded and captured in March 1865 during a **skirmish** at Bluff Spring, Florida. **Paroled** because of his wound, he saw no further combat in the war.

In September 1871, Clanton was murdered in Knoxville, Tennessee, by a drunken former Union officer.

CLARK, CHARLES (1811–1877) CSA. Born in **Ohio**, Clark graduated from **Kentucky's** Augusta College and moved to **Mississippi** to become a teacher. He was elected to the state legislature twice as a **Whig** and served in the **Mexican War** as a captain, and then colonel, of the 2nd Mississippi. Clark opposed **secession** early in his political career and was elected to the legislature twice more. His defeat in a gubernatorial race probably caused him to switch his political stand to become a secessionist **Democrat**. In 1860, Clark served as a delegate to the Democratic National Convention in **Charleston, South Carolina**, where he supported **John C. Breckinridge**.

After secession, Clark first was appointed brigadier general, and then major general, of state troops, but in May 1861, he was commissioned a brigadier general in the **Confederate army**. Clark was wounded in the shoulder while leading a **division** at **Shiloh** and had his thigh shattered while commanding a division at **Baton Rouge**. Left behind and captured in the latter battle, he was crippled permanently by the wound. **Paroled** because of his wound, Clark resigned from the **army** in October 1863.

Clark was elected governor of Mississippi by a large margin in 1863 and became a war governor who strongly supported the Confederate cause. He strove to raise troops, punish political profiteers, and maintain order. Clark also supported the use of **black troops** in the army but opposed granting them freedom for doing so. Taken into Union custody in May 1865, he was kept in **prison** for more than three months before being paroled.

After the war, Clark largely retired from politics.

CLARK, EDWARD (1815–1880) CSA. A native of **Louisiana**, Clark moved first to **Alabama** and then to **Texas** in 1842. There, he became a lawyer, was a delegate to the 1845 constitutional convention, and volunteered to fight in the **Mexican War**. After serving in a number of state offices as a **Democrat**, Clark was elected lieutenant governor in 1859.

When Governor **Sam Houston** refused to support **secession** or the Confederacy, he was removed from office in March 1861 and was replaced by Clark. Clark served as governor for only a few months, but in that time he was forced to protect the state from both the Union **army** and **Indians**, and he worked to raise troops and supplies for the Confederacy. He was narrowly defeated for reelection in the autumn of 1861 by **Francis R. Lubbock**. Clark then became colonel of the 14th Texas and served in Louisiana in 1863–64.

When the war ended, Clark at first fled to Mexico, but he later returned to Texas and resumed his law practice.

CLARK, HENRY TOOLE (1808–1874) CSA. A **North Carolina** native, Clark graduated from the University of North Carolina and studied law but became a farmer instead of opening a practice. He was elected to the state legislature in 1849 and was serving as speaker of the senate when the Civil War began.

When North Carolina's governor died in July 1861, Clark assumed the position. He strove to fund the state's growing war costs and sent a large part of North Carolina's armed forces to **Virginia**. As a result of the latter action, Union forces captured **Hatteras Inlet** and **Roanoke Island** on the North Carolina coast. This caused many people to criticize Clark unfairly and to view him as incompetent. As a result, he was defeated by **Zebulon B. Vance** in 1862. Although elected again to the legislature in 1865, Clark never took his seat because he had not been pardoned by the federal government for his secessionist activity.

CLARK, JOHN BULLOCK, JR. (1831–1885) CSA. The son of a former U.S. congressman (and future Confederate congressman), Clark was born in **Missouri** and attended Missouri University and Harvard Law School.

Clark was practicing law when the Civil War began, but he entered service in 1861 as a lieutenant in the Missouri State Guard. He soon was promoted to captain and by the time of the **Battle of Carthage** was serving as a major in the 1st Missouri Infantry. Clark also fought at **Wilson's Creek** and at the **First Battle of Springfield** and was lightly wounded in the former. Promoted to colonel, he led a **division** at **Pea Ridge**, and then he and his **regiment** were mustered into Confederate service in November 1862. Afterward, Clark commanded a **brigade** that harassed Union shipping on the Mississippi River and fought at **Little Rock, Arkansas,** in September 1863.

General **Edmund Kirby Smith** promoted Clark to brigadier general in April 1864, but the Senate did not confirm it. However, **Jefferson Davis** later renominated him. Clark served as a brigadier general at the **Battle of Jenkins' Ferry** and afterward was transferred to the cavalry. Commanding Maj. Gen. **John S. Marmaduke's** former **brigade,** he participated in **Sterling Price's Missouri Raid** in the autumn of 1864.

After the war, Clark served 10 years in the **U.S. Congress** and then became clerk of the House of Representatives.

CLAY, CASSIUS MARCELLUS (1810–1903) USA. A **Kentucky** native and Henry Clay's cousin, Clay was a Yale University graduate who came to oppose **slavery** even though he was raised in a slave-owning family. A **Whig,** he served three terms in the state legislature before being defeated in 1841 because of his antislavery views. Clay's opposition to slavery was not because he thought it was sinful but because he believed it had a harmful effect on non-slave-owning whites. As a result, many **abolitionists** denounced him. Clay served in the **Mexican War** with the 1st Kentucky Cavalry, even though he opposed the annexation of **Texas,** and was captured. In the 1850s, he helped organize the **Republican Party** and was strongly considered for the vice presidential nomination in 1860.

After campaigning for **Abraham Lincoln,** Clay was appointed U.S. minister to Russia. He returned to the United States in 1862 and was appointed major general of volunteers in April. When Clay failed to receive a command appropriate for his rank, he resigned his commission in March 1863 and returned to Russia as minister until 1869. Afterward, he was a member of the Liberal Republican, **Democratic,** and Republican Parties.

CLAY, CLEMENT CLAIBORNE (1816–1882) CSA. A native of **Alabama,** Clay was the son of an Alabama governor. After graduating from the University of Alabama and the University of Virginia Law School, he became a state legislator and judge. Clay was elected to the U.S. Senate in 1853 and 1859 but resigned his seat in February 1861 after Alabama seceded.

Turning down **Jefferson Davis's** offer to be named the Confederate secretary of war, Clay was elected to the **Confederate Congress** in November 1861. A friend and supporter of Davis, he was admired by nearly everyone. In April 1864, Davis assigned **Jacob Thompson** and Clay to Canada as agents. They worked to open unofficial peace negotiations with the Union and to strengthen the Midwestern peace movement and plotted to free Confederate **prisoners** from **Johnson's Island**. Returning to the Confederacy near war's end, Clay was arrested and held prisoner with Davis at **Fort Monroe, Virginia**, on charges of conspiring against the U.S. government and being involved in **Abraham Lincoln's assassination**. He was released in April 1866 and was never put on trial.

Clay returned to Alabama and worked as a lawyer.

CLAYTON, HENRY DELAMAR (1827–1889) CSA. Although born in **Georgia**, Clayton grew up in **Alabama**. After graduating from **Virginia's** Emory and Henry College, he became a lawyer and was elected to the Alabama legislature in 1857. Clayton was captain of a local militia **company** in 1860, but in August, the governor appointed him colonel of the 3rd Regiment, Alabama Volunteer Corps.

Unable to enter active service with his **regiment**, Clayton resigned his commission in January 1861 and rejoined his old company as a private. The next month, however, the governor appointed him colonel and commander of all state troops at **Pensacola, Florida**. In March 1861, Clayton was appointed colonel of the newly formed 1st Alabama, which trained as heavy artillerists and participated in the bombardment of **Fort Pickens, Florida**, in November. Clayton resigned his commission in January 1862, returned home to organize the 39th Alabama, and was appointed its colonel in May 1862. He participated in the 1862 **Kentucky Campaign** and was severely wounded at **Stones River** while with the **Army of Tennessee**.

Upon **Braxton Bragg's** recommendation, Clayton was promoted to brigadier general in April 1863. He led an Alabama **brigade** in the **Chickamauga** and **Chattanooga Campaigns** and was wounded again during the former. Midway through the **Atlanta Campaign**, Clayton was promoted to major general in July 1864. He commanded a **division** at **Ezra Church** and **Jonesboro** and had three horses shot from under him at the latter. During the **Franklin and Nashville Campaign**, Clayton's division did not participate in the charge at Franklin, but he did fight at Nashville. There he repulsed the Union attacks on the first day but was forced to retreat on the second. During the retreat to **Mississippi**, Clayton formed the **army's** rear guard and was praised by his superiors for his conduct. Sent to join **Joseph E. Johnston** for the **Carolinas Campaign**, he fought his last battle at **Bentonville**. Because of mental and physical fatigue and there being a surplus of high-ranking officers, Clayton retired from service in April 1865.

After the war, Clayton served as an Alabama judge and as president of the University of Alabama.

CLAYTON, POWELL (1833–1914) USA. Born in **Pennsylvania**, Clayton attended a military school and an engineering school before moving to **Kansas** in 1855 to become a civil engineer.

Clayton was in a militia **company** in early 1861 and in May entered Union service as a captain in the 1st Kansas Infantry. After fighting at **Wilson's Creek**, he was made lieutenant colonel of the 5th Kansas Cavalry in December and was promoted to colonel in March 1862. Clayton was put in command of the post at **Pine Bluff, Arkansas**, in September 1863 and in October repulsed an attack by Confederate cavalry. Promoted to brigadier general of volunteers in August 1864, he led a cavalry **brigade** in **Arkansas** and **Missouri** for the rest of the war.

Clayton remained in Arkansas after the war and was elected its **carpetbagger** governor in 1868. He fought the Ku Klux Klan, ran up the state debt, and was accused of being corrupt, but an 1871 impeachment was unsuccessful. Elected to the U.S. Senate the same year, Clayton controlled Arkansas politics until his death.

CLEBURNE, PATRICK RONAYNE (1828–1864) CSA. Born in Ireland, Cleburne (CLAY-burn) was a druggist's apprentice as a young man but failed to pass his examination because of foreign language deficiencies. He then joined the 41st Infantry Regiment but, as a corporal, bought a discharge and immigrated to the United States when he was 21. Cleburne eventually settled in **Arkansas** and became partner in an apothecary. After studying law, he opened his own practice, engaged in politics (first as a **Whig**, then as a **Democrat**), and was shot in the back over a political dispute. In 1860, Cleburne helped organize a militia **company** known as the Yell Rifles and joined it as a private.

Elected captain, Cleburne led his company to **Little Rock** in February 1861 to seize the federal arsenal there. After Arkansas seceded in May 1861, he was elected colonel of the 1st Arkansas Infantry. By year's end, Cleburne was in command of a **brigade** in **William J. Hardee's division**. After participating in the Confederate withdrawal from **Kentucky** in early 1862, he was promoted to brigadier general in March 1862.

As a **brigade** commander, Cleburne earned praise for his conduct at **Shiloh** and in late summer was put in command of a small division that led **Braxton Bragg's** army in the **Kentucky Campaign**. Cleburne's leadership was a major factor in the Confederate victory at **Richmond**, but he was wounded in the face during the battle. He recovered in time to lead his brigade in an attack at **Perryville** that broke the Union line, but he again was wounded near the ankle and had his horse killed under him.

Cleburne's bravery and leadership led to a promotion to major general in December 1862. He came to be seen by many as the best division commander in the **Confederate army** and sometimes was referred to as the "Stonewall Jackson of the West." Cleburne was greatly admired and loved by his men for his bravery and caring manner and was one of only two foreign-born men to become Confederate major generals (the other was Camille A.J., Prince de Polignac). He fought well with the **Army of Tennessee** at **Stones River** and **Chickamauga**, and at **Missionary Ridge** his division repulsed attacks against the Confederate right flank and then covered the **army's** withdrawal by holding back the Federals at **Ringgold Gap**, **Georgia**. For the second time, Cleburne earned the **Thanks of Congress** for his actions at Ringgold Gap (the first being for Richmond). While encamped at Dalton, Georgia, in 1864, Cleburne controversially proposed the use of **black troops** at a meeting that came to be known as the **Dalton Conference**. His proposal, though supported by some officers, brought rebuke from many others and may have prevented him from being further promoted. Cleburne continued to fight well during the **Atlanta Campaign**, particularly at **Kennesaw Mountain**. During the 1864 **Franklin and Nashville Campaign**, he was leading his division on horseback during the attack at Franklin when his horse was killed. Cleburne then continued on foot until he was shot and killed.

CLEM, JOHN "JOHNNY" LINCOLN (1851–1937) USA. An **Ohio** native, Clem became famous as the "Drummer Boy of **Chickamauga**," although many of his supposed wartime exploits were fabrications. In May 1861, he ran away from home when he was nine to join the **army**. When the 3rd Ohio **regiment** turned him down because of his youth, Clem claimed he informally joined the 22nd Michigan and accompanied it as an unofficial drummer boy, with officers donating his pay, the regimental tailor cutting down a **uniform** to fit him, and the soldiers providing him a shortened musket. Clem said his drum was destroyed by an **artillery** shell at **Shiloh**, and that afterwards he became known as "Johnny Shiloh." However, the entire tale is suspect because the 22nd Michigan was not mustered into service until August 1862—nearly five months after the Battle of Shiloh. Clem may have informally joined the regiment the following month, and he officially enlisted in May 1863 (his papers list him as being four feet tall and 13 years old, but he actually was 11). Clem also claimed to have served at the **Battles of Perryville** and **Stones River**, but the 22nd Michigan was at neither. He did serve at Chickamauga and claimed to have badly wounded a Confederate colonel when he demanded Clem's surrender, but no such officers were wounded at that time on that part of the field. Clem then said he was captured but managed to escape. Now known as the "Drummer Boy of Chickamauga," he served for the rest of the war, becoming Maj. Gen. **George**

H. Thomas's orderly in January 1864. Clem was captured in October 1863 and was wounded twice. He remained in the army after the war and in 1871 was commissioned a 2nd lieutenant by President **U. S. Grant**. Clem retired from the service in 1916 as a major general.

CLINGMAN, THOMAS LANIER (1812–1897) CSA. A **North Carolina** native, Clingman graduated first in his class from the University of North Carolina and became a lawyer. After serving as both a state representative and senator, he was elected to the U.S. House of Representatives in 1843 and to the U.S. Senate in 1847. A secessionist, Clingman left the Senate in March 1861 without resigning, but the Senate expelled him in July.

Early in the Civil War, Clingman served as an aide to **Joseph E. Johnston** and as North Carolina's emissary to the Confederate government. In August 1861, he was elected colonel of the 25th North Carolina Infantry. After serving in the Carolinas, Clingman's political influence won him promotion to brigadier general in May 1862. He was put in command of North Carolina's coastal region until September and in November received a **brigade** of infantry at **Wilmington**. The brigade was not one of the Confederacy's better ones, being made up of poorly disciplined **regiments** and commanded by the inexperienced Clingman. It performed poorly in a fight at **Goldsboro Bridge** in December and in the spring of 1863 was sent to defend **Wilmington**. There the regiment earned some fame for defending **Fort Wagner**, but Clingman was mostly shuffled to various areas around **Charleston, South Carolina**. Sent to **Virginia** in 1864, he finally saw substantial combat around Petersburg and **Richmond** during the **Petersburg Campaign**. Although he at times showed great bravery, Clingman's record was uneven. A severe leg wound received while defending the **Weldon Railroad** in August 1864 disabled him until very late in the war.

After the war, Clingman unsuccessfully tried to reclaim his Senate seat and then practiced law and prospected in the North Carolina mountains.

CLOYD'S MOUNTAIN, VIRGINIA, BATTLE OF (MAY 9, 1864). When the Union armies launched several offensives against the South in the spring of 1864, one was a raid by Brig. Gen. **George Crook** into southwest **Virginia**. Leading 6,500 men, Crook was to destroy the Virginia & Tennessee Railroad, the only **railroad** that connected **Richmond, Virginia**, with the west. Opposing the raid were Confederate Brig. Gen. **Albert Gallatin Jenkins** and about 2,400 men.

Jenkins positioned his small force to confront Crook as he emerged from a mountain pass through Cloyd's Mountain. On the morning of May 9, 1864, Crook launched an attack against Jenkins's right flank, followed by an attack against his right center led by future president Col.

Rutherford B. Hayes. In fierce fighting that included hand-to-hand combat, Jenkins was severely wounded in the arm, and his line began to give way. Colonel **John McCausland** then assumed command and successfully withdrew the Confederates from the field. The battle lasted only about an hour, but Crook lost 688 men to Jenkins's 538 casualties. Jenkins himself was captured and died after his arm was amputated. Afterward, Crook burned the New River Bridge, slightly damaged the crucial railroad, and then withdrew.

CLUSERET, GUSTAVE PAUL (1823–1900) USA. A native of France, Cluseret (kloo-zuh-RAY) attended the French military academy at St. Cyr and was made a chevalier for his role in suppressing an 1848 insurrection. He served in Algeria and the Crimea but resigned his captain's commission in 1858 and took command of Giuseppe Garibaldi's French Legion. After being wounded at Capua, Cluseret traveled to the United States, where he received a colonel's commission in the Union **army** in January 1862.

Cluseret served on the staffs of **George B. McClellan** and **John C. Frémont** and led an infantry **brigade** under Frémont at **Cross Keys**. Promoted to brigadier general of volunteers in October 1862, he apparently was under arrest for an unknown offense in early 1863. Superior officers thought poorly of him, and Cluseret resigned his commission in March 1863.

After briefly editing a newspaper that supported Frémont's presidential ambitions, Cluseret returned to Europe. There Britain offered a reward for his capture, accusing him of being involved in the Fenian uprisings, and France jailed him for publishing inflammatory articles. The French Commune later condemned Cluseret to be executed, but the sentence was never carried out. Afterward, he was elected four times to the French Chamber of Deputies.

COBB, HOWELL (1815–1868) CSA. A member of a very influential **Georgia** family and the brother of Confederate Brig. Gen. **Thomas Reade Rootes Cobb**, Cobb attended the University of Georgia and became a lawyer. During his antebellum career, he served in the U.S. House of Representatives and became Speaker of the House in 1849. Cobb was elected governor in 1851, but his prior support for the **Compromise of 1850** apparently led to his defeat for a U.S. Senate seat in 1854. To reclaim this lost support, he dropped his moderate stand and became more of a Southern "**fire-eater**." Cobb was reelected to the **U.S. Congress** in 1855 and was appointed secretary of the treasury by President **James Buchanan** in 1857.

Cobb resigned his cabinet post in December 1860 and actively encouraged Georgia's **secession**. He served as president of the **Montgomery Convention** that formed the **Confederate States of America** in February 1861 and swore in President **Jefferson Davis**. Although Cobb served in the Provisional **Confederate Congress**, he desired a military appointment and after helping to raise the 16th Georgia Infantry was commissioned its colonel in July 1861.

Sent to the **Virginia** Peninsula, Cobb divided his time between the **army** and Congress until the Provisional Congress disbanded in November. Promoted to brigadier general in February 1862, he performed admirably in command of a **brigade** in a small fight at Lee's Mill in April. Cobb also fought at **Malvern Hill** with the **Army of Northern Virginia**, where it was falsely reported that he had been drunk. This rumor infuriated Cobb, who always was touchy over the widely held belief that political generals were inferior to **West Point** officers. During the **Antietam Campaign**, he was ordered to hold **Crampton's Gap** against the enemy, but his men broke and fled. After being criticized for poor leadership there, Cobb asked to be transferred closer to Georgia. He then was made commander of the Military District of Middle Florida and continued in similar administrative positions until war's end. Cobb proved to be a better administrator than field commander and in September 1863 was promoted to major general. He then was put in command of the Georgia State Guard, but he and Gov. **Joseph E. Brown** clashed frequently. In April 1864, Cobb was given command of the Georgia Reserve Force and performed some service fighting in the **Atlanta Campaign**.

After the war, Cobb opened a law practice and opposed Georgia's **Reconstruction** governments.

COBB, THOMAS READE ROOTES (1823–1862) CSA. The brother of Confederate Maj. Gen. **Howell Cobb**, Cobb was a native of **Georgia** who weighed 21½ pounds at birth. He graduated first in his class from the University of Georgia and became a lawyer at age 18. Cobb served as the state senate's assistant secretary and the Supreme Court's reporter and was a strong supporter of **slavery** and **secession**. He also was a member of the state's secession convention and the Provisional **Confederate Congress**, where he helped write the **Confederate Constitution**.

At the outbreak of war, Cobb formed **Cobb's Legion** and was elected its colonel in August 1861. As a commander, he was disliked by many of his men and was quarrelsome with his superiors, intensely disliking **Robert E. Lee**, whom he believed held a low opinion of his abilities. During the first year of war in **Virginia**, Cobb was further angered when his **legion** was fragmented and dispersed.

Although he had seen very little combat, the influential Cobb was promoted to brigadier general in November 1862 and was given command of his brother's **brigade**. At **Fredericksburg**, his first battle, he was hit in the thigh by a shell fragment while defending the famous stone wall on Marye's Heights and bled to death in a field hospital. Some men claimed the fatal round was fired by Union **artillery** positioned at his mother's childhood home on "Federal Hill."

COBB'S LEGION. Influential Georgian **Thomas R. R. Cobb** organized this unit in June 1861. Cobb's Legion had 10 **companies** and included 600 infantrymen, 300 cavalrymen, and 100 artillerymen. Designed to be a self-contained, multicomponent unit, it quickly was fragmented. First, the artillerymen were detained in **Georgia** to help defend the state while the rest of the **legion** was sent to **Virginia**. For the first year of war, the legion served on the Virginia Peninsula and on the **North Carolina** coast, seeing little combat. Its first major engagement was at **Antietam**, where it suffered heavy losses while fighting with the **Army of Northern Virginia**. Cobb, who had been absent from the command at Antietam, saw his first combat when the legion defended the famous stone wall on Marye's Heights at **Fredericksburg**. There he was killed by a shell fragment.

The legion went on to fight at **Chancellorsville**, and although it had performed admirably in battle, it was permanently broken up in 1863. The infantry and cavalry were put into separate units, each retaining the name Cobb's Legion, and were brought up to regimental strength. The cavalry served under **J. E. B. Stuart**, while the infantry was put in **William T. Wofford's brigade**. The cavalry fought well at **Brandy Station** and at **Gettysburg**, while the infantry participated in **James Longstreet's** attack into Gettysburg's **"Peach Orchard"** and **"Wheatfield."** Although the infantry arrived too late to fight at **Chickamauga** with Longstreet, it did fight at Knoxville's **Fort Sanders**, where it made a costly attack. The infantrymen and cavalrymen of Cobb's Legion fought throughout the **Overland Campaign** and continued to earn praise for their abilities. The infantry surrendered at **Appomattox**, while the cavalry accompanied **Wade Hampton** to **South Carolina** late in the war.

COBURN, ABNER (1803–1885) USA. A native of **Maine**, Coburn was the son of a prominent timber tycoon and legislator. He worked for his father as a surveyor before joining his brother to work in the **railroad** industry. Coburn was elected to the legislature as a **Whig** in 1838 and served three terms. In the 1850s, he helped organize the **Republican Party** in Maine and was elected governor in 1863. Coburn was an honest governor who supported the war effort, but he failed to be reelected when his party opted to broaden its base of support and nominated a **War Democrat**.

COCHRANE, JOHN (1813–1898) USA. A native of **New York**, Cochrane was the grandson of Revolutionary War Surgeon General John

Cochran. After graduating from New York's Hamilton College, he became a lawyer and moved to New York City. There, Cochrane became a **Democrat** who strongly supported the Southern viewpoint on most political issues. Elected to the **U.S. Congress** in 1856, he served two terms and was a delegate to the 1860 Democratic National Convention at **Charleston, South Carolina**.

Despite his Southern views, Cochrane raised the 65th New York Infantry when civil war came and was appointed its colonel in June 1861. After fighting at **Seven Pines** with the **Army of the Potomac**, he was promoted to brigadier general of volunteers in July 1862 and served at **Fredericksburg** in **John Newton's division**. Cochrane resigned his commission in February 1863, supposedly because of poor health but actually because he was among the officers who bitterly criticized **Ambrose Burnside** after Fredericksburg. Cochrane's superiors also had criticized Burnside, and one had been dismissed from the service and the other was about to be when Cochrane resigned.

Cochrane returned to New York, where he was elected state attorney general. In 1864, there was a modest, but unsuccessful movement, to run him for vice president on the **John C. Frémont** ticket.

COCKE, PHILIP ST. GEORGE (1809–1861) CSA. A native of **Virginia**, Cocke graduated from **West Point** in 1832, but he only served two years in the **U.S. Army** before resigning his commission. He became a prominent Virginia planter who advocated progressive farming techniques and served as president of the Virginia Agricultural Society and on the **Virginia Military Institute's** Board of Visitors.

After Virginia seceded in April 1861, Cocke was appointed brigadier general of state troops. He entered Confederate service as a colonel and may have been the officer who first saw the strategic importance of Manassas Junction and the Manassas Gap Railroad, which linked the Junction with the **Shenandoah Valley** and allowed the rapid transfer of reinforcements during the **First Battle of Manassas**. Cocke was good friends with **Robert E. Lee** and conferred with him frequently. He fought as a **brigade** commander at First Manassas and won promotion to brigadier general in October 1861. Perhaps broken down physically and mentally from his months in the military, Cocke committed suicide on December 26, 1861.

COCKRELL, FRANCIS MARION (1834–1915) CSA. A native of **Missouri**, Cockrell graduated from Chapel Hill College and became a lawyer. He raised a militia **company** when the Civil War began and was elevated from private to company captain.

As part of the 3rd Missouri (Confederate), Cockrell first fought at **Carthage** and **Wilson's Creek** before becoming a captain in the 2nd Missouri (Confederate) in January 1862 and serving at **Pea Ridge**. Cockrell's **regiment** next was transferred to **Mississippi**, where he participated **the siege of Corinth**. Promoted to lieutenant colonel in May 1862 and to colonel in June, he was in command of the Missouri Brigade during the **Vicksburg Campaign**. Cockrell opposed **U. S. Grant's** march down the **Louisiana** side of the Mississippi River in April 1863 and then defended **Grand Gulf, Mississippi**. After fighting at **Port Gibson**, **Champion Hill**, and **Big Black River Bridge**, he was wounded during the siege of **Vicksburg** and was captured when it surrendered.

Promoted to brigadier general in July 1863 while still held **prisoner**, Cockrell was **exchanged** in September. His Missouri Brigade then served with the **Army of Tennessee** throughout the **Atlanta Campaign** and gained recognition for its role in the victory at **Kennesaw Mountain**. Cockrell lost several fingers when wounded in the hand during the campaign but rejoined his command in August. He also received three wounds at **Franklin** (Cockrell was wounded a total of five times in the war), but he recovered and became second in command of **Fort Blakely** near Mobile, Alabama. Cockrell was captured again when the fort fell in April 1865 during the **Mobile Campaign**.

After the war, Cockrell was elected to the U.S. Senate in 1874. He served as a senator for 30 years and for five years sat on the Interstate Commerce Commission.

COEHORN MORTAR. Named for its Dutch inventor, the coehorn **mortar** had a small bore, usually 4.6 inches, which made it light and maneuverable. Union forces used one that fired a 24-pound projectile, but it weighed less than 300 pounds. The coehorn mortar was used mostly in such sieges as occurred in the **Vicksburg** and **Petersburg Campaigns**.

COFFEEVILLE, MISSISSIPPI, BATTLE OF (DECEMBER 5, 1862). In December 1862, Maj. Gen. **U. S. Grant** was pushing through north-central **Mississippi** with the **Army of the Tennessee** in **Grant's Overland Vicksburg Campaign**. Union cavalry under Col. T. Lyle Dickey **skirmished** with the Confederate rear guard as Maj. Gen. **Earl Van Dorn** retreated down the Coffeeville Road through Oxford. On December 5, Dickey's cavalry engaged a sizeable Confederate force under Maj. Gen. **Mansfield Lovell** and Brig. Gen. **Lloyd Tilghman** just north of Coffeeville. Outnumbered, Dickey was forced into a fighting retreat back up the road but at dark found a strong position and made a stand that finally stopped the pursuing Confederates. In the engagement, Dickey lost 116 men, while the Confederate's suffered 50 casualties.

COFFIN, CHARLES CARLETON (1823–1896) USA. Born in **New Hampshire**, Coffin was a newspaper reporter who had been laid off from the Boston *Journal* when the Civil War began. He was in **Washington, D.C.**, in July 1861 and covered the **First Battle of Manassas** on his own. Coffin's scoop won him back his job with the *Journal*, and he became one of the war's premier **war correspondents**. Writing under the pen name "Carleton" (his middle name), Coffin covered both the eastern and western theaters. He broke the news of **U. S. Grant's** capture of **Fort Donelson** and went on to cover the **Battles of Antietam, Gettysburg, Atlanta**, the **Wilderness, Charleston, Fort Fisher**, and the fall of **Richmond, Virginia**. Coffin also covered **Abraham Lincoln's Gettysburg Address** and his tour of Richmond in April 1865. His coverage of battles and human-interest stories won him a large following.

After the war, Coffin wrote a number of children's and travel books and gave more than 2,000 lectures. He also served one term each in the **Massachusetts** State Assembly and Senate.

COLD HARBOR, VIRGINIA, BATTLE OF (JUNE 1–3, 1864). After the **Battles of the Wilderness** and **Spotsylvania** in the 1864 **Overland Campaign**, Lt. Gen. **U. S. Grant** again attempted to turn the right flank of Gen. **Robert E. Lee's Army of Northern Virginia**. He first sent Maj. Gen. **George Meade's Army of the Potomac** to the **North Anna River**, but when the Confederates blocked them there, the Federals went on another flanking march and reached the crossroad settlement of Cold Harbor on May 31.

Upon reaching the crossroads, Maj. Gen. **Philip Sheridan's** Union cavalry drove off the Confederate cavalry under Brig. Gen. **Fitzhugh Lee**. This put Grant only 10 miles northeast of **Richmond, Virginia**. On June 1, Lee attempted to dislodge Sheridan by attacking him with Lt. Gen. **Richard H. Anderson's** corps, but Sheridan repulsed the attacks, and both sides began digging entrenchments that stretched for six miles. By afternoon, Union Maj. Gen. **Horatio G. Wright's** VI Corps and Maj. Gen. **William F. Smith's** XVIII Corps had arrived, and they launched a strong attack against Anderson and **Robert F. Hoke's division**. Although a brief breakthrough was achieved, the Confederates finally drove out the Federals with a counterattack. In this vicious fight, the Federals lost 2,650 men. Confederate losses are unknown but were probably somewhat fewer.

Grant believed a vigorous dawn attack would break Lee's line and ordered Maj. Gen. **Winfield Scott Hancock's** II Corps on a forced march to Cold Harbor. After an exhausting march, Hancock did not arrive until the morning of June 2, forcing Grant to postpone the attack planned for that afternoon. Further delays made him put it off until the morning of June 3. Grant planned for his left and center to attack Lee's right and center, but it was a dangerous gamble since past battles had shown the futility of attacking well-entrenched positions. He believed that the previous month's fighting had weakened Lee's **army** to the point that a **frontal attack** could succeed. If Lee could be defeated at Cold Harbor, Grant could quickly capture Richmond and, hopefully, end the war. Unfortunately for Grant, the delay in launching the attack gave Lee time to place his other two **corps** under **Jubal A. Early** and **A. P. Hill** behind impregnable entrenchments. The Union soldiers recognized the suicidal nature of the offensive, and on the night of June 2 many men were seen pinning their names and addresses to their **uniforms** so their bodies could be identified.

At 4:30 A.M., June 3, Grant launched his attack with the 40,000 men in the corps of Wright, Hancock, and Smith. The Federals carried some advanced Confederate lines, and Hancock briefly reached the works on the Confederate right. Nowhere was Lee's main line penetrated, however, and the entrenched Confederates slaughtered the attackers. In an attack that lasted from an estimated seven to 30 minutes, Grant lost 7,000 men. Lee lost approximately 1,500.

Cold Harbor was the last battle of the Overland Campaign. After the battle, Grant refused to ask for a truce to recover his wounded and bury the dead, because apparently he did not want to admit defeat. A truce was not declared until June 7, by which time only two Union wounded reportedly were found alive. After this debacle, Grant decided to abandon his previous **tactic** of sliding around Lee's right. Instead, he disengaged, crossed the James River and attempted to take Petersburg south of Richmond in the **Petersburg Campaign**. In his memoirs, Grant admitted that the attack at Cold Harbor was one of only two that he regretted having ordered; the other was at **Vicksburg, Mississippi**.

COLD HARBOR, VIRGINIA, FIRST BATTLE OF (JUNE 27, 1862). *See* GAINES' MILL, VIRGINIA, BATTLE OF.

COLD SPRING FOUNDRY, NEW YORK. *See* WEST POINT FOUNDRY, COLD SPRING, NEW YORK.

COLFAX, SCHUYLER (1823–1885) USA. The son of a Revolutionary War general, Colfax was born in **New York** but moved to **Indiana** as a boy. After working in his stepfather's store, he became a journalist and then began his own **Whig** newspaper. Colfax became known as the "Little **Greeley** of the West" and took a moderate stand on **slavery**. He switched to the **Know-Nothing Party** when the Whigs became defunct and opposed both the **Compromise of 1850** and the **Kansas-Nebraska**

Act. Joining the **Republican Party** next, Colfax was elected to the **U.S. Congress** in 1854. He supported the **Homestead Act** and the Morrill Act and in 1860 advised president-elect **Abraham Lincoln** not to give in to secessionists. Despite his strong stand against **secession**, Colfax was in favor of giving concessions to the South in order to maintain the Union. He supported guaranteeing slavery in the South but was against the **Crittenden Compromise** because it would extend the **Missouri Compromise** Line to the Pacific Ocean.

During the Civil War, Colfax worked to raise Indiana troops and supported the Lincoln administration's **income tax, Emancipation Proclamation, conscription**, and **13th Amendment**. Elected Speaker of the House in 1863, he kept that post until he left Congress in 1869. By war's end, Colfax had become a **Radical Republican** and was instrumental in winning congressional control over **Reconstruction**. He helped pass the Civil Rights Act and 14th Amendment and played a key role in the impeachment of President **Andrew Johnson**. In 1868, Colfax was elected vice president under **U. S. Grant** but was forced to retire after one term when he was implicated in the Crédit Mobilier Scandal.

COLLIERVILLE, TENNESSEE, BATTLE OF (NOVEMBER 3, 1863). When Maj. Gen. **William T. Sherman** moved his **corps** from **Vicksburg, Mississippi**, to Chattanooga, Tennessee, in the autumn of 1863, Confederate cavalry under Brig. Gen. **James R. Chalmers** tried to disrupt the deployment by attacking the **railroad** used by Sherman. On November 3, Chalmers attacked the track at Collierville, Tennessee, because there was only a small Union garrison there. Unknown to Chalmers, his approach was discovered, and Col. **Edward Hatch** led reinforcements to the town. When the Confederates attacked, they were surprised to find Hatch's cavalry on their flanks. Believing he was outnumbered, Chalmers broke off the fight and withdrew into **Mississippi**. In the short clash, Chalmers lost 95 men, while the Federals counted 60 casualties.

COLLINS, NAPOLEON (1814–1875) USA. A native of **Pennsylvania**, Collins entered the **U.S. Navy** as a midshipman in 1834 and served on the USS *Decatur* during the **Mexican War**. A lieutenant when the Civil War began, he was assigned to the **South Atlantic Blockading Squadron** and commanded the USS *Unadilla* in November 1861 during the capture of **Port Royal, South Carolina**. Promoted to commander in July 1862, Collins was given command of the USS *Octarara* and was sent to the West Indies to pursue **blockade runners**. During this service, he first showed what would become a frequent habit of embroiling himself in controversial events when he seized a British ship without sufficient cause. Although a prize court ruled that there was some cause for his actions, the ship was returned to sea, and Collins was censored (over the objections of Secretary of the Navy **Gideon Welles**).

Collins next was assigned to the **USS** *Wachusett* and patrolled the Brazilian coast searching for Confederate **commerce raiders**. He caught up with the **CSS** *Florida* when it anchored at Bahia for repairs. Despite international law forbidding hostile action in the neutral port, Collins waited until most of the Confederate crew went ashore on the night of October 7, 1864, and then rammed the *Florida*, took control of the ship, and sailed it to Hampton Roads, Virginia. Although Collins was hailed as a hero by many people, his action was disavowed by the government, and the *Florida* was ordered returned to Brazil. Before this could be done, the ship sank under mysterious circumstances. Collins was court-martialed and ordered dismissed from the service, but many government officials privately approved his actions, and Welles refused to carry out the order.

Collins was promoted to captain in 1866, but the following year he was charged with negligence when his vessel wrecked in the Bay of Bengal. This time Welles suspended him from duty until 1869. Collins then was made an inspector of lighthouses. He was promoted to rear admiral in 1874 and died in Peru while in command of the South Pacific Squadron.

COLORADO TERRITORY. Organized in 1861, the Colorado Territory witnessed no fighting between the opposing Civil War armies, but many of its citizens fought on both sides. Officially the territory remained loyal and supplied 4,903 men to the Union cause. These soldiers saw combat at the battles of **Valverde** and **Glorieta Pass**. An equal number of men are estimated to have served the Confederacy. In addition to being involved in the Civil War, Colorado soldiers under Col. **John M. Chivington** also carried out the infamous **Sand Creek Massacre** in 1864.

COLQUITT, ALFRED HOLT (1824–1894) CSA. A native of **Georgia**, Colquitt was the son of a former Georgia senator. After graduating from the College of New Jersey (Princeton), he served in the **Mexican War** as a major on staff duty. After the war, Colquitt opened a law practice and was elected to the U.S. House of Representatives for one term in 1852. A staunch secessionist, he was elected to the state legislature in 1859 and served in Georgia's 1861 **secession** convention.

In May 1861, Colquitt was elected colonel of the 6th Georgia and was sent to **Virginia**. After fighting at **Seven Pines**, he was put in command of a **brigade** in the **Army of Northern Virginia** and led it through the **Seven Days Campaign**. Colquitt impressed Gen. **Robert E. Lee** and was promoted to brigadier general in September 1862. During the **Antietam Campaign**, his brigade fought well at Turner's Gap in **South Mountain** and at Antietam, where it suffered heavy casualties. At **Chancellorsville**, it was Colquitt's brigade that led **Stonewall Jackson's** famous flanking march. Afterward, his brigade was so depleted by casualties as to be of little use to Lee and was sent first to **North Carolina** and then **Florida**. In February 1864, Colquitt played a key role in the Confederate victory at **Olustee**, after which he was ordered back to Virginia, where he fought with Lee through the **Overland Campaign** and much of the **Petersburg Campaign**. In January 1865, Colquitt was ordered to take command of **Fort Fisher**, **North Carolina**, but he arrived just as the fort was being overrun and barely escaped capture.

After the war, Colquitt was elected governor of Georgia in 1876 and 1880. He also was elected to the U.S. Senate in 1882 and served there until his death.

COLSTON, RALEIGH EDWARD (1825–1896) CSA. Colston was born in Paris, France, but the circumstances of his birth are unknown. His mother, the divorced wife of Napoleon's Marshal Kellermann, admitted on her deathbed that she adopted him while her new husband, a **Virginia** physician, was away on an extended trip. She then presented the baby as their natural child. Colston received some education in Paris before his adopted father took him to Virginia. Graduating from the **Virginia Military Institute** (VMI) in 1846, he taught French and other courses at the institute until the Civil War.

Colston was serving as the VMI commandant, with the rank of major of state troops, when the Civil War began. In May 1861, he was appointed colonel of the 16th Virginia Infantry and assumed command of the training camp at **Norfolk, Virginia**. Promoted to brigadier general in December, Colston served for over a year in the quiet areas of southeastern Virginia and in the **Richmond** defenses. In the spring of 1863, his fellow VMI professor **Stonewall Jackson** got him transferred to the **Army of Northern Virginia**. There the inexperienced officer took command of one of Jackson's **brigades** and even temporarily led a **division**. At **Chancellorsville**, Colston apparently badly mishandled his division and earned the scorn of **Robert E. Lee**. Lee quickly relieved him of command and ignored his subsequent requests to receive another one. In July 1864, after temporarily commanding a brigade at Savannah, Georgia, Colston became commander of **Lynchburg, Virginia**. He remained there until war's end.

After the war, Colston ran two military academies and served as a colonel in the Egyptian army.

COLT REPEATING RIFLE. Famous gun maker Samuel Colt, along with his armory superintendent Elisha Root, used Colt's basic revolver design to develop a repeating **rifle** in 1855. It had a five- or six-shot **percussion cap** cylinder mounted on a long barrel and rifle stock. The weapon came in many models and calibers, with .44, .50, and .56 being the most common. It never was very popular because when a round was fired, the sparks frequently set off an adjacent chamber. Both sides used the rifle in the Civil War, with the Union buying more than 4,000 of them. **Berdan's Sharpshooters** used the Colt repeater for a while, as did some other units.

COLT REVOLVER. One of gun maker Samuel Colt's most famous weapons was the Colt revolver. A percussion revolver, it had a six-shot revolving cylinder. To load the pistol, powder was poured into each cylinder, and the ball was seated on top of it with the use of a loading arm hinged under the barrel. To prevent the weapon's discharge from sparking off an adjacent cylinder, grease was used to seal over each chamber. Each chamber then was capped with a **percussion cap**.

The revolver came in two basic models, the Army and the Navy. The name did not describe which branch of service used the model but rather denoted different calibers. The 1860 Army was a .44 caliber, while the 1851 and 1861 Navy was a .36 caliber. The revolvers were highly prized because of their reliability, but they also were expensive. Colt charged the government $13.50 each for his pistols. The Union government bought more than 100,000 of them, while many others were bought privately. Confederate soldiers either bought them before the war began or took them from dead or captured Union soldiers.

COLUMBIA, SOUTH CAROLINA, CAPTURE AND BURNING OF (FEBRUARY 16–17, 1865). During the 1865 **Carolinas Campaign**, Maj. Gen. **William T. Sherman's** forces drove off Lt. Gen. **Wade Hampton's** Confederate cavalry and entered Columbia, South Carolina, on February 16, 1865. When forward elements of Maj. Gen. **Oliver O. Howard's** XV Corps entered town, the city officially surrendered. The next day, the last withdrawing Confederate troops set fire to cotton bales and a high wind, aided by drunken soldiers, apparently scattered the flames. As a result, more than half of Columbia was burned. The burning became a source of controversy as both sides blamed the other for the destruction. Hampton accused Sherman of deliberately ordering the city's destruction, while Sherman denied it and claimed that his soldiers prevented the fire from destroying the entire city. Sherman's men occupied the city's ruins until February 20, when they continued their march.

COLUMBIAD. Developed in 1811 by Col. George Bomford, the Columbiad was a large-caliber, smoothbore **artillery** piece used mostly for coastal defense that fired shells great distances at a high trajectory. The most popular model was the 1861, which was made of cast iron by the **Thomas J. Rodman** method in order for the breech and barrel to withstand greater pressures. Columbiads were made in many different calibers up to a 20-inch bore. The 15-inch model weighed 49,100 pounds and fired a 320-pound shell 5,730 yards. Confederate manufacturers also made Columbiads but did not use the true Rodman method. They sometimes **rifled** the barrels and also used bands to reinforce the cannon's breech.

COLUMBUS (GEORGIA) IRON WORKS COMPANY. Founded on the Chattahoochee River at Columbus, Georgia, the Columbus Iron Works Company became one of the most important industrial sites in the Confederacy. It produced an assortment of iron products during the antebellum period before the five-building factory produced ordnance for the Confederacy. In September 1862, the ironworks was leased by the **Confederate navy** and became known as the Confederate States Naval Iron Works. The foundry then began producing steam engines, machinery, and ordnance for the navy and even turned out a 2.75-inch breech-loading **rifled** cannon. The works expanded by taking over other ironworks in **Alabama** and after the 1864 capture of Atlanta, Georgia, was described by **Josiah Gorgas** as being the "nucleus" of his ordnance works. On April 16, 1865, Brig. Gen. **James H. Wilson's** Union cavalry captured Columbus and destroyed the ironworks.

COMMERCE RAIDERS. With no navy in existence when it was formed, the Confederacy turned to the use of commerce raiders as an economical way to conduct naval warfare. Such raiders destroyed or captured Union merchant vessels to disrupt Union trade and drive Union insurance rates higher. The use of commerce raiders also was an economical way to force the **U.S. Navy** to disperse its fleet to hunt down the raiders.

The Confederacy employed as commerce raiders both government navy vessels and privately owned **privateers**, which were first authorized by **Jefferson Davis** in April 1861. These ships were sleek and fast and usually operated close to their home ports. The increased effectiveness of the Union **blockade** made it more difficult to bring back captured prizes, so privateering fell out of favor. By 1863, the Confederates relied more on cruisers, whose steam power and heavier armament made them more suitable for long voyages and for engaging in combat. They operated far from home, many never actually visiting a Confederate port, and usually destroyed their prey because of the difficulty in taking prizes back to port. Several of the more successful cruisers were built in Great Britain, whose law allowed the Confederates to purchase ships and armament but not to engage a crew or fit the ship with cannons while in British waters. The ships were purchased in Great Britain and then rendezvoused offshore for fitting.

Among the more successful Confederate commerce raiders (which captured or destroyed more than 200 Union ships) were the *Alabama*, *Florida*, *Shenandoah*, and *Sumter*. Union diplomats constantly complained to British officials about the raiders and forced the British to begin seizing ships suspected of violating its neutrality. After the war, the United States sued Great Britain for compensation for losses to the commerce raiders on the grounds that Britain's failure to vigorously enforce its neutrality laws led to the raiders' success. An international tribunal ruled in the 1873 *Alabama* **Claims** that the British pay the United States $15,500,000. *See also* NAVY, CONFEDERATE.

COMMITTEE OF THIRTEEN. Along with the **Committee of Thirty-three**, this U.S. congressional committee made a final attempt to avoid conflict during the **secession** crisis. In an effort to avoid disunion, the U.S. Senate established the Committee of Thirteen on December 20, 1860—the same day **South Carolina** seceded. The committee included eight **Democrats** and five **Republicans** and represented different regional and political factions. Chaired by **Kentucky's John J. Crittenden**, it first met on December 22.

The committee agreed that it would not submit any proposal to the Senate unless it had the support of a majority of both Republican and Democratic committee members. Crittenden proposed six constitutional amendments that became known as the **Crittenden Compromise**. Based on similar proposals by the late Henry Clay, the amendments guaranteed Southern **slavery** interests, while prohibiting slavery north of the old **Missouri Compromise** Line and granting **popular sovereignty** to future states. Crittenden's compromise was countered by a proposal from **Robert Toombs**, calling for the protection of slavery in all territories, the **suspension of the writ of habeas corpus** in cases of returning escaped slaves, and the requirement that all laws pertaining to slavery be approved by a majority of the Southern states. Committee member **Jefferson Davis** also proposed that slavery be specifically guaranteed by the Constitution. **William Seward** countered these Southern demands by proposing that the **Fugitive Slave Act** be enforced, that all laws that conflicted with federal law be repealed, and that the states agree to submit to congressional legislation.

After hours of discussion, a vote was taken on the Crittenden Compromise, but the five Republicans voted against it because of their opposition to reestablishing the Missouri Compromise Line. Toombs and Davis also voted against it because the compromise did not have the required Republican consent. As a result, the committee failed to make any formal recommendations to the Senate.

COMMITTEE OF THIRTY-THREE. Along with the **Committee of Thirteen**, this congressional committee was part of a final effort to avoid **secession**. When secession loomed in December 1860, **Virginia** Congressman Alexander R. Boteler recommended that the **U.S. Congress** appoint one representative from each state to serve on the committee to work out a compromise that would avoid disunion. Two proposals were made. One called for admitting the **New Mexico Territory** as a slave state, while another proposed an inalterable constitutional amendment guaranteeing **slavery** in the South, the enforcement of the **Fugitive Slave Act**, and the repeal of Northern personal liberty laws. It appeared the committee might save the nation from disunion as both houses of Congress passed the proposals by a two-thirds vote in February and March 1861 and submitted them to the states in the form of a constitutional amendment. But it was too late; the secession crisis deepened and war erupted before the amendment could be ratified.

COMMITTEE ON THE CONDUCT OF THE WAR. On December 20, 1861, this body was created by the **U.S. Congress** as a joint committee to investigate the Union disasters at **First Manassas** and **Ball's Bluff**. Chaired by **Radical Republican** Sen. **Benjamin Wade**, it consisted of Sens. **Zachariah Chandler** and **Andrew Johnson**, and Congressmen Daniel W. Gooch, **George W. Julian**, **John Covode**, and **Moses F. Odell**. Much of the committee's work was investigating corruption and scandals, but it became notorious as a watchdog of radicalism. Controlled by the Radical Republicans, the committee investigated how the war was being prosecuted and targeted for persecution any general deemed soft on the rebellion or emancipation. The committee especially opposed Maj. Gen. **George B. McClellan** and his supporters. Among those generals who ran afoul of the committee were Brig. Gen. **Charles P. Stone**, who was arrested and imprisoned for his role in the Ball's Bluff disaster, and Maj. Gen. **Fitz John Porter**, who was court-martialed and cashiered for supposed wrongdoings at **Second Manassas**. The committee was a major force in the Union war effort until it was dissolved in June 1865.

COMMUTATION. When both the Union and Confederacy resorted to **conscription**, included in their draft laws was the principle of commutation. This allowed a man whose name was chosen in the draft to pay a commutation fee to avoid military service. It was designed to allow needed skilled laborers and religious pacifists to avoid military service, but it quickly became a legal way in which the wealthy could avoid the draft. The Confederate commutation fee was $500 and only covered **conscientious objectors** and overseers on the larger plantations, while the Union fee was $300 and was available to all conscripts. Records show that half of the Union men who were conscripted and declared fit for service used the commutation to avoid service. Commutation was one way in which the Civil War became "a rich man's war and a poor man's fight."

COMPANY. The company, commanded by a captain, was the basic military unit for both the Union and Confederate armies. A company usually consisted of about 100 men raised from a local community, often by a leading citizen, and it was allowed to elect its officers and noncommissioned officers. Upon organizing, they adopted such colorful names as the Raccoon Roughs and Tiger Rifles but were given a letter designation once attached to a **regiment**. Usually 10 companies made up a regiment.

COMPANY FUND. Both the Union and Confederate armies used the company fund as a way to supplement **rations**. A military post could raise the money by such means as taxing **sutlers** or from savings obtained by running its own bakery or store. The savings then were parceled out to each **company** for buying additional rations or other small items.

COMPROMISE OF 1850. Following the **Mexican War** and the U.S. acquisition of **California** and the American southwest, the issue of **slavery** became more and more divisive. By 1850, a number of slavery-related problems faced the nation. These included whether to admit California as a free or slave state and **New Mexico** and Utah as slave or free territories; Southern demands that federal authority be used to return runaway slaves to the South; Northern demands that the unsightly slave auctions be abolished in **Washington, D.C.**; and a simmering border dispute between **Texas** and New Mexico.

The combination of issues brought an impasse to the **U.S. Congress** until Sen. Henry Clay offered a compromise. Clay proposed that California be admitted as a free state; New Mexico and Utah be admitted as territories with the right to decide the slavery issue later; a Federal **Fugitive Slave Act** be passed to return runaways; slave auctions, but not slavery, be abolished in Washington; and the border dispute be settled in favor of New Mexico in exchange for a $10,000,000 payment to Texas. When Clay was unable to get the so-called Compromise of 1850 passed as a package, Sen. **Stephen A. Douglas** carried on the fight and finally got it passed by breaking the compromise into separate bills. The Compromise of 1850 was Henry Clay's last political work (he died shortly afterward), and it briefly settled the slavery debate.

CONESTOGA, USS. Bought in Cincinnati, Ohio, by the **U.S. Navy** in June 1861, the *Conestoga* was an important part of the western Union fleet. The wooden steamer was converted into a 572-ton gunboat and saw combat on the Cumberland River, at **Forts Henry and Donelson, Island No. 10**, and on the White River, Arkansas. In March 1864, while on **Louisiana's** Ouachita (WASH-hi-taw) River, it was accidentally rammed by the USS *General Sterling Price*, which caused it to sink, killing two crewmen.

CONFEDERATE ARMY. The Provisional **Confederate Congress** created a regular **army** called the Army of the Confederate States of America on March 6, 1861, which was intended to become the nation's permanent army, but it never became a real functioning entity. Congress authorized it to contain about 10,000 men, with six **regiments** of infantry, one regiment of cavalry, one **corps** each of **artillery** and **engineers**, and bureaus of adjutant and inspector general, quartermaster general, commissary general, and a medical department. Later laws increased the number of authorized infantry and cavalry regiments, with a **Zouave** infantry unit also being approved. Colonels were to command the bureaus, while brigadier generals would be the highest-ranking officers for the field units. This regular Confederate army never reached its intended size because it quickly became apparent to the government that the volunteers of the Provisional Army of the Confederate States would be the main fighting force. As a result, only 12 cavalry and seven infantry regiments, one artillery battery, and a number of independent **companies** were ever authorized in the regular army, for a total of about 1,750 officers and men. Early in the war, those **U.S. Army** officers who resigned their commissions to join the Confederacy were first commissioned in the regular Confederate army before being assigned to positions in the provisional army.

For its main fighting force, the Confederacy depended on a temporary volunteer Provisional Army of the Confederate States that was created by congressional acts on February 28 and March 6, 1861. These volunteers first entered state militia service and then were mustered into Confederate service and placed under the authority of the president. Volunteers first joined for a specific length of time, usually a year, but in April 1862, a reorganization occurred, whereby the existing volunteers were allowed to reelect new officers but were required to reenlist for the duration of the war. The **Conscription** Act was passed at that time to supplement the army with draftees. It is estimated that 850,000–900,000 men served in the Confederate armies.

CONFEDERATE BATTLE FLAG. *See* FLAGS, CONFEDERATE.

CONFEDERATE CONGRESS. In February 1861, the seven seceding states sent delegates, chosen in convention or by the state government, to the **Montgomery, Alabama, Convention** to form a new nation. These delegates adopted a Provisional **Confederate Constitution**, which largely was the same as the U.S. Constitution and was to be in effect for one year, and declared themselves to be the Provisional Confederate Congress. Thus, the original Congress was made up of members appointed by the state governments, not elected by voters. Eventually, the Confederate Congress comprised representatives from 13 states, the 11 original members of the Confederacy and members from **Kentucky** and **Missouri**, which never officially seceded but were seen as sister states, nonetheless. There also were nonvoting representatives from the Arizona Territory and several major **Indian** nations.

The Provisional Congress elected **Jefferson Davis** as president and **Alexander Stephens** as vice president. They served for one year in provisional positions, but both were elected in November 1861 to six-year terms (with the president ineligible for reelection). The Provisional Congress also set up a working government similar to that of the United States (but without a senate), formed the **Confederate army**, and set up a financial base on which to operate. The Provisional Congress governed the Confederacy until February 17, 1862.

Elections were held in November 1861 for the regular Congress, including a Senate that was created by the permanent Confederate Constitution. The permanent Congress met on February 18, 1862, and Davis was sworn in as president on February 22.

During the war, the Congress was convened three times, but it generally was perceived as being weak and rather inefficient. Without formal political parties, members formed cliques and factions that often centered on whether one was pro- or anti-administration, thus making votes unpredictable. Congress also frequently clashed with Davis over **conscription**, the **suspension of the writ of habeas corpus**, appointment of officers, and **states rights** issues. *See also* FINANCES; TAXES.

CONFEDERATE CONSTITUTION. In February 1861, the seceding states met in the **Montgomery, Alabama, Convention**, where they appointed a committee to draw up a Provisional Constitution for the newly formed **Confederate States of America**. Using the U.S. Constitution as its guide, the committee drafted a document that closely mirrored it but with provisions to safeguard **slavery** and **states rights**. The document provided for a one-house Congress; the provisional president and vice president being elected by the states, with each state having one vote; the **Confederate supreme court** being made up of the existing district court judges; Montgomery, Alabama, being the nation's capital but with Congress having the authority to relocate it; and the Provisional Constitution being open to amendment by a two-thirds vote of Congress.

This Provisional Constitution was adopted by Congress on March 11, 1861. Another committee then went to work to draft a permanent Constitution to go into effect in one year. Again, the permanent Confederate Constitution largely was the same as the U.S. Constitution. Twelve amendments were adopted; a congressional house and senate were created; the president and vice president served six-year terms, with the president being ineligible for reelection; cabinet members could enter congressional debates on issues concerning their departments; the president had the power of line-item veto in an appropriations bill; protective tariffs were forbidden; slavery was guaranteed in the territories, but the foreign slave trade was forbidden; new states could be admitted by a two-thirds vote of both houses of Congress; and state sovereignty was explicitly recognized.

Amending this Constitution was not left up to Congress. Any three states agreeing on an amendment could force Congress to call a convention of all the states to consider the proposal. If the convention approved the amendment, it would then be submitted to the states for ratification by a two-thirds vote. This permanent Confederate Constitution was submitted to the states for ratification and went into effect when the permanent government was installed in February 1862.

CONFEDERATE MONEY. After **secession**, the **Confederate States of America** seized three U.S. mints but still was woefully short of specie. As a result, the Confederate government never issued coinage. However, there was a flood of paper money, including state, city, and county (or parish) notes. In addition, some **railroads**, banks, and other private entities also issued notes that were sometimes redeemable in goods or services. These state, local, and private notes ranged in value from five cents to $500, and by 1865 more than $200,000,000 had been issued.

Confederate Treasury Notes were the main paper currency used, with approximately $800,000,000 being issued by 1864. At first these were interest-bearing bonds that were to be redeemed six months after a peace treaty was signed with the United States, but the last issues were in non-interest-bearing bills. They came in denominations ranging from fifty cents to $500.

Because of the huge flood of paper money, inflation became a serious problem, and by the end of the war, Confederate money was virtually worthless. Whereas a Confederate dollar was valued as high as 80 cents in December 1861, it had fallen to less than two cents by the end of the war. *See also* SHINPLASTERS; GREENBACKS; FINANCE.

CONFEDERATE STATES NAVAL IRON WORKS. *See* COLUMBUS (GEORGIA) IRON WORKS COMPANY.

CONFEDERATE STATES OF AMERICA. In February 1861, the seven seceding states (**South Carolina, Georgia, Florida, Alabama, Mississippi, Louisiana**, and **Texas**) met in the **Montgomery, Alabama Convention**, and created the Confederate States of America. A provisional government was created that operated under a provisional **Confederate Constitution. Jefferson Davis** was elected the provisional president, with **Alexander Stephens** being voted provisional vice president. After **Fort Sumter** was fired on in April, **Arkansas, Tennessee, North Carolina**, and **Virginia** also seceded and joined the Confederacy. The states of **Kentucky** and **Missouri** formed Confederate governments but never officially seceded from the Union. A permanent Confederate government and constitution went into effect in February 1862.

CONFEDERATE VETERAN. As Civil War veterans became older, the publication of war histories and reminiscences became very popular. In January 1893, Confederate veteran Sumner A. Cunningham began a monthly magazine called *Confederate Veteran* to publish and promote the Southern side of the war. Until it ceased publication in December 1932, the magazine published hundreds of eyewitness accounts of battles, personal reminiscences, and news on reunions and dedications. It remains an important source of primary information on the Confederate side of the war.

CONFISCATION ACTS. In an attempt to hinder the Confederates' ability to wage war, and to punish them, the **U.S. Congress** passed two confiscation acts during the war. Introduced by Sen. **Lyman Trumbull** and backed by the **Radical Republicans**, the acts also set the groundwork for the later **Emancipation Proclamation**.

In August 1861, the First Confiscation Act went into effect. It authorized the president to confiscate any property, including slaves, that was being used to support the Rebellion. The actual confiscation was carried out through the court system. In December 1861, Trumbull introduced a Second Confiscation Act that was passed in July 1862. It allowed for the imprisonment and fining of those supporting the Rebellion and forbade them from holding political office. The president also could confiscate the property of the more important classes of Confederates, while less important Confederates were given 60 days to cease rebellious activity or have their property confiscated. The Second Confiscation Act also dealt with **slavery** and was a precursor to the Emancipation Proclamation. It declared that slaves of Rebellion supporters who fell into the hands of the Union military would be forever freed. It also authorized the president to use such slaves in any way he judged best to help end the Rebellion. This part of the act helped open the way for the use of **black troops** in the Union **army**.

Abraham Lincoln, however, did not vigorously enforce the acts because of constitutional reservations. He was able to restrict the confiscation of property to the lifetime of the offender only, thus preventing the punishment of families beyond the offending generation. While many slaves did become free by falling under the control of the Union army, little other Southern property was confiscated. Most that was, was restored to the owners during **Reconstruction**.

CONNECTICUT. Under war Gov. **William A. Buckingham**, Connecticut was a strong **Republican** state and actively supported the Union war effort. Out of an 1860 population of 460,147, it supplied the North 30 infantry and one cavalry **regiments**, plus two regiments and three battalions of **artillery**. More than 50,000 Connecticut men served in the Union **army**, while another 2,750 served in the **U.S. Navy**. Of these, approximately 20,000 became casualties. In addition to this manpower, Connecticut also produced a large amount of **rifles**, ammunition, and clothing for the war effort.

CONNER, JAMES (1829–1883) CSA. A native of **South Carolina**, Conner graduated from South Carolina College and opened a law practice. Although serving as a U.S. attorney in 1860, he actively supported **secession**. As captain of a local militia **company**, Conner participated in the bombardment of **Fort Sumter** and then in May 1861 accepted a captain's commission in the **Hampton Legion**.

At **First Manassas**, Conner took command of the **legion** at the end of the day when the ranking officers were wounded. Promoted to major, he continued to serve with the legion until June 1862, when he was appointed colonel of the 22nd North Carolina. Conner was badly wounded in the leg at **Gaines' Mill** while fighting with the **Army of Northern Virginia** and apparently did not serve in battle with the **regiment** again.

Promoted to brigadier general in June 1864, Conner was given command of a **brigade** in **A. P. Hill's corps** and took charge of the defenses at Chaffin's Bluff, Virginia. In late summer 1864, he was given command of a South Carolina brigade and fought under **Jubal A. Early** during **Philip Sheridan's Shenandoah Campaign**. Conner was wounded again in the same leg during a **skirmish** in October and had to have his leg amputated.

Although he and his brigade were transferred to South Carolina late in the war, it does not seem that Conner saw any further field service.

After the war, Connor resumed his law practice and was elected state attorney general in 1876.

CONNOR, PATRICK EDWARD (1820–1891) USA. Born in Ireland, Connor accompanied his family to the United States as a child and settled in New York City. He served in the **U.S. Army** in the **Seminole Wars** and then moved to **Texas** in 1846. Connor served as a lieutenant and captain in an independent **company** during the **Mexican War** and was wounded at Buena Vista. Afterward he became a gold miner in **California**.

In September 1861, Connor raised the 3rd California Infantry and was appointed its colonel. Put in command of the District of Utah, his main duty was to keep the mail running to California. In doing so, Connor fought **Indians** and earned the wrath of Mormons by building a fort near Salt Lake City. His victories over hostile Indians earned him a promotion to brigadier general of volunteers in March 1863.

Connor was **brevetted** major general of volunteers for his war service and continued to serve as an Indian fighter after the war. He was removed from command in 1865 after two columns were defeated by Indians when Connor failed to unite with them. He left the **army** in 1866 and settled in Salt Lake City. There, Connor opened Utah's first daily newspaper and silver mine and founded the town of Stockton.

CONNOR, SELDEN (1839–1917) USA. A native of **Maine**, Connor graduated from Tufts College and became a lawyer, but in May 1861, he entered Union service as a private in the 1st Vermont Infantry. After fighting at **Big Bethel**, the three-month **regiment** was disbanded.

In August 1861, Connor was appointed lieutenant colonel of the 7th Maine. For the next two years, he fought with this regiment in most of the **Army of the Potomac's** major battles and was slightly wounded at **Fredericksburg**. Already having served as temporary commander of the 7th Maine, Connor was promoted to colonel of the 19th Maine in January 1864. At the **Wilderness**, the regiment fought well, but Connor was severely wounded in the thigh. Although unable to serve in the field again, he was promoted to brigadier general of volunteers in June 1864 at the age of 25.

Connor left the **army** in April 1866 and was elected governor of Maine in 1875.

CONRAD'S FERRY, MARYLAND, BATTLE OF (OCTOBER 21, 1861). *See* BALL'S BLUFF, VIRGINIA, BATTLE OF.

CONSCIENTIOUS OBJECTORS. When the Civil War began, neither side had any official policy to deal with such conscientious objectors as

Dunkards, Mennonites, and Quakers. As long as volunteers were relied on, this posed no problem other than bringing upon the conscientious objectors the scorn of their more militant neighbors. When **conscription** was adopted, however, the opposing governments had to find a way to deal with pacifists.

The Union had to address the issue of conscientious objectors more than the Confederacy, because the bulk of pacifist religious groups lived in the North. The **U.S. Congress** was reluctant to pass a bill exempting religious sects from military service for fear of creating abuse in the system. An alternative was to have local conscription boards and **Abraham Lincoln** simply provide draft exemptions on an individual basis. This kept many conscientious objectors out of the **army**, while others agreed to serve in such noncombat roles as hospital nurses or stewards, paid **commutation** fees, or hired **substitutes** (the last two measures were not that popular because payment was seen as blood money). In December 1863, Secretary of War **Edwin Stanton paroled** all conscientious objectors, and two months later Congress made provisions for any conscientious objector who was drafted to be put in a noncombat position or be allowed to pay a $300 fee to be used for the relief of sick and wounded soldiers.

The Confederate government addressed the issue of conscientious objectors more swiftly than its Union counterpart. The Conscription Act of April 1862 did not make provisions for objectors, but some individual states did allow them to take noncombat positions. When the draft law was revised in October, specific provisions were made to exempt those religious sects that clearly were pacifist in nature as long as they provided a substitute or paid a $500 exemption fee (Southern pacifists looked upon this fee with the same disdain as the Northerners, and it was finally abandoned).

CONSCRIPTION. The first military draft law in the United States was the April 1862 Conscription Act passed by the **Confederate Congress**. All of America's previous wars had been fought entirely by volunteers, because people believed conscription was an infringement on personal liberty. By 1862, however, both the Confederate and Union armies were facing manpower shortages. In April, the Confederate Congress passed the first conscription law, which made all white males between 18 and 35 eligible for the draft. This was changed in subsequent laws to include those between 17 and 50. The Union enacted its first conscription act in March 1863, making all white men between 18 and 35 eligible for service.

Both sides provided for the exemption of men whose work was considered vital to the war effort. **Commutations** also were provided, as was the hiring of **substitutes** to serve in the place of the man who was drafted. Both sides also eventually made provisions for the exemption of certain religious **conscientious objectors**.

In the Union **army**, only about 6 percent of those men who were conscripted actually served. Conscription mainly was seen as a way to induce men to volunteer, since there was much stigma attached to being a draftee. The conscription acts were very unpopular on both sides. People viewed them as unfair, since so many of the wealthier or politically connected men were able to avoid service by taking advantage of the many loopholes in the law. In the North, there were bloody **draft riots**, particularly the 1863 **New York City Draft Riot**.

CONSTITUTIONAL UNION PARTY. In 1860, the United States was splitting apart over **slavery** and other issues, and the **election of 1860** was seen as the last opportunity to settle the differences peacefully. The **Democratic Party** split into Northern and Southern parties and nominated **Stephen A. Douglas** and **John C. Breckinridge**, respectively, while the **Republican Party** nominated **Abraham Lincoln**. The **border states** realized that if war broke out, their territory would be the battlefield. In an attempt to prevent disunion by giving the nation a compromise candidate, border state politicians formed the Constitutional Union Party and nominated **John Bell** of **Tennessee**. To attract as many voters as possible, Bell stood on a vague platform, calling for the people to support the Union, obey the law, and uphold the Constitution. He and his running mate, **Edward Everett**, carried only the border states of Tennessee, **Kentucky**, and **Virginia**. Lincoln won the election, largely because the moderate vote was split between Bell and Douglas.

CONTRABANDS. Use of the term *contraband* for fugitive slaves began in May 1861. Union Maj. Gen. **Benjamin F. Butler** was stationed at **Fort Monroe** on the Virginia Peninsula and refused to return slaves who had fled into Union lines to their masters. In defending his actions, Butler declared that the runaways had been used to build Confederate fortifications and therefore were "contraband of war." There was no general policy in the Union **army** dealing with such runaways until the **confiscation acts** were passed, which freed slaves who were being used by the Confederates for military purposes.

CONY, SAMUEL (1811–1870) USA. A native of **Maine**, Cony graduated from Brown University and became a legislator, judge, and state treasurer. He was a **War Democrat** during the Civil War and was reelected to the legislature in 1862 after a 23-year absence. In 1864, Cony was elected governor and strongly supported the Union war effort. After being reelected twice, Cony retired from politics because of poor health.

COOK, GEORGE SMITH (1819–1902) CSA. A native of **Connecticut**, Cook moved to **New Orleans, Louisiana**, as a boy and learned the trade of daguerreotype photography. He then opened a gallery in **Charleston, South Carolina**, and became such a respected photographer that **Mathew Brady** hired him in 1851 to manage his New York City studio. Over the next several years, Cook opened his own galleries in New York City; Philadelphia, Pennsylvania; and Chicago, Illinois; but eventually moved back to Charleston.

Cook's Civil War photographic career began in February 1861 when he made a popular photograph of Maj. **Robert Anderson** and his staff at **Fort Sumter**. Over the next months, he made many photographs of soldiers and installations and was hired by **P. G. T. Beauregard** to make photographic copies of important maps and drawings. During the war, Cook made two famous photographs (one while under fire) of Union warships attacking Charleston's defenses. These rare images depict U.S. **monitors** firing at Fort Moultrie and the actual explosion of a shell inside Fort Sumter. Cook remained in Charleston for the war's duration and made a profit by requiring that his customers' payments be made in gold. For his work around Charleston, he became known as "the photographer of the Confederacy."

After the war, Cook moved to **Richmond, Virginia**, and opened galleries in other cities as well. After his death, his sons continued as photographers and amassed a huge collection of images. The Cook Collection of more than 10,000 photographs (including hundreds of Civil War personalities) later was donated to Richmond's Valentine Museum.

COOK, JOHN (1825–1910) USA. A native of **Illinois**, Cook was the son of a congressman, after whom Chicago's Cook County is named, and the grandson of a governor. He was educated at a local college and became a merchant in Springfield. Before the Civil War, Cook was elected mayor of Springfield, county sheriff, and state quartermaster.

In April 1861, Cook was appointed colonel of the 7th Illinois Infantry. For valor while in command of a **brigade** at **Fort Donelson**, he was promoted to brigadier general of volunteers in March 1862. Afterward, Cook served against the **Sioux uprising** in **Minnesota** and then took command of the District of Illinois. He remained at this post until war's end and was **brevetted** major general of volunteers for his war service.

After the war, Cook was elected to the Illinois legislature and became the Indian agent on the Rosebud Reservation in South Dakota.

COOK, PHILIP (1817–1894) CSA. A native of **Georgia**, Cook attended several colleges before the Civil War and served in the **Seminole Wars**.

He had a law practice when the Civil War began but left it in April 1861 to join the 4th Georgia as a private.

Cook quickly was promoted to lieutenant and regimental adjutant. He served in that capacity through the **Seven Days Campaign** with the **Army of Northern Virginia** and was severely wounded at **Malvern Hill**. In August 1862, Cook was elected lieutenant colonel and won acclaim for his actions at **South Mountain** and **Antietam**. In November, he was promoted to regimental colonel. After fighting at **Fredericksburg**, Cook was wounded in the leg at **Chancellorsville**. He recuperated in Georgia and while there served one month in the state senate.

In June 1864, Cook was given command of **George Dole's** old **brigade** and was promoted to brigadier general in August. His small brigade served under **Jubal A. Early** in **Philip Sheridan's Shenandoah Valley Campaign** and then participated in the attack on **Fort Stedman** in the waning days of the **Petersburg Campaign**. In the latter battle, Cook was wounded in the arm, and he was captured when he was left behind in the hospital when **Robert E. Lee** evacuated **Richmond** and Petersburg.

After the war, Cook returned to Georgia and was elected to the **U.S. Congress** in 1873. After serving there for 10 years, he became Georgia's secretary of state.

COOKE, JAY (1821–1905) USA. A native of **Ohio**, Cooke left home when he was 14 and became associated with a prominent Philadelphia, Pennsylvania, banking and investment firm when he was 22. During the **Mexican War**, he helped finance loans with the federal government to pay for the war, and by the beginning of the Civil War, he had amassed a fortune.

Cooke became a close associate of **Salmon Chase**, **Abraham Lincoln's** first secretary of the treasury. In 1861, he approached Chase with a proposal for him to sell bonds on a commission basis to help **finance** the war. Chase agreed, and Cooke gained a monopoly on the sale of government bonds and became one of the war's main financiers. Although frequently accused of improper profiteering, he was hugely successful in the endeavor. In just the first half of 1865, Cooke's agency sold more than $850,000,000 in bonds.

COOKE, JOHN ESTEN (1830–1886) CSA. A native of **Virginia**, Cooke was a cousin of Confederate Gen. **John Rogers Cooke** and a nephew of Union Gen. **Philip St. George Cooke**, and was a lawyer-turned-author who wrote romantic stories about the South prior to the Civil War. He

COOKE, JOHN ROGERS (1833–1891) CSA • 331

joined the **Confederate army** as a private in the Richmond Howitzers but quickly joined the staff of his cousin's husband, **J. E. B. Stuart**. Throughout the war, Cooke was associated with the dashing Confederate cavalry, and he used his wartime experiences to pen numerous books and articles. Only months after **Thomas J. "Stonewall" Jackson's** death, he wrote the biography *The Life of Stonewall Jackson*. After the war, Cooke wrote additional articles and five more books related to the war. Although more romantic than accurate, Cooke's writings became popular reading.

COOKE, JOHN ROGERS (1833–1891) CSA. A native of **Missouri**, Cooke was the son of Union Gen. **Philip St. George Cooke** and a cousin of Confederate writer **John Esten Cooke**. After graduating from Harvard University, he entered the **U.S. Army** as a lieutenant in the 8th U.S. Infantry. Cooke served at various southwestern posts and in 1855 became future Confederate general **J. E. B. Stuart's** brother-in-law when Stuart married Cooke's sister.

The Civil War broke apart the family, with John Rogers Cooke and Stuart joining the Confederacy, while Philip St. George Cooke remained loyal to the Union. The younger Cooke resigned his commission and in the spring of 1861 accepted a lieutenant's commission in the **Confederate army**. After service at **First Manassas** under Brig. Gen. **Theophilus H. Holmes**, he raised a **company** of light artillerymen. In February 1862, Cooke was promoted to major and became chief of **artillery** for the **Department of North Carolina**. He was elected colonel of the 27th North Carolina in April and joined what became the **Army of Northern Virginia**. Cooke led the **regiment** at **Seven Pines** and throughout the **Battle of Cedar Mountain**, and the **Seven Days**, and **Second Manassas Campaigns**.

After performing admirably at **Antietam**, where he was wounded while sealing the Union breakthrough at "Bloody Lane," Cooke was promoted to brigadier general in November 1862. At **Fredericksburg**, he commanded a **North Carolina brigade** at Marye's Heights' famous stone wall and suffered another wound. Afterward, Cooke fought at **Chancellorsville**, **Gettysburg**, and **Bristoe Station**, where he again was wounded. He sustained yet another wound in the **Wilderness** but recovered in time to participate in the **Petersburg Campaign**. After surviving seven wounds during the war, Cooke finally was surrendered at **Appomattox**.

Cooke became director of the Virginia State Penitentiary after the war and became very active in veterans' affairs. Time finally healed the breach that war created between him and his father.

COOKE, PHILIP ST. GEORGE (1809–1895) USA. A native of **Virginia**, Cooke was the father of Confederate Brig. Gen. **John Rogers Cooke**, the uncle of **John Esten Cooke**, and the father-in-law of Confederate Maj. Gen. **J. E. B. Stuart**. He graduated from **West Point** in 1827 and had a distinguished antebellum military career that included service in the Black Hawk War, **Mexican War**, and **Utah Expedition**. Cooke also wrote a book on cavalry **tactics**, helped explore the West, and was an official observer of an Italian war. Colonel of the 2nd U.S. Dragoons when the Civil War began, Cooke remained loyal to the Union, as did one daughter and a son-in-law. However, his son John Rogers, nephew John Esten, two daughters, and son-in-law Stuart joined the Confederacy.

In November 1861, Cooke was promoted to brigadier general in the **U.S. Army** and was given command of a cavalry **brigade** at **Washington, D.C.** In January 1862, he was placed in command of the **Army of the Potomac's** Cavalry Reserve and during the **Peninsula Campaign** led a **division** that pursued his son-in-law during **Stuart's Ride** around Maj. Gen. **George B. McClellan's** army. After fighting in the **Seven Days Campaign**, Cooke saw no further field service but instead served on court-martial duty and in other administrative positions. He was **brevetted** major general of regulars in 1865 and retired from the **army** in 1875 after more than 50 years of service.

COOL SPRING, VIRGINIA, BATTLE OF (JULY 17–18, 1864). Jubal A. Early's Washington Raid in the summer of 1864 ended with the Confederates retreating back into **Virginia**. The Federals slowly pursued and on July 17 engaged the enemy when Union cavalry under Brig. Gen. **Alfred N. A. Duffié** forced its way through Snicker's Gap. The next day, Col. Joseph Thoburn took his Union cavalry **division** across the Shenandoah River to flank Early out of his position. Confederate Maj. Gen. **Robert Rodes** placed his division at the Cool Spring farm on a ridge overlooking the ford and crushed Thoburn's right flank after he crossed the river. The Federals managed to repulse three attacks before they were able to retreat across the river at dusk. In the clash, the Federals lost 422 men (some of whom drowned while retreating across the river), while the Confederates counted 397 casualties.

COOPER, DOUGLAS HANCOCK (1815–1879) CSA. Born in **Mississippi**, Cooper attended the University of Virginia but did not graduate. A planter when the **Mexican War** began, he became a captain in **Jefferson Davis's** Mississippi Rifles. Cooper was serving as **Indian** agent to the Choctaw Nation in **Indian Territory** when the Civil War began and was able to secure the support of the Five Civilized Tribes for the Confederacy.

In the spring of 1861, Cooper was appointed colonel of the 1st Choctaw and Chickasaw Mounted Rifles. This made him the only non-Indian to command a Confederate Indian unit, although the Chickasaws adopted him into their tribe. In late 1861, Cooper fought a pro-Union Indian and fugitive slave force at **Chusto-Talasah** and **Chustenahlah** and later commanded the Indian troops at **Pea Ridge**. After that battle, Cooper and Brig. Gen. **Albert Pike** clashed, partly because both wanted to be superintendent of Indian affairs. After Cooper was given command of the Confederate forces north of the Canadian River in June 1862, he informed his old friend Jefferson Davis that Pike was insane. This helped Davis to accept Pike's resignation from the **army** and opened the way for Cooper to be named commander of the Indian Territory and Indian superintendent in September 1862 (although the Senate at first rejected him on grounds of alcoholism). That same month, Cooper led his Indians at the **Battle of Newtonia, Missouri**, and the following month fought at **Old Fort Wayne**.

Although Cooper was relieved of command of the Indian Territory in January 1863 by Brig. Gen. **William Steele**, he was promoted to brigadier general in June. After fighting at **Honey Springs**, Cooper made more political enemies when his Indians lobbied to get him named as Steele's replacement. Steele was replaced, but not by Cooper, who was given command of the Indians in January 1864 but had to serve under Brig. Gen. **Samuel Bell Maxey**. Cooper's supporters continued to lobby for his promotion to Indian Territory command and superintendent, but Gen. **Edmund Kirby Smith** opposed it on the grounds Cooper could not be both an effective field commander and superintendent. Finally, in February 1865, Cooper was successful and was named commander of the Indian Territory and Indian superintendent.

After the war, Cooper remained in the Indian Territory and worked to restore peace among the Indians.

COOPER, JAMES (1810–1863) USA. A native of **Maryland**, Cooper graduated from **Pennsylvania's** Washington College and studied law under **Thaddeus Stevens** in Gettysburg. After becoming a lawyer, he was elected as a **Whig** to the U.S. House of Representatives in 1838 and served two terms. In the 1840s, Cooper was elected to the Pennsylvania legislature four times (serving one year as Speaker), served as state attorney general, and finally was elected U.S. Senator in 1849. As a senator, Cooper helped write the **Compromise of 1850** and opposed the **Kansas-Nebraska Act**.

Because of Cooper's political influence and southern birth, **Abraham Lincoln** appointed him a brigadier general of volunteers in May 1861 with permission to raise pro-Union troops in Maryland. Cooper led a

brigade in **Stonewall Jackson's Shenandoah Valley Campaign** and in the autumn of 1862 was put in command of **Camp Chase, Ohio**. He died there in March 1863.

COOPER, JOSEPH ALEXANDER (1823–1910) USA. Born in **Kentucky**, Cooper moved to **Tennessee** as a boy. After briefly serving in the 4th Tennessee during the **Mexican War**, he returned to East Tennessee and became a farmer. A **Whig**, Cooper was a delegate to the pro-Union convention in Knoxville in 1861. He then recruited men in his area to fight the Confederates and entered the Union **army** in August 1861 when he was elected a captain in the 1st Tennessee (Union).

After **skirmishing** in Tennessee and fighting at **Mill Springs, Kentucky**, Cooper was appointed colonel of the 6th Tennessee (Union) in May 1862 and led the **regiment** in the **Army of the Cumberland** in the Battle of **Stones River** and in the **Chickamauga**, and **Chattanooga Campaigns**. After temporarily commanding **brigades** in the **Army of the Ohio** and Army of the Cumberland in 1863 and 1864, he often led a brigade in the Army of the Ohio's XXIII Corps during the **Atlanta Campaign**. Cooper was promoted to brigadier general of volunteers in July 1864. For the rest of the war, he led his brigade and sometimes acted as a **division** commander, fighting in the **Franklin and Nashville** and **Carolinas Campaigns**.

Cooper was **brevetted** major general of volunteers for his gallantry at Nashville and left the army in 1866. After the war, he was collector of internal revenue at Knoxville for 10 years before moving to **Kansas** and becoming a farmer.

COOPER, SAMUEL (1798–1876) CSA. A native of **New Jersey**, Cooper was the son of a Revolutionary War veteran and graduated from **West Point** in 1815. For the next 13 years, he served in the **artillery** but in 1828 was assigned to a general's staff. Cooper continued to serve on staff assignments, rose to captain (with the **brevet** rank of major), and became an assistant adjutant general in the War Department. After seeing some combat in the **Seminole Wars**, he was promoted to lieutenant colonel and brevet colonel during the **Mexican War**. In 1852, Cooper was promoted to colonel and was appointed the **U.S. Army's** adjutant general. In that position, he became close friends with Secretary of War **Jefferson Davis** and increasingly supported the South on issues, perhaps because he married a **Virginia** woman.

In March 1861, Cooper resigned his commission, and days later was named by Davis to be the Confederacy's adjutant general with the rank of brigadier general (thus, during his career, Cooper served as adjutant general for both of the opposing armies). In August, he was named the ranking full general in the **Confederate army**, and for the duration of the war he remained in **Richmond, Virginia**, supervising the **army's** administrative details. Cooper became very unpopular with many officers and politicians because of his close relationship with Davis and his noncommittal and indecisive nature. He was viewed by many officers to be no more than a clerk and Davis's rubber stamp because he seemed content to let Davis handle the important military decisions while he routed orders, handled pay, oversaw inspections, and kept other records. Cooper managed to save much of the War Department's records at the end of the war and turned them over to federal authorities. He then retired to Virginia and became a farmer.

COPELAND, JOSEPH TARR (1813–1893) USA. A native of **Maine**, Copeland was a Harvard University graduate who studied law under Daniel Webster. Moving to **Michigan**, he became a prominent state supreme court judge and sawmill owner and had just retired from the bench when the Civil War began.

In August 1861, Copeland entered Union service as lieutenant colonel of the 1st Michigan Cavalry and served in **Stonewall Jackson's Shenandoah Valley Campaign**. Appointed colonel of the 5th Michigan Cavalry in August 1862, he served with that **regiment** in the **Army of Virginia** at **Second Manassas** before being commissioned brigadier general of volunteers in November. For the next several months, Copeland commanded a Michigan cavalry **brigade** in **Washington, D.C.**, and then was assigned to command the draft depots at Annapolis, Maryland, and Pittsburgh, Pennsylvania. He ended the war in command of **Alton Prison**.

Copeland resigned his commission in November 1865 and returned to Michigan, where he operated a hotel.

COPPERHEADS. This was the nickname given to those Northern **Democrats** known as **Peace Democrats**, who opposed **Abraham Lincoln's** vigorous war policy and preferred a negotiated settlement. The Copperheads were most active in the old northwest states of **Illinois, Indiana**, and **Ohio** and operated such clandestine organizations as the **Knights of the Golden Circle** and **Sons of Liberty**. Because of their antiwar activities and the perceived threat that they might aid the Confederacy, Lincoln's administration took strong measures to combat the Copperheads. Members were arrested, the right of **habeas corpus** was suspended, and their presses were censored. A leading Copperhead, **Clement L. Vallandigham**, was arrested and exiled into Confederate territory. These Peace Democrats succeeded in adopting a plank in the 1864 platform calling for a negotiated settlement with the Confederates, but presidential candidate **George B. McClellan** repudiated it.

CORCORAN LEGION. In November 1862, Brig. Gen. **Michael Corcoran**, an Irish native, raised a **brigade** of **New York regiments** composed mostly of Irish immigrants. Also known as the Irish Legion, the brigade consisted of the 155th, 164th, 170th, and 182nd New York regiments. The **legion** first served in the Union VII Corps and helped defend **Suffolk, Virginia**, against Confederate Lt. Gen. **James Longstreet's** siege in the spring of 1863. Afterward, it was transferred to the **Washington, D.C.**, defenses, near which Corcoran was killed in a riding accident in December 1863. In May 1864, the legion was transferred to the **Army of the Potomac's** II Corps' 2nd Division. It fought in the **Overland Campaign** and suffered particularly heavy casualties in the disastrous charge at **Cold Harbor**.

CORCORAN, MICHAEL (1827–1863) USA. Born in Ireland, Corcoran was the son of a British officer who became an Irish constable. However, because of the British repression of Ireland, he resigned his position and immigrated to New York City in 1849. Corcoran worked in the post office and city government and rose from private to colonel of the 69th New York Militia. Because of his strong Irish sentiment, he refused to march his **regiment** in the parade honoring the 1860 visit of the Prince of Wales. Corcoran was court-martialed as a result, but the Civil War brought a dismissal of the charges since his regiment was needed for Union service.

At **First Manassas**, Corcoran was wounded in the arm and was captured. He then was chosen by the Confederates to be used for reprisals if the United States carried out a threat to execute Confederate **privateers**. Finally **exchanged** in August 1862, Corcoran was promoted to brigadier general of volunteers and raised a mostly Irish **brigade** that became known as the **Corcoran Legion**. He then was sent to southeast **Virginia** and commanded a **division** in the siege of **Suffolk, Virginia**. Corcoran was transferred to the **Washington, D.C.**, defenses after the **Gettysburg Campaign** and there took command of another division. On December 22, 1863, while riding with fellow Irishman Brig. Gen. **Thomas Meagher** near Fairfax Court House, Virginia, Corcoran was killed when his horse stumbled and fell on him.

CORDUROY ROAD. Civil War roads became notorious for turning into quagmires during rain. To help make such roads passable, armies often corduroyed them. This was a practice of laying small saplings and branches across the roadbed to give support to wagons, **artillery**, and infantrymen.

CORINTH, MISSISSIPPI, BATTLE OF (OCTOBER 3–4, 1862). When Confederate Gen. **Braxton Bragg** moved north in the 1862 **Kentucky Campaign**, two Confederate commands were left behind in **Mississippi** to prevent Union forces there from being sent to reinforce **Ten-**

nessee or **Kentucky**. Major General **Earl Van Dorn** commanded approximately 7,000 men at **Holly Springs**, while Maj. Gen. **Sterling Price** had about 17,000 at **Tupelo**. Van Dorn was the senior officer and wanted to attack the Union supply lines in western Tennessee, but, instead, Price attacked Union Maj. Gen. **William Rosecrans** at **Iuka, Mississippi**, in September. When Price was forced to withdraw, he joined Van Dorn at Ripley.

Now with about 22,000 men, Van Dorn decided to attack the important rail center at Corinth. Capturing it would allow him to use the **railroads** to launch his own invasion into Tennessee or at least prevent Rosecrans from sending troops to oppose Bragg. Rosecrans was defending Corinth with approximately 23,000 men but had additional support in the area. Thus, speed and surprise were vital if Van Dorn was to capture the town before reinforcements could join the garrison.

On the morning of October 3, 1862, Van Dorn attacked the town from the north and northwest and slowly drove the Union defenders back two miles into the main defenses. In blistering heat, the Confederates became exhausted as they advanced, while the Union defenders showed a more compact front the farther back they fell. A final Confederate assault in late afternoon was canceled when Van Dorn's subordinates complained of their men's exhaustion and of a lack of water and ammunition. Rosecrans used the delay to strengthen his line, centered on a small fort named Battery Robinett that lay just northwest of town.

Although planned for early morning, Van Dorn's attack did not begin until about 10:00 A.M. Brigadier General **Louis Hébert**, whose **division** was to lead the attack, reported being too sick to continue. By the time his replacement was ready, precious hours had passed. Some of the Confederates broke through Rosecrans's line and actually entered Corinth, but the main assault was stopped at Battery Robinett. There, Van Dorn suffered heavy casualties in a series of **frontal attacks**. His men once briefly captured the position but soon were driven out by a counterattack. Realizing nothing further could be gained, Van Dorn withdrew from Corinth and retreated to Holly Springs.

In the battle, Van Dorn reported losing approximately 4,800 men (nearly half of whom were taken **prisoner**), while Rosecrans lost about 2,400 men. Van Dorn placed much of the blame for his defeat on division commander Maj. Gen. **Mansfield Lovell**, who failed to support the brief breakthrough and generally performed poorly.

CORINTH, MISSISSIPPI, SIEGE OF (APRIL 29–MAY 30, 1862). After the **Battle of Shiloh, Tennessee**, in April 1862, **P. G. T. Beauregard** withdrew the Confederate **army** to Corinth, Mississippi, a vital **railroad**

town 23 miles to the south. There, two important railroads intersected, the east-west Memphis & Charleston and the north-south Mobile & Ohio. On the Union side, Maj. Gen. **Henry Halleck** relieved **U. S. Grant** from command of the Union army and methodically built up a massive force at Shiloh to capture the important Confederate town.

An intellectual and **engineer**, Halleck slowly built up his force and then on April 29 began his advance. Fearful of a counterattack, he plodded along through muddy conditions and frequently stopped to erect fortifications. Beauregard also gathered reinforcements, including Maj. Gen. **Earl Van Dorn's Army of the West**, and eventually had about 70,000 men to stop Halleck's 120,000. Twice, Beauregard attempted to destroy elements of Halleck's command. In early May, Van Dorn was ordered to attack Halleck's isolated left wing east of Corinth near Farmington, and Maj. Gen. **Leonidas Polk's corps** massed north of town on the Mobile & Ohio railroad to strike the Union right flank. When Van Dorn proved unable to accomplish his mission, Polk's attack was called off. Each side lost about 1,000 men during these maneuvers. During the Union advance there was also frequent **skirmishing**, but by May 28, Halleck finally was close enough to begin bombarding the Confederate defenses north and east of town.

By this time, Beauregard's army was seriously weakened by disease, partly caused by a drought affecting water quantity and quality. During the monthlong Union advance, nearly as many Confederates had died from disease in Corinth as had been killed at Shiloh (Halleck also suffered, and by the end of May he had only 95,000 effectives). Beauregard also feared that Halleck might swing south of Corinth to cut his supply lines. As a result, Beauregard decided to evacuate Corinth. On the night of May 29–30, he skillfully evacuated the town without the enemy becoming aware of it. To cover the sound of the withdrawal, Beauregard shuttled empty trains back and forth in the rear, and troops cheered nonexisting reinforcements. Halleck was unaware of the evacuation until the morning of May 30, when Union troops spied smoke columns rising from abandoned Confederate supplies that had been burned. The Confederates safely reached Tupelo, Mississippi, on June 9. The siege did not enhance either commander's reputation. Halleck's performance confirmed that he was not bold enough to be a successful field commander, and **Jefferson Davis** was displeased that Beauregard abandoned such a vital town without a fight.

CORNFIELD AT BATTLE OF ANTIETAM, MARYLAND (SEPTEMBER 17, 1862). *See* ANTIETAM, MARYLAND, CAMPAIGN AND BATTLE OF.

CORPS. Next to an **army**, a corps (CORE) was the largest military organization used in the Civil War and usually comprised two to four **divisions** and included its own **artillery** force. Both armies established corps in March 1862. Corps generally were commanded by a major general in the Union army and by a lieutenant general in the **Confederate army**. Officially, corps were given numerical designations, and the Union army adopted **corps badges** to help identify a soldier's corps affiliation. The Union army used these numerical designations to identify their corps (I Corps, II Corps, etc.), while the Confederates normally referred to a corps by its commander's name (Longstreet's corps, Hardee's corps, etc.).

CORPS BADGES. The **U.S. Army's** practice of using symbols to denote unit identity came of age in the Civil War. Early in the war, Maj. Gen. **Philip Kearny** mistakenly berated some officers who he believed were in his **division**. To avoid future errors, Kearny ordered his officers to place small red flannel diamonds on their caps. This "Kearny Patch" was soon adopted by the enlisted men as well. When Maj. Gen. **Joseph Hooker** took command of the **Army of the Potomac**, he initiated an army-wide system of badges in March 1863 as a means to boost morale. Major General **Daniel Butterfield** designed the badges and gave each **corps** a different symbol. The symbols adopted for the U.S. Army's corps were as follows: I (disk), II (trefoil), III (diamond), IV (triangle), V (Maltese cross), VI (standard cross), VII (crescent and star), VIII (six-pointed star), IX (shield with anchor and cannon), X (square bastion), XI (crescent), XII (none), XIII (none), XIV (acorn), XV (cartridge box within a diamond), XVI (Maltese cross variation), XVII (arrow), XVIII (trefoil cross), XIX (Maltese cross variation), XX (five-pointed star), XXI (none), XXII (pentagon cross), XXIII (shield), XXIV (heart), and XXV (diamond on a square). Within each corps, the 1st Division was to be red, 2nd Division white, 3rd Division blue, 4th Division green, and 5th Division orange.

The badge usually was made of flannel, but metal sometimes was used, and it was normally worn on the hat or left shirt front with the **regiment's** number pinned in the middle. The badge concept spread to the western Union armies in 1864, but the **Confederate army** never adopted such badges.

CORPS D'AFRIQUE. In late 1862, Union Maj. Gen. **Benjamin F. Butler** mustered the 1st, 2nd, and 3rd **Louisiana Native Guards** into Union service in **New Orleans, Louisiana**. Major General **Nathaniel Banks** reorganized these **black troops** in July 1863 in an attempt to create a **division**. The **regiments** then were renamed the 1st, 2nd, and 3rd Regiments of the Corps D'Afrique (KOR-dah-FREEK). The 2nd Regiment spent the rest of the war guarding Ship Island in the Gulf of Mexico, while the 1st and 3rd Regiments participated in the 1864 **Red River Campaign**, performed garrison duty in **Louisiana**, and fought at **Fort Blakely, Alabama**, during the **Mobile Campaign**.

CORRICK'S FORD, VIRGINIA, BATTLE OF (JULY 13, 1861). *See* CARRICK'S FORD, VIRGINIA, BATTLE OF.

CORSE, JOHN MURRAY (1835–1893) USA. Born in **Pennsylvania**, Corse moved to **Iowa** as a boy. After attending, but not graduating from, **West Point** in the 1850s, he became a lawyer.

Corse entered Union service in July 1861 as major of the 6th Iowa but joined Maj. Gen. **John Pope's** staff for operations against **New Madrid and Island No. 10**. He was promoted to lieutenant colonel of the 6th Iowa in April 1862 and fought well at **Corinth**. Promoted to colonel in March 1863, Corse distinguished himself again in the **Vicksburg Campaign** and was promoted to brigadier general of volunteers in August 1863. After being wounded by a spent ball at **Missionary Ridge**, he was made Maj. Gen. **William T. Sherman's** inspector general for the **Atlanta Campaign**. In July 1864, Corse was given a **division** command and won fame in October when he was sent by Sherman to defend strategic **Allatoona Pass** against Confederate Gen. **John Bell Hood**. In very bloody fighting, he again was wounded and lost one-third of his men while successfully defending the pass against a Confederate **division**. In exaggerated bravado, Corse wired Sherman, "I am short of a cheekbone, and one ear, but am able to whip all hell yet" (Warner, *Generals in Blue*, 95). After leading his division through the **March to the Sea** and the **Carolinas Campaign**, he turned down a lieutenant colonel's commission in the regular **army** and left the service in April 1866 as a **brevet** major general of volunteers (awarded for his actions at Allatoona Pass).

After serving as internal revenue collector of Chicago, Illinois, Corse moved to Boston, Massachusetts, and became chairman of the state's **Democratic** committee and the city's postmaster.

CORSE, MONTGOMERY DENT (1816–1895) CSA. A native of **Virginia**, Corse served as a captain in the 1st Virginia Volunteers during the **Mexican War**. After mining gold in **California** and commanding a local militia **company**, he returned to Virginia and entered the banking business.

Prior to the Civil War, Corse organized a Virginia militia company named the Old Dominion Rifles. He was commanding a battalion of militiamen in 1861 and was appointed assistant adjutant general in Alexandria, Virginia. Commissioned colonel of the 17th Virginia, Corse fought at **Blackburn's Ford** and throughout the **Peninsula** and **Seven**

Days Campaigns. He was praised for his service and was slightly wounded at **Second Manassas** while in temporary command of a **brigade** in the **Army of Northern Virginia** and then again two weeks later at Boonsborough. At **Antietam**, Corse was wounded a third time in the foot and was captured, but a Confederate counterattack soon rescued him. Both **James Longstreet** and **Robert E. Lee** praised his conduct, and in November 1862 he was promoted to brigadier general and was given command of **George Pickett's** old Virginia brigade.

Left on garrison duty around **Richmond, Virginia**, Corse's brigade missed the **Gettysburg Campaign**, but it did see service at **Chickamauga** and **Knoxville**. He was sent back to Virginia in May 1864 and fought at the **Wilderness, Second Drewry's Bluff**, and **New Bern, North Carolina**. After serving in the **Petersburg Campaign** that winter, Corse again performed admirably in April 1865 when his brigade maintained its integrity at **Five Forks** while most of Lee's right wing was crushed. During the **Appomattox Campaign**, he was captured on April 6 at **Sailor's Creek**.

Corse was released from **Fort Warren, Massachusetts**, in August 1865 and returned to Virginia to resume banking. He lost his eyesight later in life when the ceiling of the Virginia capitol building collapsed on him and other spectators.

CORYDON, INDIANA, BATTLE OF (JULY 9, 1863). In July 1863, Confederate **John Hunt Morgan's Ohio Raid** began when Hunt led 2,500 cavalrymen into **Kentucky**. After several clashes with the enemy, Hunt disobeyed orders and crossed the Ohio River into **Indiana**, causing panic in the area. On July 9, Richard Hunt (the commander's brother) led a detachment of raiders north from Mauckport, Indiana, toward Corydon. Just south of the latter town, the Confederates engaged and captured most of the militiamen who were there under the command of Col. Lewis Jordan. After **paroling** his **prisoners**, Hunt looted stores and took up ransom money from citizens and then continued the raid toward **Ohio**. In the raid on Corydon, Richard Hunt lost 51 men, while Jordan suffered 360 casualties, almost all of whom were taken prisoner.

COSBY, GEORGE BLAKE (1830–1909) CSA. Born into a prominent **Kentucky** family, Cosby graduated from **West Point** in 1852. After being wounded in 1854 while fighting with the cavalry against **Indians** on the frontier, he served as an instructor at West Point before being sent to **Texas** to confront Indians once again.

In March 1861, Cosby offered his services to the Confederacy even though he was still a **U.S. Army** officer. His offer was accepted in April, and he was appointed a captain of cavalry. One day after being promoted to captain in the U.S. Army in May, Cosby resigned that commission. After being promoted to major, he became Brig. Gen. **Simon B. Buckner's** assistant adjutant general in October 1861. At **Fort Donelson** in February 1862, it was Cosby who carried messages between Buckner and **U. S. Grant** arranging the fort's surrender. After being held in several **prisons**, he was **exchanged** in August 1862. Promoted to lieutenant colonel, Cosby became Buckner's chief of staff for the **Department of the Gulf** and in April 1863 was promoted to brigadier general.

Cosby was given a **brigade** of cavalry and served under Maj. Gen. **Earl Van Dorn** in **Tennessee**, where he was commended for his conduct at **Thompson's Station**. During the **Vicksburg Campaign**, he served under **Joseph E. Johnston** and saw some service around Canton and the Big Black River. Despite what seemed to have been competent service, Cosby's officers and men thought little of his leadership, and in December 1863 he was relieved of command. It took eight months before he received another. In August 1864, Cosby was given a small cavalry brigade in East Tennessee, which he took to the **Shenandoah Valley** for service under **Jubal A. Early** until November. For the remainder of the war, he served in mountainous East Tennessee and southwest **Virginia**, where he opposed raids by Union Maj. Gen. **George Stoneman**.

After the war, Cosby moved to **California**, where he farmed and served on West Point's Board of Visitors. Racked by pain brought on by a stroke, he committed suicide in 1909.

COTTON DIPLOMACY. When the Civil War began, the Confederacy believed it could pressure Great Britain and France into recognizing its independence or at least break the Union **blockade** by withholding cotton exports. It was hoped that the lack of cotton would so threaten the countries' textile industries that action would have to be taken to avoid economic disaster. This so-called Cotton Diplomacy failed because there was a large surplus of cotton already on hand from the 1860 bumper crop, and the British and French quickly made up for later shortfalls with cotton from Egypt, India, and Brazil. A better policy might have been to ship as much cotton as possible to Europe early in the war to establish credit for loans and weapons purchases.

COTTONCLADS. This was the nickname given to small Confederate warships that used cotton for protection rather than iron plating or additional wood. The Confederates used 28 of these odd ships, some with cotton bales stacked around vital parts, others with cotton stuffed between two wooden bulkheads. Most of the vessels only carried one cannon and were fitted with an iron ram on the bow. Cottonclads were used to defend **Forts Jackson**

and St. Philip as part of the **River Defense Fleet** and saw combat at **Charleston, South Carolina**; **Plymouth, North Carolina**; and **Mobile Bay, Alabama**. The most famous cottonclad was the *Queen of the West*.

COUCH, DARIUS NASH (1822–1897) USA. A native of **New York**, Couch graduated from **West Point** in 1846. He fought with the **artillery** in the **Mexican** and **Seminole Wars**, earning a **brevet** for gallantry in the former, and accompanied a scientific expedition into Mexico sponsored by the Smithsonian Institution. After resigning his lieutenant's commission in 1855, Couch was engaged in the **Massachusetts** copper manufacturing business until the Civil War erupted.

In June 1861, Couch became colonel of the 7th Massachusetts and was promoted by his former West Point classmate **George B. McClellan** to brigadier general of volunteers in August. After leading a **brigade** in the **Army of the Potomac** from August 1861 to March 1862, he was given command of a **division** in the IV Corps and was praised for his actions during the **Peninsula Campaign**. Afterward, Couch tried to resign his commission because of illness, but McClellan refused to accept it. Instead, he was promoted to major general of volunteers in July 1862.

After leading a VI Corps division at **Second Manassas** and **Crampton's Gap**, Couch was given command of the II Corps in October 1862 and led it at **Fredericksburg** and **Chancellorsville**. Army politics then ended his career when he questioned whether **Joseph Hooker** was fit to lead the **army** and asked to be transferred out of his command. This criticism, plus his friendship with McClellan, seriously damaged his standing. After Chancellorsville, Couch was put in command of the **Department of the Susquehanna** in July 1863, and he led the **Pennsylvania** militia during the **Gettysburg Campaign**. He then was given a division in the **Army of the Ohio** in December 1864 and fought with distinction at **Nashville** and in the **Carolinas Campaign**.

After resigning from the army in May 1865, Couch unsuccessfully ran for governor in Massachusetts. He then moved to **Connecticut**, where he served as the state quartermaster general and adjutant general.

COUP-DE-MAIN. *Coup-de-main* (KOO-duh-MAHN) is a French military term that refers to a quick and strong surprise attack that captures an enemy's position.

COVE MOUNTAIN, VIRGINIA, BATTLE OF (MAY 10, 1864). As part of Lt. Gen. **U. S. Grant's** offensive **strategy** for May 1864, Brig. Gen. **George R. Crook** led a column of Union troops in southwestern **Virginia** to destroy the Virginia & Tennessee Railroad connecting **Tennessee** and Virginia. In conjunction with that raid, Brig. Gen. **William W. Averell**

was to lead 2,000 cavalrymen from Logan Court House, West Virginia, to destroy the enemy salt mines at Saltville, Virginia, and then join Crook's force.

Averell began his raid on May 5, but a few days later learned that Saltville was defended by Brig. Gen. **John Hunt Morgan's** cavalry. He then changed his objective to the lead mines at Wytheville and sent word to Crook that he would be delayed in joining him. Learning of the Federal plan, Morgan took his men from Saltville to reinforce Brig. Gen. **William E. "Grumble" Jones** at Wytheville. On May 10, Averell unsuccessfully attacked Jones, who was strongly positioned on Cove Mountain. Later that day, Morgan arrived, and with Jones he counterattacked and forced Averell to retreat. In the meantime, Crook had won the **Battle of Cloyd's Mountain** and withdrew back to **West Virginia**. Averell finally linked up with him on May 15. In the fight at Cove Mountain, total casualties are estimated at 300.

COVODE, JOHN (1808–1871) USA. A native of **Pennsylvania**, Covode was a self-made man. He worked his way from a blacksmith's apprentice to become a wool mill owner and **railroad** investor. Entering politics, Covode was elected to the state legislature and then to the **U.S. Congress** in 1854 as a **Whig**. Popularly known as "Honest John," he served four terms in Congress and became a **Republican**. In 1860, Covode gained national prominence by heading an investigation into allegations that President **James Buchanan** had used bribery to win the support of two congressmen for **Kansas's** proslavery Lecompton Constitution.

In December 1861, Covode was appointed to the **Committee on the Conduct of the War**. As a member of the **Radical Republicans**, he supported a vigorous war effort and the abolition of **slavery**. While on the committee, Covode participated in ruining the careers of officers deemed soft on the Rebellion while protecting those officers who were popular with the Radicals. He did not run for reelection in 1863 but won back his seat in 1866. Serving two terms, he introduced the 1867 impeachment resolution against President **Andrew Johnson**.

COWDIN, ROBERT (1805–1874) USA. A native of **Vermont**, Cowdin moved to **Massachusetts** and became a lumberman. He also joined the local militia and was serving as its colonel when the Civil War began.

In May 1861, Cowdin entered Union service as colonel of the 1st Massachusetts Infantry. He fought at **First Manassas**, where his horse was killed, and then with the **Army of the Potomac** through the **Peninsula**, **Seven Days**, and **Second Manassas Campaigns**. Cowdin was recommended for promotion because of his gallantry at **Williamsburg** and in

September 1862 was promoted to brigadier general of volunteers. For the next several months, he commanded a **division** in the **Washington, D.C.**, defenses. The Senate failed to confirm his promotion, however (perhaps because of his age), and his commission expired in March 1863. Cowdin settled in Massachusetts and became captain of a local **artillery company**.

COX, JACOB DOLSON (1828–1900) USA. Born in Montreal, Canada, Cox graduated from Oberlin College in 1851 and opened an **Ohio** law practice in 1853. As an **abolitionist**, he helped organize the state's **Republican Party** and was elected to the state senate in 1858.

In April 1861, Cox was appointed brigadier general of state troops. He entered Union service as a brigadier general of volunteers in May and served in western **Virginia** under **George B. McClellan**. Cox commanded the Kanawha Brigade from July to October 1861 and the District of Kanawha from October 1861 to March 1862. He temporarily led the **Kanawha Division** from September to October 1862 and commanded the **Army of the Potomac's** IX Corps at **Antietam**.

Although promoted to major general of volunteers in October 1862, Cox's commission was allowed to expire in March 1863 because of an overabundance of general grade officers. From April to the end of 1863, he commanded the District of Ohio and then in April 1864 was given a **division** in the **Army of the Ohio** and led it during the **Atlanta** and **Franklin and Nashville Campaigns**. Cox was reappointed a major general in December 1864 and commanded the XXIII Corps from March 1865 to war's end, during which time he won the **Battle of Wyse Fork** during the **Carolinas Campaign**.

After the war, Cox was elected governor of Ohio in 1866, but he failed to secure a renomination because of his support of President **Andrew Johnson's Reconstruction** policy and his less than enthusiastic support of black suffrage. Afterward, he served as President **U. S. Grant's** secretary of the interior (resigning in 1870 after clashing with Grant), one term in the **U.S. Congress**, and president of the University of Cincinnati.

COX, WILLIAM RUFFIN (1832–1919) CSA. Born in **North Carolina**, Cox moved as a child to **Tennessee**, where he graduated from Franklin College and the Lebanon Law School. After practicing law in Nashville, he moved back to North Carolina and became a planter.

A secessionist, Cox entered Confederate service in May 1861 as major of the 2nd North Carolina. The **regiment** served in **Virginia** and North Carolina over the next year before seeing bloody combat with the **Army of Northern Virginia** at **Gaines' Mill** and **Malvern Hill**. In

September 1862, Cox again entered heavy combat at **South Mountain** and at **Antietam's** "Bloody Lane." He took temporary command of the regiment after Antietam and was promoted to lieutenant colonel and then colonel about April 1863 (the exact dates of these commissions are questionable). While leading his regiment at **Chancellorsville**, Cox was wounded five times and earned praise from his superiors. He was out of action until the spring of 1864, when he again led the regiment during the **Overland Campaign**. At **Spotsylvania**, Cox performed admirably at the "Bloody Angle" and was praised by **Robert E. Lee**.

Promoted to brigadier general in June 1864, Cox took command of **Stephen D. Ramseur's** old **brigade** and led it in **Jubal A. Early's Washington Raid** and in **Philip Sheridan's Shenandoah Valley Campaign**. He again fought well, except at **Fisher's Hill**, where he became confused and led his brigade away from the fighting. After joining Lee for the **Petersburg Campaign**, Cox's brigade participated in the attack on **Fort Stedman** and claimed to have fired the last Confederate shots at **Appomattox**. A popular, competent officer, Cox was wounded eleven times in the war.

After the war, Cox served as a judge and was elected three times to the **U.S. Congress**.

COX'S PLANTATION, LOUISIANA, BATTLE OF (JULY 13, 1863). *See* BAYOU LAFOURCHE, LOUISIANA, BATTLE OF.

"CRACKER LINE." *See* CHATTANOOGA, TENNESSEE, CAMPAIGN; WAUHATCHIE, TENNESSEE, BATTLE OF.

CRAIG, JAMES (1817–1888) USA. Born in **Pennsylvania**, Craig moved to **Ohio** with his family and became a lawyer. In 1844, he moved again to **Missouri** and opened a practice near St. Joseph. After fighting in the **Mexican War** as a volunteer captain, Craig returned to Missouri and was elected to the state senate as a **Democrat**. In 1856, he was elected to the **U.S. Congress** and served two terms. Defeated for reelection, Craig then returned to his law practice.

In March 1862, **Abraham Lincoln** appointed Craig a brigadier general of volunteers to win Union support among the state's Democrats. He helped protect the western mail routes and was put in command of the District of Nebraska in October 1862. Craig resigned his commission in May 1863, but in May 1864, he accepted an appointment as brigadier general of the Missouri militia. He resigned that position in January 1865 and became a **railroad** executive.

CRAMPTON'S GAP, MARYLAND, BATTLE OF (SEPTEMBER 14, 1862). During the **Antietam Campaign**, **Stonewall Jackson** took part of **Robert E. Lee's Army of Northern Virginia** to capture the Union garrison at **Harpers Ferry, Virginia**. When Maj. Gen. **George B. Mc-Clellan** and the **Army of the Potomac** entered **Maryland** in pursuit of Lee, McClellan sent Maj. Gen. **William B. Franklin's** VI Corps to rescue the garrison. To reach Harpers Ferry, Franklin's 12,000 men had to cross **South Mountain** at Crampton's Gap. Defending the gap were perhaps 1,200 Confederates under Col. William A. Parham. If Franklin could push through the gap, he could attack the enemy's rear and probably destroy the Confederate **division** of Maj. Gen. **Lafayette McLaws**, which was positioned outside Harpers Ferry on Maryland Heights.

Franklin reached Crampton's Gap at about noon on September 14, 1862, and sent first one, and then another, division against the outnumbered Confederates. Confederate Brig. Gen. **Howell Cobb** arrived with his **brigade** to reinforce the defenders, but the Confederates could not hold against the relentless Union assaults. After hours of fighting, the Confederates finally broke and fled, but Cobb was able to use part of another newly arrived brigade to delay the pursuing Federals. The Confederates then rallied on two new brigades sent by McLaws and drew up in a new line away from the gap. Franklin greatly overestimated this Confederate force and failed to fight his way through to Harpers Ferry. The Union garrison there surrendered the next day.

In the daylong fight at Crampton's Gap, Franklin lost only 533 men, while the Confederates lost an estimated 1,000. Franklin's lack of aggression doomed the 12,000 Federals at Harpers Ferry who were captured by Jackson.

CRAPO, HENRY HOWLAND (1804–1869) USA. A native of **Massachusetts**, Crapo (KRAY-poh) pursued many careers before the Civil War, including teaching, surveying, insurance, and land speculating. He also served as a colonel in the state militia. In 1858, Crapo moved to **Michigan** while involved in the lumber industry and was elected mayor of Flint. A **Republican**, he was elected to the state senate in 1863 and served as a loyal supporter of Gov. **Austin Blair's** war effort. Crapo was elected governor in 1864 on the pledge to continue Blair's policies. He won reelection in 1866 and spent his second term opposing President **Andrew Johnson's Reconstruction** policies.

CRATER, VIRGINIA, BATTLE OF THE (JULY 30, 1864). In the summer of 1864, the war in **Virginia** became stalemated in the **Petersburg Campaign** as **Robert E. Lee's Army of Northern Virginia** became besieged by **U. S. Grant** and the **Army of the Potomac**. In an attempt to break through the formidable Confederate defenses, Union Lt. Col. Henry Pleasants of the 48th Pennsylvania passed on an idea by some of his men to dig a 600-foot-long mine from the Union line to a point under the Confederate works. The mine then would be packed with powder and exploded, blowing a huge hole in the enemy works that would allow a Union breakthrough.

Pleasants secured the backing of IX Corps commander, Maj. Gen. **Ambrose Burnside**. Neither **army** commander **George Meade** nor Grant were enthusiastic about the plan, but they reluctantly authorized it. Pleasants's men, mostly coal miners, began digging on June 25 and finished the mine on July 23. It measured 586 feet long and had a 75-foot-long perpendicular shaft at its end, running 20 feet beneath the Confederate works. After packing the shaft with 8,000 pounds of powder and sealing the last 38 feet of the mine to force the blast upward, a **fuse** was run to the mine's mouth.

The **black troops** of Brig. Gen. **Edward Ferrero's** division were specially trained to lead the attack once the mine was blown. However, Grant and Meade feared an **abolitionist** outcry should the attack fail and the black soldiers be slaughtered. Thus, on the day before the attack, Burnside was ordered to substitute a white **division** for Ferrero's troops. By drawing straws, Brig. Gen. **James H. Ledlie** was picked to lead the assault.

The mine fuse was set in the predawn hours of July 30, but a splice failed, and the fuse sputtered out. Two volunteers crawled into the mine and reset the fuse. The powder detonated at 4:45 A.M. in a spectacular explosion that virtually annihilated 300 men in two Confederate **regiments**. A hole approximately 170 feet long, 70 feet wide, and 30 feet deep was blown into the Confederate defenses, and Confederates on both sides of it fled in terror. Ledlie, who remained behind the lines in his bunker drinking with Ferrero, ordered his division forward. The men stumbled into the crater rather than fanning out to either side and soon were trapped. Burnside sent in two more divisions, but by then Maj. Gen. **William Mahone's** Confederate division had counterattacked and pinned down the Federals in the Crater, while **artillery** lobbed shells into the mass of soldiers. With the battle turning into a slaughter, Burnside finally sent in Ferrero's black troops, but they, too, became trapped in and around the Crater. The Confederates shot down hundreds of Federals packed into the hole and **massacred** many black soldiers who tried to surrender. By 1:00 P.M., the battered Union divisions returned to their lines.

In the disaster, Grant lost 3,798 men, while the Confederates lost approximately 1,500. An inquiry blamed Burnside, Ledlie, and Ferrero for the defeat. Ledlie resigned from the army, but, incredibly, Ferrero was **brevetted** major general of volunteers for his Petersburg service.

CRAVEN, THOMAS TINSEY (1808–1887) USA. The brother of **Tunis A. M. Craven**, Thomas Craven was born in **Washington, D.C.** He entered the **U.S. Navy** in 1822 as a midshipman and was a commander when the Civil War began.

Craven's Civil War service included commanding the Potomac River flotilla early in the war before becoming captain of the USS *Brooklyn* and serving on the Mississippi River under **David Farragut**. Promoted to commodore in 1863, Craven took command of the *Iroquois* and hunted Confederate **commerce raiders** in the Atlantic Ocean. He seized the former Confederate raider *Georgia* off Portugal even though the ship had been transferred to a British merchant. In March 1865, Craven's *Iroquois* and the accompanying *Sacramento* encountered the **CSS *Stonewall*** in a Spanish harbor. Craven declined an invitation to give battle because he did not believe his wooden ships could stand up to the **ironclad**. As a result, he was convicted in a court-martial for failing to fight and was suspended for two years. The secretary of the navy overturned the verdict, however, and Craven was promoted to rear admiral in 1866.

CRAVEN, TUNIS AUGUSTUS MacDONOUGH (1813–1864) USA. The brother of **Thomas T. Craven**, Craven was born in **New Hampshire** and entered the **U.S. Navy** as a midshipman in 1829. Before the Civil War, he helped seize **California** during the **Mexican War** and was recognized as one of the navy's leading surveyors and hydrographers.

When the Civil War began, Craven was a lieutenant in command of the USS *Crusader* and helped save Key West, **Florida**, for the Union. Promoted to commander in 1861, he commanded the *Tuscarora* in search of Confederate **commerce raiders** and blockaded the **CSS *Sumter*** at Gibraltar until it was sold in 1862. In April 1864, Craven took command of the **monitor** *Tecumseh* and fought Confederate batteries on **Virginia's** James River.

Transferred to Mobile, **Alabama**, Craven led Rear Adm. **David Farragut's** attack against **Forts Morgan** and **Gaines** in the **Battle of Mobile Bay** in August 1864. After the monitor struck a **torpedo**, he allowed his pilot to climb out of the turret first. The *Tecumseh* sank quickly, drowning Craven and most of his crew. Farragut's other ships hesitated in attacking after seeing the *Tecumseh* sink, and it was then that Farragut supposedly shouted, "Damn the torpedoes! Full speed ahead!"

CRAVEN'S FARM, TENNESSEE, BATTLE OF (NOVEMBER 24, 1863). *See* LOOKOUT MOUNTAIN, TENNESSEE, BATTLE OF.

CRAWFORD, SAMUEL WYLIE (1829–1892) USA. A native of **Pennsylvania**, Crawford graduated from the University of Pennsylvania's medical school and became a **U.S. Army** surgeon in 1851. After serving on the frontier, he was transferred to **Fort Sumter**, **South Carolina**, and there commanded an **artillery** battery during the April 1861 bombardment. The following month, Crawford left the medical field and was appointed major of the 13th U.S. Infantry.

In April 1862, Crawford was promoted to brigadier general of volunteers and led a **brigade** at **First Winchester** and **Cedar Mountain**, losing half of his men in the latter battle. Severely wounded at **Antietam** while commanding a **division** in the **Army of the Potomac**, he was out of action for months before finally being put in command of the Pennsylvania Reserve Corps in **Washington, D.C.** This unit became a division in the V Corps, and Crawford led it skillfully in the **Gettysburg**, **Overland**, and **Petersburg Campaigns**. Because of his gallantry, he was commissioned a lieutenant colonel in the regular army's 2nd U.S. Infantry in February 1864 and was **brevetted** through all grades to major general in both the volunteers and regular **army**.

Crawford remained in the army with the 2nd Infantry after the war and was promoted to colonel in 1869. He retired in 1873 and was promoted to brigadier general on the retired list in 1875.

CREW'S FARM, VIRGINIA, BATTLE OF (JULY 1, 1862). *See* MALVERN HILL, VIRGINIA, BATTLE OF.

CRITTENDEN COMMITTEE. *See* COMMITTEE OF THIRTEEN.

CRITTENDEN COMPROMISE. When the **secession** crisis erupted in December 1860, **Kentucky** Sen. **John J. Crittenden** proposed a series of resolutions in an attempt to forestall disunion. The Senate then formed the **Committee of Thirteen** to find a peaceful solution to the crisis, and Crittenden was appointed its chairman. Crittenden's resolutions were used as the basis for the committee's work and became known as the Crittenden Compromise. The compromise called for the passage of six constitutional amendments to permanently settle the **slavery** issue. These amendments would (1) revise the **Missouri Compromise** Line of 36° 30′ and extend it to the Pacific Ocean (with slavery guaranteed south of the line but prohibited north of it) but with new states entering the Union being given the right of **popular sovereignty**; (2) prohibit the U.S. Congress from abolishing slavery in the territories; (3) prohibit Congress from abolishing slavery in **Washington, D.C.**, as long as **Virginia** or **Maryland** had slaves or until a majority of Washington's citizens approved of such action (with slave owners being compensated if slavery was abolished); (4) protect the interstate transportation of slaves; (5) have the federal government compensate slave owners for slaves that were aided in escape, with the county where the escape was aided being forced to reimburse the government; and (6) prohibit any future constitutional amendments from interfering with these five amendments.

The compromise was voted down, partly because president-elect **Abraham Lincoln** let the committee know he would refuse to compromise on containing the spread of slavery. Despite the committee's failure to endorse the compromise, it was presented to the Senate in January 1861. There it failed by a vote of 25–23.

CRITTENDEN, GEORGE BIBB (1812–1880) CSA. A native of **Kentucky**, Crittenden was the eldest son of Sen. **John J. Crittenden**, the brother of **Thomas L. Crittenden**, and a cousin of **Thomas Turpin Crittenden**. He graduated from **West Point** in 1832 but resigned his commission after the Black Hawk War to study law. In 1842, Crittenden moved to **Texas** and served in a Texas unit that attacked a Mexican village and was captured. Every tenth Texan was to be executed, and the prisoners drew lots to determine their fate. When Crittenden drew a white bean that guaranteed his life, he gave it to a friend and redrew. Luckily, he drew another white bean. Crittenden was freed a year later after his father and powerful political friends lobbied for his release. He returned to Kentucky to practice law but quickly entered the **Mexican War** as a captain of a Kentucky **regiment**. Crittenden was **brevetted** once for gallantry and was promoted to major. He remained in the **U.S. Army** until June 1861, when he resigned his lieutenant colonel's commission and returned to Kentucky.

Despite his father's objections, Crittenden entered Confederate service that summer as a colonel and took command of the **Trans-Allegheny Department**. Promotion to brigadier general and major general came in August and November, respectively. By late 1861, he was in command of the District of East Tennessee with orders to invade Kentucky. In January 1862, Crittenden joined his subordinate, Brig. Gen. **Felix Zollicoffer**, who had disobeyed orders and placed his **brigade** in an exposed position across the Cumberland River at Beech Grove, Kentucky. Unable to recross the river because of a lack of boats and threatened by two advancing Union armies, Crittenden decided to attack one enemy force at **Mill Springs**. On January 19, he was badly defeated by Brig. Gen. **George H. Thomas**. Zollicoffer was killed, and Crittenden was forced to retreat to Beech Grove. Crittenden was vilified for the defeat and was accused of cowardice and drunkenness. Instead of being cashiered, however, he was transferred to Corinth, Mississippi, and was put in command of **Albert Sidney Johnston's** Reserve Corps.

In April 1862, Maj. Gen. **William J. Hardee** arrested Crittenden and Brig. Gen. **William H. Carroll** for being drunk and incompetent. Crittenden was censored in a court-martial where Gen. **Braxton Bragg** declared him incompetent. He resigned his commission in October but served the rest of the war as a volunteer aide to Brig. Gen. **John S. Williams** and others.

After the war, Crittenden returned to Kentucky, where he became the state librarian.

CRITTENDEN, JOHN JORDAN (1787–1863) USA. A native of **Kentucky**, Crittenden was the father of **George Bibb** and **Thomas Leonidas Crittenden**, and the uncle of **Thomas Turpin Crittenden**. After studying law at William and Mary College, he became a prominent Kentucky lawyer and politician and served in the War of 1812. During the antebellum period, Crittenden served in the state legislature, as Kentucky's secretary of state, as a U.S. district attorney, in the U.S. Senate, as governor, and attorney general under Presidents William H. Harrison and Millard Fillmore.

It was as a senator, however, that Crittenden was most famous. First as a **Whig**, then as a **Know-Nothing**, and finally as a **Democrat**, he was a strong Unionist but believed compromise was the only way to save the nation from **secession**. When the secession crisis erupted in December 1860, Crittenden authored resolutions designed to save the nation through compromise. When the Senate formed the **Committee of Thirteen**, he was appointed chairman, and his resolutions became known as the **Crittenden Compromise**. Radical members on the committee refused to support the compromise, and it failed.

After the compromise's failure, Crittenden returned to Kentucky and played a prominent role in getting the state to remain neutral early in the war. In May 1861, he chaired a convention held by **border states** that called for the South to reconsider secession and for the federal government to adopt a moderate course. Crittenden finally became a supporter of the Union war effort as the only way to save the nation, but he opposed **West Virginia** statehood, the use of **black troops**, and the **confiscation acts**. He saw his two sons become major generals in the opposing armies, and his nephew **Thomas Turpin Crittenden** become a brigadier general in the Union **army**.

CRITTENDEN, THOMAS LEONIDAS (1819–1893) USA. A native of **Kentucky**, Crittenden was the son of **John J. Crittenden**, the brother of Maj. Gen. **George B. Crittenden**, and a cousin of Brig. Gen. **Thomas Turpin Crittenden**. After studying law under his father, he became a state attorney and served in the **Mexican War**, first as Gen. Zachary Taylor's aide and then as colonel of the 3rd Kentucky. From 1849 to 1853, Crittenden was President Taylor's consul to Liverpool in Great Britain.

In 1860, Crittenden was appointed major general of state troops, and when the Civil War began, he took command of the pro-Union Kentucky militia. He was promoted to brigadier general of volunteers in September 1861 and led a **division** in the **Army of the Ohio** at **Shiloh**.

Promoted to major general of volunteers in July 1862, Crittenden led a **corps** in the **Army of the Cumberland** at **Stones River**. There, his gallantry earned him the **brevet** rank of brigadier general in the regular **army** after the war. Crittenden then served in the **Tullahoma Campaign** and led the XXI Corps at **Chickamauga**. In that battle, his command was crushed, and Crittenden was among those officers who were swept back to **Chattanooga, Tennessee,** by the retreating army. Although he had been one of Maj. Gen. **William Rosecrans's** main subordinates, Rosecrans preferred charges against Crittenden and other officers to deflect some of the blame for the Chickamauga disaster. Crittenden was cleared of any wrongdoing, but his career suffered, nonetheless. Transferred to the **Army of the Potomac**, he commanded a division at **Spotsylvania** and **Cold Harbor**, but he then resigned his commission in December 1864 and retired.

After the war, Crittenden served as Kentucky's state treasurer and in 1867 was commissioned a colonel in the **U.S. Army**. He remained in the army until 1881, serving mostly with the 17th U.S. Infantry.

CRITTENDEN, THOMAS TURPIN (1825–1905) USA. Born in **Alabama**, Crittenden was a cousin of **George B.** and **Thomas L. Crittenden** and a nephew of **John J. Crittenden**. He moved to **Texas** as a boy and graduated from **Kentucky's** Transylvania College. Crittenden then became a **Missouri** lawyer and served in the **Mexican War** as a lieutenant in a Missouri battalion. After the war, he moved to **Indiana** and was living there when the Civil War began.

Crittenden entered Union service in April 1861 as a captain in the 6th Indiana but a week later was promoted to colonel. He led his **regiment** at **Philippi, Carrick's Ford,** and **Shiloh**. After being promoted to brigadier general of volunteers in April 1862, Crittenden was put in command of Murfreesboro, Tennessee. On the day after he took command in July, he and his men were surprised and captured by **Nathan Bedford Forrest's** cavalry. Crittenden was held responsible for the embarrassing defeat and never again held an important command after his release from **prison** in October. He resigned his commission in May 1863.

After leaving the service, Crittenden lived in **Washington, D.C.,** and in **California** and worked in real estate.

CROCKER, MARCELLUS MONROE (1830–1865) USA. A native of **Indiana**, Crocker entered **West Point** in 1847 but left in 1849 to study law. He became an **Iowa** lawyer and then entered Union service in May 1861 as a captain in the 2nd Iowa. Four days later, Crocker was promoted to major.

After serving with his **regiment** guarding **railroads** in **Missouri**, Crocker was appointed lieutenant colonel in September 1861. He quickly left the regiment, because he was appointed colonel of the 13th Iowa later that month. After suffering heavy losses at **Shiloh**, Crocker was given command of the "Iowa Brigade" in the **Army of the Tennessee**. He was commissioned a brigadier general in November 1862 after fighting at **Corinth, Mississippi**. Crocker led a **division** during the **Vicksburg Campaign**, after which he served in **Louisiana** and at Natchez, Mississippi. His service was superb, and Maj. Gen. **U. S. Grant** claimed that he had few equals as a division commander. Crocker's division became renowned for its rapid marches and during the **Atlanta Campaign** (with Crocker absent) it became known as "Crocker's Greyhounds."

Suffering from tuberculosis, Crocker submitted his resignation in May 1864, but it was refused because he was such a valued officer. Instead, he was transferred to **New Mexico** for his health. Crocker seemed to recover and returned to **Washington, D.C.**, but there he had a relapse and died in August 1865.

CROOK, GEORGE (1828–1890) USA. A native of **Ohio**, Crook graduated from **West Point** in 1852 and served in the Pacific Northwest until the Civil War. While in **California**, he was wounded by a poison arrow in 1857 while fighting **Indians**.

Crook was appointed colonel of the 36th Ohio in September 1861 and served in western **Virginia**, where he was wounded in May 1862. Commissioned brigadier general of volunteers in August, he was put in command of an Ohio infantry **brigade** in the **Army of the Potomac** but was serving as **division** commander at **South Mountain** and **Antietam**. Given a cavalry division in the **Army of the Cumberland**, Crook led it at **Chickamauga** and then was transferred back to **West Virginia**, where he commanded the Kanawha District and won the **Battle of Cloyd's Mountain**. Afterward, Crook commanded the **Department of Western Virginia** and led the **Army of Western Virginia** during **Philip Sheridan's Shenandoah Valley Campaign**. He was awarded his fourth citation for gallantry at **Fisher's Hill** (the other three being for Lewisburg, **Antietam**, and Farmington).

Crook was promoted to major general of volunteers in October 1864 and returned to his **department** in February 1865. That month at Cumberland, Maryland, he and Brig. Gen. **Benjamin F. Kelley** were surprised by 60 Confederate **partisans** of **McNeill's Rangers**, who took them away as **prisoners** amidst their 10,000 Union troops. Crook was **exchanged** in March and participated in the **Appomattox Campaign** as commander of a cavalry division. **Brevetted** major general of regulars for his war service, he remained in the **army** and was appointed lieutenant colonel of the 23rd U.S. Infantry in 1866.

Crook became famous as an Indian fighter and peacemaker over the next 20 years. He quickly rose to the rank of major general and in 1888 was put in command of the vast Division of the Missouri.

CROSS KEYS, VIRGINIA, BATTLE OF (JUNE 8, 1862). By early June 1862, Confederate Maj. Gen. **Thomas J. "Stonewall" Jackson** had wreaked havoc in **Jackson's Shenandoah Valley Campaign**. Shortly after his victory at **First Winchester**, he had been forced to retreat up the Valley to avoid being trapped by three converging Union forces. Major General **Nathaniel P. Banks** was threatening his rear, while Maj. Gen. **John C. Frémont** was entering the Valley from the west, and Maj. Gen. **James Shields** from the east. By June 7, Frémont's and Shields's columns were closing around Jackson near Cross Keys and **Port Republic**.

Jackson made plans to defeat the separated forces by first attacking Frémont at Cross Keys and then turning on Shields about four miles to the south at Port Republic. He had Maj. Gen. **Richard S. Ewell** deploy about 5,000 men to keep Frémont at bay at Cross Keys, while the rest of Jackson's **army** crossed the Shenandoah River to face Shields at Port Republic.

Ewell placed his four **brigades** and accompanying **artillery** along a ridge bordering a field, and by June 8, the rest of Jackson's army arrived and camped within supporting distance. Shields's lead units also began arriving at Port Republic. That morning Frémont was in position with about 12,000 men and attacked Ewell's right, held by Brig. Gen. **Isaac Trimble's** brigade. Trimble repulsed the attack and, after some desultory artillery fire, counterattacked Frémont's left. With little Federal opposition, Trimble drove in the Union flank and pushed Frémont back a mile, allowing Ewell to possess the field. Leaving Trimble to watch Frémont, Jackson took the rest of the army across the river the next morning and defeated Shields at Port Republic. These twin battles ended Jackson's Shenandoah Valley Campaign. Ewell reported losing 288 men at Cross Keys, while Frémont lost 684.

CRUFT, CHARLES (1826–1883) USA. A native of **Indiana**, Cruft graduated from Wabash College in 1842 and worked as a teacher, lawyer, bank clerk, and **railroad** president before the Civil War. Being in **Washington, D.C.**, in July 1861, he witnessed the **First Battle of Manassas** as a civilian and then entered Union service in September 1861 as colonel of the 31st Indiana. First given command of a **brigade** in the **Army of the Ohio** in November, Cruft was transferred to a brigade command under **Lew Wallace** for the **Forts Henry and Donelson Campaign**. Afterward, he was severely wounded in the leg and shoulder on the first day of battle at **Shiloh**.

After serving in the **siege of Corinth, Mississippi**, Cruft was promoted to brigadier general of volunteers in July 1862 and was given a brigade command in the **Army of Kentucky**. He served well at **Richmond** during the **Kentucky Campaign** but lost most of his command captured. Cruft then took command of another brigade in **John M. Palmer's** division in the **Army of the Cumberland** and served in the **Stones River**, **Tullahoma**, and **Chickamauga Campaigns** and commanded a IV Corps **division** during the **Chattanooga Campaign**. Reverting to a IV Corps brigade command in early 1864, he served in the early part of the **Atlanta Campaign** but then returned to **Tennessee**, where he led a provisional division of mostly **black troops** at the **Battle of Nashville**. In March 1865, Cruft was put in command of the District of East Tennessee, where he remained until war's end.

Cruft left the **army** in August 1865 and was **brevetted** major general of volunteers for his war service. He then returned to his law practice and became very active in the Masonic order.

CRUISERS, CONFEDERATE. *See* COMMERCE RAIDERS.

CULLUM, GEORGE WASHINGTON (1809–1892) USA. Born in New York City, Cullum moved to **Pennsylvania** as a child. After graduating from **West Point** in 1833, he served 28 years in the **engineers** along the east coast and at West Point.

In 1861, Cullum was still a captain and joined General-in-Chief **Winfield Scott's** staff. He later joined the **U.S. Sanitation Commission** but in November 1861 was promoted to brigadier general of volunteers and became chief of staff and chief engineer for Maj. Gen. **Henry W. Halleck**, who commanded the **Department of the Missouri**. Cullum remained with Halleck after he was appointed commander of the **Department of the Mississippi** and general-in-chief. Cullum won a promotion to lieutenant colonel of regulars in May 1863.

In September 1864, Cullum was appointed superintendent of West Point. After two years, he resumed engineering duties and retired from the **army** in 1874 as a colonel and **brevet** major general. In retirement, Cullum married Elizabeth Halleck, Halleck's widow (and Alexander Hamilton's granddaughter). Perhaps Cullum's greatest service was his compilation in 1890 of the *Biographical Register of the Officers and Graduates of the United States Military Academy*, a two-volume work that gives the service records of all West Point graduates. His will provided that the Register be upgraded every 10 years.

CULP'S HILL AT BATTLE OF GETTYSBURG, PENNSYLVANIA (July 2–3, 1863). *See* GETTYSBURG, PENNSYLVANIA, CAMPAIGN AND BATTLE OF.

CUMBERLAND CHURCH, VIRGINIA, BATTLE OF (APRIL 7, 1865). During the **Appomattox Campaign**, **Robert E. Lee's Army of Northern Virginia** was retreating from Petersburg, Virginia, toward Farmville, closely pursued by the Federals. On April 7, 1865, **Andrew A. Humphreys's** II Corps of the **Army of the Potomac** crossed **High Bridge** and with **Francis C. Barlow's** division pressed the Confederate rear guard.

When **William Mahone's** Confederate **division** reached Cumberland Church, it took up a defensive position north and east of the church to keep the enemy at bay and to keep open the road to **Appomattox Court House**. After Mahone had repulsed some Union probes, he was joined by the **corps** of **John B. Gordon** and **James Longstreet**, who extended the Confederate line to the right. Fighting continued throughout the day, with Union cavalry raiding a Confederate wagon train nearby and Mahone repulsing an attack by **Nelson Mile's** cavalry division. That night, Lee refused a **surrender** request from **U. S. Grant** and continued his westward march toward Appomattox. While Confederate casualties at Cumberland Church are unknown, the Federals lost 571 men.

CUMMING, ALFRED (1829–1910) CSA. A native of **Georgia**, Cumming graduated from **West Point** in 1849. His antebellum service included frontier duty, aide to Brig. Gen. **David E. Twiggs**, and the **Utah Expedition**.

Cumming resigned his captain's commission when Georgia seceded in January 1861 and was elected lieutenant colonel of the Augusta Volunteer Battalion. He resigned that position in June to become major of the 1st Georgia. Within days, Cumming was promoted to lieutenant colonel and was placed on detached duty with the 10th Georgia, serving on the Virginia Peninsula outside **Richmond**. In October, Cumming was appointed the 10th Georgia's colonel and led it during the **Peninsula** and **Seven Days Campaigns**. Cumming's **regiment** suffered heavy losses in the latter campaign, and he was wounded by a shell at **Malvern Hill**. During the **Antietam Campaign**, he temporarily led Brig. Gen. **Cadmus M. Wilcox's** brigade in the **Army of Northern Virginia** and was wounded again at Antietam's "Bloody Lane."

While recuperating in Georgia, Cumming was promoted to brigadier general in October 1862 and was given command of a **brigade** at Mobile, Alabama. He was transferred from this unit, however, because of a law that stated brigade commanders had to be from the state most represented by the brigade's units. Cumming was sent to participate in the **Vicksburg Campaign** in May 1863 and took command of a Georgia brigade. He led it in heavy fighting at **Champion Hill** and at **Vicksburg** and was captured with the rest of the garrison on July 4, 1863. After being **exchanged**, Cumming and his brigade fought at **Lookout Mountain** and **Missionary Ridge** during the **Chattanooga Campaign**, receiving praise from **Braxton Bragg** for assisting **Patrick Cleburne** in holding the right flank at the latter and in defending **Ringgold Gap** during the **army's** withdrawal. He and his brigade won more acclaim in heavy fighting throughout the **Atlanta Campaign** as part of **Carter Stevenson's division**. After suffering his third wound at **Jonesboro**, Cumming became unfit for field service, although he was placed in command of three consolidated brigades.

Cumming returned to Georgia after the war and became a farmer.

CUMMING, KATE (1835–1909) CSA. Born in Scotland, Cumming grew up in Mobile, **Alabama**. Her Civil War service began when she collected supplies for wounded soldiers, but by April 1862 she was working as a nurse. Cumming served at **Shiloh**, **Corinth**, **Okolona**, and in the **Chattanooga Campaign**. Although outspoken and assertive, she became a hospital matron and was known for running well-organized and efficient hospitals.

After the war, Cumming wrote one of the better accounts of hospital service entitled *A Journal of Hospital Life in the Confederate Army of Tennessee* (later revised as *Kate: The Journal of a Confederate Nurse*). She never married and became a teacher and was active in the United Daughters of the Confederacy and the **United Confederate Veterans**.

CURRENCY. *See* CONFEDERATE MONEY; FINANCE, CONFEDERATE; GREENBACKS; SHINPLASTERS.

CURTIN, ANDREW GREGG (1817–1894) USA. A native of **Pennsylvania**, Curtin was a first cousin of Union Brig. Gen. **David M. Gregg** and was considered by some to have been the best of the Union wartime governors. Before the Civil War, he was a lawyer, active in the **Whig** Party, and served as Pennsylvania's secretary of state in the 1850s. In 1860, Curtin was elected governor on the People's Party ticket, although in political philosophy he was a **Republican**.

Curtin was a staunch supporter of **Abraham Lincoln's** administration and worked tirelessly for the Union war effort. He raised 427,000 troops for the Union **army**, cared for soldiers' dependents, suppressed dissent, encouraged war-related **industry**, and in the dark days of 1862 was instrumental in getting a number of governors to declare publicly their support of the administration. These achievements were made despite a bitter feud Curtin had with Lincoln's first secretary of war, **Simon Cameron**, the Republican boss of Pennsylvania. Curtin declined to run for reelection in 1864 because of poor health but was drafted and re-elected nonetheless.

After the war, Curtin served as minister to Russia, but Cameron prevented his election to several other political positions. Curtin eventually switched to the **Democratic Party** and was elected to the first of three congressional terms in 1880.

CURTIS, NEWTON MARTIN (1835–1910) USA. A native of **New York**, Curtis was a farmer, teacher, postmaster, and law student before the Civil War. He entered Union service in May 1861 as a **company** captain in the 16th New York. Curtis fought at **First Manassas** and was severely wounded in a May 1862 **skirmish** while fighting with the **Army of the Potomac** during the **Peninsula Campaign**. He was promoted to lieutenant colonel of the 142nd New York in October 1862 and to colonel in January 1863.

Curtis mostly served in administrative positions until the **Overland Campaign**, when he fought at **Cold Harbor**. He was elevated to **brigade** commander in **Benjamin F. Butler's Army of the James** during the **Petersburg Campaign** and was **brevetted** brigadier general of volunteers in October 1864 for his actions at **New Market Heights**. Curtis then accompanied Butler for an attack on **Fort Fisher**, **North Carolina**, in December 1864. After Butler's failure there, he participated in the next attack against the fort under **Quincy A. Gillmore** in January 1865. Leading his brigade, Curtis supposedly was the first Union soldier to enter Fort Fisher. He was wounded four times in the battle and lost his left eye. Curtis was also awarded the **Medal of Honor** (in 1891), was voted the **Thanks of Congress**, won promotion to brigadier general, and was **brevetted** major general of volunteers.

Curtis left the **army** in 1866 and returned to New York, where he became a state legislator and U.S. congressman. In 1906, he published his war memoirs, entitled *From Bull Run to Chancellorsville*.

CURTIS, SAMUEL RYAN (1805–1866) USA. Born in **New York**, Curtis grew up in **Ohio** and graduated from **West Point** in 1831. He served in the **U.S. Army** only a year before resigning to become a lawyer and engineer. Curtis rose to the rank of colonel in the Ohio militia and during the **Mexican War** served as Ohio's adjutant general, colonel of the 2nd Ohio, and assistant adjutant general to Brig. Gen. **John E. Wool**. After the war, he practiced law and became mayor of Keokuk, **Iowa**, and chief engineer of St. Louis, **Missouri**. In 1856, Curtis was elected to the **U.S.**

Congress and was still serving there when he was appointed colonel of the 2nd Iowa in May 1861.

In August 1861, Curtis was promoted to brigadier general of volunteers and resigned his congressional seat. During the war, he commanded a training camp near St. Louis, the Southwest District of Missouri, and the **Army of the Southwest**. Curtis's victory at the **Battle of Pea Ridge** earned him promotion to major general of volunteers in March 1863. Afterward, he commanded the **Departments of the Missouri, Kansas**, and **the Northwest**, and in 1864 played a role in turning back **Sterling Price's Missouri Raid**.

CUSHING, ALONZO HERSFORD (1841–1863) USA. A native of **Wisconsin**, Cushing was the brother of Union naval officer **William B. Cushing**. He graduated from **West Point** in 1861 and was appointed lieutenant of **artillery** in the 4th U.S. Artillery. Cushing saw service with his battery at **First Manassas** and then joined the **Army of the Potomac** for the **Peninsula Campaign**. During the **Antietam** and **Fredericksburg Campaigns**, he temporarily was assigned to the **engineers** and won a **brevet** for his actions in the latter campaign. Cushing was back with his battery for the **Chancellorsville Campaign** and was brevetted major for his service.

On July 3, 1863, Cushing's battery was positioned in the Union center at **Gettysburg** and took a pounding from Confederate batteries prior to **Pickett's Charge**. Cushing was wounded in both thighs by shell fragments but remained at his post directing his battery's counterfire. As the Confederate infantry approached his position, he had three guns rolled to the famous stone wall and continued to fire **canister** until two of the three guns were disabled, and the enemy overran his battery. Cushing was killed next to his last cannon just as he fired a round of canister. Confederate Brig. Gen. **Lewis Armistead** fell mortally wounded beside the same cannon. Because of his bravery and young age (he was only 22), Cushing became one of the heroes of Gettysburg and was brevetted lieutenant colonel posthumously.

CUSHING, WILLIAM BARKER (1842–1874) USA. The younger brother of **Alonzo Hersford Cushing**, Cushing was a native of **Wisconsin** who entered the **U.S. Naval Academy** in 1857. He resigned in March 1861, however, and was appointed acting master's mate on the USS *Minnesota*. After helping capture a **blockade runner**, Cushing was promoted to acting midshipman and then to lieutenant in July 1862.

Cushing gained fame in the Civil War for carrying out several commando-style raids against the Confederates. In October 1862, he was commanding the tugboat *Ellet*, which he used to raid and destroy an enemy saltworks near New Topsail Inlet, North Carolina. Shortly afterward, he led another raid against Jacksonville, **North Carolina**, and captured two enemy schooners but was forced to destroy his ship to prevent its capture. In the first half of 1864, Cushing carried out several additional raids that netted him a number of **prisoners** and intelligence information.

Cushing's most famous escapade was on the night of October 28, 1864, when he led a party of raiders to destroy the **CSS** *Albemarle*, a formidable Confederate **ram** anchored at Plymouth, North Carolina. He rigged a **torpedo** on his boat's boom and with 15 men set out against the *Albemarle*. Under heavy fire, Cushing managed to ram the ship with his torpedo and sink it. Only he and one other man escaped by swimming ashore, but the daring raid helped the Union fleet recapture Plymouth. For his exploit, Cushing was promoted to lieutenant commander and was voted the **Thanks of Congress**.

Cushing's last combat was while in command of the **Monticello** during the attack against **Fort Fisher**, **North Carolina**. He spent six hours under heavy fire scouting the channel leading to the fort and then led a force of sailors and **U.S. Marines** against the fort's sea face.

Cushing remained in the navy after the war and was promoted to commander in 1872.

CUSHMAN, PAULINE (1833–1893) USA. Born in **Louisiana**, Cushman grew up in **Michigan** and became an actress. Her actor-husband joined the Union **army** as a musician but died from dysentery in 1862. While performing in Louisville, **Kentucky**, Cushman was bribed by **paroled** Confederates to toast **Jefferson Davis** during the play. She first informed Union officials and then made the toast, thus earning a reputation as being a Southern sympathizer. By 1863, Cushman was performing for Confederate forces in **Tennessee** while secretly gathering intelligence information for the Union. When discovered with incriminating papers, she was tried by **Braxton Bragg** and was found guilty of spying. Although sentenced to hang in Shelbyville, Tennessee, Cushman was saved when Maj. Gen. **William Rosecrans** advanced against the town, and her captors retreated, leaving Cushman behind.

Cushman's exploits made her a popular hero in the North, and **Abraham Lincoln** appointed her an honorary major in the Union army. She then made a career out of giving lectures on her exploits and in 1865 Ferdinand L. Sarmiento published a much-exaggerated account of her life entitled *Life of Pauline Cushman*. After the war, Cushman moved to **California**, where she worked as a seamstress and faded into obscurity. After a second husband died, and she separated from a third, she committed suicide with an overdose of opium.

CUSTER, GEORGE ARMSTRONG (1839–1876) USA. Born in **Ohio**, Custer spent much of his youth living with his half-sister in Monroe, **Michigan**. He was admitted to **West Point** in 1857 amidst rumors that a young girl's father had secured the appointment to remove Custer from his daughter. Custer's academy career was a dismal one. Each year he was threatened with expulsion because of excessive demerits, and at the time of his graduation he was under detention. Custer, or "Fanny," as he was called at the academy, graduated last in the West Point class of 1861, but he was immediately dispatched to **Washington, D.C.**, where he carried orders from **Winfield Scott** to Brig. Gen. **Irvin McDowell**.

After participating in the **First Battle of Manassas**, Lieutenant Custer joined the **Army of the Potomac** and served on **George B. McClellan's** staff during the **Peninsula Campaign**, sometimes gathering intelligence by going aloft in a hot air **balloon**. He was promoted to captain in June 1862 and served on the staffs of Maj. Gens. **Philip Kearny**, **William F. Smith**, and **Alfred Pleasonton**. All of Custer's superiors thought highly of him because even though he was brash and arrogant, he also was extremely brave and capable.

After Custer conducted a particularly gallant cavalry charge at the **Battle of Aldie**, Pleasonton recommended that he be promoted from captain to brigadier general of volunteers. The promotion came in June 1863, and he was put in command of the Michigan Cavalry Brigade, commonly referred to as **Custer's Cavalry Brigade**. At age 23, Custer became one of the youngest generals in the Union **army**. Only days later, he won acclaim for leading his **brigade** against **J. E. B. Stuart's** Confederate cavalry during the **Gettysburg Campaign**. Afterward, Custer participated in all of the major cavalry battles in the eastern theater. He was **brevetted** for gallantry five times (earning brevet ranks through major general in both the volunteer and regular army), had 11 horses shot from under him, and was wounded once.

Custer became one of **Philip Sheridan's** favorite generals and in October 1864 was put in command of a **division**. He led the cavalry charge at **Yellow Tavern** that resulted in Stuart being mortally wounded and performed outstanding service in **Sheridan's Shenandoah Valley Campaign**. During the **Appomattox Campaign**, it was Custer's cavalry that finally cut off **Robert E. Lee's** escape route. After Lee's surrender, Sheridan purchased for Custer's wife the table on which the surrender document was signed.

Custer's outstanding service was rewarded when he was promoted to major general of volunteers in April 1865. In 1866, he was appointed lieutenant colonel of the 7th U.S. Cavalry and began his famous career as an **Indian** fighter. In that role, Custer was ruthless, once destroying a peaceful Cheyenne camp on the Washita River. After he led an expedition into the Dakota Black Hills, warfare erupted with the Sioux and Cheyenne. On June 25, 1876, Custer divided his column and hastily attacked a much superior Indian force at the Little Big Horn River. Custer and 265 of his men were killed in what became known as Custer's Last Stand. His body later was removed from the battlefield and was reinterred at West Point. Largely due to the influence of his widow, Custer was elevated to mythical status and ultimately became more famous for his role as an Indian fighter than Civil War general.

CUSTER'S CAVALRY BRIGADE. Consisting of the 1st, 5th, 6th, and 7th Michigan Cavalry, this unit officially was the 2nd Brigade of Maj. Gen. **H. Judson Kilpatrick's** 3rd Cavalry Division in the **Army of the Potomac**. Made up of men from Detroit and Grand Rapids, Michigan, the **brigade** was placed under the command of Brig. Gen. **George A. Custer** in June 1863. Custer nicknamed his brigade the "Wolverines" (from the "Wolverine State"), and the troopers came to idolize him (even adopting Custer's red necktie as their unofficial badge). Under Custer, the brigade became the most famous of the **army's** cavalry units and compiled an outstanding record on such battlefields as **Gettysburg**, **Yellow Tavern**, **Trevilian Station**, and **Fisher's Hill**. Custer's Cavalry Brigade suffered more casualties than any other Union cavalry brigade, with 524 men being killed or dying of disease.

CUTLER, LYSANDER (1807–1866) USA. A native of **Massachusetts**, Cutler served as a schoolteacher and businessman before the Civil War. He also was active in the state militia (obtaining the rank of colonel) and was elected to the state senate. After suffering financial ruin in the Panic of 1857, Cutler moved to **Wisconsin** and became a grain broker.

In July 1861, Cutler was appointed colonel of the 6th Wisconsin, which was destined to become part of the famous **Iron Brigade**. After serving in the **Washington, D.C.**, area early in the war, he was severely wounded in the leg at the **Battle of Groveton** while the **regiment** was attached to the **Army of Virginia** during the **Second Manassas Campaign**.

After temporarily leading the **brigade** with the **Army of the Potomac** at **Fredericksburg**, Cutler was promoted to brigadier general of volunteers effective November 1862 and commanded the Iron Brigade through heavy fighting at **Chancellorsville** and **Gettysburg**. He also temporarily led the **division** during the **Bristoe Station** and **Mine Run Campaigns**. During the **Battle of the Wilderness**, Cutler took command of the V

Corps' 4th Division when Brig. Gen. **James S. Wadsworth** was killed. He led the division through the rest of the **Overland Campaign** and at the beginning of the **Petersburg Campaign** and was **brevetted** major general of volunteers in August 1864 for his services. The division was disbanded during the Petersburg Campaign because of heavy casualties. Weakened by two wounds and exposure, Cutler asked to be relieved in September 1864 and spent the rest of the war supervising the draft in **Michigan**. He resigned from the **army** in July 1865, returned to Wisconsin, and died the following year.

CYNTHIANA, KENTUCKY, BATTLE OF (JUNE 11–12, 1864). After helping defeat the Federals at **Cove Mountain**, **John Hunt Morgan** began his last raid on May 30, 1864. With 2,700 men, he entered **Kentucky** and forced Union Brig. Gen. **Stephen G. Burbridge** to cancel his own planned raid into southwestern **Virginia** in order to pursue him. At dawn on June 11, Morgan attacked a Union supply depot at Cynthiana. Colonel Conrad Garis's 500-man guard was no match for the raiders and was driven back, but Burbridge and his 5,200 men were soon on the scene. Having set fire to the town, Morgan made the unwise decision to stand and fight Burbridge's superior force, even though his raiders were exhausted and low on ammunition. Morgan took up a defensive position two miles south of town and was attacked before dawn the next day. The Confederates held their position until running out of ammunition, but then were forced to retreat and return to Virginia. It is estimated that Morgan lost about 1,000 men at Cynthiana, while the Federals suffered 1,092 casualties.

– D –

DABNEY'S MILL, VIRGINIA, BATTLE OF (FEBRUARY 5–7, 1865). *See* HATCHER'S RUN, VIRGINIA, BATTLE OF.

DAHLGREN GUN. Several types of **artillery** pieces were designed by **John A. B. Dahlgren**. They carried the designation of Dahlgren (DAL-gren) gun and were used by both navies in the Civil War. The gun tubes first were cast in a cylindrical shape, then cooled from the outside and shapened. The guns were thick at the breech and then tapered toward the muzzle, producing a "soda bottle" appearance. The most popular Dahlgren guns included bronze 12- and 24-pounder **howitzers** and **rifles**; 9- and 11-inch iron smoothbores (the **USS** *Monitor* carried two 11-inch Dahlgrens); and 50-pounder rifles.

DAHLGREN, JOHN ADOLPH BERNARD (1809–1870) USA. Born to Sweden's consul in Philadelphia, Pennsylvania, Dahlgren (DAL-gren) entered the **U.S. Navy** in 1826 as a midshipman. Although he damaged his eyes in 1836 while following orders to observe a solar eclipse, Dahlgren remained in the navy and won fame as an ordnance officer. Assigned to the Washington Naval Yard in 1847, he was active in the navy's ordnance department; designed the **Dahlgren Gun**, bronze boat **howitzers**, and a percussion lock; and wrote several books and manuals.

By the beginning of the Civil War, Dahlgren was a commander. In April 1861, he was placed in command of the Washington Navy Yard when **Franklin Buchanan** resigned to join the Confederacy. In July 1862, Dahlgren was promoted to captain and was made chief of the navy's Bureau of Ordnance. After being promoted to rear admiral in February 1863, he requested sea duty and was placed in command of the **South Atlantic Blockading Squadron** in July. For the rest of the war, Dahlgren was stationed off **Charleston**, **South Carolina**, and **Savannah**, **Georgia**. There he engaged in **blockade** duty, assisted the **army** in the capture of those cities, and sent an expedition up **Florida's** St. John River.

After the war, Dahlgren served in the Pacific for a time and then returned to command the Washington Naval Yard until his death. He was the father of **Ulric Dahlgren**.

DAHLGREN PAPERS. When Col. **Ulric Dahlgren** (DAL-gren) was ambushed and killed on March 2, 1864, during the **Kilpatrick-Dahlgren Raid**, a set of secret documents was found on his body. These included the draft of a speech to be delivered to his men, instructions to part of his command, and a memorandum book. Among these were papers indicating that Dahlgren planned to free the 15,000 Union **prisoners** being held in **Richmond**, **Virginia**, and then burn the city and execute **Jefferson Davis** and his Cabinet. The discovery of the papers stirred a firestorm of outrage as many Confederates demanded that Dahlgren's captured men be executed as war criminals. As the outcry mounted, **Robert E. Lee** contacted Maj. Gen. **George G. Meade** for an explanation, and Meade questioned the raid's originator, Brig. Gen. **H. Judson Kilpatrick**. Kilpatrick disavowed the documents and denied any knowledge of Dahlgren's plans. Meade suspected Kilpatrick's involvement but was unable to prove his suspicions and thus kept silent. Assured that no Union officials had any connection to the Dahlgren Papers, the Confederates did not carry out threats of retaliation, but the incident increased Southerners' suspicion and hatred of the North.

For years, many people believed the papers were forgeries because Dahlgren's signature seemed to be misspelled and was in a form he did not normally use. Modern tests conducted at the National Archives proved that leaking ink caused the signature to appear misspelled—the document, indeed, was signed by Dahlgren. Whether or not higher Union officials were involved in the plot remains a mystery.

DAHLGREN, ULRIC (1842–1864) USA. The son of Union Adm. **John A. B. Dahlgren**, Dahlgren (DAL-gren) was born in **Pennsylvania** and was a Philadelphia lawyer when the Civil War began.

Dahlgren entered Union service as a captain in May 1862 and became Maj. Gen. **Franz Sigel's** aide in the **Army of the Potomac**. After serving as Sigel's chief of **artillery** at **Second Manassas**, he won fame for several escapades while serving on the staffs of other generals. Dahlgren served as an aide to **Ambrose E. Burnside** at **Fredericksburg** and then joined **Joseph Hooker's** staff. During the **Chancellorsville Campaign**, he hid in a tree and counted the Confederate units as they marched underneath him and then led a cavalry raid to **Richmond, Virginia**. Afterward, Dahlgren served on **George G. Meade's** staff during the **Gettysburg Campaign** and captured a Confederate courier bringing the crucial intelligence that no reinforcements were being sent to **Robert E. Lee** in **Pennsylvania**. When the Confederates began their retreat from Pennsylvania, Dahlgren led a small force in pursuit. He joined Brig. Gen. **H. Judson Kilpatrick's** cavalry at Hagerstown, Maryland, and was severely wounded in the foot during a street battle.

While recuperating from an amputation, Dahlgren was promoted to colonel of cavalry effective July 1863. He was assigned to Kilpatrick's command and in February 1864 participated in the **Kilpatrick-Dahlgren Raid** against Richmond. Dahlgren's 500 men were forced by high water, bad weather, and enemy resistance to retreat before reaching the city. When Dahlgren was killed in an ambush in King and Queen County on March 2, papers were discovered on him indicating his intention to burn Richmond and execute **Jefferson Davis** and other officials. Although the authenticity of the **Dahlgren Papers** were, and still are, debated, they caused the young colonel to be branded a criminal. He was buried in an unmarked grave, but the body later was exhumed and reinterred in Philadelphia.

DALLAS, GEORGIA, BATTLE OF (MAY 28, 1864). *See* NEW HOPE CHURCH AND DALLAS, GEORGIA, BATTLES OF.

DALTON, GEORGIA, BATTLE OF (MAY 7–11, 1864). *See* ROCKY FACE RIDGE, GEORGIA, BATTLE OF.

DALTON (GEORGIA) CONFERENCE (JANUARY 2, 1864). While the Confederate **Army of Tennessee** was in camp around Dalton, Georgia, during the winter of 1863–64, Maj. Gen. **Patrick Cleburne** drafted a proposal advocating the enlistment of slaves into the **Confederate army** with a promise of freedom to those who served. Cleburne saw the use of slaves as an answer to the Confederacy's serious manpower shortage and believed such a step would encourage European powers to recognize the Confederacy. After getting all four of his **brigade** commanders and 10 of his regimental commanders to sign the document, Cleburne had Lt. Gen. **William J. Hardee** arrange a meeting of the army's **corps** and **division** commanders at Gen. **Joseph E. Johnston's** headquarters on the night of January 2, 1864. All but Maj. Gen. **Benjamin F. Cheatham** attended what some came to call the Dalton Conference.

Cleburne read his document and touched off a storm of debate. Some of the generals were sympathetic to the idea of using **black troops**, but others were vehemently opposed. Major General **W. H. T. Walker** led the opposition and informed **Jefferson Davis** of the meeting. Davis was shocked and had discussion of the conference suppressed. Although the matter was discussed for years, not until 1890 was Cleburne's document rediscovered in private papers.

The Dalton Conference further poisoned the high command of the Army of Tennessee. Forces sympathetic to former **army** commander **Braxton Bragg** used the incident to attack Generals Cleburne, Cheatham, and **Thomas C. Hindman**, who were seen as instigators of the plan. Many believed it was Cleburne's proposal of recruiting slaves that prevented his being promoted beyond a division command.

DANA, CHARLES ANDERSON (1819–1897) USA. Born in **New Hampshire**, Dana was managing editor of **Horace Greeley's New York Tribune** when the Civil War began. In 1862, he left that position to become an unofficial inspector and informer for Union Secretary of War **Edwin M. Stanton**. Dana mainly served in the western theater in 1862–63, keeping an eye on Maj. Gens. **William S. Rosecrans** and **U. S. Grant**. In January 1864, **Abraham Lincoln** appointed Dana assistant secretary of war, a position he held until August 1865. After the war, he became publisher and editor of the *New York Sun* and wrote his memoirs, *Recollections of the Civil War*.

DANA, NAPOLEON JACKSON TECUMSEH (1822–1905) USA. The son of a **U.S. Army** officer, Dana was born in **Maine**. After graduating from **West Point** in 1842, he fought in the **Mexican War** and was so badly wounded at Cerro Gordo that he was left on the field for dead for 36 hours. Dana resigned his captain's commission in 1855 to become a banker in **Minnesota**.

Dana was serving as a brigadier general of state militia when the Civil War began and entered Union service in October 1861 when he was appointed colonel of the 1st Minnesota. After fighting at **Ball's Bluff**, he was promoted to brigadier general of volunteers in February 1862. While commanding a **brigade** in the **Army of the Potomac** at **Antietam**, Dana was severely wounded and spent more than a year recovering. He was promoted to major general of volunteers in November 1862 but never again had an important field command. Dana spent the rest of the war commanding the defenses of Philadelphia, Pennsylvania, and various posts on the Gulf Coast and Mississippi River. Shortly before resigning his commission in May 1865, he commanded the **Department of Mississippi**.

After the war, Dana was an active businessman and **railroad** executive.

DANDRIDGE, TENNESSEE, BATTLE OF (JANUARY 17, 1864). After his failed **Knoxville Campaign** in late 1863, Confederate Lt. Gen. **James Longstreet** put his men into winter quarters east of Knoxville around Dandridge, Tennessee. In January 1864, Lt. Gen. **U. S. Grant** ordered Maj. Gen. **Gordon Granger** to force Longstreet out of the area.

On January 14, **John Parke** advanced his **division** toward Dandridge, and Longstreet began to withdraw. The next day, Longstreet brought up reinforcements to threaten the Federal base at New Market, northwest of Dandridge. On January 16, the Confederates engaged **Samuel D. Sturgis's** cavalry near Kimbrough's Crossroads and forced it to retire back to Dandridge, where Longstreet attacked the next afternoon. Fighting continued until after dark, but neither side could gain an advantage. The Federals disengaged that night and withdrew to New Market and Strawberry Plains. In the fighting around Dandridge, the Federals lost 150 men, but Confederate losses are unknown.

DANIEL, JUNIUS (1828–1864) CSA. The son of a former **North Carolina** congressman and state attorney general, Daniel graduated from **West Point** in 1851. He spent his antebellum military career in **New Mexico** on garrison duty and occasionally fighting **Indians**. Daniel resigned from the **U.S. Army** in 1858 and became a **Louisiana** planter, only to return to his native state in 1860.

After North Carolina seceded in 1861, Daniel was elected colonel of the 14th North Carolina in June and was forced to decline similar offers from two other **regiments**. Sent to **Virginia**, he assumed command of the 45th North Carolina in April 1862. Daniel then was put in command of a North Carolina **brigade** and saw combat in the **Peninsula** and **Seven Days Campaigns**, having his horse shot from under him at **Malvern Hill**. Although praised by his superiors, Daniel was left behind to guard the peninsula while the rest of the **Army of Northern Virginia** engaged in the **Second Manassas** and **Antietam Campaigns**.

In September 1862, Daniel was promoted to brigadier general and spent the next several months in southeastern Virginia and in North Carolina. His brigade then joined the Army of Northern Virginia for the **Gettysburg Campaign** as part of **Robert Rodes's division**. At Gettysburg, Daniel was heavily engaged, and he again was praised when his unit suffered more casualties on the first day than any other Confederate brigade. He remained with the **army** through the **Bristoe Station** and **Mine Run Campaigns** and by 1864 had become one of **Robert E. Lee's** better brigade commanders. After further combat in the **Wilderness**, Daniel's brigade was one of several that were rushed in to contain the Union breakthrough at **Spotsylvania's** "Bloody Angle" on May 12, 1864. While cheering his men onward, Daniel was mortally wounded, and he died the next day.

DARBYTOWN ROAD, VIRGINIA, BATTLES OF (OCTOBER 7, 13, AND 27, 1864). During the **Petersburg Campaign**, elements of the Union **Army of the James** captured **Fort Harrison**, southeast of **Richmond, Virginia**, from the Confederate **Army of Northern Virginia** on September 29, 1864. **Robert E. Lee** quickly massed one cavalry **brigade** under **Martin W. Gary** and one infantry brigade under **Edward A. Perry** north of the Union position. Fronting the fort, to the west, were placed the **divisions** of **Charles W. Field** and **Robert F. Hoke**. Lee planned a counterattack, with Gary's and Perry's brigades attacking from the north to gain the enemy's rear, at which time Field and Hoke would launch a **frontal attack**.

Shortly after dawn of October 7, the attack was made. Gary and Perry forced **August V. Kautz's** Union cavalry division to fall back to the main works held by Brig. Gen. **Alfred Terry's** X Corps. Field's division then attacked from the west but was repulsed, and Brig. Gen. **John Gregg** was killed. Hoke's division was supposed to come up in support of Field's right, but when it failed to advance, Lee called off the attacks. Lee lost 1,350 men in the operation, while the Federals reported 399 casualties.

Within days, Lee constructed a new line of entrenchments to protect Richmond from the X Corps, which remained in the Fort Harrison area. On October 13, Terry's X Corps, with the support of Kautz's cavalry, attacked this new line but was repulsed with 337 casualties. Two weeks later, Lt. Gen. **U. S. Grant** ordered another attack against Lee's line north of the James River in conjunction with an attack on the south side. On October 27, Maj. Gen. **Benjamin F. Butler** advanced against the

Confederate works with his Army of the James. Lieutenant General **James Longstreet** commanded this part of the Confederate line and skillfully maneuvered his troops to repulse easily all of Butler's attacks. Along the Darbytown Road, Hoke's division inflicted heavy losses on the attacking enemy, with Terry's X Corps losing 526 men. In all, Butler suffered 1,603 casualties to Longstreet's 64.

DARBYTOWN, VIRGINIA, BATTLE OF (JULY 27–29, 1864). *See* DEEP BOTTOM, VIRGINIA, FIRST BATTLE OF.

DAVID, **CSS.** This was a steam-powered Confederate **torpedo** boat that was built in **Charleston, South Carolina**, in 1863 (other unknown Confederate torpedo boats in the Charleston area also were referred to as "Davids" by the **U.S. Navy**). It was 50 feet long, had a **torpedo** mounted on a 10-foot spar, and carried a crew of four. In October 1863, the *David* seriously damaged the **USS** *New Ironsides* in Charleston harbor but failed to sink it. It also struck the USS *Memphis* in March 1864, but the torpedo failed to detonate, and in October attacked the USS *Wabash* but was unable to make contact. The *David* probably was captured when Charleston fell in 1865, but its fate is uncertain.

DAVIDSON, HENRY BREVARD (1831?–1899) CSA. Davidson's middle name and birth date are uncertain, but he was born in **Tennessee** and served in the 1st Tennessee during the **Mexican War**. His service earned him an appointment to **West Point**, where he graduated in 1853. Davidson rose to the rank of captain and spent his antebellum career in the Southwest and Northwest fighting **Indians**.

Davidson was on leave when Tennessee seceded in 1861 and failed to report back to duty. He was dropped from the rolls and then entered Confederate service as a major and assistant adjutant general. At **Fort Donelson**, Davidson first served on Brig. Gen. **John B. Floyd's** staff and then became **Simon B. Buckner's** chief of **artillery**. It is not clear whether he escaped capture or was released immediately after the fort's surrender, but Davidson soon was on Brig. Gen. **William W. Mackall's** staff at **Island No. 10**. There he was captured when the stronghold fell in April 1862.

After being **exchanged** in August, Davidson was promoted to colonel and was put in command of Staunton, Virginia. He remained there until August 1863, when he was promoted to brigadier general and was put in command of a cavalry **brigade**, first under **Nathan Bedford Forrest** and then **Joseph Wheeler**. Davidson fought at **Chickamauga** and guarded **railroads** in East Tennessee and northern **Georgia** until the 1864 **Atlanta Campaign**, in which he played a small role. In late summer 1864, he was sent back to the **Shenandoah Valley** and commanded a cavalry brigade under **Jubal A. Early**, although he arrived too late to participate in any of the major battles in **Philip Sheridan's Shenandoah Valley Campaign**. Near war's end, Davidson escaped from **Virginia** with a small cavalry brigade and made his way to **North Carolina**, where he surrendered.

After the war, Davidson moved to **California**, where he served as the state's deputy secretary of state and worked for a railroad.

DAVIDSON, JOHN WYNN (1824–1881) USA. The son of a **West Point** officer, Davidson was born in **Virginia** and graduated from the academy in 1845. He served on the frontier and in **California** during the **Mexican War** and was promoted to captain in 1855. In the years preceding the Civil War, Davidson fought **Indians** in California and the Southwest and was wounded in one fight. It was claimed that he turned down a Confederate commission while in California, choosing, instead, to remain loyal to the Union.

After serving in the **Washington, D.C.**, defenses, Davidson was promoted to brigadier general of volunteers in February 1862 and earned two **brevets** for gallantry while leading a **brigade** in the **Army of the Potomac** during the **Peninsula Campaign**. Afterward, he was put in command of the **districts** of St. Louis and of Southeast Missouri and the **Army of Arkansas**. Davidson received another brevet for his role in the capture of **Little Rock, Arkansas**, and by war's end was commanding the cavalry in the **Department of Mississippi**. Having compiled a solid, if not spectacular, war record, Davidson was brevetted through the rank of major general in both the volunteers and regulars.

Davidson remained in the **army** after the war and rose to the rank of colonel of the 2nd U.S. Cavalry. He died as the result of a fall by his horse.

DAVIES, HENRY EUGENE (1836–1894) USA. A native of New York City and the nephew of Union Gen. **Thomas A. Davies**, Davies graduated from Columbia College and became a **New York** lawyer.

Davies entered Union service in May 1861 as a captain in the 5th New York and fought at **Big Bethel**. In August, he was appointed major of the 2nd New York Cavalry and served with it in the **Army of Virginia** at **Second Manassas**. Davies quickly rose through the ranks, becoming the **regiment's** lieutenant colonel in December 1862 and colonel in June 1863. His regiment became part of the **Army of the Potomac** and was heavily engaged in the fight at **Aldie** prior to **Gettysburg**, but it missed the Battle of Gettysburg.

Davies was promoted to brigadier general of volunteers in September 1863 and took command of a cavalry **brigade**. He skillfully led it, and sometimes his **division**, for the remainder of the war. Davies performed admirably in raids on **Richmond, Virginia**, and in **Philip Sheridan's Shenandoah Valley Campaign** and was **brevetted** major general of volunteers in October 1864. During the **Petersburg Campaign**, he was wounded at **Hatcher's Run** but returned to duty in time to play an important role in the **Appomattox Campaign**.

Davies was promoted to major general of volunteers in May 1865 but resigned from the **army** in January 1866 to resume his law practice. He wrote several books after the war, including a biography of **Philip Sheridan**.

DAVIES, THOMAS ALFRED (1809–1899) USA. The uncle of Union Gen. **Henry E. Davies**, Davies was a **New York** native who graduated from **West Point** in 1829, along with **Robert E. Lee** and **Joseph E. Johnston**. He served only two years in the **U.S. Army** before resigning to become an engineer. Davies was a businessman in New York City when the Civil War began and entered Union service in May 1861 as colonel of the 16th New York.

After covering the Union retreat at **First Manassas**, Davies's **regiment** served in and around **Washington, D.C.** He was promoted to brigadier general of volunteers in March 1862 and was transferred west, where he participated in the siege, and later battle, of **Corinth, Mississippi**. For the remainder of the war, Davies commanded the **districts** of Columbus, **Kentucky**, and **Wisconsin**.

When he left the **army** in August 1865, Davies was **brevetted** major general of volunteers. He returned to New York and wrote a number of works on various subjects.

DAVIS, BENJAMIN FRANKLIN "GRIMES" (1832–1863) USA. A native of **Alabama**, Davis graduated from **West Point** in 1854. He spent his antebellum military career fighting **Indians** on the frontier and was wounded in one battle.

Although a Southerner, Davis remained loyal to the Union and was appointed captain in the 1st U.S. Cavalry in July 1861. The following month, he was promoted to lieutenant colonel and was assigned to the 1st California Cavalry. After fighting with the **Army of the Potomac** at **Yorktown** and **Williamsburg**, Davis was appointed colonel of the 8th New York Cavalry in June 1862. His **regiment** was stationed at **Harpers Ferry, Virginia**, during the **Antietam Campaign**. There, Davis earned praise and a **brevet** in the regular **army** for escaping the doomed garrison with his troopers and capturing a Confederate ammunition train. Afterward, he commanded a cavalry **brigade** at **Antietam** and led his regiment at **Fredericksburg**. While in command of the **division**, Davis was killed on June 9, 1863, at **Brandy Station**.

DAVIS BOOT. The official boot adopted by the **U.S. Army** in the 1850s became known as the Davis Boot because future Confederate President **Jefferson Davis** was secretary of war at the time. The boot came to just above the ankle, was tied with a lace running through only two pairs of eyes, and was made in just a few standard sizes.

DAVIS BRIDGE, TENNESSEE, BATTLE OF (OCTOBER 6, 1862). As Confederate Maj. Gen. **Earl Van Dorn** retreated after the **Battle of Corinth**, Union Maj. Gen. **U. S. Grant** attempted to destroy his army by trapping it between two forces. While **William S. Rosecrans** pursued the enemy, **E. O. C. Ord's** 8,000 men moved down the Hatchie River's west bank to capture Davis Bridge and cut off the Confederates' line of retreat. Van Dorn's vanguard under **Sterling Price**, however, reached the bridge first on October 5.

Price positioned one **brigade** on the west bank's high ground to defend the bridge, but it was attacked by Ord and driven back with the loss of four cannons and 200 **prisoners**. Ord was wounded in the battle, but his men seized the bridge, crossed over to the east side, and were led by **Stephen A. Hurlbut** against the Confederates. Grant's plan was working, but Rosecrans moved too slowly. As a result, Price was able to hold off Hurlbut until another river crossing was found farther south that allowed the Confederates to safely cross the river that night and retire to **Holly Springs**. In the day's fighting, the Federals lost approximately 500 men, while the Confederates lost about 400.

DAVIS, CHARLES HENRY (1807–1877) USA. A native of **Massachusetts**, Davis attended Harvard University for two years and then entered the **U.S. Navy** in 1824 as a midshipman. He quickly was promoted to lieutenant in 1827 and was able to return to Harvard and graduate. Davis spent his antebellum naval career engaged in scientific work and was promoted to commander in 1854.

Davis commanded the Bureau of Detail when the Civil War began and spent the early years of the conflict planning the **blockade** and expeditions to **Hatteras Inlet, North Carolina** and **Port Royal, South Carolina**. Promoted to captain in November 1861, he participated in the Port Royal operation as Flag Officer **Samuel F. Du Pont's** chief of staff. In May 1862, Davis was promoted to flag officer and became acting commander of the Mississippi River fleet. He effectively destroyed the Confederate **River Defense Fleet** in June at the **First Battle of Memphis**. This victory enabled him to capture Memphis, Tennessee, and his position as fleet commander was made official soon afterward. In July 1862, the Confederate **ram** *Arkansas* caused havoc at **Vicksburg, Mississippi**, and Rear Adm. **David G. Farragut** and Secretary of the Navy **Gideon Welles** believed Davis was too timid in his actions against the **ironclad**. As a result, he was replaced in October by Comdr. **David D. Porter**.

Davis returned to **Washington, D.C.**, was promoted to rear admiral in February 1863, and resumed his scientific work. He later became commander of the South Atlantic Squadron and was superintendent of the Naval Observatory at the time of his death.

DAVIS' CROSS ROADS, GEORGIA, BATTLE OF (SEPTEMBER 10–11, 1863). *See* McLEMORE'S COVE, GEORGIA, BATTLE OF.

DAVIS, EDMUND JACKSON (1827–1883) USA. Born in **Florida**, Davis grew up in **Texas** and became a lawyer. In the 1850s, he became a district attorney and then a judge in the Rio Grande Valley.

Davis remained loyal to the Union when Texas seceded, with some saying his loyalty came from bitterness from being defeated as a delegate to the state **secession** convention. He traveled to Mexico and raised a loyal **regiment** of Texans called the 1st Texas Cavalry. Davis was appointed colonel of Union volunteers in October 1862 and spent much of the war establishing pro-Union areas in the **Matamoros** area. He was promoted to brigadier general of volunteers in November 1864 and spent the latter months of the war commanding a cavalry **brigade** in **Louisiana**.

After the war, Davis was active in Texas **Reconstruction** politics as a harsh **Radical Republican** and was elected governor in 1869. He was viewed by most Texans as the worst of the Reconstruction governors.

DAVIS, GEORGE (1820–1896) CSA. A native of **North Carolina**, Davis practiced law after graduating from the University of North Carolina in 1838. He was a Unionist during the **secession** crisis and served as a delegate to the **Washington Peace Conference**. After its failure, Davis decided secession was North Carolina's only recourse.

In early 1861, Davis was named to the Provisional **Confederate Congress** and later that year was elected to the Confederate Senate. He chaired the Senate Claims Committee and served on several others. Unlike many other politicians from his state, Davis was a strong nationalist and was one of only a handful of senators who voted to give a **Confed-**

erate supreme court the power to overrule state courts. Because of this nationalism, he lost his bid for reelection in 1863. In January 1864, **Jefferson Davis** appointed Davis as the Confederate attorney general. In that position, he continued to support a strong central government and even ruled some state laws unconstitutional because they conflicted with Confederate law. Davis resigned his position while the government was fleeing capture in the last days of the war and tried to escape to Europe. He was arrested in Key West, Florida, however, and was briefly imprisoned.

Upon his release from **prison**, Davis continued his law practice in North Carolina.

DAVIS GUARD MEDAL. On September 8, 1863, Lt. **Richard "Dick" Dowling** and 44 men of the Davis Guards, 1st Texas Heavy Artillery, stopped a Union invasion that consisted of 11 ships and 4,000 men at **Sabine Pass, Texas**. In recognition of this feat, Dowling and his men were awarded the only medal ever presented by the Confederates. The medal was sponsored by Sabine City, Texas, and was made from a silver dollar, which was suspended around the neck on a green ribbon. On one side was a Maltese Cross, with the letters DG, and the other side bore the inscription "Battle of Sabine Pass, September 8, 1863." **Jefferson Davis** received one of the medals and kept it until it was confiscated at the time of his imprisonment.

DAVIS, HENRY WINTER (1817–1865) USA. A native of **Maryland**, Davis was a member of an influential family that included his cousin, Judge David Davis, **Abraham Lincoln's** close adviser. After attending Kenyon College and the University of Virginia Law School, Davis became a prominent Baltimore attorney. He first was a **Whig**, then became active in the **Know-Nothing Party.** Davis was elected to the **U.S. Congress** as a Know-Nothing in 1855 but later switched parties again to the **Republicans**. By 1860, he was a powerful force in Congress and played a key role in getting Unionist **Thomas Hicks** nominated governor of Maryland. Davis's neutral stand on **slavery** angered those Marylanders sympathetic to the South, however, and in 1860 he was censured by the state legislature and was defeated for reelection

Davis wanted to be appointed to **Abraham Lincoln's** Cabinet but was overshadowed by his fellow Marylander and arch rival **Montgomery Blair**, who won the appointment to postmaster general. This rejection pushed Davis into the arms of the **Radical Republicans**, and afterward he often opposed the Lincoln administration. Davis won back his congressional seat in 1862 and became chairman of the House Foreign Relations Committee. He then teamed up with fellow Radical **Benjamin F. Wade** to oppose Lincoln's **Reconstruction** policy and coauthored the **Wade-Davis Bill**, a harsher Reconstruction plan, which Lincoln pocket vetoed. Davis was defeated for reelection in 1864 and died before the next election.

DAVIS, JEFFERSON COLUMBUS (1828–1879) USA. A native of **Indiana**, Davis served in the 3rd Indiana during the **Mexican War** and saw combat at Buena Vista. In 1848, he was commissioned a 2nd lieutenant of **artillery** and remained in the **U.S. Army** until the Civil War. At **Fort Sumter**, Davis was a captain and endured the bombardment that initiated the war.

Davis was appointed colonel of the 22nd Indiana in August 1861 and was promoted to brigadier general of volunteers in December. After commanding a **brigade** at **Wilson's Creek** and a **division** in the **Battle of Pea Ridge** and the **siege of Corinth, Mississippi**, he became involved in a bitter feud with his former commander, Maj. Gen. **William Nelson**.

During the **Kentucky Campaign** in autumn 1862, Nelson was dissatisfied with Davis's performance in defending Louisville, Kentucky, and relieved him. In September 1862, the two met in the lobby of a Louisville hotel and argued. When Nelson refused to apologize for his earlier actions, Davis threw a crumpled piece of paper in his face. Nelson then slapped Davis, and moments later, Davis shot and killed him. Although witnesses felt the shooting was murder, Davis was restored to command because of influence from his close friend, Indiana's Gov. **Oliver P. Morton**. He was never tried for the killing and went on to lead a division in the **Army of the Cumberland** in the **Stones River**, **Chickamauga**, and **Atlanta Campaigns**. Although Davis never was promoted after the shooting, he did command a **corps** during **William T. Sherman's March to the Sea**. Davis was **brevetted** major general of volunteers for his wartime service, and Sherman thought highly of him.

Davis remained in the **army** after the war and was appointed colonel of the 23rd U.S. Infantry.

DAVIS, JEFFERSON FINIS (1808–1889) CSA. Born in **Kentucky**, Davis was the uncle of future Confederate general **Joseph R. Davis**. He did not come from an old Southern aristocratic family but, in fact, was only a second-generation Southerner who belonged to a moderately successful planter family.

Davis's father moved the family to Woodville, Mississippi, when Davis was a child. He attended **Mississippi's** Jefferson College and Kentucky's Transylvania University but dropped out of the latter in 1824 to enter

West Point. Davis's West Point career was unspectacular, and he graduated in the lower half of the class of 1828. His **U.S. Army** career included the Black Hawk War, in which he took the surrender of Chief Black Hawk and escorted him to Jefferson Barracks. Davis was promoted to 1st lieutenant of dragoons and saw some service against **Indians** on the frontier, but he resigned his commission in 1835.

A month after his resignation, Davis married Sarah Knox Taylor, the daughter of Davis's former commander Zachary Taylor and the sister of future Confederate general **Richard Taylor**. Davis brought his wife back to Mississippi, where they settled at "Brierfield," a plantation outside **Vicksburg**, which Davis's brother Joseph had established for him. Within weeks, both Davis and "Knoxie" contracted a fever, probably malaria. She died in September, but Davis recovered. Grief stricken, he secluded himself on his plantation for years and developed it into a progressive model on which slaves were humanely treated. In February 1845, Davis married **Varina Howell (Davis)**, who was 18 years his junior. They had a sometimes-contentious marriage, but Varina came to be his staunch supporter and steadfastly promoted Davis during his political career and after his death. The couple had four sons and two daughters.

Davis was elected to the **U.S. Congress** as a **Democrat** in 1845, but when the **Mexican War** began, he resigned his seat and was elected colonel of the 1st Mississippi Rifles. The **regiment** joined Davis's former father-in-law, Zachary Taylor, in Mexico and saw hard service. Davis played an important role in the victory at Monterrey and then became a bona fide hero at the Battle of Buena Vista when he deployed his regiment in an unorthodox manner and annihilated a Mexican cavalry charge. Severely wounded in the foot, he turned down a commission as brigadier general and instead returned to Mississippi, where the state presented him a ceremonial sword and in 1847 appointed him to complete an unexpired U.S. senatorial term.

Davis was elected to the Senate in his own right in 1850 and became a prominent force, chairing the Military Committee and becoming an outspoken defender of Southern rights. He favored extending the **Missouri Compromise** Line as a solution to the **slavery** issue and succeeded **John C. Calhoun** as the leading Southern advocate. Davis resigned his Senate seat in 1850 to run for governor against **Henry S. Foote**. Although he campaigned hard on a Southern rights platform, he was defeated and retired to Brierfield. In 1853, however, Davis returned to **Washington, D.C.**, as President Franklin Pierce's secretary of war. He was an outstanding secretary, who advocated such modern weapons as **rifle muskets**, adopted the **Davis boot**, sent out exploration parties to survey a transcontinental **railroad**, and even experimented with camels in the desert Southwest.

After his time in the War Department, Davis was elected again to the Senate and took his seat in 1857. The spread of slavery into the western territories was the major issue of the day, and he staunchly defended Southerners' property rights. Davis believed that slavery was the only practical way for blacks and whites to coexist peacefully, that the Constitution guaranteed slave property, and that the Northern idea of **popular sovereignty** was simply tyranny by the majority. He also believed that the newly formed **Republican Party** most threatened Southern rights. Although he loved the Union, and called for moderation, Davis believed the South had to defend **states rights** against the dangerous Republicans—even by **secession**, if necessary.

When **Abraham Lincoln** won the **election of 1860**, Davis believed the administration would trample Southern rights and that secession was the only option. He sadly resigned from the Senate in January 1861 and returned to Mississippi, where he accepted appointment as major general of state troops. When the seceding states met in the February 1861 **Montgomery, Alabama, Convention**, Davis was elected provisional president of the **Confederate States of America** (he was elected as the permanent president for a six-year term in February 1862). Although he preferred a military command, Davis accepted the position.

Under Davis's leadership, the Confederacy became a credible nation, with a strong military force and functioning government. He adopted a defensive-offensive military **strategy** whereby the armies would defend as much Confederate territory as possible and only take the offensive when there was a minimum risk of defeat. Davis was a devoted nationalist, who, ironically, struggled to limit the very states rights he had championed for so long. He supported the first military **conscription** act in American history, the **suspension of the writ of habeas corpus**, putting state militia under national control, and the **Impressment Act** to obtain much needed supplies. Yet, Davis also defended free speech and never nationalized the railroads. Overall, he probably did as well as anyone possibly could have done as Confederate president.

Davis largely served as his own secretary of war, never fully trusting anyone to work independently in that position, and reduced the six secretaries who served under him to little more than clerks. Yet, he left the other cabinet members to run their departments largely unsupervised.

Davis was knowledgeable about military matters, honest, and hard working. However, he also had many personality flaws that weakened his presidency. His poor health often incapacitated him and made him testy and short tempered. Davis also lacked the skills necessary to stir emotions and tightly bind the Southern people together as did his counterpart, Abraham Lincoln. He could be petty, lacked the important political skills of compromise and tact, and wasted precious time immersing himself in minutiae that could have been handled by clerks. Davis also played favorites with generals, standing by incompetent ones whom he liked while banishing skillful ones to unimportant positions because of personal differences. The war effort was weakened by personal feuds Davis had with Gens. **Joseph E. Johnston** and **P. G. T. Beauregard** and by his keeping **Lucius Northrop** and **Braxton Bragg** well beyond their usefulness. Of all his generals, **Robert E. Lee** had the best relationship with Davis, largely because of Lee's interpersonal skills.

One of Davis's greatest military mistakes was using a system whereby the Confederacy was divided into numerous **departments**, each having a commander whose duty was to defend his department with his available force. Such a system made these commanders reluctant to cooperate and made it very difficult to send reinforcements from one department to another or to coordinate military operations that cut across departmental lines.

By war's end, Davis's flaws had alienated many generals and politicians. Still, he never gave up hope for final victory. Even when Lee was forced to evacuate **Richmond, Virginia**, in April 1865 and the Confederate government fled toward **Georgia**, Davis continued to believe that somehow the war could be continued from a base in the **Trans-Mississippi Department**. It took a concerted effort by the generals and cabinet members finally to convince him that the war was lost. Davis and his entourage were finally captured in May 1865 near Irwinville, Georgia, and he was imprisoned for two years in **Fort Monroe, Virginia**. His harsh confinement turned him into a martyr for the **Lost Cause**, and Davis became more popular after the war than he was as president. He finally was released on bond in May 1867 but was never brought to trial for treason as was threatened.

Financially and physically ruined, Davis failed at several business ventures and finally accepted an offer to live at Beauvoir, a house in Biloxi, Mississippi, that was owned by a friend. He spent his remaining years corresponding with various war figures, defending the Confederacy, and writing his two-volume *Rise and Fall of the Confederate Government*, in which he continued to attack his critics and praise his friends. Davis died in 1889 at age 82, having lived much longer than anyone expected. He was survived by two daughters and Varina, who continued to promote his legacy. All four of his sons died before him, including Joseph Evan, who was killed in 1864 when he fell from a balcony at the presidential house in Richmond.

DAVIS, JOSEPH ROBERT (1825–1896) CSA. The nephew of Confederate President **Jefferson Davis**, Davis was born in **Mississippi** and graduated from **Ohio's** Miami University. He became an attorney in Mississippi and in 1860 was elected to the state senate.

When the Civil War began, Davis was a captain in the state militia and became lieutenant colonel of the 10th Mississippi in April 1861. In August, he was promoted to colonel and joined Jefferson Davis's staff in **Richmond, Virginia**. Davis held this position until he was promoted to brigadier general in October 1862. Since the president's nephew had no military training or experience, the appointment was criticized by many as nepotism and once was rejected by the Senate. Nonetheless, Davis was given an infantry **brigade** in the **Army of Northern Virginia** and saw his first combat at **Gettysburg**, where his inexperience led to his unit being cut to pieces on the first day's battle. Two days later the brigade participated in **Pickett's Charge** and, though fighting well, again suffered extremely heavy losses. Soon after Gettysburg, Davis contracted a fever and was on sick leave until the spring of 1864, when he rejoined his brigade for the **Overland Campaign**. He also competently led his men throughout the **Petersburg Campaign** and surrendered with the **army** at **Appomattox**.

After the war, Davis returned to his Mississippi law practice.

DAVIS, SAM (1842–1863) CSA. A popular Southern martyr, Davis was a **Tennessee** native who enlisted as a private in the 1st Tennessee in April 1861. After service in **Virginia**, the **regiment** transferred west, and Davis was wounded at **Shiloh**. The young soldier then enlisted in a **company** of scouts and in November 1863 was captured while carrying intelligence information back to his lines. Accused of spying, Davis was jailed in Pulaski, Tennessee, and was interrogated as to the source of his information and the identity of the scouts' leader. His captors offered leniency if he cooperated and a hangman's noose if he did not. Davis refused to answer and insisted he was a courier rather than a spy.

After being interrogated by Brig. Gen. **Grenville M. Dodge** and others, Davis was tried for spying, convicted, and hanged in Pulaski on November 27, 1863. The commander whose identity he protected watched the hanging from his own jail cell. His young age and brave demeanor turned Davis into a Confederate hero, and even his captors were impressed with his stoic patriotism. After the war, Davis became one of the most popular Confederate war heroes, and his home in Smyrna, Tennessee, was made into a museum.

DAVIS, VARINA HOWELL (1826–1905) CSA. Born in **Mississippi**, Varina Howell had a comfortable upbringing with a private tutor and finishing school. She was described as being a gracious hostess, good conversationalist, and intensely interested in politics. Varina's family had reservations about her marrying **Jefferson Davis** in 1845 since he was 18 years her senior, but it finally relented. The marriage was contentious at first, since both were strong-willed people, but they resolved their differences and developed a very successful, supportive marriage.

During the Civil War, Varina was invaluable to the president and became his confidante and defender and was quick to attack those who criticized him. This trait, plus her obvious influence on Davis and her habit of entertaining even during times of shortages and hardships, made her a target of gossip and criticism. Varina fled **Richmond**, **Virginia**, with the government in April 1865 and was with her husband when he was captured weeks later in **Georgia**. After she worked tirelessly to win his release from **prison**, the couple finally settled at Beauvoir, a house in Biloxi, Mississippi, that was offered to them by a friend.

After her husband's death, Varina wrote her own memoirs and played a major part in promoting the memory of Jefferson Davis. She eventually donated Beauvoir to the state to become a Confederate veterans' home and moved to New York City, where she became a writer. The Davises had six children, but only one survived Varina. Their youngest son, Joseph, was killed during the war when he fell from a balcony at the presidential mansion.

DAVIS, WILLIAM GEORGE MACKEY (1812–1898) CSA. One of the more obscure Confederate generals, Davis was a **Virginia** native and the son of a **U.S. Navy** officer. He went to sea when he was 17 but eventually settled in **Alabama** and became a newspaper editor. Davis later moved to **Florida** and became a wealthy lawyer, one-term judge, and cotton speculator.

After serving in the Florida **secession** convention, Davis contributed $50,000 to the cause and then raised and equipped the 1st Florida Cavalry, of which he became lieutenant colonel in the summer of 1861. Promoted to colonel in January 1862, he was put in command of the provisional forces in east Florida. Governor **John Milton**, who felt cavalry was ill-suited for Florida's swampy terrain, questioned Davis's ability and usefulness. Apparently, Davis also was less than a competent commander, for later one inspector declared his **regiment** to be "in a state of mutiny" (Davis, ed., *The Confederate General*, vol. 2, p. 53). After being transferred to **Tennessee** in May 1861, he performed scouting duty around Knoxville and briefly commanded a **brigade** and the town. Davis also participated in the **Kentucky Campaign** that autumn in command of a Florida infantry **brigade** that included his dismounted regiment. He was promoted to brigadier general in November 1862 and temporarily took command of the **Department of East Tennessee** until April 1863. Davis then resigned his commission a month later and became involved in **blockade running** at **Wilmington, North Carolina**.

Davis resumed his law practice after the war and eventually settled in **Washington, D.C.**

DAY'S GAP, ALABAMA, BATTLE OF (APRIL 30, 1863). In April 1863, Col. **Abel D. Streight** led 1,500 men on **Streight's Raid** from northeast **Mississippi** toward a vital Confederate **railroad** in **Georgia**. Mounted on mules, his men left Tuscumbia, Alabama, on April 26 and headed to the southeast, with **Nathan Bedford Forrest's** Confederate cavalry in pursuit. On April 30, Forrest's hard-riding troopers caught up with Streight at Sand Mountain's Day's Gap. When Forrest attempted to surround Streight, the Federals ambushed one of the Confederate columns and captured two cannons. Streight lost 23 men in the fight, while Forrest suffered 65 casualties. Streight then continued on toward Rome, Georgia, but Forrest eventually caught him on May 3 near the Georgia state line and Streight was forced to surrender.

DAYTON, VIRGINIA, BURNING OF (OCTOBER 4, 1864). *See* MEIGS, JOHN RODGERS.

DAYTON, WILLIAM LEWIS (1807–1864) USA. A native of **New Jersey**, Dayton graduated from the College of New Jersey (now Princeton University) and became a lawyer and active **Whig**. He served on the state supreme court and in the 1840s was appointed to fill a U.S. Senate seat. In the Senate, Dayton opposed the **Mexican War**, the admission of additional slave states, and the **Compromise of 1850**. He helped form the **Republican Party** in 1854 and was **John C. Frémont's** running mate in the 1856 presidential election. In 1860, Dayton ran for the Republican presidential nomination but then bowed out in favor of **Abraham Lincoln**.

Lincoln appointed Dayton minister to France, even though Dayton spoke no French and had no diplomatic experience. Nonetheless, he performed his job well. Dayton had previously been an acquaintance of Louis Napoleon when the emperor lived in the United States in exile, and the two worked well together. He was able to prevent France from recognizing the Confederacy, displayed American displeasure at France's involvement in Mexico, stopped Confederate agents from purchasing material in France, put an end to France's building Confederate warships, and stopped the French practice of allowing Confederate **commerce raiders** to use French ports (his actions helped force the **CSS** *Alabama* from port to battle the **USS** *Kearsarge*). In the midst of his important work, Dayton died in Paris in 1864.

DEARING, JAMES (1840–1865) CSA. A native of **Virginia**, Dearing entered **West Point** in 1858 and quickly became a popular, although somewhat rowdy, cadet. After **Fort Sumter** was fired on, he and friend **Thomas L. Rosser** resigned from the academy and went home. Rosser joined the **Washington Artillery**, and when it passed through Lynchburg, Virginia, in June 1861, Dearing joined up as well.

At first, Dearing had no rank, but in July he was appointed a 2nd lieutenant of infantry, even though he served with the **artillery**. After fighting at **First Manassas**, he was promoted to 1st lieutenant in February 1862 and became a **company** commander. During the **army's** April 1862 reorganization, Dearing was elected captain by the Lynchburg Artillery and joined it. He won accolades for his fighting during the **Peninsula Campaign** and also served with the **Army of Northern Virginia** at **Second Manassas** and **Fredericksburg**. Promoted to major in January 1863, Dearing joined the artillery in **George Pickett's division** and fought at **Suffolk, Virginia**, where he lost some of his guns. He performed well while commanding Pickett's artillery battalion at **Gettysburg** but afterward was transferred to the cavalry and was promoted to colonel in January 1864. He again received praise for leading cavalry raids in **North Carolina** and in April 1864 was rewarded with a promotion to brigadier general.

Dearing's **brigade** served well at **Second Drewry's Bluff** and in the **Petersburg Campaign** and participated in **Wade Hampton's** famous "Beefsteak Raid" in September 1864. By the end of the war, he received command of the Laurel Brigade and led it at **Dinwiddie Court House** and **Five Forks**. Dearing was mortally wounded in a hand-to-hand cavalry clash at **High Bridge** on April 6, 1865, just three days before **Robert E. Lee's** surrender. It was claimed that Dearing engaged Union **brevet** Brig. Gen. Theodore Read in a close-quarter pistol shoot-out. Read was killed outright, and Dearing was mortally wounded. Dearing died on April 23, 1865, the last Confederate general to be killed in battle.

DEAS, ZACHARIAH CANTEY (1819–1882) CSA. A first cousin of Confederate Brig. Gen. **James Chesnut Jr.**, Deas (DAZE) was born in **South Carolina** but moved with his family to Mobile, **Alabama**, when he was a teenager. He was educated in South Carolina schools and in

France and served in the **Mexican War** as an enlisted man. Deas became a wealthy cotton broker during the antebellum period and married into one of the most prominent Mobile families.

When the Civil War began, Deas first served as an aide to **Joseph E. Johnston** during the **First Battle of Manassas** and then raised the 22nd Alabama and became its colonel in October 1861. He used $28,000 of his own money (later reimbursed) to buy **Enfield rifles** for his men. The **regiment** first served in Mobile, but it was shipped to Corinth, Mississippi, in early 1862 and fought at **Shiloh**. There, Deas became acting **brigade** commander because of casualties among the officers. He handled the brigade well, had two horses shot from under him, and was severely wounded. Deas recovered in time to lead his regiment in the 1862 **Kentucky Campaign** and was promoted to brigadier general in December 1862.

Deas fought with the **Army of Tennessee** at **Stones River**, and at **Chickamauga** he and his Alabama brigade won accolades when they overran a Union position and captured 17 cannons. After fighting at **Missionary Ridge**, he took temporary command of the **division** but later resigned his commission when the expected promotion to major general did not occur. The resignation was not accepted, because Deas led his brigade in the **Atlanta Campaign** until he became ill sometime before June 30, 1864. An unknown controversy then apparently erupted, for in July the secretary of war ordered him brought before an examining board. This never took place, however, and in August, Johnston placed Deas back in command of his brigade. He continued to earn the praise of his superiors and was badly wounded again at **Jonesboro**. Deas fought gallantly at **Franklin** and there received a third, although, slight wound. He never received his promotion to major general, but after the **Battle of Nashville**, he again became temporary commander of the division until the **army** retreated. Afterward, Deas and his brigade fought at **Wyse Fork** and **Bentonville** during the **Carolinas Campaign**. At the time of the **surrender**, he apparently had relinquished command because of illness.

After the war, Deas moved to New York City and became a cotton broker and a member of the stock exchange.

DECATUR, ALABAMA, BATTLE OF (OCTOBER 26–29, 1864). After the 1864 **Atlanta Campaign**, **John Bell Hood** took his **Army of Tennessee** into north **Georgia** to disrupt **William T. Sherman's** supply lines. Hood eventually decided to invade **Tennessee** to clear it of enemy troops and march on to **Virginia** to join **Robert E. Lee's** army. The Confederate **army** first marched to Decatur, **Alabama**, where it planned to cross the Tennessee River, but Brig. Gen. **Robert S. Granger's** 5,000-

man Union garrison held the town. From October 26 to 29, Hood probed Granger's defenses but finally decided it would be too costly to force a crossing there and moved west toward Tuscumbia. In the **skirmishing** at Decatur, Hood lost about 200 men, while Granger suffered 155 casualties. Hood crossed the river at Tuscumbia in mid-November and began the **Franklin and Nashville Campaign.**

DECLARATION OF IMMEDIATE CAUSES. This document was written by **Christopher G. Memminger** to justify **South Carolina's secession** in December 1860 and was based on the principle of **states rights**. It declared that the Union, as seen by the Founding Fathers, was a voluntary constitutional government, with each state having the right to withdraw whenever it believed its rights were being violated. Memminger stated that the North had violated the South's constitutional rights by attempting to contain **slavery** and supporting **abolitionism**. Thus, the declaration claimed that South Carolina had the right to secede and called for other Southern states to join it in forming a new nation.

DECORATIONS. Neither side in the Civil War presented decorations or medals at the beginning of the war because recognizing an individual's bravery was thought to create dissension within the ranks and was contrary to the idea of equality among volunteer soldiers. Stress was placed on unit bravery, and individual **regiments** were allowed to place the names of battles on their regimental **flags** as a way of displaying their proud service record. In keeping with the American tradition, the highest accolade an individual soldier could expect was a **brevet** (for Union officers only) or a commendation by being mentioned in his commander's after-action report. High-ranking officers on both sides also sometimes received the **Thanks of Congress** for outstanding service.

Many people disagreed with this lack of recognition, and both sides eventually did begin recognizing individual acts of bravery. The only government-authorized medal was the Union's **Medal of Honor**. The Confederates never authorized any medals, but in October 1862, the **Confederate Congress** authorized publication of a **Roll of Honor**, which was a list of soldiers who had distinguished themselves in battle. After a battle, the roll was read to the troops during parade and often was published in reports and newspapers.

There were a number of medals issued during the war, but except for the Medal of Honor, they were given out by individuals, towns, or organizations. Examples of these are the **Butler Medal**, **Davis Guard Medal**, and **Kearny Cross**. *See also* GILMORE MEDAL; FORT SUMTER AND FORT PICKENS MEDALS; XVII CORPS MEDAL.

DEEP BOTTOM, VIRGINIA, FIRST BATTLE OF (JULY 27–29, 1864). Also known as Darbytown, New Market Road, and Strawberry Plains, this action took place southeast of **Richmond, Virginia**, near Deep Bottom on the James River during the **Petersburg Campaign**. It was a Union diversionary attack in support of the explosion of the Petersburg mine that led to the **Battle of the Crater**. Lieutenant General **U. S. Grant** ordered Maj. Gen. **Winfield S. Hancock's** II Corps of the **Army of the Potomac** and two of Maj. Gen. **Philip Sheridan's** cavalry **divisions** to make a diversionary attack north of the James River to draw off Confederate forces from the area where the mine was to be exploded. Hancock was to advance toward Chaffin's Bluff, and if the attack was successful, the cavalry was to ride into Richmond or raid the Virginia Central Railroad.

The combined force crossed the James River on the night of July 26–27, with the infantry leading. Once across, an **Army of the James** cavalry division under Brig. Gen. **August Valentine Kautz** was added to Sheridan's two divisions. Advancing from a bridgehead held by the X Corps, Hancock moved out on the New Market Road on the morning of July 27 toward the Confederate defenses at Bailey's Creek. Unknown to the Federals, Gen. **Robert E. Lee** had heard rumors of the movement and had dispatched Maj. Gen. **Joseph B. Kershaw's** division to reinforce Maj. Gen. **Cadmus M. Wilcox's** division.

Brigadier General **Francis C. Barlow's** division drove in the Confederate advanced line and captured four guns, but it was halted near the creek when Kershaw counterattacked. Meanwhile, Sheridan's cavalry advanced north along the Darbytown Road but found the creek crossing heavily defended. Two of Hancock's divisions were sent to reinforce Sheridan, but no gains could be made other than a cavalry charge that seized some forward positions.

Major General **Henry Heth's** Confederate division was rushed to reinforce the Darbytown Road area, and Grant arrived on the scene that afternoon. Realizing he had underestimated the enemy's numbers, Grant ordered an **envelopment** of the Confederate northern flank the next day to allow Sheridan to continue his mission. However, Kershaw attacked Sheridan first on the morning of July 28. After losing some ground, Sheridan's dismounted troopers counterattacked and drove Kershaw back with a loss of 300 **prisoners**. Replaced by an infantry division, Sheridan then moved to the New Market Road, but the aggressive Confederate defenders prevented his advancing down it. With all approaches to Richmond effectively blocked, the operation was called off, and Hancock returned to the south side of the James River on July 29.

Lee's response to this threat had been swift, and the Confederate defenders prevented what could have been a serious cavalry raid. Confederate efforts were hampered by command confusion when Lt. Gen. **Richard H. Anderson**, commanding the I Corps, and Lt. Gen. **Richard S. Ewell**, commanding the Richmond defenses, could not agree on who should oversee the action. Confederate losses are estimated at about 700 men, while Hancock and Sheridan lost 334.

DEEP BOTTOM, VIRGINIA, SECOND BATTLE OF (AUGUST 13–20, 1864). During the **Petersburg Campaign**, Lt. Gen. **U. S. Grant** believed Confederate Gen. **Robert E. Lee** must have weakened his defensive line near Deep Bottom after learning that Lee had dispatched part of his **Army of Northern Virginia** to the **Shenandoah Valley**. Grant planned to strike this supposedly weak point early on August 14, 1864.

Grant sent Maj. Gen. **Winfield S. Hancock's** II Corps and Brig. Gen. **David M. Gregg's** cavalry **division** north of the James River to join the X Corps, which was holding a bridgehead there. The operation was supervised by Hancock and called for the infantry to make a **frontal attack** to turn the Confederates out of their Chaffin's Bluff position. Once the Confederates massed their forces to meet this attack, the cavalry was to swing around their northern flank at Fussell's Mill and head for **Richmond, Virginia**.

When Maj. Gen. **David Birney's** X Corps began the attack on the morning of August 14, it ran into heavy Confederate resistance. Instead of being weakened, the Confederate defenses along Deep Run were manned by Maj. Gen. **Charles W. Field's** entire division, with four other infantry and cavalry divisions positioned nearby for support. The attack had little success, except for capturing four guns and Gregg's cavalry making some progress along the Charles City Road.

On August 15, Lee arrived at Chaffin's Bluff to assume command of the Confederate defense, and Hancock sent Birney's **corps** to the north to turn the enemy's left flank. Gregg again attacked up the Charles City Road on August 16 as a diversion and managed to get within seven miles of Richmond and kill Confederate Brig. Gen. **John Chambliss** before being forced back. Birney, however, became confused in the thick timber and moved so far around the enemy flank that he was unable to get all of his corps into action. While Birney floundered in the woods, other X Corps divisions and part of Hancock's corps attacked the Confederate line at Fussell's Mill. The Federals overran the position, captured several hundred **prisoners**, and killed Confederate Brig. Gen. **Victor Girardey**, but they were forced back by a counterattack later in the day.

Both sides remained quiet on August 17, but late the next day Lee attacked at Fussell's Mill to push Hancock from the north side of the river. The II Corps' Brig. Gen. **Nelson Miles** aggressively counterattacked the Confederate left flank, however, and drove it in with heavy loss. This ended the action around Deep Bottom, and Hancock withdrew to the south side of the river on August 20. Out of approximately 28,000 Union soldiers engaged, Hancock lost 2,899. An estimated 20,000 Confederates were engaged with an estimated loss of 1,000 men.

DEEP RUN, VIRGINIA, BATTLE OF (JUNE 5, 1863). *See* FRANKLIN'S CROSSING, VIRGINIA, BATTLE OF.

DEFEAT IN DETAIL. This is a military term that means to defeat an enemy's army piece by piece, and it usually occurs when a force is scattered and its individual units are unable to support one another.

DEITZLER, GEORGE WASHINGTON (1826–1884) USA. A native of **Pennsylvania**, Deitzler eventually settled in **Kansas**, where he became a successful farmer and land dealer. He also was a fierce antislavery politician and was active in arming the **abolitionist** forces in **"Bleeding Kansas."** In the 1850s, Deitzler served as the territory's speaker of the house and senator and was elected mayor of Lawrence in 1860.

Deitzler entered Union service in June 1861 when he helped organize the 1st Kansas and was elected its colonel. After being severely wounded at **Wilson's Creek**, he was appointed a **brigade** commander in the **Army of the Tennessee** even though he was not fully recovered from his wound. After leading the brigade through part of the **Vicksburg Campaign**, Deitzler took sick leave and returned to Kansas. He was in **Lawrence** when it was raided by **William Quantrill** but survived by hiding in a gulch. Deitzler resigned his commission in August 1863 but then was appointed major general in the Kansas militia and helped turn back **Sterling Price's Missouri Raid** in 1864.

After the war, Deitzler eventually moved to **California** and was killed in an 1884 Arizona carriage accident.

DE LAGNEL, JULIUS ADOLPH (1827–1912) CSA. The son of a **West Point** officer, de Lagnel was born in **New Jersey** but grew up in **Virginia**. He was commissioned directly into the **U.S. Army** as a 2nd lieutenant in 1847 and served in the 2nd U.S. Artillery until the Civil War began. In command of the Fayetteville, North Carolina, arsenal when it was seized by secessionists in April 1861, de Lagnel took his **company** back to **New York**. After settling all of his official duties, he then resigned his 2nd lieutenant's commission and joined the Confederacy.

De Lagnel entered Confederate service in June 1861 as a captain in the Lee Virginia Artillery. He then joined Brig. Gen. **Robert S. Garnett's** staff in western Virginia and at the **Battle of Rich Mountain** commanded a small group of infantry and **artillery** that was attacked by a much superior Union force. De Lagnel's unit suffered heavy losses and was overrun, and he received a serious wound in his side while manning his lone gun after its crew was shot. He saved himself from capture by hiding in a thicket and then wandered three days before receiving aid at a farmhouse. De Lagnel was captured later, as he tried to return to his lines and was held **prisoner** until **exchanged** in January 1862. After commanding a naval battery on Mulberry Island on the Virginia Peninsula, he was promoted to major in the 20th Virginia Artillery Battalion.

In April 1862, de Lagnel was promoted to brigadier general but declined the appointment in July for unknown reasons. Instead, he accepted a lieutenant colonel's commission in the Ordnance Bureau and in September resumed command of the Fayetteville arsenal. De Lagnel kept that post for more than a year and then served until war's end at various other arsenals and in Ordnance Bureau positions.

After the war, de Lagnel became involved in the shipping industry and eventually settled in **Washington, D.C.**

DELAWARE. Delaware was one of the **border states**, and it cast more votes for proslavery candidate **John C. Breckinridge** in the **election of 1860** than for any other candidate. Still, most Delaware voters were moderates who opposed both **secession** and the use of force to coerce the South to remain in the Union. When war came, Delaware remained in the Union, although it did not officially free its slaves (1,800 in 1860) until the **13th Amendment** was ratified in December 1865. The state provided about 12,000 men to the Union armies, produced much of the North's gunpowder at the Du Pont mills, housed Confederate **prisoners** at **Fort Delaware**, and constructed many ships at the Wilmington shipyards.

DE LEON, EDWIN (1818–1891) CSA. A native of **South Carolina**, de Leon was a journalist friend of both **Jefferson Davis** and President **James Buchanan** and was appointed by the latter to be consul general to Egypt. In 1861, he resigned his position and returned to the South, where he convinced Davis to send him to France with $25,000 to try to sway public opinion toward the Confederacy. As a propagandist, de Leon was a failure. He clashed with Confederate minister **John Slidell** after de Leon portrayed himself as Davis's diplomatic envoy and then publicly denounced the French government when it failed to aid the Confederacy. As a result, de Leon was replaced by **Henry Hotze** in February 1864.

After the war, de Leon introduced the telephone to Egypt and wrote a number of books.

DEMOCRATIC PARTY. Formed by **Andrew Jackson** in the 1820s as a champion for the common people, the Democratic Party was the only true national party by the 1850s. Virtually all Southerners, as well as millions of Northerners, were members, while the **Republican Party** was purely a Northern party devoted to stopping the spread of **slavery**. However, the Democrats also were fractionalized between the proslavery Southerners and the Northern **Free-Soilers**, who wanted to contain the spread of slavery for economic reasons.

In 1860, the party finally split along sectional lines when the nominating convention failed to agree on a platform. Southern delegates at **Charleston, South Carolina**, and at Baltimore, Maryland, walked out in protest after the Northern delegates refused to support a platform calling for congressional protection of slavery in the territories. As a result, the Northerners formed the Northern Democratic Party and nominated **Stephen A. Douglas**, while the Southerners formed the Southern Democratic Party and nominated **John C. Breckinridge**. By splitting their vote, the Democrats enabled **Abraham Lincoln** to win the election.

During the conflict, many Northern Democrats supported war to preserve the Union and became known as **War Democrats**. Others, however, opposed the **Emancipation Proclamation** or believed preserving the Union was not worth the devastating cost in lives. These opponents became known as **Copperheads**, or **Peace Democrats**.

In 1864, the Northern Democrats nominated **George B. McClellan** for president and adopted a platform that called for a negotiated peace with the Confederacy. McClellan repudiated the peace platform but was badly defeated by Lincoln because the successful **Atlanta Campaign** and **Battle of Mobile Bay** gave voters hope that the war was nearly won. Because of its association with rebellion and tepid patriotism, the Democratic Party waned and did not fully recover from the Civil War until the early 20th century.

DEMONSTRATION. This is a military **tactic** where part of one's force feints, probes, or shifts troops in front of one part of the enemy's position to draw his attention and manpower away from where the main attack or movement is actually to take place. *See also* FEINT.

DENNIS, ELIAS SMITH (1812–1894) USA. Although apparently a competent officer, Dennis became one of the most obscure of the Union generals. Born in **New York**, he moved to **Illinois** as a young man. There,

Dennis married a prominent widow, ran a gristmill, and in the 1840s was elected to both houses of the state legislature. After serving as a U.S. marshal in **"Bleeding Kansas"** during the 1850s, he entered Union service in August 1861 as lieutenant colonel of the 30th Illinois.

Dennis was commended for his service at **Fort Donelson** and was promoted to colonel in May 1862. Another promotion to brigadier general followed in November. He served in eastern **Louisiana** during the 1863 **Vicksburg Campaign** and was **brevetted** major general of volunteers for gallantry during the 1865 **Mobile Campaign**.

After the war, Dennis briefly served as military governor of Louisiana but then left the **army** in August 1865. He remained in Louisiana to become a planter and in 1880 was elected sheriff of Madison Parish. Dennis returned to Illinois later in life.

DENNISON, WILLIAM (1815–1882) USA. A native of **Ohio**, Dennison graduated from Miami University and practiced law in Columbus. He was elected to the state senate as a **Whig** in 1848 and helped repeal the "Black Laws," which relegated blacks to a near slave existence. After helping organize the **Republican Party**, Dennison served as chairman of the 1856 Republican National Convention and was elected governor in 1859.

Dennison had an unsuccessful term of office. People came to dislike his haughty nature, and in 1861 he had little success in providing the support needed to turn the state's thousands of volunteers into an armed and trained **army**. Dennison also took control of the state's **telegraph** and **railroad** system and sometimes spent money that had not yet been appropriated. He had more success in defending the state against Confederate raiders and in supporting Unionism in neighboring **Kentucky** and western **Virginia**.

Because of his unpopularity, Dennison failed to be renominated in 1861. After chairing the 1864 Republican National Convention, he was appointed postmaster general by **Abraham Lincoln** to replace **Montgomery Blair**. Dennison kept that post until 1866, when he resigned in opposition to President **Andrew Johnson's Reconstruction** policies. He then returned to Ohio and resumed his law practice and business affairs.

DENVER, JAMES WILLIAM (1817–1892) USA. A native of **Virginia**, Denver moved to **Ohio** as a boy and became a surveyor, teacher, lawyer, and newspaper editor. He later moved to **Missouri** and organized a volunteer **company** to serve in the **Mexican War** with **Winfield Scott**. After the war, Denver settled in **California** and in the 1850s served in the state senate, as secretary of state, and in the **U.S. Congress**. He also killed a newspaper editor in a duel after the editor criticized Denver's handling of some supply trains that were sent to relieve incoming settlers. In 1857, President **James Buchanan** appointed Denver commissioner of Indian Affairs and later secretary of the **Kansas** Territory. The following year, he was appointed governor of the **Colorado Territory**, where the city of Denver was named in his honor.

Living in Ohio when the Civil War began, Denver was appointed brigadier general of volunteers in August 1861 to serve as an inspector general for the troops there. By 1862, he was commanding a **brigade** in Brig. Gen. **William T. Sherman's division** of the **Army of the Tennessee** and led it in the **siege of Corinth, Mississippi**. Afterward, Denver served mostly on garrison duty until he resigned his commission in March 1863.

After leaving the **army**, Denver eventually settled in **Washington, D.C.**, where he practiced law.

DEPARTMENT. Both the Union and Confederacy used the department as their basic military territorial organization. Each department had its own commander and military force and was sometimes subdivided into **districts**. The military force within a department sometimes was an **army** carrying the departmental name, such as the **Army of Northern Virginia**, which defended the Confederate **Department of Northern Virginia**.

Departments on both sides were very fluid. They sometimes were created, disbanded, and redrawn according to military and political necessities. As with their armies, the opposing sides generally followed different guidelines in naming their departments. The Union usually named departments after bodies of water, while the Confederacy mostly used state or regional names.

The department often proved to be a poor military system because it bred jealousy and poor coordination among the commanders. Since each commander was responsible for defending his department, there often was a reluctance to send reinforcements from one department to another or to cooperate in military campaigns involving more than one department.

DEPARTMENT NO. 1 (CONFEDERATE). Formed in the spring of 1861 under Maj. Gen. **David E. Twiggs** with headquarters at **New Orleans, Louisiana**, this was one of the Confederacy's first military **departments**. It originally included all of **Louisiana** (except for a narrow strip along the Mississippi River in the northeastern part of the state) and the southern **Mississippi** and **Alabama** panhandles (including Mobile). In October 1861, Maj. Gen. **Mansfield Lovell** replaced Twiggs, and by

December the department was reduced in size, with its eastern border extending only to the Pascagoula River. Lovell barely had 10,000 troops and was unable to prevent the capture of New Orleans, in the spring of 1862. After the city's fall, Department No. 1 was abolished in June 1862, with the territory west of the Mississippi River becoming part of the **Trans-Mississippi Department** and that part lying east of the river joining **Department No. 2**.

DEPARTMENT NO. 2 (CONFEDERATE). Organized in the spring of 1861 and sometimes referred to as the **Western Department**, this was one of the Confederacy's first **departments**. It centered on the Mississippi River and included that portion of **Louisiana** and **Mississippi** that bordered the river north of the 31st parallel, that part of **Arkansas** east of the White River that bordered the Mississippi River, and that part of **Tennessee** west of the Tennessee River. Also included in the department was a narrow strip of land in northeast Mississippi and northern **Alabama** that was bounded on the south by the Memphis & Charleston Railroad. By December 1861, Department No. 2 had been expanded to include all of Arkansas and Tennessee, that part of Mississippi lying west of the Mississippi Central Railroad, and all of **Missouri**. Further changes came in May 1862, when that part of Louisiana that lay east of the Mississippi River and all of Mississippi lying south of the 33rd parallel (except that portion that lay east of the Pascagoula and Chickasawhay Rivers) were added.

Major General **Leonidas Polk** took command of Department No. 2 in July 1861. Successive commanders were **Albert Sidney Johnston**, **P. G. T. Beauregard**, and **Braxton Bragg**. In June 1862, after the fall of **New Orleans, Louisiana**, that part of **Department No. 1** lying east of the Mississippi River was added to Department No. 2, and a month later it was extended to include all of Mississippi and Alabama, Middle and western Tennessee, northwestern Georgia, and western **Florida**. In October 1862 the department was reduced to include only Alabama, Middle and west Tennessee, and western Florida.

In November 1862, Department No. 2 became a subdepartment of **Joseph E. Johnston's Department of the West**. It disappeared entirely in July 1863, when the **Department of Tennessee** was formed.

DEPARTMENT OF ALABAMA (UNION). This **department** was created in June 1865 and consisted of the state of **Alabama**, with headquarters at Mobile. It was commanded by Maj. Gen. **Charles R. Woods** but was merged with the **Department of the South** in May 1866.

DEPARTMENT OF ALABAMA AND WEST FLORIDA (CONFEDERATE). Consisting of **Alabama** and western **Florida**, this **department**

was created in October 1861 under the command of Maj. Gen. **Braxton Bragg**. It was enlarged in December to include that part of **Mississippi** east of Pascagoula Bay. Bragg concentrated on defending **Pensacola, Florida**, and Mobile, Alabama, but early in 1862 was forced to send most of his troops to **Albert Sidney Johnston** for the attack at **Shiloh**. Bragg turned over the department to Brig. Gen. **Jones M. Withers** in February 1862 and accompanied his troops to northern **Mississippi**. The department went through several commanders over the next few months before coming under the control of Brig. Gen. **John H. Forney** in April 1862. It was absorbed into the larger **Department No. 2** in June 1862 after the Confederates abandoned Pensacola.

DEPARTMENT OF ALABAMA, MISSISSIPPI, AND EAST LOUISIANA (CONFEDERATE). In May 1864, the Confederate **Department of Mississippi and East Louisiana** was enlarged to create this new **department** under Maj. Gen. **Stephen D. Lee**. When Lee transferred to the **Army of Tennessee** in June to take over the **corps** of slain Lt. Gen. **Leonidas Polk**, the department temporarily was put into the hands of Maj. Gen. **Dabney H. Maury**. In August 1864, Lt. Gen. **Richard Taylor** assumed command and kept it until war's end. **Meridian, Mississippi**, served as headquarters, but the department's importance lay in its **railroads**; the industrial cities of Selma and Montgomery, Alabama; and the port of Mobile, Alabama. The number of Confederate defenders ranged from a high of about 16,000 in May 1864 to 12,000 when Taylor surrendered in May 1865. Major battles in the department included **Brice's Cross Roads**, **Tupelo**, cavalry operations by **Nathan Bedford Forrest** and **James H. Wilson**, and the **Mobile Campaign**.

DEPARTMENT OF ALEXANDRIA (CONFEDERATE). This **department** (sometimes also known as the Potomac Department) was created in April 1861 and included much of northern **Virginia**. Culpeper Court House first served as its headquarters under Col. **Philip St. George Cocke**, but he was replaced in May by Brig. Gen. **Milledge L. Bonham**, who moved headquarters to Manassas Junction. Confederate authorities realized the main Union thrust toward **Richmond, Virginia**, would come through this department, so in June, Brig. Gen. **P. G. T. Beauregard** took command and began assembling the Confederate **Army of the Potomac** that fought the **First Battle of Manassas** in July. After the battle, Beauregard was replaced by Gen. **Joseph E. Johnston**, who commanded the department until October, when it was absorbed into the **Department of Northern Virginia**.

DEPARTMENT OF ANNAPOLIS (UNION). As the first Union troops headed toward **Washington, D.C.**, in April 1861, secessionist citizens attacked them in the **Baltimore Riot**. Evidence of such hostility in that strategic area caused the Union government to create this **department** in April 1861 to prevent Washington from being surrounded by secessionist territory. The department was put under the command of Brig. Gen. **Benjamin F. Butler** and consisted of a strip of territory that lay 20 miles on either side of the **railroad** that ran from Annapolis to Washington. Butler secured the area for the Union, and thousands of troops were able to reach Washington safely. He relinquished command in May to Maj. Gen. **George Cadwalader**, who was succeeded in rapid succession by Maj. Gens. **Nathaniel P. Banks** and **John A. Dix**. In July 1861, the department was renamed the **Department of Maryland**, but six days later it was incorporated into the **Department of Pennsylvania**.

DEPARTMENT OF ARKANSAS (UNION). Created in January 1864, this **department** included all of **Arkansas** except **Fort Smith**, which was added to the department in April along with the **Indian Territory**. Major General **Frederick Steele**, with headquarters at **Little Rock**, commanded the department, and the VII Corps was its military force. Steele was replaced in December by Maj. Gen. **Joseph J. Reynolds**, who commanded the department until it was abolished in August 1865. The department's major military events were the **Camden Expedition** and various guerrilla activities.

DEPARTMENT OF EAST TENNESSEE (CONFEDERATE). This **department**, which included Chattanooga, Tennessee, was created in February 1862 as part of the Confederate response to the defeat at **Mill Springs, Kentucky**. Major General **Edmund Kirby Smith** assumed command in March, with his headquarters at Knoxville. During his tenure, the forces within the department were temporarily called the **Army of Kentucky**. In June, the extreme western part of **North Carolina** was added to the department. Chattanooga was withdrawn from it in late 1862, and in November 1862, it became a subdepartment of **Joseph E. Johnston's Department of the West**. Part of western **Virginia** was added in early 1863. The department's defense was hampered by its large, mountainous terrain; an inadequate number of defenders; and frequent change in commanders (nine officers in one year). In July 1863, the department was merged with the **Department of Tennessee**.

DEPARTMENT OF FLORIDA (UNION). This **department** was created in April 1861 at the outbreak of civil war and included **Florida** and the adjoining islands in the Gulf of Mexico. **Fort Pickens**, at **Pensacola**, served as headquarters, and Maj. Harvey Brown became commander when he arrived there with a relief expedition in April. In January 1862, the department was reorganized with Key West, the Tortugas, and parts of northern Florida being transferred to the **Department of Key West**. The Department of Florida was merged with the **Department of the South** in March 1862 but was reestablished in June 1865 for **Reconstruction**.

DEPARTMENT OF FREDERICKSBURG (CONFEDERATE). This **department** was created soon after **Virginia** seceded in 1861 and included a number of counties on both sides of the Rappahannock River from its mouth to Fredericksburg. It was commanded by Brig. Gen. **Theophilus H. Holmes** but in October 1861 became part of the District of Aquia.

DEPARTMENT OF GEORGIA (CONFEDERATE). This **department**, which included all of **Georgia**, was created in October 1861 after the capture of **Port Royal, South Carolina**, to protect the Georgia coast from a similar fate. Brigadier General **Alexander R. Lawton** took command with headquarters at Savannah. Lawton's department disappeared in 10 days, however, when it merged in November with the **Department of South Carolina and Georgia**.

DEPARTMENT OF HENRICO (CONFEDERATE). This **department** was created in October 1861 and encompassed Henrico (hen-RIE-koh) County, Virginia, in which **Richmond** is located. In March 1862, it was enlarged to include the city of Petersburg. Brigadier General **John H. Winder** was appointed commander and served until the department was abolished in May 1864. **Libby** and **Belle Isle prisons** fell under its jurisdiction, and Winder served as Richmond's provost marshal.

DEPARTMENT OF INDIAN TERRITORY (CONFEDERATE). *See* INDIAN TERRITORY.

DEPARTMENT OF KANSAS (UNION). This **department** was created out of the **Western Department** in November 1861 and included **Kansas, Indian Territory**, and the territories of **Colorado**, Nebraska, and Dakota. In February 1862, a small part of Colorado was transferred to the **Department of New Mexico**.

Major General **David Hunter** was appointed commander of the Department of Kansas and established his headquarters at Fort Leavenworth. The department briefly disappeared in March 1862 when it was incorporated into the **Department of the Mississippi**, but it was reestablished in May under Brig. Gen. **James G. Blunt**. New changes came in September when Nebraska and Dakota were incorporated into the **Department of the Northwest**, and the department itself again disappeared in September when it was absorbed by the **Department of the Missouri**.

In January 1864, the Department of Kansas was created a third time, with Nebraska and **Fort Smith, Arkansas**, being added to it. Major General **Samuel R. Curtis** took command, only to see the department reduced again in April when the Indian Territory and Fort Smith were merged into the **Department of Arkansas**. The Department of Kansas finally disappeared for good in January 1865 when it was reincorporated into the Department of the Missouri. The few thousand troops assigned to the department sometimes were referred to as the **Army of Kansas**.

DEPARTMENT OF KENTUCKY (UNION). Established in May 1861, this **department** consisted of that part of **Kentucky** that lay within one hundred miles of the Ohio River and was originally commanded by Brig. Gen. **Robert Anderson**. In August, it was incorporated into the **Department of the Cumberland**, but it then was recreated in February 1865 under Maj. Gen. **John M. Palmer**. The forces defending this department were referred to as the **Army of Kentucky**.

DEPARTMENT OF KEY WEST (UNION). When **Florida** seceded in January 1861, the Union military kept control of its bases on Key West. That month, the Department of Key West was created (as part of the **Department of Florida**) and was placed under Brig. Gen. **John M. Brannan**. The department included Key West, the Tortugas, and all of Florida as far north as Appalachicola in the west and Cape Canaveral in the east. It existed only a short time and was incorporated into the **Department of the South** in March 1862.

DEPARTMENT OF MARYLAND (UNION). Created in July 1861, this **department** was the former **Department of Annapolis**. Six days later it was incorporated into the **Department of Pennsylvania**.

DEPARTMENT OF MIDDLE AND EASTERN FLORIDA (CONFEDERATE). This **department** was created in August 1861 under Brig. Gen. **John B. Grayson**, with headquarters at Fernandina. It originally included the eastern coast of **Florida** but in October was expanded inland to the Choctawhatchee River. Over the next year, the department had several commanders and frequently was redrawn. In November 1861, the eastern Florida coast was taken out of the department and was incorporated into the **Department of South Carolina and Georgia**. In April 1862, the entire department was incorporated into the Department of South Carolina and Georgia, but it then was recreated only two days later under Brig. Gen. **Joseph Finegan**. Finegan established his headquarters at Tallahassee but saw much of his meager force drawn off to defend more threatened parts of the Confederacy.

In October 1862, the department was split into two **districts** of the **Department of South Carolina, Georgia, and Florida**—the District of East Florida and the District of West Florida. In February 1864, these two districts were merged to create the Military District of Florida under Maj. Gen. **James Patton Anderson**. This district remained in effect for the rest of the war and went through several commanders.

DEPARTMENT OF MISSISSIPPI (UNION). Created in November 1864, this **department** was commanded by Maj. Gen. **Napoleon J. T. Dana**. It included all of **Mississippi** and west **Tennessee**, with headquarters at Memphis, Tennessee, and its troops were to protect **William T. Sherman's** lines of communication as he advanced into **Georgia** during the **Atlanta Campaign**. Major General **Gouverneur K. Warren** took command of the department in May 1865.

DEPARTMENT OF MISSISSIPPI AND EAST LOUISIANA (CONFEDERATE). Consisting of **Mississippi** and that part of **Louisiana** lying east of the Mississippi River, this **department** was created in October 1862 to replace the District of Mississippi. In November, it became a subdepartment of **Joseph E. Johnston's Department of the West**. Lieutenant General **John C. Pemberton** then was put in command with headquarters at Jackson, Mississippi. His troops were referred to as the **Army of Mississippi**. After Pemberton was captured at the end of the **Vicksburg Campaign** in July 1863, Lt. Gen. **Leonidas Polk** assumed command of the department. In January 1864, it was restructured into the **Department of Alabama, Mississippi, and East Louisiana**.

DEPARTMENT OF NEW ENGLAND (UNION). This **department** was created in October 1861 as part of the larger **Department of the East**. Its purpose was to supervise the recruitment and transfer of volunteer troops from New England to **Washington, D.C.** Major General **Benjamin F. Butler** was put in command with headquarters at Boston, Massachusetts, but the department was abolished in February 1862.

DEPARTMENT OF NEW MEXICO (UNION). This **department** consisted of modern-day **New Mexico** (with headquarters located in Santa Fe) and already was in existence when the Civil War began. It was expanded in February 1862 to include part of southwestern **Colorado Territory** and by September was under the command of Brig. Gen. **James H. Carleton**. Western Arizona was added in January 1863, but it was removed in 1865 when Arizona became a territory. The department was abolished in June 1865.

DEPARTMENT OF NEW YORK (UNION). This **department** was created because of political disputes in **New York**. Governor **Edwin D. Morgan** was a strong supporter of **Abraham Lincoln's** administration, but his policies were sometimes thwarted by other state governing boards. To ensure the continued support of New York, the War Department appointed Morgan a major general of volunteers and in October 1861 put him in command of the newly created Department of New York. From his Albany headquarters, Morgan then had the authority to raise and equip volunteers and to appoint their officers without political interference. When Morgan resigned as governor to accept a U.S. Senate seat, the department was incorporated into the **Department of the East** in January 1863.

DEPARTMENT OF NORFOLK (CONFEDERATE). This **department** was created in May 1861 and was placed under the command of Brig. Gen. **Benjamin Huger**. It originally included only the immediate area around **Norfolk, Virginia**, but by year's end was expanded to include Albemarle Sound, North Carolina (except Roanoke Island). When Norfolk was captured by Union forces in May 1862, the department ceased to exist.

DEPARTMENT OF NORTH CAROLINA (CONFEDERATE). This **department** was created out of the **Department of Norfolk** and Brig. Gen. **Richard C. Gatlin's** North Carolina coastal command, which had been created in August 1861. By the time Gatlin was replaced by Brig. Gen. **Joseph R. Anderson** in March 1862, all of **North Carolina** had been designated the Department of North Carolina, with Goldsboro serving as headquarters. Other officers who served in command of the department were **Theophilus H. Holmes, Daniel H. Hill, James G. Martin, William H. C. Whiting, George E. Pickett**, and **Braxton Bragg**.

The department, which at times had as many as 22,000 men defending it, went through a dizzying amount of reorganization. In June 1862, its northern boundary was extended to the James River, and headquarters were transferred to **Petersburg, Virginia**. By August 1862, the command was known as the District of North Carolina and included the territory between the Roanoke River and the **South Carolina** state line. Between September 1862 and November 1864, this **district** twice became a subdepartment of the **Department of North Carolina and Southern Virginia**, only to revert to a separate department each time. By war's end, the department technically included North Carolina and southern **Virginia** and was under Bragg's command.

DEPARTMENT OF NORTH CAROLINA (UNION). This **department** included all of **North Carolina** and was created in January 1862 as a prelude to Maj. Gen. **Ambrose E. Burnside's** expedition to **Roanoke Island** and **New Bern, North Carolina**. After capturing several coastal strongholds, Burnside was transferred to **Virginia**, and in July 1862 Brig. Gen. **John G. Foster** assumed command. The troops defending the department were designated the XVIII Corps, and at one time numbered 30,000 men. In July 1863, the department was incorporated into the **Department of Virginia and North Carolina**.

In January 1865, the Department of North Carolina was recreated under the command of Maj. Gen. **John M. Schofield**. Schofield led the X and XXIII Corps (later **H. Judson Kilpatrick's** cavalry command was added) and participated in the **Carolinas Campaign**, but he was under the immediate direction of Maj. Gen. **William T. Sherman**.

DEPARTMENT OF NORTH CAROLINA AND SOUTHERN VIRGINIA (CONFEDERATE). This **department** sometimes was referred to as the Department of Virginia and North Carolina or simply the Department of North Carolina. Created in September 1862 under the command of Maj. Gen. **Gustavus W. Smith**, it consisted of three former departments (**Richmond, Southern Virginia,** and **North Carolina**) and at one time had 40,500 troops defending it. Lieutenant General **James Longstreet** took command in February 1863 when he was sent against Union forces at **Suffolk, Virginia**. When Longstreet returned to the **Army of Northern Virginia** in April, Maj. Gen. **Daniel H. Hill** assumed command. In May 1863, the department was renamed the **Department of North Carolina**, with Hill in command.

By May 1864, the Department of North Carolina and Southern Virginia had been recreated under Gen. **P. G. T. Beauregard**. It included that part of **Virginia** south of the James and Appomattox Rivers and all of **North Carolina** east of the Smokey Mountains. Most of its 8,000 troops were stationed around **Richmond** and Petersburg, Virginia. When **U. S. Grant** began the **Petersburg Campaign** in June 1864, Beauregard and his men defended the cities until **Robert E. Lee** arrived with the **Army of Northern Virginia**. The department then was incorporated into Lee's command.

DEPARTMENT OF NORTHEASTERN VIRGINIA (UNION). Created in May 1861, this **department** included that part of **Virginia** east of the Allegheny Mountains and north of the James River (except for the **Fort Monroe** area). Commanded by Brig. Gen. **Irvin McDowell**, its military force was called the **Army of Northeastern Virginia** and fought at the **First Battle of Manassas** in July 1861. Only days after the battle, the department was incorporated into the **Military Division of the Potomac**.

DEPARTMENT OF NORTHERN VIRGINIA (CONFEDERATE). This **department** was created in October 1861 under the command of Gen. **Joseph E. Johnston**. Manassas Junction served as headquarters, and the department included all of northern **Virginia**. Subdivided into three districts—the Potomac, the Aquia, and the **Valley**—its military force was known as the **Army of the Potomac (Confederate)** (although **Jefferson Davis** referred to it as the Army of the North or the Army of Richmond). During the **Peninsula Campaign** in April 1862, the **Departments of Norfolk** and **the Peninsula** were temporarily added to Johnston's command. When **Robert E. Lee** took over the department in June, the **army** became known as the **Army of Northern Virginia**. Most of the major Virginia battles occurred in this department as Lee defended **Richmond** against attack. Lee remained in command of the department until war's end.

DEPARTMENT OF PENNSYLVANIA (UNION). This **department** was created in April 1861 and included **Pennsylvania**, **Delaware**, and that part of **Maryland** not included in the **Departments of Annapolis** and **Washington**. With headquarters at Philadelphia, Pennsylvania, it was commanded by Maj. Gen. **Robert Patterson**. Patterson formed the 13,000-man **Army of the Shenandoah**, which entered Maryland to threaten the Confederates at **Harpers Ferry**, **Virginia**, and to support pro-Union citizens in western **Virginia**. The Confederates at Harpers Ferry under **Joseph E. Johnston** slipped away from Patterson, however, and joined **P. G. T. Beauregard** for the **First Battle of Manassas**. Patterson was relieved of command in July 1861, and the department was incorporated into the **Department of the Potomac** in August. In December 1864, it was revised within the **Middle Military Division**.

DEPARTMENT OF RICHMOND (CONFEDERATE). The city of **Richmond**, **Virginia**, officially was within the **Department of Henrico**, but its defenses were referred to as the Department of Richmond. Major General **Gustavus W. Smith** took command of the defenses in August 1862, but he was replaced by Maj. Gen. **Arnold Elzey**. In April 1863, the **department** formally was recognized as being part of the larger **Department of North Carolina and Southern Virginia**. During his tenure, Elzey organized a defense force from government clerks and employees, prepared Richmond's fortifications, and protected the city against several Union cavalry raids. Major General **Robert Ransom Jr.** replaced Elzey in April 1864, but he only served briefly. When Lt. Gen. **Richard Ewell** became too ill in May 1864 to lead the **Army of Northern Virginia's** II Corps, he was assigned to replace Elzey. Ewell's command was actively engaged in manning the city's defenses against the besieging Union armies during the **Petersburg Campaign**. When Richmond was evacuated on April 2, 1865, the department ceased to exist when its defenders joined the main Confederate **army** for the **Appomattox Campaign**.

DEPARTMENT OF SOUTH CAROLINA (CONFEDERATE). Consisting of **South Carolina**, this **department** was created in August 1861 and was put under the command of Brig. Gen. **Roswell S. Ripley**. With approximately 8,300 men, Ripley's main concern was the defense of **Charleston** and the South Carolina coastal region. The department was abolished in November 1861 when it was absorbed by the **Department of South Carolina and Georgia**.

DEPARTMENT OF SOUTH CAROLINA AND GEORGIA (CONFEDERATE). This **department** was created in November 1861 out of two separate departments as a result of the Union occupation of **Port Royal**, **South Carolina**. Put under the command of Gen. **Robert E. Lee**, with headquarters at **Charleston**, **South Carolina**, it included the **South Carolina** and **Georgia** coasts and eastern **Florida**. For two days only in April 1862, much of Florida also was added to the department. In March 1862, Lee was replaced by Maj. Gen. **John C. Pemberton**, and in August 1862, Gen. **P. G. T. Beauregard** replaced Pemberton. Most of their 23,000 men were positioned to defend Charleston and **Savannah, Georgia**. When the **Department of Middle and Eastern Florida** was added in March 1863, the department's name was changed to the **Department of South Carolina, Georgia, and Florida**.

DEPARTMENT OF SOUTH CAROLINA, GEORGIA, AND FLORIDA (CONFEDERATE). This **department** was created in October 1862 by consolidating the **Department of South Carolina and Georgia** and the **Department of Middle and Eastern Florida**. General **P. G. T. Beauregard** assumed command and established his headquarters at **Charleston, South Carolina**. In November 1862, the department was expanded into **Florida** as far as the Choctawhatchee River and Bay. From November 1862 to December 1863, northwestern **Georgia** was detached from it to be added to the **Department of the West**.

After Beauregard was transferred in April 1864, command fell to several different officers, including Gen. **Joseph E. Johnston** from February to April 1865. At its peak, the department had approximately 35,000 men to defend it, with most being concentrated around Charleston and **Savannah, Georgia**. Atlanta, Georgia, was within this department, but its defense during the 1864 **Atlanta Campaign** mostly was assumed by the **Army of Tennessee** and not the department's troops.

DEPARTMENT OF SOUTHERN MISSISSIPPI AND EAST LOUISIANA (CONFEDERATE). This **department** was created in June 1862 (officially as a subdepartment of **Department No. 2**) under the command of Maj. Gen. **Earl Van Dorn** and included that part of **Louisiana** east of the Mississippi River and all of Mississippi east of the Pearl River in the south and the Mississippi Central Railroad in the north. In October, this subdepartment was abolished when it was incorporated into the newly created **Department of Mississippi and East Louisiana**.

DEPARTMENT OF SOUTHERN VIRGINIA (CONFEDERATE). In April 1863, the large **Department of North Carolina and Southern Virginia** was abolished, and its territory was divided into three new, smaller **departments**. One was the Department of Southern Virginia, which included that part of **Virginia** south of the James River and east of Powhatan County. The department was placed under the command of Maj. Gen. **Samuel G. French**. In May, however, it was merged into the **Department of North Carolina** under the command of Maj. Gen. **Daniel H. Hill**.

DEPARTMENT OF SOUTHWESTERN VIRGINIA (CONFEDERATE). Also known as the Department of Western Virginia, this department was created in May 1862 and encompassed a vague area of southwestern **Virginia** adjacent to **Kentucky** "and as far west of that boundary as circumstances may allow" (Boatner, *Civil War Dictionary*, 904). Originally under Maj. Gen. **William W. Loring**, it subsequently had numerous commanding officers and went through several name changes. In November 1862, the department was renamed the **Trans-Allegheny Department**, and by the end of 1863 it was called the Department of Southwestern Virginia and East Tennessee.

The most important strategic value of the department was the East Tennessee & Virginia Railroad. To protect this vital **railroad**, the department's army fought the battles of **Droop Mountain** and **Cloyd's Mountain**. The **Battle of New Market** also was fought within the department. In February 1865, the department was renamed the **Department of Western Virginia and East Tennessee** and was placed under the jurisdiction of the **Valley District**.

DEPARTMENT OF SOUTHWESTERN VIRGINIA AND EAST TENNESSEE (CONFEDERATE). *See* DEPARTMENT OF SOUTHWESTERN VIRGINIA (CONFEDERATE).

DEPARTMENT OF TENNESSEE (CONFEDERATE). At the suggestion of Maj. Gen. **Simon B. Buckner**, commander of the **Department of**

East Tennessee, this **department** was created in July 1863 and was put under the command of Gen. **Braxton Bragg**. It included Buckner's department (which maintained its separate identity), Middle **Tennessee**, northern **Alabama**, northern **Georgia**, western **North Carolina**, and western **Virginia**. By mid-1864, the department had expanded to include eastern Alabama and part of western **Florida**, but a part of northeastern Georgia was taken away. Bragg was replaced by Gen. **Joseph E. Johnston** in December 1863, and Johnston was replaced by **John B. Hood** in July 1864. Abolished in August 1864, this department was replaced by the **Department of Tennessee and Georgia**.

The main fighting force within the Department of Tennessee was the **Army of Tennessee**, but that **army** actually took on its name before the department was created. During its existence, the department experienced heavy fighting in the **Chattanooga** and **Atlanta Campaigns**.

DEPARTMENT OF TENNESSEE AND GEORGIA (CONFEDERATE). When the **Department of Tennessee** was abolished in August 1864, the Department of Tennessee and Georgia took its place. Placed under Gen. **John B. Hood**, this new **department** included that part of western and Middle **Tennessee** that lay south of a line running roughly from Paris to Nashville, all of **Alabama**, and part of northwestern **Georgia**. By 1865, all of western Georgia and part of eastern **Florida** were added to it as well. In February 1865, the department, along with the **Department of South Carolina, Georgia, and Florida**, was placed under the supervision of Gen. **Joseph E. Johnston**. In March, Johnston put Maj. Gen. **Howell Cobb** in command of the department.

DEPARTMENT OF TEXAS (CONFEDERATE). This **department**, which included all of **Texas**, was created in April 1861 and was placed under the command of Maj. Gen. **Earl Van Dorn**. Colonel **Henry E. McCulloch** assumed command in September but within a few days relinquished it to Brig. Gen. **Paul O. Hébert**. In May 1862, the **Trans-Mississippi Department** was created, which included Texas. Texas and western **Louisiana** then were reorganized as the District of West Louisiana and Texas under Hébert, but he continued to refer to the area as the Department of Texas. In August 1862, Texas became part of the District of Texas and in November was absorbed by the District of Texas, New Mexico, and Arizona under Maj. Gen. **John B. Magruder**.

DEPARTMENT OF TEXAS (UNION). This **department** consisted of **Texas** and was in existence before the Civil War began. Commanded by Brig. Gen. **David E. Twiggs**, with headquarters at San Antonio, its troops mainly protected the frontier against **Indians**. In February 1861, Twiggs surrendered the department and its equipment to the state and then resigned his commission to join the Confederacy. For the next year, the department had no Union troops within it. In February 1862, it was abolished when Texas was made part of the **Department of the Gulf**.

DEPARTMENT OF THE CUMBERLAND (UNION). Created in August 1861, this **department** was commanded by Brig. Gen. **Robert Anderson** and consisted of **Tennessee** and **Kentucky**, except for a small area bordering Cincinnati, Ohio, and part of western Tennessee along the Mississippi River. In October, it was incorporated into the **Department of the Ohio** but was recreated in October 1862 following the **Kentucky Campaign**. This second Department of the Cumberland was under the command of Maj. Gen. **William S. Rosecrans** and included Kentucky, that part of Tennessee east of the Tennessee River, and those parts of northern **Alabama** and **Georgia** then under Union control.

In October 1863, the department came under the jurisdiction of the newly created **Military Division of the Mississippi**. Major General **U. S. Grant** commanded the division, while Maj. Gen. **George H. Thomas** assumed command of the department. In the spring of 1864, Maj. Gen. **William T. Sherman** took command of the division. He added to it parts of northern **Georgia** as he advanced southward in the **Atlanta Campaign**. In February 1865, the department was divided for purposes of **Reconstruction**, with Kentucky being incorporated into the **Department of Kentucky**. Thomas continued to command both departments until war's end.

DEPARTMENT OF THE EAST (UNION). This **department** originally referred to the U.S. military designation for all territory east of the Mississippi River. In 1861 it was headquartered in Albany, New York, under the command of Brig. Gen. **John E. Wool**. The department began a reorganization in April 1861 when **secession** and war led to the loss of the department's southern areas. By October, it ceased to exist, having been carved into smaller, more manageable departments. In January 1863, however, it was reestablished under Wool and included **New York**, **New Jersey**, and the New England states, with headquarters in New York City. When Wool retired in August, Maj. Gen. **John A. Dix** became the commander, and he served until the end of the war. The military in this department largely was involved in maintaining civil order and guarding against Confederate raiders.

DEPARTMENT OF THE GULF (CONFEDERATE). In June 1863, the Confederate District of the Gulf was given departmental status. It consisted of that territory south of the 32nd parallel, bounded on the east by the Pearl River and on the west by the Appalachicola River. Major General **Simon B. Buckner** initially commanded the **department**, but he was replaced by Maj. Gen. **Dabney H. Maury** in May. In January 1864, it was absorbed by the **Department of Alabama, Mississippi, and East Louisiana** and reverted to the District of the Gulf, with Maury still in command.

DEPARTMENT OF THE GULF (UNION). This **department** was created in February 1862 and encompassed the Gulf Coast west of **Pensacola, Florida**. After **New Orleans, Louisiana**, was captured in May, it served as departmental headquarters. Major General **Benjamin F. Butler** first commanded the department, but he was replaced in December by Maj. Gen. **Nathaniel P. Banks**. In May 1864, it was incorporated into the **Military Division of West Mississippi** but continued to operate as virtually a separate department.

Most of the military operations in the department occurred under Banks, when the **Army of the Gulf** participated in the **Bayou Teche, Port Hudson,** and **Red River Campaigns**, and in the **Texas Overland Expedition**. Banks was replaced in September 1864 by Maj. Gen. **Stephen A. Hurlbut**, who served until Banks made a brief return in April 1865. Banks then was replaced by Maj. Gen. **E. R. S. Canby**, who accepted the Confederate **surrender** in the area.

DEPARTMENT OF THE MISSISSIPPI (UNION). Created in March 1862 by the consolidation of the **Departments of the Missouri, the Ohio**, and **Kansas**, this **department** consisted of the territory west of Knoxville, Tennessee, and east of the Great Plains. A huge area, it included **Missouri, Kansas, Mississippi**, and west **Tennessee**. Placed under Maj. Gen. **Henry W. Halleck**, who established his headquarters at St. Louis, Missouri, the department included almost 130,000 men. After the battles at **Shiloh** and **New Madrid and Island No. 10** were fought within its borders, the department was reduced in August 1862 when western Tennessee and Mississippi were added to the recreated Department of the Ohio. It was reduced again in September when part of it was assigned to the **Department of the Northwest**. The Department of the Mississippi was abolished in September 1862 when the Department of the Missouri was recreated and absorbed its territory.

DEPARTMENT OF THE MISSOURI (UNION). This **department** was created in November 1861 under the command of Maj. Gen. **Henry W.**

Halleck, with headquarters at St. Louis, Missouri. It included **Missouri, Iowa, Minnesota, Illinois, Arkansas**, and that part of **Kentucky** lying west of the Cumberland River. The department briefly was incorporated into the **Department of the Mississippi** in May 1862, but it was recreated in September to include Missouri, **Kansas**, Arkansas, part of Illinois, and the borderland of **Indian Territory** (in October, Nebraska Territory and most of the **Colorado Territory** were added). Major General **Samuel R. Curtis** commanded this reconstituted department until he was replaced by Maj. Gen. **John M. Schofield** in May 1863. In January 1864, the department was reduced and was left only with Missouri (the small part of Illinois was added back a few weeks later). Major General **William S. Rosecrans** assumed command until he was replaced by Maj. Gen. **Grenville M. Dodge** in December 1864. In early 1865, Nebraska and most of Colorado, the Utah Territory, and western Dakota Territory were added to the department.

DEPARTMENT OF THE MONONGAHELA (UNION). This department was created in June 1863 to counter threats posed by Confederate cavalry raids. It was placed under the command of Maj. Gen. **William T. H. Brooks**, with headquarters at Pittsburgh, Pennsylvania. The department included western **Pennsylvania**, part of **West Virginia** (including Wheeling), and eastern **Ohio**. It never had a very strong defending force and was incorporated into the **Department of the Susquehanna** in April 1864.

DEPARTMENT OF THE NORTHWEST (UNION). This department was created in September 1862 following the **Sioux uprising** in Minnesota. It included **Wisconsin, Iowa, Minnesota**, and the Nebraska (transferred to the **Department of the Missouri** in October 1862) and Dakota territories. After his defeat at **Second Manassas**, Maj. Gen. **John Pope** was put in command of the department with his headquarters located at St. Paul, Minnesota. Brigadier General **Washington L. Elliott** temporarily served as commander from November 1862 to February 1863, and Maj. Gen. **Samuel R. Curtis** replaced Pope permanently in February 1865. Department headquarters were moved twice—to Madison, **Wisconsin**, in November 1862, and to Milwaukee, Wisconsin, in February 1863. In January 1865, the department came under the jurisdiction of the **Military Division of the Missouri**, and western Dakota was transferred to the Department of the Missouri the following month. In June 1865, the entire department was merged into the Department of the Missouri.

DEPARTMENT OF THE OHIO (UNION). This department was created in May 1861 and originally consisted of **Illinois, Indiana**, and

Ohio, but it was expanded within days to include western **Pennsylvania** and part of western **Virginia**. Other early changes included **Missouri** being added in June and Illinois being transferred to the **Western Department** in July. Major General **George B. McClellan** was placed in command of the department and fought his campaign in western Virginia within its borders. When McClellan was ordered to assume command of the **Washington, D.C.**, defenses, he was replaced in July 1861 by Maj. Gen. **William S. Rosecrans**. More changes came in September when Brig. Gen. **Ormsby M. Mitchel** replaced Rosecrans, and Ohio, Indiana, and that part of **Kentucky** adjacent to Cincinnati, Ohio, (which served as headquarters) were added to the department.

In November 1861, the department was expanded to include Ohio, **Michigan**, Indiana, and that part of Kentucky east of the Cumberland River, and headquarters were moved to Louisville, Kentucky. Major General **Don Carlos Buell** then was put in command, and under him the department's military force became known as the **Army of the Ohio**.

In March 1862, the department disappeared when part of it was assigned to the **Mountain Department** and part to the **Department of the Mississippi**. The Army of the Ohio continued to function, however. In August 1862, the department was revived under Maj. Gen. **Horatio G. Wright**, with headquarters at Cincinnati, and included Illinois, Indiana, Ohio, Michigan, **Wisconsin**, and that part of Kentucky east of the Tennessee River. Major General **Ambrose Burnside** assumed command in March 1863, and in October the department became part of the **Military Division of the Mississippi**. Other officers who commanded the department before it was merged with the **Department of the Cumberland** in January 1865 were **John G. Foster**, **John M. Schofield**, and **George Stoneman**.

DEPARTMENT OF THE PACIFIC (UNION). This **department** was created in January 1861 by consolidating the Departments of Oregon and California. It included all of modern-day **California**, **Arizona**, **Oregon**, Washington, and Idaho. With headquarters in Los Angeles, California, the department was enlarged in July to include the Department of Utah. Future Confederate Gen. **Albert Sidney Johnston** commanded it until he resigned his post in April 1861 and was replaced by Brig. Gen. **Edwin V. Sumner**. In July 1861, Utah and most of **Nevada** were added to the department, and in November modern-day Arizona was transferred to the **Department of New Mexico**. Colonel **George Wright** and Maj. Gen. **Irvin McDowell** also commanded the department during the war, and headquarters eventually were moved to San Francisco, California.

The only Civil War–related activity within the department was when the **California Column** left southern California to oppose **Henry H. Sibley's New Mexico Campaign** in 1862. In June 1865, the department was replaced by the Military Division of the Pacific.

DEPARTMENT OF THE PENINSULA (CONFEDERATE). This **department** was created in May 1861 under the command of Col. **John B. Magruder**. With headquarters at **Yorktown, Virginia**, it consisted of the Virginia Peninsula and the James and York Rivers. The **Battle of Big Bethel**, the **Peninsula Campaign**, and much of the **Seven Days Campaign** were fought within the department. Magruder's 13,000 men originally were known as the **Army of the Peninsula**, but they lost their separate identity when Magruder was placed under Gen. **Joseph E. Johnston's** command for the Peninsula Campaign in April 1862.

DEPARTMENT OF THE POTOMAC (UNION). When Maj. Gen. **George B. McClellan** assumed command of the defeated Union **army** at **Washington, D.C.**, in July 1861 following the **First Battle of Manassas**, his area of command was called the **Military Division of the Potomac**. In August the name was changed to the Department of the Potomac. McClellan's army became the **Army of the Potomac** and was the Union's main fighting force in the eastern theater. The department's boundaries shifted occasionally but basically included that part of **Virginia** over which the Army of the Potomac and the Confederate **Army of Northern Virginia** fought.

DEPARTMENT OF THE RAPPAHANNOCK (UNION). At the beginning of the 1862 **Peninsula Campaign**, Maj. Gen. **Irvin McDowell's** I Corps was detached from the **Army of the Potomac** and was left to defend **Washington, D.C.** In April, McDowell was put in command of the newly created Department of the Rappahannock, with his headquarters located at Fredericksburg, Virginia. The **department** included Washington and all of **Virginia** east of the Blue Ridge Mountains, south of the Potomac River, along the Fredericksburg & Richmond Railroad, and between the Patuxent and Potomac Rivers. McDowell's **corps** originally was to join **George B. McClellan** for the Peninsula Campaign, but Maj. Gen. **Thomas "Stonewall" Jackson's Valley Campaign** forced **Abraham Lincoln** to keep McDowell near Fredericksburg to defend Washington. Part of McDowell's command under Maj. Gen. **James Shields** was sent to the **Shenandoah Valley** to confront Jackson, but it was defeated in June 1862 at the **Battle of Port Republic**. Later that month, the department was merged into Maj. Gen. **John Pope's Army of Virginia**.

DEPARTMENT OF THE SHENANDOAH (UNION). Created in July 1861, this **department** included the **Shenandoah Valley** and two adjoining **Maryland** counties, as well as any other part of **Virginia** that happened to fall within the area of its **army's** operations. The department was incorporated into the **Department of the Potomac** in August 1861, but it then was recreated in April 1862 when the Valley was threatened during Maj. Gen. **Thomas "Stonewall" Jackson's Shenandoah Valley Campaign**. It was placed under the command of Maj. Gen. **Nathaniel Banks**, with Banks's V Corps operating out of **Winchester**. The department was abolished again in June 1862, and Banks's corps became part of **John Pope's Army of Virginia**.

DEPARTMENT OF THE SOUTH (UNION). This **department** was created in March 1862 and included **South Carolina**, **Georgia**, **Florida**, and the **Department of Key West**, with headquarters located at Hilton Head, South Carolina. Brigadier General **Thomas W. Sherman** briefly commanded it for about two weeks, but he was replaced by Maj. Gen. **David Hunter**. Hunter declared that all slaves within his jurisdiction were free, but **Abraham Lincoln** quickly disavowed his action. In August 1862, the District of West Florida was detached from the department, as was southern Georgia the following month, and northern Georgia and the Department of Key West in March 1863. In September 1862, the department's troops were designated the X Corps.

Hunter was replaced in August 1862 and was followed by a number of commanders. Major General **Quincy A. Gillmore** led the department from July 1863 to May 1864, and under him Union forces were defeated at **Olustee, Florida**, laid siege to **Charleston, South Carolina**, and captured **Fort Wagner**. In January 1865, **North Carolina** was added to the department for two weeks, and in May, Florida was detached. At war's end in June 1865, the department was abolished, and its territory was divided between the Departments of South Carolina and Georgia.

DEPARTMENT OF THE SOUTHWEST (CONFEDERATE). This was the new name given to the **Department of Mississippi and East Louisiana** when Lt. Gen. **Leonidas Polk** assumed command in December 1863. With headquarters located at Jackson, Mississippi, it included all of **Mississippi** and that part of **Louisiana** east of the Mississippi River. After opposing Maj. Gen. **William T. Sherman's Meridian Campaign**, Polk had his command merged into the **Department of Alabama, Mississippi and East Louisiana** in January 1864, and he and his men were transferred to **Georgia**.

DEPARTMENT OF THE SUSQUEHANNA (UNION). This **department** was created in June 1863 as a response to the Confederate invasion of **Pennsylvania** during the **Gettysburg Campaign**. It included that part of Pennsylvania east of Johnstown and the Laurel Hill Mountains and had Chambersburg as its headquarters. Placed under the command of Maj. Gen. **Darius N. Couch**, the department's purpose was to organize the Pennsylvania volunteers and out-of-state reinforcements that were being assembled to face the invasion. In April 1864, the **Department of the Monongahela** was added to it, but in December, the Department of the Susquehanna reverted to its original area with headquarters in Philadelphia, Pennsylvania.

DEPARTMENT OF THE TENNESSEE (UNION). An attempt to create this **department** under Maj. Gen. **George H. Thomas** was made in September 1862, but bureaucratic delays prevented its creation until October. Placed under Maj. Gen. **U. S. Grant**, it covered the vague territory of **Tennessee** and **Kentucky** west of the Tennessee River and the **Corinth, Mississippi**, area. Cairo, **Illinois**, and **Forts Henry and Donelson, Tennessee**, also were included. In October 1863, it became a subdepartment of the newly created **Military Division of the Mississippi**, and Grant was elevated to command the division. The department included the famed **Army of the Tennessee** and was subsequently commanded by **William T. Sherman, James B. McPherson, John A. Logan**, and **Oliver O. Howard**.

DEPARTMENT OF THE WEST (CONFEDERATE). This **department** was created in November 1862 under the command of Gen. **Joseph E. Johnston**. It was a huge area comprising **Departments No. 2, of East Tennessee**, and **of Mississippi and East Louisiana**, as well as northwestern **Georgia** and part of northwestern **South Carolina**. A few days later, **Atlanta, Georgia**, was added to it. Johnston's main responsibility was to protect **Vicksburg, Mississippi**, but he failed in this mission because of poor decisions made by Lt. Gen. **John C. Pemberton** at Vicksburg and Johnston's lack of aggressiveness and reluctance to interfere with the armies under his authority. The **Department of East Tennessee**, western **North Carolina**, and part of western Georgia were added to Johnston's department in July 1863. Following the **Vicksburg Campaign**, the next major operations in the department were the **Meridian, Chickamauga**, and **Chattanooga Campaigns**. When **Braxton Bragg** was defeated at Chattanooga, Johnston took command of the **army**, and the Department of the West was abolished in December 1863.

DEPARTMENT OF THE WEST (UNION). This **department** was in existence when the Civil War began and consisted of the territory between the Mississippi River and the Rocky Mountains (including **Arkansas** and **Louisiana**, but not **Texas**). Headquarters were located at Fort Leavenworth, **Kansas**. Brigadier General William S. Harney commanded the region in early 1861 when Louisiana and Arkansas seceded. In early May 1861, **Missouri** was detached and was placed in the **Department of the Ohio**. Brigadier General **Nathaniel Lyon** replaced Harney in May 1861, but the department was abolished in July when it was absorbed by the **Western Department**.

DEPARTMENT OF UTAH (UNION). This **department** already was in existence when the Civil War began and consisted of the Utah Territory, with headquarters at Fort Crittenden. Colonel **Philip St. George Cooke** was in command when the war started. In July 1861, it became a subdepartment of the **Department of the Pacific**, but it existed mainly on paper since Cooke took his troops eastward in August 1861 to help fight the Confederates. After February 1865, the department was a part of the **Military Division of the Missouri**.

DEPARTMENT OF VIRGINIA (UNION). This **department** was created in May 1861 under the command of Maj. Gen. **Benjamin F. Butler**. It consisted of the southeastern tip of the Virginia Peninsula and had **Fort Monroe** as its headquarters. Major General **John E. Wool** replaced Butler in August 1861 and was in command when Maj. Gen. **George B. McClellan** landed the **Army of the Potomac** at Fort Monroe in March 1862 to begin the **Peninsula Campaign**. **John A. Dix** and **George W. Getty** followed Wool in command.

After fighting at **Big Bethel** and in the Peninsula Campaign, the department's troops were designated the VII Corps in July 1862. In July 1863, the department was merged with the **Department of North Carolina** to form the **Department of Virginia and North Carolina**. Major General **E. O. C. Ord** commanded this new entity, but in January 1865, it was again divided and the Department of Virginia was recreated. Ord commanded the department until after the Confederate surrender at **Appomattox**, at which time Maj. Gen. **Henry W. Halleck** took over in mid-April 1865.

DEPARTMENT OF VIRGINIA AND NORTH CAROLINA (CONFEDERATE). This was another name sometimes given to the **Department of North Carolina and Southern Virginia**.

DEPARTMENT OF VIRGINIA AND NORTH CAROLINA (UNION). In July 1863, the **Department of Virginia** was merged with the **De-**

partment of North Carolina to form a new Department of Virginia and North Carolina. With headquarters at **Fort Monroe, Virginia**, it was placed under Maj. Gen. **John G. Foster** and consisted of all of **North Carolina** and that part of **Virginia** that lay within a 60-mile radius of Fort Monroe (including the territory south of the Rappahannock River and east of the Richmond, Fredericksburg & Potomac Railroad). The approximately 42,000 men in the IV and VII Corps were merged to form the XVIII Corps.

Foster was replaced by Maj. Gen. **Benjamin F. Butler** in November 1863. Under his command, the **Army of the James** was formed when the X Corps from North Carolina joined the XVIII Corps for the **Petersburg Campaign**. After service in the **Bermuda Hundred Campaign**, this **corps** was split in December 1864, with its white soldiers being designated the XXIV Corps, while the **black troops** became the XXV Corps. In January 1865, Butler was replaced by Maj. Gen. **E. O. C. Ord**, but the department again was split into separate departments for Virginia and North Carolina.

DEPARTMENT OF WASHINGTON (UNION). This **department** was created in April 1861 and consisted of **Washington, D.C., Maryland, Pennsylvania**, and **Delaware**. Found to be too large for efficient management, it was reorganized a week later to include only Washington; Georgetown; Alexandria County, Virginia; the Fort Washington area; and that part of Maryland south of Bladensburg. Colonel **Joseph Mansfield** was put in command, but in July the department was abolished, and its territory was absorbed by the **Military Division of the Potomac**.

In February 1863, the Department of Washington was recreated but only consisted of the city. Major General **Samuel P. Heintzelman** then was given command, and the XXII Corps provided defense. Major General **Christopher C. Augur** assumed command in October 1863. In June 1865, the department was enlarged to include the surrounding Maryland counties and Fairfax City, Virginia.

DEPARTMENT OF WEST FLORIDA (CONFEDERATE). This **department** officially was named the District of Middle Florida and was part of the **Department of South Carolina, Georgia, and Florida**. Its headquarters were located at Quincy, and it included the **Florida** panhandle and much of western Florida. However, when Brig. Gen. **William M. Gardner** was placed in command in October 1863, his orders mistakenly referred to it as the Department of West Florida, and Gardner continued to use the name. Gardner enforced **conscription** laws in his area and was able to raise reinforcements that were sent to the **Battle of Olustee** in February 1864. His department was abolished a few days after the battle when it was merged with the District of Eastern Florida to form the new District of Florida.

DEPARTMENT OF WEST VIRGINIA (UNION). This **department** was created in June 1863 as a subdepartment of the **Middle Department**. It consisted of that part of **Maryland** west of the Allegheny Mountains and the new state of **West Virginia**. Brigadier General **Benjamin F. Kelley** commanded it, and his VIII Corps protected the Baltimore & Ohio Railroad and West Virginia, as well as opposed Confederate forces in the **Shenandoah Valley**.

In March 1864, Maj. Gen. **Franz Sigel** took command of the department. In May, he was defeated at **New Market** and was replaced by Maj. Gen. **David Hunter**. In **Hunter's Shenandoah Valley Campaign**, a small battle was fought at **Piedmont** in June and the **Virginia Military Institute** was burned, but Hunter's **Army of West Virginia** was eventually turned back at **Lynchburg**. Brigadier General **George Crook** then took command of the department in August and served in **Philip Sheridan's Shenandoah Valley Campaign** until he was captured by guerrillas in February 1865 at his Cumberland, Maryland, headquarters. Brigadier General **John D. Stevenson**, Brig. Gen. **Samuel S. Carroll**, and Maj. Gen. **Winfield Scott Hancock** then commanded the department until war's end.

DEPARTMENT OF WESTERN KENTUCKY (CONFEDERATE). This **department** was created in September 1864 and included western **Kentucky** and part of north-central **Tennessee**. Brigadier General **Adam R. Johnson** was put in command, but he was recovering from wounds and was replaced days later by Brig. Gen. **Hylan B. Lyon**. Because the department lay within Union control, it played little role in military operations. Lyon's main responsibility was enforcing **conscription** laws and fighting guerrillas.

DEPARTMENT OF WESTERN VIRGINIA (CONFEDERATE). This was another name for the **Department of Southwestern Virginia**.

DEPARTMENT OF WESTERN VIRGINIA (UNION). This **department** was created in September 1861 western Virginia (within the **Department of the Ohio**) and included that part of **Virginia** west of the Blue Ridge Mountains. It was commanded by Brig. Gen. **William S. Rosecrans** but in March 1862 was abolished when it merged with the **Mountain Department**.

DEPARTMENT OF WESTERN VIRGINIA AND EAST TENNESSEE (CONFEDERATE). This **department** was created in February 1865 when the **Department of Southwestern Virginia and East Tennessee**

was renamed the Department of Western Virginia and East Tennessee. Lieutenant General **Jubal A. Early**, commanding the **Valley District**, was given jurisdiction over the department. *See also* DEPARTMENT OF SOUTHWESTERN VIRGINIA.

DE RUSSY, GUSTAVUS ADOLPHUS (1818–1891) USA. The son of an **army** officer, De Russy was a **New York** native who was forced to resign from **West Point** in 1838 for drinking. He was commissioned a 2nd lieutenant of **artillery** in 1847 and won two **brevets** for gallantry in the **Mexican War**.

When the Civil War began, De Russy was a captain of artillery. He first was assigned to the **Army of the Potomac's** reserve artillery and in June 1862 became chief of artillery for **Joseph Hooker's division**. De Russy won praise and two more **brevets** for his conduct at **Seven Pines** and **Malvern Hill**. After commanding the artillery positioned on the Union left wing during the **Battle of Fredericksburg**, he was appointed a colonel of volunteers in March 1863 and was put in command of the 4th New York Artillery. De Russy was promoted to brigadier general of volunteers in May 1863 and spent the remainder of the war in the **Washington, D.C.**, defenses. He returned to the regular army in 1866 as a major, with brevets of major general of volunteers and brigadier general of regulars. De Russy retired as a colonel in 1882.

DESERTION. Contrary to a popular belief that all Civil War soldiers were die-hard **Rebels** and **Yankees**, desertion was a major problem for both armies. Desertion was caused by many factors. Many men volunteered for service early in the war because of community or peer pressure, to seek adventure, or simply needing food and shelter. Deep patriotism was not always a motivating factor. **Conscripts** and **foreign-born soldiers**, particularly, were likely to desert because of a lack of conviction for the cause. Thousands of soldiers on both sides either became disillusioned with military service very quickly or were worn down by fear, hunger, and exposure. Also, many brave and patriotic soldiers—especially Confederates later in the war—were persuaded to desert because they were needed more at home to provide for their families than they were needed in the **army**. These men sometimes returned to their original units or simply joined other units closer to their homes.

Authorities tried to stop desertion through a combination of harsh punishment (including execution) and offers of **amnesty** to those who would return to duty. Neither was particularly effective. It is estimated that by late 1864, perhaps half of all Confederate soldiers were absent from their posts, while about one-third of the Union soldiers were missing. Although records are incomplete, more than 105,000 Confederate and 278,000 Union soldiers were listed as deserters during the war.

DESHLER, JAMES (1833–1863) CSA. A native of **Alabama**, Deshler graduated from **West Point** in 1854 and served mostly in the west before the Civil War. In 1861, he was a 1st lieutenant with the 10th U.S. Infantry.

Deshler left his post while on leave and never returned, prompting authorities to drop him from the rolls. He joined the Confederate service as a captain of **artillery** and served in western **Virginia** under Brig. Gen. **Henry R. Jackson** and Col. **Edward Johnson**. Deshler was praised for his actions in several **skirmishes** and was severely wounded in the legs during one December 1861 fight. He was promoted to colonel of artillery in early 1862 and served as chief of artillery for Maj. Gen. **Theophilus H. Holmes** in the **Peninsula** and **Seven Days Campaigns**. Deshler accompanied Holmes to the **Trans-Mississippi Department** in August 1862 as his chief of staff, but in October, he took command of a **Texas** infantry **brigade**. A popular commander, Deshler was sent to **Arkansas Post**, and when it was attacked in January 1863, another officer surrendered that part of the line defended by Deshler. Deshler bitterly argued that he was not ready to surrender and even continued the argument in the presence of Union Maj. Gen. **William T. Sherman** when the position was seized.

Exchanged in June 1863, Deshler was promoted to brigadier general in July and took command of the **Army of Tennessee's** reserve artillery. In August, he was ordered to take command of **Thomas J. Churchill's** brigade in **Patrick Cleburne's division**. Deshler was killed instantly on September 20, 1863, at **Chickamauga** when a shell tore through his chest. His death was greatly lamented by officers, who viewed him as a fine field officer.

DE TROBRIAND, PHILIPPE RÉGIS DÉNIS DE KEREDERN (1816–1897) USA. A native of France, de Trobriand (duh-TROH-bri-AHN) was the son of a baron and former French general. He graduated from the College de Tours and from Poitiers but immigrated to the United States in 1841 and married a New York heiress. After living for a while in Venice, Italy, de Trobriand became an American citizen and newspaper editor.

In August 1861, de Trobriand entered Union service as colonel of the 55th New York. Dubbing his **regiment** the "Lafayette Guard," he became a valuable commander in the **Army of the Potomac** and fought in most of the major eastern battles. De Trobriand led his regiment during the **Peninsula Campaign** and commanded **brigades** at **Fredericksburg**,

Chancellorsville, and **Gettysburg**, performing admirably in the latter's **Peach Orchard**. After serving in the **Bristoe Station** and **Mine Run Campaigns**, de Trobriand was mustered out of the service in November 1863. Weeks later, he was commissioned a brigadier general of volunteers in January 1864 and was placed in command of a II Corps **division**. De Trobriand fought in the latter part of the **Petersburg Campaign** and in April 1865 was **brevetted** major general of volunteers for his service during the **Appomattox Campaign**.

In 1866, de Trobriand was commissioned a colonel in the regular **army** and spent time both on the frontier and in command of **New Orleans, Louisiana**, during the latter period of **Reconstruction**. He wrote an acclaimed account of his Civil War service and in 1874 inherited the title of count.

DEVALL'S BLUFF, ARKANSAS, BATTLES OF (JULY 6, 1862, AND JANUARY 13–19, 1863). This was a site on the White River in **Arkansas** that was the location of several Civil War engagements. On July 6, 1862, the 24th Indiana attacked and defeated 400 Confederate cavalrymen there. In the battle, the Confederates lost 84 men, while the Federals suffered 22 casualties. From January 13 to 19, 1863, Union forces again operated in the area after the capture of **Arkansas Post** to clear the White River of Confederates. Union Brigadier General **Willis A. Gorman** attacked Devall's Bluff and nearby Des Arcs and captured a number of **prisoners** and some equipment.

DEVENS, CHARLES, JR. (1820–1891) USA. A native of **Massachusetts**, Devens was a graduate of Harvard University and the Harvard Law School. He became a noted lawyer, U.S. marshal, and militia general and was elected to the state senate in 1848. An opponent of **slavery**, even while a marshal, Devens once unsuccessfully tried to buy a runaway slave he was being forced to return to the owner.

Devens entered Union service in April 1861 as major of the 3rd Battalion of Massachusetts Rifles, a 90-day militia unit. He then was commissioned colonel of the 15th Massachusetts in July and fought with it at **Ball's Bluff, Virginia**, where one of his **uniform** buttons stopped a bullet. Devens was promoted to brigadier general of volunteers in April 1862 and took command of a **brigade** in the **Army of the Potomac's** IV Corps. He was wounded while leading it at **Seven Pines**. Devens then commanded a VI Corps brigade at **Fredericksburg**, and at **Chancellorsville** he was wounded again while leading a XI Corps **division**. During the latter battle, his division was one of those crushed by **Thomas "Stonewall" Jackson's** flank attack. Despite the defeat, Devens was

brevetted major general of volunteers for his Chancellorsville service. He returned to duty in May 1864 and at **Cold Harbor** commanded his division from a stretcher because of severe rheumatism. This illness forced Devens temporarily to give up command, but he returned in time to participate in the **Petersburg** and **Appomattox Campaigns**. He was brevetted major general of volunteers for his service in the latter.

After the war, Devens commanded the District of Charleston, South Carolina, before leaving the **army** in 1866. He became a justice of the Massachusetts Supreme Court and served as President **Rutherford B. Hayes's** attorney general.

DEVIL'S DEN AT BATTLE OF GETTYSBURG, PENNSYLVANIA (JULY 2, 1863). Located on the Union left flank during the 1863 **Battle of Gettysburg**, this area was a jumble of rocks and large boulders and included a hill. On the afternoon of July 2, 1863, Brig. Gen. **John Henry Hobart Ward's brigade** of the Union III Corps held the position. Attacked by Confederate Lt. Gen. **James Longstreet's corps**, Ward's men put up a stiff fight among the rocks but finally were forced out by the brigades of **Jerome B. Robertson** and **Henry L. Benning**. Heavy casualties were suffered on both sides, but the Confederates held Devil's Den for the remainder of the battle.

DEVIN, THOMAS CASIMER (1822–1878) USA. A native of **New York**, Devin was a house painter and lieutenant colonel of the 1st New York Militia Cavalry when the Civil War began. He entered Union service in July 1861 as a captain in the 1st New York Cavalry after he and one of his militia **companies** volunteered for service. Devin then was promoted to colonel of the 6th New York Cavalry (sometimes referred to as the "2nd Ira Harris Guards") in November.

Devin was placed in command of a **brigade** and was recommended for promotion after serving with the **Army of the Potomac** at **Antietam** and **Fredericksburg**. His brigade was defeated and badly shot up at **Chancellorsville** and then played an important role under **John Buford** in delaying the Confederate advance on the first day at **Gettysburg**. Devin next participated in the **Kilpatrick-Dahlgren Raid** in 1864 and in the **Overland Campaign** and then fought in **Philip Sheridan's Shenandoah Valley Campaign**, where he was slightly wounded during a **skirmish** at Crooked Run. He returned to his command in time to participate in the battles at **Third Winchester**, **Fisher's Hill**, and **Cedar Creek**. In March 1865, Devin finally was promoted to brigadier general of volunteers and was given command of a cavalry **division**. He played a key role in the victory at **Five Forks** and in the **Appomattox Campaign**.

One of the better Union cavalry commanders, Devin was **brevetted** brigadier general of regulars and major general of volunteers. In 1866, he was appointed lieutenant colonel in the **U.S. Army** and rose to the rank of colonel before he retired.

***DIANA*, CSS.** The *Diana* originally was a small steamer that was captured by **David Farragut** at **New Orleans, Louisiana**, when he took that city in April 1862. Pressed into Union service as a **tinclad**, the vessel was used in Bayou Teche later that year in operations against **Richard Taylor's** Confederates. In March 1863, Union Brig. Gen. **Godfrey Weitzel** sent the *Diana* on a **reconnaissance** mission into Grand Lake, with **companies** from the 160th New York and 12th Connecticut on board for protection. Captain Thomas L. Peterson, however, disobeyed orders and steamed up a channel of the Atchafalaya (uh-CHAF-uh-LIE-uh) near Patterson and was ambushed by a 500-man Confederate force under Maj. Hannibal H. Boone. Using the Valverde Battery and detachments from the 28th (Gray's) Louisiana and the 13th Battalion Texas Cavalry, Boone raked the *Diana* with **rifle** and **artillery** fire, killing Peterson and all but one of its officers. The ship soon ran aground and surrendered. Some Federals managed to escape, but 33 were killed and 120 were captured.

Taylor had the *Diana* repaired and manned by a company of the 28th (Gray's) Louisiana under the command of Capt. Oliver J. Semmes. He then used it in the 1863 **Bayou Teche Campaign**, where the *Diana* helped anchor the Confederate line at **Fort Bisland**. When Taylor retreated from Bisland, the ship helped hold the Federals at bay at **Irish Bend** before Semmes set it on fire and abandoned it in Bayou Teche.

DIBRELL, GEORGE GIBBS (1822–1888) CSA. A native of **Tennessee**, Dibrell was a Unionist merchant and state legislator when the **secession** crisis began. He attended the state's secession convention as a Unionist but then supported secession after the firing on **Fort Sumter**.

Dibrell entered Confederate service in June 1861 as a private in the 25th Tennessee but was elected lieutenant colonel in August. After fighting at **Mill Springs**, the **regiment** went to Corinth, Mississippi, where it was reorganized, and Dibrell lost his rank. In September, he raised the 13th Tennessee Cavalry as a **partisan ranger** regiment and was elected colonel. The following month, the regiment was designated the 13th Tennessee Cavalry, and it soon was attached to **Nathan Bedford Forrest's** cavalry command. Dibrell participated in the **Battle of Stones River**, **Forrest's raids** into Tennessee, and helped capture **Abel Streight's Raid** in May 1863. In July, Dibrell took command of Forrest's old **brigade** and led it through the **Tullahoma Campaign**. He finally was given a permanent brigade command and saw much combat in the **Chickamauga**, **Knoxville**, and **Atlanta Campaigns**. After participating in **Joseph Wheeler's Raids** in September 1864, Dibrell's brigade rode to **Saltville**, **Virginia**, and helped repel a Union raid there in October.

After opposing **William T. Sherman's March to the Sea**, Dibrell finally was promoted to brigadier general in January 1865. He led a **division** in **Wade Hampton's corps** during the **Carolinas Campaign** and then escorted the wagon train carrying the War Department's archives as **Jefferson Davis** fled to **Georgia** in April–May 1865. When Dibrell's men finally refused to go any farther, he and his command **surrendered** in May.

A well-respected and competent commander, Dibrell's popularity led to his being elected to the **U.S. Congress** five times after the war.

"DICTATOR" OR "PETERSBURG EXPRESS." This was a large, 13-inch **mortar** used by Union forces to shell the Confederate defenses during the **Petersburg Campaign**. Manned by the 1st Connecticut Heavy Artillery, it weighed 17,000 pounds and fired a 200-pound shell. The "Dictator" first was mounted on a **railroad** car and was used during the **Battle of the Crater** in July 1864. Afterward, it was placed in a permanent position on the Union line.

DILL, BENJAMIN FRANKLIN (1814–1866) CSA. A native of **Georgia**, Dill moved to Memphis, Tennessee, and became editor and co-owner with John R. McClanahan of the Memphis *Appeal*. The newspaper became staunchly pro-Confederate, and Dill moved his operation out of **Memphis** rather than be silenced when that city fell to Union forces in June 1862. He published the *Appeal* throughout the war in Grenada, Jackson, and Meridian, Mississippi; Atlanta, Georgia; Montgomery, Alabama; and finally Columbus, Georgia. When Union Maj. Gen. **James H. Wilson's** cavalry occupied Columbus in April 1865, Dill was captured, and his paper was shut down. He later returned to Memphis and, with partner McClanahan, continued to publish the *Appeal* until his death.

DINWIDDIE COURT HOUSE, VIRGINIA, BATTLE OF (MARCH 29–31, 1865). On March 25, 1865, during the **Petersburg Campaign**, Gen. **Robert E. Lee** and the **Army of Northern Virginia** attempted to break out of the siege by attacking **Fort Stedman**. After the attempt failed, Lt. Gen. **U. S. Grant** launched a counterattack with the **Army of the Potomac** against Lee's right flank at Dinwiddie Court House. Grant believed Lee had stripped the rest of his line's defensives to mass for the assault on Fort Stedman, thus leaving his flank weakened.

On March 29, Grant sent 13,000 cavalrymen under Maj. Gen. **Philip Sheridan** toward the Confederate right flank. Sheridan was supported by **Gouverneur K. Warren's** V Corps and **Andrew A. Humphreys's** II Corps. Anticipating such a maneuver, Lee hurried 19,000 men under Maj. Gens. **George Pickett** and **Fitzhugh Lee** toward the endangered flank. The Confederates **skirmished** with the advancing enemy, but by nightfall Sheridan's troopers had reached Dinwiddie Court House, about five miles south of the important crossroads of **Five Forks**. Heavy rains then set in and made movements almost impossible.

On March 30, fighting erupted around Dinwiddie Court House as Sheridan and his infantry support continued to press the Confederates. On March 31, Sheridan renewed his advance toward Five Forks, but Pickett counterattacked against his left flank and pushed him back toward Dinwiddie Court House. Warren's and Humphreys's **corps** also were stopped. Despite his momentary victory, Pickett still was greatly outnumbered and was threatened with **envelopment**. He therefore withdrew during the night back to Five Forks, setting the stage for the Confederate disaster there on April 1.

DISCIPLINE. Both sides sometimes found it difficult to maintain order since their **armies** were made up of volunteers who were not used to military discipline. At the beginning of the Civil War, officers up to the rank of colonel were elected, and they often were hesitant to enforce strict discipline because their positions depended on keeping the soldiers' goodwill. The **West Point**-trained professional officers attempted to maintain strict discipline, and as the war continued the volunteer officers also recognized the necessity of being stricter.

Discipline was maintained in the same way in both armies. For most infractions, commanding officers simply ordered summary—and often inventive—forms of punishment. Drunkenness, dereliction of duty, theft, unauthorized absence, and other such minor offenses, were punished by such means as confinement to the guardhouse, **bucking and gagging**, carrying a rail on the shoulder for hours, wearing a barrel shirt, or being forced to straddle a fence rail for hours. Often, a sign naming the offense was worn around the offender's neck. Reduction in pay or rank and confinement to quarters were less painful punishments.

More serious crimes, such as attacking an officer, murder, spying, **desertion**, or cowardice, were usually tried by court-martial. Punishment could range from incarceration to execution. Hanging was the preferred punishment for spies, whereas firing squads usually were used for other offenses. Sometimes in cases of attacking an officer or cowardice in battle, officers simply shot the offenders on the spot. The punishment of officers, as a rule, was not as drastic as it was for enlisted men. Officers often were confined to quarters, forfeited pay, or were cashiered from the service, and sometimes were publicly stripped of insignia and had their swords broken before being drummed out of camp. In many cases, however, officers were simply allowed to resign quietly or were transferred to other areas of service.

DISTRICT. Many military **departments** on both sides were subdivided into districts. Each district encompassed a particular geographic area and had a commander and defending troops. Usually, the district commanders were subject to the orders of the department commander, but some districts were separate entities.

DISTRICT EMANCIPATION ACT. Slavery in **Washington, D.C.**, always had been a source of embarrassment to the antislavery faction, and the **Compromise of 1850** had abolished the slave trade there. However, there had been no success in abolishing slavery itself in the nation's capital.

During the Civil War, with the Southern politicians gone, new efforts were made to abolish slavery in Washington, D.C. In 1862, **Massachusetts Republican** Sen. **Henry Wilson** introduced a bill to emancipate Washington's slaves, with $1,000,000 to be appropriated to compensate loyal slave owners for their losses. **Border state** leaders opposed the bill, interpreting it as a first step toward the total abolishment of slavery, and argued that the money appropriated for compensation was far less than the slaves' value. Many citizens of the city also opposed the measure for fear of having a large population of unemployed free blacks living there. Still, the bill passed in April 1862 and was signed by **Abraham Lincoln**. Soon afterward, the **U.S. Congress** also granted full civil rights to the city's free black population, except for the right to serve on juries.

DISTRICT OF COLUMBIA. *See* WASHINGTON, D.C.

DITCH BAYOU, ARKANSAS, BATTLE OF (JUNE 6, 1864). During the spring of 1864, Confederates under Brig. Gen. **John S. Marmaduke** harassed Union shipping on the Mississippi River near Lake Village, Arkansas. When Union Maj. Gen. **Andrew J. Smith** moved his XVI and XVII Corps from **Vicksburg, Mississippi**, to **Tennessee** on June 4, he decided to attack the Confederates' position.

Late on June 5, Smith landed two **brigades** under Brig. Gen. **Joseph A. Mower** a few miles east of Lake Village. The **Mississippi Marine**

Brigade skirmished with the Confederates that evening, and the next day Mower and his 3,000 men advanced along Lake Chicot toward Lake Village. Colonel Colton Greene's 3rd Missouri Cavalry (Confederate), with 600 men and six cannons, skirmished heavily with Mower and fell back to a strong natural defensive position where Ditch Bayou (actually a swamp) blocked the Union advance. A heavy rain turned the road to mud, and the swampy terrain prevented Mower from deploying all of his men. At Ditch Bayou, the Confederates held Mower at bay until they ran out of ammunition in mid-afternoon. Greene then retreated beyond Lake Village, and Mower occupied the town. After sacking the village, the Federals returned to their boats the following day. Mower lost 250 men in the small battle, while Greene suffered 37 casualties.

DIVERS, BRIDGET (dates unknown) USA. Born in Ireland, Divers's dates of birth and death are unknown. She became a **vivandière** in 1861 when her husband joined the 1st Michigan Cavalry. Divers began nursing sick and wounded soldiers, sometimes under fire, and gained the notice of **Mary Livermore** of the **U.S. Sanitary Commission**. Sometimes referred to as "Irish Biddy" or "Michigan Bridget," Divers became an agent of the Sanitary Commission and accompanied her husband throughout the war as part of **George Custer's Cavalry Brigade**. Her bravery was legendary. Divers was credited with rallying retreating men in battle and fighting alongside of them and had several horses shot from under her. After briefly being a civilian after the war, she again joined the **U.S. Army** as a laundress and served in the west during the **Indian** campaigns.

DIVISION. The division was the second largest military organization to make up an **army**. It usually consisted of two to four **brigades** and was commanded by a brigadier general in the Union army and a major general in the **Confederate army**. In theory, a division consisted of as many as 15,000 men, but casualties, sickness, **desertion**, and detached duty made most divisions number 10,000 or less. Union divisions were identified by a numerical designation, whereas Confederate ones were named for their commanding general. Normally, two to four divisions made up a **corps**.

DIX, DOROTHEA LYNDE (1802–1887) USA. A native of **Maine**, Dix spent her antebellum years as a teacher and writer and became well known while caring for the mentally ill. In April 1861, she offered her services to the Union and in June was appointed superintendent of the Union **armies'** women nurses. Although very competent, Dix also was somewhat dictatorial and was resented by many surgeons, soldiers, and nurses. One rule she followed was hiring only homely women more than

30 years of age, because she believed they would create less distraction in the hospitals. Operating out of **Washington, D.C.**, Dix was a key factor in the Union's ability to care for its sick and wounded. Besides providing competent nurses, she also secured needed medical supplies from both government and private sources. Dix accepted no pay for her four years of service, and after the war she resumed her work with the mentally ill.

DIX, JOHN ADAMS (1798–1879) USA. A native of **New Hampshire** and a **U.S. Army** officer's son, Dix received an education in the classics, Spanish, and French. In the War of 1812, his father secured him an ensign's commission, and he fought at Lundy's Lane when he was only 14. Dix remained in the army until 1828, at which time he resigned and became a prominent New York **Democratic** politician. He served as state secretary of state, adjutant general, and school superintendent, and served in the U.S. Senate from 1845 to 1850. In January 1861, President **James Buchanan** appointed Dix his secretary of the treasury. During the **secession** crisis, Dix earned fame when he issued the **American Flag Dispatch**, in which he ordered an official in **New Orleans, Louisiana**, to shoot on the spot anyone attempting to take down the U.S. **flag**.

In May 1861, **Abraham Lincoln** appointed Dix a major general of volunteers, making him and **Benjamin Butler** (who received his commission the same day) the two highest-ranking Union volunteer officers. He served in various administrative positions during the war and commanded at various times the **Departments of Annapolis, Pennsylvania, Virginia**, and **the East**. One of Dix's major wartime contributions was in quelling the **New York City Draft Riot** in 1863.

Dix resigned his commission in November 1865 and later served as U.S. minister to France and as the governor of **New York**.

"DIXIE." This word came to refer to the South, and the song by the same name became the Confederacy's unofficial anthem. The origin of the term *Dixie* is unclear. Some believe it originated in **New Orleans, Louisiana**, where the word *dix* (French for "ten") was used on some forms of money. New Orleans became known as "Dix's Land," and from that "Dixie" supposedly was derived. Others believe it originated with the Mason-Dixon line, a line surveyed in the 1760s that came to separate **Pennsylvania** (free territory) from **Delaware, Maryland**, and **Virginia** (slave territory). The song "Dixie" (originally entitled "I Wish I Was in Dixie's Land") was written in 1859 by Daniel Decatur Emmett, a **New York** minstrel performer. The song became very popular in the South when it was played at **Jefferson Davis's** 1861 inauguration.

DOCKERY, THOMAS PLEASANT (1833–1898) CSA. A native of **North Carolina**, Dockery moved to **Arkansas** at an early age. Sometime in the summer of 1861, he entered Confederate service as colonel of the 5th Arkansas State Troops. At the **Battle of Wilson's Creek**, Dockery was colonel of the 19th Arkansas and was praised for his role in the battle. He went on to fight at **Pea Ridge** and **Corinth**, and in the **Vicksburg Campaign** commanded a **brigade**. Dockery led his brigade at **Champion Hill** and **Big Black River Bridge**, where most of his men were captured. During the siege of **Vicksburg, Mississippi**, his troops manned the trenches, and he assumed command of **Martin Green's** brigade when Green was killed. Dockery was captured when the city fell on July 4, 1863.

After being **exchanged**, Dockery was promoted to brigadier general in August 1863 and was sent to the **Trans-Mississippi Department** to reorganize his brigade and to collect the Arkansas troops that had been **paroled** after their capture in the Vicksburg and **Port Hudson Campaigns**. After his brigade of mounted infantry fought at **Jenkins' Ferry**, he was placed in command of Arkansas's Reserve Corps for the rest of the war.

Dockery moved to **Texas** after the war, where he worked as a civil engineer.

DODGE, CHARLES CLEVELAND (1841–1910) USA. A native of **New Jersey**, Dodge was a member of the family that founded the copper enterprise, Phelps Dodge Corporation. He entered Union service in December 1861 as a captain in the 1st New York Mounted Rifles. Dodge served around **Norfolk** and **Suffolk, Virginia**, throughout most of the war and rapidly rose through the ranks to become colonel in August 1862.

Although his superiors often were critical of his ability, Dodge was promoted to brigadier general of volunteers in November 1862. His commanding officer preferred a colonel over Dodge and refused to put Dodge in command of the cavalry around Suffolk. This apparently caused Dodge to resign his commission in June 1863. He then served as a volunteer to help quell the **New York City Draft Riot** and was praised for his efforts by Maj. Gen. **John E. Wool**.

After the war, Dodge was involved in the family's copper business and in canal construction.

DODGE, GRENVILLE MELLEN (1831–1916) USA. Born in **Massachusetts**, Dodge graduated from **Vermont's** Norwich University in 1851 and immediately moved to **Iowa**, where he worked as a **railroad** engineer and organized a militia **company**.

Dodge entered Union service in July 1861 as colonel of the 4th Iowa and in January 1862 was in command of a **brigade** in the **Army of Southwest Missouri**. At **Pea Ridge**, he was wounded in the side and had three horses shot from under him. Promoted to brigadier general of volunteers in March 1862, Dodge was named commander of the District of Mississippi in September. He commanded **districts** in the western theater before being promoted to major general of volunteers in June 1864. During the **Atlanta Campaign**, Dodge commanded the **Army of the Tennessee's** XVI Corps and was severely wounded in the head outside Atlanta in August 1864. After recovering from this wound, he was put in command of the **Department of Missouri** in February 1865 and there fought guerrillas and **Indians** until war's end.

While serving in **Kansas**, Dodge's headquarters became known as Fort Dodge—later to be renamed Dodge City. He became chief engineer for the Union Pacific Railroad in January 1866 and then resigned from the **army** in May. Later, Dodge served as an Iowa congressman from 1867 to 1869, helped lay 9,000 miles of railroad track in the United States and Cuba, and amassed a fortune valued at $25 million.

DOLES, GEORGE PIERCE (1830–1864) CSA. A native of **Georgia**, Doles was a merchant and captain of a militia **company** before the Civil War. He and his company entered Confederate service in May 1861 as part of the 4th Georgia. Doles was then elected colonel and took his **regiment** to **Virginia**, where it became part of the **Army of Northern Virginia**. While fighting in the **Seven Days Campaign**, he was stunned by a shell at **Malvern Hill**. At **Antietam**, Doles took charge of the **brigade** after the brigade commander was wounded.

Doles was promoted to brigadier general in November 1862 and led a Georgia brigade in **Thomas "Stonewall" Jackson's** flank attack at **Chancellorsville**. At **Gettysburg**, he again won praise for his fighting on the first day. Doles was seen as one of the **army's** best brigade commanders, but at **Spotsylvania** he was harshly criticized when he failed to have **pickets** properly posted and lost several hundred men when his position was overrun by a Union assault. This humiliation may have led him to expose himself unnecessarily in fighting along the **Cold Harbor** line at Bethesda Church on June 2, 1864. There, he was killed instantly by a **sharpshooter**.

DONALDSONVILLE, LOUISIANA, BATTLE OF (JUNE 28, 1863). *See* FORT BUTLER, LOUISIANA, BATTLE OF.

DONELSON, DANIEL SMITH (1801–1863) CSA. A native of **Tennessee**, Donelson was educated by his father's brother-in-law, Andrew

Jackson, and through Jackson's influence, won an appointment to **West Point**. After graduating in 1825, he served only a few months in the **artillery** before resigning and becoming a Tennessee planter. Donelson married into a prominent family, became a brigadier general of militia, and served in the state legislature.

A secessionist, Donelson was Tennessee's speaker of the house when the state seceded in 1861. After being appointed state adjutant general, he was assigned the task of selecting sites on the upper Tennessee and Cumberland Rivers at which to build fortifications. These two fortifications were named **Forts Henry and Donelson**.

Donelson was appointed brigadier general in July 1861 and led a **brigade** at **Cheat Mountain, Virginia**. He then served under **Robert E. Lee** in **Charleston, South Carolina**, before assuming a brigade command in the **Army of Tennessee**. Donelson fought at **Perryville** and won praise at **Stones River** when his brigade broke the Union line and captured 11 cannons and one thousand **prisoners**. Illness finally forced him to relinquish field command, and in January 1863, he was put in command of the **Department of East Tennessee**. Donelson died on April 17, 1863, reportedly from chronic diarrhea. Unaware of his death, the War Department promoted him to major general that same month.

DOUBLE SHOTTING. This was the practice of placing two rounds of **canister** instead of one into an **artillery** piece. It was only done in extreme emergencies, usually when the battery was in immediate danger of being overrun.

DOUBLEDAY, ABNER (1819–1893) USA. A native of **New York** and the son of a congressman, Doubleday worked as a civil engineer before entering **West Point** in 1838. He graduated in 1842, served in the **artillery** during the **Mexican War**, and fought **Indians** in **Texas** and **Florida**.

During the **Fort Sumter** crisis, Doubleday was a captain in the garrison and firmly believed the fort should be defended. Some also credit him with firing the first Union shot in the bombardment. After the fort's surrender, Doubleday was promoted to major in the 17th U.S. Infantry and served under **Robert Patterson** in the **Shenandoah Valley** in the summer of 1861. In February 1862, he was appointed brigadier general of volunteers.

Doubleday led a **brigade** in the **Army of Virginia** at **Second Manassas** and a **division** in the **Army of the Potomac** at **South Mountain**, **Antietam**, **Fredericksburg**, and **Chancellorsville**. He was somewhat of a plodding general and earned the nickname "Forty-eight Hours," but he played a key role on **Gettysburg's** first day when he assumed command of the I Corps and kept it from retreating, after **John F. Reynolds** was killed. Afterward, Doubleday was incensed when he was passed over for permanent **corps** command and, in an effort to win recognition, wrote what was called the longest after-action report of the Union **army**. He saw no further field service in the war except for commanding part of the **Washington, D.C.**, defenses during **Jubal Early's Washington Raid** in 1864.

Brevetted major general of regulars for his war service, Doubleday remained in the army until 1873. Despite the popular belief, Doubleday had nothing to do with the creation of baseball.

DOUGLAS, HENRY KYD (1838–1903) CSA. A native of **Virginia**, Douglas entered Confederate service as a private in the 2nd Virginia, but he was promoted to lieutenant in August 1861 and joined **Thomas "Stonewall" Jackson's** staff. He served Jackson throughout **Jackson's Shenandoah Valley Campaign** and at **Antietam** but returned to his **regiment** as a captain in November. After serving at **Fredericksburg** and **Chancellorsville**, Douglas joined Maj. Gen. **Edward Johnson's** staff. Wounded and captured at **Gettysburg**, he was finally **exchanged** in March 1864. Douglas then returned to Johnson's staff until Johnson was captured at **Spotsylvania**. He next served on the staffs of **John B. Gordon** and **Jubal A. Early** and saw combat in **Philip Sheridan's Shenandoah Valley Campaign** and in the **Petersburg Campaign**. In March 1865, Douglas was placed in command of a **brigade**, but the war ended before he was promoted to brigadier general. He was wounded six times during the war. After the war, Douglas wrote the famous, albeit embellished, book *I Rode with Stonewall*.

DOUGLAS, STEPHEN ARNOLD (1813–1861) USA. USA. Born in **Vermont**, Douglas became one of the leading **Democratic Party** members of the 1850s. He moved to **Illinois** as a young man and became a lawyer and prominent politician. Douglas served in the state legislature and on the state supreme court before being elected to the U.S. House of Representatives in 1842. He next was elected to the U.S. Senate in 1847 and became an increasingly important figure as the **slavery** issue intensified. Douglas supported **homesteading**, a northern transcontinental **railroad**, and the South's right to have slaves, but he opposed the spread of slavery into the western territories. He also supported the idea of **popular sovereignty**, which called for the slavery issue in the territories to be decided by a vote of the people who lived there. Douglas got passed the **Compromise of 1850** and the divisive 1854 **Kansas-Nebraska Act**, which replaced the **Missouri Compromise** Line with popular sovereignty. By making possible the spread of slavery into the territories, he lost much Northern support.

Douglas was challenged for his Senate seat in 1858 by **Republican Abraham Lincoln** (a close acquaintance, whose wife, **Mary Todd Lincoln**, had been courted by Douglas). The campaign's **Lincoln-Douglas Debates** became some of the most famous political dialogues in American history. The **Dred Scott case** had outlawed popular sovereignty, so Douglas was pressured to develop an alternative for keeping slavery out of the territories. During the debates, he won back Northern support by introducing the Freeport Doctrine, a philosophy that called for the people of a territory to pass unfriendly legislation (such as high taxes) as a way of keeping out slavery. Douglas won the election, but his Freeport Doctrine angered many of his Southern supporters.

In 1860, Douglas was the Northern Democratic Party presidential nominee and ran on a platform of noninterference with slavery in the South but the containment of slavery through the Freeport Doctrine. After losing to Lincoln, he returned to the Senate and worked to find a compromise that would avoid civil war. Once war began, however, Douglas supported the Union war effort. He died on June 3, 1861, before playing any important role in the war itself.

DOUGLASS, FREDERICK (1817–1895) USA. Born a **Maryland** slave to a white father, Frederick Augustus Washington Bailey was taught to read and write and generally was treated well. In 1838, he escaped **slavery** to **Massachusetts** and took the name Frederick Douglass. An antislavery speech he made in 1841 impressed **abolitionist William Lloyd Garrison**, who hired Douglass to be a speaker for the Massachusetts Anti-Slavery Society. While working for the society, Douglass traveled to Great Britain and persuaded friends to buy his freedom so he could work within the United States without fear of being returned to Maryland as a runaway slave.

Douglass and Garrison eventually split because Douglass did not agree with Garrison's "moral suasion," a policy whereby abolitionists preached nonresistance and refused to work within the normal political system. In 1847, Douglass started *The North Star*, a **New York** abolitionist newspaper, and gained more recognition as an abolitionist leader. In 1859, he tacitly supported **John Brown's Raid on Harpers Ferry**, **Virginia**, but did not believe it would have any appreciable results. When Brown was captured, Douglass feared for his safety and fled to Canada and Europe. He eventually returned to the United States and during the Civil War was a strong supporter of enlisting **black troops** and making the war a fight against slavery. In this regard, Douglass was instrumental in raising the famous black regiment, the **54th Massachusetts**.

Douglass was allied with the **Radical Republicans** during **Reconstruction** and served in a number of minor government posts, including minister to Haiti.

DOVER, TENNESSEE, BATTLE OF (FEBRUARY 3, 1863). One of Maj. Gen. **Joseph Wheeler's Raids** was made in January 1863 when he was ordered by **Braxton Bragg** to disrupt Union shipping on the Cumberland River. Joined by **Nathan Bedford Forrest's brigade**, Wheeler positioned his men on the river, but the Federals learned of the ambush and stopped their ships. Wheeler then decided to attack the fortified Union post at Dover, just outside **Fort Donelson**. Forrest opposed the move, but Wheeler went ahead with his plans to first bombard the post and then attack with dismounted troopers.

On February 3, Forrest attacked prematurely with his dismounted men and suffered a defeat at the hands of the 800-man garrison under Col. **Abner C. Harding**. Although he had lost the element of surprise, Wheeler then attacked with his men, but he, too, was repulsed. The defeat at Dover caused Forrest to declare to Wheeler that while he liked him as a friend, "I will be in my coffin before I will fight again under your command"(Wills, *A Battle from the Start*, 102).

Wheeler accepted all responsibility for the defeat. In the fight, the Confederates suffered 855 casualties, while the Federals lost only 110 men.

DOW, NEAL (1804–1897) USA. A native of **Maine**, Dow was raised in a Quaker home and became a successful businessman and a leader of the temperance movement. It largely was through his influence that Maine outlawed liquor in 1851. Dow served as mayor of Portland before the Civil War and in November 1861 entered Union service as colonel of the 13th Maine (his wartime service led the Quakers to eject him from the church).

Dow was part of **Benjamin F. Butler's** command that garrisoned **New Orleans, Louisiana**, in the spring of 1862. Promoted to brigadier general of volunteers in April 1862, he commanded the former Confederate **Forts Jackson and St. Philip** and the District of **Florida**. During the **Port Hudson Campaign**, Dow was wounded twice in May 1863 and later was captured while recuperating from his injuries. He was **exchanged** for **Robert E. Lee's** son **W. H. F. "Rooney" Lee** in March 1864. Dow then resigned his commission in November because of poor health.

Dow continued to be active in the temperance movement after the war and was the Prohibition Party's presidential candidate in 1880.

DOWLING, RICHARD "DICK" WILLIAM (1838–1867) CSA. A native of Ireland, "Dick" Dowling immigrated to the United States in the 1840s and lived in **Louisiana** before settling in **Texas**. He entered Confederate service in August 1861 as a lieutenant in an infantry **company** named the Davis Guards. After participating in operations along the Rio Grande, Dowling's company became part of the 1st Texas Heavy Artillery in October 1862. While in its service, he received praise for his handling of the **artillery** at the **Battle of Galveston** on January 1, 1863.

After Galveston, Dowling was sent to **Sabine Pass, Texas**, to take charge of Fort Griffin. Later in January, two steamers under his jurisdiction captured two Union blockaders. Then on September 8, 1863, Dowling's six-gun battery and 44 men stopped a Union invasion consisting of four gunboats, seven transports, and 4,000 men. Two gunboats surrendered during the battle, and the others withdrew. The feat won Dowling great praise, and he and his men were awarded the **Thanks of Congress** and the **Davis Guard Medal**. After Sabine Pass, Dowling became a recruiter and was promoted to major before the war's end.

DRAFT. *See* CONSCRIPTION.

DRAFT RIOTS. The U.S. military tradition at the time of the Civil War was to rely almost entirely on volunteers to fill the ranks. Military **conscription** was seen as undemocratic and un-American. But in the Civil War, manpower shortages forced both the Union and Confederacy to rely finally on the draft. Opposition to the draft was especially strong in the North, particularly in the Midwest and New York City. Besides disliking the notion of conscription, many viewed the draft as unfair because of its many exemption, **substitution**, and **commutation** clauses. Others opposed the **Emancipation Proclamation** and detested fighting to free the slaves. The result was that the draft was violently opposed in virtually every Northern state, with riots breaking out in **Wisconsin, Illinois,** and **New York**. Draft officials were attacked and threatened, and mobs formed in towns to prevent the draft lottery from being performed.

The worst incident was the **New York City Draft Riot** in July 1863. The city was a center of draft opposition because its traditionally **Democratic** population opposed **Abraham Lincoln's** policies, and the large number of Irish immigrants opposed fighting to free the slaves. Democratic Gov. **Horatio Seymour** also questioned the authority of the federal government to impose a draft. When the lottery was held on July 11, a bloody three-day riot erupted. Led mostly by the Irish, the mobs attacked blacks, newspaper offices, and police. Estimates of the dead ranged from fewer than one hundred to several hundred. Troops were rushed from the **Gettysburg** battlefield, and order finally was restored.

DRANESVILLE, VIRGINIA, BATTLE OF (DECEMBER 20, 1861). This battle was brought on by Gen. **Joseph E. Johnston** and Maj. Gen. **George B. McClellan** sending **foraging** parties to the Dranesville, Virginia, area at the same time. The Confederate force left Centreville and consisted of about 150 cavalrymen, an **artillery** battery, and four infantry **regiments** under the command of Brig. Gen. **J. E. B. Stuart**. The Union column left the **Washington, D.C.**, area with five infantry regiments, some cavalry, and an artillery battery, commanded by Brig. Gen. **E. O. C. Ord**. Both commands included a large number of wagons.

Ord's force entered Dranesville at about noon on December 20, 1861, and soon was followed by Stuart. Fighting broke out, and both sides deployed their infantry and artillery in opposing lines. Stuart attacked and attempted to drive off the enemy, but he was repulsed by Ord. A rather confusing fight lasted for a couple of hours before Stuart finally withdrew at mid-afternoon. The Confederates suffered 194 casualties at Dranesville, while Ord reported losing 68 men.

DRAYTON, PERCIVAL (1812–1865) USA. A native of **South Carolina**, Drayton was the son of a prominent planter, army officer, and congressman, and was the brother of Confederate Brig. Gen. **Thomas F. Drayton**. He entered the **U.S. Navy** as a midshipman in 1827 and rose to the rank of commander by 1860. Drayton had lived in Philadelphia, Pennsylvania, most of his life, so he remained loyal to the Union when his native state seceded.

Drayton commanded the USS *Pocahontas* during the October 1861 **Battle of Port Royal**, **South Carolina**. Ironically, his brother was in command of the Confederate fort being attacked. Drayton moved his ship closer to the enemy fort than any other officer so that he would not be charged with dereliction of duty because of his brother's position. In March 1862, Drayton joined the **South Atlantic Blockading Squadron** and was promoted to captain in July. He participated in the attack on **Charleston, South Carolina**, in April 1863 and afterward was brought to the Gulf of Mexico by Adm. **David G. Farragut** and made fleet captain of the West **Gulf Blockading Squadron**.

As fleet captain, Drayton took command of Farragut's flagship, the **USS** *Hartford* in August 1864 and fought at the **Battle of Mobile Bay**. In the spring of 1865, Drayton was put in command of the Bureau of Navigation, but he died four months later.

DRAYTON, THOMAS FENWICK (1808–1891) CSA. Like his brother **Percival Drayton**, Drayton was born in **South Carolina**. His father, a prominent planter, **U.S. Army** officer, and congressman, secured him an appointment to **West Point**, from which he graduated in 1828. While there, Drayton became close friends with his classmate **Jefferson Davis**. He then served in various eastern posts before resigning from the **army** in 1836. Returning to South Carolina, Drayton became a planter and **railroad** president, served as a militia captain, and was elected to the state senate in 1853.

While his brother remained loyal to the Union, Drayton entered Confederate service in September 1861 when his friend Davis appointed him brigadier general. His subsequent record indicates it was Drayton's political connections, and not his skill, that led to this position. Drayton was put in command of the defenses of **Port Royal**, **South Carolina**, but in November 1861, he was forced to evacuate the town in the face of a naval bombardment (his brother Percival commanded one of the attacking ships).

After serving in other South Carolina **district** commands, Drayton eventually was given a **brigade** command and was transferred to the **Army of Northern Virginia**. His lackluster performance at **Thoroughfare Gap** and **Second Manassas** led his **division** commander to criticize him for being slow and perhaps even dimwitted. Drayton performed better at **South Mountain** and **Antietam**, but in the latter battle he drew more criticism when his **brigade** was forced to retire. Afterward, he was transferred to court-martial duty and then to **Arkansas** in August 1863.

Drayton was given a brigade command in **Louisiana**, but **Edmund Kirby Smith** relieved him just as the **Red River Campaign** was beginning, probably to keep him out of the field. He held various administrative posts in the **Trans-Mississippi Department** for the remainder of the war, including commanding the Sub-District of Texas and serving as president of the board of inquiry that investigated **Sterling Price's 1864 Missouri Raid**. **Robert E. Lee**, a friend, wrote that while he was a gentleman and a soldier, Drayton "seems to lack the capacity to command" (Davis, *The Confederate General*, vol. 2, 77).

After the war, Drayton became a **Georgia** farmer before moving to **North Carolina** and working in the insurance business.

DRED SCOTT DECISION. Slavery was the most divisive issue in the United States during the 1850s, and the **U.S. Supreme Court** used the Dred Scott case as a means to make a sweeping court decision on the matter. Dred Scott was a slave who belonged to **U.S. Army** surgeon John

Emerson and in 1846 was taken into **Illinois** and the **Wisconsin** Territory where slavery was illegal. After Emerson's death, Scott received **abolitionist** help to sue for his freedom on the basis that he should have been freed when he was taken into free territory.

The case dragged through the lower courts for 10 years before reaching the Supreme Court. Chief Justice **Roger Taney** handed down the much-awaited decision in March 1857. In a 7–2 ruling, the Court stated that Negroes were not citizens of the United States and could not sue in federal court; that slaves were property and therefore protected by the Constitution; and that the **Missouri Compromise** Line was in violation of the 5th Amendment. The decision also implied that territories could not use **popular sovereignty** as a means of outlawing slavery.

The decision was a major victory for the South but outraged the North because the vote was along sectional lines, with all of the majority Southern justices voting for it. The Dred Scott decision was one of the major disrupting factors prior to the Civil War, and it led to the **Republican Party** gaining significant strength in the North. Although he lost the case, Scott and his family were acquired by abolitionist friends and were freed quietly in May 1857.

DREWRY'S BLUFF, VIRGINIA. Drewry's Bluff is a 110-foot bluff on the south side of the James River a few miles downstream from **Richmond, Virginia**. The river narrows at that point, making it an ideal location for defensive works. When **Norfolk** fell to Union forces in early May 1862, Drewry's Bluff was fortified to prevent Union ships from moving up the river to Richmond. Officially known as Fort Darling, these defenses were supervised by Col. **George Washington Custis Lee** and consisted of heavy gun emplacements on top of the bluff, with sunken obstructions in the river itself. The position withstood several Union attacks and protected Richmond until the war's last days.

DREWRY'S BLUFF, VIRGINIA, FIRST BATTLE OF (MAY 15, 1862). After capturing **Norfolk, Virginia**, in May 1862, Union naval forces proceeded up the James River toward **Richmond**. The only major Confederate position on the river to stop them was the hastily fortified works known as Fort Darling at **Drewry's Bluff**. There, some heavy guns manned by sailors from the recently destroyed CSS *Virginia* were in position and supported by an infantry **brigade**. The river had also been blocked by sunken obstructions.

On May 15, five Union ships arrived at the bluff. The river obstructions prevented the larger vessels from passing by, and two small **monitors** were left to challenge the Confederates. It soon became apparent that the **USS *Monitor*** and USS *Galena* could not elevate their guns enough to reach the Confederate position. The Confederates drove off the two monitors, inflicting heavy damage on the *Galena* (which was hit 44 times and lost 24 men), and forced the entire fleet to withdraw. The Confederates lost 15 men.

DREWRY'S BLUFF, VIRGINIA, SECOND BATTLE OF (MAY 12–16, 1864). After Confederate Gen. **P. G. T. Beauregard** contained Maj. Gen. **Benjamin F. Butler's Army of the James** at the beginning of the **Bermuda Hundred Campaign** in May 1864, he decided to draw Butler out of his defensive works for a decisive battle. Beauregard sent seven **brigades** under Maj. Gen. **Robert F. Hoke** to Proctor's Creek in hope that Butler would move against them.

On May 12, Butler sent his cavalry on a raid against the Petersburg **railroads** and about 16,000 men of the XVIII and X Corps northward toward Drewry's Bluff and **Richmond, Virginia**. Butler's men pushed Hoke's defenders into their main works around Drewry's Bluff (known as Fort Darling) and by May 14 had the Confederates pinned up there. Beauregard arrived the same day with reinforcements, bringing his total to about 18,000 men, and made plans to attack the enemy's flanks the next morning, while Maj. Gen. **W. H. C. Whiting** attacked Butler's rear.

At daylight on May 16, Maj. Gen. **Robert Ransom's division** attacked Butler's right flank, held by Maj. Gen. **William F. Smith's** XVIII Corps. One Union brigade was overrun, but dense fog, disorganization, and an ammunition shortage forced Ransom to halt his advance. On Butler's left, fog also slowed Hoke, but he finally attacked Maj. Gen. **Quincy A. Gillmore's** X Corps nearly two hours after Ransom had advanced. After an initial success, Hoke was stopped by a Union counterattack and the dense fog. Whiting was hesitant and unaggressive (perhaps suffering from battle fatigue) and stopped when he encountered Union troops at Walthall's Station. As a result, Butler was able to disengage and return to his Bermuda Hundred line. Beauregard followed and "corked" Butler on the Bermuda Hundred peninsula by digging entrenchments across its neck. In the Second Battle of Drewry's Bluff, Beauregard lost 2,506 men to Butler's 4,160.

DROOP MOUNTAIN, WEST VIRGINIA, BATTLE OF (NOVEMBER 6, 1863). In early November 1863, two Union columns marched from Beverly and Charleston, **West Virginia**, toward Lewisburg to destroy the East Tennessee & Virginia Railroad. Brigadier General **Alfred N. A. Duffié's** 1,700 men had little trouble after leaving Charleston, but Brig. Gen. **William W. Averell's** 5,000-man column had to fight its way from Beverly.

In the Huntersville's area, Averell engaged about 600 Confederate cavalrymen under Col. **William L. "Mudwall" Jackson**. On November 4–5, Averell's cavalry forced Jackson to withdraw to Droop Mountain, where Brig. Gen. **John Echols** reinforced him on November 6 with about 1,700 infantry and six cannons. Averell engaged Echols with his cavalry and **artillery**, while the infantry circled around the Confederate left flank. In the early afternoon, Averell launched a flank attack against Jackson, followed by a general assault by his dismounted cavalrymen. After holding their position on the mountain's crest for an hour, the Confederates finally retreated, losing one cannon and one **flag**.

Averell and Duffié both entered Lewisburg the following day and began pursuing Echols, but soon stopped because of exhaustion and obstructed roads. The two Union columns returned to Beverly by separate routes, having failed to accomplish their mission to destroy the **railroad**.

"DRUMMER BOY OF CHICKAMAUGA." *See* CLEM, JOHN "JOHNNY" LINCOLN.

DuBOSE, DUDLEY McILVER (1834–1883) CSA. A native of **Tennessee**, DuBose graduated from the Lebanon Law School and became a lawyer in **Georgia**, where he married the daughter of **Robert Toombs**. He entered Confederate service in 1861 as a lieutenant in the 15th Georgia but soon became a member of his father-in-law's staff. Promoted to captain in 1862, DuBose continued to serve with Toombs until January 1863, when he was appointed colonel of the 15th Georgia.

DuBose led his **regiment** at **Suffolk**, **Virginia**, and fought with the **Army of Northern Virginia** at **Gettysburg**, where he earned praise for his action at **Devil's Den**. When the rest of his **division** was withdrawn on July 3, 1863, DuBose mistakenly was left behind and suffered heavy losses when he was attacked and nearly overrun. He went west with **James Longstreet's corps** that autumn, was wounded at **Chickamauga**, and fought in the **Chattanooga** and **Knoxville Campaigns** before returning to **Virginia** with Longstreet. During the **Overland Campaign**, DuBose took command of the **brigade** during the **Battle of the Wilderness** when **Henry Benning** was wounded, and won praise for his leadership at **Spotsylvania, Cold Harbor**, and **Petersburg**. He was promoted to brigadier general in December 1864 and transferred to a Georgia brigade in **Joseph Kershaw's** division. DuBose was captured at **Sailor's Creek** on April 6, 1865.

After being released from **prison** in July, DuBose returned to Georgia, reopened a law practice, and was elected to the **U.S. Congress** in 1870.

DUFFIÉ, ALFRED NAPOLEON ALEXANDER (1835–1880) USA. A native of France and the son of a count, Duffié (DOO-fee-YAY) graduated from the military academy of St. Cyr in 1854. He then served as a cavalry lieutenant in Algeria, Senegal, and the Crimea, where he was awarded four decorations. After being wounded while fighting the Austrians, Duffié came to the United States on leave and married a prominent **New York** woman.

"Nattie," as Duffié was called, resigned his French commission at the outbreak of the Civil War and entered Union service in August 1861 as a captain in the 2nd New York Cavalry. He was promoted to major in October and in July 1862 was appointed colonel of the 1st Rhode Island Cavalry. Duffié fought at **Second Manassas** with the **Army of Virginia**, and his performance at **Kelly's Ford** in March 1863 led to his promotion to brigadier general of volunteers in June 1863.

After leading a cavalry **division** in the **Army of the Potomac** during the **Chancellorsville** and **Gettysburg Campaigns**, Duffié was transferred to **West Virginia**. He was relieved of his command in October 1864 while stationed in **Maryland** because of complaints made against his men's depredations. Soon afterward, Confederate guerrillas captured Duffié near Bunker Hill, Virginia. **Philip Sheridan** recommended he be dismissed from the service for allowing himself to be captured, but when Duffié was **exchanged** in April 1865 he was sent to the **Department of the Missouri**.

After the war, Duffié served as U.S. consul to Cádiz, Spain. He died there from tuberculosis.

DUG GAP, GEORGIA, BATTLE OF (MAY 7–11, 1864). *See* ROCKY FACE RIDGE, GEORGIA, BATTLE OF.

DUKE, BASIL WILSON (1838–1916) CSA. A native of **Kentucky** and the son of a **U.S. Navy** officer, Duke attended Centre College and Transylvania Law School and then began a law practice in St. Louis, **Missouri**. Because of his involvement in the St. Louis secessionist militia, in 1861, Duke was indicted for treason and was forced to return to Kentucky. There he married the sister of **John Hunt Morgan** before traveling to **Arkansas** to serve as a volunteer aide to Col. **Thomas C. Hindman**.

Returning to Kentucky, Duke joined Morgan's Lexington Rifles as a private but in October 1861 was elected 2nd lieutenant. He fought at **Shiloh** with the 2nd Kentucky Cavalry (Confederate) and was badly wounded in both shoulders. Promoted to lieutenant colonel in June, Duke accompanied Morgan on a raid into Kentucky in July and earned a reputation for being the brains behind Morgan's cavalry. After leading the **regiment** in the 1862 **Kentucky Campaign** and on several successful **Tennessee** raids, Duke was promoted to colonel in December 1862. During one of **Morgan's Kentucky Raids** that month, he was badly wounded a second time when he was struck behind the ear by a shell fragment.

In the summer of 1863, Duke went on **Morgan's Ohio Raid**. Beleaguered by Federals, he and his men finally were captured in July when they fought a holding action on the Ohio River's **Buffington Island** to allow Morgan to escape (Morgan was captured soon afterward). **Exchanged** a year later, Duke was promoted to brigadier general in September 1864 and took command of Morgan's cavalry (Morgan having been killed). His cavalry saw hard service in southwestern **Virginia** that winter as it protected Wytheville and **Saltville** from Union raiders. In the war's final days, Duke helped escort **Jefferson Davis** to **Georgia**. After guarding the Confederate treasury wagons for a while, he led a party of cavalry away from Davis to divert Union pursuers. Duke surrendered in Augusta, Georgia, soon afterward.

After the war, Duke opened a Kentucky law practice and was elected to the state legislature in 1869. He was active in veteran affairs and wrote two popular books on his war service.

DUMFRIES, VIRGINIA, RAID ON (DECEMBER 26–28, 1862). On the day after Christmas, 1862, Confederate Maj. Gen. **J. E. B. Stuart** led 1,800 cavalrymen on a raid from **Fredericksburg, Virginia**, into the rear of Union Maj. Gen. **Ambrose Burnside's Army of the Potomac**. Crossing the Rappahannock River upstream near Brandy Station, the Confederates split into two columns to attack two Union supply bases at Dumfries (DUM-freez) and Occoquan (OK-uh-KWAN). Stuart was repulsed at Dumfries on December 27, and his subordinate, **Wade Hampton**, succeeded in capturing only a few supplies at Occoquan. Stuart continued the raid, however, and caused some havoc in the Union rear, particularly when he captured **prisoners**, mules, horses, and wagons just 12 miles from **Washington, D.C.** After successfully returning to his own lines, Stuart wired Union Quartermaster General **Montgomery C. Meigs** and complained of the poor quality of mules the Union **army** was supplying.

DUMONT, EBENEZER (1814–1871) USA. A native of **Indiana**, Dumont graduated from the University of Indiana and became a lawyer. He served in the state legislature several times and was a lieutenant colonel in the **Mexican War**.

Dumont entered Union service in April 1861 as colonel of the 7th Indiana and served under **George B. McClellan** in western **Virginia**. Promoted to brigadier general of volunteers in September 1861, he fought at **Cheat Mountain** before taking command of a **brigade** in the **Army of the Ohio** in January 1862. Dumont fought **John Hunt Morgan's** raiders in **Kentucky** and then led a **division** under **Don Carlos Buell** during the 1862 **Kentucky Campaign**. In December 1862, he left his command on sick leave and resigned his commission in February 1863 to take a seat in the **U.S. Congress**.

DUNCAN, JOHNSON KELLY (1827–1862) CSA. A native of **Pennsylvania**, Duncan graduated from **West Point** in 1849. He served with the **artillery** in the **Seminole Wars** and helped explore a **railroad** route in the Pacific Northwest before resigning his commission in 1855 to become superintendent of government construction in **New Orleans, Louisiana**. Duncan was serving on the Louisiana Board of Public Works when the Civil War began in 1861. He entered Confederate service as a colonel of artillery and was put in command of Ship Island in September. Duncan then was given command of the coastal defenses of New Orleans and was promoted to brigadier general in January 1862.

Duncan's main wartime service was commanding **Forts Jackson and St. Philip** when **David G. Farragut** attacked New Orleans in April 1862. His defense was hampered by antiquated artillery and powder and a lack of cooperation from naval officials. Duncan established his headquarters in Fort Jackson and endured a prolonged bombardment before Farragut ran his ships past the forts on April 24. After New Orleans surrendered, Duncan continued to hold out at the forts until a large part of the garrison mutinied and surrendered on April 28. He was quickly **exchanged** and was ordered to take command of a **brigade** under **Leonidas Polk**, but he died from typhoid fever in Knoxville, Tennessee, on December 18, 1862.

DUNKARD CHURCH AT BATTLE OF ANTIETAM, MARYLAND (SEPTEMBER 17, 1862). *See* ANTIETAM, MARYLAND, CAMPAIGN AND BATTLE OF.

DUNOVANT, JOHN (1825–1864) CSA. A native of **South Carolina**, Dunovant was a veteran of the **Mexican War** and served as a captain in the 10th U.S. Infantry from 1855 to 1860. An ardent secessionist, he resigned his commission when South Carolina seceded, became major of the 1st South Carolina in January 1861, and saw service at **Fort Sumter**. Promoted to colonel in July, Dunovant's heavy drinking nearly ruined him. Ordered to attack near **Secessionville, South Carolina**, in June 1862, he was too drunk to obey and was arrested. When Dunovant was convicted,

Jefferson Davis wanted him dismissed from the service, but other officers appealed to reinstate him. Davis relented and in July 1863 appointed Dunovant colonel of the 5th South Carolina Cavalry.

After serving in the siege of **Charleston, South Carolina**, Dunovant's **regiment** was sent to **Virginia** in April 1864 and served as infantry in the **Bermuda Hundred Campaign** and at the **Second Battle of Drewry's Bluff**. Afterward, the regiment mounted again and fought under **Wade Hampton** at **Haw's Shop**, where Dunovant performed competently and received a wound through the hand. After he recovered, he was recommended for promotion by a number of general officers, including **Robert E. Lee**.

Dunovant was finally promoted to brigadier general in August 1864 and took command of a cavalry **brigade**. At first he fought well in several clashes, but in September he was surprised and defeated near **Hatcher's Run**. Perhaps because of this setback and his previous conviction, Dunovant was eager to redeem himself. On October 1, 1864, two days after his defeat, he begged his commander to allow him to make a **frontal attack** on the Vaughn Road. The reluctant commander finally allowed it, and Dunovant was killed instantly by a bullet through his heart.

DU PONT, SAMUEL FRANCIS (1803–1865) USA. A native of **New Jersey**, Du Pont entered the **U.S. Navy** as a midshipman in 1815, when he was only 12. He served around the world and rose through the ranks to become captain in 1855.

When the Civil War began, Du Pont was in command of the Philadelphia Navy Yard. He then was appointed head of the Blockade Strategy Board to plan the **blockade** against the Confederacy, but in September 1861, he took command of the **South Atlantic Blockading Squadron**. In November, Du Pont led the attack that captured **Port Royal, South Carolina**, and received the **Thanks of Congress** and a promotion to rear admiral in July 1862. Over the next several months, his command captured Beaufort, South Carolina, and assisted in the capture of **Fort Pulaski, Georgia**. In command of a large attack fleet, Du Pont was repulsed in April 1863 when he attacked the defenses of **Charleston, South Carolina**. Although he blamed his defeat on the ineffectiveness of his **monitors**, he believed that **Abraham Lincoln's** administration held him responsible for the setback and asked to be relieved. Du Pont was replaced by Rear Adm. **John A. B. Dahlgren** in July and returned to his Delaware home.

Du Pont did not hold another command during the war and died just as hostilities ended. He was nephew of the founder of the Du Pont chemical company.

DURHAM STATION, NORTH CAROLINA, SURRENDER AT (MAY 3, 1865). It was near this place that Gen. **Joseph E. Johnston** surrendered his Confederate command to **William T. Sherman** in April 1865 at the end of the **Carolinas Campaign**. After learning that **Robert E. Lee** had surrendered to **U. S. Grant** on April 9, Johnston secured permission from **Jefferson Davis** to open negotiations with Sherman. The two met at James Bennett's farmhouse on April 17–18 and agreed on **surrender** terms. The terms were rejected by the U.S. government, since Sherman agreed to allow the Confederate state governments to continue to function. The two generals met again April 23–26, and Johnston agreed to the same surrender terms Grant offered Lee. Johnston's actual surrender of approximately 30,000 men took place on May 3.

DURYÉE, ABRAM (1815–1890) USA. A native of **New York**, Duryée (dur-YAY) became a wealthy importer of mahogany. He was active in the militia before the Civil War and rose to the rank of colonel in command of a militia **regiment** that was composed of New York socialites. While serving in that capacity, Duryée was wounded twice while putting down domestic riots.

Duryée entered Union service in April 1861 when he raised the 5th New York, informally known as **Duryée's Zouaves**. After fighting at **Big Bethel, Virginia**, he was promoted to brigadier general of volunteers in August and eventually was given a **brigade** in the **Army of the Potomac's** III Corps. Duryée fought at **Second Manassas** (where he was wounded twice), **South Mountain**, and in **Antietam's** cornfield (where he was wounded three times). When he returned to duty, Duryée was furious that he had been passed over for **division** command in favor of a junior officer and that his brigade had been reorganized. He immediately offered his resignation, which was accepted in January 1863. Despite his abrupt departure from service, Duryée was **brevetted** major general of volunteers in 1865.

After the war, Duryée served for a time as New York City's police commissioner.

DURYÉE'S ZOUAVES. This was the popular name for the 5th New York Infantry, which was raised by **Abram Duryée**. Duryée (dur-YAY) was a wealthy New York City mahogany importer who had been active in the antebellum militia. Before the war, he was colonel of the 7th Regiment, which became famous for its drill and large number of upper class gentlemen. Many of these socialites joined the **regiment** that Duryée organized when the Civil War began. The 5th New York adopted the French **Zouave uniform** and became a conspicuous and famous unit.

The regiment was assigned to the **Army of the Potomac's** V Corps and suffered heavy casualties at **Gaines' Mill** during the **Peninsula Campaign**. At **Second Manassas**, it again saw bloody fighting and lost nearly 300 men. In both battles, the Zouaves were recognized for sacrificing themselves to slow Confederate attacks. **Division** commander Maj. Gen. **George Sykes** called the Zouaves the best volunteer regiment he ever saw. Future Union generals who began their careers as officers in Duryée's Zouaves were **Gouverneur K. Warren**, **H. Judson Kilpatrick**, Joseph E. Hamblin, and **Henry E. Davies**. The Zouaves' terms of enlistment expired in 1863, and the regiment was mustered out of service in May.

DUTCH GAP CANAL, VIRGINIA. When Maj. Gen. **Benjamin F. Butler** began the **Bermuda Hundred Campaign** in May 1864, he found the Confederate defenses at **Drewry's Bluff** to be a major impediment to his plans. Union gunboats on the James River were unable to eliminate these defenses because river obstructions and other Confederate guns at Trent's Reach prevented the larger ships from getting close to the bluff. To remedy the situation, Butler planned to dig a canal across a peninsula formed by the river. Known as Dutch Gap, this peninsula was 174 yards wide. A canal across its neck would allow Union gunboats to avoid both the river obstructions and the enemy guns at Trent's Reach and enable them to close on Drewry's Bluff.

Butler put a large number of men, mostly **black troops**, to work on the canal from August to December 1864. Lieutenant General **U. S. Grant** did not put much hope in the project but allowed Butler to continue work on it just to keep the inept general occupied. Impatient to finish, Butler exploded 12,000 pounds of powder in the canal on January 1, 1865, but the resultant explosion only further filled it in. The canal was finally finished in April, but it was too late to be of any use.

DUVAL, ISAAC HARDIN (1824–1902) USA. A native of western **Virginia**, Duval settled in **Arkansas** and operated a trading post with his brother before moving to the western plains to become a hunter and trapper. It was claimed he led the first wagon train from **Texas** to **California** and in 1851 participated in a Cuban revolt. Duval had returned to western Virginia by 1861 and entered Union service in June as major of the 1st (West) Virginia.

In September 1862, Duval was promoted to colonel of the 9th West Virginia. He served in mountainous **West Virginia** fighting guerrillas and participated in the **Battle of Cloyd's Mountain** in 1864. Duval was promoted to brigadier general in September 1864, fought in **Philip**

Sheridan's 1864 Shenandoah Valley Campaign, and was **brevetted** major general of volunteers for his service in the **Shenandoah Valley**. During the war, he fought in more than 30 battles and **skirmishes**, had 11 horses shot from under him, and was wounded three times.

After the war, Duval became involved in politics and served as a West Virginia state representative and senator, a congressman, and the state's adjutant general.

DWIGHT, WILLIAM (1831–1888) USA. A native of **Massachusetts**, Dwight entered **West Point** in 1849, but he was dismissed in 1853 for poor grades. He became a manufacturer in Massachusetts and **Pennsylvania** and in June 1861 entered Union service as lieutenant colonel of **Daniel Sickles's** 70th New York.

In May 1862, Dwight was wounded three times and was captured at **Williamsburg** while serving with the **Army of the Potomac** in the **Peninsula Campaign**. After being **exchanged**, he was promoted to brigadier general of volunteers in November 1862 and was given a **brigade** in **Louisiana**. Dwight participated in the 1863 **Bayou Teche** and **Port Hudson Campaigns** and was **Nathaniel P. Banks's** chief of staff during the 1864 **Red River Campaign**. In the latter campaign, it was claimed that Dwight was largely engaged in collecting cotton to ship to Massachusetts's textile mills.

After the failed Red River Campaign, Dwight received a **division** command in the XIX Corps and fought in **Philip Sheridan's 1864 Shenandoah Valley Campaign**. He was arrested, however, for desparaging remarks made about other commands during the **Third Battle of Winchester** and for leaving the battle to eat lunch. Although the charges were never acted upon, Dwight was not recommended for a **brevet** promotion after the war when most other high-ranking officers received one.

After leaving the **army** in January 1866, Dwight became involved in the **railroad** industry in Cincinnati, Ohio.

DYER, ALEXANDER BRYDIE (1815–1874) USA. A native of **Virginia**, Dyer graduated from **West Point** in 1833 and fought in the **Seminole Wars** as an **artillery** officer. During the **Mexican War**, he was chief of ordnance for Stephen W. Kearny's New Mexico Expedition. After turning down one **brevet**, Dyer finally accepted another for his Mexican War service.

A captain by 1861, Dyer remained loyal to the Union and was put in command of the **Springfield (Massachusetts) Armory** in August. He quadrupled the armory's production of **rifles** and was offered the position of chief of ordnance by **Abraham Lincoln**. Dyer turned it down, out

of respect for the incumbent, **James W. Ripley**. He then was promoted
to major in March 1863, and when Ripley retired as chief of ordnance in
September 1863, Dyer accepted the position. He proved to be an excellent administrator, being more interested than Ripley in new weaponry
(even patenting a new heavy artillery shell called the **Dyer Shell**) and opposing profiteers and charlatan inventors. When his opponents, including
Col. **Hiram Berdan**, complained to the **U.S. Congress** that Dyer was incompetent, Dyer requested a court of inquiry. The investigation confirmed his competence and allowed him to run the armory as he saw fit.

Dyer was promoted to brigadier general of volunteers in September
1864 and received a brevet of major general of regulars when the war
ended. He remained at the Ordnance Bureau until 1869, when he resigned because of poor health.

DYER SHELL. Invented by **Alexander B. Dyer**, this 3-inch, or 24-pound,
artillery shell was made out of cast iron, but it had a lead cup on the bottom that expanded when the piece was fired, allowing it to fit snugly the
barrel's **rifling**. There also was a corrugated cap over the shell's point
that directed flames to the **fuse** when the cannon was fired. More than
168,000 of the shells were produced during the war.

– E –

EARLY, JUBAL ANDERSON (1816–1894) CSA. A native of **Virginia**,
Early received a good local education before entering **West Point**. After
graduating in 1837, he served with the **artillery** in the **Seminole Wars**
but then resigned from the **U.S. Army** in 1838 to study law. Early opened
a successful law practice, became an active **Whig**, and was elected to
one term in the Virginia legislature in 1840. He also served in the **Mexican War** as major of the 1st Virginia but served on garrison duty in
Mexico rather than seeing any combat.

In 1861, Early was a delegate to the Virginia **secession** convention,
where he voted against secession. When Virginia seceded, he remained
loyal to his native state and was appointed colonel of the 24th Virginia.
At **First Manassas**, Early commanded a **brigade** and played a key role
in the victory by launching a flank attack against the enemy late in the
battle.

Early was promoted to brigadier general in August 1861 and served in
the **Peninsula Campaign**, where he was badly wounded in the shoulder
at **Williamsburg**. This wound kept him out of action until **Malvern Hill**

in July 1862. Leading a brigade in **Richard Ewell's** division of the **Army of Northern Virginia**, Early was praised for his service at **Cedar Mountain**, **Second Manassas**, **Antietam**, and **Fredericksburg**, where he sealed a breakthrough on the Confederate right.

Promotion to major general finally came for Early in April 1863. Commanding a **division** in **Stonewall Jackson's** corps, he held the Fredericksburg line for several days during the **Chancellorsville Campaign** before finally being driven back by superior numbers in the **Second Battle of Fredericksburg**. During the **Gettysburg Campaign**, Early again won accolades for capturing a key fort at the **Second Battle of Winchester**, for helping rout the Union XI Corps on the first day of the Battle of Gettysburg, and for briefly seizing Cemetery Hill on the second day of the battle. After the campaign, much of Early's **division** was captured at **Rappahannock Station** in November 1863 when two of his brigades were left isolated on the north bank of the river. Despite this setback, he was given temporary command of the II Corps during the **Mine Run Campaign** when Ewell became ill.

After leading his division at the **Wilderness**, Early again was placed in command of the II Corps when Ewell became ill. This time he remained in command and was promoted to lieutenant general in May 1864. The promotion caused some ill will among the **corps'** officers, but it is clear that **Robert E. Lee** had come to prefer Early over Ewell as commander of the corps. In June 1864, Early was sent to contest Union Maj. Gen. **David Hunter's Shenandoah Valley Campaign** and, it was hoped, to threaten **Washington, D.C.**, to draw Union troops away from Lee's front. Early stopped Hunter at **Lynchburg** and then began **Early's Washington Raid**. After winning the **Battle of the Monocacy**, he reached the outskirts of Washington before being forced to retire back to the **Shenandoah Valley**.

At the end of July, Early's reputation was tarnished when he ordered his cavalry to burn **Chambersburg**, **Pennsylvania**, when its citizens failed to pay a ransom demanded for the destruction of Virginia homes. He continued to operate in the Valley afterward and in the autumn of 1864 faced **Philip Sheridan's Shenandoah Valley Campaign**. Badly outnumbered, Early's **Valley Army** was defeated at **Third Winchester** and **Fisher's Hill**, but he then launched a surprise attack against Sheridan at **Cedar Creek** in October that at first routed the Union **army**. He failed to follow up his victory and ultimately was defeated when Sheridan arrived on the field and organized a counterattack. With his command severely weakened, Early was unable to stop Sheridan from thoroughly destroying the Valley. He suffered his final defeat at **Waynesboro** in March 1865 and then rejoined Lee for the last part of the **Petersburg Campaign**. Public pressure forced Lee to relieve Early of command in late March, and he returned home.

Early was one of the most famous of Lee's lieutenants. An excellent brigade and division commander, his tenure as a corps commander was erratic. Early generally was a popular officer in the army, where he was known as "Old Jube" or "Old Jubilee," but he also had a "raspy disposition" and a biting wit. Lee fondly called him "my bad old man."

After the war, Early remained an unreconstructed **Rebel**. He briefly lived in Mexico and Canada and wrote a popular memoir of the war. Returning to Virginia in 1869 to reopen his law practice, Early became involved with the corrupt Louisiana Lottery Company and was president of the Southern Historical Society. More than anyone, he promoted the hero worship of Lee and the perpetuation of the **Lost Cause** sentiment.

EARLY'S WASHINGTON RAID (JULY 5–14, 1864). In June 1864, at the end of the **Overland Campaign**, Gen. **Robert E. Lee** sent his II Corps under Lt. Gen. **Jubal A. Early** to the **Shenandoah Valley**. Early's mission was to stop Maj. Gen. **David Hunter's Shenandoah Valley Campaign** and, if possible, to threaten **Washington, D.C.**, to draw away Union forces from Lee's front outside **Richmond, Virginia**. After halting Hunter at **Lynchburg** and driving him westward, Early moved down the Valley toward the Potomac River. His 14,000 men crossed into **Maryland** at Shepherdstown on July 5. Early then followed new orders to also send one cavalry **brigade** to **Point Lookout** to free the thousands of Confederate **prisoners** held there.

Continuing his advance, Early occupied Hagerstown and Frederick, Maryland, and forced their residents to pay $20,000 and $200,000 ransoms, respectively, to save their towns from destruction. Meanwhile, a small Union force under Maj. Gen. **Lew Wallace** took up a position near the Monocacy River outside Frederick to stop the Confederates. At the fierce **Battle of the Monocacy** on July 9, Early's men viciously attacked Wallace. Wallace was forced to retreat, but he had succeeded in delaying Early's march on Washington one crucial day.

The Confederates reached the outskirts of the city on July 11 and **skirmishing** began near **Fort Stevens** (located at Silver Spring, Maryland). By that time, elements of the **Army of the Potomac's** VI Corps had arrived from the **Petersburg** front and the XIX Corps from **Louisiana**. **Abraham Lincoln** came to the fort and witnessed the action on July 11 and 12 and reportedly had to be ordered to take cover to avoid being shot by Confederate **sharpshooters**. Early wisely decided against attacking and withdrew on the night of July 12. The Confederates burned the house of Postmaster General **Montgomery Blair** and then crossed back into **Virginia** on July 13–14. Meanwhile, the Confederate attack against Point Lookout was canceled because Union authorities learned of it and prepared a defense.

Early's raid succeeded in temporarily clearing the Federals from the Shenandoah Valley and drawing some Union troops from Lee's front, but it had no impact on the war's outcome. Early summed up the operation by declaring to one officer, "Major, we haven't taken Washington, but we've scared Abe Lincoln like hell!" (Freeman, *Lee's Lieutenants*, vol. 3, 567).

EASTPORT, USS. This steamship originally was bought by the Confederates in the autumn of 1861 to be converted into a warship. The 700-ton vessel was converted into an **ironclad** on the Tennessee River, at Cerro Gordo, Tennessee. After the fall of **Fort Henry** in February 1862, a Union flotilla steamed up the Tennessee River and captured the unfinished ship, its ironwork, and guns. Taken to Cairo, Illinois, the *Eastport* was completed in August 1862. Commanded by Lt. Samuel L. Phelps and carrying eight guns, it was one of the largest ships in the western waters.

The *Eastport* missed the **Vicksburg Campaign** because it ran aground and had to be repaired, but it was finished in time to participate in the 1864 **Red River Campaign**. Steaming down the river during the Union retreat, the *Eastport* struck a **torpedo** below Grand Ecore, Louisiana. It sank, but quickly was raised and lightened and continued downstream until it became snagged in a drift near modern-day Montgomery. Unable to save her, the sailors salvaged what was possible and then on April 26, 1864, used more than 3,000 pounds of powder to blow it up. In 1996, the wreckage was discovered and examined by a team of archaeologists.

EATON, AMOS BEEBE (1806–1877) USA. A native of **New York**, Eaton graduated from **West Point** in 1826 and rose to the rank of captain while performing routine garrison duty. He served in the **Seminole Wars** as a commissary officer and won a **brevet** during the **Mexican War** while serving as Zachary Taylor's chief commissary. After the war, Eaton became chief commissary for the **Department of the Pacific** before transferring to New York City to become a depot commissary.

Eaton was promoted to lieutenant colonel of regulars in September 1861 and was appointed the Union's assistant commissary general. A superb commissary, he efficiently handled the overwhelming job of supplying the rapidly expanding **army** and was appointed brigadier general and commissary general in June 1864. Brevetted major general for his war service in March 1865, Eaton retired from the army in 1874.

EBENEZER CHURCH, ALABAMA, BATTLE OF (APRIL 1, 1865). On March 22, 1865, Union Brig. Gen. **James H. Wilson** led 13,500 cavalrymen on **Wilson's Selma, Alabama, Raid**. On April 1, he approached Selma with two **divisions** advancing on two separate roads. Wilson was opposed by **Nathan Bedford Forrest** and about 2,000 Confederate cavalrymen. Expecting reinforcements (which never arrived), Forrest fell back to Ebenezer Church and blocked Wilson's advance near where the two roads converged. The Union cavalry divisions of **Eli Long** and **Emory Upton** repeatedly attacked Forrest that afternoon, and hand-to-hand fighting erupted at several points (during which, Forrest was wounded by a **saber**). The Confederate right was held by mostly inexperienced **Alabama** troops, and they eventually were broken and routed. Forrest then was forced to retreat toward Selma. In the hour-long battle, Forrest lost three cannons and perhaps 400 men (mostly captured), while Wilson lost 52 men.

ECHELON. Usually when making a **frontal attack**, the troops formed in a straight line and advanced. A different formation was to arrange a line in *echelon*. This is a French term meaning to position the attacking units side by side in a staggered fashion, resembling steps. The unit on one end of the line began the assault, and then one by one the others followed in their turn, much like a wave washing against the defenses rather than the entire line hitting it at once.

ECHOLS, JOHN (1823–1896) CSA. A native of **Virginia**, Echols graduated from Lexington College and studied at Harvard University before becoming a lawyer and state legislator. He was a delegate at Virginia's **secession** convention and then entered Confederate service in May 1861 as lieutenant colonel of the 27th Virginia.

As part of **Thomas J. "Stonewall" Jackson's** brigade, Echols fought well while commanding the **regiment** at **First Manassas**. He was promoted to colonel in October and was badly wounded at the **First Battle of Kernstown** in March 1862, but his actions there won him promotion to brigadier general in April. Echols was given a **brigade** in western Virginia, and in October 1862 he was placed in command of the **Department of Southwestern Virginia**, but poor health forced him to give up both commands. After serving on the board of inquiry that investigated the loss of **Vicksburg, Mississippi**, Echols was given another brigade in western Virginia. Leading a small combined force of infantry, **artillery**, and cavalry, he put up a good fight at **Droop Mountain** in November 1863 but finally was forced to retreat.

Joining Confederate forces in the **Shenandoah Valley**, Echols fought well at **New Market** but afterward relinquished command again because of poor health. In August 1864, he was placed in command of the District of Southwest Virginia and repulsed a Union raid on **Saltville**. Echols remained in command of the **district** until March 1865, when he replaced **Jubal Early** as commander of the **Department of Western Virginia**. At war's end, he was on his way to join **Robert E. Lee** with several thousand men when he heard of the **surrender** at **Appomattox**. Echols then joined **Joseph E. Johnston** in **North Carolina** and escorted the fleeing Confederate government to **Georgia**, where he finally surrendered.

After the war, Echols was involved in banking and railroading and served on the Board of Visitors for both Washington and Lee University and the **Virginia Military Institute**. A large man (he stood six feet, four inches tall and weighed 260 lbs.), he was a capable officer whose poor health limited his effectiveness.

ECTOR, MATTHEW DUNCAN (1822–1879) CSA. A native of **Georgia**, Ector attended **Kentucky's** Centre College and opened a law practice in Georgia. There he served one term in the state legislature before volunteering for service in the **Mexican War**. Ector moved to **Texas** after the war and opened a law practice there. He became a member of the Texas legislature in 1855 but resigned his seat in April 1861.

Ector entered Confederate service in April 1861 as a private but then was commissioned a lieutenant and adjutant for a cavalry **regiment** known as the South Kansas-Texas Regiment. He served as adjutant to Brig. Gen. **Elkanah Brackin Greer** at **Wilson's Creek**, led his own **company** at the **Battle of Chustenahlah**, and again served on Greer's staff at **Pea Ridge**. By April 1862, Ector was adjutant to Brig. Gen. **Joseph L. Hogg** and saw duty at the **siege of Corinth, Mississippi**. In May, he was elected colonel of the 14th Texas Dismounted Cavalry and led it with distinction at **Richmond, Kentucky**.

In October 1862, Ector was promoted to brigadier general and at **Stones River** led a **brigade** in the **Army of Tennessee** that helped rout the Union right wing. His brigade joined Gen. **Joseph E. Johnston** at Jackson, Mississippi, during the **Vicksburg Campaign** but returned to the Army of Tennessee in time to fight at **Chickamauga**. During the **Atlanta Campaign**, Ector was wounded in the left leg by a shell fragment outside Atlanta, Georgia, and lost his leg to amputation. Upon returning to duty, he may have rejoined his brigade at Mobile, Alabama, but his senior colonel led the unit in the **Battle of Spanish Fort**. Ector finally surrendered with **Richard Taylor** in May 1865.

Not a well-known general, Ector nonetheless was praised highly by his superiors in virtually every engagement in which he was a participant. He returned to his Texas law practice after the war and became a justice of the Texas Court of Appeals.

EDMONDS, SARAH EMMA (1842–1898) USA. There were an unknown number of women who disguised themselves as men and served in the Civil War, and Edmonds was one of the most famous. A native of Canada, she ran away from home to **Rhode Island** as a young woman because her father had arranged her marriage to a man she did not love. Edmonds then disguised herself as a man, took the alias "Franklin Thompson," and secured a job selling Bibles.

After being sent to **Michigan** by her employer, Edmonds tried to join the Union **army** in early 1861. She failed her first physical because she was too short but then passed and joined the 2nd Michigan in May. Trained as a nurse, Edmonds participated in the **First Battle of Manassas** and in the **Peninsula Campaign**. After a close friend was killed, she volunteered to become a spy and later claimed to have been very successful. Edmonds also claimed to have been at **Antietam**, where she supposedly buried another female imposter. When the **regiment** was transferred to **Kentucky** in the spring of 1863, she contracted malaria. Fearful that her secret would be discovered in the hospital, Edmonds deserted the army in April and joined the **U.S. Christian Commission**—as a woman.

In 1865, under the name Sarah E. Edmundson, Edmonds wrote a highly embellished account of her life as a soldier entitled *Nurse and Spy in the Union Army* (republished later under a different title). She married in 1867 and eventually revealed her true identity when she attended an 1884 regimental reunion. Encouraged to apply for a veteran's pension, Edmonds successfully lobbied the **U.S. Congress** to get her **desertion** removed from her record and finally was awarded the pension. She also was the only woman ever to be given membership in the Union veterans' organization **Grand Army of the Republic**.

EDWARDS, JOHN (1815–1894) USA. A native of **Kentucky** who received only a local education, Edwards lived in a number of states before the Civil War. His antebellum career included service as an **Indiana** legislator, a **California** justice of the peace, a member of the **Iowa** constitutional convention, the founder of the newspaper *Patriot*, and a member of the Iowa legislature (serving as speaker from 1858 to 1860).

Edwards entered Union service in May 1861 when he was appointed lieutenant colonel and aide-de-camp to Iowa's Gov. **Samuel J. Kirkwood**. In August 1862, he was appointed colonel of the 18th Iowa. Edwards spent most of his military career on garrison duty in **Arkansas**, but he did participate in the 1864 **Camden Expedition** and fought at **Jenkins' Ferry**. He was promoted to brigadier general of volunteers in September 1864 and commanded first a **brigade**, then a **division**, at **Fort Smith, Arkansas**, for the rest of the war.

After the war, Edwards served one term as an Arkansas congressman and then moved to **Washington, D.C.**

EGAN, THOMAS WILBERFORCE (1834–1887) USA. A native of **New York**, Egan's early life is obscure. He entered Union service in April 1861 as a private in the 40th New York (also known as the "Mozart Regiment") but was commissioned its lieutenant colonel in July. After fighting at **Yorktown** with the **Army of the Potomac**, Egan served courageously at **Seven Pines** and even preferred charges against his colonel for misconduct. As a result, the colonel was dismissed from the service, and Egan was commissioned colonel in June 1862.

Egan served with distinction, often as a **brigade** commander, in nearly every battle fought by the Army of the Potomac and saw his **regiment** devastated by heavy losses. Eventually other veteran New York regiments were consolidated into the 40th New York as they became too small for separate service. Egan temporarily commanded a brigade at **Chancellorsville** and during part of the **Overland Campaign**. He was badly wounded near the spine during the **Petersburg Campaign** and suffered some paralysis of the legs but returned to duty and was promoted to brigadier general of volunteers in September 1864. Egan was **brevetted** major general of volunteers for his actions at **Burgess' Mill** and while in temporary command of the **division** in November was badly wounded in the right arm. Although disabled by the wound, he returned to duty and was given a permanent division command.

Egan left the **army** in 1866 and became a deputy collector in the New York Customs House. Although he had been one of the Union's better field commanders, he died in obscurity in a New York charity hospital.

ELECTION OF 1860. By 1860, the United States was on the verge of splitting apart over **slavery** and other issues, and everyone knew the presidential election might be the last chance to save it. Most hopes lay with the **Democratic Party**, the only truly national party by 1860. However, the Democrats were divided between the proslavery Southerners and the **Free-Soil** Northerners. The **Republican Party**, on the other hand, was purely a Northern party that opposed the spread of slavery.

In 1860, the Democrats finally split along sectional lines when two nominating conventions failed to agree on a platform. Southern delegates at **Charleston, South Carolina**, and at Baltimore, Maryland, walked out in protest after the Northern delegates refused to support congressional protection of slavery in the territories. As a result, the Northerners formed the Northern Democratic Party and nominated **Stephen A. Douglas**, who pledged not to interfere with slavery in the South, while promising to support his Freeport Doctrine to prevent its spread into the territories. The Southerners formed the Southern Democratic Party and nominated **John C. Breckinridge**, who declared that the **Dred Scott decision** gave slave owners the constitutional right to take their slaves into any territory. Thus, the only national party—and the nation's last hope for avoiding disaster—ceased to exist.

The Republicans held their convention next and nominated **Abraham Lincoln**. Lincoln also promised not to interfere with slavery in the South, but he, too, was determined to prevent its spread. He also supported a higher tariff to provide better protection for Northern industrial workers.

The **border states** realized that any conflict between the North and South would consume them, so they formed the new **Constitutional Union Party** to give voters a compromise candidate that was neither pro-North nor pro-South. **John Bell** of **Tennessee** was nominated, and he adopted a platform that was vague and noncontroversial so as not to offend any voters. Bell asked that everyone support the Union, obey the law, and uphold the Constitution. This was a platform everyone could support, but it depended on one's interpretation of the Union, the law, and the Constitution.

Realizing the South's political power was waning as the North's advantage in population and states grew, Southerners feared that the North's growing majority at the polls and in the **U.S. Congress** would lead to its complete domination. The North could at will force upon the South protective tariffs, stop the expansion of slavery into the territories, or even abolish slavery itself. Despite Lincoln's promises to the contrary, Southerners were convinced that he was an **abolitionist** and if elected would try to destroy slavery. In the face of this threat, the South believed **secession** was the only remaining option that would protect them against tyranny by the majority and openly warned the nation that Lincoln's election would lead to disunion.

In the election on November 6, 1860, Lincoln carried approximately 40 percent of the popular vote, but he won 180 electoral votes. Breckinridge won 72 electoral votes, while Bell received 39, and Douglas, 12. With Lincoln's victory, the South carried out its threat when **South Carolina** seceded on December 20, 1860.

ELK CREEK, INDIAN TERRITORY, BATTLE OF (JULY 17, 1863). *See* HONEY SPRINGS, INDIAN TERRITORY, BATTLE OF.

ELKHORN TAVERN, ARKANSAS, BATTLE OF (MARCH 7–8, 1862). *See* PEA RIDGE, ARKANSAS, BATTLE OF.

ELLERSON'S MILL, VIRGINIA, BATTLE OF (JUNE 26, 1862). *See* MECHANICSVILLE, VIRGINIA, BATTLE OF.

ELLET, ALFRED WASHINGTON (1820–1895) USA. The brother of **Charles Ellet**, Ellet was a **Pennsylvania** native who became a civil engineer and worked in various places before the Civil War. He entered Union service in August 1861 as a captain in the 59th Illinois and fought with it at **Pea Ridge**. Ellet was promoted to lieutenant colonel in April 1862 and was assigned to his brother Charles as an aide-de-camp when he was ordered to obtain vessels for use as **ironclad rams**. When Charles was mortally wounded at the **Battle of Memphis** in June 1862, Alfred took command of the river fleet.

After service around **Vicksburg, Mississippi**, Ellet was promoted to brigadier general of volunteers in November 1862 and was given command of the **Mississippi Marine Brigade**, an infantry unit that operated from ships to raid enemy positions and fight guerrillas. He participated in raids along the Mississippi River and ordered the town of Austin, Mississippi, burned before the **brigade** was dissolved in August 1864. Throughout his military career, Ellet often was embroiled in conflict. This largely was a result of the awkward situation created by his fleet and brigade officially being part of the **army** but having to take orders from navy commanders. Having lost both his fleet and brigade, Ellet resigned his commission in December 1864 and returned to his engineering profession.

After the war, Ellet moved to **Kansas** and became a prominent banker and businessman.

ELLET, CHARLES (1810–1862) USA. The brother of **Alfred Washington Ellet**, Ellet was a native of **Pennsylvania** and a prominent civil engineer. He specialized in building suspension bridges and in 1849 built the world's longest such bridge across the Wheeling and Ohio Rivers.

Ellet entered Union service in April 1862 after convincing the War Department that swift, unarmed **ironclad rams** could win control of the western rivers. He first saw the value of such rams while observing the siege of Sebastopol during the Crimean War. Ellet held a peculiar position within the **army**, being subject only to the orders of Secretary of War **Edwin Stanton**, and soon had nine vessels formed into a fleet. His first opportunity to demonstrate their effectiveness came in June 1862 at the **Battle of Memphis**. Ellet's ship *Queen of the West* rammed and sank one Confederate vessel, but he was badly wounded above the knee by a pistol shot and died on June 21. Two of his rams had played an important role in the Union victory at Memphis, and Ellet was the only casualty among his men.

ELLIOTT, STEPHEN, JR. (1830–1866) CSA. A native of **South Carolina**, Elliott was a prosperous planter who was elected to the state legislature in 1859 and served as captain of a militia **artillery** company that participated in the capture of **Fort Sumter**.

Elliott's **company** entered Confederate service as infantry in June 1861 when it became part of the 11th South Carolina. He was slightly wounded in November while defending **Port Royal**, and he and his men left the **regiment** in March 1862 to become an artillery battery. After commanding the battery in some **skirmishing**, Elliott was appointed chief of artillery for the 3rd District in November 1862. There he won the admiration of **Robert E. Lee** and other superiors and was promoted to major in April 1863. Elliott proved to be a resourceful officer and acted as much as a guerrilla leader as an artillery commander. His men raided outposts, captured ships along the **Georgia** coast, and sank one Union ship with a **torpedo**. In September 1863, **P. G. T. Beauregard** placed Elliott in command of Fort Sumter. There, he earned more praise by successfully defending the fort for months against enemy ships and landing parties, even though he was badly wounded in December.

Elliott was rapidly promoted to lieutenant colonel and colonel in April 1864 and was put in command of the Holcombe Legion. He accompanied the **legion** to **Virginia** to participate in the **Petersburg Campaign** and in May was made brigadier general and was put in command of a South Carolina **brigade**. The famous Union mine at the **Crater** in July 1864 devastated part of Elliott's brigade, and he was badly wounded in the left lung while attempting to counterattack. The wound paralyzed his left arm, but Elliott returned to duty in December as commander of a South Carolina **district**. After the fall of **Charleston**, Elliott commanded a mixed brigade at **Averasboro** and **Bentonville** and was wounded again at the latter. He died from his many wounds shortly after the war ended.

ELLIOTT, WASHINGTON LAFAYETTE (1825–1888) USA. The son of a prominent **U.S. Navy** officer, Elliott was a native of **Pennsylvania**.

He entered **West Point** in 1841 but left because of poor grades during his third year and studied medicine. Because of his military training, Elliott was commissioned a 2nd lieutenant in the Mounted Rifles in 1846 and fought in the **Mexican War**. He remained in the **U.S. Army** after the war and was a captain when the Civil War began.

After fighting at **Wilson's Creek**, Elliott was appointed colonel of the 2nd Iowa Cavalry in September 1861 and served in **John Pope's** campaign against **New Madrid and Island No. 10**. While commanding a **brigade** in **the siege of Corinth, Mississippi**, Elliott led one of the first Union cavalry raids of the war when he attacked the Mobile & Ohio Railroad.

Elliott was promoted to brigadier general of volunteers in June 1862 and was transferred to **Virginia**, where he was wounded at **Second Manassas** while serving as chief of cavalry for Pope's **Army of Virginia**. For the remainder of the war, he performed such various duties as commanding the **Department of the Northwest**, leading an **Army of the Potomac** infantry **division** at **Chancellorsville** and **Gettysburg**, and commanding a cavalry division in eastern **Tennessee**. Elliott also served as chief of cavalry for the **Army of the Cumberland** during the **Atlanta Campaign** and led an infantry division at the **Battle of Nashville**. He briefly commanded the District of **Kansas** before leaving the volunteers in March 1866.

Having been promoted to major in the regular **army** and **brevetted** major general in both the regulars and volunteers, Elliott remained in the army until retiring as a colonel in 1868.

ELLIS, JOHN WILLIS (1820–1861) CSA. A native of **North Carolina** and a graduate of the University of North Carolina, Ellis became a lawyer and prominent **Democratic** politician. He served in the legislature from 1844 to 1848, was elected to the state superior court in 1848, and became governor in 1858. Ellis's programs of internal improvement won him reelection in 1860.

During the **secession** crisis, Ellis supported the creation of the Confederacy, the expansion of the state militia, and a state referendum on secession. Voters rejected calling a secession convention, however, and at first Ellis opposed seizing federal property and forceful disunion. After the fall of **Fort Sumter** and **Abraham Lincoln's** call for volunteers to put down the Rebellion, he became more radical. Ellis refused Lincoln's request for volunteers, called on citizens to resist invasion, and successfully held a convention that voted for secession in May 1861. Shortly afterward, Ellis died on July 7, supposedly from exhaustion.

ELLSWORTH, EPHRAIM ELMER (1837–1861) USA. A native of **New York**, Ellsworth moved to **Illinois** as a young man and worked as a law clerk. Having always been interested in the military (and failing to gain entrance into **West Point**), he joined a struggling militia **company** and soon revived it with his enthusiasm and leadership. Named the National Guard Cadets (later the U.S. **Zouave** Cadets), the company adopted the colorful French Algerian Zouave **uniform** and became famous for its close-quarter drill. In 1860, the Zouaves toured the northeast and drilled on the White House lawn. The popular Ellsworth was promoted to major and was placed on the Illinois National Guard commander's staff, while the Zouaves became the governor's guard. In August 1860, Ellsworth studied law under **Abraham Lincoln** and became close friends with the future president. He helped out in Lincoln's election campaign and then accompanied him to **Washington, D.C.**, for the inauguration.

When war erupted, Ellsworth raised a New York **regiment**, largely from the city's firemen, and trained and outfitted it as Zouaves. The regiment was mustered into Union service in May 1861 as the 11th New York Fire Zouaves (or **Ellsworth's Zouaves**), with Ellsworth as colonel. Sent to Washington, Ellsworth's regiment crossed the Potomac River on May 24 to occupy Alexandria, Virginia. During the movement, Ellsworth entered the Marshall Hotel to take down a Confederate **flag** that was flying from its roof. While descending the stairway, he was confronted by hotel owner, James T. Jackson, who shot and killed Ellsworth with one shotgun blast. Private **Francis E. Brownell** then killed Jackson by shooting and bayoneting him. Ellsworth's death led to national mourning, and his body lay in state in the White House. Besides being a close friend of the president, he also was the first Union casualty of the war.

ELLSWORTH'S ZOUAVES. Zouave units were popular in both the North and South at the time of the Civil War. Patterned after the French Algerian Zouaves, these units wore colorful **uniforms** and drilled in the French style. One officer who was active in such units was **Ephraim Elmer Ellsworth**, who had organized a Zouave unit in the Illinois National Guard before the war and toured the nation giving drill performances.

When civil war erupted in 1861, Ellsworth organized a **regiment** from among New York City's firemen and became its colonel. Mustered into state service in April and into Union service for two years in May, it was designated the 11th New York. The regiment adopted the Zouave uniform and drill and became a colorful part of the **Army of the Potomac**. It was popularly known as the 1st New York Fire Zouaves or simply as Ellsworth's Zouaves.

Soon after arriving in **Washington, D.C.**, Ellsworth was killed in May after tearing down a Confederate **flag** from an Alexandria, Virginia, hotel. His men went on to fight well at **First Manassas** but were not engaged in any other battles. Although rowdy in camp, they were popular and once helped extinguish a fire at the Capitol building. Even though the Zouaves enlisted for two years, the regiment was mustered out of service in June 1862.

ELMIRA PRISON, NEW YORK. This notorious Union **prison** encompassed 40 acres and was built in May 1864 by erecting a palisade around some old **army** barracks. The barracks quickly proved inadequate to house the large number of **prisoners**, and many men were force to live in tents. The ground was low and poorly drained, and a pond located on the compound caught the drainage from the prisoners' latrines. In addition to the poor drainage, the prisoners also suffered from the intense winter cold and a poor diet.

Despite the commandant's efforts to improve conditions, by November 1864 scurvy and other diseases were rampant. From August to November, the commandant recorded 775 deaths out of 2,011 patients admitted to the prison hospital. He also noted that approximately 10 percent of the prisoners were in the hospital on an average day. Conditions worsened as Confederate prisoners from other overcrowded camps were shipped to Elmira. By the end of the summer almost 10,000 were housed there, and by war's end there were approximately 12,000 prisoners. During its one-year existence, only 17 prisoners escaped Elmira, while 2,917 died.

ELTHAM'S LANDING, VIRGINIA, BATTLE OF (MAY 7, 1862). After the **Battle of Williamsburg** during the 1862 **Peninsula Campaign**, Confederate Gen. **Joseph E. Johnston** continued his retreat toward **Richmond, Virginia**, on May 6. During the withdrawal, Maj. Gen. **George B. McClellan** sent Brig. Gen. **William B. Franklin's division** by transport to the York River's Eltham's Landing to flank the Confederates. This move was made too late to cut off Johnston's retreat, but it did force him to concentrate his **army** around Barhamsville to protect his wagon train. When the Federals did not advance beyond their river entrenchments, Johnston sent **John Bell Hood's Texas brigade** forward on the morning of May 7 to keep the enemy at bay. Hood forced the Union **skirmishers** back more than a mile but then disengaged when he found that the main enemy force was protected by a river bluff and that the transports were beyond **artillery** range. With his flank secure, Johnston then continued the withdrawal of his wagon train. In the clash at Eltham's Landing, Hood lost 48 men, while Union casualties totaled 186.

ELZEY, ARNOLD (1816–1871) CSA. A native of **Maryland**, Elzey was born Arnold Elzey Jones, but, for reasons unknown, he dropped his last name while attending **West Point** and took the name of his paternal grandmother. He graduated from the academy in 1837 and served in the **artillery** in the **Seminole** and **Mexican Wars**, winning a **brevet** in the latter.

When the Civil War began, Elzey was serving as an artillery captain in command of the **Augusta (Georgia) Arsenal**. After surrendering the post to the Confederates, he resigned his commission in April 1861 and entered Confederate service as colonel of the 1st Maryland. Sent to the **Shenandoah Valley**, Elzey took command of a **brigade** and played a major role in the victory at **First Manassas**. His actions there also won him a promotion to brigadier general in August.

Elzey was slightly wounded in the hand at **Port Republic** during **Stonewall Jackson's Shenandoah Valley Campaign** and was severely wounded in the face and head at **Gaines' Mill** during the **Seven Days Campaign**. When he returned to duty in December 1862, he was promoted to major general and joined **James Longstreet's** command in southeastern **Virginia**. **Robert E. Lee** wanted Elzey appointed chief of artillery for the **Army of Northern Virginia**, but Elzey's poor health dissuaded him. Instead, he was put in command of the **Department of Richmond** in April 1863. Elzey proved to be an unpopular **department** commander because he was forced to raise a home guard from government employees and other civilians. He disliked his position, as well, and finally received a new field command in June 1864 when **John C. Breckinridge** succeeded in getting him placed in command of one of his **divisions** around Lynchburg, Virginia. In September, Elzey was appointed chief of artillery for the **Army of Tennessee**, but his poor health prevented him from accompanying the **army** in the 1864 **Franklin and Nashville Campaign**. He returned to **Richmond** in February 1865 and accompanied **Jefferson Davis** when the government fled south in April. Elzey finally was captured at Washington, Georgia, in May.

Elzey returned to Maryland after the war and became a farmer, but he died soon afterward.

EMANCIPATION PROCLAMATION. Although the Civil War is noted for having freed the slaves, that was not its original purpose. For the first year, Union forces fought solely to preserve the Union, even though some soldiers did oppose **slavery**. Although personally opposed to slavery, even **Abraham Lincoln** had always maintained that it was guaranteed by the Constitution, and that the government had no authority to arbitrarily abolish it. But emancipation inevitably became part of the war effort. Union generals **David Hunter** and **John C. Frémont** tried to force the issue early in the war by ordering slaves to be freed in their **departments**, but both were repudiated by Lincoln. The **U.S. Congress** also got involved and in 1862 abolished slavery (with compensation) in **Washington, D.C.**, by passing the **District Emancipation Act**. It later abolished slavery in the territories without compensation.

As the war dragged on and became more and more bloody, Lincoln began to view emancipation as a way to weaken the Confederacy. It would deny the enemy much of the labor supply that was being used to construct fortifications and to raise food and would create internal chaos by encouraging slaves to run away to Union lines. The Confederate infrastructure would be weakened further by forcing more troops to remain behind the lines to guard against runaways. Emancipation also would prevent the antislavery European nations from recognizing Confederate independence. In answer to critics who argued that he had no authority to free the slaves, Lincoln claimed that emancipation—as a war measure—was within his power as commander-in-chief.

Lincoln drafted the Emancipation Proclamation in July 1862, but the cabinet convinced him to delay issuing it until the Union had won a major victory so that the government would be releasing it from a position of strength rather than as an act of desperation. Viewing the **Battle of Antietam** as that needed victory, Lincoln issued the Preliminary Emancipation Proclamation on September 22, 1862. It stated that if the Confederates did not end the rebellion by January 1, 1863, all slaves then being held in Confederate territory would be free. The proclamation exempted slaves in the **border states** in order to ensure those states' continued loyalty.

Although the document actually freed slaves in areas over which Lincoln had no control, it did have the desired effect. Slaves were freed as the Union **armies** advanced or as slaves could runaway into Union lines. Thousands of Union soldiers at first protested this change in war goals, some even to the point of mutiny. But in the end, most came to recognize the military necessity of such an action. When Lincoln signed the Emancipation Proclamation on January 1, 1863, the war was changed from a war simply to preserve the Union to a war to preserve the Union without slavery.

"EMBALMED BEEF." Canned meat was one of the **ration** items Union soldiers received in the Civil War, making the war the first time American soldiers received canned supplies. *Embalmed beef* was their slang term for the canned meat.

EMORY, WILLIAM HEMSLEY (1811–1887) USA. A native of **Maryland**, Emory graduated from **West Point** in 1831 and served five years in the **artillery**. He resigned his commission in 1836 but two years later was appointed a 1st lieutenant in the Topographical Engineers. Emory was **brevetted** twice for gallantry in the **Mexican War** while serving as a lieutenant colonel of volunteers and afterward was active in mapping the west. He had risen to the rank of lieutenant colonel in the 3rd U.S. Cavalry by 1861 and was stationed in **Indian Territory** when the Civil War began.

It was claimed that Emory was the only U.S. officer who successfully brought out all of his men from secessionist territory at the beginning of the war. He was promoted to brigadier general of volunteers in March 1862 and led a **brigade** in the **Army of the Potomac** during the **Peninsula Campaign**. Emory was brevetted for his actions at **Hanover Court House** in May 1862 and then was transferred to a **division** command in **Louisiana**, where he participated in the 1863 **Bayou Teche Campaign**. Placed in command of the XIX Corps, he also served in the 1864 **Red River Campaign** and played a key role at **Mansfield** by fighting a delaying action that allowed **Nathaniel P. Banks** to withdraw the **army** safely. Emory's **corps** was transferred to **Virginia** later that year and participated in **Philip Sheridan's Shenandoah Valley Campaign**.

Emory received brevets through the rank of major general in both the volunteers and regulars during the war, but he was not promoted to major general of volunteers until September 1865. He remained in the army after the war and commanded several military **departments** before he retired as a brigadier general in 1876.

***ENCHANTRESS* AFFAIR.** In July 1861, the Confederate **privateer Jefferson Davis** captured the Union merchant ship *Enchantress*. A crew was placed on board the *Enchantress* to take charge of the prize and captured crew, but about two weeks later it was recaptured by the **U.S. Navy**. Taken to Philadelphia, **Pennsylvania**, the Confederate crewmen from the *Enchantress* were tried, convicted of piracy, and sentenced to death.

International law provided for privateers to be treated differently from pirates, but since the Union did not recognize Confederate independence, it also did not recognize Confederate privateers. To protect the privateers, Confederate Secretary of War **Judah P. Benjamin** ordered **Richmond, Virginia's**, Provost Marshal **John H. Winder** to choose Union **prisoners** for execution should the Lincoln administration carry

Abraham Lincoln. *Source:* Library of Congress

Jefferson Davis. *Source:* National Archives

Robert E. Lee. *Source:* Library of Congress

Ulysses S. Grant. *Source:* National Archives

Thomas J. "Stonewall" Jackson. *Source:* Library of Congress

William T. Sherman. *Source:* National Archives

Joseph E. Johnston. *Source:* National Archives

George B. McClellan. *Source:* National Archives

out its execution order. Winder used a lottery to select 15 officers to serve as hostages for the crew of the *Enchantress* and the *Savannah*, another captured Confederate privateer. Colonel **Michael Corcoran** was designated to share the fate of the *Enchantress's* pilot, Walter W. Smith. Federal authorities backed down from the confrontation, however, and began treating captured Confederate privateers as prisoners of war. Although unintentionally and unofficially, this position actually gave some recognition to Confederate independence.

ENFIELD RIFLE. One of the main infantry weapons used in the Civil War was the British-made Enfield **rifle**. It was highly prized by both sides but came to be identified as one of the standard Confederate arms. The 1853 model, .577-caliber Enfield rifle was designed by the Royal Small Arms Factory. However, private British companies, rather than the royal factory, produced the approximately 800,000 rifles that saw use in the Civil War. Weighing nine pounds, the Enfield was a single-shot, muzzle-loading **rifle musket** that was accurate up to 800 yards.

ENFILADE. *Enfilade* (EN-fuh-layd) is a term used to describe firing down the length of a battle line or position as opposed to firing into its front. If an **army** could position troops or **artillery** on the enemy's flank, a very destructive enfilade fire could be sent down its entire length, causing massive casualties.

ENGINEERS. During the Civil War, there were two types of **army** engineers. Topographical engineers conducted **reconnaissance** and generally made campaign maps and drawings of fortifications and installations. The regular engineers were responsible for laying out defensive positions and supervising such construction projects as field fortifications, forts, and harbor improvements. When the Civil War began, the **U.S. Army** had a Corps of Engineers for construction and a Corps of Topographical Engineers for survey work. In 1863, the topographical engineers were absorbed into the Corps of Engineers under Brig. Gen. **Joseph G. Totten**. The **Confederate army** created a Corps of Engineers that at various times was commanded by **Josiah Gorgas**, **Danville Leadbetter**, and **Jeremy F. Gilmer**. Among the Civil War officers who were trained as engineers were **Robert E. Lee**, **George G. Meade**, **P. G. T. Beauregard**, **George B. McClellan**, and **Joseph E. Johnston**.

ENRICA, **CSS.** *See ALABAMA*, CSS.

ENVELOPMENT. This is a military term referring to an advance against the enemy's flank to force him out of a fixed position. A double envelopment would be an advance against both flanks. If the envelopment went completely around the flank and actually moved into the enemy's rear, it was called a strategic envelopment or, more often, a **turning movement**.

EPROUVETTE. An eprouvette (EH-proo-VET) was a small **mortar** that was used to test the quality and strength of a quantity of gunpowder.

ERICSSON, JOHN (1803–1889) USA. A native of Sweden, Ericsson was a naval engineer and inventor who first served in his native country's military. Moving to Great Britain, he was granted 30 patents there, including a hot-air engine, a high-speed locomotive, and the screw-propelled ship. Ericsson also went bankrupt and briefly served in debtor's prison before immigrating to the United States in 1839. He next entered a partnership with American inventor Robert F. Stockton, and together they invented the *Princeton*, the **U.S. Navy's** first steam-powered ship, and a new navy cannon. The cannon accidentally exploded during an 1844 demonstration, killing, among others, the secretaries of state and navy. His reputation tarnished, Ericsson then worked as a **New York** engineer until the Civil War.

To counter the Confederate **ironclad** *Virginia*, Union naval officials in 1861 called for designs of a Union ironclad. Ericsson submitted his plans for a revolutionary type of ship that had a revolving iron turret. At first it was rejected, but in September 1861 Ericsson received a contract to build his "iron-clad battery." Finished in January 1862, it was christened the *Monitor* and became famous for its duel with the *Virginia* at **Hampton Roads**. Numerous **monitors** were built for the U.S. Navy, and Ericsson later modified the design to include two revolving gun turrets.

ERLANGER LOAN. To **finance** the war, the Confederate government turned to Europe as a source of loans. In October 1862, Confederate minister to France, **John Slidell**, secured such a loan from the French banking house of Emile Erlanger (ER-lahn-JAY) and Company. Approved by the **Confederate Congress** in January 1863, the loan called for the sale of $14.55 million in Confederate bonds. The 20-year bonds earned 7 percent interest and would be redeemed in cotton, below the market price. The loan was a speculative venture because its payment depended on a Confederate victory. Investors were willing to participate, however, because when it was made in 1862, Confederate armies were enjoying great battlefield success.

Erlanger and Company paid 77 percent face value for the loans and sold them to investors at 90 percent of value. The bonds oversold on the first day of sales in March of 1863, but demand quickly declined as the Confederates began losing the war. Despite the downturn in sales, the Confederate government realized perhaps $8.5 million from the Erlanger Loan.

ETHERIDGE, ANNA OR ANNIE (1844–?) USA. Born in **Michigan**, Etheridge grew up in **Wisconsin** and became the best known of the Union **vivandières**. She enlisted as a nurse in the 2nd Michigan in early 1861 and later also served with the 3rd Michigan and 5th Michigan.

Etheridge became known as "Michigan Annie" or "Gentle Annie (or Anna)" and served in the **Army of the Potomac** from **First Manassas** to **Appomattox**. She often was exposed to enemy fire while treating the wounded and was said to have rallied retreating troops at **Spotsylvania**. Etheridge frequently had bullets pass through her clothing and once was wounded slightly on the hand. Major General **Philip Kearny** reportedly was going to appoint her a sergeant major, but he was killed before doing so. After Kearny's death, Etheridge was awarded the **Kearny Cross** for bravery. During the **Petersburg Campaign**, **U. S. Grant** finally had her sent to a hospital at **City Point**, **Virginia**, to remove her from danger.

After the war, Etheridge was given a governmental clerk position in Detroit, Michigan.

EUSTIS, HENRY LAWRENCE (1819–1885) USA. The son of a prominent **U.S. Army** officer, Eustis was born in **Massachusetts**. After graduating from Harvard University, he entered **West Point** and graduated first in his 1842 class. As an **engineer**, Eustis constructed **Fort Warren** in Boston, Massachusetts, and taught at the academy before resigning his commission in 1849. He then taught engineering at Harvard until he entered Union service in August 1862 as colonel of the 10th Massachusetts.

Eustis was given command of a **brigade** in the **Army of the Potomac's** VI Corps in late 1862 and led it through the **Fredericksburg**, **Chancellorsville**, and **Gettysburg Campaigns**. After being promoted to brigadier general of volunteers in September 1863, he fought in the **Mine Run** and **Overland Campaigns**. The **Battle of Cold Harbor** was Eustis's last fight. He had become an opium user and was given the choice of resigning his commission or facing charges of neglect of duty and incompetence. He chose to resign in June 1864 and returned to Harvard, where he taught until his death.

EVANS, CLEMENT ANSELM (1833–1911) CSA. A native of **Georgia**, Evans attended a local law school in Augusta before opening a practice in

1852. He became a county judge in 1855 and was elected to the state senate in 1859.

During the **secession** crisis, Evans organized a volunteer **company** that became part of the 2nd Georgia. Instead of remaining with it, however, he was appointed major of the 31st Georgia in April 1862 and began serving as its commanding officer a short time later. Joining the **Army of Northern Virginia**, Evans led the **regiment** during the **Seven Days Campaign** and was slightly wounded at **Gaines' Mill**. He was in command of the Fredericksburg, Virginia, garrison for a while before being promoted to colonel in March 1863. Evans saw fierce combat over the next year while in **John B. Gordon's** brigade. During the **Chancellorsville Campaign**, his regiment helped recapture Marye's Heights during the fighting around **Fredericksburg**, and on the first day of **Gettysburg**, he was painfully wounded in the side by a shell fragment while helping to rout the Union XI Corps. Evans served in the **Bristoe Station** and **Mine Run Campaigns**, and at the **Wilderness** participated in Gordon's flank attack on May 6, 1864. Evans then took command of the **brigade** when Gordon assumed **division** command.

After earning recognition for helping contain the Union breakthrough at **Spotsylvania's** "Bloody Angle," Evans was promoted to brigadier general in May 1864. The brigade then participated in **Jubal A. Early's Washington Raid**. At the **Battle of the Monocacy**, Evans was wounded for the fifth time when a bullet hit him in the left side and drove into his body a number of sewing pins he carried in his pocket. Evans returned to duty in time to fight at **Cedar Creek**, but it took years for some of the pins to work their way out his body. Afterward, he took command of the division and led it for the rest of the war, although he never was promoted to major general. Evans's division was heavily engaged in the fight at **Fort Stedman** in March 1865 and claimed to have fired the last shots at **Appomattox**.

After the war, Evans returned to Georgia and became a Methodist minister. He also was very active in veterans organizations and in compiling the war's history.

EVANS, NATHAN GEORGE (1824–1868) CSA. Known as "Shanks" because of his skinny legs, Evans was a native of **South Carolina** who graduated from **West Point** in 1848. He served with the cavalry on the frontier, frequently fighting **Indians**, and rose to the rank of captain.

Evans resigned his commission in February 1861 and was made a major and adjutant general of South Carolina troops. After participating in the capture of **Fort Sumter**, he entered Confederate service as colonel of the 4th South Carolina and was sent to **Virginia**. At **First Manassas**,

Evans commanded his **regiment** and **Chatham Roberdeau Wheat's Louisiana Tiger** battalion. When he noticed that enemy troops were crossing Bull Run to turn the Confederate left flank, Evans moved upstream to confront them and delayed the enemy attack for several crucial hours. He also commanded the Confederate forces in the victory at **Ball's Bluff**, where he won the **Thanks of Congress** and a promotion to brigadier general in October 1861.

Evans and his so-called Tramp Brigade (so named because of its frequent travels) fought at **Second Manassas** and **Antietam** (where he temporarily commanded the **division**), suffering heavy casualties in both engagements. He then was transferred west and was part of **Joseph E. Johnston's** force near Jackson, Mississippi, during the **Vicksburg Campaign**. Evans's weakness for liquor ruined him in late 1863. He was so fond of drink that it was said an aide always kept a gallon jug nearby. Evans was court-martialed for drunkenness and disobedience and, although acquitted, lost his **brigade** and never again commanded troops in the field. He then was sent to **Richmond, Virginia**, but a fall from his horse prevented him from returning to active duty for months. Evans fled with the government when Richmond fell in April 1865 and surrendered after evading the enemy for a time.

After the war, Evans became a high school principal in **Alabama**.

EVARTS, WILLIAM MAXWELL (1818–1901) USA. A native of **Massachusetts** and a graduate of Yale University and the Harvard Law School, Evarts earned fame before the Civil War by successfully winning a slave's freedom in the Lemmon Slave Case. Active in the **Republican Party**, he headed the **New York** delegation at the 1860 national convention and supported **William H. Seward's** nomination.

When the Civil War began, Evarts served as secretary of the New York Union Defense Committee and, as an assistant U.S. attorney, prosecuted the Confederate **privateers** in the *Enchantress* **Affair**. **Abraham Lincoln** then sent him to Europe in 1863 and 1864 to help stop private companies from building **commerce raiders** for the Confederates. Because of his excellent reputation, Evarts also was considered for the position of **U.S. Supreme Court** chief justice but was passed over in favor of **Salmon P. Chase**.

After the war, Evarts served as President **Andrew Johnson's** attorney general and defense counsel during the impeachment. He also was President **Rutherford B. Hayes's** secretary of state and a U.S. senator.

EVERETT, EDWARD (1794–1865) USA. A native of **Massachusetts**, Everett was educated at Harvard University (where he later taught) and in Europe and served as editor of the *North American Review*. Before the Civil War, he was both a member of the U.S. House of Representatives and U.S. senator from Massachusetts, the governor of Massachusetts, and President Millard Fillmore's secretary of state. Everett became one of the most famous orators in America and in 1860 ran for vice president with **John Bell** on the **Constitutional Union Party** ticket.

During the war, Everett continued to deliver well-attended speeches in favor of the Union war effort and in November 1863 was the keynote speaker at the cemetery dedication at Gettysburg, Pennsylvania. Although his two-hour-long speech was well received, it later became overshadowed by **Abraham Lincoln's Gettysburg Address**.

EWELL, RICHARD STODDERT (1817–1872) CSA. Born in **Washington, D.C.**, Ewell (YOOL) was a member of a prominent, though poor, **Virginia** family. He graduated from **West Point** in 1840, served in the dragoons on the frontier, and participated in both the Santa Fe and Oregon Trail Expeditions. During the **Mexican War**, Ewell was part of **Winfield Scott's** escort, and he was **brevetted** once for gallantry. Afterward, he served in the desert southwest fighting Apaches and became a well-known frontier officer. Arizona even named a county after Ewell, but its name later was changed because of his Confederate service.

Ewell resigned his captain's commission when Virginia seceded and entered Confederate service as a lieutenant colonel of cavalry. He may have been the first Confederate casualty of the war when he was wounded in early June 1861 during a **skirmish** at Fairfax Court House, Virginia. Promoted to brigadier general that same month, Ewell commanded a **brigade** at **First Manassas**. Although not engaged, he became embroiled in a dispute with **P. G. T. Beauregard** when orders calling for him to advance against the Union left flank miscarried. Although he was blameless, some newspapers held Ewell responsible for the Confederate failure to completely destroy the Union **army**.

Despite the controversy, Ewell was promoted to major general in January 1862 and served as **Stonewall Jackson's** second in command during **Jackson's Shenandoah Valley Campaign**. Ewell's service was excellent, and his **division** largely bore the brunt of the fighting. Although less spectacularly, Ewell served well with the **Army of Northern Virginia** in the **Seven Days Campaign** and at **Cedar Mountain**. His division again played a key role in Jackson's flanking march during the **Second Manassas Campaign**, but Ewell's lower left leg was shattered by a bullet at **Groveton**. After having his leg amputated, he was out of service until May 1863, when he was promoted to lieutenant general and was given command of Jackson's II Corps.

During the **Gettysburg Campaign**, Ewell again won praise for his victory at **Second Winchester** and **Stephenson's Depot** and for helping rout the Union XI Corps on the first day at the Battle of Gettysburg. His hesitancy on July 1, 1863, however, caused him to miss an opportunity to seize Cemetery and Culp's Hills. This failure caused Ewell to become one of the main scapegoats for the Confederate defeat at Gettsyburg. Ewell once again handled his **corps** well at the **Wilderness**, but his line was broken at **Spotsylvania**. The strain of the **Overland Campaign** finally broke down his health, and he was replaced in late May by **Jubal A. Early**. Ewell unsuccessfully tried to regain command of the II Corps within a few weeks, but was disappointed when **Robert E. Lee** put him in charge of the **Department of Richmond**.

Ewell oversaw the **Richmond** defenses for the remainder of the war and was charged with burning the city's warehouses and commodities when the Confederates evacuated in April 1865. These fires were spread by looters and wind, and much of the city burned, causing Ewell to be blamed for the destruction. Ewell was captured at **Sailor's Creek** during the **Appomattox Campaign** and spent several months in **prison** at **Fort Warren, Massachusetts**.

After the war, Ewell settled in **Tennessee** and engaged in farming and stockbreeding. He was one of Lee's best division commanders, whose record as a corps commander was somewhat erratic. Ewell spoke with a slight lisp, was frequently profane, and had peculiar habits that caused him to be quite eccentric, but he also was very popular with his troops. Many soldiers believed the loss of his leg and his 1863 marriage to the widow Lizinka Brown—whom he sometimes introduced as "my wife Mrs. Brown"—took some of the fire out of the former **Indian** fighter.

EWING, CHARLES (1835–1883) USA. A native of **Ohio**, Ewing was the brother of Union generals **Hugh Boyle Ewing** and **Thomas Ewing Jr.** and was **William T. Sherman's** brother-in-law. The son of Thomas Ewing, former U.S. senator and former secretary of the treasury and of the interior, Ewing attended the University of Virginia and became a lawyer in St. Louis, **Missouri**.

Ewing entered Union service in May 1861 as a captain in the 13th U.S. Infantry. His first real combat was during the **Vicksburg Campaign**, where he was severely wounded while placing the **flag** on the Confederate works. Promoted to lieutenant colonel in June 1863, Ewing then joined Sherman's staff as assistant inspector general. He served under Sherman during the **Chattanooga** and **Atlanta Campaigns**, the **March to the Sea**, and the **Carolinas Campaign**, and was promoted to brigadier general of volunteers in March 1865. Ewing received three

brevets for his wartime service and left the **army** in 1867 to return to his law practice.

EWING, HUGH BOYLE (1826–1905) USA. A native of **Ohio**, Ewing was the brother of Union generals **Charles Ewing** and **Thomas Ewing Jr.** and the brother-in-law of **William T. Sherman**. The son of Thomas Ewing, a former U.S. senator and former secretary of the treasury and of the interior, Ewing was appointed to **West Point** but was forced to drop out during his senior year after failing the engineering exam. He participated in the **California** Gold Rush but then returned east and practiced law in **Missouri** and **Kansas**.

In May 1861, Ewing was appointed **brigade** inspector of Ohio state troops and saw service in the early campaign in western **Virginia**. He then was commissioned colonel of the 30th Ohio in August and fought with the **Army of the Potomac** at **South Mountain** (where he was credited with dislodging the Confederates) and at **Antietam**.

Ewing was promoted to brigadier general of volunteers in November 1862 and was transferred to Sherman's **corps** in the **Army of the Tennessee** for the **Vicksburg Campaign**. There he earned a **division** command, and at **Missionary Ridge** he led the attack against **Patrick Cleburne's** entrenched Confederates. After commanding Louisville, **Kentucky**, for a year, he rejoined Sherman for the last part of the **Carolinas Campaign**.

After being mustered out of service in 1866 with a **brevet** rank of major general of volunteers, Ewing served as the U.S. minister to Holland.

EWING, THOMAS, JR. (1829–1896) USA. A native of **Ohio**, Ewing was the brother of Union generals **Charles Ewing** and **Hugh Boyle Ewing** and the brother-in-law of **William T. Sherman**. The son of Thomas Ewing, a former U.S. senator and former secretary of the treasury and of the interior, Ewing served as President Zachary Taylor's private secretary. After graduating from Brown University, he opened a law practice in **Kansas**, became active in the antislavery faction in **"Bleeding Kansas,"** and served as Kansas's first chief justice.

Ewing entered Union service in September 1862 as colonel of the 11th Kansas Cavalry and led it at **Prairie Grove, Arkansas**. Promoted to brigadier general of volunteers in March 1863, he then took command of the District of the Border and earned the Confederates' hatred when he issued General Orders No. 11. This measure ordered the evacuation of four **Missouri** counties that harbored Confederate guerrillas and sympathizers. Since violators were to be executed, the order brought further misery to war-torn Missouri. After playing a key role in the defeat of

Sterling Price's 1864 Missouri Raid, Ewing resigned his commission in February 1865. For his service at **Pilot Knob**, he was **brevetted** major general of volunteers.

After the war, Ewing practiced law in **Washington, D.C.**, and turned down appointment offers for attorney general and secretary of war. He eventually returned to Kansas and served two terms in the **U.S. Congress**.

EXCELSIOR BRIGADE. Organized by **Daniel E. Sickles** in New York City at the beginning of hostilities, this **brigade** consisted of the 70th, 71st, 72nd, 73rd, and 74th New York. Sickles was appointed colonel of the 70th New York in June 1861. The brigade was sent to **Washington, D.C.**, after **First Manassas** and became part of the **Army of the Potomac**, serving first in the III Corps and later in the II Corps. After Sickles was promoted to **division** command, the brigade went through a number of commanders.

The Excelsior Brigade fought in nearly all of the battles of the Army of the Potomac and suffered heavy casualties. In early 1864, the 120th New York and 11th Massachusetts were added to the brigade, but shortly afterward the brigade was disbanded when the original members' enlistments expired in the summer of 1864. In July, the remaining members of the brigade were dispersed among other units. Only the 73rd and 120th New York remained intact for the entire war. The Excelsior Brigade suffered the fifth highest rate of battle deaths in the Union **army**, with 876 men being killed or mortally wounded.

EXCHANGE. Since neither side was prepared to handle the huge numbers of **prisoners** that were captured in the Civil War, methods had to be adopted to relieve the overburdened **prisons**. Exchange was a system whereby the two sides swapped prisoners; **parole** was when a prisoner was released upon taking an oath not to fight again until exchanged.

The two sides began exchange discussions in February 1862 and reached an agreement in July. **City Point**, **Virginia**, and **Vicksburg**, **Mississippi**, were designated as the two points of exchange. Besides a direct exchange of rank for rank, a formula that weighed the value of each soldier was also used. For example, 60 privates could be exchanged for one general, or two privates could be exchanged for one sergeant. The practice worked rather smoothly until mid-war when large numbers of **black troops** began being used by the Union **army**. In retaliation for the Confederates refusing to recognize black soldiers as prisoners of war, the Union officially stopped exchanging officers in December 1862 and all routine exchanges were stopped in May 1863. However, exchanges continued to take place by special agreement. When **U. S. Grant** became general-in-chief in March 1864, he ordered all exchanges to halt because they were advantageous to the under-manned **Confederate army**. Despite this decision, however, some exchanges of sick and wounded soldiers continued until war's end.

EZRA CHURCH, GEORGIA, BATTLE OF (JULY 28, 1864). When Maj. Gen. **William T. Sherman** finally reached the outskirts of Atlanta, Georgia, during the **Atlanta Campaign** and repelled two attacks by **John B. Hood's** Confederate **Army of Tennessee**, he began extending his right wing to the west and south of Atlanta to cut the **railroads** that were supplying the Confederate defenders. In late July 1864, Maj. Gen. **Oliver O. Howard's Army of the Tennessee** shifted positions from Sherman's left flank to his right.

On July 28, Howard was ordered to move south and cut the Macon & Western Railroad between East Point and Atlanta. Hood quickly responded and sent part of **Stephen D. Lee's** and **Alexander P. Stewart's corps** to head off Howard. Planning to hit Howard's flank as he marched south, the Confederates attacked on the afternoon of July 28 at Ezra Church, a few miles west-southwest of Atlanta. The Federals were prepared, however, and **John A. Logan's** XV Corps had formed a strong line at right angles to Howard's flank. Lee attacked first, followed by Stewart, but all of the assaults were repulsed by Logan. In the heavy fighting, it is estimated that the Confederates lost about 5,000 men to Logan's 562. Howard's progress to the south was stopped, and the railroad was saved, but the tremendous bloodletting only further weakened Hood's dwindling **army**.

– F –

FAGAN, JAMES FLEMING (1828–1893) CSA. Born in **Kentucky**, Fagan moved to **Arkansas** as a boy. He fought in the **Mexican War** as a lieutenant and served one term in the state legislature as a **Whig**. When Civil War came, Fagan raised a **regiment** that became designated the 1st Arkansas and was appointed its colonel in May 1861. He was elevated to **brigade** command after fighting at **Shiloh** and **Corinth** but did not impress **Braxton Bragg** and was transferred to the **Trans-Mississippi Department**.

Fagan was promoted to brigadier general in October 1861 and was put in command of an Arkansas cavalry brigade. He fought at **Cane Hill**, **Prairie Grove**, and **Helena**, and in July 1863 took temporary command of **Sterling Price's** division. After defending **Little Rock** in 1863, Fagan played a key role in the 1864 **Camden Expedition** by attacking and destroying a Union 240-wagon supply train at **Marks' Mills** and inflicting some 1,300 casualties on the enemy while losing only 293 men. This feat won him promotion to major general in June 1864. During **Price's 1864 Missouri Raid**, Fagan commanded a cavalry division and participated in the fight at **Pilot Knob**, but he was defeated at the **Little Blue River** and at **Westport**. His division disintegrated after the latter battle. In 1865, Fagan first commanded the cavalry in the District of Arkansas and ended the war in command of the **district**.

After the war, Fagan farmed and became a U.S. marshal in Arkansas.

FAIR GARDEN (KELLY'S FORD), TENNESSEE, BATTLE OF (JANUARY 26–27, 1864). After the 1863 **Knoxville Campaign**, Lt. Gen. **James Longstreet's** Confederate command quartered for the winter northeast of Knoxville at Russellville and Morristown, **Tennessee**. In January 1864, Union cavalry commander Maj. Gen. **John G. Foster** was ordered to attack the Confederates and force them out of the area.

Foster sent Brig. Gen. **Samuel D. Sturgis** northeast from Sevierville toward the enemy. Longstreet countered by sending Maj. Gen. **William T. Martin's** cavalry to contest the Federal advance. Fighting broke out on January 26 at Fair Garden and near Sevierville, in which the Confederates drove back Sturgis. The next day, more fighting occurred near Fair Garden at Kelly's Ford on the Big East Fork of the Little Pigeon River. Numerous charges and countercharges were made, with the Union troopers finally pushing back the Confederates and capturing two cannons and more than one hundred **prisoners**. Martin lost about 200 men, while Sturgis lost approximately 70. Sturgis withdrew on January 28 when Longstreet brought up additional reinforcements.

FAIR OAKS, VIRGINIA, BATTLE OF (MAY 31–JUNE 1, 1862). *See* SEVEN PINES, VIRGINIA, BATTLE OF.

FAIRBANKS, ERASTUS (1792–1864) USA. A native of **Massachusetts**, Fairbanks moved to **Vermont** as a young man and became a successful saw and gristmill owner. He and his brothers then expanded their business into a thriving manufacturing enterprise. Fairbanks was elected to the state legislature in 1836, served as a **Whig** presidential elector in 1844 and 1848, and was elected governor in 1852. His administration pushed educational and social reforms and brought prohibition to Vermont. After he was defeated for reelection, Fairbanks joined the **Republican Party** and won the governor's race in 1860 even though he was almost 70 years old.

A strong supporter of the Union war effort, Fairbanks not only convened a special legislative session in April 1861 to raise troops but also extended personal credit to those men who were raising **regiments**. Having promised to serve only one term when elected in 1860, he voluntarily stepped down from the office in 1862.

FAIRCHILD, LUCIUS (1831–1896) USA. Born in **Ohio**, Fairchild grew up in **Wisconsin**, where his father was the first state treasurer and the first mayor of Madison. He dropped out of college and lived in **California** for a number of years before returning to Wisconsin in 1858.

Fairchild entered Union service in April 1861 as a private in the 1st Wisconsin and was elected **company** captain in May. After fighting at Falling Waters, Maryland, he was appointed lieutenant colonel of the 2nd Wisconsin in July and became part of the famous **"Iron Brigade."** Fairchild also was appointed captain in the 16th U.S. Infantry, but he obtained leave from the regular **army** so he could keep his position in the 2nd Wisconsin. Fighting with the **Army of the Potomac**, he was praised for his actions at **Second Manassas**, **South Mountain**, and **Antietam**, and won promotion to colonel in September 1862. After service at **Fredericksburg** and **Chancellorsville**, Fairchild was badly wounded in the left arm on the first day at **Gettysburg**. Captured, he lost his arm to amputation and never again took the field.

After being **exchanged**, Fairchild resigned his commission in August 1863, but he then was appointed a brigadier general of volunteers in November. He resigned that commission, as well, and accepted the position of **Wisconsin** secretary of state, to which he had been elected while in the army. Fairchild also served as governor from 1866 to 1872 and held a number of diplomatic positions in Europe.

FALLING WATERS, MARYLAND, BATTLE OF (JULY 8–14, 1863). After the **Battle of Gettysburg**, **Robert E. Lee's** retreating **Army of Northern Virginia** reached the Potomac River on July 6, 1863, but then had to wait in entrenchments around Williamsport, Maryland, until a **pontoon bridge** could be built across the swollen river. When the bridge was completed on July 13, and the waters began to recede, the Confederates began crossing over to **Virginia** that night.

On July 14, Maj. Gen. **George G. Meade** advanced the **Army of the Potomac** against the Confederate positions but found the works at Williamsport abandoned. At Falling Waters, however, the Confederate **divisions** of **Henry Heth** and **William Pender** had not yet crossed the river. Heth's division, forming Lee's rear guard, was attacked by the

Union cavalry of **John Buford** and **H. Judson Kilpatrick**. Heth was taken by surprise and lost about 700 men taken **prisoners**, and Maj. Gen. **James Pettigrew** was mortally wounded. Meade, however, overestimated enemy losses and claimed to have inflicted 2,000 casualties on Lee. In an unusual move, Lee publicly disputed Meade's claim, but many people believed the exaggeration, and Heth's reputation was somewhat tarnished. The clash at Falling Waters was the last combat of the Gettysburg Campaign.

FARNSWORTH, ELON JOHN (1837–1863) USA. The nephew of Union general **John F. Farnsworth**, Farnsworth was a **Michigan** native who attended the University of Michigan but was forced to resign over an incident in which a student was killed. He participated in the 1857–58 **Utah Expedition** as a civilian **forage** master and entered Union service in September 1861 as a 1st lieutenant and adjutant in his uncle's 8th Illinois Cavalry.

Farnsworth was a worthy officer who was said to have participated in 41 engagements during the Civil War. He also was praised by Northerners for removing a minister from his Alexandria, Virginia, pulpit for failing to offer the customary prayer for the president's health. Promoted to captain in December 1861, Farnsworth served as acting quartermaster for the **Army of the Potomac's** IV Corps and in the spring of 1863 was appointed aide-de-camp to **Alfred Pleasonton**.

Farnsworth was promoted to brigadier general of volunteers in June 1863. This rapid rise in rank supposedly stemmed from his having uncle John Farnsworth, now a congressman, help get Pleasonton promoted, and Pleasonton returned the favor. Given command of a cavalry **brigade** during the **Gettysburg Campaign**, Farnsworth fought **J. E. B. Stuart's** cavalry at **Hanover** on July 1 and at Hunterstown on July 2. On July 3, when **Pickett's Charge** was repulsed, Farnsworth's **division** commander, **H. Judson Kilpatrick**, ordered him to attack the Confederate right to throw the enemy into confusion. It was a reckless order, and Farnsworth protested that it was suicide to attack an enemy positioned behind stone walls. Kilpatrick questioned Farnsworth's bravery and offered to lead the charge himself. Farnsworth then carried out the order. He escaped the initial charge but lost 25 percent of his men. Witnesses then claimed Farnsworth turned and rode back along the Confederate line and received five mortal wounds. Confederate soldiers claimed that after being wounded several times, Farnsworth actually killed himself.

FARNSWORTH, JOHN FRANKLIN (1820–1897) USA. An uncle of Union general **Elon J. Farnsworth**, Farnsworth was a native of Quebec,

Canada, but he moved to **Illinois** as a youngster. Becoming a lawyer, he was elected to the **U.S. Congress** in 1856 and 1858 as an **abolitionist**. After being defeated for reelection, Farnsworth entered Union service in September 1861 as colonel of the 8th Illinois Cavalry, a regiment that he had raised. Sent to **Virginia** to join the **Army of the Potomac**, he fought in the **Peninsula Campaign** and led a brigade at **Antietam**, although he was only lightly engaged there.

Farnsworth was promoted to brigadier general of volunteers in November 1862 and next fought at **Fredericksburg**. He again was elected to Congress that year and resigned his commission in March 1863 to take his seat. Farnsworth served in Congress as a **Radical Republican** until 1873.

FARRAGUT, DAVID GLASGOW (1801–1870) USA. Although a native of **Tennessee**, Farragut became the most famous Union admiral of the Civil War. He was raised as a foster son by Cmdr. David D. Porter, the father of future Union Adm. **David Dixon Porter**, and entered the **U.S. Navy** in 1810 as a midshipman (when he was nine years old). Farragut served under his adopted father in the War of 1812 and became a prize master at age 12. He then rose through the ranks from lieutenant in 1822 to captain in 1855, having in the meantime served in the **Mexican War**.

Farragut was living in **Norfolk, Virginia**, when **Virginia** seceded in April 1861. Because of his Unionism, he was forced to move north and in December was placed in command of the West **Gulf Blockading Squadron**. In April 1862, with the support of foster brother David, Farragut successfully steamed past **Forts Jackson and St. Philip, Louisiana**, and captured **New Orleans**. As a reward, he received the **Thanks of Congress** and was promoted to rear admiral in July. That summer, Farragut unsuccessfully attacked **Vicksburg, Mississippi**, and then concentrated on enforcing the Gulf Coast **blockade**.

In the spring and summer of 1863, Farragut's fleet cooperated with Maj. Gen. **Nathaniel P. Banks** in the **Port Hudson Campaign**. The following year, he was given the responsibility of capturing Mobile, Alabama, and in August sailed into the bay with several ships. When his lead ship was sunk by a **torpedo** in the **Battle of Mobile Bay**, other captains hesitated to continue. Lashed to the rigging of the **USS** *Hartford*, Farragut then supposedly yelled his famous command, "Damn the torpedoes! Full speed ahead!" (Kennedy, ed., *The Civil War Battlefield Guide*, 374). He defeated the **Confederate navy** at Mobile, and Confederate **Fort Morgan** surrendered. Farragut's victory earned him promotion to vice admiral in December 1864.

When the war ended, Farragut was operating on Virginia's James River. He was promoted to admiral in July 1866 (the first American officer to hold that rank) and commanded the European Squadron from 1867 to 1868.

FASCINE. Fascine (fuh-SEEN) was brush, sticks, or stakes tied tightly together to form a long cylindrical bundle. The fascine was used to fill in ditches, reinforce trench or fortification walls, or to protect **artillery** positions.

FEATHERSTON, WINFIELD SCOTT (1820–1891) CSA. A native of **Tennessee**, Featherston fought in the Creek **Indian** War and then moved to **Mississippi**, where he opened a law practice. A **Democrat**, he served two terms in the **U.S. Congress** from 1849 to 1853 but then was defeated for reelection.

Featherston was a secessionist and organized and commanded a volunteer **company** when Mississippi seceded. In June 1861, he was elected colonel of the 17th Mississippi. After participating in the **First Battle of Manassas**, Featherston played a key role in the Confederate victory at **Ball's Bluff**, where his men captured two cannons and more than 500 **prisoners**.

Featherston, or "Old Swet" as his men called him, was promoted to brigadier general in March 1862 and led a **brigade** at **Williamsburg**. After taking command of a Mississippi brigade, he fought well with the **Army of Northern Virginia** during the **Seven Days Campaign** and was wounded in the shoulder at **Frayser's Farm**. Returning to duty in time for **Second Manassas**, Featherston led two brigades there, but he failed to impress his superior, **James Longstreet**. He was transferred to Mississippi after the **Battle of Fredericksburg** and took command of a brigade there in February 1863. Serving in **William Loring's** division, Featherston helped stop the **Steele's Bayou Expedition** and fought at **Champion Hill**. His brigade remained with **Joseph E. Johnston** around Jackson, Mississippi, during the rest of the **Vicksburg Campaign** and opposed **William T. Sherman's Meridian Campaign** in early 1864.

Featherston was transferred to **Georgia** and fought in most of the major battles of the **Atlanta Campaign**, at times in command of the **division**. His command suffered heavy losses and later was badly shot up again at the **Battles of Franklin and Nashville, Tennessee**. Joining Johnston for the **Carolinas Campaign** late in the war, Featherston fought his last battles at **Kinston** and **Bentonville** before surrendering with the rest of Johnston's **army**.

After the war, Featherston returned to Mississippi and served in the state legislature, where he opposed the **Reconstruction** government.

FEINT. Similar to a **demonstration**, this is a military maneuver designed to draw the enemy's attention away from the main point of attack by making a limited attack at another point with a small part of one's force.

FENTON, REUBEN EATON (1819–1885) USA. A native of **New York**, Fenton went to work in logging camps as a teenager to help pay off debts his father owed from a failed business. He became a lawyer and a **Democrat** and was elected to the legislature in 1849 and to the **U.S. Congress** in 1852. Opposed to the spread of **slavery**, Fenton helped found the **Republican Party** while in Congress and continued to serve there until 1864, when he defeated Democratic incumbent **Horatio Seymour** in the governor's race.

Fenton was a strong supporter of **Abraham Lincoln's** administration and of the war effort and won reelection in 1866. A very powerful governor, he also worked to improve education and reform prisons. Fenton was elected to one term in the U.S. Senate in 1868 and then became a successful banker and businessman.

FERGUSON, SAMUEL WRAGG (1834–1917) CSA. A native of **South Carolina**, Ferguson graduated from **West Point** in 1857 and served in the **Utah Expedition** and in the Pacific Northwest before resigning his commission in March 1861. When the Civil War began, he first entered state service as a captain but then was appointed a lieutenant of Confederate cavalry.

Ferguson served as **P. G. T. Beauregard's** aide at **Fort Sumter** and **First Manassas**, and at **Shiloh** he held the rank of lieutenant colonel and temporarily led a **brigade**. In October 1862, he was appointed lieutenant colonel of the 28th Mississippi Cavalry. Rising to the rank of colonel in May 1863, Ferguson served along the Mississippi River and performed well while countering Union raids into the Mississippi Delta.

Promoted to brigadier general in July 1863, Ferguson led a cavalry brigade during the 1864 **Meridian Campaign**. During the **Atlanta Campaign**, his brigade saw frequent combat while with the **Army of Tennessee** and was the last Confederate unit to evacuate the city when it fell to **William T. Sherman**. Despite his valuable service, Ferguson clashed bitterly with his superior, **Joseph Wheeler**, and Wheeler accused him of being both incompetent and insubordinate. When Beauregard recommended Ferguson be promoted to major general, Wheeler opposed the promotion and kept him at the brigade level. After hard service during the **Carolinas Campaign**, Ferguson joined **Jefferson Davis** and the fleeing Confederate government until early May 1865.

After his surrender and **parole**, Ferguson became a **Mississippi** lawyer and served as president of the Board of Mississippi Levee Commissioners and the Rivers Commission. Later in life he settled in **Charleston, South Carolina**, as a civil engineer.

FERRERO, EDWARD (1831–1899) USA. Born in Spain to Italian parents, Ferrero moved to New York City as a child and became a dance instructor. He also became a lieutenant colonel in the state militia and in 1861 was working as a dance instructor at **West Point**.

Ferrero entered Union service in October 1861 as colonel of the 51st New York. After helping capture **New Bern, North Carolina**, he led a **brigade** at **Second Manassas** and earned a promotion to brigadier general of volunteers in September 1862. As part of the **Army of the Potomac**, Ferrero's brigade fought at **Antietam** and **Fredericksburg**. When the Senate failed to confirm his promotion after the latter battle, Ferrero was reappointed brigadier general in May 1863 and was transferred west to the **Army of the Tennessee**. After leading his brigade in the **Vicksburg Campaign**, he took command of a **division** under **Ambrose E. Burnside** during the **Knoxville Campaign**.

Returning to Virginia, Ferrero was given command of a new division of **black troops** in the Army of the Potomac's IX Corps. During the **Petersburg Campaign**, his men were especially trained to lead the attack at the **Crater** in July 1864, but at the last minute they were replaced by white troops. When ordered to support the attack, Ferrero and Brig. Gen. **James H. Ledlie** were found drinking in a rear **bombproof**. While they drank, Ferrero's division was cut to pieces. A similar affair had occurred while he was at Knoxville. Therefore, when a court of inquiry was held over the Crater disaster, it reported that Ferrero habitually remained in bombproofs during battle. Still, he was **brevetted** major general of volunteers for his service in the Petersburg Campaign.

After the war, Ferrero returned to his dance studio in New York City.

FERRY, ORRIS SANFORD (1823–1875) USA. A native of **Connecticut**, Ferry was a distinguished Yale University graduate who opened a law practice in his native state. After serving as a probate judge, state attorney, and state senator, he was elected to the U.S. House of Representatives in 1858 as a **Republican**.

When defeated for reelection, Ferry entered Union service in July 1861 as colonel of the 5th Connecticut. Promoted to brigadier general of volunteers in March 1862, he led a **brigade** during **Stonewall Jackson's 1862 Shenandoah Valley Campaign** and then was transferred to the **Army of the Potomac** on the Virginia Peninsula after the close of the **Seven Days Campaign**. Ferry served on garrison duty in southeastern **Virginia** and in **South Carolina** until 1864, when he led a **division** in the **Army of the James** in the **Bermuda Hundred** and **Petersburg Campaigns**.

After the war, Ferry was elected to the U.S. Senate in 1866. Thought to be a **Radical Republican**, he surprised many by mostly following a moderate course during **Reconstruction**.

FESSENDEN, FRANCIS (1839–1906) USA. A native of **Maine**, Fessenden was the son of Secretary of the Treasury **William P. Fessenden** and the brother of Union Brig. Gen. **James D. Fessenden**. He graduated from Bowdoin College and studied law at Harvard University before opening a law practice.

Fessenden entered Union service in May 1861 when Secretary of War **Simon Cameron** commissioned him a captain in the 19th U.S. Infantry. He was badly wounded at **Shiloh** but returned to duty in September as colonel of the 25th Maine. Fessenden left the **army** in July 1863 but then reentered in January 1864 as colonel of the 30th Maine. Taking part in the **Red River Campaign**, he fought gallantly at **Pleasant Hill** and **Monett's Ferry**, where he suffered a wound that led to his right leg being amputated.

Promoted to brigadier general of volunteers in May 1864, Fessenden remained in the service and was promoted to major general of volunteers in November 1865. He also served as commissioner for the trial of **Andersonville Prison** commandant **Henry Wirz** before leaving the army in 1866 as a brigadier general of regulars, with the **brevet** rank of major general of regulars.

After leaving the army, Fessenden twice was elected mayor of Portland, Maine.

FESSENDEN, JAMES DEERING (1833–1882) USA. A native of **Maine**, Fessenden was the son of **William Pitt Fessenden** and the brother of Union Brig. Gen. **Francis Fessenden**. A graduate of Bowdoin College, he was a partner in his father's law office when the Civil War began.

Fessenden raised, and served as captain of, a **company** of **sharpshooters** that became part of the 2nd U.S. Sharpshooters (of **Berdan's Sharpshooters**) in November 1861. In March 1862, he joined Maj. Gen. **David Hunter's** staff in **South Carolina** and organized the 1st South Carolina Volunteers, a **regiment** of **black troops**. When the regiment was disbanded during the controversy over Hunter's emancipation actions, Fessenden rejoined the general's staff and participated in the attack on **Charleston**, **South Carolina**, that summer. After being promoted to colonel in July 1862, he was injured in a riding accident and was unable to return to active duty until September. At that time, Fessenden joined Maj. Gen. **Joseph Hooker's** staff and accompanied him and his two **corps** to **Tennessee**. Fessenden was praised for his actions in the **Chattanooga Campaign** and at **Resaca** and **Peachtree Creek** during the **At-**

lanta Campaign and was promoted to brigadier general of volunteers in August 1864.

Fessenden commanded a **brigade** during **Philip Sheridan's Shenandoah Valley Campaign** and fought at **Third Winchester** and **Cedar Creek**. For the remainder of the war, he served on garrison duty in the **Shenandoah Valley**, sometimes in command of a **division**. In March 1865, Fessenden was **brevetted** major general of volunteers.

After leaving the **army** in January 1866, Fessenden returned to his law practice and served three terms in the Maine legislature.

FESSENDEN, WILLIAM PITT (1806–1869) USA. A native of **New Hampshire**, Fessenden was the father of Union generals **Francis Fessenden** and **James Deering Fessenden**. An illegitimate child, he was raised by his grandparents until his father married. Fessenden graduated from Bowdoin College, but he was refused a diploma because of his "general character." After receiving a law degree in 1827, he moved to **Maine** and became active in state politics. Originally a **Whig**, Fessenden served four terms in the legislature and was elected to the U.S. House of Representatives in 1840. He then was elected to the U.S. Senate in 1854 and became a **Republican** because of his antislavery sentiments. Reelected in 1860, Fessenden became chairman of the powerful Finance Committee.

Fessenden had a stern, insensitive personality, but he served the Union well. He opposed wasteful spending and supported **financing** the war through the sale of bonds and raising **taxes**. When the 1862 **Legal Tender Act** was passed to issue paper money, Fessenden bitterly opposed it as a dangerous move that would lead to inflation. Despite his objections to **greenbacks**, he was appointed by **Abraham Lincoln** to be secretary of the treasury in July 1864 to replace **Salmon P. Chase**. Fessenden resigned from the Senate, but he agreed to serve only as a temporary secretary. He quickly renewed the sale of bonds to finance the war and kept the Union on firm financial ground. After being safely reelected to the Senate, Fessenden resigned his cabinet post in March 1865.

During **Reconstruction**, Fessenden chaired the Joint Committee on Reconstruction but opposed his party's impeachment of President **Andrew Johnson**. He died in 1869 while in office.

FIELD, CHARLES WILLIAM (1828–1892) CSA. A native of **Kentucky**, Field graduated from **West Point** in 1849. He served with the dragoons on the frontier and was a cavalry instructor at the academy before resigning his captain's commission in May 1861.

Field entered Confederate service as a captain of cavalry but within months was appointed colonel of the 6th Virginia Cavalry. Promoted to brigadier general in May 1862, he was given command of an infantry **brigade** in the **Army of Northern Virginia** and was praised for his service in the **Seven Days Campaign** and at **Cedar Mountain** and **Second Manassas**. Field was badly wounded in the hips at the latter battle and served as head of the Bureau of Conscription while he recovered.

Promoted to major general in February 1864, Field took command of **John Bell Hood's** former **division** over the opposition of **corps** commander **James Longstreet**, who felt Field was physically unfit for the post. Contrary to Longstreet's belief, Field proved to be one of the Confederacy's best division commanders and performed excellent service throughout the **Overland** and **Petersburg Campaigns**. At the **Wilderness**, his division helped save the **army** from destruction on the second day of fighting when **A. P. Hill's** corps was pushed out of its position. When Longstreet was wounded there, Field temporarily took command of the I Corps.

After surrendering his division at **Appomattox**, Field embarked on a varied career. He served in the Egyptian army, was the doorkeeper of the **U.S. Congress**, and worked as an **Indian** reservation superintendent.

"FIGHTING McCOOKS." **Ohio's** McCook family became famous for providing 14 men to the Union **army**. Seven were brothers, sons of Maj. Daniel McCook, and the other seven were cousins. The group included generals **Alexander McDowell McCook**, **Daniel McCook Jr.**, **Edward Moody McCook** and **Robert Latimer McCook**. Robert and Daniel were killed during the war.

FILE CLOSERS. This was the name given to officers and men who were placed just behind the firing line. During battle, the file closers served as a deterrent to those who might run away and stepped forward to fill in any gaps in the main line that were created by casualties.

FINANCE, CONFEDERATE. Being a new government, the Confederacy was forced to begin the Civil War with no **currency**, **tax** structure, or other financial base, and only a few million dollars in specie that had been seized from federal mints. The Confederates financed the government and war through loans, taxes, and treasury notes (paper money).

To operate the government in February 1861, Secretary of the Treasury **Christopher G. Memminger** first was forced to take out $15 million in loans from **New Orleans**, **Louisiana**, and **Alabama** banks. He then placed the Confederacy deeply in debt by selling bonds to finance the war. Another $100 million loan, paid largely by planters using treasury notes and produce, was taken out in November. Meanwhile, efforts were made in Europe to obtain additional loans. In October 1862, the **Er-langer Loan** was secured in France, but it provided only $8.5 million. It is estimated that the Confederate government raised about $700 million—or 39 percent of its revenue—through such loans.

In April 1863, the Confederate government adopted an **income tax** to finance the war. It also adopted a **tax-in-kind**, whereby farmers were taxed 10 percent of their produce. Some other Confederate taxes were adopted, but it is estimated that they raised only about 7 percent of Confederate revenues.

Both the national and state governments also began printing treasury notes to pay for government expenses, with the Confederate government printing approximately $1.5 billion in paper money. Inflation set in almost immediately, fueled further by the government's policy of allowing citizens to use state paper money to pay property taxes. By 1864, inflation was rampant, and **Jefferson Davis** replaced Memminger with **George A. Trenholm** in July. The change did not affect inflation, however, and by 1865 the Confederate dollar's value had shrunk to 1.7 cents.

A major weakness of the Confederacy was its inability to solve its financial problems. Faced with such overwhelming difficulties, it was rather incredible that the government lasted as long as it did.

FINANCE, UNION. One regard in which the Union had a huge advantage over the Confederacy was that it had an established financial base from which to fight the war. The U.S. government paid for the war by making loans, issuing paper money, selling bonds, and raising **taxes**. Of these methods, loans and paper money far outweighed the others in importance.

The majority of the war costs were paid for by taking out short-term loans of 4–6 percent and issuing treasury notes, for a total of $2.6 billion. The use of treasury notes (or paper money) was resorted to in February 1862 when the **U.S. Congress** passed a law authorizing the issuance of non-interest-bearing government notes known as **"greenbacks."** About $433 million in such notes were issued by war's end.

The sale of government bonds was undertaken by financier **Jay Cooke**, who was given the sole right to sell U.S. bonds by Secretary of the Treasury **Salmon P. Chase**. Cooke was so successful in this enterprise that he became known as the financier of the war.

Taxes did not play a very large role in the war's financing. In August 1861, the Congress imposed both an **income tax** and a quota on states for direct taxes to be paid. The income tax ranged from 3 to 10 percent and was the first income tax in American history. Neither of these methods raised a significant amount of money, however, the direct tax providing only about $17 million and the income tax about $55 million. The most successful tax was an internal tax passed in July 1862 that taxed nearly everything—raw materials, labor, sales, and so on. The internal tax and the income tax raised $209 million in the last year of war alone.

FINEGAN, JOSEPH (1814–1885) CSA. A native of Ireland, Finegan immigrated to the United States but forever spoke in a heavy Irish brogue. After settling in **Florida** as a planter and sawmill operator, he served as a secessionist delegate to the state's 1861 **secession** convention and then was placed in charge of preparing Florida for war.

In April 1862, Finegan was appointed brigadier general of Confederate troops and took command of the **Department of Middle and Eastern Florida**. There he earned the respect of **Robert E. Lee** by transferring as many men as possible to the **Virginia** theater. After defeating a Union invasion at **Olustee** in February 1864, Finegan received the **Thanks of Congress**, and Lee requested that he join the **Army of Northern Virginia** with a **brigade** of infantry. He did so and fought particularly well at **Cold Harbor**. During the **Petersburg Campaign**, Florida officials requested that Finegan be returned there. He voluntarily requested to be reassigned and in March 1865 was placed back in command of Florida, with his brigade remaining in Virginia. Finegan's final service to the Confederacy was in helping cabinet members **John C. Breckinridge** and **Judah P. Benjamin** escape Florida to Cuba and the Bahamas, respectively, at war's end.

After the war, Finegan became a cotton broker, lawyer, and state senator.

FINLEY, JESSE JOHNSON (1812–1904) CSA. A native of **Tennessee**, Finley became a lawyer and served in the **Seminole Wars** as a company captain. Afterward, he moved frequently and served as an **Arkansas** state senator and the mayor of Memphis, Tennessee, before moving to **Florida** and becoming a state senator and judge.

Finley entered Confederate service in early 1861 when he became a Confederate judge in Florida. In March 1862, he resigned his position and enlisted in the 6th Florida as a private. Probably because of his political influence, Finley quickly rose to captain and then to colonel. After leading his **regiment** in the 1862 **Kentucky Campaign**, he was placed on court-martial duty at Knoxville, Tennessee. Finley's first real battle was with the **Army of Tennessee** at **Chickamauga**. There his regiment charged the enemy and temporarily captured an **artillery** battery on the first day of fighting and on the second day helped capture 500 **prisoners**.

Finley was promoted to brigadier general in November 1863 and took command of a Florida **brigade**. He was praised for helping form the

army's rear guard after the disaster at **Missionary Ridge** and was severely wounded at **Resaca** at the beginning of the **Atlanta Campaign**. Returning to duty outside Atlanta, Finley was severely wounded again by a shell fragment at **Jonesboro** and barely escaped capture. This wound ended his field duty, for he was unable to rejoin his troops in **North Carolina** when he recovered.

After the war, Finley returned to his Florida law practice, served two terms in the **U.S. Congress**, and became a circuit judge.

"FIRE-EATERS." This was the nickname given to the radical Southerners who staunchly defended **states rights** and **slavery** before the Civil War. They also came to believe that **secession** was the only way in which to protect Southern rights. The fire-eaters included such politicians as **William L. Yancey** and **Robert Barnwell Rhett**.

FISHER'S HILL, VIRGINIA, BATTLE OF (SEPTEMBER 22, 1864). Following his defeat at the **Third Battle of Winchester** during **Philip Sheridan's Shenandoah Valley Campaign**, Lt. Gen. **Jubal A. Early** withdrew his small **Valley Army** up the **Shenandoah Valley** to Fisher's Hill. This prominent rise is located 21 miles south of Winchester and is at a point where the Valley narrows. Fisher's Hill dominates the region and was a good place at which to make a defensive stand.

Arriving on September 20, Early positioned his 9,000-man **army** in previously constructed entrenchments and awaited Sheridan's 35,000-man army. When Sheridan arrived that afternoon, he hesitated to attack the formidable position. Instead, he planned to attack on September 22 by sending Maj. Gen. **George Crook's** corps to launch a surprise attack against Early's left flank. At the same time, Maj. Gen. **Alfred T. A. Torbert's** cavalry was to sweep far around Early's right flank and get into position to cut his line of retreat near **New Market**.

After spending September 21 dueling with the Confederates, Sheridan sent Crook's **corps** into motion on September 22. He launched the surprise attack at about 4:00 P.M. and crushed Early's left flank, which was held by cavalryman Maj. Gen. **Lindsay Lunsford Lomax**. The Confederate line then became unhinged unit by unit, from left to right, as Crook's men pressed the attack. Only darkness and some stubborn Confederate units prevented the defeat from becoming annihilation. Early lost 12 cannons and about 1,200 men, mostly taken **prisoners**, while Sheridan counted only 456 casualties. The victory would have been much more complete, but Torbert's cavalry failed to get into position to cut off Early's line of retreat. The disaster at Fisher's Hill, coupled with Early's earlier defeat at Third Winchester, began a pattern of defeat for the Confederates in the Valley.

FISHING CREEK, KENTUCKY, BATTLE OF (JANUARY 19, 1862).
See MILL SPRINGS, KENTUCKY, BATTLE OF.

FISK, CLINTON BOWEN (1828–1890) USA. Born in **New York**, Fisk
moved to **Michigan** as an infant. He became an **abolitionist** and a successful businessman and banker but was ruined by the Panic of 1857.
Moving to **Missouri**, Fisk worked as an insurance salesman until the
Civil War.

Fisk was said to have joined the pro-Union Missouri militia and in
May 1861 supposedly participated in the capture of **Camp Jackson**. The
first official record of his service, however, is found in September 1862
when he was appointed colonel of the 33rd Missouri (Union). After
forming a **brigade**, Fisk was promoted to brigadier general of volunteers
in November. He remained in Missouri and **Arkansas** for the entire war,
mostly fighting Confederate guerrillas and cavalry raiders. From July
1863 to May 1865, Fisk commanded at various times the **districts** of
Southeastern Missouri, St. Louis, and Northern Missouri. His greatest
contribution to the war effort was during **Sterling Price's 1864 Missouri
Raid**. At that time, Fisk removed pro-Confederate militiamen from his
ranks and helped defeat Price. For his war service, he was **brevetted** major general of volunteers in March 1865.

After the war, Fisk became assistant commissioner of the **Freedmen's
Bureau** and opened a school for **freedmen** in Nashville, **Tennessee**,
which became Fisk University. A reformer, he also was the unsuccessful
1888 presidential candidate for the Prohibition Party.

FIVE FORKS, VIRGINIA, BATTLE OF (APRIL 1, 1865). On March
25, 1865, during the latter part of the **Petersburg Campaign**, **Robert E.
Lee** made an unsuccessful attempt to break out of the siege by attacking
Fort Stedman with his **Army of Northern Virginia**. Correctly guessing that Lee had weakened other parts of his line to make this effort,
U. S. Grant counterattacked with the **Army of the Potomac** by sending
a massive force toward **Dinwiddie Court House** to turn Lee's right
flank. To carry out the mission, **Philip Sheridan** was given three cavalry
divisions and the support of two infantry **corps**. Lee responded by shifting Maj. Gen. **George E. Pickett** and 19,000 men to that flank.

Heavy fighting erupted around Dinwiddie Court House on March 31,
1865, and the Confederates at first were able to stall Sheridan's 50,000
men. The situation was critical, however, and Lee ordered Pickett to hold
the flank "at all hazards." Pickett found himself in a precarious position,
posted three miles beyond Lee's right flank without any support. Only
one small cavalry **brigade** and one dismounted **regiment** guarded this

gap. Pickett positioned his main force of five infantry brigades in an entrenched line around a road junction known as Five Forks. Major General **W. H. F. "Rooney" Lee's** cavalry division was placed on his right flank.

Meanwhile, Sheridan planned to attack Pickett's main line with his three cavalry divisions, while Maj. Gen. **Gouverneur K. Warren's** V Corps crushed the Confederate left flank. Sheridan attacked on April 1 with the mostly dismounted cavalry divisions of **George A. Custer** and **Thomas C. Devin**, but Warren was late getting into action and did not begin his attack until about 4:00 P.M. Despite the danger they were in and the certain knowledge that Sheridan would renew his attack that day, Pickett and Lee were absent from their commands, attending a shad bake in the rear.

On Sheridan's right, Warren discovered that the Confederate line did not extend across his front as expected; instead, he was moving into the gap between Pickett and Robert E. Lee. When his flank came under heavy fire from Pickett's **refused** left flank, Warren had his left flank turn to charge the Confederate works, and then he rode after the rest of his corps to turn it in the right direction. Sheridan was on the scene at the time and finding Warren absent from the fighting, relieved him of command. By that time, Pickett had rejoined his command and had begun shifting forces to his threatened left. But it was too little, too late. Two V Corps divisions got into Pickett's rear, and Devin's cavalry charged over his front line. The Confederates were routed and fled to the rear, losing several cannons and thousands of **prisoners**.

In the disaster, Pickett lost more than 5,000 men, mostly prisoners, while Sheridan reported 1,111 casualties. Five Forks was the beginning of the end for Lee. Having turned the Confederate right flank, Grant launched an all-out attack the next day that broke Lee's line and forced him to evacuate Petersburg and **Richmond** in what was the beginning of the **Appomattox Campaign**. Lee relieved Pickett of command a few days later, whereas Warren was eventually cleared of misconduct by a court of inquiry.

FIXED AMMUNITION. This was **artillery** ammunition in which the shell and powder charge were fixed into one piece for ease and speed of loading. Also, it could be ensured that the shell's **fuse** always pointed forward so that it would ignite at the proper time. A fused shell was lit when the muzzle blast enveloped the shell as it came out of the barrel. If pointed incorrectly, it would light as soon as the cannon was fired—inside the barrel. Some round shells—such as **solid shot**—also had a wooden disk called a **sabot** attached to its base by metal or leather bands. It served much like a bullet patch in a muzzle-loading **rifle**, making the shell fit tightly in the cannon tube for better projection and accuracy.

FLAGS. Both sides used a variety of flags in the Civil War, and they were very important to a unit's pride and identity. In addition to a national flag, a regimental flag was also used. This often was similar to the national flag, but it had the regimental name printed on it, as well as the names of battles in which the **regiment** had fought. **Company** flags bearing the company's name also were used, more often early in the war, since they usually were not replaced when worn out. State flags, **corps** flags, and **guidons** also were used, and some Irish-dominated units carried Irish flags. Company and corps flags were of different styles, each unique in its wording, color, and symbols. *See also* FLAGS, CONFEDERATE.

FLAGS, CONFEDERATE. The Confederate nation developed two basic **flags**, the national flag and the battle flag, and many people confuse the latter for the former. The first national flag, nicknamed the "Stars and Bars," was designed by Nicola Marschall and was adopted in March 1861. It consisted of three wide horizontal bars, with the upper and lower being red and the middle being white. In the upper corner was a blue square with seven white stars in a circle to represent the original seven seceding states. This flag proved impractical because it so closely resembled the U.S. flag and caused confusion in battle. A second national flag was adopted in May 1863. Nicknamed the "Stainless Banner," it had a white background, with the Confederate battle flag in the upper corner. This flag also caused problems because it appeared to be a surrender flag during calm wind. Thus in March 1865, a third national flag was approved. This flag was the same as the second national flag but with a wide red stripe arranged vertically on the end.

The original Confederate battle flag was designed by Gens. **P. G. T. Beauregard** and **Joseph E. Johnston** after the **First Battle of Manassas** because of the confusion certain flags caused there. It was patterned after a design that had been rejected for the national flag. This battle flag had a blue St. Andrew's Cross, with a narrow white border, arranged on a red background. Within the cross were 13 white stars, representing the 11 seceded states, plus **Kentucky** and **Missouri** (which had created Confederate governments). Although this flag never was made an official flag by the **Confederate Congress**, it became the most famous of all the Southern flags. Its use spread to the western theater in 1862 when Beauregard and Johnston took it with them when they transferred there.

FLANAGIN, HARRIS (1817–1874) CSA. Born in **New Jersey**, Flanagin moved to **Arkansas** as a young man and opened a law practice. He was elected as a **Democrat** to the state legislature in 1842 but only served one term before returning to his practice. In 1861, Flanagin was a delegate to the state secession convention, where he voted against **secession**.

When the Civil War began, Flanagin entered Confederate service in July 1861 as a captain in the 2nd Arkansas Mounted Rifles. After fighting at **Wilson's Creek** and **Pea Ridge**, he was promoted to colonel in May 1862 and transferred to Knoxville, Tennessee. There, Flanagin learned that the Arkansas legislature had elected him governor. As a result, he resigned his commission in November 1862, returned to Arkansas, and was sworn in as governor later that month.

Flanagin's term as war governor was made more difficult by Union occupation and a nearly bankrupt treasury. Still, he did his best to maintain state troops, encourage agriculture and manufacturing, and provide for those who lived in areas hardest hit by the war. Flanagin remained in office at **Little Rock** even after Union troops captured the city in September 1863. Afterward, he cooperated in establishing a state government that the Union government would accept but then left office in April 1864 when Unionist Isaac Murphy was sworn in as governor. When the Confederacy collapsed in 1865, Flanagin met with Confederate officials from other **Trans-Mississippi Department** states to discuss the possibility of the **department** making a separate peace with the Union. Nothing came of this, however, and Flanagin returned to his law practice.

FLANKING POSITION. This is a military term having both a strategic and tactical meaning. Strategically, it is when one force takes up a position from which it can threaten the enemy's flank if the enemy advances. Tactically, it is when a defender places part of his force on a flank, perpendicular to the main line. When the enemy attacks the main line, the force in the flanking position can **enfilade** the attackers as they advance. At **Second Manassas**, Confederate Lt. Gen. **James Longstreet's corps** was placed in a flanking position to enfilade **John Pope's army** as it attacked **Stonewall Jackson's** line. *See also* STRATEGY; TACTICS.

FLEETWOOD HILL, VIRGINIA, BATTLE OF (JUNE 9, 1863). *See* BRANDY STATION, VIRGINIA, BATTLE OF.

FLETCHER, THOMAS (1819–1900) CSA. Born in **Tennessee**, Fletcher practiced law after graduating from the University of Tennessee and then moved to **Mississippi**. After serving as a probate judge and a U.S. marshal, he moved to **Arkansas** in 1850. There, Fletcher was elected to the state senate in 1858 and served as its president three times. When Gov. **Henry M. Rector** resigned in November 1862 after being defeated for reelection by **Harris Flanagin**, Fletcher was sworn in as a temporary governor. He served only 11 days before Flanagin arrived to assume the position. Fletcher then returned to the senate and served there until it was replaced by a loyal government in April 1864.

FLORIDA. Although a relatively quiet area militarily in the Civil War, Florida nonetheless played an important role. It was carried by **John C. Breckinridge** during the **election of 1860** and became one of the original seceding states when it left the Union on January 10, 1861, by a convention vote of 62–7.

During the war, Florida provided about 15,000 soldiers (one-third of whom died) to the Confederacy out of a white population of only 77,746. Such Confederate leaders as **Stephen Mallory**, **William W. Loring**, **Edmund Kirby Smith**, and **Joseph Finegan** hailed from the state. It also is estimated that about 1,200 whites, and nearly as many blacks, served in the Union forces. Florida was a popular location for **blockade runners**, and it also provided to the Confederacy such valuable supplies as cattle, hogs, and salt.

Military activity in the state included Gov. **Madison S. Perry** ordering the seizure of St. Augustine's Fort Marion and the Pensacola Naval Yard in early 1861. Union forces kept control of **Fort Pickens** at **Pensacola**, and it became a center of activity early in the war, as well as Forts Jefferson and Taylor. The largest Florida battle of the war occurred at **Olustee** in February 1864.

FLORIDA, CSS. This was the first **commerce raider** built overseas for the Confederacy and was a sister ship to the more famous *Alabama*. Secretly constructed in Great Britain as the *Oreto*, it was a 192-foot-long, steam-powered wooden ship that displaced 700 tons and had a propeller that could be lifted out of the water when under sail. In March 1862, the *Oreto* was manned by a British crew and was taken out of Liverpool to Nassau. There, the ship was met by its first Confederate commander, Lt. **John N. Maffitt**. Maffitt departed Nassau in August, armed the ship with two 7-inch and six 6-inch **Blakely rifles**, and renamed it the *Florida*.

During its career, the *Florida* sank or captured 37 enemy ships. In October 1864, it docked in Bahia, Brazil, not far from the **USS *Wachusett***. Despite being in a neutral port, the crew of the Union vessel waited until most of the Confederates were ashore and then in the predawn hours of October 7 rammed the *Florida*, boarded it, and towed it to sea. While Brazil protested this violation of international law, the *Florida* was taken to Hampton Roads, Virginia. The United States eventually agreed to return the ship and its captured crew to Brazil, but before it could do so, the *Florida* was suspiciously rammed by a transport and sank. The United States apologized to Brazil, but it was obvious that the sinking had been intentional.

FLOYD, JOHN BUCHANAN (1806–1863) CSA. Born in **Virginia**, Floyd was the son of a former congressman and governor. After graduating first in his class at South Carolina College, he practiced law in Virginia and then moved to **Arkansas**. Floyd worked as a lawyer and planter there for a time, but he finally returned to Virginia and in 1847 was elected to the legislature as a **Democrat**. Elected governor in 1848, he constructed new **railroads** and worked to expand the right to vote. After leaving office, Floyd again was elected to the legislature in 1855. In 1857, he was recognized as one of the nation's leading Democrats and was appointed secretary of war by President **James Buchanan**. As tensions mounted in 1860, Floyd's loyalty was questioned when he began transferring large quantities of arms and ammunition to Southern arsenals. He resigned his post in late December to protest Buchanan's decision to hold **Fort Sumter**, but Floyd continued to serve until Buchanan chose a replacement.

Floyd had opposed **secession** up to the firing on Fort Sumter, but then he came to favor it. He raised a Virginia **brigade** of volunteers and in May 1861 was commissioned brigadier general of Confederate troops. Serving in western Virginia under **Robert E. Lee**, Floyd took command of the **Army of the Kanawha** in August and fought at **Carnifex Ferry**. After fighting more **skirmishes** in the mountainous terrain, he was transferred westward in December and took command of Fort Donelson, Tennessee.

In February 1862, Floyd was besieged by **U. S. Grant** in the **Forts Henry and Donelson Campaign**. He boldly attacked and was successfully cutting his way out of the trap, when he stopped and timidly withdrew back into the fort. At a meeting on the night of February 15, Floyd agreed with Brig. Gen. **Simon B. Buckner** that surrender was the only option. Being a former cabinet member, however, he feared he might be hanged as a traitor if captured. Floyd therefore turned command over to his subordinate, and he and his Virginia brigade escaped by steamer on the Tennessee River. Shortly afterward, Floyd abandoned Nashville, Tennessee, to the enemy after attempting to withdraw some of its supplies. Because of his poor performance, he was relieved of command in March. Unable to gain any Confederate assignment, Floyd returned to Virginia and was commissioned a major general of state troops. He raised some **partisan ranger** troops and was active in southwestern Virginia, but the constant exposure and exhaustion broke his health, and he died on August 26, 1863.

FLYING BATTERY. This term, although not an official designation, was used to describe very mobile **artillery**. Popularized in the **U.S. Army** during the **Mexican War**, it was a horse-drawn gun or guns that rapidly advanced, unlimbered, opened fire, and then limbered up again to move somewhere else. It was particularly effective in keeping the enemy off balance, because the enemy often could not tell how many artillery pieces were being used.

FLYING TELEGRAPH TRAIN. Used briefly in the spring of 1862, this was a highly mobile Union **telegraph** system designed by **Albert J. Myer**. Each "train" consisted of two wagons carrying two **Beardslee Telegraphs** and enough accompanying equipment to string five miles of telegraph wire. The train moved with the **army** and provided constant telegraph service between different areas. The Beardslee relied on a hand-cranked magneto for power, however, and had a range of only about five miles. When it was replaced by the standard battery telegraph in 1863, the Flying Telegraph Train was obsolete since the standard telegraph's range was greatly increased and came to use permanent wires. The Flying Telegraph Train then became just a standard telegraph train.

"FOOT CAVALRY." This was the nickname given to the Confederate infantry of **Thomas J. "Stonewall" Jackson**. During his celebrated 1862 **Shenandoah Valley Campaign**, Jackson's men sometimes marched 30 miles a day because of his standing orders of marching 50 minutes and resting 10. By mid-1862, the men of Jackson's II Corps, **Army of Northern Virginia**, were recognized as being among the swiftest of the Confederate troops.

FOOTE, ANDREW HULL (1806–1863) USA. A native of **Connecticut**, Foote dropped out of **West Point** in 1822 to enter the **U.S. Navy** as a midshipman. He earned an outstanding reputation while serving around the world and once while in China during the 1850s successfully attacked a much superior Chinese force that fired on American ships.

Commodore Foote was given command of the Union naval forces on the upper Mississippi River in August 1861. While cooperating with **U. S. Grant** in the **Forts Henry and Donelson Campaign**, his ships bombarded and captured Fort Henry, Tennessee, in February 1862. Foote then joined Grant for the attack on Fort Donelson. There his boats were badly shot up by the Confederates, and Foote was wounded in the foot by wood splinters, but the fort soon surrendered to Grant. While still on crutches,

Foote next joined Maj. Gen. **John Pope** for the operation against **Island No. 10** and in March 1862 unsuccessfully attacked the island with 17 ships. Afterward, he successfully ran two ships past the island and worked with Pope to trap the Confederates and force their surrender in April.

In poor health, Foote was forced to relinquish his command to Capt. **Charles H. Davis**. He was promoted to rear admiral in June 1862, received the **Thanks of Congress**, and was placed in command of the Bureau of Equipment and Recruiting. Unhappy with this administrative job, Foote succeeded in getting placed in command of the **South Atlantic Blockading Squadron** in June 1863, but he died from Bright's disease while en route to assume his new duties.

FOOTE, HENRY STUART (1804–1880) CSA. A native of **Virginia**, Foote practiced law in **Richmond, Virginia**, before moving first to **Alabama** and then **Mississippi**. In Mississippi, he was a popular attorney and in 1847 was elected to the U.S. Senate, where he clashed with fellow Mississippian Sen. **Jefferson Davis** over **secession**. Elected governor in 1853, Foote resigned his position in 1854 over continued disputes with the state's secessionists. After living in **California** for a while, he moved to **Tennessee** in 1858.

During the secession crisis, Foote first opposed secession but like many Unionists, embraced it after **Fort Sumter** was fired on. After Tennessee seceded, he was elected to the **Confederate Congress** despite his reputation as an outspoken Unionist and there made bitter political enemies. Foote was an ill-tempered, eccentric, and exasperating man who initiated at least 30 inquiries into government operations and consistently opposed such war measures as **conscription** and the **suspension of the writ of habeas corpus**. One fellow congressman tried to stab him on the floor with a Bowie knife, another did stab him with an umbrella, he came to blows with still another congressman, and was threatened with death by a newspaper editor. Despite being such a thorn in the side of the Davis administration, Foote was reelected by his constituents.

Just months before the war ended, Foote attempted to open his own private negotiations with the Union government but was captured by his own people before he could get across the lines. An attempt to expel him from Congress failed, and soon Foote succeeded in getting to **Washington, D.C.**, but **Abraham Lincoln** refused to deal with him.

After the war ended, Foote traveled to Europe rather than returning home. When he did finally return, he was befriended by President **U. S. Grant** and was appointed superintendent of the U.S. Mint in **New Orleans, Louisiana**.

FORAGING. Foraging was the gathering of supplies from the surrounding countryside by an **army**. It sometimes was done under orders and was supervised by an officer, especially early in the war, with civilians being given receipts for goods taken. The receipts later could be turned in to army quartermasters for reimbursement. However, foraging often was carried out by individual soldiers operating outside lawful bounds and was little more than looting. This especially was true later as war conditions worsened. *See also* BUMMERS.

FORBES, EDWIN (1839–1895) USA. A native of **New York**, Forbes specialized in animal art when he studied at the National Academy of Design. In 1862, he was hired as a **war correspondent** by *Frank Leslie's Illustrated Newspaper* and accompanied the Union armies in **Virginia** from **Stonewall Jackson's 1862 Shenandoah Valley Campaign** through **Jubal Early's 1864 Washington Raid**. Forbes was interested in illustrating not only battles scenes but everyday camp life, as well. In 1876, he published a collection of his copperplate etchings in *Life Studies of the Great Army* and in 1890 produced a two-volume work that was reprinted in 1993 as *Thirty Years After: An Artist's Memoir of the Civil War*. A stroke in the 1890s restricted Forbes to working with his left hand, but he continued to illustrate for numerous books. He was probably the best-known illustrator of the war.

FORCE, MANNING FERGUSON (1824–1899) USA. A native of **Washington, D.C.**, Force graduated from Harvard University and Harvard Law School. After moving to **Ohio** in 1850 and opening a law practice, he entered Union service in August 1861 as major of the 20th Ohio.

In September 1861, Force was promoted to lieutenant colonel. After fighting at **Fort Donelson**, he commanded the **regiment** at **Shiloh** and **Corinth**. Promoted to colonel in May 1862, he was given command of a **brigade** in the **Army of the Mississippi** XVII Corps during the **Vicksburg Campaign** and fought at **Raymond**, **Jackson**, and in the **Vicksburg** siege. Force had a splendid war record at the end of the Vicksburg Campaign and was promoted to brigadier general of volunteers in August 1863. He led a brigade in the **Meridian Campaign** before heading to **Georgia** to fight in the **Atlanta Campaign** in June 1864. At the **Battle of Atlanta**, Force was so severely wounded in the face and disfigured that at first he was thought to be mortally wounded. He recovered, however, and led his brigade in the **March to the Sea** and commanded a **division** in the **Carolinas Campaign**.

In 1866, Force was **brevetted** major general of volunteers for the Battle of Atlanta and in 1892 was awarded the **Medal of Honor** for his gallant actions there. He left the **army** in January 1866 and returned to his

Ohio law practice. Force went on to serve as a judge and congressman and was a well-known writer of history, archaeology, and law.

FORD'S THEATER. The **Washington, D.C.**, theater in which **Abraham Lincoln** was shot on April 14, 1865, was bought by John Thomas Ford in 1861. The building, located on 10th Street, originally had been built in 1833–34 and was used as a church until 1855. Ford opened a theater in the building and named it Ford's Atheneum, but it burned in 1862. The new Ford's Theater was built in 1863 and could hold nearly 1,700 people. It became one of Washington's leading theaters, and Lincoln attended several plays there. The night he was shot, a sold-out crowd was present watching *Our American Cousin*. Federal authorities closed the theater after **Lincoln's assassination**.

FOREIGN-BORN SOLDIERS. It is estimated that more than 500,000 foreign-born men served in the Civil War, with a larger number serving in the Union armies because the North had more large cities, which attracted immigrants. Hundreds of thousands of Irish and Germans immigrated to the United States during the 1840s because of European revolutions and the Irish potato famine. They settled in large numbers in New York City, **New York**; Philadelphia, **Pennsylvania**; Chicago, **Illinois**; and **New Orleans, Louisiana**. When war came, these immigrants joined the service for various reasons. Many volunteered out of patriotism for their adopted homes and to demonstrate their loyalty publicly. Some were suffering economic difficulties and enlisted as a means of securing food, clothing, and shelter. Still others only volunteered to get the **bounties** that were offered, while many others served as **conscripts**.

Numerous **regiments** were made up nearly entirely of foreign-born men, and language barriers sometimes made it difficult to assimilate them into the **army**. In the **Confederate army**, for example, some of the units formed in New Orleans were drilled entirely in French. Such units as the Union army's **Irish Brigade** and the Confederate's **Louisiana Tigers** became famous for their foreign makeup and fighting ability. Some of the more notable foreign-born officers were **Thomas F. Meagher**; **Franz Sigel**; **Carl Schurz**; **Patrick Cleburne**; and **Camille Armand Jules Marie, Prince de Polignac**.

FORNEY, JOHN HORACE (1829–1902) CSA. The brother of Confederate Brig. Gen. **William Henry Forney**, Forney was a native of **North Carolina** but grew up in **Alabama**. He graduated from **West Point** in 1852 and served on routine garrison duty, in the **Utah Expedition**, and as an instructor of infantry tactics at the academy.

In January 1861, Forney resigned his 1st lieutenant's commission and was appointed colonel of Alabama's 1st Regiment of Artillery. Sent to **Pensacola, Florida**, he trained troops, supervised the construction of defenses, and became **Braxton Bragg's** acting inspector general. Appointed captain of Confederate **artillery** in March, Forney was soon promoted to colonel of the 10th Alabama in June (his brother served as one of his captains). Sent to **Virginia**, he assumed command of a **brigade**. After being severely wounded in the right arm at **Dranesville** in December (where his brother was wounded in the shin), Forney was appointed a brigadier general in March 1862, but he had to take leave to recover from his wound.

In April 1862, Forney was put in command of the **Department of Alabama and West Florida**. Promoted to major general in October, he remained in Mobile, Alabama, until poor health forced him to give up his post in December. Forney had recovered by spring 1863 and led a **division** during the **Vicksburg Campaign**. After the city's surrender, he commanded the **parole** camps in **Mississippi** and Alabama until the **prisoners** had been **exchanged**. In May 1864, Forney was sent to the **Trans-Mississippi Department**, where he took command of **John G. Walker's** Texas division in September. His division served in **Arkansas, Louisiana**, and **Texas** before disbanding in May 1865 upon learning of the **department's** impending **surrender**.

After the war, Forney returned to Alabama and became a planter and civil engineer.

FORNEY, WILLIAM HENRY (1823–1894) CSA. The brother of Confederate Maj. Gen. **John Horace Forney**, Forney was a native of **North Carolina**, but he moved to **Alabama** as a boy. There he became a lawyer, served in the **Mexican War** as a 1st lieutenant, and was elected to the state legislature in the 1850s.

Forney entered Confederate service in June 1861 as a captain in the 10th Alabama, his younger brother's **regiment**. Sent to **Virginia**, he was wounded in the shin at **Dranesville** in December, while his brother was wounded in the arm. In January 1862, Forney was promoted to major and in May to lieutenant colonel. He was severely wounded in the right shoulder at **Williamsburg** and was taken **prisoner**. While in **prison**, Forney was promoted to colonel in June. After being **exchanged** in August 1862, he was unable to retake the field because of his wound and served on various courts and boards until joining the **Army of Northern Virginia** for the **Chancellorsville Campaign**. At **Salem Church**, Forney rallied his retreating men but was slightly wounded again in the leg. He next led his regiment at **Gettysburg** and during the fighting on the second day along the Emmitsburg Road, was shot four times, two bullets striking him in the arm and chest, one rebreaking his right arm, and another tearing off part of his heel. Left behind in a hospital, Forney was captured again. After being exchanged in August, he returned to his regiment in November at Petersburg and led the **brigade** in the **Petersburg Campaign**. With **Robert E. Lee's** support, he was appointed to brigadier general in February 1865 and served with Lee's **army** until the **surrender**. Forney was said to have been wounded 13 times in the war.

After the war, Forney opened an Alabama law practice and served in the **U.S. Congress** from 1875 to 1893.

FORREST, FRENCH (1796–1866) CSA. A native of **Maryland**, Forrest entered the **U.S. Navy** in 1811 as a midshipman. After serving at the Battle of Lake Erie in the War of 1812, he rose to the rank of captain and commanded his own ship in the **Mexican War**.

Forrest resigned his commission when **Virginia** seceded in 1861 and was appointed captain in the Virginia state navy. He entered Confederate service in June when he was appointed captain in the **Confederate navy**. Ranking third in naval seniority, Forrest was put in command of the **Norfolk, Virginia**, Navy Yard and supervised construction of the **CSS** *Virginia*. In June 1862, he was removed from command after being slow in repairing the **ironclad** following the **Battle of Hampton Roads**. Forrest then was put in command of the Office of Orders and Details. In March 1863, he finally received an active command when he was put in charge of the James River Squadron. Forrest's service was lackluster, and he was replaced in May 1864. It appears that he then was dropped from the navy's rolls.

FORREST, NATHAN BEDFORD (1821–1877) CSA. Born to a poor **Tennessee** family, Forrest grew up to become a wealthy planter and what **Robert E. Lee** called the most talented general of the Civil War. His family moved to northern **Mississippi** when he was 13, and when his father died three years later, Forrest assumed responsibility for the family. When he was 21, Forrest entered business with an uncle, and when the uncle was murdered, Forrest killed the murderer. After marrying, Forrest moved to Memphis, Tennessee, and became a prosperous trader in cotton, land, and slaves. Becoming a wealthy man, he bought two north Mississippi plantations and in 1858 was elected a Memphis alderman. Forrest resigned his position in 1859 and abandoned his business enterprises to become a Mississippi planter.

Forrest entered Confederate service in June 1861 as a private in a Tennessee volunteer **company**. Soon, the governor authorized him to raise a battalion of mounted troops. Forrest did so at his own expense and in October was elected lieutenant colonel of Forrest's Tennessee Cavalry Battalion. An imposing figure at six feet, two inches tall, Forrest shaped his command into an efficient fighting unit. At **Fort Donelson** in February 1862, his cavalry played an important role when the defenders launched a counterattack to cut their way out of the siege. When the opportunity was lost, and his superiors decided to surrender, Forrest became outraged and secured permission to lead his cavalry out of the doomed fort in a legendary nighttime ride across frozen backwater.

In March 1862, Forrest's command was reorganized as the 3rd Tennessee Cavalry, and in April he was elected colonel. At **Shiloh**, his **regiment** performed valuable service and formed the rear guard when the Confederates retreated. During one **skirmish**, Forrest was severely wounded, but he managed to escape by grabbing a shocked Union soldier and using him as a shield.

Forrest was given command of a cavalry **brigade** in June 1862. He and his "critter cavalry" raided Murfreesboro, Tennessee, in July and captured 1,200 **prisoners**. Promoted to brigadier general that month, he participated in the 1862 **Kentucky Campaign** before being relieved of command and allowed to raise another brigade in Middle Tennessee. From December 1862 to January 1863, this new brigade wreaked havoc in western Tennessee on another one of **Forrest's Tennessee Raids**. In March 1863, he and **Earl Van Dorn** captured 2,500 prisoners at **Thompson's Station, Tennessee**, and in April and May, Forrest pursued and captured the Federals involved in **Abel Streight's Raid** in northern **Alabama**. During the **Tullahoma** and **Chickamauga Campaigns**, Forrest commanded two cavalry **divisions** in the **Army of Tennessee**, and he was promoted to major general in December 1863.

Sent to defend northern Mississippi, Forrest won a stunning victory at **Okolona** over a superior enemy force in February 1864 and then raided **Kentucky**. The most controversial moment of his career came in April 1864 when he attacked **Fort Pillow, Tennessee**, which was garrisoned mostly by **black troops**. In the attack, many blacks were **massacred**, and Forrest was accused of ordering the murders. Evidence indicates that while many black soldiers undoubtedly were murdered, it probably was the result of individual acts of brutality and not by Forrest's orders. However, one of Forrest's own officers claimed to have once witnessed the general murder an unarmed free black while in a rage, so whether Forrest did all he could to avoid the massacre is open to debate.

Forrest returned to Mississippi and in June won perhaps his greatest victory at **Brice's Cross Roads**. He was defeated at **Tupelo** in July while serving under **Stephen D. Lee** and again was wounded in a skirmish at Oldtown Creek. An August raid on Memphis was followed by another into Middle Tennessee in September that netted 2,600 prisoners. That autumn Forrest struck the Tennessee River at **Johnsonville** and actually captured several gunboats with his cavalry and destroyed more than $2 million of property and supplies. He led the Confederate invasion during the **Franklin and Nashville Campaign** that November and unsuccessfully proposed to **John Bell Hood** a **flanking** maneuver against the Union position at **Franklin** rather than launching the suicidal **frontal attack**. After Franklin, Forrest raided Murfreesboro, Tennessee, and then played a critical role in forming the rear guard during the retreat from the Battle of Nashville.

In March 1865, Forrest was promoted to lieutenant general and fought his last campaign trying to stop **James H. Wilson's Selma**, **Alabama**, **Raid**. After his outnumbered cavalry was defeated at Selma in April, Forrest surrendered his command in May.

After the war, Forrest returned to his Mississippi plantation and in 1867 was elected Grand Wizard of the Ku Klux Klan. He then returned to Memphis and worked in insurance and railroading until his death. Forrest was excitable, profane, and a man of action. He threatened to strike his commander **Braxton Bragg** in one dispute and was knifed by one of his own officers in another. Yet Forrest proved to be one of the most remarkable generals of the war. He had 29 horses shot from under him, killed 30 enemy soldiers in combat, and was wounded four times. Two quotes attributed to him summed up his style of warfare: "War means fightin' and fightin' means killing" and "Get there fustest with the mostest." Known as "that devil Forrest" by his enemies, he was recognized by Lee to have been the best general of the war.

FORREST'S TENNESSEE RAIDS. Confederate cavalry leader **Nathan Bedford Forrest** proved to be one of the best raiders of the Civil War. He launched numerous forays into enemy territory, but three stand out. On July 9, 1862, while a colonel, Forrest left the Chattanooga, Tennessee, area with his **regiment** and rendezvoused with five additional **companies** at McMinnville, Tennessee. With these 1,400 men, he raided Murfreesboro, Tennessee, on July 13. There, Forrest divided his command into three columns and launched attacks against two Union encampments outside of town and the town itself. The fighting was hard, and Forrest finally resorted to trickery to force the garrison's surrender. He told one Union detachment that if he were forced to attack again he would take no **prisoners**. Forrest allowed another Union officer to view his cavalrymen, which he was riding around in circles through an opening to give the appearance of a large force. Both officers quickly surrendered. In this raid, the Confederates rode 50 miles in fewer than 15 hours, inflicted 149 casualties on the defenders, and captured 1,200 prisoners, some **artillery**, and $1 million in weapons and supplies at a cost of fewer than 100 casualties.

In December 1862, Forrest led another successful raid into **Tennessee** with 2,100 men to disrupt **U. S. Grant's railroad** supply line during **Grant's Overland Vicksburg Campaign** through northern **Mississippi**. Forrest crossed the Tennessee River at Clifton, Tennessee, on December 15–17 but was discovered by Union scouts. Grant dispatched Col. Robert G. Ingersoll's cavalry to confront the raiders, and heavy fighting erupted on December 18 around **Lexington**. Ingersoll was defeated and captured, along with 149 of his men, two cannons, and 300 **rifles**. On December 19, Forrest rode to Jackson, damaged the railroads in that area, and **paroled** his 1,200 prisoners. The Confederates then moved on to Union City and continued destroying railroads across the **Kentucky** border. After remaining in Union City December 23–25, Forrest left on Christmas Day and rode to the southeast, but flooded rivers impeded his progress. He was forced to fight off Union pursuers at **Parker's Cross Roads** on December 31 but made it back to Lexington. After further **skirmishes**, Forrest finally crossed back over the Tennessee River at Clifton on January 1, 1863. In the raid, he captured approximately 1,500 prisoners and a large quantity of arms and wrecked the vital Mississippi Central and the Mobile & Ohio Railroads. His losses were about 500 men. Forrest's raid, along with that of **Earl Van Dorn** at **Holly Springs, Mississippi**, forced Grant to abandon the Vicksburg Overland Campaign.

Forrest's third Tennessee raid began on October 19, 1863, from **Corinth, Mississippi**. After riding to Paris, Tennessee, with about 3,500 men, he turned to the east and reached Paris Landing on the Tennessee River on October 28. Forrest took up a concealed position near Fort Heiman from which to attack Union shipping and managed to capture one gunboat and one steamer. He then proceeded downriver on November 1 to the important Union supply base at **Johnsonville**. Again taking up a concealed position across the river, Forrest opened fire with his **artillery** on November 4 and devastated the base. Eighteen ships and 20 barges were destroyed, along with $2.2–$6.7 million of property and supplies. It was this raid that prompted **William T. Sherman** to brand the Confederate raider "that devil Forrest."

FORT ANDERSON, NORTH CAROLINA, BATTLE OF (MARCH 13–15, 1863). *See* NEW BERN, NORTH CAROLINA, RAIDS ON.

FORT BEAUREGARD, LOUISIANA.

Fort Beauregard was a small Confederate fort located on a high hill overlooking the Ouachita (WASH-uh-taw) River just north of Harrisonburg, Louisiana. During the war, it was the scene of several small clashes with Union ships. In May 1863, the fort stopped four Union gunboats from ascending the river in search of the Confederate gunboats *Webb* and *Queen of the West*. On September 4, 1863, the fort was abandoned by its garrison as a large Union column approached Harrisonburg.

FORT BISLAND, LOUISIANA, BATTLE OF (APRIL 12–13, 1863).

In the spring of 1863, Union Maj. Gen. **Nathaniel P. Banks** was preparing his **Port Hudson, Louisiana, Campaign**. Before laying siege to that stronghold, however, he planned a **Bayou Teche Campaign** to clear that region of Maj. Gen. **Richard Taylor's** approximately 5,000 Confederate troops. Such a move would remove enemy forces from Banks's flank while he was at Port Hudson and would deny the Confederates one of their main bases of supply.

Banks took his main force to Brashear City, Louisiana, and began moving up Bayou Teche in early April. Meanwhile, another column under Brig. Gen. **Cuvier Grover** was taken by transport across Grand Lake to cut off the Confederate line of retreat near Franklin. Confederate Brig. Gen. **J. J. Alfred Mouton's division** arrived at Bisland Plantation, below Franklin, on April 10 and began constructing a line of entrenchments on the east side of Bayou Teche to support an existing line on the west side. Taylor assembled his command at this so-called Fort Bisland and placed the gunboat *Diana* to bolster the center of his line.

Banks arrived at Fort Bisland on April 12 and probed the position with **artillery** fire throughout the day. Sharp probes and **skirmish** fire continued throughout April 13. Taylor left Mouton in command there that night and hurried toward Franklin to oversee a small force that had been sent to the rear to stop Grover. Mouton evacuated Fort Bisland on the night of April 13 and joined Taylor. The next day, Taylor stopped Grover at **Irish Bend** and managed to extricate his small command from the entrapment. In the fighting at Fort Bisland, Banks lost 224 men. Taylor's losses are unknown.

FORT BLAKELY, ALABAMA, SIEGE OF (APRIL 2–9, 1865).

After seizing control of **Mobile Bay, Alabama**, in August 1864, the Federals turned their attention to the city itself in the 1865 **Mobile Campaign**.

Two of the most important Confederate defensive works were **Spanish Fort**, located on the bay's eastern side, and Fort Blakely, positioned on the Appalachee River on the bay's northern side. In March 1865, a concerted effort was made by the Federals to gain possession of Mobile by capturing these crucial fortifications.

On March 17, Maj. Gen. **E. R. S. Canby** sent the XIII Corps northward from the bay's entrance toward Spanish Fort, while a column of 13,000 men under Maj. Gen. **Frederick Steele** moved from **Pensacola, Florida**, to converge on Fort Blakely from the north. On April 1, Steele began siege operations against Brig. Gen. **St. John R. Liddell's** 8,000 Confederate defenders at Fort Blakely. Canby attacked Spanish Fort on April 8 and forced its defenders to evacuate to Mobile. He then concentrated 45,000 men of the XIII and XVI Corps against Fort Blakely. After digging approaches to within 500 yards of the fort, Canby launched an attack on the evening of April 9. The 16,000 attacking Union soldiers, including nine **regiments** of **black troops**, were forced to cross open ground, which had been obstructed with **abatis** and buried **torpedoes** connected to trip wires. Following an intense **artillery** barrage, the Federals were met by fierce musketry, but sheer numbers prevailed, and they overran the Confederate defenders in 20 minutes. About 3,200 Confederates and 40 cannons were captured, but the rest of the defenders escaped to Mobile. Canby lost 571 men. Mobile was evacuated by the Confederates on April 11 and surrendered to Canby the next day. The assault at Fort Blakely was the last significant combat of the Civil War and was one of the larger battles in which black troops participated. Its significance, however, was overshadowed by events that occurred at **Appomattox Court House, Virginia**, that same day.

FORT BLUNT, INDIAN TERRITORY. *See* FORT GIBSON, INDIAN TERRITORY.

FORT BUTLER, LOUISIANA, BATTLE OF (JUNE 28, 1863). Located at Donaldsonville, Louisiana, Fort Butler was a star-shaped fort, with a surrounding moat that had six cannons and was manned by 180 men, mostly from the 28th Maine. Confederate Maj. Gen. **Richard Taylor** was operating in the Bayou Teche (TESH) and Mississippi River areas in the summer of 1863 to disrupt Maj. Gen. **Nathaniel P. Banks's** lines of communications during the **Port Hudson Campaign**. As part of the operation, Taylor's subordinate Maj. Gen. **J. J. Alfred Mouton** ordered the Confederate cavalry **brigades** of Brig. Gen. **Thomas Green** and Col. **James P. Major** to attack Fort Butler and capture Donaldsonville.

The Confederates surrounded the fort in the predawn hours of June 28 and attacked. The Texans managed to reach the fort's parapet, but were unable to scale it to get inside. Fierce fighting raged into the morning, with bricks sometimes being thrown as weapons. After daylight, three Union gunboats arrived and finally forced the Confederates to withdraw after shelling their position. Green, who was in overall command, lost 261 men, while Union losses were reported at only 23.

FORT CLARK, NORTH CAROLINA, BATTLE OF (AUGUST 27–29, 1861). *See* HATTERAS INLET, NORTH CAROLINA, BATTLE OF.

FORT CLIFTON, VIRGINIA, BATTLE OF (MAY 9, 1864). *See* SWIFT CREEK AND FORT CLIFTON, VIRGINIA, BATTLE OF.

FORT DARLING, VIRGINIA, BATTLES OF (MAY 15, 1862, AND MAY 16, 1864). *See* DREWRY'S BLUFF, VIRGINIA, FIRST AND SECOND BATTLES OF.

FORT DELAWARE, DELAWARE. Fort Delaware, built to control shipping on the Delaware River, was a stone fort located on an island. It became one of the most notorious **prison** camps in the Civil War. The fort was first used to hold political and naval **prisoners** and then was used mostly as a way station for Confederate prisoners on their way to **City Point, Virginia**, for **exchange**. When the exchange system slowed in 1863, the fort came to be used as a regular prison camp. At its peak in 1864, Fort Delaware held approximately 9,200 prisoners in barracks designed to hold 5,000. Also, the ground was below the river level and thus remained damp and unhealthy, with some barracks actually sinking in the mud. Union surgeons condemned the prison's overcrowding and unsanitary conditions, but Union commissary general of prisons, Col. William Hoffman, refused to take action.

Besides being fed poor and scant food, prisoners also suffered from exposure, scurvy, and smallpox. A total of 2,436 prisoners died at Fort Delaware during the war, with 327 dying in September 1863 alone. Prisoners held commandant Brig. Gen. **Albin Francisco Schoepf**, a native of Hungary, responsible for the poor conditions and nicknamed him "General Terror." The fort's last prisoners were released in August 1865, but Fort Delaware continued to be used by the **U.S. Army**.

FORT DE RUSSY, LOUISIANA, BATTLE OF (MARCH 14, 1864). Fort De Russy was a Confederate fort located on the right bank of the Red River near its mouth. On May 4, 1863, **David Porter's** Union fleet attacked the fort before it was completed, damaged and drove off two

Confederate gunboats, and a few days later leveled the uncompleted earthworks.

The fort was rebuilt by the Confederates and was the scene of more combat a year later during the **Red River Campaign** when Porter transferred Brig. Gen. **A. J. Smith's** 10,000 men from **Vicksburg, Mississippi**, to Alexandria, Louisiana. After arriving at the mouth of the Red River, Porter and Smith learned that **Nathaniel P. Banks's** army was delayed by heavy rains on its march from **Baton Rouge, Louisiana**, and decided to capture Fort De Russy themselves.

Smith disembarked at Simmesport and marched toward the fort on March 14, 1864, while Porter took some of his gunboats up the Red River. Upon reaching the fort, Smith immediately put his men into line and attacked. Confederate Lt. Col. William Byrd had fewer than 400 defenders, and they were kept pinned down by Union **skirmishers'** fire while the attacking line rolled over the fort's defensive works. In the short action, Smith lost only 38 men, while the Confederates suffered the loss of 10 guns and 317 men, virtually all of whom were taken **prisoner**. The fall of Fort De Russy allowed Porter's fleet to continue to Alexandria, where it was met later by Banks's **army**.

FORT DONELSON, TENNESSEE, BATTLE OF (FEBRUARY 13–16, 1862). *See* FORTS HENRY AND DONELSON, TENNESSEE, CAMPAIGN AND BATTLES OF.

FORT FILLMORE, NEW MEXICO TERRITORY, CAPTURE OF (JULY 25–26, 1861). This Union fort, garrisoned by 700 men of the 7th U.S. Infantry, helped control the **New Mexico Territory**. In July 1861, Confederate Lt. Col. **John Baylor** led his 2nd Texas Mounted Rifles from San Antonio, Texas, to capture New Mexico in what became known as **Baylor's "Buffalo Hunt."** With only about 250 men, Baylor advanced to Fort Fillmore, but upon his arrival on July 25, the 700-man Union garrison under Maj. Isaac Lynde came out of the fort and demanded his surrender. A **skirmish** broke out, with the Federals gaining the upper hand, but the Federals withdrew for fear of being cut off. The garrison abandoned the fort that night and was captured on July 26 by Baylor's outnumbered command.

FORT FISHER, NORTH CAROLINA, BATTLE OF (DECEMBER 24, 1864–JANUARY 15, 1865). By late 1864, **Wilmington, North Carolina**, was the only major Confederate port still open to **blockade runners**. Its entrance was guarded by Fort Fisher, a large earthen fort located at the mouth of the Cape Fear River. Construction of the fort began in April 1861, and it eventually became the largest earthen fortification in the Confederacy. Located at the tip of a peninsula, Fort Fisher had earthworks nearly 500 yards long, running across the peninsula and then down the beach for about three-quarters of a mile, thus forming the shape of a 7. Reinforced with sandbags and **revetments**, the fort's walls were 20 feet high and 25 feet thick and were protected in front by minefields. Colonel William Lamb was placed in command of the fort, and by December 1864 he had 48 guns in place.

In September 1864, **U. S. Grant** ordered a combined force of 60 ships under Rear Adm. **David Porter** and a large infantry force under Maj. Gen. **Godfrey Weitzel** to capture Wilmington. The powerful political general Maj. Gen. **Benjamin F. Butler** outranked Weitzel and—much to Grant's chagrin—successfully demanded the commanding position. Before sailing, Butler was given specific orders by Grant to besiege the fort if it could not be taken by assault.

Butler left **Fort Monroe, Virginia**, on December 13 with transports carrying 6,500 men and two **artillery** batteries under Weitzel's command. Wilmington was in the Confederate **department** commanded by Gen. **Braxton Bragg**, but its defenses were commanded by Brig. Gen. **William H. C. Whiting**. Whiting had only 800 men inside the fort under Colonel Lamb. When **Robert E. Lee** became aware of the enemy move, he dispatched 6,100 men under Maj. Gen. **Robert Hoke** from **Petersburg, Virginia**, to reinforce the Wilmington defenses.

Butler planned to detonate a ship laden with 235 tons of powder within 300 yards of Fort Fisher to annihilate the Confederate defenses and then follow up the explosion with a naval bombardment and an infantry attack. Porter had the powder ship towed toward the fort on the night of December 23, but it grounded 800 yards off the beach. Because of poor coordination, Butler did not arrive off Fort Fisher until December 24 and was not in position to attack when Porter detonated the ship later that day. The explosion, however, was harmless, and the subsequent bombardment made no dent in Fort Fisher's defenses.

On Christmas Day, Butler landed 2,200 men on the peninsula north of Fort Fisher, and Porter renewed the bombardment. The Federals charged within 50 yards of the fort but were stopped by a withering fire, and the attack was called off. Butler finally got his men out from under the Confederate guns two days later and sailed back to Fort Monroe. Disgusted with Butler's leadership and his failure to follow orders to besiege the fort, Grant relieved him of command and agreed to launch a second expedition under Porter and Brig. Gen. **Alfred H. Terry**.

Porter and Terry proved to be a formidable team and cooperated well together. On January 13, 1865, the day after arriving, Terry landed 8,000 men on the peninsula, including one **division** of **black troops**. A heavy two-day naval bombardment from Porter's 44 ships caused considerable damage to Fort Fisher, and Lamb requested reinforcements from Bragg. Out of Hoke's 6,100 men, Bragg sent only about 350—including Whiting—to the fort in time, giving Lamb about 1,200 men. Late on the afternoon of January 15, Porter landed 2,000 sailors and **U.S. Marines** on the beach at the earthwork's angle. This force suffered heavy casualties but diverted the defenders' attention when 6,000 of Terry's infantry surged forward. The Federals advanced across the minefield and stormed the fortifications while Porter kept up the bombardment from sea. After intense hand-to-hand fighting, the fort finally surrendered at about 9:00 P.M.

The attack cost Terry and Porter about 1,070 men, while the Confederates suffered about 500 battle casualties and the loss of some 1,500 **prisoners**. Among the Confederate wounded and captured were Lamb and Whiting, the latter being mortally wounded. The capture of Fort Fisher opened the way for an attack on Wilmington, which was captured on February 22, 1865.

FORT GAINES, ALABAMA. Located on Dauphin Island, Alabama, this fort and **Fort Morgan** controlled access to Mobile Bay. Fort Gaines was captured by **Alabama** state troops in January 1861 and became an important part of Mobile's defenses. Under the command of Brig. Gen. **Richard L. Page**, who was headquartered at Fort Morgan, Fort Gaines was attacked by Adm. **David G. Farragut** and Maj. Gen. **Gordon Granger** in August 1864 at the **Battle of Mobile Bay**. Granger landed 1,500 men of the XIII Corps on the western end of Dauphin Island on August 3 and marched on the fort. Granger engaged Fort Gaines on August 4–8 while Farragut's ships bombarded it from the Gulf of Mexico. After a feeble resistance, the fort's 600-man garrison surrendered on the morning of August 8.

FORT GIBSON, INDIAN TERRITORY. This U.S. fort in eastern **Indian Territory** was occupied by Confederate forces early in the Civil War, but it was abandoned after the Confederate defeat at **Pea Ridge, Arkansas**, in March 1862. In June, Union forces temporarily reoccupied Fort Gibson, and then in April 1863 a larger force returned. When Maj. Gen. **James G. Blunt** made the fort the Union's main outpost in Indian Territory, it was renamed Fort Blunt. In late summer 1864, Confederate **Indians** and a **brigade** of **Texas** cavalry under Brig. Gen. **Stand Watie** threatened the post by conducting a series of attacks on outlying positions to deny supplies to the garrison. By September, more than 10,000 Union soldiers and refugees were seeking shelter at Fort Gibson with very little food to sustain them. However, Watie was unable to maintain this pressure when his Indians left him to spend the winter in Texas.

FORT GILMER, VIRGINIA, BATTLE OF (SEPTEMBER 29, 1864). *See* FORT HARRISON, VIRGINIA, BATTLE OF.

FORT GREGG, VIRGINIA, BATTLE OF (APRIL 2, 1865). After successfully breaking the right flank of **Robert E. Lee's Army of Northern Virginia** at **Five Forks** at the end of the **Petersburg Campaign**, U. S. **Grant** ordered the **Army of the Potomac** to make a general assault against the Petersburg, Virginia, defenses on April 2, 1865. Attacking at daylight, Grant's men crushed Lee's right wing from the Jerusalem Plank Road to **Hatcher's Run**. The surviving Confederates withdrew toward Fort Gregg, an earthen fort located on the Boydton Plank Road just west of the city. Along with Fort Whitworth, located a short distance to the north, it was Petersburg's last line of defense. Both forts were named for the farms on which they were built.

When Lee decided to evacuate Petersburg and **Richmond**, Fort Gregg became crucial because it guarded the western escape route. Survivors of Maj. Gen. **Cadmus M. Wilcox's division** and **Nathaniel H. Harris's brigade** manned the fort with some **artillery**, but they had barely 600 men. Forts Gregg and Whitworth were attacked by the Union XXIV Corps divisions of Brig. Gens. **Robert S. Foster** and **John W. Turner**. In bitter fighting, the Confederates repulsed three assaults, sometimes lighting shells and tumbling them down on the attackers, but on the fourth attempt the Federals found an unfinished ditch that allowed them access to the parapet. Charging in, they overwhelmed the defenders and after a lengthy hand-to-hand fight finally secured the forts. The fight for Fort Gregg was one of the war's most bitter struggles. One Union soldier remembered, "The interior of the fort was a pool of blood. . . ." (Trudeau, *The Last Citadel*, 338). The two Union divisions lost 714 men in the bloody attacks, while virtually all of the Confederates became casualties. However, the outnumbered garrison bought enough time for Lee to finish a new defensive line behind the fort and enabled him to finish the evacuation of Petersburg that night.

FORT HARRISON, VIRGINIA, BATTLE OF (SEPTEMBER 29–30, 1864). In late summer 1864 during the **Petersburg Campaign**, Gen. **Robert E. Lee** weakened his **Army of Northern Virginia** at Petersburg, Virginia, to strengthen the **Shenandoah Valley**. Upon learning of this,

Lt. Gen. **U. S. Grant** decided to attack **Richmond's** outer defenses to prevent Lee from sending more troops. Grant planned for Maj. Gen. **Benjamin F. Butler** to launch a two-pronged assault with his **Army of the James**. Major General **E. O. C. Ord** was to cross the James River by **pontoon bridge** and attack the enemy line near Chaffin's Farm with about 2,000 men, while Brig. Gen. **David Birney** took 18,000 men across the river at Deep Bottom to attack the Confederate works at **New Market Heights**.

Ord attacked across 1,400 yards of open ground on September 29 and in bitter fighting defeated the 150 defenders and captured Fort Harrison, which dominated the Confederate positions on that part of the river. Union Brig. Gen. **Hiram Burnham** was killed in this attack. Turning north, Ord then attacked Fort Gilmer, which the Confederates had by then reinforced. In this assault, Ord was wounded, and his attack stalled, although a **brigade** of **black troops** fought very bravely and won much acclaim. At New Market Heights, Birney succeeded in capturing some outer enemy works but failed to make any serious penetration.

Lee immediately ordered Lt. Gen. **Richard Ewell** to recapture Fort Harrison. On September 30, Ewell sent two **divisions** in three desperate attempts to dislodge the Federals, but all failed, and Lee was forced to construct a new defensive line around Richmond. In the two-day battle, the Confederates lost 2,000 men to Butler's 3,300.

FORT HATTERAS, NORTH CAROLINA (August 27–29, 1861). *See* HATTERAS INLET, NORTH CAROLINA, BATTLE OF.

FORT HENRY, TENNESSEE, CAPTURE OF (FEBRUARY 6, 1862). *See* FORTS HENRY AND DONELSON, TENNESSEE, CAMPAIGN AND BATTLES OF.

FORT HINDMAN, ARKANSAS, BATTLE OF (JANUARY 10–11, 1863). *See* ARKANSAS POST, ARKANSAS, BATTLE OF.

FORT HUGER, VIRGINIA, BATTLE OF (APRIL 19, 1863). Named for Maj. Gen. **Benjamin Huger**, this Confederate fort was constructed in 1861 to protect Suffolk, Virginia. Located just north of the city on the Nansemond River, it remained in Confederate hands after Union forces captured the city in 1862. After his unsuccessful raids on **New Bern, North Carolina**, in early 1863, Confederate Lt. Gen. **James Longstreet** took three **divisions** in April to undertake a siege of **Suffolk**.

A five-gun battery was set up in Fort Huger, with two more batteries positioned in the rear, all being supported by the 55th North Carolina and **Evander M. Law's brigade**. At about dark on April 19, 270 Union soldiers landed near the fort with four small **howitzers**. They surprised the fort and after a brief struggle captured the five cannons and more than 130 artillerymen. The embarrassing raid led to duels between the colonel of the 55th North Carolina and two of Law's aides when the aides blamed the defeat on the **regiment's** failure to properly support the fort. Shots were fired, but none of the officers was hit.

FORT LAFAYETTE, NEW YORK. This Union fort was used as a **prison** during the Civil War. Early in the war, it housed people accused of disloyalty, but in August 1861, it took in several hundred Confederate **prisoners** who had been captured at **Hatteras Inlet**, **North Carolina**. During the war, Fort Lafayette was used mostly to hold Confederate officers and suspected disloyal citizens.

FORT LOUDON, TENNESSEE, BATTLE OF (NOVEMBER 29, 1863). *See* FORT SANDERS, TENNESSEE, BATTLE OF.

FORT McALLISTER, GEORGIA, BATTLE OF (DECEMBER 13, 1864). This Confederate fort was a strategic part of the defenses of **Savannah, Georgia**, in late 1864. Located on the Ogeechee River, it was constructed of earth and logs, had 22 cannons, and was manned by about 250 men. The approaches to the fort were obstructed by **abatis**, **chevaux-de-frise**, and a minefield that had been created by placing **torpedoes** with trip wires. The **U.S. Navy** under **Samuel F. Du Pont** had made previous unsuccessful attacks on the fort on January 27, February 1, and March 3, 1863.

On December 10, 1864, **William T. Sherman's armies** reached Savannah after their **March to the Sea**. With supplies running low, Sherman needed access to the sea so he could be resupplied by ship. He ordered Maj. Gen. **Oliver O. Howard** to seize Fort McAllister and to make contact with the warships offshore. To make the attack, Howard picked Brig. Gen. **William B. Hazen's division**, which went forward with 1,500 men just before dark on December 13. After a short but bloody hand-to-hand fight, the fort was taken. Hazen lost 134 men, while 71 of the Confederates were killed or wounded, with most of the rest being captured. The capture of Fort McAllister allowed Sherman access to the coast and was a key event in the capture of Savannah. Hazen was promoted to major general for his role in the attack.

FORT McREE FLORIDA. *See* FORT PICKENS, FLORIDA, SIEGE OF.

FORT MACON, NORTH CAROLINA, SIEGE OF (MARCH 23–APRIL 25, 1862). This Confederate fort was located on the tip of a coastal island south of Beaufort, North Carolina, and was part of the city's defenses. It was made of stone and had about 400 defenders and 67 guns.

After capturing **Roanoke Island** and **New Bern** in March 1862, Union Maj. Gen. **Ambrose Burnside** ordered Brig. Gen. **John G. Parke** to seize Fort Macon. When Confederate Col. Moses J. White refused Parke's surrender demand on March 23, 1862, Parke began landing troops on the island on March 29. Supported by naval gunfire from Capt. **Louis M. Goldsborough's** warships, Parke slowly invested the fort with troops and cannons. After another surrender demand was refused, Parke began bombarding Fort Macon on April 25. That afternoon the badly outgunned Confederates surrendered after suffering a small number of casualties. With Fort Macon in his possession, Burnside was able to move on Beaufort, which fell on April 26, 1862.

FORT MONROE, VIRGINIA. Sometimes incorrectly referred to as Fortress Monroe, this stone and brick Union fort was located on the Virginia Peninsula's Old Point Comfort at Hampton Roads. At various times during the Civil War, it served as headquarters for the **Department of Virginia and North Carolina**, and the **Army of the James**. Fort Monroe also was the staging area for **George B. McClellan's Army of the Potomac** in March 1862 at the beginning of the **Peninsula Campaign**.

FORT MORGAN, ALABAMA, SIEGE OF (AUGUST 5–22, 1864). This Confederate fort was located at the eastern entrance of Mobile Bay, Alabama, and was an important defensive position for that area. Construction of the 10-sided brick fort was completed in 1834 as part of the general U.S. coastal defenses, and it was named for Revolutionary War hero Daniel Morgan. After **Alabama** seized the fort in January 1861, it and **Fort Gaines** (located on a separate island 2,000 yards to the west) provided protection for **blockade runners** using Mobile Bay.

During the **Battle of Mobile Bay** in August 1864, Rear Adm. **David Farragut** ran his ships past the fort on August 5 to gain entrance to the bay. Commanded by Brig. Gen. **Richard L. Page**, Fort Morgan's 400 men heavily shelled the fleet but were unable to stop its progress. After securing the bay, the Federals then turned on Fort Gaines and captured it on August 8. Farragut's ships and Maj. Gen. **Gordon Granger's army** next kept up a constant fire on Fort Morgan and finally blasted it to rubble. The fort surrendered on August 23, and Union forces used it as a staging area in March 1865 for their drive on **Fort Blakely** during the **Mobile Campaign**.

FORT PICKENS, FLORIDA, SIEGE OF (JANUARY 10, 1861–MAY 12, 1862).

This Union stone fort, located on the western tip of **Pensacola, Florida's**, Santa Rosa Island, was built before the Civil War but had not been used since the **Mexican War**. Along with Forts McRee and Barrancas, it protected Pensacola and its important navy yard and could easily have been the starting point of the Civil War instead of **Fort Sumter**.

When threatened by secessionists, the garrisons of Forts Barrancas and McRee abandoned their positions on January 10, 1861—the day **Florida** seceded—and moved to Fort Pickens. The secessionists seized both forts, and on January 12, the Federals surrendered the Pensacola Navy Yard. Although badly outnumbered, the small Union garrison at Fort Pickens under Lt. **Adam J. Slemmer** refused surrender demands, and the fort became a point of confrontation along with Fort Sumter.

Learning that the USS *Brooklyn* was en route to relieve Fort Pickens, Southern politicians reached a compromise with President **James Buchanan** by agreeing not to attack the fort if the relief expedition was canceled. Buchanan agreed, and the *Brooklyn* anchored in the bay on January 29 but did not unload its **company** of men. When **Abraham Lincoln** was sworn in as president, he was determined to hold Forts Pickens and Sumter and ordered the *Brooklyn* to reinforce Pickens's garrison. The order was received on March 31, but the ship's captain refused to obey because it did not come from his navy superiors. After new orders were issued by the Navy Department, the 200 men finally were disembarked on April 12, and Col. Harvey Brown assumed command of the fort. When several other ships arrived with an additional 800 men on April 16, Fort Pickens was strong enough to hold out against the 5,000 Confederates being massed against it by Confederate Brig. Gen. **Braxton Bragg**.

The antagonists made several raids against each other during April and May but enjoyed no success. Bragg launched one strong surprise attack on **Santa Rosa Island** in October 1861 but was repulsed, and on November 22–23, 1861, and January 1, 1862, Fort Pickens heavily bombarded Fort McRee. Bragg evacuated Pensacola on May 9, 1862, and the town was occupied by Union troops three days later. Fort Pickens remained in Union hands throughout the war. *See also* FORT SUMTER AND FORT PICKENS MEDALS.

FORT PILLOW, TENNESSEE, BATTLE OF (APRIL 12, 1864).

Located on the Mississippi River 40 miles upstream from Memphis, Tennessee, this earthen fort was constructed by the Confederates early in the

Civil War as part of the Mississippi River defenses. When the Confederate defensive line through **Tennessee** and **Kentucky** was breached at **Forts Henry and Donelson, Tennessee**, in early 1862, the fort was abandoned. Union forces then occupied it and used the fort to protect their lines of communications running through western Tennessee.

In April 1864, Fort Pillow was under the command of Maj. Lionel F. Booth and was garrisoned by nearly 600 soldiers of the 13th Tennessee Cavalry (Union), 11th U.S. Colored Infantry, and 4th U.S. Colored Light Artillery. During one of **Forrest's Tennessee Raids** in the spring of 1864, Confederate Maj. Gen. **Nathan Bedford Forrest** moved against the fort with his cavalry. Led by Brig. Gen. **James R. Chalmers**, the Confederates attacked early on April 12 and drove the garrison into the fort. By mid-morning Forrest was in position to storm the fort and demanded its surrender. If refused, Forrest warned Booth, "I cannot be responsible for the fate of your command" (Wills, *A Battle from the Start*, 182). Feeling secure behind their breastworks, many of the **black troops** taunted the enemy during the negotiations. Booth had been killed by this time, and his subordinate, Maj. William F. Bradford, had assumed command. Bradford rejected Forrest's demand, and the Confederates attacked.

Reaching the parapet, the Confederates stood on the shoulders of comrades and were able to swarm over the wall. The Union garrison fought briefly and then panicked and fled for the river and the protection of the USS *New Era*. As racial hatred boiled over, the Confederates went on a killing spree of black soldiers who were trying to surrender. At a cost of 100 men, Forrest captured the fort and inflicted 557 casualties on the garrison, of whom 231 were killed. Most of the dead were black, and only 58 black soldiers were taken captive.

The Fort Pillow "Massacre" became one of the war's most controversial events and was investigated by the **Committee on the Conduct of the War**. There is little doubt that many black soldiers were murdered, but the role of Forrest and Chalmers is disputed. Union officials branded Forrest a murderous criminal, but evidence indicates that neither he nor Chalmers ordered the killings and, in fact, may have tried to stop it after it began. The **massacre** seems to have been the product of hatred the Confederates had toward the Tennessee Unionists and the black soldiers.

FORT POWELL, ALABAMA. This was a Confederate fort located at Grant's Pass that helped guard the entrance to Mobile Bay, Alabama. It was abandoned by its 140 defenders on the night of August 5, 1864, after Adm. **David Farragut** won the **Battle of Mobile Bay**.

FORT PULASKI, GEORGIA, BATTLE OF (APRIL 10–11, 1862). This Confederate fort was located on Cockspur Island and guarded the sea approaches to Savannah, Georgia. Named for Revolutionary War hero Count Casimir Pulaski, the initial fort construction was supervised by **Robert E. Lee**, with construction being completed in 1847. After **Georgia** militia seized the fort on January 6, 1861, it was placed under the command of Col. Charles H. Olmstead. By November 1861, Olmstead had 385 men and 48 cannons to defend it.

After Union forces occupied a nearby island in November 1861, Union Capt. **Quincy A. Gillmore** made plans to capture Fort Pulaski and close Savannah to **blockade runners**. Gillmore assembled 36 **mortars** and cannons (three of which were **Parrott rifles**) and began bombarding the fort on the morning of April 10, 1862, after Olmstead refused a surrender demand. Gillmore and Olmstead traded salvos, with the Union guns slowly breaching the fort's wall. By the afternoon of April 11, a number of the fort's guns were dismounted, and there was a dangerous threat of the powder magazine exploding. Thus, after enduring a bombardment of 5,275 shells in two days, Olmstead finally surrendered. The Confederates suffered only about a dozen casualties in the bombardment, while Gillmore had one man killed. This was the first battle that pitted **rifled** cannons against a masonry fort, and it demonstrated the vulnerability of such forts to modern weapons. The capture of Fort Pulaski effectively closed Savannah as a major port for the Confederacy.

FORT ST. PHILIP, LOUISIANA. *See* FORTS JACKSON AND ST. PHILIP, LOUISIANA, SIEGE OF.

FORT SANDERS, TENNESSEE, BATTLE OF (NOVEMBER 29, 1863). Fort Sanders, originally known as Fort Loudon, was an earthen fort built by the Confederates as part of the Knoxville, Tennessee, defenses. Located west of town, it was fronted by a deep ditch and had nearly vertical walls 15 feet high. After Union troops occupied Knoxville in September 1863, the fort was renamed Fort Sanders in honor of Brig. Gen. **William P. Sanders**, who was mortally wounded nearby.

During the **Knoxville Campaign**, Confederate Lt. Gen. **James Longstreet** attacked the fort with Maj. Gen. **Lafayette McLaws's division** on November 29, 1863. The fort was defended by 440 Federals from various **regiments** and had 12 cannons. Longstreet believed the protective ditch was only waist deep after observing a soldier walk across it, not knowing that the soldier actually was walking on a board laid across the ditch. As a result, Longstreet made no plans to send scaling ladders with the assault troops.

Bitter cold and sleet hampered movements, but the Confederates got into position on the night of November 28. At dawn the attack was made, and McLaws's men crossed **wire entanglements** and reached the ditch without serious loss. The assault then broke down, for without ladders the Confederates became trapped in the deep ditch. A thin glaze of ice also prevented them from scaling the nearly perpendicular wall. By standing on comrades' shoulders, color bearers managed to plant three **flags** on the parapet, but few Confederates found their way inside the fort. For about half an hour the attackers fought from the ditch and then withdrew, except for about 200 men who refused to leave the ditch's protection and were captured. McLaws lost 1,030 men in the attack, while the Federals counted 100 casualties. Following this battle, Longstreet suspended his attack on Knoxville after learning of **Braxton Bragg's** defeat at **Missionary Ridge** during the **Chattanooga Campaign**.

FORT SMITH, ARKANSAS. This Union fort was located on the Arkansas River on the border of **Arkansas** and **Indian Territory**. Built in 1817, it was the first fort built by the **U.S. Army** on the southwestern frontier and was intended to maintain the peace while eastern **Indians** were relocated to Indian Territory. Fort Smith eventually became the **army's** main supply base for all of its frontier forts.

Confronted by Arkansas state troops in April 1861, Capt. **Samuel D. Sturgis** evacuated his small garrison of U.S. cavalry, and the state troops seized Fort Smith on April 25. During the first half of the Civil War, the fort served the Confederates as an important supply depot and staging base from which to control Indian Territory and Arkansas, but it was not occupied continuously. Union troops captured Fort Smith on September 1, 1863, and held it for the duration of the war.

FORT STEDMAN, VIRGINIA, BATTLE OF (MARCH 25, 1865). Suffering from acute manpower and supply shortages, Confederate Gen. **Robert E. Lee** decided in March 1865 to end the **Petersburg Campaign** by breaking out of the Petersburg, Virginia, defensives before **U. S. Grant** could be reinforced by **Philip Sheridan**, who had finished his successful **Shenandoah Valley Campaign** and was on his way to join Grant. If a breakthrough could be achieved, Lee hoped also to attack Grant's supply base at **City Point** and throw the Federals off balance long enough for at least part of the **Army of Northern Virginia** to escape to **North Carolina** to join Gen. **Joseph E. Johnston's** army.

Major General **John B. Gordon** was given command of the assault force, which included the II Corps and almost half of Lee's **army**. Gordon planned to attack Fort Stedman, a major Union fortification that lay about 150 yards from the Confederate line northeast of Petersburg near the Appomattox River. The fort was manned by some **artillery** and Brig. Gen. **Orlando B. Willcox's** IX Corps **division** of the **Army of the Po-**

tomac. Gordon chose three groups of 100 handpicked troops to lead the assault. These men were armed with axes and were to slip into no-man's land before dawn of March 25, capture the Union **pickets**, and clear away obstructions. Selected officers also were to pose as Union officers in the dark and mislead and confuse the Federal defenders. The main assault then would be made. Once Fort Stedman was taken, Gordon's men were to continue toward the rear to capture additional positions and to fan out left and right to clear more of the trenches and create a gap in the Union lines through which Lee could extract the army.

At 4:00 A.M., March 25, Gordon sent his men forward. At first things proceeded well, with the obstructions being cleared and the pickets captured without sounding the alarm. The Confederates then overran Fort Stedman and seized it in a quick hand-to-hand fight. At that moment, however, the attack began to stall. Gordon's men were unable to find the fortifications that supposedly lay in the rear of Fort Stedman, and by 7:30 A.M. Willcox's and **John F. Hartranft's** divisions swarmed in to close the gap. Facing inevitable defeat, Lee finally ordered Gordon to withdraw, but that proved far more dangerous than the assault itself. Many Confederates were shot down as they ran back to their lines, while hundreds of others surrendered rather than run the gauntlet of fire. Shortly after 8:00 A.M., Gordon was back at his starting position, having lost 4,000 men, of which about half had been captured. The Federals lost 1,500 men.

The attack on Fort Stedman was the last major offensive by the Army of Northern Virginia. Grant correctly guessed that Lee had weakened other parts of his line to mount the attack and quickly launched a counterattack that broke Lee's line at **Five Forks** and set in motion the **Appomattox Campaign**.

FORT STEVENS, WASHINGTON, D.C., BATTLE OF (JULY 11–12, 1864). As the Civil War progressed, **Washington, D.C.**, became ringed by strong fortifications. One of these was Fort Stevens, located on the road to Silver Spring, Maryland. In the summer of 1864, Confederate Lt. Gen. **Jubal A. Early's Washington Raid** approached Fort Stevens on July 11. **Skirmishing** erupted at and around the fort as Early probed the area's defenses. During the skirmishing on July 11, **Abraham** and **Mary Lincoln** visited the fort and witnessed some of the fighting. Lincoln returned the next day and came under fire from Confederate **sharpshooters**, and one man standing near him was shot down. Years after the war, Capt. Oliver Wendell Holmes Jr. claimed he shouted, "Get down, you damn fool, before you get shot!" not realizing to whom he was speaking

(Foote, *The Civil War*, vol. 3, p. 459). Lincoln supposedly complied. Luckily for the capital, the **Army of the Potomac's** VI Corps had been rushed from Petersburg, Virginia, to guard the city, and its forward elements began filing into the fort on the night of July 11. Early had planned to attack on July 12 but was forced to reconsider when the VI Corps kept moving into position that morning. Unable to do more, Early withdrew that night and began his march back to **Virginia**.

FORT SUMTER, SOUTH CAROLINA. As the Southern states seceded in 1860–61, they began occupying all federal forts within their borders. By early 1861, only **Fort Pickens** at **Pensacola, Florida**, and **Fort Sumter** at **Charleston, South Carolina**, were still in Union hands. Located on a man-made island in the harbor, the latter was an unfinished pentagon-shaped brick fort with walls 40 feet high and up to 12 feet thick.

When threatened by secessionists, Maj. **Robert Anderson** evacuated Fort Moultrie on the night of December 26, 1860, and moved his approximately 80 officers and men and about 40 civilian workers to the more defensible island-fortress of Sumter. President **James Buchanan** wished to avoid war, so when the supply vessel *Star of the West* was fired upon on January 9, 1861, he took no further action to reinforce Anderson. When **Abraham Lincoln** took office on March 4, 1861, however, he decided to hold both forts. By that time Anderson was surrounded by a large Confederate force under Brig. Gen. **P. G. T. Beauregard**. A standoff continued for weeks with Anderson refusing all calls to surrender. When the Confederates learned on April 8 that a relief expedition was being sent from New York City to aid Anderson, Beauregard made one last surrender demand. Anderson again refused on April 11 but noted that he would be "starved out in a few days" (Current et al., eds., *Encyclopedia of the Confederacy*, vol. 2, 629). Beauregard had to act before the relief force arrived.

At 4:30 A.M. on April 12, Beauregard opened fire on Fort Sumter. Anderson, recognizing the futility of resistance, protected his men and only occasionally fired back. After a 33-hour bombardment in which approximately 4,000 shells were fired, Anderson surrendered the badly damaged fort. No deaths had been suffered on either side, but war was ensured when Lincoln quickly declared that the South was in rebellion and called for 75,000 volunteers to put it down. Beauregard allowed Anderson to fire a 100-gun salute to the U.S. **flag** before departing for the North, and one U.S. artilleryman was killed when a cannon accidentally exploded. His was the first death of the Civil War. Confederate troops then garrisoned **Fort Sumter**, and it became an important part of Charleston's defenses.

On April 7, 1863, a Union fleet under **Samuel F. Du Pont** attacked Fort Sumter with eight **monitors** and one **ironclad**, but it was forced to withdraw after a heavy bombardment. After capturing nearby Morris Island, Union forces positioned heavy **artillery** with which to bombard the fort. Beginning on August 17, 1863, a heavy fire was kept up on Sumter, and its artillery was mostly destroyed. Beauregard then replaced the artillerymen with infantry and continued to hold the fort. After an amphibious assault on the night of September 8 was repulsed, no further Union efforts were made to capture Fort Sumter, but it frequently was bombarded by naval and shore batteries. The Confederates finally abandoned the fort on February 18, 1865, when Charleston was evacuated. On April 14, 1865, Robert Anderson came back to Sumter and four years to the day raised the same U.S. flag he had lowered in 1861. *See also* FORT SUMTER AND FORT PICKENS MEDALS.

FORT SUMTER AND FORT PICKENS MEDALS. Two of the few medals presented in the Civil War, these were privately commissioned by the New York State Chamber of Commerce in June 1861 to honor the defenders of the two forts. The chamber struck 168 bronze medals and presented them to a number of Union servicemen in a May 1862 ceremony. The medals were designed by Charles Miller and came in four sizes and eight designs. They were disk-shaped and ranged from two and one-half to six inches in diameter. The **Fort Sumter** medal had **Robert Anderson's** portrait on one side and on the other side the inscription "The Genius or Guardian Spirit of America Rising from Fort Sumter." The **Fort Pickens** medal had a portrait of Lt. **Adam J. Slemmer** and the inscription "Cerebus, or the Monster of War, Chained to Fort Pickens." Both medals came in different sizes according to rank. *See also* DECORATIONS.

FORT WAGNER, SOUTH CAROLINA, BATTLE OF (JULY 10– SEPTEMBER 6, 1863). Located on the northern tip of Morris Island, Fort (or Battery) Wagner, was about one and one-half miles from **Fort Sumter** and formed an important part of the defenses of **Charleston, South Carolina**. An earthen **redoubt** that ran all the way across the island, the fort protected the land approaches to the island's other fortification, Battery Gregg. In July 1863, Maj. Gen. **Quincy A. Gillmore** and Rear Adm. **John Dahlgren** led a joint task force to capture Charleston. On July 10, Brig. Gen. **George C. Strong's** brigade left its base on Folly Island and in fierce fighting secured a landing on the southern end of Morris Island. Strong lost 106 men in the operation to the Confederates' 294 casualties. He then moved up the island and on July 11 unsuccessfully attacked the fort with his lone **brigade**, losing another 339 men, while the Confederates suffered only 12 casualties.

Gillmore decided not to risk another direct assault and instead put 40 large guns on the southern part of Morris Island on July 15–17 to bombard the fort. On July 18, these guns joined the naval bombardment in preparation for another assault. By this time, Fort Wagner's commander, Brig. Gen. **William B. Taliaferro**, had been reinforced and had about 1,300 men. At dusk, Brig. Gen. **Truman Seymour** launched another attack with soldiers from Strong's and Col. H. S. Putnam's brigades, with a third brigade in support. This attack was led by the **54th Massachusetts**, a **regiment** of **black troops** commanded by Col. **Robert Gould Shaw**. The attack succeeded in reaching the fort and in desperate fighting some soldiers managed to claw their way to the top of the parapet. Furious Confederate fire finally drove back the Federals, killing Shaw and Putnam, mortally wounding Strong, and seriously wounding Seymour. Seymour lost 1,515 men in the assault, while the Confederates counted 174 casualties.

After the repulse, Gillmore and the **U.S. Navy** continued to bombard the fort for seven weeks, while sappers dug approaches toward it. After reaching the fort's outer ditch, Gillmore planned another assault for September 7, but the Confederates evacuated Wagner the night before and crossed to the mainland by boat.

FORT WARREN, MASSACHUSETTS. This large granite pentagon fort sits on an island and guards the harbor of Boston, Massachusetts. At the beginning of the Civil War, it was used to confine some political **prisoners** and smugglers, but in August 1861, it became a prisoner-of-war camp to hold Confederate prisoners taken at **Hatteras Inlet**, **North Carolina**. Fort Warren was one of the better Civil War **prisons** with more room, furniture, and food than most. It largely was used to hold officers, who were given such privileges as exercising outside their cells and buying supplies at the fort's commissary. Only 12 deaths were recorded among the prisoners housed at Fort Warren.

FORT WHITWORTH, VIRGINIA, BATTLE OF (APRIL 2, 1865). *See* FORT GREGG, VIRGINIA, BATTLE OF.

FORTS HENRY AND DONELSON, TENNESSEE, CAMPAIGN AND BATTLES OF (FEBRUARY 4–16, 1862). In February 1862, Union Maj. Gen. **Henry Halleck** approved a plan by Brig. Gen. **U. S. Grant** to work in cooperation with **Andrew Foote's** fleet to clear the lower Tennessee and Cumberland Rivers by capturing the Confederate Forts Henry and Donelson. If successful, the enemy defensive line anchored at Bowling Green, Kentucky, would be pierced, and **Albert Sidney John-**

ston's Confederates would have to withdraw into **Tennessee**. By moving up the Cumberland River, Nashville and all of Middle Tennessee then might possibly fall to the Union, as well.

Foote's gunboats entered the Tennessee River and reached Fort Henry on February 4. The fort was located upstream from a river bend and commanded a long stretch of water, but it was situated on low ground and was dominated by nearby hills. Brigadier General **Lloyd Tilghman**, who had commanded the fort since November 1861, was also constructing Fort Heiman across the river, but it was still unfinished. As Foote's gunboats approached, Fort Henry was nearly indefensible and had flooded. Tilghman, therefore, sent most of the garrison to Fort Donelson, 10 miles to the east, and kept only about 100 men to man his 17 guns to give the others time to escape. Grant and Foote planned for Foote to engage the fort while Grant marched his men overland to invest it. Foote, however, attacked on February 6 and after a heavy bombardment forced Tilghman to surrender before Grant arrived.

On February 11, Grant marched his 15,000 men eastward toward Fort Donelson, located on the west bank of the Cumberland River at Dover. Foote took his seven gunboats back to the Ohio River to gain entrance to the Cumberland. At Fort Donelson, Brig. Gen. **John B. Floyd** had about 21,000 men on hand but made no attempt to engage Grant before he reached the fort. Grant arrived at Fort Donelson on February 12 and encircled it. He was reinforced by another **division** the next day, giving him approximately 27,000 men. The weather quickly turned from mild to bitterly cold, with sleet and snow setting in and the temperature dipping to 10 degrees. Many soldiers had thrown away their winter coats during the march and now suffered terribly from the cold. On February 14, Foote's fleet arrived and engaged the fort's batteries, but two of the gunboats were disabled, and Foote was wounded in the foot.

That night Floyd and his officers planned a daring breakout the next day. Massing troops on the Confederate left under cover of darkness, Floyd attacked on the morning of February 15 to open an escape route to Nashville. In heavy fighting, the Confederates managed to break through the Union right wing. Just at the moment of success, however, Floyd lost his nerve and ordered the troops to withdraw back into the fort. Grant, who was absent conferring with Foote when the attack was made, soon arrived back on the scene and launched a counterattack that permanently closed the escape route.

That night Floyd and his subordinates, Maj. Gen. **Gideon Pillow** and Brig. Gen. **Simon B. Buckner**, discussed their options. When Buckner declared that surrender was the only course of action left to them, Floyd agreed. Floyd, however, feared being taken **prisoner** since he was a former U.S. secretary of war and might be hanged. He relinquished command to Pillow, who in turn gave command to Buckner. Floyd and Pillow then escaped the doomed fort by boat, with Floyd also taking away about 2,500 men of his **brigade**. When cavalry commander Col. **Nathan Bedford Forrest** heard of the surrender plans, he was indignant and received permission to escape with his men. By splashing through frozen backwater, Forrest escaped with his cavalry and some infantrymen who begged to be taken along.

Buckner, an old **U.S. Army** friend of Grant's, asked for terms on the morning of February 16 and was incensed when Grant demanded unconditional surrender. Having no other choice, Buckner surrendered the garrison. In the engagement, Grant lost 2,832 men, while the Confederates suffered about 2,000 casualties in the fighting. In addition, Buckner surrendered 65 cannons; 20,000 muskets; and 12,000–15,000 prisoners. The fall of Fort Donelson breached the Confederate defensive line in **Kentucky**, opened the way for the Union capture of Nashville on February 23, and made a hero out of Grant, who was nicknamed "Unconditional Surrender" Grant.

FORTS JACKSON AND ST. PHILIP, LOUISIANA, SIEGE OF (APRIL 18–28, 1862). By early 1862, Union forces began concentrating in the Gulf of Mexico to attack **New Orleans**, **Louisiana**, and seize control of the lower Mississippi River. Captain **David Farragut** was placed in command of a flotilla that included 24 warships and 19 **mortar** boats (under the command of his foster brother, Lt. **David Porter**). Major General **Benjamin F. Butler** also had a large infantry force with which to assist Farragut and take control of New Orleans.

The only obstacles confronting Farragut were two brick forts located about 12 miles above Head of Passes. Fort St. Philip was on the east bank, and Fort Jackson sat diagonally across the river on the west bank. The larger of the two was Fort Jackson, a star-shaped fort with moat, completed in 1832. The forts were manned by several hundred Confederates under the command of Brig. Gen. **Johnson K. Duncan**. Duncan had about 110 cannons in the two forts, but many were antiquated, and his powder proved to be of poor quality. To block the river, a large boom made by chaining schooners together had been stretched across the water. A small **River Defense Fleet** of 12 Confederate gunboats and a number of fire rafts were also in the river, but, for the most part, they were poorly armed, and the **Confederate navy** officers proved reluctant to cooperate with Duncan. While Confederate authorities believed the forts and ships were sufficient to stop any Union attack, events proved that the defenders were badly outgunned.

Farragut was reluctant to steam past the ominous forts and decided to use Porter's mortar boats to reduce them first. Anchoring the mortar boats downriver, Porter began bombarding the forts on April 18 and concentrated his fire mainly on Fort Jackson. On the night of April 20, Farragut sent ships to the boom and cut a small hole in it to allow the fleet to pass through when it came time to attack. During the bombardment, the Confederate **ironclad *Louisiana*** arrived from New Orleans and was anchored next to Fort St. Philip. It was a formidable ship, but the engines were unfinished and it served merely as a floating battery.

After a week of bombardment, the forts were battered but still defiant, and Farragut decided to run past them in the predawn hours of April 24. The Confederates spotted the fleet, and for several hours the ships and forts dueled in a spectacular engagement. Although expecting heavy casualties, Farragut routed the Confederate fleet and placed all but three of his ships above the forts with little loss. He faced no further opposition and sailed on to capture New Orleans on April 25. After holding out for a few more days, much of Fort Jackson's garrison mutinied and surrendered on April 28 rather than fight a losing battle. Having lost the bulk of his force, Duncan then surrendered the two forts to Porter, while the captain of the *Louisiana* blew up his ship rather than surrender it.

FOSTER, JOHN GRAY (1823–1874) USA. A native of **New Hampshire**, Foster graduated from **West Point** in 1846 and entered the **engineers**. He served gallantly in the **Mexican War**, receiving two **brevets** for gallantry, and was severely wounded at Molino del Rey. Foster remained in the engineers and taught at the academy before the Civil War.

In April 1861, Foster was an officer at **Fort Sumter, South Carolina**, and was present during the bombardment. Afterward, he worked on fortifications and served on garrison duty until promoted to brigadier general of volunteers in October 1861. Foster led a **brigade** during **Ambrose Burnside's** operations against **Roanoke Island** and **New Bern, North Carolina**.

After serving as New Bern's military governor, Foster was promoted to major general of volunteers in July 1862 and commanded the **Department of North Carolina** until July 1863, when he took command of the **Department of Virginia and North Carolina**. He remained at this post until November 1863, when he joined Burnside in **Tennessee** for the **Knoxville Campaign**. Foster replaced Burnside in command of the **Army of the Ohio** in December, but a fall from his horse forced him to relinquish the position two months later. He was placed in command of the **Department of the South** in May 1864, and in February 1865, his troops captured **Charleston, South Carolina**. Afterward, Foster was placed in command of the **Department of Florida**.

Foster was brevetted brigadier general of regulars for his actions at Fort Sumter, Roanoke, and New Bern, and major general of regulars for his war service. He remained in the **army** as an engineer and was a lieutenant colonel when he died.

FOSTER, ROBERT SANFORD (1834–1903) USA. A native of **Indiana**, Foster was working as a tinner when he entered Union service in April 1861 as a captain in the 11th Indiana. The 90-day **regiment** saw some service in western **Virginia** before being disbanded. In June, Foster was appointed major of the 13th Indiana. After fighting at **Rich Mountain**, he was promoted to lieutenant colonel in October and then to colonel in April 1862. Foster fought in **Stonewall Jackson's 1862 Shenandoah Valley Campaign** and then was transferred first to the **Army of the Potomac** for the **Peninsula Campaign** and then to Suffolk, Virginia. At **Suffolk**, he commanded a **brigade** and helped defend the city against **James Longstreet's** siege in the spring of 1863.

Promoted to brigadier general of volunteers in June 1863, Foster took command of a brigade and served on Folly Island during operations against **Charleston, South Carolina**, that fall and winter. After serving for a while in **Florida**, he returned to Virginia in early 1864 and served as Maj. Gen. **Quincy Gillmore's** chief of staff. During the **Petersburg Campaign**, Foster at first commanded a brigade, but he then was given a XXIV Corps **division**, which he led in the assault on April 2, 1865, that captured **Fort Gregg**.

After the war, Foster served on the military court that tried the conspirators involved in **Lincoln's assassination** and then resigned from the **army** in September 1865 after being **brevetted** major general of volunteers. He returned to Indiana and served as Indianapolis's secretary of treasury and as a U.S. marshal.

FOUGASSE. A fougasse (foo-GAHS) was a type of land mine that was used to spray rock fragments like **shrapnel**. It was made by placing a powder charge in a shallow pit beneath a layer of rocks. A **fuse** ran from the powder to a protected location from where it could be lighted.

FOX, GUSTAVUS VASA (1821–1883) USA. A native of **Massachusetts** and the brother-in-law of **Montgomery Blair**, Fox graduated from the **U.S. Naval Academy** in 1838 and saw service during the **Mexican War**.

After resigning his lieutenant's commission in 1856, he worked in the textile industry.

During the 1861 **Fort Sumter** crisis, Blair succeeded in getting Fox appointed as a government consultant. **Abraham Lincoln** was impressed with Fox's plan to resupply the fort by steamship and sent him to **Charleston, South Carolina**, to work out the details with the garrison. Fox met with Maj. **Robert Anderson** and then returned to **Washington, D.C.**, to put the plan into effect. When the Confederates learned of this relief expedition, they opened fire on the fort. All Fox could do then was arrange transport for the captured garrison to New York City.

Lincoln offered Fox command of a naval vessel, but Fox instead accepted an appointment as the Navy Department's chief clerk. To make use of his talents, Lincoln created the position of assistant secretary of the navy in August just for him. Fox performed exceptionally well under Secretary of the Navy **Gideon Welles** and was noted for his administrative skills and tact. It was Fox who urged the adoption of **ironclad** ships, helped plan the capture of **New Orleans, Louisiana**, and helped get **David Farragut** promoted to admiral. He resigned his position in May 1866 but almost immediately was reappointed as a courier to Russia to open informal negotiations for the purchase of Alaska.

When his Russian mission was completed, Fox returned to the textile industry in Massachusetts.

FOX'S GAP, MARYLAND, BATTLE OF (SEPTEMBER 14, 1862). *See* SOUTH MOUNTAIN, MARYLAND, BATTLE OF.

FRANK LESLIE'S ILLUSTRATED NEWSPAPER. This illustrated newspaper had its beginnings with Henry Carter, who worked as an engraver for the *Illustrated London News* in 1842. After immigrating to the United States in 1848, Carter changed his name to Frank Leslie and began publishing the weekly *Frank Leslie's Illustrated Newspaper* in 1855. It became one of the most popular publications during the Civil War because Leslie hired such talented artists as James E. Taylor, **Alfred R. Waud**, and **Edwin Forbes** to travel with the Union **armies** and provide illustrations for the paper's articles. The paper continued publication until the 20th century, but it never again attained the popularity it enjoyed during the war.

FRANKLIN AND NASHVILLE, TENNESSEE, CAMPAIGN AND BATTLES OF (NOVEMBER 16–DECEMBER 27, 1864). After the fall of **Atlanta, Georgia**, in September 1864, Confederate Gen. **John Bell Hood** moved his 40,000-man **Army of Tennessee** into northern **Georgia** to draw **William T. Sherman** out of the city. When Hood attacked

Sherman's **railroad** supply line, Sherman did give chase briefly but finally returned to Atlanta to prepare for his **March to the Sea** and dispatched Maj. Gen. **George H. Thomas** to Nashville, Tennessee, to protect **Tennessee**.

While at Gadsden, Alabama, in October, Hood decided to invade Tennessee and threaten Nashville to force Sherman to abandon Georgia and to restore Confederate morale. He even entertained the possibility of marching to **Virginia** after securing Tennessee and linking up with **Robert E. Lee** for a final confrontation with **U. S. Grant's** armies. When department commander, Gen. **P. G. T. Beauregard**, was notified of the plan, he insisted on detaching **Joseph Wheeler's** cavalry to confront Sherman in Georgia and assigned Hood Maj. Gen. **Nathan Bedford Forrest's** cavalry in **Mississippi**. Hood intended to begin his invasion from Decatur, Alabama, but Forrest was delayed in joining him. He, therefore, marched farther west to Tuscumbia, Alabama, to join Forrest and to gather supplies. Forrest joined Hood on November 17 at Florence, Alabama, but the three-week delay gave Thomas time to begin preparations in Tennessee to meet the invasion. The Confederates crossed the Tennessee River near Tuscumbia on November 16–21 and entered Tennessee.

Thomas had stationed Maj. Gen. **John M. Schofield's** 30,000-man IV and XXIII Corps at Pulaski, Tennessee, to delay the invasion, while Thomas assembled a force in Nashville. When Hood's northward march threatened to turn Schofield's western flank, Schofield withdrew to Columbia on November 24. Hood arrived there on November 26 and began moving his **army** east of town on the night of November 28, to cut off Schofield's retreat at Spring Hill, a small hamlet a few miles north of Columbia. What happened next is still debated, but there is little question that the entire Confederate command system broke down. Establishing his headquarters several miles from Spring Hill, Hood sent Maj. Gen. **Benjamin F. Cheatham's corps** ahead with orders to cut the road. Cheatham, however, ran into a large Union force east of the village and positioned his corps facing the road, not across it. Thinking Cheatham was blocking the road as ordered, Hood sent more units forward with orders to extend Cheatham's line to the right. This simply extended the Confederate line farther along the road, not across it. Hood later was informed that the road was not blocked, but he never went to the front or took any personal action to see that his orders were carried out. As a result of the Confederate blunders in the Spring Hill Incident, Schofield retreated up the road that night and escape to Franklin by marching right past the Confederate campfires.

On the morning of November 30, Hood was furious with his officers and men and ordered a pursuit. That afternoon, he found Schofield with

32,000 men strongly entrenched on the south side of Franklin while the Union wagon train escaped across the Harpeth River in his rear. Despite Forrest's insistence that he could take an infantry force into Schofield's rear and trap him, Hood insisted on making a **frontal attack**. The Confederate attack at Franklin perhaps was the most spectacular of the war. Larger than **Pickett's Charge** at **Gettysburg**, it included 18 **brigades** and covered two miles of open ground. The charge was made at about 3:30 P.M. and briefly broke through Schofield's center. The Federals sealed the break, however, and in bitter, close-quarter fighting, finally repulsed the attack at about 9:00 P.M. Hood lost 6,252 men and a staggering 12 generals. These included four generals killed—**Patrick Cleburne**, **John Adams**, **Otho Strahl**, and **Hiram Granbury**. Two generals, **John C. Carter** and **States Rights Gist**, were mortally wounded, five others were wounded, and one was captured. The Army of Tennessee was nearly wrecked, with two brigades being commanded by captains afterward. Schofield lost 2,326 men, but he safely retreated to Nashville that night.

Hood detached **William B. Bate's** division to Murfreesboro to block any enemy reinforcements heading to Nashville and then followed Schofield, in hope of receiving reinforcements or luring Thomas into attacking on ground of his choosing. Hood took up a defensive position along a range of hills south of Nashville and then sent Forrest to join Bate at Murfreesboro. With Bate's **division** and two infantry brigades, Forrest attacked the town on December 7, but he was defeated by **Robert H. Milroy**.

Hood's decision to wait at Nashville gave Thomas time to assemble a large force of almost 70,000 men with which to crush the invaders. The methodical Thomas took his time despite orders from Grant to attack immediately. When he finally was ready to move, an ice storm delayed him further. Frustrated over Thomas's slowness, Grant decided to replace him and was on his way to Nashville for that purpose when Thomas finally acted. On December 15, 1864, Thomas launched a devastating assault by first feinting toward Hood's right and then unleashing a heavy attack against the Confederate left. Hood withdrew a few miles to a new position, but on December 16 Thomas renewed his attacks and succeeded in crushing Hood's left flank with his cavalry that afternoon. The Confederates fled to the south, with **Stephen D. Lee's** corps fighting as rear guard. The Battle of Nashville essentially destroyed the Army of Tennessee. Hood's losses are uncertain, but he probably lost about 6,000 men in the battle and retreat. Thomas reported losing 2,562 men.

The demoralized Confederates reached Columbia on December 18 and there, were rejoined by Forrest's cavalry from Murfreesboro. When the army's rear guard crossed the Tennessee River into Alabama on December 27, Hood assembled the survivors at Tupelo, Mississippi. Out of the 40,000 men who entered Tennessee in November, only 18,708 reported for duty at Tupelo. In January 1865, Hood was relieved of command, and the remnants of the Army of Tennessee were scattered to various points in the Confederacy, with some units being sent to join **Joseph E. Johnston** for the **Carolinas Campaign**.

FRANKLIN, LOUISIANA, BATTLE OF (APRIL 14, 1863). *See* IRISH BEND, LOUISIANA, BATTLE OF.

FRANKLIN, TENNESSEE, BATTLE OF (NOVEMBER 30, 1864). *See* FRANKLIN AND NASHVILLE, TENNESSEE, CAMPAIGN AND BATTLES OF.

FRANKLIN, TENNESSEE, RAID ON (APRIL 10, 1863). In early 1863, Confederate cavalry was active in Middle Tennessee, fighting at **Dover**, **Thompson's Station**, **Vaught's Hill**, and **Brentwood**. On April 10, Maj. Gen. **Earl Van Dorn** probed Franklin with his and **Nathan Bedford Forrest's** commands. As he advanced, **skirmishing**, Forrest was surprised by Union cavalry under Brig. Gen. **David S. Stanley**, which got into his right rear and captured one of his **artillery** batteries. After a sharp clash, Van Dorn finally concluded that the Federals held Franklin in force and withdrew to Spring Hill. In the fight, the Confederates lost 137 men, while the Federals counted about 100 casualties.

FRANKLIN, WILLIAM BUEL (1823–1903) USA. A native of **Pennsylvania**, Franklin graduated first in his **West Point** class of 1843 and served as an **engineer** on **Philip Kearny's** South Pass Expedition in 1843–45. After winning a **brevet** for gallantry in the **Mexican War**, he was stationed in **Washington, D.C.**, to oversee the construction of the Capitol dome.

In May 1861, Franklin was commissioned colonel of the 12th U.S. Infantry, with a promotion to brigadier general of volunteers coming three days later. After leading a **brigade** at **First Manassas**, he took command of a **division** in the Washington defenses. Although he was praised while leading the **Army of the Potomac's** VI Corps during the **Peninsula** (where he was brevetted to brigadier general of regulars) and **Antietam Campaigns**, Franklin's close allegiance to **George B. McClellan** earned him many enemies. At **Fredericksburg**, he was given command of the **army's** "Left Grand Division" and was accused by **Ambrose Burnside** of contributing to the disaster by disobeying orders. When Franklin became involved in the officer corps' intrigue against Burnside, Burnside demanded that he be cashiered. **Abraham Lincoln** refused, but Franklin's career was ruined when the **Committee on the Conduct of the War** supported Burnside's claims. He and Burnside were relieved of command on the same day in January 1863.

Franklin never was restored to his **corps** command. Instead, he was transferred to **Louisiana**, where in August 1863 he took command of the XIX Corps and led it in the **Sabine Pass** Expedition, the 1863 **Texas Overland Expedition**, and the 1864 **Red River Campaign**. After being wounded at **Mansfield**, Franklin was assigned to administrative duties.

Franklin resigned his volunteer commission in November 1865 and his regular commission in March 1866. He then served for many years as general manager of Colt's Fire Arms and supervised the construction of **Connecticut's** capitol building.

FRANKLIN'S CROSSING, VIRGINIA, BATTLE OF (JUNE 5, 1863). When **Robert E. Lee's Army of Northern Virginia** left its camps around Fredericksburg, Virginia, on June 3, 1863, to begin the **Gettysburg Campaign**, Maj. Gen. **Joseph Hooker** sent an **Army of the Potomac** detachment to probe Lee's position to confirm rumors that the enemy was on the move. On June 5, **John Sedgwick** sent the VI Corps' 26th New Jersey and 5th Vermont to Franklin's Crossing, near Deep Run, to cross the Rappahannock River. The entrenched Confederates of **A. P. Hill's** III Corps opened fire from the south side, but the two **regiments** crossed over in boats and captured the **rifle pits**. After meeting more Confederate resistance, the Federals then withdrew to the north bank. In the clash, the Federals lost 57 men, while the Confederates had at least 35 men taken **prisoner**. Sedgwick incorrectly reported to Hooker that Lee was still encamped on the south side of the river, not realizing that Hill's **corps** had been left behind and would march the next day. Still suspicious, Hooker sent his cavalry on a **reconnaissance** on June 9, which resulted in the **Battle of Brandy Station**.

FRASER, TRENHOLM & CO. This British company in Liverpool became an important part of the Confederacy's financial activities in Europe. A subsidiary of John Fraser & Co. in **Charleston, South Carolina**, it was established before the Civil War by **George A. Trenholm**. The company served almost as a Confederate bank and unofficial embassy. Its activities included converting currency for the Confederacy, maintaining government financial accounts, receiving government funds, helping arrange the **Erlanger Loan**, and selling Confederate cotton. Confederate agents **James D. Bulloch** and **Caleb Huse** kept offices in the company's building. The company received very little compensation for its activities, but it did run 50 **blockade runners** for its own profit.

FRAYSER'S FARM, VIRGINIA, BATTLE OF (JUNE 30, 1862). By June 30, 1862, the **Seven Days Campaign** was reaching its conclusion. **Robert E. Lee's Army of Northern Virginia** had pushed **George B. McClellan's Army of the Potomac** from the outskirts of **Richmond, Virginia**, down the Virginia Peninsula. During the campaign, Lee had tried to destroy isolated parts of McClellan's **army**, but unfamiliar terrain, poor staff work, and fumbling subordinates had frustrated him every time.

Lee made one last effort to crush a segment of McClellan's army as it retreated toward **Harrison's Landing** across a boggy morass called White Oak Swamp. Lee planned for **Thomas "Stonewall" Jackson's** command to press McClellan from the rear, while **James Longstreet, A. P. Hill, John B. Magruder**, and **Benjamin Huger** approached from the west and attacked the enemy's flank. If the attacks were coordinated, McClellan would be hit from flank and rear while he was crossing the swamp.

Once again, however, Lee's plans were spoiled. Jackson approached the swamp crossing about 11:00 A.M., but, as he had previously done in the campaign, he acted with uncharacteristic timidity and failed to make any serious attack against the Union rear guard. Across the swamp, Magruder and Huger were too slow and never reached their assigned positions in time to help, while Longstreet and Hill slugged it out alone with the Federals around Glendale and Frayser's Farm. As in the previous battles, McClellan was absent from the Union army and left no one in overall command on the battlefield. The **division** commanders were on their own and had to fight the best they could. A defensive line was formed facing west, with the divisions of **Philip Kearny** on the right, **George McCall** in the center, and **Joseph Hooker** on the left. Longstreet charged McCall's position at about 4:00 P.M. and was making progress when Hill joined in the attack. McCall's line was briefly broken, and the general was captured, but Kearny and Hooker finally contained the Confederate breakthrough. Fighting was vicious and raged past dark, but the Union line held.

Lee suffered over 3,600 casualties to McClellan's over 2,700, in this battle (which also was known as White Oak Swamp, Charles City Cross Roads, and Glendale). Although the Confederates failed to destroy McClellan's army, they continued to drive it farther away from Richmond. McClellan retreated to **Malvern Hill** that night and the next day fought the campaign's last battle.

FRAZER, JOHN WESLEY (1827–1906) CSA. A native of **Tennessee**, Frazer graduated from **West Point** in 1849 and rose to the rank of captain while performing routine garrison duty. He resigned his commission in March 1861 and entered Confederate service as a captain.

In June 1861, Frazer was appointed lieutenant colonel of the 8th Alabama and accompanied it to **Virginia**. He resigned from the **regiment** in March 1862 and accepted a colonel's commission for the 28th Alabama. Joining the regiment at **Corinth, Mississippi,** Frazer participated in the 1862 **Kentucky Campaign** but saw only rear guard action. Although he resigned his colonel's commission in late 1862, Frazer was appointed brigadier general in May 1863 and took command of a **brigade** in eastern Tennessee. In August, he became commander of Cumberland Gap and soon was threatened by **Ambrose Burnside's** Union **army** as it headed for **Knoxville, Tennessee.** Frazer received conflicting orders on whether to hold or abandon his position, and he finally decided to hold it. He soon became surrounded and was forced to surrender his 1,700 men on September 9. **Jefferson Davis** and others criticized Frazer for this, and the Senate refused to confirm his appointment to brigadier general. From **prison** at **Fort Warren, Massachusetts,** Frazer blamed his poorly trained troops for the disaster.

Frazer remained in prison until war's end and then moved to **Arkansas.** After the war, he worked as a planter and **New York** businessman.

FREDERICKSBURG, VIRGINIA, CAMPAIGN AND BATTLE OF (NOVEMBER 15–DECEMBER 15, 1862). In early November 1862, Maj. Gen. **Ambrose E. Burnside** replaced Maj. Gen. **George B. McClellan** as commander of the **Army of the Potomac** while the **army** was in camp on the north side of the Rappahannock River around Warrenton, Virginia. **Robert E. Lee's Army of Northern Virginia** was scattered, with **James Longstreet's** corps facing Burnside at Culpeper and **Stonewall Jackson's** corps in the **Shenandoah Valley.** McClellan was planning a campaign to thrust his army between the two enemy **corps** and **defeat in detail** the Confederates, but Burnside decided on a different **strategy**. He would march the army rapidly downstream to Falmouth, cross the river at Fredericksburg, and head south toward **Richmond** before Lee could bring his **corps** eastward into position to challenge him.

Burnside left his camps on November 15 and by rapid marches had his 120,000 men concentrated at Falmouth by November 19. The maneuver was a success, for Lee was at first unaware of Burnside's move and belatedly ordered his army toward Fredericksburg. The plan then fell apart.

Pontoon bridges failed to arrive, and Burnside refused to push across the river without them. He waited and gave Lee time to assemble his 75,000-man army along a seven-mile line one to two miles behind Fredericksburg. Lee placed Longstreet's corps on Marye's (muh-REEZ) Heights, with Jackson stretching to his right. Longstreet's position included a sunken road along the base of the heights that was lined with a stone wall, which gave his men a natural fortified position. **Artillery** massed farther up the hill covered the plain over which Burnside would have to cross to get to Lee.

Burnside's pontoon bridges finally arrived on November 25, but by then he was reluctant to cross the river in Lee's front. Unable to find any unguarded river crossings downstream, however, he finally decided to cross at Fredericksburg. **Engineers** began laying the pontoon bridges on December 11. Early morning fog helped cover the work and downstream progress was steady. At Fredericksburg Confederate Brig. Gen. **William Barksdale's Mississippi Brigade** contested the bridge building. Hiding in houses, the Confederates kept up a heavy fire on the Union engineers and delayed the crossing for hours. Burnside first tried to dislodge the Confederates with artillery fire but only succeeded in destroying the mostly evacuated town. Finally, infantry were rowed across the river in boats under fire, and Barksdale was forced to withdraw. The five bridges were then finished, and Burnside crossed most of his men over the river, where they promptly looted the town.

Burnside had divided the army into the Left Grand Division, under **William B. Franklin**, and the Right Grand Division, under **Edwin V. Sumner**. He planned to make a general advance on the morning of December 13, with Franklin attacking Jackson's position and Sumner attacking Longstreet. At first, a single Confederate cannon commanded by Maj. **John Pelham** confused and delayed Franklin by quickly moving from point to point, **enfilading** the Union line. When Franklin finally did attack, he had some success. Jackson's line ran through woods and low areas and did not enjoy the high hills found along Longstreet's front. A weak point was a low marshy bog that was largely left undefended. When Franklin advanced, **George Meade's division** managed to punch a hole through this gap in Jackson's line. Fierce fighting ensued, but Jackson rushed reinforcements forward, forced out Meade, and sealed the break. The battle then stagnated on the Confederate right, but it rose to a fury on Longstreet's front.

Wave after wave of Union troops assaulted Marye's Heights, only to be shot down in front of the stone wall. The **Irish Brigade** particularly won acclaim as it rushed toward the wall, but it was unable to break through. As many as 12 different **frontal attacks** were made, and all failed. Watching from the rear, Burnside was shocked at the results but gave orders for a new attack the next day. In what may have been a death wish, he announced that he would personally lead the charge. Cooler heads prevailed, however, and Burnside was persuaded to cancel the order. Thousands of Union soldiers, many of whom were desperately wounded, were forced to spend a bitterly cold night on the slopes of Marye's Heights before being withdrawn. Because of the artillery massed on the northern side of the river, Lee was powerless to pursue.

Fredericksburg was one of the Union's greatest disasters in the war and Lee's easiest victory. Burnside lost 12,653 men, while Lee counted 5,309 casualties (most of whom were on Jackson's front). Burnside recrossed the river on the night of December 15 and soon met further humiliation with his **Mud March**. Burnside blamed his subordinates for the failure at Fredericksburg and demanded that a number be cashiered from the army. Ultimately, however, it was he who was replaced by Maj. Gen. **Joseph Hooker**.

FREDERICKSBURG, VIRGINIA, SECOND BATTLE OF (MAY 3, 1863). During the 1863 **Chancellorsville Campaign**, Maj. Gen. **Joseph Hooker** planned to turn **Robert E. Lee's** position at Fredericksburg by taking most of the **Army of the Potomac** upstream and crossing the Rappahannock River. Hooker then would march around Lee's left flank and force him either to retreat or give battle on ground of Hooker's choosing. To keep Lee in place at Fredericksburg, Maj. Gen. **John Sedgwick** was placed in command of 40,000 men across the river at Falmouth.

Sedgwick crossed the river on April 30, 1863, as a **demonstration** to distract Lee from the upstream maneuver. When Lee surmised Hooker's plan, he left 10,000 men under **Jubal A. Early** to watch Sedgwick while the rest of the **Army of Northern Virginia** marched westward to battle Hooker at Chancellorsville. Early placed his men in a very thin line, running about eight miles along Marye's (muh-REEZ) Heights and other high ground outside Fredericksburg.

When Hooker encountered Lee at Chancellorsville, he ordered Sedgwick to push aside Early and strike Lee's rear to relieve some of the pressure on his front. On May 3, Sedgwick launched several attacks against **William Barksdale's Mississippi Brigade** holding Marye's Heights but was repulsed. During a truce to gather the wounded, Union officers noticed an undefended approach to Early's line. Their next attack used this approach and succeeded in forcing Barksdale and the entire Confederate line to retreat. Early fell back toward Chancellorsville and was reinforced when Lee split his **army** again and sent **Lafayette McLaws's** division to help. The Confederates made a stand at **Salem Church** that afternoon and halted the enemy. On May 4, Lee sent **Richard Anderson's** division to Salem Church as well. The three Confederate **divisions** then attacked Sedgwick late in the afternoon of May 4 and pinned him against the river, thus preventing him from joining Hooker. Sedgwick retreated across the river that night after suffering about 5,000 casualties, nearly all of whom were lost at Salem Church.

FREDERICKTOWN, MISSOURI, BATTLE OF (OCTOBER 21, 1861). In October 1861, two Union columns under Cols. **Joseph B. Plummer** and **William P. Carlin** advanced on Fredericktown, Missouri, where Confederate guerrillas under Brig. Gen. **M. Jeff Thompson** were located. On October 21, Thompson withdrew to the south to safely hide his wagon train and then returned, only to find that the enemy had occupied Fredericktown. At noon, Thompson attacked the superior Union force but was defeated by Plummer in a two-hour battle and was forced to retreat. Federal losses in the clash are unknown, but Thompson lost 62 men.

FREEDMEN. This term referred to slaves who were freed by the **Confiscation Act** of 1862, the **Emancipation Proclamation**, or the **13th Amendment**. Freedmen naturally were drawn to the Union armies as a means to guarantee their freedom. In fact, so many freedmen came within Union lines that they presented problems to authorities, who simply could not provide for such large numbers. Various measures were used to relieve this strain. Some freedmen were hired out to local planters (sometimes more or less forcibly), some were placed on confiscated land to farm, and others were accepted into the **army**. Eventually, such Northern aid societies as the New England Freedman's Aid Society were formed to help them. In March 1865, the U.S. government created the **Freedmen's Bureau** to provide federal help.

FREEDMEN'S BUREAU. During the Civil War, the problem of caring for the several million **freedmen** became nearly overwhelming, and numerous agencies and measures were tried. On March 4, 1865, the **U.S. Congress** created the Bureau for the Relief of Freedmen and Refugees (more commonly referred to as the Freedmen's Bureau) as a one-year experiment to consolidate care into one agency. Major General **Oliver O. Howard** was appointed commissioner in May 1865, and he sent the bureau into every Southern state to perform many services. It helped feed freedmen and poor whites, set up schools and hospitals, found jobs for the unemployed, oversaw working contracts with landowners, worked out labor disputes, and helped place freedmen on their own land. **Radi-**

cal **Republicans** passed a bill in February 1866 to continue the bureau's work, but President **Andrew Johnson** vetoed it. Congress successfully passed another Freedmen's Bureau bill in July and was able to override Johnson's veto. The Freedmen's Bureau went on to play an important role during **Reconstruction**.

FREE-SOIL PARTY. This was a very fractious political party that briefly existed from 1848 to 1852. It contained **Democrats**, **Whigs**, and Liberty Party members whose only common trait was the opposition of **slavery**. While some were **abolitionists** who wanted to free the slaves, most were content to allow the South to keep slaves as long as slavery did not spread into new territories recently won from Mexico. Some members opposed slavery on moral grounds and believed in at least limited rights for blacks, while others were racists who simply opposed slavery because free labor could not compete with slave labor. The latter believed slavery was a direct threat to the wage labor system of the North. The typical Free-Soiler thought slavery was wrong but did not believe in racial equality. Free-Soilers also championed **homesteading** public land and had as their slogan, "Free Soil for Free Men." The party ran Martin Van Buren for president in 1848 and split the Democratic vote enough to allow Whig candidate Zachary Taylor to win. Its 1852 candidate, John P. Hale, garnered few votes, and the party quickly disappeared. Many of the Free-Soilers joined the **Republican Party** when it was formed in 1854 as the main antislavery party.

FRÉMONT, JOHN CHARLES (1813–1890) USA. Born in **Georgia**, Frémont (fruh-MONT) was expelled from Charleston College and taught mathematics onboard a naval vessel before joining the **U.S. Army** as an **engineer** in 1838. He was very active in exploring the Rocky Mountains and earned the nickname "The Pathfinder" for discovering several important mountain passes. During the **Mexican War**, Frémont led a small force to **California** and seized control for the United States. He was elected governor by the voters and refused to relinquish control to Stephen W. Kearny when he arrived with orders to set up a government. Frémont subsequently was court-martialed and convicted of mutiny, but he was allowed to resign his commission. When admitted as a state, California elected him to the U.S. Senate, and in 1856 he ran for president on the first **Republican Party** ticket. An **abolitionist**, Frémont lost the election but became a very influential figure in the years preceding the Civil War.

Because of his political influence, Frémont was appointed major general of volunteers by **Abraham Lincoln** in July 1861, making him one of the four most senior Union generals. However, he proved to be one of the Union's most controversial and incompetent commanders. Hoping Frémont's popularity would help ensure **Missouri's** loyalty, Lincoln put him in command of the **Western Department**, with headquarters in St. Louis. Frémont was handsome, dramatic, and was admired by many, but he proved to be a poor administrator, and corruption and incompetent officers plagued his **department**.

One of Frémont's largest problems was fighting Confederate guerrillas. Believing that **slavery** strengthened the guerrillas, he issued an order on August 10, 1861, freeing all slaves in the Western Department. Greatly overstepping his authority, Frémont did not consult Lincoln and only informed the president of his actions a week later. Lincoln asked him to modify the order to conform to the **Confiscation Act** of 1861, but Frémont refused. Lincoln then quickly repudiated the order to keep the support of the slaveholding **border states**. Frémont's wife, Jessie Benton (daughter of Sen. Thomas Hart Benton) made things worse by personally visiting Lincoln in an attempt to help her husband.

In addition to his administrative blunders, Frémont also proved to be a poor general. Lincoln finally replaced him in November, but in March 1862, put him in command of the **Mountain Department**. Frémont was defeated by **Stonewall Jackson** at **McDowell** and **Cross Keys** during **Jackson's 1862 Shenandoah Valley Campaign**. Ordered to serve as a **corps** commander under **John Pope**, Frémont refused and was relieved of command in June 1862. For the rest of the war, he remained in **New York** awaiting orders that never came.

Frémont considered running for president as a **Radical Republican** in 1864 but eventually decided against it. After the war, he was involved in **railroads** and in 1873 was convicted by the French government of dishonest activities associated with a western railroad. Frémont also was appointed territorial governor of Arizona in 1878.

FRENCH, SAMUEL GIBBS (1818–1910) CSA. A native of **New Jersey**, French graduated from **West Point** in 1843. In the **Mexican War**, he won two **brevets** for gallantry, was seriously wounded at Buena Vista, and while in the hospital became friends with fellow wounded officer **Jefferson Davis**. French resigned from the **army** in 1856 and became a **Mississippi** planter. He was appointed Mississippi's chief of ordnance when the state seceded in 1861, and in October President Davis appointed him brigadier general in the **Confederate army**.

Sent to **Virginia**, French oversaw construction of much of the **Richmond** and **Petersburg, Virginia**, defenses. He took command of southern Virginia and North Carolina in July 1862 and was instrumental in preparing **Fort Fisher** to defend **Wilmington, North Carolina**. Promoted to major general in October 1862, French briefly commanded the **Department of Southern Virginia** and then was sent to Jackson, Mississippi, to command a **division** in **Joseph E. Johnston's** army during the **Vicksburg Campaign**. French's division next participated in the **Atlanta Campaign** with the **Army of Tennessee**, and it led the attack against **Allatoona, Georgia**, in October 1864. After leading his division at **Franklin**, he was forced to take sick leave because of an infected eye that had been plaguing him since the Atlanta Campaign. Afterward, French served in the **Mobile, Alabama, Campaign** and was captured there in April 1865.

After the war, French returned to Mississippi and then moved to **Florida** and remained there until his death.

FRENCH, WILLIAM HENRY (1815–1881) USA. A native of **Maryland**, French graduated from **West Point** in 1837 and served with the **artillery** in the **Seminole Wars** and as an aide to Gen. Franklin Pierce in the **Mexican War**. He earned two **brevets** for gallantry in the latter. In 1861, French was in command of a garrison at Eagle Pass, **Texas**. Refusing secessionists' demands to surrender, he evacuated his men to the mouth of the Rio Grande for transport to Key West, **Florida**.

Promoted to brigadier general of volunteers in September 1861, French was given command of an infantry **brigade** in the **Army of the Potomac** and fought in the **Peninsula** and **Seven Days Campaigns**. He then was elevated to a **division** command and led it at **Antietam**. After being promoted to major general of volunteers in November 1862, French fought at **Fredericksburg** and **Chancellorsville**, but he was left in command of **Harpers Ferry, West Virginia**, during the **Gettysburg Campaign**. After the Battle of Gettysburg, he earned the displeasure of **George G. Meade** by moving too slowly in pursuit of the enemy and allowing the Confederates to retreat into **Virginia** unmolested.

After the Gettysburg Campaign, French replaced the wounded **Daniel Sickles** in command of the III Corps. As a **corps** commander, he proved disappointing. During the **Mine Run Campaign**, French again was slow and performed poorly at **Payne's Farm**. When the **army** was reorganized in the spring of 1864, the III Corps was disbanded, and French left the volunteer service. He continued to serve in the **U.S. Army** in various administrative duties and eventually rose to the rank of colonel.

FRENCH'S FIELD, VIRGINIA, BATTLE OF (JUNE 25, 1862). *See* KING'S SCHOOL HOUSE, VIRGINIA, BATTLE OF.

FRITCHIE, BARBARA (1766–1862) USA. The subject of the famous John G. Whittier poem by the same name, the aged Mrs. Fritchie supposedly waved a Union **flag** at **Stonewall Jackson** as he marched through Frederick, **Maryland**, during the 1862 **Antietam Campaign**. Faced by the scowling enemy, she reportedly shouted, "Shoot if you must this old gray head, but spare your country's flag" (Boatner, *Civil War Dictionary*, 316–17). The Confederates were said to have admired her bravery and showed her respect. Actually, there is no proof Fritchie ever did what is claimed. More convincing evidence indicates it was Mary S. Quantrill, a relative of Confederate guerrilla **William Quantrill**, who did these things. But it was Fritchie who became associated with the story and was immortalized by Whittier.

FRONT ROYAL, VIRGINIA, BATTLE OF (MAY 23, 1862). During **Stonewall Jackson's 1862 Shenandoah Valley Campaign**, Jackson maneuvered to turn Maj. Gen. **Nathaniel Banks** out of his position at Strasburg, Virginia. Jackson's **Valley Army** was split by Massanutten Mountain, with Jackson moving down the Valley on its west side toward Strasburg and **Richard S. Ewell's division** marching to the east in the Luray Valley. Jackson first acted as if he would attack Strasburg to pin Banks into position, but then he suddenly marched eastward over Massanutten Mountain at New Market. Joining Ewell in the Luray Valley, Jackson then had close to 17,000 men to strike a small 1,000-man Union garrison at Front Royal. If successful, he would break Banks's left flank and be in a position to advance to **Winchester**, deep in Banks's rear, and force him to abandon Strasburg.

While approaching Front Royal on May 23, 1862, Jackson was met by sometime-spy **Belle Boyd**, who told him that few enemy troops were in the town. He quickly sent forward the 1st Maryland (Confederate) at about 2:00 P.M. to seize the crucial bridges across the Shenandoah River's South Fork. This Confederate **regiment** clashed with Col. **John R. Kenly's** 1st Maryland (Union). When Kenly burned one bridge and retreated, Jackson sent **Richard Taylor's brigade** forward to save the bridge. This was accomplished, and the Union troops were routed. A Confederate cavalry charge then wounded and captured Kenly and most of his men. The Federals lost 904 men, mostly taken **prisoner**, while Jackson lost only 56. The victory forced Banks to retreat and led to the **First Battle of Winchester** two days later.

FRONTAL ATTACK. This was the primary infantry **tactic** used by **armies** since colonial times. It was a direct attack against an enemy's front, as opposed to a flanking or **turning movement**. The tactic was developed when armies used inaccurate smoothbore muskets and relied more on the **bayonet** than firearms to decide a battle. During the Civil War, the use of entrenchments and accurate **rifle muskets** made the frontal attack nearly suicidal, as proved at **Gettysburg**, **Cold Harbor**, **Kennesaw Mountain**, **Franklin**, and **Fredericksburg**. Still, generals continued to order them because they were easier to control and to coordinate than flank attacks and there sometimes was the hope that the element of surprise would make a difference. One example of a successful frontal attack was the Union victory at **Missionary Ridge**.

FROST, DANIEL MARSH (1823–1900) CSA. A native of **New York**, Frost graduated from **West Point** in 1844, where he became close friends with a number of Southern cadets. He won a **brevet** for gallantry in the **Mexican War** and then served a year in Europe before resigning his lieutenant's commission in 1853 and moving to St. Louis, **Missouri**. There Frost became a manufacturer, state legislator, member of the West Point Board of Visitors, general of state militia, and an ardent secessionist.

In 1861, Frost was in command of the Missouri militia and established **Camp Jackson** outside St. Louis as a secessionist stronghold in preparation to seizing the federal arsenal. When attacked by **Nathaniel Lyon**, Frost denied being involved in such a plot, but he was forced to surrender his men in any case. He later blamed the Unionists for the **St. Louis Riot** that occurred when the **prisoners** were marched through the city.

After being **exchanged**, Frost was put in command of two **divisions** of Missouri state troops and led them at **Pea Ridge**. He then raised an **artillery** brigade and served as **Braxton Bragg's** inspector general at Corinth, Mississippi, before being appointed brigadier general in October 1862. Given a division, Frost first fought at **Prairie Grove** and then in the summer of 1863 was sent to defend **Little Rock**, **Arkansas**, and assume command of most of the infantry in the area. After the city fell to Union forces, he resumed commanding a **brigade**. In 1863, Frost became absent without leave when he left the **army** to join his family, which had fled St. Louis for Canada. In December 1863, he became the only Confederate general to be dropped from the rolls for such misconduct.

After the war, Frost returned to the St. Louis area and became a farmer.

FRY, BIRKETT DAVENPORT (1822–1891) CSA. A native of western **Virginia**, Fry attended both the **Virginia Military Institute** and **West Point** but graduated from neither. He became a lawyer, served in **California** during the **Mexican War**, and became one of William Walker's generals during his filibustering expedition in Central America.

Fry was an **Alabama** cotton manufacturer when the Civil War began and organized the 13th Alabama. Appointed its colonel in July 1861, he served in the **Peninsula Campaign** and was severely wounded in the right hand at **Seven Pines**. Fry recovered in time to fight at **South Mountain** with the **Army of Northern Virginia** and was praised for his service at **Antietam**, where his left arm was badly shattered. He recovered in time to fight at **Chancellorsville** and again was slightly wounded while in temporary command of his **brigade**. At **Gettysburg**, Fry again took temporary command of the brigade when **James Archer** was captured. During **Pickett's Charge**, he was wounded in the shoulder during the preliminary **artillery** bombardment but still accompanied his brigade in the attack. Fry's brigade was in the center of the assault and served as the guide for the other brigades. His thigh was fractured by a **rifle** ball in the attack, and he was left behind and captured.

After being **exchanged** in April 1864, Fry eventually was given command of a brigade at **Richmond, Virginia**, and fought at **Second Drewry's Bluff** in May. After rejoining the main **army**, he was promoted to brigadier general later that month and fought with his brigade in the final stages of the **Overland Campaign**. Unwell from his wounds, Fry went on sick leave in June and never returned to the army. Instead, he was sent to **Georgia** in September to command the garrison at Augusta. Fry remained at that post until war's end, at which time he escaped to Cuba rather than surrendering.

Fry later returned to the United States in 1868 and lived in several Southern states as a manufacturer.

FRY, JAMES BARNETT (1827–1894) USA. A native of **Illinois**, Fry graduated from **West Point** in 1847 and served on garrison duty in Mexico during the **Mexican War**. Afterward, he was adjutant for West Point and was in command of an **artillery** battery when the Civil War began.

At **First Manassas**, Fry was **Irvin McDowell's** chief of staff, a position he later held for **Don Carlos Buell** and the **Army of the Ohio** at **Shiloh, Corinth**, and **Perryville**. He was appointed the Union's Provost Marshal General in March 1863 and did an outstanding job fighting **desertion** and enforcing **conscription**. By war's end, Fry was **brevetted** through all of the ranks to major general of regulars. He retired from the **U.S. Army** in 1881 as a brigadier general.

FRY, SPEED SMITH (1817–1892) USA. A native of **Kentucky**, Fry graduated from Wabash College and became a lawyer. He raised a volunteer **company** and served as its captain in the **Mexican War** and was serving as a county judge when the Civil War began.

Fry entered Union service in July 1861 when he was appointed colonel of Kentucky militia. He was made colonel of the 4th Kentucky (Union) in October and at **Mill Springs** shot and killed Confederate Brig. Gen. **Felix Zollicoffer**. Promoted to brigadier general of volunteers in March 1862, Fry commanded a **brigade** in the **Army of the Ohio** at **Shiloh** and was described by **Don Carlos Buell** as being "inefficient," although he never entered the fight. At year's end, he commanded a **division** in the **Army of the Cumberland** at **Stones River**, but again he missed the battle. Afterward, Fry was placed on garrison duty and spent most of his later service in command of Kentucky's Camp Nelson. When he left the **army** in August 1865, Fry did not receive the customary **brevet**.

Fry remained in Kentucky after the war and was superintendent of Louisville's Soldiers' Home when he died.

FUGITIVE SLAVE ACT. One of the major political issues in 1850 was runaway slaves. In 1793, a federal fugitive slave act was passed allowing slave owners to recapture runaways without a warrant. This outraged **abolitionists**, who began to hide runaways and helped pass Northern personal liberty laws giving protection to runaway slaves. As part of the **Compromise of 1850**, a new, stronger federal Fugitive Slave Act was passed to placate the South. This law gave authority to U.S. marshals to track down and return runaway slaves to their masters. It also required civilians to aid the marshals when called on for help and provided punishment for those who refused assistance or helped runaways. Finally, the law denied the right of **habeas corpus** or trial by jury for runaways. The law was hated by abolitionists and other Northerners and further split the North and South.

FULLER, JOHN WALLACE (1827–1891) USA. Born in Great Britain, Fuller immigrated to **New York** as a boy. In the 1850s, he became a publisher, city treasurer, and militia officer before moving to **Ohio**.

When the Civil War began, Fuller first trained Union troops in western **Virginia** before being appointed colonel of the 27th Ohio. He led his **regiment** at **New Madrid and Island No. 10** and commanded a **brigade** in the **Army of the Tennessee** at **Iuka** and **Corinth**. In the latter battle, Fuller played a key role in repulsing the Confederate attack. His greatest moment came in December 1862 when he defeated **Nathan Bedford Forrest** at **Parker's Cross Roads** and claims to have captured more than 300 of Forrest's men. Afterward, Fuller mostly served on garrison duty, but in January 1864, he was promoted to brigadier general of volunteers. Fuller led a brigade during the **Atlanta Campaign** and temporarily had a **division** at the Battle of Atlanta, but he resumed his brigade command for the **March to the Sea** and the **Carolinas Campaign**. **Brevetted** major general of volunteers for his war service, he resigned from the **army** in August 1865 and returned to Ohio to become a merchant.

FURLOUGH. This was leave from the **army** taken by an enlisted man. Furloughs usually were for specific lengths of time, and the soldier had to leave his weapon and **accouterments** behind with his unit. Furloughs usually were difficult to receive, especially as the war dragged on, and sometimes were used as inducements in the Union army to entice veterans to reenlist early. Many veterans believed they would not live to see the end of their original enlistment and might as well reenlist early in order to go home one last time.

FUSE. Fuses were used to detonate **artillery** shells. Percussion fuses had fulminate that detonated on impact and exploded the shell. Time fuses were wooden or paper tubes with a compound that ignited when the cannon was discharged. The fuse burned at a certain rate and exploded the shell when it reached the powder charge. Time fuses were tricky, because the artillerymen had to cut the fuse just the right length in order to explode the shell at the proper time. *See also* PERCUSSION CAPS.

– G –

GABION. This was a cylindrical, open-ended basket made by weaving brush or metal strips on wooden pickets. They often were filled with rocks and earth and were used in making **revetments** and field fortifications.

GAINES' MILL, VIRGINIA, BATTLE OF (JUNE 27, 1862). Also known as the Battle of Cold Harbor or the Chickahominy, this was the bloodiest battle of the **Seven Days Campaign**. On June 26, 1862, the campaign's second day, **Robert E. Lee's Army of Northern Virginia** attacked Union Maj. Gen. **Fitz John Porter's** isolated V Corps on the north side of the Chickahominy River. Porter successfully repulsed the Confederate attacks at **Mechanicsville** and then withdrew his corps that night to Gaines' Mill as George B. McClellan decided to withdraw his entire **Army of the Potomac** down the Virginia Peninsula. On June 27, Porter put his 30,000 men in a semicircle along a plateau overlooking Boatswain's Swamp, a low, marshy area the Confederates would have to cross to attack his position. **George Sykes's** division held the right, **George W. Morell**, the left, and **George McCall** was in reserve, with batteries of **artillery** arranged behind them farther up the slope.

Lee pursued Porter with approximately 57,000 men and ordered **Stonewall Jackson** to keep his command on the far Confederate left and, with the support of **Daniel H. Hill**, to make a circuitous march to strike Porter's right flank. As at Mechanicsville, Jackson performed poorly. The secretive general told his guide to lead him to Old Cold Harbor, and the guide took him on the shortest route that went through Gaines' Mill. When Jackson realized he was approaching the center of Porter's line instead of the flank, he had to stop and countermarch to reach his proper destination.

In the meantime, Maj. Gen. **A. P. Hill** reached Porter and attacked that afternoon without waiting for Lee's other units to get into position. Hill launched numerous attacks but was repulsed each time with heavy losses. **James Longstreet** finally arrived on Hill's right, and then Daniel H. Hill, who had marched ahead of Jackson, arrived on the left. Lee ordered Longstreet to wait for Jackson to get into position on the flank before launching additional attacks, but Hill attacked on the left and was repulsed. Although battered, Porter was holding his position and finally was reinforced by **Henry W. Slocum's** VI Corps **division**. When Jackson failed to arrive, Lee went ahead and sent Longstreet into action to take some of the pressure off Daniel H. Hill's front. Longstreet also was repulsed with heavy losses.

Jackson finally arrived in position about 3:00 P.M., but he only sent a couple of **brigades** into action because he was unaware of the tactical situation and was afraid his men might be fired on by other Confederates. It was not until 7:00 P.M. that Lee finally had his entire **army** on hand. Brigadier Generals **John B. Hood's** and **Evander M. Law's** brigades launched a determined attack against Porter's center and finally broke through. The Confederates pressed Porter, but his retreat was skillfully conducted, and he escaped again. One of the battle's more tragic moments came when the 5th and part of the 2nd U.S. Cavalry were slaughtered as they launched a suicidal charge to hold back the Confederates.

Lee had won the battle but at a terrible cost, and many soldiers remembered Gaines' Mill to have been one of the hardest fought battles of the war. The Confederates lost 8,750 men, while Porter counted 6,837 casualties. Porter retreated across the Chickahominy River that night to join McClellan, and the Union army continued its retreat down the peninsula.

GAINESVILLE, TEXAS, HANGINGS. *See* "GREAT GAINSVILLE, TEXAS, HANGING."

GALLATIN, TENNESSEE, BATTLE OF (AUGUST 12, 1862). During the 1862 **Kentucky Campaign**, Confederate Maj. Gen. **Edmund Kirby**

Smith sent Col. **John Hunt Morgan's** cavalry from Sparta, Tennessee, to Gallatin to destroy an 800-foot-long **railroad** bridge there. On August 12, 1862, Morgan attacked the town, which was garrisoned by Union cavalry. At a cost of 24 men, Morgan inflicted 280 casualties on the defenders, mostly **prisoners** taken, and burned the bridge.

"GALVANIZED YANKEE." Of the thousands of Confederates taken **prisoner** during the Civil War, some 6,000 escaped confinement beginning in September 1864 by taking the **oath of allegiance** and joining the Union **army**. These so-called Galvanized Yankees were used mostly on frontier duty and were not required to fight their former comrades. They performed valuable service fighting **Indians** and providing security but were hated by other Confederates and generally were viewed with suspicion by their Union comrades.

GALVESTON, TEXAS, BATTLE OF (JANUARY 1, 1863). On October 5, 1862, the **U.S. Navy** steamed into Galveston Bay, Texas, and forced the Confederate defenders to surrender the city, although the Confederates managed to evacuate their men and guns. A number of vessels, commanded by Cmdr. William B. Renshaw, then anchored in the bay, while 260 men of the 42nd Massachusetts garrisoned the town. Confederate Maj. Gen. **John B. Magruder** converted two steamers, the *Bayou City* and *Neptune*, into **cottonclad** gunboats and assembled a small force to retake the town.

Magruder attacked before dawn on January 1, 1863. Confederate infantry quickly pinned down the 42nd Massachusetts on a wharf, while the two gunboats attacked Renshaw. One Union gunboat ran aground trying to get under way, and the **USS *Harriet Lane*** rammed the *Bayou City*. In turn, the *Neptune* rammed the *Harriet Lane*, but the *Neptune* was heavily damaged and sank. The *Bayou City* then rammed the *Harriet Lane*, and both ships became entangled. Confederate cavalry under **Thomas Green** boarded the Union ship, and in a vicious hand-to-hand fight the Union commander and first officer both were killed, and the *Harriet Lane* finally surrendered. Turning on the grounded Union vessel *Westfield*, the Confederates demanded its surrender after promising to allow the crew to abandon ship safely. Renshaw refused, evacuated most of the crew, and then climbed aboard to blow it up. Unfortunately, the ship exploded prematurely, killing Renshaw and the crewmen with him. By then Magruder had captured most of the Union infantry in town, and the remaining Union gunboats withdrew.

In the four-hour fight, Magruder recaptured Galveston, inflicted 414 casualties on the enemy, captured one Union gunboat, and caused another to be destroyed, at a cost of only 143 men. The town remained in Confederate hands and was the South's only remaining open port when the war ended.

GAMBLE, HAMILTON ROWAN (1798–1864) USA. A native of **Virginia**, Gamble graduated from Hampden-Sydney College and became a lawyer. Moving to **Missouri**, he practiced law and served as the state secretary of state in 1824–25, was elected to the state legislature as a **Whig** in 1846, and sat on the state supreme court from 1851 to 1854. In the latter position, Gamble wrote a dissenting opinion in the **Dred Scott** case and supported Scott's claim of freedom. After illness forced him to resign from the court in 1854, Gamble briefly moved to **Pennsylvania**. During the **secession** crisis, he returned to Missouri to try to ensure its loyalty to the Union.

Although he opposed **secession**, Gamble was a moderate and in June 1861 was appointed Missouri's provisional governor when Gov. **Claiborne F. Jackson** fled to form a secessionist government. He became a supporter of the Union war effort, but his moderate nature sometimes angered Unionists. Gamble occasionally refused to use state troops to reinforce Union forces in the state and allowed many secessionists to join the state militia. He also angered **abolitionists** by supporting a plan in 1863 to gradually emancipate Missouri's slaves. Gamble served as governor until his death in 1864.

GANO, RICHARD MONTGOMERY (1830–1913) CSA. A native of **Kentucky**, Gano graduated from **Virginia's** Bethany College and became a physician after attending the Louisville University Medical School. After practicing medicine for eight years, he moved to **Texas** and became a rancher and **Indian** fighter.

Gano was elected to the state legislature in 1860 but in 1861 organized and became captain of Gano's Texas Cavalry Battalion for service in Kentucky at the request of Confederate Gen. **Albert Sidney Johnston**. Gano's men captured numerous Union **prisoners** along the Mississippi River before joining **John Hunt Morgan's** cavalry at **Chattanooga, Tennessee**. The 7th Kentucky Cavalry (Confederate) was organized around Gano's battalion and became one of Morgan's best units. Gano became its colonel in September 1862 and fought in **Morgan's Kentucky Raids** and in the **Tullahoma Campaign** before illness forced him to return home.

In July 1863, Gano was put in command of the Texas state cavalry, but in October, he was placed in command of a poorly **disciplined** cavalry **brigade** to improve its usefulness. Although a competent commander, his brigade was poorly equipped and **desertions** were frequent when it was sent into **Indian Territory**. Gano served there until 1864, at which time his brigade went to **Arkansas** to help stop the **Camden Expedition**. A serious wound received in one **skirmish** kept him out of the field for a while. Returning to Indian Territory, Gano joined Brig. Gen. **Stand Watie** and led his brigade in frequent skirmishes with the enemy late that summer. He particularly was active around **Forts Gibson** and Scott and once captured a 300-wagon train. During his career, Gano was frequently praised by his superiors as an outstanding cavalry officer. In March 1865, he was finally promoted to brigadier general, but the war ended before he performed much service at that rank.

After the war, Gano returned to Kentucky, but he soon moved back to Texas and served as a minister in the First Christian Church for more than 45 years.

GARDNER, ALEXANDER (1821–1882) USA. A native of Scotland, Gardner worked his way up from reporter to editor of a Glasgow newspaper. During that time, he became acquainted with photography but how and to what degree is unknown. Gardner immigrated to New York City in 1856 and was hired by **Mathew Brady** for his popular studio. In 1858, Gardner began managing Brady's **Washington, D.C.**, studio. There, he photographed **Abraham Lincoln** during the 1861 inauguration and was ordered by Brady to follow the **Army of the Potomac** during the early part of the Civil War.

Gardner took numerous battlefield and camp life photographs. These and the Lincoln photographs became famous, but Brady, not Gardner, received credit for them since the photographs carried the name of Brady's studio. In 1863, Gardner left Brady's service and began his own studio in Washington. He hired other photographers and went to the **Gettysburg** battlefield that summer to take some of the war's most famous photographs. Afterward, Gardner stayed mostly at the Washington studio while his photographers, including **Timothy O'Sullivan** (whom he hired away from Brady) and Brady's brother James, followed the **army**.

After the war, Gardner photographed the Union armies' **Grand Review**, the **Lincoln assassination** conspirators and executions, and the execution of **Henry Wirz**. After publishing his work in the *Gardner's Photographic Sketch Book of the War* (1865), he moved west and photographed much of the Union Pacific Railroad's construction of the transcontinental line.

GARDNER, FRANKLIN (1823–1873) CSA. A native of New York City, Gardner was the son of a **U.S. Army** officer and became the brother-in-law of future Confederate Brig. Gen. **J. J. Alfred Mouton**. He graduated from **West Point** in 1843 and saw extensive combat in the **Mexican War**, winning two **brevets** for gallantry. Afterward, Gardner served in the **Seminole Wars** and on the frontier and rose to the rank of captain. He married the daughter of Louisiana's Gov. Alexander Mouton and supported the Confederate cause after **Louisiana** seceded.

Gardner abandoned his **U.S. Army** post in the spring of 1861, but he never actually resigned his U.S. commission. As a result, he was dropped from the army's rolls in May. Gardner entered Confederate service in March 1861 as a lieutenant colonel of infantry and had an embarrassing start when he was arrested for public drunkenness. He was assigned to **Braxton Bragg's** command at **Pensacola, Florida**, and again was arrested for drunkenness while in Mobile, Alabama. These charges were not pursued, and in March 1862 Gardner was given command of a cavalry **brigade**, which served at **Shiloh** but did not enter combat.

Despite his fondness for alcohol, Gardner was promoted to brigadier general in April 1862 and led an infantry brigade during the 1862 **Kentucky Campaign**. In December, he was promoted to major general and was placed in command of a **district** in the **Department of Mississippi and East Louisiana**. Establishing his headquarters at Port Hudson, Louisiana, Gardner worked diligently to strengthen that position and in March 1863 succeeded in sinking one Union ship and damaging others when **David Farragut** steamed past Port Hudson for **Vicksburg, Mississippi**.

In May 1863, Union Maj. Gen. **Nathaniel P. Banks** began the **Port Hudson Campaign**. Gardner's **department** commander, **Joseph E. Johnston**, ordered him to evacuate the town, but his immediate superior, **John C. Pemberton**, told him President **Jefferson Davis** wanted Vicksburg and Port Hudson to be held at all costs. Gardner followed Pemberton's advice and with barely almost 7,000 men skillfully defended Port Hudson through a 49-day siege against Banks's 30,000 men. Gardner was a source of strength for his soldiers. When food ran scarce, he was the first to eat mule meat and later dined on rats and dried magnolia leaves. He repulsed all of Banks's attacks, but when he learned of Vicksburg's surrender, Gardner decided it was futile to hold out any longer and surrendered the garrison on July 9, 1863. After being **exchanged** in August 1863, he took command of a district in the **Department of Alabama, Mississippi, and East Louisiana** until war's end.

After the war, Gardner became a Louisiana planter.

GARDNER, WILLIAM MONTGOMERY (1824–1901) CSA. A native of **Georgia**, Gardner graduated from **West Point** in 1846 and fought in several battles during the **Mexican War**. He was **brevetted** once for gallantry and was seriously wounded at Churubusco. Afterward, Gardner served on the frontier and rose to the rank of captain.

Gardner resigned his commission when Georgia seceded and entered Confederate service as lieutenant colonel of the 8th Georgia. At **First Manassas**, he took command of the **regiment** when **Francis Bartow** was wounded, but he also was severely wounded in the left leg. Reports that his wound was mortal proved untrue, and Gardner was promoted to brigadier general in November 1861.

Despite his promotion, Gardner was unable to take the field because of his wound and returned to Georgia. He remained there until 1863, when he took command of a **brigade** in the **Army of Tennessee**. In November 1863, Gardner was placed in command of the District of Middle Florida. He arrived at **Olustee** shortly after the battle in February 1864 and angered some superiors by breaking off the pursuit of the defeated enemy. In May 1864, Gardner was transferred to **Virginia**, where he first served on a court-martial and then was assigned to the **Richmond** defenses. Until war's end, he sometimes commanded Richmond and sometimes was in charge of most of the eastern **prisons**. Gardner was relieved of all duties in March 1865 and was ordered back to Georgia, but when he reached **Salisbury**, **North Carolina**, he assumed command of its defenses to contest the advance of Maj. Gen. **George Stoneman's** Union cavalry. Gardner's defeat there in April was one of the war's last battles.

When the war was over, Gardner returned to Georgia and later moved to **Tennessee**.

GARFIELD, JAMES ABRAM (1831–1881) USA. A native of **Ohio**, Garfield had an impoverished childhood but put himself through Williams College, taught at Western Reserve Eclectic Institute, and was elected to the state senate as a **Republican** in 1859.

Garfield entered Union service in August 1861 as lieutenant colonel of the 42nd Ohio and was promoted to colonel in November. He worked hard to learn his new profession and studied drills at night by using blocks on his table. Placed in command of a **brigade**, Garfield saw his first combat in small **Kentucky skirmishes** and was promoted to brigadier general of volunteers in January 1862.

After arriving at **Shiloh** with his **Army of the Ohio** brigade late on the second day of fighting, Garfield took part in the **siege of Corinth, Mississippi**. He then was elected to the **U.S. Congress**, but he remained with the **army** since he did not have to take his seat until December 1863. While on sick leave in late 1862, Garfield served on

Fitz John Porter's court-martial and supported the decision to cashier him. Upon his return to duty, he became **William S. Rosecrans's** chief of staff for the **Army of the Cumberland** in January 1863. When Rosecrans retreated to Chattanooga, Tennessee, after his defeat at **Chickamauga**, Garfield volunteered to return to the battlefield and assisted **George H. Thomas** in making his famous stand at **Snodgrass Hill**. This action allowed Garfield to escape the condemnation that befell Rosecrans and won him promotion to major general of volunteers in September 1863.

In December 1863, Garfield left the army and took his seat in Congress. He was reelected eight more times and in 1880 was elected to the U.S. Senate. Elected the twentieth president in 1880, Garfield was mortally wounded in 1881 by a deranged and disgruntled office seeker.

GARLAND, SAMUEL, JR. (1830–1862) CSA. A native of **Virginia**, Garland graduated from the **Virginia Military Institute** and the University of Virginia Law School. He then practiced law in Virginia and became captain of a local militia **company** that he organized.

Garland entered Confederate service in April 1861 as a captain in the 11th Virginia, but he almost immediately was elected colonel. He and his **regiment** were praised for their actions at **Blackburn's Ford**, **Dranesville**, and **Williamsburg** (in which Garland was wounded), and Garland's conspicuous conduct won him promotion to brigadier general in May 1862.

Given an infantry **brigade**, Garland led the Confederate attack at **Seven Pines** but suffered heavy losses and had two horses shot from under him. After earning more praise for his actions at **Gaines' Mill** with the **Army of Northern Virginia**, he participated in the **Antietam Campaign** and helped defend **South Mountain** as part of **Daniel H. Hill's division**. After being attacked by a much superior Union force at Fox's Gap, Garland was inspecting his line and talking with a regimental colonel, when both officers were wounded. Garland died shortly afterward. Hill described Garland as "the most fearless man I ever knew" (Davis, ed., *The Confederate General*, vol. 2, 166), and his premature death cut short a promising military career.

GARNETT, RICHARD BROOKE (1817–1863) CSA. A cousin of Confederate Brig. Gen. **Robert S. Garnett**, Garnett (GAHR-nit) was a native of **Virginia** who graduated with his cousin from **West Point** in 1841. He served in the **Seminole Wars** but missed the **Mexican War** and served most of his antebellum military career on garrison duty.

Garnett resigned his **U.S. Army** commission in May 1861 and entered Confederate service as a major of infantry. Promoted to brigadier general in November, he was sent to the **Shenandoah Valley** and took command of the **Stonewall Brigade** under **Stonewall Jackson**. At the **First Battle of Kernstown**, Garnett earned Jackson's wrath by pulling his **brigade** out of line without orders when it began running out of ammunition in the face of a superior enemy force. Jackson lost the battle and arrested Garnett on charges of neglect of duty, but no trial ever was completed because of the constant campaigning. When Jackson was mortally wounded at **Chancellorsville** in 1863, the matter was quietly dropped. The entire affair was unfortunate and unjust, and Jackson may have been trying to make Garnett the scapegoat for the Kernstown defeat (ironically, Garnett served as a pallbearer in Jackson's funeral).

Before Jackson's death, and over his bitter objections, Garnett finally was released from arrest and was given command of a brigade in **George Pickett's division**, but his reputation was tarnished and the Kernstown incident continued to haunt him. At **Antietam**, he saw action late in the battle, but he was not engaged at **Fredericksburg**. Afterward, Garnett served in **North Carolina** with **Daniel H. Hill** and in the siege of **Suffolk, Virginia**, before rejoining the **Army of Northern Virginia** for the **Gettysburg Campaign**. He saw no action in the first two days at Gettysburg, but on July 3, 1863, Garnett's brigade was a part of **Pickett's Charge**.

Garnett was sick at Gettysburg, had been injured by a horse kick a few days earlier, and had difficulty moving. Still, he insisted on leading his brigade—probably to atone for the Kernstown incident. Because of his injury, Garnett rode his horse in the attack instead of walking like other officers. Leading the brigade in the center of the line, he was last seen riding into the smoke around the "copse of trees." Garnett was never seen again, although his bloodstained horse was found later. It is not known where or how Garnett died, but his sword was discovered years later in Baltimore, Maryland.

GARNETT, ROBERT SELDON (1819–1861) CSA. A native of **Virginia**, Garnett (GAHR-nit) was a cousin of Confederate Brig. Gen. **Richard B. Garnett**. He graduated with his cousin from **West Point** in 1841 and fought in both the **Seminole** and **Mexican Wars**, winning two **brevets** for gallantry in the latter. Afterward, Garnett became commandant of cadets at West Point and taught infantry **tactics** there. While he was serving in the Pacific Northwest fighting **Indians**, his wife and child died. Devastated, Garnett took leave and was traveling in Europe during the **secession** crisis.

Garnett hurried home, resigned his major's commission in April 1861, was appointed Virginia's adjutant general, and then entered Confederate service in June 1861 as a brigadier general. He was put in command of the Confederate forces in western Virginia and was defeated at **Cheat Mountain** and Laurel Hill by a much superior enemy force. While retreating through the mountains, Garnett was mortally wounded in a small battle at **Carrick's Ford** on July 13, 1861. He was the first general, on either side, to be killed in the war.

GARNETT'S AND GOLDING'S FARMS, VIRGINIA, BATTLE OF (JUNE 27–28, 1862). During the opening days of the **Seven Days Campaign**, several Confederate **divisions** of the **Army of Northern Virginia** were left on the south side of the Chickahominy River to guard **Richmond, Virginia**, while **Robert E. Lee** attacked the right flank of **George B. McClellan's Army of the Potomac** north of the river. On June 27, 1862, while Lee was engaged at **Gaines' Mill**, Confederate Brig. Gen. **Robert Toombs** advanced his **brigade** on the south side of the Chickahominy to probe the Union lines around Garnett's Farm. Toombs was decisively defeated by **William F. "Baldy" Smith's** Union brigade and suffered 271 casualties. The next day, Toombs was ordered forward again to see if the Federals were withdrawing. He again attacked Smith, this time at Golding's Farm, and again was repulsed. In the two days of fighting, Toombs suffered 438 casualties, while Smith lost 189 men.

GARRARD, KENNER (1827–1879) USA. A cousin of Union Brig. Gen. **Theophilus T. Garrard**, Garrard was a native of **Kentucky** and left Harvard University to enter **West Point**. After graduating in 1851, he served in the Southwest and was captured by secessionists in April 1861 at San Antonio, **Texas**.

After being **paroled**, Garrard served at West Point and in other administrative positions until formally **exchanged** in August 1862. He then was appointed colonel of the **Army of the Potomac's** 146th New York and led it well at **Fredericksburg** and **Chancellorsville**. During the **Battle of Gettysburg**, Garrard took temporary command of the **brigade** when its commander was killed. Promoted to brigadier general of volunteers in July 1863, he led a brigade in the **Mine Run Campaign** before being placed in command of the Cavalry Bureau at **Washington, D.C.** Garrard was promoted to major of regulars in November 1863. In February 1864, he was transferred west and took command of a cavalry **division** in the **Army of the Cumberland**. After serving in the **Atlanta Campaign**, Garrard was transferred to command an infantry division in December 1864. He led it well at **Nashville** and was **brevetted** major general of volunteers for his conduct there. Garrard's last combat role was in the **Mobile Campaign**, where he played a key role in the capture of that city and was made its military commander. For his actions at Mobile, he was brevetted brigadier general and major general in the regular **army**.

Garrard resigned from the army in 1866 and settled in **Ohio**, where he engaged in the real estate business and was involved in civic affairs.

GARRARD, THEOPHILUS TOULMIN (1812–1902) USA. A cousin of Union Maj. Gen. **Kenner Garrard**, Garrard was a native of **Kentucky**. He was elected to the state legislature four times beginning in 1843 and served as a **company** captain in the **Mexican War**.

Garrard entered Union service in September 1861 when he was appointed colonel of the 7th Kentucky (Union). After some minor combat in Kentucky, he fought at **Perryville** at the head of three **regiments**. Promoted to brigadier general of volunteers in November 1862, Garrard was given command of a **brigade** in the **Army of the Tennessee** during the **Vicksburg Campaign** and fought at **Port Gibson** and **Champion Hill**. He was transferred to **Arkansas** after the latter battle and briefly served there before being sent back to Kentucky. After holding several **district** commands in Kentucky, Garrard was honorably discharged from the service in April 1864 for reasons that are not clear.

After leaving the **army**, Garrard returned to his boyhood Kentucky home, where he farmed and operated a saltworks for nearly 40 years.

GARRISON, WILLIAM LLOYD (1805–1879) USA. A **Massachusetts** native, Garrison became one of the leading Northern **abolitionists**. He began publishing *The Liberator* in 1831, helped organize the **American Anti-Slavery Society** in 1833, and advocated the nonviolent abolition of **slavery**. Garrison did not support the Union war effort until the **Emancipation Proclamation** changed the war's goals to include the abolishment of slavery. After the war, he continued to be a reformer and became active in the prohibition movement, women's suffrage, and the humane treatment of **Indians**.

GARROTT, ISHAM WARREN (1816–1863) CSA. A native of **North Carolina**, Garrott graduated from the University of North Carolina and became an **Alabama** lawyer. A **states rights Democrat**, he was elected to the legislature in 1845 and 1847 and served as a presidential elector in 1860.

After Alabama seceded in January 1861, Garrott was sent to North Carolina to build support for **secession** there. In the summer of 1861, he helped raise several **companies** that became part of the 20th Alabama and in September was appointed the **regiment's** lieutenant colonel. Promoted to colonel in October, Garrott first was sent to Mobile, Alabama, but in February 1862, he was ordered to reinforce Knoxville, Tennessee. He served there until joining **Edmund Kirby Smith** for the 1862 **Kentucky Campaign**. The regiment helped clear Union forces out of Cumberland Gap during the campaign and afterward reinforced **Vicksburg, Mississippi**, in January 1863. When Union forces crossed the Mississippi River in April 1863, Garrott's regiment was hurried to reinforce **Port Gibson**. During the battle there, he assumed temporary command of his **brigade** when his superior was killed. Garrott was back in command of his regiment at **Champion Hill** and then served with his men in the trenches during the rest of the **Vicksburg Campaign**.

Garrott was promoted to brigadier general in May 1863 but did not live long enough to be notified of his promotion. On June 17, while using a borrowed **rifle** to try to shoot a Union **sharpshooter**, Garrott himself was shot through the heart and killed. His men buried him in a nearby garden and promptly renamed their position Fort Garrott. Sadly, the general's remains and gravesite were destroyed when Vicksburg's Finney Street was opened in the 1890s.

GARTRELL, LUCIUS JEREMIAH (1821–1891) CSA. A native of **Georgia**, Gartrell studied at Randolph-Macon College and at Franklin College before becoming a lawyer. In the 1840s, he served two terms in the state legislature, one as a **Whig** and one as a **Democrat**. A strong advocate of **slavery**, Gartrell was elected to the **U.S. Congress** in 1857 and became a staunch secessionist.

In January 1861, Gartrell resigned his congressional seat, returned to Georgia, and raised the 7th Georgia. Elected colonel, he fought at **First Manassas**, where his 16-year-old son was killed, and caught his **brigade** commander, **Francis Bartow**, when he was shot from his horse and killed. Gartrell resigned his commission in January 1862 after being elected to the **Confederate Congress**. There he was a strong supporter of **Jefferson Davis**, chaired the House Committee on the Judiciary, and supported the **suspension of the writ of habeas corpus**. Wanting to reenter the **army**, Gartrell refused to run for reelection and instead asked Davis for a commission. He went to work raising 20 state reserve **companies** and was rewarded with a brigadier general's commission in August 1864.

Put in command of the 2nd Brigade of Georgia Reserves, Gartrell was involved in a battle near **Savannah, Georgia**, in December 1864. There he was criticized for failing to commit all of his troops to check a Union advance and for a lack of aggressiveness. Despite the criticism, Gartrell's brigade delayed the Federals long enough to allow **William J. Hardee** to evacuate the city. Gartrell was wounded by a shell fragment in the fighting and was recuperating from the wound at home in Georgia when the war ended.

After the war, Gartrell became a well-respected defense lawyer, defending Gov. Rufus Brown against criminal charges during **Reconstruction**, and headed the 1877 state constitutional convention.

GARY, MARTIN WITHERSPOON (1831–1881) CSA. A native of **South Carolina**, Gary was the brother-in-law of Confederate Brig. Gen. **Nathan G. Evans**. He graduated from Harvard University and became a prominent South Carolina criminal lawyer before being elected to the state legislature in 1860 as an ardent secessionist.

Although a colonel in the state militia, Gary raised a volunteer infantry **company** for the **Hampton Legion** in 1861 and entered Confederate service as its captain in June. At **First Manassas**, he captured a Union **artillery** battery and was in temporary command of the **legion** by the end of the fight. After leading his company at **Seven Pines**, Gary was elected lieutenant colonel in June 1862 and took command of the legion's infantry battalion. As part of **John Bell Hood's brigade** in the **Army of Northern Virginia**, his battalion distinguished itself in the **Seven Days**, **Second Manassas**, and **Antietam Campaigns**, with Gary carrying forward the **flag** in the latter fight after four color bearers were shot down. In late 1862, the Hampton Legion was made a **regiment**, and Gary was appointed its colonel in December. The regiment did not participate in the **army's** 1863 battles but did accompany **James Longstreet's corps** westward in September. After fighting at **Wauhatchie** and in the **Knoxville Campaign**, Gary was transferred to South Carolina in March 1864 to convert his command to a mounted unit.

In May 1864, Gary took command of the **Department of Richmond's** cavalry brigade and was promoted to brigadier general in June. He received praise for his actions in the **Petersburg Campaign** at **First** and **Second Deep Bottom**, **Fort Harrison**, and **Darbytown Road**. When **Robert E. Lee** evacuated the Richmond-Petersburg defenses in April 1865, Gary's cavalry formed the rear guard, and he was the last Confederate general officer to leave **Richmond**. Gary frequently clashed with Union cavalry in the **Appomattox Campaign** and in one fight personally sabered three Union troopers. He refused to accept the **surrender** at **Appomattox** and escaped with about 60 of his men. Gary reached South Carolina and helped escort **Jefferson Davis** to his mother's home. When Davis continued westward, he remained at his mother's house and was never **paroled**.

Gary was a brave, but elderly looking bald man, which prompted one soldier to exclaim he "looks like a man of eighty and acts like one of twenty." He was a very popular officer with his men and was nicknamed "the Bald Eagle of Edgefield." Gary remained an unrepentant **Rebel** and again served in the South Carolina legislature after the war.

GATLIN, RICHARD CASWELL (1809–1896) CSA. A native of **North Carolina**, Gatlin graduated from **West Point** in 1832 and served in the Black Hawk, **Seminole**, and **Mexican Wars**. In this last, he was wounded and **brevetted** for his actions at Monterrey. After Mexico, Gatlin again fought the Seminoles and served at various frontier outposts.

Gatlin was a major serving in the **New Mexico Territory** 1861 and was captured by secessionists in April 1861 while visiting **Fort Smith, Arkansas**. He was **paroled** and in May resigned his commission and was appointed North Carolina's adjutant general. Gatlin quickly was made a major general of state troops, and **Jefferson Davis** simultaneously appointed him a colonel in the **Confederate army**.

In August 1861, Davis appointed Gatlin brigadier general and placed him in command of the **Department of North Carolina**. Almost immediately Union forces captured **Hatteras Inlet**, and Gatlin began preparing other coastal areas for defense. He frequently pleaded for reinforcements and aid from the government, but Secretary of War **Judah P. Benjamin** provided little help. In January 1862, **Ambrose Burnside** captured **New Bern** and **Roanoke Island** despite Gatlin's best attempts to defend them. Apparently false accusations of drunkenness and an illness that prevented him from being at New Bern when it fell brought criticism upon him. As a result, Benjamin removed Gatlin from command in March and made him the scapegoat for New Bern's capture. After waiting in vain for another command, Gatlin resigned his commission in September 1862. He continued to serve as North Carolina's adjutant and inspector general until war's end.

After the war, Gatlin moved to **Arkansas** and farmed.

GATLING GUN. The precursor of the modern machine gun, the Gatling gun was invented by Dr. Richard Jordan Gatling. It was a six-barreled gun that was fed by a clip magazine and had a crank handle that rotated and fired the barrels at a rapid rate. The gun was made in several calibers, including the standard .58, and could fire up to 600 rounds per minute. The original model fired a paper cartridge housed inside a capped steel chamber and was less than reliable. The Union **army** refused to purchase any Gatling guns because of its radical nature, but such officers as **Benjamin Butler**, **Winfield Scott Hancock**, and **David Porter** privately acquired them during the Civil War. Butler reportedly bought 12 for $1,000 apiece. Except for some service in the **Petersburg Campaign**, the Gatling gun was not used in combat during the war. When the gun was refined and made to fire copper rimfire cartridges, the **U.S. Army** finally adopted it for use in 1866.

GEARY, JOHN WHITE (1819–1873) USA. A native of **Pennsylvania**, Geary attended Pennsylvania's Jefferson College but was forced to drop out before graduating because of his father's death. He then worked as a teacher, store clerk, surveyor, and lawyer, and served as a militia officer. During the **Mexican War**, Geary was elected lieutenant colonel and then colonel of the 2nd Pennsylvania and was wounded five times at Chapultepec. After the war, he moved to **California**, set up the first postal system there, and served as the first mayor of San Francisco. Geary also was appointed territorial governor of **"Bleeding Kansas"** in 1856, but he was forced to resign in 1857 because of his very strong and controversial antislavery stance. He returned to farm in Pennsylvania and began raising volunteer **companies** when the Civil War began.

Geary was so popular that he quickly raised 68 companies and formed the 28th Pennsylvania with 15 of them. He entered Union service in June 1861 when the **regiment** elected him colonel. Geary participated in some minor battles around **Harpers Ferry**, **Virginia**, while serving under **Nathaniel P. Banks** and received a slight wound in October. In March 1862, he was captured at Leesburg, Virginia, but soon was **exchanged**.

Promoted to brigadier general of volunteers in April 1862, Geary commanded a **brigade** at **Cedar Mountain** and was wounded in the foot and shoulder. Upon returning to duty, he was given a **division** in the **Army of the Potomac's** XII Corps and led it well at **Chancellorsville** and **Gettysburg**. In the former battle, Geary was hit in the chest by a spent cannon ball and was knocked unconscious. After Gettysburg, he was transferred west with the XI and XII Corps and fought at **Wauhatchie** (where his son was killed), **Lookout Mountain**, and **Missionary Ridge**. During the **Atlanta Campaign** and the **March to the Sea**, Geary led a division in the **Army of the Cumberland's** XX Corps. He was appointed military governor of **Savannah, Georgia**, after that city fell and was brevetted major general of volunteers in January 1865 for his war service.

Returning to Pennsylvania after the war, Geary was elected governor in 1866 and served two terms as a **Republican**.

GENERAL ORDERS NO. 11, THOMAS EWING'S. *See* EWING, THOMAS, JR.; MISSOURI.

GENERAL ORDERS NO. 28, BENJAMIN BUTLER'S. *See* BUTLER, BENJAMIN FRANKLIN; WOMAN'S ORDER.

GENERAL STERLING PRICE, **CSS.** Originally named the *Laurent Millaudon*, this vessel was seized by the Confederates in 1861 to be converted into a **ram**. It was 182 feet long, 30 feet in beam, and had a 9-foot draft. In **New Orleans**, **Louisiana**, the ship was fitted with a reinforced bow of timber and iron, backed by wooden bulkheads and compressed cotton. It also carried one 32-pounder and one 24-pounder cannons fore and aft, respectively.

Placed in the **River Defense Fleet**, the *General Sterling Price* was sent to **Fort Pillow**, **Tennessee**, in April 1862 to guard the Mississippi River approach to **Memphis**, **Tennessee**. On May 10, it was part of an eight-ship fleet that engaged the **U.S. Navy** at **Plum Rum Bend**. In the battle, the *General Sterling Price* rammed the USS *Cincinnati* and a **mortar** boat, sinking the former and disabling the latter. At Memphis on June 6, 1862, the *General Sterling Price* was part of the Confederate force that engaged the Union fleet in a wild melee. While attempting to ram one vessel, it accidentally collided with another Confederate vessel and was disabled. It then was rammed by the USS *Queen of the West* and sank in shallow water. The ship was later raised and was used by the Union fleet until war's end. In March 1864, it accidentally rammed and sank the USS *Conestoga* on **Louisiana's** Ouachita (WASH-ih-taw) River. After the war, the *General Sterling Price* was scrapped.

GEORGIA. After **John C. Breckinridge** won a plurality in Georgia in the **election of 1860**, Gov. **Joseph E. Brown** called for a **secession** convention. In a rather close vote of 166–130 on January 19, 1861, Georgia became the fifth state to secede. Although Brown often disagreed with **Jefferson Davis** on such **states rights** issues as Confederate control of **conscription** and the **suspension of the writ of habeas corpus**, he was devoted to the cause and competently led the state throughout the war.

With its large population of approximately 1,057,000 (of whom about 462,000 were slaves), Georgia proved crucial in supplying manpower to the **Confederate army**. During the war, 120,000 Georgians served the Confederacy, including **John B. Gordon**, **Alexander Stephens**, **Robert**

Toombs, and **Howell Cobb**. The state's rich agricultural land also provided much needed supplies, and **railroads** converging at Atlanta connected the far-flung Confederacy together and made Georgia the crucial link between the eastern and western theaters. The state also contained much of the South's **industry**, with numerous textile mills and a large rolling mill located in Atlanta.

Militarily, Georgia was the scene of little fighting until the 1864 **Atlanta Campaign**. Then much of the state's northern region became a battlefield. When **William T. Sherman** made his **March to the Sea** later in the year, central and southeastern Georgia also felt the hard hand of war, and **Savannah** was captured in December 1864.

GEORGIA, **CSS.** This Confederate **commerce raider** was built in Scotland in 1862 as the merchant ship *Japan* (sometimes referred to as the *Virginian*). It was purchased in Scotland in March 1863 by Confederate agent **Matthew F. Maury** and was commissioned the CSS *Georgia* in April while off the French coast. The ship was 212 feet long, 27 feet in beam, and displaced 648 tons, but it was not well suited as a raider because its iron hull quickly fouled and greatly reduced its speed. Commanded by Lt. William L. Maury, the *Georgia* carried two 100-pounder, two 24-pounder, and one 32-pounder cannons.

Maury cruised off Brazil and Africa for six months and captured nine ships but then was forced to Cherbourg, France, for repairs. Under Lt. William E. Evans, the *Georgia* sailed to Morocco in early 1864 to transfer its guns to the more suitable **CSS *Rappahannock***, but the *Rappahannock* had been detained in France and never appeared. Evans sailed the *Georgia* to Liverpool, England, and sold it to a merchant in May, but the USS *Niagara* seized it on the open sea and took it to Boston, Massachusetts, as a prize. Despite the *Georgia* being a private vessel by that time, a federal court upheld the seizure.

GEORGIA LANDING, LOUISIANA, BATTLE OF (OCTOBER 27, 1862). In October 1862, Maj. Gen. **Benjamin F. Butler**, headquartered in **New Orleans, Louisiana**, sent Brig. Gen. **Godfrey Weitzel** with 4,000 men to drive out the Confederates from the **Bayou Lafourche** (luh FOOSH) region and to establish a Union presence there. Weitzel reached Donaldsonville on October 25 and began advancing up the east bank of Bayou Lafourche. Two days later he encountered Confederate Brig. Gen. **J. J. Alfred Mouton**, who was positioned on both sides of the bayou at Georgia Landing. Weitzel drove back Mouton's men on the east bank and then crossed the bayou on a **pontoon bridge** and attacked the west bank. There the Confederates held off the Federals until a lack of ammunition forced them to retire. In the fight, the Confederates lost 229 men, while Weitzel suffered 86 casualties. Mouton withdrew to nearby Labadieville (LA-buh-dee-ville), leaving much of the Lafourche district under Union control.

GETTY, GEORGE WASHINGTON (1819–1901) USA. A native of Georgetown, D.C., Getty graduated from **West Point** in 1840 and won a **brevet** in the **Mexican War** while serving with the **artillery**. Afterward, he fought in the **Seminole Wars** and had risen to the rank of captain when the Civil War began.

In September 1861, Getty was promoted to lieutenant colonel of volunteers and became commander of four artillery batteries in the **Army of the Potomac**. After fighting in the **Peninsula Campaign**, he served as chief of artillery for **Ambrose Burnside's** IX Corps in the **Antietam Campaign**.

Getty was promoted to brigadier general of volunteers in September 1862 and led a **division** of IX Corps infantry at **Fredericksburg**. In the spring of 1863, his division was sent to protect **Suffolk, Virginia**, from **James Longstreet's** Confederate siege. Afterward, Getty commanded the Union forces at **Norfolk** and Portsmouth, Virginia, and briefly was acting inspector general of the Army of the Potomac in early 1864. He was back in command of a VI Corps division by the time of the **Overland Campaign**. Getty was severely wounded at the **Wilderness** but recovered in time to serve in the **Petersburg** and **Philip Sheridan's Shenandoah Valley Campaigns**, commanding the entire VI Corps at **Cedar Creek**. On April 2, 1865, Getty's division made the initial breakthrough of the Confederate lines at Petersburg, and he took part in the pursuit and capture of **Robert E. Lee's Army of Northern Virginia** in the **Appomattox Campaign**. During the war, Getty earned brevets of brigadier general and major general of regulars and major general of volunteers.

Getty remained in the **army** after the war and rose to the rank of colonel. In 1879, he served on the board of inquiry that overturned the court-martial conviction of **Fitz John Porter** for misconduct at **Second Manassas**.

GETTYSBURG ADDRESS. While plans were being made in 1863 to dedicate a cemetery for the Union dead at Gettysburg, Pennsylvania, the committee in charge casually invited **Abraham Lincoln** to "make a few remarks" following the main speech by **Edward Everett**. To the committee's surprise, Lincoln agreed. Contrary to a popular myth, Lincoln did not write his speech on the back of an envelope while on the train to Gettysburg but actually worked on his remarks for some weeks prior to the event because he saw it as an opportunity to boost the Union's sagging morale. The dedication took place on November 19, 1863, and Everett gave a two-hour speech. Lincoln then stood and read his brief remarks from two sheets of paper. Some newspapers and audience members dismissed the address as unremarkable, and even Lincoln supposedly remarked to a friend afterward that "It is a flat failure" (Boatner, *Civil War Dictionary*, 330). Others, however, immediately recognized it as a brilliant oration, and the Gettysburg Address became one of the most famous speeches in American history.

GETTYSBURG, PENNSYLVANIA, CAMPAIGN AND BATTLE OF (JUNE 3–JULY 14, 1863). Following the **Battle of Chancellorsville** in May 1863, **Robert E. Lee** and the **Army of Northern Virginia** held the initiative in **Virginia**. Several options were open to Lee. Some government officials and military officers pressured him to send **James Longstreet's** corps to the west to recapture **Tennessee** and help relieve **Vicksburg**, **Mississippi**, and some even recommended that Lee go to the west himself to reverse the setbacks there. Other options were staying in Virginia to rest his men and resupply or invading the North to once again take the war to the enemy. Lee rejected relieving Vicksburg because he believed he could do more good in the eastern theater, and he probably had little faith that his men would be used any more wisely than the troops already there. He also rejected staying on the defensive because he naturally favored the offensive and wanted to keep the initiative. Thus, Lee decided that an invasion of **Pennsylvania** was in order. Such a move, he argued, would take the war out of Virginia and allow him to gather supplies in rich Pennsylvania. If he could capture a major city or win a large battle on the enemy's soil, an invasion also could strengthen the growing peace movement in the North and perhaps finally win the Confederacy foreign recognition. Although **Jefferson Davis** preferred a more defensive **strategy**, he had confidence in Lee's judgment and approved the invasion.

To better handle his **army** of 75,000 men, Lee created a new III Corps and left it at **Fredericksburg**, **Virginia**, under **A. P. Hill** to mislead Maj. Gen. **Joseph Hooker's Army of the Potomac**. On June 3, 1863, the main body of the Army of Northern Virginia began marching to Culpeper, from where the campaign would begin (Hill's corps followed on June 6). Suspecting Lee was planning an offensive, Hooker sent elements of the VI Corps across the Rappahannock River on June 5 to gather intelligence, and a sharp clash erupted at **Franklin's Crossing**. Unsatisfied, he next sent Maj. Gen. **Alfred Pleasonton's** cavalry across the Rapidan River to probe Lee's position. Pleasonton surprised Maj.

Gen. **J. E. B. Stuart** at **Brandy Station** on June 9, but in a wild melee that proved to be the war's largest cavalry battle, the Confederates eventually drove off the Federals.

Concerned that Hooker had become aware of his intentions, Lee hurried Lt. Gen. **Richard S. Ewell's** II Corps to the **Shenandoah Valley** on June 10 to clear the way to the Potomac River. When Ewell approached Winchester on June 13, Hooker was notified and withdrew from Fredericksburg to Centreville. After defeating Maj. Gen. **Robert H. Milroy** at the **Second Battle of Winchester** and **Stephenson's Depot** on June 14–15, Ewell began crossing the Potomac River on June 15, and entered Pennsylvania later that day. Hill crossed into **Maryland** on June 24, followed by Longstreet's I Corps the next day.

Stuart's cavalry screened the march and engaged the Union cavalry at **Aldie**, **Middleburg**, and **Upperville**, **Virginia**. On June 24, one of the campaigns greatest controversies began to unfold. Stuart, embarrassed over the surprise he suffered at Brandy Station, received permission to raid east of the advancing army and rejoin Lee later in Pennsylvania. Stuart's orders were to leave behind two cavalry **brigades** to screen the invasion, to guard Ewell's right flank, and to remain in communication with Ewell to keep the army informed of Union activity. Stuart left his two weakest brigades with Lee and on June 25 began his **Gettysburg Raid** with three brigades that carried him around the advancing Union army. He soon became trapped behind enemy lines and was unable to maintain communications with Lee. Thus, as Lee advanced into Pennsylvania, he was deprived of the bulk of his cavalry and was virtually blind.

Hooker carefully kept his 93,500 men between Lee and Washington, D.C. and by June 28 was at Frederick, Maryland. He believed Lee outnumbered him and complained that the army was not being properly supported by the government. Hooker requested that the Union garrison at **Harpers Ferry**, **West Virginia**, be evacuated and assigned to him, but General-in-Chief **Henry Halleck** refused. An angry Hooker then submitted his resignation, which was quickly accepted by **Abraham Lincoln**. Lincoln replaced Hooker on June 28 with Maj. Gen. **George Gordon Meade**, commander of the V Corps.

By June 28, Ewell's **corps** had advanced to Carlisle and York, Pennsylvania, while Hill and Longstreet were at Chambersburg, Pennsylvania. That morning, Lee ordered Ewell to move forward and capture Harrisburg. When **Albert Jenkins's** cavalry brigade reached the outskirts of Harrisburg that day, the invasion's deepest penetration had been made. During the march through Pennsylvania, the Confederates seized numerous horses and supplies. Civilians were unharmed and generally were treated with respect, but they were forced to accept Confederate money for goods taken. Several hundred blacks, both free and runaway slaves, were also seized and returned south into slavery.

On June 28, Lee learned from spy **James Harrison** for the first time that the Union army had pushed north of the Potomac River. Alarmed that the enemy might cross west of **South Mountain** and threaten his lines of communications to the Shenandoah Valley, Lee ordered the army to concentrate at Cashtown. By massing there, east of the mountains and 10 miles west of Gettysburg, he would be able to threaten both Baltimore, Maryland, and Harrisburg, Pennsylvania, and force the enemy to remain east of the mountains and away from his line of communications.

To the east, Meade advanced northward along a 30-mile-wide front to cover Baltimore. Learning from his cavalry that Lee was at Cashtown, Meade began shifting to the west to concentrate at Gettysburg, a small town where nine roads intersected. On June 30, Brig. Gen. **John Buford's** Union cavalry **division** reached Gettysburg first. That same day, Brig. Gen. **James Pettigrew's** Confederate brigade approached town from the west in search of shoes that reportedly were there. Upon finding Union cavalry in town, Pettigrew withdrew and informed his superiors. On July 1, Hill sent **Henry Heth's** and **William Dorsey Pender's** divisions back to Gettysburg to drive out Buford. Their orders were to not bring on a general engagement, however, since Lee did not want a battle until the army was concentrated. Buford recognized the importance of the high ground west of town and took up a position to defend it. At about 8:00 A.M., Heth's division engaged Buford along McPherson's Ridge, about four miles west of town. Although outnumbered, Buford fought stubbornly, putting to good use the repeating **Spencer carbines**, with which his troopers were armed. **John F. Reynold's** I Corps arrived on the scene at about 10:30 A.M. and relieved Buford's cavalry.

The battle that no one wanted quickly escalated as both sides sent in reinforcements. Hill next sent in Pender's division, and the battle raged for hours. A Confederate **sharpshooter** killed Reynolds, and heavy fighting took place at a **railroad** cut. The Union **Iron Brigade** was cut to pieces, and Confederate Brig. Gen. **James J. Archer** became the first of Lee's generals ever to be captured in battle. Reynolds's corps finally was forced back to Seminary Ridge closer to town. **Oliver O. Howard's** XI Corps arrived shortly after noon and went into action on the right of the I Corps, stretching the battle line north of town. Both sides suffered heavy losses, and the fight was stalemated by mid-afternoon.

By chance, Ewell's II Corps approached the field from the northeast along the Heidlersburg Road. He quickly placed **Robert Rodes's** division to extend Hill's left and then sent **Jubal Early's** division in a crushing attack against Howard's right flank. The XI Corps was routed, and when Hill renewed his attack, the entire Union line collapsed. The Confederates pursued the Federals through Gettysburg, capturing several thousand **prisoners**. By that time, **Winfield Scott Hancock** had arrived with orders from Meade to take command of the field. Hancock rallied the retreating Union soldiers atop Cemetery and Culp's Hills, just south of town. Observing this, Lee ordered Ewell to advance and seize the hills if practicable, but Ewell failed to do so. Ewell later was criticized greatly for his failure, but he had good reasons for not advancing. His corps was disorganized after the battle, there were thousands of prisoners to take charge of, **Edward Johnson's** division had not yet arrived, and there was a false report of an enemy column approaching his left flank. Ewell decided to wait for Johnson's division and to check out the report of an approaching enemy before committing to an advance. By the time this was done, darkness had fallen, and it was too late to attack the high ground.

When Meade arrived that night, Hancock told him that it was excellent defensive ground. He decided to stay and fight and arranged his arriving corps in a defensive line resembling an inverted fishhook. Culp's Hill, to the northeast, was the hook's barb, while the shank curved at Cemetery Hill and ran south along Cemetery Ridge. The eye of the hook was the far left (or southern) flank, which was anchored on two rugged hills known as Little Round Top and Big Round Top.

The Confederates paralleled Meade's line, with Ewell on the left, Hill in the center, and Longstreet on the right. Lee planned for Longstreet to attack the Union left flank the next day, with Ewell advancing against Culp's and Cemetery Hills and Hill against the center. Longstreet, however, disapproved of attacking such a strong position and advised disengaging from Gettysburg, circling behind the Union army, and forcing Meade to attack on ground of Lee's choosing. Lee, reluctant to turn his back on the enemy without a decisive fight, rejected the advice and insisted the battle continue. Final plans for the attack were not made until late morning on July 2, and it took time for Longstreet to move his corps into position without being seen. After the war, Longstreet became another scapegoat for Lee's failure at Gettysburg when critics assailed him for being too slow to get this attack started.

At about 4:00 P.M., Longstreet sent **Lafayette McLaws's** and **John Bell Hood's** divisions against **Daniel Sickles's** III Corps, which held Meade's left flank. Without orders, Sickles had advanced his corps far beyond the main Union line to take advantage of higher ground in his front. As a result, he abandoned the Round Tops just as the Confederates attacked. Advancing in **echelon**, Longstreet smashed Sickles's corps and slowly pushed it back in vicious fighting in the **Wheatfield**, **Devil's Den**, and the **Peach Orchard**. Brigadier General **Gouverneur K. Warren** realized that Little Round Top controlled the battlefield and ordered Col. **Strong Vincent** of the Union V Corps to move his brigade to the top of the hill. There Col. **Joshua Lawrence Chamberlain** and his 20th Maine put up a stubborn defense and repulsed numerous attacks by **Evander Law's** Confederate brigade. The Union line was battered by Longstreet's assault but held as elements of the I, V, VI, and XI Corps were rushed into the gap formed by Sickles's untimely advance. In the bloody fighting, Hood was severely wounded in the arm, and Brig. Gen. **William Barksdale** was killed. On the Union side, Sickles lost a leg, Vincent and Brig. Gen. **Stephen H. Weed** were mortally wounded, Brig. Gen. **Samuel K. Zook** was killed, and the 1st Minnesota lost 215 out of 262 men.

On the Union right, Ewell bombarded the Federal line with heavy **artillery** fire when he heard Longstreet attack and then assaulted Culp's and Cemetery Hills. In heavy fighting, Johnson's division gained a foothold on Culp's Hill, but it was prevented from seizing the high ground because of the stubborn defense of **Samuel Carroll's** lone brigade. Early's division managed briefly to seize two batteries atop Cemetery Hill, but a Union counterattack and the lack of Confederate supports forced it to withdraw after dark. In the center, Hill failed to put any significant pressure on the Union line. During the heavy fighting, Meade was able to take advantage of his **interior line** and skillfully shifted needed reinforcements to the most threatened areas.

That night Meade's officers supported remaining on the defensive, and Meade correctly predicted that Lee would attack his center the next day and warned Hancock to be ready. Lee believed Meade had weakened his center to reinforce the flanks that day and decided to make his main attack there on July 3. He also ordered Stuart, who finally arrived on the field on July 2 after engaging the Union cavalry at **Hanover**, to raid behind Meade's line and for Ewell to continue his assault against Culp's Hill.

At daybreak of July 3, Union forces attacked Ewell's men on Culp's Hill, and a fierce but indecisive battle raged there until about noon. Longstreet again opposed making a **frontal attack** against the Union center but was ordered to assemble a strike force around **George Pickett's** fresh division. Approximately 13,000 men in eleven brigades from Pickett's, Pettigrew's, and **Isaac Trimble's** divisions were assembled for the attack. At 1:00 P.M., the Confederates opened a heavy artillery bombardment against the Union line, which lasted about two hours, but most of the shells overshot the target and did little harm to the Federal batteries and frontline troops. At about 3:00 P.M., the Confederate infantry surged forward against a stone wall near a copse of trees. **Pickett's Charge** was one of the war's most dramatic moments as the Confederates advanced from Seminary Ridge across a mile of open ground. Raked by artillery fire and musketry, hundreds of men were shot down, but the assault continued. A few hundred soldiers managed to reach the Union line and engage in fierce hand-to-hand fighting, but Hancock (who was seriously wounded) stood firm and was able to repulse the charge. Pickett lost more than half his men, including Brig. Gen. **Richard Garnett** killed, Brig. Gen. **Lewis Armistead** mortally wounded and captured, and Trimble and Kemper wounded and captured. At the same time, cavalry actions took place on both flanks. East of the battlefield on Meade's far right, Stuart was repulsed in heavy fighting against **David M. Gregg's** Union cavalry division. On the far left, **H. Judson Kilpatrick** ordered a foolish suicidal attack against Hood's division. Brigadier General **Elon J. Farnsworth** protested the order but led his brigade forward and was killed along with many of his men.

Still seeking to gain an advantage, Lee remained in place on July 4 hoping in vain that Meade would attack him. He finally began retreating that night and reached Williamsport, Maryland, on July 6, where he found that heavy rains had swollen the Potomac River and flooded the fords. While a **pontoon bridge** was built, the Confederates prepared defensive positions protecting the river crossings. Meade approached cautiously and some **skirmishing** erupted at **Williamsport** as he probed for weaknesses in the enemy defenses. Lee finally crossed safely to Virginia on the night of July 13–14. The last clash of the campaign came on July 14 when Kilpatrick's cavalry attacked Lee's rear guard division under Henry Heth at **Falling Waters, Maryland**. Heth successfully crossed over the river, but he lost more than 700 men, including Brig. Gen. James J. Pettigrew, mortally wounded.

Gettysburg was the largest battle of the Civil War and the largest ever waged in the Western Hemisphere. Losses vary according to different sources, but more than 50,000 casualties were suffered in the battle, with Lee losing perhaps 28,000 men to Meade's 23,000. The campaign also became one of the war's most controversial, with Confederates especially searching for the causes of Lee's defeat. Stuart, Ewell, and Longstreet all became scapegoats for their failures, but Lee bore ultimate responsibility for insisting on fighting a battle where the enemy enjoyed a great tactical advantage. One point many Confederates failed to grasp was that at Gettysburg, Meade and the Army of the Potomac performed magnificently and essentially had outfought them. Gettysburg later was seen by some to be a major turning point in the war, with Lee's retreat occurring on the same day **U. S. Grant** captured Vicksburg, Mississippi. Sometimes called the "high water mark of the Confederacy," Gettysburg marked the pinnacle of Confederate power.

GETTYSBURG, PENNSYLVANIA, RAID, STUART'S (JUNE 25–JULY 2, 1863). After being surprised and nearly defeated at **Brandy Station, Virginia**, on June 9, 1863, Confederate Maj. Gen. **J. E. B. Stuart** was eager to reclaim his reputation. When **Robert E. Lee** began the **Gettysburg Campaign** a few days later, Stuart requested permission to raid behind the Union **Army of the Potomac**. Lee was reluctant to have Stuart ride off at the start of a major campaign but as usual gave him discretionary orders. Stuart received permission for the raid on June 22, but he was ordered by Lee to leave enough cavalry behind to screen the **army** as it advanced into **Pennsylvania**. Stuart's orders were to guard the **Army of Northern Virginia's** right flank as it advanced northward; stay in communication with **Richard S. Ewell**, who led the advance; keep Lee informed of the enemy's whereabouts; and gather supplies. Stuart left his two weakest **brigades** with Lee and took his other three with him in the predawn hours of June 25, 1863.

The raid quickly bogged down. The Union Army of the Potomac advanced sooner than Lee expected, and Stuart became trapped behind it, unable to remain in communication with Ewell or to let Lee know the enemy's position. Stuart did manage to capture 125 wagons at Rockville, Maryland, on June 28, but they only slowed him down as he tried to ride ahead of the advancing enemy and rejoin Lee. The next day, Stuart's troopers destroyed part of the Baltimore & Ohio Railroad at Hood's Mill, Maryland. After clashing with Union cavalry at Westminster, Maryland, later on June 29, Stuart arrived at **Hanover, Pennsylvania**, on June 30. There he was attacked by the Union cavalry brigades of **Elon J. Farnsworth** and **George Custer**, but he successfully fought them off in bitter fighting.

Stuart finally rejoined Lee at Gettysburg, Pennsylvania, on July 2 after the unexpected Battle of Gettysburg had begun. His failure to follow orders and leaving Lee blind as he entered Pennsylvania have been seen as contributing factors to Lee's defeat at Gettysburg.

GHOLSON, SAMUEL JAMESON (1808–1883) CSA. Born in **Kentucky**, Gholson grew up in **Alabama** and became a lawyer after receiving a local education. He moved to **Mississippi** to open a law practice and in the 1830s was elected twice to the state legislature and once to the **U.S. Congress**. In 1838, Gholson was appointed a Mississippi federal judge and held that position until the Civil War.

A devoted secessionist, Gholson was a delegate to the state **secession** convention and resigned his judgeship once Mississippi seceded in 1861. He entered Confederate service as a private in the 14th Mississippi but quickly was elected **company** captain. By the end of 1861, Gholson had been appointed regimental colonel and then brigadier general of state militia. While serving as a militia general, he was wounded in the right lung and was captured at **Fort Donelson**. After being **exchanged**, Gholson fought at **Iuka** and **Corinth** and received a severe wound in the left leg at the latter battle.

In April 1863, Gholson was appointed major general of state militia and recruited troops in northeastern Mississippi, but he often clashed with regular Confederate officers who also were trying to raise men there. By October, he was commanding state troops in the area and led some of them in cooperation with **Nathan Bedford Forrest** against **William Sooy Smith's Expedition**. Gholson pursued Smith after the Union defeat at **Okolona** in February 1864, and Forrest recommended him for promotion to brigadier general in the **Confederate army**.

Gholson's appointment was made in June 1864, and he was given command of a cavalry **brigade** under **James R. Chalmers**. His brigade **skirmished** with the enemy around **Vicksburg** and **Jackson, Mississippi**, and he received another severe wound in one clash. Gholson's brigade then was sent to reinforce the **Army of Tennessee** in **Georgia**, but he remained in Mississippi. In December 1864, Gholson received his fourth wound in a fight at Egypt and was captured and lost his left arm to amputation.

After the war, Gholson was again elected to the Mississippi legislature and served as speaker of the house until ousted by **Radical Republicans** during **Reconstruction**. He then resumed his law practice and was elected to the legislature for a final time in 1878.

GIBBON, JOHN (1827–1896) USA. A native of **Pennsylvania**, Gibbon moved to **North Carolina** as a boy. He graduated from **West Point** in 1847 and served in the **Mexican** and **Seminole Wars**. After serving as an **artillery** instructor and quartermaster at the academy, he wrote the *Artillerist's Manual*, which was published by the **U.S. Army** in 1860 as its basic artillery manual. When the Civil War began, Captain Gibbon was serving with the 4th U.S. Artillery.

Although three of his brothers joined the **Confederate army**, Gibbon remained loyal to the Union and in October 1861 was appointed chief of artillery for **Irvin McDowell's** division in the **Army of the Potomac**. Promoted to brigadier general of volunteers in May 1862, he took command of the unit that became famous as the **"Iron Brigade."** Its service at **Groveton, Second Manassas, South Mountain,** and **Antietam** made it one of the most famous **brigades** of the war. Gibbon was promoted to a I Corps **division** command in November 1862 and was severely wounded at **Fredericksburg**. Upon returning to duty, he took command of a II Corps division. Gibbon was praised for his actions while in temporary command of the **corps** at **Gettysburg**, where he again was severely wounded. After commanding draft depots in **Ohio** and Pennsylvania, he resumed command of his II Corps division for the **Overland Campaign**. Gibbon saw combat in all of the campaign's battles and in June 1864 was promoted to major general of volunteers. He was put in command of the new **XXIV Corps** in January 1865 and led it through the **Petersburg** and **Appomattox Campaigns**. At Appomattox, Gibbon was appointed one of the commissioners to receive the Confederate **surrender**. He received **brevets** of brigadier general and major general of regulars for his war service.

After the war, Gibbon served as colonel of the 36th, and later 7th, U.S. Infantry and saw service fighting **Indians** in the west. His unit arrived at Little Big Horn in June 1876 to save the survivors of **George Armstrong Custer's** command and to bury the dead. He later successfully fought the Nez Percé and was promoted to brigadier general of regulars in 1885. After retiring from the **army**, Gibbon became commander in chief of the **Military Order of the Loyal Legion**.

GIBBS, ALFRED (1823–1868) USA. A native of **New York**, Gibbs was the grandson of Oliver Wolcott, secretary of the treasury under Presidents George Washington and John Adams. After attending Dartmouth College, he graduated from **West Point** in 1846 and fought in the **Mexican War**, where he was wounded and won two **brevets** for gallantry. After the war, Gibbs first served as a staff officer and then was sent to the frontier, where he was wounded fighting Apache **Indians**.

Gibbs was captured by **John R. Baylor's** Confederates near **Fort Fillmore, New Mexico,** in July 1861. **Paroled,** he was **exchanged** more than a year later and was appointed colonel of the 130th New York in September 1862. After serving around Suffolk, Virginia, Gibbs's **regiment** was reorganized as the 1st New York Dragoons (also known as the 19th New York Cavalry). He then guarded **railroads** and in November 1862 was put in command of the **Army of the Potomac's** Cavalry Reserve Brigade. After experiencing considerable combat during the 1864 **Overland Campaign**, Gibbs's **brigade** was sent to participate in **Philip Sheridan's Shenandoah Valley Campaign**. In October 1864, he was promoted to brigadier general of volunteers. After leading his brigade at

Five Forks, Gibbs played a key role in encircling the Confederate **Army of Northern Virginia** during the **Appomattox Campaign**.

At the end of the war, Gibbs was brevetted major general in both the volunteers and regulars for his war service. He remained in the **U.S. Army** and became major of the 7th U.S. Cavalry in 1866.

GIBSON, RANDALL LEE (1832–1892) CSA. Born in **Kentucky**, Gibson grew up in **Louisiana**. He graduated from Yale College in 1853 and earned a law degree from the University of Louisiana in 1855. After traveling in Europe and serving for a time as an attaché to the U.S. embassy in Madrid, Spain, Gibson returned to Louisiana and became a planter.

Gibson was Gov. **Thomas O. Moore's** aide when the Civil War began, and in May 1861 he was appointed captain in the 1st Louisiana Heavy Artillery. He resigned that position in September to become colonel of the 13th Louisiana. Gibson served in **Kentucky** and **Mississippi** and by early 1862 commanded a small **brigade**. At **Shiloh**, his brigade was part of **Daniel Ruggles's division** and made four attacks against the "Hornets' Nest" on the first day and on the second day captured an **artillery** battery. **Braxton Bragg**, however, thought Gibson was a coward and criticized him in his after-action report. Gibson demanded a court of inquiry, but the War Department refused to convene one. At **Perryville**, Gibson was praised for his actions, and in November he took command of the consolidated 13th and 20th Louisiana **regiments**. At **Stones River** with the **Army of Tennessee**, he again was praised for his service when he took temporary command of the brigade when **Daniel W. Adams** was wounded. In March 1863, Bragg removed Gibson from command and placed him on **conscription** and recruitment duty. Gibson protested to the secretary of war, however, and won back his **regiments**. At **Chickamauga**, he again took command of the brigade when Adams was wounded and captured.

Gibson had consistently been praised by every superior except Bragg, and in February 1864 he received promotion to brigadier general. During the **Atlanta Campaign**, his brigade distinguished itself at **Resaca** and **New Hope Church**, and he received specific praise at **Jonesboro** for taking up a **flag** and leading his men in an attack. Gibson's brigade missed the fight at **Franklin**, but at **Nashville** it helped protect the Confederate flank. On the second day of battle at Nashville, the brigade repulsed several enemy attacks and then helped form the rear guard to protect the retreating **army**. Detached from the Army of Tennessee in February 1865, Gibson's brigade was sent to **Spanish Fort, Alabama**. He commanded the fort during the **Mobile Campaign** and was highly praised by his superiors for his stubborn defense.

After surrendering with **Richard Taylor's** army in May 1865, Gibson returned to Louisiana and practiced law. He was elected to the **U.S. Congress** in 1872, but the **Radical Republicans** denied him his seat. Elected again in 1875, Gibson remained in Congress until 1882. He was a U.S. senator from 1883 to 1892, found a new location for Louisiana State University at **Baton Rouge**, and helped create Tulane University.

GILBERT, CHARLES CHAMPION (1822–1903) USA. A native of **Ohio**, Gilbert graduated from **West Point** in 1846 and served in the **Mexican War**. In the 1850s, he taught at the academy and was promoted to captain in 1855 while serving on the southwestern frontier.

After being severely wounded at **Wilson's Creek** while leading a **company** in the 1st U.S. Infantry, Gilbert was appointed inspector general of the **Department of the Cumberland**. He then served as the **Army of the Ohio's** inspector general during the **Battle of Shiloh** (where he won a **brevet** to major) and in the **siege of Corinth, Mississippi**.

After the **Battle of Richmond, Kentucky**, Gilbert was appointed acting major general of volunteers and was put in command of the **Army of Kentucky**. An appointment to brigadier general of volunteers came in September 1862. When his **army** was absorbed by the **Army of the Ohio**, Gilbert assumed command of the III Provisional Corps and led it at **Perryville**. There, he won another brevet to lieutenant colonel of regulars but also was criticized for failing to support the troops on his left. As a result, Gilbert was relieved of his command and never again led troops in the field. The Senate failed to confirm his appointment to brigadier general, and when the commission expired in March 1863, he was not reappointed. In July, Gilbert was appointed major of the 19th U.S. Infantry, and he held various administrative positions until war's end.

Gilbert remained in the **U.S. Army** after the war and rose to the rank of colonel.

GILBERT, JAMES ISHAM (1823–1884) USA. Born in **Kentucky**, Gilbert grew up in **Wisconsin**. Before the Civil War, he worked as an **Indian** trader, merchant, real estate agent, and livery stable operator. Gilbert eventually moved to **Iowa** and founded the town of Lansing in 1851.

Gilbert entered Union service in October 1862 as colonel of the 27th Iowa. His **regiment** defended **Minnesota** against Indian attacks until it was moved to **Tennessee** in November 1862. Gilbert served in the **Meridian Campaign**, but he did not see any combat until the 1864 **Red River Campaign**, when he served in **Andrew Jackson Smith's** XVI Corps. He was praised for his service at **Fort De Russy** and **Pleasant**

Hill and won a **brigade** command in June 1864. After again fighting well at **Nashville**, Gilbert was promoted to brigadier general of volunteers in February 1865. He led a brigade during the **Mobile Campaign** and was **brevetted** to major general of volunteers.

After the war, Gilbert engaged in the lumber business in Iowa and became a miner in **Colorado**.

GILGAL CHURCH, GEORGIA, BATTLE OF (JUNE 15–17, 1864). *See* LOST MOUNTAIN-BRUSHY MOUNTAIN LINE, GEORGIA, BATTLE OF.

GILLEM, ALVAN CULLEM (1830–1875) USA. A native of **Tennessee**, Gillem graduated from **West Point** in 1851 and served in the **Seminole Wars** and on the frontier. He was promoted to captain in July 1861 and helped defend Fort Taylor, **Florida**, against the Confederates. Gillem then was made brigade quartermaster and fought at **Mill Springs** as **George H. Thomas's** quartermaster. At **Shiloh**, he served as quartermaster for **Don Carlos Buell's Army of the Ohio** and commanded Buell's siege **artillery**. Gillem was appointed colonel of the 10th Tennessee (Union) in May 1862 and served for a time as provost marshal of Nashville, Tennessee. Military governor **Andrew Johnson** was impressed with his service and secured him an appointment as Tennessee's adjutant general in June 1863. Promoted to brigadier general of volunteers in August 1863, Gillem led the fight against Confederates in East Tennessee in 1864, and it was troops under his command who killed **John Hunt Morgan**. He served as vice president of the state's January 1865 constitutional convention and was elected to the state legislature in April. Gillem also led a cavalry **division** under **George Stoneman** during the **Carolinas Campaign** and captured Salisbury, North Carolina, near war's end.

Brevetted brigadier general and major general of regulars for his war service, Gillem was appointed colonel of the 28th U.S. Infantry in 1866 and in 1868 was made military commander of **Arkansas** and **Mississippi**. He remained in the **U.S. Army** and later fought the Modoc **Indians** in the Pacific Northwest.

GILLMORE, QUINCY ADAMS (1825–1888) USA. A native of **Ohio**, Gillmore graduated first in the **West Point** class of 1849. Before the Civil War, he built fortifications, taught at the academy, and headed New York City's Engineer Agency.

As a 1st lieutenant, Gillmore was appointed chief **engineer** for the 1861 **Port Royal**, **South Carolina**, expedition. He then was promoted to captain and in February 1862 was sent to Savannah, Georgia, to participate in the attack on **Fort Pulaski**. There, Gillmore accepted the fort's surrender on April 11, after concentrating Tybee Island's **rifled** guns to batter down its wall.

Gillmore's success at Fort Pulaski led to his promotion to brigadier general of volunteers in April 1862. After serving in **Kentucky**, he was promoted to major general of volunteers in July 1863 and was given command of the X Corps and the **Department of the South**. At **Charleston**, **South Carolina**, Gillmore captured **Fort Wagner** in September 1863, bombarded **Fort Sumter** to rubble, and shelled the city with the cannon known as the **"Swamp Angel."** In May 1864, his **corps** was assigned to **Benjamin Butler's Army of the James** and participated in the **Bermuda Hundred Campaign**. Butler blamed Gillmore for his failure in the campaign and sent him to **Washington, D.C.** There, Gillmore helped defend the city against **Jubal Early's Washington Raid** in July, but an injury he received when his horse fell seriously impaired his service. In February 1865, he was placed back in command of the Department of the South and kept that position until war's end.

Gillmore received **brevets** of brigadier general and major general of regulars for his war service and was promoted to major of regulars. After the war, he remained in the **U.S. Army**, worked to improve fortifications on the Atlantic coast, and rose to the rank of colonel. *See also* GILLMORE MEDAL.

GILLMORE MEDAL. This was a bronze medal commissioned by Maj. Gen. **Quincy Adams Gillmore** to honor those enlisted men who distinguished themselves in operations around **Charleston**, **South Carolina**, in the summer of 1863. The medal pictured the ruins of **Fort Sumter**, with the date "Aug. 23d 1863" on one side and Gillmore's signature and the words *For Gallant and Meritorious Conduct* on the other. Each medal also had clasps with the soldier's name, rank, and **regiment**, and a certificate was issued detailing why the soldier deserved the award. Four hundred medals were struck, and Gillmore asked that regimental commanders submit names of soldiers they thought were deserving of one. *See also* DECORATIONS.

GILMER, JEREMY FRANCIS (1818–1883) CSA. A native of **North Carolina**, Gilmer graduated from **West Point** in 1839 and entered the **engineers**. He served as chief engineer for occupation forces in **New Mexico** during the **Mexican War** and built Fort Marcy. After the war, Gilmer worked on several fortifications, including building **Forts Jackson** and **Pulaski**, and was serving as a captain in charge of constructing the defenses of San Francisco, **California**, when civil war came.

Gilmer resigned his commission in June 1861 and with the help of his brother John Adams Gilmer, a Confederate congressman, was appointed a captain of engineers in the **Confederate army**. In September, he was promoted to lieutenant colonel. Assigned to **Albert Sidney Johnston**, Gilmer picked the site for **Fort Donelson, Tennessee**, and worked on the construction of it and **Fort Henry**. He escaped with the garrison when Fort Henry was captured in February 1862 and then successfully escaped Fort Donelson by accepting an offer to accompany the departing **Gideon Pillow**. Gilmer next became head of Johnston's engineering department and was wounded while serving with him at **Shiloh**. In July 1862, he took command of **Robert E. Lee's** engineering corps in the **Army of Northern Virginia** and by October was chief of the Bureau of Engineering in **Richmond, Virginia**. In this position, Gilmer was regarded as the Confederacy's leading engineer and was involved in all of the Confederacy's major defense projects.

In August 1863, Gilmer was promoted to major general and was made second in command of **P. G. T. Beauregard's Department of South Carolina, Georgia, and Florida**. He actively oversaw the defenses of **Charleston, South Carolina**, and earned the temporary command of the District of Georgia and the Third District of South Carolina, where he worked on the defenses of Savannah and **Atlanta, Georgia**. Gilmer returned to his post as chief of the Bureau of Engineering in April 1864. For the rest of the war, he made inspections and worked tirelessly overseeing the Confederacy's defenses.

After the war, Gilmer worked as an engineer and became president of the Savannah Gas Light Company.

GILMORE, JOSEPH ALBREE (1811–1867) USA. A native of **Vermont**, Gilmore first worked as a store clerk before opening his own store in **New Hampshire**. After great success in business, he became a **railroad** superintendent in 1856. Gilmore switched from the **Whig** to the **Republican Party** and first was elected to the New Hampshire state assembly and then to the senate, where he became president in 1859.

In 1863, Gilmore ran for governor, but no candidate received a majority. The election was thrown to the legislature, and he was chosen even though he had won fewer popular votes than the **Democratic** candidate. As a war governor, Gilmore protested **conscription** and demanded that federal provost marshals be removed from New Hampshire. He then actively recruited volunteers for military service and was able to meet the state's quota without resorting to a draft. Gilmore was reelected in 1864 and then retired in 1865.

GIRARDEY, VICTOR JEAN BAPTISTE (1837–1864) CSA. Born in France, Girardey moved to **Georgia** as a child. After moving to **New Orleans, Louisiana**, he became an officer in a local militia **company** and was involved in seizing the U.S. Arsenal at **Baton Rouge** in January 1861.

Girardey entered Confederate service in April 1861 as a 2nd lieutenant in the 1st Louisiana Infantry Battalion. After service at **Pensacola, Florida**, the battalion was sent to **Virginia** and engaged in one of the war's first **skirmishes** at Newport News. Girardey resigned his commission in October 1861 to become 1st lieutenant and staff officer to Brig. Gen. **Albert G. Blanchard** at Portsmouth, Virginia. After seeing service at **Seven Pines**, he became Brig. Gen. **Ambrose R. Wright's** assistant adjutant general in June 1862 and was promoted to captain in July. Girardy's service in the **Seven Days**, **Second Manassas**, and **Chancellorsville Campaigns** with the **Army of Northern Virginia** won him much praise from his superiors, but he resigned his commission a second time in July 1863 to take care of some family matters. The War Department refused to accept the resignation, however, and instead gave him eight months leave. While at Augusta, Georgia, Girardey raised underage youths to guard the **Augusta arsenal**. This organization became the 27th Georgia Infantry Battalion, and Girardey was asked to serve as its lieutenant colonel, but he was ordered back to Virginia. He served on the staffs of **Richard H. Anderson** and **William Mahone** and continued to win recognition for his outstanding abilities.

By 1864, Girardey was recommended for a **brigade** command and after temporarily leading two brigades at the **Battle of the Crater** during the **Petersburg Campaign**, he finally was promoted to brigadier general in August. Girardey was the only Confederate ever promoted from captain to brigadier general, a jump of four grades. He then took command of Wright's brigade but was killed on August 16, 1864, at **Second Deep Bottom** when skirmish fire along the Darbytown Road hit him in the head.

GIST, STATES RIGHTS (1831–1864) CSA. A native of **South Carolina** and the son of a future state governor, Gist graduated from South Carolina College and Harvard Law School. He became a lawyer and was appointed brigadier general of state militia in 1859.

Soon after **secession**, Gist was promoted to major general of state troops and was appointed the state's adjutant and inspector general. After being involved in the capture of **Fort Sumter**, he joined Brig. Gen. **Barnard Bee's** staff as a volunteer aide with the rank of colonel, but during the **First Battle of Manassas**, he temporarily led the 4th Alabama.

Returning to South Carolina to raise troops, Gist was appointed brigadier general in the **Confederate army** in March 1862 and was sent to James Island at **Charleston, South Carolina**. In December 1862, he led 5,000 men to **Wilmington, North Carolina**, to help defend it against the Union forces that had gained a foothold on the Atlantic coast. Gist moved back and forth between Wilmington and South Carolina for a time before returning to James Island in early 1863. After playing a minor role in the defense of Fort Sumter in April, he was given a **brigade** and was ordered to join **Joseph E. Johnston** at **Jackson, Mississippi**, during the **Vicksburg Campaign**. Gist served there in **William H. T. Walker's** division throughout the siege and then accompanied Walker to **Georgia**. During the **Chickamauga Campaign**, he temporarily led an **Army of Tennessee division** on the second day and helped form the rear guard during the November retreat from **Missionary Ridge**. Gist led his brigade throughout the **Atlanta Campaign** and was wounded at the **Battle of Atlanta**. His brigade then was attached to **Benjamin F. Cheatham's** division, and Gist rejoined it upon his recovery. During the 1864 **Franklin and Nashville Campaign**, he led his brigade in the attack at Franklin. When his horse was killed, Gist continued on foot until he was shot in the chest. He died that night in a hospital.

GLADDEN, ADLEY HOGAN (1810–1862) CSA. A native of **South Carolina**, Gladden was a cotton broker who served in the **Seminole Wars** and was wounded while colonel of the famous Palmetto Regiment during the **Mexican War**. He moved to **New Orleans, Louisiana**, after the war, but when South Carolina seceded, he accepted a commission as lieutenant colonel of the 1st South Carolina.

Gladden resigned his commission in January 1861 to serve in the **Louisiana secession** convention. He then accepted the position of colonel of the 1st Louisiana Regulars. Gladden was sent to **Pensacola, Florida**, and in September 1861 was promoted to brigadier general. In Pensacola, he temporarily commanded two different **brigades** and the post itself. In November, **Braxton Bragg** commended Gladden's defense of Fort McRee against Union shelling from **Fort Pickens**. Bragg wanted to take Gladden with him when he was transferred to northern **Mississippi**, but the War Department refused. Instead, Bragg was able to give him command of **Leroy P. Walker's** brigade in Mobile, Alabama, in early 1862 when Walker was transferred. Bragg was pleased with Gladden's service at Mobile and expanded his responsibilities to include Pensacola. By early March 1862, Gladden was sent to **Tennessee**, where he took command of two brigades under **Leonidas Polk**.

On the first day of battle at **Shiloh**, Gladden commanded a mostly **Alabama** brigade in **Jones M. Withers's division**. He was badly wounded in the arm by a shell fragment and died on April 12 after having the arm amputated. Gladden had the distinction of being one of the few field officers that the critical Bragg consistently praised.

GLASGOW, MISSOURI, BATTLE OF (OCTOBER 15, 1864). After the **Battle of Pilot Knob** during **Sterling Price's 1864 Missouri Raid**, Price was forced to abandon his plan to attack St. Louis, Missouri, and headed west, instead. On October 15, a detachment of his **army** attacked Union-occupied Glasgow on the Missouri River. After enduring an **artillery** bombardment and faced with encirclement, Union Col. Chester Harding surrendered his small garrison. The Confederates **paroled** more than 500 **prisoners** and then rejoined Price's main column with the supplies and weapons that had been seized.

GLENDALE, VIRGINIA, BATTLE OF (JUNE 30, 1862). *See* FRAYSER'S FARM, VIRGINIA, BATTLE OF.

GLOBE TAVERN, VIRGINIA, BATTLE OF (AUGUST 18–21, 1864). *See* WELDON RAILROAD, VIRGINIA, UNION OPERATIONS AGAINST.

GLORIETA PASS, NEW MEXICO TERRITORY, BATTLE OF (MARCH 26–28, 1862). Beginning in February 1862, Confederate Brig. Gen. **Henry H. Sibley** led his 2,600-man **Army of New Mexico** on **Sibley's New Mexico Campaign** to capture the territory for the Confederacy. By March 10, his **army** had captured Santa Fe. Sibley had remained behind at Albuquerque, but he ordered his men to advance toward Fort Union. Located 150 miles to the northeast, Fort Union was on the Santa Fe Trail and controlled the route to the **Colorado** gold mines.

From Fort Union, Col. **John P. Slough** took 1,340 men and advanced to meet the Confederates on March 22. On March 26, Maj. **John M. Chivington's** 1st Colorado Volunteers, acting as Slough's advance guard, surprised and captured part of the 2nd Texas Mounted Rifles a few miles west of Glorieta Pass. Confederate Maj. Charles L. Pyron made several defensive stands around Apache Canyon but repeatedly was flanked when Chivington's men climbed the canyon walls. Pyron finally withdrew to Cañoncito, where he had previously camped, and called for reinforcements. He had lost 94 men in the fight at Apache Canyon, mostly taken **prisoner**. Chivington had lost only 19 men, but he also withdrew 12 miles and rejoined Slough at Kozlowski's Ranch.

Both sides renewed the advance on March 28. Lieutenant Colonel **William R. Scurry** of the 4th Texas Mounted Volunteers left his supply train with a small guard and one cannon at Cañoncito and took 1,200 men and eight cannons along the Santa Fe Trail toward Glorieta Pass. To the east, the Union column divided before reaching the pass, with Chivington taking 430 men to the west to strike the Confederate camp at Cañoncito. At 11:00 A.M., Scurry came upon Slough resting at Pigeon's Ranch, one mile east of Glorieta Pass. Both sides formed battle lines along the Santa Fe Trail just west of the ranch and **skirmished** until 2:00 P.M. At that time, Scurry flanked Slough and forced him to withdraw to the ranch. Continuing the attack, the Confederates again turned the Union right flank and forced Slough to fall back to a third line a half mile to the rear. There the Federals held their line until dark, but, outnumbered and exhausted, they retreated to Kozlowski's Ranch that night. The Confederates lost 133 men in the fight, while Slough suffered 113 casualties.

While the Confederates were winning the battle at Glorieta Pass, Chivington was destroying their base at Cañoncito. Surprising the small guard, he captured Scurry's 80-wagon train and destroyed it before retiring to rejoin Slough. Left with no food, ammunition, or medicine, Scurry was forced to retreat to Santa Fe two days later. Although the fight at Glorieta Pass was small, it was decisive because it forced the Confederates to abandon their New Mexico Campaign.

GODWIN, ARCHIBALD CAMPBELL (1831?–1864) CSA. The exact date of Godwin's birth is unknown, but he was a native of **Virginia** and either was orphaned as a child or was sent to his grandmother's to live. He moved to **California** as a young man, became wealthy from a gold strike and ranching, and almost won the 1860 gubernatorial nomination.

When Virginia seceded in early 1861, Godwin returned to his native state and entered Confederate service as a captain and assistant provost marshal of **Libby Prison**. He then was sent to establish and command the **Salisbury Prison** in **North Carolina** and in the spring of 1862 was promoted to major. In July 1862, Godwin raised the 57th North Carolina and was appointed its colonel. His **regiment** became part of **Evander Law's** brigade in the **Army of Northern Virginia**, and he won praise at **Fredericksburg** when he attacked and recaptured some lost ground. After fighting at **Second Fredericksburg**, Godwin saw heavy combat at **Gettysburg**. On the first day, he was hotly engaged around the **railroad** cut northwest of town, and on the second day he participated in **Jubal Early's** assault on Cemetery Hill that briefly captured two enemy batteries. During the latter action, Godwin took temporary command of the

brigade when Col. Isaac Avery was killed. He remained in temporary command of the brigade for several months. At **Rappahannock Station** in November 1863, Godwin's and **Harry T. Hays's** brigades were over- whelmed and captured as they manned an isolated position on the north bank of the Rappahannock River. Godwin again won praise in that ac- tion for his tenacious defense and for threatening to shoot anyone who tried to surrender.

After being **exchanged** in the summer of 1864, Godwin was promoted to brigadier general in August and was given permanent command of his brigade. Only weeks later, he was killed by a shell at the **Third Battle of Winchester** on September 19, 1864.

GOGGIN, JAMES MONROE (1820–1889) CSA. A native of **Virginia**, Goggin dropped out of **West Point** and moved to **Texas**, where he joined the Texas army as a lieutenant. He eventually resigned his commission, moved to **California** in 1848, and became rich managing an overland stage mail service.

By the time the Civil War began, Goggin had moved once again, this time to **Tennessee**, where he worked as a cotton broker. When Virginia seceded, he returned to his native state and entered Confederate service in July 1861 as a major in the 32nd Virginia. After serving on the Vir- ginia Peninsula, Goggin became assistant adjutant general for **Lafayette McLaws** and was praised by McLaws for his service with the **Army of Northern Virginia** in the **Peninsula**, **Seven Days**, **Antietam**, **Freder- icksburg**, and **Chancellorsville Campaigns**. After the **Chickamauga** and **Knoxville Campaigns**, McLaws highly recommended Goggin for promotion to brigadier general. This did not occur, however, and when McLaws was removed from his **division** command, Goggin remained to serve the new commander, **Joseph B. Kershaw**. Goggin was put in tem- porary command of **James Conner's brigade** when Conner was wounded in October 1864. He led the brigade at **Cedar Creek** and fought well early in the battle, but his brigade was thrown back in con- fusion when **Philip Sheridan** counterattacked that afternoon. It appears that Goggin finally received his promotion to brigadier general in De- cember 1864. However, either he declined to accept the commission, or **Jefferson Davis** withdrew the appointment, for Goggin continued to serve as a major on Kershaw's staff until he was captured in April 1865 at **Sailor's Creek**.

After the war, Goggin returned to Texas.

GOLD HOAX (MAY 18, 1864). After Union forces had suffered heavy casualties in the 1864 **Overland Campaign** and seemed no closer to

Richmond, Virginia, newspaper editor **Joseph Howard Jr.** of the Brooklyn *Eagle* saw an opportunity to manipulate the gold market. He first speculated in gold and then had a reporter help him duplicate an Associated Press news release declaring that **Abraham Lincoln** had asked for a day of prayer and fasting and for 400,000 more volunteers because of the recent military reverses. Howard then sent the false dispatch to seven leading New York City newspapers, but most of them were suspicious of the story and only the *World* and the *Journal of Commerce* printed it.

The dismal news affected Wall Street, and gold prices increased 10 percent before it was learned that the story was false. Still, Howard made a nice profit on his speculation. Lincoln was furious and had the **army** seize the two newspapers and the Independent Telegraph line that wired the false story. Howard was arrested on May 20 and was imprisoned for three months, but he exonerated the newspapers. Lincoln was criticized for his heavy-handed response to the hoax and worried it would hurt his reelection. Moreover, he had, indeed, planned to call for more soldiers, but the outcry created by the Gold Hoax forced him to postpone it for two months.

GOLDING'S FARM, VIRGINIA, BATTLE OF (JUNE 28, 1862). *See* GARNETT'S AND GOLDING'S FARMS, BATTLE OF.

GOLDSBORO BRIDGE, NORTH CAROLINA, BATTLE OF (DECEMBER 17, 1862). In December 1862, Union Brig. Gen. **John G. Foster** was ordered from New Bern, North Carolina, to destroy the vital Wilmington & Weldon Railroad bridge across the Neuse River to disrupt the supply line of **Robert E. Lee's Army of Northern Virginia**. With 10,640 men, Foster defeated Confederate Brig. Gen. **Nathan G. Evans** at **First Kinston** and engaged another enemy force at **White Hall** before reaching Goldsboro on December 17. Foster attacked **Thomas L. Clingman's** defenders on the south bank and drove them across the river. He then burned the bridge and destroyed a substantial amount of track in the area before returning to New Bern. The Confederates soon had the damage repaired, and trains again were crossing the river. In the short clash at Goldsboro Bridge, total casualties are estimated to have been 220.

GOLDSBOROUGH, JOHN RODGERS (1809–1877) USA. A native of **Washington, D.C.**, Goldsborough was the brother of Union Adm. **Louis Malesherbes Goldsborough**. He entered the **U.S. Navy** in 1823 as a midshipman, fought pirates while serving under David Porter Sr., and rose through the ranks to become commander in 1855.

When the Civil War began, Goldsborough commanded the USS *Union* and initiated the Union **blockade** of **Savannah, Georgia**. He later was put in command of the *Florida* and in 1862 was promoted to captain and was named the senior naval officer of the squadron that was blockading **Charleston, South Carolina**. Goldsborough then was transferred to the *Colorado* and from March to September 1863 commanded the blockading squadron off **Mobile, Alabama**. In November 1863, he was relieved of sea duty and was appointed inspector of ordnance at the Portsmouth, New York, Navy Yard. Goldsborough remained at that post until war's end.

After the war, Goldsborough commanded the *Shenandoah* on a cruise to Japan and Korea from 1865 to 1868. Promoted to commodore during the mission, he spent the rest of his navy career in command of the Mare Island Navy Yard and the station at Mound City, **Illinois**. Goldsborough retired from the navy in 1877.

GOLDSBOROUGH, LOUIS MALESHERBES (1805–1873) USA. A native of **Washington, D.C.**, Goldsborough was the brother of Union Capt. **John Rodgers Goldsborough** and entered the **U.S. Navy** as a midshipman in 1816. He served in both the **Seminole** and **Mexican Wars** and was superintendent of the **U.S. Naval Academy** for four years.

When the Civil War began, Goldsborough was a captain commanding a ship off the coast of Brazil. He was appointed commander of the Atlantic Blockading Squadron, but when it was divided, Goldsborough took charge of the **North Atlantic Blockading Squadron** in September 1861. He earned the **Thanks of Congress** for leading the fleet that captured **Roanoke Island, North Carolina**, in February 1862 but then was criticized for being absent during the **Battle of Hampton Roads** and for failing to cooperate with the **Army of the Potomac** during the **Peninsula Campaign**. Goldsborough was relieved of command at his own request in July 1862 after the James River Flotilla was made a separate command from his squadron. He was promoted to rear admiral the day after making the request and for the rest of the war performed administrative duties in Washington.

In July 1865, Goldsborough was sent to Europe to command a squadron to destroy the surviving Confederate **commerce raiders**. He remained in the navy after the war and retired in 1871.

GOODRICH'S LANDING, LOUISIANA, BATTLE OF (JUNE 29–30, 1863). By the summer of 1863, northeast **Louisiana** was the scene of much **freedmen** activity. The Union **army** was enlisting large numbers of **black troops**, some of whom saw combat at **Milliken's Bend** early in the month, while other freedmen were being put to work on lessee plantations. To disrupt these activities, Col. **William H. Parsons** led a Confederate force into the area from southeast **Arkansas**. One of Parson's targets was a Union encampment near Goodrich's Landing that was providing protection for the nearby leased plantations. This encampment was defended by just over 100 men of the 1st Arkansas Infantry (African Descent), who had constructed a fortified position atop an **Indian** mound.

After Parsons was reinforced by Brig. Gen. **James C. Tappan's brigade**, he demanded the surrender of the black soldiers on June 29. The **regiment's** three white officers quickly agreed, with the understanding they would be treated as **prisoners** of war; their men, however, were surrendered unconditionally. After taking the 116 prisoners, Parsons destroyed the nearby leased plantations and then engaged the 1st Kansas Mounted Infantry near Lake Providence the following day. The Confederates were forced to withdraw after Brig. Gen. **Alfred W. Ellet's Mississippi Marine Brigade** was landed at Goodrich's Landing. During this operation, Parsons lost six men while inflicting approximately 150 casualties on the enemy.

GOODWIN, ICHABOD (1794–1882) USA. Born in **Maine**, Goodwin worked as a business clerk and seaman before becoming the wealthy owner of a **New Hampshire** trading house. A **Whig**, he was elected to the state legislature six times and served as a delegate to three national conventions. After unsuccessful attempts to win a congressional and governor's seat, Goodwin became a **Republican** and was elected governor in 1859 and 1860.

Goodwin and **Abraham Lincoln** had a good relationship, and Lincoln even made some speeches promoting Goodwin's reelection. When the Civil War began and Lincoln called for volunteers, the New Hampshire legislature was not in session. Goodwin borrowed $680,000 from banks and outfitted two **regiments** and then gained the legislature's approval when it did convene. Although a candidate for reelection in 1861, he did not have the support of the **Radical Republicans** who had won control of the party. Goodwin retired from politics and later served as president of several **railroads**.

GORDON, GEORGE HENRY (1823–1886) USA. A native of **Massachusetts**, Gordon graduated from **West Point** in 1846. He served with distinction in the **Mexican War**, where he was wounded twice and was **brevetted** once for gallantry at Cerro Gordo. Gordon resigned from the

U.S. Army in 1854 and became a lawyer after studying at Harvard University.

When civil war erupted, Gordon raised the 2nd Massachusetts and was appointed its colonel in May 1861. After serving as a **brigade** commander under **Nathaniel P. Banks** during **Stonewall Jackson's 1862 Shenandoah Valley Campaign**, he was promoted to brigadier general of volunteers in June 1862. Gordon fought at **Cedar Mountain, Chantilly, Chancellorsville, South Mountain**, and **Antietam**, and at times commanded a XII Corps **division** in the **Army of the Potomac**. During the **Fredericksburg Campaign**, he protected the upper Potomac River and then was sent to command the reserve division at **Suffolk, Virginia**, during **James Longstreet's** siege. Afterward, Gordon led a division on Folly Island near **Charleston, South Carolina**, and then saw service in **Florida, Arkansas**, and **Alabama**. In November 1864, he was transferred to the **Department of Virginia** and in February 1865 was put in command of its Eastern District. Gordon remained in that position until war's end and earned a brevet of major general of volunteers.

After the war, Gordon wrote several books on his wartime experiences, practiced law in Massachusetts, and helped found the Military Historical Society of Massachusetts.

GORDON, GEORGE WASHINGTON (1836–1911) CSA. A native of **Tennessee**, Gordon graduated from Nashville's Western Institute in 1850 and became a surveyor before entering Confederate service in June 1861 as a drillmaster for the 11th Tennessee. After accompanying the **regiment** to eastern Tennessee, he was elected a **company** captain and then became lieutenant colonel in July. Gordon was captured in a **skirmish** at Tazewell, Tennessee, and after being **exchanged** was appointed the regiment's colonel in October 1862.

The 11th Tennessee was part of **James E. Rains's** brigade in the **Army of Tennessee** and fought at **Stones River**, where Gordon was severely wounded while leading an attack. His regiment later served in various **brigades** and saw service in the **Chickamauga, Chattanooga**, and **Atlanta Campaigns**. After the **Battle of Kennesaw Mountain**, Gordon took command of the brigade and was promoted to brigadier general in August 1864. As part of **John C. Brown's division**, his brigade participated in the **Franklin and Nashville Campaign**. At Franklin, Gordon led his men into the Union defenses farther than any other Confederate unit, but he was wounded and captured in the process. He was kept a **prisoner** in **Fort Warren, Massachusetts**, and was not released until July 1865.

After the war, Gordon became a Tennessee lawyer and a **Mississippi** planter. He also served in various state and federal political positions, including the **U.S. Congress** from 1907 to 1911; was a founder of the Southern Historical Society; and twice served as commander in chief of the **United Confederate Veterans**.

GORDON, JAMES BYRON (1822–1864) CSA. A native of **North Carolina**, Gordon graduated from **Virginia's** Emory and Henry College. He became a prosperous North Carolina businessman and was elected to the state legislature in 1850.

Gordon entered Confederate service as a private in a volunteer **company** when North Carolina seceded but was quickly elected 1st lieutenant. When the company became part of the 1st North Carolina Cavalry in July 1861, he was appointed major. The **regiment** became part of **J. E. B. Stuart's** brigade and in late 1861 fought at **Dranesville, Virginia**. Gordon was promoted to lieutenant colonel in the spring of 1862 and fought in the **Peninsula** and **Seven Days Campaigns**. As part of **Wade Hampton's** brigade in the **Army of Northern Virginia**, the regiment and Gordon earned praise for their service at **Second Manassas**, **Antietam**, the **Dumfries Raid**, **Brandy Station**, and **Gettysburg**. Gordon took command of the regiment during this last campaign when his colonel assumed **division** command from a wounded Hampton. Stuart commended Gordon's actions during the retreat from **Pennsylvania** when he led a counterattack that routed a Union cavalry **brigade**.

Gordon earned promotions to colonel in late July 1863 and to brigadier general and brigade command in September. During the **Bristoe Station Campaign**, he was wounded in a **skirmish** but remained in the field, and during the **Mine Run Campaign** his horse was killed under him. Gordon led his brigade against **Philip Sheridan's** Union troopers during the **Overland Campaign** and was mortally wounded in a skirmish on May 12, 1864. He died in **Richmond, Virginia**, on May 18.

GORDON, JOHN BROWN (1832–1904) CSA. A native of **Georgia**, Gordon established an impressive record at the University of Georgia, but he inexplicably dropped out his senior year. He then became a lawyer, but his practice did poorly, and in 1856 he went to work for his father superintending a northeast **Alabama** coal mine.

When civil war erupted, Gordon raised a volunteer **company** named the "Raccoon Roughs" and was elected its captain. During the next four years, he became one of the Confederacy's best and most popular field commanders. When his company became part of the 6th Alabama, Gordon was elected major in May 1861. Assigned to **Richard S. Ewell's brigade** in **Virginia**, the **regiment** was at **First Manassas**, but it was never engaged. Gordon was promoted to lieutenant colonel in December 1861 and to colonel in April 1862, after which the regiment became part of **Robert Rodes's** brigade. When Rodes was wounded at **Seven Pines**, Gordon took command of the brigade and fought well with the **Army of Northern Virginia** at **Gaines' Mill** and **Malvern Hill**. During the **Antietam Campaign**, he was back in command of his regiment. Gordon again fought well at **South Mountain** and at Antietam, receiving five wounds in the latter battle.

After winning promotion to brigadier general in November 1862, Gordon was given command of a brigade in **Jubal Early's division**. When the Senate failed to confirm his appointment, he was reappointed brigadier general in May 1863. Gordon fought at **Second Fredericksburg**, and at **Gettysburg** he was praised for routing the Union XI Corps' right flank on the first day. Already a rising star within the **army**, he earned more praise during the **Overland Campaign** when he launched a successful flank attack in the **Wilderness**. While leading a division, Gordon also sealed the Union breakthrough at **Spotsylvania's** "Bloody Angle" with a determined counterattack.

Gordon's impressive record won him promotion to major general in May 1864 and command of **Edward Johnson's** former division. Accompanying Jubal **Early's Washington Raid** that summer, he fought at the **Monocacy** and then at **Third Winchester** during **Philip Sheridan's Shenandoah Valley Campaign**. At **Cedar Creek**, Gordon led the brilliant flank attack against the Union army, but then Early failed to press his advantage. Early blamed Gordon for the defeat, for not controlling his men more effectively, and the two officers became bitter enemies. In December 1864, **Robert E. Lee** placed Gordon in command of the II Corps, but he was never promoted to lieutenant general. Lee came to have the utmost confidence in him during the **Petersburg Campaign**, and in March 1865, he put Gordon in command of the attempted breakout at **Fort Stedman**. Gordon led his **corps** in the **Appomattox Campaign** and was chosen by Lee to ride at the head of the army during the **surrender** ceremony.

After the war, Gordon was elected to the U.S. Senate in 1873, 1879 (he resigned midway through his term), and 1891, and was elected Georgia's governor in 1886. He was very active in writing about the Civil War and served as the first commander in chief of the **United Confederate Veterans**. A year before his death, Gordon published his popular memoirs, *Reminiscences of the Civil War*.

GORGAS, JOSIAH (1818–1883) CSA. A native of **Pennsylvania**, Gorgas graduated from **West Point** in 1841 and served in the **U.S. Army's** Ordnance Department. He spent one year in Europe studying the **artillery** and in the **Mexican War** earned a promotion to 1st lieutenant while in command of the ordnance depot at Vera Cruz. After the war, Gorgas commanded a number of arsenals and married the daughter of a former **Alabama** governor. This union probably led to his supporting the Confederacy during the Civil War.

When **Fort Sumter** was bombarded in April 1861, Gorgas resigned his captain's commission and entered Confederate service as major and chief of the Ordnance Department. As head of this department, he became one of the most important officers in the **Confederate army**, performing invaluable service keeping the armies supplied with arms and ammunition. Gorgas dispatched agents to Europe to purchase needed weapons and ammunition, used captured U.S. machinery to establish government arsenals, and contracted with such private firms as the **Tredegar Iron Works** to make cannons and other weapons. He also opened mines for such precious material as lead and copper and initiated the collection of human waste to produce saltpeter for making gunpowder. Largely due to Gorgas's herculean efforts, the Confederacy never lost a battle because of a lack of arms or ammunition.

Although a habitual complainer, Gorgas also maintained good relations with both military and governmental officials, all of whom highly praised his efforts. By November 1864, he had risen to the rank of colonel and was promoted that month to brigadier general. Gorgas was in **Richmond, Virginia**, when it was evacuated in April 1865 and accompanied the government to **North Carolina**, but he then left the party in Charlotte and returned to Alabama.

After the war, Gorgas briefly was superintendent of an Alabama ironworks and then became headmaster of the University of the South. In 1868, he was appointed president of the University of Alabama but poor health forced him to resign that position to become the university's librarian.

GORMAN, WILLIS ARNOLD (1816–1876) USA. A native of **Kentucky**, Gorman moved to **Indiana** as a young man and became a lawyer. He was elected to the state legislature three times and entered the **Mexican War** as a major. Rising to the rank of colonel, Gorman was severely wounded in the war and in 1848 was made the military governor of Puebla, Mexico. He was elected to the **U.S. Congress** in 1848 and served there until appointed territorial governor of **Minnesota** in 1853. After four years, Gorman returned to Indiana and again was elected to the legislature.

Gorman entered Union service in April 1861 as colonel of the 1st Minnesota. After fighting at **First Manassas**, he was promoted to brigadier general of volunteers and led a **brigade** at **Ball's Bluff**. As part of **John Sedgwick's division** in the **Army of the Potomac**, Gordon's brigade also fought at **Seven Pines** and at **Antietam**. He was praised by his superiors in all of these fights and in November 1862 was put in command of the District of Eastern Arkansas. Gorman later was replaced as **district** commander, but he remained in the district until he left the **army** in May 1864.

Gorman returned to Indiana after resigning his commission and became the city attorney for St. Paul.

GOVAN, DANIEL CHEVILETTE (1829–1911) CSA. A native of **North Carolina**, Govan (GUV-en) moved with his family to **Tennessee** as an infant and then settled in **Mississippi**. After attending, but not graduating from, the University of South Carolina, he accompanied his relative **Benjamin McCulloch** to **California** during the Gold Rush. When McCulloch was elected sheriff of Sacramento County, he appointed Govan his deputy. Govan returned east in 1852 and eventually became an **Arkansas** planter.

In 1861, Govan raised a volunteer **company**, was elected its captain, and entered Confederate service in June as part of the 2nd Arkansas, of which he was elected lieutenant colonel later that month. After being posted in **Kentucky**, he was promoted to colonel in January 1862. Govan led his **regiment** at **Shiloh** and participated in the 1862 **Kentucky Campaign** as part of **St. John R. Liddell's brigade**. His regiment then fought at **Perryville**, **Stones River**, and in the **Tullahoma Campaign** with the **Army of Tennessee**. When Liddell was promoted to a **division** command in August 1863, Govan took command of the brigade, which by then was part of **Patrick Cleburne's** division. He led it at **Chickamauga** but afterward reverted to regimental command when Liddell resumed command of the brigade. Govan temporarily led the brigade again at **Missionary Ridge** and **Ringgold Gap** in November 1863 while Liddell was on leave.

Govan was promoted to brigadier general in February 1864 and led his brigade through vicious fighting during the **Atlanta Campaign**, including **Resaca**, **Pickett's Mill**, and **Kennesaw Mountain**. During the **Battle of Atlanta**, he claimed to have captured 700 **prisoners** and eight cannons but lost over half his men in the process. At **Jonesboro**, Govan's position was overrun by the enemy, and he and hundreds of his men were captured. **Exchanged** a few weeks later, he rejoined his brigade and led it during the **Franklin and Nashville Campaign**. After fighting at Franklin, Govan was wounded at Nashville. He recovered in time to join his men for the **Carolinas Campaign** and surrendered there with **Joseph E. Johnston**.

After the war, Govan returned to his Arkansas plantation and briefly served as a federal **Indian** agent.

GRACIE, ARCHIBALD, JR. (1832–1864) CSA. A native of **New York**, Gracie was educated in Europe and graduated from **West Point** in 1854. He resigned from the **U.S. Army** after only two years' service and joined his father's cotton brokerage in **Alabama**. Although his father and family remained loyal to the Union and returned to New York when the Civil War began, Gracie supported the Confederacy, probably because he had lived in the South for so long, had married a Southern girl, and was the commander of a local militia **company**.

In January 1861, Gracie led his men in the capture of the federal arsenal near Mobile. His company then became part of the 3rd Alabama, but in July Gracie was appointed major of the 11th Alabama. After serving for months in **Virginia**, he was recalled to Alabama to raise a new **regiment**. In May 1862, Gracie was elected colonel of the unit that ultimately became the 43rd Alabama. Sent to eastern **Tennessee**, he was given command of a **brigade** under **Edmund Kirby Smith** during the 1862 **Kentucky Campaign**.

Gracie was promoted to brigadier general in November 1862 and took command of Cumberland Gap. His brigade served in **William Preston's** division of the **Army of Tennessee** at **Chickamauga** and in **Bushrod Johnson's** division at **Bean's Station**, where Gracie was severely wounded in the arm. Gracie accompanied Johnson's **division** to Petersburg, Virginia, in the spring of 1864 and saw combat at the **Second Battle of Drewry's Bluff**. He continued to serve around Petersburg during the **Petersburg Campaign** and temporarily commanded the division late in the year. While observing the Union works on December 2, 1864, Gracie was killed instantly by an exploding shell.

GRAHAM, CHARLES KINNAIRD (1824–1889) USA. A native of **New York**, Graham entered the **U.S. Navy** as a midshipman when he was 17. After serving in the **Mexican War**, he resigned from the navy in 1848 and became both a lawyer and engineer, although he never practiced law. Before the Civil War, Graham helped design New York City's Central Park, and he constructed the Brooklyn Navy Yard's dry docks.

Graham entered Union service in the spring of 1861 when he and several hundred navy yard workmen joined **Daniel Sickles's Excelsior**

Brigade. He was appointed colonel of the 74th New York in May and led it in numerous battles with the **Army of the Potomac** during the **Peninsula** and **Seven Days Campaigns**. Poor health finally forced Graham from the field and on recruiting duty for about a year, but he was promoted to brigadier general of volunteers in March 1863. He returned to the **army** that spring and led a **brigade** in **David Birney's division** at **Chancellorsville**. Graham was wounded in the head and captured at **Gettysburg's Peach Orchard**, but he was **exchanged** in September. In November, he was put in command of the army's gunboats that were assigned to **Benjamin Butler's** command. Near Fredericksburg, Virginia, and acting under Butler's orders, Graham shelled and burned the home of Confederate Secretary of War **James A. Seddon's** brother in retaliation for the Confederates having burned the home of Postmaster General **Montgomery Blair** in **Maryland**. At war's end, Graham was **brevetted** major general of volunteers.

Graham returned to his engineering profession in New York City after the war and held several city engineering positions.

GRAHAM, LAWRENCE PIKE (1815–1905) USA. A native of **Virginia**, Graham was commissioned a 2nd lieutenant in the dragoons in 1837, and in the **Seminole Wars** he rose to the rank of captain. During the **Mexican War**, he was **brevetted** major for gallantry at Palo Alto and Resaca de la Palma.

A major when the Civil War began, Graham was promoted to brigadier general of volunteers in August 1861 and took command of a **brigade** in **Darius Couch's** division. After temporarily leading the **division** at **Yorktown**, he fell ill and left the **Army of the Potomac**. Upon recovering from the illness, Graham was made chief of cavalry at an instruction camp near Annapolis, **Maryland**, and performed other various administrative duties. He was mustered out of the volunteer service in August 1864. During the war, Graham was promoted to lieutenant colonel and colonel in the regular **U.S. Army** and was brevetted brigadier general of regulars. He retired from the **army** in 1870 and became a noted Shakespeare scholar.

GRAHAM, WILLIAM ALEXANDER (1804–1875) CSA. A native of **North Carolina**, Graham graduated from the University of North Carolina and became a well-known lawyer after studying under Thomas Ruffin. Active in politics, he served in the state legislature (1833–40) and the U.S. Senate (1840–43 and 1855–61), was governor (1845–49), and served as the U.S. secretary of the navy (1850–52). Graham also ran unsuccessfully for vice president on the **Whig** ticket in 1852.

An opponent of **secession**, Graham helped organize the **Constitutional Union Party** in 1860 and participated in the 1861 **Washington Peace Conference**. It was not until **Abraham Lincoln** called for volunteers to suppress the Rebellion that he supported secession (five of his sons also served as Confederate officers). As a delegate to the state's secession convention, Graham attempted to portray the state's action as revolution rather than the constitutionally questionable act of secession. Elected a Confederate senator, he assumed his new duties in May 1864. In the **Confederate Congress**, Graham consistently opposed **Jefferson Davis's** strong war measures, including the **suspension of the writ of habeas corpus**, **conscription**, and the recruitment of **black troops**. By war's end, he was calling for Davis to negotiate a peace that would allow the South to rejoin the Union with the same status as the Northern states. When this failed, Graham urged the Confederate states to make their own separate peace with the Union on the best terms they could get.

Graham emerged from the war well respected by many North Carolinians, and he was elected to the state senate in 1865. **Reconstruction** policies forbade him from taking his seat, however, and he resumed his law practice.

GRANBURY, HIRAM BRONSON (1831–1864) CSA. A native of **Mississippi**, Granbury was educated at Mississippi's Oakland College. He then moved to **Texas** as a young man and became a lawyer. From 1856 to 1858, Granbury served as chief justice of McLennan County.

When Texas seceded, Granbury organized and was elected captain of a volunteer **company** that became part of the 7th Texas. He was elected major in October 1861 and was praised for his performance during the attempted **Fort Donelson** breakout. Taken **prisoner** when the fort was captured, Granbury was **exchanged** in August 1862 and was promoted to colonel of the 7th Texas that same month. Sent to Port Hudson, Louisiana, he served in **John Gregg's brigade** and helped repulse Union gunboats in March 1863. The following month, Granbury was among those Confederates who pursued the Union cavalry in **Benjamin Grierson's Raid**. Afterward, he fought with Gregg's brigade at **Raymond** and **Jackson, Mississippi**, during the **Vicksburg Campaign**. At **Chickamauga** with the **Army of Tennessee**, Granbury was severely wounded, but he remained with his **regiment**. Transferred to **James A. Smith's** Texas brigade, he assumed command of the brigade when Smith was wounded at **Missionary Ridge** during the **Chattanooga Campaign** and was praised for his service with the rear guard both during the retreat and at **Ringgold Gap**.

Granbury was promoted to brigadier general in March 1864 and led his Texas brigade in **Patrick Cleburne's division** through the **Atlanta Campaign**. Praised again by his superiors for leading a charge at **New Hope Church**, he also fought at **Peachtree Creek** and **Jonesboro**. At the **Battle of Franklin**, Granbury was killed within a few yards of the Union line while leading his brigade in the Confederate attack.

GRAND ARMY OF THE REPUBLIC (GAR). This was the main Union veterans' organization that was first established in Springfield, **Illinois**, in April 1866 by former Union generals **Richard J. Oglesby** and **John A. Logan** and former surgeon Dr. Benjamin F. Stephenson. The GAR was a social organization that aided disabled veterans and the families of deceased veterans, won pensions and other benefits for veterans, and promoted patriotism. The organization soon spread nationwide and was strongly allied with the **Republican Party** because the Republicans were seen as the party that saved the Union. This association led to the popular saying that GAR actually stood for "Generally All Republicans." It was a powerful political block in the late 19th century and peaked in 1890 with 427,981 members. Not only did the GAR succeed in winning Union veteran pensions, it also helped establish a national holiday known as Decoration Day (now known as Memorial Day).

GRAND COTEAU, LOUISIANA, BATTLE OF (NOVEMBER 3, 1863). *See* BAYOU BOURBEAU, LOUISIANA, BATTLE OF.

GRAND GULF, MISSISSIPPI, BATTLE OF (APRIL 29, 1863). After months of frustration, Union Maj. Gen. **U. S. Grant** was ready in April 1863 to cross the Mississippi River in the **Vicksburg Campaign**. He marched his **Army of the Tennessee** down the west side of the Mississippi River toward Hard Times, Louisiana, and Adm. **David Porter** successfully ran his ships past the **Vicksburg, Mississippi**, batteries to get in position to ferry the **army** across the river at Grand Gulf, Mississippi.

On the morning of April 29, Porter attacked the Confederate fortifications at Grand Gulf with seven gunboats to open the way for Grant's crossing. The Confederate defenders under Brig. Gen. **John S. Bowen**, however, fought skillfully. Porter successfully silenced a lower battery known as Fort Wade, but Fort Cobun, the upper battery, was on a high bluff, and the gunboats could not elevate their cannons high enough to hit it. In a hard-fought five-and-one-half-hour battle, the USS *Tuscumbia* was knocked out of action, and the fleet was forced to withdraw. The failure to silence the Confederate battery at Grand Gulf forced Grant to change his crossing site farther downstream to Bruinsburg, Mississippi.

The Federals crossed the river on April 30 and engaged the Confederates at **Port Gibson** the following day. In the Battle at Grand Gulf, Porter lost 80 sailors, but Confederate losses are unknown.

GRAND REVIEW (MAY 23–24, 1865). On May 18, 1865, the U.S. War Department ordered that a grand review be held in **Washington, D.C.**, for the Union's principal **armies**. In one of the war's most dramatic spectacles, Maj. Gen. **George G. Meade's** 80,000-man **Army of the Potomac** and **William T. Sherman's** 65,000-man **Army of the Tennessee** and **Army of Georgia** marched through Washington on May 23 and 24, respectively. President **Andrew Johnson** and thousands of spectators turned out to watch. Sherman's men had worn their shoes and **uniforms** to tatters during the **Carolinas Campaign**, and Sherman was concerned that his men would not match the neatly attired Army of the Potomac. As a result, he made sure that all of his men received new uniforms and shoes for their review.

GRANGER, GORDON (1822–1876) USA. A native of **New York**, Granger graduated from **West Point** in 1845 and served in the **Mexican War**, where he won two **brevets** for gallantry. Afterward, he served on the frontier until the Civil War, rising to the rank of 1st lieutenant in the Mounted Rifles.

In April 1861, Granger was appointed lieutenant colonel of **Ohio** volunteers and the following month was promoted to captain in the 3rd U.S. Cavalry. After serving on **Samuel Davis Sturgis's** staff at **Wilson's Creek**, he was appointed colonel of the 2nd Michigan Cavalry in September 1861. Granger commanded the **Army of the Mississippi's** cavalry at **New Madrid** and was promoted to brigadier general of volunteers in late March 1862.

Granger continued to lead the Union cavalry at **Island No. 10** and in the **siege of Corinth, Mississippi**, in the spring of 1862 and was promoted to major general of volunteers in September. During the **Tullahoma Campaign**, he led the Reserve Corps in **William Rosecrans's Army of the Cumberland**. Granger's greatest contribution to the Union war effort came at **Chickamauga** when, without orders, he marched his **corps** to the assistance of **George H. Thomas**, who was fighting off the Confederates at **Snodgrass Hill** while the rest of the **army** retreated to Chattanooga, Tennessee. Granger lost more than 40 percent of his corps, but he helped Thomas save the army. He then led the IV Corps in the **Chattanooga Campaign** and afterward fought in the **Knoxville** and **Mobile Campaigns**. Granger ended the war with brevets of brigadier general and major general of regulars.

Granger remained in the army after the war and was promoted to colonel in 1866. He died in 1876 while still on duty and serving as commander of the 15th U.S. Infantry.

GRANGER, ROBERT SEAMAN (1816–1894) USA. A native of **Ohio**, Granger graduated from **West Point** in 1838, served in the **Seminole Wars**, taught at the academy, and won a promotion to captain in the **Mexican War**. Serving in **Texas** when the Civil War began, he was captured by the Confederates in April 1861 but was **paroled**. Granger was not **exchanged** until August 1862, but he was promoted to major in September 1861 while awaiting exchange.

While serving in administrative positions, Granger was appointed brigadier general of **Kentucky** troops in September 1862 and brigadier general of volunteers the following month. His war service mainly was on garrison duty in Kentucky, **Tennessee**, and northern **Alabama**, where he tried to protect lines of communications against Confederate raiders. Granger was **brevetted** brigadier general of regulars for his service during the 1864 **Franklin and Nashville Campaign** and major general of volunteers and regulars for his war service.

After the war, Granger served as superintendent of recruitment and retired as a colonel.

GRANT, LEWIS ADDISON (1828–1918) USA. A native of **Vermont**, Grant taught school in **New Jersey** and **Massachusetts** before becoming a Vermont lawyer in 1855. He entered Union service in August 1861 as major of the 5th Vermont and became one of the best **brigade** commanders in the **Army of the Potomac**.

Promoted to lieutenant colonel in September 1861, Grant commanded the **regiment** at **Williamsburg** and during the **Seven Days Campaign**. At **Savage's Station**, his regiment suffered one of the highest casualty rates of the war for a single battle. After being promoted to colonel in September 1862, Grant was placed in command of the famous **Vermont Brigade** and was wounded while leading it at **Fredericksburg**. During the fighting at **Salem Church** in May 1863, he was wounded again, but his brigade captured three **Confederate flags**, for which Grant was awarded the **Medal of Honor** in 1893. After being held in reserve at **Gettysburg**, he participated in the **Bristoe Station** and **Mine Run Campaigns**.

Promoted to brigadier general of volunteers in April 1864, Grant often was in **division** command during the war's last year. He fought throughout the **Overland Campaign** and then was sent to **Washington, D.C.**, to help defend the city against **Jubal Early's Washington Raid** in July 1864. Joining **Philip Sheridan's Shenandoah Valley Campaign**,

Grant next fought at **Third Winchester**, **Fisher's Hill**, and **Cedar Creek**. In this last battle, he performed valuable service by helping stabilize the Union line after it was smashed by the Confederates early in the battle. Grant was **brevetted** major general of volunteers for his action there. From the **Shenandoah Valley**, Grant's brigade was sent to the **Petersburg Campaign**, where he was wounded again when the Union **army** broke through the Confederate defenses on April 2, 1865. He returned to duty later in the day, however, and was present with his command at the **Appomattox surrender**.

After the war, Grant turned down a commission in the **U.S. Army**, moved west, and eventually settled in **Minnesota**. From 1890 to 1893, he served as the U.S. assistant secretary of war.

GRANT, ULYSSES SIMPSON (1822–1885) USA. A native of **Ohio**, Grant became the most successful Civil War general and general-in-chief of the Union armies. Born Hiram Ulysses Grant, he accidentally was given the middle name Simpson when the congressman who appointed him to **West Point** incorrectly used the maiden name of Grant's mother. Grant grew up in a middle-class family and never considered a military career until his father secured him an appointment to West Point. At the academy, he was not a strong student but neither was he the failure that he has often been portrayed. "Sam" Grant, as he became known (because his initials reminded friends of "Uncle Sam"), excelled in mathematics and horsemanship and graduated 21st out of 39 cadets in 1839.

Assigned to the infantry, Grant fought in the **Mexican War** (although he condemned the war as unjust) under both Zachary Taylor and **Winfield Scott** and won two **brevets** for gallantry at Molino del Rey and Chapultepec. He rose to the rank of captain but became frustrated in the peacetime **U.S. Army** and its slow promotion. When Grant apparently began drinking too much while stationed in **California**, he was given the choice of resigning his commission or being court-martialed. He chose resignation in 1854.

Grant was a loving husband to his wife, Julia Dent Grant, and a caring father to their four children, but he failed in all other endeavors. Before the Civil War, he tried and failed to make a living at farming, rent collecting, and selling firewood and finally had to take a clerking position in his family's store. When the Civil War began, Grant tried unsuccessfully to join **George B. McClellan's** staff, but he finally was commissioned colonel of the 21st Illinois in June 1861. This appointment was largely due to the influence of Illinois Congressman **Elihu B. Washburne**, who became Grant's sponsor. Grant quickly turned his **regiment** from an ill-disciplined mob into a well-trained unit and was promoted to brigadier general of volunteers in July.

Grant commanded several western **districts** early in the war, and in November 1861, he led an attack on **Belmont, Missouri**. He captured the town early in the operation but then was forced to retreat when Confederate reinforcements arrived from across the Mississippi River. Grant's name exploded on the scene in February 1862 when he, with the cooperation of **Andrew Foote's** fleet, moved against the Confederate defenses in **Tennessee**. After Foote captured **Fort Henry**, Grant led his force against **Fort Donelson**, forced its surrender, and earned the nickname "Unconditional Surrender" Grant. This proved to be one of the war's most strategic victories, because it forced the Confederates to abandon **Kentucky** and most of Tennessee. Moving up the Tennessee River to near the **Mississippi** state line, Grant then encamped his army at **Shiloh** to await reinforcements from Nashville, Tennessee.

On April 6, 1862, Grant was surprised when Confederate Gen. **Albert Sidney Johnston** attacked. Although he fought tenaciously and won the battle the next day (with help from **Don Carlos Buell**), Grant was criticized for being caught off guard and was falsely accused of being drunk. His superior, **Henry Halleck**, reduced him to second-in-command and took over the **Army of the Tennessee** for the **siege of Corinth, Mississippi**. Grant languished in this position until he was put back in command of the Army of the Tennessee in October 1862.

In December 1862, Grant advanced from Tennessee through north-central Mississippi in **Grant's Overland Vicksburg Campaign**, while sending **William T. Sherman** to attack **Vicksburg, Mississippi**, from the Mississippi River. Grant was forced to retreat after Confederate cavalry raided his line of communications, and Sherman was repulsed. During this campaign, Grant became frustrated with the traders and speculators who flooded his **department** and violated established trade rules in the war zone. As a result, he issued a controversial order on December 17, 1862, expelling all Jews (whom he believed to be engaged in the trade) from the department. This General Orders No. 11 was criticized bitterly by Jews and non-Jews alike, and protests reached **Washington, D.C. Abraham Lincoln** ordered it rescinded in January 1863, but the anti-Semitic episode did not reflect well on Grant.

In January 1863, Grant took his **army** down the river and began in earnest the **Vicksburg Campaign**. He first unsuccessfully attempted to bypass the city through Grant's Canals and the **Steele's Bayou** and **Yazoo Pass Expeditions**. Grant then marched below Vicksburg in April, was ferried over the river by **David Porter's** ships, and marched inland.

Defeating the Confederates at **Port Gibson**, **Raymond**, **Jackson**, **Champion Hill**, and **Big Black River Bridge**, Grant invested Vicksburg and finally forced its surrender on July 4, 1863.

Promoted to command the **Military Division of the Mississippi** in October 1863, Grant next went to Chattanooga, Tennessee, to relieve the **Army of the Cumberland** that was besieged there. After opening up the "Cracker Line," he defeated the Confederates at **Lookout Mountain** and **Missionary Ridge** in the November **Chattanooga Campaign** and forced **Braxton Bragg's Army of Tennessee** to retreat. By this time, Grant was the only consistently successful Union general, and in March he was promoted to lieutenant general and was appointed general-in-chief.

Grant developed the **strategy** that finally defeated the Confederates. He devised simultaneous offenses that would overwhelm the enemy's ability to move reinforcements along its **interior lines**. Sherman and **George G. Meade** would attack Atlanta, Georgia, and **Richmond, Virginia**, respectively, while **David Hunter** and **Benjamin F. Butler** would threaten the **Shenandoah Valley** and Richmond. Another minor expedition was that of **Nathaniel P. Banks** in the **Red River Campaign**. Since **Robert E. Lee's Army of Northern Virginia** was the most important **Confederate army**, Grant accompanied Meade's **Army of the Potomac** against Lee in **Virginia**.

In May 1864, Grant launched the **Overland Campaign** to destroy Lee and capture Richmond. Very bloody battles at the **Wilderness**, **Spotsylvania**, and **Cold Harbor** soon earned him the nickname of "Butcher." Although Grant did lose 60,000 men in 30 days, he was not totally insensitive to his losses. He realized that the war had become one of attrition and while he could replace his losses, Lee could not, and the Confederate army would eventually bleed itself to exhaustion. In a bold move in June, Grant withdrew from Lee's front northeast of Richmond and marched southward across the James River to attack Petersburg and cut off Lee's supply line. The Confederates were able to hold off Grant long enough for Lee to reach Petersburg. This led to the long **Petersburg Campaign** that lasted from June 1864 to April 1865. During the siege, Grant continually pressured Lee's line and slowly extended his left flank to cut Lee's last **railroads** feeding the city. Fighting was continuous until Grant finally launched a massive assault on April 2, 1865, that forced Lee to abandon his lines. He then pursued Lee in the **Appomattox Campaign** and finally forced his **surrender** on April 9.

During **Reconstruction**, Grant became embroiled in the dispute between President **Andrew Johnson** and the **Radical Republicans** when Johnson appointed him secretary of war in 1867 to replace the suspended

Edwin Stanton. Grant remained a popular figure, however, and was elected president in 1868 and 1872 on the **Republican Party** ticket. Unfortunately, his administration was filled with corrupt officials and his reputation was tarnished. Finding himself impoverished in 1884 after an unwise investment, Grant was persuaded by Mark Twain to write his memoirs as a way to regain financial stability. While writing, he discovered he suffered from terminal throat cancer (he smoked up to 20 cigars a day during the Civil War) and finished his *Personal Memoirs* only days before his death. The memoirs sold 300,000 copies and provided financial relief for Grant's widow.

GRAPE SHOT. During the Civil War, grape shot often was mentioned as an **artillery** projectile, but it actually had been discontinued largely in favor of **canister**. Only some **howitzers** and **Columbiads** still fired grape shot in the war. Like canister, grape shot was a projectile that contained numerous iron balls (nine and 21 were common) to gain a shotgun-like effect against attacking troops. The balls normally were held in place by two iron plates, connected with a bolt, and surrounded by iron rings. Another method, called "quilted grape," consisted of an iron plate with a bolt, around which the grape shot was stacked. Then a canvas bag was pulled over the projectile, and the balls were held in place by wrapping the bag with rope or string. When fired, both types of projectiles came apart, scattering the grape shot. Grape shot was most effective out to several hundred yards but could be used as far as 800 yards.

"GRAY GHOST OF THE CONFEDERACY." *See* MOSBY, JOHN SINGLETON.

GRAY, HENRY (1816–1892) CSA. A native of **South Carolina**, Gray graduated from South Carolina College and became a lawyer. He then moved to **Mississippi**, where he became friends with **Jefferson Davis**, practiced law, and served as a district attorney and one-term legislator. Moving to **Louisiana**, Gray changed his political affiliation from **Whig** to **Democrat** and was elected to the legislature. In 1859, **Judah P. Benjamin** defeated him by one vote in the legislature for a U.S. Senate seat.

When the Civil War began, Gray joined a Mississippi **regiment** as a private, but Davis persuaded him to raise a regiment in Louisiana. He formed the 28th Louisiana (Gray's) and was appointed its colonel in May 1862. After serving in northeast Louisiana for a time, the regiment joined **Richard Taylor's** command on Bayou Teche as part of **J. J. Alfred Mouton's brigade**. Gray fought in the **Bayou Teche Campaign** at **Fort Bisland** and **Irish Bend**, winning high praise from Taylor for the latter battle. Assuming command of the brigade in April 1863, he maneuvered and **skirmished** in south Louisiana throughout 1863 and then wintered in the northeastern part of the state. During the **Red River Campaign**, Gray led his brigade in a charge at **Mansfield** that drove back **Nathaniel P. Banks's** Union **army**.

Upon Taylor's recommendation, Gray was promoted to brigadier general in April 1864, although his superior **Edmund Kirby Smith** was hesitant because, he wrote, Gray's habits "are not good" (Davis, ed., *The Confederate General*, vol. 3, 27). After fighting at **Yellow Bayou** at the end of the Red River Campaign, Gray's brigade was sent to southern **Arkansas**. In October 1864, he was elected to the **Confederate Congress** and left the army to take his seat.

After the war, Gray served one term in the state senate.

GRAYBEARD REGIMENT. This was the nickname given to the 37th Iowa because it was made up of men at least 45 years old, with one soldier being 80. It was authorized by Gov. **Samuel J. Kirkwood** as a way to supply soldiers for garrison and guard duty to free up more able-bodied men to fight. Entering service in December 1862 with 914 men, the **regiment** served until May 1865. During its existence, the Graybeards served as guards at **Alton**, **Rock Island**, and **Camp Morton prisons** and provided guards for the Memphis & Charleston Railroad.

GRAYSON, JOHN BRECKINRIDGE (1806–1861) CSA. A cousin of **John C. Breckinridge**, Grayson was a native of **Kentucky**. After graduating from **West Point** in 1826, he served in the **Seminole Wars** and was a captain and **Winfield Scott's** chief commissary in the **Mexican War**. In Mexico, Grayson won two **brevets** for his gallantry. He continued to serve in the **U.S. Army's** commissary department at various posts after the war and helped organize the Historical Society of **New Mexico**. In July 1861, Grayson resigned his major's commission and entered Confederate service in August as a brigadier general. Placed in command of the **Department of Middle and Eastern Florida**, his health quickly deteriorated, and he died in October from tuberculosis.

"GREAT GAINESVILLE, TEXAS, HANGING" (OCTOBER 1862). During the 1861 **secession** crisis, many north **Texas** residents were either German immigrants or recent arrivals from the North and Midwest and thus opposed secession. After 11 north Texas counties voted against secession, these Unionists often were harassed by their neighbors, and some even were killed. In August 1862, German Unionists attempting to escape to Mexico were chased down by the Confederates and were **massacred** at the **Nueces River**. Later that year, an even worse atrocity was carried out at Gainesville.

The latter incident was the result of Unionist opposition to the 1862 Confederate **conscription** act. These men formed a secret Peace Party and held meetings to discuss ways in which to oppose the draft and the Confederacy. When it was learned that the Unionists were planning a violent uprising in the area in October 1862, enraged secessionists arrested a large number of the men in Cooke County, killing two who tried to escape. In an atmosphere tinged with rancor and rumors, a vigilante court was convened in the county seat of Gainesville, and many of the Unionists were sentenced to death. Over a weeklong period, 40 Unionists were hanged, with 19 being executed in one day. Other arrests followed in nearby Grayson, Wise, and Denton Counties, where six more men were executed. What became known as the "Great Gainesville Hanging" was the war's single worst case of Confederate attacks on Unionists. After the war, a number of the secessionists who were involved in the incident were tried for murder, but none was convicted.

"GREAT LOCOMOTIVE CHASE." *See* ANDREWS' RAID.

GREELEY, HORACE (1811–1872) USA. A native of **New Hampshire**, Greeley worked as a printer before moving to New York City in 1831. There he became a nationally known newspaperman after he founded the **New York** *Tribune* in 1841.

By the Civil War, the *Tribune* was the nation's largest newspaper, with a circulation of nearly 300,000. Using his paper to promote his **Republican** views on politics, morals, and society, Greeley became a very public figure. A staunch opponent of **slavery**, he opposed the **Compromise of 1850, Kansas-Nebraska Act**, and **Crittenden Compromise**. He also strongly supported the Union war effort and joined the **Radical Republicans** to demand immediate emancipation of the slaves. Despite his strong loyalty, Greeley's eccentric nature and sometimes erratic actions earned him enemies. He supported **Abraham Lincoln's** reelection belatedly because he did not at first think he could win, at one time believed foreign mediation of the war was desirable, and in 1864 tried to negotiate directly with the Confederacy to end the war.

After the war, Greeley also supported amnesty for **Jefferson Davis** and, with others, promised to pay bail for his release from custody. This latter act caused his newspaper's circulation to be cut in half. In 1872, Greeley ran for president on a ticket supported by **Democrats** and Liberal Republicans, but he was defeated.

GREEN, MARTIN EDWIN (1815–1863) CSA. A native of **Virginia**, Green moved to **Missouri** as a young man and ran a sawmill with his brothers. In 1861, he organized a cavalry **company** and was elected colonel of Green's Cavalry Regiment in the Missouri State Guard. Green led his **regiment** at **Lexington** and was elevated to a **division** command in December 1861. After leading his division at **Pea Ridge**, but seeing little action there, he was transferred to **Mississippi** in April 1862 and was given command of a **brigade** in **Sterling Price's** division.

Green was promoted to brigadier general in July and fought at **Corinth** and **Davis Bridge** that October. Sent to help defend **Vicksburg, Mississippi**, he was praised for his performance at **Port Gibson** during the **Vicksburg Campaign**. At **Champion Hill**, Green's brigade was one of the last units to leave the field, and, after the disaster at **Big Black River Bridge**, he was told by his superior to file a report so it would be known that his brigade was not the first to abandon the trenches there. In the Vicksburg defenses, Green rarely left his trenches and was admired for returning to duty on June 27, 1863, only two days after being wounded. While inspecting his position that day, Green was killed instantly when he was shot through the head by a **sharpshooter**.

GREEN, THOMAS (1814–1864) CSA. A native of **Virginia** and the brother-in-law of Confederate Brig. Gen. **James P. Major**, Green moved to **Tennessee** as a child and was educated at the University of Nashville and **Kentucky's** Princeton College. He then moved to **Texas**, where he fought in the Texas Revolution at San Jacinto. Green was appointed assistant adjutant general of the Texas **army** in 1836 and later served in the Texas legislature and as secretary of the senate. He also fought in numerous campaigns against **Indians** and Mexicans and served in the **Mexican War** as a captain. Appointed clerk of the Texas supreme court in 1841, he still held that position when the Civil War began.

Green entered Confederate service in August 1861 as colonel of the 5th Texas Cavalry. He accompanied **Henry H. Sibley's New Mexico Campaign**, led the army at **Valverde** when Sibley became ill, and fought at **Glorieta Pass**. After the unsuccessful invasion, Green was sent to Galveston, Texas. At the **Battle of Galveston**, his troopers boarded two Confederate gunboats and captured the USS *Harriet Lane*. In the spring of 1863, Green joined **Richard Taylor's** command in south **Louisiana**. After fighting in the **Bayou Teche Campaign**, he was promoted to brigadier general in May and took command of a Texas cavalry **brigade**.

Green was active in south Louisiana for the rest of the year, fighting at **Fort Butler**, **Bayou Lafourche**, **Stirling's Plantation**, and at **Bayou Bourbeau** during the **Texas Overland Expedition**. During these engagements, his ability was highly praised by Taylor. Green commanded Taylor's cavalry during the 1864 **Red River Campaign**, and he played a significant role in the Confederate victory at **Mansfield**. When the Union army retreated, Taylor sent him to stop **David Porter's** Union gunboats on the Red River. At **Blair's Landing** on April 12, Green led his dismounted troopers against the grounded gunboat *Osage*. Green, who some falsely claimed had been drinking, was killed instantly when he was hit in the head by **canister**.

GREENBACK RAID (OCTOBER 13, 1864). *See* MOSBY, JOHN SINGLETON.

GREENBACKS. When the Civil War began, gold and silver coins were the standard money of the day. **Abraham Lincoln's** administration, however, could not **finance** the war by using specie alone. Thus, in February 1862 the **Legal Tender Act** was passed authorizing the issuing of non-interest-bearing government notes. This type of paper money became known as greenbacks because of the green print on them. Although it did create some inflation (by August 1862, a one dollar greenback was worth 91 cents in gold), the experiment was successful. Approximately $433 million in greenbacks were issued during the war. The federal government passed a bill to retire the notes in December 1865, but it failed to do so because the paper money was so popular with the people.

GREENBRIER RIVER, VIRGINIA, BATTLE OF (OCTOBER 3, 1861). About two weeks after the **Battle of Cheat Mountain, Virginia**, 5,000 Union soldiers under Brig. Gen. **Joseph J. Reynolds** marched east from Cheat Mountain on a **reconnaissance** toward Brig. Gen. **Henry R. Jackson's** Confederate camp on the south fork of the Greenbrier River. Leaving on the night of October 2, 1861, Reynolds reached Jackson's Camp Bartow the next morning. After opening fire with **artillery**, Reynolds attacked first Jackson's left wing across the river and then his right, but he was repulsed. The Federals withdrew after losing 44 men in the fighting. Jackson's 1,800-man command counted 52 casualties.

GREENE, GEORGE SEARS (1801–1899) USA. A native of **Rhode Island**, Greene graduated from **West Point** in 1823 and served as an academy engineering instructor and on garrison duty. Resigning from the **U.S. Army** in 1836, he worked as a civil engineer and helped build Croton Reservoir in New York City's Central Park.

Greene entered Union service in January 1862 as colonel of the 60th New York and was promoted to brigadier general of volunteers in April. One of the Union **army's** oldest generals, he nonetheless earned an enviable record. Greene led a **brigade** at **First Winchester** and **Cedar Mountain** and a **division** at **Second Manassas** and **Antietam**. He was back in command of an **Army of the Potomac** brigade for the **Chancellorsville Campaign** and then had his greatest moment at **Gettysburg**. On the battle's second day while the Confederates battered the Union line, all of the Union brigades defending Culp's Hill were withdrawn except Greene's brigade. Late in the day and into the night, Greene singlehandedly fought off repeated enemy attacks and held the important hill. Transferred west with the XII Corps in the autumn of 1863, he was severely wounded in the face during the **Battle of Wauhatchie**. This wound kept Greene off duty until the latter part of the **Carolinas Campaign**, when he rejoined his command and served under **William T. Sherman**.

Greene was **brevetted** major general of volunteers for his war service and left the army in April 1866 to resume his engineering career. He helped found the American Society of Civil Engineers and served as its president from 1875 to 1877. At the time of his death, Greene was the oldest living West Point graduate.

GREENHOW, ROSE O'NEAL (1817?–1864) CSA. A native of **Maryland**, Greenhow was a well-known **Washington, D.C.**, socialite and the widow of Dr. Robert Greenhow, a former State Department employee. She was pretty, charming, and intelligent, and counted numerous government officials as friends and acquaintances.

When the Civil War began, Greenhow immediately joined a Confederate spy network that reported to **P. G. T. Beauregard** and used her contacts within the Union government to gather intelligence information. In July 1861, she discovered the marching orders for Brig. Gen. **Irvin McDowell** and was able to alert Beauregard just prior to the **First Battle of Manassas**. This warning enabled the Confederates to reinforce Beauregard with **Joseph E. Johnston's** command from the **Shenandoah Valley**. Discovered by Union agent **Allan Pinkerton**, Greenhow was placed under house arrest in August 1861. However, she was still able to smuggle information to the Confederates by using visitors as couriers. Incarcerated with her young daughter in the **Old Capitol Prison** in January 1862, Greenhow finally was **paroled** in June on the condition she leave and never return to Union territory. She arrived in **Richmond, Virginia**, to a heroine's welcome.

Greenhow traveled to Europe in August 1863 as an unofficial Confederate representative and published a book about her adventures. While she was returning to the Confederacy aboard a **blockade-runner** in October 1864, her ship ran aground near **North Carolina's** Cape Fear River while being chased by a Union warship. Greenhow was being transported to shore in a launch when it floundered in the surf. Weighed down by $2,000 in gold, she drowned and was buried with full military honors.

GREER, ELKANAH BRACKIN (1825–1877) CSA. A native of **Tennessee**, Greer moved to **Mississippi** as a young man and fought in the **Mexican War** with **Jefferson Davis's** 1st Mississippi Rifles. He moved to **Texas** after the war and became a prosperous planter and merchant. Greer also was an avid supporter of **states rights** and became Grand Commander of the Texas **Knights of the Golden Circle**.

In July 1861, Greer entered Confederate service as colonel of what became the 3rd Texas Cavalry. He led a charge at **Wilson's Creek** and was slightly wounded at **Pea Ridge** while commanding a **division**. In the latter battle, Greer also became the **army's** senior officer when both of his superiors were killed.

After commanding a cavalry **brigade**, Greer was promoted to brigadier general in October 1862. In June 1863, he was put in charge of conscripts in the **Trans-Mississippi Department** and established his headquarters in his hometown of Marshall, Texas. In that position, Greer clashed with state officials when he tried to replace able-bodied men working for the officials with unfit men so the former could be **conscripted**. His responsibility of **impressing** slaves for Confederate use also caused problems with local planters. The War Department sent a new officer to replace Greer in November 1864, but **department** commander **Edmund Kirby Smith** refused to replace him on the grounds that he was performing his duties well. The War Department insisted, however, and Greer was replaced in December. His last Confederate service was in March 1865 when he was put in command of the Reserve Corps in Texas.

After the war, Greer returned to Marshall, Texas.

GREGG, DAVID McMURTRIE (1833–1916) USA. A native of **Pennsylvania**, Gregg was the first cousin of Gov. **Andrew Gregg Curtin**. He graduated from **West Point** in 1855 and served in the dragoons on the frontier and in **California**.

In January 1862, Gregg was promoted from captain to colonel and was transferred east to take command of the 8th Pennsylvania Cavalry.

He fought well with the **Army of the Potomac** in the **Seven Days** and **Antietam Campaigns** and was promoted to brigadier general of volunteers in November 1862. Gregg led a **division** in one of **George Stoneman's Raids** during the **Chancellorsville Campaign** and repulsed **J. E. B. Stuart's** cavalry in a battle on the far Union right at **Gettysburg**, although **George A. Custer** received most of the credit. After ably leading a cavalry division in the **Bristoe Station, Mine Run,** and **Overland Campaigns**, he was **brevetted** major general of volunteers in August 1864. Gregg then suddenly resigned his commissions in the volunteer and regular service in February 1865. Why such a capable and successful officer would do so is still a mystery. He then settled in Pennsylvania after briefly serving as the U.S. consul in Prague, Yugoslavia, in 1874.

GREGG, JOHN (1828–1864) CSA. A native of **Alabama**, Gregg moved to **Texas** after graduating from La Grange College and studying law at Tuscumbia University. He was elected a district judge when he was 28 and served as a secessionist delegate at the Texas **secession** convention. Gregg then was elected to the Provisional **Confederate Congress**.

After **First Manassas**, Gregg resigned his congressional seat, returned to Texas to raise the 7th Texas, and was elected colonel in September 1861. Sent to **Fort Donelson, Tennessee**, he and the **regiment** were captured when the fort surrendered in February 1862. After being **exchanged**, Gregg was promoted to brigadier general in September 1862 and was given command of an infantry **brigade**.

Gregg's brigade saw some combat at **Chickasaw Bayou** near **Vicksburg, Mississippi**, and then was sent to **Port Hudson, Louisiana**. Before the siege there began, he was moved again to help defend Vicksburg and fought at **Raymond** during the **Vicksburg Campaign**. Gregg joined **Joseph E. Johnston's** command for the rest of the campaign and fought at **Jackson** after the capture of Vicksburg. Joining the **Army of Tennessee** for the **Battle of Chickamauga**, Gregg received a serious wound while participating in **James Longstreet's** attack that broke the Union line. Afterward, he was placed in command of **John Bell Hood's Texas Brigade**. While with the **Army of Northern Virginia** at the **Wilderness**, Gregg was praised for saving **Robert E. Lee's** right wing by viciously counterattacking the Federals on the second day. In that battle, Gregg's men refused to make their attack until Lee withdrew from the front line. Gregg received high praise throughout the **Overland Campaign** and then joined the **Richmond, Virginia**, defenses. On October 7, 1864, during fighting along the **Darbytown Road** in the **Petersburg Campaign**, he was killed instantly by a **rifle** shot.

GREGG, MAXCY (1814–1862) CSA. A member of a wealthy, prominent **South Carolina** family, Gregg attended South Carolina College but refused his diploma because of his unwillingness to share top honors with another student. He then became a lawyer and served as an officer in the **Mexican War**, but he saw no combat.

A radical **fire-eater**, Gregg enthusiastically supported **secession** and served as a delegate at the state's secession convention. He entered state service in January 1861 when he was commissioned colonel of the six-month 1st South Carolina. After participating in the bombardment of **Fort Sumter**, Gregg was sent to **Virginia**, where he became a hero for winning one of the first **skirmishes** with the enemy. His men's enlistments expired within a few months, however, and he missed the **First Battle of Manassas**.

In December 1861, Gregg was promoted to brigadier general and took command of a South Carolina **brigade** that became part of **A. P. Hill's** famous **Light Division** in the **Army of Northern Virginia**. He was praised for his service at **Gaines' Mill**, but he did not see any more serious combat until **Second Manassas**. There, Gregg's brigade again won wide acclaim for holding **Stonewall Jackson's** left flank against repeated Union assaults. At **Antietam**, he was in Hill's column that arrived from **Harpers Ferry, Virginia**, just in time to save **Robert E. Lee's army** from disaster and was severely bruised by a **rifle** ball that struck him on the hip. The volley that struck Gregg was the same one that killed Brig. Gen. **Lawrence O. Branch**. At **Fredericksburg**, Gregg's brigade was held in reserve behind the gap that was inexplicably left in Jackson's line. When the enemy poured through this hole, Gregg was caught unprepared because the courier sent to warn him was killed. Thinking the advancing soldiers were friends, he ordered his men not to fire. A Union volley unhorsed Gregg with a bullet that pierced his side and lodged in his spine. When his men counterattacked and drove back the enemy, Gregg was seen painfully pulling himself up on a sapling, waving his hat, and cheering them onward. He died on December 15, 1862.

GRESHAM, WALTER QUINTIN (1832–1895) USA. A native of **Indiana**, Gresham worked as a lawyer before the Civil War and was elected to the state legislature as a **Republican** in 1860. In that position, he feuded with Gov. **Oliver P. Morton** over patronage and thus was turned down when he sought a commission at the beginning of the war. Gresham then raised a volunteer **company** and was appointed lieutenant colonel of 38th Indiana in September 1861.

In March 1862, Gresham was commissioned colonel of the 53rd Indiana. He participated in the **siege of Corinth, Mississippi**, in the spring of 1862 and marched with **U. S. Grant's Army of the Tennessee** through northern **Mississippi** in **Grant's Overland Vicksburg Campaign**. Afterward, Gresham saw combat during the **Vicksburg Campaign** and was promoted to brigadier general of volunteers in August 1863. After serving with **William T. Sherman** in the **Meridian Campaign**, he was sent to **Georgia** for the **Atlanta Campaign**. There Gresham commanded a **division** in the Army of the Tennessee's XVII Corps and was wounded in the knee at **Peachtree Creek**. This wound ended his field service, and he was mustered out of the **army** in April 1866 with a **brevet** of major general of volunteers.

After the war, Gresham served as President Chester A. Arthur's postmaster general and secretary of the treasury. In the former position, he helped end the notoriously corrupt Louisiana Lottery Company by refusing to let it sell tickets through the mail. Gresham also served as President Grover Cleveland's secretary of state.

GRIERSON, BENJAMIN HENRY (1826–1911) USA. A native of **Pennsylvania**, Grierson taught music in **Ohio** and **Indiana** after receiving an education at an Ohio academy. When the Civil War began, he was managing an **Illinois** store.

Grierson entered Union service in May 1861 as a captain and volunteer aide to **Benjamin M. Prentiss**. Commissioned major of the 7th Illinois Cavalry in October, he rose to colonel in April 1862 and led it in a number of **skirmishes** in **Tennessee** and **Mississippi** while the **regiment** was scattered at three different posts. Grierson's regiment also helped chase Confederate raider **Earl Van Dorn** in December 1862 after Van Dorn attacked **Holly Springs, Mississippi**, in **U. S. Grant's Overland Vicksburg Campaign**.

During the **Vicksburg Campaign**, Grierson was given command of a cavalry brigade and was sent on the celebrated **Grierson's Raid** through Mississippi to divert Confederate attention away from Grant's crossing of the Mississippi River. He left La Grange, Tennessee, in mid-April 1863 and rode 800 miles in 16 days through Mississippi to **Baton Rouge, Louisiana**, destroying **railroads** and enemy property and skirmishing with Confederates. The raid earned Grierson promotion to brigadier general in June 1863, and in the 1950s it was the subject of the movie *The Horse Soldiers*, starring John Wayne. After his raid, Grierson participated in the **Port Hudson** and **Meridian Campaigns** and fought at **Brice's Cross Roads** and **Tupelo**. After launching another raid into Mississippi in 1864, he rode to southern **Alabama** and participated in the **Mobile Campaign** in early 1865. During the latter half of the war, Grierson sometimes commanded a **division** and at times even the **Army of the Mississippi's** cavalry **corps**.

Brevetted major general of volunteers for his service, Grierson remained in the **army** after the war and was promoted to major general of volunteers in March 1866. He left the volunteer service a few weeks later but in July was appointed colonel of the 10th U.S. Cavalry, one of the regiments of **black troops** that became known as Buffalo Soldiers. Grierson remained in the **U.S. Army**, mostly serving in the Southwest and sometimes fighting **Indians**, and won brevets of brigadier general and major general of regulars. He retired in 1890 as a brigadier general.

GRIERSON'S RAID (APRIL 17–MAY 2, 1863). One of the few successful Union cavalry raids in the first half of the Civil War, this raid was led by Col. **Benjamin H. Grierson**. Grierson's mission was to ride through the heart of **Mississippi** to divert Confederate attention away from **U. S. Grant's** crossing of the Mississippi River during his **Vicksburg Campaign**. The raid was part of a two-prong thrust to disrupt Confederate activity. Major General **Stephen A. Hurlbut** in Memphis, Tennessee, was planning Grierson's Raid into Mississippi at the same time Maj. Gen. **William S. Rosecrans** was planning **Streight's Raid** into northern **Alabama** to cut a Confederate **railroad** in northwest **Georgia**. Grierson left La Grange, Tennessee, on April 17, 1863, with 1,700 men from the 6th and 7th Illinois Cavalry, 2nd Iowa Cavalry, and Battery K of the 1st Illinois Light Artillery. On April 26, Streight left Tuscumbia, Alabama, and rode toward northwest Georgia. Streight later was captured by **Nathan Bedford Forrest**, but Grierson's Raid was successful.

Grierson's immediate target was Newton Station, Mississippi, an important depot on the Southern Railroad about 60 miles east of Jackson. Not long after entering Mississippi, the column was hard pressed by the Confederates. Grierson sent about one-third of his men with the 2nd Iowa's Col. **Edward Hatch** to the east to threaten the Mobile & Ohio Railroad and to draw the enemy away. Hatch later turned north and managed to ride back to La Grange, while Grierson continued south. He captured Newton Station with little trouble on April 24 and destroyed tracks, **telegraph** wires, and supplies. To avoid capture by pursuing Confederate troops, Grierson then rode south to **Baton Rouge, Louisiana**, rather than retracing his route to La Grange. After cutting the New Orleans, Jackson, & Great Northern Railroad, he successfully reached Baton Rouge on May 2.

During the 16-day raid, Grierson destroyed 50 miles of railroad tracks, as well as telegraph lines and enemy supplies, and fought numerous **skirmishes**. His command rode 800 miles, inflicted approximately 600 casualties on the enemy (mostly captured and **paroled** soldiers), captured 1,000 horses and mules, and destroyed 3,000 **stands of arms**. Grierson lost only 27 men. Confederate pursuit ordered by Lt. Gen. **John C. Pemberton** was ineffective, and Grierson skillfully diverted enemy attention away from Grant's critical river crossing south of Vicksburg. In the 1950s, the movie *The Horse Soldiers*, starring John Wayne, gave a fictional portrayal of the raid.

GRIFFIN, CHARLES (1825–1867) USA. A native of **Ohio**, Griffin graduated from **West Point** in 1847 and served with the **artillery** in the **Mexican War**. Afterward, he served in the Southwest and then taught artillery **tactics** at the academy. As civil war approached in January 1861, Captain Griffin was ordered to raise an artillery battery from the regular soldiers stationed at West Point. Originally called the "West Point Battery" and later part of the 5th U.S. Artillery, Griffin's command fought with distinction at **First Manassas**. Despite losing all but one of his guns there, he was **brevetted** major of regulars.

After serving in the **Peninsula Campaign** with the **Army of the Potomac**, Griffin was promoted to brigadier general of volunteers in June 1862. He fought in the **Seven Days Campaign** as part of **Fitz John Porter's** V Corps and served in a support role at **Second Manassas**. Afterward, Griffin vigorously defended Porter during his court-martial, but he retained his command despite that support. He led a V Corps **division** at **Fredericksburg** and **Chancellorsville** but missed fighting at **Gettysburg** because of sickness. Always popular with his men, Griffin was pulled from his horse and was carried to his tent on their shoulders in glee when he finally arrived at Gettysburg on the third day of battle.

After service in the **Bristoe Station Campaign**, Griffin led his division throughout the **Overland Campaign**. At the **Wilderness**, he enhanced his reputation for being a hot-tempered officer when he cursed and fumed at **George G. Meade** because other commanders had not supported his line. **U. S. Grant** thought he should have been arrested for insubordination, but Meade overlooked it. Griffin led his division in the **Petersburg Campaign**, and at **Five Forks** on April 1, 1865, he was put in command of the V Corps when **Philip Sheridan** relieved **Gouverneur K. Warren**. Promoted to major general of volunteers the next day, he led the **corps** to **Appomattox** and there was appointed a commissioner to arrange the formal **surrender** of **Robert E. Lee's** army.

Griffin's war service earned him brevets of major general in both the **U. S. Army** and volunteers. He remained in the **army** after the war and was appointed colonel of the 35th U.S. Infantry in 1866, but he died of yellow fever in Galveston, Texas, the next year.

GRIFFIN, RICHARD (1814–1862) CSA. A native of **Pennsylvania**, Griffin graduated from Ohio University and moved to **Mississippi**, where he became a teacher. During the **Mexican War**, he served as adjutant of **Jefferson Davis's** 1st Mississippi Rifles and became one of Davis's close friends. After Mexico, Griffin became a banker and a U.S. marshal, and he was serving in his second term as state treasurer when the Civil War began.

Griffin first was appointed adjutant general of the **Army of Mississippi** in early 1861 and then was commissioned a state brigadier general. He entered Confederate service in May 1861 as colonel of the 12th Mississippi and became part of **Richard S. Ewell's** brigade in **Virginia**. Soon, Davis created a new position for his friend by transferring another general out of Virginia. Griffin was promoted to brigadier general in November 1861 and received command of a Mississippi **brigade**. During the 1862 **Peninsula Campaign**, his brigade served in **Lafayette McLaws's** and **John B. Magruder's divisions**. Griffin, however, saw no heavy combat until he entered the **Seven Days Campaign** with the **Army of Northern Virginia**. At **Savage's Station**, he was mortally wounded by Union **artillery** fire and died sometime after midnight in **Richmond, Virginia**, with Davis at his side.

GRIFFIN, SIMON GOODELL (1824–1902) USA. A native of **New Hampshire**, Griffin received a local education and worked as a teacher and lawyer before the Civil War. He was serving in the state legislature when the war began and entered Union service in June 1861 as a **company** captain in the 2nd New Hampshire.

Griffin fought at **First Manassas** in **Ambrose Burnside's brigade** but in October 1861 resigned his position to become lieutenant colonel of the 6th New Hampshire. After serving in Burnside's expedition to **Roanoke Island, North Carolina**, in early 1862, he was promoted to colonel in April. Griffin led his **regiment** at **Second Manassas** and suffered heavy losses at **Antietam** and **Fredericksburg** while with the **Army of the Potomac**. In May 1863, he was put in command of a IX Corps brigade and was sent to participate in the **Vicksburg Campaign**. Afterward, Griffin was sent to New Hampshire to recruit, but he returned to **Virginia** to lead a brigade in the **Overland Campaign**. Promoted to brigadier general of volunteers in May 1864, he at times commanded a **division** during the **Petersburg Campaign** and fought at the **Crater**. Griffin ended the war with a **brevet** of major general of volunteers, and it was claimed he had not missed one day's duty during the entire war.

Griffin returned to New Hampshire after the war, where he engaged in manufacturing and served three terms in the legislature.

GRIMES, BRYAN (1828–1880) CSA. A native of **North Carolina**, Grimes graduated from the University of North Carolina and became a planter. He also was a delegate to the North Carolina **secession** convention and voted for secession.

Grimes was appointed major of the 4th North Carolina in May 1861 and was sent to **Virginia**, where the **regiment** fought at **Williamsburg** during the **Peninsula Campaign**. Promoted to lieutenant colonel in May 1862, he lost at **Seven Pines** the first of seven horses that were killed under him during the war and was the only officer in his regiment to emerge from the battle unhurt. Promoted to colonel in June, Grimes served in **George Burgwyn Anderson's brigade** of the **Army of Northern Virginia** during the **Seven Days Campaign**. He fought at **South Mountain's** Fox's Gap during the **Antietam Campaign**, but a horse kick forced him to miss the Battle of Antietam. Grimes took temporary command of the brigade after Anderson was killed at Antietam and led it at **Fredericksburg**. After being wounded at **Chancellorsville**, he fought well at **Gettysburg** and served in the **Bristoe Station** and **Mine Run Campaigns**. At **Spotsylvania**, Grimes won great praise for his service near the "Bloody Angle," when he took command of the brigade after **Stephen D. Ramseur** was wounded, and at Harris Farm a week later.

These fights earned Grimes a promotion to brigadier general in June 1864 and command of the slain **Junius Daniel's** North Carolina brigade. He accompanied **Jubal Early** to **Lynchburg** that month but missed **Early's Washington Raid** because of sickness. During **Philip Sheridan's 1864 Shenandoah Valley Campaign**, Grimes performed admirably at **Third Winchester** (where he temporarily took command of the **division** when **Robert Rodes** was killed), **Fisher's Hill**, and **Cedar Creek**. At this last battle, Ramseur was killed, and Grimes assumed command of the division and led it for the rest of the war. He took his division to join the **Petersburg Campaign** and there was promoted to major general in February 1865, becoming the last officer to attain that rank in the **Army of Northern Virginia**. He fought at **Fort Stedman** the following month and then served in the **Appomattox Campaign**. At Appomattox, Grimes disagreed with **surrender** and considered taking his division to **North Carolina**, but he relented when told it would not only dishonor himself, but **Robert E. Lee**, as well.

After the war, Grimes resumed life as a planter and served as a trustee for his alma mater. One of Lee's best brigade commanders, he was murdered in 1880 by two brothers he tried to evict from the county as undesirables.

GRISWOLD AND GUNNISON. This company was owned by Samuel Griswold and A. W. Gunnison and was one of the Confederacy's most important manufacturers of pistols. Little is known of Gunnison, but Griswold was a prosperous cotton gin owner in Griswoldville, **Georgia**, before the Civil War. During the war, the two started an arms company and in May 1862 received a contract from the Confederate government to produce copies of the 1851 Navy **Colt revolver** (with round barrels and brass frames) for $40 each. The first orders filled were of poor quality because of defective iron, but eventually Griswold and Gunnison produced about 100 pistols a month for the government. After supplying the Confederacy with about 3,600 pistols, Griswold and Gunnison saw their factory destroyed in November 1864 after **William T. Sherman** captured the town following the **Battle of Griswoldville**.

GRISWOLDVILLE, GEORGIA, BATTLE OF (NOVEMBER 21–22, 1864). This clash occurred during **William T. Sherman's March to the Sea** and was the largest battle of that campaign. On November 21, 1864, **H. Judson Kilpatrick's** Union cavalry captured Griswoldville and a trainload of medicine and burned the **railroad** depot and some buildings. The next day, **Joseph Wheeler's** Confederate cavalry attacked the 9th Pennsylvania Cavalry but was repulsed after the **Pennsylvania** troopers lost 21 men. Afterward, **Charles C. Walcutt's** Union infantry **brigade** arrived and took up a defensive position about a mile beyond town on a ridge overlooking an open field. Late in the afternoon, Walcutt was attacked three times by Pleasant J. Phillips's **Georgia** militia **division**. The inexperienced Confederates, mostly young boys and old men, attacked with "more courage than discretion" (Boatner, *Civil War Dictionary*, 362) and were badly defeated. Estimates of Confederate losses in these attacks range from 500 to 600, while Walcutt lost 62 men. One Union soldier wrote, "I hope we will never have to shoot at such men again. They knew nothing at all about fighting. . . ." (Foote, *The Civil War*, vol. 3, 646–47).

GROSE, WILLIAM (1812–1900) USA. Born in **Ohio**, Grose moved to **Indiana** as a boy and became a lawyer. Becoming involved in politics, he ran unsuccessfully for the **U.S. Congress** in 1852 and was a delegate to the 1856 **Republican** National Convention.

Grose was a judge when the Civil War began and entered Union service in October 1861 as colonel of the 36th Indiana. The following month, he was put in command of an **Army of the Ohio** brigade and led it at **Shiloh**. Grose then joined the **Army of the Cumberland** in November 1862 and led a XIV Corps **brigade** at **Stones River**, a XXI Corps brigade at **Chickamauga**, and a IV Corps brigade in the **Chat-**

tanooga and **Atlanta Campaigns** (he also sometimes led the **division** in the latter). Promoted to brigadier general of volunteers in July 1864, he also fought in both of the major battles of the **Franklin and Nashville Campaign**. Grose resigned his commission in January 1866 and left the **army** with a **brevet** of major general of volunteers.

Grose became an internal revenue collector after the war and served in the Indiana legislature.

GROVER, CUVIER (1828–1885) USA. A native of **Maine**, Grover was the brother of an **Oregon** governor. He graduated from **West Point** in 1850 and served on the 1853–54 Northern Pacific Railroad Expedition and in the **Utah Expedition**. In November 1861, Grover was a captain in command of Fort Union, **New Mexico Territory**. When a Confederate force demanded his surrender during **Henry H. Sibley's New Mexico Campaign**, he burned his supplies and marched his men to safety.

Grover was appointed brigadier general of volunteers in April 1862. Joining the **Army of the Potomac**, he led a **brigade** in **Joseph Hooker's** division during the **Peninsula** and **Seven Days' Campaigns** and won two **brevets** in the regular **army** for gallantry. Transferred to **John Pope's Army of Virginia**, Grover's brigade suffered heavy casualties in the **Second Manassas Campaign** at **Groveton**. Afterward, Grover was sent to the **Department of the Gulf**, where he took command of a **division** under **Nathaniel Banks**. After fighting in the **Bayou Teche Campaign**, he commanded Banks's right wing during the **Port Hudson Campaign**. Grover then was sent back to **Virginia** with the XIX Corps and served in **Philip Sheridan's 1864 Shenandoah Valley Campaign**. At **Third Winchester**, he became embroiled in controversy after his division was routed by a Confederate counterattack. Grover continued in command, however, and fought well at **Fisher's Hill** and **Cedar Creek**, where he was wounded. He was brevetted brigadier general of regulars for his service in the **Shenandoah Valley** and ended the war with a brevet of major general of regulars.

Remaining in the **U.S. Army** after the war, Grover rose to the rank of colonel of the 1st U.S. Cavalry.

GROVETON, VIRGINIA, BATTLE OF (AUGUST 28, 1862). During the **Second Manassas Campaign**, **Stonewall Jackson** was sent around the right flank of **John Pope's Army of Virginia** to force him to withdraw from his Rappahannock River line. If successful, **Robert E. Lee** would follow his route with the rest of the **Army of Northern Virginia**, link up with Jackson, and defeat Pope. Jackson destroyed Pope's supply base at Manassas Junction on August 26–27, 1862, and then took up a hidden position near Brawner's Farm north of the Warrenton Turnpike at Groveton, a few miles east of the Manassas battlefield. Pope then took action to drive off what he thought were Confederate raiders in his rear.

Uncertain of Jackson's position, Pope ordered his units to concentrate at Centreville. On August 28, **Rufus King's** division marched east along the Warrenton pike toward Centreville. As the **division** passed Groveton about 5:30 P.M., Jackson opened fire with **artillery** and then attacked with **William B. Taliaferro's** division and part of **Richard S. Ewell's** division. King's lead **brigade**—known as the Black Hat Brigade—under **John Gibbon** quickly faced left and met the attack. A vicious, close-quartered fight raged for two hours on an open hillside at a range of barely 100 yards. In this, its first fight, Gibbon's brigade earned the nickname **"Iron Brigade,"** as it stood toe-to-toe with Jackson's men and lost one-third of its strength. The brigade fought largely unsupported except for two **regiments** sent forward from **Abner Doubleday's** brigade. King's division suffered about 1,000 casualties. Although outnumbering the enemy at least two to one, the Confederates also suffered heavy losses, but the precise number is unknown. The **Stonewall Brigade** lost 40 percent of its men, and two **Georgia** regiments lost 70 percent. Numerous field officers also were lost, including both **Isaac Trimble** and Ewell wounded. Shot in the left knee, Ewell's leg was amputated later that night, and he was out of action for months. In all, about one in three combatants was shot that evening.

Finally, well after dark, the Federals slowly withdrew. That night, Jackson positioned his divisions along a nearby unfinished **railroad** grade. Now realizing that Jackson was in his rear, Pope withdrew from the Rappahannock and attacked Jackson on August 29–30 in the Second Battle of Manassas.

GUARD HILL, VIRGINIA, BATTLE OF (AUGUST 16, 1864). In August 1864, Union Maj. Gen. **Philip H. Sheridan** took command of the **Middle Military Division** with orders to clear **Jubal A. Early's** Confederates out of the **Shenandoah Valley** and to deny the Confederates the use of the Valley's supplies. On August 10, Sheridan left **Harpers Ferry, West Virginia**, with his 40,000-man **Army of the Shenandoah** to engage Early's 18,500 men at Winchester in what was the beginning of **Sheridan's Shenandoah Valley Campaign**. Early retreated to **Fisher's Hill**, while Sheridan took up a position on **Cedar Creek**. When Confederate reinforcements under **Richard H. Anderson** arrived at Front Royal on August 14 threatening Sheridan's rear, Sheridan sent **Wesley Merritt's** cavalry **division** to guard the area.

Anderson responded to Merritt's presence by sending **William T. Wofford's** and **Williams C. Wickham's brigades** across the Shenandoah River to Guard Hill. On the afternoon of August 16, Wickham's cavalry attacked the advance guard of **Thomas C. Devin's** brigade at Cedarville, but Devin's troopers finally forced the Confederates to withdraw across the river. In this confused hand-to-hand fight, Devin captured 139 of Wickham's men. While this fight was going on near Cedarville, **George A. Custer's** brigade attacked Wofford at Guard Hill and forced him back across the river. In the fighting, the Confederates lost 480 men, while the Federals suffered only 71 casualties. Realizing that a sizeable Confederate force was threatening his flank, Sheridan withdrew from Cedar Creek that night and fell back to Harpers Ferry.

GUIDON. A guidon (GUY-din) was a small, forked **flag** carried by cavalry units that showed the regimental number.

GULF BLOCKADING SQUADRON. Created in May 1861, this was the Union naval squadron under Capt. **William Mervine** that was responsible for **blockading** the Gulf of Mexico coastline. At first it was a nearly impossible task since the squadron had only 17 ships. Secretary of the Navy **Gideon Welles** blamed Mervine for its ineffectiveness and replaced him with Capt. **William W. McKean** in September. McKean sealed off the Mississippi River and concentrated on closing the major ports of Mobile, Alabama, and Galveston, Texas. His force increased to 20 ships by November, and he cooperated with the **army** in attacking Confederate Gulf outposts.

In December 1861, the squadron was divided into an eastern and western squadron. The East Gulf Blockading Squadron, commanded by McKean, was responsible for blockading ports east of **Pensacola, Florida**, including the Florida Atlantic coast, Cuba, and the Bahamas. **David G. Farragut** took command of the West Gulf Blockading Squadron in February 1862 and was responsible for ports west of Pensacola and the capture of **New Orleans, Louisiana**.

GUNTOWN, MISSISSIPPI, BATTLE OF (JUNE 10, 1864). *See* BRICE'S CROSS ROADS, MISSISSIPPI, BATTLE OF.

– H –

HABEAS CORPUS, SUSPENSION OF THE WRIT OF. A writ of habeas corpus is a legal procedure through which someone who is detained can be brought before a judge quickly to determine whether the detention is legal. The U.S. Constitution allows its suspension when the public safety requires it.

On April 27, 1861, **Abraham Lincoln** suspended the writ of habeas corpus along the route between **Washington, D.C.**, and Philadelphia, **Pennsylvania**, to facilitate the shipment of troops to the capital and to prevent **Maryland** from **seceding**. In September 1862, he suspended habeas corpus throughout the North as a wartime measure. This allowed the government to arrest and detain suspected disloyalists without having to prove a case against them. At first, the public supported such action, but as more and more people were arrested, it became a great controversy since it was being used in states that had remained loyal. Lincoln saw the suspension as a tool with which to intimidate people to remain loyal. Attorney General **Edward Bates** gave an opinion in favor of Lincoln in July 1861, but Lincoln **paroled** the **prisoners** and granted them amnesty in February 1862 to mollify the public. As the war dragged on, the **U.S. Congress** passed the Habeas Corpus Act in March 1863 specifically authorizing suspension and protecting military officers from prosecution for carrying out their duties. Arrests of suspected disloyalists resumed and continued to the end of the war.

In the Confederacy, **Jefferson Davis** also suspended habeas corpus but to a lesser degree because of **states rights** philosophy and congressional restrictions. The **Confederate Congress** first approved suspension in February 1862 to maintain civil order and to enforce the **conscription** act. Congress passed three acts suspending habeas corpus, the last one in February 1864, but each one expired after a certain period of time. Confederates became increasingly discontented with such measures because they saw them as an attempt by the central government to seize tyrannical powers. Although Davis requested another suspension in November 1864, Congress refused.

HACKLEMAN, PLEASANT ADAM (1814–1862) USA. A native of **Indiana**, Hackleman was the son of a **U.S. Army** officer. He became a prominent lawyer and served as the county probate judge, clerk for the state legislature, and county clerk. After twice running unsuccessfully for the **U.S. Congress**, Hackleman was a delegate to the 1860 **Republican** National Convention and the 1861 **Washington Peace Conference**.

Hackleman entered Union service in May 1861 as colonel of the 16th Indiana. Serving in western **Maryland** and the **Shenandoah Valley**, he participated in the operation that ended in the disaster at **Ball's Bluff, Virginia**. Promoted to brigadier general of volunteers in April 1862, Hackleman was transferred west to take command of a **brigade** in

Thomas A. Davies's division in **Tennessee**. At the **Battle of Corinth**, **Mississippi**, on October 3, 1862, Hackleman was praised for courageously rallying Union troops, but he was mortally wounded (in this his first battle) and died that night.

HAGOOD, JOHNSON (1829–1898) CSA. A native of **South Carolina**, Hagood graduated from the South Carolina Military Academy in 1847. Afterward, he practiced law and became a brigadier general and deputy adjutant general in the state militia.

During the 1861 **Fort Sumter** crisis, Hagood was elected colonel of the 1st South Carolina and was present during the fort's bombardment. His **regiment** then was sent to **Virginia**, and he served as a volunteer aide to Col. **Joseph B. Kershaw** during the **First Battle of Manassas** rather than leading his own regiment. Returning to South Carolina with his men, Hagood led a **brigade** at **Secessionville** and then was put in command of the Second Military District of South Carolina.

Promoted to brigadier general in August 1862, Hagood served along the South Carolina coast and was in command of **Fort Wagner** when it was attacked in July 1863. In February 1864, he was put in command of the Seventh Military District of the **Department of South Carolina, Georgia, and Florida**. When **P. G. T. Beauregard** was ordered to Petersburg, Virginia, in April, Hagood's South Carolina brigade went along and was praised for stopping **Benjamin Butler's** advance in the May 1864 **Bermuda Hundred Campaign**. After fighting at the **Second Battle of Drewry's Bluff**, Hagood joined the **Army of Northern Virginia** and fought with it at **Cold Harbor**. His brigade served well in the **Petersburg Campaign**, losing 65 percent of its men, but late in the year Hagood was sent to **North Carolina**, where he participated in the **Carolinas Campaign**. After fighting at **Wyse Fork** and **Bentonville**, he surrendered with the rest of **Joseph E. Johnston's army** in April 1865.

Hagood returned to South Carolina after the war and worked with **Wade Hampton** to end **Reconstruction**. He also was elected comptroller general and governor.

HAHN, MICHAEL (1830–1886) USA. Born in Bavaria, Hahn immigrated to **New Orleans, Louisiana**, as an infant. There he graduated from the University of Louisiana Law School and came to oppose **slavery** and **secession**. Hahn supported **Stephen A. Douglas** in the **election of 1860** and, after **Abraham Lincoln's** election, he personally toured the state speaking out against secession.

Hahn quickly took the **oath of allegiance** after New Orleans was captured in April 1862, became a **Republican**, and was elected to the **U.S.**

Congress later that year. Taking his seat in February 1863, he supported Lincoln's policies on war and **Reconstruction** but was reluctant to grant immediate equal rights to **freedmen**. In February 1864, Hahn was elected the Unionist governor of Louisiana, and Lincoln appointed him state military governor the following month. Hahn also bought and edited the newspaper *Daily True Delta* and supported suffrage for freedmen, but he had little power as governor since Union generals were in control of the state. Elected to the U.S. Senate in January 1865, he later was refused his seat because of the Reconstruction feud between President **Andrew Johnson** and the **Radical Republicans**.

After the war, Hahn began a second newspaper in 1867 and became a planter. Later, he was elected state registrar of voters and served as superintendent of the U.S. Mint in New Orleans and also was a district judge. Hahn was elected to Congress in 1884 and died while in office.

HALL, MARIA (dates unknown) USA. Little is known of Hall's early life, but in the summer of 1861 she tried to become one of **Dorothea Dix's** nurses. Dix, however, turned her down because she was too young and pretty. Hall then became a nurse in **Washington, D.C.'s**, Indiana Hospital in July 1861. In July 1862, she served aboard a hospital transport with the **Army of the Potomac** at the Virginia peninsula and worked with **Eliza Harris**. Hall then joined the **U.S. Sanitary Commission** and saw service at the **Antietam** battlefield and at **Maryland's** Smoketown General Hospital. In the summer of 1863, she transferred to the U.S. Naval Academy Hospital in Annapolis, **Maryland**, and became a hospital superintendent in the spring of 1864.

HALLECK, HENRY WAGER (1815–1872) USA. A native of **New York**, Halleck ran away from home as a boy and was adopted by his grandfather. An exceptionally bright youngster, he attended Union College (where he was Phi Beta Kappa) and **West Point**. At the academy, Halleck was appointed an assistant professor while still a cadet and graduated third in his 1839 class. Assigned to the **engineers**, he worked on fortifications and wrote a report on national defense that was published by the **U.S. Congress**. Halleck then gave a series of lectures at the Lowell Institute in Boston, Massachusetts, which were published into a popular book entitled *Elements of Military Art and Science*. He served in **California** during the **Mexican War** and translated into English **Henri Jomini's** work on Napoleon, which was published in 1864. Such academic endeavors earned Halleck the nickname "Old Brains." In California, he also served as secretary of state and in other administrative positions and was awarded one **brevet**.

After the Mexican War, Halleck continued his engineering duties, studied law, and helped draft the California constitution. He resigned his captain's commission in 1854 to enter the legal profession and refused an appointment to both the state supreme court and the U.S. Senate to pursue business and legal interests. Halleck published several books on mining and international law and became quite wealthy. In 1855, he married one of Alexander Hamilton's granddaughters and became brother-in-law to future Union general **Schuyler Hamilton**.

Halleck's reputation was such that when the Civil War began, he was recommended by **Winfield Scott** for an appointment to major general of regulars. The appointment was made in August 1861, making him the fourth ranking general in Union service. In November, Halleck replaced **John C. Frémont** as commander of the **Department of the Missouri** and quickly brought badly needed order to that **department**. Although he largely restricted himself to administrative duties, he won much recognition when **U. S. Grant**, **Samuel R. Curtis**, and **John Pope** won impressive victories within his jurisdiction. Halleck was seen as a very successful commander and his department was enlarged and renamed the **Department of the Mississippi**. His only field experience, however, proved disappointing. In the spring of 1862, he took command of Grant's **army** after the **Battle of Shiloh** and led it in a **siege of Corinth, Mississippi**, that was so cautious and plodding that the Confederates were able to evacuate the town successfully.

Despite Halleck's lack of field experience, **Abraham Lincoln** appointed him general-in-chief in July 1862 and brought him to **Washington, D.C.**, to direct all of the Union forces. In that position, he was a great disappointment to Lincoln, and the president came to refer to him as "little more than a first rate clerk" (Warner, *Generals in Blue*, 196). While performing administrative duties skillfully, Halleck did little to plan and carry out a winning **strategy**, ducked responsibility, and became focused on unimportant details. His cold, judgmental, and aloof personality also earned him enemies. In March 1864, when Grant was promoted to lieutenant general and general-in-chief, Halleck was made chief of staff and became responsible for the day-to-day administration of the armies rather than directing strategy—in short, continuing to work as he had previously.

After the war, Halleck commanded the **Department of the Pacific** and the Division of the South.

HAMILTON, ANDREW JACKSON (1815–1875) USA. A native of **Alabama**, Hamilton became a lawyer and in 1847 moved to **Texas**. He became state attorney general in 1849, served in the state legislature from 1851 to 1853, and was elected to the **U.S. Congress** in 1859 as a Unionist. Hamilton was the only Texas congressman who did not resign his seat when the **secession** crisis began.

Hamilton returned to Texas in March 1861 and was reelected to his seat as an antisecessionist. Because of his politics, he became a marked man in Confederate Texas and had to flee to Mexico in 1862. Making his way to **Washington, D.C.**, Hamilton was appointed a brigadier general of volunteers in November 1862 and was made military governor of Texas by **Abraham Lincoln**. Since Texas was still in Confederate hands, he set up his office in **New Orleans, Louisiana**. Major General **Nathaniel P. Banks** accused Hamilton of rushing the Union advance into Texas and thus was partly responsible for the Union defeat at **Galveston, Texas**. To pay off his creditors, Hamilton also succeeded in getting cotton speculators onboard Union ships at Galveston and allowed them the first opportunity to acquire Texas cotton. These activities led Banks and other officers to have a very low opinion of him. ·

Hamilton's commission as brigadier general was never confirmed by the Senate and expired in March 1863. Lincoln then reappointed him, and in June 1865 President **Andrew Johnson** reappointed him as Texas's military governor. Hamilton resigned his commission that month, but he served as military governor until August 1866. During **Reconstruction**, he brought order to Texas and opposed the disenfranchisement of former Confederates. Hamilton later was appointed to the Texas supreme court and unsuccessfully ran for governor in 1869.

HAMILTON, CHARLES SMITH (1822–1891) USA. A native of **New York**, Hamilton graduated from **West Point** in 1843. He fought in the **Mexican War**, was wounded at Molino del Rey, and earned a captain's **brevet** for gallantry. Hamilton resigned from the **U.S. Army** in 1853 and moved to **Wisconsin**, where he farmed and ran a flour-milling business.

Hamilton entered Union service in May 1861 as colonel of the 3rd Wisconsin, a **regiment** he raised, and three days later was promoted to brigadier general of volunteers. After service in the **Shenandoah Valley**, he took command of a **division** in the **Army of the Potomac's** III Corps and led it at **Yorktown**. George B. McClellan, however, declared Hamilton unfit for command and replaced him in April 1862 with **Philip Kearny**. Transferred west, he received a division in the **Army of the Mississippi** and served well at **Iuka** and **Corinth**.

Supposedly through the influence of his **West Point** classmate **U. S. Grant**, Hamilton was promoted to major general of volunteers in September 1862. He then, however, accused Grant of being a drunk, criticized other officers, and tried to win command of the XVII Corps. Grant's protest of these actions led to Hamilton resigning his commission in April 1863.

Oddly, in 1869 President Grant appointed Hamilton U.S. marshal of Milwaukee, Wisconsin. He also became active in the **Grand Army of the Republic** and served as president of the University of Wisconsin's board of regents and commander of the **Military Order of the Loyal Legion**.

HAMILTON, SCHUYLER (1822–1903) USA. A native of **New York**, Hamilton was Alexander Hamilton's grandson and the brother-in-law of **Henry Halleck**. After graduating from **West Point** in 1841, he served on the frontier and as an instructor of infantry **tactics** at the academy. During the **Mexican War**, Hamilton was awarded two **brevets** and was critically wounded twice—once when he was shot in the stomach and once when a lance was thrust completely through his chest and lung. After serving as **Winfield Scott's** aide after the war, Hamilton resigned his lieutenant's commission in 1855 and lived in **California** before becoming a **Connecticut** farmer.

In April 1861, Hamilton entered the 7th New York National Guard as a private, but he was promoted to lieutenant colonel in May and became Scott's secretary. In August, he was promoted to colonel, and when Scott retired in November, he was transferred to the **Department of the Missouri** and became Halleck's assistant chief of staff.

Commissioned a brigadier general of volunteers in November, Hamilton commanded a **division** at **New Madrid and Island No. 10** (where he reportedly suggested digging the canal that allowed **John Pope** to bypass the island) and Halleck's left wing during the **siege of Corinth**, **Mississippi**. Malaria forced him on sick leave during the latter campaign, but he was promoted to major general of volunteers in September 1862. Because he was too ill for service, Hamilton resigned from the **army** in February 1863 and returned to his Connecticut farm.

HAMLIN, CYRUS (1839–1867) USA. A native of **Maine**, Hamlin was the son of **Hannibal Hamlin**. He became a lawyer and entered Union service in April 1862 as a captain and **John C. Frémont's** aide-de-camp. After fighting at **Cross Keys**, Hamlin was appointed colonel in February 1863 and was given command of a **regiment** of **black troops**, partly because he was an advocate of enlisting black soldiers. His regiment was mustered into service at **Port Hudson, Louisiana**, in September and became the 80th U.S. Colored Troops. The regiment was part of the **Corps d'Afrique**, and Hamlin became one of its **brigade** commanders. He sometimes commanded a **division** of black troops and was promoted to brigadier general of volunteers in December 1864. At war's end, Hamlin was commanding the post at Port Hudson and was **brevetted** major general of volunteers for his war service.

Hamlin remained in **Louisiana** after the war and died there of yellow fever.

HAMLIN, HANNIBAL (1809–1891) USA. The father of **Cyrus Hamlin**, Hamlin was a native of **Maine**. A lawyer, he was very active in state politics and served six terms in the state legislature, two terms in the U.S. House of Representatives, three terms in the U.S. Senate, and once as governor. During his early political career, Hamlin was a **Democrat**, but he abandoned that party because of his opposition to the **Kansas-Nebraska Act** and joined the **Republicans**. In 1860, he was chosen as **Abraham Lincoln's** running mate because he was a moderate easterner, a former Democrat, and the friend of powerful Republican **William H. Seward**.

Hamlin's term as vice president, however, was unsatisfying since Lincoln took little note of his counsel, especially when Hamlin urged immediate emancipation and the enlistment of **black troops**. Offended, Hamlin enlisted as a private in the Maine Coast Guard and even attended its annual summer encampment in 1864. Still, he wanted to serve in Lincoln's second administration, but Lincoln did not show any public support for his renomination. As a result, **Andrew Johnson** received the position.

After the war, Hamlin again was elected to the U.S. Senate in 1868 and served as minister to Spain in 1881–82.

HAMMOND, WILLIAM ALEXANDER (1828–1900) USA. A native of **Maryland**, Hammond graduated from New York University Medical College in 1848 and became a **U.S. Army** surgeon the following year. After publishing a widely read treatise on nutrition, he resigned his position in 1860 to accept a professorship at the University of Maryland.

In 1861, Hammond reentered the **army** as an assistant surgeon but with no seniority because he had previously resigned from the service. He worked as an inspector of camps and hospitals and quickly gained respect for his efficiency. Through the influence of Maj. Gen. **George B. McClellan** and the **U.S. Sanitation Commission**, Hammond was made brigadier general of regulars in April 1862 and was appointed surgeon general. He proved an excellent choice for the Medical Department and quickly brought order to the department, won greater appropriations, promoted worthy officers, organized the **Ambulance Corps**, accumulated valuable data on soldiers and wounds, and established the Army Medical Museum. Hammond's no-nonsense ways caused him to clash with Secretary of War **Edwin Stanton**. When Stanton ordered him out of **Washington, D.C.**, and named an acting surgeon general in his place, Hammond demanded a court-martial. The powerful Stanton won the contest, and Hammond was found guilty of ungentlemanly conduct and was dismissed from the army in August 1864.

After the war, Hammond continued to receive accolades in the medical field. He was a leader in the treatment of mental disorders and published numerous medical works. In 1879, Hammond was cleared of the 1864 conviction, was restored to brigadier general, and was placed on the retired list.

HAMPTON LEGION. This Confederate unit was raised in the spring of 1861 by wealthy **South Carolina** planter **Wade Hampton**, who received over twice the number of volunteers he could accept. He also paid for most of its equipment, including six **Blakely rifles**. With soldiers from some of the state's most prominent families, the Hampton Legion consisted of six **companies** of infantry, four of cavalry, and one **artillery** battery. Hampton was elected colonel in July 1861.

At **First Manassas**, the **legion** was nearly surrounded, and Lt. Col. Benjamin J. Johnson was killed, and Hampton was wounded. Still, it fought on and was praised for its role in the fierce engagement, where it lost 121 men out of about 600 engaged. Mixed units like the Hampton Legion were not very efficient, and the artillery battery and cavalry companies were transferred to separate units after First Manassas. The battery became Hart's South Carolina Battery, and the cavalry was attached to **Thomas L. Rosser's brigade**. The six infantry companies that were left formed a battalion, although it kept the name Hampton Legion.

Attached to **John Bell Hood's Texas Brigade** in the **Army of Northern Virginia** in 1862, the battalion fought under the command of Lt. Col. **Martin W. Gary** in the **Seven Days**, **Second Manassas**, and **Antietam Campaigns**. Transferred to **Micah Jenkins's** brigade after Antietam, the Hampton Legion remained in **Virginia** during the **Gettysburg Campaign** but then left the state to fight at **Chickamauga** and **Knoxville**. In the spring of 1864, the unit was converted to mounted infantry and became part of a cavalry brigade under Gary, who was promoted to brigadier general. During the **Petersburg Campaign**, it served on the north side of the James River and surrendered at **Appomattox** in April 1865. Four officers from the Hampton Legion became generals during the war.

HAMPTON ROADS, VIRGINIA, BATTLE OF (MARCH 8–9, 1862). In early March 1862, Union forces were concentrating around **Fort**

Monroe, Virginia, for the beginning of the Peninsula Campaign. An important part of the Confederate defenses was the CSS *Virginia*, an ironclad made from the sunken hulk of the USS *Merrimac*. Captain Franklin Buchanan, commanding the Confederate defenses around Norfolk, took the *Virginia* out of Norfolk on March 8 to attack the Union fleet anchored at Hampton Roads.

Approaching the enemy near Newport News, Buchanan first rammed the USS *Cumberland* and sank it in shallow water, although its ram broke off inside the enemy ship. He then went after the *Congress*, but its captain ran it aground to escape the deep-drafted ironclad. Buchanan opened fire and set it ablaze. During the battle Buchanan was wounded in the thigh by small arms fire while shooting at Union infantry on shore with a rifle. Lieutenant Catesby ap Roger Jones took command and withdrew.

On March 9, Jones steamed back to Hampton Roads to finish off the Union vessels. By then, however, the USS *Monitor*, the North's unique ironclad, had arrived and was protecting the USS *Minnesota*. The two ironclads engaged in a hotly contested duel that lasted several hours. While the *Virginia* was larger and carried more guns, the *Monitor* was faster and more maneuverable. The result was a stalemate as the two ships fought at point-blank range. About noon, a Confederate shell temporarily blinded Lt. John L. Worden, commander of the *Monitor*, and the *Virginia* suffered rudder damage. Both ships withdrew.

This first battle between ironclads resulted in a stalemate, but the *Monitor* had saved the *Minnesota*. Neither ship suffered extensive damage, proving the protective value of the iron plates that revolutionized warships. When Union forces captured Norfolk on May 9, the Confederates were unable to withdraw the *Virginia* upriver because of its deep draft and had to destroy it to prevent it from falling into enemy hands.

HAMPTON ROADS CONFERENCE (FEBRUARY 3, 1865). This conference was a result of a late 1864 peace initiative by Francis P. Blair Sr. to the Confederate government in Richmond, Virginia. Blair convinced Abraham Lincoln to allow him to approach Jefferson Davis with a plan for the Confederacy and the United States to join forces to drive Maximilian out of Mexico. Blair believed that if this could be accomplished, the two sides would never resume their own war. While Davis refused the naive scheme, he did agree to hold further talks at Hampton Roads in February 1865.

Davis correctly predicted that Lincoln would offer the Confederacy no peace terms except ending the war and the restoration of the Union. Davis agreed to the conference with the knowledge that it would fail and thus used it to convince wavering Confederates and his administration's critics that there was no option but to fight for complete victory. On February 3, 1865, Confederate envoys **Alexander H. Stephens**, **Robert M. T. Hunter**, and **John A. Campbell** met with Lincoln and Secretary of State **William H. Seward** aboard a boat at Hampton Roads, Virginia. While the Confederates tried to discuss Blair's original plan and arrange a cease-fire, Lincoln refused to discuss either and insisted on reunion without **slavery**. Lincoln did promise leniency for the Confederate leaders and the possibility of slave owners being compensated $400 each for the slaves they lost to emancipation. The conference then ended, with both Lincoln's and Davis's political positions having been bolstered, since each could claim the opposing side was unreasonable in its peace plans. **Radical Republicans** did protest Lincoln's seemingly lenient plans for **Reconstruction**. The Confederates briefly enjoyed a resurgence of patriotism, but this was quickly suppressed as the Confederacy began to crumble.

HAMPTON-ROSSER CATTLE RAID (SEPTEMBER 16, 1864). *See* "BEEFSTEAK RAID."

HAMPTON, WADE (1818–1902) CSA. A native of **South Carolina** and a member of one of the state's wealthiest families, Hampton graduated from South Carolina College in 1836. He became a prosperous planter and served in both houses of the legislature from 1852 to 1861. Hampton eagerly supported **secession** and raised and outfitted the **Hampton Legion** when war came in 1861. Elected colonel in July, he fought at **First Manassas** and was slightly wounded in the head. In January 1862, Hampton was given command of a **brigade** in **William H. C. Whiting's** division. After earning praise for an engagement at **Eltham's Landing** during the **Peninsula Campaign**, he was promoted to brigadier general in May.

Hampton was wounded in the foot at **Seven Pines** but was commended for his leadership and bravery. His brigade was dissolved after the battle, but he temporarily led Samuel V. Fulkerson's brigade in the **Army of Northern Virginia** during the **Seven Days Campaign**. In July 1862, Hampton was given one of two cavalry brigades under **J. E. B. Stuart**. He served Stuart well, but their egos and state rivalries caused friction. Hampton was an extraordinarily brave trooper, having killed bears with a knife before the war, and he frequently was in the midst of combat. At **Brandy Station**, he led his men in battle and again was slightly wounded. Two weeks later, Hampton led another charge at **Upperville** that dispersed the Union cavalry, and at **Gettysburg** he suffered two **saber** wounds and one **shrapnel** wound during hand-to-hand combat on the third day of battle. For his gallantry, he was promoted to major general in September 1863 and was given command of one of Stuart's **divisions**.

When Stuart was killed in May 1864 during the **Overland Campaign**, Hampton eventually earned the command of the Army of Northern Virginia's cavalry in August through his outstanding leadership. He continued to perform well in the **Petersburg Campaign**, fighting at **Reams' Station** and **Burgess' Mill** (where one son was mortally wounded and another wounded) and securing much needed food in the **"Beefsteak Raid."** Sent to **North Carolina** in January 1865 to join **Joseph E. Johnston**, Hampton was promoted to lieutenant general in February. He served with Johnston until the **surrender** in April.

Hampton returned to South Carolina after the war and rebuilt his plantations. A strong opponent of the **Reconstruction** government, he was elected governor in 1876 and 1878 and to the U.S. Senate in 1878 and 1884. Hampton was one of only three non-**West Point** Confederates who rose to the rank of lieutenant general, the other two being **Richard Taylor** and **Nathan Bedford Forrest**.

HANCOCK, CORNELIA (1839–1926) USA. A Quaker native of **New Jersey**, Hancock volunteered to nurse Union wounded at **Gettysburg** but was rejected by **Dorothea Dix** because she was too young and pretty. She went anyway and soon won the respect of doctors and patients alike. Afterward, Hancock worked at the Contraband Hospital in **Washington, D.C.**, and was horrified at how poorly black patients were treated. At the beginning of the 1864 **Overland Campaign**, her services were requested at the **Army of the Potomac's** II Corps hospital at Brandy Station, Virginia, and she treated the wounded there and at several other hospitals during the campaign. Hancock remained with the **army** until war's end and actually celebrated the Confederate **surrender** at **U. S. Grant's** headquarters a few days after **Appomattox**. After the war, she served as a teacher for **freedmen** in **South Carolina** and remained active in social work until her death. Hancock's very informative Civil War letters were published under the title *South after Gettysburg*.

HANCOCK, WINFIELD SCOTT (1824–1886) USA. One of twin brothers, Hancock was a native of **Pennsylvania**. He graduated from **West Point** in 1844 and was **brevetted** for gallantry in the **Mexican War**. Afterward, Hancock served in **Kansas**, the **Utah Expedition**, and **California**.

When the Civil War began, Hancock immediately returned east and **George B. McClellan** had him appointed brigadier general of volunteers in September 1861. His brigade in the **Army of the Potomac's** II Corps fought well in the **Peninsula Campaign**, and at **Williamsburg** he earned the nom de guerre "Hancock the Superb." Hancock later took charge of the **division** at **Antietam** when the commander was mortally wounded.

Promoted to major general of volunteers in November 1862, Hancock was praised for his conduct at **Fredericksburg** and **Chancellorsville**, and he covered the **army's** retreat in the latter battle. He assumed command of the II Corps after Chancellorsville and earned great respect at **Gettysburg**, where he was ordered to the battlefield by **George Meade** on the first day to assume command of the Union forces there. Dismissing claims of seniority by **Oliver O. Howard**, Hancock brought order out of chaos and saved the high ground by drawing up his forces in a strong position atop Cemetery and Culp's Hills. When Meade arrived that night, Hancock strongly endorsed continuing the fight there. He commanded the left wing during the next two days and repulsed both **James Longstreet's** and **George Pickett's** attacks. During **Pickett's Charge**, Hancock was severely wounded by a bullet that shattered his saddle pommel and sent a nail and debris into his inner thigh. He was out of action for months but returned to command the II Corps late in 1863.

Hancock led his **corps** in the **Overland Campaign** and was brevetted major general of regulars for **Spotsylvania**, but he quickly suffered setbacks at both **Cold Harbor** and Petersburg. His corps suffered heavy casualties in the former, and at the latter he deferred command to an officer already on the field. This decision prevented a timely attack being made and helped lead to the long **Petersburg Campaign** by allowing the Confederates time to consolidate their defensive positions. After being commissioned brigadier general of regulars in August 1864, Hancock's Gettysburg wound reopened in November and forced him to give up corps command. After commanding the **Veteran Volunteer Corps** for a while, he commanded the **Middle Military Division** from February 1865 until war's end.

Hancock was one of the Union's best field commanders and remained in the army after the war. He rose to the rank of major general of regulars in 1866, later commanded the **Department of the East**, and in 1880 was the unsuccessful **Democratic** presidential nominee.

HANOVER COURT HOUSE, VIRGINIA, BATTLE OF (MAY 27, 1862). During the 1862 **Peninsula Campaign**, Maj. Gen. **George B. McClellan** ordered **Fitz John Porter** to use the **Army of the Potomac's** V Corps to drive out a Confederate force located at Hanover Court House, located about 18 miles north of **Richmond**, **Virginia**, because the enemy there could threaten the Union right flank and rear as it advanced on Richmond. The Confederates in question were the 4,500 men of **Lawrence Branch's brigade** who were protecting the **railroad** about four miles south of Hanover. Porter took **George W. Morell's division** and two additional brigades on May 27, 1862, and marched northward. Thinking the enemy was at Hanover, he at first marched past Branch's position. Porter's rear guard then was attacked by Branch, and a vicious battle erupted near a crossroads. Porter sent back reinforcements and finally drove Branch to the west. Porter lost 355 men and claimed to have inflicted 930 casualties on the enemy, but Branch reported losing only 243 men.

HANOVER, PENNSYLVANIA, BATTLE OF (JUNE 30, 1863). This clash took place during **J. E. B. Stuart's Gettysburg Raid** when Confederate cavalry entered Hanover, Pennsylvania. Stuart's 13th Virginia Cavalry charged the troopers of **Elon J. Farnsworth's** Union **brigade**. The Virginians at first drove the enemy out of town, but Farnsworth counterattacked and forced the Confederates to retreat. In the counterattack, Stuart barely escaped capture by jumping his horse over a wide ditch. In the battle, Farnsworth lost 53 men to Stuart's 135 (about half of whom were captured).

HANSON, ROGER WEIGHTMAN (1827–1863) CSA. A native of **Kentucky**, Hanson fought in the **Mexican War** and won some recognition there. Disabled in a postwar duel, he became nicknamed "Bench-leg" and then participated in the **California** Gold Rush before returning home to practice law. A **Whig**, Hanson was elected to the state legislature in 1853 and 1855. He first was against **secession** but finally embraced it when he became convinced that a Union victory would endanger **states rights**.

In August 1861, Hanson was appointed a colonel in the **Confederate army** and was given command of the 2nd Kentucky (Confederate). Sent with his **regiment** to **Fort Donelson, Tennessee**, he fought well during the attempted breakout there but was captured when the fort capitulated. **Exchanged** in August 1862, Hanson was given command of the **"Orphan Brigade"** in October. After successfully cooperating with **John Hunt Morgan's** cavalry to capture **Hartsville, Tennessee**, in early December, he was promoted to brigadier general. At **Stones River**, Hanson's **brigade** in the **Army of Tennessee** participated in the disastrous assault made by **John C. Breckinridge's division** against the Union left. He was so incensed at the orders to attack that he had to be restrained from violently confronting **Braxton Bragg**. During the attack, Hanson was wounded in the left knee by **artillery** fire, and he died a few days later.

HARDEE HAT. William J. Hardee was a member of the 1855 **U.S. Army** board that studied a new style of hat that was adopted in 1858. Known as the Hardee Hat, it was black with a high round crown and broad rim. The right side was usually rolled up and was held in place with a brass eagle, while the left side sported a black plume. The hat remained standard military issue until the Civil War, and some units adopted it during the war.

HARDEE, WILLIAM JOSEPH (1815–1873) CSA. A native of **Georgia**, Hardee (har-DEE) came from a prominent family and had private tutors early in life. He graduated from **West Point** in 1838 and served in the 2nd U.S. Dragoons until 1855. Hardee studied cavalry **tactics** in France during the 1840s, fought in the **Mexican War** (where he won two **brevets** and was wounded), and published the manual *Rifle and Light Infantry Tactics* in 1855. Known as **Hardee's** *Tactics*, this publication became the primary training manual for U.S. infantry and was used by both sides during the Civil War. Rising to the rank of major, Hardee served at West Point from 1856 to 1860 as commandant of cadets and in 1860 was appointed lieutenant colonel of the 1st U.S. Cavalry.

Hardee resigned his commission in January 1861 and entered Confederate service as a colonel of cavalry in March 1861. Appointed brigadier general in June, he first served at Mobile, Alabama's, **Fort Morgan** and then was put in command of the Upper District of Arkansas. In September, Hardee took his **brigade** to **Kentucky** and in October was promoted to major general and was given command of a **division** in what became the **Army of Tennessee**.

After leading a **corps** at **Shiloh** (where he was wounded) and in the **siege of Corinth**, Hardee commanded the Confederate left wing at **Perryville** during the **Kentucky Campaign**. He became one of the Confederacy's first lieutenant generals in October 1862 and fought well at **Stones River** when the Union right wing was crushed. Known as "Old Reliable," Hardee became one of the **army's** more dependable corps commanders, but he also was a leading critic of **Braxton Bragg**. After the **Tullahoma Campaign**, he wished to remove himself from Bragg and briefly served in **Mississippi** under **Joseph E. Johnston**. Hardee then rejoined Bragg's army at Chattanooga, Tennessee, and took over **Leonidas Polk's** corps. After fighting at **Missionary Ridge** during the **Chattanooga Campaign**, he assumed temporary command of the army when Bragg resigned in late 1863. Hardee declined to be considered for permanent command, however, and thus returned to his corps when **Joseph E. Johnston** took over.

Hardee provided dependable leadership during the **Atlanta Campaign** and was incensed when **John Bell Hood** was promoted over him for army command after Johnston was relieved in July 1864. He tried to transfer elsewhere but was refused by **Jefferson Davis**. As a result, Hardee and Hood frequently were at odds and did not work well together. Hardee finally did receive his transfer after the fall of Atlanta and assumed command of the **Department of South Carolina, Georgia, and Florida**, with headquarters at **Savannah, Georgia**. He evacuated his men in December 1864 upon the approach of **William T. Sherman** at the end of the **March to the Sea** and retreated into **South Carolina**. During the **Carolinas Campaign**, Hardee fought at **Bentonville**, where his only son, Willie, was mortally wounded while serving under him. He was surrendered with the rest of Johnston's troops in April 1865.

After the war, Hardee settled in **Alabama**, where he became a planter and businessman.

HARDEE'S *TACTICS*. Officially titled *Rifle and Light Infantry Tactics*, this manual was written by **William J. Hardee** and was published in 1854. After the **Mexican War**, it was recognized that traditional Napoleonic **tactics** were dangerous against the **rifle** and other modern weaponry. Speed and flexibility were more important than slow, methodical, massed formations. Secretary of War **Jefferson Davis** authorized Hardee to begin work on a new training manual in 1853. The text was based on a French tactical manual and stressed speed over mass. For example, Hardee doubled the speed of advancing troops by requiring them to march 180 steps per minute (33 inches to the step). The manual became the standard training text for soldiers on both sides in the Civil War.

HARDEMAN, WILLIAM POLK (1816–1898) CSA. A native of **Tennessee**, Hardeman moved to **Texas** as a young man. He served in the Texas Revolution, fought **Indians**, and served in the **Mexican War** under **Ben McCulloch**. By 1861, Hardeman was a planter and was selected as a delegate to the state **secession** convention.

Hardeman entered Confederate service as a captain in the 4th Texas Cavalry and won recognition at **Valverde** during **Henry Hopkins Sibley's 1862 New Mexico Campaign** when he led the attack that won the battle. Known to his men as "Gotch," he rose through the ranks to become lieutenant colonel and colonel. Hardeman commanded the regiment at the **Battle of Galveston, Texas**, in January 1863 and then was sent to **Louisiana**, where he eventually joined **Thomas Green's** cavalry. He fought in south Louisiana at **Fort Bisland** and **Bayou Bourbeau** and by the end of 1863 was in command of Green's Texas **brigade**. Hardeman led the brigade during the 1864 **Red River Campaign** and saw combat at **Mansfield** and **Pleasant Hill**. When Green was killed at **Blair's Landing**, he temporarily took command of **Richard Taylor's** cavalry. After further service in Louisiana and **Arkansas**, Hardeman was promoted to brigadier general in March 1865 upon the recommendation of Gen. **Edmund Kirby Smith**.

After the war, Hardeman worked as a surveyor in Mexico, farmed in Texas, served as the legislative assistant sergeant at arms, was a state **railroad** inspector, and became supervisor of the Texas Confederate Soldiers' Home.

HARDIE, JAMES ALLEN (1823–1876) USA. A native of **New York**, Hardie attended **Pennsylvania's** Western Collegiate Institute and the Poughkeepsie Collegiate School before graduating from **West Point** in 1843. His antebellum military career included garrison duty, working as an assistant professor at the academy, and service in **California** during the **Mexican War** as major of the 1st New York. After the war, Hardie rose to the rank of captain in the **U.S. Army** and was serving as adjutant general of the Department of Oregon when the Civil War began.

Promoted to lieutenant colonel and aide-de-camp to **George B. McClellan** in September 1861, Hardie served as the **Army of the Potomac's** adjutant general during the **Peninsula**, **Seven Days**, and **Antietam Campaigns**. After McClellan was relieved of command, he remained with the **army** and served as a liaison between **Ambrose Burnside** and **William B. Franklin's** "Left Grand Division" at **Fredericksburg**.

Hardie was appointed brigadier general of volunteers to rank from November 1862, but his name was never submitted to the Senate for confirmation, and the appointment was revoked in January 1863. In February, he was promoted to major in the regular army and assistant adjutant general and personally delivered the orders replacing **Joseph Hooker** with **George G. Meade** in army command just days prior to **Gettysburg**. Promoted to colonel and inspector general in March 1864, Hardie held that position until war's end. In March 1865, he was **brevetted** brigadier general and major general of regulars for his war service.

Hardie remained in the army after the war and served as an inspector general.

HARDIN, MARTIN DAVIS (1837–1923) USA. Hardin was a native of **Illinois** and the son of militia Maj. Gen. John J. Hardin, who was killed in the **Mexican War**. He graduated from **West Point** in 1859 and was assigned to the **artillery**.

When the Civil War began, Hardin first served under **Henry Jackson Hunt**, the **Army of the Potomac's** chief of reserve artillery. After service in the **Peninsula** and **Seven Days Campaigns**, he was promoted to lieutenant colonel in July 1862 and was placed in command of the 12th Pennsylvania Reserves. Hardin led the **regiment** at **Groveton** and was wounded twice at **Second Manassas**. Promoted to colonel in September, he was given temporary **brigade** command but was back with his regiment at the **Battle of Gettysburg**. Recognized for his talented leadership, Hardin was given permanent command of a V Corps brigade after Gettysburg and led it during the **Bristoe Station** and **Mine Run Campaigns**. In December 1863, he was wounded by guerrillas near Catlett's Station while inspecting his **picket** line and lost his left arm to amputation. Hardin recovered from the operation, rejoined his brigade during the 1864 **Overland Campaign**, and was wounded again at the **North Anna River**. While recuperating from this wound, he was promoted to brigadier general of volunteers in July 1864. Given command of the defenses north of the Potomac River around **Washington, D.C.**, Hardin helped repulse **Jubal A. Early's Washington Raid** that same month. For his war service, he was **brevetted** through all ranks to brigadier general of regulars.

Hardin remained in the **army** after the war and was appointed major of the 43rd U.S. Infantry in 1866. In 1870, he was retired as a brigadier general because of disability from his war wounds. Hardin then became a lawyer and was very active in the **Military Order of the Loyal Legion**. Living in obscurity in **Florida** at the time of his death, he was one of the last Civil War generals to pass away.

HARDING, ABNER CLARK (1807–1874) USA. Harding was born in **Connecticut** but grew up in **New York**. After reading law, he moved first to **Pennsylvania** and then to **Illinois** to practice his new profession. Becoming involved in local and state politics, Harding in succession was active in the **Democratic, Whig, Free-Soil**, and **Republican Parties**. He abandoned his law practice in 1851 because of failing eyesight and became a very successful businessman.

Harding entered Union service in August 1862 as a private in the 83rd Illinois, but he was quickly elected its colonel. Sent to garrison Fort Donelson at **Dover, Tennessee**, Harding was attacked in February 1863 by Confederate cavalry under **Joseph Wheeler** and **Nathan Bedford Forrest**. He refused a surrender demand and then soundly defeated the Confederates when they attacked. Harding was promoted to brigadier general of volunteers in March 1863 for his excellent leadership, but his poor eyesight forced him to resign his commission in June. He then was elected to the **U.S. Congress** in 1864 and 1866.

HARDTACK. This was a standard **ration** item for soldiers on both sides of the Civil War. It was a large, quarter-inch-thick cracker that was made from unleavened flour and resembled a large modern saltine cracker.

HARKER, CHARLES GARRISON (1835–1864) USA. Born in **New Jersey**, Harker was orphaned as a child and began working as a store clerk when he was about 13. His employer was a congressman who secured him an appointment to **West Point**. After graduating in 1858, Harker served in the Pacific Northwest and then was transferred east when the Civil War began.

After training **Ohio** troops, Harker was promoted to captain of regulars in October 1861 and then was appointed colonel of the 65th Ohio in November. At **Shiloh**, his **regiment** was part of **James A. Garfield's brigade**, but he led his own brigade in **Thomas Wood's division** at **Perryville**. Harker was praised for his service with the **Army of the Cumberland** when he helped halt the Confederate attack on the first day of battle at **Stones River** and then participated in **George H. Thomas's** defense of **Snodgrass Hill** at **Chickamauga**. He went on to fight in both the **Chattanooga** and **Knoxville Campaigns**. A brave commander, Harker frequently was on the firing line and had four horses shot from under him during the war.

Having been recommended for promotion after Stones River, Harker received his appointment to brigadier general of volunteers in April 1864. During the **Atlanta Campaign**, he led a brigade in **John Newton's** division and was wounded slightly at **Resaca**. In June, Harker was mortally wounded by a **sharpshooter** while leading his brigade in the attack at **Kennesaw Mountain**.

HARLAND, EDWARD (1832–1915) USA. A native of **Connecticut**, Harland graduated from Yale University and became a lawyer. He entered Union service in May 1861 as a captain in the 90-day 3rd Connecticut. After fighting at **First Manassas**, Harland was appointed colonel of the 8th Connecticut in September and led it in **Ambrose Burnside's** expedition to **Roaknoke Island** and **New Bern, North Carolina**, in early 1862. At **Antietam**, he commanded a **brigade** in **Isaac P. Rodman's division** of the **Army of the Potomac** and fought at Burnside's Bridge. After being lightly engaged at **Fredericksburg**, Harland was sent to southeastern **Virginia** and was commissioned brigadier general of volunteers in April 1863. He commanded several

districts and subdistricts of the **Department of North Carolina** until war's end.

Harland resigned his commission in June 1865 and returned to his Connecticut law practice. He was elected to both houses of the legislature, served as a probate judge, became the state adjutant general, and was a member of the state pardon board and a bank president.

HARPERS FERRY RIFLE. This was the popular name for the **rifle musket** that was made at the **Harpers Ferry, Virginia,** Armory. Produced from 1841 to 1855, it originally was known as the Mississippi Rifle because of its fame in the **Mexican War** with **Jefferson Davis's** Mississippi Rifles. The **rifle** was about 49 inches long, weighed nearly 10 pounds, and had brass fixings. It originally was in .54 caliber, but was increased to .58 **minié ball** in 1850. The later model also was fitted for the saber **bayonet** and had an adjustable rear sight. From 1846 to 1855, just over 100,000 rifles were made by the Harpers Ferry Armory, **Remington, Springfield,** and other contractors.

HARPERS FERRY, VIRGINIA (OR WEST VIRGINIA). Located at the confluence of the Potomac and Shenandoah Rivers, Harpers Ferry, **Virginia,** was the scene of **John Brown's Raid,** and it played a major role in the Civil War period. Its importance lay in its federal armory and arsenal (containing 17,000 **rifles**), the Baltimore & Ohio Railroad, and its strategic location guarding the lower **Shenandoah Valley.**

On April 17, 1861, the day **Virginia** seceded, **Henry A. Wise** received permission from the governor to seize Harpers Ferry and its important weapons and machinery. While Wise's small command was approaching the town on April 18, the U.S. garrison learned of the danger, torched the armory and arsenal, and retreated across the Potomac River to **Maryland.** Most of the rifles and the two arsenal buildings were destroyed, but Wise salvaged nearly all of the machinery, which was sent to **Richmond, Virginia,** and Fayetteville, North Carolina, and became the nucleus of the Confederate small-arms **industry.**

During the 1862 **Antietam Campaign,** Gen. **Robert E. Lee** sent **Stonewall Jackson** from Frederick, Maryland, to capture Harpers Ferry's 12,000-man Union garrison to secure the Confederate line of communications through the Shenandoah Valley. On September 10, **John G. Walker's** division headed for Loudoun Heights, south-southeast of Harpers Ferry across the Shenandoah River; the **divisions** of **Lafayette McLaws** and **Richard H. Anderson** marched for Maryland Heights, northeast of town across the Potomac River; and Jackson took his own division and those of **Alexander Lawton** and **A. P. Hill** to School House

Ridge west of town. Union commander Col. **Dixon S. Miles** learned of the approaching enemy when Brig. Gen. **Julius White** withdrew his 2,500-man garrison from Martinsburg, Virginia, to Harpers Ferry to escape Jackson's advance. Although he was the superior officer, White allowed Miles to continue in command because of his knowledge of the land.

Miles concentrated his men on Bolivar Heights, just west of town. Not believing the enemy could drag **artillery** to the top of Loudoun and Maryland Heights, he did not defend the former at all and put only two **regiments** on the latter. Jackson marched 51 miles in 72 hours but still was behind the three-day schedule Lee had given him. By nightfall of September 13, however, he had invested the town, with the enemy only contesting the approach to Maryland Heights. Jackson's men then dragged cannons to the top of the heights and began bombarding Harpers Ferry on the afternoon of September 14. Caught in a hopeless situation, cavalry Col. **Benjamin F. "Grimes" Davis** secured permission to lead his 1,300 troopers out of the trap by a road the Confederates inexplicably left unguarded. The next morning his men captured **James Longstreet's** large reserve ammunition wagon train.

That same morning, Miles was mortally wounded by a shell and White quickly surrendered. Jackson captured approximately 12,000 **prisoners** (the largest surrender of **U.S. Army** troops until World War II); 13,000 rifles; 73 cannons; and other equipment at a cost of only 286 casualties. He then left Hill to **parole** the prisoners while he rapidly marched to join Lee for the Battle of Antietam.

HARPERS FERRY, VIRGINIA, BATTLE OF (SEPTEMBER 13–15, 1862). *See* HARPERS FERRY, VIRGINIA; ANTIETAM, MARYLAND, CAMPAIGN AND BATTLE OF.

HARPERS FERRY, VIRGINIA, JOHN BROWN'S RAID ON (OCTOBER 16–18, 1859).

After receiving the secret financial support of several prominent **abolitionists**, **John Brown** and 18 abolitionist followers attacked **Harpers Ferry, Virginia**, on October 16, 1859, to steal **rifles** with which to arm runaway slaves and form a new free black nation in the Appalachian Mountains. Without opposition, Brown seized control of the town and took several hostages, including the great-grandnephew of George Washington. The raiders also killed one man who tried to escape (ironically a free black man), but a citizen and passengers of a train that Brown mysteriously released managed to alert the militia of the attack. By October 17, hundreds of militiamen had Brown surrounded in the town's brick fire engine house.

The U.S. government sent Lt. Col. **Robert E. Lee** and 90 **U.S. Marines** to take charge of the situation. With Lt. **J. E. B. Stuart** accompanying him as an aide, Lee arrived in town on October 18. By that time several of Brown's men and civilians had been killed in the fighting. After negotiations failed to be productive, Lee sent the Marines into the fire house. Brown was wounded, two of his men were killed, and the hostages were rescued. In all, 10 of Brown's men were killed in the raid (including two sons), as were four citizens and one Marine. Brown and the eight survivors were convicted of treason against **Virginia**, insurrection, and murder in a Charles Town trial in late October. Brown was hanged there on December 2, with **Thomas J. "Stonewall" Jackson** attending the execution while in command of the **Virginia Military Institute** cadets who served as guards (**John Wilkes Booth** also witnessed the hanging).

The raid greatly increased sectional tension in the United States. Southerners viewed Brown and his supporters as typical abolitionists who intended to end **slavery** through violent insurrection and murder. Northerners mostly condemned Brown's methods but praised his goal of freeing the slaves. He quickly became a martyr in the North, and the song "John Brown's Body" (the tune of which was used later for the **"Battle Hymn of the Republic"**) became a popular Union marching tune. Some believed Brown was mentally unstable since many of his close family members had spent time in mental institutions, but there is no direct evidence that such was the case.

HARPER'S WEEKLY. First published in 1857 by Harper and Brothers publisher Fletcher Harper, this weekly illustrated newspaper became immensely popular nationwide before the Civil War. It used woodcut engravings to illustrate news stories, cartoons, and jokes, and serialized novels. During the war, *Harper's Weekly* strongly supported the Union war effort and hired such artists as **Alfred R. Waud**, Thomas Nast, and **Winslow Homer** as illustrators. The publication remained popular until the use of photography made it rather obsolete. In 1916, *Harper's Weekly* was absorbed by the *Independent*.

HARRIET LANE, USS. This 180-foot, 639-ton side-wheel steamship was built in New York City in 1857 and was christened for President **James Buchanan's** niece, who served as his White House hostess. It originally was used as a revenue cutter and in April 1861 was sent to resupply **Fort Sumter**. After witnessing the fort's bombardment, the *Harriet Lane* helped **blockade** the **Virginia** coast, and then in August 1861, it participated in the capture of **Hatteras Inlet**, **North Carolina**. It also was part of **David G. Farragut's** fleet at **Forts Jackson and St. Philip** in April

1862 and helped capture **New Orleans, Louisiana**. Sent to **Galveston, Texas**, the *Harriet Lane* was captured on January 1, 1863, when the Confederates attacked and recaptured the town. The ship then was confiscated by the Confederate government and was sold to a businessman the following year. The owner converted it into the **blockade runner** *Lavinia*. While anchored at Havana, Cuba, in January 1865, it was burned by Union agents. Raised after the war, the *Lavinia* was renamed the *Elliott Richie*, and as a merchant vessel, it finally was abandoned off the coast of Brazil in 1884.

HARRIS, ELIZA (?–1867) USA. A native of **Pennsylvania**, Harris helped organize the Ladies' Aid Society of Philadelphia at the beginning of the Civil War and distributed its supplies in the field. She then joined the **U.S. Sanitary Commission** and was instrumental in raising money for it by writing descriptive stories of the commission's work for the Pennsylvania press. From **First Manassas** through **Gettysburg**, Harris served mostly with the **Army of the Potomac,** nursing the wounded, handing out supplies, and inventing a well-known gruel known as **panada**. After Gettysburg, she went west and served in **Tennessee** from the **Chickamauga Campaign** until May 1864. Harris ended her war career working with runaway slaves and Southern white refugees and in treating the released Union **prisoners** from **Andersonville**.

HARRIS, ISHAM GREEN (1818–1897) CSA. A native of **Tennessee**, Harris worked as a clerk while he studied law. He passed the bar in 1841 and in 1847 was elected to the state legislature as a **Democrat**. After serving as a presidential elector for Lewis Cass in 1848, Harris was elected to the U.S. House of Representatives in 1849 and 1851. He declined to run a third term after the **Whig** legislature gerrymandered him out of his district. Harris resumed his law practice, was appointed to the Tennessee supreme court in 1855, and in 1856 served as a presidential elector for **James Buchanan**.

A secessionist, Harris was elected governor in 1857 and 1859. He supported **John C. Breckinridge** for president in 1860 and after the bombardment of **Fort Sumter** refused **Abraham Lincoln's** call for volunteers and encouraged Tennessee to secede. Harris even signed an agreement placing Tennessee under the authority of the Confederate president before the state actually left the Union.

After **secession**, Harris was a strong supporter of the war and raised 100,000 men for the Confederacy in 1861. He was reelected governor in 1861 but had few political responsibilities after Nashville and much of the state fell into Union hands after the capture of **Forts Henry and**

Donelson in early 1862. Harris volunteered as an aide-de-camp and served in most of the western battles on the staffs of Generals **Albert S. Johnston**, **Braxton Bragg**, and **Joseph E. Johnston**. He was considered for command of a cavalry **brigade** in late 1864 but refused to resign as governor to accept it. In recognition of Harris's service, the **Confederate Congress** voted him a courtesy seat late in the war.

When the war ended, the Tennessee legislature offered a $5,000 reward for Harris's arrest for treason, and he fled to Great Britain. He was able to return to the United States in 1867 and opened a law practice in Memphis, Tennessee. Harris was elected to the U.S. Senate for three consecutive terms after **Reconstruction** and died in office.

HARRIS, NATHANIEL HARRISON (1834–1900) CSA. A native of **Mississippi**, Harris graduated from the University of Louisiana and became a lawyer. In April 1861, he organized and became captain of a volunteer **company** that was mustered into Confederate service in May as part of the 19th Mississippi. The **regiment** arrived too late on the field to participate in the **First Battle of Manassas** but did see combat during the **Peninsula Campaign** as part of **Cadmus Wilcox's** brigade. Harris temporarily led his regiment at **Williamsburg** and was slightly wounded there. He also fought at **Seven Pines** and led the regiment during the latter half of the **Seven Days Campaign** with the **Army of Northern Virginia**, receiving another wound at **Frayser's Farm**. Harris quickly rose through the ranks and was appointed colonel in April 1863. After the regiment became part of **Winfield S. Featherston's brigade**, he was wounded severely at **Second Manassas**, but returned to duty to lead his men through the **Fredericksburg**, **Chancellorsville**, **Gettysburg**, **Bristoe Station**, and **Mine Run Campaigns**.

After brigade commander **Carnot Posey** was killed in November 1863, Harris was promoted to brigadier general in February. He fought well in **William Mahone's division** during the **Overland Campaign**, especially when he helped contain the Union breakthrough at **Spotsylvania's** "Bloody Angle." During the **Petersburg Campaign**, Harris's brigade saw a great deal of combat and lost over half its men at the **Weldon Railroad**. On April 2, 1865, the brigade again was praised for holding its line long enough for the **army** to evacuate the Petersburg defenses.

After surrendering at **Appomattox**, Harris returned to his Mississippi law practice. He later lived in South Dakota and **California**.

HARRIS, THOMAS MALEY (1817–1906) USA. A native of western **Virginia**, Harris was a physician before the Civil War. He helped recruit the 10th West Virginia and was appointed its lieutenant colonel in March

1862. Promoted to colonel in May, Harris fought in **Stonewall Jackson's 1862 Shenandoah Valley Campaign** before returning to **West Virginia** and joining **William W. Averell's brigade**. After fighting at **Cloyd's Mountain**, he was given command of a brigade under **George Crook** in July 1864 and led it during **Jubal Early's Washington Raid**. In **Philip Sheridan's 1864 Shenandoah Valley Campaign**, Harris commanded a **division** and fought at **Third Winchester** and **Cedar Creek** and won a **brevet** to brigadier general of volunteers for the latter fight. In December 1864, his division was attached to the **Army of the James** near Petersburg, Virginia. There, Harris was promoted to brigadier general of volunteers in March 1865. He performed valuable service during the later part of the **Petersburg Campaign** and was rewarded in 1866 with a brevet of major general of volunteers.

After **Appomattox**, Harris served on the commission that tried the conspirators in **Abraham Lincoln's assassination** before leaving the **army** in 1866. He then resumed his medical practice, served one term in the West Virginia legislature, and became the state's adjutant general.

HARRISBURG, MISSISSIPPI, BATTLE OF (JULY 14–15, 1864). *See* TUPELO, MISSISSIPPI, BATTLE OF.

HARRISON, JAMES (1834–1913) CSA. A **Maryland** actor, Harrison sometimes worked with **John Wilkes Booth** before the Civil War. Although he enlisted in the **Confederate army** as a private in 1861, Harrison soon became a trusted spy. Little is known of his activities during the war, except that he continued acting in **Richmond, Virginia**, while engaged in his spying duties. Harrison usually was employed by Lt. Gen. **James Longstreet**, although one of Longstreet's officers discouraged this because of the spy's fondness for liquor and women. Harrison's greatest contribution was informing **Robert E. Lee** that the **Army of the Potomac** was marching toward him a few days prior to the **Battle of Gettysburg**. Lee trusted Harrison enough to alter his campaign plans and order the **Army of Northern Virginia** to concentrate at Cashtown. Longstreet also tried to employ Harrison during the **Knoxville Campaign**, but by then the spy had dropped out of sight. After the war, Harrison continued to act, but he never wrote of his intelligence gathering activities.

HARRISON, JAMES EDWARD (1815–1875) CSA. The older brother of Confederate Brig. Gen. **Thomas Harrison**, Harrison was born in **South Carolina**, but he grew up in **Alabama** and **Mississippi**. He served two terms in the Mississippi state senate before joining his brother in **Texas** in 1857.

Speaking both Choctaw and Creek, Harrison was appointed a Texas **Indian** commissioner and in 1861 was part of a commission that tried to win Confederate support among the Five Civilized Tribes. He participated in the Texas **secession** convention in 1861, helped raise the 15th Texas in early 1862, and was appointed its lieutenant colonel in May. The **regiment** became part of W. R. Bradfute's **brigade** and was sent to **Fort Smith, Arkansas**, where the brigade was described as being poorly **disciplined**, equipped, and organized. Harrison assumed command of the brigade by May 1863 and was sent to south **Louisiana**, where he fought under Brig. Gen. **Thomas Green**. After service in the 1864 **Red River Campaign**, he was highly recommended for both promotion and a brigade command by Gen. **Edmund Kirby Smith**. Harrison received his appointment to brigadier general in January 1865 and was ordered to take command of William H. King's brigade and the District of Texas, New Mexico, and Arizona. He ended the war stationed near Houston, Texas.

After the war, Harrison returned to his home in Waco, Texas, and served as a trustee of Baylor University.

HARRISON, THOMAS (1823–1891) CSA. The younger brother of Confederate Brig. Gen. **James Edward Harrison**, Harrison was born in **Alabama**. He moved to **Mississippi** as a child and then to **Texas** as a young man. After studying law, Harrison returned to Mississippi, opened a practice, and fought in the **Mexican War** with **Jefferson Davis's** Mississippi Rifles. Afterward, he moved back to Texas and was elected to one term in the legislature in 1850.

In early 1861, Harrison became a militia captain and in September entered Confederate service when his **company** became part of **Terry's Texas Rangers**. When the unit was sent to **Kentucky** and was formally designated the 8th Texas Cavalry in November, Harrison was elected major. When the regiment's colonel was wounded at **Shiloh**, Harrison took command and on April 8, 1862, led it in rear guard action under the direction of **Nathan Bedford Forrest**. Harrison's **regiment** became part of Forrest's **brigade** in June and fought with him in some of **Forrest's Tennessee Raids**. After the **Battle of Perryville**, Harrison was promoted to colonel in November 1862 and took permanent command of the regiment. Known as "Old Iron Sides" by his men because he always escaped injury, his luck ran out at **Stones River** when he was slightly wounded in the hip while serving with the **Army of Tennessee**. After participating in **Joseph Wheeler's** February 1863 **Tennessee** raid, Harrison was given command of the brigade. He performed **picket** duty and **skirmished** in

Middle Tennessee and served in the **Chickamauga** and **Knoxville Campaigns**. During the **Atlanta Campaign**, Harrison's brigade was in **William Y. C. Humes's division**. It fought in most of the campaign's engagements and helped defeat **Edward M. McCook's** Union raiders. The brigade also participated in **Wheeler's raid** against **William T. Sherman's** supply line in August–September 1864 and was part of the Confederate force that opposed Sherman's **March to the Sea**. Harrison was promoted to brigadier general in February 1865, fought throughout the **Carolinas Campaign**, and was wounded again at **Monroe's Cross Roads, North Carolina**. He was still recuperating from this wound when the war ended.

After the war, Harrison returned to Texas, resumed his law practice, and served as a district judge.

HARRISON'S ISLAND, VIRGINIA, BATTLE OF (OCTOBER 21, 1861). *See* BALL'S BLUFF, VIRGINIA, BATTLE OF.

HARRISON'S LANDING LETTER. Never reluctant to give advice, Union Maj. Gen. **George B. McClellan** requested permission on June 20, 1862, to present to **Abraham Lincoln** his views on a variety of subjects. When Lincoln visited McClellan and the **Army of the Potomac** at **Harrison's Landing, Virginia**, on July 8 at the end of the **Seven Days Campaign**, McClellan delivered his letter.

McClellan advised Lincoln never to abandon the war effort no matter how many defeats the Union suffered. He also wrote that the Union should wage war by "the highest principles known to Christian civilization" (Sears, *George B. McClellan*, 227) and to confine the war to military and political objectives and not to molest civilians. Civilian property (including slaves) was to be protected, looters punished, and slave owners compensated for slaves that were being employed in the Union war effort. McClellan strongly opposed emancipation because he said it would harm the war effort by angering many soldiers who were fighting only to save the Union. He also argued against confiscating secessionists' property or requiring Southerners to swear **oaths of allegiance**. On military matters, McClellan advised forming a few very large **armies** to defeat the Confederacy rather than having numerous smaller ones and stated the need for a general-in-chief to direct them (he offered to accept this position).

Lincoln made few comments about the letter, but it reinforced his reservations about the general and angered the **Radical Republicans** because of its conservative approach to the war. Lincoln did adopt McClellan's proposal of a general-in-chief, however, but he appointed **Henry Halleck** to the position rather than McClellan.

HARRISON'S LANDING, VIRGINIA. After the **Battle of Malvern Hill** during the **Seven Days Campaign**, **George B. McClellan** withdrew his **Army of the Potomac** to Harrison's Landing, Virginia, on July 2, 1862. The landing was on the Berkeley Plantation, the birthplace of President William Henry Harrison. There, McClellan took up a strong defensive position covering the James River landing, with his flanks protected by two creeks. When **Robert E. Lee's Army of Northern Virginia** approached the position, **James Longstreet** wanted to attack, but **Stonewall Jackson** opposed him, fearing a repeat of the Malvern Hill defeat. Lee agreed with Jackson, and the Seven Days Campaign ended with McClellan pinned against the river. When **Abraham Lincoln** visited McClellan at Harrison's Landing on July 8, 1862, McClellan presented him with the **Harrison's Landing Letter**. On August 3, Lincoln ordered McClellan to withdraw from the Virginia Peninsula and send his troops to **Washington, D.C.**, to reinforce **John Pope's Army of Virginia**. Pope blamed his defeat at **Second Manassas** on McClellan's slowness to do so.

HARROW, WILLIAM (1822–1872) USA. Born in **Kentucky**, Harrow grew up in **Illinois** and became a lawyer and friend of **Abraham Lincoln**. He was living in **Indiana** when the Civil War began and became captain of a militia **company**.

Harrow entered Union service in May 1861 when his company became part of the 14th Indiana. He was promoted to major in June, and the **regiment** was sent to western **Virginia**. Harrow then was promoted to lieutenant colonel in February 1862 and led the regiment at the **First Battle of Kernstown**. Promoted to colonel in April, he next fought at **First Winchester**. Harrow resigned his commission in July but reentered service in August when he was reappointed colonel of the 14th Indiana. As part of **Nathan Kimball's** brigade, he fought at **Antietam** with the **Army of the Potomac** and lost more than half of his men.

Harrow was promoted to brigadier general of volunteers in April 1863 and led a **brigade** at **Gettysburg**. When **division** commander **John Gibbon** was wounded, Harrow assumed command and helped repulse **Pickett's Charge**. He again resigned his commission later that summer when the division was taken from him, but Lincoln revoked the resignation. After service in the **Mine Run Campaign**, Harrow was transferred west and led a XV Corps division in the **Army of the Tennessee** during the 1864 **Atlanta Campaign**. His division then was broken up in September 1864, and he found himself left out of the war. When neither **George H. Thomas** nor **William T. Sherman** would give him a command, Harrow was ordered to **Washington, D.C.**

Harrow resigned his commission in April 1865, returned to Indiana, and practiced law until he was killed in a train wreck.

***HARTFORD*, USS.** Built in 1858 in Boston, Massachusetts, the *Hartford* was 225 feet long, with a 44-foot beam, and displaced 2,900 tons. Armed with 20 9-inch **Dahlgrens**, two 20-pounder **Parrott rifles**, and two 12-pounder smoothbores, it served as the flagship for the **U.S. Navy's** East India Squadron before the Civil War. Returning to the United States when the war began, the *Hartford* became **David G. Farragut's** flagship in the West **Gulf Blockading Squadron**. In April 1862, it was slightly damaged by a fire raft while running past **Forts Jackson and St. Philip**. After the capture of **New Orleans, Louisiana**, the *Hartford* steamed up the Mississippi River and engaged the Confederate batteries at **Vicksburg, Mississippi**. It patrolled the river for the next year and participated in the 1863 **Port Hudson Campaign**. In August 1864, Farragut commanded his fleet at the **Battle of Mobile Bay** from aboard the *Hartford* and from it supposedly shouted his famous order, "Damn the torpedoes! Full speed ahead!" It remained at Mobile, Alabama, until late in the year and then steamed to New York City.

HARTRANFT, JOHN FREDERICK (1830–1889) USA. A native of **Pennsylvania**, Hartranft received an engineering degree from New York's Union College in 1853, served as a Pennsylvania deputy sheriff, and became a lawyer in 1860.

A colonel of a local militia **regiment** when the Civil War began, Hartranft entered Union service in April 1861 when his unit was designated the 90-day 4th Pennsylvania. Its term of duty expired just before **First Manassas**, and the regiment left the field in the face of the enemy despite pleas from Hartranft and army commander **Irvin McDowell**. Hartranft remained on duty at Manassas and earned the **Medal of Honor** (in 1886) for his volunteer service with Brig. Gen. **William B. Franklin**. After the battle, he organized the 51st Pennsylvania and was appointed its colonel in November 1861. Hartranft accompanied **Ambrose Burnside's** expedition to **North Carolina** in early 1862 and participated in operations at **Roanoke Island** and **New Bern**. He also fought at **Second Manassas** with the **Army of Virginia** and then joined the **Army of the Potomac** for the **Antietam Campaign**. The regiment fought at **South Mountain**, and at Antietam was one of the units that battled its away across Burnside's Bridge. After Antietam, Hartranft commanded a **brigade** in both the IX Corps and the **Army of the Ohio** before returning to his regiment in the **Army of the Tennessee** during the **Vicksburg Campaign**. After leading a **division** under Burnside in the **Knoxville**

Campaign, he was transferred back to the Army of the Potomac and led a brigade in the 1864 **Overland Campaign**. After fighting at **Spotsylvania**, Hartranft was commissioned brigadier general of volunteers in May 1864 and was given a division during the **Petersburg Campaign**. He played a key role in repulsing the Confederate attack on **Fort Stedman** and was **brevetted** major general of volunteers for his service there.

After **Appomattox**, Hartranft was appointed special provost marshal for the trial of **Abraham Lincoln's assassination** conspirators and was known for his kindness to the defendants, particularly to **Mary Surratt**. He left the **army** in 1866 after a distinguished and varied military career, returned to Pennsylvania, and became a powerful politician. Hartranft served as state auditor general, was a two-term governor, became postmaster of Philadelphia, and worked as the collector of the port of Philadelphia.

HARTSUFF, GEORGE LUCAS (1830–1871) USA. Born in **New York**, Hartsuff moved to **Michigan** as a boy. He graduated from **West Point** in 1852 and served with the **artillery** in the **Seminole Wars**, where he was severely wounded twice. Afterward, Hartsuff taught at the academy and was serving as a **brevet** captain in the adjutant general's office when the **secession** crisis began.

Hartsuff served in the expedition that reinforced **Fort Pickens, Florida**, in March 1861 and then became **William S. Rosecrans's** chief of staff in July 1861. He served with Rosecrans until appointed brigadier general of volunteers in April 1862. Hartsuff then took command of a **brigade** in **Irvin McDowell's corps** and fought at **Cedar Mountain** and **Second Manassas** with the **Army of Virginia**. Joining the **Army of the Potomac**, he then was severely wounded during the **Battle of Antietam**. For the next several months, Hartsuff served on boards and commissions until he was promoted to major general of volunteers in November 1862. In April 1863, he took command of the XXIII Corps and led it until his wounds forced him off duty in November. Hartsuff did not return to duty until March 1865, when he assumed command of the Bermuda Hundred line during the **Petersburg Campaign**.

Hartsuff earned brevets of brigadier general and major general of regulars for his war service and after the war resumed his duties in the adjutant general's department as a lieutenant colonel. He remained in the **U.S. Army** and served at various posts until his wartime wounds forced him to retire in 1871. Hartsuff died from pneumonia, caused by scar tissue formed by the wound he had received in the Seminole Wars.

HARTSVILLE, TENNESSEE, BATTLE OF (DECEMBER 7, 1862). In December 1862, the Cumberland River crossing east of Nashville, Tennessee, at Hartsville was guarded by the 2,400-man **brigade** of Union Col. Absalom B. Moore. On December 6, Confederate raider **John Hunt Morgan** led 2,100 men from Baird's Mill to surprise the enemy at Hartsville. After crossing the river that night in sleet and snow, Morgan attacked before daylight on December 7. Although many of the Federals formed a battle line, one unit ran away in the darkness, and Morgan surrounded Moore's position and captured most of the brigade. With his **prisoners** and captured supplies, he then recrossed the river and withdrew to **Murfreesboro**. The raid was one of Morgan's most successful. He inflicted 2,096 casualties on the enemy while losing only 139 men. Morgan was promoted to brigadier general four days later and shortly afterward launched one of **Morgan's Kentucky Raids** that became famous as the Christmas Raid.

HARTVILLE, MISSOURI, BATTLE OF (JANUARY 9–11, 1863). After the **Battle of Prairie Grove** in December 1862, Confederate Maj. Gen. **Thomas C. Hindman** sent **John S. Marmaduke's** 2,000-man cavalry command on a raid from **Arkansas** into **Missouri**. After Marmaduke was defeated at the **Second Battle of Springfield**, **Missouri**, on January 8, 1863, Col. Joseph C. Porter's cavalry **brigade** rode out of Pocahontas, Arkansas, and successfully captured the Union garrison near Hartville, Missouri. Porter then joined Marmaduke east of Marshfield, but by then Marmaduke was being threatened by 700 Union soldiers under Col. Samuel Merrill. To keep his line of retreat to Arkansas open, Marmaduke attacked Merrill on January 11 and forced him back toward Hartville. Although outnumbered, Merrill took up a strong defensive position and repulsed the Confederates in a four-hour battle. Marmaduke then retreated back to Arkansas. In the fighting around Hartville, the Confederates lost 329 men, while the Federals lost only 78.

HARVEY, LOUIS POWELL (1820–1862) USA. Born in **Connecticut**, Harvey moved to **Ohio** as a child and attended Western Reserve College for two years. He then taught school and tutored in **Kentucky** and Ohio before settling in **Wisconsin**, where he taught school and became editor of a **Whig** newspaper. Harvey also became a successful **Republican** politician because of his reputation for honesty. He was a member of the 1847 constitutional convention and was elected to the state senate in 1853 and 1855, and secretary of state in 1859.

In 1861, Harvey was elected governor. Very interested in the soldiers' welfare, he appointed state agents to look out for their well-being and often traveled to camps and hospitals himself to check on his men. In April 1862, after a little over three months in office, Harvey was accompanying an expedition up the Tennessee River to bring supplies to those Wisconsin soldiers who had been wounded at **Shiloh**. While visiting hospital ships, he slipped into the river as he stepped from one boat to another and drowned.

HASCALL, MILO SMITH (1829–1904) USA. Born in **New York**, Hascall moved to **Indiana** as a young man and worked as a store clerk and teacher. He graduated from **West Point** in 1852 but resigned from the **U.S. Army** after only a year of service. Returning to Indiana, Hascall then became a lawyer, **railroad** contractor, and district attorney.

Hascall entered Indiana military service in the spring of 1861 as a private, but he quickly was appointed captain and aide to state militia Brig. Gen. Thomas A. Morris. He accompanied Morris to western **Virginia** and temporarily led a **regiment** at **Philippi** in June 1861. Days later, Hascall was appointed colonel of the 17th Indiana, and in December, he was given command of a **brigade** in **Thomas J. Wood's** division of the **Army of the Ohio**. Arriving too late to fight at **Shiloh**, he did participate in the **siege of Corinth, Mississippi**.

Hascall was promoted to brigadier general of volunteers in April 1862 and led a brigade at **Perryville**, although he was not actively engaged. At **Stones River** with the **Army of the Cumberland**, he temporarily took command of the **division** when Wood was wounded. In 1863, Hascall spent months in command of the District of Indiana, but he returned to field duty in time to serve in the **Knoxville Campaign** late in the year. During the 1864 **Atlanta Campaign**, he commanded a division in the **Army of the Ohio's** XXIII Corps and afterward was recommended for promotion by **John M. Schofield**. When the recommendation was not acted on, Hascall resigned his commission in October 1864 and returned to Indiana.

As a civilian, Hascall engaged in banking before moving to **Illinois** and entering the real estate business.

HASKIN, JOSEPH ABEL (1818–1874) USA. A native of **New York**, Haskin graduated from **West Point** in 1839 and lost his left arm while charging Chapultepec in the **Mexican War**. **Brevetted** twice for gallantry in the war, he afterward served at various posts in the South and Southwest.

In January 1861, Captain Haskin was in command of the arsenal at **Baton Rouge, Louisiana**. When secessionists demanded its surrender on January 10, he at first refused and prepared to defend the post. After realizing he was hopelessly outnumbered, however, Haskin surrendered the arsenal. He returned to the North and served on garrison duty before being ordered to **Washington, D.C.** Haskin was promoted to major of regulars in February 1862 and to lieutenant colonel in June, and he commanded the city's northern defenses from 1862 to 1864. In 1864, he was appointed chief of **artillery** for the **Department of Washington.** Haskin was in command of **Forts Stevens** and Slocum in July 1864 and played a key role in repulsing **Jubal Early's Washington Raid.** His efforts won him promotion to brigadier general of volunteers in August and a brevet of brigadier general of regulars the following year.

After the war, Haskin served as a lieutenant colonel of regulars and commanded several fortifications. He received a disability retirement from the **army** in 1870 for the wound he suffered in the Mexican War.

HATCH, EDWARD (1832–1889) USA. A native of **Maine,** Hatch left **Vermont's** Norwich University before graduating, went to sea for a while, and then settled in **Iowa** and worked in the lumber industry.

Hatch entered Union service in August 1861 as a captain in the 2nd Iowa Cavalry. He was promoted to major in September and to lieutenant colonel in December and participated in operations at **New Madrid and Island No. 10** and in the **siege of Corinth, Mississippi.** Promoted to colonel in June 1862, Hatch led a **brigade** at the **Battle of Corinth,** but he was back with his **regiment** for **Benjamin Grierson's Raid** during the **Vicksburg Campaign.** In the winter of 1863–64, he was engaged in various cavalry operations in northern **Alabama** and **Tennessee** and was severely wounded in a December **skirmish** at Moscow, Tennessee.

Commissioned brigadier general of volunteers in April 1864, Hatch commanded the cavalry depot at St. Louis, Missouri, until he recovered from his wound and then led a cavalry **division** in western Tennessee and northern **Mississippi.** During this time, he also fought under **Andrew J. Smith** against Confederate cavalryman **Nathan Bedford Forrest.** In late 1864, Hatch was accused of looting the home **Jacob Thompson,** former Confederate secretary of the interior, while Mrs. Thompson watched. In November–December 1864, his division was part of **James H. Wilson's** cavalry command and again fought Forrest during the **Franklin and Nashville Campaign.** He later was **brevetted** major general of volunteers for his actions in the campaign.

Hatch left the volunteer service in 1866 and was commissioned colonel of the 9th U.S. Cavalry. He remained in the **U.S. Army** on garrison duty and fighting **Indians** until his death, winning brevets of brigadier general and major general of regulars for his postwar service.

HATCH, JOHN PORTER (1822–1901) USA. A native of **New York,** Hatch graduated from **West Point** in 1845 and won two **brevets** while fighting in the **Mexican War** under **Winfield Scott**. He served in the west and Pacific Northwest afterward and was chief of commissary for the **Department of New Mexico** when the Civil War began.

Transferred east, Hatch was given command of a cavalry **brigade** in **George B. McClellan's Army of the Potomac**. Promoted to brigadier general of volunteers in September 1861, he was appointed chief of cavalry for **Nathaniel P. Banks** and fought in **Stonewall Jackson's 1862 Shenandoah Valley Campaign**. Although a brave officer, Hatch twice failed on missions to cut the Virginia Central Railroad before the **Second Battle of Manassas** and was transferred from the cavalry to command an infantry brigade. He led this brigade in the **Army of Virginia** at Second Manassas and **Chantilly**. Hatch then was given command of a **division** in the Army of the Potomac's I Corps and was severely wounded while leading it at **South Mountain**. His actions there won him the **Medal of Honor** in 1893. After recovering from his wound, Hatch served in various administrative positions, including commanding the **Departments of Florida** and **the South**. For his war service, he was brevetted brigadier general of regulars and major general of volunteers.

When the war ended, Hatch remained in the **U.S. Army** as a major in the 4th U.S. Cavalry and fought **Indians** out west. He retired in the 1880s as a colonel.

HATCHER'S RUN, VIRGINIA, FIRST BATTLE OF (OCTOBER 27, 1864). *See* BURGESS' MILL, VIRGINIA, BATTLE OF.

HATCHER'S RUN, VIRGINIA, SECOND BATTLE OF (FEBRUARY 5–7, 1865). Two days after the **Hampton Roads Conference** during the **Petersburg Campaign**, Lt. Gen. **U. S. Grant** renewed his efforts to extend the **Army of the Potomac's** line around **Robert E. Lee's** right flank at Petersburg, Virginia. This was done to cut the important Boydton Plank Road and to capture Confederate wagon trains that brought supplies to Lee's **Army of Northern Virginia**.

On February 5, 1865, **Henry E. Davies's** cavalry **division** headed south and west, supported on the north by **Gouverneur K. Warren's** V Corps and **Andrew A. Humphreys's** II Corps. Davies reached the plank road at Dinwiddie Court House but did not find the huge enemy wagon train reported to be there and retired back to Warren's position. Humphreys stopped at Hatcher's Run and took up a position around the Vaughn Road crossing of the creek and at Armstrong's Mill. His line roughly was parallel to and less than a mile from the Boydton Plank Road, and his northern flank was **refused** to the east, but a gap existed where the line made this turn. Warren positioned his **corps** near Dabney's Mill, a couple of miles south of Humphreys. Facing Humphreys were the Confederate **divisions** of **Henry Heth** and **John Pegram**, with **Clement A. Evans's** division moving into position to support them.

About 5:00 P.M. on February 5 in bitterly cold and icy weather, Heth's division repeatedly attacked the gap in Humphreys's line but was repulsed by **Thomas A. Smyth's** Union division. The ferocity of the Confederate assault unnerved the Federals, and that night Warren and Davies fell back to extend Humphreys's line to the south. The following day, Warren advanced toward Dabney's Mill, but he was attacked by Pegram's Confederate division, which also had advanced. The battle raged around a large mound of sawdust as Evans came up to support Pegram, and a VI Corps division reinforced Warren. The Confederates pushed back the Federals, but Pegram was killed in the fighting. On February 7, Warren forced back the Confederate **picket** line, and that night the Federals withdrew across Hatcher's Run.

The expedition cost Grant 1,512 men out of approximately 35,000 engaged. The Confederates' losses are unknown. Although Grant failed to cut the Boydton Plank Road permanently, he did force Lee to stretch further his already thin defensive line to counter the move.

HATCHIE BRIDGE, TENNESSEE, BATTLE OF (OCTOBER 6, 1862). *See* DAVIS BRIDGE, TENNESSEE, BATTLE OF.

HATTERAS INLET, NORTH CAROLINA, BATTLE OF (AUGUST 27–29, 1861). Hatteras Inlet, North Carolina, was an important Southern port for **blockade runners**. To protect the vital area, the Confederates constructed Forts Hatteras and Clark in a manner that allowed their guns to control the inlet through crossfire.

In August 1861, Maj. Gen. **Benjamin F. Butler** planned an expedition against the forts using Flag Officer **Silas H. Stringham's** seven warships and 880 men of the 9th and 20th New York, 2nd U.S. Artillery, and Coast Guard. The Federals arrived on August 27 and attacked the next day. Stringham bombarded Fort Hatteras, while Butler's men rushed ashore in launches. The boats were battered by heavy surf, and some men drowned, but the Confederates were forced to abandon Fort Clark. Fort Hatteras was reinforced that night by Flag Officer **Samuel Barron**, but he was unable to salvage the situation. After suffering a continuous bombardment, he surrendered the fort, 670 men, and 35 cannons on the afternoon of August 29. The Union victory closed an important Confederate port, boosted Northern morale after the previous month's disaster at **First Manassas**, and won Butler some acclaim.

HATTERAS, **USS.** Intended to be a passenger ship, the side-wheeler *Hatteras* was built in 1861 and was 210 feet long and displaced 1,126 tons. The **U.S. Navy** bought the ship in September 1861 and converted it into a warship carrying eight guns of various calibers. In its first year of service on **blockade** duty in the Gulf of Mexico, the *Hatteras* captured 14 **blockade runners**. While stationed off **Galveston, Texas**, on January 11, 1863, Cmdr. Homer C. Blake gave chase to **Raphael Semmes's** Confederate **commerce raider** *Alabama*, but in a 13-minute battle, the *Alabama* sank the *Hatteras*. Two men were killed, and the others were taken onboard the *Alabama* to be released later in Jamaica.

HATTON, ROBERT HOPKINS (1826–1862) CSA. Born in **Ohio**, Hatton moved to **Tennessee** as a boy and graduated from Cumberland University. Afterward, he taught school, studied law, and opened a law practice. Entering politics as first a **Whig** and then a **Know-Nothing**, Hatton was elected to the state legislature in 1855. He ran unsuccessfully for governor in 1857 but was elected to the **U.S. Congress** in 1859. A Unionist, Hatton worked to get the **Crittenden Compromise** accepted and argued against **secession**. His position changed, however, after the firing on **Fort Sumter** when **Abraham Lincoln** called for troops to suppress the Rebellion.

Casting his lot with the Confederacy, Hatton raised a **company** of volunteers and entered Confederate service in May 1861 as colonel of the 7th Tennessee. As part of **Sam Anderson's brigade**, he fought at **Cheat Mountain** and served with both **Robert E. Lee** and **Stonewall Jackson** in western **Virginia**. In February 1862, the brigade was transferred to **Joseph E. Johnston's** command and fought at **Yorktown** during the **Peninsula Campaign**. When Anderson resigned his commission, Hatton took over the brigade and was appointed brigadier general in May 1862. As part of **W. H. C. Whiting's division**, he was leading his men through dense woods at **Seven Pines** when he suddenly encountered enemy troops and was killed.

HAUPT, HERMAN (1817–1905) USA. A native of **Pennsylvania**, Haupt graduated from **West Point** in 1835, but he served only three months in the **U.S. Army** before resigning his commission to become a **railroad** engineer and to teach engineering, architecture, and mathematics at Gettysburg's Pennsylvania College. While there he also wrote the authoritative *General Theory of Bridge Construction* in 1851. In the 1850s, Haupt served as general superintendent and on the board of directors of the Pennsylvania Railroad.

In April 1862, Haupt was called on by Secretary of War **Edwin Stanton** to oversee the construction and use of Union military railroads. He was appointed a colonel and was assigned to Maj. Gen. **Irvin McDowell** as an aide-de-camp. Although Haupt was frequently contentious, his work with the railroads was a major factor in the Union victory. He built blockhouses to defend crucial bridges from Confederate raiders, armed and trained workers to defend their trains, and worked miracles in quickly rebuilding damaged or destroyed lines. Haupt was promoted to brigadier general of volunteers in September 1862, but he refused the commission because he did not want military rank to interfere with his ability to conduct private business. Instead, he offered to continue his work without rank or pay. When the government insisted that he accept the promotion, Haupt resigned in September 1863.

Haupt returned to private life and worked as an engineer and general manager for several railroad companies. Appropriately, he was riding a train when he suffered a fatal heart attack.

HAVELOCK. This piece of attire was named for its designer, Sir Henry Havelock of the British army. It was a white **kepi** cover that draped down over the back of one's neck to provide protection from the sun. The havelock was used by both sides early in the Civil War, but it soon was abandoned because it reduced circulation around the head and neck.

HAVERSACK. This was a large canvas sack that was worn over the right shoulder and contained a soldier's **rations**. It was about a foot square and had a waterproof lining and a folding flap that buckled down.

HAWES, JAMES MORRISON (1824–1889) CSA. A native of **Kentucky**, Hawes graduated from **West Point** in 1845 and served with the dragoons in the **Mexican War**. After earning one **brevet**, he returned to teach **tactics** and mathematics at the academy. In 1850, Hawes was sent to France for two years to study and observe French cavalry tactics at the Saumur. Upon his return to the United States, he served in the **Utah Expedition** and in **"Bleeding Kansas."**

Hawes resigned his captain's commission in May 1861 and entered Confederate service as a captain. In June, he was promoted to major, and two weeks later was made colonel of the 2nd Kentucky Cavalry (Confederate). After making one raid into **Kentucky** to burn bridges that autumn, Hawes resigned his commission to accept an appointment of major in the regular **Confederate army**.

Upon the recommendation of **Albert Sidney Johnston**, Hawes's former commander in the **U.S. Army**, Hawes was promoted to brigadier general in March 1862. He led the advance to **Shiloh** with his cavalry and then was given an infantry brigade in **John C. Breckinridge's division**.

When **Braxton Bragg** took over the **Army of Tennessee**, he expressed a lack of confidence in Hawes, and Hawes asked to be transferred to a cavalry **brigade** in **Arkansas**. He remained in the **Trans-Mississippi Department** for the remainder of the war, alternating between infantry and cavalry brigades. During the **Vicksburg Campaign**, Hawes led a brigade in **John G. Walker's** division and participated in **Richard Taylor's** operation against **Milliken's Bend, Louisiana**, but he failed to carry out his assignment to attack Young's Point. Taylor was very critical of his leadership, and Hawes was transferred to **Texas**, where he took command of a cavalry brigade under **John B. Magruder**. Put in command of Galveston, Texas, he displeased Magruder by displaying a lack of readiness and for trying to arrest the mayor and city council for treason. Magruder relieved Hawes of command in April 1865.

Hawes returned to Kentucky after the war and prospered in the hardware business.

HAWES, RICHARD (1797–1877) CSA. A native of **Virginia**, Hawes moved to **Kentucky** as a boy, graduated from Transylvania University, and opened a law practice. He served in the Black Hawk War and was elected three times to the state legislature in the 1830s and twice to the **U.S. Congress** as a **Whig**. By the Civil War, Hawes had become a **Democrat** and was a moderate secessionist.

During the **secession** crisis, Hawes was appointed to a committee by the legislature to strengthen the state's neutrality. Despite this work, he supported Kentucky's secession and was appointed major of the 5th Kentucky (Confederate). After fighting at **Shiloh**, Hawes was named the provisional Confederate governor of Kentucky and during the **Kentucky Campaign** was inaugurated by **Braxton Bragg** on October 4, 1862. Four days later, the **Battle of Perryville** was fought, and Hawes retreated from Kentucky with the rest of the **Confederate army**. He bitterly criticized Bragg for the failed invasion that prevented him from carrying out any duties as governor.

After the war, Hawes returned to Kentucky and served as a county judge.

HAWKINS, JOHN PARKER (1830–1914) USA. A native of **Indiana** and the brother-in-law of Union Maj. Gen. **Edward R. S. Canby**, Hawkins graduated from **West Point** in 1852. He served in the infantry in the Pacific Northwest and was quartermaster for the 2nd U.S. Infantry when the Civil War began.

Hawkins was transferred to the Commissary Department and served as a captain in various **Missouri** commissary positions before becoming chief commissary for the **Army of the Tennessee**. In April 1863, he was appointed brigadier general of volunteers and in August was named commander of the District of Northeastern Louisiana. In that position, Hawkins was in charge of a brigade of **black troops** on garrison duty. In March 1864, he was given a **division** of black soldiers and garrisoned **Vicksburg, Mississippi**. Hawkins's division was transferred to the Gulf Coast, and in March 1865, he participated in the **Mobile Campaign**. In 1865, he was **brevetted** major general in both the regular and volunteer armies for his war service.

After being mustered out of the volunteers in 1866, Hawkins resumed his rank of captain in the Subsistence Department. He rose to the rank of brigadier general in 1892 and commanded the department before retiring in 1894.

HAW'S SHOP, VIRGINIA, BATTLE OF (MAY 28, 1864). After the stalemate along the **North Anna River** during the 1864 **Overland Campaign**, **U. S. Grant** disengaged and once again tried to move around the right flank of **Robert E. Lee's Army of Northern Virginia**. Two of **Philip H. Sheridan's** cavalry **divisions** under **David M. Gregg** and **Alfred T. A. Torbert** were screening the advance of the **Army of the Potomac**. After crossing the Pamunkey River, the dismounted Union troopers headed for an important crossroads at Haw's Shop, but just west of it at Enon Church, they encountered the entrenched Confederate cavalry of **Fitzhugh Lee** and **Wade Hampton**. The Federals advanced on May 28 but were halted by **M. Calbraith Butler's brigade**. Reinforced by **George A. Custer's** brigade, they attacked again near dusk and successfully drove off the enemy and captured the vital crossroads. In the battle, the Confederates lost approximately 400 men, while the Federals suffered 344 casualties.

HAWTHORNE, ALEXANDER TRAVIS (1825–1899) CSA. A native of **Alabama**, Hawthorne studied at **Georgia's** Evergreen Academy and Mercer University and at Yale University. Moving to **Arkansas**, he became a lawyer and entered Confederate service in June 1861 as lieutenant colonel of the 6th Arkansas.

After being promoted to colonel in October, Hawthorne fought at **Shiloh**, but he was not reelected when the **army** was reorganized in May 1862. He apparently retained his rank, because in June he was listed as a **brigade** commander in **William J. Hardee's corps**. In November, Hawthorne was in Arkansas commanding a **regiment** identified as Hawthorne's Arkansas Regiment. At the **Battle of Helena** in July 1863, he led the initial Confederate attack and forced the Federals back but did not receive any support. When the Confederates retreated, Hawthorne won much praise from his superiors when he volunteered to cover the withdrawal with only nine volunteers. Promoted to brigadier general in February 1864, he led a brigade in **Thomas Churchill's division** at **Pleasant Hill** during the **Red River Campaign** and then returned to Arkansas and fought well at **Jenkins' Ferry**. Hawthorne remained in Arkansas for the remainder of the war.

When the war ended, Hawthorne joined **Edmund Kirby Smith's** party traveling to Mexico and then moved to Brazil, where he established a Confederate community near Rio de Janeiro. Returning to the United States in 1874, he became a Baptist minister.

HAY, JOHN MILTON (1838–1905) USA. A native of **Indiana**, Hay graduated from Brown University in 1858 and began working in his uncle's Springfield, Illinois, law firm, located next door to **Abraham Lincoln's** office. When Lincoln won the presidency in 1860, his secretary, **John G. Nicolay**, persuaded him to hire Hay as an assistant secretary.

For the first two years of the administration, Hay worked closely with Lincoln on correspondence and in dealing with politicians, but in late 1863, he served as a volunteer aide-de-camp on Maj. Gen. **Quincy A. Gillmore's** staff in **South Carolina**. Lincoln appointed Hay a major and assistant adjutant general in 1864 so he could serve as a liaison between the White House and the **army**. In that position, Hay served in **Florida** trying to raise support for the Union among the civilian population and later was brevetted lieutenant colonel and colonel of volunteers.

Hay left the administration in March 1865 to accept an appointment to the U.S. legation in Paris, France. Over the next five years, he served in Paris; Vienna, Austria; and Madrid, Spain. Returning to the United States, Hay served as assistant secretary of state, ambassador to Great Britain, and secretary of state under Presidents William McKinley and Theodore Roosevelt. Despite this distinguished record, he is mostly remembered for coauthoring with Nicolay in 1890 the 10-volume biography *Abraham Lincoln: A History*.

HAYES, JOSEPH (1835–1912) USA. A native of **Maine**, Hayes finished his studies at Harvard University in 1855, but he did not receive his diploma until 1862. Afterward, he lived in **Wisconsin**, **Iowa**, and **Massachusetts**, working as a banker, civil engineer, and real estate broker, respectively.

Hayes entered Union service in July 1861 as major of the 18th Massachusetts. Joining the **Army of the Potomac's** V Corps, he fought in the **Peninsula** and **Seven Days Campaigns** and was promoted to lieutenant colonel in August 1862. After **Second Manassas**, **Antietam**, and

Fredericksburg (where his **regiment** charged Marye's Heights three times), Hayes was promoted to colonel in March 1863. He then led his regiment at **Chancellorsville** and **Gettysburg** and commanded a **brigade** in the **Bristoe Station** and **Mine Run Campaigns**. On the first day of the **Battle of the Wilderness** in May 1864, Hayes was severely wounded in the head while leading his regiment.

Hayes was recommended for promotion by his superiors and was appointed brigadier general of volunteers in May 1864. During the **Petersburg Campaign**, he participated in the August battles around the **Weldon Railroad**. While fighting near Globe Tavern, Hayes was captured and was held a **prisoner** for six months, although the Confederates **paroled** him and put him in charge of distributing supplies to Union prisoners. After being **exchanged**, he took command of a V Corps brigade late in the **Appomattox Campaign**. **Brevetted** major general of regulars for the Weldon Railroad operation, Hayes turned down a regular **U.S. Army** commission and left the service.

After the war, Hayes worked as a miner and stockbroker, but his head wound was said to have caused him depression. He eventually became a recluse before dying in a private sanatorium.

HAYES, RUTHERFORD BIRCHARD (1822–1893) USA. A native of **Ohio**, Hayes graduated from Harvard Law School and then returned home to open a law practice and become active in **Republican** politics. He entered Union service in June 1861 as major of the 23rd Ohio and served mostly in western **Virginia** early in the war. Promoted to lieutenant colonel in October, Hayes's first major battle was with the **Army of the Potomac** at **South Mountain**, where he was severely wounded in the arm. He was promoted to colonel in October 1862 and returned to western Virginia. There, Hayes commanded a **brigade** and helped defend the area against **John Hunt Morgan's** raiders. In 1864, he fought at **Cloyd's Mountain** and in **David Hunter's Shenandoah Valley Campaign**. During **Philip Sheridan's Shenandoah Valley Campaign**, Hayes commanded a brigade at **Third Winchester** and **Cedar Creek** and then temporarily took over a **division**. He was promoted to brigadier general of volunteers in October 1864 and eventually rose to permanent division command. A brave, if not distinguished commander, Hayes frequently led his men in the attack and was wounded four times. He was **brevetted** major general of volunteers when the war ended and left the **army** in June 1865.

Hayes had been elected to the U.S. House of Representatives in 1864, but he refused to leave the army to take the seat. He entered in the **U.S.**

Congress after leaving the service and was reelected in 1866. Hayes then resigned his seat in 1867 to run successfully for governor of Ohio. After serving two terms, he won the 1876 Republican presidential nomination and eventually was declared the winner of the disputed 1876 election. As president, Hayes ended **Reconstruction**.

HAYS, ALEXANDER (1819–1864) USA. A native of **Pennsylvania**, Hays became close friends with **U. S. Grant** while he was a cadet at **West Point**. After his 1844 graduation, he won one **brevet** in the **Mexican War** but then resigned his commission in 1848 to enter the iron business. Hays also mined gold in **California** and was working as a Pennsylvania construction engineer when the Civil War began.

In April 1861, Hays was appointed major of the 12th Pennsylvania, but the following month, he was commissioned captain in the 16th U.S. Infantry. That October, he was appointed colonel of the 63rd Pennsylvania and gallantly led it in **Philip Kearny's** division of the **Army of the Potomac** through numerous battles in the **Peninsula** and **Seven Days Campaigns**. After being severely wounded at **Second Manassas**, Hays was promoted to brigadier general of volunteers in September 1862.

When he returned to duty, Hays was given a **brigade** command in the **Washington, D.C.**, defenses. In June 1863, he was given command of a II Corps **division** and at **Gettysburg** played a key role in repulsing **Pickett's Charge**. When the II and III Corps were reorganized in 1864, Hays lost his division and reverted to a brigade command. On the first morning of the **Battle of the Wilderness**, he was shot in the head and killed near the intersection of the Brock and Orange Plank Roads. Rumor had it that he had leaned down from the saddle to untangle a canteen strap when his head moved into the bullet's path. Hays had already been brevetted through the rank of colonel in the **U.S. Army** and received a brevet of major general of volunteers posthumously.

HAYS, HARRY THOMPSON (1820–1876) CSA. A native of **Tennessee**, the orphaned Hays was raised by a **Mississippi** uncle. After graduating from **Maryland's** St. Mary's College, he became a lawyer in **New Orleans, Louisiana**, and was active in **Whig** politics.

Hays entered Confederate service in June 1861 when he was elected colonel of the 7th Louisiana. He saw combat at **First Manassas** as part of **Jubal Early's brigade** and then distinguished himself in **Stonewall Jackson's Shenandoah Valley Campaign** while in **Richard Taylor's** brigade. In the Valley, Hays was severely wounded while leading an attack at **Port Republic**.

When Taylor was promoted and sent west, Hays was commissioned brigadier general in July 1862 and took command of one of two **Louisiana Tiger** brigades in the **Army of Northern Virginia**. He soon earned a reputation as being a hard drinking, hard fighting officer. Joining his brigade just prior to **Antietam**, he led it into the cornfield and lost 60 percent of his men in 30 minutes of combat. The brigade was only lightly engaged at **Fredericksburg**, but during the **Chancellorsville Campaign**, it helped Jubal Early hold back the Federals at **Second Fredericksburg**. The next day at **Salem Church**, Hays's men overran two Union lines before finally being stopped by a third. His greatest moment came at **Gettysburg**, where his brigade played a key role in routing the Union XI Corps on the first day of battle and captured more **prisoners** than it had men. On July 2, 1863, Hays led an attack on Cemetery Hill at dusk that captured two enemy **artillery** batteries, but he then was forced to retreat when no one moved to his support. In November 1863, his brigade was overrun by a massive Union assault at **Rappahannock Station**. More than 700 men were captured, but Hays escaped through a hail of gunfire. After temporarily commanding Early's **division** during the **Mine Run Campaign**, he fought in the **Overland Campaign**. Because of heavy losses, the 1st Louisiana Brigade and the 2nd Louisiana Brigade were consolidated under his command after the **Battle of the Wilderness**. On May 9, 1864, Hays was severely wounded by a **sharpshooter** at **Spotsylvania**. When he returned to duty, he was transferred to **Louisiana** to reassemble absentee soldiers. **Edmund Kirby Smith** appointed him a major general in May 1865, but the appointment came too late to be confirmed by the Senate.

After the war, Hays served as sheriff of Orleans Parish, but during **Reconstruction** in 1866, **Philip Sheridan** removed him from office, after a New Orleans riot occurred against **freedmen**. He then practiced law until his death.

HAYS, WILLIAM (1819–1875) USA. Born in **Virginia**, Hays eventually moved to **Tennessee**. He graduated from **West Point** in 1840 and served in the **artillery** during the **Mexican War**, where he won two **brevets**. Hays also fought in the **Seminole Wars** and was a captain serving on routine garrison duty when the Civil War began.

After spending some time in the **Washington, D.C.**, defenses, Hays was promoted to lieutenant colonel in September 1861 and was given command of a **brigade** of **horse artillery** in the **Army of the Potomac's** Artillery Reserve in May 1862. He ably led this brigade during the **Peninsula** and **Seven Days Campaigns** and then was given command of the reserve artillery in September 1862.

After **Antietam** and **Fredericksburg**, Hays was promoted to brigadier general of volunteers in late December 1862, and while leading a brigade in **William French's** division at **Chancellorsville**, he was captured with his staff. **Exchanged** less than two weeks later, he took temporary command of the II Corps at **Gettysburg** after **Winfield S. Hancock** and **John Gibbon** were wounded. In November 1863, Hays became provost marshal of the southern District of New York and kept that position until February 1865, when he took a II Corps **division**. After leading his division in the **Petersburg** and **Appomattox Campaigns**, he was relieved by **Andrew A. Humphreys** on April 6, 1865, when he was found sleeping late at his headquarters after being ordered to be vigilant. The incident ruined Hays's military career.

Although he had been brevetted lieutenant colonel and brigadier general of regulars, Hays never advanced beyond the rank of major in the **U.S. Army**, but he remained in the service until his death.

HAZEL GROVE AT BATTLE OF CHANCELLORSVILLE, VIRGINIA (MAY 3, 1863). *See* CHANCELLORSVILLE, VIRGINIA, CAMPAIGN AND BATTLE OF.

HAZEN, WILLIAM BABCOCK (1830–1887) USA. Born in **Vermont**, Hazen moved to **Ohio** as a child. After graduating from **West Point** in 1855, he fought **Indians** in the Pacific Northwest and in **Texas**, being wounded in the latter. When the Civil War began, Hazen was a lieutenant and instructor of infantry **tactics** at the academy. He was promoted to captain in May 1862 and through the influence of childhood friend **James A. Garfield** was appointed colonel of the 41st Ohio in October. The following month, Hazen was given command of a **brigade** in the **Army of the Ohio**. He received high praise for his service at **Shiloh** and later at **Stones River** while with the **Army of the Cumberland**. In the latter battle, Hazen suffered heavy casualties while repelling a number of Confederate attacks at the Round Forest. After the war, he erected the Civil War's first battlefield monument to commemorate his men there.

Hazen was promoted to brigadier general of volunteers in April 1863 and continued to enhance his reputation in the **Chickamauga** and **Chattanooga Campaigns**. He led his brigade throughout the **Atlanta Campaign** until he was given command of a XV Corps **division** in August 1864. Hazen's division participated in the **March to the Sea** and led the crucial attack on **Fort McAllister** during operations against **Savannah, Georgia**. He then served through the **Carolinas Campaign** and was promoted to major general of volunteers in April 1865. Hazen received **brevets** of brigadier general and major general of regulars for his wartime service.

Remaining in the **U.S. Army** after the war, Hazen served as colonel of the 38th and 6th U.S. Infantry, fought Indians, helped expose **army** corruption during President **U. S. Grant's** administration, and served as an observer in the Franco-Prussian War. He held the rank of brigadier general and was the army's chief signal officer when he died.

HÉBERT, LOUIS (1820–1901) CSA. A native of **Louisiana**, Hébert (AY-bear) was a first cousin of Confederate Brig. Gen. **Paul Octave Hébert** and the brother-in-law of Brig. Gen. **Walter H. Stevens**. A member of a prominent Louisiana planter family, he was educated at Jefferson College and graduated from **West Point** in 1845. After serving only one year in the **engineers**, Hébert resigned his commission and became a planter. He also became a colonel in the Louisiana militia and served in the state senate (1853–55), as the state's chief engineer (1855–59), and on the Board of Public Works (1860–61).

Hébert entered Confederate service in May 1861 when he was elected colonel of the 3rd Louisiana. At **Wilson's Creek**, his **regiment** was highly praised for attacking the enemy and capturing five cannons. After the battle, Hébert was given command of a **brigade** under **Sterling Price** and was captured while leading it at **Pea Ridge**. After being **exchanged**, he was promoted to brigadier general in May 1862.

Hébert returned to his brigade in **L. Henry Little's** division, and when Little was killed at **Iuka**, he assumed command and kept the **division** fighting. Sickness then forced him to relinquish his division for the attack on **Corinth, Mississippi**. Afterward, Hébert resumed his brigade command and joined the **Vicksburg, Mississippi**, defenses at **Snyder's Bluff** for the winter of 1862–63. Part of **John Forney's** division, Hébert's brigade fought well during the **Vicksburg Campaign** and was captured with the rest of the city's garrison. After being exchanged, he was placed in command of the heavy **artillery** at **Fort Fisher, North Carolina**, in April 1864 and served the rest of the war in that position and as chief engineer for the **Department of North Carolina**.

After the war, Hébert taught school and was a Louisiana newspaper editor.

HÉBERT, PAUL OCTAVE (1818–1880) CSA. A native of **Louisiana**, Hébert (AY-bear) was a first cousin of Confederate Brig. Gen. **Louis Hébert**. He belonged to a prominent Louisiana family and graduated first in his class at Jefferson College and first in the **West Point** class of 1840. Hébert taught engineering at the academy and worked on Mississippi River defenses before resigning his commission in 1845 to become Louisiana's surveyor general. During the **Mexican War**, he served as Gen. Isaac Johnson's aide-de-camp before becoming lieutenant colonel of the 14th U.S. Infantry and serving under Franklin Pierce. Hébert was highly praised for his service and won one **brevet**. In 1852, he was elected Louisiana's governor as a **Democrat** and improved the state's transportation and education systems. After leaving office, Hébert also helped win former academy classmate **William T. Sherman** appointment to superintendent of the Louisiana Seminary of Learning and Military Academy.

When the Civil War began, Hébert was commissioned colonel of the 1st Louisiana Artillery and later brigadier general of state troops. In August 1861, he was appointed brigadier general of Confederate troops and after temporarily commanding the **Trans-Mississippi Department** in the spring of 1862, he was placed in command of the District of West Louisiana and Texas that autumn. Hébert's main focus was on the defense of **Galveston, Texas**, but he was hampered by a lack of troops and equipment and the government's taking from him what few men he had. When Galveston was captured in October 1862, he tried to raise and train more recruits, but they, too, were taken away. During the **Vicksburg Campaign**, Hébert commanded North Louisiana, but he could do little to interfere with Union operations in the area. In late 1864, he was given command of the Eastern Subdistrict of Texas and held it until May 1865, when he assumed command of the Trans-Mississippi Department. The day after receiving this command, Hébert surrendered it to **Gordon Granger** on May 26, 1865.

Hébert returned to Louisiana after the war and angered many residents by becoming a **Republican** during **Reconstruction**. His political connections won him various government engineering positions, and he became a brother-in-law of former Confederate Brig. Gen. **James P. Major** when Major married his sister.

HECKMAN, CHARLES ADAMS (1822–1896) USA. A native of **Pennsylvania**, Heckman attended Minerva Seminary and worked as a store clerk before serving in the **Mexican War** as a sergeant in the Regiment of **Voltigeurs**. After the war, he moved to **New Jersey** and became a **railroad** conductor.

Heckman entered Union service in April 1861 as a captain in the 1st Pennsylvania and served under **Robert Patterson** in the **Shenandoah Valley** before being appointed lieutenant colonel of the 9th New Jersey in October. He participated in the operations against **Roanoke Island** and **New Bern, North Carolina**, and was wounded at the latter. After being wounded a second time in a **skirmish**, Heckman was promoted to colonel in February 1862 and served on garrison duty in **North Carolina** until promoted to brigadier general of volunteers in November 1862.

Heckman served in operations around **Charleston, South Carolina**, before being transferred to the **Army of the James**. In **Virginia**, he garrisoned **Norfolk** and Portsmouth until the spring of 1864. Transferred to a frontline **brigade** during the **Petersburg Campaign**, Heckman was wounded a third time at **Port Walthall** in early May. His first major battle was at **Second Drewry's Bluff**, where his brigade was badly handled, and Heckman was captured. Heckman was sent to Charleston with other **prisoners** and was kept in an exposed position by the Confederates in an attempt to stop Union shelling of the city. **Exchanged** in September, he was given command of an XVIII Corps **division** despite his lack of experience. That same month, Heckman led his division in the costly assault against **Fort Harrison** and assumed command of the **corps** when **E. O. C. Ord** was wounded. His leadership was criticized, however, and Heckman was partly blamed for the defeat. He temporarily commanded the XXV Corps in early 1865, but because he had performed poorly in the only two real battles in which he was engaged, Heckman was sent back to New Jersey in March 1865 by **U. S. Grant**. He resigned his commission two months later.

After the war, Heckman worked as a train dispatcher.

HEINTZELMAN, SAMUEL PETER (1805–1869) USA. A native of **Pennsylvania**, Heintzelman graduated from **West Point** in 1826 and spent the next 20 years on garrison, quartermaster, and recruitment duty. He won one **brevet** for gallantry in the **Mexican War** and another in the 1850s for service in the southwest.

When the Civil War began, Heintzelman was a major in the 1st U.S. Infantry. He was commissioned colonel of the 17th U.S. Infantry in May 1861 and was promoted to brigadier general of volunteers three days later. After commanding the force that captured Alexandria, Virginia, in May 1861, Heintzelman was given command of a **division** under **Irvin McDowell**. At **First Manassas**, he was wounded while trying to rally his broken division during the Union defeat.

Largely basing his choices on seniority, **George B. McClellan** chose Heintzelman as one of the **Army of the Potomac's** first **corps** commanders and placed him at the head of the III Corps in March 1862. A promotion to major general of volunteers followed in May. He proved to be an overly cautious corps commander during the **Peninsula Campaign**, and his exaggerated estimates of Confederate numbers helped convince McClellan to lay siege to **Yorktown**. Despite his cautious nature, Heintzelman's corps played a key role in the campaign, and his two divisions under **Joseph Hooker** and **Philip Kearny** emerged as two of the **army's** best. The corps fought well at **Williamsburg, Seven Pines**, and in the **Seven Days Campaign**, but Heintzelman's leadership was lackluster. Still, he received brevets of brigadier general and major general of regulars for his service. During the **Second Manassas Campaign**, Heintzelman continued to demonstrate mediocre leadership and spent the **Antietam Campaign** in the **Washington, D.C.**, defenses. Although personally brave and often gallant, he did not have the ability to command large units. Heintzelman was relieved of command in October 1862 and spent the next two years in Washington before being appointed to command the **Northern Department** in January 1864. He spent the last six months of war on court-martial duty.

Heintzelman remained in the **U.S. Army** after the war and rose from colonel to major general before retiring in 1869.

HELENA, ARKANSAS, BATTLE OF (JULY 4, 1863). Having been captured by Union troops in July 1862, Helena, Arkansas, was garrisoned by 4,000 men under **Benjamin Prentiss** during the 1863 **Vicksburg Campaign**. To help the Confederates trapped in **Vicksburg, Mississippi**, **Theophilus H. Holmes**, commander of the Confederate District of Arkansas, attacked Helena to divert Union attention away from Vicksburg.

Sterling Price's division and **John S. Marmaduke's** cavalry—totaling about 7,500 men—attacked Helena in the predawn hours of July 4, 1863. Heavy rain delayed the Confederates and gave Prentiss time to bring up the gunboat *Tyler* and prepare a strong defense. The attack at first enjoyed some success when the Confederates captured some works and cannons. But then the Union **artillery** and the *Tyler's* guns played havoc with the attackers and pinned them down. By mid-morning, those Confederates who could still move retreated. Holmes lost about 1,600 men in the failed attack (mostly taken **prisoners**), while Prentiss lost 239 men. The battle occurred on the day Vicksburg surrendered and thus had no effect on the campaign. Accusations of misconduct during the fight led to a duel between Marmaduke and Brig. Gen. **Lucius M. Walker** a few months later, in which Walker was mortally wounded.

HELM, BENJAMIN HARDIN (1831–1863) CSA. A native of **Kentucky**, Helm was a brother-in-law of **Abraham Lincoln's** wife, **Mary Todd Lincoln**, and a cousin of Confederate Brig. Gen. **John T. Wood**. He graduated from **West Point** in 1851 and served briefly with the cavalry on the frontier before illness forced him to resign his commission in 1852. After studying law at the University of Louisville and Harvard Law School, Helm joined his father's Kentucky practice. In the 1850s, he was elected to one term in the state legislature as a **Whig** and served as a state attorney, and in 1860 he was appointed assistant inspector general of the state guard.

Although not a strong secessionist, Helm refused Lincoln's offer of a major's commission in the Union **army** and instead raised the 1st Kentucky Cavalry (Confederate) and entered Confederate service in October 1861 as the **regiment's** colonel. After service in Kentucky, he was promoted to brigadier general in March 1862 and helped guard the army's flank in northern **Alabama** during the **Battle of Shiloh**. At the end of the battle's first day, he erroneously notified **P. G. T. Beauregard** that **Don Carlos Buell's Army of the Ohio** was heading for Decatur, Alabama, rather than Shiloh. Helm's error did not harm his career, however, and in late April he took command of an infantry **brigade** in **John C. Breckinridge's division**. Helm was severely injured late that summer when his horse fell and crushed his right thigh as Breckinridge was advancing on **Baton Rouge, Louisiana**. This injury forced him to miss the battle. After recovering, Helm was placed in command of Chattanooga, Tennessee, and then an Alabama **district**.

In February 1863, Helm took command of the 1st Kentucky Brigade, better known as the **"Orphan Brigade."** He was well liked by his men, and he formed them into an outstanding unit. During the 1863 **Vicksburg Campaign**, Helm's brigade served in the Jackson, Mississippi, area under **Joseph E. Johnston**. Afterward, it was sent to join **Braxton Bragg's Army of Tennessee** for the **Battle of Chickamauga**. On the second day of battle, Breckinridge's division attacked a strong Union position. Three times Helm sent his brigade forward, and during the fighting he was shot from his horse, receiving a bullet in his right side. Taken from the field, he died that night. After Helm's death, his widow went to **Washington, D.C.**, and stayed for a while with the Lincolns in the White House, causing consternation in the North. In December 1862, widow Emily Helm took the **oath of allegiance** and was granted amnesty.

HELPER, HINTON ROWEN (1829–1909) USA. A native of **North Carolina**, Helper became more notorious in the South than **Harriet Beecher Stowe**. In 1857, he wrote *The Impending Crisis of the South: How to Meet It*. This book criticized **slavery** as an institution that prevented the South from modernizing, and it attempted to persuade the South's non–slave owners of its ill effects. Helper argued that slavery benefited only the aristocratic slave owners while preventing the development of a more diverse economy that would benefit the common people. Despite his antislavery stance, Helper also was a white supremacist who supported the emancipation of slaves and their colonization outside of the United States.

Some 14,000 copies of the book were sold, and it became wildly popular in the North. Antislavery forces praised it, while Southerners lashed out at Helper for being a traitor to his native land. In the South, the book was banned and burned, but it still produced a greater outcry than did *Uncle Tom's Cabin* a few years earlier. The **Republican Party** printed 100,000 copies of *The Impending Crisis* during the **election of 1860** to strengthen **Abraham Lincoln's** platform. In 1861, Helper was appointed by Lincoln to be the U.S. consul in Buenos Aires, Argentina.

HENDERSON'S HILL, LOUISIANA, BATTLE OF (MARCH 21, 1864). Early in the 1864 **Red River Campaign**, Richard Taylor's attempts to stop **Nathaniel P. Banks's** Union invasion of **Louisiana** were hampered by a lack of cavalry. Taylor finally was joined on March 19 by Col. William G. Vincent's 2nd Louisiana Cavalry, which was sent to Henderson's Hill, about 20 miles northwest of Alexandria near Bayou Rapides and Cotile. After **skirmishing** with the enemy, Vincent was reinforced by a four-gun battery under William Edgar.

On March 21, Maj. Gen. **A. J. Smith** sent out a **reconnaissance** force under **Joseph A. Mower** that included an infantry **division**, an **artillery** battery, and one cavalry **brigade**. In a pouring rain, Mower led his men through a deep swamp that night and learned Vincent's countersign by capturing Confederate **pickets**. After surrounding the camp, the Federals attacked and completely overwhelmed the surprised Confederates in the dark. Mower did not lose a man, but he captured 250 **prisoners**, four cannons, and 200 horses.

HENRY RIFLE. The standard **rifle** for soldiers on both sides of the Civil War was the muzzle-loading **rifle musket**. But in 1863, the Union **army** began supplying some of its men with the new Henry repeating rifle. Invented in 1860 by B. Tyler Henry, superintendent of Oliver Winchester's New Haven Arms Company, it was a tube-fed lever-action rifle that fired a .44-caliber rim-fire metallic cartridge. The 15-shot weapon gave Union soldiers a tremendous advantage in firepower and caused the Confederates to refer to it as the rifle the Yankees loaded on Sunday and fired all week. The government bought 1,731 rifles and nearly a half million rounds of ammunition between July 1863 and November 1865. In addition, individual states purchased thousands more for issue to their soldiers. Some of **William T. Sherman's** men used Henry's in the **Atlanta** and **Carolinas Campaigns** and in the **March to the Sea**, while other rifles saw action with the 1st Maine Cavalry in **Virginia**. Today, Henry is still honored on all Winchester rim-fire ammunition with the letter *H* stamped on the base of each one.

HEROES OF AMERICA. *See* PEACE SOCIETIES, CONFEDERATE.

HEROLD, DAVID E. (1842–1865) CSA. Herold was an acquaintance of **John Surratt** and became one of the conspirators in **Abraham Lincoln's assassination**. A native of **Maryland**, he was given the task of helping **Lewis Paine** escape south through Maryland after Paine killed Secretary of State **William Seward**. After hiding guns along the escape route, Herold met up with **John Wilkes Booth** instead of Paine (who failed in his assignment) and accompanied him on his escape attempt. When surrounded by Union troops in a tobacco warehouse at Port Royal, Virginia, Herold asked for and was given the chance to surrender. Booth cursed him for it, refused to follow suit, and was shot and killed (or committed suicide). Herold was convicted for his role in the assassination and was hanged on July 7, 1865.

HERRON, FRANCIS JAY (1837–1902) USA. A native of **Pennsylvania**, Herron attended the University of Pittsburgh before moving to **Iowa** as a young man to join his brothers in establishing a bank. There he also became captain of a militia **company** and offered its services to President-elect **Abraham Lincoln** in January 1861.

Herron entered Union service in May 1861 as a captain in the 90-day 1st Iowa. After fighting at **Wilson's Creek**, he was mustered out of service in August but reentered the **army** in September as lieutenant colonel of the 9th Iowa. At **Pea Ridge**, Herron commanded the **regiment** and was wounded and captured, but his actions won him the **Medal of Honor** in 1893.

After being **exchanged** in March 1862, Herron was promoted to brigadier general of volunteers in July. In December, he commanded two **divisions** and led them on a remarkable 125-mile march in three days to reinforce Brig. Gen. **James G. Blunt** and help win the **Battle of Prairie Grove, Arkansas**. Herron was promoted to major general of volunteers in March 1863 for his service at Prairie Grove, making him the youngest major general on either side at that time. During the **Vicksburg Campaign**, his division saw service with the **Army of the Tennessee** in the latter stages of the siege. In August 1863, Herron was assigned to the **Department of the Gulf**, and he served out the remainder of the war in **Louisiana** and **Texas** in command of various **districts**. When the war ended, he commanded the XIII Corps in Brownsville, Texas, and was one of the army's most respected officers.

Herron left the army in June 1865 and returned to Louisiana to practice law and become involved in **Reconstruction** politics. In the 1870s, he moved to **New York**.

HETH, HENRY (1825–1899) CSA. A native of **Virginia**, Heth (HEETH) attended Georgetown College and declined an appointment to the **U.S. Naval Academy** before entering **West Point**. After graduating last in the class of 1847, he served in the **Mexican War**, but he saw no combat until engaged in frontier **Indian** warfare in the 1850s. During his antebellum service, Heth also wrote a manual on marksmanship that the **U.S. Army** adopted.

Heth resigned his captain's commission in April 1861 and entered Confederate service as a captain. He quickly rose in rank to lieutenant colonel and became Virginia's acting quartermaster general. In the autumn of 1861, Heth helped organize Brig. Gen. **John B. Floyd's** command for operations in western Virginia. During that time, he was appointed colonel of the 45th Virginia.

Heth was promoted to brigadier general in January 1862, but his small western Virginia command was defeated in an insignificant May battle. His only other substantial service that year was accompanying **Edmund Kirby Smith** in the **Kentucky Campaign** as a **brigade** commander. After the Senate rejected his nomination to major general in October, Heth secured a transfer to the **Army of Northern Virginia** in January 1863. There his career was aided by his friendship with **Jefferson Davis** and **Robert E. Lee** (Heth was said to be one of the few officers whom Lee called by his first name). Assigned to a brigade in **A. P. Hill's Light Division**, Heth was wounded at **Chancellorsville**. He was promoted to major general in late May 1863 and was given command of a **division** in Hill's III Corps even though he had little field experience. Heth's division began the **Battle of Gettysburg** (on July 1, 1863) when it entered town looking for shoes. Advancing without proper **reconnaissance**, the division was badly mauled, and Heth's skull was fractured when a bullet struck him through his padded hat. He was recovered sufficiently to resume command during the retreat but suffered a humiliating defeat when one of his brigades was captured at **Falling Waters**, **Maryland**, when the **army** recrossed the Potomac River. Although his role in this affair is not clear, Heth spent much time after the war defending his actions during the Gettysburg Campaign. Fortunately, Heth's ability improved. He fought at **Bristoe Station** and served competently during the **Overland Campaign**, although his division was roughly handled on the second day of the **Wilderness**. During the **Petersburg Campaign**, Heth distinguished himself in several actions, once carrying the colors into the Union works at **Reams' Station**.

After the **surrender** at **Appomattox**, Heth remained in Virginia, but he struggled financially after trying his hand at several careers. He died of Bright's disease shortly after writing his memoirs.

HICKS, THOMAS HOLLIDAY (1798–1865) USA. A native of **Maryland**, Hicks grew up on a farm with only a basic education. He became a local constable when he was 21, sheriff when 26, and state legislator when 32. Initially a **Democrat**, Hicks switched to the **Whig** Party in the 1830s and served as a presidential elector in 1836. Over the next 20 years, he served in the legislature, on the governor's council, as Dorchester County's registrar of wills, and in the state constitutional convention. When the Whig Party dissolved in the early 1850s, Hicks joined the **Know-Nothing Party** and was elected governor in 1857.

In early 1861, Hicks resisted pressure to call a special legislative session to debate **secession**. This habitual slowness to make decisions angered some politicians, but others praised his reluctance to act rashly. After the Civil War began, Hicks remained loyal to the Union despite a large number of prosecessionists in the Baltimore area. During the April 1861 **Baltimore Riot**, his life was threatened more than once, but he waited until April 26 before finally calling a special legislative session to meet in the pro-Union city of Frederick. Hicks recommended neutrality in the war, and the legislature agreed on the grounds that secession was unconstitutional. By that time, enough Union troops were in the state to ensure its loyalty. Hicks's actions in keeping Maryland neutral until it could be occupied by Union troops was his greatest contribution to the Union war effort.

When he left office in 1862, Hicks was offered a brigadier's commission, but he declined and was appointed to the U.S. Senate after a Maryland senator died in office. He was prevented from being a very active senator because of illness and an 1863 ankle injury that led to the amputation of one of his feet. Hicks was reelected to the Senate in 1864, but he died in early 1865 from complications of the amputation.

HIGGINS, EDWARD (1821–1875) CSA. A native of **Virginia**, Higgins grew up in **Louisiana** and entered the **U.S. Navy** in 1836 as a midshipman. He resigned a lieutenant's commission in 1854, but he continued to operate a mail packet until 1858.

Higgins entered Confederate service in April 1861 as a captain in the 1st Louisiana Heavy Artillery. When Maj. Gen. **David E. Twiggs** assumed command of **New Orleans, Louisiana**, in June, he made Higgins an aide-de-camp. In that position, Higgins was praised for his efforts in converting steamships to gunboats. After organizing the 1st Confederate Light Battery in October, he was made its captain but resigned in January 1862 to convert steamboats into state gunboats. Appointed lieutenant colonel of the 22nd Louisiana in February 1862, Higgins first worked at repairing the broken river boom blocking the Mississippi River at **Forts Jackson and St. Philip** and then was placed in command of the forts in March. He also was promoted to colonel of the 22nd Louisiana in April.

Although technically in command of both forts, Higgins supervised Fort St. Philip during the April 1862 Union attack, while his superior, Brig. Gen. **Johnson K. Duncan**, remained in Fort Jackson. Duncan highly praised Higgins's service in the unsuccessful defense that ended with them taken **prisoners**. After being **exchanged** in August 1862, Higgins rejoined his **regiment**, which was serving as an **artillery** unit in the **Vicksburg, Mississippi**, defenses at **Snyder's Bluff**. There he repulsed the **USS *Benton*** in December when it came up the Yazoo River. A controversy over who should be the regiment's field officers led to Higgins being displaced in January 1863, but **John C. Pemberton** appointed him commander of Vicksburg's river batteries. He served well throughout the siege and sank the USS *Cincinnati* in May but was captured when the city fell. After being exchanged in October 1863, Higgins was promoted to brigadier general in November and was given command of the harbor defenses of Mobile, Alabama. Sickness forced him off duty for several months in early 1864, and his "irascible" temper turned many of his officers against him. When Higgins left his post without permission in September, Maj. Gen. **Dabney H. Maury** relieved him of command, and he never again held a field command during the war.

After the war, Higgins lived first in Norfolk, Virginia, working in the import and insurance business and then moved to **California**, where he became an agent for the Pacific Mail Steamship Company.

HIGH BRIDGE, VIRGINIA, BATTLE OF (APRIL 6–7, 1865). During **Robert E. Lee's** retreat from **Petersburg, Virginia**, in the **Appomattox Campaign**, U. S. **Grant** ordered **E. O. C. Ord's Army of the James** to burn the bridges across the Appomattox River at Farmville and High Bridge to disrupt Lee's line of retreat. The latter was a 60-foot-high **railroad** bridge, with a wagon bridge running parallel and below it. Ord's chief of staff, brevet Brig. Gen. Theodore Read, assembled approximately 900 men from the 54th Pennsylvania, 123rd Ohio, and part of the 4th Massachusetts Cavalry to carry out the orders.

Leaving Burkeville at 4:00 A.M. on April 6, 1865, Read encountered Brig. Gen. **Thomas Rosser's** Confederate cavalry about two miles from the bridge. He first repulsed an attack by Rosser, but then was overwhelmed by a second determined assault. Nearly 800 of the Union infantry surrendered, and every Union cavalry officer, including Read, was killed, and Confederate Brig. Gen. **James Dearing** was mortally wounded. Since the bridge was not destroyed, the Confederate survivors of the **Battle of Sailor's Creek** crossed the Appomattox River that night. Major General **William Mahone's** division covered the crossing while Maj. Gen. **John B. Gordon's** men crossed over the wagon bridge. Mahone failed to destroy the bridges in a timely fashion, however. As a result, High Bridge had just been burned when **Francis Barlow's** Union **division** arrived on April 7. While Union infantry fought off Confederate **skirmishers** on the lower wagon bridge, Col. Thomas L. Livermore led a party of men who extinguished the fire on the higher railroad bridge. Saving High Bridge enabled the Union forces to cross the Appomattox River quickly and keep the pressure on Lee's retreating **Army of Northern Virginia**.

"HIGH WATER MARK OF THE CONFEDERACY" OR "HIGH TIDE OF THE CONFEDERACY." *See* GETTYSBURG, PENNSYLVANIA, CAMPAIGN AND BATTLE OF.

HILL, ADAMS SHERMAN (1833–1910) USA. A native of **Massachusetts**, Hill graduated from Harvard Law School in 1855, but rather than practicing law, he became a night editor for the **New York *Tribune*** in 1858. Transferring to the paper's **Washington, D.C.**, bureau in 1861, he witnessed the fight at **Blackburn's Ford** in July 1861. There Hill panicked and fled back to Washington and filed a grossly inaccurate story in which he claimed the Union **army** had been defeated and had suffered 500 dead. Although Hill never again was sent to the field, he did perform excellent service in supervising **war correspondents** and in reporting on events in Washington. He rose from assistant bureau chief in August 1861 to bureau chief in January 1863 and courted many confidential government sources, including **Abraham Lincoln** and **Charles Sumner**.

In his supervision of the war coverage, Hill insisted on impartial reporting. This brought him into conflict with *Tribune* owner, **Horace Greeley**, who preferred partisan reporting. Hill finally resigned his position in December 1863 and together with **Henry Villard** and Horace White formed the Independent News Room. Competing with the Associated Press in supplying stories to city newspapers, Hill was forced to use the Independent Telegraph Company to wire his stories since the Associated Press had an exclusive contract with the larger American Telegraph Company. Partly because of his competition with the Associated

Press, Hill briefly was detained by officials in connection with the 1864 **Gold Hoax**. The hoax involved a falsified Associated Press story that was sent over the Independent Telegraph Company's wires. Officials thought Hill might have been involved in the hoax to discredit the Associated Press, but he and the **telegraph** company quickly were cleared of any wrongdoing.

Hill remained a reporter until 1872, when he began teaching rhetoric at Harvard University. He became head of Harvard's English Department and wrote two books on English and rhetoric.

HILL, AMBROSE POWELL (1825–1865) CSA. A native of **Virginia**, Hill was from a prosperous family and graduated from **West Point** in 1847. After serving briefly with the **artillery** in the **Mexican War**, he was posted to garrisons in **Texas** and **Florida**. In 1855, Hill joined the U.S. Coastal Survey and four years later married the widowed sister of **John Hunt Morgan** (earlier, he competed with **George B. McClellan** for the hand of McClellan's future wife).

In March 1861, Hill resigned his commission and in April was appointed colonel of the 13th Virginia. He proved to be an excellent organizer and trainer and in February 1862 was promoted to brigadier general. Hill first won acclaim at **Williamsburg** during the **Peninsula Campaign**, when his **brigade** launched a successful attack against the Federals.

Promoted to major general in May 1862, Hill was given command of a large **division** that became known as the **Light Division** and became perhaps the best division commander in the **Army of Northern Virginia**. Known as "Little Powell," he often wore a bright red shirt into battle and earned the admiration of his men. During the **Seven Days Campaign**, Hill's division played a leading role at **Mechanicsville**, **Gaines' Mill**, and **Frayser's Farm** and suffered very heavy casualties. Afterward, he continued to win laurels when his division arrived in time to save the day for **Stonewall Jackson** at **Cedar Mountain** and held the line at **Second Manassas** against repeated Union attacks.

Remaining under Jackson, Hill soon ran afoul of the temperamental general and was placed under arrest at the beginning of the **Antietam Campaign** for failing to follow Jackson's marching orders. Jackson agreed to allow Hill to lead his division during the campaign, however, and he made a forced march from **Harpers Ferry**, **Virginia**, to arrive in time to save the **army** from being defeated at Antietam. At **Fredericksburg**, Hill's reputation was somewhat tarnished when a gap was left in his line, and the enemy briefly broke through. Afterward, he participated in Jackson's flank attack at **Chancellorsville** and was slightly wounded in the same incident that mortally wounded Jackson.

Shortly after Chancellorsville, Hill was promoted to lieutenant general and was given command of the new III Corps. His tenure as **corps** commander was erratic, and it seems corps command was slightly above his ability. Chronic kidney illness, a result of gonorrhea he contracted during his cadet days, also weakened his effectiveness. Hill initiated the **Battle of Gettysburg** and was heavily engaged in the first day's fight but then was largely left out of the battle. At the end of the campaign, his aggressiveness saved the army's **artillery** when he successfully counterattacked the enemy at **Falling Waters, Maryland**. During the **Bristoe Station Campaign**, Hill's reputation was damaged, and he was rebuked by **Robert E. Lee** when he rashly attacked the enemy at Bristoe Station and had two brigades mauled by a Union corps hidden behind a **railroad** embankment. His performance during the **Overland Campaign** also was inconsistent. Hill fought fiercely in the **Wilderness**, but his refusal to let his men re-form after the first day's fight nearly led to disaster when the enemy counterattacked the next morning. Illness forced him to miss **Spotsylvania**, and he performed poorly at the **North Anna River**, but then he provided good service at **Cold Harbor**. Hill seemed to gain back his old drive and fought brilliantly throughout the **Petersburg Campaign**, repulsing many enemy attacks and winning several impressive victories.

Although severely ill, Hill attempted to rally his corps after the Federals smashed the Confederate line at **Five Forks** in April 1865. On April 2, while riding to his men, he inadvertently encountered the advancing enemy and was shot and killed.

HILL, BENJAMIN HARVEY (1823–1877) CSA. A native of **Georgia**, Hill graduated first in his class from the University of Georgia and became a lawyer. After being elected to the state legislature in 1851, he frequently changed his party affiliation and at different times belonged to the **Whig, Know-Nothing, Constitutional Union**, and **Democratic Parties**. Believing in compromise, Hill opposed **secession** as a member of the Georgia secession convention in January 1861 until it became inevitable. He then supported it and was elected to the Provisional **Confederate Congress**.

Hill also was elected twice to the Confederate Senate. He chaired the Judiciary Committee and was a strong supporter of **Jefferson Davis**, although he sometimes criticized **conscription, impressment**, and the **suspension of the writ of habeas corpus**. Because of his support for

Davis, Hill often bitterly clashed with Gov. **Joseph E. Brown**. At war's end, when victory was unlikely, he finally began urging Davis to negotiate an end to hostilities. Hill took his position so late that it was later said that he was the last to accept secession and the last to accept defeat. Federal authorities arrested him when the war ended, and he was imprisoned for three months in New York's **Fort Lafayette**.

After being **paroled** by President **Andrew Johnson**, Hill returned to Georgia and switched from being a vocal critic of **Reconstruction** to finally accepting it. His about-face caused the Democrats to abandon him, but he was elected to the U.S. House of Representatives in 1875 as a **Republican**. There Hill again switched positions and proudly defended the **Lost Cause** and Davis. In his last political maneuver, he again joined the Democrats and was elected to the U.S. Senate in 1877. Hill died in office.

HILL, BENJAMIN JEFFERSON (1825–1880) CSA. A native of **Tennessee**, Hill was a merchant who was elected to the state senate in 1855. After Tennessee seceded, he was appointed colonel of the 5th Infantry of state troops in September 1861. Hill was commissioned a colonel when the **regiment** entered the **Confederate army** in November as the 35th Tennessee (for two years the regiment was referred to as the 5th [Hill's] Tennessee).

The regiment was sent to **Kentucky** and became part of **Patrick Cleburne's brigade**. Hill fought well at **Shiloh** and in the **siege of Corinth, Mississippi**, in the spring of 1862 and was commended by Cleburne and **P. G. T. Beauregard**. During the beginning of the 1862 **Kentucky Campaign**, he led the brigade when Cleburne took command of a **division**. At **Richmond**, Hill again fought well and was wounded three times. He remained with his men and a few weeks later fought at **Perryville**, where Cleburne was back in brigade command. Hill's regiment went on to fight at **Stones River** and **Chickamauga** with the **Army of Tennessee**, and his **corps** commander recognized Hill's "extraordinary merit" in the latter battle. In October 1863, the 48th Consolidated Tennessee was added to his command. At **Missionary Ridge**, Hill's unit held its position and even captured some Union soldiers and **flags**. After serving under Cleburne in the rear guard actions that followed, he was appointed the Army of Tennessee's provost marshal. Hill held this position until August 1864, at which time he returned to his regiment for the remainder of the **Atlanta Campaign**.

Hill was promoted to brigadier general in November 1864, and during the **Franklin and Nashville Campaign**, he commanded a cavalry unit that participated in the raid against the **railroad** between Nashville and

Murfreesboro. In early 1865, he was given command of a cavalry brigade under **Nathan Bedford Forrest** and helped oppose **James Wilson's Selma Raid** late in the war. After fighting at Selma, Alabama, Hill finally surrendered. Hill returned to Tennessee after the war, engaged in business, and opened a law practice.

HILL, DANIEL HARVEY (1821–1889) CSA. A native of **South Carolina**, Hill graduated from **West Point** in 1842. Assigned to the **artillery**, he saw hard service in the **Mexican War** under both Zachary Taylor and **Winfield Scott** and won two **brevets** for gallantry. Resigning his lieutenant's commission in 1849, Hill became a math professor at **Virginia's** Washington College and at **North Carolina's** Davidson College. During this time, **Stonewall Jackson** became his brother-in-law by marrying the sister of Hill's wife. In 1859, Hill was appointed superintendent of North Carolina's Military Institute.

A **secession** supporter, Hill was appointed colonel of state troops in April 1861 and commanded a training camp until he was elected colonel of the 1st North Carolina in May. Sent to **Virginia**, he earned recognition for the small battle at **Big Bethel** and was promoted to brigadier general in July. Various service in Virginia and North Carolina followed, along with a promotion to major general in March 1862. Hill was given command of a **division** for the **Peninsula Campaign** and performed valuable service at **Williamsburg, Seven Pines**, and during the **Seven Days Campaign** with the **Army of Northern Virginia**. Both **Robert E. Lee** and Jackson highly praised Hill's leadership, and he was given command of the **Department of North Carolina** in July 1862. However, Hill seems to have lacked the necessary administrative skills to run a **department** and in August was brought back to his division in Virginia. His subsequent career was somewhat erratic.

Hill was an aggressive fighter and was personally brave, but his constant complaining and criticisms angered many officers—including Lee. During the **Antietam Campaign**, he earned both praise and condemnation. Some speculated, probably unfairly, that he was to blame for Lee's **Lost Order**, and others criticized him for not defending the **South Mountain** gaps more vigorously. At Antietam, Hill fought bravely at the "Bloody Lane" and held Lee's center against overwhelming odds. After minor combat at **Fredericksburg**, he offered his resignation in January 1863 because of poor health (he suffered from a painful spinal ailment). Instead of accepting his resignation, Lee again sent Hill to command the Department of North Carolina in February.

In July 1863, Hill was promoted to lieutenant general and was transferred to a **corps** command in the **Army of Tennessee**. After fighting at **Chickamauga**, he engaged in a bitter feud with **Braxton Bragg** and accused Bragg of incompetence. As a result, Hill was relieved of command in October. Perhaps because of his abrasive personality, his promotion to lieutenant general was never confirmed by the Senate, and he reverted to major general. Hill performed various service for the remainder of the war, holding positions in **Charleston, South Carolina**; Virginia; and **Georgia** before finally being given a North Carolina command under **Joseph E. Johnston** in early 1865. After fighting at **Bentonville** in the **Carolinas Campaign**, he surrendered with Johnston's **army** in April 1865.

After the war, Hill first published the pro-Southern magazine *The Land We Love* and then the newspaper *The Southern Home*. In the 1870s and 1880s, he served as president of Arkansas Industrial University and Middle Georgia Military and Agricultural College.

HILL'S PLANTATION, ARKANSAS, BATTLE OF (JULY 7, 1862). In the summer of 1862, Confederate forces in **Arkansas** under Maj. Gen. **Thomas C. Hindman** attempted to disrupt Union shipping on the White River, which supplied **Samuel R. Curtis's Army of the Southwest**. After the Confederates shelled Union ships at **St. Charles** in mid-June and low water prevented the vessels from reaching him, Curtis was forced to move south from Batesville to meet the supply ships at Clarendon.

The Confederates **skirmished** with Curtis as he marched down the White River, and on July 7, Hindman ordered Brig. Gen. **Albert Rust** to make a stand at the Cache River. Rust's tardiness, however, allowed the enemy to reach the river first, and he engaged a small Union force under Col. **Charles E. Hovey** a few miles south of the river at Hill's Plantation. Although outnumbered, Hovey's men repulsed several attacks by William H. Parson's Confederate cavalry and held their position until reinforcements arrived and forced Rust to withdraw. In the fight, the Confederates lost about 250 men, while the Federals suffered 63 casualties. Curtis finally reached Clarendon, only to find the supply ships had already left. He then marched to **Helena** and occupied it on July 12.

HILTON HEAD, SOUTH CAROLINA, BATTLE OF (NOVEMBER 7, 1861). *See* PORT ROYAL, SOUTH CAROLINA, BATTLE OF.

HINCKS, EDWARD WINSLOW (1830–1894) USA. A native of **Maine**, Hincks worked as a printer before moving to **Massachusetts** in 1849. There, he was elected to the legislature, and by the time he entered Union service in 1861, he had dropped the *c* from his name (he used it again after the war).

Hincks was commissioned a 2nd lieutenant in the 2nd U.S. Cavalry in April 1861, but four days later he was made colonel of the 8th Massachusetts Militia. He soon resigned his regular **U.S. Army** commission and in August resigned his position with the militia to become colonel of the 19th Massachusetts. After guarding and repairing **railroads** in **Maryland**, Hincks fought at **Ball's Bluff**, **Virginia**, in October. He then was transferred to the **Army of the Potomac**, with which he fought through the **Peninsula** and **Seven Days Campaigns**. At **Frayser's Farm**, Hincks was highly praised by his superiors, but he also suffered a wound. Two more wounds received at **Antietam** left him partially disabled and in pain for the remainder of his life.

Hincks was promoted to brigadier general of volunteers in April 1863 while recuperating from his second wound. He then performed court-martial and recruiting duty until March 1864, when he was placed in command of Maryland's **Point Lookout prison**. In April, Hincks was given command of an XVIII Corps **division** of **black troops** in **Ambrose Burnside's Army of the James**. Although frequently absent from duty because of illness and his old wounds, he performed competently during the early part of the **Petersburg Campaign**. Hincks's health problems forced him from the field in July 1864, however, and he returned to recruiting duty with a **brevet** of major general of volunteers.

In June 1865, Hincks resigned from the volunteers, but in July 1866 he accepted a lieutenant colonel's commission in the regular **army**. He retired as a colonel in 1870 and supervised two different soldiers' homes.

HINDMAN, THOMAS CARMICHAEL (1828–1868) CSA. A native of **Tennessee**, Hindman (HINED-mun) grew up in **Alabama** and **Mississippi** and graduated from a high school in **New Jersey**. During the **Mexican War**, he helped raise a **company** of volunteers and was appointed a lieutenant in the 2nd Mississippi. Hindman became a Mississippi lawyer after the war and was elected to the legislature in 1854 as a **Democrat**. Moving to **Arkansas** in 1856, he prospered as a lawyer and in 1858 was elected to the **U.S. Congress**. Reelected in 1860, Hindman became a proponent of **secession** and urged Arkansas to secede in early 1861.

When secession came in May, Hindman resigned his congressional seat, returned home to recruit the 2nd Arkansas, and was commissioned its colonel in June. He raised the money needed to equip his men by confiscating northern-bound cargoes on Mississippi River steamers. After serving with an informal unit known as Hindman's Legion in Tennessee, Hindman was sent to southern **Missouri** to get the Arkansas state troops there to enlist in the **Confederate army**. Although unsuccessful in his mission, he was promoted to brigadier general in September and took command of a **brigade** in **Kentucky**.

At **Shiloh**, Hindman commanded a **division** in **William J. Hardee's corps** and was knocked senseless at the "Hornets' Nest" by a shell that killed his horse. Promoted to major general a week after the battle, he briefly took command of a division in **Braxton Bragg's** corps before being sent back to Arkansas in May 1862 to command the newly created **Trans-Mississippi Department**. Union forces had the **department's** forces on the defensive, and Hindman declared martial law to maintain order. This and his rigid enforcement of the **conscription** act made him unpopular with many people, but he did relieve some enemy pressure on the department by moving his men toward Missouri. Because of his unpopularity, Hindman was removed by **Jefferson Davis** and was replaced by **Theophilus H. Holmes**.

Hindman was given command of a corps under Holmes and in December 1862 was defeated when he attacked the enemy at **Prairie Grove**. He never liked serving under Holmes and in January 1863 was relieved of the disagreeable duty. In August, Hindman took command of a division in **Leonidas Polk's** corps in the **Army of Tennessee**. Prior to the **Battle of Chickamauga**, he became one of the generals Bragg criticized for failing to trap the Union **army** near **McLemore's Cove**. Still, Bragg praised Hindman's actions at Chickamauga when he attacked with **James Longstreet** on the second day of battle and helped rout the Union army, losing more men than any other of Longstreet's divisions. During the fighting, he suffered a concussion from an exploding shell. Absent on leave during the **Chattanooga Campaign**, Hindman returned in December to assume command of **John C. Breckinridge's** corps and kept it until he was relieved by **John Bell Hood** in February 1864. During the **Atlanta Campaign**, he led a division in Hood's corps and fought tenaciously at **Resaca**, **New Hope Church**, and **Kolb's Farm** until early July, when he was wounded severely in the eye near **Kennesaw Mountain**. Unable to retake the field, Hindman performed various administrative duties in Arkansas and Mississippi for the rest of the war.

When the war ended, Hindman was one of those Confederate officers who fled to Mexico. He returned to Arkansas in 1867 and was active in opposing **Reconstruction**. In September 1868, Hindman was shot and killed by unknown assailants while sitting in his living room. Friends suspected the killers to have been either **Radical Republicans** or someone whom Hindman had angered during his harsh reign over the Trans-Mississippi Department during the war.

HINKS, EDWARD WINSLOW (1830–1894) USA. *See* HINCKS, ED-WARD WINSLOW.

HITCHCOCK, ETHAN ALLEN (1798–1870) USA. A native of **Vermont**, Hitchcock was the grandson of Revolutionary War hero Ethan Allen. He graduated from **West Point** in 1817 but earned his considerable reputation through administrative skills and the publishing of books on such various topics as philosophy, alchemy, and fairy tales. Hitchcock's military career included service in the **Seminole Wars**, on the frontier, and in the **Mexican War**, where he was **Winfield Scott's** inspector general. He was **brevetted** colonel and brigadier general for his service in Mexico and in 1851 was promoted to colonel of the 2nd U.S. Infantry. When Secretary of War **Jefferson Davis** refused to grant Hitchcock sick leave in 1855, he resigned his commission and moved to **Missouri**, where he wrote many of his books.

When the Civil War began, Hitchcock strongly supported the Union, but he initially turned down an appointment to major general of volunteers. In February 1862, he accepted the commission, and it was falsely rumored that he was to replace **U. S. Grant** at **Fort Donelson**. Hitchcock was called to **Washington, D.C.**, where Secretary of War **Edwin Stanton** considered him as a replacement for **George B. McClellan** at the head of the **Army of the Potomac**. Hitchcock was shocked at the notion and dissuaded Stanton with the excuse that he physically was unfit for field command. Stanton agreed and finally placed him on court-martial duty and in November 1862 made him a commissioner for the **exchange** of **prisoners**. A friend of both **Abraham Lincoln** and Stanton, Hitchcock was appointed Commissary General of prisoners in November 1865.

Hitchcock left the **U.S. Army** in 1867 and lived in **South Carolina** and **Georgia**.

H. L. HUNLEY, CSS. The first **submarine** to sink a warship was the Confederates' *H. L. Hunley*. Designed by Horace L. Hunley, it was one of several Confederate submarines built for **privateering** after the government offered prize money equal to 20 percent of the value of any Union warship sunk. Hunley already had helped build two submarines before constructing the *H. L. Hunley* in Mobile, Alabama. Originally called the *Fish Boat*, it was about 30 feet long, four feet wide, and five feet deep. A sophisticated boat, the submarine had two small conning towers, as well as diving planes and ballast tanks. With a crew of nine, it was powered by eight men turning a hand crank attached to the propeller, while one man controlled steering and depth. After experimenting with a towed mine, or **torpedo**, it was decided to attach the torpedo to a spar on the bow. The submarine would submerge, ram its target to attach the torpedo, and then reverse to a safe distance before detonating the torpedo with a cord attached to a primer.

After trial runs in Mobile, the *H. L. Hunley* was taken by train to **Charleston, South Carolina**. There, the government seized it and replaced its civilian crew with **Confederate navy** volunteers. In August 1863, the submarine accidentally sank during a trial run, drowning five men. After being raised, another volunteer crew was assembled, including Hunley. The boat sank again in October, drowning Hunley and seven more men. After the submarine had been raised a second time, Lt. George E. Dixon assembled yet another crew of volunteers and secured permission from **P. G. T. Beauregard** to attack the **USS *Housatonic***.

On the night of February 17, 1864, Dixon successfully sank the warship, but he never returned to dock. How the *H. L. Hunley* sank is unknown, but in 1995 it was discovered hundreds of yards from where the *Housatonic* went down. The submarine was raised in 2000 and during its examination, the remains of crew members were found inside.

HOBSON, EDWARD HENRY (1825–1901) USA. A native of **Kentucky**, Hobson worked in his father's store until the **Mexican War**, when he served with the 2nd Kentucky and was promoted to lieutenant for gallantry at Buena Vista. When the Civil War began, Hobson was a bank president, but he left that position to raise the 13th Kentucky (Union) and was appointed its colonel in January 1862.

As part of Jeremiah T. Boyle's **brigade**, Hobson served at **Shiloh** and then spent the rest of the war in Kentucky holding various **district** commands. He was promoted to brigadier general of volunteers in April 1863 and in July played a conspicuous role in capturing many of **John Hunt Morgan's** Confederate raiders at **Buffington Island** during **Morgan's Ohio Raid**. Ironically, in June 1864 Hunt captured Hobson and his **regiment** during a raid on **Cynthiana, Kentucky**. Morgan agreed to an informal arrangement to allow Hobson and some other officers to remain free to try to arrange an **exchange** of **prisoners**. Failing in this, Hobson was to return to Morgan. However, Morgan was defeated soon afterward and had to **parole** his remaining prisoners. Hobson then was left in an uncertain situation because he had not been paroled. He was ordered back to duty by his superiors and was even criticized for agreeing to the informal arrangement with the enemy.

After the war, Hobson was active in **Republican** politics and the **Grand Army of the Republic** and served as a district internal revenue collector.

HODGE, GEORGE BAIRD (1828–1892) CSA. A native of **Kentucky**, Hodge graduated from the **U.S. Naval Academy** in 1845 and served five years in the **U.S. Navy** before resigning his lieutenant's commission in 1850 to practice law. A **Democrat**, he was elected to the Kentucky legislature in 1859 and served as a delegate to the 1860 Democratic National Convention in **Charleston, South Carolina**. Although initially opposed to **secession**, Hodge came to support **states rights** and the Confederacy.

When the Civil War began, Hodge enlisted in a Kentucky **regiment** as a private, but he quickly left the **army** to become a Kentucky representative in the Provisional **Confederate Congress**. He subsequently was elected (by Kentucky's Confederate soldiers) to the First Confederate Congress. Hodge actively supported **Jefferson Davis's** war effort and between sessions served on **John C. Breckinridge's** staff with the rank of captain. After distinguishing himself at **Shiloh**, he was promoted to major in May 1862.

Back in Congress, Hodge pressured Davis to liberate Kentucky and supported **Braxton Bragg's 1862 Kentucky Campaign**. Probably because of his political influence, Hodge was promoted to colonel in May 1863 and was put in command of a small cavalry **brigade** under **Simon Buckner**. He served in eastern **Tennessee** and Kentucky making raids and performing other duties until he was ordered to **Richmond, Virginia**, in October. The following month, Davis appointed Hodge brigadier general, but anti-administration politics caused the Senate to refuse to confirm his appointment.

Hodge performed good service while leading a cavalry brigade under **Joseph Wheeler** during one of **Wheeler's Raids**, and Davis reappointed him brigadier general in August 1864. He was sent to command the District of Southwest Mississippi and East Louisiana, but again the Senate refused to confirm his appointment. In January 1865, Hodge was charged with incompetence and cowardice, and though acquitted, **department** commander **Nathan Bedford Forrest** removed him from his **district** command. He spent the remaining months of war in **Mississippi** without a command.

After the war, Hodge returned to Kentucky and served two terms in the legislature.

HODGERS, JENNIE. *See* CASHIER, ALBERT D. J.

HOGE, JANE CURRIE BLAIKIE (1811–1890) USA. A native of **Pennsylvania** and a graduate of Young Ladies' College, Hoge moved to **Illinois** with her husband in 1848. After two of her sons joined the Union **army**, she worked to get Midwestern aid societies to coordinate their efforts for the soldiers. She and friend **Mary A. Livermore** led the way in organizing the **U.S. Sanitary Commission** in the Midwest, and in January 1862 Hoge was appointed the Commission's Chicago, Illinois, agent.

Hoge worked tirelessly at speaking engagements to raise supplies and money for the commission and did a remarkable job improving the hospitals under her supervision. She also organized the first **Sanitary fair** in October 1863 and raised more than $75,000. However, Hoge had a detached and cold personality that prevented her from becoming as beloved as other Sanitary Commission agents.

After the war, Hoge published her memoirs, *The Boys in Blue; or, Heroes of the "rank and file,"* one of the first female wartime memoirs. She spent her postwar life as president of the Women's Board of Foreign Missions and working as a Chicago social worker.

HOGG, JOSEPH LEWIS (1806–1862) CSA. A native of **Georgia**, Hogg grew up in **Alabama** and became a prosperous planter, lawyer, militiaman, and politician before moving to **Texas** in 1839. A supporter of **Sam Houston**, he became active in Texas politics and was elected to the Texas assembly in 1843. In 1845, Hogg also attended the convention that led to the annexation of Texas by the United States. Afterward, he was elected to the state senate, but he resigned his seat when the **Mexican War** began and joined a Texas **regiment** as a private. Hogg was defeated in an election for colonel, but he remained with the regiment as a private and fought at Monterrey. After the war, he practiced law, engaged in banking, and served in the state senate.

As a member of the 1861 secession convention, Hogg voted for **secession** but then was defeated in a bid for the **Confederate Congress**. He was appointed colonel of state troops in early 1861 and served on recruiting duty. In February 1862, Hogg was promoted to brigadier general and was given command of a mixed **brigade** of infantry, cavalry, and **artillery**. Sent to Corinth, Mississippi, he fell ill with dysentery and died in May 1862. It was claimed that Hogg's service as a Confederate general was so brief that he never donned a Confederate **uniform**. His son, James Stephen Hogg, served as Texas governor in the 1890s.

HOKE, ROBERT FREDERICK (1837–1912) CSA. A native of **North Carolina**, Hoke attended the Kentucky Military Institute before becoming manager of his family's ironworks and cotton mill. When his native state seceded, he left his business interests and entered Confederate service as a lieutenant in the 1st North Carolina.

Hoke was praised for his actions at **Big Bethel** and in September 1861 was appointed major of the 33rd North Carolina. This was followed in January 1862 with a promotion to lieutenant colonel. As part of **Lawrence Branch's** brigade, Hoke fought at **New Bern**, **North Carolina**, where he took command of the **regiment** when his colonel was captured. He then led the regiment through the **Seven Days**, **Second Manassas**, and **Antietam Campaigns** with the **Army of Northern Virginia**. Having been praised in all of his actions, Hoke was promoted to colonel of the 21st North Carolina after **Antietam**. At **Fredericksburg** he won further praise when he assumed temporary command of **Isaac Trimble's** brigade and led a counterattack that sealed a breakthrough on **A. P. Hill's** front.

Promoted to brigadier general in April 1863, Hoke was given permanent command of the **brigade**. After being wounded at **Second Fredericksburg** during the **Chancellorsville Campaign**, he returned to North Carolina and led an assault in April 1864 that captured **Plymouth** and nearly 3,000 Union **prisoners**. This action won Hoke the **Thanks of Congress** and a promotion to major general that same month. His **division** was sent to **Virginia**, where it saw heavy combat at **Second Drewry's Bluff** in May 1864 and at **Cold Harbor** in June. After participating in the **Petersburg Campaign**, Hoke returned to North Carolina and fought at **Fort Fisher**. His last battle was at **Bentonville**, where he commanded **Braxton Bragg's** division during the **Carolinas Campaign**.

After the war, Hoke served as a director of the North Carolina Railroad Company.

HOLDEN, WILLIAM WOODS (1818–1892) CSA. *See* PEACE SOCIETIES, CONFEDERATE.

HOLLINS, GEORGE NICHOLS (1799–1878) CSA. A native of **Maryland**, Hollins joined the **U.S. Navy** as a midshipman at age 14 and served against the Barbary Pirates and in the War of 1812 (in which he was captured). He remained in the navy and rose to the rank of captain and command of the USS *Susquehanna* by the time of the Civil War.

Hollins resigned his commission when hostilities began, but the navy rejected his resignation and ordered his arrest. Avoiding capture, he made his way to Montgomery, Alabama, and advised the Confederacy in organizing a **Confederate navy**. Appointed a commander in June 1861, Hollins became famous nine days later when, disguised as a woman, he boarded and captured the Chesapeake Bay steamer *St. Nicholas*. Converted into a

commerce raider under Hollins's command, the ship captured three Union vessels in 11 days. Placed in command of the **New Orleans, Louisiana**, Naval Station in July, Hollins organized a ragtag fleet of Mississippi River gunboats and drove off the Union force **blockading** the river.

In October, Hollins was promoted to flag officer and was put in command of defenses on the upper Mississippi River. There, he fought at **New Madrid and Island No. 10** and **Memphis**. In the spring of 1862, Hollins asked permission to take his fleet downriver to New Orleans to defend the city against **David Farragut**. Secretary of the Navy **Stephen Mallory** refused, believing the main threat to New Orleans came from upstream. Disagreeing with his superior, Hollins left his fleet at Memphis, Tennessee, and proceeded to New Orleans against orders. Mallory then demoted him to captain and ordered him to **Richmond, Virginia**, thus depriving New Orleans of a competent naval officer at the moment of crisis. Hollins served on various courts and boards for the rest of the war and then returned to civilian life in Maryland.

HOLLY SPRINGS, MISSISSIPPI, RAID ON (DECEMBER 20, 1862). During **U. S. Grant's Overland Vicksburg Campaign** in December 1862, the Federals established a large supply depot at Holly Springs as they pushed through north-central **Mississippi**. Confederate Lt. Gen. **John C. Pemberton** requested help from **Braxton Bragg** in **Tennessee** to stop the invasion. Bragg dispatched **Nathan Bedford Forrest's** cavalry on a raid into western Tennessee to disrupt the Union supply line, while Pemberton's cavalry under Maj. Gen. **Earl Van Dorn** undertook a similar raid in northern Mississippi.

With 3,500 men, Van Dorn left Grenada, Mississippi, on December 17 and rode east of Grant's position until he was behind the Union line and then turned west toward Holly Springs. Grant was not alerted to the presence of the raiders until December 19 and then warned the garrison at Holly Springs to be vigilant. That night, Van Dorn divided his column east of town and attacked next morning from three directions. The surprise was complete despite Grant's warning, and 1,500 **prisoners** (mostly members of Col. Robert C. Murphy's 8th Wisconsin) and a huge amount of supplies fell into Van Dorn's hands. The Confederates **paroled** the prisoners and burned a hospital and approximately $1.5-million worth of supplies. Van Dorn then rode north and west before circling back and safely reaching Grenada on December 28.

The raid destroyed Grant's most important supply base and forced him withdraw to Tennessee on December 21. Grant's first attempt to capture

Vicksburg, Mississippi, was over, and Murphy was cashiered from the service for his poor performance at Holly Springs.

HOLMES, THEOPHILUS HUNTER (1804–1880) CSA. A native of **North Carolina**, Holmes graduated near the bottom of the 1829 **West Point** class. He then served on the frontier and in the **Seminole** and **Mexican Wars**, winning **brevets** in both conflicts. During the **secession** crisis, Holmes was on recruitment duty in **New York** and was ordered to dispatch 200 men on the *Star of the West* to reinforce **Fort Sumter**. After the fort fell in April 1861, he resigned his major's commission and in June entered Confederate service as a brigadier general.

After service (but no combat) at **First Manassas**, Holmes was promoted to major general in October. He commanded the Aquia District in the **Department of Northern Virginia** until March 1862, when he was sent to command the **Department of North Carolina**. In late June, Homes was sent back to Virginia and led an **Army of Northern Virginia division** with mediocre skill during the **Seven Days Campaign**. The nearly deaf Holmes uttered one of the war's more ludicrous sayings at the **Battle of Malvern Hill** when behind the lines he cocked his head and declared, "I thought I heard firing" (Davis, ed., *The Confederate General*, vol. 3, p. 116).

In July 1862, Holmes replaced **Thomas C. Hindman** in command of the **Trans-Mississippi Department**, but he proved to be a poor choice. Difficult to get along with, he took a provincial view of the war and was reluctant to take any measures to help areas outside of his jurisdiction. After being promoted to lieutenant general in October, Holmes successfully resisted efforts to have him send men from his **department** to reinforce **Mississippi** during the **Vicksburg Campaign**. Despite keeping his forces intact, Holmes's department still suffered defeat at **Prairie Grove, Arkansas**, in December and the loss of **Arkansas Post** in January 1863. His inability to defend the department hurt the morale of soldiers and civilians alike, but he was kept in command largely because he had a close friendship with **Jefferson Davis**.

Holmes recognized that he was unable to defend his department and had asked to be relieved in October 1862, but steps were not taken to do so until January 1863. At that time **Texas** and western **Louisiana** were put in a new department under **Edmund Kirby Smith**, and Holmes's responsibility was cut back. In February, Kirby Smith's command was expanded to include all of the Trans-Mississippi, and Holmes was reduced to commanding the District of Arkansas. Holmes's only major combat came in July 1863 when he unsuccessfully attacked **Helena, Arkansas**. Illness forced him to temporarily relinquish command during the late summer of 1863, when **Little Rock, Arkansas**, was seized by the enemy. By 1864, Holmes realized that numerous influential officers and politicians were pressuring Davis to remove him from command. He resigned his position in March rather than being dismissed and ended the war commanding reserve troops in North Carolina.

After the war, Holmes farmed in North Carolina.

HOLT, JOSEPH (1807-1894) USA. A native of **Kentucky**, Holt attended St. Joseph's and Centre Colleges before opening a law practice. He later moved to **Mississippi** and prospered as a lawyer before returning to Kentucky. There, Holt became a newspaper editor, popular speaker, and a formidable force in **Democratic** politics. In President **James Buchanan's** administration, he served as commissioner of patents, postmaster general, and secretary of war. Although Holt had lived in Mississippi and previously held strong Southern beliefs, he remained loyal to the Union when civil war came.

Abraham Lincoln appointed Holt colonel and the Union **army's** judge advocate general in September 1862. In this position, he arrested civilians suspected of disloyal activity without writs of **habeas corpus**. In June 1864, Holt was promoted to brigadier general in the regular army and was appointed head of the newly created Bureau of Military Justice. He tried such civilians as **Clement L. Vallandigham** before military tribunals; supervised the trials of **Fitz John Porter** and **Henry Wirz**; and became famous as the government prosecutor of **Lincoln's assassination** conspirators. Holt's zeal won him the admiration of the **Radical Republicans**, but it was discovered later that many witnesses perjured themselves and that Holt may sometimes have suppressed evidence. Controversy also emerged over the execution of **Mary Surratt**. Holt carried the verdicts to President **Andrew Johnson**, including the commission's recommendation that Johnson commute Surratt's sentence. Johnson claimed he never saw the recommendation, while Holt maintained that he did.

Holt remained judge advocate general until his retirement from the **U.S. Army** in December 1875.

HOLTZCLAW, JAMES THADEUS (1833-1893) CSA. A native of **Georgia**, Holtzclaw grew up in **Alabama** and attended the East Alabama Institute. He declined an appointment to **West Point** in 1853 and became a lawyer, instead.

A lieutenant in the state militia, Holtzclaw participated in the capture of the **Pensacola, Florida**, Navy Yard in 1861 and was appointed major of the 18th Alabama in August. While stationed in Mobile, Alabama, in

December, he was promoted to lieutenant colonel. At **Shiloh**, Holtzclaw was badly wounded in the right lung, but he miraculously survived and rejoined the **regiment** after it was sent back to Mobile. He was promoted to colonel in May 1862 and, after serving on garrison duty in Alabama, accompanied his **brigade** to the **Army of Tennessee** to participate in the **Tullahoma Campaign.** At **Chickamauga**, Holtzclaw's regiment suffered very heavy casualties, and he was forced to relinquish command after being injured when thrown from his horse. When brigade commander **Henry D. Clayton** was wounded in the battle, Holtzclaw assumed command and led the brigade in the **Battles of Lookout Mountain** and **Missionary Ridge** during the **Chattanooga Campaign.** After the retreat from Chattanooga, he saw further combat when the brigade helped repel a Union **reconnaissance** at **Tunnel Hill** in February 1864.

After fighting through much of the **Atlanta Campaign**, Holtzclaw was promoted to brigadier general in July 1864 and was given command of Clayton's brigade after Clayton was promoted to a **division** command. He apparently was away from his brigade, perhaps on sick leave, during the battles of **Atlanta** and **Jonesboro** but led it at **Ezra Church.** During the 1864 **Franklin and Nashville Campaign**, the brigade did not arrive in time to participate in the Battle of Franklin, but it did see combat on the second day at Nashville and sometimes served as the **army's** rear guard during the retreat. In January 1865, Holtzclaw's brigade was detached to Mobile and served at **Fort Blakely** and **Spanish Fort.** When Union forces attacked Spanish Fort in April, his brigade fought well until the fort was evacuated. Holtzclaw and his men then surrendered with the rest of the **department** the following month.

After the war, Holtzclaw resumed his Alabama law practice and late in life briefly served on the state **railroad** commission.

HOMER, WINSLOW (1836–1910) USA. A native of **Massachusetts**, Homer was apprenticed to a lithographer as a young man and in 1859 began studying at New York's National Academy of Design. He helped pay his expenses by working as an illustrator for *Harper's Weekly.* Beginning in 1861, Homer became a well-known illustrator at *Harper's* after sketching **Abraham Lincoln's** first inauguration and the **Army of the Potomac** encamped around **Washington, D.C.** In 1862, the magazine sent him to cover the **Peninsula Campaign** as a special agent. Afterward, Homer set up his own office in New York City and until war's end frequently sketched the **army** in the field. Although Homer illustrated camp scenes more often than battlefields, *Harper's* frequently used his works, and in 1864 he was elected an associate to the National Academy.

Homer continued to supply illustrations to the magazine after the war but began to concentrate more on paintings. One 1865 work entitled *Prisoners at the Front* became a classic. Throughout the postwar years, Homer's paintings of land- and seascapes made him one the country's most famous painters.

HOMESTEAD ACT OF 1862. Homesteading, or the practice of gaining free land from the government by living on it and making improvements over a certain number of years, was one of the many issues that divided the North and South before the Civil War. Northerners supported it and made it an important part of their political ideology, as seen in the **Free-Soil Party**. Southerners feared homesteading because it could lead to Northerners populating the western territories and installing antislavery governments. When these territories were admitted to the Union, it would upset the precarious balance of power between free and slave states. As a result, Southerners were able to block homesteading legislation until 1860, when a weak bill was passed but vetoed by President **James Buchanan**.

In the **election of 1860**, **Abraham Lincoln** adopted the homesteading platform and in May 1862 had the **U.S. Congress** pass the Homestead Act after the Southern states seceded. Going into effect in January 1863, the bill allowed any citizen over 21, or any veteran who had served two weeks, or any citizen under 21 who headed a household, to claim 160 acres. The applicant had to pay a $10 fee, live on the land for five years, and make improvements to receive a title to the property. Widely popular in the North, the act led to 1,261,000 acres being homesteaded by mid-1864.

HONEY HILL, SOUTH CAROLINA, BATTLE OF (NOVEMBER 30, 1864). In late November 1864, **William T. Sherman** was advancing on **Savannah, Georgia**, during his **March to the Sea**. To prevent Confederate reinforcements from reaching the city, Maj. Gen. **John G. Foster** took 5,500 men by boat on the Broad River from Hilton Head, South Carolina, to Boyd's Neck. From this position 35 miles northeast of Savannah, Foster could cut the **railroad** from **Charleston** and prevent enemy reinforcements from reaching Savannah.

Foster's command began arriving at Boyd's Neck on November 29. Brigadier General **John P. Hatch** assumed command of the expedition and took an infantry **brigade**, some sailors, and an **artillery** battery forward and reached Grahamville, South Carolina, the next morning. An additional brigade reached him later that morning. At Grahamville, Hatch found about 1,400 Georgia militia under Maj. Gen. **Gustavus W. Smith**, who had responded to **William J. Hardee's** plea for help, even though they were not required to fight outside their state. Hardee asked Smith to hold Grahamville long enough for him to bring in additional reinforcements.

On the morning of November 30, Hatch advanced and pushed the enemy back three miles to a line of earthworks on a rise known as Honey Hill. Rugged terrain and earthworks prevented him from flanking the position, so he launched a **frontal attack**. Three times the Federals attacked, but the Confederate artillery beat them back. Learning that Hardee was bringing up more troops, Hatch finally broke off the engagement and retired to the Broad River. He lost 746 men in the battle, while Smith counted only 50 casualties.

HONEY SPRINGS, INDIAN TERRITORY, BATTLE OF (JULY 17, 1863). In the summer of 1863, Union Brig. Gen. **James G. Blunt** and Confederate Brig. Gen. **Douglas H. Cooper** opposed each other in **Indian Territory**. On the night of July 15, Blunt advanced 3,000 men— mostly **Indians** and **black troops**—across the Arkansas River to strike south toward Cooper's 5,000 men near Elk Creek. When contact was made at mid-morning on July 17, Cooper's mostly Indian soldiers were hampered by poor powder and weapons. Still, they managed to hold off Blunt until rain made the Confederate's poor ammunition worthless. Discovering that his left flank was threatened, Cooper began an orderly withdrawal to find dry ammunition, but two of his **regiments** misunderstood the orders and withdrew completely. When Blunt threatened to turn his flank at an Elk Creek crossing, Cooper's orderly withdrawal broke down. Many of his men fled, but Cooper fought an effective rear guard action with some of his Choctaw Indians and forced Blunt to withdraw.

Honey Springs, or Elk Creek, as it sometimes is called, was the decisive battle in Indian Territory. Cooper's defeat allowed the Union to control most of the territory, and shortly afterward, some 15,000 pro-Confederate civilians fled the area and sought protection with Cooper south of the Red River. In terms of casualties, the battle was insignificant. Blunt lost only 60 men, mostly **prisoners**, while Cooper's casualties are unknown.

HOOD, JOHN BELL (1831–1879) CSA. A native of **Kentucky**, Hood came from a distinguished family and received an appointment to **West Point** by a congressman uncle. He graduated at the bottom of his 1853 class and was assigned to the infantry in **California**. Transferring to the 2nd U.S. Cavalry in 1855, Hood won some distinction fighting **Indians** in **Texas**, but he resigned his lieutenant's commission in April 1861 to join the Confederacy.

Hood entered Confederate service in the spring of 1861 as a lieutenant of cavalry, but in October he was appointed colonel of the 4th Texas. After being promoted to brigadier general in March 1862, he was placed in command of **Hood's Texas Brigade** in the **Army of Northern Virginia**. As a **brigade** commander, the six foot, two inch Hood had no equal. Ironically, his success came largely from launching vicious **frontal attacks**—the very thing that led to his downfall as an **army** commander.

Hood first earned fame when he broke through the Union lines at **Gaines' Mill** during the **Seven Days Campaign**. He then assumed a **division** command when his superior was forced on sick leave. Hood led the division with great skill at **Second Manassas**, but **Nathan G. Evans** placed him under arrest in a dispute over some captured ambulances. **Robert E. Lee** released him from arrest just before the **Battle of Antietam**, and his outstanding service there earned him a promotion to major general in October 1862.

Taking a division in **James Longstreet's** I Corps, Hood was badly wounded in his left arm on the second day at **Gettysburg** and lost the use of the limb. He recovered in time to accompany Longstreet to **Chickamauga**, where he took command of the **corps** while Longstreet directed one of the Confederate wings. In the battle, Hood was so badly wounded in the right leg that it was amputated at the hip. He recuperated in **Richmond, Virginia**, and became engaged to the well-known South Carolinian Sally Buchanan Campbell Preston.

Hood was promoted to lieutenant general in February 1864 and was given command of a corps in the **Army of Tennessee**. His crippling wounds did not deter him; he simply had himself tied to his horse. During the **Atlanta Campaign**, Hood did not perform up to his reputation, and it seemed that either his wounds had taken the fire out of him, or he simply did not have the talent for a large command. He also became a bitter critic of **Joseph E. Johnston's** defensive **strategy** and often privately criticized Johnston, perhaps trying to win command of the army for himself. If so, it worked, for **Jefferson Davis** appointed Hood to replace Johnston in July 1864 and gave him the temporary rank of general.

Hood was the last and youngest Confederate full general, but he proved unfit for the task. Lee had advised Davis earlier that while Hood was an aggressive fighter, he did not have the other necessary skills needed to command an army. Hood quickly took the offensive and nearly wrecked his army by making unsuccessful frontal attacks at **Peachtree Creek, Atlanta, Ezra Church**, and **Jonesboro**. With his strength dwindling, he was unable to prevent **William T. Sherman** from moving south and cutting his last supply lines into Atlanta. After evacuating the city in

September 1864, Hood moved north to cut Sherman's supply line and force him to retreat. When Sherman refused to chase him for long, Hood made plans to invade **Tennessee** and perhaps force Sherman to evacuate **Georgia**. Poor planning and coordination caused delays for weeks in northern **Alabama**, but he finally began the **Franklin and Nashville Campaign** in November 1864.

On the night of November 29, Hood seemingly had a Union force under **John Schofield** trapped at Spring Hill, Tennessee, but the enemy escaped in what became known as the Spring Hill incident. It has been debated ever since whether Hood's confusing orders and physical and mental condition (perhaps even a drug-induced stupor caused by painkillers) were to blame for the missed opportunity, or his subordinates simply let him down. Furious over the blunder, he rashly ordered a massive frontal attack against Schofield at Franklin the next day and suffered a defeat. Afterward, Hood followed the enemy to Nashville and camped outside the city, unable to inflict any damage on them and unwilling to withdraw. In December, **George H. Thomas** launched a heavy attack that crushed Hood and sent him reeling back to northern **Mississippi**. The defeat at Nashville virtually annihilated the Army of Tennessee, and Hood resigned his temporary rank of general in January 1865. His engagement to Preston also was broken off, and Hood never again held a field command.

After the war, Hood married, became prosperous in insurance and business in **New Orleans, Louisiana**,and wrote his memoirs, *Advance and Retreat* (which were published posthumously). He died in an 1879 yellow fever epidemic, along with his wife and eldest child. Hood was one of several Civil War generals who, while excellent brigade and division commanders, simply were promoted beyond their ability.

HOOD'S TENNESSEE INVASION OF 1864. *See* FRANKLIN AND NASHVILLE, TENNESSEE, CAMPAIGN AND BATTLES OF.

HOOD'S TEXAS BRIGADE. In November 1861, the **Texas** Confederate volunteers in **Virginia** were formed into the Texas Brigade under Col. **Lewis T. Wigfall**. The **brigade** originally consisted of the 1st, 4th, and 5th Texas Infantry and the 18th Georgia. When Wigfall was elected to the Senate, **John Bell Hood** was promoted to brigadier general in March 1862 and took command of the brigade. Although Hood commanded the unit for less than six months, it forever carried his name.

The Texans proved to be a reckless lot who did not conform well to military **discipline**. However, they had absolute loyalty to Hood and were one of the finest brigades in the **Army of Northern Virginia**. The brigade first gained recognition in May 1862 when it attacked and drove back a Union force at **Eltham's Landing** during the **Peninsula Campaign**. After the **Battle of Seven Pines**, the **Hampton Legion** infantry **companies** temporarily were assigned to the brigade. The following month, while in **W. H. C. Whiting's** division, the brigade won more acclaim when it successfully broke through the Union lines at **Gaines' Mill** after several other Confederate assaults had failed.

After the **Seven Days Campaign**, Hood was elevated to **division** command. The 18th Georgia's Col. **William Tatum Wofford** took temporary command of the brigade and led it through the **Second Manassas** and **Antietam Campaigns**. At Antietam, the Texans counterattacked the same **New York** troops they had faced at Gaines' Mill and captured their cannons but lost two-thirds of the brigade's members. In October 1862, the Hampton Legion companies and the 18th Georgia were replaced by the 3rd Arkansas, which remained with the brigade for the rest of the war. Colonel **Jerome B. Robertson**, of the 5th Texas, was promoted to brigadier general in November 1862 and assumed permanent brigade command. At **Gettysburg**, Robertson was wounded and Col. Phillip A. Work assumed temporary command before Robertson returned to duty.

The Texans went west with **James Longstreet's corps** in the fall of 1863 and fought at **Chickamauga** and **Wauhatchie**. Longstreet and division commander **Micah Jenkins** became dissatisfied with Robertson, and Longstreet temporarily relieved him of command just before the **Knoxville Campaign** and then had him court-martialed in January 1864. Brigadier General **John Gregg**, a Texan who had been serving in the western theater, replaced Robertson. Returning to Virginia, the Texans again earned fame at the **Wilderness** when they refused to launch a counterattack to seal a Union breakthrough until **Robert E. Lee** removed himself from the front. The attack was successful, but it cost the brigade more than 400 men out of 711 engaged. After the **Overland Campaign**, the brigade was engaged in the **Petersburg Campaign**, and in October 1864 Gregg was killed in fighting along the **Darbytown Road**. He temporarily was replaced by Col. Clinton M. Winkler until Col. Fredrick S. Bass recovered from wounds and was able to take charge. When the brigade's senior colonel, Robert Powell, was **exchanged** from **prison**, he took brigade command until war's end.

The brigade fought in 38 engagements and suffered very heavy casualties. In less than three months from Gaines' Mill to Antietam, it lost 1,780 men, and at Gettysburg the 1st Texas lost more than 82 percent of its men—reportedly the highest percentage loss of any Confederate unit in one day of battle.

HOOKER, JOSEPH "FIGHTING JOE" (1814–1879) USA. A native of **Massachusetts**, Hooker attended Hopkins Academy and then graduated from **West Point** in 1837. After serving in the **Seminole Wars** and as West Point's adjutant, he was recognized as a gallant officer in the **Mexican War**. Fighting under both Zachary Taylor and **Winfield Scott**, Hooker won three **brevets** for gallantry, but he then lost Scott's support when he testified in favor of **Gideon Pillow**, an officer Scott charged with disloyalty. Hooker resigned from the **U.S. Army** in 1853 and became a **California** farmer. He also served as a colonel in the state militia, and when civil war erupted he offered his services to the Union.

Perhaps because of Scott's influence, Hooker's offer at first was rejected. After personally witnessing the defeat at **First Manassas**, he wrote a letter to **Abraham Lincoln** criticizing the way the battle had been fought, while at the same time bragging about his own abilities. Lincoln must have been impressed, for in August 1861, Hooker was appointed brigadier general of volunteers and was assigned to the **Washington, D.C.**, defenses. Joining **George B. McClellan's Army of the Potomac**, he commanded a **division** in the **Peninsula Campaign** and was praised for his hard fighting at **Williamsburg**, where a horse was killed under him. A typographical error in a newspaper headline describing the fighting forever gave Hooker the nom de guerre "Fighting Joe Hooker."

Appointed major general of volunteers in May 1862, Hooker fought well through the **Seven Days** and **Second Manassas Campaigns**. At **Antietam**, he commanded the I Corps and began the battle by attacking **Stonewall Jackson's** men in the famous cornfield. Hooker was wounded in the foot during the battle, but he earned a promotion to brigadier general in the regular **army**. Returning to duty in time for the **Battle of Fredericksburg**, he was one of several officers who afterward bitterly criticized **Ambrose Burnside**. Hooker even sent Lincoln a letter advising that perhaps it was time for a military dictator to seize control of the Union. Despite the letter, Lincoln named Hooker as Burnside's replacement in January 1863.

Hooker was an egotistical, opinionated, hard-drinking, and immoral officer whose headquarters was said to resemble a brothel, but Lincoln was willing to overlook his faults to make use of his proven fighting capabilities. It became widely believed that the term *hookers*, meaning prostitutes, originated with Hooker, but the word actually was used before he became famous. He did, however, make it popular when he segregated Washington's prostitutes into one district that became referred to as "Hooker's Division." Despite his flaws, Hooker's tenure as army commander began with promise. He restored morale to the Army of the Potomac by supplying much-needed equipment, having each corps adopt **corps badges**, reorganizing the troops by eliminating some oversized units, and placing the cavalry into one **corps**. By the spring of 1863, the army contained 134,000 men and was in top condition.

On May 1, 1863, Hooker began the **Chancellorsville Campaign**. After sending **George Stoneman's** cavalry on a raid toward **Richmond, Virginia**, he left part of his army at Fredericksburg to occupy the Confederate **Army of Northern Virginia**. Hooker then took most of his men upstream to cross the Rappahannock River and move into **Robert E. Lee's** rear. The bold maneuver at first was successful, and Hooker boasted it was not a question of whether, but simply when, he would reach Richmond. When Lee moved to intercept him and the two armies made contact, Hooker lost his nerve and took up a defensive position around Chancellorsville. This allowed Lee time to shift reinforcements to the area and launch a devastating flank attack with Stonewall Jackson's corps. After fierce fighting, Hooker finally withdrew across the river. His lack of aggressiveness in the campaign puzzled many officers. Some attributed it to his swearing off liquor for the duration of the campaign, but more likely it was from being stunned by a shell that exploded near his head at headquarters on the critical second day of battle.

When Lee began the **Gettysburg Campaign** in June 1863, Hooker demanded that the garrison at **Harpers Ferry, West Virginia**, be evacuated and sent to him as reinforcements. When the War Department refused, he submitted his resignation. To Hooker's surprise, Lincoln accepted the resignation on June 28 and put **George G. Meade** in command of the army. However, in January 1864, Hooker received the **Thanks of Congress** for his actions at the beginning of the Gettysburg Campaign.

In September 1863, Hooker was put in command of the XI and XII Corps, which were sent west to reinforce Chattanooga, Tennessee. His old fighting spirit returned, and he successfully captured **Lookout Mountain** in November during the **Chattanooga Campaign**, earning a brevet of major general in the regular army. Hooker's two corps were consolidated into the **Army of the Cumberland's** XX Corps for the **Atlanta Campaign**. Again he served well and expected to be named commander of the **Army of the Tennessee** after **James B. McPherson** was killed at the **Battle of Atlanta**. Instead, **William T. Sherman** appointed **Oliver O. Howard**. Hooker asked to be relieved, and his request was honored on July 28, 1864. In October 1864, he was put in command of the **Northern Department**, a position he kept until war's end.

Hooker retired from the army in October 1868 after suffering a stroke. Like many other officers on both sides of the Civil War, he was an excellent brigade, division, and corps commander but seems not to have had the ability to lead an army successfully.

HOOVER'S GAP, TENNESSEE, BATTLE OF (JUNE 24–26, 1863). In June 1863, Maj. Gen. **William S. Rosecrans** began his **Tullahoma Campaign** to force **Braxton Bragg's Army of Tennessee** out of Middle Tennessee and to prevent him from reinforcing **Vicksburg, Mississippi**. While **feinting** against Shelbyville, Rosecrans massed his **Army of the Cumberland** against the mountain gaps that anchored Bragg's right flank. **Alexander M. McCook** moved against Liberty Gap, Maj. Gen. **George H. Thomas** attacked Hoover's Gap, and on the far Union left, **Thomas L. Crittenden** was to advance through Bradyville.

On June 24, Col. John T. Wilder's mounted infantry led Thomas's advance and occupied Hoover's Gap in a driving rain. Wilder managed to hold his position against several Confederate counterattacks by **Alexander P. Stewart's division**, putting to good use the new **Spencer rifles** that he had supplied his men. Thomas's main infantry force arrived the next day, and fighting at the gap continued until Bragg realized his flank was about to be turned and withdrew on June 26. Rosecrans's brilliant maneuver forced the Confederates out of Middle Tennessee and back to Chattanooga, Tennessee. In the fight at Hoover's Gap, Thomas lost 583 men. Confederate losses are unknown.

"HORNETS' NEST" AT BATTLE OF SHILOH, TENNESSEE (APRIL 6, 1862). *See* SHILOH, TENNESSEE, CAMPAIGN AND BATTLE OF.

HORS DE COMBAT. In the Civil War, a wounded man was sometimes said to have been rendered *hors de combat* (or-duh-kohm-BAH). A French term, it means "out of combat."

HORSE ARTILLERY. Horse artillery was lighter and more mobile than field **artillery**. While all field artillery was horse-drawn, horse artillery usually was a relatively small-bore cannon—often a 6-pounder—that was used by cavalry.

HORSESHOE RIDGE AT BATTLE OF CHICKAMAUGA, GEORGIA (SEPTEMBER 20, 1863). *See* SNODGRASS HILL AT BATTLE OF CHICKAMAUGA, GEORGIA.

HOT SHOT. This **artillery** projectile was used to set ships and fortifications on fire. It was a solid iron ball that was heated red-hot in a furnace.

Tongs were used to load it into the gun tube, with a wet wadding separating the shot from the gunpowder. It was used effectively in the Confederate bombardment of **Fort Sumter**.

HOTCHKISS, JEDEDIAH (1828–1899) CSA. A native of **New York**, Hotchkiss moved to **Virginia** to teach and founded the Loch Willow Academy with his brother. A self-taught cartographer, he closed the school when war broke out in 1861 and volunteered to serve as a cartographer for Confederate Brig. Gen. **Robert S. Garnett** in western Virginia. Thus began the career of the most famous topographical **engineer** of the war. Hotchkiss served the entire war as a hired civilian, although many sources incorrectly identify him as an officer.

After serving under **Robert E. Lee** at **Rich Mountain**, Hotchkiss joined **Stonewall Jackson's** staff in March 1862 as chief topographical engineer for the **Valley District**. His knowledge of the terrain and detailed maps played a key role in all of Jackson's campaigns from the **Shenandoah Valley** to **Chancellorsville**. Hotchkiss also often positioned troops in battle and at Chancellorsville found the road network that allowed Jackson to make his celebrated flank attack.

After Jackson's death, Hotchkiss continued serving the **Army of Northern Virginia's** II Corps under **Richard S. Ewell** and **Jubal A. Early**, but he often was on detached duty with Lee's headquarters. He played a major role at **Cedar Creek** during **Philip Sheridan's 1864 Shenandoah Valley Campaign** when his detailed knowledge of the terrain allowed Early to make his surprise attack on the Union camps. At war's end, Hotchkiss was not with the **army** when it surrendered at **Appomattox**, so he surrendered himself. He briefly was placed under arrest, but **U. S. Grant** released him and returned his map collection.

Grant paid Hotchkiss for the use of his maps in his own after-action reports, and many of Hotchkiss's maps were included in the atlas accompanying *The War of the Rebellion: A Compilation of the Official Records of the Union and Confederate Armies* (more than half of the Confederate maps in the atlas are his). His wartime diary also has been published under the title *Make Me a Map of the Valley*. After the war, Hotchkiss taught for a while and wrote frequently about the war.

HOTCHKISS PROJECTILE. This was an **artillery** shell designed for use in **rifled** cannons. The shell had a lead ring around its base, with a cast-iron cup on the bottom. When the cannon fired, the blast pushed the iron cup into the lead, which expanded and gripped the rifling in the gun tube, sending the shell spinning out the tube for greater range and accuracy. Both sides used the projectile during the war.

HOTZE, HENRY (1833–1887) CSA. A native of Switzerland, Hotze (HOT-suh) immigrated to the United States as a young man and began working for the *Mobile* (Alabama) *Register* in 1855 after becoming a naturalized citizen. His diplomatic manners and excellent work at the *Register* led to his being appointed secretary and chargé d'affaires of the U.S. legation in Brussels, Belgium, in 1858–59.

When the Civil War began, Hotze supported his adopted Southern homeland and entered Confederate service as a private in the 3rd Alabama. He was placed on detached service with the adjutant general's office in May 1861 and was sent on a mission to Great Britain. Upon his return, Hotze left the **army** in November to become a commercial agent for the Confederate State Department. He was ordered back to London in January 1862 to spread propaganda to help win European recognition for the Confederacy. Hotze became friends with many high-ranking officials, wrote speeches for pro-Confederate Parliament members and articles for London newspapers, and circulated various other Confederate material. In May 1862, he founded his own weekly journal, the *Index*, and published it until August 1865. Although it had a small circulation of only 2,250, the paper became very influential and was read by many government officials.

Through his unassuming manner and the help of Confederate envoy **James Mason**, Hotze became the most effective and well-known Confederate propagandist in Europe. His superiors thought so highly of his work that his budget was increased from $750 to $30,000 by war's end. Hotze, however, also was a realist and by 1864 knew the Confederacy had little chance of success. In addition, the British became increasingly hostile to **slavery** despite Hotze's best efforts to defend the institution. As a result, his influence began to wane toward war's end.

When hostilities ended, Hotze moved back to Switzerland.

HOUSATONIC*, USS.** Launched at the Boston, Massachusetts, Navy Yard in November 1861, the *Housatonic* was a screw-driven, 207-foot sloop that displaced 1,240 tons. Armed with an assortment of **Parrott rifles**, **Dahlgrens**, smoothbores, and **howitzers**, it joined the **South Atlantic Blockading Squadron** off **Charleston**, **South Carolina**, in September 1862. There it helped **blockade** the city, chased **blockade runners**, and occasionally landed small parties to raid Confederate coastal defenses. On the night of February 17, 1864, the *Housatonic* was **torpedoed** by the Confederate **submarine *H. L. Hunley. Struck on the starboard side, it sank quickly in shallow water with the loss of five crewmen. The first warship ever sunk by a submarine, the *Housatonic* was partly salvaged after the war.

HOUSTON, SAM (1793–1863) USA. A native of **Virginia**, Houston grew up in **Tennessee**, where he became intimate with the Cherokee **Indians**. He entered the **U.S. Army** in 1813 as an ensign and served until 1818, fighting with Andrew Jackson in the Creek Indian War and the War of 1812. After becoming a lawyer, Houston embarked on a Tennessee political career that included service as Nashville's district attorney, a congressman from 1823 to 1827, and governor from 1827 to 1829.

Moving to **Texas**, Houston commanded the Texas revolutionary **army** that won independence from Mexico at the 1836 Battle of San Jacinto. He then was elected the Republic's first president in 1836 and served two terms. Houston also was elected to the legislative assembly, and when Texas was annexed by the United States, he served as a U.S. senator from 1846 to 1859. His strong Unionism, however, hurt him politically and caused him to lose support in the legislature. Still, Houston remained popular with the people and surprised his enemies by being elected governor in 1859.

Houston vigorously opposed **secession** but was forced by law to grant the legislature the right to hold a secession convention. When secession passed on February 1, 1861, Houston tried to prevent Texas from joining the Confederacy by arguing that Texas had reverted to an independent republic. This idea was popular with some people, but the majority ignored him, and Texas joined the fledgling Confederate nation. It soon was required that all state officials take an **oath of allegiance** to the Confederacy. Houston attended the statehouse session but three times refused to answer when his name was called. His uncompromising stand caused his opponents to declare that the governor's office was vacant, and they appointed the lieutenant governor to take his place. Houston resigned in March 1862 and refused an offer by **Abraham Lincoln** to send troops to keep him in office. Instead, he retired to his farm and died two years later.

HOVEY, ALVIN PETERSON (1821–1891) USA. A native of **Indiana**, Hovey (HUV-ee) was a distant cousin of Union Brig. Gen. **Charles E. Hovey**. He served as an apprenticed brick mason in his youth before becoming a schoolteacher. Hovey then became a lawyer and during the **Mexican War** served as a lieutenant in a local volunteer **company** that was never called to service. After serving in the state's constitutional convention, he became a circuit judge and in 1854 became the youngest man at that time to be appointed to the state supreme court. After serving as a U.S. district attorney, Hovey unsuccessfully ran for the **U.S. Congress** as a **Republican**.

Hovey's political connections led to his being appointed colonel of the 24th Indiana in July 1861. After duty in **Missouri**, he led the **regiment** at **Shiloh** in **Morgan Smith's brigade** and performed well enough to be promoted to brigadier general of volunteers in late April 1862. Given command of a **division**, Hovey served with the **Army of the Tennessee** in **John McClernand's** XIII Corps at **Arkansas Post** and in the **Vicksburg Campaign**. In the latter, his division shouldered much of the fighting at **Champion Hill**. In December 1863, Hovey was sent back to Indiana to help organize recruits and to serve as a liaison between **U. S. Grant** and Gov. **Oliver P. Morton**. He later returned to the field and led a XXIII Corps division during the early part of the **Atlanta Campaign**. In June 1864, Hovey was granted leave, and **William T. Sherman** was so angry at its timing that he had Hovey's division disbanded. Hovey was **brevetted** major general of volunteers in July and commanded the District of Indiana until war's end. In that capacity, he was responsible for raising new recruits. In doing so, Hovey asked only for bachelors to volunteer, prompting his men to be nicknamed "Hovey's Babies."

After the war, Hovey served as the U.S. minister to Peru from 1865 to 1870 and then returned to his Indiana law practice. He was elected to Congress in 1886 and was elected governor in 1888. He died in office.

HOVEY, CHARLES EDWARD (1827–1897) USA. A native of **Vermont**, Hovey (HUV-ee) was a distant cousin of Union Brig. Gen. **Alvin Peterson Hovey**. After putting himself through Dartmouth College by teaching in the summer, he became a respected educator and served as the principal or superintendent of several schools, a member of the first state school board, president of the state teachers' association, and founder of the first state teachers' college at Normal, Illinois.

When civil war erupted, Hovey organized the 33rd Illinois, mainly from teachers and students at the Normal school. He was commissioned colonel in August 1861 and led the **regiment** in some minor **Missouri skirmishes** later that year. In September 1862, Hovey was promoted to brigadier general of volunteers and served well in the capture of **Arkansas Post** (where he was wounded in the arm), but his commission expired in March 1863 when the Senate failed to confirm him. He apparently left the service in May and received a **brevet** of major general of volunteers in March 1865.

After the war, Hovey moved to **Washington, D.C.**, and became successful as a pension lobbyist.

HOWARD, JOSEPH, JR. (1833–1908) USA. Howard was a native of **New York**, but little is known of this unscrupulous man's early life except that he was a reporter for the **New York** *Times*. He first became prominent in early 1861 when he falsely wrote that President-elect **Abraham Lincoln** slipped through Baltimore, Maryland, to **Washington, D.C.**, disguised in a Scotch cap and military overcoat to avoid an assassination plot. Howard covered the **First Battle of Manassas** and in 1862 sneaked into Maj. Gen. **Philip Kearny's** funeral (where reporters were banned) and wrote an account of it. His stories were so popular that he became one of the first reporters to receive a regular byline.

Howard eventually moved to the Brooklyn *Eagle* and became its city editor. In May 1864, he pulled off the **Gold Hoax** with fellow reporter Francis A. Mallison. After buying up gold, Howard wrote a false story that Lincoln was going to call for 400,000 more volunteers because the war was going so badly. When the story was published by two newspapers, it caused gold prices to soar, and Howard stood to make a fortune. The government, however, cracked down on the **telegraph** line and newspapers involved in the bogus story and soon arrested Howard and Mallison. Howard admitted his part in the scheme and exonerated the newspapers. He and Mallison were held **prisoner** for three months in **Fort Lafayette**, **New York**, until Howard's father appealed to **Henry Ward Beecher**. Beecher asked Lincoln to release the men, and the president did so. Ironically, Lincoln was preparing to ask for 300,000 more volunteers, but the outcry caused by the Gold Hoax caused him to delay the request for two months.

After the war, Howard worked for several newspapers and became president of the New York Press Club.

HOWARD, OLIVER OTIS (1830–1909) USA. A native of **Maine**, Howard taught school during vacations to put himself through Bowdoin College. After graduating in 1850, he entered **West Point** and graduated fourth in the 1854 class. Much of Howard's antebellum military career was at the academy, where he taught mathematics. He was serving there as a lieutenant of ordnance when the Civil War began.

In June 1861, Howard resigned his regular commission after being elected colonel of the 3rd Maine. He led a **brigade** at **First Manassas**, but his unit was routed from the field with many others. Nonetheless, Howard was promoted to brigadier general of volunteers in September. Attached to the **Army of the Potomac**, he again commanded a brigade in the **Peninsula Campaign** and lost his right arm to amputation after suffering two wounds at the **Battle of Seven Pines** (in 1893 he received the **Medal of Honor** for his actions there). Howard rejoined the **army** shortly after its defeat at **Second Manassas** and was given command of the rear guard for the march back to **Washington, D.C.** At **Antietam**, his superior, **John Sedgwick**, was wounded, and Howard temporarily took command of the **division** during the battle.

Howard was promoted to major general of volunteers in November 1862 and led a division in the **Battle of Fredericksburg**. Placed in command of the largely German XI Corps in March 1863, his career was dealt a blow at **Chancellorsville**. Holding the Union right flank, Howard failed to follow **Joseph Hooker's** orders to secure his position and thus was crushed when **Stonewall Jackson** attacked late in the afternoon. Just weeks later, his **corps** again was routed by the Confederates on the first day at **Gettysburg**. When **John Reynolds** was killed there, Howard assumed command of the field and personally rallied the I Corps on Cemetery Hill. There he got into a short but intense losing argument with **Winfield Scott Hancock** over seniority when Hancock arrived with orders from **George G. Meade** to take command of the field. Although his actions at Gettysburg were not brilliant, Howard received the **Thanks of Congress** for holding the crucial high ground.

In September 1863, the XI and XII Corps were sent west to reinforce Chattanooga, Tennessee. After participating in the **Chattanooga Campaign**, the two corps were consolidated into the **Army of the Cumberland's** XX Corps in the spring of 1864, and Howard was given command of the army's IV Corps. During the **Atlanta Campaign**, he was given command of the **Army of the Tennessee** in July 1864 when **James B. McPherson** was killed at the **Battle of Atlanta**. After the fall of Atlanta, Howard commanded the right wing during **William T. Sherman's March to the Sea** and participated in the **Carolinas Campaign**. He was promoted to brigadier general of regulars in December 1864 and for his war service was brevetted major general of regulars.

Howard's Civil War career was rather odd. A very religious man who was a devoted **abolitionist**, he undoubtedly was committed to the cause and personally was very brave. But his tactical ability was questionable. As historian Ezra J. Warner wrote, "no officer entrusted with the field direction of troops has ever equaled Howard's record for surviving so many tactical errors of judgment and disregard of orders, emerging later not only with increased rank, but on one occasion with the thanks of Congress" (Warner, *Generals in Blue*, 237).

In May 1865, Howard was appointed the first commissioner of the **Freedmen's Bureau** and genuinely tried to help the **freedmen**, but he was unable to control the fraud and corruption that riddled the organization. Corruption within the bureau led to a court of inquiry in 1874, but Howard was exonerated. Howard then helped organize Howard University and served as its president from 1869 to 1874. Afterward, he served as the superintendent of West Point and was promoted to major general in 1886. Howard retired from the **U.S. Army** in 1894, moved to **Vermont**, and stayed active in religious and educational activities.

HOWE, ALBION PARRIS (1818–1897) USA. A native of **Maine**, Howe graduated from **West Point** in 1841 and served as an instructor there. During the **Mexican War**, he was assigned to the **artillery**, fought under **Winfield Scott**, and was awarded one **brevet** for gallantry. After the war, Howe served on various garrison duty and had risen to the rank of captain in the 4th U.S. Artillery by the Civil War.

During the early days of war, Howe served under **George B. McClellan** in western **Virginia** and then commanded an infantry **brigade** in McClellan's **Army of the Potomac** through the **Peninsula Campaign**. Promoted to brigadier general of volunteers in June 1862, he won a brevet for his actions at **Malvern Hill**. Howe's brigade arrived too late to fight at **Antietam**, and he was only lightly engaged while leading a **division** at **Fredericksburg**. During the **Chancellorsville Campaign**, his division helped seize Marye's Heights at **Second Fredericksburg**, and he was awarded another brevet. Held in reserve with the VI Corps at **Gettysburg**, Howe saw little combat there. In November 1863, however, he won yet another brevet when his division helped capture two Confederates brigades at **Rappahannock Station**.

Despite his numerous brevets, Howe's superiors apparently were dissatisfied with his service. In early 1864, he was transferred to **Washington, D.C.**, where he took command of the Artillery Depot and supervised the Office of the Inspector of Artillery. Howe remained in Washington for the rest of the war and ended the conflict with brevets through the rank of major general in both the volunteer and regular service.

In 1865, not only was Howe a member of the honor guard for **Abraham Lincoln's** funeral, but he also served on the commission that tried **Lincoln's assassination** conspirators. He remained in the **army** after the war, retiring in 1882 as colonel of the 4th U.S. Artillery.

HOWE, JULIA WARD (1819–1910) USA. A native of **New York**, Howe came from a prominent family and was married to **abolitionist** Samuel Gridley Howe. While touring Union camps with **Massachusetts** Gov. **John A. Andrews**, she heard Union troops singing the marching tune "John Brown's Body." After the tour, Howe wrote a new set of lyrics for the tune, which was bought for $4.00 and was published in *Atlantic Monthly* in February 1862. This **"Battle Hymn of the Republic"** became one of the most popular songs from the Civil War.

HOWITZER. This **artillery** piece was between a field gun and a **mortar**. Howitzers were designed to fire a projectile in a relatively high trajectory, so that shells could be fired over walls or entrenchments, but they also could be fired in a flatter trajectory against advancing troops. Coming in standard sizes of 12-, 24-, and 32-pounders, howitzers usually were made of bronze and had short gun tubes. The mountain howitzer was a light model that could be broken down and packed on a mule for easy mobility.

HUGER, BENJAMIN (1805–1877) CSA. Descended from French Huguenots, Huger (YOO-jee) was a native of **South Carolina** who graduated from **West Point** in 1825. For the most part, he served in the ordnance department and was **brevetted** three times while serving as **Winfield Scott's** chief of ordnance during the **Mexican War**.

After commanding various arsenals in South Carolina during the **secession** crisis, Huger resigned his captain's commission in April 1861 and was appointed brigadier general of **Virginia** troops in May. In June, he was appointed brigadier general in the **Confederate army**, with a promotion to major general coming in October. After being placed in command of the **Department of Norfolk** in May 1861, Huger was investigated by the **Confederate Congress** for contributing to the loss of **Roanoke Island, North Carolina**, in February 1862, by failing to reinforce the garrison.

In May 1862, Huger evacuated **Norfolk, Virginia**, and destroyed the CSS *Virginia* and Navy Yard as **George B. McClellan's Army of the Potomac** threatened the city during the **Peninsula Campaign**. He led a **division** at **Seven Pines** and throughout the **Seven Days Campaign** but was criticized for being slow and unaggressive. As a result of these accusations and the dissatisfaction of **Joseph E. Johnston** and **Robert E. Lee**, Huger was relieved of command shortly after the campaign ended. In August, he was appointed an inspector of **artillery** and ordnance. This position carried little responsibility, largely because Huger's superior, **Josiah Gorgas**, had disliked him ever since Gorgas served under him during the Mexican War. In March 1863, Gorgas effectively banished Huger by appointing him inspector of the **Trans-Mississippi Department**.

After the war, Huger farmed in **North Carolina** and **Virginia**.

HUMES, WILLIAM YOUNG CONN (1830–1882) CSA. A native of **Virginia**, Humes graduated from the **Virginia Military Institute** in 1851 and taught school before moving to **Tennessee** and becoming a lawyer. He entered Confederate service in June 1861 as a lieutenant in Col. **John P. McCown's** Artillery Corps of Tennessee. When his captain was killed in November 1861, Humes was promoted to captain and took command of the **company**. During the Union operations against **New Madrid and Island No. 10** in early 1862, he commanded the island's **artillery** and was captured when the Confederates surrendered. **Exchanged** in September 1862, Humes took command of a company in the Tennessee Light Artillery in January 1863 and served at Mobile, Alabama, until **Joseph Wheeler** asked that he be assigned to him as chief of artillery. He joined Wheeler in March and was wounded in an October raid.

Wheeler highly praised Humes's service and secured him a promotion to brigadier general in November 1863. In April 1864, he was given command of a small cavalry **division**, which he led in the **Army of Tennessee** during the **Atlanta Campaign**. Humes saw hard service throughout the campaign and performed particularly well at **Pickett's Mill**. After Atlanta fell, his division joined one of **Wheeler's Raids** into northern **Georgia** and Middle Tennessee. During the **March to the Sea**, Humes's cavalry frequently **skirmished** with the enemy, and in one engagement his horse was killed under him. Throughout 1864, Wheeler consistently praised Humes and recommended him for promotion to major general. Some sources claim he received the promotion in March 1865, but there is no documented proof of it. While battling **William T. Sherman** in the **Carolinas Campaign**, Humes was wounded twice, the last time at **Monroe's Cross Roads** in March 1865. It is not clear when he returned to duty, although some sources claim he participated in the **Battle of Bentonville** a week later.

After surrendering with the rest of **Joseph E. Johnston's army** in April 1865, Humes returned to his Tennessee law practice.

HUMPHREYS, ANDREW ATKISON (1810–1883) USA. A native of **Pennsylvania** and the grandson of the designer of the USS *Constitution*, Humphreys graduated from **West Point** in 1831. He first was assigned to the **artillery**, but after seven years, he was transferred to the **engineers** and performed much service on the Mississippi River.

A captain of engineers when the Civil War began, Humphreys was promoted to major in August 1861 and in December joined **George B. McClellan's** staff as chief topographical engineer for the **Army of the Potomac**. He was promoted to colonel in March 1862 and to brigadier general of volunteers the following month. After serving with McClellan through the **Peninsula** and **Seven Days Campaigns**, Humphreys was given a V Corps **division** of new recruits just days before the **Battle of Antietam**, but he was held in reserve during the battle. He first led his men into combat at **Fredericksburg**, where he earned a **brevet** for gallantry.

After **Chancellorsville**, his men's enlistments expired, so Humphreys was given command of a III Corps division. At **Gettysburg**, he was brevetted brigadier general in the regular **army** for his role in holding back **James Longstreet's** attack on the second day.

A few days after Gettysburg, Humphreys was made major general of volunteers and **George G. Meade's** chief of staff. He skillfully served Meade through the **Overland** and **Petersburg Campaigns** until November 1864, when he replaced **Winfield Scott Hancock** in command of the II Corps. Humphreys competently led the **corps** through the remainder of the war and was awarded a third brevet, to major general of regulars, for **Sailor's Creek** during the **Appomattox Campaign**.

In August 1866, Humphreys was appointed brigadier general in the regular army and was made its chief engineer. Afterward, he wrote two books on the war and was active in various engineering organizations before retiring in 1879.

HUMPHREYS, BENJAMIN GRUBB (1808–1882) CSA. One of 16 children, Humphreys was a native of **Mississippi**. He entered **West Point** in 1825, but he was expelled in 1827 for his role in an 1826 Christmas Eve incident known as the Eggnog Riot. Humphreys returned to Mississippi, became a planter and lawyer, and served in both the state assembly and senate.

Although opposed to **secession**, Humphreys raised a volunteer **company** in May 1861 and entered Confederate service as a captain in a unit that became the 21st Mississippi. He was promoted to colonel in September. As part of **William Barksdale's brigade** in the **Army of Northern Virginia**, Humphreys led his **regiment** through the **Peninsula**, **Seven Days**, **Antietam**, **Fredericksburg**, **Chancellorsville** (where he defended Marye's Heights in the **Second Battle of Fredericksburg**), and **Gettysburg Campaigns**, often winning praise from his superiors. When Barksdale was mortally wounded during the bitter fighting at Gettysburg on July 2, 1863, Humphreys assumed command of the brigade and only reluctantly obeyed orders to withdraw.

In August 1863, Humphreys was promoted to brigadier general and received the brigade command permanently. He accompanied **James Longstreet** to **Georgia** in September 1863 and fought in the **Chickamauga** and **Knoxville Campaigns**. When **division** commander **Lafayette McLaws** was court-martialed by Longstreet after the failed attack at Knoxville, Humphreys served on the court-martial board. Still, he remained on good terms with McLaws, and McLaws praised him for his Knoxville service. After returning to **Virginia**, Humphreys's brigade saw combat in the **Overland** and **Petersburg Campaigns** and won particular notice at the **Wilderness** and **Spotsylvania**. After he reinforced **Jubal A. Early** in the **Shenandoah Valley** in late summer 1864, Humphreys was wounded "in both breasts" (Davis, ed., *The Confederate General*, vol. 3, 133) at **Berryville, Virginia**, on September 3. Instead of returning to the brigade when he recovered in February 1865, he was transferred west to take command of the **district** composed of southern Mississippi and eastern **Louisiana**.

After the war, Humphreys was pardoned by President **Andrew Johnson** and was elected governor of Mississippi in October 1865. After **Radical Republicans** succeeded in removing him from office in 1868, he worked as a planter and insurance agent.

***HUNLEY*, CSS.** *See H. L. HUNLEY, CSS.*

HUNT, HENRY JACKSON (1819–1889) USA. A native of **Michigan** and the son and grandson of **U.S. Army** officers, Hunt was the brother of Union Brig. Gen. **Lewis Cass Hunt**. He grew up in **Ohio** but was orphaned at age 10. Hunt graduated from **West Point** in 1839 and served with the **artillery** under **Winfield Scott** in the **Mexican War**, where he was wounded once and **brevetted** twice. After the war, Hunt served on a board with **William F. Barry** and **William H. French** to revise artillery **tactics**. This work was adopted by the **army** in 1860 and was used as a guide for both armies' artillery in the Civil War.

A captain in the 2nd U.S. Artillery when civil war began, Hunt was promoted to major of the 5th U.S. Artillery in May 1861. He first won recognition at **First Manassas** when his battery helped cover the Union retreat. In September, Hunt was appointed colonel and took command of the artillery in the **Washington, D.C.**, defenses and trained the **Army of the Potomac's** reserve artillery, which he commanded during the **Peninsula** and **Seven Days Campaigns**. He won more fame when his guns shattered the Confederate assaults at **Malvern Hill**.

During the **Antietam Campaign** in September 1862, Hunt was promoted to brigadier general of volunteers and was appointed chief of artillery by **George B. McClellan**. After handling his guns well at Antietam, he played an important role at **Fredericksburg**. There, Hunt's massed cannons covered the Union crossing of the Rappahannock River (destroying much of the town in the process) and dissuaded **Robert E. Lee** from counterattacking after the Union assault on Marye's Heights was repulsed. Afterward, Hunt did not get along well with new army commander, **Joseph Hooker**, and thus was not so active at **Chancellorsville**. Restored to a more active role by **George G. Meade**, Hunt's cannons were instrumental in repulsing **Pickett's Charge** at **Gettysburg**, and he won a brevet of major general of volunteers. Hunt continued to serve as the army's chief of artillery through the **Overland Campaign**, and in June 1864, **U. S. Grant** placed him in charge of siege operations during the **Petersburg Campaign**. He remained with the Army of the Potomac until war's end.

Hunt was one of most valuable Union officers, and his excellent wartime service won him a brevet of major general of regulars. After the war, he remained in the army as a lieutenant colonel of artillery and was seen as the leading expert in his field until he retired in 1883. Afterward, Hunt wrote articles on the war and served as governor of the Washington Soldiers' Home.

HUNT, LEWIS CASS (1824–1886) USA. A native of **Wisconsin**, Hunt was the son and grandson of **U.S. Army** officers and the brother of Union Brig. Gen. **Henry Jackson Hunt**. He graduated from **West Point** in 1847 and served in Mexico, the Pacific Northwest, and in an Anglo-American expedition against San Juan Island. At the time of the Civil War, Hunt was a captain in the 4th U.S. Infantry.

While serving in the **Peninsula Campaign** with the **Army of the Potomac**, Hunt was promoted to colonel of the 92nd New York in May 1862 and was wounded while leading it at **Seven Pines**. Put out of action for months, he was **brevetted** for his bravery and was assigned to the **Department North Carolina** when he returned to duty.

Hunt was promoted to brigadier general of volunteers in November 1862 and was given command of a **brigade** in **John G. Foster's division**. He fought at **First Kinston** and **Goldsboro Bridge** and won another brevet. After receiving a promotion to major in the regular **army** in June 1863, Hunt was sent to **Connecticut** to command a draft rendezvous. He held this position and various other administrative posts until March 1864, when he was put in command of the New York City harbor defenses. Hunt served in that position until war's end, when he was brevetted colonel and brigadier general in the regular army for his wartime service.

Remaining in the army, Hunt died on active duty as colonel of the 14th U.S. Infantry.

HUNTER, DAVID (1802–1886) USA. The grandson of a signer of the Declaration of Independence, Hunter was born in **Washington, D.C.**, but little is known of his early life. He graduated from **West Point** in 1822 and served in the infantry and dragoons before resigning his captain's commission in 1836. After working six years in **Illinois** real estate, Hunter rejoined the **U.S. Army** as a major and paymaster and saw service in the **Mexican War** and **"Bleeding Kansas."** While in the latter, he began corresponding with President-elect **Abraham Lincoln** and impressed Lincoln with his views on the **secession** crisis. Lincoln invited Hunter to ride to Washington with him on the inaugural train, and the two became quite close. Based solely on this personal relationship, Lincoln appointed Hunter colonel of the 3rd U.S. Cavalry in May 1861. Three days later, he promoted him to brigadier general of volunteers, making the inexperienced—and rather incompetent—Hunter the fourth-ranking Union volunteer general. Hunter led a **division** at **First Manassas** and was wounded in the shoulder. When he returned to duty, he was promoted to major general of volunteers in August 1861 and was sent to **Missouri**.

In November 1861, Hunter replaced **John C. Frémont** as commander of the **Western Department** and soon was placed over the **Department of Kansas**. After constantly complaining about affairs in his **department**, he was transferred to **South Carolina** in March 1862 and was given command of the **Department of the South**. Hunter's leadership generally was poor. While he did get credit when forces within his command captured **Fort Pulaski, Georgia**, in April, he enjoyed no success around **Charleston, South Carolina**, and was defeated at **Secessionville** in June. While commanding the department, Hunter also ran afoul of Lincoln, when in May he announced that slaves within his department were free. Lincoln quickly disavowed the announcement, but Hunter did raise the 1st South Carolina Colored Infantry, one of the **army's** first **regiments** of **black troops**.

While on leave in late 1862, Hunter served on a board of inquiry into the surrender of **Harpers Ferry, Virginia**, and presided over the **Fitz John Porter** court-martial that arose out of the **Second Manassas Campaign**. Returning to Charleston, he again failed to capture the city with his X Corps and was removed from command in June 1863. For the next year, Hunter had no command, but he did impress **U. S. Grant** while visiting the **Army of the Tennessee** during the **Chattanooga Campaign**. When **Franz Sigel** was defeated at **New Market, Virginia**, in May 1864, Grant put Hunter in command of the **Department of West Virginia**, which included the **Shenandoah Valley**. Sweeping through the Valley, **Hunter's 1864 Shenandoah Valley Campaign** cut a swath of destruction. His men plundered, burned dozens of homes and barns, and burned the **Virginia Military Institute** at Lexington. Confederates came to despise Hunter because of his strong **abolitionism** and his wanton destruction in the Valley. After enjoying initial success in the campaign and defeating the enemy at **Piedmont**, he was stopped at **Lynchurg** by **Jubal A. Early** and retreated into **West Virginia** without a major fight. This retreat was highly criticized, for it allowed the Confederates to enter the Valley and launch **Jubal Early's Washington Raid** that summer. After meeting with Grant, Hunter resigned his command in August 1864 to allow **Philip H. Sheridan** to take over the department. He did not hold any other field command during the war.

In 1865, Hunter rode Lincoln's funeral train back to Illinois and then presided over the military trial of **Lincoln's assassination** conspirators. After being **brevetted** brigadier and major general in the regular army for his wartime service, Hunter retired in 1866 as a colonel of cavalry. He then lived in Washington until his death.

HUNTER, ROBERT MERCER TALIAFERRO (1809–1887) CSA. A native of **Virginia**, Hunter attended the University of Virginia and became a lawyer. He was elected to the state legislature as an independent in 1834 but later joined the **Whig Party** and was elected to the U.S. House of Representatives in 1836. Reelected in 1838, Hunter served as Speaker of the House in his second term and continued to serve in Congress until defeated in 1842. Switching to the **Democratic Party**, he was sent back to Congress in 1844 and to the U.S. Senate in 1846. Hunter became a follower of **John C. Calhoun** and supported his 1844 presidential campaign. During the 1850s, he was a popular moderate who looked for compromises and believed **secession** was only an action of last resort. Hunter continued to look for a compromise solution to the secession crisis after **Abraham Lincoln** was elected president in 1860 and served on the **Committee of Thirteen**. He did not resign from the Senate until March 1861.

In May 1861, Virginia appointed Hunter to the Provisional **Confederate Congress**, where he chaired the Finance Committee. When Secretary of State **Robert Toombs** resigned in July, **Jefferson Davis** appointed Hunter as his replacement, but he served only seven months. During that time, Hunter worked to secure foreign recognition and sent ministers **James Mason** and **John Slidell** to Europe, but these two soon were captured in what became known as the *Trent* **Affair**.

In February 1862, Hunter resigned his position and returned to the Senate, where he served as president pro tem and on the finance and foreign relations committees for the rest of the war. As a senator, Hunter worked to create an effective **tax** system, fought inflation, and generally tried to help the economy. He usually supported the administration but strongly opposed the recruitment of **black troops** and only voted for the bill because he was instructed to do so by the Virginia legislature. In February 1865, Hunter was appointed a peace commissioner to meet with Lincoln and **Edwin M. Stanton** at the failed **Hampton Roads Conference**.

Afterward, he supported Davis in trying to wage a more vigorous war effort, but he finally realized there was no hope of victory. One of Hunter's last official acts in the Senate was to cosponsor a failed resolution asking Davis to seek an armistice to open a dialogue with the Union.

After the war, Hunter was imprisoned several months in **Fort Pulaski, Georgia**, during which time Union troops destroyed most of his property. Upon being released, he opposed the Virginia **Reconstruction** government and served as Virginia's treasurer from 1874 to 1880.

HUNTER'S RAID (MAY 26–JUNE 18, 1864). *See* SHENANDOAH VALLEY CAMPAIGN, DAVID HUNTER'S.

HUNTON, EPPA (1822–1908) CSA. A native of **Virginia**, Hunton taught school until he passed the bar exam and began his own law practice in 1843. In 1848, he became the commonwealth attorney for Prince William County, a position he held until the outbreak of the Civil War.

In 1861, Hunton served in the state **secession** convention as a secessionist. He had considerable political influence and had served as a militia brigadier general, so in May 1861 he was commissioned colonel of the 8th Virginia. Although not completely organized, the **regiment** fought at **First Manassas**. In late 1861, Hunton showed the first signs of the chronic illness that would plague him throughout the war, when he became afflicted by throat hemorrhage, hemorrhoids, and fistulas. Although confined to bed in October, he returned to duty and led his regiment with distinction at **Ball's Bluff**. Hunton frequently was absent sick until March 1862, and during that time his home and property were destroyed by Union forces.

After missing **Seven Pines** because of illness, Hunton temporarily took command of **George Pickett's** brigade in the **Army of Northern Virginia** at **Gaines' Mill** after Pickett was wounded and led the men in the final attack that drove back the enemy. After the **Seven Days Campaign**, he returned to his sickbed but rejoined the regiment in time to lead it at **Second Manassas**, **Antietam**, **Fredericksburg**, and **Suffolk**. At **Gettysburg**, Hunton was leading his men in **Pickett's Charge** when he was shot through the right leg. Of the regiment's 105 men who began the attack, he and four others were all that were left afterward.

In August 1863, Hunton was promoted to brigadier general and was given command of a **brigade**. After fighting in the **Overland Campaign**, he participated in the **Petersburg Campaign** but was stationed near the James River and saw little combat until the spring of 1865. The brigade then became heavily engaged in the final days of the siege and suffered heavy casualties at **Five Forks** and in the **Appomattox Cam-**

paign. On April 6, 1865, Hunton and most of his command were captured during the **Battle of Sailor's Creek**. He was held **prisoner** in **Fort Warren, Massachusetts**, along with **Richard S. Ewell** and other prominent generals until July.

Released after taking the **oath of allegiance**, Hunton returned to Virginia and rebuilt his law practice. Beginning in 1872, he was elected to the U.S. House of Representatives four times and served in the U.S. Senate from 1892 to 1895. During the contested 1876 presidential election, Hunton was the only Southern congressman seated on the commission that investigated the election.

HURLBUT, STEPHEN AUGUSTUS (1815–1882) USA. A native of **South Carolina**, Hurlbut became a prosperous lawyer and served as a militia officer during the **Seminole Wars**. Moving to **Illinois** in 1845, he became active in **Republican** politics and was serving in the state legislature when the Civil War began.

Because of his political connections, Hurlbut was appointed brigadier general of volunteers in June 1861 (he was the only South Carolinian to become a Union general). After service in Illinois, he was given command of a **division** in **U. S. Grant's** army in February 1862 and led it at **Shiloh** and in the **siege of Corinth, Mississippi**. Hurlbut commanded the XVI Corps at Memphis, Tennessee, during the 1863 **Vicksburg Campaign**, and in September 1864, he was placed in command of the **Army of the Gulf**. In both of these positions, he engaged in corrupt activities that made him rich. While stationed in **New Orleans, Louisiana**, Hurlbut finally was charged with corruption, but he was allowed to take an honorable discharge in June 1865 rather than face a court-martial.

After the war, despite being frequently accused of corruption and drunkenness, Hurlbut enjoyed a successful public life. He became the first president of the **Grand Army of the Republic**, was elected to the **U.S. Congress** in 1872 and 1874, and served as minister to Colombia and Peru under Presidents Grant and **James A. Garfield**, respectively. While in the latter country, Hurlbut again was accused of being corrupt.

HUSE, CALEB (1831–1905) CSA. A native of **Massachusetts**, Huse graduated from **West Point** in 1851 and served with the **artillery** in **Florida** and as a chemistry/geology professor at the academy. In 1859, he received a leave of absence and toured Europe, where he examined the European armament industries. Upon his return to the United States in May 1860, Huse accepted a position as commandant of the University of Alabama's cadets. Since the position carried with it a colonel's commission in the state militia, he had to receive permission from the **U.S. Army** to accept the job.

When the **army** ordered Huse to return to duty in February 1861, he instead resigned his lieutenant's commission and in April was appointed a captain in the **Confederate army**. He was sent to Great Britain and was promoted to major and in May was appointed the chief Confederate European agent for purchasing arms. Working out of the Liverpool offices of **Fraser, Trenholm & Co.**, Huse traveled through Europe buying up weapons and ordnance. He succeeded in gaining for the Confederacy the full production capability of the London Armory Company and acquired 20 artillery batteries and 100,000 **rifles** from Austria. Despite this success, Huse was accused of corruption because he often clashed with Confederate diplomats. He was exonerated in an investigation, however, and was able to continue his work. During the war, Huse bought millions of dollars worth of weapons, ordnance, medicine, and other crucial supplies. Along with **James D. Bulloch**, he helped keep the Confederate armies in the field.

Huse remained in Europe after the war and did not return to the United States until 1868. He then failed in several business ventures but finally established a successful New York prep school.

$$- I -$$

ÎLE À VACHE, HAITI, EXPERIMENT (APRIL 1863–MARCH 1864). Since **Abraham Lincoln** did not believe that blacks and whites could live together in harmony within the United States, he had always supported emancipation and voluntary colonization as the answer to the **slavery** dilemma. After issuing the **Emancipation Proclamation**, he also wanted to calm fears that emancipation would lead to a massive migration of **freedmen** to Northern states. As a result, he attempted to establish a colony for freedmen on the Haitian island of Île à Vache (ILL-uh-VAHSH) in April 1863.

This idea first came about in October 1862, shortly after Lincoln issued the preliminary Emancipation Proclamation. A speculator named Bernard Kock offered to settle 1,000 freedmen to grow cotton on an island he had leased in the West Indies, if the U.S. government would pay for their passage, provide supplies, and pay Kock $50 per person transported. Lincoln refused the offer after investigating Kock and finding that he had a less than stellar reputation. Shortly afterward, Charles K. Tuckerman and Paul S. Forbes, two wealthy New Yorkers, proposed a similar plan, and Lincoln agreed, except he limited the number of freedmen to 500. Unknown to Lincoln, Tuckerman and Forbes had hired Kock to oversee the operation.

The colonization attempt was a dismal failure. After sailing from **Fort Monroe, Virginia**, in April 1863, 468 freedmen landed on the island to find that none of the promised houses, hospital, or schools had been built. No progress was made, even after Kock was removed in July at Lincoln's insistence. When Tuckerman and Forbes abandoned the unprofitable scheme, the freedmen began starving. An investigation ordered by Lincoln showed the true dismal conditions of the colony, but it was not until March 1864 that the 368 survivors were transported back to the United States. The Île à Vache venture was Lincoln's last attempt to colonize freedmen.

ILLINOIS. Illinois, admitted in 1818 as the 21st state, played a key role in the Civil War era. Populated with a large number of **Free-Soilers**, it was instrumental in forming the **Republican Party** in 1854 and was the setting for both the 1858 **Lincoln-Douglas Debates** (**Abraham Lincoln** and **Stephen Douglas** were residents of the state) and the 1860 Republican National Convention. When Lincoln called for volunteers in April 1861, Gov. **Richard Yates** responded vigorously, and the state ultimately provided 259,092 men to the Union war effort. This included 150 infantry **regiments**, 17 cavalry units, 10 **artillery** units, one regiment of **black troops**, and thousands of sailors and marines. Of the state's servicemen, 34,834 died during the war. Illinois also gave the Union 63 generals, including **U. S. Grant, John A. Logan, James H. Wilson, Benjamin Grierson, John A. McClernand**, and **John Buford**.

IMBODEN, JOHN DANIEL (1823–1895) CSA. A native of **Virginia**, Imboden (IM-boh-den) attended Washington College before becoming a teacher, lawyer, and two-term state legislator. A supporter of **secession**, he organized the Staunton Artillery when civil war came and was elected its captain in April 1861.

After serving with **Joseph E. Johnston** around **Harpers Ferry, Virginia**, Imboden fought well at **First Manassas** and helped stop the Union onslaught against Henry House Hill. He also served on the board that investigated why the **Confederate army** did not pursue the defeated Federals. In the spring of 1862, Imboden went back to his native **Shenandoah Valley** and organized the 1st Virginia Partisan Rangers, which fought in **Stonewall Jackson's 1862 Shenandoah Valley Campaign**. After he officially was commissioned a colonel in July, his **regiment** was redesignated the 62nd Virginia Mounted Infantry. While in command of his regiment, some cavalry **companies**, and an artillery battery, Imboden cooperated with **Albert Jenkins's** raid into western Virginia in August–September 1862.

After raising some additional units, Imboden was promoted to brigadier general in April 1863 and was given command of a mixed **brigade** of infantry, cavalry, and **artillery** that operated independently under the direction of **Robert E. Lee**. In April 1863, **William E. Jones** and Imboden launched **Jones's and Imboden's Raid** deep into **West Virginia**. In 37 days, Imboden traveled 400 miles, destroyed eight bridges, and captured 3,000 cattle. Joining Lee and the **Army of Northern Virginia** for the **Gettysburg Campaign**, his brigade again raided into West Virginia to guard Lee's left flank and then guarded Lee's wagon train when he retreated back to Virginia. Although having a reputation for being unreliable, the brigade fought well as part of the rear guard, especially when it helped repulse a Union attack at **Williamsport, Maryland**.

Imboden was put in command of the **Valley District** in late July, but he modestly refused to seek a promotion, claiming that his rank was as high as he was qualified. During his tenure as **district** commander, his reputation for being a weak disciplinarian continued. Not only was his district plagued by **desertion**, but Imboden also allowed deserters from other units to join him. His immediate superior, **Jubal A. Early**, requested a court of inquiry, but Lee refused to convene one. Imboden's service was lackluster for the remainder of the war. He did capture the Union garrison at Charlestown, West Virginia, in October, but his failure to move swiftly during the May 1864 **Battle of New Market** allowed the enemy to escape. Over the following months, Imboden fought in **David Hunter's Shenandoah Valley Campaign**, **Early's Washington Raid**, and **Philip Sheridan's Shenandoah Valley Campaign**. After suffering from typhoid fever in late 1864, he was relieved of his field command and ended the war guarding a **prison** at Aiken, South Carolina.

Imboden practiced law and became a miner after the war and discovered a coal vein that became known as the "Imboden seam." After marrying five times, he died in Damascus, Virginia, a town he founded.

IMPRESSMENT ACT, CONFEDERATE. A chronic shortage of supplies forced the Confederates to begin an impressment policy early in the Civil War. At first the **armies**, and sometimes state governments, took what they needed and only paid owners after they had filed a claim for their losses. A formalized system was adopted on March 26, 1863, when the **Confederate Congress** passed the Impressment Act. This law originally allowed the government only to impress goods needed to feed and sustain the military, but it was amended in April 1864 and March 1865 to allow it to take anything needed for public use, except breeding live-stock. Each state established a board of commissioners that mediated disputes between impressment agents and civilians, set prices for goods impressed, and published lists of prices to keep up with inflation. **Jefferson Davis** and each governor were allowed to appoint one commissioner to the board.

Impressment agents scoured the countryside inspecting farms and businesses for potential goods and worked with the owners to set fair prices for commodities impressed. Owners either were paid immediately in **Confederate money** or with certificates for later redemption. Protests soon began because impressment was seen as a violation of **states rights** and because there were many flaws in the system. Soaring inflation prevented the prices paid by the government from equaling the actual market value of the goods, and the law did not seem to be applied equally. Civilians living closest to the armies suffered much more impressment than people living farther away from the front. Many unscrupulous men also pretended to be agents and used counterfeit certificates to steal goods. Even goods legitimately obtained often spoiled before they could be delivered, because either the agents did not make transportation arrangements, or the deteriorating Confederate **railroad** system could not handle the traffic.

The impressment of slaves was handled a little differently from that of other goods. Slaves had frequently been impressed for military labor before the Impressment Act, but afterward their impressment had to conform to the law. Slave owners were paid $30 a month, or some other agreed upon price, and they were reimbursed if the slave died during the work period. As with impressments of commodities, there was much protest over slave impressment. Owners argued that the government did not take good care of their slaves, was always late in payment, and kept slaves longer than the agreed upon time.

The Confederate government impressed hundreds of millions of dollars' worth of supplies and slaves during the war. Exactly how much is unknown, but one source estimates 17 percent of the Confederacy's purchasing power came through impressment, a total exceeding $500 million. Opposition to the practice further weakened Confederate morale, and by war's end the policy had largely been abandoned in favor of paying market value for goods seized.

INCOME TAX, CONFEDERATE. Despite a desperate need to raise money to **finance** the war, the **Confederate Congress** did not institute an income tax until April 1863. Prior to that, eight states had passed such a **tax** to support the states' war efforts. In January 1863, Secretary of the

Treasury **Christopher G. Memminger** proposed a 10 percent income tax and a 1 percent property tax to raise $60 million in the first year. The Congress responded favorably, but the House and Senate disagreed on how large the tax should be. A compromise was finally reached, and an income tax bill was passed on April 24, 1863. The bill exempted annual wages up to $1,000, with a 1 percent tax for the first $1,500 over that, and a 2 percent tax beyond that (military salaries were exempted). Other income was taxed from 5 to 15 percent. This low rate brought too little money into the treasury to be effective, and Memminger tried to raise the rate substantially higher, but Congress refused to cooperate. As a result, the Confederate income tax offered little relief to the financially strapped government.

INCOME TAX, UNION. From the beginning of war, the Union used taxation as a means to **finance** the war effort. Tariffs and real estate and excise **taxes** were passed in July 1861, and the nation's first income tax was passed by the **U.S. Congress** on August 5, 1861. Originally, this law placed a 3 percent tax on annual incomes in excess of $800. This rate gradually was increased until the act of June 30, 1864, put the rate at 5 percent on annual incomes between $600 and $5,000. This law also placed the tax rate at 7.5 percent on incomes from $5,000 to $10,000 and 10 percent on incomes more than $10,000. The income tax brought in $2 million the first year and approximately $20 million the next. Although it was not actually put into effect until the 1863 fiscal year, the income tax remained a part of the federal budget until it was repealed in 1872.

After the Civil War, the tax's constitutionality was challenged in court, but the **U.S. Supreme Court** upheld its legality. A second income tax that was passed in 1894, however, was struck down by the Court in 1895, leading to the adoption of the modern income tax through the ratification of the 16th Amendment in 1913.

INDEPENDENCE, MISSOURI, FIRST BATTLE OF (AUGUST 11, 1862). On August 11, 1862, Confederate Col. J. T. Hughes attacked the Union garrison at Independence, Missouri, with two columns of Missouri State Guard, one of which included **William C. Quantrill** and his guerrillas. After a short fight, in which Hughes was killed, Union Lt. Col. James T. Buel surrendered 150 of his men. Colonel G. W. Thompson, who had assumed command of the Confederates, **paroled** the Federals and moved on toward Kansas City, Missouri. Confederate losses in the clash are unknown, but the Federals lost a total of 344 men.

INDEPENDENCE, MISSOURI, SECOND BATTLE OF (OCTOBER 22, 1864). During **Sterling Price's 1864 Missouri Raid**, the Confederates defeated a Union force at the **Little Blue River** on October 21 and continued to advance west toward Independence, Missouri. The next day, Union cavalry under Maj. Gen. **Alfred Pleasonton** began attacking Price's rear guard under Brig. Gen. **William L. Cabell**. At Independence, Pleasonton captured a number of **prisoners** and two cannons. Pushing through town, he then was attacked by **John S. Marmaduke's** cavalry and was forced back. In these clashes at Independence, the Confederates lost 140 men, but Pleasonton's casualties are unknown.

INDIANA. Indiana was one of the largest Northern states and was vital to the Union war effort. Although containing some **Copperheads** in its southern half, Indiana was populated for the most part by intensely loyal citizens. When **Abraham Lincoln** made his initial call for 75,000 volunteers in April 1861, the state answered with almost twice its quota, and by war's end 196,363 Indiana men had served. This included 129 infantry **regiments**, 14 units of cavalry, and 27 units of **artillery**. Of these men, 7,243 were killed in battle, and 17,785 died of disease. Some of the Union generals who hailed from Indiana were **Ambrose Burnside, Jefferson C. Davis, Robert Milroy**, and **Lew Wallace**.

In 1861, Gov. **Oliver P. Morton** floated a loan with a **New York** bank and used the money not only to create a state arsenal and training camps but also to raise equipment and provide for soldiers and their families. The only military action within the state came in July 1863 during **John Hunt Morgan's Ohio Raid**, when 3,000 Confederate troopers raided Indiana. They were quickly chased into **Ohio**, however.

INDIANS. The Five Civilized Tribes—Cherokee, Choctaw, Chickasaw, Creek, and Seminole—of **Indian Territory** played the most important Indian role in the Civil War. Having been removed from their homelands in the 1830s, they had for the most part adopted the white-American ways of farming, Christianity, dress, and even slaveholding. Other tribes, such as the Quapaws, Senecas, Seneca-Shawnees, Wichitas, Caddos, and Comanches, played a lesser role in the war. Of course, thousands of other Indians lived in the warring states, but their scattered nature prevented them from forming armed units. Exceptions to this were a **North Carolina** Cherokee battalion, the 1st Mississippi Choctaw Infantry Battalion, and some small **Louisiana** Koasati and Alabama units.

Most of the Indians sided with the Confederacy, largely because the Confederates offered more concessions, the Union had a history of broken treaties, and many Indians were slave owners. The **Republicans'** outcries for seizing more Indian land for white settlement in the **election of 1860** was also a factor, as was the Union abandonment of several forts in Indian Territory early in the war.

In March 1861, **Albert Pike** was sent by the Confederate government
to negotiate alliances with the tribes in Indian Territory. Pike made
treaties that summer with the Choctaws, Creeks, Seminoles, and Chickasaws, but the Cherokees under Chief John Ross were divided in loyalties, and Ross was determined to stay neutral. In return for an Indian al-
liance, the Confederates agreed to assume the financial obligations of the
federal government, guaranteed **slavery**, promised that Indian land
would not be organized into territories, allowed the Indians the use of
Confederate courts, and admitted one nonvoting Indian delegate per tribe
to the **Confederate Congress**. Other treaties later were signed with the
Wichitas and Caddos.

After the Union defeat at **Wilson's Creek**, Ross finally agreed to sign
a Cherokee treaty with the Confederates. Once the Cherokees signed,
Pike was able to negotiate similar treaties in October 1861 with the Quapaws, Senecas, Osages, and Eastern Shawnees. To oversee Indian affairs,
the Confederate government established the Bureau of Indian Affairs
within the War Department in March 1861 and assigned six agents to
work with the Indians.

About 3,000–4,000 Indians served the Confederacy during the war,
with a similar number serving the Union. The two leading figures were
Stand Watie, a pro-Confederate Cherokee, and Chief Opothleyahola, a
pro-Union Creek. The Indians played a significant military role only in
Indian Territory and in the battles of **Pea Ridge** and **Poison Spring**.
They were good guerrilla fighters and scouts but often deserted because
they were too independent to accept strict **discipline**. In Indian Territory,
Indians played a crucial role in the many raids and **skirmishes** that dis-
rupted that area. By 1864, the Confederates had one **division** of Indians
serving in Indian Territory and **Texas**, composed of three **brigades** of
Cherokee, Choctaw-Chickasaw, and Creek-Seminole troops. After the
war, those Indians who had supported the Confederacy found their loyalty came at a high price when all of the existing federal treaties with
them were declared void. *See also* BATTLES OF CABIN CREEK,
CHUSTENAHLAH, CHUSTO-TALASAH, HONEY SPRINGS, MID-
DLE BOGGY, AND OLD FORT WAYNE, INDIAN TERRITORY;
KIRKSVILLE AND NEWTONIA, MISSOURI; SAND CREEK MAS-
SACRE, COLORADO; SIOUX UPRISING, MINNESOTA.

INDIAN TERRITORY. That area comprising most of modern-day Okla-
homa was known as Indian Territory during the Civil War. The Confederates formed it into a formal military **Department of Indian Territory**
in November 1861 under **Albert Pike**, but it was abolished in May 1862

when it became part of the **Trans-Mississippi Department**. Pike resigned as **department** commander in November 1862, and the position was left vacant until **Samuel B. Maxey** took command in December 1863. Maxey was replaced in February 1865 by **Douglas H. Cooper**.

In 1860, the territory had a population of about 64,000, mostly **Indians** who had been pushed out of their homelands before the Civil War. These included the Five Civilized Tribes (Cherokee, Choctaw, Chickasaw, Creek, and Seminole), Quapaws, Senecas, Shawnees, Osages, Comanches, Caddos, and Wichitas. Most of the Indians supported the Confederacy because of broken U.S. treaties and more enticing Confederate promises and the fact that many of the Indians were slave owners. Cherokee **Stand Watie** was a major leader of these pro-Confederates. Still, several tribes—most notably the Cherokees, Creeks, and Seminoles—were divided, with many tribal members fighting for the Union. Most of Creek Chief Opothleyahola's people supported the Union.

A large number of the troops that fought in battles at **Chusto-Talasah**, **Chustenahlah**, **Old Fort Wayne**, **Cabin Creek**, and **Middle Boggy** were Indians. Some of these fights forced Opothleyahola's followers to abandon Indian Territory and fall back into **Kansas**. The Union victory at **Pea Ridge** in early 1862, however, changed things. The Confederates under Pike fell back to near **Texas**, and Union forces—including many Indians—temporarily advanced back into the territory before retreating to Kansas again.

In April 1863, a second Union advance was made into the Indian Territory, with an entire Indian **brigade** participating in the movement. After occupying **Fort Gibson**, the Federals under **James G. Blunt** attacked a Confederate force under Cooper at **Honey Springs** in July and forced the Confederates to retreat into Texas. This Union victory liberated most of Indian Territory from Confederate control. Afterward, such Confederate commanders as Watie, **Richard M. Gano**, and **William Quantrill** were reduced to launching raids into the territory. When the Confederate Trans-Mississippi Department surrendered in May 1865, the Confederate Indians quickly laid down their arms. Watie surrendered the last organized Confederate units in July.

Indian Territory was ravaged by the Civil War, although it was seen as a relatively unimportant backwater theater by both sides. For the Indians, the war proved to be an internecine conflict that left tribes and families split and hostile for decades. Thousands lost family members, homes, and property and were displaced by the fighting. It is estimated that as much as 20 percent of the Indian population of the Indian Territory may have died during the war. Also those tribes that had signed treaties with the Confederates found themselves punished after the war. The U.S. government declared that all federal treaties with those tribes were void and forced the Indians to sign new treaties in 1866–67. These new treaties made the Indians give up additional land and allowed the building of **railroads** across tribal land.

INDUSTRY. When the Civil War began, the Union had a huge advantage over the Confederacy in industrial capacity, producing more than 92 percent of the nation's gross national product in 1860. In 1860, the Union also boasted 110,274 industrial establishments to the Confederacy's 18,026 (the states of **New York** and **Pennsylvania** individually had more industry than all of the seceding states combined). In **railroads**, the Union had approximately 20,000 miles of track in 1860 as compared with about 9,000 miles for the seceding states. Northern states had 24 times the number of locomotives as the South and produced 20 times the amount of pig iron and 17 times the amount of textiles. In addition, the North greatly outproduced the South in weapons manufacturing through its **Springfield, Colt**, and **Remington** Companies. While the South did have the great **Tredegar Iron Works** and some other heavy industry in **Virginia** and **Georgia**, it was no match for the North's industrial might.

For years it generally was believed that the Civil War pushed the United States into an industrial revolution and greatly increased its industrial might as the North was placed on a war footing. Such industries as weapons, textiles, and coal did enjoy huge growth as the **army** demanded more material, but modern research also shows that many industrial areas actually experienced a decline. Railroad expansion greatly slowed, as did the production of pig iron and copper. During the 1860s, the total commodity output of the United States was only one-third of what it had been in the 1850s, and output per capita actually declined. With a few exceptions, there were no great technological leaps made during the war; industry continued to use the same production methods used in the previous decades. In short, there is much conflicting evidence as to how the Civil War affected American industry.

"INFERNAL MACHINES." This term generally was given to any weapon that was hidden from view or was seen as being inhumane or treacherous. Such things as **torpedoes**, land mines, **submarines**, and incendiary devices were at times referred to as "infernal machines." Because of its inferiority in manpower and weapons, the Confederacy was more active in developing "infernal machines" than the Union was.

INGALLS, RUFUS (1818–1893) USA. A native of **Maine**, Ingalls graduated from **West Point** in 1843 and won a **brevet** for his service in northern **New Mexico** during the **Mexican War**. Afterward, he joined the quartermaster department, where he served for the remainder of his long military career.

Before the Civil War, Ingalls had served in posts around the country and was a captain at **Fort Pickens, Florida**, when the war began. In September 1861, he was promoted to lieutenant colonel and later that year was appointed chief quartermaster for the **Army of the Potomac**. Ingalls was promoted to major in the regular **army** in January 1862 and brigadier general of volunteers in May 1863. A testament to his ability is that he served four army commanders in this capacity until **U. S. Grant** appointed him chief quartermaster for the Army of the Potomac and the **Army of the James** in June 1864. Ingalls kept this position until war's end. For his war service, he was brevetted all ranks in the regulars and volunteers through major general.

In July 1866, Ingalls was appointed assistant quartermaster general with the staff rank of colonel. He served in various quartermaster positions until 1882, when he was made quartermaster general of the army with the rank of brigadier general. Ingalls remained at this post until retiring in 1883 after 40 years of service. He was one of those critical, but lesser known officers, who kept the Union war machine running until victory was achieved.

INTERIOR LINES. This is a military term referring to one belligerent having the advantage over the other by being able to transport men and supplies more quickly from one point to another over a shorter distance. It usually happens when one **army's** position is within a curved boundary — as was the Union position at **Gettysburg**. The side with the interior line can shift men and material from point to point over a straight line or radius, while the opposing side has to travel around the arc of the circle. Not only does geography dictate the interior line; so do transportation systems. One army may hold a geographical interior line; but it does no good unless there is also a road, river, or **railroad** system that allows it to shift men and material quickly to the needed point. Tactically, the Union held the interior line at Gettysburg and was able to rapidly deploy reinforcements to meet successfully the Confederate attacks. The Confederates held a similar position at **Antietam**. Strategically, the Confederates generally had the advantage of the interior line. *See also* STRATEGY; TACTICS.

INVALID CORPS. During the Civil War, thousands of wounded men were so badly injured that active field duty was impossible but not so badly as to render them useless to the war effort. At first, feeble soldiers were detached from their units to work in hospitals while recuperating from sickness or wounds. In April 1863, the Union formalized this practice by creating an Invalid Corps made up of sick and wounded officers and men with good service records. The **corps** was organized like any other military unit and had two battalions. One was composed of men healthy enough to shoulder weapons and serve on garrison duty, while the other contained the weaker or handicapped soldiers fit only for hospital duty. Many soldiers disliked serving in the Invalid Corps because they were forced to wear lighter colored blue **uniforms** than their field-service comrades, and the corps' initials were the same as those used by the government to stamp condemned equipment, that is, "Inspected—Condemned." To boost morale, therefore, the corps was renamed the Veteran Reserve Corps in March 1864, and it adopted the same uniforms as other Union soldiers. By the time the corps was abolished in 1866, more than 60,000 men had served in it. They performed valuable duty guarding forts and depots, working in hospitals, and even in putting down the **New York City Draft Riot** and helping repulse **Jubal A. Early's Washington Raid**.

The Confederacy organized its own Invalid Corps in 1864. Invalid soldiers had to serve in it in order to be paid and were forced to return to their own units when their health was restored. Unlike its Union counterpart, it was never organized like a military organization but did perform some valuable service.

IOWA. Iowa had a long history of **abolitionism** because of its rather large Quaker population. Therefore, when Gov. **Samuel J. Kirkwood** sent out **Abraham Lincoln's** call for 75,000 volunteers in April 1861, Iowans responded with enthusiasm. In short order, 10 times the needed men volunteered. This enthusiasm did not wane until the depressing days of 1864, at which time Gov. **William M. Stone** for the first time had to implement **conscription** to fill the state's quota of recruits. The state provided 46 infantry **regiments**, four **artillery** batteries, nine cavalry regiments, and thousands of individual recruits (including 440 **black troops**) who fought in many of the large western battles. In all, more than 76,000 men—or approximately one-half of the state's eligible men—served in the Union **army**. Iowa sent a larger percentage of its eligible men off to war than any other Northern state. Of these, 13,001 died (3,540 in battle) and more than 8,500 were seriously wounded.

IRISH BEND, LOUISIANA, BATTLE OF (APRIL 14, 1863). In April 1863, **Nathaniel P. Banks** prepared for his **Port Hudson, Louisiana, Campaign** by launching the **Bayou Teche Campaign** with 15,000 men to drive out the approximately 5,000 Confederates under Maj. Gen.

Richard Taylor that might threaten his flank. Banks's advance included two movements. Two **divisions** moved up the Teche from Brashear City to attack Taylor at **Fort Bisland**, while Brig. Gen. **Cuvier Grover** took his 5,000-man division by transport on April 12 across Grand Lake to land in Taylor's rear at Irish Bend.

On April 13, Taylor fought a delaying action at Fort Bisland and then withdrew during the night toward Franklin. The next day he drew up a battle line at Irish Bend to stop Grover's advance long enough for his trains to escape northward. With about 1,000 men, Taylor exchanged heavy **artillery** fire with the advancing enemy that was floundering in a muddy sugarcane field. With aid from his one gunboat, *Diana*, and troops freshly arrived from Fort Bisland, he attacked, drove off Grover, and continued the retreat. The *Diana* was destroyed to prevent its capture, and Taylor burned a bridge behind him to prevent pursuit. On April 14, the Confederate *Queen of the West* also was destroyed by the Union fleet on Grand Lake. Banks eventually followed Taylor into central **Louisiana**, but he failed to destroy him. In the Battle of Irish Bend (also called Indian Bend or Nerson's Wood), Grover lost 353 men. The number of Confederate casualties is unknown, except that 21 dead were left on the field and 35 wounded men were captured.

IRISH BRIGADE. Irish immigrants fought on both sides of the Civil War, dominating some **regiments** and **brigades**. The most famous was the Union Irish Brigade in the **Army of the Potomac**. This brigade was organized in the autumn of 1861 by Brig. Gen. **Thomas F. Meagher** and originally consisted of the Irish-dominated 63rd, 69th, and 88th New York. While the brigade was serving in the **Peninsula Campaign** as the 2nd Brigade of Maj. Gen. **Edwin V. Sumner's** division, the non-Irish 29th Massachusetts was added to it. The brigade received an additional Irish regiment, the 116th Pennsylvania, in October 1862, and in November the 29th Massachusetts was replaced by the Irish 28th Massachusetts. Heavy casualties so weakened the brigade by June 1864 that it was consolidated with the **division's** 3rd Brigade and became the Consolidated Brigade. The Irish Brigade regained its identity as the 2nd Brigade in November, however, when it was reorganized with the 7th New York Heavy Artillery, 28th Massachusetts, and 63rd, 69th, and 88th New York. In early 1865, the 4th New York Heavy Artillery replaced the 7th regiment. All of the regiments except the 4th New York were mustered out of service in June 1865; it was mustered out in September.

Meagher led the brigade until he resigned in late 1863. Subsequent commanders were Robert Nugent, **Thomas A. Smyth**, Patrick Kelly (killed in the **Petersburg Campaign**), Richard Byrne (mortally wounded at **Cold Harbor**), and Richard C. Duryea. The Irish Brigade became famous for its outstanding fighting ability and was conspicuous in battle because each of its Irish regiments carried a green **flag**. The unit saw combat in nearly every battle fought by the Army of the Potomac and performed particularly well at **Antietam** and **Gettysburg**. It was most remembered for a heroic attack against the stone wall on Marye's Heights at **Fredericksburg**. There the Irishmen faced ferocious Confederate fire in a brave but doomed assault.

IRON BRIGADE, CONFEDERATE. *See* SHELBY'S IRON BRIGADE.

IRON BRIGADE (OR BLACK HAT BRIGADE) USA. The only **Army of the Potomac brigade** composed entirely of Western men, the Iron Brigade was organized in **Washington, D.C.**, in the autumn of 1861. Commanded originally by Brig. Gen. **Rufus King**, it included the 2nd, 6th, and 7th Wisconsin, and the 19th Indiana. **John Gibbon** took command in May 1862 and adopted a unique black slouch hat for the men, which led to the unit being referred to as the Black Hat Brigade.

The brigade's first engagement was at **Groveton**, where it slugged it out with a superior Confederate force in an open field for two hours and lost 751 men, or one-third of its strength. Shortly afterward, the 24th Michigan was added to the brigade, which by now was designated the 1st Brigade, 1st Division, I Corps. It lost 318 men at **South Mountain** and days later charged into **Antietam's** cornfield and suffered another 348 casualties. It was at South Mountain that **corps** commander **Joseph Hooker** originally referred to the brigade as his "Iron Brigade". The name stuck when a **war correspondent** used the term in a newspaper article. After being only lightly engaged at **Fredericksburg** and **Chancellorsville**, the brigade went into action on the first day at **Gettysburg** and lost 1,212 men (two-thirds of its strength) while trying to slow the Confederate advance. The 24th Michigan suffered the highest number of casualties, losing 399 out of 496 men, or 80 percent of its strength (each **regiment** lost over 70 percent of its men). The brigade continued to serve, but after Gettysburg, it never again had the same effectiveness or special identity. Its regimental makeup was changed to include eastern regiments, and some of the original regiments either mustered out or were consolidated with others.

IRONCLAD OATH. This **oath of allegiance** originally was required of all civilian and military officeholders through an act passed by the **U.S. Congress** on July 2, 1862. It stated that the person was loyal to the U.S.

Constitution and had never supported the Rebellion or voluntarily taken up arms against the government. During **Reconstruction**, the oath was required to regain the right to vote and to run for political office. **Radical Republicans** used it to keep former Confederates from entering politics since most Southerners refused to swear that they had not voluntarily joined the **Confederate army**. The ironclad oath could be waived on an individual basis but only by a two-thirds vote of Congress.

IRONCLADS. Ironclads were any warship having iron plating to protect its vital parts and are seen as the forerunners of modern-day battleships. They originated in Great Britain and France but first saw extensive combat in the Civil War. Confederate Secretary of War **Stephen Mallory** quickly recognized that the South did not have the resources to compete with the Union in numbers of ships built. Thus, he decided to concentrate on building the more invincible ironclads to counter the Union's advantage in numbers. The Confederates' *Virginia* was the first ironclad of the war, quickly followed by the Union *Monitor*. Their epic encounter at **Hampton Roads** proved the superiority of ironclads over traditional wooden vessels and made the latter obsolete.

The Confederates began construction on about 50 ironclads during the war, but only 22 actually were finished. The Union built 60 ships of the **monitor** class and many other more traditional ironclads. Because their heavy weight greatly reduced speed and maneuverability, ironclads were more useful on inland waterways than on the open ocean. Often, Confederate ironclads, such as the *Arkansas*, had inferior engines and were used as little more than floating batteries.

ISLAND NO. 10, MISSOURI, CAPTURE OF (APRIL 7, 1862). See NEW MADRID AND ISLAND NO. 10, MISSOURI, CAPTURE OF.

IUKA, MISSISSIPPI, BATTLE OF (SEPTEMBER 19, 1862). When Confederate Gen. **Braxton Bragg** began the **Kentucky Campaign** in late summer 1862, he ordered Maj. Gen. **Sterling Price's** 14,000-man **Army of the West** to occupy Union forces in northern **Mississippi** to prevent them from reinforcing **Don Carlos Buell** in **Tennessee**.

Marching from **Tupelo**, **Mississippi**, Price drove off a Union garrison at Iuka on September 14 and occupied the town. Major General **U. S. Grant** believed Price was preparing to advance into Tennessee to reinforce Bragg and was determined to stop him. He ordered **E. O. C. Ord** to take his three **divisions** (8,000 men) from Burnsville and strike southeast toward Iuka, while **William S. Rosecrans's** two divisions (9,000 men) marched eastward on Price from Jacinto. Ord was to attack Price's front on the morning of September 19, while Rosecrans hit the Confederate rear to cut Price's line of retreat. Rosecrans's march did not go well, however, and he did not arrive in the Iuka area until September 19. Grant postponed the attack until the next day.

Meanwhile, on the night of September 18, Price was ordered by Maj. Gen. **Earl Van Dorn** to join him southwest of Jacinto at Rienzi for an attack against Corinth. Leaving some men to face Ord, Price began moving Brig. Gen. **Lewis H. Little's** division to the southwest on September 19 in accordance with Van Dorn's orders. That afternoon, Little's men attacked Rosecrans's advance, and a battle began south of Iuka. The Confederates launched heavy attacks that drove back Rosecrans's divisions, and late in the day, Little was killed while bringing up more troops. Fighting lasted until dark, but the Federals held their ground. As the battle raged south of Iuka, Ord remained motionless northwest of town. An **acoustic shadow** prevented him from hearing the fight, and as a result, Price was able to withdraw nearly all of his men from that sector and send them against Rosecrans. Price planned to continue the battle the next day, but he finally was convinced that Ord's force was a potent threat in his rear. He withdrew along a road that Rosecrans had failed to block and escaped to join Van Dorn.

Price lost 1,516 men in the battle, while the Federals counted 790 casualties. Although the Confederates suffered substantially higher casualties, the Federals were embarrassed by Price's escape. Rosecrans, who was criticized for failing to block the escape route Price used, never quite believed Ord's claim of not hearing the battle. Soon after Van Dorn and Price joined forces, they launched an attack against **Corinth** the next month.

IVERSON, ALFRED, JR. (1829–1911) CSA. The son of a U.S. senator, Iverson was a native of **Georgia**. He dropped out of school to serve in the **Mexican War** and was appointed a 2nd lieutenant at the age of 17. After the war, Iverson briefly studied law under his father but then began working for **railroads**. In 1855, he was commissioned a 1st lieutenant in the 1st U.S. Cavalry and raised a **company** of volunteers for the **regiment**. Over the next six years, Iverson served in **"Bleeding Kansas,"** in the **Utah Expedition**, and fought **Indians**.

Iverson resigned his commission in March 1861, entered Confederate service as a captain, and was sent to **North Carolina** to command the companies guarding the mouth of the Cape Fear River. There he organized enough additional companies to form the 20th North Carolina and was appointed its colonel in August 1861. Iverson's regiment fought in the **Seven Days Campaign** with the **Army of Northern Virginia** and captured an enemy battery at **Gaines' Mill**. Although wounded in the fight, he recovered in time to participate in the **Antietam Campaign**. During the fighting at **South Mountain**, Iverson's **brigade** commander, **Samuel Garland**, was killed, and Iverson led the brigade at Antietam.

Iverson was promoted to brigadier general in November 1862. He saw little combat at **Fredericksburg**, did not perform particularly well at **Chancellorsville**, and had his reputation badly tarnished at **Gettysburg**. On that battle's first day, Iverson did not handle his men well, and the brigade was nearly destroyed. The experience shattered his nerves, and the brigade adjutant had to take temporary command. **Robert E. Lee** had little confidence in Iverson after Gettysburg and had him transferred to Georgia in October. There he took command of the state troops at Rome until February 1864, when he was put in command of a cavalry brigade under **Joseph Wheeler**. Iverson partially redeemed himself in July when his men defeated a superior Union cavalry force near Macon during one of **George Stoneman's Raids**. Pursuing the enemy, he later captured Stoneman himself and hundreds of his men. It was one of the Confederacy's greatest cavalry victories, but it largely was overshadowed by the defeats in the **Atlanta Campaign**. Iverson remained in command of his cavalry brigade until February 1865, when he was given command of a **division** for the **Carolinas Campaign**.

After the war, Iverson moved to **Florida** and grew oranges.

– J –

JACKSON, ALFRED EUGENE (1807–1889) CSA. A native of **Tennessee**, Jackson attended Washington and Greenville Colleges before becoming a farmer and merchant. By the 1850s, he had a sizeable empire of stores, farms, and gristmills.

Jackson entered Confederate service in September 1861 as a major, joined Brig. Gen. **Felix K. Zollicoffer's** staff as quartermaster, and apparently served Zollicoffer until the general was killed at **Mill Springs** in January 1862. Afterward, he was made a Tennessee paymaster and served in that capacity until he was appointed brigadier general in October. This initial appointment was canceled, but apparently Jackson's political connections led to his being reappointed brigadier general in April 1863.

Given command of a mixed **brigade** of infantry, cavalry, and **artillery**, Jackson scattered his men across eastern Tennessee to protect the

Tennessee & Virginia Railroad. He could do little but **skirmish** with the enemy when **Ambrose E. Burnside** invaded eastern Tennessee in September 1863 and occupied Knoxville. After patrolling against guerrillas and skirmishing with Union **foraging** parties, Jackson was ordered to **Saltville, Virginia**, where he defeated Union raider **Stephen G. Burbridge** in a bloody October fight. Illness then forced him to give up his field command, and he apparently was employed in staff duties under **John C. Breckinridge** until war's end.

After the war, Jackson farmed in **Virginia** and eventually resettled in Tennessee.

JACKSON, CLAIBORNE FOX (1806–1862) CSA. A native of **Kentucky**, Jackson moved to **Missouri** as a young man and became involved in business, banking, and politics. He served in the state assembly from 1836 to 1848 and the senate from 1848 to 1852. At first an ally of Thomas Hart Benton, Jackson's support of spreading **slavery** into the territories finally led to a break between them. In 1857, he was appointed the state's first banking commissioner and became the state **Democratic Party** chairman. In 1860, Jackson was elected governor. During the presidential campaign, he publicly remained loyal to the Northern Democrats supporting **Stephen A. Douglas**, while privately was sympathetic to the Southern Democrats supporting **John C. Breckinridge**.

After being inaugurated in January 1861, Jackson more openly sided with the secessionists. He called on the legislature to hold a **secession** convention, which in February voted to remain neutral; entered into secret talks with Southern politicians; and began preparing the militia. When **Abraham Lincoln** called for volunteers after the bombardment of **Fort Sumter**, Jackson rejected the appeal and began plotting with secessionists to seize the U.S. arsenal in St. Louis. Assembling his prosecession militia into training camps, he received four cannons from **Jefferson Davis**. Before Jackson could take action, however, Capt. **Nathaniel Lyon** surrounded **Camp Jackson** and forced the secessionists to surrender. After the **St. Louis Riot**, the legislature gave Jackson control of the militia. He quickly appointed **Sterling Price** to command a new Missouri State Guard and called for 50,000 volunteers. Jackson then retreated to southwestern Missouri with his secessionist supporters but was removed from office by a new state convention.

After the Confederate victory at **Wilson's Creek**, Jackson convened a pro-Confederate legislative session at Neosho in October. The legislators voted to secede and join the Confederacy, but it was never seen as an official act by many citizens and had little meaning since Union forces occupied most of the state. When Union forces pushed Price out of Missouri, Jackson headed a government in exile in **Arkansas** and briefly stayed in **Texas** before dying from pneumonia in late 1862.

JACKSON, CONRAD FEGER (1813–1862) USA. A native of **Pennsylvania**, Jackson was prominent in the state militia and is said to have fought in the **Mexican War** as a captain. Afterward, he worked for the Reading Railroad and remained active in the militia.

Jackson entered Union service in July 1861 when his militia **company** became part of the 9th Pennsylvania Reserves, and he was commissioned the regiment's colonel. Sent to **Washington, D.C.**, the **regiment** (also known as the 38th Pennsylvania) became part of **E. O. C. Ord's** brigade and fought at **Dranesville**. Attached to **Truman Seymour's** brigade, the regiment next fought in the **Seven Days Campaign** with the **Army of the Potomac**. In the latter part of the campaign, Jackson took temporary command of the **brigade** after Seymour took command of the **division**.

Jackson was promoted to brigadier general of volunteers in July 1862 and led the brigade at **Second Manassas**, although he was forced to relinquish command on the battlefield because of illness. He returned to duty in time to fight at **Fredericksburg** and had a horse shot from under him there. While directing his men on foot, Jackson was killed by a shot through the head.

JACKSON, HENRY ROOTES (1820–1898) CSA. A native of **Georgia**, Jackson graduated first in his class from Yale University in 1839. After opening a Georgia law practice, he served as a U.S. district attorney from 1843 to 1847. Jackson fought in the **Mexican War** as colonel of the 1st Georgia and then was appointed to the state superior court in 1849. In 1853, he was appointed U.S. minister to Austria and remained in that position until returning to his law practice in 1858. As an attorney, Jackson won some fame by assisting the government in the unsuccessful 1859 prosecution of the captain and owners of the slave ship *Wanderer*.

In 1860, Jackson was a delegate at both failed **Democratic** National Conventions and in 1861 was a prosecession delegate at the state **secession** convention. Governor **Joseph E. Brown** then appointed him colonel and aide-de-camp and had him capture the **Augusta arsenal** and several ships. Jackson first entered Confederate service as a judge of Confederate courts in Georgia but resigned this position to accept a brigadier general's commission in June 1861.

Sent to **Virginia**, Jackson first served in the western part of the state and replaced the slain **Robert S. Garnett** at the head of the **Army of Northwestern Virginia** in July. After serving well for a few crucial weeks, he was replaced by **William W. Loring** and assumed command of a small **division**. Jackson fought well at **Cheat Mountain** but then resigned his commission in December to accept command of Georgia's state forces. Appointed major general of state troops that same month, he commanded the 1st Division at Savannah. When the **Confederate army** absorbed this division, Jackson served as an aide to **William H. T. Walker** for a time.

In September 1863, Jackson again was commissioned a Confederate brigadier general and performed various services in Georgia (including commanding the District of Georgia) until he was given command of **Clement H. Stevens's** former **brigade** in July 1864. Serving in **William B. Bate's** division of the **Army of Tennessee**, he fought at **Jonesboro** before accompanying **John B. Hood** on his move into northern Georgia and **Alabama**. In October, Jackson personally led his men in a counterattack at **Decatur, Alabama**, and the following month his brigade led the division into battle at **Franklin**. He destroyed the **railroad** around Murfreesboro while Hood confronted Nashville but rejoined the **army** before the climatic battle there. At the **Battle of Nashville**, Jackson barely escaped death when a shell exploded under his horse and killed it. On the second day of battle at Nashville, he was captured when he became bogged down in mud trying to reach his horse. Jackson was imprisoned at **Fort Warren, Massachusetts**, until July 1865.

After the war, Jackson resumed his Georgia law practice and served as President Grover Cleveland's minister to Mexico from 1885 to 1887. He also served as president of the Georgia Historical Society from 1875 to 1898, was a trustee of the Peabody Educational Fund, and served as a director for a banking and **railroad** company.

JACKSON, JAMES STRESHLY (1823–1862) USA. A native of **Kentucky**, Jackson was educated at several colleges, including the law department at Transylvania University. He began a practice in 1845 but left it during the **Mexican War** to enlist as a private in the 1st Kentucky Cavalry. Jackson was promoted to 3rd lieutenant but supposedly resigned his commission to avoid a court-martial after fighting a duel with his colonel. Elected to the **U.S. Congress** in 1860, he served only until December 1861, at which time he resigned his seat to become colonel of the 3rd Kentucky Cavalry (Union), a **regiment** he had raised.

After seeing service, but not combat, at **Shiloh**, Jackson was promoted to brigadier general of volunteers in July 1862. Placed in command of the **Army of Kentucky's** cavalry, he seems to have served well but once again missed combat at **Richmond** by arriving on the field the day after the battle. In September, Jackson was transferred to command the 10th Division of the **Army of the Ohio's** I Corps. At the **Battle of Perryville**, he was killed while positioned near his **artillery**.

JACKSON, JOHN KING (1828–1866) CSA. A native of **Georgia**, Jackson graduated with honors from the University of South Carolina in 1846 and opened a law practice two years later. Becoming active in the state militia, he rose through the ranks to become lieutenant colonel by the time of the Civil War.

Jackson entered Confederate service in May 1861 when he was elected colonel of the 5th Georgia. Sent to **Pensacola, Florida**, he impressed his superior, **Braxton Bragg**, when he led an October attack against **Santa Rosa Island**. Jackson took command of Pensacola when Bragg was transferred and, upon Bragg's recommendation, was promoted to brigadier general in January 1862.

Sent first to **Tennessee** and then to **Mississippi**, Jackson skillfully led an infantry **brigade** at **Shiloh**. Afterward, he guarded **railroads** in **Alabama** and participated in the **Kentucky Campaign** but saw no combat. As part of **John C. Breckinridge's division** in the **Army of Tennessee**, Jackson fought at **Stones River** and lost approximately 300 men. After further guard duty in Alabama, he went into action at **Chickamauga** as part of **Benjamin Cheatham's** division. There Jackson's men fought very well and captured three cannons, but one of his **regiments** lost 61 percent of its men. Jackson's reputation as a capable commander was tarnished during the **Chattanooga Campaign** when he commanded a small division that held **Lookout Mountain**. In the November 1863 battle, Jackson's brigade commanders complained that he could not be found and that he did not issue orders or inspect his line. After the defeat, Jackson nearly challenged some of these officers to duels. Resuming his brigade command, he fought at **Missionary Ridge** but was accused by a neighboring brigade commander of being absent from the firing line. After fighting through much of the **Atlanta Campaign**, Jackson's brigade was broken up, and he was sent to Georgia with two of his regiments. He briefly commanded the District of Florida, and after **Savannah** fell, he established supply depots in **South Carolina**.

After the war, Jackson returned to his Georgia law practice and also worked as a bank lobbyist.

JACKSON, MISSISSIPPI, BATTLES OF (MAY 14 AND JULY 12–16, 1863). By May 1863, Maj. Gen. **U. S. Grant's Army of the Tennessee**

had crossed the Mississippi River and was maneuvering to capture **Vicksburg, Mississippi**, during the **Vicksburg Campaign**. After defeating the Confederates at **Port Gibson**, Grant pushed his column toward Jackson rather than marching directly on Vicksburg. Jackson not only was the state capital, but it also was a major depot in **John C. Pemberton's** supply line, and if it could be taken and the **railroad** destroyed, the enemy in Vicksburg would be cut off from reinforcements and supplies.

General **Joseph E. Johnston**, the Confederate **department** commander, was en route from **Tennessee** to assume command of the **Mississippi** forces. He arrived in Jackson on May 13 and found that only 6,000 troops defended the city. After midnight, Johnston ordered Jackson evacuated and assigned Brig. Gen. **John Gregg** the duty of delaying Grant until the withdrawal was completed. On the morning of May 14, **James B. McPherson's** XVII Corps approached Jackson from the west-northwest on the Clinton Road, while **William T. Sherman's** XV Corps marched from the southwest on the Mississippi Springs Road. In a heavy downpour, the Union columns met stiff resistance at mid-morning from Confederates blocking both roads. When the rain stopped at 11:00 A.M., **Marcellus M. Crocker's** XVII Corps **division** attacked along the Clinton Road and pushed back Col. Peyton H. Colquitt's Confederate **brigade**. Sherman also forced back the enemy under Col. Albert P. Thompson.

Sporadic fighting continued until about 3:00 P.M., when Johnston informed Gregg that the evacuation was completed and he could withdraw. Gregg did so and marched north on the Mississippi Central Railroad to join Johnston. Sherman, accompanied by Grant, entered the city at about 4:00 P.M. In the fighting, Grant lost 300 men, while the Confederates probably lost about 400. Johnston has been criticized for failing to fight for the capital, for he had enough troops in the area to assemble up to 12,000 men at Jackson by May 15. If Pemberton had cooperated to the east, Grant's 20,000 or so soldiers could have been trapped between two Confederate forces. The day after Jackson was captured, Grant took part of the **army** toward Vicksburg, while Sherman's **corps** remained behind to destroy supplies, public buildings, and the railroad. Much private property, including the Catholic church, also was destroyed.

During the siege of Vicksburg, Johnston assembled 32,000 men around Jackson to threaten Grant's rear and possibly raise the siege. He actually advanced toward Pemberton on July 1 but had not yet forced a crossing of the Big Black River when the city fell. When Vicksburg surrendered on July 4, Grant ordered Sherman with 11 divisions from three corps to attack Johnston.

Sherman, who was already in Grant's rear protecting it from Johnston's aborted advance, moved out on July 5 and quickly forced Johnston to fall back from the Big Black River to Jackson's earthworks. On July 12, Sherman attacked with **Jacob G. Lauman's** XIII Corps division, but Lauman's unit was badly shot up and lost more than 500 men. For the next several days, heavy **skirmishing** was frequent as Sherman inched closer to Johnston's defenses. Fearing the enemy would surround him, Johnston evacuated the city on the night of July 16 and retreated to Morton. Sherman occupied Jackson the next day and returned to Vicksburg on July 24. During the Union occupation, the city once again suffered from widespread looting and burning. Sherman lost 1,132 men in the campaign, while Johnston suffered approximately 600 casualties

JACKSON, NATHANIEL JAMES (1818–1892) USA. A native of **Massachusetts,** Jackson moved to **Maine,** became active in the state militia, and worked as a mill superintendent. He entered Union service in May 1861 as colonel of the 90-day 1st Maine. The **regiment** was mustered out of service in August without seeing any combat, but Jackson was appointed colonel of the 5th Maine the following month.

Jackson led his regiment in the **Army of the Potomac** during the **Seven Days Campaign** and was wounded at **Gaines' Mill.** Recovering in time to fight at **South Mountain** and **Antietam,** he was promoted to brigadier general of volunteers in late September 1862. As part of **John W. Geary's** XII Corps **division,** Jackson garrisoned **Harpers Ferry, Virginia,** during the **Fredericksburg** and **Chancellorsville Campaigns.** An unknown accident suffered there kept him off duty for more than a year. When he had recovered sufficiently for light duty, Jackson was placed in command of a **conscript** rendezvous at New York City until September 1864. At that time, he was transferred to Georgia, and in November **William T. Sherman** put him in command of a division in the **Army of the Cumberland's** XX Corps. Jackson led his division through the **March to the Sea** and the **Carolinas Campaign.** Near war's end, he was relieved of command when a reorganization left him without a position. **Brevetted** major general of volunteers for his service at Gaines' Mill, Jackson left the **army** in August 1865.

Jackson's postwar career is obscure.

JACKSON, THOMAS JONATHAN "STONEWALL" (1824–1863) CSA. A native of western **Virginia,** Jackson was a second cousin of Confederate Brig. Gen. **William L. Jackson** and became one of the most famous Confederate generals. An uncle raised him after his father died and his mother was unable to provide for him. Entering **West Point** as an alternate candidate, Jackson struggled with his studies because of his lack of a formal education. By dedication and discipline he managed to graduate seventeenth in the class of 1846. Jackson served in the **Mexican War** with the **artillery** under **Winfield Scott** and won two **brevets** for gallantry. He enjoyed Mexico after the war and even learned to speak Spanish while there. After three years of garrison duty in **New York** and **Florida**, Jackson then resigned from the **U.S. Army** and accepted a teaching position at the **Virginia Military Institute** (**VMI**).

Jackson found a home at VMI and worked hard teaching mathematics and artillery **tactics**. Although his teaching methods were dull and unimaginative, the cadets came to respect his dedication and military skill. Jackson accepted the Presbyterian faith with zeal while there and became so religious that some people viewed him as a zealot. He also married Elinor Junkin, a minister's daughter, in 1853, but she died in childbirth 14 months later. In 1857, Jackson married close friend Mary Anna Morrison (the sister of Daniel H. Hill's wife).

While at VMI, Jackson also became known as an eccentric who perhaps suffered from psychosomatic disorders. He often went on bland diets to cure his stomach ailments, soaked his eyes in buckets of cold water, refused to eat pepper because it made his leg ache, rarely sat because it was bad for his posture, and often kept an arm raised to even out his blood flow. Because of this, the cadets viewed him as an oddity and referred to him as "Tom Fool," but he maintained their respect because of his strict code of honor and dedication. In 1859, Jackson participated in one of the antebellum period's major divisive events when he commanded the VMI cadets who acted as guards at **John Brown's** hanging.

When civil war came two years later, Jackson left VMI to command a contingent of cadets who served as drillmasters at **Richmond, Virginia**. After briefly commanding **Harpers Ferry, Virginia**, he was appointed a Confederate brigadier general in June 1861 and was given command of the 1st Virginia Brigade. Jackson's first battle was at **First Manassas**, where his **brigade** arrived from the **Shenandoah Valley** in time to make a stand atop Henry House Hill and blunt the Union advance. Seeing the Virginians drawn up in a strong line, Brig. Gen. **Barnard Bee** reportedly cried out to his men, "There stands Jackson like a stone wall! Rally around the Virginians!" (Current, ed., *Encyclopedia of the Confederacy*, vol. 1, p. 151.) Jackson's famous nickname "Stonewall" was born; however, the Confederate soldiers rarely referred to him as such, and Jackson insisted the name applied to the **Stonewall Brigade**, not himself. Soldiers generally referred to him simply as "Old Jack."

In October 1861, Jackson was promoted to major general and was given command of the Shenandoah Valley. That winter he launched an unsuccessful expedition to Romney, Virginia, and was criticized by subordinates for poor management. Jackson made up for it in the spring of 1862 when he fought a spectacular six-week campaign in the Valley. Outnumbered four-to-one, his small **army** outmaneuvered and outfought three different Union forces, marched several hundred miles, and won five battles in **Stonewall Jackson's Shenandoah Valley Campaign**. Most importantly, Jackson occupied thousands of Union soldiers and prevented them from reinforcing **George B. McClellan** for the **Peninsula Campaign**. Because of their rapid movement in the Valley, Jackson's infantry became nicknamed **"foot cavalry."**

After the Shenandoah Valley Campaign, Jackson reinforced **Robert E. Lee's Army of Northern Virginia** outside Richmond for the **Seven Days Campaign**. There he failed to live up to his reputation when he did not get into position to fight at **Mechanicsville** and was late at **Gaines' Mill**. Jackson's unusual slowness on these days and a lack of initiative at **Savage's Station** have been blamed on fatigue.

Jackson's old enthusiasm soon returned, and in August he moved north against **John Pope's Army of Virginia**. At **Cedar Mountain**, he rashly gave battle without proper **reconnaissance** and was nearly defeated, but he finally won the day largely through his personal leadership. During the **Second Manassas Campaign**, Lee sent Jackson on a long flanking maneuver into Pope's rear and then followed with the rest of the army. Jackson destroyed the Union supply base at Manassas Junction, ambushed an enemy column at **Groveton**, and then held out against repeated Union assaults at Second Manassas until Lee could arrive and win the battle. Jackson then advanced to cut Pope's line of retreat and engaged the enemy in the unsuccessful fight at **Chantilly**.

During the **Antietam Campaign**, Jackson again was sent on an independent mission. He successfully captured Harpers Ferry, along with 12,000 Union **prisoners**, and then rapidly joined Lee at Antietam. There, Jackson commanded the left wing and skillfully fought off repeated attacks by a superior enemy force. After Antietam, Lee organized the Army of Northern Virginia into two **corps**, and in October Jackson was promoted to lieutenant general and was given command of the II Corps. At **Fredericksburg**, his corps held Lee's right wing, and he inexplicably left a gap in his line. The enemy broke through and temporarily threatened Jackson's position, but his men finally sealed the break with a vicious counterattack.

When **Joseph Hooker** moved beyond Lee's flank during the 1863 **Chancellorsville Campaign**, Lee sent Jackson to confront the threat.

After concentrating the army there, Lee then sent Jackson's entire corps around the Union right flank. Jackson smashed the Union XI Corps on May 2, 1863, and sent it reeling, but darkness, mounting confusion, and enemy resistance forced him finally to halt his attack. That night, Jackson and his staff rode beyond the lines to reconnoiter for a possible night attack. Mistaken for Union cavalry upon its return, the party was fired upon by Confederate soldiers. Jackson was hit once in the right hand and twice in the left arm. His arm was amputated, and it appeared he would recover, but Jackson developed pneumonia and died on May 10. His wife, Anna, and infant daughter reached him just before he died. Lapsing in and out of consciousness, Jackson's reported last words were, "Let us cross over the river and rest under the shade of the trees." (Roberston, *Stonewall Jackson*, 753).

Jackson was one of Lee's most trusted subordinates. When informed of Jackson's wound, Lee replied that while Jackson had lost his left arm, Lee had lost his right. Jackson performed best when in independent command—such as in the Shenandoah Valley, Second Manassas, and Antietam Campaigns—and he won some spectacular victories. But he was also a difficult superior to serve under. Subordinates frequently complained of Jackson's unbending ways and his complete secrecy, and more than one found himself under arrest for not living up to Jackson's high standards. Jackson also could act rashly, and his dependence on the attack frequently put him at risk, as occurred at **First Kernstown** and Cedar Mountain. Despite these flaws, he was the most feared Confederate general of his time and was responsible for some of the Confederacy's most stunning victories.

JACKSON, WILLIAM HICKS (1835–1903) CSA. A native of **Tennessee**, Jackson attended West Tennessee College before entering **West Point**. He graduated in 1856, and while serving in **Texas** fighting **Indians** with the 1st Regiment of Mounted Riflemen, he once saved the life of future Union Brig. Gen. **William W. Averell**.

Jackson resigned his lieutenant's commission in May 1861 and entered Confederate service in August as captain of an artillery **company** he had organized in the 1st Tennessee Light Artillery. Known as "Red," he first served along the Mississippi River and in November fought at **Belmont** as **Gideon J. Pillow's** aide when his **artillery** could not be put into action. Jackson even led a counterattack during the battle and was severely wounded. In April 1862, he was promoted to colonel of the 7th Tennessee Cavalry and soon was given command of a two-regiment **brigade**. Over the next several months, Jackson participated in several successful raids, fought at the **Battle of Corinth**, and performed valuable service screening **John C. Pemberton's** retreat from **Holly Springs, Mississippi**, during **U. S. Grant's Overland Vicksburg Campaign**. In December, he led one of **Earl Van Dorn's** brigades that destroyed Grant's supply depot at Holly Springs and forced him to abandon the campaign.

Jackson's service in the Holly Springs raid led to his promotion to brigadier general in January 1863. Taking command of one of Van Dorn's **divisions**, he fought at **Thompson's Station** in March 1863 and then became part of **Joseph E. Johnston's** command at Jackson, Mississippi, during the **Vicksburg Campaign**. After **Vicksburg** fell, Jackson contested an October Union raid toward Canton by **James B. McPherson** and forced the enemy to retreat. In February 1864, he was praised for fighting **William T. Sherman** during the **Meridian Campaign** and two months later was sent to **Georgia** to reinforce the **Army of Tennessee**. Throughout the **Atlanta Campaign**, Jackson guarded the Confederate left flank and frequently clashed with the enemy. During the **Franklin and Nashville Campaign**, his division served under **Nathan Bedford Forrest**. It unsuccessfully blocked the enemy's escape route in the Spring Hill Incident and then served with Forrest at Murfreesboro while Hood confronted Nashville. Rejoining the **army** after its defeat at Nashville, Jackson helped form the rear guard as Hood fell back to **Mississippi**. His last campaign was against **James H. Wilson's Selma, Alabama, Raid** in April 1865.

After the war, Jackson became a planter and a famous horse breeder in Tennessee. He was elected president of the National Agriculture Congress and the Tennessee Bureau of Agriculture.

JACKSON, WILLIAM LOWTHER "MUDWALL" (1825–1890) CSA. A native of western **Virginia**, Jackson was a second cousin to **Stonewall Jackson** and became nicknamed "Mudwall." After opening a law practice, he entered politics and became his county's commonwealth attorney, a two-term legislator, superintendent of the state's library fund, a one-term lieutenant governor, and a circuit judge.

In April 1861, Jackson resigned his judgeship and entered Confederate service as a private. His political stature led to his being appointed lieutenant colonel and commander of the 31st Virginia in June 1861. Sent to western Virginia, Jackson served under **Robert S. Garnett** and fought in several small battles before giving up his command to join Stonewall Jackson's staff as a volunteer aide. He remained with his cousin through **Stonewall Jackson's 1862 Shenandoah Valley Campaign** and the **Army of Northern Virginia's** 1862 campaigns, but in February 1863, he was sent into Union-occupied western Virginia to raise a **regiment**. Jackson accomplished his mission, formed the 19th Virginia Cavalry, and was appointed its colonel in April. Assigned to **Albert G. Jenkins's** brigade, he participated in a raid against the Baltimore & Ohio Railroad later that month but was left behind in **West Virginia** when the rest of Jenkins's **brigade** fought in the **Gettysburg Campaign**. Jackson remained there for months recruiting, but in the spring of 1864, he took command of a cavalry brigade under **John C. Breckinridge**. His brigade fought at **Cloyd's Mountain**, helped defend **Lynchburg** against **David Hunter's Shenandoah Valley Campaign**, and accompanied **Jubal A. Early's Washington Raid**.

In the autumn of 1864, Jackson fought with Early in **Philip Sheridan's Shenandoah Valley Campaign** and was promoted to brigadier general in January 1865. A few days after the **surrender** at **Appomattox**, he disbanded his brigade and headed for Mexico but finally was **paroled** at Brownsville, **Texas**, in July. Afterward, Jackson moved to **Kentucky**, where he practiced law and became a circuit judge.

JAMESON, CHARLES DAVIS (1827–1862) USA. A native of **Maine**, Jameson was a successful lumberman and manufacturer before the Civil War. He also served as a militia colonel and became prominent in **Democratic** politics, serving as a delegate to the 1860 Democratic National Convention at **Charleston, South Carolina**, and being nominated for governor in 1861 and 1862.

Entering Union service in May 1861 as colonel of the 2nd Maine, Jameson served at **First Manassas** as part of **Erasmus D. Keyes's division** and helped cover the retreat. For this action, he was promoted to brigadier general of volunteers in September and was given command of a brigade in the **Army of the Potomac**. While serving under **Philip Kearny** in the **Peninsula Campaign**, Jameson was commended for his actions at **Seven Pines**, where his horse was shot from under him. Stricken with an unidentified fever after the battle, he was returning home on sick leave when he died en route.

JAYHAWKERS. This was a nickname that had two meanings during the Civil War. In much of the Confederacy, Jayhawkers were bands of **deserters**, **conscript** dodgers, and criminals who robbed, harassed, and otherwise preyed on civilians. In some areas, Jayhawker activity was so oppressive that Confederate cavalry was sent to drive them out. In **Kansas** and **Missouri**, the term *Jayhawkers* was given to pro-Union soldiers from Kansas, such as those who fought under **James H. Lane**. Besides fighting Confederate guerrillas, these Jayhawkers also terrorized the prosecessionist civilians in Missouri.

JENKINS, ALBERT GALLATIN (1830–1864) CSA. A native of western **Virginia**, Jenkins attended the **Virginia Military Institute** before graduating from **Pennsylvania's** Jefferson College and Harvard Law School. After leaving Harvard in 1850, he established a Virginia law practice and plantation and was elected twice to the **U.S. Congress** beginning in 1856. When Virginia seceded, Jenkins resigned his seat and organized a volunteer **company** of cavalry.

Jenkins entered Confederate service as a captain in the 8th Virginia Cavalry and was praised for making several successful raids into western Virginia. He rose through the ranks in late 1861 and early 1862 to lieutenant colonel and colonel, but he resigned his commission in February 1862 after being elected to the **Confederate Congress**.

Jenkins served in Congress until August 1862, when he was appointed a brigadier general. Later that month, his cavalry **brigade** launched a successful raid into **Ohio** that captured several hundred **prisoners** and won Jenkins great acclaim. Following another raid into **West Virginia** in March 1863, he was assigned to the **Army of Northern Virginia** for the **Gettysburg Campaign**. Over the next several weeks, it became obvious that while Jenkins was a successful raider, his poorly **disciplined** troopers were not very useful as regular cavalry. While leading **Robert E. Lee's** invasion into Pennsylvania, his men **deserted**, confiscated food and livestock from civilians, and generally were unruly. During the second day of battle at Gettysburg, Jenkins was stunned by an **artillery** shell that was fired from several miles away. Sent back to West Virginia after the campaign, he was captured at **Cloyd's Mountain** after being badly wounded in the arm. A Union surgeon amputated the limb, but Jenkins died days later.

JENKINS' FERRY, ARKANSAS, BATTLE OF (APRIL 30, 1864). After reaching Camden, Arkansas, in the 1864 **Camden Expedition**, Union Maj. Gen. **Frederick Steele** learned that Maj. Gen. **Nathaniel P. Banks** had abandoned the **Red River Campaign** after his defeat at **Mansfield, Louisiana**, and that Confederate Gen. **Edmund Kirby Smith** had reinforced Maj. Gen. **Sterling Price** in **Arkansas**. When enemy cavalry destroyed a supply train, Steele began retreating.

In drenching rain and deep mud, the column slogged its way back toward **Little Rock**, with Kirby Smith in pursuit. On April 30, while Steele was crossing Saline River on a **pontoon bridge** at Jenkins' Ferry, Confederate Brig. Gen. **John S. Marmaduke** engaged the Union rear guard. For most of the day, Steele's 4,000-man rear guard fought off the pursuing Confederates. When the last of the Union troops crossed the river, the pursuit and campaign ended. Steele lost 528 men in the battle, while Kirby Smith suffered 443 casualties.

JENKINS, MICAH (1835–1864) CSA. A native of **South Carolina**, Jenkins graduated first in his class from the South Carolina Military Academy in 1854. The next year, he became cofounder of King's Mountain Military School.

A secessionist, Jenkins entered Confederate service in April 1861 when he was elected colonel of the 5th South Carolina, a **regiment** he helped raise. After fighting at **First Manassas**, he organized a new regiment in April 1862. Jenkins was appointed colonel of the Palmetto Sharpshooters that month and fought in the **Peninsula Campaign** in **Richard H. Anderson's brigade**. At **Williamsburg** and **Seven Pines**, he temporarily led the brigade and earned special commendation for his aggressive attack at the latter. During the **Seven Days Campaign**, Jenkins served with the **Army of Northern Virginia**. He ably led the regiment at **Gaines' Mill** and the brigade at **Frayser's Farm** and captured an enemy battery in the latter battle.

Jenkins was promoted to brigadier general in July 1862 and was given command of Anderson's brigade. He was severely wounded at **Second Manassas** but recovered in time to see light service at **Fredericksburg**. The brigade accompanied **James Longstreet** for the **siege of Suffolk** in early 1863 and remained there after Longstreet rejoined the Army of Northern Virginia. Missing the **Gettysburg Campaign**, Jenkins's next battle was **Chickamauga**, where he served in **John B. Hood's** division. The brigade arrived too late to enter the fight, but Jenkins took temporary command of the **division** after Hood was wounded. After helping besiege **Chattanooga, Tennessee**, he was defeated when he launched a vicious night attack at **Wauhatchie**. Jenkins also saw heavy combat during the **Knoxville Campaign**, but the division's effectiveness was erratic. The defeat at Wauhatchie and operations around Knoxville led to a bitter dispute between Jenkins and his subordinate **Evander Law** over who was responsible for the failures. Over Longstreet's protests, Jenkins was replaced by **Charles Field** in March 1864 and resumed command of his brigade.

Returning to Virginia, Jenkins's last fight was at the **Wilderness**. On the second day of battle, his brigade was sent into action to exploit a successful flank attack made by Longstreet. While accompanying Longstreet at the front, Jenkins and the party were mistakenly fired upon by the Confederates. Longstreet was seriously wounded, and Jenkins was mortally wounded in the head. Continuing to order his men to the front while in delirium, he died that night.

JERICHO MILL, VIRGINIA, BATTLE OF (MAY 23, 1864). *See* NORTH ANNA RIVER, VIRGINIA, BATTLE OF.

JERUSALEM PLANK ROAD, VIRGINIA, BATTLE OF (JUNE 21–23, 1864). *See* WELDON RAILROAD, VIRGINIA, UNION OPERATIONS AGAINST.

"JOHNNY SHILOH." *See* CLEM, JOHN "JOHNNY" LINCOLN.

JOHNSON, ADAM RANKIN "STOVEPIPE" (1834–1922) CSA. A native of **Kentucky**, Johnson moved to **Texas** as a young man and became a surveyor, mail contractor, and **Indian** fighter. He returned to Kentucky when the Civil War began and entered Confederate service in 1861 as a scout for **John Hunt Morgan** and **Nathan Bedford Forrest**. Johnson served under Forrest at **Fort Donelson** and escaped with the rest of the cavalry.

In June 1862, Johnson was sent back to Kentucky to raise a **partisan ranger** unit and while there, invaded **Indiana** in July with only 35 men. Attacking Newburgh, he convinced the garrison to surrender by mounting two stovepipes on a wagon and pretending they were cannons. The trick worked, and the enemy surrendered; ever after, Johnson was known as "Stovepipe" Johnson. The recruits he raised were organized into the 10th Kentucky Cavalry (Confederate) in August 1862, with Johnson being appointed colonel. That same month, he captured Hopkinsville and Clarksville, Tennessee, along with numerous **prisoners**. By now a renowned raider, Johnson joined Morgan's command that autumn, but he turned down an offer to command one of his **brigades**. After some brief service in Texas (probably to recruit), he finally did accept command of a Kentucky cavalry brigade in February 1863. Johnson led it on **Morgan's Ohio Raid** and escaped when Morgan was captured. After the raid, he took command of the remnants of Morgan's **division** and joined the **Army of Tennessee** for the **Battle of Chickamauga**.

When Morgan returned to duty in early 1864 after escaping from **prison**, Johnson was given command of a subdistrict in southern Kentucky. He successfully raised more recruits, but in August, he was accidentally shot in the face by one of his men during an August raid on Grubbs Cross Roads, Kentucky. It was claimed that Johnson was blinded, but a wartime photograph shows his eyes intact and crude goggles protecting them, so he may have retained some sight. Taken prisoner, Johnson was briefly held at **Fort Warren, Massachusetts**, before being **exchanged**. He was promoted to brigadier general in September 1864 but was unable to take the field because of his disability.

Johnson returned to Texas after the war, founded the town of Marble Falls, and was one of the last Confederate generals to die.

JOHNSON, ANDREW (1808–1875) USA. Born in **North Carolina**, Johnson moved to eastern **Tennessee** as a young man and became a tailor in Greeneville. His youth was rather impoverished, and he did not acquire a good education until his teacher wife educated him. Becoming a Jacksonian **Democrat**, Johnson was a champion of the working class and disliked both the slave-owning aristocrats and the **abolitionists**. With the strong support of the mountaineers, he embarked on a remarkable political career, becoming a two-time alderman, mayor, legislator (1835–37, 1839–41), state senator (1841–43), U.S. congressman (1843–53), governor (1853–57), and U.S. senator (1857–61). As a senator, Johnson at first was a moderate who defended **slavery** in **Washington, D.C.**, while at the same time opposing **secession**. As the secession crisis deepened, however, it became apparent that above all else Johnson was a dedicated Unionist like many of his east Tennessee neighbors. He bravely campaigned against secession in the spring of 1861 and often received death threats because of it. When Tennessee did secede, Johnson refused to resign his Senate seat and became the only Southern senator to remain loyal to the Union. Although forced to leave Tennessee with his family, he became a Northern hero for his unswerving allegiance to the Union.

Johnson supported **Abraham Lincoln's** war policies and was rewarded in March 1862 by being appointed brigadier general of volunteers and the military governor of Tennessee. For the next three years, he tried to establish a loyal government that could control the entire state. Although secessionists hated Johnson, many of the east Tennessee people supported his measures. One of his greatest disappointments was the Union's inability, and often unwillingness, to liberate that region of Tennessee.

As time passed, Johnson became increasingly radical because many of the moderate Tennesseans opposed his efforts to restore the state to the Union. He required **oaths of allegiance** from civilians, became a supporter of emancipation and the enlistment of **black troops**, and wanted to restrict the vote to loyalists. Johnson also campaigned for Northern politicians seeking reelection and won a popular following in the North. As a result of this popularity, he was chosen as Lincoln's running mate in June 1864.

After Lincoln won reelection, Johnson tried to restore Tennessee before leaving for Washington. In February 1865, a small number of Unionist voters ratified amendments to the state constitution that outlawed slavery and made most state positions governor-appointed. Elections were held in March to choose a new governor and legislature, and in April Gov. **William G. Brownlow** supervised the installation of a new state government.

Johnson resigned as military governor of Tennessee on March 3, 1865, the day before he was sworn in as vice president. On inauguration day he appeared drunk, and his speech was incoherent. Enemies claimed he was an alcoholic, while supporters blamed the incident on a small amount of alcohol that overly affected him because he was seriously weakened from typhoid.

Johnson assumed the presidency on April 15, 1865, after **Lincoln's assassination** and promptly shocked his **Radical Republican** allies by initiating a very lenient **Reconstruction** policy. Most ex-Confederates were pardoned after taking **loyalty oaths** and were allowed to vote and run for political office. Southern states that abolished slavery, repealed secession acts, and repudiated Confederate debts were to be allowed back into the Union. As a result, within months after war's end the former Confederate states were back in the hands of the same politicians who had seceded four years earlier. For months Johnson and the Radicals battled over control of Reconstruction. Johnson opposed black suffrage and the 14th and 15th Amendments and finally was impeached when he suspended **Edwin Stanton** as secretary of war in 1868. Johnson was acquitted in the Senate by one vote and served out the remainder of his term. Afterward, he returned to Tennessee and in 1874 became the only former president to be elected to the U.S. Senate.

JOHNSON, BRADLEY TYLER (1829–1903) CSA. A native of **Maryland**, Johnson graduated from Princeton University in 1849 and became a prominent state attorney, public speaker, and chairman of the state **Democratic** Committee during the 1850s. A secessionist, he turned down an officer's commission in the **Virginia** army in 1861 and instead helped future Confederate generals **Arnold Elzey** and **George H. Steuart** raise the 1st Maryland (Confederate). The three were appointed colonel, lieutenant colonel, and major, respectively, in the spring of 1861.

After fighting at **First Manassas**, all three men were promoted in late July, with Johnson being appointed the **regiment's** lieutenant colonel. When Steuart was promoted to brigadier general in March 1862, Johnson was commissioned colonel and led the regiment through **Stonewall Jackson's 1862 Shenandoah Valley Campaign**. At **Front Royal**, he led the attack that captured a number of men from the 1st Maryland (Union). After fighting in the **Seven Days Campaign** with the **Army of Northern Virginia**, the regiment was disbanded, and Johnson was given temporary command of **John R. Jones's brigade**. He led it well at **Second Manassas**, and Jackson recommended his promotion to brigadier general. Politics intervened, however, because there already were a number of Maryland generals, and there was no appropriate unit for Johnson to command. As a result, he languished in administrative duties until the **Gettysburg Campaign**, when he temporarily took command of Jones's brigade during the retreat to Virginia.

After being given command of the Maryland Line in November 1863, Johnson performed well while helping repulse the **Kilpatrick-Dahlgren Raid** in March 1864. Still, no promotion came until **William E. "Grumble" Jones** was killed in June 1864. That month, Johnson was given command of Jones's cavalry brigade and, in a long overdue promotion, finally was made brigadier general. During **Jubal A. Early's Washington Raid**, he unsuccessfully attempted to free Confederate **prisoners** from **Point Lookout**, **Maryland**. Johnson then accompanied **John McCausland** on a raid into **Pennsylvania**, during which McCausland burned **Chambersburg** after it failed to pay a $100,000 ransom. Although McCausland was following orders from Early, Johnson objected to the destruction and later criticized the operation in his report. Both Johnson and McCausland were then pursued by Union cavalry and defeated at **Moorefield**, **West Virginia**, in August. Johnson continued to serve under Early during **Philip Sheridan's Shenandoah Valley Campaign**, but he was left without a command when the cavalry was reorganized in late 1864. Placed in charge of the **Salisbury Prison**, **North Carolina**, he remained at that post until war's end.

After the war, Johnson opened a law practice in **Richmond**, **Virginia**, and was elected to the state senate. Later, he moved back to Maryland, where he wrote biographies of George Washington and **Joseph E. Johnston**, as well as a number of works on the Civil War.

JOHNSON, BUSHROD RUST (1817–1880) CSA. A native of **Ohio**, Johnson was a Quaker and a member of an antislavery family. After becoming a teacher, he moved with the family to **Indiana** as a young man. While there, Johnson rejected his family's pacifism and won an appointment to **West Point**. After graduating in 1840, he served in the infantry at a number of posts and was promoted to 1st lieutenant. During the **Mexican War**, Johnson fought under Zachary Taylor but was forced to resign in 1847 after becoming involved in a scheme to run contraband goods into Mexico aboard U.S. ships. He resumed his teaching career at **Kentucky's** Western Military Institute and the Military College of the University of Nashville, becoming superintendent at both places.

Despite his Quaker background and northern birth, Johnson sided with his adopted **Tennessee** home when civil war came and offered the state his services. Having been active in the militia, he first entered service in June 1861 as a colonel of Tennessee militia. As chief of **engineers**, Johnson helped construct **Fort Henry**, briefly commanded Fort Donelson, and raised and trained troops.

Appointed brigadier general in the **Confederate army** in January 1862, Johnson served at **Fort Donelson** but escaped through the lines after the surrender. He then was given command of a **brigade** in **Benjamin Cheatham's** division and was wounded at **Shiloh**. Upon returning to duty, Johnson received a new brigade and led it at **Perryville**, where he had five horses shot from under him. At **Stones River** with the **Army of Tennessee**, his brigade was broken up and repulsed by heavy Union fire on the first day. The incident apparently did not hurt Johnson's career, for he was leading a provisional **division** by the **Battle of Chickamauga**. There his division led the Confederate attack that broke the Union line and forced the enemy to retreat. Johnson then was given command of **Simon B. Buckner's** division and accompanied **James Longstreet** in the **Knoxville Campaign**.

After being transferred to **Virginia**, Johnson was promoted to major general in May 1864. Given command of a division in the **Department of North Carolina and Southern Virginia**, he served well at **Second Drewry's Bluff** and during the **Petersburg Campaign**. During the latter, part of his command was blown up by the Union mine that started the **Battle of the Crater**. During the **Appomattox Campaign**, most of Johnson's division was captured at **Sailor's Creek**, but he again managed to escape. With his division destroyed, he was relieved by **Robert E. Lee** and surrendered at Appomattox without a command.

Johnson returned to Tennessee after the war and in 1870 founded the University of Nashville with fellow Confederate general **Edmund Kirby Smith**. After it failed in 1874, he eventually settled in **Illinois** and farmed.

JOHNSON, EDWARD "ALLEGHENY" (1816–1873) CSA. A native of **Virginia**, Johnson moved with his family to **Kentucky** at an early age. He graduated from **West Point** in 1838 and served with the infantry in the **Seminole Wars** and on the frontier. As a 1st lieutenant, Johnson also fought in the **Mexican War** and won two **brevets** for gallantry. He remained in the **U.S. Army** afterward and was promoted to captain in 1851.

Johnson resigned his commission in June 1861 and entered Confederate service as a lieutenant colonel of infantry. In July, he was appointed colonel of the 12th Georgia and was sent to western Virginia, where he fought at **Cheat Mountain**. Numerous **skirmishes** also were fought around his Camp Allegheny, which earned Johnson the nickname "Allegheny" Johnson. One of the more colorful Civil War generals, he was a very profane officer and sometimes led his men into battle wielding a club, which led to another nickname—"Old Clubby" (one soldier claimed the club actually was a fence rail he had snatched up, and another claimed the nickname was given to him later when a wound left him with a deformed foot, or clubfoot). Johnson also was boisterous, had an odd-shaped head ("like the pope's tiara") (Davis, ed., *The Confederate General*, vol. 3, p. 187), and tended to wink when excited.

In the spring of 1862, Johnson joined forces with **Stonewall Jackson** and received a severe foot wound at **McDowell** that left him lame. One soldier claimed Johnson was rolling on the ground laughing at a humorous remark when an enemy bullet struck his upheld foot. "Goddamn that Yankee!" (Davis, p. 187). Johnson reportedly yelled. While recovering from the wound, he was appointed major general in April 1863 and was given Jackson's old **division**. Johnson played a key role in capturing thousands of Union **prisoners** at **Stephenson's Depot**, fought tenaciously at **Gettysburg's** Culp's Hill, and had a horse killed under him at **Mine Run**. During the **Overland Campaign**, his division saw heavy combat at the **Wilderness** and was positioned at the apex of **Spotsylvania's** "Mule Shoe." On the morning of May 12, 1864, Johnson's division was overrun by the Union assault on the "Bloody Angle," and Johnson and most of his men were captured in the opening moments of the battle. After being **exchanged** that summer, he was sent west and took a division in **Stephen D. Lee's corps**. Johnson served in the final days of the **Atlanta Campaign**, and during the **Franklin and Nashville Campaign** he was captured a second time at Nashville.

After being released from **prison** in July 1865, Johnson became a Virginia farmer.

JOHNSON, GEORGE W. (1811–1862) CSA. A native of **Kentucky**, Johnson opened a law practice after graduating from Transylvania University, but he eventually became a farmer and planter. He also became involved in politics and was elected to the state legislature in 1838, 1839, and 1840. A wealthy, prominent slave owner in 1861, Johnson was sympathetic to **secession** but at first supported Kentucky's neutrality. He personally delivered Gov. **Beriah Magoffin's** letter to **Jefferson Davis** asking the Confederacy to respect that neutrality. When Union troops entered the state in September 1861, however, Johnson joined Confederate Brig. Gen. **Simon B. Buckner's** staff as a volunteer aide.

In November 1861, Johnson helped organize the convention in Russellville that passed a secession ordinance. He also was elected governor of a provisional government, which was admitted to the Confederacy in December. After Confederate troops retreated from Kentucky in early 1862, Johnson could do little to govern the state. He served at **Shiloh** as a volunteer aide to **John C. Breckinridge** and had a horse killed under him on the first day. That night, Johnson insisted on joining the 1st Kentucky (Confederate) as a private and was mortally wounded the next day. Left on the field, he was taken to a Union hospital ship and died two days later.

JOHNSON, HERSCHEL VESPASIAN (1812–1880) CSA. A native of **Georgia**, Johnson became close friends with **Alexander Stephens** while attending the University of Georgia. After graduating in 1834, he became a successful lawyer and planter and in 1847 was appointed to serve out the remaining term of a U.S. senator. After returning to Georgia, Johnson was elected a circuit judge in 1849 and governor in 1853. Previously, he had been an outspoken defender of **slavery** and **states rights**, but as governor he took a more moderate stand. Johnson supported the **Kansas-Nebraska Act** and opposed **secession**. After serving two terms, he retired to his farm but in 1860 was nominated as **Stephen A. Douglas's** vice presidential running mate. This cost Johnson much support in Georgia, but it did not ruin his political career.

In 1861, Johnson was elected to the state secession convention, where he joined Stephens and other moderates who spoke out against secession and urged patience to see what might develop on the national scene. When Georgia seceded, however, Johnson supported the state's war effort. In 1862, the legislature appointed him to fill out the remaining term of a Confederate senator. Johnson was elected to the same position the following year.

As a senator, Johnson strongly supported states rights and largely opposed **impressment**, the use of **black troops**, and most **taxes**. He also proposed an unsuccessful constitutional amendment that would have allowed states to secede from the Confederacy. Serving in the Senate until war's end, Johnson supported few of **Jefferson Davis's** policies, but he did privately support the president as the best man for the job.

Ruined financially by the war, Johnson asked for and received a presidential pardon from **Andrew Johnson** and served as president of the 1865 Georgia constitutional convention. In 1873, he was appointed to the state superior court and remained in that position until his death.

JOHNSON, REVERDY (1796–1876) USA. A native of **Maryland**, Johnson graduated from St. John's College and in 1816 opened a law practice and served as Maryland's deputy attorney general for one year. In 1821, he was elected to the state senate and served there for eight years. Afterward, Johnson resumed his law practice, but in 1845, he was elected to the U.S. Senate as a **Whig**. He supported the **Mexican War** but opposed taking any territory from the Mexicans. Johnson resigned his Senate seat in 1849 to become President Zachary Taylor's attorney general, but he resigned the position after one year.

By the outbreak of the Civil War, Johnson was one of the country's most respected legal minds. He won a case that upheld Cyrus McCormick's reaper patent and was the defense attorney in the famous **Dred Scott** case. Politically, Johnson opposed **slavery** and **secession**, but he was sympathetic to the South. He strongly believed in compromise and attended the 1861 **Washington Peace Conference** to try to find a peaceful solution to the crisis. After working to keep Maryland in the Union, Johnson was elected to the U.S. Senate in 1862 as a **Democrat**. During the Civil War, he was a moderate who opposed the **Emancipation Proclamation** but supported the **13th Amendment**. Johnson remained a public figure at war's end when he served as defense counsel for **Lincoln's assassination** conspirator **Mary Surratt**.

During **Reconstruction**, Johnson at first opposed the **Freedmen's Bureau** and black suffrage, but he supported the 14th Amendment and voted to acquit President **Andrew Johnson** in the impeachment trial. He resigned his Senate seat in 1868 to become minister to Great Britain but left that position a year later. Returning to the United States, Johnson practiced law until his death.

JOHNSON, RICHARD W. (1827–1897) USA. A native of **Kentucky**, Johnson had no middle name. He graduated from **West Point** in 1849 and served on the frontier, first with the infantry and then with the 2nd U.S. Cavalry. By the beginning of the Civil War, Johnson was a captain of cavalry.

Apparently because he was a loyal officer from the vital **border states**, Jones was promoted to brigadier general of volunteers in October 1861. Given a **brigade** in **Alexander McCook's** division, he helped capture Nashville, Tennessee, in early 1862 but was on sick leave during the **Battle of Shiloh**. That summer, Johnson pursued Confederate raider **John Hunt Morgan**. In an unfortunate twist of fate, however, Morgan captured Johnson near **Gallatin, Tennessee. Exchanged** in December, he was given command of a **division** in the **Army of the Cumberland**

and led at the **Battle of Stones River** and in the **Tullahoma** and **Chicka-mauga Campaigns**. During the **Atlanta Campaign**, Johnson was wounded at **New Hope Church**. Upon returning to duty, he briefly commanded the XIV Corps in August 1864 before being given command of the cavalry in the **Military Division of the Mississippi** in November. Johnson's cavalry division subsequently was attached to **James H. Wilson's** command, and Johnson led it at the **Battle of Nashville**. By the time Johnson was mustered out of volunteer service in January 1865, he had earned **brevets** through the rank of major general in both the regulars and volunteers.

Resuming his regular rank of major, Johnson remained in the **U.S. Army**, but his war wounds forced his retirement in 1867 with the rank of major general (reduced to brigadier general in 1875). Afterward, he taught military science at the Universities of Missouri and Minnesota and wrote a number of works on the military.

JOHNSON'S ISLAND, OHIO. Forced to house large numbers of Confederate **prisoners**, Union officials in October 1861 chose a 300-acre island in Sandusky Bay, Lake Erie, as the site for a **prison** camp. Originally designed to hold 1,000 prisoners, it first was thought that the 40-acre camp was capable of holding all of the prisoners seized by Union forces. Built by Lt. Col. William Hoffman, the camp was enclosed by a plank fence and had 13 two-story barracks to house the prisoners. Other buildings, such as warehouses, guard barracks, and hospital, completed the compound.

Prisoners began arriving in early 1862 and soon overwhelmed the facilities. Housing mostly officers, the camp mushroomed to a population of 9,423 in January 1865, but it usually held only a few thousand men. Conditions were harsh as prisoners suffered from intense cold during the winter and lived in squalid conditions because the shallow bedrock prevented the digging of adequate latrines. Confederate authorities sometimes planned to use nearby Canada to raid the camp and free the prisoners, but they never succeeded. A plot involving **John Yates Beall** was the most serious, but it ended when Beall was hanged by Federal authorities. The last remaining Confederate prisoners were released in September 1865, and the camp soon was abandoned.

JOHNSONVILLE, TENNESSEE, RAID (OCTOBER 19–NOVEMBER 10, 1864). In late 1864, a major Union supply base in **Tennessee** was the port town of Johnsonville on the Tennessee River. It became the objective of one of **Nathan Bedford Forrest's Tennessee Raids** in October 1864.

Leaving **Corinth, Mississippi**, on October 19, Forrest made his way to Paris Landing, Tennessee, on the Tennessee River. The raiders blocked the river with **artillery** on October 28, **skirmished** with Union gunboats, and managed to capture two ships. Moving downstream, Forrest began deploying his men on the west bank of the river opposite Johnsonville on November 3. When he opened fire with eight cannons at mid-afternoon on November 4, the 22 Union guns supporting the 2,000-man garrison returned fire. Completely surprised by the attack, the commander of the Union boats ordered three gunboats and seven transports run aground and burned to keep them out of enemy hands. This rash act, in combination with the Confederate bombardment, set fire to the docks and warehouses. To add to the confusion, Union soldiers, sailors, and civilians began looting their own burning warehouses. Forrest continued firing into numerous steamers and completely wrecked the dock area before withdrawing and making his way back to Corinth on November 10.

The raid was Forrest's most successful and reinforced his reputation as the Confederacy's premier raider. The Federals suffered only eight casualties, but Forrest calculated their material loss at four gunboats, 14 transports, 20 barges, 26 cannons, 150 **prisoners**, and $6.7 million in damages. One Union officer, however, estimated the raid-inflicted damages to amount to only $2.2 million.

JOHNSTON, ALBERT SIDNEY (1803–1862) CSA. A native of **Kentucky**, Johnston attended Transylvania University before entering **West Point**. After graduating eighth in the 1826 class, he embarked on an impressive career, including service as the commanding general's adjutant during the Black Hawk War. Johnston resigned his commission in 1834 to care for his terminally ill wife, however, and moved to **Texas** in 1836. There he joined the Texas Revolution as a private, but within a year, he was the ranking general, and he served as the republic's secretary of war before Texas entered the Union. During the **Mexican War**, Johnston commanded the 1st Texas Rifles and served on Zachary Taylor's staff at the Battle of Monterrey. Reentering the **U.S. Army** in 1849, he was appointed paymaster for Texas with the rank of major. In 1855, Johnston was promoted to colonel and was placed in command of the newly formed 2nd U.S. Cavalry, with **Robert E. Lee** serving as his lieutenant colonel. After commanding the 1857 **Utah Expedition**, he was **brevetted** brigadier general and was put in command of the **Department of the Pacific**.

Johnston was in **California** when Texas seceded in 1861. Although he personally did not support **secession**, he sided with his native state and wrote his second wife, "Texas has made me a rebel twice" (Davis, ed., *The Confederate General*, vol. 3, 189). Johnston was one of the most respected and well-known officers in the old **army** and his resignation and trip back east garnered great attention. Traveling with a small band of men, he made his way from California to **Virginia**, trying to avoid not only Apache **Indians** but also federal authorities, who might arrest him. Johnston's arrival in Virginia was hailed across the Confederacy, and close friend **Jefferson Davis** (who had been a classmate at West Point) appointed him the second-ranking Confederate general in August 1861.

Placed in command of **Department No. 2** in September, Johnston established a defensive line running through Kentucky and **Tennessee**. Although praised as the Confederacy's leading general, he showed little foresight in his preparations. Concentrating on defending the Mississippi River and Bowling Green, Kentucky, Johnston saw his defensive line shattered when **U. S. Grant** captured **Forts Henry and Donelson** in February 1862. Forced to retreat, he abandoned Kentucky and most of Tennessee and fell back to **Corinth, Mississippi**. Many politicians criticized Johnston's performance, but Davis retorted that if Johnston was not a general then the Confederacy had none.

At Corinth, Johnston concentrated his forces and launched a counterattack against Grant at **Shiloh**. While he was leading an attack near the Peach Orchard on the first day of battle, a bullet pierced his leg and severed an artery. Johnston bled to death in minutes. His short Civil War career makes it difficult to judge his effectiveness. Johnston clearly did not plan well at Forts Henry and Donelson, but he launched a spectacular surprise attack at Shiloh that came close to winning a major victory. Whether or not he would have led the Confederates to victory is debatable.

JOHNSTON, GEORGE DOHERTY (1832–1910) CSA. Born in **North Carolina**, Johnston moved to **Alabama** as a child. He attended Howard College and received a law degree from **Tennessee's** Cumberland University. Opening a law practice in Alabama, Johnston was elected mayor of his hometown in 1856 but resigned in 1857 to take a legislative seat he had won.

Johnston entered Confederate service in May 1861 as a 2nd lieutenant in the 4th Alabama. After fighting at **First Manassas** in **Barnard Bee's** brigade, he was promoted to major of the 25th Alabama and saw combat at **Shiloh**. Johnston was promoted to lieutenant colonel immediately after the battle and accompanied the **regiment** in the **Kentucky Campaign** that autumn. After being commissioned regimental colonel in October 1862, he led the unit in all of the battles fought by the **Army of**

Tennessee, but little is known of his activities. Johnston suffered heavy losses at **Stones River** and **Chickamauga** and fought particularly well in the **Atlanta Campaign** at **New Hope Church** and **Peachtree Creek**. In the latter fight, he captured two Union **flags** and more **prisoners** than he had men.

Johnston's service during the Atlanta Campaign won him a promotion to brigadier general in July 1864 and command of **Zachariah C. Deas's** former **brigade**. Only three hours after being notified of his promotion, he led the brigade into action at **Ezra Church**, where his leg was shattered by a bullet. Rather than leaving, Johnston stayed on the field for a time and supported the broken limb with his bridle. While still on crutches, he led the brigade in the **Franklin and Nashville Campaign**. When **William A. Quarles** was wounded at Franklin, Johnston was given command of his brigade. He led it at Nashville and helped form the rear guard during the retreat. In early 1865, Johnston's brigade participated in the **Carolinas Campaign**, and on the second day of the **Battle of Bentonville**, he assumed command of the **division**. Afterward, he was transferred west for duty under **Richard Taylor**, but the war ended before he arrived.

After the war, Johnston returned to Alabama and practiced law before becoming commandant of cadets at the University of Alabama in 1868. He later served as superintendent of the South Carolina Military Academy, was a member of the U.S. Civil Service Commission, and was elected to the state senate.

JOHNSTON, JOSEPH EGGLESTON (1807–1891) CSA. A native of **Virginia** and the son of a Revolutionary War veteran, Johnston attended a private academy before entering **West Point** in 1825. After graduation in 1829, he was assigned to the **artillery** and remained in that service for the next nine years, except for a one-year stint as a civilian engineer. Having been promoted to 1st lieutenant in 1836, Johnston fought in the **Seminole Wars** and was severely wounded in the head. His skillful service in **Florida** won him promotion to captain and a transfer to the topographical **engineers**. Johnston served with distinction in the **Mexican War** under **Winfield Scott**, was wounded again, and won promotion to lieutenant colonel of **voltigeurs** in 1848. In 1855, he was appointed lieutenant colonel of the 1st U.S. Cavalry and remained with it until 1860, when he was named the **U.S. Army's** quartermaster general with the staff rank of brigadier general. During his antebellum career, Johnston also married Lydia McLane, the daughter of a former congressman, U.S. minister to Great Britain, and President Andrew Jackson's secretary of the treasury and secretary of state.

In April 1861, Johnston resigned his commission and was appointed a major general of Virginia troops, with responsibility for organizing and training new recruits at **Richmond**. Because of an abundance of major generals, however, he quickly was reduced in rank to brigadier general and in May was appointed brigadier general of Confederate troops. Sent to **Harpers Ferry**, Johnston faced **Robert Patterson's** Union **army** in the **Shenandoah Valley** that summer, but he successfully moved his small army by train to reinforce **P. G. T. Beauregard** at Manassas. At **First Manassas**, Johnston outranked Beauregard and technically was in command of the army there, but he allowed Beauregard to retain tactical command on the field because of his familiarity with the situation. After the battle, Johnston assumed command of all Confederate forces in Northern Virginia and in August was promoted to full general.

This promotion helped create a long-running feud between Johnston and **Jefferson Davis**. Confederate law stated that generals would be ranked in seniority according to the rank they held in the old army. Johnston believed his former rank of staff brigadier general earned him the highest seniority in the **Confederate army**. Davis, however, based his seniority on his permanent field grade rank of lieutenant colonel and thus placed Johnston fourth on the seniority list. This feud was made worse in March 1862, when Johnston suddenly abandoned Manassas and much of Northern Virginia and withdrew behind the more defensible Rappahannock River. For the rest of the war, the Confederate high command was weakened because these two proud men continually argued over **strategy**, logistics, and responsibility.

During the 1862 **Peninsula Campaign**, Johnston moved his **Army of the Potomac (Confederate)** to the Virginia Peninsula to confront **George B. McClellan's** Union **Army of the Potomac**. There he stayed on the defensive and slowly retreated toward Richmond. Under pressure from Davis, Johnston finally attacked McClellan in May at the **Battle of Seven Pines**, but he was severely wounded by a bullet to the shoulder and **shrapnel** to the chest. Davis quickly placed **Robert E. Lee** in command of the army—which became known as the **Army of Northern Virginia**—and refused to restore Johnston to its command when he recovered.

When Johnston reported for duty, Davis placed him in command the **Department of the West** in December. Johnston was bitter over not regaining the Virginia command and continued to bicker with Davis over strategy. He also showed a reluctance to assume responsibility, telling Davis that he could not defend both **Tennessee** and **Mississippi** and demanding that the president decide which state he was to abandon. When **U. S. Grant** crossed the Mississippi River during the 1863 **Vicksburg**

Campaign, Johnston was sent to Jackson, Mississippi, to take command of the area. He at first was defeated and driven out of **Jackson**, but he then returned to the area and raised a sizeable army to threaten Grant's rear. Johnston also ordered **John C. Pemberton** to break out of the encirclement at **Vicksburg**, but again he showed his aversion to offensive action by never moving against the enemy. Vicksburg surrendered, the Federals forced Johnston out of Jackson, and the Johnston-Davis feud worsened.

By late 1863, Davis was convinced that Johnston was useless as a commander, but the general had strong military and political support. Because he took care of his soldiers' needs and was personable and dashing, Johnston always had the trust and support of his men and many politicians. As a result, when **Braxton Bragg** was removed from command of the **Army of Tennessee** in December 1863, Davis was pressured into naming Johnston his replacement.

Beginning in May 1864, Johnston faced **William T. Sherman** in the **Atlanta Campaign**. Using the natural strengths of northern **Georgia's** rugged terrain, he fought a defensive campaign as he retreated from one fortified position to another. Johnston's defense was skillful, but he retreated closer and closer to Atlanta without ever taking any offensive action against the enemy. When he retreated to the outskirts of Atlanta and was unable to provide Davis with any specific plan to save the city, Davis replaced him with **John Bell Hood** on July 17.

In February 1865, Johnston was put in command of the **Departments of Tennessee and Georgia** and **of South Carolina, Georgia, and Florida**, with the command of the **Department of North Carolina** being added the following month. Given responsibility for stopping Sherman's **Carolinas Campaign**, he directed the remnants of the Army of Tennessee in the war's last months. During this time, Johnston launched an attack at **Bentonville**, which proved to be only his second offensive action of the war (the other being at Seven Pines). Defeated, he continued to retreat and finally surrendered to Sherman on April 26 at **Durham Station**.

After the war, Johnston worked in transportation, insurance, and the communications industry. He was elected to the **U.S. Congress** in 1878 and 1884 and was appointed a federal **railroad** commissioner by President Grover Cleveland. Johnston also wrote several articles on the war and in 1874 published his memoirs entitled *Narrative of Military Operations Directed during the Late War between the States*. Johnson served as an honorary pallbearer at Sherman's funeral. Standing bare-headed in a cold wind, he ignored pleas to cover up, declaring that Sherman would do the same if the roles were reversed. Johnston died five weeks later, reportedly from illness caused by cold wind, but actually from heart failure. Always a very popular officer, Johnston for many years was viewed as one of the Confederacy's best generals. More modern scholarship, however, has heavily criticized him for his lack of aggressiveness and for failing to assume the responsibilities of command. One anecdotal story seems to capture his personality. Before the Civil War, Johnston was praised for being the best marksman in the army, but while on a quail hunt one of his companions noted that he never actually shot at a bird. On each occasion, he complained that conditions were not right for taking the shot, as if he were afraid of missing and damaging his reputation. Perhaps a similar concern for his military reputation prevented him from taking risks on the battlefield.

JOHNSTON, ROBERT DANIEL (1837–1919) CSA. A native of **North Carolina**, Johnston graduated from the University of North Carolina in 1857 and then studied law at the University of Virginia from 1860 to 1861. He opened a law practice in his native state and became a 2nd lieutenant in the local militia.

Johnston's **company** was mustered into state service in the spring of 1861 as part of the 23rd North Carolina, and he was elected its captain in July. Sent to **Virginia**, the **regiment** became part of **Jubal A. Early's brigade**, and Johnston was promoted to lieutenant colonel in April 1862. Five days after seeing heavy combat at **Williamsburg** in May 1862, Johnston was elected regimental colonel. In his next fight at **Seven Pines**, he was wounded in the arm, face, and neck. The 23rd North Carolina became part of **Samuel Garland's** brigade in the **Army of Northern Virginia**, and Johnston returned to duty in time to lead it at **Antietam's** "Bloody Lane." After serving in reserve at **Fredericksburg**, he temporarily was put in command of the 12th North Carolina for the **Chancellorsville Campaign**. Returning to the 23rd North Carolina, Johnston led it into heavy combat at **Gettysburg**, where he again was severely wounded.

Johnston was promoted to brigadier general in September 1863 and assumed command of the brigade. He led it in the 1864 **Overland Campaign** and was praised for personally carrying the 23rd North Carolina's **flag** forward in a counterattack at **Spotsylvania's** "Bloody Angle." Johnston received his third wound in this battle, but he recovered in time to lead the brigade in the **Shenandoah Valley** at **Third Winchester**, **Fisher's Hill**, and **Cedar Creek**. At Third Winchester, Johnston performed particularly well by fighting a delaying action that helped Early's **army** escape. Returning to the Army of Northern Virginia, he served in the **Petersburg Campaign** and briefly led the **division** in early 1865. In March 1865, Johnston was sent to command the area around the Roanoke River in North Carolina and remained there until war's end.

After the war, Johnston resumed his North Carolina law practice. In 1887, he moved to **South Carolina** to become a bank president, and he eventually relocated to Virginia.

JOMINI, DE BARON ANTOINE HENRI (1779–1869). This Swiss military theorist had the greatest influence on the military **strategy** of Civil War officers. Jomini (ZHJOE-mee-nee) quit his job as a bank clerk at age 17 and joined Napoleon's **army**. He rose to the rank of general and published several authoritative works on strategy. These works dominated military thinking in the 19th century and greatly influenced such **West Point** officers as **George B. McClellan** and **Henry W. Halleck**. Jomini believed that war should be limited between the opposing armies and that wars and campaigns could be won through maneuver. He stressed such principles as concentrating a superior force against the enemy, using **interior lines**, surprising the enemy, relying on the **turning movement**, and maintaining the initiative.

JONES, CATESBY AP ROGER (1821–1877) CSA. A native of **Virginia**, Jones entered the **U.S. Navy** as a midshipman in 1836. He served in the Pacific during the **Mexican War** and thus did not see any combat, but he was promoted to lieutenant in 1849. In the 1850s, while stationed at the Washington Navy Yard, Jones assisted **John A. Dahlgren** in developing the **Dahlgren gun**.

Jones resigned his commission when Virginia seceded in 1861 and entered the Virginia navy as a captain. In June, he was appointed a lieutenant in the **Confederate navy** and was given command of the batteries at Jamestown Island. Soon, Jones was working with **John M. Brooke** developing the ironclad *Virginia*, and by year's end he was made executive officer of the vessel. During the fight with the **USS Monitor** at **Hampton Roads** in March 1862, Jones took command of the *Virginia* when **Franklin Buchanan** was wounded. After the historic battle, he resumed his duties as executive officer until the ship was destroyed in May.

With the loss of the *Virginia*, Jones was put in command of a land battery defending the James River and assisted in repelling the enemy at the **First Battle of Drewry's Bluff**. Later in 1862, he was put in command of the CSS *Chattahoochee* and served with it near Columbus, Georgia, before being placed in charge of the naval works at Charlotte, **North Carolina**. Promoted to commander in 1863, Jones then took command of the Selma (Alabama) Iron Works in May and produced many large caliber guns for Confederate defenses.

After the war, Jones entered a partnership with John M. Brooke and another former Confederate officer. The trio bought up surplus government war material and sold it for a profit to foreign countries. In June 1877, Jones was shot to death by an **Alabama** neighbor during an altercation over an argument that had occurred between their children.

JONES, DAVID RUMPH (1825–1863) CSA. A native of **South Carolina**, Jones graduated from **West Point** in 1846 and was assigned to the 2nd U.S. Infantry. During the **Mexican War**, he served in **Winfield Scott's army** and won one **brevet** for gallantry. After being promoted to 1st lieutenant in 1849, Jones served in **California** and as an instructor at West Point before being transferred to the adjutant general's department in 1853. Fort the next eight years, he served in various administrative positions in the west and northwest. During this time, Jones married a niece of Zachary Taylor and became a cousin by marriage to future Confederate Lt. Gen. **Richard Taylor**.

Jones resigned his commission in February 1861 and entered the **Confederate army** the following month as a major. Becoming **P. G. T. Beauregard's** chief of staff, he participated in the bombardment of **Fort Sumter, South Carolina**, and carried the final surrender demand to Maj. **Robert Anderson**. When these terms were accepted, it was said that Jones personally lowered the U.S. **flag** from the fort.

Jones was promoted to brigadier general in June 1861 and was given command of a **brigade** near Manassas, Virginia. After fighting at **First Manassas**, he was given a South Carolina brigade in **James Longstreet's** division and spent several months garrisoning Northern Virginia. In February 1862, Jones was given command of **Samuel Garland's** brigade and led it to the Virginia Peninsula for the **Peninsula Campaign**. After taking charge of a two-brigade **division** on the peninsula in March 1862, he was promoted to major general the following month.

During the **Seven Days Campaign**, Jones served under **John B. Magruder** and participated in several battles. In the **Army of Northern Virginia's** reorganization following the campaign, his division was given another brigade. Jones performed very well in the **Second Manassas Campaign**, especially at **Thoroughfare Gap** and in Longstreet's counterattack. In September 1862, he also served well while defending the **South Mountain** gaps during the **Antietam Campaign**. At Antietam, Jones's division defended the Confederate right flank against

Ambrose E. Burnside's attack. During the fighting, his brother-in-law, Col. Henry W. Kingsbury of the 11th Connecticut, was killed while battling Jones's men at Burnside's Bridge.

Jones had a solid war record by October 1862, but, unfortunately, he suffered a heart attack that month and was unable to return to the **army**. He died in **Richmond, Virginia**, on January 15, 1863. Some of Jones's friends believed the sorrow caused by Kingsbury's death contributed to his own demise.

JONES, JOHN MARSHALL (1820–1864) CSA. A native of **Virginia**, Jones graduated from **West Point** in 1841 with a low class ranking and the earned nickname "Rum." Assigned to the infantry, he served on various garrison duty and spent the **Mexican War** assigned to the academy. Jones rose to the rank of captain in 1855 and spent the rest of his antebellum career at various posts and on a western topographical expedition and the **Utah Expedition**.

During the **secession** crisis, Jones took a leave of absence and accepted a major's commission in the Confederate **artillery** in March 1861, two months before his resignation from the **U.S. Army** was accepted. In September, he was promoted to lieutenant colonel and joined **John B. Magruder's** staff as adjutant. Jones was transferred to Maj. Gen. **Richard S. Ewell's** staff in January 1862 and served as his assistant adjutant general through **Stonewall Jackson's Shenandoah Valley**, the **Seven Days**, and the **Second Manassas Campaigns**. After Ewell was wounded at **Groveton**, Jones became **Jubal A. Early's** inspector general in December. He served under him at **Fredericksburg** and **Chancellorsville**, but he rejoined Ewell as adjutant when the general returned to duty in early 1863.

It was very unusual for a West Point graduate to remain so long in a staff position at a time when the Confederacy desperately needed trained line officers. Although his superiors regularly praised his conduct, Jones's slow rise through the ranks may best be explained by his nickname "Rum." After apparently remaining sober for a number of months, he finally was appointed brigadier general in May 1863 after promising **Robert E. Lee** to resign if his drinking became a problem. Jones replaced **John R. Jones** (creating some confusion for historians) as commander of a **brigade** in Jackson's old **division** in the **Army of Northern Virginia**. A strict disciplinarian, Jones soon earned his men's respect, but he was badly wounded in the thigh while leading the brigade at **Gettysburg's** Culp's Hill. He recovered in time to serve in the **Bristoe Station** and **Mine Run Campaigns** and received a second wound, to the head, at **Payne's Farm**.

On May 5, 1864, Jones's brigade was holding Ewell's line near the Orange Turnpike at the **Wilderness** when the Union V Corps attacked its right flank. Jones was behind the line at the time but quickly rode forward to rally his shattered command. As his men streamed to the rear, he calmly sat on his horse watching the approaching enemy until he was shot dead. Many soldiers believed he was humiliated by his inability to stem the rout and accepted death as his fate.

JONES, JOHN ROBERT (1827–1901) CSA. A native of **Virginia**, Jones graduated with distinction from the **Virginia Military Institute** in 1848. He became a successful teacher and administrator while working at several academies (including his alma mater) in Virginia, **Florida**, and **Maryland**.

When the Civil War began, Jones organized a Virginia militia **company** and served as its captain. The company became part of the 33rd Virginia in June 1861 and was assigned to the soon-to-be-called **Stonewall Brigade**. After fighting at **First Manassas**, Jones was promoted to lieutenant colonel in August and became a favorite of **Stonewall Jackson** that autumn while serving in western Virginia. When the **regiment** was reorganized in the spring of 1862, he was defeated in elections for colonel, lieutenant colonel, and major. Jackson intervened on Jones's behalf, however, and in June convinced **Jefferson Davis** to promote him to brigadier general. Much to the men's disgust, he then was given command of a **brigade** in Jackson's old **division**.

Jones led his brigade through the **Seven Days Campaign** with the **Army of Northern Virginia** and was wounded near its conclusion. His wound kept him out of the **Second Manassas Campaign**, but he rejoined the **army** in time to serve as the division's temporary commander at **Antietam**. After a shell exploded near him, Jones claimed he had been stunned, relinquished command, and moved to the rear. When rumors circulated at **Fredericksburg** that the general hid behind a tree during the fighting, the men began to question his bravery. Because of these rumors, Jones became the first general in **Robert E. Lee's** army to be court-martialed for cowardice. Jackson, and the army, tried to protect his reputation, however, and Jones was acquitted. In the next fight at **Chancellorsville**, he again went to the rear complaining of an ulcerated leg. This time, Lee replaced Jones with his namesake **John Marshall Jones**. Despite having no command, Jones apparently accompanied the army in the **Gettysburg Campaign** (perhaps under arrest) and was captured in Maryland on July 4, 1863. The Confederates failed to **exchange** him, however, and he remained in **prison** until war's end.

Jones returned to Virginia after the war and sold farm equipment until becoming commissioner in chancery of the county court in 1887.

JONES, SAMUEL (1819–1887) CSA. A native of **Virginia**, Jones graduated from **West Point** in 1841. Assigned to the **artillery**, he served on the Canadian border during the so-called Aroostook War and in **Florida** before returning to the academy in 1846 to teach mathematics and **tactics**. After being promoted to 1st lieutenant in 1847, Jones left West Point in 1851 and served at various posts in the 1850s. He was promoted to captain in 1853 and had been serving in **Washington, D.C.**, since 1858 as assistant to the **army's** judge advocate when the Civil War began.

Jones resigned his commission in April 1861 and joined the **Confederate army** as a major of artillery. He soon was promoted to lieutenant colonel and served as Virginia's assistant adjutant general before becoming colonel and **P. G. T. Beauregard's** chief of artillery in July. After serving well at **First Manassas**, he was promoted to brigadier general in August and took command of a **brigade** guarding the Potomac River.

In January 1862, Jones was sent to **Pensacola, Florida**, to relieve **Braxton Bragg** in command there. Two months after arriving, he was promoted to major general and relieved Bragg from command of the **Department of Alabama and West Florida**. Thus began a career unmatched in terms of transfers and personality clashes. Because of his abrasive personality and apparent incompetence, Jones was unable to satisfy any of his superiors over the next two years and was transferred all over the Confederacy. His commands included **divisions** in **Earl Van Dorn's Army of the West** and Bragg's **Army of the Mississippi** and command of Chattanooga, Tennessee; the **Department of East Tennessee**; the District of Middle Tennessee; the **Department of Western Virginia**; Savannah, Georgia; the **Department of South Carolina, Georgia, and Florida**; and the District of Florida.

After the war, Jones returned to Virginia, where he farmed until 1880. He then was given a clerkship in the Adjutant General's Office in Washington, D.C., and later worked in the Judge Advocate General's Office.

JONES, WILLIAM EDMONDSON "GRUMBLE" (1824–1864) CSA. A native of **Virginia**, Jones graduated from **West Point** in 1848 and was assigned to the Mounted Rifles. He served mostly in **Oregon** until taking a leave of absence in 1852 to marry. While returning to duty with his bride, Jones's ship sank off the **Texas** coast, and his wife drowned after being swept from his arms. He was said to have been changed forever by the tragic accident. Jones resumed his duties and was promoted to 1st lieutenant in 1854 but then resigned his commission three years later. After visiting Europe, he returned to Virginia and farmed.

When the Civil War began, Jones was captain of a local militia **company**, which he led into Confederate service in July 1861. As part of **J. E. B. Stuart's** 1st Virginia Cavalry, he fought at **First Manassas** and replaced Stuart as regimental colonel when Stuart was promoted to brigadier general in September. Jones had a sour disposition, hated Stuart, and was widely known as "Grumble" Jones. His men much preferred Lt. Col. **Fitzhugh Lee** over him, and when the **regiment** was reorganized in the spring of 1862, Jones was replaced by Lee.

In June 1862, Jones replaced **Turner Ashby** as colonel of the 7th Virginia Cavalry. Although a strict **disciplinarian**, he was respected by his men for leading them well and for allowing them to be lax in military dress and customs. Throughout the war, Jones became very adept at turning undisciplined irregular cavalry into effective fighters and was said to have been the "best outpost officer" in the **army**. However, his men came to recognize that their colonel detested Stuart and anyone associated with him and noted how Jones even would outright lie to discredit his former commander. On the other hand, Jones loved **Stonewall Jackson**, and the two formed a close bond.

After serving under Jackson in **Jackson's 1862 Shenandoah Campaign**, **Cedar Mountain**, and **Second Manassas**, Jones was promoted to brigadier general in October 1862. He officially commanded the Laurel Brigade but remained on detached duty in the **Shenandoah Valley**, where through Jackson's influence he was appointed to command the **Valley District** in December. In January 1863, Jones made an unsuccessful raid into **West Virginia**, but he made up for it in the spring when he joined **John D. Imboden** for **Jones's and Imboden's Raid**. It was one of the most successful cavalry raids of the war, and the Confederates nearly reached the Ohio River, inflicting heavy casualties on the enemy while suffering the loss of only a few men. Jones's **brigade** then joined Stuart's command in the **Army of Northern Virginia**, against both his and Stuart's objections. After fighting very well at **Brandy Station**, he was rather lackluster in the **Gettysburg Campaign**, and Stuart courtmartialed him for being disrespectful. Convicted, Jones was removed from command and was sent to southwestern Virginia in October.

Jones served under **James Longstreet** in the **Knoxville Campaign** and performed very well defending southwestern Virginia against enemy raids. In the spring of 1864 he took his brigade to the Shenandoah Valley to contest **David Hunter's Shenandoah Valley Campaign**. On June 5 at **Piedmont**, Jones was shot in the head and killed while trying to rally his men.

JONESBORO, GEORGIA, BATTLE OF (AUGUST 31–SEPTEM-BER 1, 1864). In late summer 1864, **William T. Sherman's** armies were having little success capturing Atlanta, Georgia, in the **Atlanta Campaign**. In an attempt to break the stalemate, Sherman sent his cavalry to cut the last Confederate supply lines into Atlanta. These raids led to battles at **Ezra Church** and **Lovejoy's Station**, but they failed to cut the **railroads** feeding **John Bell Hood's Army of Tennessee**. As a result, Sherman withdrew his main force from north and west of Atlanta and sent it southward to cut the Macon & Western Railroad between Rough and Ready and Jonesboro.

Leaving the XX Corps north of Atlanta, Sherman shifted the rest of his force on the night of August 25. Hood at first believed that a raid against Sherman's own supply line by **Joseph Wheeler** was forcing the enemy to withdraw. When he finally realized Sherman's **strategy**, Hood sent **William J. Hardee** south on the night of August 30 to defend the railroad with his and **Stephen D. Lee's corps**. On August 31, Hardee attacked west of Jonesboro with his corps (under **Patrick Cleburne**) on the left and Lee on the right. Cleburne was to open the attack and envelop the Union right flank, with Lee joining in when he heard Cleburne's guns. Lee, however, mistook **skirmishing** for Cleburne's attack and advanced too soon. **William B. Hazen's** XV Corps **division**, with the support **Charles R. Wood's** XVII Corps division, repulsed Lee, while on the Union right, **H. Judson Kilpatrick's** cavalry blunted Cleburne's assault.

That night, Hood learned of another Union column approaching Rough and Ready and withdrew Lee to counter it. This deployment seriously weakened Hardee's position at Jonesboro, but he remained in place and entrenched along the railroad. While part of his command destroyed the railroad near Rough and Ready, Sherman gathered reinforcements at Jonesboro. The Union XIV Corps attacked the Confederates on September 1 and after bitter fighting overran a weak **salient** manned by **Daniel C. Govan's brigade** in the Confederate center. Hardee then was forced to retreat to Lovejoy's Station.

With his last supply line now cut, Hood evacuated Atlanta that night. When Sherman learned that the XX Corps had occupied Atlanta on September 2, he decided not to pursue the retreating Confederates. In the fighting around Jonesboro, Hood lost approximately 2,000 men, while Sherman suffered 1,149 casualties.

JONES'S AND IMBODEN'S RAID (APRIL 20–MAY 27, 1863). One of the lesser known, but more successful, cavalry raids in the Civil War was made by Confederate Brig. Gens. **William E. "Grumble" Jones** and

John D. Imboden. Jones, commander of the **Valley District**, took his cavalry **brigade** from near Harrisonburg, Virginia, on April 20, 1863, to strike the Baltimore & Ohio Railroad in **West Virginia**. In cooperation, Imboden left Monterey, Virginia, with 3,500 cavalry and infantry to capture Beverly, West Virginia, before joining Jones near Grafton or Clarksburg. Imboden also was to destroy the **railroad** and collect horses, cattle, and mules.

Jones successfully destroyed a number of railroad bridges in West Virginia before riding north, where he threatened Wheeling and nearly reached the Ohio River to menace Pittsburgh, Pennsylvania. He then destroyed a vital railroad bridge at Fairmont before linking up with Imboden at Weston. At a cost of only a dozen men, Jones had inflicted a large number of Union casualties, destroyed vital bridges, and sent panic through West Virginia and southwestern **Pennsylvania**. Although he had been hampered by heavy rains, Imboden also had been successful, covering 400 miles in 37 days, destroying eight bridges, and capturing approximately 3,000 head of cattle.

JORDAN, THOMAS (1819–1895) CSA. A native of **Virginia**, Jordan graduated near the bottom of his 1840 **West Point** class (one of his roommates was **William T. Sherman**). Assigned to the infantry, he fought in the **Seminole** and **Mexican Wars** and in the latter won promotions to captain and quartermaster. After Mexico, Jordan again fought the Seminoles before being sent to the Pacific Northwest to fight **Indians** in **Oregon**.

Jordan resigned his commission in May 1861 and was commissioned lieutenant colonel of Virginia troops. Assigned to **P. G. T. Beauregard** at Manassas, he was promoted to colonel in July and became Beauregard's adjutant general. After service at **First Manassas**, Jordan accompanied Beauregard to the **Army of the Mississippi** and became its assistant adjutant general in March 1862. At the **Battle of Shiloh**, he played a particularly significant role while serving as the **army's** chief of staff. Jordan was credited with writing out **Albert Sidney Johnston's** attack orders, positioning troops during the battle, and recommending that Beauregard withdraw on the battle's second day.

Promoted to brigadier general in September 1862, Jordan continued to serve as chief of staff, first under Beauregard and then **Braxton Bragg**. After participating in the **Kentucky Campaign**, he was assigned to Beauregard in September and was sent to the **Department of South Carolina and Georgia**. There, Jordan served as Beauregard's adjutant general, inspector general, and chief of staff. He performed his duties well during the defense of **Charleston**, **South Carolina**, and in May

1864 was made commander of a **South Carolina** military **district** after **Samuel Jones** replaced Beauregard in command of the **department**. Within weeks, however, Jordan was transferred to **Richmond, Virginia**. He spent several months there before finally being assigned to Beauregard as an aide-de-camp in February 1865. Jordan spent the war's last months with Beauregard in the **Carolinas Campaign**.

Having already published one book on the Southern economy, Jordan resumed his writing career after the war with an article for *Harper's Weekly* in late 1865 that criticized former Confederate president **Jefferson Davis**. The following year, he became editor of the Memphis *Appeal* (working under former Confederate general Albert Pike), and two years later he coauthored with J. P. Pryor *The Campaigns of Lieutenant-General N. B. Forrest, and of Forrest's Cavalry*. An adventurer as well as a writer, Jordan became involved in the Cuban revolutionary movement in 1869 and served as chief of staff and commander of the rebels there. After some battlefield success, he finally returned to the United States in 1870 and became editor of a **New York** publication that championed the free silver philosophy.

JUDAH, HENRY MOSES (1821–1866) USA. A native of **Maryland**, Judah graduated near the bottom of his 1843 **West Point** class and was assigned to the infantry. After winning two **brevets** for gallantry in the **Mexican War**, he was stationed in the Pacific Northwest and was promoted to captain in 1853.

Judah was posted in **California** when the Civil War began. In September 1861, he was appointed colonel of the 4th California Infantry but resigned that position in November 1861 and traveled to **Washington, D.C.**, where he served in the city's defenses. In March 1862, Judah was promoted to brigadier general and was sent west to become inspector general for **U. S. Grant's Army of the Tennessee**. After the **Battle of Shiloh**, he resigned his post and was given command of a **division** during **Henry Halleck's siege of Corinth, Mississippi**. Judah then resigned that position in July and served as inspector general for the **Army of the Ohio** from October 1862 to February 1863. He next took command of a XXIII division in the Army of the Ohio in June 1863 and helped pursue **John Hunt Morgan's** raiders that summer. Judah's actions apparently displeased his superiors, however. Although he commanded another division in early 1864, he spent the rest of the war either commanding troops in rear areas or on administrative duty. When the war ended, Judah was commanding a **brigade** in the **Department of the Cumberland**.

Judah had been promoted to major of the 4th U.S. Infantry in 1862 and remained in the **U.S. Army** at that rank (with the brevet rank of colonel) after being mustered out of the volunteer service in August 1865. He died in 1866 while in command of the garrison at Plattsburg Barracks, New York.

JUG TAVERN, GEORGIA, BATTLE OF (AUGUST 3, 1864). During the **Atlanta Campaign**, in late July 1864, **William T. Sherman** launched **Stoneman's and McCook's Raid** to free Union **prisoners** at **Andersonville** and to destroy Confederate **railroads** supplying Atlanta, Georgia. **George Stoneman** and one of his three **brigades** were captured by pursuing Confederate cavalry on July 31, but the other two brigades escaped. Confederate cavalry under Col. William C. P. Breckinridge gave chase as the Union brigades of Cols. Horace Capron and Silas Adams headed for Athens, Georgia. On August 2, Capron and Adams became separated while maneuvering against Athens. Capron reached Jug Tavern that night and allowed his men a short rest before moving on to rejoin Sherman's command. Breckinridge, however, attacked before daylight on August 3 and routed Capron's command. Capron and some men got away, but as many as 250 of his men were killed or captured.

JULIAN, GEORGE WASHINGTON (1817–1899) USA. A native of **Indiana**, Julian was raised as a Quaker and became a self-educated **abolitionist**. He began working as a teacher at age 18 but then read the law and passed the bar exam in 1840. In 1845, Julian was elected to the state legislature as a **Whig**, but he was a politician who had no qualms about changing party allegiances. When the Whigs failed to take a strong antislavery stance, he joined the **Free-Soil Party** in 1849 and won election to the **U.S. Congress** in 1850. When Julian opposed the **Compromise of 1850**, his more conservative constituents voted him out of office in the next election. He next was the party's unsuccessful vice presidential candidate in 1852. Julian then became active in the People's Party and finally joined the **Republican Party** in 1856.

Julian returned to Congress in 1861 and became a strong ally of fellow **Radical Republicans Benjamin F. Wade** and **Zachariah Chandler**. During the Civil War, he criticized **Abraham Lincoln** for not taking immediate steps to end **slavery**, advocated the confiscation of secessionist property and the enlistment of **black troops**, and proposed granting political and civil rights to **freedmen**. As a member of the **Committee on the Conduct of the War**, Julian wielded great power and influence in the federal government and became the nemesis of such **Democratic** generals as **George B. McClellan** and **Fitz John Porter**.

After the war, Julian supported women's suffrage and the 14th Amendment and opposed monopolies and corruption. He also opposed the scandal-riddled administration of President **U. S. Grant** and helped organize the Liberal Republican Party in 1870. Julian's abandonment of the Republicans led to his being defeated for reelection in 1871 and being expelled from the party. He then joined the Democrats but never again was elected to office.

– K –

KANAWHA DIVISION. In the summer of 1862, Union Brig. Gen. **Jacob D. Cox** commanded four **brigades** on the Great Kanawha River in western Virginia. Two of these brigades, which he took east in August to lead in the **Second Manassas** and **Antietam Campaigns**, joined the **Army of the Potomac's** IX Corps and became known as the Kanawha (Kan-NOW-wha) Division. The 1st Brigade consisted of the 12th, 23rd, and 30th Ohio; 1st Ohio Independent Battery; and two independent **companies** of West Virginia cavalry. The 23rd Ohio was commanded by future president **Rutherford B. Hayes** and included future president Sgt. William McKinley. The brigade was commanded first by **Eliakim P. Scammon** and then by **Hugh Ewing**. The 2nd Brigade had the 11th, 28th, and 36th Ohio; Simmonds's Kentucky Battery (Union); Schambeck's Illinois Cavalry; and the 3rd Independent Company of Ohio Cavalry. This brigade was first commanded by Augustus Moore and then by **George Crook**. Cox led the **division** at Second Manassas, but he then took command of the **corps** when **Jesse Reno** was killed at **South Mountain**. Scammon took command of the division and led it at Antietam and returned it to **West Virginia** after the campaign.

KANE, THOMAS LEIPER (1822–1883) USA. A native of **Pennsylvania**, Kane was educated locally and in Europe. He studied law under his father, who was a federal judge, but the two clashed over the 1850 **Fugitive Slave Act**. Kane was a dedicated **abolitionist** who became a U.S. commissioner, but his father strictly enforced the law requiring commissioners to aid in the return of runaway slaves. When the younger Kane resigned his position, his father viewed it as an insult to the court and jailed him for contempt. After Kane was released on order of the **U.S. Supreme Court**, he became active in the **Underground Railroad** and later accompanied the Mormons on their move to Salt Lake City, Utah. There, Kane convinced Brigham Young that he should not resist U.S. authority and thus helped peacefully end the 1857–58 **Utah Expedition**. Returning east, Kane founded the town of Kane, Pennsylvania, just prior to the Civil War.

When the Civil War began, Kane raised a **regiment** of volunteers among local hunters. Officially designated the 13th Pennsylvania Reserves, the regiment was more popularly known as the **"Pennsylvania Bucktails"** (later designated the 42nd Pennsylvania). Kane entered Union service in June 1861 as lieutenant colonel after having turned down a colonel's commission because of his lack of military experience. During the small December 1861 battle at **Dranesville, Virginia**, he was slightly wounded. Six months later, he was wounded again and was captured at Harrisonburg during **Stonewall Jackson's Shenandoah Valley Campaign**.

Exchanged in August 1862, Kane was promoted to brigadier general of volunteers in September and was given command of a **brigade** in the 1st Division of the **Army of the Potomac's** XII Corps. After missing the **Battle of Fredericksburg**, he fought at **Chancellorsville** but was forced to relinquish command shortly afterward because of pneumonia. It was claimed that Kane left his hospital sickbed to rejoin his brigade at **Gettysburg**, arriving in time to resume command on the second day of battle. Although he saw only limited action at Culp's Hill and was forced to give up command because of his health, he was **brevetted** major general of volunteers in 1865 for his service there.

Poor health forced Kane to resign his commission in November 1863. He returned to Pennsylvania and became a businessman and the first president of the state's board of charities.

KANSAS. Kansas played an important role in American history before the Civil War began. Created as a territory by the 1854 **Kansas-Nebraska Act**, it became a battleground between pro- and antislavery factions. Despite Kansas's population being overwhelming antislavery, numerous proslavery "Border Ruffians" rode in from neighboring **Missouri** to engage in a ferocious guerrilla war. The territory was consumed by violence in the 1850s, leading to its nickname **"Bleeding Kansas."** Kansas was where **abolitionist John Brown** first gained notoriety for murdering proslavery men, and it was the catalyst of the 1856 Brooks-**Sumner** Affair in the U.S. Senate.

Kansas was admitted as a state in January 1861 and remained staunchly loyal to the Union. With a sparse population of fewer than 100,000, it did not provide many troops but did send a large percentage of its men into service. Approximately 20 percent of the population, or 20,097 men, served the Union, with 8,498 becoming casualties. Both numbers represent the highest percentage of service and casualties among Northern state populations. Many of the antislavery men joined partisan units known as **Jayhawkers** to protect their families and to take revenge on Border Ruffians who raided the territory earlier. Many regulars and Jayhawkers fought under **James H. Lane**.

The state became a battleground between these Union forces and such Confederate **partisans** as **William C. Quantrill** and **William "Bloody Bill" Anderson**. The town of **Lawrence** was raided and sacked by Quantrill and Anderson in August 1863, with 150 men and boys being murdered. Two months later, Quantrill **massacred** approximately 100 Union soldiers at **Baxter Springs**. Clashes also occurred at **Mine Creek and Marais des Cygnes River** during **Sterling Price's 1864 Missouri Raid**. *See also* 1ST KANSAS COLORED VOLUNTEERS.

1ST KANSAS COLORED VOLUNTEERS. This **regiment** generally is regarded as the first regiment of **black troops** to have seen combat in the Civil War. Recruitment began in **Kansas** in August 1862 mostly among free blacks, and two months later the **companies** engaged in a **skirmish** at Island Mound, **Missouri**. By January 1863, six companies had been raised and were designated the 1st Kansas Colored Volunteers under Col. James M. Williams. Four new companies were added in May. During its existence, the regiment fought entirely west of the Mississippi River and was engaged in 12 actions, including **Cabin Creek**, **Honey Springs**, and **Poison Spring**. In December 1864, it was redesignated the 79th U.S. Colored Troops. The regiment is ranked 21st among Union regiments for the highest percentage of members killed in action.

KANSAS-NEBRASKA ACT (MAY 22, 1854). This act by the **U.S. Congress** became one of the major issues that divided the North and South before the Civil War. Introduced by Sen. **Stephen A. Douglas**, it was intended to pave the way for a northern transcontinental **railroad**, open the Great Plains for settlement, strengthen Douglas's presidential aspirations, and lay to rest the issue of **slavery** when creating new territories.

Douglas was determined to secure a transcontinental railroad beginning in Chicago, Illinois, but doing so would require crossing the empty expanse of the Great Plains. To lure railroads into undertaking such expensive projects, the government often presented large land grants to help finance the construction. Federal law, however, only allowed such grants to be made in organized territories. Therefore, Douglas first had to form into territories the land over which the railroad would cross. Forming the territories not only would allow the railroads to get their needed land grants, but it also would help bring law and order to the area and promote settlement.

Complicating the matter was the slavery issue. The 1820 **Missouri Compromise** stipulated that new territories carved from the Louisiana Purchase north of the Missouri Compromise Line would automatically be free territories. Southerners, however, would not support the legislation unless the compromise was abolished and replaced with **popular sovereignty**. Douglas agreed, apparently because he believed that slavery would never succeed in the Great Plains and that popular sovereignty was a fairer, more democratic way to solve the slavery issue. Therefore, his Kansas-Nebraska Act not only organized the territories of **Kansas** and **Nebraska**, but it also repealed the Missouri Compromise Line in favor of popular sovereignty.

The bill created a storm of controversy. Ironically, many Southerners supported this Northern-sponsored legislation because it opened the possibility of spreading slavery farther north. Most Northerners were horrified for the same reason. Douglas was able to get the bill passed on May 22, 1854, but it cost him much political support and had far-reaching implications. The bill's passage further polarized the sections and led to the creation of the antislavery **Republican Party** later that year. It also led to **"Bleeding Kansas,"** as pro- and antislavery forces fought in Kansas to win the territory for their side.

KAUTZ, AUGUST VALENTINE (1828–1895) USA. A native of Germany, Kautz immigrated to the United States with his family as an infant. Settling in **Ohio**, he received a local education and served as a private in the **Mexican War**. Kautz then graduated from **West Point** in 1852 and was wounded twice while fighting **Indians** in the Pacific Northwest.

Soon after the Civil War began, Kautz was appointed captain in the 6th U.S. Cavalry and served in the **Washington, D.C.**, defenses. After service with the **Army of the Potomac** in the **Peninsula** and **Seven Days Campaigns**, he was appointed colonel of the 2nd Ohio Cavalry in September 1862 and was sent to **Kansas**. Late that year, Kautz was placed in command of **Camp Chase, Ohio**, and he led a cavalry **brigade** in the pursuit of Confederate raider **John Hunt Morgan** in the summer of 1863. While at Camp Chase, he also wrote a manual for **company** clerks that was reprinted 12 times during the war.

Kautz was given command of a cavalry **division** in the **Army of the James** in April 1864 and was promoted to brigadier general of volunteers the following month. He served in the **Petersburg Campaign** and fought at **Reams' Station** and in a number of other battles. Kautz's performance as a cavalry commander, however, did not impress his superiors, even though he was awarded three **brevets**. In March 1865, he was placed in command of a division of **black troops** in the XXV Corps and was among the first Union soldiers to enter **Richmond, Virginia**, in April 1865. Afterward, Kautz served on the military court that tried the **Abraham Lincoln assassination** conspirators.

Kautz was mustered out of the volunteers in January 1866, but he remained in the **U.S. Army** as lieutenant colonel of the 34th U.S. Infantry. He served mostly on the frontier and rose to the rank of brigadier general before retiring in 1891.

KEARNY MEDAL AND KEARNY CROSS. In honor of Maj. Gen. **Philip Kearny** (KAR-nee), a gold Maltese cross was designed in November 1862 to be presented to officers of his **division** who distinguished themselves in battle while under Kearny's command. The medal was worn around the neck on a ribbon, and a cross was positioned beneath a circle that had the Latin inscription *Dulce et decorum est pro patria mori* ("It is sweet to die for one's fatherland"). Another gold circle was in the middle with the name *Kearny* on it, and the name of the recipient was inscribed on the back of the medal. Although the medal was never officially adopted by the War Department, approximately 317 were made by the **New York** firm, Ball, Black, & Co.

In March 1863, Kearny's successor, **David B. Birney**, ordered that another cross be presented to gallant enlisted men. Known as the Kearny Cross, it was a bronze patté worn around the neck on a ribbon and had the inscription "Kearny Cross" on one side and "Birney's Division" on the other. Interestingly, two women—**Anna Etheridge** and **Marie Tebe**—were among the first to receive the cross. It is not known how many crosses were issued during the war, but the number was greater than the number of Kearny Medals. *See also* DECORATIONS; MEDAL OF HONOR.

KEARNY, PHILIP (1815–1862) USA. A native of **New York** and a member of a prominent family (he inherited a million dollars from his grandfather), Kearny (KAR-nee) was the nephew of **Mexican War** hero Stephen W. Kearny. After graduating from Columbia University in 1833, he practiced law before being commissioned a 2nd lieutenant in the 1st U.S. Dragoons in 1837. Kearny then embarked on an impressive military career. An excellent horseman, he attended the French cavalry school at Saumur in 1839, fought with the **Chasseurs** d'Afrique in Algiers in 1840 (where he was awarded France's Legion of Merit), and served as aide-de-camp to generals-in-chief Alexander Macomb and **Winfield Scott**. During the Mexican War, Kearny was part of Scott's escort cavalry and lost his left arm after being wounded at Churubusco. He was **brevetted** major and later served in **California** before resigning his captain's commission in 1851. Kearny traveled the world after leaving the **U.S. Army** and in 1859 served in Italy as part of Napoleon III's Imperial Guard. There he participated in several cavalry charges while holding his horse's reigns in his teeth. After further service in the Crimean War, Kearny returned to the United States when the Civil War began and entered Union service as a brigadier general of volunteers in August 1861.

Kearny first took command of a **brigade** in **William Franklin's** division, but during the **Peninsula Campaign**, he led the 3rd Division in the **Army of the Potomac's** III Corps. He fought well through the Peninsula and **Seven Days Campaigns** and was promoted to major general of volunteers in July 1862. Kearny was one of the more gifted Union **division** commanders and originated the Kearny Patch, the forerunner of **corps badges**. Scott referred to him as "the bravest man I ever knew" (Warner, *Generals in Blue*, p. 259). While commanding the III Corps' 1st Division in the **Battle of Chantilly** during the **Second Manassas Campaign**, he mistakenly rode into the Confederate lines and was shot and killed after refusing to surrender. **Robert E. Lee** greatly respected the fallen officer and sent Kearny's horse and personal effects to his widow. Afterward, the **Kearny Medal and Kearny Cross** were adopted to present to members of his division who distinguished themselves in battle.

KEARSARGE, **USS.** This Union warship was launched in September 1862 and displaced 1,031 tons, carried eight guns, and had a crew of 162. Commanded by Charles W. Pickering, the *Kearsarge* first assisted in **blockading** the CSS *Sumter* at Gibraltar. **John A. Winslow** replaced Pickering in April 1863 and began cruising the Atlantic Ocean in search of Confederate **commerce raiders**. In June 1864, he learned that the **CSS *Alabama*** was in Cherbourg, France, and headed there to engage it. On June 19, the *Alabama* accepted the challenge, and a short fight erupted in the English Channel. Winslow had better guns and had taken the precaution of protecting his ship's engines by hanging board-covered chains over the side. In little over an hour, the *Kearsarge* sank the *Alabama*. Fifteen of Winslow's crewmen were later awarded the **Medal of Honor** for the battle. Afterward, the *Kearsarge* continued in naval service until it was wrecked off Central America in 1894.

KEIM, WILLIAM HIGH (1813–1862) USA. A native of **Pennsylvania**, Keim was educated at Mt. Airy Military Academy and became active in the state militia. He was elected mayor of Reading in 1848 and in 1858 was appointed to fill out the unfinished term of a **Democratic** congressman. Keim did not run for reelection, but in 1860, he was appointed the state's surveyor general.

In April 1861, Keim was appointed major general of militia and was given command of a **division** in the **Department of Pennsylvania**. He served under **Robert Patterson** in the **Shenandoah Valley** in the weeks preceding **First Manassas**, but he and his division were mustered out of service on the day of the battle. Keim then was appointed brigadier general of volunteers in December 1861 and led a **brigade** in **Silas Casey's** division of the **Army of the Potomac's** IV Corps during the **Peninsula Campaign**. After serving at **Yorktown** and **Williamsburg**, he died in May 1862 from "camp fever."

KELLEY, BENJAMIN FRANKLIN (1807–1891) USA. A native of **New Hampshire** and the future father-in-law of Union general **Jeremiah C. Sullivan**, Kelley moved to western **Virginia** as a young man and became a **railroad** agent. He entered Union service in May 1861 when he was appointed colonel of the 1st (West) Virginia, a **regiment** he had raised.

Kelley led his men at **Philippi** the following month and was badly wounded. When he returned to duty, he was appointed brigadier general of volunteers to rank from May 1861 and protected the vital Baltimore & Ohio Railroad in **West Virginia** and **Maryland**. Kelley and his men frequently **skirmished** with enemy raiders and guerrillas and pursued the retreating Confederates during the **Gettysburg Campaign**. In 1864, he fought in numerous small battles, including the fight at **Moorefield**, **West Virginia**, for which he was awarded a **brevet** of major general of volunteers. While in camp at Cumberland, Maryland, in February 1865, Kelley and his superior, Maj. Gen. **George Crook**, were captured by **McNeill's Rangers** during a nighttime raid. **Exchanged** in March, Kelley resigned his commission in June.

After the war, Kelley held a number of federal political appointments, including revenue collector; superintendent of the Hot Springs, Arkansas, military reservation; and examiner of pensions.

KELLY, JOHN HERBERT (1840–1864) CSA. A native of **Alabama**, Kelly was orphaned at age six and was raised by a grandmother. He was admitted to **West Point** in 1857 but resigned in December 1860 as the **secession** crisis deepened.

Kelly entered Confederate service in early 1861 as a 2nd lieutenant of **artillery** and was assigned to **Fort Morgan**, **Alabama**. Later that year, he was promoted to captain and after serving on **William J. Hardee's** staff, he was appointed major of the 9th Arkansas Battalion in September. At **Shiloh**, Kelly commanded **Sterling A. M. Wood's brigade skirmishers** and lost half his battalion but was rewarded with a promotion to colonel and command of the 8th Arkansas. As part of **St. John R. Liddell's** brigade, he next fought at **Perryville** and was said to have personally captured the colonel of the 22nd Indiana. At **Stones River** with the **Army of Tennessee**, Kelly again was in heavy combat and was wounded in the arm. By **Chickamauga**, he had been given an infantry brigade in **William Preston's** division. In very heavy fighting at **Snodgrass Hill**, the brigade captured a Union position, held out against three counterattacks, and finally forced the enemy to surrender. Kelly had one horse killed under him in the battle and lost more than one-third of his men.

Kelly was appointed brigadier general in November 1863, making him (at age 23) the youngest Confederate general at the time. During the winter encampment in northern **Georgia**, he was one of the officers who signed **Patrick Cleburne's** document advocating the enlistment of **black troops** that was presented at the **Dalton Conference**. Kelly's controversial position apparently did not hurt his career, however, for he was given command of a cavalry **division** under **Joseph Wheeler** in May 1864. During the **Atlanta Campaign**, Kelly carried out the duties of a major general and served Wheeler well. While on one of **Wheeler's Raids** into Tennessee, he was mortally wounded on September 2 during a **skirmish** at Franklin. Kelly probably died the next day.

KELLY'S FORD, TENNESSEE, BATTLE OF (JANUARY 26–27, 1864). *See* FAIR GARDEN, TENNESSEE, BATTLE OF.

KELLY'S FORD, VIRGINIA, BATTLE OF (MARCH 17, 1863). In February 1863, Confederate cavalry under Brig. Gen. **Fitzhugh Lee** embarrassed Union Brig. Gen. **William W. Averell** by capturing 150 of his men in a surprise raid against an outpost at Hartwood Church, Virginia. The two having been close friends before the war, Lee left a message asking Averell to repay the visit sometime and to bring some coffee. Stung by the raid, Averell looked for revenge.

When scouts reported Lee's cavalry in the vicinity of Kelly's Ford the following month, Averell took his 2,100-man **brigade** up the Rappahannock River and crossed to the south bank at Kelly's Ford on March 17. After capturing a small number of Confederate **pickets**, he pushed on but within a mile ran into Lee's 800-man brigade. Averell assumed the defensive about noon, managed to repulse Lee's attacks, and killed the famous young artillerist **John Pelham**. Both sides enjoyed some success trading counterattacks, but after five hours of fighting Averell decided to withdraw.

This fight was one of the first times the Union cavalry held its own against Confederate troopers and was an indication of its growing effectiveness. In the battle, Averell lost 78 men to Lee's estimated 170 casualties. Before retiring, Averell left some coffee and a note to Lee asking how he enjoyed the visit.

KELLY'S FORD, VIRGINIA, BATTLE OF (NOVEMBER 7, 1863). *See* RAPPAHANNOCK STATION, VIRGINIA, BATTLE OF.

KEMPER, JAMES LAWSON (1823–1895) CSA. A native of **Virginia**, Kemper graduated from Washington College in 1842 and opened a law practice. He served in the **Mexican War** as a captain and quartermaster of the 1st Virginia but saw no combat. Returning to his Virginia practice, Kemper was elected to the legislature in 1853. During his five-time tenure, he served as chairman of the committee on military affairs and speaker of the house and was president of the **Virginia Military Institute's** Board of Visitors. At first Kemper opposed **secession**, but he came to embrace it after **Abraham Lincoln** called for volunteers to suppress the Rebellion.

Kemper briefly served as a brigadier general of state troops, but he entered Confederate service in May 1861 as colonel of the 7th Virginia. He soon was serving as quartermaster for **P. G. T. Beauregard's Army of the Potomac** and saw service at **First Manassas**. Following the battle, Kemper's **regiment** became part of **A. P. Hill's** brigade and served with it in the **Peninsula Campaign**. He was praised for his service at **Williamsburg** and was given command of the **brigade** when Hill was promoted to **division** command in May 1862. The brigade engaged in heavy combat at **Seven Pines**, and Kemper's outstanding leadership won him promotion to brigadier general in June.

As part of **James Longstreet's** division, Kemper's brigade served in the **Seven Days Campaign** with the **Army of Northern Virginia**, but it only saw combat at **Frayser's Farm**. During the **Second Manassas Campaign**, he assumed command of the division after Longstreet was promoted to wing commander. Kemper was back in command of his brigade for the **Antietam Campaign** and fought at **Turner's Gap** and on the Confederate right wing at Antietam. Placed in **George Pickett's** division in October 1862, he reinforced the line at Marye's Heights' stone wall during the **Battle of Fredericksburg**. After service in **North Carolina** during early 1863, Kemper's brigade accompanied Pickett to **Gettysburg** and participated in **Pickett's Charge**. In the attack, Kemper was badly wounded in the groin and was captured after being left behind during the retreat. Although **exchanged** in September, he no longer was fit for field duty. Kemper served the remainder of the war as commander of Virginia's Reserve Forces and head of the **Conscription** Bureau and was promoted to major general in September 1864.

Returning to his law practice after the war, Kemper reentered politics and was elected governor of Virginia in 1873.

KENLY, JOHN REESE (1818–1891) USA. A native of **Maryland**, Kenly became a lawyer and was a member of the "Eagle Artillery" militia unit. He rose to the rank of major during the **Mexican War** and received the Thanks of the Maryland legislature for his actions at Monterrey. After the war, Kenly resumed his Baltimore law practice.

In June 1861, Kenly entered Union service as colonel of the 1st Maryland (Union). Sent to the **Shenandoah Valley**, Kenly was wounded, and most of the **regiment** was captured when it faced the 1st Maryland (Confederate) at **Front Royal** during **Stonewall Jackson's Shenandoah Valley Campaign. Exchanged** in August, he was promoted to brigadier general of volunteers and was given command of a Maryland **brigade**.

Assigned to the **Army of the Potomac** after the **Battle of Antietam**, the brigade was stationed at **Harpers Ferry, Virginia**, to protect the Baltimore & Ohio Railroad. During the **Bristoe Station** and **Mine Run Campaigns**, Kenly commanded the I Corps' 3rd Division, but he lost his position when the **corps** was disbanded in early 1864. Afterward, he was put in command of the District of Delaware and helped pursue the Confederates after **Jubal A. Early's 1864 Washington Raid**. Kenly's service apparently was less than outstanding, for a wagon train he was guarding at Winchester, Virginia, was raided and partially destroyed by the enemy. After a court of inquiry, he was placed in command of the District of the Eastern Shore, Maryland, in December and remained there until war's end.

After being **brevetted** major general of volunteers for his wartime service, Kenly left the army in August 1865 and retired in Maryland, where the legislature again voted him its thanks for his military service.

KENNEDY, JOHN DOBY (1840–1896) CSA. A native of **South Carolina**, Kennedy attended South Carolina College for a time but then dropped out and studied law. He was admitted to the bar in December 1860, practiced law, and in January 1861 was appointed captain in **Joseph B. Kershaw's** 2nd South Carolina.

After serving at **Fort Sumter**, the **regiment** was sent to **Virginia** and fought at **First Manassas**, where Kennedy received the first of his six wounds (he also was said to have been struck by 15 spent balls during the war). When Kershaw was promoted to **brigade** command in January

1862, Kennedy was appointed regimental colonel. He led the regiment in the **Peninsula** and **Seven Days Campaigns**, but fever forced him to relinquish command after the **Battle of Savage's Station**. Kennedy returned to duty with the **Army of Northern Virginia**, participated in the capture of **Harpers Ferry, Virginia**, during the **Antietam Campaign**, and received another wound at Antietam. At **Fredericksburg**, his regiment fought behind the famous stone wall on Marye's Heights. He then fought at **Chancellorsville, Salem Church**, and **Gettysburg**, receiving a third wound Gettysburg's **Peach Orchard**. Later in 1863, Kennedy accompanied **James Longstreet's corps** to **Georgia** but apparently was not well enough to lead his regiment at **Chickamauga**. However, he did sometimes command the brigade in the **Chattanooga** and **Knoxville Campaigns** (receiving another wound in the latter). Kennedy led his men through the **Overland Campaign** and the early part of the **Petersburg Campaign**, but he apparently was frequently absent when the brigade was sent to the **Shenandoah Valley** to serve with **Jubal A. Early** during **Philip Sheridan's Shenandoah Valley Campaign**. In January 1865, the brigade was transferred from the Petersburg area to South Carolina. Kennedy was appointed brigadier general in February 1865, and his brigade became part of **Lafayette McLaws's** division. After fighting at **Averasboro** and **Bentonville** in the **Carolinas Campaign**, he surrendered with the rest of **Joseph E. Johnston's army** in April 1865.

After the war, Kennedy resumed his law practice and was elected to the **U.S. Congress** in December 1865, but he was denied his seat because of his refusal to take the **Ironclad Oath**. He continued to be active in **Democratic** politics, however, and served two terms in the legislature, one term as lieutenant governor, and was appointed U.S. consul general to Shanghai, China.

KENNER, DUNCAN FARRAR (1813–1887) CSA. A native of **Louisiana**, Kenner was a brother-in-law of Confederate generals **Richard Taylor** and **Allen Thomas**. After graduating from Ohio's Miami University in 1831, he traveled the world for four years. Although he studied law under **John Slidell**, Kenner became a planter and horse breeder rather than a lawyer and by 1861 was one of Louisiana's largest slave owners. Becoming active in **Whig** and **Democratic** politics, he served in both houses of the legislature and was a delegate at two constitutional conventions, serving as convention president in 1852.

Kenner was a Louisiana representative at the **Montgomery, Alabama, Convention** in February 1861 and played a leading role in establishing the **Confederate States of America**. He also was appointed to the Provisional **Confederate Congress** and later was elected without opposition to both regular congresses. As chairman of the House Ways and Means Committee, Kenner had considerable influence in the Confederate government. He believed in a strong nation and often conflicted with his **states rights** colleagues by advocating a protective tariff, higher **taxes,** and confiscation laws, while opposing the right of **secession** from the Confederacy. One of Kenner's most controversial positions was his belief that the Confederacy had to abolish **slavery** to gain the European aid needed for victory. In 1864, **Jefferson Davis** sent him to Great Britain on a secret mission to gain diplomatic recognition. He managed to slip into New York City and sail to Europe, but his mission failed when the British prime minister refused the offer.

Kenner returned to Louisiana after the war and rebuilt his sugar plantation. He also helped organize the Sugar Planters' Association and the Sugar Experiment Station and served as the first president of each. An opponent of **Republican Reconstruction,** Kenner later was appointed to the U.S. Tariff Commission by President Chester A. Arthur, served on the Louisiana Levee Board, and was president of the Louisiana Jockey Club.

KENNESAW MOUNTAIN, GEORGIA, BATTLE OF (JUNE 27, 1864). After weeks of maneuver and battle in the 1864 **Atlanta Campaign,** Confederate Gen. **Joseph E. Johnston** withdrew his **Army of Tennessee** from around **New Hope Church and Dallas, Georgia,** and fell back to a strong position along the **Lost Mountain-Brushy Mountain line.** After constant **skirmishing** with **William T. Sherman's** superior force, he abandoned these positions in mid-June 1864 and occupied a strong line anchored on Kennesaw Mountain. Facing west, this new line stretched from Kennesaw Mountain on the north to **Kolb's Farm** on the south. **William W. Loring's** corps held the mountain, while **William J. Hardee** was in the center, and **John B. Hood** held the left. Facing them were **James B. McPherson's Army of the Tennessee** on the Union left, **George H. Thomas's Army of the Cumberland** in the center, and **John Schofield's Army of the Ohio** on the right.

Sherman became frustrated over his inability to inflict a decisive blow against the enemy and was angry at how his men had become reluctant to attack entrenched positions. Heavy rains also prevented him from making any **turning movement,** which had been so successful previously. Believing that Johnston had stretched his line dangerously thin and to show his armies that they still sometimes had to attack fortified lines, Sherman unwisely ordered his men to make a **frontal attack** on the Confederates' Kennesaw Mountain line. Schofield was to advance against Johnston's right on June 26–27 to force him to lengthen and weaken his line, and then McPherson and Thomas would attack on the left and center on the morning of June 27.

Schofield advanced at his appointed time and captured some outlying Confederate works. Early on June 27, McPherson sent in **John A. Logan's** XV Corps against the southwestern base of Kennesaw Mountain. In desperate hand-to-hand fighting, Logan's men captured some of Loring's outer positions but then were shot to pieces when they continued on against the main Confederate line at Pigeon Hill. An hour after Logan began his attack, Thomas advanced two **divisions** from the IV and XIV Corps against Hardee's **corps**. They, too, had initial success against the enemy's outer works but were slaughtered by the well-entrenched divisions of **Patrick Cleburne** and **Benjamin Cheatham**. Union losses were particularly heavy at the "Dead Angle," a position on Cleburne's front. Successive Union assaults were all thrown back in furious fighting.

Of an estimated 16,000 Federals engaged, about 3,000 became casualties, including Brig. Gen. **Charles G. Harker**, who was mortally wounded. Losses among the nearly 18,000 Confederates are uncertain but probably were close to 1,000. Many of the casualties were victims of heat stroke as the temperature soared to around 100 degrees. Sherman did not make another direct assault, but he never admitted that the attack had been a mistake. On July 2, he sent McPherson and **George Stoneman's** cavalry sweeping around Johnston's right flank, forcing him to abandon the Kennesaw Mountain line and withdraw to Smyrna.

KENTUCKY. Kentucky was an important **border state** because it was strategically located on both the Mississippi and Ohio Rivers and was rich in agriculture and livestock. Ironically, both **Abraham Lincoln** and **Jefferson Davis** were born in Kentucky, as was the 1860 Southern **Democratic** presidential candidate, **John C. Breckinridge**.

When Lincoln called for volunteers in April 1861 to suppress the Rebellion, pro-Confederate Gov. **Beriah Magoffin** refused. Magoffin also ignored Confederate demands for Kentucky's **secession**, and the pro-Union legislature declared the state's neutrality in May. Because of Kentucky's strategic importance and large population (1,155,684 in 1860), both sides at first respected its neutrality for fear of pushing the state into the enemy's camp. A majority of the state's people and the legislature supported the Union, but there was a large pro-Confederate minority (the Confederate battle **flag** and the second and third national flags contained a star for Kentucky). During the war, approximately 100,000 Kentuckians served the Union, while 25,000–40,000 served the Confederacy. Of these men, some 30,000 died.

Kentucky's neutrality was violated in September 1861 when Confederate Maj. Gen. **Leonidas Polk** advanced from **Tennessee** without orders and occupied the important river town of Columbus. The Union countered the move by occupying Paducah. Soon, Confederate Gen. **Albert Sidney Johnston** had a long defensive line running through Kentucky from the Cumberland Gap, to Bowling Green, to **Forts Henry and Donelson, Tennessee**.

With Confederate troops now occupying much of the state, secessionists held a November convention at Russellville and passed a secession ordinance. The secessionist government then was admitted to the Confederacy in December under Gov. **George W. Johnson**. The Union victory at **Mill Springs** and the capture of Forts Henry and Donelson in early 1862, however, forced the Confederates to withdraw from Kentucky. The Union maintained firm control over the state for the rest of the war, except for Confederate cavalry raids and **Braxton Bragg's** and **Edmund Kirby Smith's** unsuccessful **Kentucky Campaign** later in 1862.

Secessionist Governor Johnson was killed at **Shiloh** and was replaced by **Richard Hawes**, who returned to Kentucky with Bragg in 1862 in an unsuccessful attempt to take control of the state. The legitimate governor, Magoffin, resigned in August 1862 and was replaced by **James F. Robinson**. Union Democrat **Thomas E. Bramlette** was elected in 1863, but he nearly broke with the Lincoln administration in 1864 over the enlistment of **black troops**. Many Kentuckians bitterly opposed the use of black soldiers, but more than 20,000 Kentucky blacks did serve the Union. Lincoln offered to compensate slave owners for the loss of slaves to the military, but the people refused to cooperate. As a result, **slavery** lingered in Kentucky until the adoption of the **13th Amendment** in late 1865.

KENTUCKY CAMPAIGN (AUGUST 14–OCTOBER 26, 1862). In the summer of 1862, the Confederacy was threatened on several fronts but seized an opportunity to launch simultaneous invasions in the west and east. At Corinth, Mississippi, Union Maj. Gen. **U. S. Grant** had 60,000 men to threaten **Vicksburg, Mississippi**, and in northern **Alabama**, Maj. Gen. **Don Carlos Buell's** 54,000-man **Army of the Ohio** was menacing Chattanooga, Tennessee. To face these threats, the Confederates had Gen. **Braxton Bragg's Army of the Mississippi** with about 45,000 men at Tupelo, Mississippi, and Maj. Gen. **Edmund Kirby Smith's** 16,000 men in the **Department of East Tennessee**.

In late July, Bragg decided to move swiftly to join Kirby Smith in Middle Tennessee. This would threaten the Union supply lines and not only force Grant and Buell to withdraw, but it might also present an opportunity to **defeat** them **in detail**. Bragg left 16,000 men at Tupelo under Maj.

Gen. **Sterling Price** to cooperate with Maj. Gen. **Earl Van Dorn** for an invasion of western Tennessee. On July 23, he started his **army** for Chattanooga and began arriving there on July 29. From Chattanooga, Bragg planned to join forces with Kirby Smith for an invasion of Middle Tennessee and **Kentucky**.

Kirby Smith foiled Bragg's plan, however, because he was the commander of a separate **department** and was not entirely under Bragg's jurisdiction. Kirby Smith had planned to move against Union-held Cumberland Gap in August, but at the urging of **John Hunt Morgan**, he decided instead to invade Kentucky, where it was believed large numbers of recruits were eager to join the **Confederate army**. When Kirby Smith left Knoxville, Tennessee, with 10,000 men on August 14 and headed for Kentucky, Bragg was unable to join him. Still hoping for a successful invasion, Bragg decided to move as well. On August 28, he advanced 30,000 men northward on a parallel course about 100 miles to the west and entered the Bluegrass State via Carthage, Tennessee, and Glasgow, Kentucky. When **Robert E. Lee** began the **Antietam Campaign** soon afterward, it appeared the Confederacy was poised to strike a decisive blow against the Union.

On August 30, Kirby Smith attacked and defeated 6,500 Federals under Maj. Gen. **William Nelson** at **Richmond, Kentucky**. Two days later, he was in Lexington. Naming his column the **Army of Kentucky**, Kirby Smith then could have joined Bragg and formed a considerable invasion force, but instead he allowed the army to spread out from Cumberland Gap to Lexington.

To destroy the **railroad** bridge across the Green River, elements of Bragg's army attacked the 4,000-man Union garrison at **Munfordville, Kentucky**, on September 14 and captured it after three days of sporadic fighting. Bragg then marched to Bardstown. Meanwhile, Buell had received reinforcements from Grant and had withdrawn into Kentucky on a nearly parallel course west of Bragg. If Bragg had used his cavalry more effectively, he would have been aware of Buell's location and perhaps could have broken up his long column. Instead, he did nothing, and Buell reached Louisville on September 29 and received 30,000 reinforcements. Another 45,000 Union troops were massed at Cincinnati, Ohio, under Brig. Gen. **George Morgan**. The tide now had turned, for not only were the Confederates badly outnumbered, but they also were scattered across the Kentucky countryside.

Bragg visited Kirby Smith at Lexington and installed Gov. **Richard Hawes's** secessionist government at Frankfort to attract support for the Confederate cause. The dream of thousands of new recruits proved to be overly optimistic, however, for those Kentuckians who supported the Confederacy had already volunteered. As a result, the invasion brought little to the Confederacy in terms of manpower.

On October 1, the Federals advanced against the Confederates in four columns. Bragg ordered **Leonidas Polk**, whom he had left in command at Bardstown, to cooperate with Kirby Smith in an attack on Buell's column that was approaching Frankfort from Louisville. Polk, however, claimed he was outnumbered and retreated, thus widening the distance between himself and Kirby Smith. Bragg then was forced to abandon Frankfort and rejoin the main army, bringing with him the newly installed Confederate government.

After the Confederates concentrated at Danville and Versailles, Buell attacked **William J. Hardee's** command at **Perryville** on October 7. When Polk again hesitated in carrying out orders to reinforce Hardee and attack, Bragg took personal command and ordered a hasty assault at Perryville on October 8. Buell at first was beaten back, but he had reinforcements close at hand and finally repulsed Bragg. The battle was a tactical stalemate, with Bragg suffering over 3,000 casualties to Buell's approximately 4,211, but a number of factors convinced Bragg it was time to withdraw. His foe now was larger and concentrated, while he had enjoyed little success in cooperating with Kirby Smith. Also, Price and Van Dorn had been defeated at **Iuka** and **Corinth, Mississippi**, and would not be able to support him by invading Tennessee. Finally, a lack of supplies and drought conditions made it difficult to feed the army, and the lack of recruitment showed that Kentucky was not ready to join the Confederacy.

Bragg withdrew from Perryville on the night of October 8, united with Kirby Smith at London, Kentucky, and retreated through Cumberland Gap to Tennessee on October 26. The invasion had been a dismal failure and together with Lee's retreat from **Maryland** ended what was perhaps the Confederacy's best chance of bringing the Union to the negotiating table. The campaign also ended Buell's career. His pursuit of the retreating Confederates was so feeble that he was removed from command of the Army of the Ohio.

KEPI. Kepi refers to a variety of **forage** caps used by both sides in the Civil War. They had rounded crowns with leather visors and somewhat resembled modern-day baseball caps.

KERNSTOWN, VIRGINIA, FIRST BATTLE OF (MARCH 23, 1862). When **George B. McClellan** began his **Peninsula Campaign** in March 1862, Maj. Gen. **Nathaniel P. Banks's** V Corps was sent into the **Shenandoah Valley** to confront **Thomas J. "Stonewall" Jackson**. Jackson soon was ordered to occupy Banks to prevent him from sending any reinforcements to McClellan's **Army of the Potomac**. Before Jackson could act, however, two of Banks's **divisions** were sent out of the Valley, leaving only **James Shields's** division near Strasburg. When Jackson learned that Shields was moving toward Winchester, he struck with his 4,500 men. Marching 42 miles in two days, he reached Kernstown on March 23. Cavalry commander **Turner Ashby** had **skirmished** with the Federals the previous day and wounded Shields but incorrectly concluded that the retreating Shields had left only a **brigade**-size force north of Kernstown. As a result of the faulty intelligence, Jackson rashly attacked what turned out to be Shields's entire 9,000-man division, under the tactical command of Col. **Nathan Kimball**.

Jackson sent Samuel Fulkerson's and **Richard Garnett's** brigades to attack the Union right flank, while the rest of his force made a **feint** against the main line. Fulkerson and Garnett reached a stone wall and were attacked repeatedly by the brigades of **Erastus B. Tyler** and Kimball. After two hours of fighting and receiving no orders from Jackson, Garnett was forced to retreat when he ran out of ammunition. This exposed Fulkerson's flank, and he, too, had to fall back. Jackson met the retreating men and, after vainly trying to rally them, was forced to withdraw.

In this rare defeat, Jackson lost 718 men to Shields's 590. He blamed Garnett for the debacle and preferred charges against him that were unsettled at the time of Jackson's death. Ironically, the tactical defeat proved to be a strategic victory. Jackson's attack unnerved the Union high command, and large numbers of men were sent into the Valley to suppress him. Kernstown was the beginning of **Jackson's Shenandoah Valley Campaign**, where he prevented 60,000 Union soldiers from reinforcing McClellan.

KERNSTOWN, VIRGINIA, SECOND BATTLE OF (JULY 24, 1864).
Following **Jubal A. Early's Washington Raid** in July 1864, the Confederates withdrew into the **Shenandoah Valley** to near Strasburg, and Union Brig. Gen. **George R. Crook's** VII Corps was stationed near Winchester to keep watch on them. Heavy cavalry **skirmishing** on July 23 forced Crook to advance to Kernstown, but at the end of the day, he left a **picket** line there and withdrew back to Winchester. Realizing that his 14,000 men outnumbered Crook's 9,500, Early advanced down the Valley Pike the next morning to engage the enemy.

Crook rushed his infantry south and took up a defensive position at Kernstown. At about noon, Early sent **John B. Gordon's division** against the main Union line, which was held by James A. Mulligan's division, with **Rutherford B. Hayes's** brigade in support. At the same time, **Stephen Ramseur's** division moved toward the Union right flank, and **John C. Breckinridge** took the **divisions** of **Gabriel Wharton** and **Robert Rodes** around the enemy left flank. Gordon's attack forced back Joseph Thoburn's division, which had been moved up on Mulligan's right. While Crook was being hard-pressed by Gordon, Ramseur moved onto the Union right flank and **enfiladed** Mulligan's line. Soon afterward, Breckinridge sent Wharton against Hayes's brigade on the Union left flank. When Wharton and Gordon attacked simultaneously, the Federal line collapsed. The Union retreat soon became a rout, and Confederate cavalry attacked Crook's wagon train. By the time Crook withdrew across the Potomac River, 72 wagons and 12 caissons had been abandoned or burned by the Federals. Early's losses in the battle are unknown but are estimated to have been around 600. Crook lost 1,185 men, of whom 479 were taken **prisoner**. The humiliating defeat led Union authorities to appoint Maj. Gen. **Philip H. Sheridan** to command the Valley area two weeks later.

KERSHAW, JOSEPH BREVARD (1822–1894) CSA. The son of a former congressman, Kershaw was a native of **South Carolina**. After receiving a local education, he read law and was admitted to the bar in 1843. Kershaw served in the **Mexican War** as a 1st lieutenant but resigned his commission because of illness. He then returned to his law practice and served two terms in the legislature. After **John Brown's Raid**, Kershaw became active in the militia, rising to the rank of colonel, and in December 1860 was a delegate to the state's **secession** convention.

Kershaw first served in the militia around **Charleston** and raised the 2nd South Carolina in early 1861. After the fall of **Fort Sumter**, he was appointed colonel in April and led the **regiment** to **Virginia**, where it fought at **First Manassas** in **Milledge L. Bonham's brigade**.

Appointed brigadier general in February 1862, Kershaw took command of Bonham's South Carolina brigade and led it at **Williamsburg** and during the **Seven Days Campaign** with the **Army of Northern Virginia**. After missing the **Second Manassas Campaign**, his brigade (part of **Lafayette McLaws's** division) played a key role in capturing **Harpers Ferry**, **Virginia**, during the **Antietam Campaign** and fought well in Antietam's West Woods. At **Fredericksburg**, Kershaw's brigade reinforced the stone wall on Marye's Heights and suffered heavy losses while beating back numerous Union assaults. During the fighting, he was the senior officer present and commanded the defenders along the wall.

When the rest of **James Longstreet's corps** was sent to **Suffolk, Virginia**, Kershaw remained with the **army** and fought at **Chancellorsville** and **Salem Church** in May 1863. At **Gettysburg**, he led McLaws's attack through the **Peach Orchard** and **Wheatfield** on the second day and lost more than half of his men. Kershaw was acting **division** commander two months later at **Chickamauga** and led Longstreet's attack that shattered the Union line. After serving in the **Knoxville Campaign**, he took command of McLaws's division in December 1863 after Longstreet removed McLaws for his failures in the campaign. On the second day at the **Wilderness**, Kershaw helped repulse the Union attack that threatened **Robert E. Lee's** right wing and then miraculously escaped injury in the incident that wounded Longstreet and killed **Micah Jenkins**. He fought well at **Spotsylvania** and was rewarded with a promotion to major general in June 1864. After fighting in the **Petersburg Campaign**, Kershaw reinforced **Jubal Early** in the **Shenandoah Valley** and fought at **Cedar Creek**. He returned to Petersburg in November and was captured at **Sailor's Creek** in April 1865 during the **Appomattox Campaign**.

Released from **Fort Warren, Massachusetts**, in August 1865, Kershaw returned to South Carolina and reentered politics. He was elected to the state senate later in the year and became a circuit judge in 1877.

KESSLER'S CROSS LANES, VIRGINIA, BATTLE OF (AUGUST 26, 1861). After their defeat at **Rich Mountain, Virginia**, in the summer of 1861, Confederate forces abandoned Charleston and retreated to the Gauley River. On August 26, Brig. Gen. **John B. Floyd** crossed the river and attacked Col. **Erastus Tyler's** 7th Ohio stationed at Kessler's Cross Lanes. Floyd drove Tyler away from the crossroads and then withdrew to Carnifex Ferry to protect the river crossing there. In the crossroads fight, Floyd lost 40 men while Tyler reported 132 casualties.

KETCHUM, WILLIAM SCOTT (1813–1871) USA. A native of **Connecticut** and the son of a **U.S. Army** officer, Ketchum graduated near the bottom of his 1834 **West Point** class. He spent most of his antebellum service, including the **Mexican War**, on the frontier and in the quartermaster department.

Ketchum was a major in the 4th U.S. Infantry when the Civil War began and was promoted to lieutenant colonel of the 10th U.S. Infantry in November 1861. He never led men into combat, and most of his war service involved inspections, recruitment, and other administrative positions as a special agent of the War Department. Ketchum was promoted to brigadier general of volunteers in February 1862 and colonel of the 11th U.S. Infantry in May 1864. By war's end, he had received **brevets** to major general of regulars.

After being mustered out of the volunteers in April 1866, Ketchum remained in the **army** and served in the adjutant general's office. He resigned his commission in 1870 and died the following year in a boarding house under mysterious circumstances. Ketchum's landlady, who owed him money, was arrested for poisoning him, but she was acquitted of murder.

KETTLE RUN, VIRGINIA, BATTLE OF (AUGUST 27, 1862). When **Stonewall Jackson** made his famous **turning movement** into the rear of **John Pope's Army of Virginia** in the 1862 **Second Manassas Campaign**, he first seized Bristoe Station on August 26. When he pressed on toward the Union supply depot at Manassas Junction, he left **Richard S. Ewell's** division behind to guard the rear against any approaching Federals. Ewell was ordered not to bring on a general engagement and to join Jackson at Manassas if hard pressed.

Early on the morning of August 27, Ewell sent Henry Forno's **brigade** of **Louisiana Tigers** and the 60th Georgia down the **railroad** to destroy the bridge at Kettle Run. **Skirmishing** erupted as Forno ran into a Union advance guard, but he destroyed the bridge and retired back toward the station. That afternoon, **Joseph Hooker's** Union **division** was sent by Pope to chase off what were thought to be Confederate raiders. Hidden in thick pine timber, Forno ambushed Hooker's column near Bristoe Station and sent it retreating toward Kettle Run. In the brief encounter, Hooker lost 408 men, while the Louisianians and Georgians suffered 132 casualties. Ewell then joined Jackson at Manassas Junction, and together they fought the Federals at **Groveton** the next day.

KEYES, ERASMUS DARWIN (1810–1895) USA. A native of **Massachusetts**, Keyes (KEEZ) moved to **Maine** with his family as a youngster. After graduating from **West Point** in 1832, he served as an instructor at the academy, was **Winfield Scott's** military secretary three times (although he missed serving in the **Mexican War**), and rose to the rank of lieutenant colonel while serving in the infantry, **artillery**, and cavalry.

At the beginning of the Civil War, Keyes was on Scott's staff, but he was promoted to colonel of the 11th U.S. Infantry in May 1861. After leading a **brigade** in **Daniel Tyler's** division at **First Manassas**, he was promoted to brigadier general of volunteers in August and in November took command of **Don Carlos Buell's** old **division**. When **Abraham Lincoln** named the first **corps** commanders for the **Army of the Potomac** in March 1862, Keyes was among them. He led the **army's** IV Corps during the **Peninsula** and **Seven Days Campaigns**, but his service was not considered outstanding. Nonetheless, Keyes was **brevetted** brigadier general of regulars for his conduct at **Seven Pines** and was appointed major general of volunteers in May.

Keyes was left behind in the **Department of Virginia** when the rest of the army was sent to northern **Virginia** for the **Second Manassas** and **Antietam Campaigns**. For the next year, he sometimes simultaneously commanded the IV Corps and the VII Corps on the Virginia Peninsula, but his command largely existed only on paper since most of his men had been transferred elsewhere. During the **Gettysburg Campaign**, Keyes was ordered to threaten **Richmond, Virginia**, to force the Confederates to divert troops from the invasion to protect the capital. He accomplished little and was criticized by his **department** commander for failing to follow orders effectively. Keyes's IV Corps was abolished in August 1863, and he held various administrative positions until he resigned from the army in May 1864.

Keyes moved to **California**, where he became successful in the financial and wine industries.

KIERNAN, JAMES LAWLOR (1837–1869) USA. A native of Ireland, Kiernan was the brilliant son of a military surgeon and attended Dublin's Trinity College. He immigrated to the United States as a young man and graduated from the New York University Academy of Medicine in 1857 at the age of 19. Kiernan opened a medical practice in New York City and with his brother-in-law published the *Medical Press*.

Although Kiernan became a general, little is known of his Civil War service. He entered the Union **army** in 1861 as an assistant surgeon with the 69th New York and accompanied the **regiment** to **First Manassas**. In March 1862, Kiernan was appointed surgeon for the 6th Missouri Cavalry (Union) and served with it at **Pea Ridge**. It is claimed that after the battle he tired of the medical practice and was appointed the regiment's major. Kiernan reportedly was badly wounded in the left lung at **Port Gibson, Mississippi**, during the **Vicksburg Campaign** and was captured after being left for dead but then managed to escape. His official record indicates he resigned his position as regimental surgeon in May 1863, but it does not mention him ever having been major. In August 1863, Kiernan was appointed brigadier general of volunteers and was made commander of the post at Milliken's Bend, Louisiana. Poor health forced him to resign his commission in February 1864.

After the war, Kiernan briefly served as a consul in China and became an examining physician for the pension bureau.

KILPATRICK-DAHLGREN RAID (FEBRUARY 28–MARCH 3, 1864). This cavalry raid was proposed to **Abraham Lincoln** by **H. Judson Kilpatrick** in February 1864 to free the Union **prisoners** being held at **Libby Prison** and **Belle Isle** in **Richmond, Virginia**. Kilpatrick, an ambitious and often reckless officer, may have been trying to regain his reputation, which was tarnished after he ordered a disastrous cavalry charge at **Gettysburg**.

With 4,000 troopers, Kilpatrick set out on the night of February 28 and approached the city from the north. At Spotsylvania on February 29, Col. **Ulric Dahlgren**, son of famous naval officer **John Dahlgren**, separated from the main column with 500 men to attack Richmond from the south. As the Federals approached the city in bitterly cold sleet and rain, the Confederates became aware of the raid, and defenses were prepared. Kilpatrick hesitated to attack the city once he reached its outskirts on March 1, and a small 300-man Confederate cavalry force under **Wade Hampton** caught up with him. Slashed from the rear, he decided to abandon the raid and rode east toward the Union lines on the Virginia Peninsula.

Meanwhile, Dahlgren's column attacked Richmond from the west because high water prevented it from reaching the city's south side. It was driven back by a small home guard under **George W. Custis Lee**. Becoming separated from his main column, Dahlgren and about 100 men were ambushed on March 2 in King and Queen County. Dahlgren was killed, and most of his men were captured. On Dahlgren's body were found the **Dahlgren Papers** detailing a plan to assassinate **Jefferson Davis** and his Cabinet and to burn the city. Union officials claimed the papers were forgeries, but they almost certainly were genuine.

Overall, the raid was a dismal failure, and Kilpatrick lost 340 men, 583 horses, and a large amount of arms and equipment. Because of the Dahlgren Papers, however, it did succeed in deepening Confederate hostility for their Northern enemies.

KILPATRICK, HUGH JUDSON (1836–1881) USA. A native of **New Jersey**, Kilpatrick dropped the name Hugh when he entered **West Point** in 1856. He graduated in 1861 and was commissioned a 2nd lieutenant of **artillery** in May but days later was appointed captain of the 5th New York. Although he was serving with volunteers at the time, Kilpatrick became the first regular **army** officer to be wounded in the war at **Big Bethel**. In September, he was appointed lieutenant colonel of the 2nd New York Cavalry and fought with the **regiment** in numerous **skirmishes** and at **Second Manassas**. Thus, began a famous cavalry career that earned Kilpatrick the nickname "Kill Cavalry," because of his reckless disregard for the well-being of both troopers and horses.

Kilpatrick was appointed colonel in December 1862 and in February 1863 was given command of a cavalry **brigade** in the **Army of the Potomac**. He participated in one of **George Stoneman's Raids** during the May 1863 **Chancellorsville Campaign** and fought at **Brandy Station** the following month. Just days later, Kilpatrick was promoted to brigadier general of volunteers. Shortly before the **Battle of Gettysburg**, he was given command of the cavalry corps' 3rd Division. On the last day of the battle, Kilpatrick rashly ordered a disastrous cavalry charge against the Confederate right that resulted in the death of Brig. Gen. **Elon John Farnsworth**. Wishing to regain his tarnished reputation probably prompted him to propose the **Kilpatrick-Dahlgren Raid** in early 1864. After it failed, Kilpatrick was transferred west.

In April 1864, Kilpatrick took command of the **Army of the Cumberland's** 3rd Cavalry Division and was badly wounded at **Resaca** the following month. After returning to duty in July, he engaged in a number of fights with the Confederate cavalry while guarding **William T. Sherman's** supply line during the **Atlanta Campaign**. Despite Kilpatrick's reckless nature, he had Sherman's support, and his was the only cavalry **division** that accompanied Sherman on his **March to the Sea** and the **Carolinas Campaign**. A notorious womanizer, Kilpatrick was said to have barely escaped capture by **Wade Hampton's** Confederates during the latter campaign at **Monroe's Cross Roads** by rushing out in his underwear from the headquarters bed he shared with a Southern girl. By war's end, he had been **brevetted** through all ranks to major general of both regulars and volunteers, and he was promoted to major general of volunteers in June 1865.

Kilpatrick resigned from the regulars in December 1865 and from the volunteers in January 1866. Afterward, he twice was appointed U.S. minister to Chile and died at his post.

KIMBALL, NATHAN (1822–1898) USA. A native of **Indiana**, Kimball became a teacher in **Missouri** after attending DePauw University for a few years. He soon abandoned that profession, however, and became a physician. Kimball served in the **Mexican War** as a captain in the 2nd Indiana and was said to have rallied his **company** at Buena Vista after the enemy routed the **regiment**. After the war, Kimball returned to his Indiana medical practice.

Kimball entered Union service in June 1861 when he was appointed colonel of the 14th Indiana. He led the regiment at **Cheat Mountain** that autumn, and when **James Shields** was wounded on March 22, 1862, he took command of the **division** the next day and defeated **Stonewall Jackson** at **First Kernstown**. Promoted to brigadier general of volunteers in April, Kimball was given command of a **brigade** in **William H. French's** division of the **Army of the Potomac's** II Corps. Kimball lost more than 600 men at **Antietam** and then was wounded himself at **Fredericksburg**. Upon returning to duty, he was transferred west and led a provisional division in the XVI Corps during the latter part of the **Vicksburg Campaign** and in the campaign against **Little Rock, Arkansas**. Kimball led a brigade during the **Atlanta Campaign** and in August 1864 was given command of a division in the **Army of the Cumberland's** IV Corps. After leading his division in the **Franklin and Nashville Campaign**, he helped repress disloyal activities by the **Knights of the Golden Circle** in southern Indiana.

Brevetted major general of volunteers for his service, Kimball left the **army** in August 1865 and returned to Indiana. There he served as the **Grand Army of the Republic's** state commander and was a two-term state treasurer and a one-term legislator. In 1873, President **U. S. Grant** appointed Kimball surveyor general of Utah. He moved there and was serving as postmaster of Ogden when he died.

KING, JOHN HASKELL (1820–1888) USA. A native of **New York**, King moved to **Michigan** with his parents as a boy. He entered the **U.S. Army** at 17 when he was appointed a 2nd lieutenant in the 1st U.S. Infantry. King served in the **Seminole Wars** and rose to the rank of captain in 1846. During the **Mexican War**, he served on the frontier and was in **Texas** when the Civil War began. There King won some notoriety when, threatened by secessionists, he safely led nine **companies** of regulars out of the state.

Appointed major of the 15th U.S. Infantry in May 1861, King served in the regulars for most of the war. He led a battalion drawn from the 15th and 16th U.S. Infantries at **Shiloh**, participated in the **siege of Corinth, Mississippi**, and was wounded while leading a battalion from the 15th Infantry at **Stones River**. Promoted to brigadier general of volunteers in April 1863, King led a **brigade** of regulars in **Absalom Baird's** XIV Corps **division** of the **Army of the Cumberland** at **Chickamauga**. After being badly shot up on the first day, his brigade assisted **George H. Thomas** on the second day in making his stand on **Snodgrass Hill**. In 1864, King fought in all of the major battles in the **Atlanta Campaign**, sometimes while in command of the IV Corps' 1st Division. In July 1864, he was given command of a brigade of regulars in the District of the Etowah and led it until war's end.

King received **brevets** of major general in both the regulars and volunteers for his war service. In July 1865, he was appointed colonel of the 9th U.S. Infantry and served at various frontier posts before retiring in 1882.

KING, RUFUS (1814–1876) USA. A member of a prominent **New York** family, King first attended Columbia College (where his father was president) and then entered **West Point**. He graduated in 1833 but resigned his commission in 1836 to become a civil engineer. For the rest of the antebellum period, King owned and edited a number of newspapers in New York and **Wisconsin**. He also served as New York's adjutant general for four years, helped frame the 1848 Wisconsin constitution, became superintendent of schools for Milwaukee, Wisconsin, and was a regent of the state university.

Abraham Lincoln appointed King minister to the Vatican in 1861, but King volunteered for military service instead. He was appointed brigadier general of volunteers in May 1861 and raised the famous **Iron Brigade**. King, however, never commanded the **brigade** during its most famous period. Instead, he was given command of a **division** in March 1862, first in the I Corps and then the III Corps of the **Army of the Potomac**. King did not perform well during the **Second Manassas Campaign**, when he withdrew without orders from Gainesville, Virginia, where he had been placed to keep **James Longstreet** from joining **Stonewall Jackson** at Manassas. That movement forced another division to withdraw from **Thoroughfare Gap** and allowed the Confederates to join forces at Manassas. King remained away from his division during the battles of **Groveton** and **Second Manassas** and was accused by some of being drunk. **Corps** commander **Irvin McDowell** convened a court of inquiry that found King guilty of disobeying orders and using bad judgment in abandoning Gainesville. In a strange move, he then was appointed to the court of inquiry investigating **Fitz John Porter's** role in the Union defeat at Second Manassas. Thus one disgraced general sat in judgment of another being accused of helping lose the very same campaign. King never held another important field command but did briefly lead a division in the **Washington, D.C.**, defenses. Suffering from epilepsy, he resigned his commission in October 1863.

Lincoln reappointed King minister to the Vatican the month he resigned, and he served there until 1868. During his tenure, he helped capture and extradite **Lincoln's assassination** conspirator **John H. Surratt**. Afterward, King became a deputy collector of customs in New York City.

KING'S SCHOOL HOUSE, VIRGINIA, BATTLE OF (JUNE 25, 1862). Also known as the Battle of Oak Grove, French's Field, Henrico, and the Orchards, this was the first clash of the **Seven Days Campaign**. **Robert E. Lee** had massed his **Army of Northern Virginia** north of the Chickahominy to strike the **Army of the Potomac's** V Corps near **Mechanicsville, Virginia**, on June 26, 1862. Major General **George B. McClellan**, however, advanced south of the river on June 25 to seize some high ground in front of his line on which to place siege guns to bombard **Richmond**.

On the morning of June 25, the Union advance began when **Joseph Hooker** took his **division** across White Oak Swamp, with **Philip Kearny's** and **Israel B. Richardson's** divisions supporting him. **Benjamin Huger's** Confederate division, supported by **Robert Ransom's brigade**, stopped Hooker's advance, and he was forced to call on Kearny for reinforcements. Renewed Union attacks finally forced the Confederates to fall back to their main lines, but there they held fast. McClellan lost 516 men in the attacks and only gained 600 yards of ground. The Confederates lost 316 men. Lee briefly was concerned that the attack signaled Union awareness of his plan, but it did not alter his campaign, and he carried out the attack against Mechanicsville the next day.

KINSTON, NORTH CAROLINA, FIRST BATTLE OF (DECEMBER 14, 1862). In December 1862, Union Brig. Gen. **John G. Foster**, commander of the **Department of North Carolina**, led approximately 10,600 men from New Bern to destroy a **railroad** bridge across the Neuse River at Goldsboro. Confederate Brig. Gen. **Nathan G. Evans** attempted to stop Foster at Kinston with his 2,000-man **brigade**.

Making a stand north of the Neuse River along a creek on December 13, Evans was outflanked by the enemy and was forced to fall back to within two miles of the railroad bridge. He then dug **rifle pits** and was attacked again by Foster on December 14. In a confused fight, Foster's men were mistakenly hit by their own **artillery** fire but successfully turned Evans's left flank. The Confederates retreated across the railroad bridge and burned it before all of the men were across. Approximately 400 Confederates were captured, while Foster lost about 160 men. Evans retreated toward Goldsboro, and the Federals looted and burned Kinston.

KINSTON, NORTH CAROLINA, SECOND BATTLE OF (MARCH 8–10, 1865). *See* WYSE FORK, NORTH CAROLINA, BATTLE OF.

KIRBY, EDMUND (1840–1863) USA. A native of **New York**, Kirby was the son of a **U.S. Army** officer, the grandson of former army Maj. Gen. Jacob Brown, and the second cousin of Confederate Gen. **Edmund Kirby Smith**.

Kirby graduated from **West Point** in 1861 and was appointed 2nd lieutenant of **artillery** in May. Within days he was promoted to 1st lieutenant and served with the 1st U.S. Artillery at **First Manassas**. Afterward, Kirby took command of the battery and led it in the **Peninsula, Seven Days**, and **Fredericksburg Campaigns** with the **Army of the Potomac**. At **Chancellorsville**, he was placed in command of the 5th Maine Battery after it lost all of its officers in the battle. While he was trying to withdraw the battery, Kirby's thigh was fractured by a bullet, but he refused to be removed from the field until the guns had been withdrawn. Surgeons amputated his leg, but infection had already set in. When **Abraham Lincoln** visited Kirby in the hospital, the dying officer's only regret was that his widowed mother would be left destitute. Moved by the officer's predicament, Lincoln appointed the young lieutenant to brigadier general of volunteers to give his mother a substantial pension. Kirby died on May 28, 1863, the day of his promotion.

KIRBY SMITH, EDMUND (1824–1893) CSA. Edmund Kirby Smith was a native of **Florida** and was a cousin of Union Brig. Gen. **Edmund Kirby**. To distinguish himself from the many other Smiths in the **U.S. Army**, he signed his name E. Kirby Smith and generally has been referred to as Kirby Smith. After graduating from **West Point** in 1845 (where he was nicknamed "Seminole"—his family called him Ned or Ted), Kirby Smith fought in the **Mexican War** and won two **brevets** for gallantry. Remaining in the **army**, he taught mathematics at the academy from 1849 to 1852 and was appointed captain of the 2nd U.S. Cavalry in 1855. Stationed in **Texas**, Kirby Smith was wounded in 1859 while fighting **Indians** and rose to the rank of major in early 1861.

When Texas seceded in early 1861, Kirby Smith evacuated his command rather than surrender his post to secessionist **Ben McCulloch**. Having fulfilled his duty, he then resigned his commission and joined the Confederacy as a lieutenant colonel. Sent to **Virginia**, Kirby Smith first commanded the Confederates holding Lynchburg, but in May, he became adjutant to Gen. **Joseph E. Johnston** at **Harpers Ferry**. After being promoted to brigadier general in June, he fought at **First Manassas** and was severely wounded by a bullet that tore through his body from the right collarbone to the left shoulder.

Kirby Smith was promoted to major general in October 1861 and assumed command of the District of East Tennessee in March 1862. That summer he and **Braxton Bragg** agreed to invade **Tennessee** and, if possible, **Kentucky**. Kirby Smith led his 10,000-man **Army of Kentucky** north in August in the opening phase of the **Kentucky Campaign**, defeated the Federals at **Richmond**, and occupied Frankfort, Kentucky. When the campaign failed, Kirby Smith became disillusioned and contemplated resigning his commission, but he remained in the army when he learned in October that he had been promoted to lieutenant general.

In January 1863, Kirby Smith was placed in command of the **Southwestern Army**, but in March these orders were expanded to include command of the entire **Trans-Mississippi Department**. For the rest of the war, he struggled to continue the war in what became an increasingly isolated part of the Confederacy. After the fall of **Vicksburg, Mississippi**, the Trans-Mississippi was virtually cut off from the main Confederacy, and Kirby Smith was forced to rely on his own wits, manpower, and supplies. From Shreveport, Louisiana, he ruled his **department** with absolute authority, and it became known as **"Kirby Smithdom."** In recognition of the tremendous responsibilities Kirby Smith held, **Jefferson Davis** appointed him full general in February 1864.

Overall, Kirby Smith did as well as anyone could have done under the circumstances. His soldiers under the command of **Richard Taylor** turned back the 1864 **Red River Campaign** by winning the **Battle of Mansfield**. Taylor, however, came to despise Kirby Smith when he sent most of Taylor's infantry to **Arkansas** to stop **Frederick Steele's Camden Expedition** after the **Battle of Pleasant Hill**. Taylor believed he could have won an even greater victory if his superior had not interfered. Kirby Smith accompanied the troops to Arkansas and assumed command there, but the enemy was already retreating. He did, however, attack Steele's retreating column at **Jenkins' Ferry**. Afterward, the feud with Taylor intensified, and Taylor wrote bitter letters to his superior. The controversy did not end until Taylor was transferred east of the Mississippi River.

In the last months of war, Kirby Smith assumed the responsibility of appointing general grade officers in his department and other tasks reserved for the president and War Department. The government approved some of these appointments, and others, it did not. As a result, there were a number of Confederate officers who performed the duties of generals and were addressed as such but who never officially held that rank. Kirby Smith's last major military action was authorizing **Sterling Price's 1864 Missouri Raid**. When **Robert E. Lee** and **Joseph E. Johnston** surrendered their armies in April 1865, Kirby Smith's command disintegrated as his soldiers **deserted** rather than fight for a losing cause. While wanting to continue the struggle, he found himself a general without an army and finally surrendered his department on June 2 at Galveston, Texas.

After a brief stay in Mexico and Cuba, Kirby Smith returned to the United States in the autumn of 1865. He served as president of an insurance company and of a **telegraph** company, but both ventures failed. Kirby Smith then served as president of the University of Nashville from 1870 to 1875 and taught mathematics at the University of the South from 1875 to 1893. He was the last full Confederate general to die.

"KIRBY SMITHDOM." After Federal forces captured the Mississippi River in the summer of 1863, the Confederate **Trans-Mississippi Department** was cut off and isolated from the rest of the Confederate nation.

Department commander Gen. **Edmund Kirby Smith**, with little guidance or help from the government, was forced to rule over a nearly autonomous area. As a result, the Trans-Mississippi Department was sometimes referred to as "Kirby Smithdom."

KIRK, EDWARD NEEDLES (1828–1863) USA. A native of **Ohio**, Kirk taught school and became a lawyer before settling in **Illinois**. He helped recruit the 34th Illinois in the summer of 1861 and entered Union service in September when he was appointed its colonel. After serving in **Kentucky**, Kirk was placed in command of a **brigade** in the **Army of the Ohio's** 2nd Division in January 1862. He led it and was wounded in heavy fighting on the second day at **Shiloh**. Kirk's brigade later was assigned to the I Corps and pursued the **Confederate army** during the **Kentucky Campaign**, but he did not see any combat.

Promoted to brigadier general of volunteers in November 1862, Kirk and his brigade were assigned to the XIV Corps. While fighting with the **Army of the Cumberland** at **Stones River** on the first day of battle, he was severely wounded. Sent home to Illinois, Kirk died from his wounds in July.

KIRKLAND, RICHARD ROWLAND (1841–1863) CSA. Kirkland was a 19-year-old sergeant in the **Army of Northern Virginia's** 2nd South Carolina at the **Battle of Fredericksburg**. After his unit helped slaughter the attacking Union soldiers in front of Marye's Heights' stone wall, he asked for and received permission to carry water to the wounded enemy soldiers who were begging for help. His comrades expected him to be shot by the Federals, but they held their fire as he climbed over the wall. For an hour and a half, Kirkland carried water to the wounded men and was cheered by an admiring enemy. After having survived all of the **army's** battles since **First Manassas**, he was killed at the **Battle of Chickamauga**. Kirkland became known as the "Angel of Marye's Heights," and a statue was erected in his honor in Camden, South Carolina.

KIRKLAND, WILLIAM WHEDBEE (1833–1915) CSA. A native of **North Carolina**, Kirkland entered **West Point** in 1852 but left after three years, apparently to accept a 2nd lieutenant's commission in the **U.S. Marine Corps**. He remained in the Marines until he resigned his commission in August 1860.

Kirkland was commissioned a captain in the **Confederate army** in March 1861, but he returned to North Carolina when it seceded, helped raise the 11th North Carolina, and was elected its colonel in July. After fighting at **First Manassas** in **Milledge Bonham's** brigade, the **regiment** was redesignated the 21st North Carolina in November. Kirkland failed to win reelection as colonel in the spring of 1862, but when the winner refused to accept the position, he was reappointed. During **Stonewall Jackson's Shenandoah Valley Campaign**, Kirkland was badly wounded at **First Winchester**. By the time he recovered from the wound, a new colonel had already been appointed for the regiment, so he was sent west to become Maj. Gen. **Patrick Cleburne's** chief of staff in the **Army of Tennessee**. Kirkland fought with Cleburne at **Stones River** and then returned to **Virginia**. In April 1863, he again was named colonel of the 21st North Carolina and led it at **Gettysburg** as part of **Robert Hoke's brigade** in the **Army of Northern Virginia**.

Kirkland was promoted to brigadier general in August 1863 and was put in command of a brigade in **Henry Heth's** division. He was wounded again at **Bristoe Station** and remained out of action for eight months. Upon returning to duty, Kirkland was given a brigade in Hoke's **division** in May 1864, but he was wounded again at **Cold Harbor** the following month. When he returned to duty, he found his old brigade had a new commander, and he had to be transferred to a new brigade. Kirkland first served in the **Richmond, Virginia**, defenses and then was sent to North Carolina in December. He fought at **Fort Fisher**, **Wilmington**, and **Bentonville**, and surrendered with **Joseph E. Johnston's army** in April 1865.

After the war, Kirkland lived in **Georgia** and **New York** before becoming a resident in a **Washington, D.C.'s**, soldiers' home.

KIRKSVILLE, MISSOURI, BATTLE OF (AUGUST 6–9, 1862). In the summer of 1862, **Missouri** was racked by guerrilla and cavalry raids as both sides fought for its control. In August, 1,000 Federals under Col. **John McNeill** pursued Confederate Col. Joseph C. Porter's 2,500-man **brigade** for a week before bringing it to bay at Kirksville, Missouri. McNeill attacked Porter on August 6 and successfully occupied the town. Porter remained in the area, but his brigade was destroyed on August 9 when McNeill was reinforced and attacked again. The victory helped secure Union control over northeast Missouri. In the fight, the Confederates lost 368 men (many of whom were taken **prisoner**), while the Federals lost 88.

KIRKWOOD, SAMUEL JORDAN (1813–1894) USA. A native of **Maryland**, Kirkwood worked as a druggist in **Washington, D.C.**, before moving to **Ohio** in 1835. There he became a lawyer and **Democrat**, served as his county's prosecutor, and was a delegate to the state's constitutional convention. Kirkwood moved to **Iowa** in 1855, became a farmer and miller, and eventually joined the **Republican Party** because of his opposition to the **Kansas-Nebraska Act**. He was elected to the state senate in 1856 and governor in 1859.

Fiercely pro-Union, Kirkwood quickly responded to **Abraham Lincoln's** call for volunteers and worked diligently to place Iowa on a war footing. Reelected in 1861, he filled the state's quota of recruits without ever having to resort to **conscription**. Kirkwood also supported Lincoln's policy of recruiting **black troops** and sometimes used black recruits to take the place of whites. By war's end, he had raised 50 **regiments** from Iowa. During the war, he also **financed** the war through bonds, provided relief for soldiers' families, and opposed **Copperhead** activities. Prevented constitutionally from running for a third time, Kirkwood supported and helped elect fellow Republican **William M. Stone** in 1863.

After the war, Kirkwood completed an unfinished U.S. Senate term in 1866–67, served as a **railroad** president, was elected to the U.S. Senate in 1877, and was President James A. Garfield's secretary of the interior.

KNAPSACK. This was the name of the Civil War backpack. Used by both sides, it usually was made of heavy canvas, sometimes of rubber, and was worn like a modern pack. The knapsack proved to be hot and heavy, and many soldiers, particularly Confederates, discarded it in favor of putting their goods inside a rolled-up blanket that was worn across the shoulder.

KNIGHTS OF THE GOLDEN CIRCLE. This pro-Confederate organization was created in the South in 1854 by **George W. L. Bickley**. Its original mission was to promote the annexation of northern Mexico for the purpose of extending **slavery**. The **secession** crisis breathed new life into the organization, and it began creating chapters, known as "castles" in the South and **border states**, and supported secession. During the Civil War, the Knights engaged in such pro-Confederate activities as intelligence gathering and sabotage. As **Copperheads** became more active in opposing the war, it was commonly believed that Knights castles also were being organized in the North. Two other secret societies, the **Order of American Knights** and the **Sons of Liberty**, are sometimes associated with the Knights, but they were separate organizations. Although the actual membership is unknown, there probably were not very many Knights; they seemed omnipresent because the Knights generally were blamed for all Northern antiwar incidents.

KNIPE, JOSEPH FARMER (1823–1901) USA. A native of **Pennsylvania**, Knipe (NIPE) worked as a shoemaker before joining the **U.S. Army**

as a private in 1842. He participated in putting down **Rhode Island's** Dorr Rebellion, a minor uprising aimed at achieving universal suffrage, and fought in the **Mexican War**. Knipe left the **army** in 1847 and worked with a **railroad** until the Civil War.

Knipe first entered Union service in 1861 as a **brigade** inspector of state militia, but he was appointed colonel of the 46th Pennsylvania in October. He led the **regiment** in **Stonewall Jackson's Shenandoah Valley Campaign** and later was wounded at **Cedar Mountain**. At **Antietam**, Knipe assumed command of his brigade in the **Army of the Potomac's** XII Corps and led it for the next eight months.

Knipe was promoted to brigadier general of volunteers in April 1863 and fought at **Chancellorsville**. Afterward, however, he gave up his brigade command because he still had not recovered fully from his wound. When the Confederates invaded Pennsylvania during the **Gettysburg Campaign**, he returned to duty and led a brigade of Pennsylvania militia. In the autumn of 1863, Knipe accompanied **Joseph Hooker** to **Tennessee** to reinforce Chattanooga. During the **Atlanta Campaign**, he led a brigade in the **Army of the Cumberland's** XX Corps and sometimes temporarily commanded the **division**. In November 1864, Knipe was transferred to the cavalry and was given command of a division in **James H. Wilson's** cavalry **corps**. He performed well pursuing the defeated Confederates after the **Battle of Nashville** and captured 6,000 **prisoners**.

Knipe remained in the cavalry and was serving in the **Department of the Gulf** at war's end. After leaving the army in August 1865, he worked at a number of minor government positions in **Washington, D.C.**; **Kansas**; and Pennsylvania.

KNOW-NOTHING PARTY. Officially called the American Party, this political party was formed in **New York** as a secret society in 1849. Its members were sworn to secrecy and were trained to respond "I know nothing" when questioned about the organization—thus giving it the nickname of "Know-Nothing Party." The organization was xenophobic, opposed the growing number of immigrants, and was anti-Catholic. Its platform called for electing only American-born politicians and a 21-year residency requirement for citizenship. The party had some local success in the northeast and unsuccessfully supported former president Millard Fillmore for president in 1856. Already weakened by internal disputes over **slavery**, the Know-Nothing party died out after the 1856 election.

KNOXVILLE, TENNESSEE, CAMPAIGN (NOVEMBER 4–DECEMBER 14, 1863). Following Gen. **Braxton Bragg's** victory at

Chickamauga, his **Army of Tennessee** laid siege to Chattanooga, Tennessee. Bragg had difficulty getting along with Lt. Gen. **James Longstreet**, who appeared to be politicking for Bragg's command. Thus, in November 1863 Bragg convinced **Jefferson Davis** to send Longstreet's **corps** to attack the Union garrison at Knoxville, Tennessee. Such a move would not only remove Longstreet from the Army of Tennessee, it would also prevent **Ambrose Burnside's** 20,500 Federals at Knoxville from reinforcing Chattanooga.

Although he disapproved of weakening the **army** during the siege of Chattanooga, Longstreet took 17,000 men, including **Joseph Wheeler's** cavalry, and left for Knoxville on November 4. The march was exhausting and supplies were scarce. Longstreet sent Wheeler's cavalry ahead of the infantry on November 13 to seize the high ground across the Holston River from Knoxville. Wheeler reached Knoxville two days later, but he eventually returned to Longstreet after he was unable to take the heavily fortified high ground. When Longstreet crossed the Little Tennessee River near Loudon on November 14, Burnside left Knoxville for Loudon to withdraw elements of the IX and XXIII Corps that were stationed there.

The next day, the Union and Confederate columns traveled on parallel routes to the northeast, with Longstreet trying to cut off the Union retreat at Lenoir. Burnside got there first on November 16 and avoided the trap. Longstreet then tried to intercept Burnside at **Campbell's Station**, an intersection where the two roads used by the armies converged. Longstreet sent **Lafayette McLaws's division** on the road parallel to the Union march, while **Micah Jenkins's** division pressed them from the rear. Burnside rushed **John F. Hartranft's** division forward and reached the station 15 minutes before McLaws. Taking up a strong defensive position, Hartranft repulsed McLaws's attacks and held the vital crossroads, allowing the entire Union column to pass by safely and reach Knoxville the next day.

Longstreet pursued and, on November 17, clashed with Union cavalry on the outskirts of Knoxville. In this fighting, Union Brig. Gen. **William P. Sanders** was killed. The Confederates then besieged the city and made plans to take Knoxville by assault. Burnside's men were heavily fortified in a number of forts and earthworks. The main work, **Fort Sanders**, was located northwest of town and was targeted for Longstreet's main assault. Several attacks were planned and canceled over the next few days as Longstreet waited for reinforcements and weighed his options. While planning the assault, the Confederates observed Union soldiers walking through a ditch that circled the fort, which appeared to be only a few feet deep. Actually, the ditch was up to eight feet deep; the Union soldiers had been using a walkway that the Confederates did not see. Thus, when Longstreet's men attacked, they did not carry any ladders. In the meantime, a thick layer of ice had formed, making the walls too slick to climb.

McLaws's division attacked Fort Sanders at dawn on November 29. The attack quickly bogged down as the troops became trapped in the deep ditch and were slaughtered by the Federals, who lit cannon shells and rolled them down on the enemy. After only 20 minutes, Longstreet recalled the men. He then received a telegram informing him of Bragg's defeat in the **Chattanooga Campaign** and ordering him to return to the army. In the disastrous attack on Fort Sanders, Longstreet lost 813 men, while Burnside suffered only 13 casualties.

Longstreet did not immediately abandon his campaign. Instead, he remained at Knoxville to prevent the Federals from reinforcing the Union armies facing Bragg. In early December, Longstreet learned that **U. S. Grant** had dispatched **William T. Sherman** with the XV and IV Corps to reinforce Burnside. He then quickly left Knoxville on the night of December 4 and marched northwest to Rogersville, pursued timidly by a Union column under Maj. Gen. **John G. Parke**. At Rogersville, Longstreet was reinforced by **Robert Ransom's** division from **Virginia**. Seeing an opportunity to strike, he attacked Parke's lead division under **James M. Shackelford** at **Bean's Station** on December 14. Defeated, Shackelford retreated and the Knoxville Campaign ended, although **skirmishing** continued for some time afterward.

Longstreet kept his men in winter quarters at Russellville until March 1864, when he was ordered to return to Virginia. Over the entire campaign, he lost 1,296 men, while the Federals lost 681.

KOCK'S PLANTATION, LOUISIANA, BATTLE OF (JULY 13, 1863). *See* BAYOU LAFOURCHE, LOUISIANA, BATTLE OF.

KOLB'S FARM, GEORGIA, BATTLE OF (JUNE 22, 1864). After abandoning the **Lost Mountain-Brushy Mountain** line during the 1864 **Atlanta Campaign**, **Joseph E. Johnston's Army of Tennessee** fell back to **Kennesaw Mountain**. Continuing his **strategy** of outflanking the Confederates, **William T. Sherman** sent **John M. Schofield's Army of the Ohio** around Johnston's left flank to threaten his line of communication.

On June 21, Johnston moved **John Bell Hood's corps** from his right flank to near Kolb's Farm on the threatened left. Encountering Hood on June 22, the Federals began entrenching but were attacked at about 5:00 P.M. **Carter L. Stevenson's division** drove back the Union advance guard but then was hit hard by Federal **artillery** and was forced to retire.

A second Confederate advance by **Thomas C. Hindman's** division was blocked by a dense swamp. The Confederates then entrenched and anchored the threatened left flank. In the fighting, it is estimated that the Confederates lost about 1,000 men, while the Federals suffered approximately 350 casualties.

KRZYZANOWSKI, WLADIMIR (1824–1887) USA. A native of Poland, Krzyzanowski (kriz-uh-NOV-ski) was forced to immigrate to **New York** in 1846 after participating in the failed European revolutions of that decade. He became a civil engineer and, when the Civil War began, used his influence within the immigrant society to raise the German-Polish 58th New York in October 1861.

Appointed colonel, Krzyzanowski (known in the **army** as "Kriz") first served in the **Washington, D.C.**, defenses and then was assigned to **John C. Frémont's** command in the **Shenandoah Valley**. After serving with Frémont at **Cross Keys**, he was given command of a **brigade** in the 3rd Division of the **Army of the Potomac's** I Corps in June 1862. Krzyzanowski led the brigade at **Second Manassas** and then returned to the Washington defenses.

Krzyzanowski was appointed brigadier general of volunteers in November 1862, but the Senate never confirmed the appointment (fellow immigrant **Carl Schurz** claimed it was because no senator could pronounce his name), and in March 1863 he reverted to colonel. He continued to lead a brigade in the XI Corps' 3rd Division and was badly defeated at **Chancellorsville** and **Gettysburg**. Krzyzanowski then accompanied **Joseph Hooker** west in the autumn of 1863 and fought in the **Chattanooga Campaign**. When the XI and XII Corps were consolidated into the XX Corps in early 1864, he was transferred to northern **Alabama** to guard the vital **railroad** supplying **William T. Sherman's armies** during the **Atlanta Campaign**. For his war service, Krzyzanowski was **brevetted** brigadier general of volunteers in March 1865 and was mustered out of the service in October.

After the war, Krzyzanowski served in a number of minor government positions.

– L –

LAFOURCHE CROSSING, LOUISIANA, BATTLE OF (JUNE 20–21, 1863). After Confederate Maj. Gen. **Richard Taylor** failed to disrupt the Federal supply line at **Milliken's Bend, Louisiana**, during the 1863 **Vicksburg Campaign**, he returned to south **Louisiana** with his command. There, while Maj. Gen. **Nathaniel P. Banks** was occupied in the **Port Hudson Campaign**, Taylor threatened **New Orleans** by sending cavalry under Col. **James P. Major** to raid the **Bayou Lafourche** (luh-FOOSH) area in late June 1863.

William H. Emory, commanding the Union garrison at **New Orleans**, dispatched Lt. Col. Albert Stickney to Brashear City with orders to stop the enemy raid. Arriving at Lafourche Crossing on the morning of June 20, Stickney delayed Major's advance until more reinforcements arrived. By the next morning, the Federals were in a strong position behind earthworks, a levee, and a **railroad** embankment. When the Confederates attacked, they were repulsed by Stickney's men and finally withdrew toward Thibodaux (TIB-uh-doe). In the fight, Major lost 219 men, while Stickney suffered 49 casualties. Despite the defeat, Taylor continued to pressure the Federals in south Louisiana that summer, with clashes following at **Fort Butler** and Bayou Lafourche.

LA GLORIETA PASS, NEW MEXICO TERRITORY, BATTLE OF (MARCH 26–28, 1862). *See* GLORIETA PASS, NEW MEXICO TERRITORY, BATTLE OF.

LAIRD RAMS. In 1862, Confederate naval agent **James D. Bulloch** contracted the British company of John Laird & Sons to build two **ironclad rams** for the Confederacy. Constructed between April 1862 and August 1863, the steam-powered rams displaced 1,423 tons each and were 224.5 feet long. The ships had two turrets housing a nine-inch **Armstrong gun** in each, two 32-pounders on deck, and an iron ram that protruded seven feet from the bow. To be named the *North Carolina* and *Mississippi*, the rams would be among the most formidable ships afloat.

To hide their true destination, Bulloch arranged for the ships to be sold to a French firm that claimed they were for the Egyptian navy. United States minister **Charles Francis Adams Sr.** realized their true identities, however, and bitterly complained to the Foreign Office and threatened to sever diplomatic ties with Great Britain if the ships were allowed to sail. Great Britain reexamined its neutrality policies and decided it would not be in its best interest to allow the rams to leave. With Great Britain threatening to seize the ships, the French firm sold the rams to the British government in May 1864, and they entered the royal navy as the *Scorpion* and *Wivern*.

LAKE CHICOT, ARKANSAS, BATTLE OF (JUNE 6, 1864). *See* DITCH BAYOU, ARKANSAS, BATTLE OF.

LAMAR, LUCIUS QUINTUS CINCINNATUS (1825–1893) CSA. A native of **Georgia**, Lamar graduated from Emory College in 1845 and became a lawyer in 1847. After marrying the daughter of Emory's president, he moved to **Mississippi** when his father-in-law was appointed president of the University of Mississippi in 1849. There, Lamar practiced law and taught mathematics at the university. After a brief return to Georgia, where he served one term in the legislature, Lamar eventually settled in Mississippi permanently. Although a Unionist, he eloquently defended **states rights** and **slavery**, was elected to the **U.S. Congress** in 1857 and 1859, and was a delegate at the 1860 **Democratic** National Convention in **Charleston, South Carolina**. At the convention, Lamar sided with the moderate Southerners who opposed **secession** but then came to embrace it after the **election** of **Abraham Lincoln**. He resigned his congressional seat in early 1861 and returned to Mississippi, where he drafted the state's secession ordinance.

Lamar entered Confederate service in June 1861 as lieutenant colonel of the 19th Mississippi, a **regiment** he helped raise. Sent to **Virginia**, he was soon stricken by an ailment that left him unconscious and partially paralyzed, and he had to return to Mississippi. Lamar was back with his regiment in time to fight at **Williamsburg**, where he took command of the regiment when the colonel was killed. He was promoted to colonel in May 1862, but another attack of paralysis once again forced him back to Mississippi. Lamar resigned his commission in November 1862 but then served as **Jefferson Davis's** special commissioner to seek Russian diplomatic recognition.

Lamar traveled to Europe in March 1863, but the Senate never approved his appointment, and the Russians showed their true sympathies when their fleet made a port call in New York City. Returning to **Richmond, Virginia**, in late 1863, he became a strong supporter of Davis and was sent by the president to Georgia to lobby for more state cooperation with the central government. In December 1864, Davis appointed Lamar judge advocate for the **Army of Northern Virginia's** III Corps, a position he kept until war's end.

After the war, Lamar resumed teaching at the University of Mississippi, but he was forced to resign his position by **Radical Republicans** during **Reconstruction**. His most important service came afterward as a popular politician who urged reconciliation between the sections. Lamar served in the House of Representatives from 1872 to 1877, the Senate from 1877 to 1885, as secretary of the interior from 1885 to 1888, and on the **U.S. Supreme Court** from 1888 to 1892.

LANDER, FREDERICK WEST (1821–1862) USA. A native of **Massachusetts**, Lander became a prominent **railroad** engineer who surveyed five transcontinental routes. When the **secession** crisis began, he was sent on a special mission to **Texas** to offer Unionist Gov. **Sam Houston** federal aid if needed. Houston declined, and Lander returned north, where he served as **George B. McClellan's** aide at **Philippi** and **Rich Mountain**.

Appointed brigadier general of volunteers in August 1861, Lander was given command of a **brigade** in **Charles P. Stone's** division in October. A day after the **division's** defeat at **Ball's Bluff**, he was seriously wounded in the leg during a **skirmish** at nearby Edwards Ferry. Upon returning to duty, Lander was given command of Stone's division in January 1862. He successfully defended Hancock, Maryland, against **Stonewall Jackson** that same month and in February personally led an attack against a small enemy outpost at Bloomery Gap in western **Virginia**. Lander requested sick leave following this engagement but did not receive it. Stricken with pneumonia, he died after 20 hours of morphine treatments. Besides being a famous engineer and apparently a competent officer, Lander also wrote numerous patriotic poems during the war and was married to Jean Margaret Davenport, a very popular British actress.

LANE, JAMES HENRY (1833–1907) CSA. A native of **Virginia**, Lane graduated second in his class from the **Virginia Military Institute** (VMI) in 1854 and then graduated from the University of Virginia in 1857. Over the next few years, he taught such subjects as mathematics, natural philosophy, and military studies at VMI, Florida State Seminary, and the North Carolina Military Institute.

At the beginning of the Civil War, Lane helped raise troops and served as a drillmaster in **North Carolina** before being elected major of the 1st North Carolina in May 1861. Sent to Virginia, he commanded the **reconnaissance** force that led to the fight at **Big Bethel** and in September was promoted to lieutenant colonel. That same month, Lane was appointed colonel of the 28th North Carolina and became part of **Lawrence O. Branch's brigade**. He led his new **regiment** with courage in the **Peninsula** and **Seven Days Campaigns**, suffering wounds at **Frayser's Farm** (where he was injured in the face) and **Malvern Hill**. At **Antietam** with the **Army of Northern Virginia**, Lane took command of the brigade when Branch was killed and covered the **army's** retreat back into Virginia.

Lane was appointed brigadier general in November 1862. Highly respected and beloved by his men, he had been referred to as the "Little Major" because of his small stature and now became known as the "Little General." At **Fredericksburg**, his brigade held that part of **A. P. Hill's** line that was temporarily broken by the enemy. The following year, Lane was in the forefront of **Stonewall Jackson's** flank attack at **Chancellorsville**, and it was his brigade that fired the unfortunate volley that mortally wounded Jackson. He was heavily engaged at **Gettysburg** on the first day, and in **Pickett's Charge** (where his horse was killed under him) he temporarily commanded the **division** after **William D. Pender** was mortally wounded, and **Isaac Trimble** was captured. During the **Overland Campaign**, Lane fought well at **Spotsylvania's** "Bloody Angle" and suffered a severe groin wound at **Cold Harbor** that kept him off duty for the rest of the year. Returning to the army during the **Petersburg Campaign**, he surrendered with the Army of Northern Virginia at **Appomattox**.

After the war, Lane taught at the Virginia Agricultural and Mechanical College, Missouri State University, and the Alabama Agricultural and Mechanical College (modern-day Auburn University). One of the Confederacy's most respected brigade commanders, he was a member of the honor guard for **Jefferson Davis's** funeral.

LANE, JAMES HENRY (1814–1866) USA. A native of **Indiana**, Lane became a lawyer and served in the **Mexican War** as colonel of the 5th Indiana. Using his military record to win votes, he quickly became a self-serving politician after the war. As a **Democrat**, Lane was elected lieutenant governor in 1849 and then to the **U.S. Congress** in 1853, but he did not run for reelection when his vote for the **Kansas-Nebraska Act** angered his constituents. Instead, he moved to **Kansas**, joined the antislavery forces when he saw they formed a majority, and became a prominent figure in **"Bleeding Kansas."** Lane personally carried the free-state constitution to **Washington, D.C.**, and unsuccessfully challenged **Stephen A. Douglas** to a duel when the Senate rejected it. Returning to Kansas, he became associated with **John Brown** and sometimes led raids against proslavery forces. This activity led him later to claim that he saved Kansas for the antislavery faction. Just as he was rebuilding a political base, Lane killed a neighbor in an 1858 duel. It took him two more years to regain enough support to be elected to the U.S. Senate as a **Republican** in 1861.

Lane gained the trust and admiration of **Abraham Lincoln** when he organized about 50 Kansas politicians into the "Frontier Guards" and quartered his quasi-military unit in the White House to guard it. In appreciation, Lincoln recognized Lane as the leader of Kansas and gave him enough political patronage to dominate state politics. Returning home, Lane organized a 1,500-man Kansas Brigade of **Jayhawkers** that plundered farms, killed innocent civilians, and freed slaves in nearby **Missouri**. The secessionists retaliated by burning Lane's house, and he was nearly murdered during **William Quantrill's** raid on **Lawrence, Kansas**, in 1863. Lane urged Lincoln to make war against **slavery**, and in January 1863 he organized the **1st Kansas Colored Volunteers**, the first **regiment** of **black troops** to see combat in the war. When it appeared that his enemies were going to defeat him for reelection to the Senate in 1864, Lane helped stopped **Sterling Price's Missouri Raid** and gained enough support to win the election.

After the war, Lane angered his constituents by supporting President **Andrew Johnson's** veto of the 1866 Civil Rights Act. Faced with dwindling support at home and accusations that he was involved in corruption, he committed suicide on July 1, 1866.

LANE, WALTER PAYE (1817–1892) CSA. A native of Ireland, Lane immigrated to **Ohio** as a child but then moved to **Kentucky** when he was a teenager. There he became acquainted with Stephen F. Austin and migrated to **Texas** in 1836. Volunteering for service in the Texas Revolution, Lane's gallantry at San Jacinto won him promotion to 2nd lieutenant. Afterward, he served both as an **Indian** fighter (being wounded in 1838) and as a privateer and rose to the rank of major while fighting in the **Mexican War**. Following the war, Lane earned and lost several fortunes while gold mining in the west and in Peru, and he finally settled in Texas as a businessman.

When the Civil War began, Lane was elected lieutenant colonel of the 3rd Texas Cavalry in June 1861. He fought at **Wilson's Creek** (where his horse was shot from under him), **Chustenahlah**, **Pea Ridge** (where he commanded a brigade), **Iuka**, and **Corinth**. In all of these battles, Lane was highly praised for his bravery, especially for leading a gallant charge at Corinth. By 1863, he had become colonel of the 1st Texas Partisan Rangers and served in **James Major's brigade** in several small battles in south **Louisiana**. During the 1864 **Red River Campaign**, Lane was wounded while leading his men at **Mansfield**. He was promoted to brigadier general in March 1865, but by then the war was virtually over.

After the war, Lane returned to his business interests in Texas, wrote his memoirs, and became active in veterans' activities.

LAUMAN, JACOB GARTNER (1813–1867) USA. A native of **Maryland**, Lauman moved with his family to **Pennsylvania** as a child. He later settled in **Iowa** and was a businessman there when the Civil War began.

Lauman entered Union service in July 1861 as colonel of the 7th Iowa and was severely wounded while serving under **U. S. Grant** at the **Battle of Belmont**. At **Fort Donelson**, he commanded a **brigade** in **Charles F. Smith's** division and was praised for penetrating the Confederate works. Rewarded with a promotion to brigadier general of volunteers in March 1862, Lauman led a brigade in **Stephen A. Hurlbut's** division at

Shiloh and lost 458 men while fighting around the "Hornets' Nest." After serving on **Tennessee** garrison duty, he was given command of a **division** in the **Army of the Tennessee's** XVI Corps in January 1863.

In May 1863, Lauman's division reinforced Grant during the **Vicksburg Campaign**. He then served in **William T. Sherman's** XV Corps until June, at which time he was transferred to **Edward O. C. Ord's** XIII Corps. Accompanying Sherman for the siege of **Jackson, Mississippi**, that summer, Lauman was accused of attacking a strong Confederate position without orders and causing one of his brigades to lose more than half of its men. When Ord instructed Lauman to reassemble the survivors, he claimed the brigadier "did not how to do it" (Faust, ed., *The Historical Times Illustrated Encyclopedia of the Civil War*, 426). Ord, supported by Grant, quickly relieved Lauman of command. He was sent back to Iowa to await new orders, but none came. Despite this inglorious end to what had been an admirable career, Lauman was **brevetted** major general of volunteers for his war service.

Lauman resigned from the **army** in August 1865 and resumed his business career in Iowa.

LAUREL HILL, VIRGINIA, BATTLE OF (JULY 7, 1861). *See* RICH MOUNTAIN, VIRGINIA, BATTLE OF.

LAW, EVANDER McIVOR (1836–1920) CSA. A native of **South Carolina**, Law graduated from the South Carolina Military Academy in 1856. Afterward, he taught at his alma mater and at Kings Mountain Military Academy before cofounding **Alabama's** Military High School.

When the Civil War began, Law organized a volunteer **company** from among his students and became its captain. When the company was mustered into Confederate service as part of the 4th Alabama in May 1861, he became lieutenant colonel. At **First Manassas**, the **regiment's** colonel was killed, and Law was badly wounded. When Law returned to duty, he was promoted to colonel in October. At **Seven Pines** and during the **Seven Days Campaign**, he commanded **William H. C. Whiting's brigade** and was praised by **Stonewall Jackson** for breaking the Union lines at **Gaines' Mill**. The brigade became part of **John B. Hood's** division of the **Army of Northern Virginia** and continued to be led by Law. At **Second Manassas** it participated in the counterattack that drove the enemy from the field, and at **Antietam** suffered heavy casualties in the famous cornfield.

Law finally was promoted to brigadier general in October 1862. He saw little combat at **Fredericksburg** and was with **James Longstreet** at **Suffolk, Virginia**, during the **Chancellorsville Campaign**. At Gettysburg, the brigade experienced heavy fighting around Little Round Top, and Law had to take command of the **division** when Hood was wounded. Following **Gettysburg**, Law and fellow brigade commander **Micah Jenkins** began feuding. Longstreet wanted to give the division to the more senior Jenkins even though Law had been with the division longer. The controversy ended when Hood returned to duty, but it flared again at **Chickamauga**, when Jenkins failed to reach the battlefield in time, and Law assumed division command while Hood led a **corps**. Despite Law's competent performance, Longstreet then gave the division to Jenkins during operations around **Chattanooga, Tennessee**, and the **Knoxville Campaign**. After Jenkins twice accused Law of failing to support him properly, Law submitted his resignation in December 1863 and requested a transfer to the cavalry. Although Longstreet preferred charges against Law and threatened to resign if he was not court-martialed, their superiors ignored the matter and left the two officers in their positions.

Returning to **Virginia** with Longstreet, Law led his brigade in the **Overland Campaign** and played a key role in the victory at **Cold Harbor**, but he was severely wounded in the battle and was transferred to the cavalry upon returning to duty. Sent to South Carolina, he took command of a brigade in **Wade Hampton's** cavalry in March 1865. Law was promoted to major general that same month and took temporary command of **Matthew C. Butler's** division at the **Battle of Bentonville**.

After the war, Law helped organize the Alabama Grange and was very active in education, becoming associated with Kings Mountain Military Academy and founding the South Florida Military Institute (later the South Florida Military and Educational Institute). He also served on educational boards, was a newspaper editor, and became active in veterans' affairs. Law was the last Confederate major general to die.

LAWLER, MICHAEL KELLY (1814–1882) USA. A native of Ireland, Lawler immigrated to the United States with his parents as a child. The family eventually settled in **Illinois**, where he married the daughter of one of the area's largest landowners and became a prosperous farmer. Lawler also was active in the militia and served in the **Mexican War** as a captain of the 3rd Illinois. After the war, he farmed and ran a store in Illinois.

Lawler entered Union service in June 1861 as colonel of the 18th Illinois. A very strict disciplinarian, he ruled over his **regiment** by physically battering and threatening his officers and men. Charges were brought against Lawler for the abuse, but his superior, **Henry Halleck**, acquitted him. Wounded while leading his regiment at **Fort Donelson**, he returned to duty after **Shiloh** and was promoted to brigadier general of volunteers in November 1862.

During the **Vicksburg Campaign**, Lawler commanded a **brigade** in the 4th Division of the **Army of the Tennessee's** XIII Corps. He fought at **Port Gibson**, **Champion Hill**, and **Big Black River Bridge**, and was praised at **Vicksburg** for leading an assault on May 22, 1863, that captured over 1,100 **prisoners**. After participating in operations against **Jackson, Mississippi**, Lawler was transferred to the **Department of the Gulf**, where he held various brigade and **division** commands until war's end.

After being **brevetted** major general of volunteers for his war service, Lawler left the **army** in January 1866 and became a horse trader in the South before returning to his Illinois farm.

LAWRENCE, KANSAS, RAID ON (AUGUST 21, 1863). The town of Lawrence, Kansas, was noted for its **abolitionism** and thus was despised by the Confederate guerrillas who operated in **Missouri** and **Kansas**. Confederate guerrilla **William C. Quantrill** led 450 raiders (including future outlaws Jesse and Frank James) against Lawrence on August 21, 1863, supposedly in retaliation for the collapse of a Union **prison** in Kansas City, Missouri, that killed several of his female relatives. In three hours of murder and mayhem, the raiders killed 150 men and boys, burned much of the town, and nearly captured Brig. Gen. **James H. Lane**. Quantrill lost only one man. The raid on Lawrence was one of the most brutal **massacres** of the war and prompted Union Brig. Gen. **Thomas Ewing Jr.** to issue his General Orders No. 11, which forced the evacuation and burning of four secessionist Missouri counties.

LAWTON, ALEXANDER ROBERT (1818–1896) CSA. A member of a prominent **South Carolina** family, Lawton graduated from **West Point** in 1839, but he served less than two years in the **artillery**. Resigning his commission in 1841 to study law at Harvard University, he graduated in 1842 and then opened a **Georgia** practice. Lawton became a **railroad** president in 1849 and served in the state assembly (1855–56) and state senate (1859–60).

Commanding the 1st Georgia Militia during the **secession** crisis, Lawton captured **Fort Pulaski, Georgia**, in January 1861, two weeks before the state actually seceded. This led to his being appointed a Confederate brigadier general in February. Lawton first held various **district** and **department** commands in Georgia but in June 1862 was given command of a **brigade** in **Stonewall Jackson's** division. He did not arrive in **Virginia** in time to participate in **Jackson's 1862 Shenandoah Valley Campaign**, but he did win some praise for his service under Jackson at **Gaines' Mill** with the **Army of Northern Virginia**. During the **Second Manassas Campaign**, Lawton was in **Richard Ewell's** division and took command when Ewell was wounded at **Groveton**. He then led the **division** at **Antietam** and was seriously wounded while fighting in the famous cornfield.

Antietam proved to be Lawton's last field command because **Jefferson Davis** appointed him quartermaster general in August 1863 to replace **Abraham C. Myers**. This placed Lawton in the middle of a political struggle between Davis and his opponents, who refused to confirm the appointment for months. Although hampered by poor health, Lawton served well in his new role and kept his position until war's end. He was one of the last officials to leave **Richmond, Virginia**, in April 1865 and accompanied the fleeing government until the War Department was disbanded in May.

After the war, Lawton reentered state politics. He served in the legislature in 1870, was vice president of the state constitutional convention in 1877, and led the state's **Democratic** delegation at the 1880 and 1884 national conventions. Lawton also was appointed U.S. minister to Austria in 1887.

LEADBETTER, DANVILLE (1811–1866) CSA. A native of **Maine**, Leadbetter graduated third in the **West Point** class of 1836 and briefly served in the **artillery** before transferring to the **engineers**. He performed engineering duty in **New York** and **Alabama**, where he repaired **Fort Morgan** and began construction of **Fort Gaines**. Resigning his captain's commission in 1857, Leadbetter was appointed Alabama's chief engineer.

When Alabama seceded in January 1861, Leadbetter was appointed lieutenant colonel of state troops and an aide to the governor. In March, however, he was commissioned a major of Confederate engineers and was sent first to Mobile, where he inspected defensive works and worked on Fort Gaines, and then to **Richmond, Virginia**, where he commanded the Corps of Engineers. In late 1861, Leadbetter was promoted to colonel and was stationed in eastern **Tennessee** to guard the **railroad** between Bristol and Chattanooga.

Promoted to brigadier general in March 1862, Leadbetter was transferred to **Chattanooga** in April, but he was unable to prevent Union forces from seizing the railroad bridge over the Tennessee River. As a result, **Edmund Kirby Smith** placed **Henry Heth** in command of the city in July, and Leadbetter was given a **brigade** under Heth. After accompanying Kirby Smith in the 1862 **Kentucky Campaign**, he was appointed **Mobile's** chief engineer in November. There, Leadbetter used his engineering skills to make the city one of the most strongly fortified in the Confederacy.

Leaving Mobile in October 1863, Leadbetter was appointed chief engineer for the **Army of Tennessee** and supervised the construction of defenses on **Missionary Ridge**. The poor placement of some of these works helped lead to the Union victory there in November, but Leadbetter's responsibility in the matter is not clear. During operations at Missionary Ridge, **Braxton Bragg** sent Leadbetter to join **James Longstreet** during the **Knoxville Campaign**. It was upon his advice that Longstreet made the predawn attack on **Fort Sanders**. Leadbetter rejoined the Army of Tennessee as its chief engineer in December and served in that capacity until poor health forced him to resign from the **army** in April 1864. He returned to Mobile and stayed there until war's end, apparently serving as an adviser to Maj. Gen. **Dabney H. Maury**.

After the war, Leadbetter lived in Mexico and Canada.

LEDLIE, JAMES HEWETT (1832–1882) USA. A native of **New York**, Ledlie attended Union College, became a **railroad** engineer, and entered Union service in May 1861 when he was appointed major of the 90-day 19th New York. The men mutinied when they were not discharged when their 90 days expired, and 23 were sent to **prison**. Ledlie was appointed lieutenant colonel of the troubled **regiment** in September and in December received permission to change the regiment's designation to the 3rd New York Light Artillery. He was appointed colonel that same month.

Sent to **North Carolina**, Ledlie was promoted to brigadier general in December 1862 and took command of an **artillery** brigade in the XVIII Corps. The Senate failed to confirm his original appointment, but Ledlie appealed to **Abraham Lincoln** and former neighbor and friend **William H. Seward** and was reappointed brigadier general in October 1863. This second appointment, unfortunately, was confirmed, and he proved to be one of the worst Union generals. Ledlie was praised by his superior for a battle at **White Hall**, but Union soldiers accused him of shooting down many of his own men. In May 1864, he was given command of a **brigade** in the IX Corps' 1st Division. Ledlie served with the **Army of the Potomac** at **Spotsylvania**, **North Anna River** (where he disobeyed orders and launched an attack that was repulsed), and **Cold Harbor**, and was given command of the **division** in June.

In the **Petersburg Campaign**, Ledlie's division suffered very heavy casualties in one attack that was made while he remained in the rear drinking. This performance was repeated in July at the **Crater**, where his division was chosen to lead the Union assault. Again, the general remained behind in his **bombproof** drinking rum with another division commander while his men were slaughtered. Sent on extended sick leave in August, Ledlie did not return to the **army** until December 1864. Acting on orders from **U. S. Grant**, who labeled Ledlie a coward, **George G. Meade** virtually read Ledlie out of the army the day after he arrived and sent him home to await orders that never came. One of Ledlie's subordinates reported that his removal from command "was a heavy loss to the enemy" (Sifakis, *Who Was Who in the Civil War*, 378). Ledlie resigned his commission in January 1865.

After the war, Ledlie resumed his career in railroading and business.

LEE, ALBERT LINDLEY (1834–1907) USA. A native of **New York**, Lee graduated from Union College in 1853 and became a lawyer. He moved to **Kansas** to open a law practice and in 1861 became a member of the state supreme court.

Lee resigned his judicial seat and entered Union service in October 1861 as major of the 7th Kansas Cavalry. After serving in Kansas and **Missouri**, he was promoted to colonel in May 1862. Transferred to the east bank of the Mississippi River, Lee took command of a cavalry **brigade** and served in **U. S. Grant's Overland Vicksburg Campaign**. In the spring of 1863, Lee was made chief of staff for **John A. McClernand's** XIII Corps in the **Army of the Tennessee** and was promoted to brigadier general of volunteers in April. He served in that capacity until May 1863, when he took command of a **division** from the wounded **Peter J. Osterhaus** and led it in the **Vicksburg Campaign**. Just two days after assuming command, Lee was wounded in the face and head while leading one of his brigades in an attack at Vicksburg. He did not resume duty until after Vicksburg had surrendered and then briefly led a XIII Corps division before assuming command of the **Department of the Gulf's** cavalry division in September 1863. Lee led the cavalry in **Nathaniel P. Banks's** failed **Red River Campaign** but did not perform exceptionally well. After **Edward R. S. Canby** took command of the **department**, he fell out of favor and was ordered to report to **Washington, D.C.**, for new orders in early 1865. The adjutant general, however, returned Lee to the Department of the Gulf, but Canby never found a new assignment for him. This led Lee to resign his commission in May 1865.

After the war, Lee became a businessman in the United States and Europe.

LEE, EDWIN GRAY (1836–1870) CSA. A native of **Virginia** and the great-grandson of Richard Henry Lee, Edwin Gray Lee was a second cousin of **Robert E. Lee**. He attended the College of William and Mary but left before graduating and finished his schooling at the Alexandria Boarding School in 1855. Lee then studied law and opened a practice in western Virginia. Joining the militia, he participated in the capture of

John Brown in 1859 and was praised by Robert E. Lee for his actions. The following year, Lee married the daughter of future Confederate Brig. Gen. **William Nelson Pendleton**.

When Virginia seceded, Lee entered state service with the rest of his militia **company** (although he had just been diagnosed with tuberculosis the previous year) and became a 2nd lieutenant and adjutant of the 2nd Virginia. The 2nd Virginia was part **Thomas J. Jackson's** soon-to-be-called **Stonewall Brigade**, and Jackson appointed Lee as his aide-de-camp with the rank of 1st lieutenant. After serving at **First Manassas**, Lee was appointed major of the 33rd Virginia. He was promoted to lieutenant colonel in April 1862 and fought with the **regiment** in **Jackson's Shenandoah Valley Campaign** and with the **Army of Northern Virginia** in the **Seven Days Campaign**, **Cedar Mountain**, and **Second Manassas**. Promoted to colonel in August, Lee led the regiment at **Antietam**, but he was captured soon afterward while visiting his sick father. He was **exchanged** in time to fight at **Fredericksburg**, but by then his delicate health was ruined, so he resigned his commission.

While recuperating at home, Lee continued to serve by leading raids against Union positions on the upper Potomac River. He accepted a command position at Drewry's Bluff in early 1864 and saw some combat there at **Second Drewry's Bluff** during the **Bermuda Hundred Campaign**. In May, Lee was ordered back to the **Shenandoah Valley** to take command of Staunton. He was promoted to brigadier general in September, but his weak constitution forced him on extended sick leave two months later.

The Senate rejected Lee's appointment to brigadier general in February 1865, but **Jefferson Davis** sent him to Canada as a special agent and successor to **Jacob Thompson** and **Clement Clay**. However, by the time he arrived in Montreal in April 1865, the war was virtually over. Lee's only real service there was to provide funds for Confederates in exile and to help **John Surratt** escape to Europe after he was implicated in **Abraham Lincoln's assassination**.

Lee remained in Canada until 1866 but then returned to Virginia. He later moved to **Texas** for his health and worked as a writer.

LEE, FITZHUGH (1835–1905) CSA. A native of **Virginia**, Lee was the grandson of Henry "Light Horse Harry" Lee and the nephew of both **Robert E. Lee** and **Samuel Cooper**. After attending private schools, he entered **West Point** but clashed with his uncle, who was superintendent. Lee was very outgoing and rather irresponsible, and found the strict rules difficult to abide by. Constantly amassing demerits, he was nearly court-martialed and dismissed from the academy by the elder Lee, but he finally graduated near the bottom of his class in 1856.

Assigned to the cavalry, Lee served as an instructor at Carlisle Barracks, Pennsylvania, before being sent to fight **Indians** in **Texas**. There he nearly died in 1859 when he was wounded through the lungs by an arrow while fighting Comanches. Lee then was sent to West Point as an instructor in late 1860 and was promoted to 1st lieutenant in early 1861. In May 1861, he resigned his commission after Virginia seceded and was appointed 1st lieutenant and aide to Brig. Gen. **Richard S. Ewell**.

After service with Ewell at **First Manassas**, Lee was appointed lieutenant colonel of the 1st Virginia Cavalry in August 1861. He was promoted to colonel in April 1862 and in June accompanied **J. E. B. Stuart** on **Stuart's Ride around George B. McClellan** during the **Peninsula Campaign**. Lee's service greatly pleased Stuart and earned him a promotion to brigadier general in July, although some officers questioned whether the young officer really deserved it.

Commanding one of Stuart's **brigades**, Lee fought in all of the **Army of Northern Virginia's** campaigns. At first Stuart criticized Lee being slow in operations during the **Second Manassas Campaign**. However, Lee then redeemed himself by making successful raids on **John Pope's** headquarters, fighting well at **South Mountain**, and covering the **army's** retreat during the **Antietam Campaign**. In March 1863, he led his brigade in a hard-fought battle at **Kelly's Ford**, and later at **Chancellorsville** opened the way for **Stonewall Jackson's** famous flank attack by discovering that the Union right flank was "in the air." After fighting at **Brandy Station**, Lee accompanied Stuart on his controversial ride around the Union army during the **Gettysburg Campaign** and fought with Stuart on Gettysburg's third day. During the campaign, he had four of his horses shot from under him.

In September 1863, Lee was promoted to major general and was given command of one of Stuart's **divisions**. During the **Overland Campaign**, he performed valuable service by delaying the Union march to **Spotsylvania** and for temporarily assuming command of the cavalry when Stuart was mortally wounded at **Yellow Tavern**. After fighting at **Trevilian Station**, Lee was sent to reinforce **Jubal Early** during **Philip Sheridan's Shenandoah Valley Campaign** in August 1864. He was shot in the thigh at **Third Winchester** and did not return to his division until January 1865. In February, Lee was given command of all of the cavalry north of the James River, but in April 1865 his reputation was tarnished when he joined **George Pickett** for a shad bake behind the lines as the Union army crushed their divisions at **Five Forks**. Robert E. Lee removed Pickett from command because of the incident, but he kept Lee.

At **Appomattox**, Lee refused to be a part of the **surrender** and slipped through the lines but finally surrendered a few days later.

After the war, Lee farmed, was active in state politics, and became a leading proponent of the **Lost Cause**. He was elected governor in 1885 and unsuccessfully ran for the U.S. Senate in 1893. Afterward, President Grover Cleveland appointed Lee consul to Cuba, a position he resigned when the Spanish-American War began. He was appointed major general of volunteers during the war (but did not see any combat) and thus earned the honor of serving as a major general in both the **Confederate** and **U.S. Armies**. In February 1901, Lee was appointed brigadier general in the U.S. Army, but he was honorably discharged a month later.

LEE, GEORGE WASHINGTON CUSTIS (1832–1913) CSA. A native of **Virginia**, Custis Lee was the eldest son of **Robert E. Lee**. He graduated first in the **West Point** class of 1854 and entered the **engineers** but resigned his 1st lieutenant's commission in May 1861 after Virginia seceded.

Lee entered Confederate service in July 1861 as a captain of engineers, but he was promoted to colonel of cavalry in August and was made **Jefferson Davis's** aide-de-camp. He remained in this position for the rest of the war, although he much preferred to have a field command. Davis often used Lee as a special agent to carry out sensitive assignments and in June 1863 promoted him to brigadier general. Lee declined an appointment to command the District of Southwest Virginia in early 1864 and in October was promoted to major general. During the war's last months, he was put in charge of organizing clerks and mechanics for the defense of **Richmond, Virginia**. Known as the Local Defense Troops, this hodgepodge command was assigned to **Richard S. Ewell** when the city was evacuated in April 1865. During the **Appomattox Campaign**, Lee was captured with Ewell and several other generals at **Sailor's Creek**, but because of his mother's illness, he was **paroled** instead of being taken to **prison**.

After the war, Lee taught mathematics at Washington College, where his father was president, and assumed that position when the elder Lee died in 1870. Lee served as the college's president until 1897.

LEE, ROBERT EDWARD (1807–1870) CSA. The Confederacy's most famous general was a native of **Virginia** and the son of Revolutionary War hero Henry "Light Horse Harry" Lee. He graduated from **West Point** in 1829 without any demerits and ranked second in his class. Joining the **engineers**, Lee compiled a legendary antebellum military record. His engineering projects included work on the Mississippi River at St. Louis, Missouri; building Fort Carroll at Baltimore, Maryland; and performing other services in **Georgia**, Virginia, and **New York**. In 1831, Lee married Mary Custis, great-granddaughter of George Washington's wife, Martha Custis, and came to call Arlington House in Alexandria, Virginia, his home.

During the **Mexican War**, Captain Lee served on **Winfield Scott's** staff and was seen as Scott's protégé. He performed **reconnaissance** missions that led to the victories at Cerro Gordo and Churubusco, was slightly wounded at Chapultepec, and won three **brevets** for gallantry. At war's end, Scott proclaimed Lee to be "the very best soldier that I ever saw in the field" (Thomas, Robert E. Lee, 140). After the war, Lee served as superintendent of West Point and was appointed lieutenant colonel of the 2nd U.S. Cavalry in 1855. While home on leave in 1859, he took command of a detachment of **U.S. Marines** and captured **John Brown** during **Brown's Harpers Ferry Raid**. In March 1861, Lee was appointed colonel of the 2nd U.S. Cavalry in **Texas**, but he quickly was recalled to **Washington, D.C.**, as the **secession** crisis deepened.

The political crisis was also a personal dilemma for Lee. Although he opposed both secession and **slavery** (believing slavery harmed whites more than blacks) and loved the Union, Lee was loyal to Virginia above all else. Scott offered him command of the Union armies, but Lee refused the day after Virginia seceded and resigned his commission on April 20, 1861. Governor **John Letcher** quickly appointed him major general in command of state troops, two days before Lee's resignation was accepted by the **U.S. Army** on April 25.

After organizing Virginia's forces, Lee was appointed a Confederate brigadier general in May 1861 and served as **Jefferson Davis's** adviser. In July, he was made commander of the **Department of Northwestern Virginia** and was appointed a full general in August, ranking third in seniority among the Confederate generals. Lee's first field command proved disappointing. Confronted by a large enemy force and supported by less than cooperative subordinates, he was defeated at **Rich Mountain**. Lee then was sent to command the **Department of South Carolina, Georgia, and Florida** in November. There he put his troops to work building fortifications and earthworks, which caused the men to refer to him as "Granny Lee" and "Spades Lee."

In the spring of 1862, Lee was recalled to **Richmond, Virginia**, to once again serve as Davis's adviser. When **Joseph E. Johnston** was wounded at **Seven Pines**, Davis appointed him commander of the **army** on June 1. Renaming it the **Army of Northern Virginia**, Lee quickly became the Confederacy's most successful general. In late June, he boldly split his forces across the Chickahominy River and counterattacked the

Union **Army of the Potomac**. In the bloody **Seven Days Campaign**, Lee continually hammered away at the enemy and forced **George B. McClellan** to retreat from Richmond. He saved the capital, but the campaign demonstrated Lee's willingness to take huge gambles and his preference for the offense, which would cost him many thousands of casualties over the next three years.

After his Seven Days victory, Lee turned northward to confront **John Pope's Army of Virginia**. Dividing the army into two wings (later becoming **corps**) under **James Longstreet** and **Stonewall Jackson**, Lee once again split his command in the face of a superior enemy and sent Jackson on a swift march into Pope's rear. Jackson destroyed Pope's supply base at Manassas Junction and then fought a defensive battle at **Second Manassas** until Lee could join him with Longstreet's men. Launching a crushing counterattack, Lee again defeated the enemy and sent Pope's army streaming back to Washington.

Now having the initiative, Lee invaded **Maryland** in the **Antietam Campaign** to liberate the state, gain supplies, take the military pressure off Virginia, and hopefully win foreign recognition. After crossing the Potomac River, he again divided his army into separate columns and sent most of the men with Jackson to capture **Harpers Ferry**, **Virginia**, while Longstreet gathered supplies. When McClellan discovered Lee's **Lost Order**, the Union army began concentrating against his scattered force. In one of his most controversial decisions, Lee decided to fight at Antietam Creek on September 17, 1862, rather than withdraw to Virginia. With his back to the Potomac, Lee placed the army in a desperate situation. Even after Jackson's men arrived from the capture of Harpers Ferry, he was badly outnumbered and could hope for little more than a stalemate. Lee skillfully maneuvered his small force and fought an impressive defensive battle but gained nothing for the thousands of men he lost and had to retreat two days later. Antietam showed Lee's great **tactical** skill, but it also highlighted one of his weaknesses. No matter what the odds, he always preferred to fight, believing the war could be won sooner by achieving one great victory rather than dragging it out in a long defensive struggle. Pride in his army also made Lee reluctant to leave the field to the enemy without a fight. As a result, Lee sometimes fought when he should have retreated and conserved his strength.

Following Antietam, Lee won another major victory at **Fredericksburg**, where his army held an impregnable position on Marye's Heights and slaughtered **Ambrose Burnside's** attacking troops. In the spring of 1863, he won what was considered his greatest victory, even though much of the army was on detached duty in southeast Virginia under

Longstreet. When he learned that **Joseph Hooker** was crossing upstream from Fredericksburg and threatening his rear, Lee split his army in two. Leaving a small force behind at Fredericksburg to watch the enemy across the Rappahannock River, Lee took Jackson's corps and confronted Hooker at **Chancellorsville**. Dividing his force a second time, he held the line against Hooker with a small detachment while Jackson made a daring march against the Union right flank. Jackson smashed the Union flank but that night was mortally wounded by his own men. Furious fighting continued the next day as Lee fruitlessly sent his **divisions** against the entrenched Federals. When he learned that the enemy at Fredericksburg had crossed the river and was threatening his rear, Lee divided the army a third time. Leaving part of it to continue pressuring Hooker, he took the rest to stop the enemy at **Salem Church**. The entire Union army soon abandoned the campaign and retreated across the river. Chancellorsville was a stunning victory for Lee, but it came at a very high cost and did not alter the war's strategic situation. While winning the battles, Lee was losing the war by having his army slowly bled to exhaustion.

After Chancellorsville, Lee reorganized the army and added a third corps under **A. P. Hill** (**Richard S. Ewell** assumed command of Jackson's corps). With two-thirds of his corps commanders new to their duties, Lee launched his second Northern invasion in June 1863 when he began the **Gettysburg Campaign**. He hoped to take the war out of Virginia to allow farmers to gather their crops, to gain needed supplies in the North, and to strengthen the Northern peace movement. Lee was hampered in the campaign by the absence of his cavalry chief, **J. E. B. Stuart**, who became trapped behind enemy lines while on a raid. Without his "eyes," Lee blundered into the Union army at Gettysburg.

Gettysburg was Lee's most controversial battle and showed how his loose command style sometimes was harmful. Lee believed his duty was to bring the army into contact with the enemy and to develop a general tactical plan. He then allowed his corps commanders great discretion in carrying out the plan and was reluctant to interfere with them while they do so. Previously, with Longstreet and Jackson, this style generally worked well. But at Gettysburg, two of his corps commanders were new, and Longstreet was less than enthusiastic for the fight. As a result, Lee was defeated, in part because his tactical plans were poorly carried out and in part because the Federals fought a skillful defensive battle that won them the victory. Still, if Lee had maintained closer control over the army and seen to it that orders were followed properly, the result perhaps would have been different. By 1863, there also was evidence of heart disease, and poor health may have contributed to his failing to keep firm control over the army at Gettysburg. For the remainder of the war, Lee frequently was ill and began losing some of his enormous stamina.

Lee was forced to send Longstreet's corps to the west after Gettysburg and was too weak to inflict any great damage on the enemy. The **Bristoe Station** and **Mine Run Campaigns** of late 1863 were ones of maneuver rather than of great battles.

In the spring of 1864, Lee faced **U. S. Grant** in the bloody **Overland Campaign**. Too weak for offensive action, he was forced to remain on the defensive, while occasionally launching tactical counterattacks. Lee's outnumbered army fought with great skill and continually blocked the enemy at the **Wilderness**, **Spotsylvania**, **North Anna River**, and **Cold Harbor**. Losses were heavy as both armies began adopting trench warfare, but the Confederates continued to maintain high morale and a firm belief that Lee would eventually triumph. This dedication was seen on two occasions at the Wilderness and Spotsylvania when his men refused to attack until Lee removed himself from danger on the front lines. Despite his defensive success, Lee finally was forced to weaken his army by sending **Jubal Early's** II Corps to defend the **Shenandoah Valley**. In June 1864, the Federals withdrew from Cold Harbor and marched far to the south to attack Petersburg. For crucial days, Lee was uncertain of Grant's intentions and only barely moved his army to Petersburg in time to save the city.

By July, Lee was forced to defend a long line of trenches protecting Richmond and Petersburg. Earlier in the year, he had prophesied that if the war ever came to a siege, it would only be a matter of time before the Confederacy lost. For nine months Lee held out against the superior Union army in the **Petersburg Campaign**, but his defensive line was continually stretched as Grant shifted farther and farther around Lee's right flank. Food and supplies ran short, and the Confederates suffered great hardships. Many of Lee's men finally decided the war was lost and **desertions** increased, but his most dedicated soldiers suffered through the siege. By the spring of 1865, Lee believed his only hope was to break out of the siege and join **Joseph E. Johnston's** army in **North Carolina**. When his breakout attempt failed at **Fort Stedman**, Grant counterattacked at **Five Forks** and then broke through the Petersburg lines on April 2. Lee evacuated the cities, and a running battle ensued in the **Appomattox Campaign** as Lee sought safety to the west. Finally, however, he was cut off at Appomattox Court House and was forced to surrender on April 9, 1865.

Lee had become an icon for the Confederacy because of his character and many victories. His bravery, humility, and concern for his men won him the undying loyalty and love of both his soldiers and country. As the war progressed, the fate of the Confederacy came to be tied to the fate of Lee's Army of Northern Virginia. As long as Lee held out and won battles, Confederate morale largely remained high. But when Lee was forced to surrender at Appomattox, Confederate resistance virtually collapsed.

Following the **surrender**, Lee returned to Richmond and cooperated with federal authorities. The U.S. government had seized his home at Arlington, and converted its grounds into a federal cemetery. Financially ruined, Lee finally was appointed president of Washington College at Lexington, Virginia, and for the next five years he served as a very able and popular administrator. After suffering an apparent stroke, he died in Lexington on October 12, 1870.

LEE, SAMUEL PHILLIPS (1812–1897) USA. A native of **Virginia**, Lee was a distant relative of **Robert E. Lee**. He joined the **U.S. Navy** at an early age and spent his youth at sea. A rather rough individual, Lee was suspended from duty on a cruise, fought two duels before the Civil War, and once killed a fellow passenger on a Mississippi steamboat. After commanding the USS *Washington* during the **Mexican War**, he was promoted to commander. Lee was on his way to join the East India Squadron with the *Vandalia* when he learned of **Fort Sumter's** surrender and without orders returned to the United States from South Africa and joined the naval **blockade** against the Confederacy.

Lee took command of the *Oneida* in early 1862 and helped blockade the Atlantic coast. In July 1862, he was promoted to captain and was given the rank of acting rear admiral and command of the **North Atlantic Blockading Squadron**. Lee became quite wealthy during his blockade duty, amassing prizes of over $100,000. However, the **army** complained of his lack of cooperation, and in October 1864, he was transferred west to take command of the Mississippi Squadron.

After the war, Lee remained in the navy and became a rear admiral in 1870.

LEE, STEPHEN DILL (1833–1908) CSA. A native of **South Carolina**, Lee was distantly related to **Robert E. Lee's** family. After graduating from **West Point** in 1854, he served in the **artillery** during the **Seminole Wars** and on the frontier. Lee resigned his 1st lieutenant's commission in February 1861 and became a captain of South Carolina artillery.

During the **Fort Sumter** crisis, Lee served on **P. G. T. Beauregard's** staff and then went to **Virginia** with the **Hampton Legion** artillery. After being promoted to major in November 1861, he fought at **Seven Pines** and was **John B. Magruder's** chief of artillery during the **Seven**

Days Campaign. Lee was appointed lieutenant colonel in June 1862 and quickly was promoted to colonel the following month. After briefly commanding the 4th Virginia Cavalry, he led an artillery battalion in **James Longstreet's corps** of the **Army of Northern Virginia** at **Second Manassas**. There, Lee was praised for mauling columns of attacking Union soldiers.

After service at **Antietam**, Lee was promoted to brigadier general in November 1862 and was transferred west. He played a key role in the Confederate victory at **Chickasaw Bayou** near **Vicksburg, Mississippi**, and briefly led an infantry **brigade** in early 1863 before becoming **John C. Pemberton's** chief of artillery in May during the early part of the **Vicksburg Campaign**. During the siege, Lee commanded a brigade in **Carter Stevenson's division** and was among those captured when Vicksburg surrendered. He quickly was **exchanged** and in August was promoted to major general.

Lee next led the Confederate cavalry in **Mississippi** and eastern **Louisiana** that opposed **William T. Sherman's Meridian Campaign** and was given command of the **Department of Alabama, Mississippi, and East Louisiana** in May 1864. After fighting at **Tupelo**, he joined the **Army of Tennessee** for the **Atlanta Campaign** and led **John Bell Hood's** former corps. Lee stayed with the **army** for the 1864 **Franklin and Nashville Campaign** and was wounded while covering the retreat from Nashville. In March 1865, he was appointed lieutenant general and became the youngest lieutenant general in the **Confederate army**. He served the last few months of war with **Joseph E. Johnston** in the **Carolinas Campaign**.

After the war, Lee worked in insurance, served in the Mississippi senate, was president of the Mississippi Agricultural and Mechanical College, helped preserve the Vicksburg battlefield, and helped found and served as president of the **United Confederate Veterans**.

LEE, WILLIAM HENRY FITZHUGH "ROONEY" (1837–1891) CSA. A native of **Virginia**, Lee was the second son of **Robert E. Lee**. Known as "Rooney," he attended Harvard University but dropped out before graduating. Lee tried to gain entrance to **West Point**, but he failed because earlier a horse had bitten off the tips of his fingers. Instead, he received a direct commission as 2nd lieutenant in the 6th U.S. Infantry in 1857. Lee served in the **Utah Expedition** and in **California** before resigning his commission in 1859 to become a planter.

Lee entered Confederate service in May 1861 as a captain of cavalry but promotion to major came shortly afterward. Joining **William Loring's** staff, he served in western Virginia in late 1861 as Loring's chief of cavalry. In January 1862, Lee was promoted to lieutenant colonel of the 9th Virginia Cavalry and helped organize cavalry units along the Rappahannock River. In April 1862, he was appointed colonel of the **regiment** and led it during **J. E. B. Stuart's Ride** around the Union **Army of the Potomac** during the **Peninsula Campaign**. As part of the **Army of Northern Virginia**, Lee served with Stuart during the **Seven Days** and **Antietam Campaigns** and in the **Chambersburg, Pennsylvania, Raid**.

After numerous recommendations, Lee was promoted to brigadier general in November 1862 and took command of a new **brigade** under Stuart. A very large man (well over six feet tall), he proved to be a brave and energetic cavalry officer. Lee fought **George Stoneman's** raiders during the **Chancellorsville Campaign** and at **Brandy Station**, where he received a serious thigh wound. While recuperating at his home, he was captured and imprisoned until **exchanged** in March 1864. During his incarceration, Lee's wife died of tuberculosis.

Promoted again in April 1864, Lee became the Confederacy's youngest major general. He led a cavalry **division** during the **Overland Campaign**, and in the **Weldon Railroad** operations, he commanded all of the **army's** cavalry. In January 1865, Lee was given command of all of the cavalry on the south side of the James River and began reporting directly to his father. His men fought well at the **Five Forks** disaster and covered Lee's retreat during the **Appomattox Campaign**. Rooney Lee then surrendered with his father at Appomattox.

After the war, Lee remarried and resumed the life of a planter. He also served one term in the state senate, was president of the Virginia Agricultural Society, and was elected to the **U.S. Congress** in 1887. Lee was serving his third congressional term when he died.

LEECH & RIGDON. This company was one of the Southern firms that produced firearms during the Civil War. Located in Memphis, **Tennessee**, it was founded in 1861 and was owned by Thomas Leech and Charles H. Rigdon. Operating under the name of Memphis Novelty Works, the company first began producing edged weapons. After Memphis was evacuated, Leech and Rigdon relocated their firm to the Confederate armory in Columbus, **Mississippi**, and became known simply as the Novelty Works. They later relocated again to Greensboro, **Georgia**, in the autumn of 1862 and finally went out of business in December 1863. Leech & Rigdon was the Confederacy's second largest producer of revolvers, providing 1,500 pistols (copies of **Colt's** Model 1851) for the **Confederate army**. Some of these pistols were completed by Rigdon after the firm's dissolution, but they still carried the name of Leech & Rigdon.

LEE'S FAREWELL TO THE ARMY OF NORTHERN VIRGINIA.

On April 10, 1865, the day after he surrendered the **Army of Northern Virginia** at **Appomattox**, **Robert E. Lee** issued a farewell to his men. The address became one of the most famous Civil War writings because of its eloquence. The next day, Lee quietly left the **army** for **Richmond, Virginia**, without any fanfare. The text of Lee's farewell is as follows:

> After four years of arduous service marked by unsurpassed courage and fortitude, the Army of Northern Virginia has been compelled to yield to overwhelming numbers and resources.
>
> I need not tell the brave survivors of so many hard fought battles, who have remained steadfast to the last, that I have consented to this result from no distrust of them. But feeling that valor and devotion could accomplish nothing that could compensate for the loss that must have attended the continuance of the contest, I determined to avoid the useless sacrifice of those whose past services have endeared them to their countrymen.
>
> By the terms of the agreement officers and men can return to their homes and remain until **exchanged**. You will take with you the satisfaction that proceeds from the consciousness of duty faithfully performed, and I earnestly pray that a Merciful God will extend to you His blessing and protection.
>
> With our inceasing admiration of your constancy and devotion to your country, and a grateful remembrance of your kind and generous consideration for myself, I bid you all an affectionate farewell. (Thomas, *Robert E. Lee*, p. 367).

LEE'S LOST ORDER. *See* LOST ORDER.

LEESBURG, VIRGINIA, BATTLE OF (OCTOBER 21, 1861). *See* BALL'S BLUFF, VIRGINIA, BATTLE OF.

LEGAL TENDER ACT OF 1862.

One of the largest problems facing the Union during the early months of war was **financing**. In 1861, paper money had to be backed by gold in the U.S. Treasury. As the war dragged on, however, the federal gold reserve quickly became depleted as war costs increased, and people began hoarding specie out of fear of economic collapse. By late 1861, the gold reserve was virtually exhausted, and the Union's money supply was severely restricted. In December, most major banks suspended paying specie for the redemption of bank notes.

New York Congressman Elbridge G. Spaulding proposed in January 1862 to make paper money, without any specie backing, legal tender in the United States (except for paying tariffs or interest on the national debt). The legality of such a move was questionable, but Attorney General **Edward Bates** ruled that it was constitutional. Intense congressional debate followed, but the government's $350 million debt convinced the **U.S. Congress** to pass the Legal Tender Act, and **Abraham Lincoln** signed it in February 1862. The bill provided for $150 million of Treasury notes, known as **greenbacks**, to be issued. It greatly improved the Union's ability to finance the war, and later acts in July 1862 and March 1863 increased the amount of greenbacks to $300 million. Unfortunate byproducts of the act were inflation, speculation, and fluctuations in greenback value as the Union **armies'** battlefield success ebbed and flowed. In 1871, the **U.S. Supreme Court** ruled that the Legal Tender Acts were constitutional.

LEGGETT, MORTIMER DORMER (1821–1896) USA. A native of **New York**, Leggett moved with his family to **Ohio** at age 15. After helping on the family farm, he attended a teachers' academy, Western Reserve College, and Willoughby Medical School before studying the law and passing the bar exam in 1844. Leggett became very active in Ohio education and helped found the state's primary school system. He also served as school superintendent for three towns, practiced law with future Union Maj. Gen. **Jacob D. Cox**, and taught law at Ohio Law College.

Leggett entered Union service in early 1861 as a civilian aid to his friend **George B. McClellan**. After serving under McClellan in western **Virginia**, he raised a **regiment** of volunteers and was appointed colonel of the 78th Ohio in January 1862. Leggett led the regiment at **Fort Donelson** and **Shiloh** (but was not heavily engaged) and participated in the **siege of Corinth, Mississippi**. In December 1862, he was given command of a **brigade** in **John A. Logan's** division of the **Army of the Tennessee's** XVII Corps.

Leggett was promoted to brigadier general of volunteers in April 1863 and led his brigade in the **Vicksburg Campaign**, but during the siege, he was given command of a different brigade in the same **division**. In November 1863, he assumed command of the division and during the **Atlanta Campaign** was praised for capturing Bald Hill, an important position just outside Atlanta from which Union **artillery** could shell the city. At the next day's **Battle of Atlanta**, Leggett stubbornly defended the hill against numerous Confederate attacks, and it became referred to as **Leggett's Hill**. **Brevetted** major general of volunteers for his role in the campaign, Leggett temporarily commanded the **corps** after Atlanta fell. He accompanied **William T. Sherman** on the **March to the Sea** and the **Carolinas Campaign** and was promoted to major general of volunteers in August 1865.

Leggett resigned his commission in September 1865 and returned to his Ohio law practice. From 1871 to 1874, he served as a commissioner of patents and in 1884 organized a successful electric company that became part of the General Electric Company.

LEGGETT'S HILL, GEORGIA, BATTLE OF (JULY 21, 1864). By July 20, 1864, **William T. Sherman** was on the outskirts of Atlanta, Georgia, during the **Atlanta Campaign**. **James McPherson's Army of the Tennessee** faced the city from the east, with **Francis P. Blair's** XVII Corps holding the left of his line. One of the main Confederate defensive positions in front of Blair was Bald Hill, held by **Patrick Cleburne's division** and from which the Confederates rained down accurate fire on the Federals. McPherson ordered Blair to take the hill, but Blair gave the assignment to Brig. Gen. **Mortimer D. Leggett's** division.

With **Manning F. Force's brigade** in the lead and **Walter Q. Gresham's** division supporting on the right, Leggett advanced at sunrise on July 21 behind a heavy **artillery** barrage. Leggett's men took the hill but lost about 350 men, with Gresham's division suffering similar casualties. The Federals heavily fortified what now was referred to as Leggett's Hill and brought up cannons with which to shell Atlanta. The next day, the Confederates heavily attacked Leggett's Hill during the **Battle of Atlanta**, but Leggett stubbornly defended it.

LEGION. A legion was a military unit that contained infantry, **artillery**, and cavalry units. Some of the more famous Civil War legions were **Cobb's Legion** and the **Hampton Legion**.

LeMAT REVOLVER. This was a unique pistol used by some Confederates. Developed in 1856 by Dr. Jean LeMat of **New Orleans, Louisiana**, it had two barrels. The top barrel fired .44-caliber bullets from eight chambers, while the lower barrel fired a single .60-caliber shotgun round. Flipping a stud on the hammer determined which barrel fired. The pistol was built in France, and some were presented as gifts to such Confederate generals as **J. E. B. Stuart** and **P. G. T. Beauregard** (who was said to have been a partner with LeMat). Although they became famous side arms, the pistols actually were not very well made—some entire lots were condemned—and they were rarely used in combat.

LETCHER, JOHN (1813–1884) CSA. A native of **Virginia**, Letcher first attended Randolph-Macon College and then graduated from Washington College in 1833. He became a **Shenandoah Valley** lawyer and newspaper editor and strongly supported **states rights**. In state politics, Letcher championed government reform and sought a balance of power between the old tidewater aristocracy and his poorer western area. As a delegate to the 1850–51 constitutional convention, he helped win universal suffrage for white men. Because of his growing popularity, Letcher was elected to the **U.S. Congress** as a **Democrat** in 1850 and served four terms. There he supported **slavery**, but not the more radical Southern politicians.

In 1859 Letcher was elected governor. As a moderate, he supported **Stephen A. Douglas** for president in 1860 and helped organize the **Washington Peace Conference** when the **secession** crisis deepened. Although Letcher did not favor immediate secession, he did support legislation to strengthen the state militia. It was only after the firing on **Fort Sumter** and **Abraham Lincoln's** call for troops to suppress the rebellion that Letcher finally supported secession.

Virginia was the South's most important state, and Letcher played an important role in mobilizing its resources for the Confederacy. He was the first governor to turn over state troops to Confederate authority and appointed such key officers as **Robert E. Lee** and **Stonewall Jackson** to their first positions. Unlike many governors, Letcher fully cooperated with **Jefferson Davis** and the Confederate government in the war effort. Even when he disagreed with Davis on such issues as **impressment** and **conscription**, Letcher still cooperated in order to win the war, because he believed that such unconstitutional matters could be challenged after independence had been won. Such cooperation cost him political support, however, as many state politicians and citizens believed he was surrendering too much autonomy to the national government of the Confederacy.

Letcher was defeated for a seat in the **Confederate Congress** in 1864 and had to retire to his home when his term expired that year. Letcher was financially ruined by the war, his home was destroyed during **David Hunter's Shenandoah Valley Campaign**, and he was imprisoned for six weeks by Union authorities at war's end. Upon his release, he resumed his law practice and served one term in the state legislature.

LEVENTHORPE, COLLETT (1815–1889) CSA. A native of Great Britain who came from a very distinguished family, Leventhorpe received his education at Winchester College and was commissioned an ensign in the 14th Regiment of Foot when he was 17. Rising to the rank of captain, he served in Ireland, the West Indies, and Canada before selling his commission in 1842 and immigrating to the United States. Settling in **North Carolina**, Leventhorpe married a local girl and prospered as a businessman.

Leventhorpe entered Confederate service in November 1861 when he was elected colonel of the 34th North Carolina. The six-foot, six-inch-tall officer put his skills to good use and soon had the **regiment** well trained (during the war, Leventhorpe's regiments were so well trained that they were sometimes barred from entering drill competitions). Leventhorpe's superiors took note of his ability and placed him in command of a North Carolina **brigade**, which served in the Cape Fear region for several months and opposed Union gunboats on the Roanoke River. In April 1862, Leventhorpe took leave of his brigade when he was elected colonel of the 11th North Carolina. Sent to **Wilmington, North Carolina**, he again was given command of a brigade and commanded the Wilmington area until August. In September 1862, Leventhorpe's **regiment** was sent to southeastern **Virginia** to defend the Blackwater River, where twice in December he repulsed Union columns advancing from Suffolk. That same month he was sent to Goldsboro, North Carolina, to oppose the advance of **John G. Foster** from New Bern. After Foster captured **Kinston**, Leventhorpe attacked one of his brigades at **White Hall** and roughly handled it.

After fighting at the siege of **Washington** in the spring of 1863, Leventhorpe's regiment was assigned to **James J. Pettigrew's** brigade of the **Army of Northern Virginia**. On the first day of **Gettysburg**, the regiment drove back the Union **Iron Brigade**, but it suffered heavy casualties, including Leventhorpe being wounded. When the Confederates retreated, the colonel was left behind and was captured and a Union surgeon was forced to cauterize his wound using nitric acid without an anesthetic.

Exchanged in March 1864, Leventhorpe resigned his commission because of his wound and was appointed brigadier general of North Carolina state troops. He then took command of the forces guarding the Wilmington & Weldon Railroad at Kinston, North Carolina. **Robert E. Lee** characterized Leventhorpe as the best officer in the **department** and recommended his promotion to brigadier general of Confederate troops. In February 1865, Leventhorpe was so appointed, but for unknown reasons refused to accept the commission. He continued to guard **railroads** in North Carolina until war's end.

After the war, Leventhorpe involved himself in several businesses and lived in **New York** and North Carolina.

LEWIS, JOSEPH HORACE (1824–1904) CSA. A native of **Kentucky**, Lewis graduated from Centre College in 1843 and became a lawyer and **Whig** politician. He served three terms in the state legislature, unsuccessfully ran twice for the **U.S. Congress**, and was active in the state militia.

During the **secession** crisis, Lewis led many of his fellow militiamen across the state line to Camp Boone, Tennessee, to join the **Confederate army**. He entered Confederate service in November 1861 when he was appointed colonel of the 6th Kentucky (Confederate), one of the **regi-**

ments that formed the famous **"Orphan Brigade."** Lewis was commended for his actions while leading the regiment at **Shiloh's** "Hornets' Nest" and went on to fight at **Baton Rouge**, **Stones River**, and in the **Tullahoma Campaign**. With the **Army of Tennessee** on the second day of **Chickamauga**, Lewis assumed command of the **brigade** after **Ben Hardin Helm** was killed.

Lewis was promoted to brigadier general in October 1863 and led the Orphan Brigade for the rest of the war. After fighting at **Missionary Ridge** (where he lost most of his **artillery**), he fought throughout the **Atlanta Campaign** and lost so many men at **Jonesboro** that the brigade was no longer effective as an infantry unit. The War Department converted the Orphan Brigade into a mounted unit, but a lack of equipment led to it being split between mounted and infantry commands. Lewis commanded the mounted portion of the brigade, while the infantry remained in **Georgia**. As part of **Joseph Wheeler's** cavalry, his brigade served in **Pierce M. B. Young's** division during the **Carolinas Campaign** and served as escort for the fleeing Confederate government in May 1865 before surrendering in Georgia.

After the war, Lewis returned to his Kentucky law practice. He was elected to the legislature in 1868 and to Congress in 1870. After serving three terms in Congress, Lewis was appointed to the state court of appeals and later was made chief justice.

LEWIS, WILLIAM GASTON (1835–1901) CSA. A native of **North Carolina**, Lewis graduated from the University of North Carolina in 1854. He then taught school and worked as a surveyor in **Minnesota** and as a **railroad** engineer in North Carolina.

Lewis entered Confederate service in April 1861 as a 3rd lieutenant in the 1st North Carolina. After fighting at **Big Bethel**, he was elected major of the 33rd North Carolina in January 1862. Lewis won acclaim for his actions at the **Battle of New Bern**, but in April he left the **regiment** when he was appointed lieutenant colonel of the 43rd North Carolina. As part of **Junius Daniel's brigade**, Lewis remained in North Carolina until the brigade was sent to **Virginia** in May 1863. After fighting at **Second Winchester** with the **Army of Northern Virginia**, he assumed command of the regiment when Col. Thomas S. Kenan was wounded on **Gettysburg's** Culp's Hill. After participating in the **Bristoe Station** and **Mine Run Campaigns**, Lewis's regiment was sent back to North Carolina in the spring of 1864, where it joined **Robert Hoke's** command for an attack against **Plymouth** in April. There, Lewis took charge of Hoke's old brigade and earned a promotion to colonel when the commander was killed. Sent back to Virginia, Lewis's brigade became part of **Robert**

Ransom's division and fought well at the **Second Battle of Drewry's Bluff** in May.

Lewis was promoted to brigadier general in June and was assigned to **Stephen D. Ramseur's division**. In June 1864, he accompanied **Jubal A. Early's Washington Raid**, but during Early's retreat back into Virginia, Lewis's brigade was defeated by the enemy at the **Second Battle of Stephenson's Depot**. It appears Lewis took a leave of absence after this incident and was replaced in brigade command. He returned to duty in November and led the brigade through the latter months of the **Petersburg Campaign**. Only two days before the **surrender** at **Appomattox**, Lewis was wounded and captured at Farmville, Virginia.

After the war, Lewis returned to North Carolina, where he worked as a civil engineer and for many years was the state engineer.

LEWIS'S FARM, VIRGINIA, BATTLE OF (MARCH 29, 1865). *See* QUAKER ROAD, VIRGINIA, BATTLE OF.

LEXINGTON, MISSOURI, BATTLE OF (OCTOBER 19, 1864). After their defeat at **Pilot Knob** in **Sterling Price's 1864 Missouri Raid**, the Confederates moved westward across **Missouri** and captured a Union garrison at **Glasgow** on October 15. Despite this small victory, Price found himself being trapped by Union forces that were gathering in his front and rear.

On the border of Missouri and **Kansas**, Maj. Gen. **Samuel R. Curtis** assembled a large command and sent Maj. Gen. **James G. Blunt** with 2,000 men toward Lexington, Missouri, to delay the Confederates. On October 19, Price's vanguard under Brig. Gen. **Joseph Shelby** pushed Blunt back through town, but the Federals successfully withdrew toward the Little Blue River. The number of casualties suffered in this small engagement is unknown. Although beaten, Blunt did slow the Confederate advance and gain intelligence as to its strength. Two days later, the opposing forces collided again at the **Little Blue River**.

LEXINGTON, MISSOURI, SIEGE OF (SEPTEMBER 13–20, 1861). After the Confederate victory at **Wilson's Creek**, Confederate Maj. Gen. **Sterling Price** led his 7,000 men against the 3,500-man Union garrison at Lexington, Missouri. Price's cavalry drove in the **skirmishers** of Union Col. James A. Mulligan on September 13, 1861, and then awaited the arrival of the main Confederate force. Mulligan, who entrenched on the north side of town near the Missouri River, had in his possession the state's great seal and $900,000 that had been seized from the local bank. He was under orders to hold Lexington "at all hazards" (Faust, ed., *Historical Times Illustrated Encyclopedia of the Civil War*, 435).

Price attacked on September 18 after first pounding Mulligan's position with an **artillery** barrage. Attacks and counterattacks continued throughout the day, with neither side gaining much advantage. The next day, Price renewed his artillery barrage and dispatched 3,000 men under **Mosby M. Parsons** to intercept a 1,000-man relief column coming to Mulligan's aid from Mexico, Missouri. The Confederates forced this column, under **Samuel D. Sturgis**, to retreat, thus dooming Mulligan. Price renewed his attack on September 20 using portable hemp bales for protection and finally forced Mulligan to surrender his garrison. Of the 3,500 Union soldiers, 159 were killed or wounded and the rest were taken **prisoner**. Price lost approximately 100 men.

LEXINGTON, TENNESSEE, BATTLE OF (DECEMBER 18, 1862). In December 1862, Confederate cavalryman **Nathan Bedford Forrest** raided western **Tennessee** to disrupt **U. S. Grant's** supply lines during the **Overland Vicksburg Campaign**. To stop Forrest, Col. Robert G. Ingersoll assembled approximately 700 men and a battery of **artillery** at Lexington, Tennessee. When Forrest approached on December 17, Ingersoll took up a defensive position blocking the two roads that approached the town from the east, but for unknown reasons, the commander of Ingersoll's force protecting the road on his right flank failed to destroy the bridge across Beech Creek. On December 18, Forrest probed Ingersoll's left and then charged across the bridge on the Union right. Three charges were repulsed, but the Confederates finally overran the Union position. Ingersoll and 149 of his men were captured, but Forrest's losses are unknown.

LEXINGTON, **USS.** This wooden steam side-wheeler was built in Pittsburgh, Pennsylvania, in 1860 as a commercial vessel. Bought by the U.S. government in May 1861, it was converted into a gunboat and saw hard service on the western waters. The *Lexington* was 177 feet long, displaced 448 tons, and originally carried two 32-pounders and four 8-inch **Dahlgren guns**. It fought at **Belmont**, **Forts Henry and Donelson**, **Island No. 10**, **Shiloh**, **Arkansas Post**, **Milliken's Bend**, and in the **Red River Campaign**. After war's end, the *Lexington* was sold at auction in August 1865.

LIBBY PRISON. This famous Confederate prison in **Richmond, Virginia**, was originally a warehouse belonging to the firm of Libby and Son Ship Chandlers & Grocers. The Confederate government acquired the property in March 1862 and converted it into a **prison**. Located on the James River, the prison was a three-story brick building (with a basement) about 300 feet long and 100 feet wide. Commanded by Thomas P. Turner, it originally housed a few political **prisoners** but soon was used exclusively for prisoners of war. Libby came to house Union officers and is estimated to have held about 125,000 prisoners during the war. At its peak in May 1863, approximately 3,000 prisoners were housed in its cramped confines. Lying on the floor in rows at night, the men were packed so tightly that they could only roll over as a mass upon command of a squad leader. The cold, damp atmosphere, rats, and poor ventilation were common complaints, but deaths were few because the officers were allowed to buy additional food and supplies.

On February 9, 1864, 109 inmates tunneled out of Libby in one of the largest mass escapes of the war. Forty-eight were recaptured. The escape led to tighter security, and guards began shooting at inmates who even showed themselves at the barred windows. After the March 1864 **Kilpatrick-Dahlgren Raid**, which was designed to free the prisoners, Confederate authorities buried several hundred pounds of powder beneath the prison as a deterrent to future raids.

After the war, Libby was briefly used to house Confederate inmates, including former commandant Thomas P. Turner. Made famous by Union veterans' writings, the prison was dismantled in 1888–89 and was reconstructed in Chicago, Illinois, as a tourist attraction, but it was later demolished.

LIBERTY, MISSOURI, BATTLE OF (SEPTEMBER 17, 1861). By September 1861, **Missouri** was split between pro-Union and secessionist forces. On September 15, secessionist leader D. R. Atchison led a force from Lexington toward Liberty to join the Missouri State Guard located there. At the same time, Lt. Col. John Scott led the 3rd Iowa and some other Unionists from Cameron toward Liberty. At mid-morning of September 17, the two forces clashed as Scott approached Blue Mills Landing. **Skirmishing** increased throughout the day, but Scott finally was forced to withdraw. In the clash, Scott lost 56 men, while Atchison suffered 70 casualties.

LIDDELL, ST. JOHN RICHARDSON (1815–1870) CSA. A native of **Mississippi**, Liddell (lid-DEL) was admitted to **West Point** in 1832 but resigned under uncertain circumstances one year later. Some claim poor grades were behind the resignation, while others say he wounded a fellow cadet in a duel. Liddell then became a planter on **Louisiana** land his wealthy father bought for him. There, Liddell became involved in a deadly feud with a neighbor. The feud's origin is uncertain, but may have involved a female friend of Liddell's who shot and wounded the man. Liddell killed two of the man's friends, but he was acquitted in an 1854 murder trial.

By the time of the Civil War, Liddell was a close acquaintance of such Southern personalities as **Jefferson Davis**, **Braxton Bragg**, and **William J. Hardee**. While on his way to **Richmond**, **Virginia**, to try to receive a commission, he was offered a place on Hardee's staff as a volunteer aide. Liddell went on to **Virginia** and was present at **First Manassas**, but he then returned to Hardee and joined his staff with the rank of colonel. While serving with Hardee in **Kentucky**, Liddell was sometimes used by **Albert Sidney Johnston** to carry confidential messages to Richmond. Liddell remained on Hardee's staff until May 1862, when he was given command of a small two-regiment **brigade** at Corinth, Mississippi.

Liddell was promoted to brigadier general in June 1862 and was given a brigade of infantry. He fought at **Perryville** and earned the praise of both **Leonidas Polk** and Hardee for pouring a deadly fire on the enemy. As part of **Patrick Cleburne's division**, he fought well with the **Army of Tennessee** at **Stones River**, where he broke two Union lines and was credited by Cleburne for protecting his left flank. Liddell once again showed great skill during the **Tullahoma Campaign**, when his and another brigade held Liberty Gap for several days against two Union divisions. At **Chickamauga**, he commanded a small division and captured nearly 1,000 **prisoners** before being forced back by a flank attack. Liddell was heavily engaged on both days of the battle and lost almost half of his men. Two months later, when the Army of Tennessee was forced off **Missionary Ridge** in the **Chattanooga Campaign**, he was on leave but quickly returned to his men in time to assist Cleburne in forming the rear guard.

After Missionary Ridge, Liddell became discontented with the internal politics of the army and requested a transfer to Louisiana. He was sent there in December 1863 and in January 1864 assumed command of the subdistrict of North Louisiana. For several months, Liddell's small command chased **Jayhawkers** and draft evaders, but in April he cooperated with **Richard Taylor** in the **Red River Campaign**. Liddell **skirmished** frequently with Union gunboats, but he clashed with Taylor over **tactics** and requested a transfer after the campaign ended. He was sent to command the eastern defenses of Mobile Bay, Alabama, in September and remained there until war's end. While there, Liddell repulsed a Union raid against the Montgomery & Mobile Railroad in November and in the spring of 1865 defended **Spanish Fort**. He was captured in April when **Fort Blakely** fell to the Union in the **Mobile Campaign**.

After the war, Liddell returned to his Louisiana plantation. On February 14, 1870, he was shot seven times and killed aboard a steamboat by the man with whom he had had the antebellum feud and his two sons. The man and one of the sons were later killed by a mob.

LIGHT DIVISION. This famous Confederate **division** in the **Army of Northern Virginia** was created in the spring of 1862 outside **Richmond, Virginia**. The origin of the division's name is unclear. Some thought it was called the Light Division because it marched very rapidly, while others believed it referred to the fact that the men traveled light, with very little personal gear. It originally contained the **brigades** of **Charles W. Field, Maxcy Gregg, Joseph R. Anderson, James J. Archer, Lawrence O. Branch**, and **William D. Pender** and was commanded by Maj. Gen. **A. P. Hill**. The division saw very hard fighting during the **Seven Days Campaign** and, as part of **Stonewall Jackson's** II Corps, became one of the **army's** most dependable units. Perhaps its most famous moment came at **Antietam** when it rapidly marched from **Harpers Ferry, Virginia**, and arrived on the battlefield just in time to blunt a Union attack that was threatening the army's right flank.

Hill rose to prominence as the **division's** commander and in May 1863 was selected to command the new III Corps. Pender then commanded the division until he was mortally wounded on the second day at **Gettysburg**. **Isaac G. Trimble** assumed command, but he was wounded and captured on the third day. **Cadmus M. Wilcox** was appointed permanent commander of the division in August 1863 and led it through the **Overland** and **Petersburg Campaigns**.

LIGHTBURN, JOSEPH ANDREW JACKSON (1824–1901) USA. A native of **Pennsylvania**, Lightburn moved with his family to western **Virginia** as a boy and in 1842 unsuccessfully competed with nearby resident **Stonewall Jackson** for an appointment to **West Point**. He joined the **U.S. Army** as a private in 1846 and rose to the rank of sergeant while serving mainly on recruiting duty for the next five years.

Lightburn was a strong Unionist and in 1861 was elected a delegate to the Wheeling convention that led to the creation of **West Virginia**. He entered Union service in August when he was appointed colonel of the 4th West Virginia. In March 1862, Lightburn was given command of a **brigade** in the **Mountain Department** and saw some minor combat. He then took command of the District of the Kanawha in August but in December was transferred west.

Lightburn was given command of a brigade in the XV Corps' 2nd Division and was promoted to brigadier general in March 1863. After fighting with the **Army of the Tennessee** in the **Vicksburg Campaign**, he at times temporarily led the **division** but was back with his brigade for the **Battle of Missionary Ridge**. Lightburn's brigade saw service throughout the **Atlanta Campaign**, suffering heavy casualties at **Kennesaw Mountain** and winning praise at the **Battle of Atlanta** for recapturing some cannons. During the latter part of the campaign, Lightburn sometimes commanded the division. While besieging Atlanta in August, he was wounded in the head and remained off duty until January 1865. At that time, Lightburn was given command of a division that operated in West Virginia and in the **Shenandoah Valley**.

Lightburn resigned his commission in June 1865 and became a Baptist minister.

LILLEY, ROBERT DOAK (1836–1886) CSA. A native of **Virginia**, Lilley graduated from Washington College and sold surveying instruments invented by his father. He happened to be in **Charleston, South Carolina**, in April 1861 and witnessed the bombardment of **Fort Sumter**. Lilley then returned to Virginia, became captain of a volunteer **company** he raised, and joined the 25th Virginia.

The regiment served in western Virginia and fought at **Rich Mountain** before being assigned to **Jubal Early's brigade** in early 1862 and participating in **Stonewall Jackson's Shenandoah Valley Campaign**. After service in the **Seven Days Campaign** with the **Army of Northern Virginia**, Lilley was commended by Early at **Cedar Mountain** for taking up the **flag** and rallying the **regiment** after it had been broken by an enemy attack. He was commended again at **Second Manassas** for his skillful command of the **skirmishers**. After service at **Antietam** and **Fredericksburg**, Lilley was promoted to major in January 1863 and was stationed in western Virginia before returning to the Army of Northern Virginia and fighting at **Gettysburg** in **John M. Jones's** brigade. Promoted to lieutenant colonel in August 1863, he served in the **Mine Run** and **Overland Campaigns** and was appointed brigadier general in late May 1864.

Given command of the wounded **John Pegram's** brigade, Lilley participated in **Jubal Early's Washington Raid**. During the retreat, his brigade was routed at **Rutherford's Farm** with the rest of **Stephen D. Ramseur's division**. While attempting to rally his men there, Lilley was wounded three times and was captured. Surgeons were forced to amputate his arm, but then they left him behind when the Union forces retreated, and he was rescued. After recovering from his wounds, Lilley was put in command of the **Valley District's** reserve forces in November 1864 and kept that position until war's end.

After the war, Lilley became the financial agent of Washington College and became very active in the Presbyterian Church.

LINCOLN, ABRAHAM (1809–1865) USA. A native of **Kentucky**, Lincoln grew up in a modest frontier family and received little formal education. When he was seven, the family moved to **Indiana**, where Lincoln's father remarried after his first wife died, and Lincoln's stepmother encouraged him to read. Except for briefly attending a rural school, Lincoln was self-educated.

Lincoln moved to **Illinois** when he was 21 and worked at various jobs. Standing six feet, four inches tall, he was an impressive figure and was said to have been one of the strongest men in the neighborhood. During the Black Hawk War, Lincoln became captain of the local militia **company** by reportedly winning a wrestling match with his competitor. After managing a store and working as a postmaster, he began studying law and entered **Whig** politics. Lincoln was defeated in an 1832 legislative race, but he won in 1834 and established a prosperous Springfield law practice with William Herndon while serving four terms in the legislature. In 1842, he married **Mary Todd Lincoln**, a member of a prominent Kentucky slave-owning family. Although Mary proved to be difficult at times, and her emotional instability often weighed heavily on Lincoln, they were deeply committed to one another.

In 1846, Lincoln was elected to the **U.S. Congress**. In his one term in the House of Representatives, he opposed both the **Mexican War** and the spread of **slavery** into the territories. Partly because of his opposition to the war, Lincoln was defeated for reelection and returned to his law practice. He joined the newly formed **Republican Party** in 1856 and challenged **Stephen A. Douglas** for his U.S. Senate seat in 1858. The **Lincoln-Douglas Debates** became one of the most famous political dialogues in American history, and Lincoln made an impressive showing through his eloquence and good use of frontier wit and humor. Although Douglas won the election, Lincoln gained national attention as a leader of the antislavery movement. His national reputation was enhanced in February 1860 when he made a speech at Cooper Union calling for the federal government to use its power to stop the spread of slavery into the western territories.

When the Republican National Convention was held in Chicago, Illinois, in July 1860, Lincoln was a contender for the nomination. Holding the convention in his home state gave him an advantage, and the leading candidates made ill-advised statements that portrayed them as too radical. As a result, Lincoln won the nomination on the third ballot. In the campaign, he supported a high tariff and **homesteads** and promised not to interfere with slavery in the South. Lincoln's opposition to the spread of slavery caused Southerners to label him incorrectly an **abolitionist**. Fearful that he secretly intended to destroy slavery, Southerners threatened to secede if the Republicans won. By carrying the populous Northern states in the **election of 1860**, Lincoln won handily in electoral college votes, although he only carried about 40 percent of the popular votes.

By the time Lincoln was inaugurated on March 4, 1861, the **Confederate States of America** had been formed by the seceding states, and the Confederates were seizing all federal property in their territory. **Fort Sumter, South Carolina**, refused to surrender to the Confederates and quickly became the flashpoint for hostilities. Although he was advised by many politicians to let the Confederates go in peace, Lincoln decided his constitutional duty required him to hold the fort, and he sent an expedition to resupply it. The Confederates bombarded Fort Sumter on April 12, and civil war began.

Congress was out of session during the Fort Sumter crisis, leaving Lincoln to act decisively. He declared the seceding states were in rebellion, called for 75,000 volunteers to put it down, and ordered a **blockade** of Southern ports. Lincoln also ordered the **suspension of the writ of habeas corpus** in those areas threatened by the secessionists. The North was galvanized by his actions, but several other Southern and **border states** seceded and joined the Confederacy. Not until July 4 did Lincoln call Congress into special session to consider action against the **rebels**.

Lincoln proved to be an excellent war president. An exceptional politician, he successfully worked with various political and military factions, and he sometimes kept the Union war effort going almost single-handedly through his astonishing tenacity. One of Lincoln's great strengths was his ability to learn from mistakes. He was not afraid to experiment to win the war, and he appointed and relieved generals until he finally found one who could give him victory. By war's end, Lincoln had become one of the Union's most able strategists.

When the war began, Lincoln's goal was to save the Union, not to abolish slavery, although he personally believed it was a great evil. He skillfully courted the slave-owning border states but clashed with **Radical Republicans** until he was convinced that emancipation was a weapon that could help win the war. Lincoln's **Emancipation Proclamation** was designed to destroy the slave labor system that helped support the Confederacy by encouraging slaves to run away to the Union lines. The proclamation also led to the recruitment of thousands of **black troops** into the Union **army** and kept the border states loyal because it only affected those areas in armed rebellion against the government.

Lincoln's personality also helped achieve victory. Such eloquent speeches as Lincoln's inaugural addresses and the **Gettysburg Address** gave meaning to the war and kept up morale. Soldiers appreciated his unwavering commitment to the cause, and their votes largely won him reelection in 1864. Lincoln's homespun humor irritated many politicians, but it also made him popular with the people. Privately, however, he faced much personal grief and probably suffered from depression. His

12-year-old son, Willie, died in 1862, and Lincoln had constant problems with Mary. Four of her stepbrothers and two brothers-in-law fought for the Confederates. When one of the latter, Confederate Brig. Gen. **Benjamin H. Helm**, was killed, Mary invited her widowed sister to live in the White House. Because of Mary's Southern birth, many politicians accused her of being a spy, and Lincoln appeared before the **Committee on the Conduct of the War** to deny the allegations. Mary's emotional outbursts and her compulsive spending also put a strain on the marriage, but Lincoln always remained loyal to her.

When Lincoln ran for reelection in 1864, the war was stalemated, and people were demoralized over the huge number of casualties. To gather bipartisan support, he ran on the newly created **Union Party** ticket, which included both Republicans and **War Democrats**. Lincoln at first did not think he would win against **Democrat George B. McClellan**, but the successful **Atlanta Campaign** and the capture of **Mobile Bay, Alabama**, gave the Northern people new hope. With the support of most soldiers (who either voted in camp or were given leave to vote), Lincoln carried all but three states and won a huge electoral college victory.

Lincoln began **Reconstruction** with the **Ten Percent Plan** midway through the war and appeared to be taking a lenient position toward the Southern people. Unfortunately, he did not live to see the process completed. Lincoln was mortally wounded by **John Wilkes Booth** on April 14, 1865, while attending a play at **Ford's Theater** in **Washington, D.C.** He died the next day, less than a week after **Robert E. Lee** surrendered at **Appomattox**.

Lincoln stands next to George Washington as America's greatest president. A self-made man, he showed remarkable political and military talent and was much better suited as a war president than his opponent, **Jefferson Davis**. **Lincoln's assassination** on Good Friday after victory was won also made him a martyr and ensured his place among the nation's greatest figures.

LINCOLN-DOUGLAS DEBATES. When powerful **Democratic** Sen. **Stephen A. Douglas** of **Illinois** ran for reelection in 1858, he was challenged by the popular former legislator and **Republican Abraham Lincoln**. Douglas's popularity had been hurt by his **Kansas-Nebraska Act**, and Lincoln saw an opportunity to defeat him. The two candidates agreed that the campaign would center around seven debates held in various Illinois towns. These so-called debates actually were dialogues, since the candidates did not field questions from the audience or reporters but took turns speaking and rebutting one another. Lincoln used the Kansas-Nebraska Act to portray Douglas as part of the proslavery conspiracy that was trying to spread **slavery** into new territories. He argued that the nation could not live half free and half slave and that the Republican Party was trying to contain slavery so that it would die a natural death. Douglas played on the racial prejudice of his constituents and accused Lincoln of favoring social and political rights for blacks. He pointed out that the nation had endured half free and half slave for decades and could continue to do so.

The most famous debate took place at Freeport, where Lincoln asked Douglas if the people of a territory could exclude slavery if they wished. If Douglas answered yes, he would be in violation of the **Dred Scott decision** and would anger the Southern voters whose support he would need to win the presidency in 1860. If he answered no, he would anger most Illinois voters and probably lose the election. Douglas's response became known as the Freeport Doctrine, and it won back much support. While admitting that territories could not outlaw slavery, he argued that high **taxes** or peace bonds could be used to make it too expensive to bring slaves into a territory.

Most observers believed Lincoln won the debates with his insightful arguments and frequent use of humor, but he lost the election because of Douglas's skillful use of the race issue. Lincoln, however, gained much needed national exposure and respect, which helped him in his 1860 presidential bid.

LINCOLN, MARY TODD (1818–1882) USA. A member of a prominent **Kentucky** slave-owning family, Mary Todd was well educated in local academies and became a much-desired Southern belle. She moved in with a sister living in Springfield, Illinois, in 1839 and met **Abraham Lincoln** when he was a young lawyer. The two became engaged, but Lincoln stood Mary up at the altar. Despite her family's misgivings, she accepted Lincoln's explanation that he simply was too nervous at the time, and the couple finally married in 1842. Their 23-year marriage was often turbulent, but undoubtedly there was much love and respect between them. Much of the bad publicity that later was given to Mary actually came from Lincoln's law partner, William Herndon, who detested her and made her look as shrewish as possible in his writings.

Mary's White House years proved to be unhappy ones. She was plagued with migraine headaches, was often paranoid, and spent thousands of dollars on compulsive shopping trips to New York City. Her feelings also were hurt when local socialites looked down on her frontier upbringing and criticized her habits. Mary became very suspicious and often publicly ranted at people who somehow earned her wrath. When her 12-year-old son, Willie, died in 1862, she went into deep depression and sometimes held séances to contact his spirit (she lost another son, Edward Baker, before the war). Adding to her depression was the fact that four of her stepbrothers and two brothers-in-law fought for the Confederacy. When one sister's husband, Confederate Brig. Gen. **Benjamin Helm,** was killed, Mary invited the widowed sister to stay with her at the White House. Such behavior led to rumors that Mary was a Confederate spy, and Lincoln once appeared before the **Committee on the Conduct of the War** to deny the accusations. Although Lincoln never wavered in his loyalty, his overwhelming duties prevented him from giving Mary the support she needed during these trying times.

After **Lincoln's assassination**, Mary was so distraught she could not attend the funeral. At a time when there were no presidential pensions, she lived in constant fear of poverty and pressured the **U.S. Congress** to provide her a pension. Congress obliged Mary in 1870 with a yearly pension of $3,000, but it did little to calm her fears. When her youngest son, Tad, died in 1871, it was more than she could stand. Mary began acting increasingly irrational until her surviving son, Robert, finally committed her to an insane asylum in 1875. She was outraged and took legal action that led to her release a few months later. Mary and Robert never fully reconciled, and she remained a lonely woman, although her fears of poverty were eased when Congress gave her a one-time payment of $15,000 and increased her yearly pension to $5,000.

LINCOLN'S ASSASSINATION (APRIL 14, 1865). The Lincoln assassination conspiracy started as a plan to kidnap **Abraham Lincoln** and hold him hostage for the release of Confederate **prisoners** of war. Actor **John Wilkes Booth**, a pro-Confederate **Maryland** native, hatched the plot in 1864 and gained the assistance of **David Herold**, **George Atzerodt**, **Samuel Arnold**, **Michael O'Laughlin**, **Lewis Powell**, and **John H. Surratt**. Booth intended to capture Lincoln at the Soldiers Home, a retreat outside **Washington, D.C.**, where the president stayed to escape the capital's stifling summer heat and humidity. This plan, however, was foiled by Lincoln's ever-present armed escort.

After **Robert E. Lee's** surrender at **Appomattox** on April 9, 1865, Booth changed his plan from kidnapping to murder. Booth's new plan called for Powell and Atzerodt to assassinate Secretary of State **William H. Seward** and Vice President **Andrew Johnson**, respectively, and for Booth to kill Lincoln. The night of April 14 was chosen because it had been announced that Lincoln would be attending **Ford's Theater** to watch the play *Our American Cousin*. Since Booth was an actor, he was familiar with the theater and would arouse no suspicion being there.

That night, Atzerodt became frightened and failed to attack Johnson. Powell entered Seward's house under the pretense of delivering medicine to the secretary, who was suffering from a carriage accident and confined to bed. Powell wounded Seward with a knife and then slashed several others in the household while making his escape.

At Ford's Theater earlier in the day, Booth broke the door lock to Lincoln's box seat and drilled a hole in the door so he could see his victims. Waiting for a humorous line that always produced loud laughter, he slipped into the box at about 10:30 P.M. and shot Lincoln once behind the left ear with a .44-caliber derringer. Booth then seriously cut Maj. Henry Rathbone, who accompanied the Lincolns with his fiancée, Clara Harris, and broke his leg when he jumped to the stage. After yelling, "*sic semper tyrannis*" ("thus ever to tyrants"), he escaped to a horse tied in the alley. A doctor in the crowd restored Lincoln's breathing with artificial resuscitation, and the unconscious president was taken across the street to a boarding house. There he died the next morning at 7:22 A.M. without ever regaining consciousness.

Booth and Herold escaped into **Virginia** after Dr. **Samuel Mudd** set Booth's broken leg in Maryland. On April 26, Union cavalry cornered them in a tobacco barn on Richard Garnett's farm. Herold surrendered, but Booth refused to come out. The barn was set ablaze, a shot was fired, and Booth was carried out mortally wounded. Sergeant Boston Corbett claimed to have fired the shot from his carbine and was celebrated as the man who killed Booth, but an autopsy showed that Booth was killed by a pistol shot. He probably committed suicide.

Federal authorities quickly arrested anyone who had been associated with Booth, including **Mary Surratt**, the mother of John Surratt and owner of the boarding house in which the conspirators met. Tried by a military court, Powell, Herold, Atzerodt, and Mrs. Surratt were convicted and hanged for their role in the assassination. Mrs. Surrat was the first woman executed by the U.S. government, and a controversy erupted over whether or not President **Andrew Johnson** ever saw a recommendation to spare her life. Arnold, O'Laughlin, and Mudd were sentenced to life in prison, while **Edward Spangler** (a theater stage hand) was sentenced to six years. John Surratt was extradited from Egypt in 1866 but was acquitted of murder. O'Laughlin died in prison, while Arnold and Mudd were pardoned in 1869.

LINCOLN'S INAUGURATIONS. Abraham Lincoln's first inauguration on March 4, 1861, was marked by fear and suspicion that secessionists might try to disrupt the proceeding. As a result, the ceremony was heavily guarded by both troops and plainclothes detectives. Lincoln traveled to the unfinished Capitol in a noontime procession, riding in an open carriage with outgoing President **James Buchanan**. After attending Vice President **Hannibal Hamlin's** swearing-in, Lincoln walked onto a platform at the east portico to address the crowd. While Sen. **Stephen A. Douglas** held his hat, Lincoln declared that the seceding states must return to the Union and that no concessions would be made toward them. He warned the Southerners "in *your* hands, my dissatisfied fellow countrymen, and not in *mine*, is the momentous issue of civil war. . . ." Then, following a suggestion by **William Seward**, Lincoln closed in a more conciliatory tone. "We must not be enemies. . . . The mystic chords of memory, stretching from every battlefield, and patriot grave, to every living heart and hearthstone, all over this broad land, will yet swell the chorus of the Union, when again touched, as surely they will be, by the better angels of our nature" (Donald, Lincoln, p. 283–84). When his speech was over, Lincoln was sworn into office by Chief Justice **Roger Taney**.

Four years later, on March 4, 1865, Lincoln's second inauguration was held in a more optimistic atmosphere. The war was coming to a victorious close, and Lincoln used the occasion to set the stage for reunion. He first attended the inauguration of Vice President **Andrew Johnson** in the Senate chamber, at which time Johnson appeared to be drunk. Embarrassed at Johnson's appearance, Lincoln quietly ordered that he not be allowed to speak to the crowd assembled outside. He then walked to a platform at the now completed Capitol's east entrance and made one of his greatest speeches. Although Lincoln carefully avoided mentioning the Confederacy, he blamed the war on **slavery** and hoped the conflict would soon end. "Yet," he warned, "if God wills that it continue, until all the wealth piled by the bond-man's two hundred and fifty years of unrequited toil shall be sunk, and until every drop of blood drawn with the lash shall be paid by another drawn with the sword . . . so still it must be said, 'the judgments of the Lord are true and righteous altogether.'" The speech was one of the shortest inaugural addresses in history—only 703 words—and it closed with the reassuring promise, "With malice toward none; with charity for all; with firmness in the right, as God gives us to see the right, let us strive on to finish the work we are in; to bind up the nation's wounds; . . .to do all which may achieve and cherish a just, and a lasting peace, among ourselves, and with all nations" (Donald, 567–68). Among the crowd at the second inauguration was **John Wilkes Booth**, who assassinated Lincoln a month later.

LITTLE BLUE RIVER, MISSOURI, BATTLE OF (OCTOBER 21, 1864). In mid-October 1864, **Sterling Price's Missouri Raid** forced

Union Maj. Gen. **James G. Blunt** out of **Lexington**, **Missouri**, and back to the Little Blue River. Blunt wanted his superior, **Samuel R. Curtis**, to make a defensive stand on the river, but Curtis declined when many of his **Kansas** volunteers refused to fight that far from their homes. Curtis at first ordered Blunt to retreat to Independence but then allowed him to return to the Little Blue River to support Col. Thomas Moonlight's command, which had been left there.

On October 21, **John S. Marmaduke's** Confederate cavalry engaged Moonlight before Blunt arrived. Moonlight repulsed the enemy attacks for a time but then retreated when Marmaduke was reinforced by **Joseph Shelby's division**. Burning the bridge before he left, Moonlight withdrew to the west and joined Blunt. Blunt then fought a delaying action, but he finally was forced to withdraw to **Independence**, where Union cavalry clashed with the Confederates the next day. Casualties suffered at the Little Blue River are unknown, but the Confederate victory made the Kansas militia willing to enter Missouri and make a defensive stand at the **Big Blue River** on October 22.

LITTLE, LEWIS HENRY (1817–1862) CSA. A native of **Maryland** and the son of a congressman, Little attended St. Mary's College. He received a 2nd lieutenant's commission in 1839 and served in the **Mexican War**, where he was **brevetted** for gallantry and was promoted to captain. After the war, Little served in the **Utah Expedition** and in **Arkansas**.

Sent to Jefferson Barracks near St. Louis, Missouri, in February 1861, Little's loyalties were torn during the growing **secession** crisis. When he was ordered to **Wisconsin** to raise troops to suppress the Rebellion, he resigned his commission in May. Little then reluctantly accepted a colonel's commission in the pro-Confederate Missouri militia later that month and became **Sterling Price's** aide. When Price was forced into southwestern **Missouri**, Little left him and went to **Richmond, Virginia**, where he was commissioned a colonel in the **Confederate army**.

In November 1861, Little was given command of a Missouri **brigade** under Price. After fighting well at **Pea Ridge**, he was promoted to brigadier general in April 1862 and was sent to **Corinth, Mississippi**. In June, Little took command of Price's **division** and three months later advised against attacking **Iuka, Mississippi**. Confined to an ambulance because of diarrhea and weakness during much of the march to Iuka, Little mounted his horse and rode to the front when the fighting began. While talking with Price and other officers, he was killed instantly by a bullet to the head.

LITTLE ROCK, ARKANSAS. Located on the Arkansas River, this capital of **Arkansas** had a population of 3,727 in 1860. One of its important assets was a U.S. arsenal, which was seized by **secessionists** in February 1861. Although the city served as headquarters for the **Trans-Mississippi Department** early in the war, the Confederates did not view it as strategically important and did not allocate many resources to defend it. In March 1863, the **department's** headquarters were moved to Shreveport, Louisiana.

After **Vicksburg, Mississippi**, was captured in July 1863, Maj. Gen. **Frederick Steele** took 12,000 men from **Helena** and marched on Little Rock in August. The city was defended by 7,700 men under **Sterling Price** but had little in the way of fortifications. After being defeated at **Bayou Fourche**, Price evacuated the city, and Steele captured it on September 10. Little Rock remained in Union hands for the remainder of the war.

LITTLE ROUND TOP AT BATTLE OF GETTYSBURG, PENNSYL-VANIA (JULY 2, 1863). *See* GETTYSBURG, PENNSYLVANIA, CAMPAIGN AND BATTLE OF.

LIVERMORE, MARY ASHTON RICE (1820–1905) USA. A native of **Massachusetts**, Livermore was educated at a New England female academy and taught there after graduation. For years she and her minister husband, Daniel P. Livermore, were active in reform issues and helped establish education facilities for the state's factory workers. The Livermores moved to Chicago, **Illinois**, in 1857, and became the owners and editors of the *New Covenant*, a religious and reform-oriented newspaper. Livermore was the only female reporter who covered the 1860 **Republican** National Convention.

When the Civil War began, Livermore's writings encouraged women to become active in soldiers' relief activities. In 1862, she helped form a **U.S. Sanitary Commission** branch in Chicago and became a national director. Throughout the war, Livermore was in charge of raising money and supplies for the commission and used her writing skills to expose negligence and to create sympathy for sick and wounded soldiers.

After the war, Livermore championed women's suffrage and was active in female educational issues. She also wrote her memoirs, *My Story of the War*.

LOCKWOOD, HENRY HAYES (1814–1899) USA. A native of **Delaware**, Lockwood graduated from **West Point** in 1836 and served in the **Seminole Wars** before resigning his 2nd lieutenant's commission in 1837. After farming for a while, he became a math professor at the **U.S. Naval Academy** in 1841 and served onboard a navy frigate during the **Mexican War** before returning to the academy to teach a variety of subjects.

Lockwood entered Union service in May 1861 as colonel of the 1st Delaware, but he was promoted to brigadier general of volunteers in August. For the first two years of war, he served on the **Maryland and Virginia** coasts, at times commanding **Point Lookout prison** and the District of the Eastern Shore. During the **Gettysburg Campaign**, Lockwood was put in command of an infantry **brigade** and reinforced the **Army of the Potomac's** XII Corps. After seeing combat on Culp's Hill, he was sent to reinforce the **Harpers Ferry, West Virginia**, area. In December 1863, Lockwood returned to his coastal **district** and sometimes temporarily commanded the **Middle Department**. In the spring of 1864, he reinforced the Army of the Potomac during the **Overland Campaign** and led a **division** at **Cold Harbor. U. S. Grant**, however, must have been dissatisfied with Lockwood's service, for he sent the general back to Maryland. For the rest of the war, he commanded Baltimore and the surrounding area, except for a brief period when he brought troops to **Washington, D.C.**, to defend it against **Jubal Early's Washington Raid**.

Lockwood was mustered out of service in August 1865 and returned to his teaching position at the Naval Academy. In 1870, he was assigned to the Naval Observatory in Washington and remained there until his retirement in 1876.

LOGAN, JOHN ALEXANDER (1826–1886) USA. A native of **Illinois**, Logan became one of the Union's best nonprofessional officers. As a young man, he attended **Kentucky's** Louisville University and became a lawyer. After serving in the **Mexican War** as a 2nd lieutenant of Illinois volunteers, Logan entered state politics as a **Democrat**. He was elected to the legislature four times in the 1850s, served as a presidential elector in 1856 and 1860, and began a two-term career in the U.S. House of Representatives in 1859.

Logan's family had Southern origins, and a brother-in-law joined the Confederacy, so he supported the South on some issues. As a politician, he tried to prohibit free blacks from entering Illinois, and he supported a strong **Fugitive Slave Act**. Some people suspected his loyalties, but in June 1861 Logan impressed Col. **U. S. Grant**. Although Grant at first was nervous as to what Logan would say, he allowed the politician to speak to his **regiment**, and Logan convinced most of the men to reenlist. Next month, Congressman Logan followed the **army** to **First Manassas** and actually joined in the fighting with a **Michigan** regiment before helping the wounded.

Logan entered Union service in September 1861 when he was appointed colonel of the 31st Illinois, a regiment he had raised. Known as

"Black Jack" because of his dark eyes, hair, and complexion, he had a horse killed under him at **Belmont** and was wounded at **Fort Donelson**. Promoted to brigadier general of volunteers in March 1862, Logan had to resign his congressional seat in April to accept the commission. He commanded a **brigade** during the **siege of Corinth, Mississippi**, and was given a **division** in the **Army of the Tennessee's** XIII Corps in November 1862.

Promoted to major general of volunteers in March 1863, Logan led a division in **James B. McPherson's** XVII Corps during the **Vicksburg Campaign**. He later was awarded the **Medal of Honor** for the role his troops played in attacking the city after a mine was exploded under Confederate lines. After **Vicksburg** was captured, Logan was given command of the XV Corps and led it with great skill through the **Atlanta Campaign**. He was wounded at **Dallas** and temporarily commanded the Army of the Tennessee after McPherson was killed at **Atlanta**. **William T. Sherman** decided the permanent position should go to a **West Point** graduate, even though he admitted Logan was "perfect in combat." Logan was very disappointed when the appointment went to **Oliver O. Howard** and resented West Pointers the rest of his life.

Logan briefly returned to Illinois to campaign for **Abraham Lincoln** in the 1864 election and then went to **Washington, D.C.** In December 1864, Grant sent him on a special mission to remove **George H. Thomas** from command at **Nashville, Tennessee**, for being too slow to attack the Confederates outside the city, but Logan learned of Thomas's victory at Nashville while on his way and canceled the trip. He then joined his **corps** for operations against **Savannah, Georgia**, and for the **Carolinas Campaign**. Because of his distinguished service, Logan was given the honor of leading the Army of the Tennessee during the **Grand Review** at war's end.

Logan left the army in August 1865 after declining an appointment to brigadier general in the **U.S. Army**. He joined the **Republican Party**, served in Congress from 1867 to 1871, and sat on the committee that voted to impeach President **Andrew Johnson**. Logan also served in the Senate from 1871 to 1877 and from 1879 to 1886 and unsuccessfully ran for vice president in 1884. He was being considered as a presidential candidate when he died.

LOGAN, THOMAS MULDRUP (1840–1914) CSA. A native of **South Carolina**, Logan graduated first in the South Carolina College class of 1860. After serving as a private in the Washington Light Artillery during the bombardment of **Fort Sumter**, he helped raise a **company** in the **Hampton Legion** and entered Confederate service in the spring of 1861 as a 1st lieutenant.

After seeing heavy combat at **First Manassas**, Logan was promoted to captain in July 1861. He fought in the **Seven Days Campaign** with the **Army of Northern Virginia** and was wounded at **Gaines' Mill** but rejoined his company in time to fight again at **Second Manassas**. Logan won much acclaim and a promotion to major for capturing a battery at Manassas and for fighting well at **Antietam**. Before the end of 1862, he was promoted to lieutenant colonel and joined **Micah Jenkins's brigade**. Logan participated in the siege of **Suffolk, Virginia**, during the spring of 1863 and then went west with **James Longstreet** to reinforce **Braxton Bragg's Army of Tennessee**. He commanded a unit of **sharpshooters** during the siege of **Chattanooga, Tennessee**, and in the **Knoxville Campaign**. When Longstreet unsuccessfully attacked Knoxville's **Fort Sanders** in November, Logan's sharpshooters led the way.

After returning to **Virginia** in the spring of 1864, Logan served on detached duty with **P. G. T. Beauregard** at **Drewry's Bluff** and played an important role as a courier during the second battle there. He was promoted to colonel in May 1864 and was given command of the Hampton Legion, but he was severely wounded in a **skirmish** at Riddell's Shop the following month. After returning to duty, Logan was transferred to the Carolinas, where he took command of a brigade of cavalry under **Wade Hampton**. When he was promoted to brigadier general in February 1865, he was the youngest general in the **Confederate army**. Logan served throughout the **Carolinas Campaign** and led one of the last Confederate charges of the war at **Bentonville**.

After the war, Logan became a prosperous **railroad** tycoon in Virginia and formed what became known as the Southern Railway. He won and lost several fortunes and often was associated with John D. Rockefeller.

LOGAN'S CROSS ROADS, KENTUCKY, BATTLE OF (JANUARY 19, 1862). *See* MILL SPRINGS, KENTUCKY, BATTLE OF.

LOMAX, LINDSAY LUNSFORD (1835–1913) CSA. A native of **Rhode Island** and the son of a **U.S. Army** officer, Lomax graduated from **West Point** in 1856. After serving on the frontier with the 2nd U.S. Cavalry, he resigned his 1st lieutenant's commission in April 1861 and was appointed captain of **Virginia** state troops. As **Joseph E. Johnston's** assistant adjutant general, Lomax served at **First Manassas** and then was transferred west, where he joined **Benjamin McCulloch's** staff. When McCulloch was killed at **Pea Ridge**, Lomax became the acting adjutant and inspector general of **Earl Van Dorn's Army of West Tennessee**.

Lomax was promoted to colonel in February 1863 and was placed in command of the 11th Virginia Cavalry. As part of **William E. "Grumble"**

Jones's brigade, he served with distinction at **Brandy Station** and **Gettysburg** with the **Army of Northern Virginia**. Upon recommendation by **Robert E. Lee**, Lomax was promoted to brigadier general in July 1863 and took command of a cavalry brigade.

Serving in **Fitzhugh Lee's** division, Lomax fought well through the **Overland Campaign**, particularly at **Yellow Tavern**. In August 1864, he was promoted to major general and was given **Robert Ransom's** former cavalry **division** and served under **Jubal A. Early** during **Philip Sheridan's Shenandoah Valley Campaign**. Greatly outnumbered, Lomax did not perform as well in the Valley, and his division was crushed while holding Early's left flank at **Fisher's Hill**. Shortly afterward, he suffered another disaster when he was defeated and captured at **Tom's Brook**. Lomax escaped from his captors and was given command of Early's cavalry in late October and command of the **Valley District** in March 1865. Learning of Lee's **surrender**, he took his cavalry to **North Carolina** and surrendered there with Johnston.

After the war, Lomax farmed in Virginia and served as president of the Virginia Polytechnic Institute from 1885 to 1899. He also helped compile the *War of the Rebellion* and was a commissioner of Gettysburg National Military Park.

LONE JACK, MISSOURI, BATTLE OF (AUGUST 15–16, 1862). In August 1862, **Missouri** was the scene of several raids and such small battles as **Kirksville** and **Independence**. Another minor battle occurred when Union Maj. Emory S. Foster led 800 men from Lexington to attack Confederate Col. J. T. Coffee's 1,600 men at Lone Jack. Foster attacked shortly after dark on August 15 and drove the Confederates from the area. Coffee was reinforced by 3,000 men that night and counterattacked the next day. The battle lasted five hours, with many charges and countercharges being made. When Foster became a casualty, Capt. M. H. Brawner took command of the Federals and finally retreated to Lexington. During the two-day battle, the Federals lost 272 men, but Confederate casualties are unknown.

LONG, ARMISTEAD LINDSAY (1825–1891) CSA. A native of **Virginia**, Long graduated from **West Point** in 1850 and served with the **artillery** at numerous posts. In May 1861, he was given a position on the staff of his father-in-law, Brig. Gen. **Edwin V. Sumner**, but he resigned his 1st lieutenant's commission the following month and joined the Confederacy.

Appointed a major of Confederate artillery, Long joined Brig. Gen. **William W. Loring's** staff and served as Loring's chief of artillery and acting inspector general in western Virginia. There he met **Robert E.**

Lee and joined his staff in **South Carolina** in the autumn of 1861. When Lee became **Jefferson Davis's** military adviser in early 1862, Long accompanied him to **Richmond, Virginia**, and became Lee's military secretary with the rank of colonel.

Long remained Lee's military secretary until September 1863, but he often, as at **Fredericksburg**, helped supervise the **Army of Northern Virginia's** artillery. Upon Lee's recommendation, he was appointed the II Corps' chief of artillery in September and was promoted to brigadier general. Long commanded the **corps'** artillery throughout the **Overland Campaign** and accompanied **Jubal A. Early's Washington Raid** in July 1864. Becoming ill in August, he gave up his command and did not return to duty until late in the year. After serving with Early at **Waynesboro** in March 1865, Long rejoined Lee for the **Petersburg Campaign** and surrendered with the **army** at **Appomattox**.

After the war, Long became chief engineer for the James River & Kanawha Canal Company, and when he became blind, President **U. S. Grant** appointed his wife postmistress of Charlottesville, Virginia. Long was very active in writing about the war and in 1886 he and a collaborator published *Memoirs of Robert E. Lee, His Military and Personal History*.

LONG, ELI (1837–1903) USA. A native of **Kentucky**, Long graduated from the Frankfort Military Academy in 1855 and was commissioned a 2nd lieutenant in the 1st U.S. Cavalry the following year. Serving on the frontier, Long was promoted to captain in May 1861 and in August joined the 4th U.S. Cavalry.

Long was **brevetted** for gallantry during a small battle in October 1862 and was wounded at **Stones River** while with the **Army of the Cumberland**. In February 1863, he was appointed colonel of the 4th Ohio Cavalry and took command of a cavalry **brigade** in the **army's** 2nd Cavalry Division the following month. Long led the brigade in the **Tullahoma** and **Chickamauga Campaigns** and was brevetted a second time for helping relieve the besieged Union garrison during the **Knoxville Campaign**.

After fighting through most of the **Atlanta Campaign**, Long was promoted to brigadier general of volunteers in August 1864. He was given command of a cavalry **division** in November and accompanied **William T. Sherman** on the **March to the Sea**, winning a third brevet for **Lovejoy's Station**. In April 1865, Long accompanied **James H. Wilson's Selma, Alabama, Raid** and was badly injured when he received his fifth wound at Selma. He was brevetted for his gallantry there and at war's end was brevetted major general in both the volunteer and regular army for his wartime service.

Long left the volunteers in January 1866 and commanded the District of New Jersey until he retired in 1867 with the rank of major general (this was reduced by law in 1875 to brigadier general). Long then practiced law until his death.

LONGSTREET, JAMES (1821–1904) CSA. A native of **South Carolina**, "Pete" Longstreet grew up in **Georgia** and entered **West Point** in 1838. After rooming with future Union Maj. Gen. **William Rosecrans**, he graduated near the bottom of his class in 1842. A large man at six feet, two inches in height, Longstreet served in the **Mexican War** as a regimental adjutant and was wounded once and **brevetted** twice at Chapultepec. After the war, he married a cousin of **Ulysses S. Grant's** wife, was promoted to captain, and fought **Indians** in **Texas**. During the **secession** crisis, Longstreet was a major in the paymaster's department in **New Mexico**, but he resigned his commission in June 1861 and offered his services to the Confederacy.

Commissioned brigadier general in June 1861, Longstreet commanded a **brigade** at **First Manassas** and then was given a **division** when he was promoted to major general in October. Soon afterward, he was devastated when three of his children died from scarlet fever in January 1862. Up to that time, Longstreet had always been a friendly, outgoing man, but friends noticed that he became more reserved after the children's deaths.

In the **Peninsula Campaign**, Longstreet amassed a checkered record. He fought well at **Williamsburg** but then became confused at **Seven Pines** and threw the Confederates into disarray by taking a wrong road. Longstreet performed admirably in the **Seven Days Campaign**, and afterward **Robert E. Lee** placed him in command of one wing of the **Army of Northern Virginia**. At **Second Manassas**, Longstreet disagreed with Lee's first orders to counterattack, arguing that the time was not yet right, and events proved he was right. When he did attack, the Union **army** was routed from the field. This event, however, foreshadowed future incidents when Longstreet again would disagree with Lee's **tactics** and embroil himself in controversy. A few weeks after Manassas, Longstreet was in the thick of the fighting at **Antietam**, and his tenacious defense caused Lee to refer to him as "my old warhorse!" (Wert, *General James Longstreet*, 200). When Lee reorganized the army into two **corps** in October 1862, he placed Longstreet at the head of the I Corps. Longstreet's promotion to lieutenant general came at the same time, and his commission was dated to make him the Confederacy's senior lieutenant general and second ranking officer in the Army of Northern Virginia.

At **Fredericksburg**, Longstreet held Marye's Heights' famous stone wall and slaughtered the attacking Federals. Impressed with the strength of the tactical defense, he became one of the war's first generals to make use of earthworks and entrenchments and became increasingly reluctant to launch **frontal attacks**. This mind-set would bring him into conflict with Lee at **Gettysburg**.

In the spring of 1863, Longstreet was sent to southeastern **Virginia** to gather supplies and besiege **Suffolk** and thus missed the **Chancellorsville Campaign**. Rejoining Lee, he next became involved in one of the war's biggest controversies at **Gettysburg**. On the second day of battle, Longstreet disagreed with Lee's decision to attack the Union's main line of defense. Recognizing the strong defensive position the Federals held, he argued that Lee should disengage, move behind the Union army to a strong position, and make the enemy attack him on ground of his choosing. Although Longstreet did not disobey orders to attack at daylight as later was claimed, he probably did not move as swiftly as possible to launch the attack. His corps battered the enemy at Little Round Top, the **Peach Orchard**, and **Wheatfield** but was unable to win a decisive victory. The following day, Longstreet again argued with Lee not to launch **Pickett's Charge** because he believed such an attack was hopeless. After losing the argument, however, he carried out Lee's wishes and came close to breaking the Union line. Because no one dared criticize Lee during the postwar period, Longstreet was later blamed unfairly for causing Lee to lose Gettysburg through his slowness and lack of cooperation.

After Gettysburg, Longstreet was sent to reinforce the **Army of Tennessee** in Georgia, and his men launched the attack that routed the Union army on the second day at **Chickamauga**. Longstreet wanted command of the army for himself and became one of **Braxton Bragg's** greatest critics. As a result, Bragg sent him to attack Knoxville, Tennessee, while the rest of the army besieged **Chattanooga, Tennessee**. During the **Knoxville Campaign**, Longstreet misjudged the enemy's defenses and unsuccessfully attacked **Fort Sanders**. Afterward, he made Maj. Gen. **Lafayette McLaws** the scapegoat for the failure and had the division commander court-martialed.

Longstreet rejoined Lee in Virginia in the spring of 1864 after the failed Knoxville Campaign. At the **Wilderness**, his corps arrived just in time to save Lee's right wing from being crushed on the second day and then launched a successful flank attack against the enemy. While riding along the front, Longstreet's party was mistakenly fired upon by Confederates, and he was badly wounded by a bullet that passed through his neck and shoulder and paralyzed his arm. Rejoining the army in October, he fought throughout the remainder of the **Petersburg Campaign** and surrendered with Lee at **Appomattox**.

After the war, Longstreet believed in reconciliation and joined the **Republican Party**. He worked as a cotton factor and in insurance and held many federal positions, including minister to Turkey. Longstreet's involvement with the Republican Party branded him a **scalawag** and made him hated by many of his old comrades, and **Jubal A. Early**, **John B. Gordon**, and other former officers began attacking his war record—particularly his role at Gettysburg. Longstreet did not help his defense when he wrote a number of clumsy, poorly argued articles and his memoir, *From Manassas to Appomattox*. As a result, he became the major scapegoat for the Confederacy's defeat and was portrayed as a slow, plodding officer. It was an inglorious end for one of the Confederacy's most dedicated and best combat commanders.

LOOKOUT MOUNTAIN, TENNESSEE, BATTLE OF (NOVEMBER 24, 1863). In November 1863, **U. S. Grant** arrived in Chattanooga, Tennessee, to lift the siege of **William S. Rosecrans's Army of the Cumberland** by **Braxton Bragg's** Confederate **Army of Tennessee** in the **Chattanooga Campaign**. Grant had replaced Rosecrans with **George H. Thomas** and devised an elaborate plan to break out. While **William T. Sherman** and Thomas attacked the Confederates on **Missionary Ridge**, Maj. Gen. **Joseph Hooker's** two divisions would push past Lookout Mountain and capture Rossville Gap, an important mountain gap southeast of Chattanooga on Bragg's extreme left flank. Hooker could threaten Bragg's left and rear from Rossville Gap and hopefully draw off some of Bragg's men from Missionary Ridge.

Lookout Mountain is a seemingly impregnable 1,100-foot-high mountain running southwest to northeast, terminating southwest of Chattanooga on a bend of the Tennessee River. Brigadier General **John K. Jackson** held tactical command of the mountain defenses and had two Confederate **brigades** of about 2,700 men on its slope—**Edward C. Walthall's** brigade blocking the narrow passage between the mountain and the river and **John C. Moore's** brigade manning a defensive line farther up the slope. Maj. Gen. **Carter L. Stevenson's** small **division** held the top of the mountain.

After Thomas captured **Orchard Knob** on November 23, 1863, Grant revised his plan. He added another division to Hooker's command and ordered him to attack and capture Lookout Mountain rather than simply push past it to Rossville Gap. By doing so, Hooker would not be leaving

Confederates in his rear when he reached the gap to operate against Bragg's left and rear.

On the morning of November 24, Hooker attacked with the divisions of **John W. Geary**, **Charles Cruft**, and **Peter J. Osterhaus**. The Federals first advanced against the Confederate position around Cravens's Farm (or the "White House"), and a spirited battle lasted through the morning. Hooker sent in **William P. Carlin's** brigade as reinforcements, while Brig. Gen. **Edmund W. Pettus** reinforced the Confederates. After several hours of fighting, the Confederates finally fell back to a second position. There they held out until mid-afternoon, but then Bragg ordered Stevenson to withdraw all the men from the mountain and to fall back to Missionary Ridge. The last Confederates left at 8:00 P.M.

Dense fog and drizzle hid the fight from the main Union line fronting Missionary Ridge. All day, Grant and others could hear the battle roaring up the mountain but could see nothing, thus leading to the name "Battle above the Clouds." The following morning, the 8th Kentucky (Union) climbed to the top of Lookout Mountain and raised the U.S. **flag** for all to see. Hooker then moved on to Rossville Gap, and the Federals drove Bragg off Missionary Ridge. Casualties suffered in the battle are uncertain. The battle became controversial among the Confederates because a number of officers bitterly condemned Jackson for his lack of leadership during the fight, claiming that he never came down from the mountaintop to direct affairs on the slope.

LORING-JACKSON FEUD. In January 1862, **William W. Loring's** brigade was placed under **Stonewall Jackson** for operations around Romney, in western **Virginia**. The campaign did not go well, and afterward Jackson left Loring's command at Romney while he took his men back to more comfortable quarters at Winchester. Living in harsh conditions, Loring believed that Jackson had intentionally slighted his **brigade** and went outside of regular military channels to complain directly to the War Department. He claimed that his brigade was being left dangerously exposed and unsupported and should be withdrawn from Romney immediately.

Supporting Loring, Secretary of War **Judah P. Benjamin** wired Jackson to withdraw Loring to Winchester. Furious at such interference with his command, Jackson followed orders, but in late January, he requested reassignment to the **Virginia Military Institute** and threatened to resign his commission if his request was not honored. He also wrote Gov. **John Letcher** seeking his support. Fortunately for the **army**, Letcher and Gen. **Joseph E. Johnston** intervened and worked out a compromise. Jackson remained on duty, while Loring was promoted to major general and was transferred out of Jackson's command in February to take over the **Department of Southwestern Virginia**.

LORING, WILLIAM WING (1818–1886) CSA. A native of **North Carolina**, Loring moved to **Florida** with his family as a child. There he fought in the **Seminole Wars** with a militia unit when he was only 14 and received a 2nd lieutenant's commission when 18. After attending preparatory school in Alexandria, Virginia, and Georgetown College, Loring became a lawyer and served in the Florida legislature from 1842 to 1845. During the **Mexican War**, he was commissioned a captain in the Mounted Rifles and earned much praise for his service. Loring rose to the rank of major, was **brevetted** twice for gallantry, and was wounded twice. His arm was so badly damaged at Chapultepec that it was amputated without anesthetics while Loring stoically smoked a cigar. He later claimed the loss of his arm was the proudest moment of his life because it marked him as a war veteran.

Loring remained with his **regiment** after the war and rose to the rank of colonel in 1856. He served on the frontier, fought **Indians**, and became one of the best-known frontier officers. After an inspection of European military powers, Loring returned to the United States in March 1861 during the **secession** crisis. When he resigned his commission in May to join the Confederacy, he was by far the youngest colonel in the **U.S. Army**.

Loring already had been commissioned a colonel in the **Confederate army** in March, two months before his resignation from the U.S. Army was accepted. In May 1861, he was appointed brigadier general and was sent to western **Virginia**, where he served at **Cheat Mountain** under **Robert E. Lee**. A friendly and popular officer with subordinates, Loring soon proved to be an argumentative and testy man with his superiors. In early 1862, he served under **Stonewall Jackson** in western Virginia, but the two officers became embroiled in the **Loring-Jackson Feud**. Jackson left Loring's **brigade** in very uncomfortable quarters at Romney, while Jackson's men wintered in Winchester. Believing such treatment was an insult, Loring went outside of military channels and complained directly to **Richmond, Virginia**, prompting Jackson to file charges against him. The War Department sided with Loring, which caused Jackson to threaten to resign. The feud finally ended when Loring was promoted to major general in February 1862 and was transferred to command the **Department of Southwestern Virginia**.

In November 1862, Loring was sent west to lead a **division** under **John C. Pemberton** in **Mississippi**. As a division commander, he became known as "Blizzards" because of his habit of crying out in battle, "Give them blizzards, boys!" Loring won acclaim at Fort Pemberton in March 1863 when his small force turned back the Union **Yazoo Pass Expedition**. He soon began quarreling with Pemberton, however, as they blamed each other for the defeat at **Champion Hill**, where Loring's division became cut off from Pemberton's **army** and escaped to join **Joseph E. Johnston** at Jackson. Loring remained with Johnston and led his division through the **Meridian** and **Atlanta Campaigns** and temporarily commanded a **corps** in the **Army of Tennessee** when **Leonidas Polk** was killed. He also served under **John Bell Hood** during the latter part of the Atlanta Campaign and was wounded at **Ezra Church**. When he returned to duty, Loring rejoined his division for the **Franklin and Nashville Campaign**. After the defeat at Nashville, his division rejoined Johnston for the last part of the **Carolinas Campaign**. By war's end, Loring was the Confederacy's senior major general still on active duty.

After the war, Loring worked as a New York City banker and became a brigadier general in the Egyptian army in 1869. After fighting in Abyssinia in 1875–76, he was decorated and promoted by the Khedive and was designated as pasha. In 1879, Loring returned to the United States, where he lectured about his Egyptian experiences and worked in politics and **railroads**.

LOSSES. Determining the number of casualties suffered in the Civil War is difficult. Confederate records often were kept sporadically, and many were lost or destroyed during the war. The Union kept better records, but sometimes (as in the 1864 **Overland Campaign**) officers intentionally underreported losses for political reasons. Because of these problems, estimates of casualties vary widely. A reasonable estimate would be 360,000 dead for the Union and 260,000 for the Confederacy. Of these, approximately 110,000 Union soldiers were killed or mortally wounded in battle, while at least 75,000 (and perhaps many more) Confederates suffered the same fate. The Union also had approximately 275,000 men wounded, and 211,411 captured. The Confederates had about 226,000 men wounded and 220,000 captured. The majority of deaths in the Civil War were caused by disease, thousands of which occurred in **prison** camps. There were also thousands of civilian deaths caused by disease, malnutrition, and wounds, but there is no accurate way to determine the number.

LOST CAUSE. This phrase originated from a book entitled *The Lost Cause*, a history of **secession** and the Confederacy published in 1866 by

Edward A. Pollard. As time passed, the term *Lost Cause* took on almost religious significance for Southerners as they came to terms with their past. Secession was hailed as a constitutional duty, and the Confederacy was portrayed as being the true champion of the Founding Fathers' dream of self-government. The Confederacy—and the Old South—were seen as idyllic times when the Southern people lived in harmony with their slaves and government but were trampled by a tyrannical invading power. In the Lost Cause mythology, all Southern soldiers were brave and chivalrous, while their enemy was inhuman and brutal. The Confederacy had been defeated by overwhelming Northern industrial might and population, or else God was testing the South in a Job-like manner to see if it was worthy of greater blessings. While Southerners may have lost the Civil War, they largely won the peace by convincing themselves that their culture and heritage were superior to the North's.

LOST MOUNTAIN-BRUSHY MOUNTAIN LINE, GEORGIA, BATTLE OF (JUNE 9–18, 1864). During the 1864 **Atlanta Campaign**, Gen. **Joseph E. Johnston's Army of Tennessee** held its position around **New Hope Church** until June 4. It then withdrew to the east to a new defensive line to protect Marietta, Georgia, with its left anchored on Lost Mountain, its center on Pine Mountain, and its right on Brushy Mountain. After repairing his **railroad** and resupplying his **armies, William T. Sherman** advanced against this new defensive position on June 9.

Skirmishing took place over several days as Sherman positioned his forces, and on June 14 Confederate Lt. Gen. **Leonidas Polk** was killed by a shell while atop Pine Mountain. Realizing his forward position at Pine Mountain was dangerously exposed to attack, Johnston withdrew from there on the night of June 14 and consolidated his line from Lost Mountain to Brushy Mountain. On June 15, **Joseph Hooker's** XX Corps attacked the Confederate center at the Lost Mountain-Brushy Mountain line but was repulsed by **Patrick Cleburne's** Confederate **division**. Union **artillery** fire **enfiladed** Cleburne's line, however, and the Confederate center, held by **William J. Hardee's corps**, was forced to withdraw behind Mud Creek.

The next day, Sherman sent **John M. Schofield's Army of the Ohio** against Johnston's left at Lost Mountain, while **James B. McPherson's Army of the Tennessee** pressured the right at Brushy Mountain. Johnston was forced to withdraw his left flank that night, leaving Hardee holding an exposed **salient** at Mud Creek. When Union artillery began bombarding this weak position on June 18, Johnston abandoned the Lost Mountain-Brushy Mountain line after midnight and withdrew to **Kennesaw Mountain**.

LOST MOUNTAIN, GEORGIA (JUNE 27, 1864). *See* KENNESAW MOUNTAIN, GEORGIA, BATTLE OF.

LOST ORDER. Officially designated Special Order No. 191, the Lost Order was **Robert E. Lee's** written orders for the **Antietam Campaign**. Written when Lee entered **Maryland** in September 1862, the order specified how and on what time schedule the **Army of Northern Virginia** would disperse to capture **Harpers Ferry, Virginia**, and gather supplies. **Stonewall Jackson** and three columns were ordered to converge on Harpers Ferry, while **James Longstreet** and a fourth column gathered supplies in the Maryland countryside. Seven copies of the order were made, to be distributed to the various commanders.

On September 13, while encamped at Frederick, Maryland, Union Pvt. Barton W. Mitchell of the 27th Indiana found a copy of the order lying on the ground wrapped around three cigars. The order made its way to Sgt. John M. Bloss and Col. **Silas Colgrove**, with the colonel delivering it to **George B. McClellan's** headquarters. The discovery gave McClellan a tremendous **tactical** advantage, for knowing the whereabouts of Lee's **army** and its time table, he could attack and **defeat in detail** the Confederates. Waving the order to subordinates, McClellan boldly declared that if he could not now defeat Lee he would be willing to go home. Incredibly, however, he delayed his pursuit 16 hours, giving Lee time to concentrate his army at Antietam for the coming battle.

Who lost the order has been debated ever since. The copy that was found was made for Maj. Gen. **Daniel H. Hill**, but Hill denied losing it. In fact, Jackson made another copy of the order and had it delivered to Hill since Hill had been operating under Jackson's authority. The Lost Order probably was lost by some anonymous courier who was delivering the paper to Hill from Lee's headquarters. Since Hill received another copy of the order from Jackson, no one—but the courier—would have known that a copy had been lost.

LOUDOUN RANGERS. This Union **partisan ranger** unit was composed largely of Germans living northwest of Leesburg, Virginia. Authorized by Secretary of War **Edwin Stanton**, the rangers were mustered into Union service in June 1862 to guard the region against Confederate guerrillas. Under the command of Samuel C. Means, and later Daniel M. Keyes, the rangers frequently fought **John S. Mosby's** Confederates but usually were bested in the clashes. In April 1865, the rangers were captured nearly to a man by Mosby's command when the Confederates raided their camp.

LOUISIANA. In January 1861, Gov. **Thomas O. Moore** convened a **secession** convention in **Baton Rouge**, and it voted 113–17 for secession on January 26, 1861. After existing a few weeks as the Republic of Louisiana, the state helped form the **Confederate States of America** in the **Montgomery, Alabama, Convention**. Louisiana played an important role during the Civil War, mainly because of **New Orleans** and the Mississippi River, but with an 1860 population of 708,000, it also supplied the Confederacy with considerable manpower.

Approximately 66,000 Louisianans (or 65 percent of its eligible white men) served in the **Confederate army** or state militia, and about 15,000 died of wounds or disease. Soldiers, like the **Louisiana Tigers**, played important roles in the **Army of Northern Virginia** and the **Army of Tennessee**, and such Louisiana officers as **Braxton Bragg, P. G. T. Beauregard**, and **Richard Taylor** rose to prominent positions. Thousands of other men, mostly **black troops**, supported the Union. Most notable among these were the **Louisiana Native Guards**, three **regiments** of free blacks and former slaves who fought bravely in the **Port Hudson Campaign**.

Unfortunately for Louisiana, most of its soldiers were sent elsewhere when the war began, leaving the state largely undefended when **David G. Farragut** attacked **Forts Jackson and St. Philip** and captured New Orleans in April 1862. New Orleans was the Confederacy's largest city and perhaps its most important financial and industrial center, and its capture was a tremendous loss. It became the Union capital of the state, and **Benjamin Butler** ruled over it during his controversial 1862 administration. Although Butler became known as the "Beast" to Confederates, the Union received strong support during the occupation by many foreign-born citizens, who made up nearly 40 percent of the city's population.

Baton Rouge surrendered a few days after New Orleans, and a Confederate attempt to recapture the city failed in August. In 1863, **U. S. Grant** invaded northeast Louisiana during the **Vicksburg Campaign**, while **Nathaniel P. Banks** fought the **Bayou Teche** and Port Hudson Campaigns. After bloody sieges, Vicksburg and Port Hudson surrendered in July, giving the Union control of the Mississippi River. Later that year, Banks made his unsuccessful **Texas Overland Expedition** across south Louisiana. A year later, he invaded northwest Louisiana in the **Red River Campaign** to capture cotton and the Confederate capital at Shreveport, where Gov. **Henry Allen** had established an important industrial center. This campaign laid waste to many towns and houses, but Banks was defeated by Taylor's small **army** at **Mansfield** and was forced to retreat. Afterward, no other major campaigns took place in the state.

Louisiana was devastated by the war, and more than 600 engagements were fought on its soil. Much of northeast Louisiana was flooded by

Grant's Canals during the Vicksburg Campaign, the Bayou Teche and **Lafourche** districts were burned out and destroyed, and numerous towns (such as Alexandria) were burned by Union troops.

Louisiana also played a key role in **Reconstruction**. In 1863, **Abraham Lincoln** used Louisiana as a laboratory for his **Ten Percent Plan** since Union forces controlled much of the state's population in New Orleans and Baton Rouge. A loyal government was installed in 1864, and a new constitution was adopted that abolished **slavery**. Lincoln was assassinated, however, before the state could be readmitted to the Union.

LOUISIANA, CSS. This **ironclad** was one of three the Confederacy built in **New Orleans, Louisiana**, to break the Union **blockade** (the others were the CSS *Manassas* and *Mississippi*). Construction on the *Louisiana* began in October 1861, but work was hampered by labor strikes and a lack of material. When **David G. Farragut** attacked New Orleans in April 1862, the ship was not yet finished. It was covered with heavy iron and was armed with an assortment of **rifled** and smoothbore guns, but its rudder, engines, and propeller were not fully operational. Nonetheless, Confederate authorities sent the *Louisiana* to reinforce **Forts Jackson and St. Philip** on the Mississippi River below the city.

Because of its unfinished condition, the ironclad was anchored near Fort St. Philip and was used as a floating battery. When Farragut ran past the forts on April 24, the *Louisiana's* commander, Charles F. McIntosh, was mortally wounded and was replaced by John K. Mitchell. After the forts surrendered on April 28, Mitchell destroyed the ship by setting it on fire and putting it adrift. When it exploded in the midst of the Union fleet while flags of truce were in force, **David D. Porter** accused Mitchell of treachery. As a result, Mitchell and his officers were sent to **prison** camps instead of being **paroled** like the other Confederate **prisoners**.

LOUISIANA NATIVE GUARDS. Antebellum **New Orleans, Louisiana**, had a large population of free men of color who had a long tradition of military service. The city's black militia had served Spain during the Revolutionary War and with Andrew Jackson at the Battle of New Orleans. Many of these men were well-educated, wealthy, slave owners, while others were artisans and craftsmen who formed an important part of New Orleans society. When the Civil War began, these black militiamen offered their services to the Confederacy, probably to protect their economic and social status. For propaganda reasons, Gov. **Thomas Moore** accepted them into the state militia, complete with black line officers, but they were refused entry into the **Confederate army**.

When Union forces occupied the city in the spring of 1862, however, the militiamen showed their true loyalties by immediately disbanding and offering their services to **Benjamin Butler**. In September 1862, Butler mustered the 1st Regiment of the Native Guards into Union service, making it the first sanctioned **regiment** of **black troops** in the Union **army**. By November, the 2nd and 3rd Regiments were also mustered in, but these consisted mostly of former slaves. The three regiments had white colonels, but all of the line officers in the 1st and 2nd Regiments were black, while the 3rd Regiment had both black and white officers.

The Native Guards suffered from blatant discrimination. They received inferior pay, rations, and arms and frequently were harassed by white soldiers. When **Nathaniel P. Banks** replaced Butler in command of New Orleans, he forced all of the 3rd Regiment's black officers to resign, and by war's end only two black officers were on duty with the three regiments. Still, the men served well. In May 1863, the 1st and 3rd Regiments became some of the first black units to see combat in the war when they attacked the Confederate defenses in the **Port Hudson Campaign**. Their bravery and heavy losses (169 casualties) caused many Union soldiers and officers to accept black combat soldiers in the army. After serving in the 1864 **Red River Campaign**, the regiments were redesignated the 73rd, 74th, and 75th U.S. Colored Troops. The 73rd Infantry participated in the assault on **Fort Blakely** in the **Mobile Campaign**, where it was the first regiment to mount the Confederate works and captured seven cannons.

LOUISIANA TIGERS. The name "Louisiana Tigers" originated in 1861 from a **company** of **Zouaves** in **Chatham Roberdeau Wheat's** Battalion called the Tiger Rifles. Wheat's Battalion became so notorious for thievery, brawling, and drunkenness in **Virginia** that it soon became known as the Tiger Battalion. When other **Louisiana** units showed similar behavior, all Louisiana soldiers in Virginia became referred to as Tigers. Stories of their misbehavior were legion, and soon many Virginians feared the Tigers entering their neighborhoods as much as the enemy. Despite their notoriety, the Tigers also were among the best fighters in the **Army of Northern Virginia**. At **Salem Church**, **Jubal A. Early** best summed up the attitude officers held about the Tigers. As he watched the 1st Louisiana Brigade break through two Union lines, he threw his hat to the ground and shouted out, "Those damned Louisiana fellows may steal as much as they please now!" (Jones, *Lee's Tigers*, 155).

The original **regiments** and battalions that went to Virginia eventually were organized into 10 regiments. These were placed into two **brigades** in the II Corps and fought in nearly every major battle of the eastern theater. The 1st Louisiana Brigade came to include the 5th, 6th, 7th, 8th, and 9th Louisiana Volunteers, while the 2nd Louisiana Brigade had the 1st, 2nd, 10th, 14th, and 15th Louisiana Volunteers. Under **Richard Taylor**, the 1st Louisiana Brigade played the key role in **Stonewall Jackson's Shenandoah Valley Campaign** by winning the victories at **First Winchester** and **Port Republic**. The 2nd Louisiana Brigade, under **William E. Starke**, held Jackson's line at **Second Manassas** by throwing rocks when its ammunition ran out. Under **Harry T. Hays**, the 1st Brigade again captured Winchester during the **Second Battle of Winchester** and at **Gettysburg** broke through the Union lines atop Cemetery Hill before being forced to retreat because of a lack of support. Much of the 1st Brigade was captured in late 1863 at **Rappahannock Station**, but most of the men were **exchanged** and played a significant role at **Spotsylvania's** "Bloody Angle." During the **Overland Campaign**, losses were so heavy the two brigades were consolidated into one. After leading the attack at Petersburg's **Fort Stedman**, Col. Eugene Waggaman surrendered the Louisiana Tigers at **Appomattox**. Of the approximately 12,000 men who served in the Tiger units during the war, only 373 were left at Appomattox. *See also* PECK, WILLIAM R.; STAFFORD, LEROY A.; YORK, ZEBULON.

LOVEJOY'S STATION, GEORGIA, RAID ON (AUGUST 18–23, 1864). During the **Atlanta Campaign** in mid-August 1864, **William T. Sherman** learned that **Joseph Wheeler's** Confederate cavalry had left the Atlanta area to operate in northern **Georgia**. Sherman took advantage of this by sending his cavalry under **H. Judson Kilpatrick** to raid the Atlanta & West Point Railroad and the Macon & Western Railroad south of Atlanta.

Kilpatrick took 4,700 troopers and set out from Sandtown on August 18. He destroyed some Atlanta & West Point track at Fairburn before learning from an intercepted telegram that Confederate troops were approaching. Kilpatrick then rode on to Jonesboro the next day and destroyed a quantity of supplies there. On August 20, the Union troopers reached the Macon & Western Railroad at Lovejoy's Station, but they soon were attacked by Confederate infantry. When Kilpatrick was hit in the rear by **William H. Jackson's** Confederate cavalry **division**, he cut his way out of near encirclement and returned to Sherman on August 23 by riding around Atlanta to the east and north. In the raid, Kilpatrick lost 237 men, while the Confederates suffered 240 casualties. The only major damage to the **railroad** was carried out by a small Union detachment led by Lt. Col. Robert Klein, which destroyed about three miles of track near Lovejoy's Station. Kilpatrick bragged to Sherman that he had put the railroad out of service for 10 days, but the Confederates had it back in operation two days later. The raid's failure convinced Sherman to move his main infantry force south of Atlanta to cut the enemy's supply line permanently.

LOVELL, MANSFIELD (1822–1884) CSA. The son of the nation's first surgeon general, Lovell (LUV-ul) was born in **Washington, D.C.** He moved to **New York** as a boy and graduated near the top of the **West Point** class of 1842. Lovell then fought with the **artillery** in the **Mexican War**, where he was wounded twice and **brevetted** once. He resigned his 1st lieutenant's commission in 1854 and worked at an ironworks before becoming superintendent of street improvements in New York City. Street commissioner **Gustavus W. Smith** then made him a deputy street commissioner.

After the Civil War began, Smith and Lovell traveled to Smith's native state of **Kentucky** in the summer of 1861. Upon the recommendation of **Joseph E. Johnston**, both men were appointed Confederate generals, with Lovell receiving his appointment to brigadier general in September. At first, Lovell was given command of **Louisiana's** coastal defenses under Maj. Gen. **David E. Twiggs** at **New Orleans**. Twiggs, however, asked to be relieved from command of **Department No. 1** before Lovell arrived. Thus, **Jefferson Davis** promoted Lovell to major general in October and put him in command of the **department**. Charged with defending New Orleans, he was hampered by a lack of troops and resources and Davis's refusal to let him command the naval forces on the Mississippi River. To make matters worse, Davis began stripping the department of men and ships in February 1862 to strengthen the defenses of **Tennessee** and the upper Mississippi River. As a result, Lovell had little to work with when **David G. Farragut** attacked New Orleans in April. When Farragut passed **Forts Jackson and St. Philip** and reached New Orleans, Lovell evacuated the city rather than fight what would have been a losing battle. He then made a wise decision to rush reinforcements to protect **Vicksburg, Mississippi**, from the advancing Union fleet and probably saved it from being captured as well.

Davis made Lovell the scapegoat for the loss of New Orleans and replaced him with **Earl Van Dorn** in June. In September, Van Dorn appointed Lovell to command one of his **divisions**, which Lovell led without distinction at the **Battle of Corinth**. In mid-October 1862, Van Dorn put Lovell in command of one of his **corps**. Stationed in northern **Mississippi**, he won a small battle at **Coffeeville** but then was relieved of command in December when **John C. Pemberton** took over the **Department of Mississippi and East Louisiana**. Lovell waited in vain for new orders and was the subject of an April 1863 inquiry into the loss of New Orleans (he was cleared of any wrongdoing).

Johnston requested Lovell's service as a corps commander for the **Army of Tennessee** in January 1864, but Davis refused. **Braxton Bragg** later requested Lovell's service as Johnston's chief of artillery, but nothing came of that either. It had become quite clear that Davis unfairly blamed Lovell for the loss of New Orleans and was determined not to use him again. Lovell served as Johnston's volunteer aide in the **Atlanta Campaign**, during which the War Department again refused Johnston's request to put him in charge of a division and **John Bell Hood's** request to give Lovell a corps. After the Atlanta Campaign, Lovell moved to **South Carolina**. In April 1865, Johnston finally secured his services in the **Carolinas Campaign** by appealing to General-in-Chief **Robert E. Lee** to put him in command of Confederate troops in South Carolina. By then, however, the war essentially was over.

After the war, Lovell was a **Georgia** rice planter before returning to New York City to work as a surveyor and civil engineer.

LOWE, THADDEUS SOBIESKI CONSTANTINE (1832–1913) USA.

A native of **New Hampshire**, Lowe was fascinated by aeronautics at an early age. He built his first hot air **balloon** in 1858 and the following year unsuccessfully attempted to cross the Atlantic Ocean in one. By 1861, "Professor" Lowe was fairly well known as a balloonist.

Just a week after the fall of **Fort Sumter**, Lowe rode a balloon 900 miles in nine hours from **Ohio** to **South Carolina**, where he promptly was arrested as a Union spy. Released the next day, he offered his services to the Union and began using gas balloons around **Washington, D.C.** In June, Lowe first used a **telegraph** from a balloon, in July reconnoitered Confederate positions along the Potomac River from the air, and in September directed **artillery** fire from a balloon. Impressed, **Abraham Lincoln** had appointed Lowe chief of **army** aeronautics in August.

In the spring of 1862, Lowe accompanied **George B. McClellan's Army of the Potomac** in the **Peninsula Campaign** and eventually had seven balloons in service using portable coal-gas generators. McClellan was impressed with Lowe's daily scouting trips and greatly supported the use of balloons to gather intelligence. Lowe remained with the army after the campaign and saw additional service at **Fredericksburg**. It is estimated that his balloons flew more than 3,000 missions during their time with the army. In the spring of 1863, however, **Joseph Hooker** reduced Lowe's pay, staff, and support, and placed him under the command of the army's chief **engineer**. This caused Lowe to resign his position in May 1863.

After leaving the army, Lowe remained active in the scientific community, discovering a way to produce artificial ice and building an electric train up a **California** mountain that still bears his name. The Lowe Observatory now stands on top of the mountain.

LOWREY, MARK PERRIN (1828–1885) CSA. A native of **Tennessee**, Lowrey moved to **Mississippi** as a boy. He served in the **Mexican War**, but saw no combat, and then worked as a brick mason before becoming a Baptist minister.

In December 1861, Lowrey was elected captain of a local 60-day militia **company** that became part of the 4th Mississippi State Troops. He was elected colonel and took the **regiment** to **Kentucky** as part of Reuben Davis's brigade before the men's enlistments expired. Returning to Mississippi in January 1862, Lowrey organized the 32nd Mississippi and was elected its colonel in April.

Serving in **Sterling A. M. Wood's brigade**, Lowrey's regiment fought at **Shiloh** with the **Army of the Mississippi** and helped defend **Corinth, Mississippi,** afterward. During the **Kentucky Campaign,** he assumed command of the brigade at **Perryville** when Wood was wounded but was wounded himself in the left arm shortly afterward. Lowrey was out of action for two months but returned to duty in time to engage in some **skirmishing** at **Stones River** with the **Army of Tennessee**. During the 1862–63 winter encampment, he also served as a minister to his men and during a two-week period in the spring of 1864 baptized 50 soldiers. Lowrey again temporarily commanded the brigade during part of the **Tullahoma Campaign** and by the end of July 1863 had the 45th Mississippi consolidated with his regiment. At **Chickamauga**, he was highly praised by **division** commander **Patrick Cleburne**. When Wood resigned his commission in October, Lowrey was promoted to brigadier general and was given permanent command of the brigade.

In November 1863, Lowrey's brigade fought very well with Cleburne at **Missionary Ridge** and **Ringgold Gap**. That winter, he was one of the officers who signed Cleburne's proposal to enlist **black troops**, which led to the **Dalton Conference**. Lowrey's reputation was enhanced during the **Atlanta Campaign**, when he launched a counterattack that saved Cleburne's right flank at **New Hope Church**. At the **Battle of Atlanta**, he again was credited for saving the Confederate line by rushing his men into a gap that had opened between two Confederate brigades. Lowrey's record was so impressive, he was given command of Cleburne's division in August 1864 and led it at **Jonesboro** when Cleburne temporarily was given **William J. Hardee's corps**. During the **Franklin and Nashville Campaign**, Lowrey's brigade participated in the Spring Hill Incident and fought at Franklin. In the latter battle, he lost about half of his men and again temporarily led the division when Cleburne was killed. At Nashville, Lowrey first held the Confederate right, but on the second day of battle was put in command of **Benjamin F. Cheatham's** former division and was sent to the far left. There his horse was killed under him. Lowrey continued to lead the division through much of the **Carolinas Campaign** but then resigned his commission in March 1865 and returned to Mississippi. He later stated that while willing to fight to the end with his brigade, he resigned because he did not want to "mourn with strangers the funeral of 'The **Lost Cause**'" (Faust, ed., *Historical Times Illustrated Encyclopedia of the Civil War*, 452).

After the war, Lowrey resumed his ministry and in 1873 established the Blue Mountain Female Institute (later renamed Blue Mountain College). He served as its president and professor, became president of the Mississippi Baptist Convention, and was a member of the University of Mississippi's Board of Trustees.

LOWRY, ROBERT (1830–1910) CSA. A native of **South Carolina**, Lowry moved as a boy first to **Tennessee** and then to **Mississippi**. He was raised by an uncle, with whom he later became a partner in the mercantile business. As a young man, Lowry moved to **Arkansas**, where he became a lawyer, but he returned to Mississippi five years later. He then became involved in politics before the Civil War and was elected to both the state and house senate.

Lowry was a practicing attorney when the Civil War began. An avid secessionist, he joined a local **company** as a private, became a member of the 6th Mississippi, and was elected major when the **regiment** was reorganized in August 1861. At **Shiloh**, Lowry was wounded twice, and the regiment suffered heavy losses. He was elected colonel in May 1862 and led the regiment in the **Battle of Corinth** that October. Lowry was praised for his actions at **Port Gibson**, and he also fought at **Champion Hill**, although there is no record of his activities there. As part of **William W. Loring's division**, he became separated from the **army** at Champion Hill and thus was not trapped at **Vicksburg, Mississippi**. Afterward, Lowry was attached to **Joseph E. Johnston's** command around Jackson, Mississippi, during the remainder of the **Vicksburg Campaign**. During the **Atlanta Campaign**, he served in **John Adams's brigade** with the **Army of Tennessee** and sometimes temporarily commanded **Winfield Scott Featherston's** brigade. Lowry performed particularly well at **Kennesaw Mountain**, where he commanded **skirmishers** who repulsed two Union attacks. He later took command of the brigade when Adams was killed at Franklin and led it at Nashville.

Lowry was promoted to brigadier general in February 1865. He served under Johnston during the **Carolinas Campaign** and fought at **Bentonville** before surrendering with Johnston's army in April 1865.

After the war, Lowry returned to Mississippi, served as a state senator from 1865 to 1866, and was active in opposing **Republican Reconstruction**. Elected governor in 1881, he was very popular and was reelected in 1885 without opposition. Lowry later served as commander of the state's **United Confederate Veterans**.

LOYALTY LEAGUES. *See* UNION LEAGUE OF AMERICA.

LOYALTY OATHS. Loyalty oaths were used by Union officials to ensure the good behavior of Confederate civilians. As Union **armies** began occupying Confederate territory early in the war, commanders often required civilians to swear an oath and sign a document declaring that they had never, and would never, support the Confederacy. In 1862, **Abraham Lincoln** changed the oaths to promise only future loyalty in the hope that a mild policy would encourage Southerners to abandon the Rebellion. The loyalty oaths' success was uneven. Numerous Confederate **deserters** took them as a way to be released from **prison**. They and many civilians faithfully abided by their oaths, but others took them simply to win freedom of movement, have their property protected, or to acquire supplies from the Union army and continued to support the Confederacy. *See also* OATH OF ALLEGIANCE.

LUBBOCK, FRANCIS RICHARD (1815–1905) CSA. A native of **South Carolina**, Lubbock turned down an appointment to **West Point** and became a businessman. He moved to **Texas** in 1836, became a druggist and rancher, and sometimes fought **Indians** and Mexicans while serving in the Texas militia. Entering politics, Lubbock served as the Republic's clerk of the House of Representatives, comptroller, and a district clerk. He was elected the state's lieutenant governor in 1857, was a delegate to the 1860 **Democratic** National Convention at **Charleston, South Carolina**, and was elected governor in 1861.

As a war governor, Lubbock raised a **regiment** to defend the frontier against Indian attacks, created the Texas State Military Board to raise arms and equipment for the state's soldiers, **financed** the war by selling cotton through Mexico, helped organize wartime **industries**, and secured thousands of slaves to work on military fortifications. He decided not to run for reelection in 1863, was appointed lieutenant colonel, and joined **John B. Magruder's** staff. Lubbock later joined **John A. Wharton's** staff and saw some combat in the latter part of the **Red River Campaign**. In July 1864, he was promoted to colonel and served as **Jeffer-**

son **Davis's** adviser for the remainder of the war. Lubbock was captured in May 1865 with Davis in **Georgia** and was imprisoned for several months at **Fort Delaware**.

Upon his release from **prison**, Lubbock returned to Texas and served as a state tax collector, state treasurer, and member of the Board of Pardons.

LUCAS, THOMAS JOHN (1826–1908) USA. A native of **Indiana**, Lucas worked as a watchmaker until 1847, when he served in the **Mexican War** as a 2nd lieutenant in the 4th Indiana. He entered Union service in May 1861 as lieutenant colonel of the 16th Indiana and served with it at **Ball's Bluff**. Lucas was promoted to colonel in May 1862 and led the **regiment** to the western theater, where it lost 800 men (mostly taken **prisoner**) and was nearly annihilated at the **Battle of Perryville** during the **Kentucky Campaign**.

After the men were **exchanged**, the regiment was assigned to the **Army of the Tennessee's** XIII Corps. During the **Vicksburg Campaign**, Lucas was wounded three times, and in September 1863, he was given command of a cavalry **brigade** in Brig. Gen. **Albert L. Lee's** division. He led the brigade through the 1864 **Red River Campaign** and was promoted to brigadier general of volunteers in November. Sent to the Gulf coast near Mobile, Alabama, Lucas first led a cavalry brigade and then a **division** in operations in west **Florida**, south **Georgia**, and **Alabama**. He was **brevetted** major general of volunteers in March 1865 for his service during the **Mobile Campaign**.

Lucas served in **New Orleans, Louisiana**, after the war and was mustered out of the volunteers in January 1866. He returned to Indiana and served in the U.S. Revenue Service from 1875 to 1881 and as postmaster from 1881to 1885.

LUNETTE. A lunette (loo-NET) was a type of military fortification that had two or three sides and was open to the rear.

LYNCHBURG, VIRGINIA, BATTLE OF (June 17–18, 1864). Following the **Battle of Piedmont**, Union Maj. Gen. **David Hunter** launched **Hunter's Shenandoah Valley Campaign** to destroy the **railroads** supplying **Robert E. Lee's Army of Northern Virginia** defending **Richmond, Virginia**. By mid-June 1864, he had reached Lexington and was moving toward Lynchburg. On June 13, Lee dispatched **Jubal A. Early's** II Corps from **Cold Harbor** to assist Maj. Gen. **John C. Breckinridge's** two **brigades** and **Virginia Military Institute** cadets defend Lynchburg.

On June 17, Breckinridge held Hunter at bay until Early arrived by train that afternoon and night. The next day Hunter's 18,000 men faced

Early's 13,000, but the outnumbered Confederates held strong earthworks. After some feeble movement against the works, Hunter withdrew after dark when it became apparent the position was too strong to take by assault. He then made the mistake of retreating into **West Virginia** rather than back up the **Shenandoah Valley**, thus taking his command out of the war for a month and allowing the Confederates to launch **Early's Washington Raid**. In the fighting around Lynchburg, Hunter lost approximately 700 men to Early's 200.

LYON, HYLAN BENTON (1836–1907) CSA. A native of **Kentucky**, Lyon was orphaned at age eight. He graduated from **West Point** in 1856, served in the **artillery** during the **Seminole Wars**, and was fighting **Indians** in the Washington Territory when the **secession** crisis began. Taking a leave of absence, Lyon returned east and resigned his 1st lieutenant's commission in April 1861.

Lyon entered Confederate service as a 1st lieutenant of artillery, but late in 1861, he was appointed captain of Cobb's (Kentucky) Battery. In February 1862, he was elected lieutenant colonel of the 8th Kentucky (Confederate) and served as its commanding officer at **Fort Donelson**. Captured when the fort fell, Lyon was held **prisoner** for seven months. After being **exchanged** in September, he was promoted to colonel, and his **regiment** was converted to mounted infantry. Sent to **Mississippi**, Lyon was praised for his role in the Confederate victory at **Coffeeville** and afterward led a **brigade** at **Champion Hill** during the **Vicksburg Campaign**. He escaped the battlefield with **William W. Loring's division** and was put in command of the Confederate cavalry operating outside Port Hudson, Louisiana, but there is no record of his performing any duty there during the **Port Hudson Campaign**. After the campaign, Lyon requested cavalry duty and was assigned to **Joseph Wheeler** in November 1863. He led a small detachment in **Tennessee** and then temporarily was put in command of the **Army of Tennessee's** artillery, most of which he was able to save during the defeat at **Missionary Ridge**.

In June 1864, Lyon was given command of a cavalry brigade in **Abraham Buford's** division of **Nathan Bedford Forrest's** command and led it well at **Brice's Cross Roads**. Promoted to brigadier general later in June, he was sent behind enemy lines to raise recruits for Forrest's cavalry. Lyon returned to his brigade in time to participate in **Forrest's Tennessee Raids** that autumn and was praised by Forrest for his actions at **Johnsonville**. The following month, he led his own raid into Tennessee to cut Union communications with Nashville. His 800 men captured several steamships on the Cumberland River and then entered Kentucky. Unfortunately for Lyon, however, 500 of his men **deserted** when they learned of the Confederate defeat at Nashville. In January 1865, Lyon was surprised and captured by Union cavalry while staying in a civilian's house. Incredibly, he pulled a pistol from beneath his pillow, shot dead one trooper, and escaped from the house half-dressed. Lyon ended the war in command of the Union-occupied **Department of Western Kentucky**.

After the war, Lyon briefly went into exile in Mexico, but he returned to Kentucky in 1866 and became a farmer. He also was active in veterans' affairs and became the state's prison commissioner.

LYON, NATHANIEL (1818–1861) USA. A native of **Connecticut**, Lyon graduated from **West Point** in 1841 and served in both the **Seminole** and **Mexican Wars**. He disagreed with the latter conflict but still was **brevetted** once for gallantry and was wounded at Chapultepec. Afterward, Lyon served in **California** and **"Bleeding Kansas."** He had been a **Democrat** and a moderate who did not believe the government should interfere with **slavery** in the South, but his **Kansas** experiences turned him into a **Republican** and a staunch Unionist.

When the **secession** crisis began, Lyon was a captain in the 2nd U.S. infantry in command of the U.S. arsenal at St. Louis, Missouri. Missouri was divided between those loyal to secessionist Gov. **Claiborne F. Jackson** and those who supported the pro-Union legislature. When Jackson called out his secessionist militia, Lyon believed the governor was preparing to seize control of the city and arsenal. He then disguised himself as a woman and scouted out the encampment. Convinced of the militia's intent, Lyon surrounded **Camp Jackson** with his soldiers and captured the militiamen. He then paraded his **prisoners** through the city, touching off the bloody **St. Louis Riot**. Despite this incident, Lyon saved St. Louis, and probably the state, for the Union.

Lyon was promoted from captain to brigadier general of volunteers in May 1861 and was put in command of the **Department of the West**. To avoid further bloodshed, he met with Jackson and other secessionists, but when the governor demanded that he be given control of federal troops in the state, Lyon made his famous reply, "This means war!" (Warner, *Generals in Blue*, p. 286.) Lyon then began operations against the Confederates in Missouri. After some minor **skirmishing**, he was killed on August 10 while leading an attack against **Ben McCulloch's** Confederates at **Wilson's Creek**. In December, Lyon was voted the **Thanks of Congress** posthumously for saving Missouri for the Union.

LYTLE, WILLIAM HAINES (1826–1863) USA. A native of **Ohio** and the son of a congressman, Lytle became a lawyer as a young man. He fought in the **Mexican War** with the 2nd Ohio and rose in rank from 2nd lieutenant to captain. Afterward, Lytle resumed his practice and became involved in state politics. He was elected twice to the legislature, ran unsuccessfully for lieutenant governor, and in 1857 was appointed major general of militia by Gov. **Salmon P. Chase**. In addition to his political activity, Lytle also became a well-respected poet during the antebellum years.

Lytle entered Union service in May 1861 as colonel of the 10th Ohio and was badly wounded in the leg during his first battle, at **Carnifex Ferry**. After recovering from the wound, he recruited in **Kentucky** for a while, but in December 1861, he was given command of a **brigade** in the **Army of the Ohio**. At **Perryville**, Lytle was badly wounded and was left for dead on the field. Captured by the Confederates, he was not **exchanged** until February 1863. Lytle was promoted to brigadier general of volunteers in November 1862 and in April 1863 took command of a brigade in the 3rd Division of the **Army of the Cumberland's** XX Corps. After serving in the **Tullahoma Campaign**, he was killed on the second day of **Chickamauga** while opposing the Confederate attack that successfully broke the Union line.